Vegetarian Cooking for Everyone

Vegetarian Cooking for Everyone

DEBORAH MADISON

Broadway Books

NEW YORK

BROADWAY

Broadway Books titles may be purchased for business or promotional use or for special sales.
For information, please write to: Special Markets Department,
Bantam Doubleday Dell Publishing Group, Inc., 1540 Broadway, New York, NY 10036.

BROADWAY BOOKS and its logo, a letter B bisected on the diagonal, are trademarks of
Broadway Books, a division of Bantam Doubleday Dell Publishing Group, Inc.

Library of Congress Cataloging-in-Publication Data
Madison, Deborah.
Vegetarian cooking for everyone / by Deborah Madison ; photographs
by Laurie Smith. — 1st ed.
p.   cm.
Includes index.
ISBN 0-7679-0014-6
1. Vegetarian cookery.   I. Title.
TX837.M23618   1997
641.5′636—dc21   97-11138
CIP

Photographs by Laurie Smith
Illustrations by Catherine Kirkwood
Designed by Vertigo Design

04 20 19

This book is dedicated with love, to my mentors and friends

ALICE

LINDSEY

and

MARION

and to my husband, PATRICK

Contents

Acknowledgments

My knowledge of food has been formed over a significant part of a lifetime, shaped by friends, family, and farmers; teachers and students; writers and chefs; and those with whom I've shared time in the kitchen and at the table. When it comes to cooking, inspiration and instruction spring from many sources, for food touches all of life. I am indebted to many individuals, both intimates and strangers, who have, in their own unique ways, been a part of the creation of this book.

The physical creation of *Vegetarian Cooking for Everyone* depended on the skills of many particular individuals. It could not exist without their participation. I am blessed to have as my agent Doe Coover, who has been a deep well of good nature, sound advice, warmth, and encouragement. Harriet Bell, my editor, has offered, along with her clarity and let's-get-to-work enthusiasm, genuine warmth and support, which I treasure. In addition to guiding this book to completion, she has proved a great pleasure to work with, as has the staff of Broadway Books—Bill Shinker, Roberto de Vicq de Cumptich, Daisy Alpert, Rebecca Holland, Janice Race, Trigg Robinson, and Joyce Sherrod. Chris Benton took on the unenviable task of copy-editing this unwieldy manuscript with good grace and accuracy—and I know it was frustrating—and Alison Lew and Renata de Oliveira of Vertigo Design created the beautiful pages.

I am especially grateful to my husband, Patrick McFarlin, who has given so much to this project. He has eaten virtually all of the dishes in this book and washed up after a good many meals. Without Patrick, there would much less joy in my cooking.

Laurie Smith, with camera and infant in hand and in all kinds of weather, brought my food to life with her beautiful photographs. Catherine Kirkwood's fine hand has illuminated foods and techniques often better than my words have done. Judy Espinar and her staff at The Clay Angel deserve undying thanks for an endless supply of gorgeous serving dishes, which are such a delightful and important part of the meal.

Many people have contributed not only inspiration but hands on help and instruction. I've shared many meals both behind the stove and at the table with Dan Welch, David Tanis, Randy Breski, Clifford Wright, Martha Rose Shulman, and Russ Parsons, and I thank them all. Kathi Long has been a trustworthy assistant, friend, and valued source of information. Throughout the years, Marion Cunningham has been there on the other end of the phone to answer questions and share ideas; Lindsey and Charles Shere have been ever-supportive friends and more; and I am eternally grateful to Alice Waters for her generosity and her commitment to Chez Panisse, which has nourished me in more ways than one for many years. I would like to thank Richard Baker for giving me that push into the restaurant world with the creation of Greens. Life has not been the same since.

Others I wish to thank are the farmers of the Santa Fe Farmers' Market and farmers' markets everywhere, whose produce ensures my love of cooking season after season. Fran McCullough has been a vital part of this book from the beginning—a good friend and traveling companion, always ready for a culinary adventure. Oldways Preservation and Trust made possible many highly informative trips abroad, providing firsthand experiences with foods otherwise only imagined or tasted from afar. While my mother, Winifred Madison, provided the example of culinary curiosity in the kitchen, my father, John Madison, gave me a sense of American cooking and the importance of the garden. Michael Madison, my botanist brother, has always been there to explain some of the particularities of the plant world. For sharing their recipes and expertise, my thanks go to Joe Evans, Shelly Batt, Jody Apple, Christine Hickman, Sherman Rubin, Ann Katzen, Rob Coffland, Nancy Radke, Ann Clark, Odessa Piper, Cheryl and Bill Jamison, Kathy Cary, Christopher Hirsheimer, Bharti Kirschner, Kitty Morse, Joanne Neft, Kimberly Sweet, Elizabeth Schneider, Sylvia Thompson, Lynn Alley, Luca Pioltelli, Michael Katz, and Yamuna Devi.

Lastly, I wish to thank all those cooking school directors who have invited me to teach in their schools throughout the years. It's through teaching that I've been able to meet my readers, and their questions and curiosity inspired me to write this book.

Introduction

DURING THE MANY YEARS THAT I HAVE TAUGHT COOKING, I HAVE NOTICED THAT OF MY STUDENTS, ALL ARE ENTHUSIASTIC, MANY ARE QUITE SOPHISTICATED AND KNOW THEIR WAY AROUND THE KITCHEN, BUT MORE THAN A FEW REGARD cooking as a quirky process that's hard to grasp. Unnerved, they fail to notice that while indeed there are unpredictable things about food, most of the time cooking is guided by common sense and even logic. My students' questions have revealed, most wonderfully, how and when they are at a loss when it comes to how food works. They have helped me understand that, more than recipes, it's acquiring a sense of food and cooking that allows a person to move about a kitchen with confidence and pleasure instead of anxiety. My students have taught me a great deal and it is they, most of all, who inspired me to write this book. While I've learned much of what I know by eating, cooking, and reading widely, I know that many vegetarians are reluctant to buy cookbooks centered around meat, as so many are. If they go just to the vegetable section, they're likely to feel that too little of the book pertains to their needs and the slim part that does, fails to answer their basic questions about what's what in the kitchen, especially in the world of vegetables. What I wanted to write was a compendium of basic information along with a wide range of recipes for those who want to learn to cook well without meat. And this is what this book is meant to be.

The world of food and our knowledge of it are much larger today than even 5, 10, or 20 years ago. Since no one really wants a 10-pound book that contains *everything,* my book does have its limits. Today every food field has its experts. Entire volumes deal with nothing but muffins, rice, stir-fries, or soups. Many authors can tell you far better than I can the secrets of growing levain for home-baked country bread, something I'd rather buy. Since they are the true experts, I defer to them. Similarly, I bow to those authors who have spent a lifetime cooking a particular cuisine. Turn to their books if you're really serious about Mexican food, Vietnamese noodles, or an obscure corner of some other cuisine. I've certainly included recipes from other countries, especially those foods that I've experienced in my travels, for other lands traditionally have much more experience exploring the possibilities of plant foods than we do. But because I have a real affection for the dishes and flavors of our own tradition, which I feel are often neglected in favor of more exotic cuisines, I have included a great many time-honed American recipes. While the recipes in this book are those that I like to cook, my aim has also been to choose those that provide encouragement for new cooks as well as recipes to challenge those who are more experienced.

If you are a committed vegetarian, you can cook every recipe in this book. If you're a vegan, you can cook most of them. If you're a lapsed vegetarian or, like me, you don't attach a label to your eating style, you can still cook everything in this book and serve it with meat, fish, or fowl. This book is really a source for those who want lots of vegetable recipes and information, for the person who is suddenly cooking for a child who has decided to be a vegetarian, for a spouse who suddenly has to change his or her diet for health reasons, for a caterer's client who simply wants to eat more vegetables, or for any of us who wants to explore more of the foods that exist outside the realm of meat. This is also a book for those who like to eat and who want to make food that's worth the time it takes to cook it. This is vegetarian cooking for everyone.

Who and What Are Vegetarians

Some 12 to 16 million Americans call themselves vegetarians, but the word *vegetarian* has many different meanings. For some the meaning is narrow and strict: vegans eat nothing that comes from an animal, including eggs, milk, and honey. At the other extreme are those who call themselves vegetarian but mean only that they don't eat red meat. I could buy a yacht if I had a dollar for every time someone has told me, "I'm a vegetarian; I only eat fish and chicken." While such a definition may offend those who are more strict with their own habits, I believe it is sincerely spoken and points to the rather broad way in which the word *vegetarian* is used, a word that suggests some degree of limitation when it comes to eating animal foods. There are also some people who don't consider themselves vegetarians at all, but just happen to eat mainly a plant-based diet for a variety of reasons, such as preference, taste, health.

While moral reasons have long been at the root of many people's decision not to eat meat, today many Americans are motivated by health. What we have learned about diet-related diseases strongly suggests that diets relying heavily on meat can no longer be considered healthy, and that a better approach is to give a smaller place to animal foods and to include more dishes and meals without meat.

For some, the ecological effects of large-scale factory farming are reason enough not to take part in eating factory-raised meats. The presence of hormones and genetically altered material in our meat and dairy foods, the extremely harsh conditions under which animals are raised, and the deleterious effects that factory farming has on a fragile environment have caused many people to rethink the place of meat. However, many of the same problems exist in the parallel world of plant foods: the chemical-based practices of conventional agriculture have greatly diminished soil, water, and wildlife, the quality of the food we eat, and the health of those who farm. This affects everyone, vegetarian or otherwise, and also needs rethinking. Regardless of what we eat, we can make a choice and vote with our fork for foods that are grown and raised in a manner that supports a more sustainable approach to how we treat our land and our resources.

I don't, in fact, exclude animal foods from my world—I occasionally want to eat meat, fish, or fowl, and I've never been able say "No thanks, I don't eat that" to any food that someone has prepared for me. Today, balance in life is more desirable than limitation. However, vegetables and their cousins, all those other wonderful plant foods, are my first loves and most of the time I happily make a meal from what others place on the side of their plate without thinking of it as vegetarian. Simply put, I enjoy good food and good cooking of all persuasions, and at its best, eating is an inclusive experience that draws people together. When it comes to forming a philosophy or a political position about what to eat, I leave that to each one of you to work out. But whether you place your vegetables at the center of your plate, reserve that place for meat, or find comfort somewhere in between, enjoy, eat well, and raise a glass to life!

The Foods We Cook: Buying Locally

In the kitchen, raw materials have always been my inspiration. Plant life is visual, tactile, aromatic, fetching, and mysterious—beans that look like jewels; subtle grains; the strange beauty of seaweeds; the ingenuity of man-made foods like coils of pasta, myriad cheeses, and the different hues and fragrances of oils. It was fascination with this edible circus that started me cooking as a teen, more than 30 years ago, and today it's still the food itself that suggests a recipe, a menu, or an excuse for a gathering. Regardless of what you choose to eat, nothing is more important than starting with ingredients that are of the best quality, for our final results will never be better than what we start with. A hidden advantage of using good ingredients is that they allow us to cook simply and eat well. Because our efforts in the kitchen today are hard won, hopefully the meals we make will substantiate our lives by tasting good and by infusing us with a feeling of connection to those who grow the food and to those with whom we share them.

For me, the best meal is the one in which I know where everything was grown and who grew it. In our largely urban country this may seem like an absurd value, but that's only because we're out of the habit of being connected with our food. It is possible to regain that sense of connection, and knowing where our food comes from enriches our lives immeasurably by linking us to the place where we live and to those with whom we share a landscape, a culture, and a history. Agribusiness may be big business, but there are still many farmers working small farms who market their produce directly to us through farmers' markets and subscription farming.

The food our local farmers bring to our tables is always the most vital and delectable because of its sheer proximity to market and the high quality of farming techniques generally used. It is a true joy to cook with, and that is why I always seek out farmers' markets and other direct sources, including my own small garden. The fruits and vegetables, nuts, beans, and other foods I find at my farmers' market, along with the conviviality of seeing my neighbors twice weekly, have been the truest source of inspiration in my kitchen, and I am confident that they will be in yours, if they aren't already. Farmers' markets are proliferating in our country—see if there's one near you and support your local farmers.

When farmers' markets close for the season or none are in your area, there are supermarkets, specialty stores, and natural food stores selling quality food. I personally find natural food stores to be annoyingly pretentious and overly expensive. I don't always enjoy the experience of shopping in them, but I've referred to them often, for they are a good source for organic produce, bulk foods such as French green lentils, sea vegetables, heirloom beans, hormone-free eggs and dairy, and so forth.

Buying and Eating Organically

Since World War II the face of agriculture changed through the development of pesticides and chemical fertilizers, both by-products of the war. Agriculture that depends on these products is now referred to as *conventional*, even though, in the thousands of years man has farmed, its era is but a blip in time. It's often contrasted to other farming orientations, which for these purposes can be loosely labeled as organic, although individually they involve different styles and approaches. Basically, organic farming takes an approach that is chemical-free and sustainable.

While pesticides and chemical fertilizers have eliminated many pests and increased plant yields, they have also left damaging chemical traces in our food, soil, and water. Among the fruits and vegetables considered by the EPA to be highest risk for causing cancer due to their toxicity levels are tomatoes, potatoes, oranges, apples, wheat, soybeans, beans, carrots, corn, and grapes—foods that are supposed to be good for us. For the most part, pesticides are undetectable to our immediate senses, which makes it hard to think about them when standing in front of supermarket shelves brimming with vegetables and fruit. But if you've ever seen a crop duster spraying pesticides over a field and smelled its acrid dust, you will not find it appealing to imagine the residue on your food. While you can wash some of it off, some of it is systemic. And while peeling may help eliminate surface chemicals, you're also giving up important sources of flavor and fiber when you do so. Better to seek out organically grown produce. Incidentally I think, as do many others, that organically grown food simply tastes better, as well as being better for all concerned. But like any other fruit or vegetable, organically grown produce tastes best when it's the right variety for the soil, when it's picked at the right time, and handled with care and eaten soon after harvesting.

You can know for sure that what you buy is organic when the farmer is certified either by the state or an independent agency, such as the CCOF (Certified California Organic Farmers). Often state standards are higher than federal standards, but some states don't have a certification program. In such cases farmers can use private certification programs from other parts of the country. Some small states have banded together as a region, as they have in New England, to create their own program.

Organically grown food does not use chemicals and inorganic materials, such as fertilizers, at any point in the farm cycle. In addition, certified organic food must be grown in a way that ensures the long-term health of the soil through crop rotation, use of cover crops, and myriad other agricultural practices, an entirely different orientation toward the land than conventional farming. The farmers must report their practices, paperwork, and soil work to inspectors to become certified, so certification involves an enormous commitment for a farmer and often a sizable expense. Organic food often costs more to produce and buy, and unless you buy it directly from the farmer, the farmer doesn't always benefit from the high prices that are asked for at natural food stores. If you're not sure if the food labeled "organic" actually is, ask your retailer to show you proof. Even stores that purport to be natural food markets can make errors.

Produce may also be labeled "pesticide free." While the good news is that pesticides haven't been used, this tells you nothing about other practices the farmer may use. "Transitional" refers to produce grown on farms that are in transition from conventional chemical-based farming to organic. This category exists because soil and water can retain chemical residues for several years, so the resulting produce cannot be certified even though the farmer is following organic practices. If not abused, this term, usually three years in duration, can help a farmer through the difficult transition of changing farming methods.

It's only twenty years or so that health food stores offered their organic but shriveled beets and wilted lettuce. That image should by now be fully replaced with the vital plethora of gorgeous looking organic produce that can now be found nearly everywhere. We have all learned a great deal about growing and handling produce in this time and I look forward to a time when, as the new standard, it is available to everyone.

Becoming a Cook

THOSE WHO LOVE TO COOK OFTEN WAIT FOR THE WEEKENDS TO INDULGE THEIR PASSION. BUT PUTTING A MEAL, NO MATTER HOW SIMPLE, ON THE TABLE ON WEEKDAY EVENINGS IS A STRUGGLE FOR MANY OF US. WE HAVE SO MANY OTHER options for sustenance that cooking and eating together, one of the most basic human activities, has become an occasional event. For the first time in history, we can ask, "Why cook?"

Practically speaking, if you're concerned about the quality of the food you eat, cooking should be of vital importance, for it's the only way you can really know what you're eating. If money is a consideration, your home-cooked food will cost less than eating out or buying packaged food. There's also satisfaction in taking responsibility for what we eat instead of turning it over to others. Further, cooking a meal produces immediate results, unlike many of our jobs. After a long day of routine work many people find the creative act of cooking a relaxing change of pace that restores their energy. It's a gift to be able to cook for others—and it's wonderful to be cooked for.

A home-cooked meal is more than just food. Placing a meal on the weekday table is important to the quality of our lives. It's natural to talk over dinner, and that's where family members and friends are most likely to find out what's going on in one another's lives. Something always happens at the table.

There is also the fundamental joy in cooking, born of the pleasure of using our senses—rustling our fingers through a bunch of herbs, listening to the sizzle of onions, watching the colors brighten while vegetables cook, inhaling the fragrance of olive oil the moment it hits the pasta. This sensual involvement draws us into the process of cooking and teaches us about it. That sizzling sound tells us our heat is high enough; the scent of the herbs tells us whether we need to use a lot or a few; the fragrance of the oil

5

assures us of its quality. Because these small but often stellar moments occur even when cooking the simplest things, both the beginning cook and the expert can experience them. To make cooking accessible and enjoyable, here are a few notes on kitchen savvy. Even experienced cooks may find some useful information.

Developing Your Kitchen Savvy

THE INTUITIVE PROCESS: All cooks should know from the start that cooking is an inexact business. Foods differ from one part of the country to another, from one part of the season to the next; stoves are different; pans conduct heat in different ways; your taste is different from mine. Directions like "season to taste" acknowledge the fact that nothing is the same twice. Is your salt sea salt or mild kosher salt? Do you love salt or find you don't need much? You're the only one who can answer these questions, so you have to jump into cooking—smell, touch, and taste, then adjust as needed. This is what cooking is about, regardless of how thoroughly a recipe tries to give exact measurements and cooking times. As in learning a language, you stumble at first, but all of a sudden your ear—or tongue—opens up and you find yourself discerning sounds or tastes you hadn't noticed before.

SHOPPING: Go for what looks appealing and fresh rather than shopping strictly from a list. Pay attention when you shop. Produce is not handled well in this country, and it's frustrating to find, once you're home, that your pepper has a spoiled spot. At the same time produce doesn't have to be picture perfect. Size, uniformity, and absence of flaws result from standards imposed by the food industry and the FDA. Beyond the uniformly perfect produce we see displayed, there's a wild and raunchy bunch of vegetables and fruits that are undersized or too big, twisted instead of straight, marred by hail or pecked by a bird—and all perfectly good to eat.

TIMING: Ultimately experience will be your best teacher, but timing the parts of your meal is an important skill, especially when you're entertaining. In lieu of experience, these tips can help you serve a meal without jumping up from the table a hundred times or ending up dismayed and discouraged.

First sit down and review your menu to anticipate glitches. Make sure you don't have those unconscious repetitions of ingredients or styles (I'm always guilty of this!), that you aren't cooking everything in the oven at different temperatures or serving four dishes that need essential last-minute attention.

Review each recipe and note things like: Does the dish have a part that *has to be* or *can be* made ahead of time? How long does each dish take to cook? If brown rice takes 40 minutes, don't forget to allow for that!

Unless you're a very intuitive or experienced cook, it helps to visualize (we can say that in Santa Fe) what your cooking afternoon is going to be like and make a list of what has to be done and when. This really will make everything go more smoothly.

Try not to have more than one or two things to do at the last minute, such as dress the salad or time that soufflé, so that you can enjoy the meal with everyone else.

SETTING THE TABLE: Setting a table complements your efforts in the kitchen and is part of eating well. Try to have everything you need on the table when you sit down. Jumping up for salt and pepper breaks the flow of conversation. Cloth napkins feel good and don't waste paper, and having a napkin ring for each person means napkins can be used for several meals. Taking a moment to put butter in its dish and condiments in bowls provides a considerate feeling. Having heated plates, especially for pasta and soup, helps keep food warm throughout the meal. And you might consider turning off the phone and TV during dinner if you don't already.

DON'T APOLOGIZE: When it comes to cooking for others, I have learned—am *still* learning, in truth—that it's best to keep your doubts and disappointments to yourself. When you cook, you're surrounding yourself with tastes and smells, so your food doesn't always deliver the vivid impression to you that it does to others. Apologizing only makes others uneasy, whereas with nothing said, they might be completely content. I once had restaurant customers raving about my "smoked" mushroom soup. Smoked mushrooms? I checked the pot and found, to my dismay, that the soup had scorched. I wanted to say "You liked *that?"* But they were happy, so, with difficulty, I swallowed my embarrassment.

Making It Possible

To be honest, many vegetarian dishes require more time to prepare than meat-based dishes do. For starters, many vegetables need to be sorted, pared, trimmed, and washed, but not all vegetables demand a lot of time to prepare or cook. A scrubbed sweet potato takes 10 to 20 minutes in the pressure cooker or microwave, and asparagus cooks in minutes. Time-consuming dishes are generally those with many parts or those that involve a lot of handwork like rolling or stuffing, dishes where there are no leftovers to speed things along, and dishes involving unfamiliar techniques. Following are 10 tips for making cooking, especially vegetarian cooking, manageable, possible, and even efficient.

1. LEARN TO USE A KNIFE. Basic knife skills are essential to making cooking pleasant and quick. Use the right knife, keep it sharp, and give yourself plenty of room to work.

2. LEARN TO WORK IN A NONLINEAR FASHION. Cooking doesn't progress in a straight line but meanders from here to there. For example, you always put the pasta water on to boil first, even though cooking the pasta is the last step. If the onions for a soup are going to cook for 15 minutes, use that time to prepare the rest of the ingredients or another dish. This is one reason it's important to read your recipes through before starting. If you can see the whole picture, you have an enormous advantage, because several things always are going on simultaneously when you cook. Like tying a shoe, it's one of those things that is hopelessly complicated to describe but crucial to learn and once you do, it becomes second nature.

3. LEARN TO MAKE A FEW THINGS WELL. Learning too many new dishes at once makes cooking trying. It's better to build your cooking vocabulary dish by dish, since the foods that are easiest to make are invariably the ones you already know how to cook. So decide what you like to eat, then practice cooking that type of dish—stir-fries or braises, for example—until you feel confident. Once you understand the basics, you'll be able to cook creatively and easily, for most types of dishes follow the same pattern. Then go on to something new. Or do as a friend does: Cook the same three meals as long as your friends and family will let you.

4. SIMPLIFY THE MENU. Consider making one- or two-dish meals standard. They're less taxing, and there are fewer dishes to wash. The popularity of the stir-fry speaks to exactly this. Other simple meals might be a baked potato and a salad; soup and toast; an omelet; or a salad that's filled with vegetables. Fruit for dessert isn't just healthy; it's easy. In winter, try dried fruits and a few nuts.

5. DEVELOP A ROUTINE. In spite of the overwhelming choices we have of what to eat, having something of a routine saves time spent thinking about what to make for dinner. Besides, as eaters we enjoy repetition, both in restaurants and at home. It's reassuring and involving: "I liked last week's version better. What about you?" or "We're having my favorite dish!"

6. HAVE DO-AHEADS. Working days in advance of a meal can become confusing, but doing a few easy things ahead does pay off later. For example, having prewashed salad greens often makes the difference between eating a salad and not. Or having some steamed beets, boiled potatoes, or cooked beans on hand and a few chopped onions ready to go makes getting a meal started much easier.

7. PLAN ON LEFTOVERS. Certain foods can return to the table in another form, and often it takes little extra time to double a recipe. Leftover polenta can be fixed in all kinds of ways; beans, lentils, and chickpeas can go into salads, soups, stews, purees; whole grains can be frozen and later added to soups. Leftover rice, quinoa, and couscous can be shaped into croquettes or made into salads. Soups usually taste better on the second or third day.

8. USE A FEW MACHINES. These can helpfully speed things up or usefully slow things down. A pressure cooker makes short work of long-cooking foods, cooking them in about one-third the time. Slow cookers slow everything down enough that food can cook while you're at work or asleep.

9. USE A FEW GOOD-QUALITY CONVENIENCE FOODS. Maybe your region has a specialty food, like tamales, that can be bought frozen and set aside for those nights when you just can't cook. Good organic canned tomatoes make a fast sauce, or you can improve a commercial sauce by adding fennel seeds, rosemary, mushrooms, olives. Canned chickpeas and black beans are a good resource, as are a few frozen vegetables—lima beans, black-eyed peas, okra, and peas. Condiments like capers, olives, Thai curry pastes, coconut milk, and roasted peppers can accomplish a lot in the kitchen. Tofu is not only a staple for many; it couldn't be easier to cook. A spoonful of extra virgin olive oil adds a splendid finish to plain foods of good quality, such as a plate of asparagus. And when it comes to ordering in that pizza, then, if you're up to it, dress it up with cilantro and diced chile, olives, and so on.

10. ENLIST HELP. About the time you think your children are able, get them started on some simple kitchen tasks. Eventually a child can be put in charge of the whole dinner once a week, from planning the menu to cooking it. Having kids work in the kitchen is undoubtedly a struggle at first, but later it can be a great gift, for the parent will get some relief and the child can take pride in making a meaningful contribution—and will leave home with a truly practical skill.

Composing a Vegetarian Menu

Replacing meat with something that's like it is one way of approaching vegetarian food, and long before the adventurous life of the sixties, the Seventh-Day Adventists were producing meat analogues—nutlets instead of cutlets. Since then, Americans have opened up to new ways of eating that have considerably relaxed the vegetarian approach to menu planning. When I first started cooking vegetarian food, there was a deep striving to find that "main dish"—the center on which the diner focused. There has always been some dread of the meatless plate imagined as the blank space in the middle surrounded by vegetables. Over the years I've tried many menu approaches. Here are the ones that work for me and why they do.

HAVE SOMETHING IMPRESSIVE IN THE CENTER OF THE PLATE: When I was chef at Greens in San Francisco, I felt that my job was to provide our many customers with food that not only tasted wonderful but was visually striking as well. Their eyes would be drawn to these centerpieces, which other dishes would flatter and complement just the way side dishes complement meat. If its form was at least familiar, I felt, the customer would feel relaxed about the meal. After all, when it comes to food, we're at least as conservative as we are adventurous, if not more so. The kinds of foods that best fill this center role are generally layered, rolled, stuffed, stacked, or wrapped—food that has had something done to it. For example, you could have chard and a spicy couscous dish, or you could roll the couscous in the chard leaves, then present them with a sauce, and that would make all the difference between supper and dinner out. But many of the dishes that work well in this capacity are time consuming to make. Getting the couscous inside the chard is indeed an extra step—*then* it needs a sauce. But it's precisely this effort that produces a dish that has focus, clarity, and enough interest that the diner's eye isn't restlessly seeking for something to be "it." I think this was a much more important consideration in the seventies and eighties than it is today, but it still has relevance.

A SIMPLER APPROACH: Today expectations about what should be at the center of the plate are much more relaxed than they used to be. A simple gratin can take the place of an impressive eight-layered crêpe cake, provided you don't just plop it on the plate but make a conscious presentation. My notion of what can be in the center now includes gratins, vegetable ragouts, pastas, stir-fries, and even a roasted sweet potato. By nature some of these dishes are formless—stir-fries and stews, for example, take up the whole plate. But you can give them focus by setting your stir-fry on a noodle cake or serving your stew with a popover or over polenta. The simple act of nestling spaghetti in a wide-rimmed pasta plate gives it visual tidiness and keeps it warm as well.

SERIAL EATING—NO MAIN DISH: Following the example of the Mediterranean mezze table and Chinese dim sum, many people like a meal that consists of a succession of small dishes. There is neither focus nor climax, but it manages to work. This approach is simply a structured grazing or the tendency to order several appetizers from the restaurant menu instead of a main course. The buffet is another example. At its most informal extreme, you just put all your interesting leftovers on the table.

DISHES FOR LIGHTER EATING: Simply put, we've become happier with less. Soup, salad, a stuffed baked potato, a vegetable sauté, a quesadilla, an omelet—all make perfectly fine, light weekday entrées that are eminently doable. Taking care with setting the table and presenting the food can often balance its simplicity, so that a simple soup, salad, cheese plate, and dessert can be as satisfying for a company meal as something more elaborate.

THE ROLE OF ACCOMPANIMENTS: Accompaniments accomplish several things: They round out the main dish by complementing its taste or texture (the stir-fry *needs* noodles or rice); they extend time at the table so that you're dining instead of just fueling; and they offer a progression of textures and flavors. Often the accompaniment is obvious because it provides contrast and balance, like a starchy food with a vegetable main dish or a salad with a gratin. The foods that fill this role are simply prepared vegetables, beans, and grains.

AVOIDING REPETITION: Is everything you're serving white or based on onions? Does it all involve last-minute timing? It's amazingly easy to repeat ingredients and techniques without even noticing—until it's nearly on the table. When you're sketching out your menu, be sure to look at the entire meal before starting, especially if it's rather an important dinner, not just supper. Notice if you've chosen onion salad, onion soup, and onion gratin and plan to make a few changes if you have. (If it's too late, you can always call such a meal an onion festival.)

COMPOSITION—CHANGING LEVELS OF INTENSITY: First courses and appetizers are small but rich or intense so that a few small bites both ease our hunger and stimulate our interest. The next course needs to drop a little in intensity and be a little larger. A simple soup is often this ideal next step—it provides some spacing, like a comma or a dash. (A complex soup, garnished and accompanied with a crouton, could well be the main course of a casual meal.) Then we need to go on to something heartier but not so rich that you can't comfortably eat a portion: the main course. A salad might follow, providing a cleansing freshness and lull before the final sweet note of dessert.

This progression is for a classic meal. If you're eating a succession of small dishes, these considerations aren't so important. Maybe everything is at the appetizer level of intensity, but the portions are small and varied. For everyday meals with children, you might keep these pointers somewhere in the back of your mind—they're undoubtedly not nearly as crucial as simply getting dinner on the table. For that, we need strategies, leftovers, some fast foods, and some things we know how to do well that everyone likes.

Menus for Holidays and Special Occasions

Regardless of your religious or cultural heritage, most holidays have traditional foods that don't involve meat, so vegetarians are not entirely excluded from what everyone else is eating. In fact, one way to approach the traditional holiday meal is just to make all those side dishes—they're usually more than ample and wonderfully varied—and ignore the traditional turkey, ham, lamb, or brisket. Generally, it's those candied yams, cranberries, and stuffings that people love best at Thanksgiving. Long gone, fortunately, are the days when vegetarians attempted to make turkeys out of tofu.

The other approach is to regard holidays and other special occasions as times of celebration and honor these days by making those foods that are special to you. These might include complicated dishes, such as ravioli or lasagne from scratch; foods that are richer than those we usually eat, such as a sizzling risotto gratin; or foods that are costly, such as truffles or a galette made with lots of wild mushrooms.

Of course, the other things that make holidays special are the solemnity, sentimentality, or joy of the occasion, the people around us, the care with which we prepare our homes and tables, and what's in our hearts. In my experience, the food ends up being important, but often not quite as important as we imagined it would be.

Wine with Vegetables

The idea of pairing wine with food may at first seem less obvious than when meat is the anchor on the plate—some wines are just too big and too grand to be supported by vegetarian fare. But there are plenty of wines that are fine to drink with vegetables—good ones too, so you needn't restrict yourself to Sauvignon Blanc or Fumé Blanc, the wines so often designated for vegetarian dishes.

In our home, we're apt to buy a case of well-priced *vin de pays*, one that's lively and interesting but on the light and fruity side, and drink that as our "house" wine. This is the kind of wine that goes well with most of the food we cook and one we're happy to drink on a daily basis. For special dinners, I'll focus more on the wine, choosing those that will go particularly well with the food I'm planning to serve. And I always keep some very good wines and champagnes on hand for occasions when something really special comes along, like a gift of great cheeses or the arrival of a dear friend—after all, friends as well as foods warrant opening a good bottle.

One of the reasons a daily wine works well for me is that left to my own devices rather than the demands of recipe testing, I tend to cook with many of the same ingredients over and over. I'm not apt to make a Thai stir-fry one night, a curry the next, followed by a Tuscan-inspired meal the third,—meals that each have their own demands when it comes to wine. Rather, I generally cook foods that enjoy an easy affinity for light-to medium-bodied reds from Italy, the South of France, Spain, or California and Oregon. If your food tastes change from day to day, a single wine may not work so easily.

One of the first things that become clear about pairing wine and vegetables is that the wines will be lighter than those you serve with meats. Not only meat's robust flavor but its fats seem to support bigger wines, which is one reason that cheese, though not meat but a fairly high-fat animal product, goes so beautifully with those fuller-bodied reds that are harder to place in the vegetarian menu. Vegetables that are naturally sweet, such as winter squash, caramelized onions, and carrots, go well with wines that offer sweetness as well, such as Johannisberg Riesling and Gewurztraminers, while more acidic foods—fresh goat cheeses, feta, tomatoes, and asparagus—are better suited to those wines that also enjoy higher acidity, such as Sauvignon Blanc, Fumé Blanc, Zinfandel, and Pinot Noir.

Some people feel that very dry wines are best with vegetables because they balance their natural sweetness, but I find a little more sweetness in wine works to harmonize rather than argue with their concentration of sugar. Not all vegetables have a pronounced sweet component; artichokes, asparagus, and tomatoes, for example, are more acidic. As tempting as it is to try, it's not easy to make rules about matching a vegetable with a particular wine, because what ultimately matters is how that vegetable is prepared and what it is partnered with and seasoned with, all factors that can change the balance of sweetness and acidity. Cream and cheese with asparagus completely change its nature, just as beets with ginger and chile are different than beets with butter, or raw tomatoes versus as tomatoes cooked with garlic, olives, mushrooms, and capers. Underlying herbs can influence a dish, too. Rosemary, thyme, bay, and sometimes sage set a flavor tone that is much more hospitable to fuller-bodied, softer red wines than, say, cilantro, chervil, parsley, and dill, which are happier with more acidic whites or a lighter red.

When it comes to serving wine with salads, consider making dressings that are low in acid by using low-acid vinegars, such as balsamic and rice wine vinegar, citrus juices, or simply a greater proportion of oil to acid than usual so the salad doesn't fight with wine. A little crème fraîche whisked into the dressing can replace some of the vinegar while providing the needed sharpness. The fat softens its effects on the wine. A good way to make a wine choice is to consider using the salad ingredients themselves as ways to build a connection to a particular wine. Nuts (and nut oils), cheeses, olives, mushrooms and other vegetables (either grilled or fresh), herbs, spices, and even fruits can suggest a linkage to particular wines.

Matching and harmonizing wines with food creates a union of tastes that's larger and more exciting than either of the single elements, and that's one of the reasons for trying to pair wines with food. But wine preferences are like any other—a personal matter. What tastes good to you may differ from my own inclinations and that really doesn't matter as long as you enjoy what you drink. And one way to find out what you enjoy is to experiment. If you want to build a good wine and food vocabulary for yourself, it helps to jot down what wine and food combinations worked (or didn't work) for you.

RED WINES: There are a number of reds that are friendly with vegetarian food, among them Riojas, Zinfandels, Australian Shiraz, Côtes-du-Rhône, Merlots, lighter Cabernets, and syrah-based wines. In short, wines that are warm and soft, a little spicy, yet not too big. Pinot Noirs can be especially full, yet they're a good match for foods that end up on the grill or dishes that contain the concentrated juices of summer vegetables. Zinfandel can provide a wonderful brightness that harmonizes with lively Mediterranean flavors such as capers, sharp cheeses, olives, or contrasts well with heavier elements like earthy grains. If you like to cook food that's representative of a particular part of the world it makes sense to turn to the wines of that area. Tuscany's Chianti or Sangiovese wines, for example, are natural choices to serve with the foods and flavors of that region.

WHITES AND ROSÉS: Many people find a more comfortable match is to be made between white wines and vegetables, than with reds. Though I'm partial to reds, I think both can work quite well, and rosés shouldn't be left out of the picture either. In fact, they are especially flattering since they possess both the fruitiness of a red and the refreshing crispness of a white wine, a dual personality that allows them to pair nicely with many dishes, including Asian dishes. Chardonnays, even the more full-bodied oaky ones, have their place with certain foods, such as those that include cream and mild-flavored, buttery cheeses. Sauvignon Blanc, Rieslings, and Gewurztraminers are often called upon when dishes featuring intense and spicy ingredients are offered—food featuring chiles, wasabi, cilantro, spicy herbs, curry, or those difficult wine vegetables—asparagus and artichokes. The sweeter varietals, however, are good with sweeter vegetables. Chenin Blanc, Rieslings, and Chardonnays shine with winter roots and winter squash, while drier wines fight them. Vegetables on the bitter end of the spectrum, such as robust greens like broccoli rabe, can pair with drier whites, like Pinot Grigio.

To suggest some wines with certain foods, I've assembled the following list of vegetables and flavor clusters that are commonly found. These suggestions, however, need to be taken with a grain of salt, for, like food, wine is subject to personal preferences and likes and dislikes, and wines themselves change.

WINES BY FLAVOR CLUSTERS: Particular combinations of ingredients and seasonings appear over and over again. Here are guides for those clusters of seasonings that appear in this book:

Hearty winter soups and stews featuring lentils, roots, tomatoes, garlic, mushrooms: Côtes-du-Rhône, Rioja, and Zinfandel if the dish is on the spicy side or prepared with capers and olives

Hearty summer gratins and pastas featuring eggplant, leeks, goat cheese, mozzarella: Merlot, Sauvignon Blanc, Zinfandel, Pinot Noir, Gamay

Dishes featuring garlic and tomato: Zinfandel, Chianti, Merlot

Dishes featuring rosemary, tomato, hearty cheeses: Zinfandel, Cabernet

Dishes featuring basil and pesto: Sauvignon Blanc, Fumé Blanc

Dishes featuring cheese, olives, tomatoes, garlic, such as a polenta gratin or pastas: Zinfandel, Chianti, Merlot

Spicy foods, rich foods, Asian foods featuring wasabi, ginger: Gewurztraminer, Pinot Grigio, Trebbiano, Sauvignon Blanc, White Zinfandel

Creamy sauces, soft cheeses, vegetable custards, cheese flans: Gewurztraminer, Chardonnay, Chenin Blanc, Côtes-du-Rhône, Sauvignon/Fumé Blanc depending on the vegetable or cheese

Dishes featuring curry spices: Riesling, Chenin Blanc

Dishes featuring chiles and spicy foods: Riesling, Gewurztraminer

Dishes featuring Szechuan spices, especially with eggplant: Malvasia, Riesling, Chenin Blanc

Dishes featuring North African seasonings such as cumin, coriander, saffron: Light-bodied reds such as Rioja and Portuguese wines

Asian dishes featuring lemongrass, cilantro, lime, kaffir lime: Chenin Blanc, Vouvray, Pinot Grigio, Trebbiano, Riesling

Dishes with lemony accents or those emphasizing parsley: Sauvignon Blanc or Fumé Blanc

Aged Parmesan, dry Jack, or Asiago: Chardonnay, fino-style sherry

Other hearty cheeses: Petite Syrah, Merlot, Zinfandel, Côtes-du-Rhône, Chardonnay

Milder soft cheeses: Chardonnay, Pinot Noir

Nuts: Chardonnay, sherry

Berries and cherries: Beaujolais, Pinot Noirs

Dried fruits: Grenache, Gamay for cherries, currants, raisins; Zinfandel, especially for figs and prunes

Apples and pears: Riesling, Chardonnay, Gewurztraminer, Sauvignon Blanc

Melons: Gewurztraminer, Riesling

The Knife: Your Most Important Tool

The importance of knowing how to use a knife applies to anyone who cooks, but especially to those who are cooking lots of vegetables, because they require paring, trimming, chopping, slicing—all knife work.

While food processors have become as common as knives and they're undoubtedly useful machines, they tend to mangle vegetables like parsley and onions. Often you can chop something more quickly by hand than you can in the machine (and the cleanup is easier), and you can cut more interesting shapes, such as a roll cut. Also, food processed in a machine never reveals the hand of the cook. I always find it much more interesting to see the person in the way he or she cuts vegetables; it's one of the things that makes hands-on cooking so vital.

When I watch people cook in their homes, I understand why they don't enjoy it: they're usually using a dull knife that's wrong for the job and trying to work on a tiny board that was probably intended for cheese. Their work is laborious, slow, and frustrating, but with the right sharp knife and plenty of room to work, they could be sailing through the prep work without strain.

WHAT YOU NEED: Of the vast selection of cutlery sold, you need only three or four knives: a few inexpensive paring knives for peeling, a 6-inch knife that's small enough to use for paring jobs but large enough for limited slicing, and a 10-inch chef's knife for chopping and slicing. A heavy cleaver is helpful for cutting into dense winter vegetables; an inexpensive small serrated knife is useful for slicing tomatoes; a larger serrated one is used for bread.

CHOOSING THE RIGHT KNIFE: Most people like stainless-steel knives because they don't react chemically with foods and the blades don't rust. Carbon-steel knives slice beautifully and sharpen easily, but they stain many foods. They also need to be washed and wiped dry immediately after each use. Ceramic knives from Japan are very thin and ever sharp, ideal for fine work but expensive and brittle.

When it comes to shape, chef's knives have a triangular blade that's pointed at the tip and wide at the base so that your knuckles don't scrape the counter. This shape ensures contact with a large surface area, so they're very efficient for chopping. The Japanese vegetable knife, which is squared off rather than pointed, is similarly well designed for slicing, cutting, and chopping. Curved blades are terribly inefficient since only a fraction of the curve comes into contact with the board at any one time. Paring knives, however, can have straight or curved blades. The curved blades are good for going around surfaces such as on potatoes or pears. I never like to pay a lot for a paring knife—they're too easy to lose, and the cheap ones work fine.

KEEPING KNIVES SHARP: A dull knife makes work difficult and can be dangerous since you need to use a lot of pressure. A sharp knife slices through foods as if they're warm butter. Many home cooks have a hard time keeping their knives sharp, but with the electric and manual knife sharpeners now available it isn't hard to keep a good edge on a blade. Magnets hold the blade at the correct angle for sharpening so that you don't end up with a knife that's crooked or out of whack. Don't wait until your knives are impossibly dull before sharpening them. Frequent fine tunings, as often as each time you use your main knife or once a week with a steel or magnetic knife sharpener, help keep those blades honed.

More traditionally, you can use a whetstone to sharpen a knife. Whetstones are used with running water or oil. A diamond steel is used to hone the sharpened edge of a knife and keep it sharp through hours of prep.

An alternative to sharpening your own knives is to find someone who sharpens them professionally—often a cutlery shop does this. It will wear them down a little faster over time, but you will have well-honed blades that are sharpened evenly. If you've let your knives get seriously dull, go to the professionals. Regardless of how you sharpen your knives, store them carefully in a slotted container or knife rack so that they aren't all jumbled together, a damaging arrangement.

HOW TO HOLD A KNIFE: Grasp the handle of the knife in whatever hand you're most comfortable with. Hold it firmly enough that you have some control, but not so that your hand feels tight or tense. With your other hand, hold whatever is to be sliced, curving your fingers under your knuckles. This way you actually use your fingers as a guide for the blade rather than relying entirely on sight. Don't worry about cutting yourself—you'd have to tilt the knife at an extremely unlikely angle. Try it—you'll see! Once you get the hang of letting your curved fingers guide your cutting hand, you can hold your head upright, giving an occasional glance at your hands, instead of bending your head forward. This prevents strain from building in the shoulders and neck.

PRACTICE! Beginners often feel timid and work very slowly. One of the things you'll gain from becoming proficient is speed, and to help build proficiency you need to loosen up your arm and wrist. So take something of little consequence—the outer leaves of a lettuce or something that will be pureed—give yourself plenty of room, and just cut like crazy. Don't worry about how it comes out; just get your arm in motion. As you practice, you'll soon begin to gain control over what you're doing. Remember to keep your fingers tucked under your knuckles.

CUTTING BOARDS: Giving yourself plenty of room to work is absolutely essential. A small cutting board hampers your action, constantly confining you to an area that won't hold what you're doing. Wood is much kinder to your knife, but plastic is lighter. (Secure a lightweight board by placing it on top of a damp dish towel.) Plan to have at least two roomy boards. Use one board for garlic, onions, and vegetables and the other for fruits. The smell of garlic really does linger on a board if it's not washed well between uses. There's nothing more disappointing than eating a fruit salad that tastes like garlic.

The Rest of Your Kitchen Equipment

Once you have your knives and something to chop on, you need bowls to put things in—especially plenty of small ones—a strainer, a variety of spoons, a few pots and pans, and a vegetable peeler to make a very bare-bones working kitchen. Sometimes such kitchens are the most fun to work in, but as you discover your own cooking inclinations and style, you will begin to outfit your kitchen to suit your cooking style and your budget. Both undoubtedly will change many times during your life.

In general, choose the best-quality pots and pans you can afford; they last a long time if treated well, and good tools are a pleasure to use. As a rule, heavier pots and pans cook food most evenly since they're less likely to have hot spots. Still, some of my favorite pans have been cheap, lightweight nonstick skillets from the supermarket, which are good for many foods and inexpensive to replace. Always read the instructions when you buy a pan so you'll know how to season, use, and maintain its surface.

As for the materials your equipment is made from, plain aluminum discolors foods and imparts an off taste. Cast-iron pans can also discolor foods like eggs and artichokes, but they're heavy and sturdy, and many today are lined with a nonreactive surface. Stainless steel is always a good choice, as is anodized aluminum, neither of which reacts with food. Tin-lined copper, especially if it's heavy, is the Cadillac of pots and pans, but it's expensive and requires special care to avoid scratching the surface, not to mention retinning. Some high-quality cookware sandwich layers of copper, stainless steel, and aluminum, taking advantage of the best each metal has to offer.

WHERE TO FIND IT: If you don't have much money to spend, see what you can find at garage sales and flea markets. You'll be amazed at what people discard. Restaurant supply stores often have a selection of tools many stores don't have and at a lower price. Supermarkets also carry a decent selection of basic equipment, some of which is inexpensive and works perfectly fine. Thrift stores and antiques stores are good sources for equipment that's made in the good old-fashioned way—heavy-gauge bread pans, good cast iron, crockery bowls, and Dutch ovens are some of my favorite finds.

The Equipment I Use Most in My Kitchen

Infinite pieces of equipment can find their way into a kitchen, depending on your culinary needs or fondness for acquiring things. Some especially functional pieces are described in chapters of the book where they are most likely to be used, but here are some pieces, both large and small, that I feel are essential for making your efforts productive and worthwhile.

BLENDER: Still good after all these years and relatively inexpensive, a blender is used for pureeing a soup, making a crêpe batter or a smoothie, pulverizing bread into crumbs, and many other things. An immersion blender—a hand-held blender on a stick—is wonderfully efficient since you use it directly in the pot.

CITRUS ZESTER: Makes fine shreds of citrus zest in a moment and can be used to score a cucumber.

DOUBLE BOILER: Once a standard item in every kitchen, a double boiler is still enormously practical since it allows you to cook foods such as polenta and flour-based sauces without constant stirring. You also can improvise by setting a bowl over a pot of boiling water. The boiling water should never touch the bottom of the bowl or pot.

FOOD MILL: This inexpensive, old-fashioned device is ideal for pureeing soups, sauces, and vegetables. Using a food mill means you don't have to seed and peel apples and tomatoes before making a sauce since it separates them out for you.

HEAVY-DUTY ELECTRIC MIXER: A heavy-duty mixer that comes with a dough hook, paddle, and wire whip is an investment but well worth it. It's terrific for making batters, pasta, and bread, for beating and whipping foods, and has attachments available for other kitchen functions.

MEASURING CUPS AND SPOONS: Especially for beginners, measuring is important. After a while you'll find that you can eyeball amounts quite accurately. Get sturdy spoons and cups. Measuring spoons come in sets, from 1/8 teaspoon to 1 tablespoon. When measuring dry ingredients like baking soda, level off the spoons with a knife.

There are two kinds of measuring cups, one for dry ingredients and one for wet. Dry measuring cups are calibrated to the rim so that when measuring flour, for example, you can dip it into the flour sack and sweep the excess off the top. Measuring cups for liquids have a pouring lip and extra uncalibrated space at the top so that you can carry wet ingredients without spilling them. For accuracy they should be read at eye level. You'll want at least one set of dry measuring cups and one wet measuring cup of 2- to 4-cup capacity.

MORTAR AND PESTLE: Crushing and hand-grinding foods in a mortar opens up their flavors impressively. Mortars are very efficient in spite of being hand tools. Choose a small one if you think you'll use it just for garlic or pounding spices; you can always get a larger one. Wooden mortars retain the odors of whatever you grind in them, whereas metal, ceramic, and marble ones don't. If you choose wood, dedicate it to either garlic and savory herbs and spices or to sweet spices.

If you don't have a mortar and pestle, you can, to some degree, approximate its effect by chopping garlic mixed with salt, then turning the knife over and using the dull side to break down the fibers.

NUT AND CHEESE GRATERS: A small hand-held cheese grater is good for passing at the table along with a hunk of cheese so that everyone can grate his or her own. A hand-held rotary grater makes feather-light shreds of cheese and nuts—essential for fine baking. An upright box grater is a standard piece of equipment for every kitchen. It can be used for coarse or fine grating, whether cheese or vegetables.

PEPPER AND SPICE MILLS: Essential for freshly ground pepper, which is how pepper should be. If possible, have one each for white and black pepper and also one for coarse sea salt. An electric spice mill (or coffee grinder) is great for powdering toasted whole spices, which really brings out their flavors. Use it just for spice only, though; coffee easily picks up the lingering aromas of cumin or coriander.

PRESSURE COOKER: This underutilized timesaver makes short work of beans, soups, and hefty vegetables. The new pressure cookers are fail-safe and easy to use. They don't have jigglers, and they won't blow up. They make it possible to have real food in minutes and are especially useful at high altitudes, where everything takes longer to cook. Be sure to read the instructions that come with the model you buy. A good source of pressure cooker recipes is *Great Vegetarian Cooking Under Pressure* by Lorna J. Sass.

SLOW COOKER: The ultimate in unattended cooking: cereal cooks while you sleep; beans and soups while you work. Be sure to look at the instructions; slow cookers have their own unique cooking requirements.

SALAD SPINNER: If you want dry salad greens, parsley, or shredded potatoes, you need a salad spinner, although you can get by without one if you have a mesh bag and can go outdoors to swing it or are patient with towels. There are different kinds of spinners, and some drain right into the sink—be sure that's what you want when you choose one.

SCALE: Americans are not as geared to weight as they are to volume, but a scale tells you in an instant how much you have of a vegetable, a chunk of chocolate or an odd piece of butter, a piece of cheese (important for dieters), or the weight of a piece of dough that's to be divided into rolls. Although most ingredients are given in volume with occasional equivalent weight measurements, weight is really more accurate. Scales also can convert to and from metric weights. I use a scale almost every day. If you decide to buy one, make sure it's easy for you to read.

SHEET PANS AND COOKIE SHEETS: Those with $1/2$-inch sides (called *sheet pans* or *jelly-roll pans*) are essential in the kitchen for baking croutons, roulades, biscuits, breads, and so forth. Have at least two. You can also use them for cookies, even though proper cookie sheets don't have sides. Restaurant supply stores sell good, sturdy pans called *half-sheets* that fit into home ovens.

SPATULAS AND SPOONS: You'll want at least one big wide flat metal spatula for turning pancakes and lifting cookies off a pan and an offset spatula—one with a crook in it—for smoothing icings and batters without dragging your knuckles through them. Be sure to have a nylon spatula that won't scratch the surface of your nonstick pans. Wooden spoons stay cool in your hand and don't clang when they come into contact with metal pots, bowls, and pans. They're inexpensive, so you can have a lot of them in different sizes. Be sure to have one with a flat bottom for stirring sauces. Large metal spoons, especially one that's slotted, are also useful.

STEAMING BASKET: This inexpensive gadget fits into virtually any size pot—essential if you like to steam vegetables and other foods. There are fancier steaming units and Chinese bamboo steamers, but the basket is efficient and basic.

SPRING-LOADED TONGS: Tongs are a must. They work as an extension of your hand and are used for grilling, turning things in a pan, picking up items that won't balance on a spatula, and reaching over hot surfaces. They're also a handy household tool— great for reaching into hard-to-get-to corners. You can find tongs at restaurant supply stores; they range in size from 8 to 18 inches. A shorter pair is most useful in the kitchen; longer ones allow you to stand back from the smoke and heat of a grill.

SAUTÉ PANS AND FRYING PANS: You can cook virtually everything in these, and many meals for four to six can be cooked in a single 10- or 12-inch pan. American sauté pans have sloping sides and are popular with restaurant cooks. Frying pans and French sauté pans have straight sides and are heavier, not meant to be picked up. Having a skillet with a cover is helpful for slow cooking, where it's important to retain moisture. A 6- or 7-inch skillet is useful for tasks like toasting pine nuts, melting butter, or frying an egg.

TIMER: Even though you'll end up judging doneness by eye and touch, a timer helps free your mind so that you can turn to other tasks until its ring summons you back.

Basic Cooking Methods

Following are descriptions for the basic cooking methods you'll be using in all recipes.

BOILING: Boiling is a fast, efficient way to cook many things. You need a lot of water so that foods cook quickly without great loss of nutrients. A good boil means that large bubbles burble and break on the surface. Add salt just before you add your food, about 1 teaspoon to a quart, then add vegetables gradually enough to maintain the boil but not too slowly or the first to enter will be overcooked. Keep the pot uncovered so that sulfurous odors of the cabbage family can escape and the colors of green vegetables can stay bright. Taste the vegetables as they cook and drain them before they're fully done since they'll continue cooking in their own heat. Remember that at higher altitudes foods take longer to boil because the temperature of the water is lower.

BLANCHING OR PARBOILING: To soften a vegetable before going on to another step, to leach out bitterness, or to make skins easy to remove, vegetables are plunged into a pot of boiling water for a brief time. This is referred to as *blanching* or *parboiling.* Once they're blanched, the vegetables may be removed to a towel, rinsed under cold running water, or plunged into a bowl of ice water, a technique called *shocking,* to stop the cooking.

BRAISING: Braising is the slow cooking of vegetables in a small amount of water or vegetable stock. Aromatics may be added, and wine, vinegar, or lemon is sometimes included for the edge they provide and for their ability to keep tender vegetables firm. Often a vegetable base, such as diced carrots, onions, and celery, is cooked alongside the larger vegetables. Traditionally it's discarded at the end, but I always find it a nice addition to a dish, either as a garnish or pureed and used to thicken a sauce.

Braises can be made on top of the stove or in the oven. If a lot of juice remains, remove the lid and simmer until it's reduced to a thick sauce or a glaze. Toward the end you can add flavor by stirring in butter and fresh herbs.

BROILING: Cooking food under direct heat browns it. Quickly cooked foods, like sliced eggplant, tofu, or croutons, can be cooked through under the broiler, while longer-cooking foods are only finished there. Keep food between 4 and 6 inches from the heat source.

COOKING WITH ACIDULATED WATER: Water made acidic with lemon juice or vinegar prevents artichokes, celery root, Jerusalem artichokes, and salsify from discoloring. For acidulated water, add $1/4$ cup lemon juice or vinegar to 2 quarts water. To make a blanc, which mellows the taste of the lemon, add 1 tablespoon each flour and olive oil to the mixture.

DEEP FRYING: There's an art to frying, and in countries where it is practiced well the fried foods are light, not greasy. I have experimented with measuring the oil before and after frying foods and found that no more oil was absorbed in deep frying than if the same food had been shallow fried—and sometimes less.

A light, neutral vegetable oil, such as peanut, adds no taste to the food and heats to a high temperature before it begins to smoke—the temperature called the *smoke point*. Food fried in olive oil, as it is in Spain, is delicious. Use an oil with lots of flavor, but not your finest extra virgin. Here's how to deep-fry.

1. Use a heavy-bottomed deep skillet or pot so that the heat is well distributed and oil won't spatter—it does rise when you add ingredients. A cast-iron skillet or Dutch oven is ideal, as is a deep fryer.

2. Use enough oil so that the food floats rather than sits—and enough so that the oil retains its heat—the same thing you want from a pot of boiling water.

3. Hot oil is absorbed less than oil that is merely warm. It should be heated to just below the point where smoke begins to rise from the pan—look for a haze over the surface. Don't heat the oil until it's smoking since excessive heat breaks it down and it's risky to cook with. Temperatures differ for different oils, but they generally range between 370°F and 390°F. In lieu of using a thermometer, drop a piece of bread in the oil. It should brown and crisp in less than a minute.

4. To keep the oil hot and fried food light, add room-temperature food in small batches. Cold food brings the temperature down, and while the oil is reheating, it's being absorbed into the food. Make sure your food is dry—wet food spatters.

5. After frying, drain the food on paper towels or paper bags. Let the oil cool, then pour it through a coffee cone or paper towel. Afterward, store it in a wine bottle or other container in a cool, dark place. Oil that has been used for frying vegetables can be reused three or four times. Smell it before using it—to make sure that it's free of off odors.

GRILLING: Grilling seems to make all foods—especially vegetables—taste particularly good.

PUREEING: Whether making a soup, a puree of vegetables or cooked beans, or baby food, there are various tools for the job.

> **Immersion Blender:** This blender on a stick is easy to use: Simply immerse it in a pot of soup or vegetables and puree. A regular blender is also good for soups.

> **Food Mill:** This handy tool breaks up soft vegetables and forces them through the holes in the disk set in the bottom of the mill while strings, peels, seeds, and other hard-textured bits are left behind. It keeps purees light and doesn't overwork them.

> **Potato Masher:** Another old-fashioned tool—essentially a perforated disk or wire coil on a handle—that breaks down potatoes into a smooth puree without turning them gluey.

> **Food Processor:** Its fierce action turns potatoes to glue, but it works fine with some other vegetables, such as carrots and broccoli, quickly producing silken purees. You'll need to stop and scrape down the sides.

ROASTING AND BAKING: Roasting vegetables at high heat in an open pan glazes the surfaces, sears the bottoms, and gives them a rich, concentrated flavor. Baking is gentler than roasting, frequently using lower temperatures and a covered or uncovered dish. Always preheat the oven for at least 10 minutes.

SAUTÉING: Cooking vegetables in small amounts of hot oil over high heat, *sauté* refers to a method, a pan, and a kind of dish.

To sauté, use a large skillet with sloping sides that's light enough to pick up in one hand. Vegetables need plenty of room to move around so that they can brown and sear. Piled on top of each other, they'll merely steam. If using garlic, add it toward the end of the process so it doesn't burn.

First heat the pan, then add the oil. When it's hot, add the vegetables. Grasp the handle of the pan with one or both hands, then slide it back and forth, adding a jerk as you draw it toward you. This motion makes the vegetables jump in the pan so that they turn and new surfaces are exposed to the heat. When people watch line cooks working in a restaurant, they see a lot of this sliding/jerking action. It's not that hard to learn—though you'll undoubtedly lose a few onions in the process. If you can't master the pan action, use a wooden spoon or tongs to move the vegetables around in the pan. The motion needn't be continuous—there has to be some sustained contact with the pan for vegetables to brown.

Many low-fat cookbooks suggest sautéing in water instead of in oil, but water doesn't heat to the temperature fat does and it can't sear and add flavor. If any browning does occur, it's because the natural sugars have been drawn out and caramelized.

SIMMERING: When foods are simmered, it means that they're cooked at a gentle rather than a rolling boil.

STEAMING: Vegetables cooked over a small amount of water retain more nutrients, and the small amount of vitamin-rich water isn't difficult to incorporate into soups and sauces. Unlike boiling, steaming is always done with a lid. It is not the best method for green beans and peas, which lose their sparkle when steam condenses and drips back

OVEN TEMPERATURES

Very Slow	250°F or below	
Slow	300°F	
Moderately Slow	325°F	
Moderate	350°F	
Moderately Hot	375°F	
Hot	400°F	
Very Hot	425°F or higher	

Always preheat your oven for 10 to 20 minutes to allow it to come to the required temperature, unless otherwise indicated. The higher the temperature, the longer it takes to preheat the oven. If you're using a baking stone for pizza, bread, or other dishes, put it in a cold oven, and allow 25 to 30 minutes for it to heat through.

over them, but most other vegetables are good candidates for steaming, whether small and tender or large and dense.

Use a collapsible stainless-steel steaming basket that sits over boiling water. Sprigs of herbs, crushed seeds, and spices added to the water bathe the vegetables in a subtly perfumed steam—especially good with vegetables that absorb flavors well, like potatoes.

STIR-FRYING: Another type of sautéing that takes place at high temperature in a wok.

Cutting and Chopping Techniques

Slicing, dicing, chopping, and *mincing* are words that describe how we transform raw materials with a knife. Even though the shapes are very basic, how you cut them affects the whole feeling of a dish. Some people, including me, tend to cut things into small, precise pieces, while others use big, bold strokes. One way isn't better than the other. I'm always delighted when people make my recipes according to their own cutting inclinations. I often don't recognize the dish by its look, although I do recognize its taste, and sometimes I think it looks much better. You, too, will have your own approach, but in the meantime, here are explanations of cutting terms:

SLICED ONIONS, HALF-MOONS: Cut an onion in half through the root end, remove the skin, then lay it flat side down. With your knife aligned from the root end to the stem end, slice the onion into half-moons, following its curve. Thin slices are $^1/_8$ to $^1/_4$ inch thick, thick ones about $^1/_2$ inch thick.

DICED ONIONS: Lay the halved, peeled onion on a cutting board and slice into it horizontally, making parallel cuts. For a fine dice, make your cuts about $^1/_4$ inch apart; for a large dice, about $^1/_2$ inch apart. Make similar cuts going from the top down, then slice the onion crosswise. The squares of onion will fall away, completely diced.

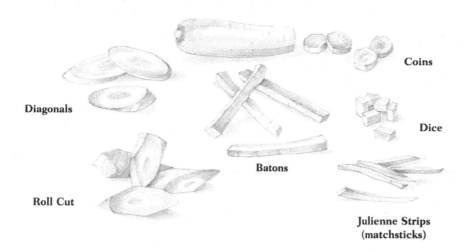

Coins

Diagonals

Dice

Batons

Roll Cut

Julienne Strips
(matchsticks)

COINS, MEDALLIONS, OR ROUNDS: For carrots, zucchini, and other long vegetables, slice them straight across in even parallel slices to produce coin-shaped pieces.

DIAGONAL SLICES: Slice long vegetables at an angle so that you'll end up with oblong pieces. The steeper the angle, the longer the slice. This technique is often used with Asian eggplants, carrots, asparagus, and zucchini.

ROLL CUT: This cutting technique, which yields substantial and interesting shapes, is used with long, thin vegetables: carrots, asparagus, skinny zucchini, and so on. First make a diagonal cut, then roll your vegetable between one-quarter and one-third around and make another cut. Repeat this rolling and cutting motion for the length of the vegetable.

JULIENNE STRIPS: These are long skinny shapes, like old-fashioned wooden matchsticks. Slice your vegetable, if it's a long one like a carrot, into long diagonals, then stack them up and slice them lengthwise into strips. Or cut your vegetable into lengths as long as you want your final piece to be, then cut the lengths into slabs as thick as you want them, then cut the slabs into strips. *Batons* are cut the same way, but into larger pieces that can be picked up and used for dipping or in stir-fries.

DICE: Cut vegetables into cubes between ⅓ and ½ inch across. You can do this as described for onions or make julienne strips or batons, then slice crosswise.

LARGE DICE: Squares ½ to 1 inch across.

FINE DICE: Squares about ¼ inch across.

MINCE: Usually used for garlic and ginger. Cut into very small, indistinct pieces by quickly moving your knife back and forth over the food.

CHOP: Basically the same as dice but without the implied precision of squares. A certain irregularity of shape and size is okay.

COARSE CHOP: Larger, more imprecise pieces—usually applies to vegetables that are going to be pureed.

SHREDDED: Usually applied to cabbage to be used in coleslaw or salad. Cut a cored wedge crosswise into thin slices with a knife to resemble shredded paper.

CHIFFONADE: Another term for fine strips, usually referring to leafy greens. Roll a number of leaves up together to make a "cigar," then slice them thinly crosswise. Make sure you cut all the way through so that the final strips aren't joined to each other.

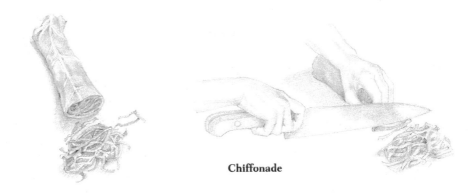

Chiffonade

High-Altitude Cooking

Having lived at an elevation of 7,000 feet for almost 10 years, I am familiar with the special set of conditions that the many people who live above 3,000 feet have to cook in. The higher the elevation, the lower the atmospheric pressure, which affects temperature, leavening, and the way foods behave.

TEMPERATURE: Each 500-foot increase in elevation means a drop of 1°F in the temperature at which water boils. If you vacation in the mountains, you may notice that your coffee never seems really hot or that foods takes longer to cook than you're used to. Hungry campers have all noticed this—watching a pot of spaghetti that boils energetically but doesn't seem to cook.

Anything that's boiled or steamed takes longer to cook at high altitude than it does at sea level. How long, exactly, is a matter of trial and error. You may have to boil a few eggs before you find out exactly how long it takes to cook them perfectly. In many instances it helps to use a pressure cooker, which raises the temperature of the boiling water and steam so that the timing is almost the same as pressure cooking at sea level.

BAKING TIPS: Angel food, sponge cakes, soufflés, and other air-leavened dishes soar in their pans, while butter cakes are a little more difficult to manage at high altitudes. Local extension services can provide you with tips that apply to your area, but it's helpful to keep a record of what changes you make in your normal routines so that you can, over time, understand what works best. In the meantime, here are some practical tips:

Oven Temperature: If you live higher than 3,000 feet, raise the oven temperature 25°F. The higher oven temperature helps to set the structure of fast-rising baked goods so that they won't fall.

Moisture: At high altitudes the air is very dry, so the flour is also dry and more absorbent. If you're baking bread, you may find that you can't incorporate all the flour called for. Adding oil or an extra egg to breads not only provides more liquid so that it can absorb more flour but also helps prevent dryness in a finished product. In cakes, increase liquid as follows:

3,000 to 5,000 feet, add 2 tablespoons liquid per cup called for

5,000 to 7,000 feet, add 3 tablespoons liquid per cup called for

over 7,000 feet, add 3 to 4 tablespoons liquid per cup called for

Leavenings and Sugar: While I adjust most ingredients more or less by feel, when it comes to leavenings, I keep the baking soda the same and reduce the baking powder and sugar as follows:

3,000 to 5,000 feet, reduce baking powder by ⅛ teaspoon; reduce sugar by 1 tablespoon per cup called for

5,000 feet and above, reduce baking powder by ¼ teaspoon; reduce sugar by 2 tablespoons per cup called for. To ensure stability in cakes, add 1 to 2 tablespoons additional flour.

When making cakes that are risen with beaten egg whites, beat the eggs a little less than you would at sea level so that the whites form only soft peaks.

Reducing yeast is optional unless you are baking large batches; then it's essential. Reducing the yeast by one-quarter to one-half the total amount results in a bread with a firmer, stronger texture. The full amount can give you a fluffy, airy bread, which may be disappointing. Yeast doughs tend to rise more quickly at higher altitudes.

Foundations of Flavor:
Seasonings in the Kitchen

WHEN WE PAUSE TO TAKE A CLOSER LOOK, WE DISCOVER THAT MANY OF THE BASIC INGREDIENTS WE USE EVERY DAY IN THE KITCHEN ARE MORE COMPLICATED THAN THEY APPEAR. VIRTUALLY ALL RECIPES CALL FOR SALT TO DEVELOP flavor, while just about as many ask for a bit of pepper to warm them up, yet there's far more to salt and pepper than just white and black powders. Oils and vinegars are both colorful and essential players in anyone's kitchen, while other ingredients, such as herbs, spices, and seasonings, provide the essential underpinnings of flavor that give a unique personality to a dish. Even more than vegetables themselves, it's these small, intensely flavored ingredients and how they're combined that give a culture's food its unique stamp. This is so true that certain combinations immediately signal to us the national origin of a dish—the lemon and oregano of Greece, for example. For the vegetarian cook especially, the importance of herbs, spices, and seasonings can't be overstated, and being familiar with basic ingredients and foundations of flavor is a tremendous advantage for any cook. Discerning their differences is what truly makes the difference between a so-so dish and one that's really good.

BASIC INGREDIENTS

It gets quite wordy to keep saying things like "1 medium onion, about 4 ounces, or 1 cup," or "1 cup milk, skim, low-fat, whole, or soy milk"—so in the recipes I just say "1 onion" or "1 cup milk." The rest, being a constant, is implied. When more specific information is needed, it's given—"1 large onion" or "1 cup milk, preferably whole milk." Here are some of the constants you can assume to be true throughout this book:

BUTTER means lightly salted or unsalted butter.

CAPERS are always drained and rinsed.

CREAM is referred to by different names in various parts of the country. Rather than attempting to accommodate each regional difference, I have limited myself to the word *cream* for light or heavy. If you live where creams are distinguished by the amount of butterfat and labeled accordingly, you will be familiar with their properties in cooking and be able to choose what will work best for your taste. If you're planning to whip cream, you should use "heavy" or "whipping" cream; light cream will not whip.

EGGS are large, preferably from flocks that are not given hormones or antibiotics and are not caged. Such eggs are usually labeled as such and are available at natural health food stores.

FLOUR, unless otherwise described, is all-purpose unbleached white or whole-wheat pastry flour.

GRATED CHEESE is assumed to be freshly grated. Parmesan is not Parmigiano-Reggiano unless its quality is necessary for taste, although it certainly could be used in any of the recipes. Never use the so-called Parmesan that comes in a green can or box.

MILK can be whole, low-fat, skim, or soy unless otherwise specified. I have used 1 percent milk in almost all recipes where milk is called for. Rice milk and almond milk should be used only where their sweetness is desired.

OLIVE OIL means a flavorful, full-bodied oil with the fruity aroma of olives, regardless of how it's labeled. Many relatively inexpensive oils called extra virgin impart their flavor to food when used in cooking. Your best estate-bottled extra virgin oil is to be used as a seasoning.

SALT means sea salt.

VEGETABLE OIL can be safflower, canola, light peanut oil (as opposed to roasted peanut oil), corn oil, sunflower seed, or light sesame.

VEGETABLES are assumed to be washed and trimmed, with bad parts discarded, and dried when appropriate.

1 CARROT means a medium or average one, weighing about 4 ounces, about 7 inches long. Carrots are peeled, unless fresh from the garden, then they're scrubbed.

1 GARLIC CLOVE, unless otherwise stated, is medium, neither from a super-large head nor from the center of the head.

1 ONION means a medium yellow onion, weighing 4 to 6 ounces, yielding about 1 cup chopped or sliced. Small onions weigh about 3 ounces, large ones about 8 ounces and sometimes more.

Herb- and Vegetable-Based Seasonings

AROMATICS: This bundle of herbs, also known as a *bouquet garni,* consists most commonly of parsley sprigs, a bay leaf, and a few thyme sprigs tied with string or gathered in a cheesecloth bag. (I just put them into the dish loose most of the time and fish them out before serving.) Bouquet garni is used to flavor soups, braises, stews, and many other dishes. I usually make mine rather generous—8 long, full branches of parsley, 4 to 6 brushy sprigs of thyme, and 2 small bay leaves—and add any other herb that's appropriate to the dish, such as a sprig of tarragon if tarragon is called for in the recipe, and so forth.

FINES HERBES: This is a classic mixture of chopped fresh herbs, usually parsley, chervil, tarragon, and chives. Use it to season vegetable sautés and braises, beans, butter, and egg dishes of all kinds. It consists of the following herbs in more or less this proportion.

¼ cup parsley leaves

1 tablespoon chervil leaves

2 teaspoons tarragon leaves

2 teaspoons finely sliced chives

Chop the parsley, chervil, and tarragon leaves together, then add the chives. Chopped watercress, grated lemon zest, and minced garlic expand this herbal collection very nicely. When chervil is unavailable, which is most of the time, increase the tarragon to a tablespoon.

PERSILLADE: Use 1 plump garlic clove to about ¼ cup parsley leaves—or more as suits the dish or your taste for garlic. Chop them together, preferably at the last minute, then scatter over hot foods for the full effect of both ingredients. Try it with sautéed mushrooms and artichokes, fried eggplant, grilled vegetables, and warm beans. Persillade is often just described in a recipe as 1 clove garlic chopped with 3 to 4 tablespoons parsley.

GREMOLATA: Add the grated or chopped zest of ½ lemon to the persillade.

Butter

Butter is a big part of our culinary tradition, a taste we are used to, recognize, and like. Being an animal product *and* a fat has made it something of a pariah, but there are ways to use butter intelligently. You can cook with a mixture of butter and oil or simply use it where it counts most. For example, make your muffins with oil, then eat them with butter on top, where the flavor is clearly discerned and appreciated.

American butter used to be salted to preserve it, but today salt is added to give it flavor. However, many people prefer the delicacy of lightly salted or unsalted (or sweet) butter. I prefer to use unsalted or lightly salted butter and add salt to food separately, but if you haven't any on hand, you can certainly make do with salted as I often do.

Butter contains some water, fat, and milk solids. Most butter is 80 percent butterfat, but European-style premium butters are slightly higher—82 percent. Some small organic dairies are producing American-made premium butters. Plugra, a brand whose name means "more fat" in relation to water, is available to the restaurant industry and can be found in better groceries around the country. These butters are so sweet and delicious that if you're a moderate person, a little is truly satisfying. But if your love of butter is immoderate, watch out! When you melt higher-fat butter, you will see it's very clear and pure, with little separation of water and milk solids. Reduced-fat or so-called light butter is extra-watery—you can see that when you melt it. Because its fat content is so low, it should never be used in baking.

Keep the larger part of an unused pound of butter in the freezer, particularly if it's unsalted. Always wrap butter well. Like all fats, it picks up odors from other foods like a sponge. Good butter should smell sweet and pure.

CLARIFIED BUTTER: Clarifying is the simple process of melting butter so that you can separate the fat from the milk solids. It's the solids that burn, so if you want to fry in butter, clarifying is necessary.

Cut the butter into chunks, put it in a small, heavy pan, and melt it over low heat. When the foam has risen to the top and the milk solids have fallen to the bottom, turn off the heat. Skim off the foam, then pour the butter carefully through a strainer lined with cheesecloth. Or decant it by eye, leaving the solids behind in the pan. One stick or 8 tablespoons butter will yield 5 to 6 tablespoons clarified. It keeps, refrigerated, almost indefinitely.

FLAVORED CLARIFIED BUTTER: Taking advantage of fat's ability to absorb flavors, add a bay leaf, thyme sprigs, crushed peppercorns or cumin seeds, red pepper flakes, or other herbs and spices to the melting butter. Strain them out before storing.

GHEE: Once the butter has melted, lower the heat even more and continue cooking until there's a crusty covering on top, the butter beneath is perfectly clear and deep gold, and the milk solids are light brown, 40 minutes to 1 hour. Ghee provides Indian cooking with one of its distinctive flavors.

BROWN BUTTER: Cook the butter longer still, until the milk solids are browned and the butter is brown rather than gold. The aroma should be toasty and nutty. Brown butter is delicious on many vegetables and can be used in baking.

FLAVORED BUTTERS: See the "Sauces and Condiments" chapter for recipes for flavored butters and butter sauces.

A WORD IN FAVOR OF FAT

In spite of our struggles with it, fat is one of our most important ingredients when it comes to making food taste good—and right. (If you're used to cooking eggs in butter, they won't taste *right* when cooked in olive oil, as any homesick traveler knows.) Fat both contributes and carries flavor. It also provides a certain voluptuous sensation in the mouth that makes us feel satisfied when we encounter it. Most of the metaphorical language associated with fat throughout history is positive; fat has been both good and, until recently, comparatively rare. Today perhaps it is far too plentiful, but we need enough fat in our diet to use fat-soluble vitamins, to make hormones, and to keep our immune systems in good order.

Because fat is simultaneously important and troublesome, it's essential that we use those fats that give us the greatest measure of satisfaction. A highly refined, tasteless oil has the same number of calories and fat grams as a rich-tasting roasted peanut oil, a redolent nut oil, a fruity olive oil, or the sweetest butter. The true flavor of good oil or butter satisfies in a way that tasteless foods don't, and in smaller amounts. In every respect, good-quality fats are worth their higher cost.

Capers and Caper Berries

The pickled buds of the Mediterranean caper bush provide small tart nuggets of flavor in vinaigrettes and sauces of melted butter. Typically they're found jarred in a vinegar solution (give them a rinse before using), but those that come packed in salt are the best; soak them in a few changes of tepid water to get rid of their saltiness. Caper berries are extremely big, plump capers with their stem attached. They make a dramatic and pungent garnish on a composed salad plate or plate of hors d'oeuvres.

Cheese

Cheese, more than many other foods, relates to place and traditon. As with wine, the characteristics of different cheeses are determined by climate and geography, season, aging, tradition, and the cheesemaker's personal style of crafting this unique food. The endlessly varied and fascinating world of cheese offers many pleasures for the palate. If you are loath to give up such an interesting and satisfying food, here are some ways to fit cheese into today's general guidelines for healthier eating.

- Don't serve rich cheeses for appetizers, when people are hungry and ready to dive into food—they're too filling and they can't be savored as well then as they can later in the meal.

- Enjoy cheese as a course in itself for dessert, with fruit, or with a salad. Or use cheese as an element that enriches the flavor of a dish—the classic veiling of good Parmesan on a pasta, for example.

- Always serve cheese at room temperature when its flavor and texture are at their best. Cold cheese is missing most of its essence. Neutral-tasting breads and crackers allow the nuances of the cheese to be enjoyed rather than covered, but some specialty breads, such as walnut bread, beautifully complement particular cheeses, such as aged Cheddar, mature goat cheese, or creamy triple cream.

- True gustatory pleasure is satisfying in itself, and low-fat remakes of classic dishes lack the soul of the original. When cheese is a featured ingredient, as in pasta with Gorgonzola, use the real thing and the full amount, but place the dish more judiciously—as a first course, say, rather than the main event. A fine cheese can make a dish memorable.

CHEESE ALTERNATIVES: There are now quite a few nondairy cheese substitutes on the market. They're made mainly from soy milk, along with Irish moss (seaweed), tapioca, rice, oats, oil, spices, seasonings, and other ingredients. Most use calcium caseinate, a protein derived from cow's milk, to make them stretchy and elastic, but that keeps them from being acceptable to vegans. While some may use these cheeses to avoid cholesterol and fat, even the conservative *Vegetarian Journal* points out that most cheeses are not that high in cholesterol anyway and that the fat content of cheese alternatives keeps them out of the heart-healthy ballpark. As for taste and texture, they don't taste like cheese, and they don't melt well.

Chiles

Many people crave the rush that comes from eating hot foods, but you don't have to be a chile head to enjoy chile. Even small amounts give an exciting warmth and tingle to the tongue. Today, we have a vast vocabulary of chiles to cook with, from chipotles to cayenne to tiny but ferociously hot Thai bird peppers. Chiles have been written about extensively in the last few years, and would-be aficionados should refer to more extensive sources to learn more about chiles. Meanwhile, here are some tips on working with chiles.

The veins and seeds, which contact each other in the pod, are the hottest parts of the chile. If you don't want the optimum amount of heat, shake out the seeds and slice off the veins. If you plan to be handling a lot of chile and you're not accustomed to it, put on a pair of rubber gloves. I never do, and I've never had a problem—or one that didn't go away quickly—but people vary in sensitivity to the volatile chile oils, so caution is always wise. At the very least, avoid touching your eyes, nose, and mouth when your fingers are covered with chile oils—whether they're gloved or not.

Before being used, dried chiles are toasted in a pan over low heat, roasted in a slow oven, or they're covered with boiling water to soften, then pureed in a blender, depending on their intended use. Whether you use chile ground or whole, take care not to burn it by adding it to too hot a pan, for once burned it turns bitter. And stand back when you add chile to the pot or grind it, for the rising mist of volatile oils can make you cough a lot.

Ground or whole, chile eventually loses its potency, so don't buy so much that you'll have it around for years. A year is its optimum shelf life. New Mexican chile farmers tell me that they store their ground chile in the refrigerator, not the freezer, to preserve its life.

PAPRIKA: We forget that paprika is, in fact, chile. Readily available, the best is from Hungary, where it's the national seasoning. Paprika is labeled "hot" or "sweet," reflecting the basic flavor components of the pepper used. Not just something to sprinkle on deviled eggs for color, paprika is a warm and delicious seasoning to use in more generous amounts.

GROUND RED CHILE, NEW MEXICAN CHILE: This is simply dried finely ground New Mexican chile pods without any additions. (Chili powder is a blend of chile, spices, and powdered garlic.) Paprika and cayenne, also ground red chiles, may be used when ground red chile is called for in small amounts, but their flavors will differ from that of New Mexican red chile.

CHIPOTLE CHILES: This smoked jalapeño chile comes packed in adobo sauce, dried, or ground. Chipotle chile combines the hot, smoky, and sweet chile essence in one ingredient and makes an excellent seasoning for soups, sauces, and salsas—but it is hot. You can temper its heat by mixing it with pureed or ground guajillo chiles. Whether in sauce or dried, if you grind it into a puree or powder first, it's easier to use in small quantities. The powder is great on fried eggs if you like your eggs "from hell." Chipotles can be found at Mexican groceries, supermarkets, and fancy food shops.

RED PEPPER FLAKES: These crushed dried red chiles with seeds add that edge of heat and spice to many dishes without turning them into hot food. Add a few pinches to warming oil to release their flavor. Pepper flakes should be red. If they're brownish, they're old and should be thrown out.

CAYENNE: Cayenne is the name of the small hot red chile ground for cayenne powder. As with all hot chiles, add it in small increments until you find the right amount.

SMALL DRIED RED PEPPERS: There are many kinds—chile pequín, bird peppers, árbol, and so on. The general rule is, the smaller the chile, the hotter its bite. Add them whole to a dish or, for more heat, break them in two first. Remember, the seeds and veins are the hottest parts of the chile. Take them out or not, as you dare.

Chutneys

A wide range of Indian chutneys are available at natural food stores as well as Indian and Asian markets. Lime, eggplant, mango, and others add a fillip to an otherwise simple curry and keep for months in the refrigerator. Read the labels carefully. Some are loaded with chemicals and taste that way. Recipes for homemade chutneys are in "Sauces and Condiments."

Citrus Fruit

Zest and Juice

The outer skin of citrus fruit is called the *zest*. The perfumed, volatile oils of the fruit reside in the zest rather than the juice. An inexpensive tool called a *zester* removes thin shreds of zest in moments. You can also remove it in strips with a vegetable peeler, then mince it with a knife, or grate the fruit on the fine holes of a grater. I usually pull the zest off with a zester, then chop it. I don't try to get it too fine because I enjoy biting into a bit of orange or lemon, but you may prefer to chop yours very finely. Just avoid taking up the white pith beneath the zest since it tends to be bitter, and be sure to use clean fruit.

The acid nip of lemon and lime juice often brings everything into balance at the end of preparing a dish. Bottled lemon and lime juices simply don't taste good; the added chemicals come through. Use freshly squeezed juice instead. To get the most juice out of a lemon or lime, press down on it while rolling it back and forth on the counter, then juice it. A good juicy lemon contains $1/4$ cup juice; a lime, 1 to 2 tablespoons.

Peeling and Sectioning Citrus Fruit

To neatly peel an orange or a grapefruit for salads, compotes, and desserts, first take two slices off the polar ends so that the fruit will stand. Then, using a very sharp, small knife, begin cutting in a zigzag motion down the side, from top to bottom, removing a strip of skin and the white pith that lies beneath it. You'll have to really angle your knife at the top and bottom. Continue this motion around the entire fruit until it's peeled, then pick it up in your hand and cut away any pith you missed. At this point you can slice the fruit into rounds or sections.

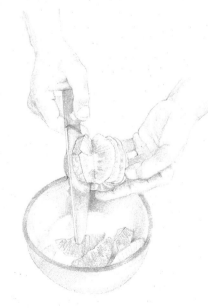

To section an orange or a grapefruit, hold the peeled fruit firmly in your hand over a bowl. You'll see the edges of the membranes that separate the sections facing you; they look like white lines. Slide your knife downward, as close to the membrane as you can get, then do the same on the opposite side of the same section of fruit. When the cuts meet at the bottom, the fruit section will slide away into the bowl. Repeat this with the remaining sections. When done, squeeze the juice from what's left into the bowl.

Coconut Milk

Fragrant, naturally sweet coconut milk gives body to the sauces of Thai and Indian dishes. Most supermarkets now carry at least one brand, but Asian markets usually have many brands from all over East Asia. Avoid coconut milk that's labeled "sweetened." This is used only for making mixed drinks. Like cow's milk, coconut milk separates, with the thick "cream" floating to the top. You can lift the cream off and use it to garnish a dish or shake the can so that milk and cream are blended. *Light* coconut milk, like skim milk, is lacking the cream.

Crème Fraîche

Although it doesn't perfectly duplicate the true flavor of the French version, this crème fraîche doesn't curdle when added to soups and sauces, and it's more delicately flavored than many commercial sour creams. It's a real treat when made with fresh cream that hasn't been ultrapasteurized.

To make 1 cup crème fraîche, stir together 1 cup cream and 1 teaspoon buttermilk. Cover and set in a draft-free place for 24 hours. By then it should be set and ready to use, but even if it's a little wobbly, it will continue to thicken in the refrigerator, where it should be stored. Crème fraîche keeps for about 2 weeks.

Croutons and Bread Crumbs

Homemade croutons and bread crumbs make good use of bread that might otherwise be discarded. Small croutons, either thin slices or cubes to float on soups or are tossed in salads. Larger ones can serve as a base for savory toppings, as in crostini and bruschette. Fresh bread crumbs coat foods that are to be fried or add a crunchy cover to gratins. Dried bread crumbs add body and substance to a filling or a timbale. Crisped bread crumbs add textural interest to pasta, polenta, and vegetable sautés.

CROUTONS: Slice baguettes, sourdough, or country-style bread about ¼ inch thick. Place on a sheet pan and bake at 375°F until crisp and golden. Small croutons can be floated in a soup, larger ones broken in half, set in the bottom of a soup plate, and covered with soup. Either can be tucked into the leaves of a salad.

GARLIC-RUBBED CROUTONS: You can, if you wish, brush the croutons first with olive oil or melted butter and rub them with a halved clove of garlic when they emerge from the oven.

CRISPED CROUTONS: Remove the crust and cut the bread into small cubes. Toss with melted butter or olive oil to coat lightly, then spread on a sheet pan and toast in a moderate oven until crisp and lightly colored, 10 to 15 minutes. Or crisp them in a skillet over medium heat, stirring often so that they cook evenly. You can also toast them without the fat if preferred.

SEASONED CROUTONS: While still warm, toss crisped croutons with sea salt and pepper, a little lemon juice, chopped thyme, savory, or marjoram, or spices, such as ground red chile, paprika, curry powder, or toasted cumin or fennel seeds.

BREAD CRUMBS: Japanese bread crumbs, sold at Asian markets or even your own supermarket, are free of chemicals (unlike American brands) and are crisp and white. They make a visually exciting, crunchy coating for fried foods, such as croquettes of risotto or vegetables. Other than these, I generally make my own as follows.

Fresh Bread Crumbs: Remove the crusts, tear bread into large pieces, and work in a food processor or blender until the crumbs are as fine as you want. Store extra in the freezer in an airtight container. One slice sandwich bread yields ½ cup loosely packed crumbs.

Dried Bread Crumbs: Lay bread slices on a sheet pan and set in the oven at 200°F until they're dry, crisp, and golden, 30 to 45 minutes. Let cool, then grind in a food processor until fine. They will keep for weeks in an airtight container. Two slices bread yield a scant ½ cup bread crumbs.

Crisped Bread Crumbs: Toss fresh bread crumbs in enough melted butter or olive oil to coat lightly, about 2 tablespoons for 1 cup crumbs. Fry in a skillet over medium heat, stirring frequently, until golden and crisp, 5 to 7 minutes, or toast in a 350°F oven until golden, about 10 minutes. Stir every few minutes so that they brown evenly.

Picada: A lively seasoning of fried bread, almonds, and garlic, picada is used in Spanish dishes as a thickener and flavoring. Picada is also a good addition to pasta and plain vegetables.

To make ½ cup picada, toast ¼ cup peeled almonds in a 350°F oven until they're pale gold, 8 to 10 minutes. Remove and set aside. Meanwhile, slowly fry one slice of white country-style bread in 2 tablespoons olive oil until golden on both sides. Grind the bread, almonds, and 2 large garlic cloves and pinch of salt in a food processor to make a crumbly paste.

HERB-SCENTED BREAD CRUMBS: These simple bread crumbs can add so much to pasta or vegetables. Try them tossed with spaghetti or with simply prepared asparagus, steamed potatoes, sautéed corn, and roasted squash.

To make approximately 1¾ cups, toss 1½ cups fresh bread crumbs with enough olive oil to moisten, about 2 tablespoons, then toast in a skillet over medium-high heat until crisp and golden. Remove the crumbs to a plate. Add another tablespoon olive oil to the pan along with 1 tablespoon chopped garlic, 3 tablespoons chopped sage, rosemary, thyme, or marjoram. Sauté just until the garlic begins to color, and stir in the bread crumbs. Season to taste with salt, pepper, and ½ teaspoon sherry vinegar.

Curry Seasonings

CURRY POWDER: Authentic Indian recipes call for combinations of spices that best complement a given dish, making each one unique rather than tasting of the same seasoning. If you're into Indian cooking you'll undoubtedly be using Indian cookbooks and composing your spice mixtures as you go. If you're just using a curry powder to season a sauce, however, prepared curry powders are fine. Look for good ones at Indian markets and buy small amounts so that they don't turn stale.

CURRY PASTES: Prepared red, green, and yellow Thai curry pastes of fine quality can be purchased at Asian markets and natural food and specialty stores. A spoonful mixed into unsweetened coconut milk makes an instant sauce for tofu, noodles, rice, or a stir-fry.

GARAM MASALA: This mixture of warm spices is usually added as a seasoning at the end of an Indian dish rather than at the start. Since garam masala can be a little more difficult to find than good prepared curry powder, here is a general recipe. (For the most fragrant powder, start with whole spices and toast them.)

Put 1 tablespoon cardamom seeds, 1 tablespoon coriander seeds, 2½ teaspoons cumin seeds, 1¼ teaspoons black peppercorns, and ½ teaspoon whole cloves in a small dry skillet over low heat. Sliding the pan back and forth so that they don't burn, toast them until they smell fragrant, after a few minutes. Let cool, then grind in a spice grinder until powdered. Remove to a bowl. Grind one 3-inch cinnamon stick as fine as you can, then sift it, through a fine strainer, into the bowl. Grate in ½ whole nutmeg or add ¾ teaspoon ground to the bowl.

Edible Flowers

SOME FLAVORFUL EDIBLE FLOWERS
Arugula • Borage • Calendula • Chive • Daylily • Hyssop • Lavender • Marigold • Mint • Nasturtium • Rose • Rosemary • Sage • Squash and zucchini • Thyme • Violet

A salad with a confetti of flowers is undeniably charming, as is an herb butter laced with spicy nasturtiums or candied rose petals and violets on a cake. More than mere decoration, some flowers convey the flavor of the host plant, especially herbs. They're also serviceable; certainly many people have eaten stuffed squash blossoms, scarcely thinking of them as flowers. Though decorative, many edible flowers don't contribute much taste. My own preference is for those blossoms that contribute flavor or are an obvious part of the plant to use, such as arugula or sage that's in bloom.

Choose unsprayed garden blossoms and shake them gently to knock out any small insects. Float or swish them back and forth in a bowl of water, then shake dry. Separate those that grow in a cluster at the base, like chive blossoms. Pluck off petals of flowers like calendulas and marigolds. Unless they're small to begin with, finely slice, chop, or tear the blossoms. While pretty, a large flower or petal really isn't all that pleasant to eat.

Galangal

A form of Thai ginger that's sold in dry, hard rounds resembling wood chips, galangal is used as a warm, aromatic flavoring for soups and stews.

Herbs

Over time the word *herb* has referred to a wide range of plants, including salad greens, spice-bearing shrubs and trees, and medicinal as well as culinary plants. In today's common usage *herb* refers mostly to plants whose uses are culinary or medicinal. The line that divides herbs and spices is a wavy one, but generally herbs are leafy and associated with savory foods, while spices are dry and hard—seeds, berries, and barks—and suggest an alliance with sweet and pungent foods. Sometimes a plant provides both herb and spice, as in the case of coriander: the green leaf is the herb, called *cilantro;* the seed is the spice, called *coriander.*

Through travel, plain curiosity, and the arrival of new populations to our shores, the American repertoire of herbs and spices continues to grow.

Fresh Herbs or Dried?

Fresh herbs are the greatest joy to cook with. As your hands move through their leaves, the air around you fills with their scents. Their flavors are alive, their leaves and flowers varied and charming. However, dried herbs are often a necessary stand-in. Because the flavor-bearing volatile oils concentrate as the water in the leaves evaporates, dried herbs are usually considered more potent. The rule of thumb for dried herbs is to use a third of the fresh amount. I find this is true, however, only if the herbs were dried recently, so unless that's the case I generally use half. When using dried herbs, crumble some between your fingers to release the aromatic oils, then inhale to see how much aroma there is. If it's big and bold, use the conservative amount. If not, use more. When cooking with dried herbs, add them at the beginning of the process; fresh herbs, which are more volatile, are generally more effective added at the end.

Not all herbs dry successfully. Chervil, parsley, and cilantro turn flat and grassy when dried, whereas basil, sage, tarragon, and marjoram hold their flavors rather well.

Dried herbs are always preferable in their whole or cut leaf form, for powdered versions quickly lose their potency. Crushing, rubbing, pounding, or even powdering the leaves between your fingers or in a mortar is important for releasing their flavors. This is true of fresh herbs as well.

BUYING AND STORING HERBS: Fresh herbs usually come in sealed plastic bags, and depending on the herb, they'll keep well left in them and refrigerated, washed, if at all, just before using. Store dried herbs in their tightly covered jars in the cupboard and plan to replace them yearly or sooner if they've lost their punch. If you've had dried herbs for a long time, throw them out and start over. The same is true for spices and mixtures like curry powders.

A Lexicon of Herbs

BASIL: Flirting with anise and other flavor hues, basil is the main ingredient of pesto, the constant companion of tomatoes, *the* herb of summer. The type we use most is the Italian culinary variety, Genovese, but there are others with complex shadings of curry, cinnamon, and lemon. Opal basil has the classic aroma, but the leaves are a rich burgundy. Basil goes well with virtually all summer vegetables and even some fruits, like peaches. Keep it well wrapped in paper towels, then in a plastic bag in the vegetable bin of the refrigerator. Unless well protected, it will blacken and wilt.

BAY LEAF: Used dried, or fresh should you have a bay laurel tree, this leaf is important for laying down a strong, deep aromatic base to soups and stews. Where many herbs and vegetables are sweet, bay leaves are pungent, deep, sober, authoritative. Imported bay leaves—Turkish ones are my favorite—from the *Laurus nobilis* are the leaves to use, not California bay, which are fiercely aggressive. Heating a bay leaf in olive oil before sautéing flavors the oil (and scents the kitchen), as does dropping one into a pot of boiling water waiting for artichokes.

CHERVIL: A delicate, leafy green herb, favored in French cuisine and one of the fines herbes, chervil, with its flavors of parsley and anise, makes a refined addition to salads, creamy soups, leeks, and egg dishes. Parsley is often suggested as a substitute, but parsley chopped with fennel greens makes a closer flavor approximation. In the end, chervil stands uniquely alone. Because it dries poorly, fresh is the only way to use it. It's also best added at the last minute, for its subtle flavor quickly disappears when cooked.

CHIVES: These greens bring a leafy version of onion (or garlic if using garlic chives) to vegetables, salads, eggs, cheese, and soups. Snip them with scissors or slice them neatly straight across—chopping merely mangles them. Use chives fresh and add them at the end of cooking. The clusters of purple blossoms can be detached at the base and used as a garnish. Garlic chives are slightly larger, flatter, and perfumed with garlic.

Cilantro

Parsley

Lovage

CILANTRO (CHINESE PARSLEY, FRESH CORIANDER): Now firmly present in America, cilantro is an "in your face" herb, the herb that people either love or hate. While I love it, I sympathize with those who don't, because once present in a dish, it's virtually impossible to disguise. The seed form, coriander, isn't nearly as potent. If you crush and inhale the two side by side, you can detect the thread of scent that links them. In a pinch, coriander can partially replace the fresh herb, but not the other way around. Cilantro provides the warm, spicy, distinctive flavor in Asian, Mexican, and Indian cooking.

DILL: Everyone knows dill and its familiar sunny perfume. The feathery green leaves and the flat seeds contribute much the same flavor. Associated with Scandinavian cooking, potatoes, beets, carrots, and yogurt sauces, dill also combines in a most interesting way with parsley, cilantro, and basil, a mix called *sabzi,* used in Afghanistan and the eastern Mediterranean.

EPAZOTE: This semiwild herb is favored in New Mexico as well as Mexico and Central and South American countries. It's frequently used with beans for both its flavor and its legendary power to make them more digestible. Its smell is unappealing when raw, but it softens with cooking, leaving a lingering flavor whose subtle presence makes an important difference. Epazote grows on you.

LEMON BALM: Soft and gentle both in the garden and in the teapot, lemon balm makes a delicate herb tea and a good addition to salads of greens and herbs. Lemon verbena is another lemon-scented herb, this one with clear, sparkly flavor. The leaves, finely sliced or chopped, make a distinctive addition to fruit and lettuce salads and an exquisite infusion for tea or ice cream.

LOVAGE: An herb that resembles giant flat-leaf parsley, lovage has a bright and bracing flavor similar to celery, only wilder—like wild celery, in fact. An approximation can be made by mixing celery leaves and flat-leaf parsley. Lovage is wonderful with potatoes, tomatoes, and corn and torn into salads, but it needs to be handled judiciously for it's bold and assertive. A few leaves are ample for any recipe. Its hollow stems make a perfect straw for Bloody Marys or tomato juice. One plant will supply your neighborhood.

MARJORAM: Marjoram is another sweet summer herb. I use it as often as basil and frequently in its place (though about two-thirds as much) since it harmonizes with the same foods. Although often compared to its cousin oregano, marjoram is a great deal sweeter and more aromatic, without the resinous tones of oregano.

MINT: There are so many kinds, including chocolate, but I stick with the more classic culinary varieties—spearmint, peppermint, and orange bergamot. Mint goes into salads and vegetable dishes more often than you might guess, and, of course, it makes a wonderful tea. Dried mint is surprisingly flavorful and can be used successfully in place of fresh.

OREGANO: Except for true Greek oregano, which is hard to find fresh, I think this is one herb that gains in flavor when it's dried. Oregano's soul mate is lemon, and in Greek cooking the two are often juxtaposed. Mexican oregano, a different plant from the European cultivar, is stronger, more resinous and aggressive. It's very good in Mexican dishes, especially with beans. Toasting dried oregano leaves briefly in a dry pan brings out richer flavor notes.

PARSLEY: Parsley has become so ubiquitous we sometimes forget it's an herb, not a garnish. Robust and earthy, parsley has a clean bright flavor that infuses stocks, soups, and stews with unparalleled depth. Parsley can be enjoyed quite in its own right, as the primary ingredient of parsley salads. The flat-leaf varieties tend to be more flavorful than the curly and are easy to find. Dried parsley has a grassy taste and no merit. Parsley root or Hamburg parsley—the vegetable version of parsley—is very good eating when grated into salads, added to soups, or chopped into stews.

CHOPPING PARSLEY

Mud and sand often are hidden in the leaves, especially in the folds of curly parsley leaves, so a good washing is important. Vigorously swish the parsley bunch around in a large bowl of water, run your fingers through the leaves, then rinse the stems. If the water is muddy, fill the bowl with fresh water and repeat. Still keeping the bunch intact, dry it in a salad spinner. (It's impossible to sprinkle wet parsley, and wringing it dry in a towel rids it of much of its flavor and nutrients.) Grasp the dried bunch by the stems, tilt the head downward toward the cutting board, and shave off the leaves with a sharp knife. Or pluck them off by hand. (Be sure to save the stems for vegetable stocks.) Pick out the larger remaining stems, but don't worry about the rest. Using a chef's knife, start chopping. As you work, keep dragging the leaves that migrate to the edge back into the middle of the board with your knife so that all is evenly chopped. Cover chopped parsley with a damp paper towel and refrigerate until you need it. Although it's best used within a few hours, you can keep it overnight, covered with a damp towel inside a covered container in the refrigerator.

ROSEMARY: Strong, with the potential to overwhelm, rosemary is fresh in the summer, but its taste harmonizes well with winter foods, such as roasted vegetables, white beans, and split peas. In summer its long sticklike branches can serve as skewers for vegetables. Throw some, fresh or dried, on the grill to make an appetite-enticing aromatic smoke.

SAGE: Associated with stuffings and often thought of as a wintery, musty-tasting herb— old powdered sage is indeed a musty item—in its fresh form sage has a delicate taste with clear tones of mint. Fresh sage leaves enhance many foods that we tend to associate more with herbs like basil and marjoram, such as asparagus, corn, and peas. It also has a striking affinity for winter squash and pumpkin. Fresh sage leaves, used alone or mixed with chamomile, make a soothing, minty tea. Pineapple sage has scarlet, pineapple-perfumed flowers and leaves that can go right into salads. Float morsels of crisp fried sage leaves in soups—especially white bean or pumpkin soups—crumble them over roasted squash and onion dishes, or insert a few into a grilled Fontina sandwich. The sage family is large and eccentric, and not all of it is suitable for cooking. Be careful of wild sages, especially the artemisias—they can be bitter.

SALAD BURNET: A pretty perennial herb that you'll have to plant since stores don't carry it, salad burnet has the distinct flavor of cucumbers. Young sprigs are lovely tossed in a salad or paired with cucumbers in a sandwich.

SAVORY: So closely associated with fresh beans that it's nicknamed the bean herb, savory (both the annual summer and perennial winter varieties) is compatible with other vegetables, too. Like thyme, it lends an earthy note to vegetables that's grounding, rather than sunny and bright, the way marjoram and basil are.

SORREL: The large, soft leaves suggest none of the acidic surprise they give the tongue. Sorrel's bright, lemony tartness is perfect paired with eggs and potatoes. It wakes them right up. Sorrel leaves literally melt into a puree when heated in a pan with a little butter, making a more or less instant sauce. A cup of leaves disappears into little more than a few teaspoons, so it pays to have a few plants in the garden if you like sorrel. If you're buying them packaged for a salad, examine the leaves carefully to make sure they haven't begun to disintegrate in the dampness of the packaging.

SORREL PUREE

Using 4 cups or about 5 ounces of sorrel leaves, if the leaves are large or coarse, pull the stems down the entire length of the leaves and discard them. Coarsely chop the leaves. Melt 2 tablespoons butter in a skillet over medium heat. Add the leaves with a few tablespoons water and cook for 6 to 8 minutes, pushing them about with a fork to break them up. Add more water, as needed, so that they don't fry. Season with a pinch of salt and store in a covered container in the refrigerator. Makes about ¼ cup. Use over a period of several weeks.

TARRAGON: French tarragon is full of the pungent licorice-lemon flavor that goes so well with mushrooms and potatoes, vinegars and vinaigrettes, and eggs. Tarragon is so distinctive that I find it difficult to pair with any other herb except parsley and chives. After years of romancing the new basils, lovage, and other exotics, I've recently rediscovered tarragon and found it to be a delightful addition to my repertoire.

THYME: One of the essential herbs practically around the world, thyme is included in many recipes for its mostly earthy nature. Whole sprigs can be added to soups and stews, or the leaves can be plucked off the stems, then chopped. Lemon thyme provides a little of the uplifting aroma of citrus and makes a delicious infusion to drink as tea. There are many varieties of thyme that hint of this and that perfume, but in the end basic culinary thyme is most useful in the kitchen. Fortunately, fresh thyme from the market holds up well, but I can't imagine cooking without a border of these aromatic, low-growing shrubs close by.

Nuts and Seeds

Nuts have long played an important part in our diet. Only recently—and mostly in the United States—have we spurned them for being too fatty, but vegetarians in particular should keep in mind that they are a good source of protein. Recent studies have revealed that they are filled with nutrients essential to a healthy diet. They have far more fiber than chips, far less saturated fat than cheese, and the same fatty acids found in fish oil. The health benefits of eating nuts should let everyone relax and enjoy these foods, not only as tasty morsels but in their other forms—nut butters, peanut sauces, moles, tahini, coconut milk, and almond milk.

Because of their high oil content, nuts and seeds quickly turn rancid unless properly cared for. Not only is rancid oil harmful, but it just doesn't taste good. Rancidity can be detected by its off smell when cold, and its fishy smell when heated, and stale taste.

Nuts in their shells are least likely to be rancid because they are naturally protected from the oil-corrupting influences of light and air. While cracking nuts may be viewed as impractical in today's fast-paced world, it makes a pleasant fall or winter evening's activity. A bowl left on the counter provides a healthy nibble for anyone who wants to pause for a few minutes and crack a few.

If I can't buy nuts in their shells, I buy raw nuts still in their skins. The skins, which act as a protective coating, aren't hard to remove. I also make sure they're unroasted. Roasted nuts are more likely to have been fried than roasted and they often contain salts, MSG, and sugars. Dry-roasted nuts also may have added flavorings as well as a slow turnover.

All nuts and seeds are best stored in the refrigerator or freezer. Cold retards the spoilage of their oils so they will remain fresh longer.

TO BLANCH AND PEEL ALMONDS: Drop whole, shelled almonds into a pan of boiling water for 1 minute, then lift them out and pinch off the skins. If they don't come off easily, return them to the water for another minute and try again. Don't soak almonds longer than necessary, or they'll become waterlogged and splotchy looking.

TO PEEL HAZELNUTS: Spread nuts in a single layer on a sheet pan and bake at 300°F until the skins begin to crack, 15 to 20 minutes. Remove, wrap them in a towel for a minute, then vigorously rub them a handful at a time in the towel. This will take off all the loosened skins, but the difficult patches will remain, which can be removed with a knife or left on. If the skins are really stubborn, return them to the oven for another 5 minutes. A little skin won't hurt the flavor.

TO PEEL PISTACHIOS: The green meat of the pistachio is revealed only when the skin is removed. Cover the nuts with boiling water and let stand for 5 minutes. Drain, then rub the nuts with a towel. The loosened soft skins should slip right off. Remove more stubborn pieces with a knife. Discard any nuts that are blackened or moldy looking. To recrisp them, bake at 300°F until dry, about 15 minutes. Don't overbake them, or their colors will fade.

TO BLANCH AND ROAST WALNUTS: This simple process greatly improves the flavor of shelled walnuts that aren't freshly cracked and renders them less irritating for those who are sensitive to their skins. Bring a pan of water to a boil, add walnuts, and let them stand for 1 minute. Drain and wick up the excess moisture with a towel. Spread them out on a sheet pan, then toast in a 300°F oven until they've dried out, about 20 minutes. Remove them as soon as they're dry.

Oil

Oils are described by what they're made from and how they're made. When it comes to the process, there are two main approaches, resulting in what are known as *unrefined* and *refined oils*.

UNREFINED, PARTIALLY REFINED, OR PURE OILS: These are the oils I use and recommend because of their character, intensity, and superior nutritional value. Partially refined or pure oils are made by cooking cleaned seeds or nuts at low temperatures to make the oil accessible, then pressing it out by using a screw press, or expeller. The resulting oil is rich with aroma and nutrients. Cold-pressed oil is pressed between slowly turned stones, the artisanal method of making olive oil, for example. Today even cold-pressed oils are heated, but not to the excessive temperatures that refined oils are. Pure or partially refined oils may show cloudiness or deposits of natural waxes, especially when they've been refrigerated. These harmless substances are reintegrated into the oil when it's heated; they don't indicate any kind of spoilage. Your nose will tell you when oil is bad. These oils are more expensive than refined oils, but they are a far better product in every way and worth the extra cost.

REFINED OILS: This is the method used for extracting most oils today. A mash made of the seeds is treated with hexane, a solvent, to pull out the oil. To make the oil into a tasteless, odorless product, lecithin, vitamin E, minerals, and other important nutrients are removed. The oil is then bleached (which removes its carotenes), steamed to remove odors, then further clarified. In the end, refined oil is essentially a lubricant, contributing fatty acids with no flavor, aroma, or food value. This is the bulk of the oil that's found in our supermarkets and in processed foods. In spite of its chemical treatment, it can still have unpleasant off odors.

RANCIDITY IN OIL: All fats eventually become rancid with exposure to air, and unrefined oils turn rancid more quickly than refined ones. Nut oils are the most unstable of all. When oil is off, you can tell because its odor is stale, fishy, or soapy—especially when heated. Rancid oil is unhealthy to eat and should be thrown out. When oil is good, it will smell sweet and reflect its source—olives, peanuts, walnuts, sesame seeds, and so on. Unfortunately so many of the oil-bearing foods we eat are slightly rancid that rancidity is a taste many people have unknowingly grown accustomed to. But once you can identify it, you may be surprised at how often you encounter it. You can find it in a package of sunflower seeds, salted peanuts, the nuts in a candy bar, and many other places.

STORAGE: The three enemies of oil are oxygen, heat, and light. To keep oils fresh, keep them capped, cool, and away from light. It's also a good idea to buy oils in small quantities and store them, once opened, in the refrigerator. (Olive and sesame oils, which are fairly stable, can be kept in a dark, cool cupboard.) For convenience, you might keep a small amount of the oils you use daily on the counter in a bottled jar and refill it as needed.

Types of Oil

AVOCADO: Rich, thick, with a buttery feel but not much flavor. Use it in baking, some sautéing, or with citrus and avocado salads.

CANOLA: The new health food favorite, canola is heavy, golden, and viscous, yet low in saturated fat. Many use it in combination with butter or olive oil or to replace butter in baked goods, like quick breads and pancakes.

CITRUS OILS: Almost more like perfume than oil, these should be used by the droplet to add the essence of orange, lemon, and lime to pastries, smoothies, and vinaigrettes.

CORN OIL: You can occasionally find a golden unrefined corn oil that has a strong hint of corn in its aroma. I use it to underscore the presence of corn.

OLIVE OIL: The oil of the Mediterranean, olive oil has gained much media attention for its beneficial qualities, but it's also a delicious oil. In countries where it is the principal fat, it is even used in desserts. There's sometimes confusion about the different designations for olive oils and what they mean. Fruitiness is a quality I look for regardless of what the label says. By *fruitiness* I mean an aroma that clearly conveys the scent of the fruit, in this case olives. Fruity olive oils are usually also a rich green or golden color.

Extra virgin olive oil comes from the first, cold pressing of the olives. Its acidity is below 1 percent, and it is pronouncedly redolent of olives. Fine estate-bottled extra virgin olive oil should not be used for cooking since direct heat alters it, but used to flavor foods (try some drizzled over warm asparagus, green beans, or tomatoes) and for salad dressings. For sautéing, look to those oils designated as extra virgin (it used to be called *virgin),* which have the correct acidity level but are sold at a fraction of the cost of estate-bottled oils. Although relatively inexpensive, these are fruity and have good color. This is my principal cooking oil. A fine example is Colavita.

Pure or light olive oil is refined, deodorized olive oil to which flavor is introduced by adding a little extra virgin oil. It's suitable where you want a fairly bland oil for cooking.

PEANUT OIL: The common refined version is perfect for frying. It hasn't much character, which in this case is what you want. Roasted peanut oil, which is saturated with the perfume of roasted peanuts, is excellent for introducing powerful flavor to stir-fries as well as in certain dressings. (Loriva, available at supermarkets and specialty stores, is the best American brand I know.)

SAFFLOWER OIL: One of the more neutral cooking oils, safflower oil is often rather plain, although a good-quality brand like Loriva or Omega Nutrition has a floral, nutty flavor that's very agreeable.

"SALAD" OILS: The main virtue of these mass-produced supermarket oils, sometimes also labeled vegetable oil, is that they're utterly tasteless, which is sometimes desirable for frying or using to oil a pan. But I find they often have an off taste and salads are the last things they should be used for.

SESAME OIL: There is a refined, light version, suitable for cooking, with subtle flavor and a trace of nuttiness, and a toasted version, dark with a pronounced perfume. Dark sesame oil is used as a seasoning, spooned over a stir-fry, added by the drop to a bowl of miso soup, and even featured in certain salad dressings. Chili oil is sesame oil that has been steeped with chile to make it hot; use it in small amounts to taste.

SOY OIL: I have always found this bland oil to be particularly unstable unless highly refined. Take a good whiff of it to be sure it's not rancid.

SUNFLOWER SEED OIL: I'm very fond of this oil, especially when it's made from roasted seeds (Loriva again). It has more character than most all-purpose oils, yet it isn't overwhelming. Use for cooking or for salads.

WALNUT, HAZELNUT, AND OTHER NUT OILS: Although principally for salads, you can drizzle these over hot foods that are flavor-compatible, such as hazelnut oil over artichokes, toasted macadamia oil over basmati rice, etc. You can also use them in baked goods where oil is called for. Always keep these oils refrigerated.

MISCELLANEOUS OILS: Oils can be pressed from all nuts and seeds, and some of the more unusual oils available are pumpkin seed, a delicious dark green oil, pistachio, flax oil, pine nut, and almond. If you're curious, try them; they may have a place in your cooking vocabulary, at least as a flavoring for warm vegetables and grains or in vinaigrettes.

Pepper

There's nothing like the fragrance of freshly milled pepper, and that's how it should always be used. The flat, stale taste of preground pepper doesn't compare with fresh, and it's on just such a small point that the difference between something all right and something really good depends. Pepper is not only for savory dishes; it also has its place with sweets. A little pepper gives a warm vibrant note to poached fruits, mousses, and even pastries—the best-known example being pfeffernüsse. Pepper is the fruit of a vine, *Piper nigrum*. Green, black, and white pepper all come from the same plant. The difference in color is accounted for by maturity.

GREEN PEPPERCORNS: Picked green, these must be eaten right away, preserved in brine, or frozen. If not, they turn black. They are intensely aromatic and so soft they can be mashed into a paste or scattered over food.

BLACK PEPPERCORNS: The pepper is picked green but left to dry until shriveled and black. Their flavor is stronger than either green or white peppercorns. Two of the most notable types are Tellicherry and Malabar. Black pepper is complex with sweet, fruity, warm, and hot nuances.

WHITE PEPPERCORNS: Picked when fully ripe and red, the berries are soaked until soft, then the outer skin is sloughed off. White pepper is what remains. It's milder than black pepper and used where the mildness—or whiteness—is desired.

Other plants are used as pepper, although they aren't true pepper.

SICHUAN PEPPER (SZECHUAN OR ANISE PEPPER): Used in Chinese cooking, Sichuan pepper has become quite popular. It looks like a tiny, reddish dried flower rather than corns. It's intensely aromatic and very complex—slightly numbing on the tongue.

PINK PEPPERCORNS: Another well-known pepperlike berry that is not related botanically to pepper but is used along with true pepper, mainly for its color. Some people have an allergic reaction to the berries, which causes the throat to contract.

Salt

Salt contributes its own flavor and brings out the flavors of the foods themselves. It enhances all foods, including sweets. Salt is also used to draw out moisture and bitter juices from vegetables and as a preservative, such as in making pickles and preserving capers.

Although we think of salt as pure sodium chloride, it comes to us from the earth and the sea as a complex substance that's filled with trace minerals. It's then processed, altered, diminished, or enhanced just like other foods. In their natural states, salts have different flavors, textures, and colors, and they naturally attract moisture and clump when the air is damp. To make salt white, even grained, and pourable, it's refined with chemicals that eliminate most of the trace minerals, then fortified with additives. A glance at the label on a salt box may surprise you; salt is not always so pure as we assume. Here are some common forms of salt.

TABLE SALT: Refined and fine grained, table salt has chemical additives to keep it free flowing in all weather. ("When it rains, it pours.") Compared to other salts, its flavor is harsh and not particularly interesting.

IODIZED SALT: Iodine is often removed during the processing of salts; when it's added back, we get iodized salt—important in the "goiter belt" parts of the country where there's not enough iodine in the diet.

SEA SALT: Coarse or fine grained, sea salt is more complex and saltier tasting than other salts. The complexity comes from its higher mineral content, which in turn reflects the composition of sea water. The most commonly available sea salt is from the Mediterranean; it comes in coarse crystals and as table salt. You can keep the crystals in a pepper mill and grind them directly onto your food, like pepper. Sea salt is what I've used to make all the recipes in this book.

KOSHER SALT: Kosher salt is less salty tasting than sea salt. Unlike table salt, it's ragged and rough. Chefs like it because they can grab it with their fingers and hold on to it, whereas fine salt just ebbs away.

OTHER SALTS: Most countries have their own salts that are treasured for their unique flavors—salt mixed with pink clay from Hawaii and black Indian salt with a pronounced sulfurous odor, for example. Many can be found at natural food stores, and some of the finer salts, like the English Malden salt or the wildly expensive Fleur de Sel from France, are available at gourmet stores. You might find some of these other salts interesting and enjoyable. Taste them on your tongue and compare, then remember to adjust your recipes accordingly. Some are very salty indeed. You'll develop a feel for a preferred salt after a short while.

SALTING TO TASTE AND WHEN TO SALT

Salt is a matter of personal taste, so it's virtually impossible for anyone to ascertain the right amount of salt for someone else. I have suggested amounts as a starting point in many recipes, but in the end it really has to be "salt to taste." Practiced cooks know by feel how much salt to use, but even if you're new to cooking you'll quickly develop a feel for how much is enough, especially if you really do taste as you cook. More precise measurements are given for baked goods, which are difficult to taste before they're cooked and impossible to alter afterward.

Since salt draws out the flavors of foods, it has the best chance of doing its work if you add it at the beginning of the cooking process—with the exception of beans and large grains. When salt is added only at the end, it adds mostly a salty taste, whereas if you salt each component of a recipe, the final dish should be sufficiently seasoned, needing perhaps only a pinch to fine-tune it. When you cook this way, you'll find yourself reaching into the salt dish more often, but in the end you probably won't use any more salt than usual, and maybe even less, since the flavors of the ingredients are maximized from the beginning.

Tamarind

The sweet-sour pulp attained from the large pods of the leguminous tamarind tree, tamarind is an important seasoning in Indian cooking. It's easiest to use in its paste form since wresting it from its pods and seeds is a rather time-consuming process. Tamarind paste can be found in Asian, Indian, and Mexican markets.

Tomato Products

There's no disputing the great convenience of canned tomatoes. Most of the year they're better than fresh ones, and there are many good brands on the market. I am especially fond of the organic brands, such as Muir Glen and Eden Foods, for their good taste and texture. Diced canned tomatoes from Muir Glen are always well cut and nice looking. With a can of tomatoes you can make a vibrant, simple sauce within minutes.

Tomato puree is sweet and very smooth. It makes an uninteresting sauce, but it can be used in an emergency to fortify one that's lackluster.

Tomato paste is the most concentrated tomato product. It's used in small amounts to bring a spot of flavor, acidity, and color to a dish or to bolster a weak sauce. Often a little dab is just enough to bring discursive elements into more harmonious play. Paste that comes in a tube is wonderfully efficient. Simply use what you want, put the cap back on, and refrigerate. It won't come back to greet you filmed with mold.

Sun-dried tomatoes, either dry-packed, packed in oil, or in paste form, also can add a great deal of body to a sauce. The best ones are plump and tender, swimming in their jars of olive oil. They can be thinly slivered and added to other dishes as a seasoning, but they're meant to be used in small, not large, quantities. Dried tomatoes that aren't oil packed are leathery and concentrated. They soften as they cook, so add them at the beginning of any recipe.

Tortilla Strips and Chips

Stale corn tortillas don't absorb as much oil as fresh ones. If yours are fresh, spread them out on the kitchen counter to dry for 30 minutes. For chips, cut them into sixths. For strips, cut them into quarters, stack them up, then slice them into skinny strips. Heat a few tablespoons of vegetable oil in a skillet over fairly high heat. When it's hot enough to quickly sizzle a piece of tortilla, add a handful and fry them just until golden and crisp. Remove to paper toweling and fry the rest.

For a low-fat version, brush the tortillas lightly with oil before slicing; spread them on a sheet pan and bake at 425°F until crisp.

For a nonfat version, Martha Rose Shulman recommends this method in her book *Mexican Light* (Bantam, 1996): Place 4 to 10 triangles or twice as many strips on a plate and microwave for 1 minute on high power. Turn them over and microwave for another 40 seconds. Check to make sure they're not too brown. If they need further crisping, cook for another 30 seconds or longer. Cool on a rack.

Vinegars are important for vinaigrettes and salad dressings, but they're also used in other dishes to bring flavors that are almost "there" into sharper relief. When added to bitter greens, they have a way of softening their edge. Vinegars are essential for pickling, and a little added to vegetable stews helps keep the texture of tender vegetables from becoming mushy. Many vinegars can be used interchangeably because they're used in such small amounts, but they definitely have their own personalities.

APPLE CIDER VINEGAR: With its nicely balanced, lively taste, apple cider vinegar is an interesting, mildly fruity vinegar traditionally popular in American cooking. The organic, unfiltered type has the most character.

BALSAMIC VINEGAR: Low-acid, sweet, and complex, good-quality balsamic vinegar can, by the drop, bring out the most in fruits, such as cherries, strawberries, poached quince, and others. It also complements onions, tomatoes, eggplant, and many other vegetables.

DISTILLED VINEGARS: These provide acidity but lack any noteworthy flavor notes. However, distilled vinegar is inexpensive and useful where you need lots of it—for example, when you're making pickles.

RED WINE VINEGAR: Red wine vinegars vary in body and strength from average to high acid. Aged red wine vinegars are quite strong. A few drops enliven greens, such as spinach, chard, dandelions, and kale.

RICE WINE VINEGAR: This Japanese vinegar is mild and rather sweet. You can use it generously because of its low acidity. It's delicious with Asian noodles, cucumbers, and in dressings where its sweetness is welcome. There are both plain and flavored rice wine vinegars.

SHERRY VINEGAR: This delicious Spanish vinegar is superb with sweet vegetables like onions, rich dishes, or bitter greens. Sizzled with butter in a skillet, it makes a fast, big-tasting sauce for frittatas, onions, or seared radicchio.

WHITE WINE VINEGAR: Generally milder and a little less aggressive than red wine vinegars. Champagne vinegar is one of the most delicate. A few drops will often throw the flavors of a dish into relief, the way lemon juice does.

Drained Yogurt and Yogurt Cheese

Creamy, thick, and slightly tart, yogurt cheese can take the place of sour cream or be used as a soft cheese for appetizers or desserts. It's not necessarily slimming. Labneh, the authentic thick yogurt cheese, is made with rich, creamy yogurt, but when you make your own you can use whatever yogurt you like as long as it's free of gums and gelatins (which prevent the whey from separating). Draining yogurt involves exactly the same process as making the cheese, only it doesn't go on for so long. Losing the whey sweetens the flavor of the yogurt, especially non-

fat yogurts, and gives it a little more body. Fine-mesh strainers for making yogurt cheese are available, but most hold only a cup and take quite a while to drain.

To make 1 to 2 cups yogurt cheese, stir 1 quart yogurt until it's smooth, then pour it into a strainer lined with a double layer of cheesecloth. Fold the ends over the top and set the whole unit over a bowl to drip. For faster draining, tie the ends of the cheesecloth around the handle of a spoon and let it hang over a deep bowl. (Make sure it doesn't end up sitting in its own liquid.) Let it drip until the cheese is as firm as you want. If you want slightly thickened or drained yogurt, 25 to 30 minutes is enough time to lose a good portion of the whey.

Scrape the thickened yogurt off the cheesecloth and store it in a covered container in the refrigerator. The whey can be used in baking bread, muffins, and quick breads. The drained yogurt can be flavored with various additions—lemon zest, fresh herbs, salt and pepper, garlic, etc.

Sauces and Condiments

IN THE LANGUAGE OF FOOD, SAUCES ARE THE ADJECTIVES. THEY EMBELLISH, ENRICH, AND ENHANCE OTHER FOODS, RAISING THEM TO GREATER POSSIBILITIES. SAUCES MOISTEN (MAYONNAISE ON BREAD), ADD A BRIGHT ACIDIC TOUCH (tomato sauce on pasta), or enrobe and enrich (a creamy sorrel sauce or beurre blanc). Knowing how to make even a few sauces, such as a classic mayonnaise and a proper béchamel, will give your cooking finesse, allowing you to transform plain and simple foods into dishes that have more excitement, and deeper dimension. Sauces are sometimes viewed as intimidating, the secret realm of chefs rather than the province of the home cook. But sauces are like anything else—some have a trick or two that can be mastered with practice, and others are utterly straightforward. And these sauces are mostly of the latter persuasion.

Sauces and condiments are quite unlike the other foods we eat. Too concentrated, too acidic, too garlicky, or too rich to eat in large amounts, they're used in small quantities to add polish to a dish. It's their intensity that brings other foods to life—the glistening flourish of a caper-filled salsa verde on steamed carrots that would otherwise be dull, the aromatic hues of an herb-infused butter that suddenly makes a baked potato unusual. A garlic-laden mayonnaise significantly transforms a bowl of chickpeas.

Condiments, pickles, and chutneys are so sharp and vinegary they're often served on the side, more like a garnish. Many condiments last for weeks or even months in the refrigerator. They're a wonderfully convenient pantry item—a spoonful of this or that sauce or condiment can magically round out a dish or a meal, giving it a unique stamp of personality.

Sauces Made with Butter

EVEN *if you're a devoted fan of all the pleasurable oils that grace our shelves, as I certainly am, nothing quite replaces the flavor and smell of butter. It graces all forms of vegetables and in turn is enhanced by the numerous items it marries so well with—sage and other herbs, capers, vinegar, wine and shallots, mustard, and so forth. You may not feel any reason to go beyond letting a pat of pure butter melt over your vegetables, but the sizzle of sage butter or a touch of beurre blanc is far more exciting. Experimenting with the flavored butters in this chapter will show you how to bring out an unsuspected wealth of possibilities in your vegetables and grains. And you can have the best of both worlds when you use the Herb-Butter and Olive Oil Sauce—a classic that trades in some of its buttery essence for a successful merging with fruity oil.*

Warm Sage and Garlic Butter

THIS *fast sizzling sauce is particularly compatible spooned over winter squash, ravioli, or a warm slice of baked ricotta.*

MAKES ABOUT ⅓ CUP

2 tablespoons butter

2 tablespoons extra virgin olive oil

1 tablespoon chopped sage or 1 teaspoon dried

2 garlic cloves, finely chopped

1 tablespoon finely chopped parsley

Salt and freshly milled pepper

Heat the butter and oil in a small skillet over high heat. When bubbling, add the sage and fry for about 30 seconds. Add the garlic and cook until it has perfumed the oil. Remove from the heat, stir in the parsley, and season with a pinch of salt and plenty of pepper.

Beurre Blanc

STIR *a spoonful of this classic French sauce into a vegetable ragout just before serving or serve with asparagus.*

MAKES ABOUT 1 CUP

⅓ cup white wine vinegar or champagne vinegar

⅓ cup dry white wine

2 tablespoons finely diced shallot

Salt and freshly milled white pepper

½ pound butter, cut into small pieces

Put the vinegar, wine, shallot, and ½ teaspoon salt in a small, heavy saucepan and simmer until only 3 tablespoons remain. Remove from the heat and cool until tepid. Return to very low heat and whisk in the butter piece by piece until all is incorporated. Remove from the heat and season with a little pepper. Strain (or not) and serve.

If you're making the sauce in advance or have leftover cold beurre blanc, rewarm it by setting it over low heat and whisking until warm. If the butter begins to melt and separate, it's because the heat is too high. Pull the pan off the stove and continue whisking until it has cooled and come back together. If this doesn't help, pour a little into a cold bowl and start whisking in the remaining sauce gradually. The coolness will help solidify the butter again.

Beurre Rouge: Use red wine vinegar and red wine in place of the white.

Beurre Blanc with Herbs: When the sauce is done stir in 2 to 3 tablespoons finely cut chives, chopped basil, or tarragon.

Herb-Butter and Olive Oil Sauce

1/4 cup finely chopped parsley

2 tablespoons thinly sliced chives

1 tablespoon minced tarragon

1 garlic clove

Salt

2 tablespoons capers, rinsed

1 teaspoon grated lemon zest

1 shallot, minced

5 tablespoons butter at room temperature

3 tablespoons extra virgin olive oil

Fresh lemon juice

A SAUCE inspired by one of my favorite cooks, Ann Clark, try it on steamed vegetables.

MAKES ABOUT 1/2 CUP

Blanch the herbs for 1 minute in a cup or so of boiling water, then drain in a fine strainer and blot dry. Pound the garlic and 1/4 teaspoon salt in a mortar to a paste. Beat the herbs, garlic, capers, lemon zest, shallot, and butter with a wooden spoon, then gradually mix in the olive oil. Taste and season with a pinch of salt and lemon juice to taste.

Flavored Butters

These are all made the same way. Start with butter at room temperature, add the ingredients, and mix them together with a wooden paddle or spoon. They can be transferred to a crock or set on a sheet of wax paper, rolled into a cylinder, and frozen until firm. Once frozen, the flavored butter can be sliced into thin disks and floated on soups or used in a number of other ways, as suggested in the recipes that follow.

Herb Butter

1/4 pound butter

2 tablespoons chopped thyme

3 tablespoons chopped marjoram

1 shallot, finely diced

1/2 teaspoon grated lemon zest

Pinch salt

UNIVERSALLY good, this butter can be tossed with virtually any vegetable, rice, or cooked dried beans.

MAKES 1/2 CUP

Olive-Rosemary Butter

1/4 pound butter

1/2 cup finely chopped Niçoise olives

1 tablespoon minced rosemary

1 teaspoon minced thyme

1/2 teaspoon grated lemon zest

Pinch salt

A PUNGENT butter that's excellent with grilled vegetables or as a dynamic flavoring for a white bean or potato soup.

MAKES 1/2 CUP

Blossom Butter

1/4 pound butter

2 tablespoons finely chopped mixed herbs—opal basil, marjoram, chives, thyme

3 tablespoons chopped edible blossoms—sage, rosemary, borage, calendula, or nasturtium

Salt and freshly milled white pepper

STREAKS and flecks of color mark this delectable butter.

MAKES 1/2 CUP

Nasturtium Butter Use nasturtium blossoms along with 2 tender nasturtium leaves, finely sliced. This butter has a peppery flavor that lifts up so-so soups and is delicious in a cucumber sandwich.

Saffron Butter

SAFFRON goes with all those Provençal vegetables—fennel, eggplant, tomato, potato.

MAKES ½ CUP

2 pinches saffron threads, pulverized

¼ pound butter

1 large shallot, finely diced

2 teaspoons finely chopped marjoram or basil

1 tablespoon finely chopped parsley

½ teaspoon grated orange or lemon zest

Pinch cayenne

Salt and freshly milled pepper to taste

Cover the saffron with 2 teaspoons hot water and let steep until the color emerges, after a few minutes. Work it into the butter with the remaining ingredients.

Mustard Butter

MUSTARD-FLAVORED butter always suits those strong members of the cabbage family.

MAKES ½ CUP

1 garlic clove, put through a press

¼ pound butter

1 tablespoon Dijon mustard or to taste

1 large shallot, finely diced, or 2 tablespoons minced scallion

2 tablespoons chopped parsley

Salt and freshly milled pepper

Spicy Moroccan Butter

USE this complex and exotic butter with sweet potatoes or stir into a chickpea soup for a burst of flavor.

MAKES ½ CUP

½ bunch scallions, white parts only

2 garlic cloves, coarsely chopped

1 tablespoon sweet paprika

2 teaspoons ground cumin

½ teaspoon ground coriander

Cayenne to taste

2 tablespoons chopped parsley

2 tablespoons chopped cilantro

1 teaspoon chopped mint

Salt

¼ pound butter

Juice of 1 lime

Pound the scallions, garlic, ground spices, herbs, and ⅛ teaspoon salt in a mortar to form a slightly rough paste. (Or puree in a small food processor.) Stir this paste into the butter with the lime juice.

Chile Butter

THIS spicy butter goes particularly well with sweet vegetables, such as carrots, beets, sweet potatoes, and corn.

MAKES ½ CUP

1 large jalapeño, 2 serrano chiles, or 1 New Mexican long green chile, roasted

Finely chopped zest of 1 lime

¼ pound butter

1 teaspoon lime juice or more to taste

2 tablespoons chopped cilantro

1 scallion, including an inch of the green, thinly sliced

Few pinches salt

¼ teaspoon ground coriander

Mince the chiles with the lime zest, then beat into the butter and add the remaining ingredients. Roll into a log, wrap in plastic wrap, and refrigerate until needed.

Béchamel and Other Roux-Based Sauces

SAUCES thickened with an amalgam of flour and butter, or roux, have often been scorned, mainly because they're seldom properly cooked. However, they can be quite delicious and very useful. Béchamel or white sauce, provides the smooth layer in lasagne, the base for a soufflé, or the blanket that covers a gratin. A thin béchamel can take the place of cream in a number of situations. Any roux-based sauce can be smooth and silky if you allow it to cook for at least 25 minutes. If you use a double boiler, the sauce can cook while you do other things in the kitchen.

THE ROUX AND THE LIQUID: The roux, the mixture of flour and fat, thickens the sauce. Usually the fat is butter and the liquid is milk, but you can also make a sauce using oil and a good vegetable stock.

PREVENTING LUMPS: If you add warm liquid to a warm roux or cold liquid to a cold roux, you won't get lumps in your sauce. Stir briskly with a whisk as you quickly add all the liquid at once. Once the sauce thickens, switch to a flat-edged wooden spoon and be sure to run it around the edges of the pan as well as the bottom as you stir so that nothing sticks and burns. If you use a double boiler, you have to stir only occasionally during the 25-minute cooking time.

FINAL SEASONINGS: Finished sauces can be flavored with vegetable purees, roasted garlic, concentrated tomato sauces, fresh herbs, curry, and grated cheeses.

Béchamel Sauce

2 cups milk

1/4 cup finely diced onion

Aromatics: 1 bay leaf, 3 parsley sprigs,
   2 thyme sprigs

3 1/2 tablespoons butter

3 1/2 tablespoons flour

Salt and freshly milled white pepper

Grated nutmeg

ALTHOUGH it's not traditional, I always steep a little onion and some aromatics in the milk to make a better-tasting sauce. This recipe makes a sauce of medium thickness.

MAKES 2 CUPS

Heat the milk with the onion and aromatics in a heavy saucepan over medium heat. Turn it off just before it boils and set aside for 15 minutes to steep.

In another saucepan, make the roux by melting the butter, adding the flour, and stirring constantly over medium heat for 2 minutes. Quickly pour the milk through a strainer into the roux and whisk until thickened. Stir until the sauce comes to a boil. Set the pan over very low heat or transfer to a double boiler. Cook for 25 to 30 minutes, stirring occasionally. Season with salt, pepper, and nutmeg to taste. If you're not ready to use the sauce right away, lay a piece of plastic wrap directly on the surface to prevent a skin from forming.

   Herb Béchamel: To the finished sauce, add 1/3 to 1/2 cup chopped herbs: chervil, thyme, and tarragon, or chopped parsley mixed with other herbs of your choice.

   Rich Béchamel: Add 1/2 cup or more cream to the finished sauce.

   Nondairy Béchamel: Replace the butter with olive or vegetable oil. For liquid, use soy milk or a vegetable stock, pages 196 to 198, that best complements the dish.

   Cheese Béchamel: When the sauce is finished, stir in 1/2 to 1 cup grated sharp Cheddar, Swiss, or Gruyère and season with a pinch of cayenne and 2 to 3 teaspoons Dijon mustard. A cheese sauce is traditional—and good—with cauliflower, cabbage, and broccoli.

Walnut Béchamel Sauce

GOOD *with pasta and rice, especially when combined with greens. Pale new-crop walnuts make an ivory-colored sauce. Older, dark-colored walnuts will tint the sauce purplish pink.*

MAKES ABOUT 3 CUPS

3 cups milk

½ cup finely chopped walnuts

¼ cup minced leek or scallion, white part only, or shallot

2 garlic cloves, crushed or put through a press

2 bay leaves

2 tablespoons butter

2 tablespoons flour

Salt and freshly milled white pepper

Grated nutmeg

2 tablespoons chopped chervil, parsley, or marjoram

Bring the milk, walnuts, leek, garlic, and bay leaves to a near boil. Remove from the heat and let steep for 30 minutes. Melt the butter in another saucepan over medium heat. Stir in the flour and cook for 2 minutes, stirring frequently. Whisk in the milk mixture all at once, then bring to a boil. Reduce the heat and cook slowly for 25 minutes, stirring frequently. Season with salt, pepper, and nutmeg to taste. When done, pull out the bay leaves and stir in the herb. If you wish your sauce to be perfectly smooth, pass it through a food mill or puree in a blender.

Sorrel Sauce

TART *sorrel is always right with egg-based dishes such as timbales, roulades, and pudding soufflés. If I have a windfall of sorrel—say twice as much as given here—I don't make the roux but rely on the bulk of the herb to thicken the sauce.*

MAKES ABOUT 3 CUPS

3 tablespoons butter

3 tablespoons finely diced shallot or onion

3 cups packed sorrel leaves, large stems removed

2 cups Basic Vegetable Stock, page 196, or Mushroom Stock, page 197

1½ tablespoons flour

1 cup crème fraîche, cream, or half-and-half

Salt and freshly milled pepper

Melt 1½ tablespoons of the butter in a saucepan, add the shallot, and cook over high heat, stirring frequently, until it begins to brown around the edges, after a few minutes. Add the sorrel by handfuls. When the leaves have collapsed and turned olive green, add the stock and bring to a boil. Lower the heat and simmer for 5 minutes. Cool slightly, then puree.

Melt the remaining butter in the same pan over low heat, stir in the flour, and cook for 2 minutes. Whisk the pureed sorrel into the flour, then whisk in the crème fraîche. Season with salt and pepper to taste, then cook for 25 minutes in a double boiler over very low heat, stirring frequently. Taste for salt and pepper when done.

Green Herb Sauces

THESE *shimmering sauces are essentially top-quality olive oil made green with fresh herbs, seasoned variously with garlic, shallots, a little lemon or vinegar to perk up the flavors, and enriched with pounded nuts, capers, cheese, or hard-cooked eggs. Green herb sauces provide a verdant finishing touch for a diverse assortment of foods, from grilled vegetables to pizzas, soups, pastas, grains, cheeses, scrambled eggs, and omelets. Although they'll keep in the refrigerator for several days, their color begins to fade as soon as the acid is added. Lemon or lime juice can be added as the sauce is used, but a salsa verde really is best fresh.*

Salsa Verde

2 shallots, finely diced

1/2 cup finely chopped parsley

1/3 cup chopped mixed herbs—tarragon, chervil, thyme, marjoram, dill

2 to 3 tablespoons capers, rinsed

Grated zest of 1 lemon

1 small garlic clove, minced

3/4 cup extra virgin olive oil

2 to 3 teaspoons champagne vinegar or fresh lemon juice

1 hard-cooked egg, optional

Salt and freshly milled pepper

CHOOSE those herbs that best complement the dish or the meal.

MAKES ABOUT 1 CUP

Combine all the ingredients except the egg, salt, and pepper. Mash the egg yolk until smooth, adding a little of the sauce to thin it. Finely chop the white. Stir the yolk and the white back into the sauce, season with salt and pepper, and adjust the amount of vinegar if needed. If you're planning to serve the sauce later, wait to add the vinegar or lemon juice so that the green will remain bright.

Salsa Verde with Walnuts and Tarragon

1/2 cup walnuts, finely chopped

2 small garlic cloves, finely chopped

1 cup finely chopped parsley, about 1 large bunch

2 tablespoons finely chopped tarragon

2 tablespoons chopped rinsed capers

1 cup extra virgin olive oil

1 teaspoon good-quality red wine vinegar or to taste

Salt and freshly milled pepper

EVERYTHING in this sauce should be very finely chopped—by hand for the best texture and taste.

MAKES ABOUT 1 1/2 CUPS

Combine the nuts, garlic, parsley, tarragon, and capers in a small bowl. Stir in the oil and vinegar, then season with salt and pepper to taste.

Chermoula (Moroccan Green Sauce)

THE Moroccan marinade for fish is also wonderful with vegetables— especially sweet ones like beets, carrots, and winter squash.

MAKES ABOUT ³/₄ CUP

4 garlic cloves, coarsely chopped

Salt

²/₃ cup finely chopped cilantro

¹/₃ cup finely chopped parsley

1¹/₂ teaspoons sweet paprika

¹/₂ teaspoon ground cumin

¹/₈ teaspoon cayenne

¹/₄ cup extra virgin olive oil

Juice of 2 large lemons or to taste

Pound the garlic with 1 teaspoon salt in a mortar until smooth. Add the cilantro and parsley and pound a little more to bruise the leaves and release their flavor. Stir in the spices, olive oil, and lemon juice.

Cilantro Salsa

IF you make this in a blender, the sauce will be thick and creamy, flecked with green. If you chop everything by hand and stir it into the oil, it will be more like the traditional salsa verde, the herbs suspended in oil. Use this as a dip, in pita sandwiches, with hard-cooked eggs, or spooned over grilled vegetables.

MAKES ABOUT ²/₃ CUP

1 jalapeño chile, seeded

1 large bunch cilantro, stems removed

¹/₂ cup mint leaves

2 garlic cloves

¹/₂ cup plus 2 tablespoons extra virgin olive oil

Juice of 1 lime

¹/₂ teaspoon ground cumin

¹/₂ teaspoon ground coriander

Salt

For a creamy sauce, coarsely chop the chile, cilantro, mint, and garlic, then puree in a food processor with ¹/₄ cup water and the oil. Add the lime juice, cumin, coriander, and salt. Taste and correct the spices.

To make the sauce by hand, very finely chop everything, then stir in ¹/₄ cup water, the oil, and the spices.

Parsley-Caper Sauce

SHARP and lemony, this sauce brightens warm or cold vegetables, fried cheese, vegetable fritters, and grains and beans.

MAKES ABOUT ¹/₂ CUP

¹/₂ cup finely chopped parsley

2 tablespoons small capers, rinsed

1 shallot, finely diced

1 teaspoon grated lemon zest

¹/₃ cup extra virgin olive oil

1 tablespoon white wine vinegar or champagne vinegar

2 teaspoons fresh lemon juice or to taste

Salt and freshly milled pepper

Whisk everything together, seasoning with salt and pepper to taste. Let stand for 10 minutes, then taste again and adjust the seasonings, adding more vinegar or lemon juice if needed. Serve right away.

Pesto

1 or 2 plump garlic cloves

Salt

3 tablespoons pine nuts

3 cups loosely packed basil leaves, stems removed, leaves washed and dried

1/2 cup freshly grated Parmesan, preferably Parmigiano-Reggiano

2 to 3 tablespoons grated pecorino Romano to taste

2 tablespoons soft butter, optional

1/2 cup extra virgin olive oil

By Hand Smash the garlic with 1/2 teaspoon salt and the pine nuts to break them up, then add the basil leaves a handful at a time. (If you're impatient, you can speed things up by tearing the leaves into smaller pieces first.) Grind them, using a circular motion, until you have a fairly fine paste with very small flecks of leaves. Briefly work in the cheeses and butter, then stir in the olive oil. Taste for salt.

In a Food Processor Use the same ingredients but in the following order: Process the garlic, salt, and pine nuts until fairly finely chopped, then add the basil and olive oil. When smooth, add the cheeses and butter and process just to combine.

ALTHOUGH we have taken this most popular of sauces to places where it has never gone before, pesto may still be best on pasta.

The food processor makes it very easy to make pesto, but I think it's well worth making by hand. The slowed-down process of hand grinding the leaves in a mortar lets you see the extraordinary transformation that takes place as garlic, salt, nuts, and basil are worked into a paste, all the while inhaling magnificent scents. If you have a choice at your market, use Genovese (Italian) basil.

MAKES ABOUT 1 CUP

Tomato-Basil Pesto

2 garlic cloves, coarsely chopped

Salt

1 1/2 cups loosely packed basil leaves

1/3 cup extra virgin olive oil

1/2 cup freshly grated Parmesan

2 to 3 tablespoons tomato paste

Pound the garlic with 1/2 teaspoon salt in a mortar until smooth. Chop the basil in a food processor and gradually add the oil to make a coarse puree. Remove and stir into the garlic with the cheese and tomato paste. Taste for salt.

USE this red pesto to season soups, spread on grilled cheese sandwiches, or drop into a ramekin of baked eggs.

MAKES ABOUT 3/4 CUP

Mayonnaise

BOTTLED *mayonnaise is a serviceable item, but homemade mayonnaise is subtle and fine with a velvety texture, neither excessively salty nor sweet. It serves as the foundation for the many wonderful sauces that complement vegetables so well. Mayonnaise is to be enjoyed by the spoonful, not the cupful, and a little bit goes a long way.*

Making Mayonnaise

Mayonnaise is simple to make but if something does go wrong, and your sauce breaks, or disintegrates into a loose, oily mass, it can be fixed.

1. Have ingredients at room temperature. If the egg is cold from the refrigerator, rinse a bowl with hot water, dry it thoroughly, and add the yolk. Or cover the whole egg with hot water for 5 minutes before beginning.

2. Set your bowl on a damp, twisted, curled-up towel to help hold it in place.

3. Begin whisking the oil into the yolk drop by drop. Once the mayonnaise has begun to emulsify or thicken, after a third or more of the oil has been added, add the rest of the oil in a thin, steady stream.

4. The finished mayonnaise will be thick, which is fine for a sandwich, but it can be thinned to saucelike consistency by stirring in near-boiling water or additional lemon juice. Use a thinner mayonnaise as a dressing to coat or drizzle over vegetables.

5. If your mayonnaise breaks, don't despair. Instead, whisk in 1 or 2 teaspoons boiling water. If that doesn't bring it back, start over with a new yolk and use the broken sauce as the oil, whisking it in drop by drop until you have a new emulsion.

Basic Mayonnaise

MAKES ABOUT 1 CUP

1 large egg yolk at room temperature

1 teaspoon Dijon mustard

Salt

2 to 3 teaspoons fresh lemon juice, white wine vinegar, or tarragon vinegar

¾ cup peanut oil or mild olive oil

2 tablespoons extra virgin olive oil

By Hand Rinse a 1-quart bowl with hot water and dry and set it on the counter with a towel wrapped tightly around the base to keep it stable. Add the egg yolk and whisk it vigorously back and forth until thick and sticky, then stir in the mustard, a pinch of salt, and the lemon juice. Whisk in the peanut oil by droplets until the egg and oil have begun to thicken (when one-third to one-half the oil has been added), then whisk in the remaining oil in a thin, steady stream. Add the extra virgin oil at the end and season to taste with additional salt and a little lemon juice. To thin, whisk in lemon juice or vinegar by drops or 1 to 2 tablespoons boiling water as needed. Cover and refrigerate until ready to use.

In a Blender Put a *whole* egg, the mustard, and a pinch of salt in the blender with ¼ cup oil and turn it on. Add the remaining oil in a steady steam until all is incorporated, then add the lemon juice. Thin with additional lemon juice or boiling water.

In a Food Processor Use a whole egg, two yolks, or a whole egg plus a yolk. Plan to use an additional ½ cup oil and adjust the other ingredients accordingly, to taste. Start with the egg, mustard, and a pinch of salt and, with the machine running, add the oil in a steady stream until all is incorporated. Add the lemon juice and thin with fresh lemon juice or boiling water.

Mayonnaise with Cooked Yolks: As a precaution against the possibility of using salmonella-contaminated eggs, cooked yolks can be used in place of raw ones, though the texture will be a little coarser and heavier. Start with 2 hard-cooked or soft-cooked (3-minute) yolks, then proceed as described, either by hand or by food processor.

Garlic Mayonnaise (Aïoli): Aïoli, a garlic-infused Provençal sauce, can be served confidently with any vegetable but especially green beans, potatoes, chickpeas, asparagus, cooked carrots, fennel, and cauliflower. It's heavenly with grilled foods, in a sandwich, or spooned into a soup or pasta. I suggest this sauce more than any other throughout this book. Coarsely chop 4 to 6 firm, unblemished garlic cloves. Put them in a mortar, add a pinch of salt, and pound until a smooth paste forms, which will happen quite quickly. (If you don't have a mortar, chop the garlic and salt together until smooth.) Stir it into the mayonnaise, add lemon juice to taste, then thin with hot water or leave it thick, depending on its intended use.

Herb Mayonnaise: Select ⅓ to ½ cup herb leaves—basil, chervil, parsley, lovage, marjoram, chives, and tarragon, singly or in combination. If using lovage, use just 1 teaspoon, for it's very robust. Dip the leaves into boiling salted water for 5 seconds, then rinse under cold water and pat dry. Finely chop the leaves and stir into the mayonnaise. Use with potatoes, carrots, green beans, on vegetable salads and sandwiches.

Fresh Dill and Lemon Mayonnaise: Add ¼ cup chopped dill, 1 teaspoon finely grated lemon zest, and lemon juice to taste to 1 cup mayonnaise. Good with eggs and most vegetables, especially new potatoes.

Orange Mayonnaise: Stir 2 teaspoons finely grated orange zest into 1 cup mayonnaise and thin with fresh orange juice to the desired consistency. Use with asparagus, broccoli, fennel, and cauliflower.

Saffron Mayonnaise: Saffron infuses mayonnaise with its yellow-orange color and intriguing flavor. Grind 2 large pinches saffron threads in a small mortar, then add 1 tablespoon boiling water. Steep for several minutes to release the color, then stir it into the mayonnaise. Serve with grilled potatoes, roasted peppers, tomatoes, fried or grilled fennel, chickpeas—in fact, with most Mediterranean vegetables and legumes.

Tarragon Mayonnaise with Capers: To 1 cup mayonnaise, stir in 2 tablespoons *each* chopped tarragon, snipped chives, and chopped parsley; 1 tablespoon chopped capers; and 2 tablespoons finely chopped cornichon pickle. Serve with cucumbers, as a dip for celery hearts, or with fried vegetables.

Roasted Red Pepper Mayonnaise: Roast, peel, and finely dice 1 large red bell pepper. Stir it into the Garlic Mayonnaise made with just 2 garlic cloves and season with several pinches cayenne plus lemon juice to taste. Use this salmon-pink sauce to bind layers of vegetable frittatas or to serve with the Saffron Noodle Cake.

Red Chile Mayonnaise: Stir 1 or more teaspoons ground red chile, to taste, into 1 cup mayonnaise. (Remember, the heat will increase as it sits.)

Green Chile Mayonnaise: Add several minced and seeded jalapeño, an unseeded serrano chile, or a large Anaheim chile, grilled, peeled, seeded, and finely minced.

Chipotle Mayonnaise: For a smoky-hot mayonnaise, stir in a little pureed canned chipotle chile. Add chopped scallions, garlic, and cilantro, if desired, to taste.

Tofu "Mayonnaise"

THIS ersatz mayonnaise serves as a substitute for egg-based sauces. It can be seasoned as in the variations suggested for egg-based mayonnaise but more highly to compensate for the blandness of tofu. Thinned with additional water or olive oil, it can be used as a salad dressing for vegetables.

MAKES ABOUT 1 CUP

4 ounces soft silken tofu
1/3 cup mild olive oil
2 tablespoons extra virgin olive oil
2 tablespoons fresh lemon juice

2 teaspoons Dijon mustard
3 scallions, white parts only, thinly sliced
1 teaspoon grated lemon zest
Salt and freshly milled white pepper

Puree the tofu, 1/4 cup water, olive oils, lemon juice, and mustard in a blender or food processor until smooth. Add the scallions and lemon zest and season with salt and pepper to taste.

Tofu Garlic "Mayonnaise": Pound 4 to 6 garlic cloves with 1/2 teaspoon salt in a mortar until it becomes a paste. Add the paste once the sauce is emulsified.

Tomato Sauces

THEIR acidity, bright color, ease of preparation, and affinity for so many dishes account for the popularity of tomato sauces. They're often just the thing to provide a needed punch of flavor or color to set off a dish. Tomato sauces are basically of two kinds—briefly cooked to preserve the fresh, bright flavor of the tomato, or long-simmered with many ingredients. Whether you're making a simple basic sauce or a chunky one with olives, capers, and mushrooms, fresh or canned tomatoes can be used.

USING CANNED TOMATOES: Since truly flavorful tomatoes enjoy such a short season, canned tomatoes are usually the better choice for sauces. Several brands are quite good, and the best ones aren't necessarily Italian or expensive. I like canned organic tomatoes by Eden Foods and Muir Glen, but I also use the boxed Italian Pomi tomatoes. When choosing canned tomatoes, read the label to see what else, if anything, is with them. Cayenne, onions, and peppers may add a dimension to your sauce that you don't really want. You can choose from whole canned tomatoes, crushed tomatoes in puree, and diced tomatoes in water. If you rely on canned tomatoes, try several brands side by side to see which one you prefer and how much they differ.

USING FRESH TOMATOES: The delight of a sauce made with fresh tomatoes is its summery essence, but there's no point in using fresh fruits if they aren't perfect to start with—ripe and perfumed. The ideal tomato for sauce is one with little juice, which allows the watery juices to evaporate rapidly. Thick-fleshed not-very-juicy Romas, San Marzanos, and other plum-shaped varieties are sauce tomatoes. You certainly can use juicier varieties, but they will require more time to cook down. Longer cooking benefits tomatoes that are very tart or mixtures of many ingredients whose flavors need time to marry.

USING A FOOD MILL: A food mill is a great timesaver for making tomato sauces. Just wash, chop, and cook the tomatoes—the skins and seeds will be removed quickly by this simple mechanical device. If you want a chunky sauce, you'll have to peel, seed, and chop the tomatoes first since the food mill will effectively puree them.

CORRECTING FOR LACKLUSTER FLAVOR: If your sauce seems a little weak, you can strengthen it by adding a tablespoon or two of tomato paste or puree.

ACIDITY: Since all tomatoes have some acidity, cook them in a pot that won't react, such as enamel-lined cast iron, glass, or stainless steel. Aluminum does nothing for their taste. Excessive acidity or tartness can be corrected with the addition of a little sugar. Yellow tomatoes can be used for sauce, but since they tend to be very low in acid and are usually quite juicy, they don't always provide the desired tartness and need more time on the stove to thicken. You may want to add a little vinegar or lemon at the end.

Fresh Tomato Sauce

3 pounds ripe tomatoes, quartered

3 tablespoons chopped basil or
   1 tablespoon chopped marjoram

Salt and freshly milled pepper

2 tablespoons extra virgin olive oil or
   butter

Put the tomatoes in a heavy pan with the basil. Cover and cook over medium-high heat. The tomatoes should yield their juices right away, but keep an eye on the pot to make sure the pan isn't dry. You don't want the tomatoes to scorch. When the tomatoes have broken down after about 10 minutes, pass them through a food mill. If you want the final sauce to be thicker, return it to the pot and cook over low heat, stirring frequently, until it's as thick as you want. Season with salt and pepper to taste and stir in the oil.

Tomato Sauce Concassé

2½ to 3 pounds ripe tomatoes

2 tablespoons butter

1 small white onion, finely diced

Salt and freshly milled pepper

Make an X on the bottom of each tomato with a small, sharp knife. Plunge them into a pot of boiling water until the skins roll back, 10 to 15 seconds, then peel, seed, and finely chop them. Heat the butter in a wide skillet over medium heat, add the onion, and cook until wilted, about 5 minutes. Add the chopped tomatoes and simmer, stirring occasionally, until the watery juices have cooked off, 15 to 30 minutes, depending on the tomatoes. Season with salt and pepper to taste.

FREEZING TOMATO SAUCE

Making sauce to freeze for the winter isn't a big production—or a time-consuming one. When tomatoes are in season, I make the Fresh Tomato Sauce using 4 to 5 pounds tomatoes or whatever is convenient. When it's cool, I ladle it into plastic freezer bags in 1- or 2-cup portions and lay the bags on the freezer floor until they harden. This makes slim packages that are easy to store upright, taking little space. When you warm the sauce, you can season it with crushed garlic or an herb that goes with the dish you're making.

THIS quick little sauce is one I make on a regular basis during the brief time good tomatoes are in the market. It takes about 20 minutes from start to finish, depending on the type of tomatoes used. This sauce offers simple, pure tomato flavor. It's delicious tossed with linguine.

MAKES ABOUT 2½ CUPS

HERE the finished sauce retains the texture of diced tomatoes because it's not run through a food mill.

MAKES ABOUT 2 CUPS

Tomato Sauce with Herbs: Add 2 tablespoons chopped basil or parsley or 2 teaspoons chopped marjoram or rosemary to the onions.

Tomato Sauce with Cream: Stir in ¼ cup cream or crème fraîche at the end.

Tomato Sauce with Pepper Flakes: Sauté the onion in olive oil with ½ teaspoon red pepper flakes, then add the tomatoes and cook as described.

Cherry Tomato Sauce

CHERRY tomatoes often have better flavor than their larger counterparts, particularly early in the season.

MAKES ABOUT 1 CUP

1 pint cherry tomatoes, stems removed
Salt and freshly milled pepper
Pinch sugar

2 teaspoons extra virgin olive oil or butter
1 teaspoon finely chopped herb— tarragon, basil, lovage, rosemary, marjoram

Put the tomatoes in a saucepan or skillet with ⅓ cup water over high heat. Cover and cook until the tomatoes begin to split, adding water in small amounts if the pan becomes dry. When most of the tomatoes have burst open, pass them through a food mill or push through a sieve to remove the skins and seeds. Season with salt, pepper, and sugar to correct the acidity if necessary. Stir in the oil and the herb.

Oven-Roasted Tomato Sauce

A GOOD treatment both for tomatoes at their peak and for those that aren't quite at perfection— roasting concentrates their flavor. The oven temperature isn't really crucial, so take advantage of an oven that's being used for something else.

MAKES ABOUT 2 CUPS

2½ pounds Roma tomatoes, halved lengthwise
1 onion, thinly sliced

4 thyme or marjoram sprigs
2 to 3 tablespoons olive oil
Salt and freshly milled pepper

Preheat the oven to 375°F. Put the tomatoes in a single layer in a baking pan with the onion and thyme, drizzle the oil over all, and season with salt and pepper. Bake until they're soft, shriveled, and falling apart, 45 minutes to 1 hour. Remove the thyme branches and puree or pass through a food mill. Taste for salt and season with pepper.

Grilled Tomato Sauce

GRILLING or broiling tomatoes brings out flavor by caramelizing their sugary juices.

MAKES ABOUT 2 CUPS

2 pounds ripe tomatoes
3 tablespoons olive oil
½ small onion, finely diced

Salt and freshly milled pepper
Pinch sugar if needed

Rub the tomatoes lightly with oil, then grill, broil, or sear them in a heavy skillet, turning them frequently, until blistered and charred. Puree them, skin and all. Don't worry about the black flecks. Meanwhile, heat the remaining oil in a skillet over medium heat, add the onion, and sauté until translucent, about 5 minutes. Add the pureed tomatoes and cook, stirring frequently, until the sauce has thickened. Season with salt, a little pepper, and sugar to correct the acidity if needed.

Grilled Tomato Sauce with Basil Puree Puree 1 cup packed basil leaves with 2 garlic cloves, 3 tablespoons extra virgin olive oil, and water if needed. Add to the grilled tomato sauce and season with a little balsamic or red wine vinegar to taste. Use warm or at room temperature with pasta and as a sauce for grilled vegetables. (This makes a wonderful base for a vinaigrette.) Makes 2$\frac{1}{2}$ cups.

Grilled Tomato Sauce with Garlic

2$\frac{1}{2}$ pounds ripe tomatoes

About 3 tablespoons vegetable oil

1 teaspoon dried oregano, preferably Mexican

15 garlic cloves, unpeeled

Salt

PAN-ROASTED garlic and tomatoes make a richly concentrated sauce to use with corn dishes, grilled vegetables, beans, polenta, and enchiladas.

MAKES ABOUT 3 CUPS

Toss the tomatoes with a little oil to coat them, then grill, broil, or sear in a heavy skillet until wrinkled and charred in places. Toast the oregano in a dry skillet until fragrant, then remove to a dish. Toss the garlic cloves with enough oil to coat lightly, then put them in the same skillet. Cover and cook over medium heat, shaking the pan occasionally, until browned on the outside and tender when pressed. Peel the garlic when cool enough to handle.

Puree the tomatoes and garlic in a blender until smooth. Heat 2 tablespoons oil in a wide, deep skillet over medium-high heat. Pour in the tomato sauce and add the oregano. Simmer the sauce, stirring frequently, until it's thickened, about 10 minutes. Season with salt to taste.

Grilled Tomato Sauce with Chiles: Toast 2 ancho chiles in a 300°F oven until puffed and fragrant, about 3 minutes. Remove the stems, seeds, and veins, tear the pods into pieces, and puree in a blender with the tomatoes and garlic.

Quick Canned Tomato Sauce

1 28-ounce can diced tomatoes, drained, or crushed tomatoes in puree

$\frac{1}{4}$ cup finely diced onion

1 garlic clove, peeled and smashed

2 to 4 tablespoons olive oil or butter

Salt and freshly milled pepper

TOMATOES are in season for such a brief moment that I often end up using canned tomatoes for sauce. This one can't be surpassed for ease and is perfectly fine when made with good-quality tomatoes.

MAKES ABOUT 3 CUPS

Combine the tomatoes, onion, garlic, and oil in a wide skillet. Simmer for 20 to 30 minutes, stirring occasionally, until the excess water is cooked off and the oil has separated. Season with salt and pepper to taste. The tomatoes will have broken down, but if you want a smooth sauce, pass it through a food mill or quickly puree it in a blender.

Variations: Use any of those suggested on page 62 for Tomato Sauce Concassé.

Red Wine Tomato Sauce

USE this as seasoning as well as a sauce. Stir a spoonful into hearty grain dishes, serve with Herb-Crusted Tofu and Lentil and Caramelized Onion Croquettes, or toss with pasta and chickpeas for a substantial cold-weather pasta.

MAKES ABOUT 4 CUPS

2 tablespoons olive oil

2 small onions, finely minced or grated

2 small bay leaves

6 thyme sprigs or $^1/_2$ teaspoon dried

1 teaspoon dried oregano

1 teaspoon dried savory

Pinch red pepper flakes

3 large garlic cloves, minced

1 cup dry red wine

1 28-ounce can crushed tomatoes in puree

Salt and freshly milled pepper

Heat the oil in a wide skillet. Add the onions, herbs, and pepper flakes and cook over medium heat, stirring frequently, for 15 minutes. Add the garlic during the last few minutes. Raise the heat, add the wine and $^1/_2$ cup water, and simmer until reduced by half, 12 to 15 minutes. Add the tomatoes and $^1/_2$ teaspoon salt. Simmer until the sauce has thickened, about 35 minutes. Taste for salt and season with pepper.

Variation with Olives: This sauce is good with sturdy pasta, such as rigatoni, and grilled or fried polenta. Pit and finely chop 1/3 cup Kalamata, Niçoise, or oil-cured olives. Add them for the last 20 minutes of the cooking along with 1 tablespoon capers and 2 tablespoons chopped parsley.

Tomato Sauce with Dried Mushrooms

LONGER simmering builds a complex and mellow flavor in this sauce.

MAKES ABOUT 2$^1/_2$ CUPS

$^1/_2$ to 1 ounce dried porcini

2 tablespoons olive oil

1 small onion, finely diced

1 large garlic clove, sliced

4 thyme sprigs or $^1/_4$ teaspoon dried

1 bay leaf

2 teaspoons chopped rosemary or $^1/_2$ teaspoon dried

Salt and freshly milled pepper

1 28-ounce can crushed tomatoes in puree

2 tablespoons tomato paste

$^1/_2$ teaspoon balsamic or red wine vinegar

Cover the mushrooms with 1 cup warm water, let stand for 30 minutes, then squeeze dry and chop. Strain the soaking water and reserve. Warm the oil in a wide skillet with the onion, garlic, and herbs. Cook over medium-high heat for about 5 minutes, stirring frequently. Add the mushrooms and cook for 5 minutes more. Season with salt and pepper. Pour in half the mushroom-soaking liquid and cook until completely evaporated, scraping the pan to work in any caramelized bits of onion. Add the tomatoes, tomato paste, and remaining mushroom liquid. Lower the heat and simmer for 30 minutes. Add vinegar at the end to taste.

Yogurt Sauces

SMOOTH *and creamy with a pleasant edge of tartness, yogurt-based sauces can be used as dips, or cooling accompaniments to a wide range of foods: fresh or grilled vegetables—most notably cucumbers, beets, tomatoes, fennel, and carrots; falafel, grain-based dishes, chickpeas, and lentils; and as a condiment for curries and vegetable fritters.*

The success of any yogurt sauce depends on the quality of the yogurt. Use plain yogurt that has not been stabilized with gums and gelatins for a sweet natural flavor with a mild tang. I recommend using whole-milk or low-fat yogurt—both taste so much better than most nonfat yogurts, which tend to have a thin, slightly sour taste. Draining off the whey enriches the flavor of nonfat yogurt, but still it can't make the memorable sauce that a richer yogurt does. (To drain yogurt, see page 47.) If you can find goat's milk yogurt, try it mixed with cow's milk yogurt or a little sour cream.

Another crucial element is the treatment of the garlic, an essential ingredient in most of these sauces. Pounding it in a mortar with a little sea salt until you have a mushy paste results in something very different from garlic that's minced, whether by hand or in the food processor. Though it seems easier to reach for the garlic press, pounded garlic gains a subtle sweetness—a trade-off that's worth the small extra effort.

These sauces keep well for 4 or 5 days when refrigerated. As they stand, their flavors mellow and deepen.

Yogurt Sauce with Cucumbers, Cumin, and Mint

2 cups yogurt, drained, for 1 hour

1 small cucumber, peeled if waxed

2 scallions, including a few inches of the greens, minced

2 tablespoons finely chopped mint

¼ to ½ teaspoon ground cumin

1 tablespoon extra virgin olive oil

¼ teaspoon salt or to taste

Freshly milled white pepper to taste

SERVE this cooling sauce with grains, vegetable fritters, and bean croquettes.

MAKES ABOUT 1½ CUPS

Stir all the ingredients together in a bowl and let stand at least 15 minutes for the flavors to develop.

Yogurt Sauce with Cayenne and Dill

WHEN my friend Clifford Wright made this sauce for me, I couldn't stop eating it. Endlessly enjoyable, you'll see this sauce suggested throughout the book.

MAKES 1¹/₂ CUPS

1 cup yogurt

¹/₂ cup Yogurt Cheese, page 47, or sour cream

1 large garlic clove

Salt

2 teaspoons chopped dill

³/₄ teaspoon cayenne or hot paprika

Whisk the yogurt and yogurt cheese together. In a mortar, mash the garlic to a paste with ¹/₂ teaspoon salt; measure 1 teaspoon, then add it to the yogurt with the dill and cayenne. If you have time, refrigerate for 1 hour before serving.

Yogurt Tahini Sauce

THE tahini gives this sauce a rich, round taste that cuts the sharpness of the yogurt. Use in pita sandwiches and on grilled vegetables.

MAKES 1¹/₂ CUPS

1 garlic clove

Salt

2 tablespoons tahini

1 cup yogurt

2 tablespoons fresh lemon juice and grated zest of lemon

Pound the garlic and ¹/₄ teaspoon salt together in a mortar to make a mushy paste. Stir in the tahini, then gradually stir in the yogurt and lemon zest. Season with lemon juice to taste.

Raita with Cucumber and Spices

THIS classic, cooling accompaniment to spicy or rich Indian dishes also can be used as a dip for vegetables—it makes a fragrant sauce for baked potatoes, yams, and roasted shredded eggplant.

MAKES ABOUT 3 CUPS

1 jalapeño chile, seeded and coarsely chopped

3 garlic cloves, coarsely chopped

1 tablespoon chopped cilantro stems

1 tablespoon grated ginger

Salt

2¹/₂ cups yogurt, drained for 30 minutes

1 cucumber, peeled if waxed, and grated

¹/₂ cup grated carrot

2 tablespoons ghee

1 tablespoon coriander seeds

1 tablespoon black mustard seeds

1 tablespoon cumin seeds

Juice of 1 lime or to taste

Pound or puree the chile, garlic, cilantro, and ginger with a few pinches salt to make a fairly smooth paste, then stir it into the drained yogurt with the cucumber and carrot. Heat the ghee in a small pan over medium-high heat. Add the coriander, mustard, and cumin seeds and sizzle until the mustard seeds begin to turn gray, after a minute or so. Swirl this into the yogurt mixture. Add lime juice to taste, starting with ¹/₂ lime. Let stand for 1 hour or so for the flavors to develop.

Sauces with Nuts and Seeds

NUTS *and seeds are luxurious foods because of their richness and inherent goodness, so it follows that sauces based on nuts and seeds make relatively plain foods extremely satisfying. Peanut sauces grace noodles; Middle Eastern tarator sauces based on sesame and other nuts nap all kinds of grains, legumes, and vegetables; and hazelnuts and almonds form the background of the glorious Romesco Sauce. Depending on the stability of the other ingredients, most nut-based sauces keep well for at least several days.*

Tahini with Lemon and Garlic

1 plump garlic clove, coarsely chopped
Salt

$^1/_3$ cup tahini
Juice of 1 large lemon

Pound the garlic to a paste with $^1/_4$ teaspoon salt in a mortar, then stir it into the tahini. Begin stirring in about $^1/_2$ cup water until the sauce is as thin as you want it, then add the lemon juice to taste. Taste for salt and add more if needed.

THIS silky Lebanese sauce can be drizzled over braised greens, chickpeas, lentils, and falafel or served as a dip or with pita bread and sliced cucumbers.

MAKES ABOUT $^1/_2$ CUP

Sesame Sauce with Tofu

4 ounces silken tofu
$^1/_4$ cup tahini
1 large garlic clove, coarsely chopped
Juice of $^1/_2$ lemon, plus more to taste

1 teaspoon dark sesame oil
Salt
Chopped parsley

Puree the tofu, tahini, garlic, 2 tablespoons lemon juice, and the sesame oil in a blender or food processor, adding just enough water to thin the sauce to the desired consistency. Taste and season with salt and lemon juice if needed. Serve in a bowl, garnished with the parsley.

THE tofu disappears in this sauce, but you can still enjoy its benefits.

MAKES ABOUT 1 CUP

Tarator Sauce

$^1/_2$ cup pine nuts, almonds, walnuts, or hazelnuts
1 slice sturdy white bread, crusts removed
1 garlic clove

Salt
2 tablespoons fresh lemon juice
Finely chopped parsley
Paprika or cayenne

Toast the pine nuts in a small skillet until golden. For other nuts, lightly roast in a moderate oven for 6 to 8 minutes.

Moisten the bread with water and set aside to soak. In a mortar, mash the garlic, $^1/_4$ teaspoon salt, and the nuts until smooth. Squeeze the bread and add it to the mixture with

THE particular nut used in tarator (nut) sauces can vary. My favorite is made with pine nuts, which have a haunting but subtle flavor. Excellent on grilled eggplant.

MAKES ABOUT 1 CUP

½ cup water. Work by hand, in a blender, or in a food processor until the sauce is smooth and thin, adding more water if needed. Season with lemon juice and taste for salt. Tarator sauce will thicken as it sits, so you may need to thin it out again just before serving. Pour into a bowl and sprinkle with a little chopped parsley and a dash of paprika. Keeps for 2 or 3 days.

Walnut Sauce

FOR a superb sauce, use the new-crop walnuts that arrive in the fall. Excellent tossed with fresh pasta (dilute it first with the cooking water), spooned over broiled eggplant, grilled zucchini, fennel, and cooked greens, especially chard.

MAKES ABOUT 1 CUP

¾ cup freshly cracked walnuts

1 small garlic clove

Salt and freshly milled white pepper

2 to 3 tablespoons extra virgin olive oil or roasted walnut oil

Grind the walnuts, garlic, and ¼ teaspoon salt in a mortar or food processor until smooth, then gradually add the oil. Thin to the desired consistency with about ¼ cup boiling water. The sauce will thicken a little as it cools. Taste for salt and season with pepper.

Rich Sesame Sauce or Marinade

TRY this scrumptious sauce over grains or grilled vegetables or as a marinade for tofu and tempeh.

MAKES ABOUT 1 CUPS

2 tablespoons Dijon mustard

3 tablespoons honey

6 tablespoons soy sauce

6 tablespoons mild olive, sunflower seed, or sesame oil

2 tablespoons dark sesame oil

¼ cup sesame seeds, toasted in a small pan

4 to 6 garlic cloves to taste, peeled and smashed

1 teaspoon ground ginger

¼ teaspoon freshly milled pepper

Put all the ingredients in a blender and puree until smooth.

Variation with Peanuts: Roast or fry raw peanuts until golden and use ½ cup light peanut oil flavored with 2 tablespoons roasted peanut oil.

Peanut Sauces

RICH and pungent peanut sauces are intriguing. They greatly enhance the simplest foods, such as simmered, fried, or grilled tofu, tempeh, grilled yams, Chinese noodles, brown rice, and spring rolls. These sauces will keep for several days, but the garlic flavor does grow with time.

Quick Peanut Sauce

3 tablespoons unsweetened peanut butter

2 tablespoons rice wine vinegar

1 tablespoon chopped cilantro

1 plump garlic clove, minced or put through a press

2 teaspoons soy sauce or to taste

1 teaspoon light brown sugar

1/2 teaspoon chile oil

Salt

THIS is truly quick and definitely good, especially with Golden Tofu and brown rice.

MAKES ABOUT 1/2 CUP

Combine all the ingredients except the salt, adding 2 to 4 tablespoons warm water to make it the consistency you wish. Add 1/4 teaspoon salt and then taste.

Peanut-Tofu Sauce

1 or 2 garlic cloves to taste, minced or put through a press

1 tablespoon chopped shallot or scallion

1/4 cup unsweetened peanut butter

5 ounces silken tofu

1 teaspoon Lan Chi Chilli Paste with soybean or 1 serrano chile, minced

1/2 teaspoon salt or tamari to taste

IF you're looking for ways to eat more tofu, try it here.

MAKES ABOUT 1 CUP

In a food processor or blender, puree all the ingredients with enough water to loosen the mixture. Taste for salt and season as needed.

Thai Peanut Sauce

3 tablespoons Thai peanut paste

1 teaspoon Thai red chili paste

1 cup unsweetened coconut milk

1 scallion, including half of the greens, thinly sliced

MAKE this tasty sauce when you're lacking the time and ingredients to make a real satay sauce from scratch. You can rely on it to make a simply prepared tofu dish into a respectable dinner.

MAKES ABOUT 1 CUP

Work the peanut and red chili pastes into the coconut milk until smooth, then heat in a small saucepan until boiling. Turn off the heat and stir in the scallions. Taste and increase the heat if you like by adding more chili paste.

Romesco Sauce

nut Bechamel Sauce

THE combined essences of grilled peppers, tomatoes, chile, and roasted nuts make this Catalan sauce utterly vivid. Serve it with warm chickpeas or large white beans and/or virtually any grilled vegetable. Spread it on garlic-rubbed croutons and cover with sliced green olives and parsley for a delicious appetizer to serve with a glass of sherry.

MAKES ABOUT 1 CUP

1 slice country-style white bread
Olive oil for frying
¼ cup almonds, roasted
¼ cup hazelnuts, roasted and peeled
3 garlic cloves
1 to 2 teaspoons ground red chile or red pepper flakes to taste
4 Roma tomatoes

1 tablespoon parsley leaves
Salt and freshly milled pepper
1 teaspoon sweet paprika
1 red bell pepper, roasted
¼ cup sherry vinegar
½ cup plus 2 tablespoons extra virgin olive oil, preferably Spanish

Fry the bread in a little olive oil until golden and crisp. When cool, grind the bread, nuts, garlic, and chile in a food processor. Add everything but the vinegar and oil and process until smooth. With the machine running, gradually pour in the vinegar, then the oil. Taste and make sure the sauce has plenty of piquancy and enough salt.

Other Sauces

RED wine, red chile, and pureed vegetables comprise sauces that flatter foods such as pasta, enchiladas or posole, egg dishes, and so forth. Certainly many other sauces fail to fit neatly into the categories already mentioned in this chapter, but there are a few stand-alone renegades that I enjoy making regularly on a seasonal basis. Here they are.

Red Chile Sauce

ALSO known as chile colorado, red chile sauce is mainly dried red chile and water, although different seasonings are added depending on where in the Southwest you are. Make sure you're using ground chile, not chili powder, which includes other ingredients. This smooth brick-red sauce is served with enchiladas and burritos, and used as a flavoring for posole or beans.

MAKES ABOUT 2½ CUPS

2 tablespoons vegetable oil
2 tablespoons finely diced onion
1 large garlic clove, finely chopped
1 teaspoon dried oregano, optional

2 tablespoons flour
½ teaspoon ground cumin, optional
½ cup ground red chile
Salt

Heat the oil with the onion, garlic, and oregano in a heavy saucepan. Cook over medium heat until the onion begins to color a little, about 6 minutes. Add the flour and cumin and cook for at least 2 minutes, stirring constantly. The flour will brown slightly. Mix the chile and 2½ cups warm water and pour it all at once into the roux, whisking as you do so. Keep stirring until the sauce thickens, then lower the heat and cook, stirring occasionally, for 15 minutes. Season with salt to taste. If it tastes a little harsh, just a few drops of vinegar will soften it.

Red Pepper Sauce

3 large red bell peppers, roasted

2 tablespoons olive oil

1 onion, minced

3 tablespoons basil or 1½ teaspoons dried

1 tablespoon chopped marjoram or 1 teaspoon dried

Salt

½ cup dry white wine

¼ cup tomato puree

1 tablespoon tomato paste

2 cups water or Basic Vegetable Stock, page 196, made with summer vegetables

2 to 3 teaspoons white wine vinegar

1 tablespoon butter, optional

SERVE this silky sauce with grilled vegetables, roulades, frittatas, or pastas or wherever its sweet brightness is called for.

MAKES ABOUT 2½ CUPS

Coarsely chop the peeled peppers. Warm the olive oil in a medium skillet with the onion and half the herbs. Add the peppers and ½ teaspoon salt and cook over medium heat until the onion is soft, about 10 minutes. Add the wine and cook until it's syrupy, then add the tomato puree, paste, and water. Simmer, covered, for 25 minutes. Puree, then pass through a food mill. Season to taste with the vinegar and stir in the butter (it rounds the flavors and gives the sauce a silky sheen). Reheat before serving and stir in the remaining herbs at the last minute.

Curry Sauce

1 onion, chopped

½ cup dry white wine

1 tablespoon butter

Salt and freshly milled pepper

2 teaspoons curry powder

1 tablespoon flour

1½ cups heated Basic Vegetable Stock, page 196, or water

1 cup whole milk or a mixture of cream and milk

SERVE this thin golden sauce over rice or use it as the base for a creamed curried vegetable soup, adding a cooked pureed vegetable such as broccoli or asparagus.

MAKES ABOUT 2 CUPS

Put the onion, wine, butter, ½ teaspoon salt, and a few grinds of pepper in a saucepan and simmer, covered, for 4 to 5 minutes. Remove the lid and cook until the wine becomes syrupy, then add the curry powder and flour. Cook for 3 minutes, stirring frequently, over low heat, then whisk in the stock all at once. Cook over low heat or in a double boiler, partially covered, for 25 minutes. Puree, then return to the heat, stir in the milk, and cook until heated through. Taste for salt and pepper.

Mustard-Cilantro Sauce

BECAUSE of their
assertiveness, mustard-
based sauces always
complement broccoli and
cauliflower and are good
with tofu and tempeh,
too.

MAKES ABOUT ½ CUP

½ cup sour cream or whole-milk yogurt

¼ cup Dijon mustard

2 tablespoons fresh lime juice

2 to 3 teaspoons light brown sugar

¼ cup finely chopped cilantro

Salt and freshly milled pepper to taste

Put all the ingredients in a bowl along with 2 tablespoons water and stir until smooth. Cover and let stand for 1 hour or so for the flavors to mellow. Before serving, taste the sauce on the vegetable or tofu and make any adjustments—more tartness, more sweetness—if necessary.

Fresh Horseradish Sauce

FRESH horseradish root
makes the nose tingle.
This sauce can be made
vegan by using pureed
silken tofu and possibly
increasing the flavorings.
Serve with vegetable
fritters, baked potatoes,
cabbage, and beets.

MAKES ABOUT 1 CUP

1 3-inch chunk horseradish root

1 cup drained yogurt, sour cream, or
cream, whipped

2 tablespoons finely snipped chives

1 tablespoon sugar or to taste

Salt

White wine vinegar

Peel the horseradish, removing any green. Coarsely chop it, then partially puree in a food processor or blender with enough water to loosen the mixture. It should retain some texture—not be a puree. Drain it to get rid of the water, then combine with the yogurt, chives, sugar, a pinch of salt, and a few drops of vinegar.

Goat Cheese Sauce

THIS couldn't be easier to
make, and it makes a
glorious finish to roasted
root vegetables and
summer's vegetables,
especially those assembled
in the Eggplant Torta.

MAKES ABOUT 1½ CUPS

¾ cup soft goat cheese

1 cup cream, half-and-half, whole milk,
or Roasted Vegetable Stock, page 198

1 garlic clove smashed in a mortar with
½ teaspoon salt

Freshly milled white pepper

2 teaspoons minced rosemary, basil, or
thyme

Working directly in a medium skillet, mash the cheese with the liquid and garlic until partially smooth. Just before serving, simmer it over medium heat, stirring to blend and melt the cheese. The longer you cook the sauce, the thicker it will be. (Or you can make it thinner by adding more liquid.) Taste for salt, season with pepper, stir in the herbs, and serve.

Warm Gorgonzola Sauce: Make the sauce using Gorgonzola dolcelatte in place of the goat cheese. Though you can use a stock, I think this tastes much better made with light or heavy cream, and rosemary and thyme are preferable to basil. Try this spooned over a baked potato or stirred into a simple risotto.

Asian Dipping Sauces

USE these versatile sauces with potstickers and dumplings, as a marinade or sauce for tofu and tempeh, and with grilled vegetables, especially eggplant.

Hoisin Sauce with Chili Paste and Tangerine Zest

3 tablespoons dark soy sauce

2 tablespoons dark sesame oil

1 tablespoon hoisin sauce

2 teaspoons Lan Chi Chilli Paste with Garlic

1 tablespoon sugar

2 teaspoons finely chopped tangerine or orange zest

1 tablespoon minced ginger

2 tablespoons chopped cilantro

A DARK, luscious, aromatic sauce.

MAKES ABOUT ½ CUP

Stir all the ingredients together in a bowl. Taste and adjust the seasonings if necessary.

Sesame-Soy Sauce

2 tablespoons soy sauce

1 tablespoon roasted sesame oil

1 tablespoon finely chopped scallion

A VERY simple sauce for tofu and blanched vegetables.

MAKES ABOUT ¼ CUP

Stir all the ingredients together.

Peanut-Soy Sauce with Ginger and Scallions

2 tablespoons soy sauce

1 teaspoon minced ginger

1 tablespoon chopped scallion, white part only

1 tablespoon roasted peanut oil

HEATING the oil brings out the flavors of the ginger and scallion.

MAKES ABOUT ¼ CUP

Combine the soy sauce, ginger, and scallion in a small bowl. Heat the oil in a small skillet over medium heat until hot but not smoking, then whisk it into the soy sauce mixture.

Rice Wine Vinegar with Garlic

½ cup rice wine vinegar

1 small garlic clove, slivered

THIS sweet vinegar is good with dumplings and spring rolls.

MAKES ABOUT ½ CUP

Combine the vinegar and garlic and let stand for at least 15 minutes before using.

THESE foods are hot and spicy, vinegary and acidic, or sweet. In some cases, several intense elements come together in a single bite. Like sauces, condiments enhance other foods, but their flavors tend to be so distilled or concentrated that their place in a meal is more likely to be on the side than on the top of foods. In properly sealed jars, traditional pickles and chutneys keep more or less indefinitely, but the recipes here are for quickly made, more briefly stored varieties that don't involve canning—or the large quantities that canning usually entails. Having a few condiments, pickles, or chutneys at your disposal enables you to make simple, plain foods special while easily expanding your repertoire as a cook.

Pepper Sauce

PEPPER sauce—vinegar made hot by pickling hot peppers—is an essential southern condiment, used for sprinkling over greens or wherever you want the acid nip of the vinegar combined with the bite of pickled peppers.

MAKES ABOUT 1 CUP

4 ounces chiles—serrano, cayenne, tabasco, or other small, straight chiles

1 cup white vinegar

Wash the peppers in cold water until clean, then drain in a colander. Drop them into a bottle that has been freshly washed in hot, soapy water and rinsed clean. It should have a narrow neck so that the vinegar can be released in drops. Bring the vinegar to a boil in a small pan, then transfer it to a measuring cup and pour it into the bottle until full. Let it sit, uncapped, until cool. The peppers will absorb some of the vinegar. Add more vinegar to fill the bottle, then cap and set aside in the cupboard. The vinegar will be ready to use in 6 weeks.

Golden Mustard Barbecue Sauce

FRIENDS and barbecue experts Bill and Cheryl Jamison gave me this recipe with grilled or smoked vegetables especially in mind. They write that "this mustard-based sauce, common in South Carolina and Georgia, offers a tangier alternative to the sweet tomato-based barbecue sauces that have become the supermarket standard." Two to 3 teaspoons brown sugar can be added for those who like it sweet.

MAKES 2 CUPS

³/₄ cup white vinegar

³/₄ cup prepared yellow mustard

¹/₂ onion, minced

¹/₄ cup canned crushed tomatoes

1 tablespoon paprika

6 garlic cloves, minced

1¹/₂ teaspoons salt

¹/₂ teaspoon cayenne

¹/₂ teaspoon freshly milled black pepper

Mix the ingredients, plus ¹/₃ cup water, in a saucepan and bring to a simmer. Reduce the heat to low and cook until the onions are tender and the mixture thickens, approximately 15 to 20 minutes. Use the sauce warm or chilled. It keeps, refrigerated, for several weeks.

Harissa

12 dried red New Mexican chiles

3 guajillo chiles

4 plump garlic cloves, coarsely chopped

Salt

1 tablespoon caraway seeds

1 1/2 teaspoons coriander seeds

1 1/2 teaspoons cumin seeds

1 tablespoon olive oil, plus extra for storage

Cayenne, optional

I ALWAYS like to have a jar of this condiment in the refrigerator. Pounding it in a mortar provides a heady, sensual delight for the cook, but for speed you may prefer to use a food processor.

MAKES ABOUT 1 CUP

Wipe off the chiles with a damp cloth, break off the stems, shake out as many seeds as you can, and pull out any large veins. (If you're sensitive to chiles, wear gloves—these are the hot parts.) Discard any gray or yellowed areas on the skin—they may have a moldy taste. Tear the chiles into pieces, put them in a bowl, then cover with boiling water and let stand for at least 30 minutes to soften. Remove from the bowl, then snip them into smaller pieces with scissors.

In a food processor: Grind the chiles with the garlic, 1/2 teaspoon salt, the caraway, coriander, cumin, and oil until a smooth paste forms. Add a little of the chile soaking water to loosen the mixture.

By hand: This can also be done by hand in a mortar with a heavy pestle, but plan to spend some time with it and don't expect your sauce to be perfectly smooth. The chile skins are tough. Pound the garlic to a paste with 1/2 teaspoon salt, the caraway, coriander, and cumin. Add the chile and keep pounding until you have a smooth paste. Taste for salt and stir in the oil.

If you want more heat, add cayenne to taste. Pack into a clean jar, cover the surface with oil, and refrigerate.

Herb Salts

THESE *aromatic mixtures of toasted seeds and salt bring life to plain foods. The toasted seeds release their aromatic oils and saturate the salt with flavor, making the salt go further and providing a strong flavor accent without adding fat. While they don't go bad, after a week or two they begin to lose their potency.*

Use herb salts as dips for crudités and as seasoning for vegetables and grains. Grind them coarsely, leaving bits of seeds, or finely. You can also put whole toasted seeds and salts in a pepper mill and grind them as you use them. Sea salt and kosher salt tastes best and seem to cling best to the seeds.

Grinding Tools

The suribachi is the Japanese mortar and pestle. It's distinguished by ridges on its ceramic surface that catch the seeds, spices, and salt as they're being ground. This very effective, inexpensive tool can be found at Japanese markets and frequently at natural food stores.

A mortar and pestle is always an effective tool, but if using one made of ceramic, marble, or stone, the bottom should be slightly rough to catch the ingredients so that they don't fly away.

The electric coffee or spice mill cuts rather than pounds the seeds and spices. It works best if you avoid making your herb salt too fine. Designate the mill for spices only. Coffee will pick up any residual flavors, and there always are some.

Gomashio

GOMASHIO, *a Japanese condiment, is delicious over rice and other grains, including hot breakfast cereals like oatmeal, cornmeal, and rice cream.*

MAKES ABOUT ⅓ CUP

⅓ cup white or black sesame seeds or a mixture

2 teaspoons sea salt or kosher salt

Roast the sesame seeds and salt in a heavy skillet over medium heat until fragrant and light gold, about 3 minutes. Grind them in a suribachi or in a small spice grinder. Leave plenty of texture; it shouldn't be a powder.

Toasted Nori with Sesame Seeds

USE *just as you would gomashio. Mix it with leftover white or brown rice and form it into rice balls for a bag lunch item.*

MAKES ABOUT ½ CUP

2 sheets nori (Japanese seaweed)

½ cup white sesame seeds

2 teaspoons sea salt or kosher salt

1 teaspoon red pepper flakes

Toast the nori by passing each sheet repeatedly over a hot burner until it becomes crisp and the color dulls. Put the sheets together and, using scissors, slice them into thin strips, then into small squares. Toast the seeds and salt in a dry skillet over medium heat until the seeds begin to color, then grind them just enough for the salt to adhere. Combine with the nori and pepper flakes. Cool, then store in a covered jar so that they'll stay crisp.

Sichuan Pepper Salt

SPRINKLE *this Chinese condiment on raw cabbage, asparagus, or Asian pear-apples, but especially on corn and eggs, where it really shines.*

MAKES ABOUT ⅓ CUP

2 tablespoons Sichuan peppercorns

1 teaspoon black peppercorns

¼ cup sea salt or kosher salt

Toast the peppercorns and salt in a heavy skillet over medium heat until the peppers are fragrant and the salt has begun to lose its whiteness, about 4 minutes. Grind or pound in a mortar to break up the peppers, then pass through a sieve to separate out the hulls. The black pepper gives spice and warmth to the perfumed Sichuan peppercorns.

Indian Salt with Mixed Spices

3 tablespoons sesame seeds

2 tablespoons coriander seeds

1 tablespoon cumin seeds

2 tablespoons sea salt

1/4 teaspoon cayenne or freshly milled black pepper

Toast the seeds in a dry skillet over medium heat until fragrant. Let them cool briefly on a plate, then grind with the salt and cayenne to make a fine or coarse dipping salt.

IN her classic World of the East, Madhur Jaffrey suggests this combination in what she calls a "dry dip." It has a gutsy flavor and is indeed a good dip for vegetables.

MAKES ABOUT 1/2 CUP

Sea Salt with Fennel Seeds and Thyme

1/4 cup fennel seeds

1 1/2 teaspoons dried marjoram

1 teaspoon dried thyme

4 teaspoons sea salt

Toast the fennel seeds in a dry skillet over medium heat until they release their aroma and begin to darken slightly, 4 to 5 minutes. Cool, then grind with the herbs and salt.

USE this mixture with carrots, cucumbers, and fennel or to season soups and stews.

MAKES ABOUT 1/3 CUP

Relishes

As their name implies, relishes lend a pleasing, zestful element to a plate of food. They don't last quite as long nor are they as vinegary as pickles, although they can be canned and are sometimes lightly pickled. I think of relishes as fresh and spritely condiments, whether they're raw or cooked. Some relishes are at their peak for but a few hours while others can linger for weeks and even months in the refrigerator, to be brought out at a moment's notice.

Pepper Relish with Anise Seeds

1 pound bell peppers, a variety of colors

3 large garlic cloves

Salt and freshly milled pepper

3 tablespoons extra virgin olive oil

1 bay leaf

1 red onion, finely diced

1/2 teaspoon fennel or anise seeds

1 tablespoon tomato paste

1 tablespoon red wine vinegar

1 tablespoon chopped basil or parsley

Seed and finely dice the peppers. Pound the garlic with 1/4 teaspoon salt until mushy. Heat the oil with the bay leaf in a medium skillet over medium heat. Add the onion and fennel seeds and cook for 5 minutes, stirring occasionally. Add the garlic and peppers, lower the heat, and cook for 10 minutes. Stir in the tomato paste, add a few tablespoons water, then cover and cook until the peppers are tender, 5 minutes more. Add the vinegar, raise the heat to high, and reduce until syrupy. Taste for salt, season with pepper, and stir in the basil. Serve warm, at room temperature, or chilled.

A GREAT side dish or topping for crostini, this pepper mélange can also find its way into frittatas, pizzas, and pasta salads or be spooned over polenta and tofu. It keeps, refrigerated, for a week or more.

MAKES 2 CUPS

Cherry Tomato and Olive Relish

ONLY the sweetest, most flavorful tomatoes work in this relish. Use it to accompany mashed potato cakes, grilled polenta, or spooned over Skillet Cheese.

MAKES ABOUT 2½ CUPS

1 pint cherry tomatoes, halved or quartered if large

1 or 2 yellow tomatoes, seeded and finely diced

24 Niçoise olives, pitted and halved

1 tablespoon capers, rinsed

1 tablespoon chopped parsley

2 teaspoons chopped marjoram

5 basil leaves, thinly sliced

1 tablespoon extra virgin olive oil

Fresh lemon juice to taste

Salt and freshly milled pepper

Put the tomatoes in a bowl with the olives, capers, and herbs. Moisten with the olive oil, then season to taste with lemon juice, salt, and pepper. Serve right away or let stand, but try to serve within 1 hour or so.

Corn-Tomato Relish

TRY this with black bean cakes or spooned over Savory Corn Waffles. Best used within the day.

MAKES ABOUT 2 CUPS

Kernels from 2 ears corn, about 1½ cups

1 Roma tomato, seeded and diced

¼ small red or white onion, finely diced

1 or 2 serrano chiles to taste, finely chopped

Juice of 1 lime or to taste

Salt

1 tablespoon chopped cilantro

Blanch the corn in a small pot of boiling water for about 30 seconds; drain and shake dry. Toss the corn with the tomato, onion, and chile. Add lime juice to taste, season with salt, and stir in the cilantro. Cover and refrigerate for 30 minutes or until ready to use.

Variation with Peppers: Add 2 tablespoons *each* finely diced red, green, and yellow bell peppers—or just one kind—to the salsa and stir in 1 tablespoon olive or sunflower seed oil.

Variation with Black Beans: Add ½ cup cooked but fairly firm black beans to the salsa, with another chile and extra lime juice to taste. Chopped basil and marjoram would both be good in this relish.

Pickled Onions

THE easiest pickle in the world to make, these make a gorgeous garnish for sandwiches, salads, cold pastas, or just to serve on the table. The redder the onions, the pinker the pickle. Refrigerated, they keep for weeks, but as time passes they lose some of their crunch.

MAKES ABOUT 1 QUART

1 pound red onions, peeled but left whole

1½ cups white wine vinegar

2 bay leaves

4 marjoram or thyme branches

Several small dried red chiles, optional

1 tablespoon sugar

1 teaspoon black or mixed peppercorns, bruised

Salt

Bring a teakettle of water to a boil. Slice the onions crosswise, ¼ inch thick or thicker. Separate the rings and put them in a colander, then pour the boiling water over them. Mix the other ingredients plus 1½ cups cold water and several pinches salt in a large bowl and stir to dissolve the sugar. Add the onions, submerging them in the liquid by placing a plate on top. If there isn't enough liquid, add equal amounts of vinegar and water. The color will begin to develop in about 15 minutes. You can use the onions then or chill them first. Store in a covered jar in the refrigerator.

Pickled Carrots and Garlic with Cumin

4 carrots

1 small head garlic

Salt

1 jalapeño chile, sliced into rounds, or 1 whole chile de árbol

³/₄ cup apple cider vinegar

1 teaspoon cumin seeds

¹/₂ teaspoon sugar

¹/₂ teaspoon black peppercorns

THIS spunky little pickle will keep, refrigerated, for several weeks.

MAKES 2 CUPS

Peel the carrots and slice them diagonally or crosswise about ³/₈ inch thick. Separate the garlic cloves and peel them. Don't use any that are bruised or sprouting.

Boil the carrots in salted water to cover for 3 minutes, then drain. Combine the remaining ingredients plus ³/₄ cup cold water and ¹/₂ teaspoon salt in a bowl. Stir to dissolve the salt and sugar, then add the carrots. Refrigerate overnight before serving.

Tomato-Onion Relish

1 small red onion, finely and neatly diced

2 ripe tomatoes, 1 red and 1 yellow

1 tablespoon chopped parsley or basil

Several pinches red pepper flakes or 1 serrano chile, minced, optional

Vinegar to taste

Salt and freshly milled pepper

SPOON over grilled vegetables, grilled polenta, or garlic croutons. Refrigerating the onion reduces its pungency and makes it crisp and cold. Best used within the day.

MAKES ABOUT 1 CUP

Put the onion in a bowl with cold water and a few ice cubes to cover. Refrigerate for at least 30 minutes, then drain. Meanwhile, halve, seed, and finely dice the tomatoes, reserving the inner core for another use. Combine the onion, tomatoes, parsley, and red pepper flakes in a bowl. Season to taste with a vinegar that you like—sherry, balsamic, apple cider—a pinch salt, and pepper. Add a few tablespoons cold water for a more saucelike texture.

Sweet and Sour Onions with Dried Fruits

1 pound boiling onions, pearl onions, shallots, or a mixture

2 teaspoons butter

1 tablespoon golden raisins

1 tablespoon dried cherries

1 tablespoon light brown sugar

1 small rosemary sprig

2 tablespoons diced tomatoes, fresh or canned

2 tablespoons red wine vinegar

Salt and freshly milled pepper

BOILING onions are much faster to prepare than the tiny pearl onions, and shallots are also delectable. Serve warm or at room temperature. This relish will keep for several weeks in the refrigerator.

MAKES ABOUT 2¹/₂ CUPS

Boil the onions for 1 minute, then drain and remove the skins. Shallots needn't be parboiled. If shallots show natural divisions, pry them apart, then peel.

Heat the butter in a heavy medium skillet. Add the onions and cook over medium heat, shaking the pan every few minutes, until they're nicely browned, about 15 minutes. Add 2 cups water and the remaining ingredients except the vinegar, salt, and pepper. Cover and simmer until the onions are tender—25 minutes or more, depending on the size. Uncover, raise the heat, add the vinegar, and cook until the liquid has evaporated, leaving behind a thick glaze. Season with salt and pepper.

Gingered Cranberry Sauce

THE *traditional sauce for the holidays, spiked with ginger and clove. This can be made several days in advance.*

MAKES ABOUT 2¹/₂ CUPS

1 12-ounce bag cranberries

³/₄ cup sugar

1 2-inch knob ginger, peeled and thinly sliced into rounds

4 cloves

Grated zest of 2 oranges

Sort through the cranberries, removing any that are mushy, then rinse them well. Combine the remaining ingredients plus ³/₄ cup water in a large saucepan and bring to a boil. Add the cranberries and cook over medium heat until they begin to pop. They needn't all pop—it's nice to have a lot of them whole. Remove from the heat, cool to room temperature, then refrigerate. Serve chilled.

Cranberry Relish with Walnuts

THIS *is the way I prefer my cranberries. If orange seems dull to you, try tangerines, a Meyer lemon, or a few drops of orange oil in its place.*

MAKES ABOUT 3 CUPS

1 12-ounce bag cranberries

1 orange or 2 tangerines

¹/₂ to ³/₄ cup sugar as needed

Salt

1 teaspoon orange flower water, optional

3 tablespoons finely chopped walnuts or pecans

Sort through the cranberries, removing any that are mushy, then rinse well. Chop the orange into large chunks and remove the seeds. Grind the orange and cranberries in a food processor, using short pulses, or in an old-fashioned hand mill (meat grinder). There should be some texture. Turn into a bowl; stir in ¹/₂ cup sugar and a pinch salt and taste. If it's not sweet enough, add more sugar. Season with the orange flower water and stir in the chopped walnuts. Serve chilled. This relish should keep for 5 to 7 days.

Sweet and Sour Quinces with Dried Fruit

A PRETTY, *glistening condiment to serve in the winter months. The acidity and sweetness contrast well with the rich flavors and creamy textures of winter foods, such as the Winter Squash Galette.*

MAKES ABOUT 1¹/₂ CUPS

2 ripe yellow quinces, about 1 pound

Salt

¹/₂ cup granulated sugar

¹/₂ cup light brown sugar, packed

¹/₄ cup apple cider vinegar, preferably unfiltered

1 teaspoon coriander seeds

4 cloves

¹/₄ teaspoon black peppercorns

¹/₃ cup dried cherries or cranberries

¹/₃ cup dark raisins, preferably monukka

¹/₃ cup diced dried apricots or pears

Balsamic vinegar to taste

Cut the quinces into eighths, like apples. Peel and core each piece, then slice crosswise into small pieces slightly less than ¹/₂ inch long. Put the quinces, 2 cups water, and 1 teaspoon salt in a saucepan and boil for 5 minutes. Add the sugars, cider vinegar, and spices, then cook over low heat, covered, until the quinces turn pink, 1 to 1¹/₂ hours. If needed, add more water. Add the dried fruits and cook until they're soft, 12 to 15 minutes. Taste and season with ¹/₂ teaspoon or so of balsamic vinegar if more tartness and sweetness are needed. Store in a clean jar in the refrigerator for several months.

Apple-Pear Chutney

3 apples

2 pears, preferably Anjou or Bosc

1 large yellow quince, if available

1 cup light honey

1/2 cup apple cider vinegar, preferably
unfiltered

1/4 cup balsamic vinegar

1 3-inch cinnamon stick

5 cloves

10 peppercorns

Several slices ginger, optional

BY the time this chutney is done, the vinegar is so mild that it can be served with either savory or sweet dishes—from roasted root vegetables to the Nutmeg Pie or a slice of Manchego cheese.

MAKES ABOUT 2 CUPS

Peel, core, and thinly slice the fruits. Combine the remaining ingredients in a medium saucepan and bring to a boil. Simmer each fruit separately in the syrup until transparent, about 15 minutes, then remove to a bowl or clean glass jar. The quince will take longest. When done, pour the syrup and spices over all, cover, and refrigerate. The chutney will keep for several months.

Apricot and Dried Fruit Chutney

1 1/2 cups whole dried apricots, chopped

1/2 cup golden raisins

1/4 cup currants

1/4 cup dried cherries or cranberries

3 1/2 cups apple juice or water

1/2 cup apple cider vinegar, preferably
unfiltered

2 tablespoons julienne strips of ginger

1/2 teaspoon fennel or anise seeds

1/2 teaspoon black peppercorns

1/2 teaspoon coriander seeds

1/4 teaspoon red pepper flakes

Pinch salt

Balsamic vinegar to taste

MAKES ABOUT 2 1/2 CUPS

Put everything except the balsamic vinegar in a heavy saucepan and bring to a boil. Lower the heat and simmer until the fruit is soft but not mushy and the liquid is reduced to a syrup, about 45 minutes. Stir in 1/2 teaspoon or so balsamic vinegar to taste. Serve right away if desired, but the flavors will merge as it sits. Stored in the refrigerator, the finished chutney should keep for many weeks.

Preserved Lemons

A staple seasoning in North African cuisine, lemons preserved in salt are both a condiment and an ingredient, adding a soft, briny accent to salads and tagines that's altogether different from fresh lemon. The skin is what's used, but Kitty Morse, author of *Come With Me to the Casbah,* uses the soft flesh as well, in vinaigrettes, soups, and other dishes. You can buy these at Middle Eastern delis, but they're not hard to make and they're a pleasure to have in the kitchen.

To make preserved lemons, first sterilize a clean jar large enough to hold the number of lemons you plan to use by submerging it in a pot of boiling water for a full minute. Carefully lift it out with a pair of tongs, allowing the water to drain out, then set it upside down on a clean towel to drain.

You'll need enough lemons to fit in the jar plus extras for juice. Rinse them under warm water, then cut four lengthwise slits in each lemon, going from near the top almost to the bottom, but don't cut all the way through the fruit. Rub sea salt or kosher salt generously into the slits, then put the lemons in the jar, packing them tightly. Add fresh lemon juice to within $1/2$ inch from the top, then cover and put in a cool dark place or the refrigerator to cure for 3 weeks. Sometimes a white film develops over the lemons—just rinse it off. Preserved lemons will keep, refrigerated, for 6 months or longer.

Greetings from the Cook:
Appetizers and First Courses

THIS COLLECTION OF TASTY SMALL ITEMS ASSUAGES OUR HUNGER AT DAY'S END, WHEN WE MAY NOT BE QUITE READY TO EAT OR COOK A MEAL BUT NEED A LITTLE PICK-ME-UP OR A BITE TO TAKE THE EDGE OFF THE APPETITE.

Welcoming appetizers ease the wait for food and keep a clamoring family at bay. A small bite before dinner extends hospitality to guests, setting a tone of conviviality and drawing everyone into a circle of friendship and exchange. When it comes to making these intriguing morsels, there's a wealth of possibilities for the vegetarian cook. Many traditional cuisines have long featured vegetable-based appetizers knowing that meat was to follow.

Hors d'oeuvres can be as informal as a plate of Black Olives with Orange and Fennel or a bowl of Salted Almonds, a dish of celery stalks and sea salt, or a cracker spread with cream cheese and coated with glistening toasted sesame seeds. At the other extreme, your offerings can be as formal as the elaborate Silky Mushroom Pâté with a Scallion-Walnut Topping, which clearly introduces a meal of some importance. In between is a host of items—from a Spicy Eggplant Spread with Thai Basil to salsas, spring rolls, small sandwiches and crostini, warm one-bite pastries, golden wedges of artichoke, and many more delicious little nibbles that are likely to dovetail with your cupboard's contents and your culinary inclinations.

Appetizers

Today appetizers needn't be numerous or complicated. People tend to want just a bite of this or that, pacing themselves so that they don't fill up before dinner. There are many items you can have on hand for such moments—a basket of crudités with a sauce for dipping, seasoned olives, or roasted nuts. Marinated vegetables or little vegetable salads also make good appetizers to serve with rounds of bread or croutons. Cheeses, if any, should come from the lighter end of the spectrum—a square of Baked Ricotta with Thyme or Warm Feta Cheese with Sesame Seeds—saving a rich, buttery Explorateur for dessert.

Regardless of what you offer, make it easy to eat with the fingers or provide plates and forks—and offer napkins either way.

First Courses

The first course helps set the pace of a meal and extends the time spent at the table, especially important for entertaining. Often a first course is more complex than an appetizer, but it can also be as simple as a bowl of soup or a few hors d'oeuvres like olives, crudités, and a dip artfully arranged as an antipasto. Although larger than appetizers, first courses are small enough to feature those favorite foods we no longer eat in main-course quantities, such as a rich pasta or a creamy Goat Cheese Flan, page 589.

First courses can be drawn from recipes throughout the book. Many vegetable dishes—a steamed artichoke, a stuffed vegetable, or a crisply fried food—are good candidates. A slice of a savory galette, a small pizza, or hand-formed ravioli make good first courses, as do soups and salads, especially composed salad plates that draw together a number of diverse elements.

Olives

NIBBLING *from a bowl of olives while sipping a glass of wine is simple, elegant, and easy on the cook. Ethnic markets are where you're likely to find the widest variety of unusual olives, sold in bulk and at the best prices. Some olives are shipped in their brine, which continues to cure as well as to protect them. Ask for some of the brine to be included with the olives (after the olives are weighed) and store them in your refrigerator, where they'll keep for weeks. Or toss them with olive oil when you get home and refrigerate to keep them longer. Olives that are old or poorly stored eventually become spongy and soft. While there are many kinds of olives and ways of curing them, here are some of the most commonly available ones.*

CRACKED GREEN OLIVES: These firm, tart cracked olives, produced in Morocco, Sicily, and California, are made from unripened olives. Tangy, sharp, and with meat that is difficult to free from the pits, they're frequently cooked in stews but can be seasoned with red pepper, garlic, and herbs such as rosemary, cumin, fennel seed, and lemon. They're also good fried or simmered in tomato sauce.

GAETA: These small black Italian olives are somewhat wrinkled and have a mild, sweet flavor. They marry well with rosemary and provide richness to olive pastes.

KALAMATA: These large, meaty, rich-tasting purplish black olives are packed in brine. If they taste too salty, rinse them briefly. Usually imported from Greece, Kalamata-style olives are also grown in California and Peru. This versatile olive can be seasoned, baked with wine and herbs, and used for olive pastes.

NIÇOISE: Tiny brownish black French olives have large pits in proportion to their flesh, but they're flavorful and soft. Olive pastes made from Niçoise olives are smooth and rich tasting, but it takes time to pit enough olives to make it in any quantity. Good for nibbling, they also make a bright garnish for vegetable salads and crudité plates.

NYONS: Also from France, these small olives come packed in jars, often with bits of stems and olive leaves included. They are browner and rounder than Niçoise olives and have a slight bitter edge to their intense olive flavor.

OIL-CURED BLACK OLIVES: These wrinkled little olives are first cured with salt, then with oil. They are usually Moroccan, but sometimes sold under an Italian label, and are produced in California as well. Their flavor is very meaty and concentrated, and they go well with paprika, garlic, and lemon. When added to stews and ragouts they plump up grandly and impart a soft but earthy flavor to the surrounding broth or sauce.

STUFFED GREEN OLIVES: Their tartness, paired with the sweet morsel of pimiento, almond, or garlic, makes these olives especially good for hors d'oeuvres. They're a special feature in certain vegetable salads, especially those including cauliflower, and in olive sandwiches.

Seasoned Olives

These can be stored for 2 to 3 weeks in the refrigerator, but the garlic will become stronger with time. I usually remove any garlic slices and add fresh ones when I next serve them. Before serving olives marinated in olive oil, let them come to room temperature to allow the oil to return to its liquid state.

Olives with Roasted Cumin and Paprika

1½ cups Kalamata, oil-cured, or cracked green olives

1 teaspoon cumin seeds

2 garlic cloves, thinly sliced

2 teaspoons paprika

Several pinches red pepper flakes

2 tablespoons extra virgin olive oil

Juice of 1 lemon

MAKES 1½ CUPS

Taste the olives; rinse them if they're excessively salty. Place them in a bowl. Toast the cumin seeds in a small skillet until fragrant, then bruise them with a pestle or the back of a wooden spoon to release their flavor. Add the cumin seeds and the remaining ingredients to the olives and toss. Let stand 1 hour or more before serving.

Black Olives with Orange and Fennel

THE olives are the perfect garnish for a salad of oranges and fennel.

MAKES 2 CUPS

2 cups black olives—oil-cured, Niçoise, Kalamata, or a mixture

6 small bay leaves

¼ teaspoon fennel seeds

2 garlic cloves, thinly sliced

Zest of ½ small orange in large strips

Extra virgin olive oil to moisten

Combine everything in a bowl. Let stand for 1 hour or more for the flavors to develop. Store in a covered container in the refrigerator for up to 2 to 3 weeks.

Mixed Olives with Rosemary and Thyme

A SELECTION of olive varieties looks as pretty as beach stones. If using oil-cured olives, add them just before serving since they tend to stain the green ones with inky streaks.

MAKES 2 CUPS

2 cups mixed olives—Kalamata, Niçoise, Nyons, cracked green, oil-cured, etc.

6 or more thyme or lemon thyme sprigs

Several small rosemary sprigs

4 bay leaves, broken into pieces

1 large garlic clove, thinly sliced

Extra virgin olive oil to moisten

Combine everything in a serving dish. Let stand at room temperature at least 2 hours for the flavors to develop, and then serve. Store in a covered container in the refrigerator for up to 2 weeks.

Fried Green Olives

A DELICIOUS Spanish tapa, these olives are best fried in a fruity olive oil and served hot.

SERVES 4 TO 6

8 ounces green Spanish olives

1 egg, beaten

Flour as needed

2 cups olive oil

Dip the olives in the egg, then toss them in a plateful of flour to coat. Heat the oil in a skillet until it begins to haze. Add the olives in batches and fry over high heat until golden. Give the pan a few shakes while they're cooking to turn the olives. Drain on paper towels and serve hot.

86   VEGETARIAN COOKING FOR EVERYONE

Baked Olives

2 cups Kalamata olives

1/2 cup dry red or white wine

3 tablespoons olive oil

3 garlic cloves, 1 sliced, 2 coarsely chopped

1 bay leaf

2 tablespoons marjoram or 1 teaspoon dried oregano

1 tablespoon chopped parsley

Freshly milled pepper

Several pinches red pepper flakes

THIS is a Greek way—via Sicily—with olives. Just the aroma elicits sighs and exclamations. They can be served immediately, but I prefer to let them stand for several hours for the flavors to develop.

MAKES 2 CUPS

Preheat the oven to 375°F. Rinse the olives if salty and put them in a baking dish large enough to hold them in a single layer. Add the wine, half the oil, the sliced garlic, and the bay leaf. Cover and bake until they're fragrant and swollen, about 45 minutes.

Meanwhile, pound the chopped garlic in a mortar with the marjoram, parsley, and a few grinds of pepper. When the olives come out of the oven, poke each one with a fork or the tip of a knife, then stir in the garlic-herb paste, the remaining oil, and the red pepper flakes.

Olive Paste

1 cup olives, such as Niçoise, Kalamata, or green, pitted

1/4 cup capers, rinsed

2 small garlic cloves

2 teaspoons chopped thyme leaves or 1/2 teaspoon dried

1 to 2 tablespoons extra virgin olive oil

Freshly milled pepper

Fresh lemon juice

SPREAD on croutons, pungent olive paste sets off all kinds of foods— fresh mozzarella, tomatoes, roasted peppers, grilled eggplant, and hard-cooked eggs. Olive paste keeps more or less indefinitely in the refrigerator.

MAKES ABOUT 3/4 CUP

In a food processor, make a smooth paste of the olives, capers, garlic, and thyme if using dried. Add the olive oil while the machine is running. Season with pepper and add lemon juice and thyme if using fresh.

Hot and Spicy Tapenade

1/2 pound mixed olives, mostly Kalamata

1/4 cup capers, rinsed

1/4 cup extra virgin olive oil

2 to 3 garlic cloves to taste, finely chopped

Grated zest and juice of 1 large lemon

1 teaspoon chopped green peppercorns, drained

1 teaspoon red pepper flakes

ONE of my favorite cooks, Dan Welch, always has a lot of this spicy tapenade around his kitchen. This spread goes everywhere— even on pasta (with lots of parsley), in sandwiches or simply spread on croutons and covered with mild goat or fresh mozzarella cheese.

MAKES ABOUT 2 CUPS

If the olives are excessively salty, rinse them in several changes of water. Remove the pits, then chop them by hand and mix with the remaining ingredients. Stored in the refrigerator, this will keep well for up to 2 weeks.

Roasted Nuts and Salted Seeds

ROASTED nuts and seeds make a perfect accompaniment to one or two simple crudités and everyone loves them.

OVEN ROASTING: Preheat the oven to 300°F. Toss the nuts or seeds with just enough oil to coat lightly—1 teaspoon should be ample for 2 cups—then spread the nuts on a sheet pan and bake until golden, from 10 to 20 minutes. At this moderate temperature the nuts will dry out as they brown, making them crunchy once cooled. This is especially true for nuts that have been boiled first, as almonds are in order to remove their skins.

OILS: Olive oil and vegetable oils can be used in all cases, but highly aromatic oils, such as peanut, walnut, or hazelnut, emphasize the natural flavors of those particular nuts.

SEASONINGS: Use rough-edged kosher salt and ground sea salt, which happily stick to the nuts, whereas table salt is too fine and coarse crystals of sea salt are too large. For chile, use cayenne, ground red chile, or powders you've made yourself from dried chiles, such as chipotles. Spice mixtures like garam masala and curry are also good seasonings with nuts and seeds.

STORING: If not eaten within a few days, roasted nuts can be kept in a tightly covered container in the freezer, where they'll keep for several months—an appetizer at the ready. To refresh them, return them to the oven for a few minutes and then cool.

Salted Almonds

THE skins can be left on or not, but blanched almonds with their pale straw-gold color are far prettier. Serve with sherry, olives, and a simple crudité.

MAKES 2 CUPS

2 cups whole almonds, blanched, or not

1 teaspoon olive oil

1 teaspoon sea or kosher salt

1 teaspoon ground red chile or cayenne, optional

Preheat the oven to 300°F. Toss the nuts with the oil and roast on a sheet pan until light golden, about 25 minutes. Stir a few times so that they color evenly. When done, add the salt and chile and swish them around. Taste and add more salt or chile if desired.

Roasted Chile-Peanuts

THE turmeric gives the peanuts a rich golden color, but don't add too much. It can be bitter in quantity.

MAKES 2 CUPS

2 cups shelled raw peanuts

1 teaspoon roasted peanut or vegetable oil

2 to 3 teaspoons ground red chile or 1 teaspoon cayenne

½ teaspoon turmeric

1 teaspoon sea or kosher salt

Preheat the oven to 300°F. Toss the peanuts with the oil, spread on a sheet pan, and roast until golden, about 25 minutes. Shake the pan a few times so that they color evenly. Toss them with the chile, turmeric, and salt.

Roasted Peanuts with Chipotle Chile Powder: Chipotle chiles are smoked jalapeños, and they're hot! Toss the hot roasted peanuts with a little chipotle powder, starting with 1/2 teaspoon, and omit the cayenne and red chile.

Beer Nuts: These should be sour, salty, and hot. Toss the roasted chile-peanuts with the juice of 1 large lime. Add enough chile to give them a nice crusty coating. Since they're moist with the lime juice, plan to eat them within the day.

Roasted Cashews with Garam Masala

2 cups raw cashew nuts

1 teaspoon vegetable oil

1 tablespoon Garam Masala, page 36

1 teaspoon sugar

1 teaspoon salt

YOU also can use a mixture of cashews, almonds, and pecans with these seasonings. The pecans are especially good since their crevices catch the seasonings.

MAKES 2 CUPS

Preheat the oven to 300°F. Toss the nuts with the oil and roast on a sheet pan until lightly browned all over, 15 to 20 minutes. Remove and toss with the garam masala, sugar, and salt.

Salt and Pepper Walnuts

1 cup walnut halves or pieces

1 teaspoon walnut oil

Kosher or sea salt and freshly milled white pepper

IF you're serving these as an appetizer, aim for perfect halves and save the smaller pieces for salads.

MAKES 1 CUP

Preheat the oven to 325°F. Bake the nuts on a sheet pan until they smell toasty, about 10 minutes. Toss with the oil, salt, and pepper to taste.

Lacquered Almonds

1 cup whole almonds, blanched

1/4 cup honey or 2 tablespoons *each* honey and molasses

1/2 cup sugar

1/4 teaspoon salt

THIS Chinese technique brings a sweet or salty flavor to nuts by simmering them in syrup or brine before drying them out. Traditionally they're then fried, but when baked very slowly they emerge a burnished mahogany with a lustrous glaze.

MAKES 1 CUP

Simmer the almonds in boiling water to cover for 2 minutes, then drain. Bring 2 cups water and the remaining ingredients to a boil, stirring to dissolve the sugar. Add the nuts and simmer for 15 minutes.

Preheat the oven to 250°F. Drain the nuts, discarding the syrup, and spread them on a sheet pan. Put them in the oven and turn off the heat. Let dry for 2 hours, until glazed and no longer tacky. Cool completely before storing.

Sweet, Salty, and Spicy Pecans

THESE *are immensely popular. Serve them with skewers of cucumber or honeydew melon before or after dinner.*

MAKES 1 CUP

1 cup pecan halves

1 teaspoon canola oil

1 1/2 tablespoons sugar or more
   to taste

1/2 teaspoon kosher or sea salt

1 teaspoon ground red chile

Preheat the oven to 300°F. Spread the pecans on a sheet pan and roast until fragrant, about 25 minutes. Stir a few times so that they color evenly. Heat the oil in a skillet over medium heat, add the nuts, and stir to coat. Sprinkle with the sugar and salt and cook, stirring continually, over medium heat, until the sugar melts and starts to caramelize and coat the nuts, about 5 minutes. Turn off the heat but keep stirring until the nuts begin to cool, then toss with the chile and turn them onto a plate to finish cooling.

Salted Sunflower Seeds

ADDING the salted water coats the seeds with a salty glaze. If you wish to avoid the salt, simply toast them in the oil—or a dry pan—until golden.

MAKES 1 CUP

1 cup hulled sunflower seeds

1 teaspoon sunflower seed or vegetable oil

1/2 teaspoon salt

In a heavy skillet over medium heat, toast the seeds in the oil, stirring frequently until golden, about 5 minutes. Dissolve the salt in 1/4 cup water, pour it into the hot pan, and shake the pan until the water completely evaporates. Continue to toast until the seeds are dry, about 3 minutes.

NUT PACKAGES

Nuts are so irresistible, it makes sense to store them in something that's a challenge to get into. Shake them with their salt and seasonings in a paper bag, twist the bag, and leave them there until ready to serve. Or wrap them in a square of twisted parchment paper. If you're giving a large cocktail party, leave the packages in strategic places around the room. Everyone loves opening presents, and the noisy rustling of the paper works as a great icebreaker.

Brine-Soaked Nuts and Seeds This Native American method is similar to the Mongolian method of curing peanuts—the salt is brought directly into the nuts or seeds by a long soaking, after which they're roasted slowly. These are delicious in salads with wild or robust greens.

   Cover raw sunflower seeds, peanuts, pine nuts, or whatever you're using with cold water. Add enough salt so that it's good and salty, but not so much so that you can't stand to taste it, and soak overnight. The next day, pour off the water and toast the seeds on a sheet pan in a 250°F oven until they're dried, about 1 hour.

From the Garden: Crudités

CRUDITÉS—*meaning raw, not crude—are simply cut-up vegetables offered as appetizers. Crudités also refers to the plates of small vegetable salads that are sometimes served as a first course in France. In either case, crudités are a refreshing, healthy offering. The keys to making crudités delightful are to seek out vegetables that are absolutely fresh, cut them artfully but not fussily, and gather them into easy arrangements. Using unexpected vegetables adds surprise. And just a single vegetable or two will do—you needn't gather a gardenful.*

Put them in a napkin-lined basket, a silver dish, a rustic platter, or a fine china plate—whatever your fancy. If you have a garden, garnish your offering with tender pea shoots, sprigs of bean blossoms, sprays of herbs, and other garden delights.

A dish of sea salt flatters all vegetables and keeps things simple, but many sauces are also delicious if you care to be more elaborate. And while many vegetables are fine eaten raw, others are improved with a brief blanching in boiling salted water. Rinse under cold water then set on a towel to dry.

ASPARAGUS: Trim the tough ends, then simmer the stalks in salted water until tender. Serve with sea salt, Orange Mayonnaise, Thai Peanut Sauce, Cilantro Salsa, or Hoisin Sauce with Chili Paste and Tangerine Zest.

BEANS: Using any tender variety of bean—green, yellow, or purple—trim, blanch just until tender-firm, and rinse. Serve with salt, mayonnaise flavored with Pesto, Tarator Sauce, or Garlic Mayonnaise. Accompany with a dish of olives.

BELGIAN ENDIVE: Trim the bottom, then separate the leaves and fan them out on a platter. Cover the base of each leaf with a small bit of flavored mayonnaise, a mound of finely shredded vegetable salad, or a morsel of soft herb-flavored cheese.

CABBAGE: Slice into thick, short ribbons, pile them on a plate, and serve with sea salt or a seasoned herb salt. Kohlrabi, apples, and turnips would be good on this plate, too. For dipping, have a bowl of Fresh Horseradish Sauce or Mustard-Cilantro Sauce.

CARROTS: Leave very small carrots whole and uncooked with their fresh greens still attached. Serve them with a bowl of Salsa Verde, Spicy Yogurt Dressing, or Indian Salt with Mixed Spices.

CAULIFLOWER AND BROCCOLI: Cut the crowns into florets; the broccoli stems can be peeled and sliced in batons. Parboil just long enough to soften and take off their raw edge. Serve chilled or at room temperature with Curry Mayonnaise with Mango Chutney, Gomashio, or Mustard-Cilantro Sauce.

CELERY: The inner stalks are preferable, but the outer ones can be used if peeled. Cut them into manageable lengths, crisp in ice water, and serve them in a dish or an old-fashioned celery glass. Have a bowl of whole walnuts to crack, unsalted butter to spread in their hollows, or Green Goddess Dressing for dipping.

CUCUMBERS: Peel unless they're organic, then cut into long spears and slice away the seeds. Use yellow lemon cucumbers, quartered lengthwise, or ridged Armenian cucumbers sliced on the diagonal. Serve with Yogurt Sauce with Cayenne and Dill, Tarator Sauce, or Toasted Nori with Sesame Seeds.

FENNEL: Slice into thin wedges or long batons and accompany with a dish of Salted Almonds, Sea Salt with Fennel Seeds and Thyme, and a bowl of green olives.

JÍCAMA: Peel and cut into cubes or batons. Squeeze lime juice over all or serve with wedges of lime, a bowl of red pepper flakes, and crushed roasted peanuts for dipping.

KOHLRABI AND TURNIPS: Peel, then cut into wedges or slice into paper-thin rounds. Serve with sea salt. If very young and tender, leave the skins on. These are very pretty mixed with radishes.

PEAS: String sugar snap or snow peas, then dip into boiling water just until they brighten. Cool under running water. They're delicious just like this or dipped into Spicy Yogurt Dressing or Green Goddess Dressing. You can stuff them—people do—but it's rather fussy for something that's so good plain.

PEPPERS: Use all colors, cut them into sturdy strips, and remove their veins and seeds. Have a trio of sauces for dipping—Saffron Mayonnaise, Romesco Sauce, Thai Peanut Sauce, or choose just one.

RADISHES: Multicolored Easter egg radishes, white icicles, Spanish black radishes, and daikon can all be used. Leave a few fresh leaves on the tops of small radishes and serve whole; cut larger ones into strips or paper-thin rounds. Crisp them in ice water, then drain, pile in a bowl, and serve with salt and thin slices of French bread or dark bread lightly buttered or spread with cream cheese.

TOMATOES: Slice large ones into wedges or serve clusters of currant tomatoes, whole cherry and pear tomatoes, or a glistening arrangement of all. Accompany with Herb or Garlic Mayonnaise, Cilantro Salsa, or Salsa Verde.

TURNIPS: Cut small and tender turnips into wedges or paper-thin rounds, sprinkle them with salt, accompany with sprigs of lemon thyme, a dish of salted seeds, or Mustard-Cilantro Sauce for dipping.

PINZIMONIO

A bowl of fragrant green Tuscan olive oil, salt, and pepper—nothing could be easier to make than pinzimonio. It's served with a variety of vegetables but is particularly good with fennel, celery, and sweet bell peppers. Slice small fennel bulbs into wedges, celery hearts into sticks with the leaves attached, and sweet bell peppers into curved batons. Arrange the vegetables on a platter. Prepare for each person a shallow bowl of extra virgin olive oil, just slightly warmed and seasoned with salt and freshly ground pepper; or let each person make his or her own bowl. The vegetables are dipped in the seasoned oil.

Dips, Spreads, and Salsas

THE sour cream–based spreadables so many of us grew up with are replaced here by spreads and dips made with roasted vegetables, highly seasoned beans, and richly flavored vegetable purees. Spread on croutons or scooped with chips and crisps, they provide alluring predinner bites. Thick spreads can also replace butter on the table or fill a sandwich. Thinned, they become dips for chips or crudités. Salsas not only serve as dips for chips but play roles in other dishes, such as quesadillas.

Cottage Cheese and Watercress Dip

1 cup cottage cheese

½ cup sour cream or Yogurt Cheese, page 47

1 cup watercress leaves, finely chopped

Salt and freshly milled white pepper

I FOUND this delicious spread or dip in an old collection of Pennsylvania Dutch recipes. Try it with arugula or parsley in place of the watercress, too.

MAKES ABOUT 1 CUP

If the cottage cheese is very moist, drain it in a sieve lined with two layers of cheesecloth for 1 hour or so. By hand or in a food processor, mix the cottage cheese, sour cream, and watercress, then season to taste with salt and pepper. (If you use a food processor, the dip will come out pale green.)

Curry Mayonnaise with Mango Chutney

½ cup mango chutney, preferably Major Grey's

1 cup mayonnaise

4 scallions, including some of the greens, finely chopped

1 tablespoon curry powder

Juice of 2 to 3 limes

Cayenne

¼ cup yogurt or sour cream, optional

THIS recipe from Carolyn Wyman is one of the best dips I know for crudités. It's terrific with everything, but especially with hearty vegetables such as broccoli and cauliflower. If you use bottled mayonnaise, add yogurt or sour cream to even out its salty-sweet taste.

MAKES ABOUT 1¼ CUPS

Chop the chutney if it's chunky and stir it into the mayonnaise along with the scallions, curry, and enough lime juice to make a tart but harmonious balance. Stir in a pinch or two or more cayenne and the yogurt. Cover and refrigerate for at least 1 hour. Taste before serving to make sure the balance is right and add a bit more lime juice if it seems too sweet.

Spicy Peanut Dip

THIS *dip makes even the most mundane crudités irresistible. If you can, get your peanut butter at a natural food store equipped with a machine that grinds peanuts into butter while you wait.*

MAKES ABOUT 1 CUP

1 cup unsweetened peanut butter

1 bunch scallions, including a few inches of the greens, coarsely chopped

½ cup chopped cilantro

2 serrano chiles, coarsely chopped

1 tablespoon soy sauce

Juice and zest of 2 limes

1 teaspoon turmeric

Combine all the ingredients in a food processor and blend until smooth but flecks of green still remain. Add warm water to thin the sauce if needed. Taste and adjust the soy sauce and lime, adding more of either to get the balance right.

Guacamole

REGARDLESS *of the seasonings—with or without lime, garlic, or cumin—guacamole should be a little chunky, never puree smooth. You can spread guacamole on warm tortillas with crumbly white Mexican cheese, use it in sandwiches, as a topping for nachos, and as a side for corn waffles.*

MAKES ABOUT 2 CUPS, SERVING 6 TO 8

⅓ cup finely diced white onion or scallion, including some of the greens

¼ cup chopped cilantro

2 medium tomatoes, seeded and finely diced

1 to 2 serrano chiles, finely diced

Salt

3 large avocados, preferably Hass

Juice of 1 or 2 limes

Set aside a few tablespoons of the onion, cilantro, and tomato for garnish. Grind or chop the remaining onion, cilantro, and chile with ½ teaspoon salt to make a rough paste. Peel and mash the avocado with a fork. Add the onion mixture and tomatoes and season with lime juice and salt to taste.

If you're not serving the guacamole right away, press a piece of plastic wrap directly on the surface to keep it from browning. To serve, heap the guacamole into a bowl and garnish with the reserved onion, cilantro, and tomato.

> *Avocado and Pea Guacamole:* To make a lighter guacamole or to extend avocados when they're scarce, replace a portion with fresh or frozen peas. Briefly cook the peas, puree, and season exactly as you would guacamole. This is very good in its own right.

THE HASS AVOCADO

Of the various avocados available, the Hass is preferred. Small and dark green with pebbly, rough skin, its flesh is buttery and dense. Other varieties, such as Fuertes, may be larger, but they have less flavor and can be watery. However, they're usually in season when Hass avocados are scarce. Guacamole made with Fuertes might need a little more seasoning.

Artichoke Pesto

4 medium artichokes, trimmed and quartered, page 330, or 1 package, frozen

3 tablespoons extra virgin olive oil

3 large strips lemon zest

1 tablespoon finely diced shallot or onion

2 garlic cloves, thinly sliced

Aromatics: 1 bay leaf, 4 parsley sprigs, 2 thyme sprigs

1/4 cup freshly grated Parmesan or dry Jack, optional

Salt and freshly milled pepper

A SUBTLE spread for crostini and canapés. Fresh artichokes are plentiful in spring and again in the fall. Although you can also use frozen, they do have that ascorbic acid flavor that fights with the artichoke's subtle nature.

MAKES ABOUT 1 CUP

Thinly slice the trimmed artichokes. In a medium skillet, warm 2 tablespoons of the oil with the lemon zest. Add the shallot and garlic and cook over medium heat for about 3 minutes. Add the artichokes and aromatics, season with 1/2 teaspoon salt, and add water barely to cover. Bring to a boil, then lower the heat and simmer, covered, until the artichokes are tender and a few tablespoons liquid remain, about 12 minutes.

Remove the aromatics and lemon zest. Puree the artichokes with any remaining pan juices, the cheese, and the last tablespoon of olive oil. Season with salt and pepper to taste. Store in a clean jar, covered with a layer of olive oil, in the refrigerator, where it will keep for several weeks.

Roasted Red Pepper Spread

1 large red bell pepper, roasted

1 small garlic clove

1 tablespoon extra virgin olive oil

Few drops red wine vinegar

Salt and freshly milled pepper

SPREAD this on crackers or croutons and top with grilled onions, rounds of eggplant, thinly sliced cheese, or chopped herbs.

MAKES ABOUT 1/2 CUP

Puree the pepper, garlic, and oil in a blender or by hand in a mortar. Season to taste with the vinegar, salt, and pepper.

Eggplant Spreads and Purees

EGGPLANT *has a reputation for absorbing large quantities of oil, which it's quite capable of doing, but it doesn't do that here—the eggplants are roasted and the oil is used for flavoring. Serve these spreads chilled or at room temperature with flatbreads, pita crisps, crackers, or croutons or as little vegetable salads.*

Eggplants in season make the sweetest spreads, with no trace of bitterness. While any eggplant can be roasted, those weighing 6 ounces or more are more efficient to handle than very small ones. The standard teardrop-shaped American eggplant or the round European varieties, such as Rosa Bianca, are good choices. After roasting, very large eggplants often exude bitter juices as they cool. Simply discard the juice.

Roasted Eggplant Puree

THIS *basic roasted eggplant, as simple as it is, is absolutely delicious, especially when still a little warm. Here the eggplant is coarsely chopped, making an eggplant caviar. But if you prefer, you can shred the flesh with your fingers or puree it in a food processor until smooth.*

MAKES ABOUT 1½ CUPS

1 pound eggplant

2 tablespoons extra virgin olive oil

2 garlic cloves, put through a press or pounded with salt

Salt and freshly milled pepper

Chopped parsley

Preheat the oven to 425°F. Slash the eggplant in several places so it won't explode. Put it in a pan and bake until it's soft to the point of collapsing, 30 to 40 minutes. Let cool for 15 minutes or so. Discard any bitter juices that may collect. Peel off the skin, then finely chop the flesh. Stir in the olive oil, garlic, and season with salt and pepper to taste. Mound it on a plate, garnish with the parsley, and serve with crackers or pita bread.

Eggplant Jam: This produces a rich, dark spread flecked with bits of skin. From a large eggplant, remove long ribbons of the skin about 1 inch wide and 1 inch apart. Slice the eggplant into rounds a scant ½ inch thick, then brown them on both sides in olive oil. As the eggplant becomes tender, begin mashing it with a fork until it has a thick jamlike consistency. At this point you can add any of the seasonings used in the following recipes.

Baba Ghanoush (Roasted Eggplant with Tahini)

EVERYONE *knows this delectable spread—and for good reason. It's a summer staple in my kitchen, enjoyed at lunch with salads of sliced tomatoes and cucumbers and, as often as not, again at dinner.*

MAKES ABOUT 1½ CUPS

1 large or 2 medium eggplants, about 1¼ pounds

3 garlic cloves, coarsely chopped

¼ cup tahini

Juice of 1 large lemon

Salt

Extra virgin olive oil

Chopped parsley

Roast the eggplant as described for the Roasted Eggplant Puree, preceding recipe, but let the skin harden and char in places to give the dish a smoky flavor. Alternatively, grill it slowly over the coals until soft. Peel the eggplant, then puree it in a blender or food processor with the garlic and tahini. Season with lemon juice and salt to taste. Mound the puree in a bowl and make an depression in the top with the back of a spoon. Pour olive oil into the hollow and sprinkle with parsley.

Roasted Eggplant with Dill, Yogurt, and Walnuts

1 large or 2 medium eggplants, about
   1 1/4 pounds

3 garlic cloves

1/3 cup walnuts or pine nuts

Salt and freshly milled pepper

1/2 cup chopped dill

3 tablespoons extra virgin olive oil

1/3 to 1/2 cup drained yogurt

ELIZABETH Rozin, one of my favorite cookbook authors, inspired this unusual green-flecked puree. It's easy to make with a mortar and pestle, which gives it a pleasing, slightly irregular texture, or you can use a food processor.

MAKES ABOUT 1 1/2 CUPS

Make four or five short incisions in the eggplant. Thinly slice one of the garlic cloves and insert a slice in each incision. Roast the eggplant as described in Roasted Eggplant Puree, page 96.

Meanwhile, toast the nuts on a small sheet pan until fragrant, watching them carefully since the oven is hot. Coarsely chop. Pound the remaining garlic with 1/2 teaspoon salt in a large mortar until smooth. Add the dill and olive oil and work it into a paste. Peel the eggplant, add the flesh to the mortar, and pound just enough to make a coarse puree. Stir in the yogurt, fold in the nuts, and season with salt and pepper to taste.

Spicy Eggplant Spread with Thai Basil

1 pound eggplant, any variety

1 1/2 tablespoons light brown sugar

2 tablespoons rice wine vinegar

1 tablespoon mushroom or dark Chinese
   soy sauce

2 to 3 serrano chiles, finely minced

3 tablespoons dark sesame or roasted
   peanut oil

3 garlic cloves, minced

3 tablespoons chopped basil

Salt

Small basil leaves

2 tablespoons black sesame seeds,
   toasted in a small skillet

FRAGRANT Thai, anise, or cinnamon basil is perfect in this sweet, spicy puree, but regular basil will also be delicious here.

MAKES ABOUT 2 CUPS

Roast the eggplant as described for Roasted Eggplant Puree, page 96, allowing the skin to char in places to give the dish a smoky flavor. Remove to a colander to cool. Peel—don't worry about stubborn flecks of skin—and coarsely chop the flesh.

Mix the sugar, vinegar, soy, and chiles together. Heat a wok or skillet over high heat and add the oil. When it begins to haze, add the garlic and stir-fry for 30 seconds. Add the eggplant and stir-fry for 2 minutes, then add the sauce and fry for 1 minute more. Remove from the heat and stir in the chopped basil. Taste for salt.

Mound the eggplant in a bowl and garnish with the basil leaves and sesame seeds. Or spread on croutons or crackers and garnish each individually.

Bean Dips and Spreads

BEING *rather neutral, beans provide a blank canvas that can be painted with bright or subtle flavors. I generally find that bean dips are most appealing when they're warm or at room temperature. Cold, they stiffen and their full flavors are dimmed. (To warm a cold puree, add more bean broth or water until the desired consistency is reached, then reheat in a double boiler or small skillet.) Leftovers can be refrigerated for up to 4 or 5 days. Canned beans, drained and rinsed, work particularly well in purees.*

Serve bean purees with tortilla chips, pita crisps, or spread over little croutons.

Black Bean–Smoked Chile Dip

USE *this spicy spread for nachos, following recipe, or in a quesadilla, as well as for a dip.*

MAKES ABOUT 2 CUPS

2 cups cooked black beans
1/2 cup water or bean broth
1 tablespoon sunflower or safflower oil
1/4 cup sliced scallion, including some of the greens
1 teaspoon ground coriander

1 teaspoon ground cumin
1/4 cup chopped cilantro
1 teaspoon pureed chipotle chile or 1/2 teaspoon cayenne
Juice of 2 or 3 limes
Salt

Warm the beans in the water. Heat the oil in a small skillet. Add the scallion and spices and cook over medium heat until tender, about 10 minutes. Stir in the cilantro and turn off the heat.

Coarsely puree the beans, scallion mixture, and chile in a food processor. Taste; if you want it hotter, add more chile in small increments. Add lime juice and salt to sharpen the flavors.

Individual Nachos

MAMMOTH *platters of chips galvanized with hot, stringy cheese are not among our culinary stars, but the same idea applied to tortilla chips one at a time has some merit. These are light and tasty with bright, clear flavors.*

SERVES 4 TO 6

Black Bean–Smoked Chile Dip, preceding recipe, or Refried Beans, page 320, warmed
4 corn tortillas, cut into sixths and baked until crisp

Pico de Gallo, page 102, or a favorite bottled salsa
1/2 crumbled queso fresco or feta
Cilantro sprigs

Place a spoonful of warmed beans on the base of each chip, cover with a little salsa and crumbled cheese, then garnish with a cilantro sprig and serve.

Individual Nachos with Guacamole: Mound a spoonful of Guacamole, page 94, on the base of each chip, then add a few crumbles of feta if desired, a dab of Tomatillo Salsa, page 103, and a cilantro sprig.

PITA CRISPS

Put stale pita bread to good use by making your own pita crisps to serve with eggplant and chickpea dips. Preheat the broiler. Separate a pita bread into two circles and brush the rough inside lightly with olive oil or water. Cut into wedges, spread them on a cookie sheet, and sprinkle sesame seeds over the tops. Broil just until toasty brown, a minute or so. Serve warm or let cool. Cumin or fennel seeds, sea salt, red pepper flakes, and black pepper can be sprinkled on in place of the sesame seeds.

Spicy Chickpea Puree

1 teaspoon cumin seeds

¹/₂ teaspoon coriander seeds

¹/₄ teaspoon fennel seeds

1 to 2 garlic cloves

Salt

¹/₈ to ¹/₄ teaspoon cayenne

1 ¹/₂ cups cooked chickpeas

2 tablespoons olive oil, plus extra to finish

¹/₂ cup cilantro leaves

Juice of 1 lemon

Use this green-flecked spicy spread in place of hummus for a change of pace. For the deepest flavor, take an extra moment to toast and grind the spices. You can make the entire dish in a mortar or in a blender.

MAKES ABOUT 1 ¹/₂ CUPS

Toast the cumin, coriander, and fennel seeds in a small skillet over low heat, shaking the pan frequently. As soon as they release their aroma, after a few minutes, turn them onto a plate to cool.

By hand: In a large mortar, mash the toasted seeds, garlic, ¹/₂ teaspoon salt, and cayenne until broken down. Add the chickpeas, oil, and cilantro and mash until smooth. Season the puree with lemon juice and salt to taste.

In a blender or food processor: Coarsely chop the garlic, ¹/₂ teaspoon salt, the cayenne, oil, and cilantro with ¹/₄ cup water. Add the spices and chickpeas and puree until smooth.

Pile the puree into a dish, make a depression in the middle, and add a spoonful of olive oil.

Silky Mushroom Pâté with Scallion-Walnut Topping

MUSHROOM pâtés of old were tasty but chunky affairs. This silky and luxurious version, inspired by a recipe in Gourmet, is impressive, especially on a buffet table. It also keeps long enough (up to 5 days) to have on hand during the busy holiday season.

This pâté isn't difficult to make, and you'll be proud of the results. But there are a few steps to keep track of, so be sure to read the recipe over before you start. You'll need a 6- to 8-cup terrine or a narrow (10- × 4-inch) bread pan.

SERVES 15 TO 20

1 ounce dried porcini, about 1 cup

2 medium leeks, white parts only, chopped

1 pound white mushrooms, thinly sliced

¼ to ½ pound shiitake or cremini mushrooms, thinly sliced

6 tablespoons butter, plus extra for the pan

1 large garlic clove, minced

½ cup walnuts

Salt and freshly milled pepper

2½ teaspoons chopped thyme or 1 tablespoon chopped marjoram

3 eggs

1 cup cream

¼ cup fine dry bread crumbs

1½ tablespoons fresh lemon juice

Cover the dried porcini with 1½ cups warm water and set aside to soak. Meanwhile, prepare the leeks and mushrooms. Butter the pan for the pâté, then line it—including the ends—with parchment or wax paper and butter again. Preheat the oven to 350°F. Now, returning to the mushrooms, lift the porcini from the water, gently squeeze them dry, then chop them. Carefully decant the liquid into a small saucepan, leaving any sediment behind, bring to a boil, and simmer until only 2 tablespoons remain.

Melt 2 tablespoons of the butter in a wide skillet. Add the leeks, garlic, and walnuts and cook over medium heat, stirring occasionally, until the leeks are tender, about 6 minutes. Season with salt and transfer to a blender.

Melt 2 more tablespoons butter in the same skillet over fairly high heat. When the butter foams, add three-quarters of the white mushrooms and a pinch of the thyme. Sauté until they begin to color, after a few minutes. Add these to the blender. Melt another 2 tablespoons butter and repeat with the remaining white mushrooms, shiitakes, and chopped porcini, plus another pinch of thyme. Set aside.

Add the eggs and cream to the blender, then puree until the mixture is completely smooth. Pour the mixture into a bowl and fold in the reserved sautéed mushrooms, remaining thyme, reduced mushroom water, bread crumbs, lemon juice, 1½ teaspoons salt, and several twists of the peppermill.

Transfer the mixture to the prepared pan and cover the top tightly with aluminum foil. Set it in a baking pan and add hot water to come halfway up the sides. Bake in the center of the oven for 1 hour and 10 minutes. It should be browned on top and starting to pull away from the sides. Remove and refrigerate until completely chilled, at least 6 hours, but allow it to return to room temperature before serving.

To serve, gently pull at the paper lining to ease the pâté from the sides of the pan or run a hot knife along the edges. Set a platter over the pâté, then invert. Ease the pan off the pâté, then peel off the paper. Any rough-looking spots can be smoothed with a hot knife. Prepare the scallion-walnut topping and spoon it over the top just before serving. Serve with crackers, thin toast, or fresh bread that has plenty of character.

Scallion-Walnut Topping

1 1/2 tablespoons butter

1/3 cup walnuts, chopped

2 bunches scallions, including half of
  the greens, thinly sliced

4 tablespoons chopped parsley

Salt and freshly milled pepper

Melt the butter in a medium skillet over fairly high heat. When foamy, add the walnuts and cook, stirring frequently, until they begin to color a little, about 3 minutes. Add the scallions and parsley and cook until the scallions are bright green and tender, about 3 minutes. Season with salt and plenty of pepper. Spoon this mixture over the pâté just before serving.

White Bean, Sage, and Roasted Garlic Spread

1 1/2 cups navy beans or cannellini,
  soaked and drained

5 garlic cloves

10 sage leaves

2 bay leaves

3 tablespoons olive oil

1 whole head garlic, outermost papery
  husk removed

Salt and freshly milled pepper

Juice of 1 lemon

1 tablespoon chopped thyme

THE smell of the cooking beans is so rich and savory, it's tempting to forgo the puree and just eat them as a dish in their own right. Serve as a dip for celery or fennel or spread on croutons and garnish with a sage leaf or a tiny sprig of thyme.

MAKES ABOUT 2 CUPS

Boil the beans in a large pot with water to cover by 2 inches for 10 minutes. Lower the heat and add the 5 garlic cloves, sage leaves, bay leaves, and 2 teaspoons of the oil. Simmer, covered, until the beans are tender, about 1 1/2 hours. (Or bake them in a 350°F oven for the same amount of time.) Remove the bay leaves and drain, reserving the broth.

Meanwhile, preheat the oven to 350°F. Rub the head of garlic with a little of the remaining oil, put it in a small baking dish, and add 1/3 cup water. Cover and bake until soft and lightly caramelized, about 45 minutes. Cool, then squeeze out the softened garlic. Puree the beans in a food processor with all the garlic, the remaining oil, 1 teaspoon salt, and enough bean broth to give the beans a soft, spreadable consistency. Season to taste with lemon juice and pepper and taste again for salt. Stir in the thyme leaves and serve warm.

Variation with Basil Puree: For this summer version, omit the sage and roasted garlic and add 1 cup basil leaves and 2 garlic cloves pureed in 1/3 cup extra virgin olive oil.

White Bean Pâté: Oil a small, deep bowl or a narrow bread pan with plastic wrap, add the puree, and smooth it down. Turn it out onto a serving dish and peel away the plastic. Smooth the top with a spatula dipped in hot water, then garnish with sage or basil leaves.

Salsas

A LIVELY dip for chips, salsas—really the Spanish word for sauce—also are used with quesadillas, nachos, savory corn waffles, and enchiladas, and they're wonderful stirred into scrambled eggs or a bowl of beans, or spooned over vegetable fritters. The world of salsa has expanded enormously. Here are a few basic ones that can be used with all the dishes suggested above.

Pico de Gallo

ALSO known as salsa Mexicana and salsa cruda, this is what comes with the chips in Mexican restaurants. (Cruda means raw, not crude.) For best results, chop very finely; large chunks of tomato are hard to catch on a chip.

MAKES ABOUT 2 CUPS

2 large ripe tomatoes, finely diced

2 garlic cloves, finely chopped

3 serrano chiles, finely diced, or 1 jalapeño, seeded and diced

1/4 cup finely diced white onion

2 tablespoons chopped cilantro

Salt

Juice of 1 lime or 2 teaspoons apple cider vinegar

Combine the tomatoes with their juices, garlic, chiles, onion, cilantro, and 1/4 teaspoon salt in a bowl. Add the lime juice and taste for salt. If the tomatoes weren't very juicy, add 1 tablespoon water. Let stand 20 minutes or so before serving.

Variation with Chipotle Chile: Omit the fresh chile and stir in 1/2 teaspoon pureed chipotle chile. Increase until it's as hot as you like it.

Tomato-Avocado Salsa

YOU can emphasize the avocado or the tomato, make it mild or hot, but do use it within an hour or so.

MAKES ABOUT 1 1/2 CUPS

1 avocado, peeled and diced

1 ripe firm tomato, seeded and finely chopped

2 to 3 scallions, including half of the greens, thinly sliced

1 jalapeño chile, seeded, or 2 serranos, finely diced

1 garlic clove, minced

Salt

Few drops sherry vinegar or apple cider vinegar

1 tablespoon chopped cilantro

Combine the avocado, tomato, scallions, chile, and garlic in a bowl. Add 1/4 teaspoon salt and the vinegar to bring up the flavors. Stir in the cilantro and let the salsa stand for 20 minutes before serving for the flavors to merge.

Tomatillo Salsa

8 ounces tomatillos, husked

2 serrano chiles, quartered lengthwise

½ small white onion, sliced

5 cilantro sprigs

Salt

Put the tomatillos in a saucepan with water to cover. Bring to a boil, then lower the heat and simmer until they're dull green, about 10 minutes. Drain. Puree in a blender with the chiles, onion, cilantro, and about ¼ teaspoon salt. Chill before serving, unless you're serving it with enchiladas—then it should be warm.

SALSAS made from green husked tomato-like fruits have a pleasantly tart bite. A little pureed chipotle chile is also very good in this salsa.

MAKES ABOUT 1½ CUPS

Green Chile and Mint Salsa

2 serrano chiles, finely diced

½ green bell pepper, finely diced

2 tablespoons finely diced white onion or scallion

½ cup chopped cilantro

2 to 4 tablespoons chopped mint

Juice and grated zest of 2 limes

Salt

Combine the vegetables and herbs in a bowl and toss them with the lime juice, zest, and ¼ teaspoon salt. Add 2 to 3 tablespoons water, cover, and refrigerate for 30 minutes before using if time allows.

USE this where you want a minty bite—in eggs, quesadillas, grain-based salads, or over grilled vegetables, especially corn and onions.

MAKES ABOUT ¾ CUP

Little Bites
CROSTINI, CANAPÉS, CROUTONS

REGARDLESS of what name they go by—crostini, canapés, croutons—small sandwiches are what many of us look to when we need an appetizer or an accompaniment to round out a soup-and-salad meal. They're pretty to look at, far simpler to make than individual pastries, and easy to improvise. They require so little in the way of toppings that often a tablespoon or two of a spread, a sprig of herbs, a sliced mushroom, and a dab of mayonnaise to hold everything fast are all that's needed. When friends drop by at the end of the day, I often find myself putting together a plate of little sandwiches to have with a glass of wine.

Because of their diminutive nature, small sandwiches can support an intensity and richness that might be overpowering in a large sandwich.

CANAPÉS: These old-fashioned cocktail or tea sandwiches consist of bread buttered (flavored butters shine here) or covered with a spread and topped with fresh vegetables like cucumbers and radishes, sprigs of herbs, or grated vegetable salads. Despite their fifties image, canapés achieve a contemporary feeling since they convey freshness and flavor without being filling. Choose a soft but not squishy bread—white sandwich bread, whole wheat, rye, even a pita or other specialty bread. Slice thinly, remove the crusts if they're hard, cover thinly with butter or other spread, and top. Cut them into small squares or fingers. In addition to sandwich bread you can use an assortment of crackers.

CROSTINI AND CROUTONS: The Italian and French names for little crusts, or golden rounds of toasted bread. Baguettes are perfect for crostini, although larger pieces of bread can be toasted and then cut into smaller pieces. Slice sweet or sour French bread a little less than $\frac{1}{2}$ inch thick and toast in a moderate (350°F) oven, turning it once, until lightly browned and crisp but still soft in the middle. Remove, then brush with olive oil. If desired, rub with a clove of garlic. If large, cut in half or into small pieces.

Radish Canapés Radish canapés make a colorful and spicy bite, particularly when made with the different-colored Easter egg radishes or the mild French breakfast radishes. Spread sliced baguette with unsalted butter, then cover with thinly sliced radishes. Sprinkle with sea salt and garnish with some nice-looking radish leaves, radish sprouts, or sprouted cress.

Cucumber and Herb Canapés Cover whole-wheat or multigrain bread with Yogurt Cheese, page 47, sour cream, or mayonnaise, then sprinkle with chopped herbs, such as salad burnet, lovage, nasturtium leaves, watercress, lemon verbena, or parsley. Layer thinly sliced cucumbers on top and season with a pinch of salt or one of the herb salts on pages 75 to 77 and freshly milled white pepper.

Guacamole Toasts with Pickled Onions Cover toasted or fresh sourdough bread with guacamole and top with diced Pickled Onions, page 78, or thinly sliced onion rings, cilantro sprigs, and finely diced jalapeños. Serve with a wedge of lime.

Pita Triangles with Eggplant Spread and Roasted Peppers Make Pita Crisps, page 99, or cut fresh pita bread into triangles. Top with a spoonful of an eggplant spread, pages 96 to 97, a strip of roasted pepper, and a leaf of parsley or basil. Arrange on a plate and serve with accompanying bowl of olives and fresh celery or fennel.

Frittata Sandwiches Good made small or large enough to make a meal. Cut thin frittatas, pages 574 to 578, into pieces the same size as slices of French, Italian, or American bread. Spread the bread with a thin film of mayonnaise or Romesco Sauce, page 70, then add the frittata.

Crostini with Tomatoes and Basil Wait for summer's tomatoes for these crostini. Choose ones that more or less fit the bread and slice into rounds. Lay over small garlic-rubbed toasts, interspersed with green or opal basil leaves. Gently press them into the toast, season with salt and pepper, and drizzle with extra virgin olive oil.

Crostini with Diced Tomatoes and Fontina Cheese For two to four toasts, mix a diced ripe tomato with a teaspoon of minced shallot or scallion, a pinch of salt, and a little pepper. Stir in a tablespoon or two of small cubes of diced Fontina or ricotta salata. Add a teaspoon of olive oil and a few drops of balsamic vinegar and spoon over crostini.

Crostini with Fresh Mozzarella, Tomatoes, and Olive Paste Bocconcini (bite-sized mozzarella cheeses) and cherry tomatoes are ideal for crostini. Cover toasted bread with Olive Paste, page 87. Overlap layers of tomato and thinly sliced fresh mozzarella interspersed with basil or arugula, then drizzle with extra virgin olive oil or Salsa Verde, page 55, and a few drops of red wine vinegar.

Warm Croutons with Shaved Cheese Parmesan, aged Monterey Jack (dry Jack), Asiago, aged goat, and other hard cheeses can all be used, to varying effect. Using a vegetable peeler, pull off long, thin shards from a block of cheese, preferably at room temperature. Make the croutons and lay the cheese on them while still hot. The heat softens the cheese and brings out its aroma. Drizzle olive oil over the surface and add a little freshly milled pepper. If using the dry Jack or Asiago, spread the croutons thinly with mustard, Mustard Butter, page 52, or Tomato-Basil Pesto, page 57.

Crostini with Olive Paste, Ricotta, and Marjoram The olive paste provides the salt and intensity for this mild cheese. Spread toasted baguette or country bread with a thin layer of Olive Paste, page 87, and a thick layer of ricotta. Season with freshly cracked pepper and drizzle with extra virgin olive oil. Broil to warm the cheese, then cover with chopped marjoram or crumbled dried oregano. Serve warm.

Crostini with White Bean, Sage, and Roasted Garlic Spread This topping is richly flavored and aromatic. Spread warm White Bean, Sage, and Roasted Garlic Spread, page 101, over warm garlic toasts and arrange several of these on a platter. Cover with chopped parsley or fried sage leaves, or top with finely diced Pickled Onions, page 78, and capers. Garnish the plate with sprigs of sage leaves.

Crostini with Artichoke Spread and Chervil Grill or toast white sandwich bread or sweet baguette, then brush lightly with olive oil or butter and cover with Artichoke Pesto, page 95. Garnish with chopped chervil, tarragon, or chives and a little white pepper.

Crostini with Green Olives and Romesco Sauce Serve this lively, pretty appetizer, one of my favorites, with a glass of sherry and a dish of Salted Almonds, page 88. Spread Garlic-Rubbed Croutons, page 34, with a generous layer of Romesco Sauce, page 70, then cover with sliced green Spanish olives and sprinkle with minced parsley.

Sesame Cream Cheese Crackers This is one of those appetizers you can have ready in seconds. My favorites are crisp rye and sesame crackers, but any good whole-grain cracker will do. Spread them with cream cheese, then sprinkle them liberally with toasted sesame seeds. Add a pinch of sea salt, coarsely cracked pepper, or red pepper flakes and serve.

Cheese Toasts

THESE *warm, fragrant toasts are just the tease they should be—arousing but not sating the appetite. Pass them around while warm or serve them tucked among the leaves of a salad. For cheese, a good strong Cheddar is fine, but so is a creamy Jack or Fontina, a mild goat, Tilsit, or smoked cheeses—whatever's on hand at the moment.*

MAKES 10 TO 12 LITTLE TOASTS

1 egg, separated, or 1 egg white

1 teaspoon Dijon mustard

Pinch cayenne

3/4 cup grated cheese

1 teaspoon minced scallion or shallot

Salt and freshly milled pepper

12 slices baguette or 3 slices sandwich bread, quartered

Preheat the oven to 400°F. Combine the egg yolk with the mustard and cayenne, then stir in the cheese, scallion, and a little salt. Beat the white until it holds soft peaks and fold it into the mixture. Spread the mixture on the bread and bake until puffed and golden, about 5 minutes. Add pepper and serve.

Chile Cheese Toasts Use Cheddar, Muenster, or Jack. Spread a thin layer of pureed chipotle chile or harissa on the bread, then add the cheese mixture and bake as described. Garnish with chopped cilantro.

Feta Toasts with Marjoram and Tomato Cream 1/2 cup feta with enough milk to soften. Season with pepper and spread on the bread. Sprinkle with chopped marjoram, add a slice of Roma tomato, and drizzle with olive oil. Broil or bake in a 400°F oven until the cheese is soft.

Cheese Toasts with Pesto Spread Pesto or Tomato-Basil Pesto, page 57, over the bread, then top with crumbled goat cheese or Cheddar. Bake at 400°F or broil until the cheese is soft and fragrant.

Warm Crostini with Blue Cheese and Walnuts

SERVE these with a glass of sherry, a bowl of pumpkin soup, or a salad of pears and endive. The butter melts into the crisp toast; the cheese stays on top. It's heady and very aromatic.

MAKES 8

8 slices baguette or country bread, about 2 × 3 inches

4 ounces Roquefort, Maytag, or Danish blue

3 tablespoons butter at room temperature

1 teaspoon cognac

1/4 cup finely chopped walnuts

Freshly milled pepper

Finely chopped parsley

Toast the bread under the broiler until nicely browned on one side, then a little less so on the second. Cream the cheese and butter until smooth, then work in the cognac and three-quarters of the walnuts and season with pepper. Spread on the paler side of the toasts, then broil until the cheese is bubbling. Remove, dust with the remaining nuts, and garnish with parsley. Serve warm.

MANY vegetables can go inside a spring roll, and the packages usually come with recipes. Here are three very different fillings. The first two are served with hot mustard, which is simply dry mustard mixed with water. The third has its own peanut dipping sauce.

Spring Rolls with Napa Cabbage and Tofu

2 tablespoons dry mustard

2 slices ginger plus 1 tablespoon minced

Salt

4 cups thinly shredded Napa cabbage, about 1 pound

1 bunch scallions, preferably fat ones, including 3 inches of the greens, sliced

1 cup broccoli florets cut into small pieces

1 10-ounce package extra-firm tofu, finely diced

1 tablespoon minced garlic

2 teaspoons dark sesame oil

1 teaspoon sugar

½ teaspoon rice wine vinegar

12 egg roll wrappers

12 cilantro sprigs

Peanut oil for frying

A RECIPE from Eileen Yin-Fei Lo's book From the Earth, Chinese Vegetarian Cooking *was the point of departure for this filling, which makes a light and unusual salad when tossed with an orange vinaigrette.*

MAKES ABOUT 12

Mix the mustard with 3 tablespoons water and set aside.

Heat 2 quarts water with the sliced ginger and 1 tablespoon salt. When it boils, add the cabbage, scallions, and broccoli and cook for 1½ minutes. (The water won't return to a boil.) Drain the vegetables, rinse them with cold water, then wrap them in a clean towel and squeeze several times until dry. Combine them with the tofu, minced ginger, and garlic. Sprinkle with sesame oil, sugar, vinegar, and ¾ teaspoon salt. Toss well and taste the mixture to be sure it's seasoned sufficiently.

Lay one egg roll wrapper on the counter at a diagonal, with a corner facing you. Heap 3 tablespoons of the filling crosswise, near the base. Lay a cilantro sprig on top. Fold up the lower corner, fold in the outer corners, then wrap. Repeat, using the rest of the filling. Place the egg rolls on a plate and cover with wax paper, then with plastic, until ready to cook.

To cook, heat ½ inch peanut oil in a medium skillet until hot enough to quickly sizzle a corner of an egg roll. Add two egg rolls and fry until golden, about 2 minutes. Turn and fry the second side, then remove to paper toweling to drain. Continue frying the rest. Serve hot with the mustard sauce.

Spring Rolls with Shiitake Mushroom Filling

USUALLY *dried mush-rooms are used in spring rolls, but I rather like using fresh ones. Where I live, the mung bean sprouts are always broken and limp, so I use big, fresh sunflower seed or spicy radish sprouts instead.*

MAKES 8 TO 10

1 tablespoon cornstarch

1 1/2 tablespoons soy sauce

1 1/2 tablespoons roasted peanut oil

8 to 10 fresh shiitake mushroom caps, thinly sliced

1 bunch scallions, preferably thick ones, including 3 inches of the greens, sliced diagonally

1 tablespoon minced ginger

1 large carrot, julienned, about 3/4 cup

3 cups very thinly sliced Napa cabbage

Salt

1 cup large bean sprouts

Mix the cornstarch, soy sauce, and 1/3 cup water in a small bowl and set aside.

Heat the oil in a wok or a wide skillet. When a haze appears, add the mushrooms, scallions, ginger, and carrot and stir-fry for 3 minutes. Add the cabbage, sprinkle with 1 teaspoon salt, and stir-fry until bright green and starting to turn limp, about 2 minutes. Stir in the cornstarch mixture and stir-fry until the vegetables are coated and the pan is dry, 1 to 3 minutes. Turn off the heat. Taste for salt and transfer the vegetables to a bowl to cool.

Form the spring rolls as described in the preceding recipe. Use about 2 tablespoons filling and cover it with sprouts before rolling. Fry in hot peanut oil as described. Eat while crisp and hot with or without a dipping sauce.

Vietnamese Spring Rolls

I BUY these rolls for lunch whenever I visit Vancouver's bustling Granville Island Market. I make them at home for an appetizer or light lunch and serve with a glass of Riesling. It takes a few practice tries to learn how to fold the rice paper around the filling, but your fingers will soon become nimble.

MAKES 12 LARGE, SERVING 6 TO 12

2 ounces cellophane noodles

1 carrot

1 cup mung bean sprouts, blanched briefly

2 cups finely shredded Napa cabbage

5 scallions, quartered lengthwise and sliced

1/2 cup coarsely chopped cilantro

1/3 cup coarsely chopped mint

1/4 cup thinly sliced Thai or Italian basil leaves

1/2 teaspoon sugar

3 garlic cloves

Salt

2 serrano chiles, thinly sliced

Juice of 2 limes

12 large or 24 small round Vietnamese rice papers

24 butter or Boston lettuce leaves

Peanut Dipping Sauce, recipe follows

Soak the noodles in hot water to cover until soft and pliable, about 30 minutes. Snip them into 2-inch lengths and drain. Make the sauce and set it aside.

Using a vegetable peeler, peel the carrot right down to the core, making long, thin strips. Combine them with the noodles, bean sprouts, cabbage, scallions, herbs, and sugar. Smash the garlic in a mortar or food processor with a pinch of salt and chiles to make a paste, then stir in the lime juice. Toss with the vegetables.

Fill a bowl with warm water and spread a clean towel on the counter. Working with one paper at a time, slip it into the water and soak until soft and pliable, about 10 seconds, then remove and set on the towel. Mound some of the vegetable mixture at one end of the rice paper, roll it over once, fold over the sides, and roll to the end, making a neat little package. When all are done, slice the large rolls in half and stand them, cut side up, on a plate lined with lettuce leaves. Leave small rolls whole. Use the lettuce as an additional wrapper, to keep all the ingredients neatly contained. If the spring rolls aren't to be served right away, cover them with a barely damp towel and refrigerate. Serve with the sauce.

Peanut Dipping Sauce

3 tablespoons red wine vinegar

3 tablespoons water or Vegetarian Nuoc Cham, page 603

1 teaspoon Asian chili oil

1 garlic clove, minced

3 tablespoons roasted peanuts, chopped

1 teaspoon sugar

Combine all the ingredients and let stand 10 minutes before using.

Other Vegetable Appetizers

MORE *succulent than crudités simply because more has been done to them, cooked and marinated vegetables also make delicious appetizers. Many are extremely simple to make from scratch while others can be drawn from leftovers such as Peperonata, Roasted Pepper Strips and Onions, Caramelized Onions, Slow-Baked Tomatoes, or the Tunisian Tomato and Pepper Stew. You can perk up leftovers with a dash of vinegar, some grated lemon zest, or a spoonful of capers. Sometimes nothing at all is needed but a crouton or piece of bread to hold the vegetable while mopping up its savory juices.*

Artichokes Leaf by Leaf Served warm or chilled, artichokes can be a first course, or, when shared, an appetizer. And sharing a giant artichoke can certainly be an icebreaker.

Clip the leaves with scissors if they have thorns; slice off the top third and even the bottom so that it stands. Rub the cut parts with lemon, then steam over boiling water until a leaf comes easily free when tugged, about 45 minutes.

Don't just limit yourself to melted butter and plain mayonnaise. Serve with any number of sauces, allowing about 1/4 cup per person, in individual bowls. Try extra virgin olive oil seasoned with sea salt and freshly ground pepper; one of the flavored mayonnaises, yogurt sauces, Cilantro Salsa, Salsa Verde, or Herb-Butter and Olive Oil Sauce in the sauce chapter; or Green Goddess Dressing, page 190. Have an extra bowl on the table for the finished leaves.

Golden Artichoke Wedges

THESE *succulent little nuggets are just the thing to offer to guests who are standing around the kitchen before dinner. Serve them with lemon wedges or a silky home-made mayonnaise for dipping.*

SERVES 4

4 medium artichokes, trimmed and
  quartered, page 330, or 12 babies
Juice of 1 lemon
1/2 cup flour
2 eggs

Salt and freshly milled pepper
1 cup olive or vegetable oil
Sea salt and lemon wedges
Tarragon Mayonnaise with Capers,
  page 59, optional

Slice the trimmed artichokes into wedges a little less than 1/2 inch thick, dropping them into the lemon juice mixed with water to cover as you work. When all are done, drain and pat dry. (If using the babies, trim the base and top, then slice lengthwise into thirds.)

Put the flour on a plate. Beat the eggs with a few pinches salt and a little pepper in a shallow bowl. Dip the artichokes into the egg, then toss them in the flour to coat lightly.

Heat the oil in a medium skillet until hot enough to sizzle a bread crumb. Fry a few artichokes at a time over high heat until golden, 3 to 4 minutes. Pile them on a plate, sprinkle with the sea salt and a squeeze of lemon juice, and serve, with or without a bowl of mayonnaise for dipping.

Eggplant Rounds with Shallots and Basil

SMALL Asian and slender Italian eggplants fit better on a crouton if you want to serve little open-faced sandwiches. The eggplant will keep, refrigerated, for several days, but bring it to room temperature before serving.

SERVES 4 TO 6

1 pound small eggplants
Olive oil
Salt and freshly milled pepper
2 large shallots, finely diced

2 garlic cloves, thinly sliced
Balsamic vinegar
15 basil leaves, torn into small pieces,
  plus small leaves for garnish

Slice the eggplants into 1/2-inch rounds or ovals. Brush both sides with oil, set on a sheet pan, and broil on both sides until golden. Or, if you prefer, grill them. (Don't worry if the surfaces look dry; they'll soften later.) While they're still hot, make a layer on a plate, season with salt and pepper, and sprinkle with shallots, garlic, and a few drops of vinegar. Scatter the torn basil over the top, then cover with another layer of eggplant and repeat. When done, cover with plastic wrap and let stand for 15 minutes. Pile on a plate or serve on croutons and garnish with basil leaves.

Sweet and Sour Eggplant

1 pound eggplant

Salt and freshly milled pepper

1/4 cup olive oil

1 red onion, finely diced

4 tomatoes, seeded and diced

3 tablespoons red wine vinegar or sherry
vinegar

1 tablespoon honey

2 teaspoons chopped mint

1/3 cup thinly sliced or crumbled feta or
ricotta salata

THE honey, vinegar, and salty cheese make an intriguing mixture of tastes on the tongue.

SERVES 4

Slice the eggplant into 1/2-inch rounds, then into 1/2-inch strips. Unless very fresh, sprinkle with salt and let stand 30 minutes or longer. Rinse and pat dry. Heat 2 1/2 tablespoons of the oil in a wide skillet over medium heat. When a haze forms over the oil, add the eggplant and sauté, stirring frequently, until browned all over, about 12 minutes. Taste for salt and season with pepper. Heat the remaining 1 1/2 tablespoons oil in a wide skillet, add the onion, and sauté over medium heat until beginning to color. (The amount of onion will be small for the skillet, but you'll need the surface area to quickly evaporate the vinegar in the next step.) Add the tomatoes, vinegar, and honey, raise the heat, and cook, shaking the pan frequently, until the vinegar is evaporated. Add the mint and eggplant and mix gently. Let cool, fold in the cheese, and serve.

Jícama and Cucumbers with Chile and Lime

1/2 small jícama, about 8 ounces

2 cucumbers

Grated zest and juice of 2 limes

1 jalapeño chile, seeded and finely diced

Salt

A LARGE tuber covered with a papery tan skin, jícama's appearance doesn't even hint at its white flesh, which is crisp, juicy, and sweet.

SERVES 4 TO 6

Peel the jícama and cut into bite-sized cubes. Peel the cucumbers if they've been waxed; otherwise score the skins with a fork, then quarter them lengthwise and dice into cubes. If they're very mature, scrape out and discard the seeds first. Toss everything together and taste for salt and lime. Refrigerate until very cold, or serve right away on little plates with toothpicks or small forks.

Marinated Mushrooms with Tarragon

THIS easy dish can be assembled up to 2 hours in advance. A great appetizer, these mushrooms are also good tossed in a spinach salad. When fresh tarragon isn't available, cumin makes an excellent alternative.

SERVES 3 TO 4

2 garlic cloves

Salt and coarsely cracked pepper

4 to 6 scallions, including some of the greens, thinly sliced

2½ tablespoons red wine vinegar

4 teaspoons chopped tarragon or ½ teaspoon cumin seeds

¼ cup extra virgin olive oil

8 ounces white mushrooms, stem ends trimmed

2 pinches red pepper flakes

Finely chop the garlic with ½ teaspoon salt or smash it in a mortar until smooth. Combine with the scallions, vinegar, and tarragon in a bowl, then whisk in the oil. (If using the cumin, toast the seeds in a small pan until they smell fragrant, then cool and grind to a powder.) Unless the mushrooms are very small, cut them into quarters, slightly angling each cut to make a more interesting shape. Pour the dressing over the mushrooms and toss with the pepper flakes. Taste for salt and season with pepper. Cover and refrigerate until ready to serve.

Fennel à la Grecque

PALE fennel is lovely prepared this way, but many vegetables are good candidates for treating à la Grecque, such as celery, mushrooms, carrots, pearl onions, cauliflower florets, tender turnips, and radishes. In fact, a bouquet of several pickled vegetables can be very fetching on a composed salad plate.

SERVES 4 TO 6

1 teaspoon coriander seeds

½ teaspoon peppercorns

¼ teaspoon fennel seeds, bruised

3 to 4 fennel bulbs, approximately 1 pound, quartered

1 onion, thinly sliced

3 large garlic cloves, crushed

1 bay leaf

Salt

2 teaspoons extra virgin olive oil

½ cup dry white wine

Juice of 1 lemon

Gently bruise the coriander, pepper, and fennel to release their flavors. Combine everything in a noncorrosive pan with water to cover and bring to a boil. Lower the heat and simmer, covered, until the fennel is tender but still a little firm when pierced with a knife, 15 to 20 minutes, depending on the size of the pieces. Remove the fennel to a dish. Raise the heat, reduce the cooking liquid by about one-third, then pour it over the fennel. Cover and refrigerate. Serve chilled, the pieces left whole or thinly sliced.

Using Other Vegetables: Leave small carrots whole or cut larger ones into 3-inch lengths; trim celery into 3-inch lengths; leave small mushrooms and radishes whole; quarter larger mushrooms; separate cauliflower into florets and parboil for 1 minute; scrub young turnips and peel and quarter older ones; parboil and peel boiling onions. Remove individual vegetables as they become tender.

Golden Roasted Potatoes with Chile Mayonnaise

2 large russet potatoes, about 1 pound	Salt
Vegetable oil	Red Chile Mayonnaise, page 60

Preheat the oven to 400°F and lightly oil a baking dish.

Neatly peel the potatoes with a paring knife and cut them lengthwise into quarters or sixths if very large. Toss them with just enough oil to coat and season with salt. Bake until they're tender and covered with a golden crust, about an hour, turning them a few times so that they color evenly. Serve with the mayonnaise.

JODY Apple, a bold and fearless cook from New Mexico, serves these golden potatoes with mayonnaise made red with her homegrown chiles.

SERVES 4

Cheese and Egg Appetizers

YES, they're filling, but cheese and eggs have a place when the meal that follows is small or light. Leave the buttery triple-cream cheeses for a cheese course or dessert and offer lighter cheeses for appetizers. Remember, cold dulls the taste of most foods, especially cheeses, so make sure they're served at room temperature.

Goat Cheese Rounds with Pepper and Herbs

1 11-ounce log goat cheese, such as Montrachet	Coarsely milled black pepper
6 thyme or 3 small rosemary sprigs	Extra virgin olive oil
2 garlic cloves, sliced	

Slice the cheese into ½-inch rounds and set them in a serving dish. Pull the leaves off half the thyme sprigs or chop a teaspoon of rosemary and scatter it over the cheese. Tuck in the garlic, grind on the pepper, and intersperse the remaining herbs among the rounds. Drizzle generously with oil, cover, and let stand several hours if time allows. Serve at room temperature, accompanied by crackers or good crusty sourdough or rustic country bread.

MEASUREMENTS aren't crucial; the point is to bathe the cheese in herbs and a fruity olive oil— which can be used in a salad dressing or in cooking.

SERVES 6 TO 8

Goat Cheese Log Dusted with Herbs

PRESENT *the log whole on a small platter or use the same treatment with small rounds and logs of cheese. Serve at room temperature with bread or crackers.*

SERVES 6 TO 8

¼ cup finely chopped mixed herbs—
thyme or lemon thyme, parsley,
marjoram, summer savory, and
rosemary

Freshly milled black pepper

1 11-ounce log or round of goat cheese

Toss the herbs with several grinds of pepper. Scatter this mixture on a cutting board and roll the cheese in it until well coated.

Bocconcini with Red Pepper Flakes

THESE bite-sized balls of fresh mozzarella can be found in Italian markets, delicatessens, and even many supermarkets. They make a succulent tidbit to pop into your mouth. Allow two for each person.

Bocconcini

Extra virgin olive oil

Red pepper flakes

Coarsely milled black pepper

Coarsely chopped parsley,
plus sprigs for garnish

Drain the cheese and place in a serving dish. Drizzle the olive oil generously over it, then add a pinch or two of pepper flakes, pepper, and parsley. Gently toss everything together. Let stand for 1 hour or serve right away, garnished with long sprigs of the dark green parsley. Serve with toothpicks.

Bocconcini Rounds: Slice the cheeses into rounds, overlap them on a small platter, and dress with Lemon Vinaigrette, page 184, or Parsley-Caper Sauce, page 56.

Bocconcini with Tomatoes: Toss whole red and yellow cherry, currant, or pear tomatoes with the bocconcini, torn basil leaves, and extra virgin olive oil. Or thread pieces of cheese, tomatoes, and basil leaves on short skewers, drizzle with olive oil, and add freshly cracked pepper.

Fried Kasseri Cheese

TRADITIONALLY appetizers, these golden cubes of melting cheese also make a succulent garnish for rice and legumes, such as Rice with Spinach, Lemon, and Dill, effectively turning a side dish into a main course.

SERVES 4 TO 6

8 ounces kasseri

½ cup flour or fine semolina for
dredging

¼ cup olive oil or clarified butter

1 tablespoon chopped parsley

Freshly milled pepper

Lemon wedges

Cut the cheese into 1-inch cubes and toss them in the flour. Heat the oil in a medium skillet over medium heat until hot. Add the cheese, fry for a few seconds, then turn, letting it brown on all sides before it melts. If the cheese sticks, scrape up the stuck parts—they're delicious—and serve them too. Scatter the parsley on top along with pepper to taste. Serve accompanied by lemon wedges.

Warm Feta Cheese with Sesame Seeds

8 ounces feta, in two chunks
2 tablespoons butter
2 tablespoons olive oil
2 bay leaves

Freshly milled pepper
Juice of 1 large lemon
2 teaspoons chopped marjoram
1 tablespoon toasted sesame seeds

COVERED with toasted sesame seeds, this cheese makes a crunchy, succulent first course or addition to a salad. Serve with fresh bread to mop up the juices.
SERVES 4 TO 6

If the feta tastes too salty, soak it in water for 20 minutes, then drain. Slice into slabs ⅜ inch thick. Thicker, it won't warm through; thinner, it'll fall apart. Warm the butter and olive oil with the bay leaves in a wide skillet over medium heat until the bay releases its aroma. Add the cheese in a single layer, season with pepper, and heat until it softens and begins to bubble. Turn it over and cook the second side for 1 minute. Add the lemon juice and let it sizzle for a few seconds, then remove the cheese to a plate. Scrape up any golden, crisp bits of cheese that have stuck to the bottom of the pan and include them too. Sprinkle with the marjoram and sesame seeds and serve.

Baked Ricotta with Thyme

1 pound ricotta
Extra virgin olive oil

8 thyme sprigs, plus 1 teaspoon leaves
Freshly cracked pepper

BAKED ricotta with its firm texture, golden surface, and delicate milky taste, is best served warm, plain, or covered with the Herb-Scented Bread Crumbs. Leftovers look uninspiring but are excellent crumbled over pasta or diced and added to soups, where they turn into tender dumplings.
SERVES 6 OR MORE

If the ricotta is very moist, drain it in a colander lined with two layers of cheesecloth and a weight on top—a can of tomatoes will do—for 1 hour.

Preheat the oven to 375°F. Lightly oil a 2- or 3-cup shallow baking dish and evenly spread the ricotta in it. Brush the top with oil, scatter with the thyme sprigs, and season with pepper. Bake, uncovered, until the top is golden and the sides start to pull away from the dish, 45 minutes to 1 hour. If there's any milky residue, carefully pour it off. Scatter the thyme leaves over the top and let cool for 10 minutes. Cut into squares or diamonds and serve.

EGGS AS APPETIZERS

Peel hard-cooked eggs, halve them lengthwise, and set each half on a radicchio leaf. Spoon Olive Paste or Hot and Spicy Tapenade, page 87, on top of the yolk. Alternatively you can mash the yolks with the olive paste, then spoon it back into the whites.

Frittatas are quite good at room temperature and can be made a few hours ahead of time. Here are three ways to serve them:

- Make them ½ inch thick or less, cut into small squares or diamonds, and serve on thinly sliced baguette with a dab of mayonnaise.

- Make them thicker, cut into bite-sized pieces, and pile them onto a platter. Serve as a finger food or offer toothpicks.

- For an elaborate first course, make very thin frittatas (the same or different flavors) and layer them with a binding of seasoned mayonnaise. Slice into wedges and serve. For example, layer thin red pepper, zucchini, and olive frittatas with a binding of saffron mayonnaise between them.

Sandwiches: *A Casual Thing*

SANDWICHES ARE FOUND AROUND THE WORLD IN ONE FORM OR AN-
OTHER, BUT WE HAVE A SPECIAL FONDNESS FOR THEM HERE AT HOME, WHERE
THEY SEEM TO RESPOND READILY TO ALL OF OUR WHIMS. HOT OR COLD, OPEN OR CLOSED,
dainty or mammoth, traditional or contemporary, sandwiches remain *the* informal,
portable meal. Smaller varieties—neat open-faced croutons, canapés, and crostini—can
be appetizers (see the "Greetings from the Cook" chapter) and accompaniments to soups
and salads, while larger sandwiches have the heft to make a meal. For adults as well as
children, sandwiches are still lunch and sometimes dinner too, so they should be nourishing as well as good to eat.

Sandwiches are casual, and that is part of their charm. Here's one area where
people who otherwise want to measure compulsively will forge ahead confidently on
their own. Really, making a sandwich is nothing more than putting together the tastes
you like, perhaps keeping in mind to vary the textures so that your sandwiches are interesting to eat. To make assembling an interesting sandwich an easy matter, try to keep
a few basic sandwich elements on hand that are popular at your house.

Some sandwiches travel better than others. Cheese and mustard on sturdy
bread is a good traveler, and a pan bagnat can sit around for hours, but chopped vegetables in a pita pocket can't go anywhere unless they go separately. Some sandwich vegetables suffer with time—tomatoes turn soggy; lettuce and sprouts wilt. Keeping some
of these more fragile elements wrapped separately to be slipped into the sandwich just
before eating makes a lunch sandwich more enjoyable. Otherwise, a thin coating of mayonnaise or olive paste or a layer of lettuce next to the bread helps keep a sandwich from
getting soggy by lunchtime.

Building a Great Sandwich

JUST four things are needed to build a sandwich—bread, a filling, a flavoring, and a garnish.

BREAD: Good bread makes the most ordinary sandwich simply delicious, while poor-quality bread disintegrates and ruins the best of fillings. Bread should be fresh, full of flavor, and strong enough to stand up to its fillings. Sandwich breads are the traditional American high, light loaves—heavenly when fresh. But foccacia and country breads have become new favorites, along with pita bread, tortillas, rolls, and other special breads such as olive, herb, cheese, rye, pumpernickel, and quick breads. Each bread contributes its individual personality to a sandwich—and often suggests its own fillings. A cheese bread makes an exciting cover for a tomato sandwich; fig or raisin breads are delicious with cream cheese and fresh figs; rosemary bread works well with goat cheese and braised spinach; and so on.

FILLINGS AND TOPPINGS: There are endless ones to choose from—spreads, cheeses of all kinds, grilled and fresh vegetables, salads, eggs in various forms, falafel, tofu, and tempeh. For children who want a sandwich that looks like what their friends are eating, there are meat look-alikes, such as bacon, hot dogs, and bologna made from tofu and tempeh. While I personally don't care for these ersatz foods, I do know how desperately children want to be like other kids. As a child I usually threw away my mother's healthy sandwiches so as not to stand out from the white-bread-and-bologna crowd.

SAUCES AND CONDIMENTS: These make sandwiches succulent, moist, and intensely flavorful. It's the thin swipe of spicy mustard or flavored mayonnaise that adds the finishing touch and puts a good sandwich over the top. Beyond the usual mustard and mayonnaise, olive pastes, Romesco Sauce, harissa, pesto, chutneys, and other seasonings make unusual and excellent flavorings for sandwiches.

GARNISHES: A sandwich always looks better on the plate when it has a little something on the side. And it's nicer to eat that way, too, pacing your bites with nibbles of this and that. Instead of the usual chips, try grated vegetable salad, coleslaw, crisp radishes, sliced tomatoes, or a little green salad.

The Vegetarian Classic—Avocado and Cheese with Sprouts

Scribbled on the blackboards of vegetarian restaurants for decades, this sandwich works because of the contrasting textures and tastes. Spread whole-wheat or multigrain bread with a thin layer of mayonnaise and mustard. Add iceberg or romaine lettuce, thinly sliced Monterey Jack cheese, sliced avocado, and sliced tomato. Season with salt and pepper and a squeeze of lemon juice. Add a covering of sprouts. (Try some of the more interesting sprouts, such as leek, radish, or sunflower, but don't put too many in—just enough to make the sandwich fresh and crunchy.) Top with the second slice of bread, press down lightly, and slice in two. A side of pickles would be nice.

Avocado Sandwich with Green Chile and Spicy Olive Paste

One of my food pals, Dan Welch, is known for his outrageous sandwich combinations, including this one. It's hot, tangy, and messy—not for the timid or the neat. Toast a large slice of country bread or focaccia, then cover it with a generous layer of Hot and Spicy Tapenade on page 87. Next overlap slices of avocado and tomato and crumble some fresh goat cheese over the top. Slide it under the broiler and heat it just long enough to soften the cheese. Remove and sprinkle with diced jalapeño chile (with seeds) and finish with a dash of red wine vinegar. Serve with lots of napkins and a bottle of cold beer.

Avocado Club Sandwich with Chipotle Mayonnaise Club sandwiches always include a third piece of bread, so slice the bread thinly, or the finished sandwich might be too thick. Season several tablespoons of mayonnaise with pureed chipotle chile, chopped cilantro, and lime juice to taste. Toast 3 thin pieces of bread and spread each slice with the mayonnaise. Cover one slice with a crisp lettuce leaf and 3 slices avocado and season with salt and pepper. Add the second piece of toast, mayonnaise side up, and cover with 3 slices Swiss cheese, sliced tomato, and another layer of lettuce. Set the third piece of toast, mayonnaise side down, over the lettuce and press down gently. To be ultra-traditional, trim the crusts, then cut the sandwiches diagonally to make 4 triangles and secure each with a skirted toothpick. Serve with pickled vegetables or a mound of finely shredded cabbage tossed with salt and lime juice on the side.

Avocado Club with Tempeh Strips Baconlike tempeh strips, homemade, page 608, or store-bought provide some of the texture and smoke that bacon does. Add tempeh strips to the club sandwich and, if you don't eat eggs, use Tofu "Mayonnaise," page 60, and soy-based cheese.

Cucumber Sandwiches with Spicy Greens An interesting twist on the traditional tea sandwiches. Spread white or wheat bread with mayonnaise, page 58, and top with thinly sliced cucumber and sprigs of arugula, nasturtium leaves, or garden cress. Season with salt and white pepper, then top with a second piece of bread. If spicy greens aren't available, mix the mayonnaise with horseradish.

Cucumber Sandwiches with Garden Herbs Spread white or wheat bread with Herb and Blossom Butters, page 51, or Yogurt Cheese, page 47, and cover with thinly sliced cucumber. Tuck herb leaves among them: borage leaves and their sky-blue flowers, torn lovage leaves, delicate salad burnet, chives, lemon thyme leaves, or garlic chives. Use sprigs of herbs and their flowers, when available, to garnish the plate.

Cucumbers and Cream Cheese with Radish Sprouts Spread whole-wheat bread or toast with a layer of cream cheese, ricotta, Boursin, or goat cheese, then top with sliced cucumber and radish sprouts. Spread a little mayonnaise on the second piece of bread or toast and cover. Slice in two and serve with Cherry Tomato and Olive Relish, page 78.

Cucumbers with Spicy Chickpea Spread Cucumbers make a moist and juicy foil for Spicy Chickpea Puree on page 99. For two sandwiches, toast 4 slices white, wheat, or dark rye bread or leave it fresh. In a small bowl, combine a seeded and minced jalapeño chile, 1 tablespoon chopped cilantro, and 1 tablespoon fresh lime juice. Spread a moderate layer of the chickpea puree on two slices of the bread, cover with thinly sliced cucumbers, and spoon the sauce over all. Top with the remaining toast.

CUCUMBERS

During the summer many varieties of cucumbers are seen at farmers' markets. All are good on sandwiches, especially when they're fresh and juicy. It's a good idea to taste a cucumber first to see if it's bitter. If it is, rubbing the two cut surfaces together until they foam seems to sweeten it. If cucumbers are unsprayed, unwaxed, and thin skinned, they needn't be peeled. And unless they're very mature, they needn't be seeded.

Grilled Portobello Mushroom Sandwich These giant mushrooms make a succulent, meaty sandwich. For two sandwiches you'll need a large portobello mushroom. Dislodge the stem, then slice the cap at an angle about $\frac{1}{3}$ inch thick. Brush both sides of each slice with olive oil and season with salt and pepper. Grill, broil, or sear, on both sides until browned. Spread 2 slices of bread or toast with mayonnaise—Garlic Mayonnaise is especially good—then top with sliced tomatoes, the mushrooms, and arugula, lettuce, or red mustard leaves. Add the top slices of bread, cut in two, and serve.

TO SWEETEN
HOT ONIONS

If you love onion sandwiches, but can't get naturally sweet onions like Vidalias, slice them and put them in a bowl of water with some ice cubes. Refrigerated for 30 minutes or more, they'll become crisp and lose their pungency.

Grilled Onions on Toast with Romesco Sauce For two people, grill 2 medium or 1 very large red onion. Toast 4 slices country bread, spread them with Romesco Sauce, page 70, sprinkle with chopped parsley, and add the grilled onions. Season with salt and top with the remaining toast. Simple but superb.

Sweet Onions on Black Bread The combination of sweet onion and dark bread is classic. Peel and slice thinly into rounds. Lightly butter 2 thin slices dark rye or pumpernickel. Cover one slice with the onions, season with salt and pepper, add a few drops mild vinegar, and cover with the second slice of bread.

Sweet Onions on Toast Toast 2 slices country, multigrain, or light rye bread, then spread each slice with plain or flavored mayonnaise. Sprinkle chopped parsley or dill over the mayonnaise on one slice, add thinly sliced sweet onion, and top with the second slice of toast.

Tomato and Avocado Sandwich on Toast Although utterly simple, this sandwich manages to be crisp, succulent, and juicy all at once. Cover toasted whole-wheat or multigrain bread with overlapping slices of ripe tomato, then with sliced avocado. Season with salt and pepper and a squeeze of lemon or a spoonful of Lemon Vinaigrette, page 184. Cover with a crisp romaine leaf and top with a second piece of toast. For additional excitement, spread the toast with Cilantro Salsa, page 56, or Harissa, page 75.

Tomato Sandwich with Greens and Herb Mayonnaise Use a substantial country or whole-wheat bread and spread it with Fresh Dill and Lemon Mayonnaise or Herb Mayonnaise, page 59. Add sliced tomato, freshly cracked pepper, and arugula, red mustard leaves, or a handful of "gourmet lettuces." Top with another slice of bread and serve.

Tomato Sandwich with Olive Paste, Mozzarella, and Arugula A lusty sandwich if the tomatoes are juicy and you're generous with the olive paste. Spread country or sourdough bread or garlic-rubbed toast with a layer of Olive Paste, page 87. Cover with overlapping layers of fresh mozzarella and thick-sliced tomato. Add a pinch of salt and plenty of arugula leaves, then top with another slice of bread and serve.

Fried Green Tomato Sandwich I don't know why this sandwich didn't occur to me sooner—it's such a great combination of tastes and textures. For two sandwiches, slice 2 large green tomatoes $\frac{3}{8}$ inch thick. Dip them into cornmeal seasoned with salt and pepper, then fry them in a thin layer of vegetable oil over medium-high heat on both sides until golden and tender but not mushy. Toast 2 sourdough rolls or squares of focaccia, halved horizontally, then spread with Garlic Mayonnaise, page 59, or Green Goddess Dressing, page 190. Add thinly sliced feta or fresh mozzarella, the tomatoes, and a final layer of greens, such as arugula, watercress, or a few large basil leaves. Top with the second slice of bread, then cut in half and serve.

Cheese Sandwiches

CHEESE *is a natural with bread, it's versatile, and it's very satisfying. Although cheese has been frowned upon because of its fat content and calories, it's still a good source of protein, not to mention calcium. Vegans and those who are allergic to dairy foods can approximate these sandwiches by using soy-based cheese.*

Cheese, Apple, and Watercress Sandwich For this bright, fresh sandwich, spread 2 slices nutty sandwich bread such as oat, multigrain, or whole wheat with mayonnaise. Add thinly sliced Gruyère or Jack, thinly sliced unpeeled apple, and watercress. Top with the second slice of bread, cut in half, and serve.

Smoked Mozzarella Sandwich with Olive Paste and Roasted Peppers
An impressive open-faced sandwich with big, bold flavors. Toast a piece of country bread, then cover it with a layer of Olive Paste, page 87, and thin overlapping slices of smoked mozzarella. Broil just long enough to soften the cheese, then crisscross with strips of roasted peppers. Spoon a little Pesto, page 57, or Salsa Verde, page 55, over the top and shower with freshly milled pepper. Serve with a fresh, lightly dressed green salad.

Open-Faced Sandwich with Blue Cheese, Pears, and Roasted Nuts
Blue cheese, pears, and roasted nuts are always right together, whether in a dessert, a salad, or a sandwich. For cheese try Maytag, Gorgonzola dolcelatte, Danish blue, or Cambazola; for fruit, a crisp Asian pear-apple or tender juicy Comice or Bartlett. Accompany with a salad of frizzy endive (frisée) or Belgian endive dressed with a Walnut Oil or Hazelnut Oil Vinaigrette, page 185.

Lightly toast semolina or country bread, then cover with thinly sliced cheese. Sprinkle roasted walnuts or hazelnuts over the cheese and season with pepper and a little chopped chervil, tarragon, or parsley. Cover with sliced pears.

Limburger Sandwich This is a cheese that seems to be appreciated by people like my father—in other words, those of an earlier generation, though if it were better known, I think many people of my generation would like it too. After making this sandwich for a photo shoot for *Saveur* magazine, the photographer and I sat down to feast on the props. We found this sandwich so delicious that I asked editor Christopher Hirsheimer for permission to use it here. Limburger is definitely a fragrant cheese, but it should be a little firm and have a good, clean scent that is appealing, not overwhelming.

Spread French bread or a white country bread with butter. Add a few butter lettuce leaves, sliced tomato, and several good slices of Limburger. Top with very thinly sliced white or red onion and roasted crushed walnuts. Top with bread and enjoy this wonderful robust combination of elements.

Classic American Grilled Cheese Put 3 or 4 thin slices of cheese between 2 slices of sturdy white or whole-wheat sandwich bread. Melt 2 or 3 teaspoons butter in a skillet just large enough to hold the sandwich, add the sandwich, and cook over medium-low heat until golden on the bottom. Remove, add more butter to the pan, and cook on the second side until golden and the cheese is melted. Cover the pan to hasten the cooking. Slice in half and serve. Serve this favorite with a side of pickled vegetables, Sweet and Sour Quinces with Dried Fruit, page 80, or a mound of coleslaw. In the fall, wash it down with a glass of cold apple cider.

With its soft, runny cheese and crisp toast, the grilled cheese sandwich is a favorite—and for good reason. As the variations suggest, all types of breads and cheeses, not just white bread and orange Cheddar, can be used. Cook grilled cheese sandwiches over moderate heat so that the cheese melts and the bread toasts at the same time. Butter is the traditional cooking fat, but olive oil works with some cheeses.

Grilled Cheddar on Rye with Onion Use light or dark rye bread and a good aged Cheddar. Slice a small tomato into rounds and a small onion into thin wedges. Sauté the onion in 2 teaspoons oil in a small skillet over high heat until golden, about 7 minutes. Season with salt and pepper. Build the sandwich this way: bread, a thin covering of cheese, the tomato, onion, another covering of cheese, and a second slice of bread. Cook on both sides in butter or olive oil.

Grilled Fontina or Teleme with Sage Leaves Fontina, creamy soft rice rind Teleme, and fresh sage seem to be made for each other. Halve a square of focaccia or cut 2 slices of country bread. Cover one piece with sliced Fontina or Teleme cheese. Sauté 6 fresh sage leaves in ½ teaspoon olive oil or butter until dark green and set them on the cheese. Cover with a few more slices of cheese and the second piece of bread. Cook on both sides in butter or olive oil. Delicious served with a fennel or mushroom salad.

Grilled Cheese with Salsa Pico de Gallo, page 102, Tomato-Avocado Salsa, page 102, Tomatillo Salsa, page 103, and Green Chile and Mint Salsa, page 103, are all good matches with grilled cheese. Layer Muenster, Monterey Jack, or mild Cheddar between slices of white or wheat bread and cook in butter or oil. When done, remove the top and spoon on as much salsa as the sandwich will hold. Return the top and serve with plenty of napkins. Made with tortillas, you have a quesadilla.

Grilled Cheese with Chile and Cilantro Thinly slice Cheddar, Monterey Jack, or Muenster cheese. Spread 2 slices of bread with a layer of Harissa, page 75, or pureed chipotle chile. Top one piece with a few slices of cheese, then add fresh cilantro sprigs and sliced tomato, another slice of cheese, and the second slice of bread. Grill and serve with a side of Pickled Onions, page 78, or Pickled Carrots and Garlic with Cumin, page 79.

Grilled Cream Cheese Sandwiches Cream cheese can be grilled, too, and it's very good this way since its delicacy sets off the flavor of the bread. Use a serious, nutty, multigrain bread; otherwise, pair it with savory condiments such as Tomato-Basil Pesto, page 57, or Salsa Verde, page 55, or with sweet ones—a tart marmalade, fruit butters, and fresh fruits. Try making grilled cream cheese sandwiches with a fruit bread. They make an unusual brunch or breakfast offering. Just spread softened cream cheese between 2 slices of bread and fry in a small amount of butter over medium heat on both sides until the cheese has softened.

Quesadillas

Quesadillas, the grilled cheese sandwich of Mexico, make a great spur-of-the-moment snack, lunch, or accompaniment to salads or soups, especially those made of beans and corn. They're also a good party food. Cheese is a part of quesadillas—it's even part of the word—but it needn't be used with a heavy hand. A light covering gives the quesadilla a satisfying taste—and helps hold everything together. Many things can go into quesadillas besides cheese, so here's a place where you can really improvise.

Basic Quesadillas

FOLDED: Start with good, fresh flour or corn tortillas. Set a heavy skillet over medium heat. When it's hot, add a tortilla. (If using corn tortillas, which tend to be a little dry, add a little oil to the pan.) When the bottom is hot, flip it over, then cover lightly with grated cheese—Jack, Cheddar, Muenster, queso fresco, goat cheese, or Mexican Chihuahua. When the cheese is quite soft but not entirely melted, sprinkle it with chopped cilantro or add a few epazote leaves and any other fillings you might be using. Fold it in half, cook a minute or two more, then serve hot.

FLAT: Follow the directions above, but instead of folding the tortilla, cover the topping with a second tortilla. Once the cheese has softened, flip the whole thing over and cook for a few minutes more. Remove and cut into wedges. Serve with Pico de Gallo or Tomatilla Salsa. If you're feeding a crowd, start making the quesadillas when your guests arrive and keep them in a warm oven until you have enough to serve.

Some other things to put into a quesadilla are diced tomato and avocado, chopped scallions, grilled or pickled onions, chopped olives or Hot and Spicy Tapenade, scrambled or fried eggs, diced serrano or jalapeño chiles, sautéed zucchini and/or zucchini blossoms, sautéed mushrooms, and strips of roasted poblano chiles.

Quesadilla with Smoky Black Bean Spread and Salsa

Black Bean–Smoked Chile Dip,
    page 98, about 1/3 cup per tortilla

2 corn tortillas

Vegetable oil

Grated Monterey Jack, queso fresco,
    or goat cheese

Coarsely chopped cilantro

Pico de Gallo, page 102

Diced serrano chile

OF course you can use a ready-made pinto bean spread, but these spicy black beans are a little different.

MAKES 1 QUESADILLA

Spread the bean dip on a tortilla and place it in a lightly oiled skillet over low heat. Scatter the cheese and cilantro over the beans and add a spoonful of salsa and diced chiles. Top with a second tortilla. Flip it over and warm the second side. When heated through, slide the quesadilla to a plate and cut into wedges.

Quesadilla with Roasted Pepper Strips (Rajas) The Roasted Pepper Strips and Onions on page 404 make a soft, succulent filling for quesadillas. Spread 1/2 cup or more over the bottom tortilla; add a little grated cheese or a few dabs of sour cream if you wish and chopped cilantro. Either fold it in half or cover with a second tortilla, flip the whole thing over, and cook on the second side. Cut into wedges and serve with a pile of pickled vegetables.

Whole-Wheat Quesadilla with Monterey Jack and Cilantro Salsa
If you can find whole-wheat tortillas, use them here. Set a tortilla on a heavy, ungreased skillet over medium heat. Grate Jack cheese generously over the top. When the cheese has melted, drizzle with Cilantro Salsa, page 56, then fold the tortilla in half and serve with a plate of sliced serrano chiles or Pico de Gallo, page 102.

SANDWICH CHEESES

Beyond the familiar Cheddar, Monterey Jack, and Muenster, there's a whole spectrum of cheeses to use on sandwiches.

CREAM CHEESE: Traditionally used with fruit and nut breads, it also makes a good savory filling and works in grilled cheese sandwiches. "Natural" cream cheese, free of gums and gelatins, is more delicate and spreadable than the foil-wrapped variety. Look for it at health food stores.

FETA: Greek, French, Bulgarian, and Israeli fetas have slightly different personalities, but overall they provide a sharp accent for less intense fillings such as a chopped vegetable salad, cucumbers, and tomatoes. Dried oregano, mint, and fresh marjoram complement feta. For very salty feta, soak the cheese in cold water for 5 minutes.

FONTINA: Italian Fontina is creamy, with fruit and nut overtones. Danish and domestic versions are a bland rendition, but they're more available and less expensive. An excellent melting cheese, Fontina is ideal for grilled cheese sandwiches with sage and grilled onions.

GOAT CHEESE: Whether sharp and assertive or fresh and soft, goat cheese always adds tang and character to a dish. It can be mixed with a little milk, ricotta, or cream cheese to make it even milder and more spreadable or used as is. It's very good with sourdough bread, roasted peppers, and eggplant. Rosemary, thyme, garlic, and olive oil are its natural partners. Fresh goat cheese makes an excellent grilled cheese sandwich.

GRUYÈRE: Gruyère makes the perfect grilled cheese sandwich. Thinly sliced Gruyère accompanied by mustard, fine butter, or mayonnaise on French bread is simple goodness.

HAVARTI, PLAIN OR WITH DILL: Often overlooked but easy to find, Havarti is a rather mild soft cheese with a bit of tang. Try it on dark and rye breads with cucumbers and mustard, horseradish, or sour cream.

MOZZARELLA: Delicate and delicious raw or melted, fresh mozzarella can be paired with tomatoes, olive paste, roasted peppers, and basil. Unlike the processed version, this cheese does not turn rubbery when heated but melts into tender strands.

RICOTTA: Not usually thought of as a sandwich cheese, ricotta makes a delicate filling with less fat than most cheeses. Like cream cheese, which it can replace, ricotta can go in a sweet or savory direction with the addition of herbs, honey, or fruits. If the ricotta is very moist, drain it in a colander lined with cheesecloth.

RICOTTA SALATA: A salted, pressed, dense ricotta, this cheese is similar to feta but neither as salty nor as crumbly. Try it thinly sliced and combined with salad greens, tomatoes, cucumbers, avocado, and grilled vegetables.

TELEME: A soft cheese that practically flows at room temperature, teleme is buttery but tangy. Teleme that's labeled "rice washed" or "rice rind" is the best. It makes a wonderful, runny grilled cheese sandwich.

YOGURT CHEESE: Thick and tangy, this low-fat cheese can be spread on bread or toast. It goes well with the same foods yogurt is good with—cucumbers, tomatoes, eggplant, hummus, or spicy chickpea spread. You can find it in Middle Eastern markets or make your own, page 47.

Pita Sandwiches

FRESHLY baked pita bread—tender, pliable, and fragrant with the scent of wheat—is one of the most delicious containers for fillings, albeit a fairly fragile one. With its nourishing taste and ancient feel, pita bread is worth making at home on occasion—page 672. Otherwise, look to Middle Eastern and Mediterranean bakeries for fresh pita.

Unless it's very fresh, pita bread requires some special handling. Defrost frozen pita slowly, at room temperature or in the refrigerator. If the bread seems dry, moisten it with water, wrap in aluminum foil, and heat it briefly in the oven. Halve and carefully open the pita. Spread the sauce inside the pocket first, then fill and drizzle more sauce on top. Don't put too much filling in the sandwich, or it'll burst. And most important, assemble it just before you plan to eat. Moist fillings quickly soften the bread.

Pita sandwiches will tempt you to improvise, but here are some specific combinations that I enjoy.

Pita with Falafel, Tomatoes, Tahini, and Lemon

3 to 4 falafel patties, made from a
   prepared mix
1 7-inch pita bread
Yogurt Tahini Sauce, page 66

2 ripe tomatoes, seeded and diced
Shredded lettuce
Green Chile and Mint Salsa, page 103

THIS classic Middle Eastern combination is one of my favorites. It's especially good when the bread and falafel are both fresh and warm. While falafel can be made by soaking and pureeing cooked chickpeas, I use a convenient mix.

MAKES 1 SANDWICH

Make the falafel according to the packaged instructions. Open the pita bread and spread a little sauce inside. Add the falafel, then the tomatoes and lettuce. Spoon more sauce over the top. Serve with a dish of the green chile relish on the side.

Pita with Broiled Eggplant Broil or grill rounds of eggplant. Tuck them into pita bread and spoon in Yogurt Sauce with Cayenne and Dill, page 66. Serve with a dish of olives or diced Preserved Lemon, page 82.

Pita with Fried Zucchini Fry sliced zucchini in a little olive oil in a skillet over medium-high heat until golden, and season with salt and pepper. Dice a tomato and mix it with a little chopped parsley, cilantro, and/or dill. Spread pita bread with Tarator Sauce, page 67, add the zucchini, then add the tomato-herb mixture. Top with extra sauce and serve.

Pita with Herb Salad and Pine Nuts I like this best with whole-wheat pita. Make Herb Salad (Sabzi), page 143, and toss it with a few pine nuts or roasted walnuts. Line pita bread with Tarator Sauce, page 67, and add the salad and a few sliced tomatoes if they're in season. Spoon a little extra sauce over the top and serve.

Pita with Chopped Salad and Spicy Chickpea Puree This sandwich is one of my favorite summer lunches. Don't fill it too full, or you'll have to gulp it down. Line pita bread with Spicy Chickpea Puree, page 99, then add a little salad of chopped cucumbers and tomatoes and drizzle with Lemon Vinaigrette, page 184, or lemon juice.

Sandwiches in Rolls

ROLLS also make good containers for fillings and unlike tender pita breads, rolls are sturdy, making them good little travelers. Be sure that you use a good hard roll or one made from strong bread dough, like the Sandwich Focaccia with Rosemary or Focaccia Sandwich Rolls.

Focaccia with Tomato, Ricotta Salata, and Salad Greens This sandwich is inspired by a breakfast sandwich I like at Campanile in Los Angeles, but it's a great sandwich any time of day.

The tender salad greens and the seeded bread make it special. If you're not up to making bread, use a Vienna or other plain roll with strong texture. If you are, make the Focaccia with Fennel Seeds, page 670, shaping it into 3-ounce rolls. Slice the rolls in half and cover with a layer of ricotta salata or fresh mozzarella, sliced tomato, and sliced cucumber. Toss a handful of small salad greens with a pinch of salt, extra virgin olive oil, a squeeze of lemon, and freshly milled pepper. Add to the sandwich, close the top, and serve.

Pan Bagnat

MADE in a sturdy roll, this Provence-inspired sandwich should be moist with olive oil and the good juices from the vegetables.

MAKES 4 SANDWICHES

4 large rolls, about 6 ounces each, sourdough or any good hard roll

Extra virgin olive oil

1 garlic clove

1 cup finely diced celery heart

2 ripe tomatoes, seeded and chopped

5 white mushrooms, chopped

6 marinated artichoke hearts, chopped

½ cup pitted Niçoise olives

2 tablespoons capers, rinsed

½ cup cubed ricotta salata, Gruyère, or goat cheese, optional

1 tablespoon chopped parsley, marjoram, or tarragon

Salt and freshly milled pepper

Red wine vinegar

Slice the rolls crosswise a third of the way down from the top. Pull out some of the bread, leaving a solid bottom. Brush the insides with oil and rub with the garlic, then mince the clove and put it in a bowl with the vegetables, olives, capers, cheese, and herb. Toss with oil to coat and season with salt and pepper. Add vinegar to taste. Fill the bottoms, add the tops, and wrap tightly. Let stand 1 hour or more.

Pan Bagnat with Saffron-Basil Vinaigrette

4 small tomatoes, seeded and diced

1 small cucumber or 2 little zucchini, diced

1 small fennel bulb or 3 small celery ribs, diced

1 large shallot, finely diced

1 large red pepper, roasted and chopped

6 marinated artichoke hearts, diced

8 Kalamata olives, pitted and chopped

¼ cup toasted pine nuts

Saffron Vinaigrette with Basil, page 188

Salt and freshly milled pepper

4 6-ounce rolls

4 rounds of fresh mozzarella, optional

THIS filling can go into a pita sandwich, too. If so, plan to eat it right away.

MAKES 4 SANDWICHES

Toss the vegetables, olives, and pine nuts with enough vinaigrette to moisten well. Season with salt and pepper. Prepare the roll as described in the preceding recipe. Partially fill it with the vegetables, add a round of cheese to each, and top with more filling. Replace the top of the roll and eat right away or let stand 1 hour before serving.

Grilled Vegetable Heroes

1½ pounds eggplant—small globe, Asian, or full-sized Western varieties

Salt and freshly milled pepper

About ⅓ cup olive oil

2 large red or yellow bell peppers

2 large red onions, sliced into ½-inch rounds

2 sweet or sourdough baguettes, each cut into thirds

Garlic Mayonnaise, page 59

3 ripe tomatoes, thickly sliced

Splash of red wine vinegar

THESE succulent summer sandwiches are a bit of a production, so set aside time to make them the main event of a picnic or backyard supper. You needn't feel constrained by the suggestions made here. Other good vegetables to grill are zucchini, scallions, leeks, mushrooms, and fennel (see the Vegetables chapter).

MAKES 6 SANDWICHES

Slice the eggplants into rounds a little less than ½ inch thick. Unless they're garden fresh, sprinkle with salt, let stand 30 minutes or longer, then pat dry. Brush the slices with oil, season with pepper, then grill or broil until browned and a little crusty on the bottom. Turn and grill on the second side for about 4 minutes. Flatten the peppers, grill until the skins separate, then steam and peel them as described on page 403. Cut the peppers into wide strips. Brush the sliced onions with oil and grill on both sides until browned. Season with salt and pepper, then turn them carefully and grill to brown the other side.

Slice the bread in half. Spread with the mayonnaise and cover the bottom layer with the vegetables, including the tomatoes. Douse lightly with vinegar and top.

Egg Sandwiches

NOW *that eggs have been liberated from their cholesterol quarantine, maybe egg salad sandwiches will return to their rightful place on our tables. They're nutritious, sustaining, and make a nice change from cheese sandwiches in the lunch box. They're especially good made with farm-raised eggs with bright yellow yolks. A basic egg salad can be varied in a hundred different ways—simply adding herbs and other flavorings to the mayonnaise will change its character. The versatile egg tastes good on white breads, full-flavored grains, dark ryes, and country breads. Toast the bread or not, make the sandwiches open faced or closed. And don't forget that you can also use egg salad as a spread on crackers or on a salad plate.*

Egg Salad

MAKES 2 SANDWICHES

3 hard-cooked eggs
2 or more tablespoons mayonnaise
Salt and freshly milled pepper

Chopped parsley
2 teaspoons minced chives or 1 scallion, finely chopped

Mash the eggs with the mayonnaise, leaving as much or as little texture as you like. Season with salt and pepper to taste and stir in the parsley and chives.

Other additions might include finely diced celery or green or yellow bell pepper, minced green chile, chopped watercress, diced jícama, or water chestnuts. All add crunch and color to the egg salad and expand its volume. A few drops vinegar or lemon give eggs a little sharpness if you've gone light on the mayonnaise.

REDUCING YOLKS

If you want to reduce the number of yolks in your egg salad, use one yolk to two or three whites or eliminate them altogether. With no yolks, the sandwich will be lacking in flavor and color, so you'll need to help it out with extra herbs. If eggs are completely problematic for you, try the Tofu Salad Spread made Tofu "Mayonnaise."

Egg Salad with Herbs Almost all herbs have an affinity for eggs. Use Herb Mayonnaise or Tarragon Mayonnaise with Capers, page 59, or add a few tablespoons chopped fresh herbs—marjoram, dill, chervil, tarragon, and arugula are particularly pleasing—to the eggs themselves. Nasturtium leaves and flowers, branches of salad burnet, flowering tips of lemon thyme, and garden cress are pretty as well as delicious.

Egg Salad Sandwiches with Olive Paste Spread bread, toast, or crackers with a thin layer of Olive Paste, page 87, then mound the egg salad on top. The pungent olives really perk up the eggs.

Egg Salad with Capers and Onions Mix the basic egg salad with 2 tablespoons finely diced onion or shallot, an equal amount of parsley, and 1 tablespoon rinsed capers. Spread on toast or crackers.

Egg Salad with Sprouts or Seedlings Sprouts with strong flavors, like leek, radish, and mustard, mounded on top of the egg salad provide a fresh and assertive counterpoint to eggs. The same is true of garden seedlings such as arugula, leeks, radish, and scallions. Finely chop them and sprinkle them over the egg salad.

Fried Egg Sandwich A great fast sandwich to make on the fly or when cooking has to be simple. Fry an egg (or just the whites) any way you like—with a soft runny yolk or a firm one. Season with salt and pepper and tuck it between two slices of toast. Keep it simple or add hot sauce, a slice of cheese, or a layer of sun-dried tomato paste or spicy Harissa, page 75.

Frittata Sandwich Frittata sandwiches make a good solid item to pack for lunch or take on a picnic. Make any thin small frittata, pages 574 to 578, sandwich it between 2 slices of bread, toast, or split focaccia covered with a little mayonnaise, and that's that.

Tofu Salad Spread

1 pound Chinese-style firm tofu

⅓ cup finely diced celery

⅓ cup finely diced green bell pepper

⅓ cup finely diced carrot

2 tablespoons minced onion or scallion

1 large garlic clove, put through a press

2 tablespoons chopped parsley

2 tablespoons chopped marjoram or
   1½ teaspoons dried

2 teaspoons chopped thyme or
   ½ teaspoon dried

⅛ teaspoon turmeric

2 pinches cayenne

½ cup mayonnaise

1 tablespoon capers, rinsed, or chopped
   sour pickles

2 to 3 teaspoons Dijon mustard

Salt and freshly milled pepper

Wine or apple cider vinegar

TOFU salad spread is surprisingly good on its own, but it's most appreciated as a replacement for egg salad. Use it in sandwiches just as you would egg salad, or as a spread for crackers.

MAKES ENOUGH FOR 3 TO 4 SANDWICHES

Break the tofu into large chunks and twist it in a towel to get rid of the liquid. When it's as dry as possible, put it in a bowl with the rest of the ingredients and mash them together with a fork. At first it will taste bland, but the flavors will get stronger as the salad sits. Refrigerate for 1 hour before using if time allows.

Marinated Tofu Sandwich

THIS has gutsy character—especially for tofu—and the marinade is also good with tempeh. Tofu that's been frozen and thawed develops a porous texture that really soaks up the marinade.

MAKES 3 OR 4 SANDWICHES

1 block Chinese-style firm tofu, drained or frozen, page 595

Hot Mustard Marinade, page 597

1 tablespoon vegetable or canola oil

Bread, toasted

Mustard and mayonnaise

Lettuce and tomato

Chopped cilantro

Cut the tofu into 4 to 8 slices, place in a pie plate, and cover with the marinade. Marinate for as little as 15 minutes or as long as a few days if refrigerated. Heat a little oil in a non-stick pan, add the tofu slices, and cover the pan. Don't worry about scraping off the marinade—it makes a glaze as it cooks. Fry over medium-high heat on both sides until browned. Add more of the marinade to the pan if it seems dry. When done, set the tofu on toast, spread with mustard and mayonnaise, and cover with lettuce, tomatoes, and cilantro. Cut the sandwiches in half and serve.

Tempeh on Rye

BRAISING tempeh in its seasoning, then letting it brown in the remaining oil improves its flavor and is more effective than marinating it. Even if you're not a fan of meat pretenders, this robust sandwich is hefty and satisfying and tastes good in its own right.

MAKES 3 SANDWICHES

1 8- or 10-ounce package tempeh

1 large garlic clove, thinly sliced

2 tablespoons vegetable oil

1 teaspoon paprika

½ teaspoon dried dill

½ teaspoon caraway seed

1 bay leaf

2 tablespoons apple cider vinegar

1 tablespoon soy sauce

Salt and freshly milled pepper

6 slices light rye bread

3 slices Swiss cheese

1 cup sauerkraut, drained and warmed

Prepared horseradish and mustard

Cut the tempeh crosswise in half, then cut each half piece into 3 very thin slabs. In a skillet wide enough to hold the tempeh in a single layer—though this isn't absolutely crucial—heat the garlic and oil over medium heat until the garlic begins to color. Add the tempeh pieces and turn them once to coat them with the oil, then add the paprika, dill, caraway, bay, vinegar, and soy sauce. Season with pepper to taste. Add water to cover and simmer until the water has reduced to a glaze, about 20 minutes. (If it cooks down sooner, add more water as needed—tempeh does need to cook.) Allow the tempeh to fry for several minutes in the oil that remains in the pan, turning it a few times. Taste a corner, then season with salt, if needed, and more pepper.

Toast the bread. Lay the cheese on 3 slices and broil until it begins to melt. Add the tempeh and sauerkraut. Cover the rest of the bread with horseradish and mustard, cover the sandwiches, and serve.

TLT—Tempeh, Lettuce, and Tomato Prepare the Tempeh Strips in a Smoky Molasses Marinade, page 608, or use commercially prepared baconlike tempeh. Cover toasted bread with mayonnaise, regular or tofu-based, and add crisp lettuce, the tempeh, and thick slices of tomato. Season with salt and freshly milled pepper, close the sandwich, and serve.

Supper Sandwiches

THE following knife-and-fork sandwiches are fine fare for supper—lunch, too, if you eat at home, but they're definitely not the kind to carry to work. These sandwiches are warm, full of vegetables, and satisfying to eat. Similar to Italian bruschetta and, to a degree, those homey American classics such as creamed mushrooms on toast and Welsh rarebit.

The basic technique is straightforward. Start with a slice of country bread. Place it under a broiler or, if a grill is going, over the coals until browned around the edges, crisp on the outside, but still soft inside. Rub one side with the cut surface of a large garlic clove, perfuming the bread with its juice, then brush extra virgin olive oil on top. I often lay a thin slice of Gruyère, Parmesan, or Fontina right on top of the hot bread. This small enrichment makes all the tastes resonate, in a particularly satisfying way, but of course those avoiding dairy foods can omit it. Then add vegetables, including their juices, so that the final rendering is an exciting mingling of crisp edges with soft toast, tender cheese, and succulent, moist vegetables.

Braised Spinach with Tomatoes and Sautéed Onion on Focaccia

Olive oil as needed
2 garlic cloves, 1 sliced, 1 halved
1 bunch spinach, stems removed
Salt and freshly milled pepper
Red pepper flakes
1 small onion, thinly sliced

2 big squares focaccia, about 6 by 6 inches, or 4 large slices sourdough bread
2 small tomatoes, sliced
6 ½-inch rounds goat cheese
Balsamic or red wine vinegar

MAKES 2 LARGE SANDWICHES

Heat 1 tablespoon oil with the sliced garlic in a medium skillet over medium-high heat until the garlic begins to color, then add the spinach and sprinkle with salt and several pinches pepper flakes. Raise the heat and sauté until wilted and tender, after a few minutes. Remove to a colander to drain.

Discard any juices left in the pan, add 2 teaspoons oil and the onion, and sauté over high heat until golden, about 5 minutes. Toast or broil the focaccia, then rub with the halved garlic clove.

Pile the spinach on the bottom halves of the focaccia, then top with the onion, tomato, and cheese. Drizzle with olive oil and season with pepper. Broil until the cheese begins to color in spots, about 5 minutes. Sprinkle generously with vinegar, add the tops, and press down to secure them.

Bruschetta with Broccoli Rabe

IF broccoli rabe isn't available, try this with escarole, chard, kale or a mixture of greens.

MAKES 4 BRUSCHETTA

1 hefty bunch broccoli rabe or 2 bunches chard, trimmed

Salt and freshly milled pepper

1½ tablespoons olive oil

2 garlic cloves, 1 chopped, 1 halved

Few pinches red pepper flakes

4 large slices country or sourdough bread

Thinly sliced Fontina

Olive Paste, page 87

Extra virgin olive oil

Cook the greens in a pot of boiling salted water until nearly tender, about 5 minutes, then drain. Heat the oil in a medium to large skillet with the chopped garlic and pepper flakes. When the garlic begins to color, add the greens and simmer with a cup of water until completely tender. Season with salt and pepper.

Toast the bread, then rub it vigorously with the halved garlic. Lay the cheese on the hot toast, spread it with olive paste, then cover with the greens. Drizzle a little extra virgin olive oil over the top and serve.

Bruschetta with Grilled Eggplant and Tomato

THE eggplant can be grilled well ahead of time, but have it warm rather than chilled when you make the sandwich.

MAKES 4 BRUSCHETTA

4 plump Asian eggplants, strips of peel removed if desired

Olive oil

4 slices country bread

Salt and freshly milled pepper

½ cup crumbled goat cheese or feta

2 teaspoons chopped marjoram or thyme

2 ripe tomatoes, seeded and finely diced

Red wine vinegar to taste

Cut the eggplant into diagonal slices about ⅜ inch thick. Score one side of each piece diagonally with the tip of a knife to allow the heat to penetrate quickly. Brush both sides with oil, then grill or broil on both sides until tender, 7 to 10 minutes on each side. Toast the bread. Divide the eggplant among the pieces, season with salt and pepper, and cover with the cheese. Broil until the cheese starts to bubble and color in places, about 7 minutes, then remove and set on individual plates. Sprinkle with the herb and spoon the tomatoes over the top. Finish with a few drops vinegar.

Mushroom and Spinach Bruschetta

½ ounce dried porcini, about ½ cup

8 ounces large white mushrooms

2 tablespoons olive oil

2 plump garlic cloves, 1 finely chopped, 1 halved

Pinch red pepper flakes

1 bunch spinach, stems discarded, leaves coarsely chopped

1 tablespoon butter

Salt and freshly milled pepper

2 large slices country bread

Scant ½ cup grated Fontina or Gruyère

I WOULDN'T hesitate to serve these to company, they're so full of flavor and so eminently satisfying. Add a soup or a salad—both if you've time—and fruit or a dessert.

MAKES 2 BRUSCHETTA

Soak the porcini in ¾ cup warm water and set them aside. Slice the fresh mushrooms about ⅓ inch thick, making irregular angular cuts.

Heat the oil in a wide nonstick skillet. Add the fresh mushrooms and sauté over high heat, stirring occasionally, until browned, 5 to 7 minutes. Meanwhile, lift the dried mushrooms from their soaking water, coarsely chop them, and add them to the pan with the chopped garlic, pepper flakes, and spinach. Sauté for 1 minute, then add the soaking water and cook until the spinach is wilted and a little juice is left in the pan. Stir in the butter and season well with salt and pepper.

Toast the bread, then rub with the halved garlic and cover them with the cheese. Set them on two plates, spoon the vegetables and their juices on top, and add a grinding of black pepper.

Bruschetta with Peperonata

Peperonata, page 404, or Sautéed Peppers, page 402

4 slices sourdough or country bread

1 garlic clove, halved

Thinly sliced or grated Fontina or Gruyère

1 heaping tablespoon thinly sliced basil

HERE'S another way to use this highly versatile summer vegetable braise.

MAKES 4 BRUSCHETTA

If you're using leftover peperonata that's been refrigerated, warm it up in a skillet, adding some water or a splash of white wine to thin it and make a little sauce. Toast the bread, rub with garlic, and cover with the cheese. Set on plates, spoon the peperonata over the top, and garnish with the basil.

Creamed Leeks on Walnut Toast

AN *American-style*
that's homey yet extrava-
gant. Although a walnut
bread is particularly
good with the leeks,
don't let its absence deter
you. Any rustic bread,
including a rye bread,
will go well.

MAKES 2 SANDWICHES

4 small or 2 large leeks, trimmed and
   sliced into ¼-inch rounds

1½ tablespoons butter

Salt and freshly milled pepper

⅓ cup dry white wine

½ cup half-and-half or crème fraîche

2 teaspoons chopped tarragon, parsley,
   or rosemary

¼ cup grated Parmesan, Gruyère, or
   crumbled goat cheese

2 slices Walnut Bread, page 668,
   toasted and lightly buttered

Wash the leeks well, but don't dry them. Melt the butter in a wide skillet, add the leeks, and toss with a little salt. Add the wine, cover, and cook over medium heat until the leeks are tender, about 20 minutes. Add the cream and herbs and simmer until slightly thickened. Turn off the heat, stir in the cheese, then spoon the leeks over the toast. Add pepper and serve.

Caramelized Onions and Walnuts on Toast Spread toasted bread with a little butter, olive oil, or softened goat cheese. Top with warm Caramelized Onions, page 396, mixed with chopped roasted walnuts and a little chopped rosemary or thyme. Serve warm. (If you don't eat cheese, know that this is also good without it. Instead, you might use a little Olive Paste, page 87, for pungency.)

Once you've made the caramelized onions, you can present them in many other ways. You can accent them with a number of pungent cheeses, layering thin slices over the hot toast or grating them on top—Gruyère, Swiss, Fontina, dry Jack, and fresh or more mature goat cheeses come to mind. Slivers of roasted pepper or pitted Niçoise olives might be combined with the onion. Sage, rosemary, and thyme all flatter, as does a burst of Italian parsley.

OTHER TOPPINGS
FOR SUPPER
SANDWICHES

Baby Artichoke and
Scallion Sauté,
page 332

Slivered Asparagus
Sauté with Shallots,
page 335

Cabbage with Juniper
Berries, page 348

Kale with Olives,
page 381

Mushrooms with
Tarragon and Cream,
page 389

Salads for All Seasons

WE USUALLY THINK OF SALADS AS SOMETHING FRESH, LIGHT, LEAFY, AND COOL THAT PRECEDES A MAIN COURSE, AND GREEN SALADS DO JUST THAT WHEN THEY'RE SERVED AT THE BEGINNING OF A MEAL. THEY CAN ALSO PROVIDE A refreshing pause at the end, however, and that's just a small example of the versatility that makes salads so appealing as well as difficult to define. Salads may start with simple collections of tender leaves, but they can go on to become complex arrangements of varied ingredients. Composed salads, which include a number of elements on a plate, can be first courses when served small or main courses when served generously. Hearty salads based on grains, legumes, and pasta might well be presented as the main feature of a meal. And, of course, fruits, eggs, cheese, and an array of condiments also have a role to play in salads. On the very rare occasion that a person says he or she doesn't like salad, I've found that what the person *really* dislikes is vinegar, so perhaps it's the sharp acidic note of this single ingredient that unifies such a disparate collection of foods into "salad."

Not only do salad ingredients range widely, but so do temperatures. Cold and cool are not the only degrees for salad. Some salads use contrasting temperatures to good effect—a warm crouton or a warm dressing tossed with chilled greens tantalizes the senses, for heat brings out the fruity side of the vinegar and the full possibilities of the oil, while hot dressings temper aggressive greens like dandelions or soften other greens, like spinach.

Vinaigrettes and dressings, those richly endowed amalgamations of aromatic oils, vinegars, mustards, garlic, and herbs, are key players in the world of salads. Even with only lettuce to work with, you can make an infinite number of salads simply by changing the dressing.

Leafy Salad Greens: Lettuce, Herbs, Spinach, and Cabbages

LETTUCE is one of the most lovely, pure, and beguiling foods to handle. Its delicate leaves hold a wealth of flavor, texture, coolness, and color. Exciting heirloom and new varieties of salad greens are increasingly becoming available through specialty growers and farmers' markets. As lettuce has become chic, it has also become practical. Now mixes of "gourmet greens," ready to dress and serve, are available even at ordinary supermarkets.

Salad greens also include chicories, herbs, spinach, cabbages, wild greens, and more. Here is a basic lexicon to give you the general idea of family groups and their possibilities.

CRISPHEADS: These are the lettuces that crunch, most famous of which is iceberg. Crispheads offer texture, which Americans like as much as, and indeed confuse with, taste. Older crisphead types, from which our standard is descended, are actually quite flavorful, such as the French Reine de Glace. But iceberg is the lettuce to use when you want texture or a salad that will support a heavy dressing or when you're going camping.

ROMAINE OR COS LETTUCES: Romaine or cos lettuce is prized for its long, graceful leaves at the heart and its snappy texture. It also has good, strong flavor and is the most nutritious of the lettuces—signaled by its dark green leaves. Romaine can be quite diminutive and have red or rouge-tipped leaves, but the standard variety is a good lettuce to use with a heavy dressing, such as avocado or blue cheese.

LOOSELEAF LETTUCES: These are soft, open heads of loosely joined tender leaves. Red leaf and green leaf are common varieties. Red and green oakleaf lettuces have sharply indented leaves, while the frizzy, gaudy red Lollo Rossa is a new favorite. Looseleaf lettuces require lighter dressings than iceberg and romaine.

BUTTERHEADS: These are soft, buttery-textured leaves that form a loose and curvaceous rosette—Boston, Bibb, and butter lettuce are well-known examples; exotic varieties are etched with bronze and red. These lettuces are tender and exceptionally elegant, the perfect lettuce for a refined dinner salad.

GARDEN SALAD, MESCLUN, GOURMET LETTUCE MIX: These names refer to mixtures of small leaves, usually no longer than 3 inches, of lettuces and other greens such as arugula, red mustard, frisée, mâche, baby spinach, and sometimes tatsoi and mizuna. *Mesclun* is the Provençal word for fairly specific mixtures; farmers here tend to make more personal mixes, which are sold clean and ready to use. While the pound price is high, lettuce is light; if it's in good condition, there's virtually no waste, of either lettuce or effort.

CHICORIES: ENDIVE, ESCAROLE, FRISÉE, DANDELION, AND RADICCHIO: These interesting greens range from slight to pronounced bitterness. They take well to fragrant nut oils, shallots, sharp vinegars, and pairings with citrus, apples and pears, walnuts and hazelnuts, and blue cheeses. They also stand up well to hot dressing, which sweetens their bitterness.

SPINACH: There are basically two types of spinach leaves: smooth and crinkled. The smooth type is preferable for salads unless the crinkled leaves are very young—tender little leaves with slender stems are best for raw salads. If spinach has been in the field for a while—you can tell by its thick stems and leathery-looking leaves—it's better for cooking. Spinach is best with a robust or heated dressing.

CABBAGE: In addition to green and red Dutch cabbages, Savoy and Napa cabbage make excellent salads. Fine slicing and a brief wilting in boiling water make raw cabbage more appealing to many.

HERBS: Herbs provide many wonderful possibilities for salads. Arugula; sorrel; torn basil, lovage, and parsley leaves; curly cress and watercress—the tender leaves of any garden herb, really—add so much. A salad composed entirely of herbs has big, exciting flavors that often need only a little lemon juice and olive oil for dressing.

WILD GREENS: Like herbs, wild greens can be very attractive and interesting in a salad. Some common backyard greens that I enjoy using are lamb's-quarters, miner's lettuce, amaranth, purslane, and mâche. Garden thinnings and volunteer seedlings, which sometimes behave as if they were wild, also qualify as salad ingredients.

Care and Handling of Salad Greens

Always handle salad greens gently—they bruise when roughly handled. Never open a head of lettuce by twisting it from the stem; this causes dark bruises and subsequent spoilage.

TRIMMING: Slice the head at its base with a sharp knife and let the leaves fall open. Discard those outside leaves that look thick and leathery—they've been exposed to the elements while protecting the rest—or use them for soup stocks. With a sure, light touch, gently tear or cut leaves that are too large to eat whole. A small, sharp knife or nimble fingers will do little harm, unlike a heavily wielded knife or aggressive tearing. With Belgian endive and escarole, the cut or torn edges discolor after an hour or so.

WASHING: It's most practical to wash greens after they've been trimmed. Plunge them into a large basin of cold water, gently swish them about with your hands, and, if very dirty, let them soak for at least 5 minutes. Lift the greens out of the water, leaving the debris behind. Take a close look, especially at the base of the leaves, to make sure they're really clean. Chicories, which are in the field for a long time, are often gritty at the base, and sandy spinach frequently needs a second washing.

DRYING: Drying greens is important; if the salad isn't dry, the vinaigrette will get watered down, wasting what may be your most expensive oil. Also, if you plan to store washed greens, they won't spoil if they're well dried. If you don't have a salad spinner, dry lettuce between towels or swing it outdoors in a perforated bag. To store, roll washed and dried greens loosely in a kitchen towel, put the towel in a plastic bag, and refrigerate in the vegetable bin.

CUTTING STYLES

Some people are inclined to cut everything into small, evenly diced fragments; others like big uneven chunks, slices, wedges, or something in between. We naturally have our own styles. How things are cut affects the look and character of a dish but seldom affects the taste. Therefore I've left the details of cutting sizes up to your own discretion, unless, for some reason, they do make a difference.

Putting a Salad Together

Some salads call for roasted nuts. Use any of the nuts in the "Greetings from the Cook" chapter that are appropriate, such as basic roasted nuts or the Salt and Pepper Walnuts.

Pine nuts, sesame seeds, and sunflower seeds can be toasted right in an ungreased skillet. Heat a small pan with the nuts in it and slide it back and forth occasionally so that the nuts brown evenly.

Peanuts can be pan-fried in a little oil or roasted in the oven.

AMOUNTS: Because salads are often made by eye, feel, and taste, there's no real need to measure greens. Besides, greens don't lend themselves to measurement—you certainly don't want to cram them into a cup. Roughly speaking, a good handful of lettuce and a few teaspoons of vinaigrette make a generous dinner salad. Many vinaigrette recipes make about ½ cup because the amounts are easier to handle than minuscule measurements and the unused portion can be used over the next few days.

TOSSING: Give yourself a bowl with lots of room. I always toss my greens first with a pinch of salt, then add the dressing and toss until the leaves are coated evenly. Your hands are the best tool since they won't bruise the greens and you'll know by touch when you have enough dressing.

ADDING FLOWERS: If you're including edible flowers, add them after the salad is dressed so that they don't collapse or wilt under the oil. Scatter them over the finished salad, toss once more, and serve.

PRESENTATION: Most salad bowls are deep, but since salads are among the prettiest dishes we serve, you might consider a wide, shallow bowl or platter to show them off. On plates, lightly mound the leaves in a tangle so that they have a lively look. A salad that lies flat on the plate looks dispirited. Take a moment to turn a few of the prettier leaves to show their brighter sides, but quickly and without fussing.

Mixed Green Salad

THIS simple salad is equally appropriate at the start or the close of a meal. The lettuce could be garden lettuces of mixed varieties or a single type only. Chopped herbs or tiny sprigs add unexpected bursts of flavor to a salad.

SERVES 4 TO 6

4 to 6 handfuls salad greens

Salt and freshly milled pepper

½ teaspoon Dijon mustard

1½ tablespoons white or red wine vinegar or 1 tablespoon fresh lemon juice

5 tablespoons extra virgin olive oil

Chopped herbs—chervil, small basil leaves, chives, or parsley leaves

Carefully sort through the greens, then trim, wash, and dry them well. In a small bowl, combine ¼ teaspoon salt, the mustard, and the vinegar and let stand at least 10 minutes to dissolve the salt. Whisk in the oil to make a smooth sauce or shake everything together in a jar. Taste the vinaigrette on a leaf. Add more oil if it's too tart or a little vinegar if it's too oily. Though you can make your vinaigrette ahead of time, don't actually dress the salad until you're ready to serve it—it will quickly grow limp.

Using your hands, toss the greens with the herbs and a few pinches of salt. Add 3 tablespoons dressing and toss until they're coated lightly but evenly. Taste and add more dressing, if desired. Grind a little pepper on the leaves, toss again, and serve.

Sprouts on Salads

Keep an eye out for these infant plants. All sprouts are nutritious, and some are quite delicious. Long white and short pink radish sprouts are as peppery tasting as a radish. Fine, threadlike leek sprouts topped with their black seeds taste every bit like a leek, while sprouted basil tastes like basil. Sunflower sprouts don't taste like much, but with their large fleshy leaves and white stems they look striking on a salad of dark green spinach. Sprouts from the garden, otherwise known as *thinnings,* make great additions to a salad. They don't look like much, but they're full of flavor. Beet, leek, lettuce, arugula, and carrot are just a few possibilities.

Red Lettuces with Radish Sprouts

4 good handfuls red-leaf salad greens

1 large shallot, finely diced

1½ tablespoons red wine vinegar

Salt

3 tablespoons extra virgin olive or sunflower seed oil

1 tablespoon walnut oil

1 cup red radish sprouts

Sort through the greens, then trim, wash, and dry them well. Combine the shallot, vinegar, and ¼ teaspoon salt in a bowl and let stand for 10 to 15 minutes. Whisk in the oils. Toss the greens with a few pinches salt, add the dressing, distribute the radish sprouts on top, and toss until the leaves are coated evenly.

PART of a salad's character comes from the mix of greens. Here's one based on red-leaf lettuces, such as Lollo Rossa, red romaine, red-tipped butterheads, or some slender leaves of Treviso radicchio. Pink radish sprouts add a peppery tingle to the mix.

SERVES 4 TO 6

Tender Tatsoi with Sesame Oil Vinaigrette

8 cups tender tatsoi leaves and/or salad greens

2 scallions, including some of the greens, thinly sliced

1 tablespoon thinly sliced garlic chives or regular chives

2 teaspoons rice vinegar

2 tablespoons sesame oil

1 tablespoon dark sesame oil

½ teaspoon Sichuan Pepper Salt, page 76, or sea salt

1 tablespoon toasted sesame seeds

Sort through the greens, then trim, wash, and dry them well. Toss the greens with the scallions and chives. In another bowl, whisk together the vinegar, oils, and salt. Taste the dressing on a leaf and adjust the oil or vinegar if necessary. Pour over the salad, toss well, add the sesame seeds, toss again, and serve.

TINY spoon-shaped tatsoi leaves make an unusual salad, especially with the addition of floral Sichuan Pepper Salt and fragrant dark sesame oil. If your tatsoi is not so small and tender, combine it with mixed salad greens and use it as an accent.

SERVES 4

Watercress with Slivered Endive

I LOVE this simple yet distinctive salad with its shower of endive slivers. It's a wonderful first course for a winter meal. Follow it with a cheese or vegetable soufflé, an omelet, gratin, or even a hearty soup.

SERVES 4

2 bunches watercress

2 Belgian endives

Lemon Vinaigrette, page 184

Carefully sort through the greens, then trim, wash, and dry them well. Trim the watercress by removing the larger stems and broken branches. Wash and spin dry. Halve the endives, remove the cores, then slice them diagonally into slender slivers. Make the vinaigrette. Taste and adjust the balance if needed.

Toss the watercress with enough dressing to coat lightly, then distribute it among salad plates, piling it lightly. Toss the endive with vinaigrette to coat lightly, then scatter it over the watercress and serve.

Winter Greens with Fennel and Mushrooms

STURDY chicories— Belgian endive, frisée, radicchio, and dandelion marry well with crisp fennel and earthy mushrooms, while a fruity extra virgin olive oil ties everything together. Pears, by the way, are also stellar in this salad; use them in place of the mushrooms.

SERVES 4 TO 6

4 good handfuls mixed greens— radicchio torn into small pieces, slivered endive, tender frisée sprigs, dandelion, butter lettuce

1 fennel bulb, trimmed and very thinly sliced

6 firm white mushrooms, thinly sliced

Salt and freshly milled pepper

Shallot Vinaigrette, page 183

A piece of Parmesan or dry Jack at room temperature

Carefully sort through the greens, then trim, wash, and dry them well. Toss the greens, fennel, and mushrooms in a salad bowl with a few pinches of salt. Toss with enough vinaigrette to coat well and season with pepper. Divide among plates and shave the cheese into long shards over each serving.

Salad with Warm Goat Cheese Croutons

THE warm, near-melting goat cheese paired with greens, popularized by Alice Waters at Chez Panisse, is one of the best combinations imaginable. Use a mixture of small garden lettuces and frisée if available.

SERVES 6

6 ounces soft white goat cheese

3 tablespoons milk or cream

1 garlic clove, minced

2 teaspoons coarsely chopped thyme leaves, plus extra for garnish

Salt and freshly milled pepper

6 large or 12 small baguette slices

8 to 10 cups salad greens

Shallot Vinaigrette, page 183

Smooth the goat cheese with the milk, then stir in the garlic, thyme, and a little pepper. Broil the bread just until the tops are lightly colored, then spread the cheese mixture thickly over the untoasted side and set aside. Toss the salad greens with a pinch of salt, then with the vinaigrette, and arrange on individual plates. Broil the croutons until the cheese begins to slump and bubble, about 3 minutes. Sprinkle on the thyme, then set the cheese toasts right on top of the greens. Grind black pepper over the top and serve.

Variation with Figs: Include some arugula in the lettuce mix. Slice 12 ripe figs into halves or rounds and dress them separately with a little Lemon Vinaigrette, page 184, or Shallot Vinaigrette, page 183. Dress and serve the greens, placing the figs among them. Set the warm croutons on top.

Dandelion Greens with Garlic Croutons and Hard-Cooked Egg

1 large bunch dandelion greens, about 1 pound

2 large, thin slices sourdough bread

1 large garlic clove, halved

Salt and freshly milled pepper

1 large shallot, finely diced

4 teaspoons sherry vinegar or aged red wine vinegar

5 tablespoons extra virgin olive oil

2 hard-cooked eggs, quartered

COMMERCIAL dandelion greens, available in early spring, need the assertive tastes of garlic and good, strong vinegar to match their own aggressive nature, even though they're far milder than wild ones. The hot dressing wilts them just enough to sweeten their flavor. Spinach and escarole are also good treated this way.

SERVES 4

Carefully sort through the greens, then trim, wash, and dry them well. Trim and discard the long stems of the greens, then chop the remaining leaves into bite-sized pieces. There should be about 6 cups. Toast the bread in the oven until crisp, then rub it with garlic and break each piece into quarters.

Pound the same clove of garlic with $1/4$ teaspoon salt in a mortar until smooth, then whisk in the shallot, vinegar, and oil. Heat the vinaigrette in a small skillet until it sizzles, then pour it over the dandelion greens while tossing them with tongs. Add the croutons and plenty of pepper and toss again. Serve garnished with the eggs.

Variation with Roasted Walnuts: In place of the croutons, substitute $1/2$ cup Salt and Pepper Walnuts, page 89.

Variation with Garlic Croutons and Gruyère: Add several paper-thin slices of Gruyère to each salad. The buttery cheese, the garlicky bread, and the strong greens make a stupendous combination. Spinach is also delicious this way.

Romaine Salads

Romaine hearts, the crisp, pale, perfect leaves at the center of a head of romaine lettuce, are strong enough to support denser, heavier dressings. These salads make a light meal or, in smaller portions, a substantial first course. Iceberg lettuce would also work here, but romaine has better flavor and a fine appearance when the leaves are left whole. The heart constitutes only about a third of the head. Use the outer leaves in another salad or in soup stock.

Romaine Hearts with Parmesan and Lemon Vinaigrette

THIS will remind you of a Caesar salad.

SERVES 4 TO 6

2 heads romaine lettuce

1 garlic clove

Salt and freshly milled pepper

1 teaspoon finely grated lemon zest

2¹/₂ tablespoons fresh lemon juice

1 teaspoon Dijon mustard

6 tablespoons extra virgin olive oil

¹/₂ cup freshly grated Parmesan or more to taste

³/₄ cup small toasted croutons

Slice the bottoms off the lettuce and remove most of the leaves until you get to the hearts. Wash if needed and put the hearts in a spacious, wide bowl.

Pound the garlic with ¹/₂ teaspoon salt in a mortar until smooth. Whisk in the lemon zest and juice, the mustard, then the oil. Pour the dressing over the leaves and roll them over each other until coated. Sprinkle most of the cheese over the leaves, add the croutons, and toss again until the leaves are coated. Divide the salad among four large plates, add the remaining cheese, and finish with pepper.

Romaine Hearts with Chives and Pecans Omit the cheese and croutons but add 2 tablespoons snipped chives and ¹/₂ cup roasted pecans to the romaine. If you have chive blossoms, cut through the base of one or two clusters and scatter the blossoms on top.

Romaine Hearts with Blue Cheese Dressing Toss the hearts with Blue Cheese Dressing, page 189. With sliced pears or apples and roasted walnuts, this makes a perfect fall salad.

Romaine Hearts with Feta Dressing and Tomatoes Chop the romaine and toss with Feta Dressing with Marjoram and Mint, page 190. Slice 3 ripe tomatoes— a mixture of varieties is nice—into wedges or chunks, toss them with the greens, and finish with plenty of pepper.

Romaine Hearts with Green Goddess Dressing Everyone will tell you that this is divine when you serve it. Make either version of Green Goddess Dressing, page 190; toss with the romaine and ¹/₂ cup or so small diced croutons, crisped in olive oil.

PURSLANE AND LAMB'S-QUARTERS

The succulent creeper purslane and the upright *Chenopodium*, lamb's-quarters or wild spinach, are among the first plants to volunteer in freshly turned soil and are persistent residents of established gardens as well. Although usually regarded as weeds in the suburbs, in the country these plants are recognized as food. In northern New Mexico, where I live, both plants are sold in the farmers' market by traditional farmers. Purslane, almost lemony and crunchy when raw, is added raw to salads, sautéed, or cooked with beans. Lamb's-quarters, which are related to spinach and chard, can be included in salads when the leaves are small and tender or cooked like spinach.

Aside from being unusual and delicious, purslane and lamb's-quarters are both richly endowed with antioxidant vitamins C and E, beta carotene, and other protective substances. Purslane is a rare plant source of omega-3 fatty acids. If you have a garden, chances are you already are growing purslane and lamb's-quarters. Instead of weeding them out, try mixing them in a salad.

Herb Salads

Salads emphasizing fresh herbs are vigorous and fill the mouth with big, robust flavors. A little goes far, and because of their intensity they're excellent paired with milder foods or as a contrast to rich ones. Parsley, so ubiquitous but overlooked in this capacity, makes an especially healthful—as well as good—salad. Improvising with your own garden gleanings can provide you with an ever-changing salad on the table. With so much flavor, the dressing need be only a light coating of olive oil and a squeeze of lemon.

Herb Salad (*Sabzi*)

3 cups small spinach leaves

1 cup arugula

¼ cup flat-leaf parsley leaves

¼ cup cilantro leaves

¼ cup dill sprigs

6 mint leaves, torn into small pieces

Several celery or lovage leaves, torn

2 scallions, including a few inches of the greens, thinly sliced

Salt

1 tablespoon extra virgin olive oil or as needed

Fresh lemon juice

SABZI *refers to greens or potherbs, usually a Middle Eastern combination of dill, parsley, and mint. Serve* sabzi *with a warm cheese-filled turnover or falafel or add it to a pita sandwich along with tomatoes and feta or ricotta salata.*

SERVES 3 TO 4

Carefully sort through the greens, then wash and dry them well. Tear or cut the spinach and arugula into bite-sized pieces and toss with the herbs, scallions, and a few pinches of salt. Drizzle on enough oil to lightly coat the leaves, then squeeze on a little lemon juice and toss again.

A Salad with Garden Herbs

SERVE *this salad or its variation with the Rice and Ricotta Tart, roasted potatoes, or small cheese toasts. It also provides an exuberant accompaniment to a cheese soufflé or vegetable timbale.*

SERVES 3 TO 4

2 cups lettuce leaves

2 cups spinach leaves

4 marjoram sprigs

2 tablespoons basil leaves

½ cup celery leaves

½ cup flat-leaf parsley leaves

Several lemon verbena sprigs

1 cup small purslane sprigs

Salt

Extra virgin olive oil

Fresh lemon juice or apple cider vinegar

Herb blossoms if available

Carefully sort through the leaves, then wash and dry them well. Tear or cut the lettuce and spinach into bite-sized pieces. Strip the marjoram leaves from their stems. Keep the marjoram leaves whole, tear the basil leaves unless they're the tiny *piccolo fino* variety, and keep the celery, parsley, and lemon verbena leaves in fairly large pieces. Toss everything with a pinch or two of salt, then with just enough oil to coat. Season with lemon juice to taste, then toss again with the herb blossoms.

Fall Salad with Walnuts and Walnut Oil Dress the salad with walnut oil and a few drops sherry vinegar. Add ½ cup of the season's new-crop walnuts in large pieces and 1 tablespoon snipped chives.

Parsley Salad with Parmesan

FLAT-LEAF parsley has better flavor, so choose it over the curly type if possible. Include parsley salad on a composed salad plate or sprinkle it over hot pizza, grilled eggplant, a baked potato, or warm chickpeas. The heat brings out its flavor and softens the leaves. You'll need no more than ½ cup per person.

SERVES 4 TO 6

2½ cups parsley leaves

1 tablespoon chopped marjoram

1 tablespoon chopped mint

Salt and freshly milled pepper

Sherry Vinaigrette, page 189, or Lemon Vinaigrette, page 184

Thin shavings of Parmesan or dry Jack

Pluck the parsley leaves from the stems, then wash and dry well. Toss with the herbs, a few pinches salt and pepper to taste, then with a few tablespoons vinaigrette or enough to coat lightly. Serve covered lightly with thin shavings of cheese.

Parsley Salad with Oil and Lemon Toss parsley leaves with 2 tablespoons extra virgin olive oil and 1½ to 2 teaspoons fresh lemon juice. Season with salt and freshly milled pepper.

Arugula Salads

Those who have come across arugula and fallen in love with it don't want an arugula accent; they (we) want an entire salad of it. As arugula matures, the leaves get big, peppery, and hot, and those should be used sparingly. For an all-arugula salad, look for small, soft leaves with a mild but definite bite. Discard the long stems, but keep any cream-colored blossoms for a fine edible garnish. Pungent olives, hard-cooked eggs with the yolk still a little moist, grilled onions, and fresh figs with salty cheeses all form happy alliances with arugula. Vinaigrettes featuring extra virgin olive oil and walnut and hazelnut oils are a good match for arugula's warm flavor, as are assertive aged red wine and sherry vinegars and lemon juice.

Impromptu Arugula Salad Allow 1 1/2 to 2 cups arugula per person. Carefully sort through the leaves, then wash and dry them well. Tear any large leaves in half or thirds, put them all in a spacious bowl, and toss with a few pinches of salt. Drizzle on enough extra virgin olive oil to coat lightly and evenly when tossed. Squeeze on a little lemon juice, then toss again and taste. Serve the leaves heaped into a high, light pile.

Arugula Salad with Hard-Cooked Eggs and Croutons For four servings, boil 2 or 3 eggs and separate the yolks and whites. Finely chop the whites and scatter them over the preceding arugula salad, then crumble or sieve the yolks over all. Add 2 large, thin Garlic-Rubbed Croutons, page 34, to each plate. Or quarter the eggs and include them among the greens and croutons.

Arugula Salad with Grilled Onion Vinaigrette Add grilled red onions, diced and tossed with balsamic vinegar and seasoned with pepper, to the salad. The sweet onion contrasts well with the spicy greens.

Arugula with Pecorino Romano and Toasted Walnuts

8 to 10 cups arugula, 4 large handfuls, stems discarded, any large leaves torn

Salt

Walnut Oil Vinaigrette, page 185

1/2 cup or more coarsely grated pecorino Romano

1/2 cup cracked walnuts, roasted

AN excellent salad for fall, when walnuts are new and fresh.

SERVES 4

Toss the arugula with a little salt and enough vinaigrette to coat lightly. Add the cheese and walnuts, toss again, and serve.

Arugula with Tomatoes and Olive Croutons

THIS *combination offers*
strong flavor and color
contrasts—even more so
if you use both red and
yellow tomatoes.

SERVES 4

2 or 3 ripe tomatoes or 1 cup cherry
   tomatoes

8 Garlic-Rubbed Croutons, page 34

Olive Paste, page 87

8 to 10 cups arugula, stems discarded,
   any large leaves torn

3 tablespoons Balsamic Vinaigrette,
   page 184

Halve the tomatoes, remove the seeds, and cut them neatly into small pieces or simply cut the cherry tomatoes in half. Spread the croutons with the olive paste. Toss the greens with enough vinaigrette to coat lightly. Add the tomatoes and toss again. Serve with the croutons tucked among the leaves.

Spinach Salads

The best-tasting spinach salads are those made with tender small leaves, whether smooth or crinkled. Remember to take special care to wash spinach thoroughly and make sure it's clean by tasting a few leaves. Fine sand, which is hard to see, often clings to the leaves, and nothing can devastate a salad more thoroughly than gritty greens.

Wilted Spinach Salad

TOSSING *spinach leaves*
quickly in a hot oil or a
heated vinaigrette makes
them shiny and brings
out their flavor as well as
reducing the fuzzy feel
that spinach sometimes
leaves in the mouth.
Essentially the same
salad as in The Greens
Cookbook, *this is still*
one of my favorites, and
it's a template for all
wilted salads.

SERVES 4

1 cup Pickled Onions, page 78, or
   1 small red onion

8 cups small spinach leaves

12 thin Garlic-Rubbed Croutons,
   page 34

1 garlic clove, finely chopped

4 ounces crumbled goat cheese, feta, or
   ricotta salata, optional

12 Kalamata olives, pitted and cut into
   large pieces

1 tablespoon thinly sliced mint leaves

2 tablespoons sherry vinegar

Salt and freshly milled pepper

6 tablespoons olive oil, fragrant but not
   your very best

If you're using the raw onion, quarter and thinly slice it crosswise, then cover with ice water. Refrigerate for 30 minutes, then drain and pat dry.

Carefully sort through the leaves, then wash and dry them well. In a large bowl, toss together everything except the oil with several pinches salt. Heat the oil until almost smoking, then pour it over the salad, quickly turning the leaves with a pair of tongs as you do so. The spinach should sizzle, brighten, and soften. Taste and correct the levels of salt and vinegar. Add pepper to taste and serve, dividing the croutons evenly among the plates.

Spinach and Tomato Salad with Basil-Walnut Dressing

1 small red onion, sliced into paper-thin rounds

4 ripe tomatoes

8 cups small spinach leaves, sliced into wide ribbons

8 white mushrooms, thinly sliced

$\frac{1}{4}$ cup basil leaves, torn or thinly sliced

Salt

Basil-Walnut Dressing

$\frac{1}{2}$ cup walnuts

2 garlic cloves

Salt and freshly milled pepper

Scant $\frac{1}{2}$ cup olive oil

3 tablespoons red wine vinegar or 2 tablespoons sherry vinegar

1 tablespoon chopped basil or 1 teaspoon dried

THE crinkly Bloomsdale spinach makes a good support for this thick, garlicky dressing.

SERVES 4

Cover the onion with cold water and refrigerate for 30 minutes. Meanwhile, make the dressing. Using a small food processor or a mortar and pestle, grind or pound the walnuts, garlic, and $\frac{1}{2}$ teaspoon salt to a chunky paste. Gradually whisk in the oil, then add the vinegar. Stir in the basil and season with pepper. If the dressing thickens too much before serving, thin it with water to a lighter consistency.

Slice the tomatoes into eighths or large chunks and reserve 12 pieces for garnish. Put the spinach in a spacious bowl with the remaining tomatoes, the mushrooms, and the basil. Drain the onion, towel off the excess moisture, and add to the spinach. Toss with a few pinches salt, then add the dressing and toss well. Garnish with the reserved tomato.

Spinach Salad with Sunflower Seeds and Sprouts

6 cups small spinach leaves

$\frac{1}{3}$ cup sunflower seeds, toasted

2 tablespoons chopped parsley, dill, or basil

Salt and freshly milled pepper

1 tablespoon red wine vinegar

1 small garlic clove, minced

3 tablespoons sunflower seed oil

6 scallions, including an inch of the greens, thinly sliced

2 cups sunflower sprouts

2 ripe tomatoes, seeded and chopped

1 avocado, sliced

Crumbled feta, optional

SPROUTS on salad are a vegetarian cliché, but sprouted sunflower seeds, with their fleshy large leaves and stems, are far from commonplace. If you want to wilt this salad, toss the leaves and herbs with the garlic, vinegar, and scallions, then heat the oil as described in Wilted Spinach Salad.

SERVES 2 TO 4

Toss the spinach with the sunflower seeds, parsley, a pinch of salt, and some pepper. Put another pinch of salt, the vinegar, and the garlic in a small bowl; whisk in the oil and add the scallions. Pour the vinaigrette over the greens and toss. Loosely arrange the greens on a large platter, then add the sprouts, tomatoes, avocado, and feta to taste.

Vegetables can be
dressed as freely as let-
tuce, a great advantage
when you're in a hurry
or feel you can't make
one more thing. For ex-
ample, instead of mak-
ing a lemon vinaigrette
for green beans, simply
toss them in good olive
oil, season them with
salt and pepper, and add
a squeeze of lemon juice
to taste. In the "Vegeta-
bles" chapter, pairings of
herbs and seasonings
are suggested for each
vegetable to help you
improvise a vegetable
salad.

Vegetables and Fruits Dressed as Salads

Virtually all vegetables and many fruits have strong affinities for vinaigrettes and other salad dressings. While not every fruit and vegetable has been given its own recipe, here are examples to give you a sense of what's possible. Botanically related foods usually respond well to the same kinds of seasoning: Mustardy dressings work with broccoli as well as cauliflower, both brassicas; blue cheese is delicious with pears and apples, both pome fruits.

COOKED AND RAW VEGETABLES: Common sense tells you which vegetables can be dressed raw or cooked. Some, like beets and carrots, can go both ways. When cooked, vegetables are usually steamed or boiled, but there's no reason not to roast or grill them, especially if it's convenient. In fact both roasting and grilling concentrate flavor. Roasted potatoes or grilled eggplants with a vinaigrette are simply delicious. Although fresh is always better, many leftover vegetables can be turned into salads.

DRESSING VEGETABLES: Vegetables are most aromatic dressed while warm, but they can be eaten warm, tepid, or chilled. If you dress green vegetables well in advance of serving them, the acid from the lemon or vinegar will gradually dull their color, making them dull. Either wait to dress them or add the acidic element just before serving.

DRESSING FRUITS: Since fruits are generally eaten uncooked, it's especially important that they start out full of flavor. Salty and pungent dressings bring out the sweetness of fruit—even a little fresh lime or lemon juice or some black pepper on a piece of melon dramatically sets off its sweetness.

Warm Asparagus Salad on Arugula with Walnut Vinaigrette

A ROASTED walnut oil makes a stunning match for arugula and the first pencil-thin asparagus. Here the asparagus is boiled, but this is a wonderful way to treat Roasted Asparagus, as well.

SERVES 2 TO 4

1 large shallot, finely diced
1½ tablespoons champagne vinegar or white wine vinegar
Salt
3½ tablespoons roasted walnut oil

1 pound thin asparagus trimmed
3 to 4 handfuls arugula, stems discarded, leaves torn into small pieces
1 hard-cooked egg

Combine the shallot, vinegar, and ⅛ teaspoon salt in a small bowl. Let stand for 15 minutes to dissolve the salt, then whisk in the oil.

Simmer the asparagus in boiling salted water until tender; then drain and remove to a clean towel.

Dress the arugula with 1 tablespoon of the vinaigrette and set it on a platter. Lay the warm asparagus directly on top and spoon the remaining dressing over the top. Finely chop the egg white, scatter it over the top, followed by the yolk, rubbed through a sieve. Serve at once.

Avocado, Jícama, and Orange Salad

8 ounces jícama

1 large or 2 small avocados

2 navel oranges

4 large radishes

About 24 small spinach leaves

Juice of 2 limes or Lime-Cumin Vinaigrette, page 187

Salt

1 jalapeño chile, seeded and finely diced, or ground red chile

Handful sunflower sprouts

JÍCAMA is a large, roundish tuber with a papery brown skin. It looks dull, but underneath its skin the flesh is white, sweet, and crunchy. Serve this salad with enchiladas.

SERVES 4 TO 6

Peel the jícama; thinly slice it into rounds, then slice again into narrow strips. Peel and slice the avocado. Cut the oranges either into round slices or into sections. Thinly slice the radishes, then cut into narrow strips.

Line a platter with the spinach leaves. Lightly scatter the jícama over it and intersperse with the avocado, oranges, and radishes. Squeeze lime juice or spoon the vinaigrette over all. Season with salt, sprinkle with chile, and garnish with the sunflower sprouts.

Warm Green Bean Salads

1½ pounds slender green, yellow wax, or Romano beans

3 to 4 tablespoons extra virgin olive oil as needed

1 tablespoon fresh lemon juice, to taste

Chopped herbs—parsley, chervil, basil, or tarragon

LITTLE green beans, yellow wax, or wide Romano beans tossed warm with a vinaigrette make a stellar summer salad. If you want to mix varieties, boil each type separately so that they all are cooked perfectly.

SERVES 4

Tip and tail the beans. Boil the beans in plenty of salted water, uncovered; drain while they're still a little on the firm side. Shake off the excess water, then lay them on a clean kitchen towel to dry for a few minutes. Toss the beans while warm with enough oil to coat well. Then add the lemon juice and herbs. Serve immediately. (If you plan to serve them later, either dress them just before serving or add the acid at the last minute.)

GOOD VINAIGRETTES FOR BEANS

Lemon Vinaigrette, page 184 • Shallot Vinaigrette, page 183 • Tomato Vinaigrette with Olives, page 188 • Walnut Oil Vinaigrette, page 185 • Creamy Herb and Shallot Dressing, page 186

Beet Salads

I'm convinced that beets are best enjoyed in salads. The tang of a vinaigrette tames their earthy sweetness in a way that makes them easily likable. Once cooked, beets keep for a week in the refrigerator. Even after they're dressed, they keep well for days. All varieties can be used in salads, and mixtures of red, golden, and striped Chioggias are dazzling. When mixing different colors, be sure to keep the red ones away from everything else since they stain. Beets stand up to strong flavors such as bright acids, salty cheeses and olives, peppery greens, and pungent seeds.

Beet Salad with Ricotta Salata and Olives

SERVES 4 TO 6

1 1/2 to 2 pounds beets, steamed or
   roasted and peeled

1 small garlic clove

Salt

2 teaspoons fresh lemon juice, to taste

2 tablespoons extra virgin olive oil

2 handfuls arugula

4 ounces ricotta salata, thinly sliced

8 Kalamata olives

Cut the beets into wedges or large dice, keeping different colors separate. Pound the garlic with 1/4 teaspoon salt in a mortar until smooth, then whisk in the lemon juice and olive oil. The dressing should be a little on the tart side. Toss the beets in enough dressing to coat lightly. Arrange them on a platter and garnish with arugula. Just before serving, tuck the cheese and olives among the greens. If any dressing remains, spoon it over the cheese.

Roasted Beets with Anise Vinaigrette

THE Spanish combination of anise with beets is just as right as the more familiar dill and orange. Roasting adds another layer of flavor to beets, tempering their sweetness.

SERVES 4 TO 6

1 1/2 pounds beets

Olive oil

Salt and freshly milled pepper

1 teaspoon anise seeds

1 garlic clove

2 teaspoons sherry vinegar

2 tablespoons extra virgin olive oil

Preheat the oven to 375°F. Peel the beets and cut them into 1/2-inch dice. Toss in enough olive oil to coat lightly and season with salt and pepper. Spread the beets on a sheet pan—make sure they have plenty of room so they don't just steam—and bake until the juices begin to caramelize and the beets are tender but firm, about 25 minutes.

In a mortar, crush the anise seeds with the garlic and a little salt. Whisk in the vinegar and the extra virgin olive oil. Pour the vinaigrette over the beets and marinate for several hours or overnight.

Variation with Shaved Fennel: Core a fennel bulb and slice it paper-thin on a box grater or mandoline. Arrange the fennel loosely around the beets and garnish with watercress sprigs or fennel greens.

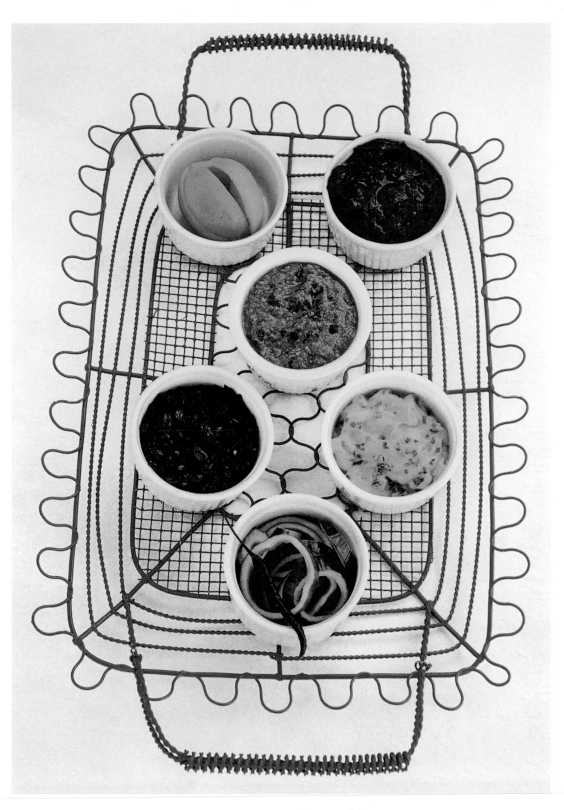

CLOCKWISE FROM TOP LEFT: **Preserved Lemons** *page 82,*
Harissa *page 75,* **Saffron Mayonnaise** *page 59,* **Pickled Onions** *page 78,*
Olive Paste *page 87,* and **Romesco Sauce** *page 70*

CLOCKWISE FROM TOP LEFT: Olives with Roasted Cumin and Paprika *page 85,*
Salted Almonds *page 88,* and Crudités (sliced fennel, sliced turnips, radishes)

FACING PAGE • LEFT TO RIGHT: Quesadilla with Smoky Black Bean Spread and Salsa, *page 123*
and Smoked Mozzarella Sandwich with Olive Paste and Roasted Peppers *page 121*

Leeks in Mustard Vinaigrette *page 158*

FACING PAGE • FRONT TO BACK:
Beet Salad with Ricotta Salata and Olives *page 150* **and Avocado, Jícama, and Orange Salad** *page 149*

FRONT TO BACK: **Tomato Salad of Many Colors** *page 162,* **Mixed Green Salad** *page 138*

Leeks poaching in a stock

FOLLOWING PAGE: **Lentil Minestrone** *page 225*

Beets with Lemon, Cilantro, and Mint

1 1/2 pounds beets, cooked and peeled

Finely grated zest of 1 lemon plus 2 tablespoons juice

2 tablespoons finely diced red onion

2 tablespoons chopped parsley

2 tablespoons chopped cilantro

1 tablespoon chopped mint or 1 teaspoon dried

1/2 teaspoon ground coriander

Salt and freshly milled pepper

6 tablespoons extra virgin olive oil

4 handfuls salad greens, such as spinach, frisée, and/or red-leaf lettuce

1/4 cup oil-cured black olives or Olives with Roasted Cumin and Paprika, page 85

THESE herbs also flatter the versatile beet. Serve with Yogurt Cheese or Havarti with dill and dark bread to make a salad meal.

SERVES 4 TO 6

Cut the beets into quarters or sixths. Whisk together the lemon zest and juice, onion, herbs, coriander, 1/4 teaspoon salt, pepper to taste, and the oil in a small bowl. Taste the dressing on a beet and correct the seasonings if needed. Toss the beets with enough dressing to coat lightly. Toss the greens with the remaining dressing and arrange them on salad plates. Add the beets and olives and serve.

Broccoli and Roasted Pepper Salad with Tomato Vinaigrette

2 yellow or red bell peppers, roasted

1 1/2 pounds broccoli with the stems

Tomato Vinaigrette with Olives, page 188

1 tablespoon chopped marjoram or parsley

Salt and freshly ground pepper

1/2 cup crumbled feta cheese

BROCCOLI always tastes best with strong, lively accompaniments; here it's the pungent feta and the olives in the dressing that provide that punch. Green beans, cauliflower, and broccoli Romanesco are also good prepared this way.

SERVES 4 TO 6

Dice the peeled peppers into 1/2-inch squares. Separate the broccoli into small florets. Peel and dice the stems. Blanch both the stems and florets in boiling salted water until tender; drain and shake off any excess water.

In a large bowl, toss the broccoli and peppers with the vinaigrette and marjoram. Taste for salt, allowing for the feta, season with pepper, and toss again with the feta. Serve warm or at room temperature.

Cabbage Salads

Cabbage salads, coleslaw and its cousins, are an entirely agreeable way to eat this healthful and inexpensive vegetable. Once dressed, cabbage keeps refrigerated for hours, which is one reason coleslaw is a popular picnic food. Unlike lettuce salads, a leftover of coleslaw makes a great bag lunch item. As a change from the smooth heavy heads of cabbage, try using the crinkled Savoy or lighter Napa cabbage. Both are more tender and mild. They don't hold up for quite as long, but they do make a fairly sturdy and quite delicious salad.

Coleslaw with Buttermilk-Horseradish Dressing

*A TANGY slaw that can
be made with all green
or red and green ribbons
of cabbage.*

SERVES 4 TO 6

4 cups thinly sliced green or red and
    green cabbage, about 1 pound

1 green bell pepper, finely sliced or
    grated

1 small onion, grated

Salt

Buttermilk Dressing with Horseradish,
    page 190

Chopped dill

Toss the cabbage, pepper, and onion in a bowl with ½ teaspoon salt. Toss with the dressing. Cover and refrigerate for 1 hour or until needed. Taste for salt and serve garnished with the chopped dill.

Cabbage Slaw with Spicy Greens

SERVES 4 TO 6

3 or 4 handfuls arugula, garden cress,
    watercress, or red mustard greens

1½ pounds green cabbage, very thinly
    sliced

1 large cucumber, peeled, seeded, and
    diced

1 small white onion or 1 bunch
    scallions, including an inch or so of
    the greens, thinly sliced

3 tablespoons chopped parsley

Salt

Winter Herb Vinaigrette, page 186

Chop the greens or cut them into ribbons and put them in a bowl with the cabbage, cucumber, onion, and parsley. Toss with ½ teaspoon salt. Add the dressing and toss again. Chill for 30 minutes or longer before serving.

Napa and Savoy Cabbage Salad with Peanut-Ginger Dressing

1 small Napa cabbage, about ³/₄ pound

2 medium carrots, julienned

1 cucumber, peeled and seeded

1 bunch scallions, including a few inches of the greens

¹/₂ small Savoy cabbage, about ¹/₂ pound, thinly sliced

2 tablespoons finely chopped mint leaves

1 tablespoon finely sliced basil leaves, preferably Thai or anise basil

Peanut Dressing with Thai Basil, page 189

¹/₂ cup roasted peanuts or Roasted Cashews with Garam Masala, page 89

THE dressing is warmed to bring up the aromatic quality of the oil, but the salad isn't wilted. Use a fragrant roasted peanut oil, such as Loriva.

SERVES 6

Quarter the Napa cabbage, including the base, and thinly slice it crosswise. Parboil the carrots for 1 minute, then refresh under cold water. Slice the cucumber and scallions into long, thin pieces and toss with the Napa and Savoy cabbage and the herbs. Heat the dressing in a small skillet until the aromas are released, then immediately pour it over the greens while tossing with a pair of tongs. Add the nuts, toss again, and serve.

Warm Red Cabbage Salad with Pecans

1 garlic clove, finely chopped

1 tablespoon sherry vinegar

3 tablespoons olive oil

1 red onion, quartered and thinly sliced

1 small red cabbage, about 1¹/₄ pounds, quartered and thinly sliced

Salt and freshly milled pepper

3 ounces crumbled goat cheese or mild feta

1 red apple, quartered and thinly sliced

¹/₄ cup pitted and chopped Kalamata olives

1 tablespoon *each* chopped parsley and marjoram

¹/₂ cup pecans or walnuts, roasted

THOUGH included in slightly different form in The Greens Cookbook, this recipe has held up well. It can be served as a salad or as a vegetable.

SERVES 4 TO 6

Heat the garlic, vinegar, and oil in a wide skillet, add the onion, and cook for 30 seconds. Add the cabbage, season with ¹/₂ teaspoon salt, and cook over high heat, tossing constantly with tongs. When the leaves begin to soften and change from red to pink, remove from the heat. Add the remaining ingredients and toss just enough to combine them, then remove from the heat. Season with plenty of pepper and serve warm.

Spicy Cooked Carrot Salad with Paprika, Feta, and Olives

THIS *salad is inspired by the flavors of Tunisia's popular salad of cooked carrots. There the carrots are very finely diced, but I find larger pieces are more appealing.*

SERVES 4 TO 6

1 pound carrots

1 garlic clove, minced

Salt

2 teaspoons hot paprika or Harissa, page 75

1 tablespoon red wine vinegar or fresh lemon juice

3 tablespoons olive oil

2 tablespoons chopped parsley

¹/₃ cup crumbled or thinly sliced feta cheese

12 oil-cured black olives, pitted and diced

Boil the carrots in salted water until tender but not soft, then drain and rinse with cold water. Slip off the skins and slice them into rounds or dice into small pieces.

Smash the garlic with ¹/₄ teaspoon salt, then add the paprika, vinegar, and whisk in the oil. Toss the carrots with the vinaigrette, parsley, and most of the cheese and olives. Taste for salt. Mound the carrots on a plate and garnish with the remaining cheese and olives.

Cooked Carrot Salad with Cilantro Salsa

COOKED *carrots (or beets) tossed with this pungent sauce—or any salsa verde, for that matter—are delicious and beautiful together.*

SERVES 4 TO 6

1 pound carrots, cooked

¹/₄ cup Cilantro Salsa, page 56

Salt

Mint sprigs and oil-cured black or Niçoise olives for garnish

Peel and dice the carrots, then toss with the salsa. Taste for salt. Serve chilled or at room temperature, garnished with the mint and olives.

Grated Vegetable Salads

Grated vegetables—carrots, beets, kohlrabi, celery root, and turnips—make refreshing salads that have all the virtues we want these days: They're bright and fresh, quick and easy to make, they keep well, and they require little dressing. An assortment of colorful vegetables mounded on a plate and garnished with a few shiny olives makes an ideal first course for richer winter meals, but it's right at other times of the year as well. Spooned into the curve of a small radicchio leaf or perched on the end of an endive leaf, they even can be passed around as appetizers.

Grated vegetable salads can be served as soon as they're made but also will be fine sitting for a few hours in the refrigerator until needed. Because they're so sturdy, they also make excellent picnic and brown-bag lunch fare.

WHAT TOOL TO USE: A Japanese box grater (benriner cutter), a French mandoline, and an American four-sided box grater are all good tools. To get nice long shreds on a box grater, roll the vegetable in your hand as you move it down the side—the greater exposed surface gives longer shreds. If you want slightly larger pieces, slice the vegetables by hand into fine julienne strips, then blanch them in boiling salted water for about 1 minute to soften. Rinse under cold water and towel-dry before dressing.

Carrot Salad with Parsley and Mint

1 pound carrots

1 tablespoon champagne vinegar, white wine vinegar, or fresh lemon juice

Salt and freshly milled white pepper

2 tablespoons olive oil

1 tablespoon finely chopped parsley or lovage

2 teaspoons finely chopped mint leaves

SERVES 4 TO 6

Peel, then grate the carrots. Mix the vinegar with ¼ teaspoon salt, then whisk in the oil. Toss with the carrots, parsley, and mint and season with pepper to taste. Serve right away or cover and chill for 1 hour.

Carrot Salad with Caper Sauce and Dill Prepare cooked or grated carrots and toss with Parsley-Caper Sauce, page 56, replacing 2 tablespoons of the parsley with chopped dill.

Grated Carrot or Beet Salad with Cumin Grate or hand-cut carrots or beets, blanch them briefly in boiling salted water, then drain and towel-dry. Dress while warm with Lime-Cumin Vinaigrette, page 187, plus 1 teaspoon orange flower water if you like.

Grated Kohlrabi and Celery with Mustard Vinaigrette Thickly peel 12 ounces kohlrabi or turnips and cut into fine julienne strips. Thinly slice or grate 3 or 4 inner celery ribs. Toss with enough Mustard Vinaigrette, page 186, to moisten.

Cauliflower Salad with Green Olives and Capers

1 small firm head cauliflower or broccoflower, about 12 ounces

2 cups watercress or inner escarole leaves

1 hard-cooked egg

Sherry Vinaigrette, page 185

2 scallions, including an inch of the greens, thinly sliced

1 cup diced celery heart with leaves

1 small green bell pepper, thinly sliced

1 small cucumber, peeled, seeded, and chopped

12 pimiento-stuffed Spanish green olives, halved

1 tablespoon capers, rinsed

½ cup parsley leaves

PEOPLE always love this salad. The dressing has strong, lively tastes and the vegetables plenty of texture. The real secret to making it shine is to slice the cauliflower as thinly as possible.

SERVES 4

Slice off very thin slices of cauliflower, working your way around the head. Quarter, then thinly slice the cauliflower. Be sure to include the stalks, too, peeled and thinly sliced. Remove the large stems from the watercress and coarsely chop the rest. If you're using escarole, select the pale inner leaves and tear or cut them into small pieces.

Smash the hard-cooked egg yolk with the garlic and salt when you make the vinaigrette. Keep the dressing a little on the tart side.

Dice the egg white and toss it with the vegetables and greens, olives, capers, and parsley. Add the vinaigrette and toss again.

Celery Root and Apple Salad with Mustard Vinaigrette

EVERYONE seems happy to see old-fashioned celery root salads make their winter appearance. A little goes far, and the salad can be made hours before serving. Include this on a plate of small salads for a first course or mound it at the base of an endive leaf.

SERVES 4 TO 6

⅓ cup Mustard Vinaigrette, page 186

1 celery root, 14 to 16 ounces

1 large Granny Smith apple, quartered, cored, and sliced into slivers

Watercress sprigs for garnish

Make the vinaigrette. Thickly peel the celery root as you would an orange, page 33, slice it into ⅛-inch-thick rounds, then stack the slices and cut them into long, thin julienne strips. Drop the celery root into a large pot of boiling salted water for 1 minute. (Don't wait for the boil to return, or it will be overcooked.) Drain, rinse with cold water, and pat dry. Toss with the apple and vinaigrette, then mound the salad on a platter and garnish with fat sprigs of watercress.

> **Variation with Walnuts:** Use walnut oil instead of olive oil in the vinaigrette and toss ¼ cup chopped toasted walnuts with the celery root. Hazelnut oil and hazelnuts are another possibility.

CUCUMBER SALADS

Subtle differences among types aside, all cucumbers more or less taste alike, and all can be used in salads. In addition to the standard Kirbys, there are small yellow lemon cucumbers, scalloped Armenian cucumbers, fuzzy Italian varieties, pickling cucumbers, and of course the pricey hothouse prima donnas sealed in their plastic wrappings. If the skins are unwaxed, you don't have to peel them unless they're very thick, and seeds need be removed only if they're very large. Cucumbers can be decoratively scored by running a fork or citrus zester down the skins, leaving white stripes in the green.

Cucumber and Yogurt Salad

CALLED tzatziki or cacik, depending on where in the eastern Mediterranean it's being made, this is a hot weather dish. Thick drained yogurt makes the best version. Serve it alone or with other vegetable salads, such as roasted peppers or carrots with Lime-Cumin Vinaigrette.

MAKES ABOUT 2 CUPS

2 cups yogurt, preferably whole milk

2 small or 1 large cucumber, peeled unless garden fresh, seeded, and diced

Salt and freshly milled white pepper

2 garlic cloves

2 teaspoons chopped mint

2 teaspoons chopped dill

2 to 3 teaspoons white wine vinegar

1 tablespoon extra virgin olive oil

Set the yogurt to drain, page 47, for 30 minutes. Meanwhile, in a colander, sprinkle the cucumbers lightly with salt and drain for 30 minutes.

Squeeze the cucumbers and blot with a towel. Pound the garlic with a few pinches salt in a mortar until smooth. Combine the yogurt, cucumbers, garlic, and herbs, then season with a little pepper and the vinegar. Taste for salt, drizzle the oil over the top, and serve.

In-a-Pinch Cucumber Salad

2 cucumbers or 1 long hothouse
    cucumber

Salt and freshly milled white pepper

2 to 3 teaspoons extra virgin olive oil

Champagne vinegar or fresh lemon juice

1 teaspoon fresh dill or several pinches
    dried dill, finely chopped watercress,
    or chopped parsley

NOTHING could be simpler to prepare than these cucumbers. Although summer's cucumbers are far better than winter's waxed ones, I often turn to this dish for a quick raw salad when winter greens are scarce.

SERVES 4

Unless you're using the hothouse variety, peel the cucumbers. Cut them in half lengthwise, scoop out the seeds, leaving a nicely shaped shell with smooth sides, and thinly slice. Toss the cucumbers with a few pinches salt, pepper to taste, and enough oil to coat lightly. Add a few drops vinegar and the herb of your choice.

FENNEL SALADS

Tender fennel bulbs make a sweet spring or fall salad, but the secret to success is to slice the fennel paper-thin on a box grater, benriner, or mandoline. First trim off the stalks and run a vegetable peeler over the outer leaves. Halve the bulb lengthwise; if the core looks tender, and it should for small bulbs, leave it in. Slice the halves crosswise.

Garnishes for fennel salad can include thin croutons spread with olive paste, thin shavings of Parmigiano-Reggiano, pecans or walnuts, or frisée, watercress, or arugula leaves. Serve fennel salads as a first course or include them on a composed salad plate.

Fennel with Oil and Lemon Trim the fennel, then slice paper-thin. Toss with a few pinches salt, then with extra virgin olive oil or white truffle oil to coat lightly. Squeeze a little lemon juice over the top, toss, and taste. Season with white pepper and serve garnished with finely chopped fennel greens.

Fennel with Tarragon Vinaigrette

2 small fennel bulbs, 3 to 4 ounces each

1 tablespoon crème fraîche

2 tablespoons extra virgin olive oil

2 to 3 teaspoons fresh lemon juice

1½ teaspoons minced lemon zest

2 teaspoons chopped tarragon or fennel
    greens

1 tablespoon finely chopped parsley

Salt and freshly milled pepper

2 cups watercress, frisée, or mixed small
    salad greens

SERVES 4

Trim the fennel bulbs, then slice paper-thin. Whisk the crème fraîche, oil, and 2 teaspoons lemon juice together; add the lemon zest, herbs, and salt and pepper to taste. Toss with the fennel. Taste and add more lemon juice if needed. Serve mounded on a plate, over or surrounded by the greens.

Fennel, Pear, and Endive Salad Plan to serve this lovely salad for fall or winter shortly after you make it, otherwise the pears and endive will brown. Slice 1 plump Belgian endive diagonally into narrow strips. Toss it and 6 walnuts, broken into small pieces, with the fennel. Halve and core 2 ripe but firm pears, such as Bartlett or Comice, then slice lengthwise. Toss quickly with the fennel, dress as described, and arrange the salad on plates.

Leeks in Mustard Vinaigrette

ONE of my favorite first courses to eat and to serve, this is inspired by my friend cookbook author Ann Clark. Serve them as Ann does—warm, in a soup plate, with country bread to mop up the juices. Leftovers can be sliced and mounded on bread or croutons for a pass-around appetizer.

SERVES 4 TO 6

6 to 8 leeks, including an inch of the pale greens
Aromatics: 1 bay leaf, 5 parsley branches, 4 thyme sprigs

1 large carrot, thinly sliced
1 celery rib, thinly sliced
Mustard Vinaigrette, page 186

Halve the leeks lengthwise to 1 inch above the root end. Soak them in a large bowl of water for 15 minutes, then rinse gently under running water. Put them, in a single layer, in a large skillet with the aromatics, vegetables, and water to cover. Simmer until they're tender when pierced with a knife, 20 to 25 minutes, depending on their size. Gently transfer the leeks to a platter or individual plates with some of the broth, spoon the vinaigrette generously over the top, and serve with fresh bread. Be sure to use the remaining broth for soup stock or risotto.

Grilled Mushroom Salad with Watercress

THIS impressive little salad is good for the fall and winter months. Here the mushrooms are broiled or grilled, but you also could sear them in a skillet.

SERVES 2 TO 4

1 large shallot, finely diced
Salt and freshly milled pepper
1 tablespoon aged red wine vinegar
2 large portobello mushrooms, stems removed
Olive oil for the mushrooms

3 tablespoons walnut or extra virgin olive oil
1 bunch watercress, large stems discarded, washed and dried
3 tablespoons walnuts, roasted and chopped

Put the shallot in a bowl with ¼ teaspoon salt and the vinegar and set aside. Meanwhile, brush the mushroom caps with olive oil and season with salt and pepper. Grill or broil for about 4 minutes on each side, then cut into wide strips. Whisk the walnut oil into the vinegar mixture and season with pepper. Toss the mushrooms with 1 tablespoon of the dressing and use the rest to dress the watercress and walnuts. Divide the greens among salad plates and arrange the mushrooms loosely among them.

Roasted Pepper Salads

Sweet roasted peppers have many uses in the summer kitchen, one of which is their transformation into small, colorful salads. Like many of the little vegetable salads in this chapter, they also serve well as appetizers, toppings for crostini and crackers, or elements on a composed salad plate. Some things that go well with roasted peppers are capers and olives, basil and marjoram, fine extra virgin olive oil, balsamic vinegar, lemon juice, and cheeses, like Fontina, goat cheese, and feta. Saffron, cumin, chiles, fennel, and preserved lemon match the sweetness and smokiness of grilled peppers. Roasted peppers keep for a week or so in the refrigerator, so these salads can be put together at a moment's notice if the peppers are at hand. (To roast, peel, and seed peppers, see page 403.)

Grilled Peppers with Saffron Vinaigrette Grill and peel a selection of different-colored bell peppers, allowing ¹/₂ pepper per person. Be sure to reserve any juices that collect in the bowl while they're steaming. Slice the peppers into halves or quarters, scrape out the seeds, and layer the peppers on a platter. Make Saffron Vinaigrette with Basil, page 188, adding any reserved pepper juices. Toss the peppers with vinaigrette to moisten and serve garnished with sprigs of basil and Niçoise olives.

Roasted Peppers with Preserved Lemon and Cumin Preserved Lemons, page 82, add a whole new dimension to peppers. For 4 roasted red or green bell peppers, use ¹/₂ preserved lemon. Cut away and discard the inside of the lemon and dice the skin into small pieces. Peel the peppers, then cut them into strips or squares. Toss the peppers with the lemon, ¹/₂ teaspoon toasted ground cumin, 1 to 2 tablespoons extra virgin olive oil, and some chopped parsley. Arrange on a platter and garnish with oil-cured black olives and glossy sprigs of flat-leaf parsley.

Grilled Pepper Salad with Fontina Slice grilled and peeled yellow, red, and orange bell peppers into quarters. Put them in a bowl and toss with a few tablespoons extra virgin olive oil and balsamic vinegar to taste. Arrange overlapping layers of peppers on a platter with thin strips of Fontina, at room temperature, placed between them. Garnish with finely chopped parsley.

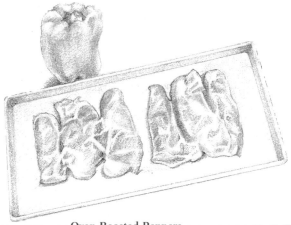

Oven Roasted Peppers

Salad Potatoes

For salads, use boiling potatoes or waxy yellow-fleshed potatoes, such as fingerlings. Once cooked, both can be sliced without crumbling apart.

To cook the potatoes, first scrub them well, then put them in a pot with salted cold water to cover. Bring to a boil. Lower the heat and simmer until they're tender when pierced with a knife. When cool enough to handle fairly easily, rub off the skins; doing this under a trickle—not a gush—of cold water makes them easier to handle. Slice the potatoes about $1/3$ inch thick, then dress them. Potato salads usually are eaten at room temperature or even cold, but the flavors are sensational when they're warm.

Picnic Potato Salad with Marjoram and Pickled Onions

A STRAIGHTFORWARD potato salad that's just the kind to take on a picnic. By the time the potatoes are cooked, the onions will have turned bright pink and mellowed.

SERVES 10 TO 12

1 large dark red onion, finely diced

$1/2$ cup apple cider vinegar

Salt and freshly milled pepper

$1/2$ cup olive oil

3 pounds boiling or waxy potatoes

2 tablespoons Dijon mustard

3 large garlic cloves, pounded or put through a press

3 tablespoons capers, rinsed

1 bell pepper, any color, finely diced

4 celery ribs or 1 fennel bulb, finely diced

3 tablespoons chopped marjoram

1 tablespoon chopped thyme or lemon thyme

Put the diced onion in a strainer. Bring a kettle of water to a boil and pour it slowly over the onion. Shake the onion dry and put it in a large salad bowl. Add the vinegar, 1 teaspoon salt, several grinds of pepper, the oil and set aside.

Cook the potatoes, then peel and slice them. While still warm, add them to the onion along with the mustard, garlic, and capers. Toss gently with a soft rubber spatula. Add the bell pepper, celery, and herbs and toss once more. Taste for salt and grind in plenty of pepper.

Potato Salad with Green Beans and Hard-Cooked Eggs Boil 8 ounces green beans in salted water until tender; drain, rinse under cold water, and pat dry. Toss the beans with a little olive oil. Arrange the potato salad in a wide, shallow Spanish casserole or gratin dish and scatter the beans on top. Garnish with 3 or 4 hard-cooked eggs cut into quarters or halves. Tip the dish to get a little dressing and spoon it over the yolks so they don't dry out. Cover with chopped tarragon or basil and their blossoms if available. Toss just before serving, or carefully lift out so that each portion has a judicious amount of potatoes, beans, and eggs.

Warm Potato Salad with Garlic Mayonnaise

2 pounds boiling or waxy potatoes
½ cup Garlic Mayonnaise, page 59

1 cup chopped parsley

GREEN beans are also delicious prepared this way—and the two can be done together.

SERVES 6

Boil, peel, and slice the potatoes. While still warm, toss them with the mayonnaise and the parsley. Serve right away.

Peruvian Potatoes with Peanut Sauce and Garnishes

2 pounds Peruvian blue or Yellow Finn potatoes
2 ears corn, cut into 2-inch segments
Pickled Onions, page 78
3 hard-cooked eggs, quartered
Kalamata or Alfonso olives
3 handfuls spicy greens, such as red mustard or arugula

Peanut Sauce
¼ cup roasted peanut oil
1 cup skinned Spanish peanuts
1 small onion, chopped
1 garlic clove, coarsely chopped
2 jalapeño chiles, halved and seeded, or ground red chile to taste
¾ cup crumbled ricotta salata
1 cup milk
½ teaspoon turmeric
Salt

KATHI Long, a Santa Fe chef whose husband is Peruvian, showed me this exceptionally pretty potato salad from his native country.

SERVES 6

Boil the potatoes, then peel and slice into thick rounds. Boil the corn briefly in unsalted water and drain. To make the sauce, heat half the oil in a small skillet and fry the peanuts over medium heat, stirring frequently, until browned, 3 to 4 minutes. Put them in a blender and return the pan to the heat with the remaining oil. Add the onion and garlic and cook until soft and translucent, about 5 minutes. Add them to the blender with the rest of the ingredients and puree until smooth. Season with salt to taste. Arrange the potatoes and corn on individual plates or a large platter with the onions, eggs, olives, and greens. Spoon the peanut sauce over the potatoes and serve with extra sauce on the side.

Tomato Salads

Ripe summer tomatoes make some of the best—and easiest—summer salads. They needn't be dressed, although tomatoes that are low in acid benefit from a squeeze of fresh lemon juice or a splash of balsamic vinegar, while more acidic tomatoes are enhanced with a thread of fruity extra virgin olive oil. Spicy Indian mustard oil is also interesting. Tomatoes needn't be peeled unless their skins are tough and leathery or you want the refinement of smooth, slippery, fruitlike flesh.

Remember, tomatoes are best warm from the sun or at least at room temperature. Refrigeration deadens them, so keep them on a counter until you're ready to use them. However, some salads are refrigerated an hour or so before serving, partly for the benefit of the accompanying ingredients.

When it comes to seasonings, many herbs and their perfumed blossoms form a natural alliance with tomatoes: dill and its yellow flowers, marjoram, chives and their purple blossoms, the various thymes, the blue star-shaped borage flowers; violet rosemary blossoms, purple sage, tarragon, and so forth. All would be excellent on this salad.

Tomato Salad of Many Colors Today an exotic variety of tomatoes is being grown—bright green striped Zebras, tiny currant-sized ones, bright yellow, matte gold, and orange as well as red. A mélange of tomatoes with basil, the classic tomato herb—or one of the other herbs just listed—is truly spectacular fare. Slice a colorful array and lay them on a platter. Add torn or thinly sliced basil leaves, using the classic Italian basil or opal basil. Drizzle with a thread of extra virgin olive oil and add a few drops of balsamic vinegar, a pinch of salt, and freshly milled pepper.

Tomato and Avocado Salad Cut 2 large tomatoes around the equator, remove the seeds, and dice them into large pieces. Toss with 1 avocado, cut in good-sized chunks, and a few chopped scallions, parsley or cilantro, a pinch of salt, and freshly cracked pepper to taste. Squeeze a little lime or lemon juice over all and serve with warm tortillas and queso fresco or feta.

Tomato and Sweet Onion Salad When you can get genuine sweet Vidalia, Walla Walla, or Maui onions as well as ripe, luscious tomatoes, this is the salad to make. Peel whole onions, then slice them into thin rounds. Slice the tomatoes into rounds as well. On a platter, overlap layers of onions and tomatoes so that both can easily be picked up at once. Serve right away or chill before serving.

Tomato and Mozzarella Salad The simplicity and clarity of the components are what make *insalata caprese* a classic that never grows tiresome, but its success depends on top-quality ingredients. The tomatoes should have a slightly tart edge to contrast with the mildness of the cheese. Slice fresh mozzarella and ripe but firm tomatoes into rounds and overlap them on a plate. Drizzle extra virgin olive oil over the top and season with salt and freshly milled pepper. Tear basil leaves over the top or tuck them in between the tomatoes and cheese.

Tomato Salad on Grilled Eggplant Rounds

2 eggplants, 8 to 12 ounces each

Olive oil

Salt and freshly milled pepper

3 ripe tomatoes or 1½ cups cherry tomatoes

1 shallot, finely diced

3 tablespoons finely sliced green or opal basil leaves

1 tablespoon capers, rinsed

1 tablespoon extra virgin olive oil

Aged red wine vinegar

THIS makes a stunning little salad that's fast and easy to make. For an especially handsome effect, use yellow or mixed-colored tomatoes and purple basil. Look for small Italian eggplants.

SERVES 4

Slice the eggplants into rounds about ⅓-inch thick. Brush both sides with olive oil and grill or broil until browned and tender, 5 to 6 minutes on each side. Divide them among four plates and season with salt and pepper. While the eggplant is cooking, dice the tomatoes into nice-looking pieces or halve the cherry tomatoes and toss them with the shallot, basil, capers, a pinch of salt, and the extra virgin oil. Add pepper and a little vinegar to taste. Spoon the tomatoes over the eggplant and serve.

Chopped Salad with Feta Dressing

2 scallions, including some of the greens

1 red bell pepper

1 cucumber, peeled if waxed, halved, and seeded

1 celery rib

12 cherry tomatoes, halved

¼ cup chopped parsley

10 Kalamata olives, pitted and chopped

Feta Dressing with Marjoram and Mint, page 190

1 avocado, diced

Salt and freshly milled pepper

SIMILAR in ingredients to a Greek salad, but with an entirely different feel. For a nondairy version, use the Olive Oil Vinaigrette. This salad makes a great filling for a pita sandwich, or serve with Lentils and Rice with Fried Onions.

MAKES ABOUT 2 CUPS

Finely or coarsely chop the vegetables as you like, then toss them with the tomatoes, parsley, olives, and dressing. Add the avocado last so that it doesn't end up mushy. Taste and add salt if needed (both the feta and the olives are salty) and pepper.

Farmers' Market Salad

1 carrot, scrubbed and finely diced

1 cucumber, peeled if waxed, seeded, and diced

2 tomatoes, chopped

1 celery rib, finely diced

4 large green olives, pitted

Small cubes of cheese, such as a goat Cheddar or ricotta salata

1 tablespoon toasted sunflower seeds or pine nuts

Torn leaves of basil, marjoram, lovage, or whatever herb is available

1 teaspoon olive oil or sunflower seed oil or to taste

Salt and freshly milled pepper

Fresh lemon juice or red wine vinegar to taste

THIS is a dish I look forward to eating day after day throughout the summer when vegetables are at their peak. I use whatever the farmers' market is offering. Here's an example.

SERVES 1

Gently toss everything with the oil. Season with salt and pepper and add a little lemon juice to taste.

Greek Salad

MANY greens are far more interesting—and traditional—than the mounds of iceberg lettuce that seem to be a part of every American Greek salad. Do give them a try.

SERVES 4 TO 6

About 2 cups salad greens—watercress, romaine hearts, oakleaf lettuce, escarole, purslane, and other wild greens—torn into pieces

4 ripe tomatoes, cut into wedges

1 large cucumber, halved, seeded, and thinly sliced

1 green bell pepper, thinly sliced into rings

1 small mild onion, thinly sliced

8 peperoncini

2 tablespoons capers, rinsed

12 Kalamata olives

4 ounces feta cheese, cubed or crumbled

1 teaspoon dried oregano, preferably Greek

1/3 cup coarsely chopped parsley

Salt and freshly milled pepper

1/4 cup extra virgin olive oil

1 lemon, cut into wedges

Line a platter with the greens. Arrange the tomatoes, cucumber, and green pepper on the platter. Scatter the onion rings over them and intersperse the peperoncini, capers, and olives with the cheese. Sprinkle the oregano and parsley over the salad, then season with salt and pepper. Drizzle the oil over all and garnish with the lemon wedges.

Toasted Pita Bread with Vegetables and Herbs (*Fattoush*)

THOUGH this salad is always delicious made with these common vegetables, consider adding the seeds of a small pomegranate, a handful of purslane sprigs or watercress, or some freshly shelled peas.

SERVES 3 TO 4

1 small cucumber, peeled, seeded, and diced

Salt

2 7-inch pita breads

3 ripe tomatoes, chopped

1 small green pepper, diced

6 scallions, including some of the greens, finely chopped

1/3 cup chopped parsley

2 tablespoons chopped cilantro

1 tablespoon finely chopped mint

1/4 cup extra virgin olive oil

Juice of 1 large lemon

1 garlic clove, finely chopped

1 1/2 teaspoons ground sumac, if available

Put the cucumber in a colander, toss with 1 teaspoon salt, and set aside to drain. Preheat the oven to 350°F. Open the breads and bake them on a sheet pan until crisp and light brown, about 10 minutes. Break them into bite-sized pieces and set aside. Press the excess water out of the cucumbers, then rinse quickly and blot dry. Put them in a bowl with the rest of the vegetables and the herbs.

In a screw-top jar, shake together the oil, lemon juice, garlic, sumac, and 1/4 teaspoon salt. Pour it over the salad, then toss well. Add the bread, toss again, and serve.

Composed Salad of Winter Vegetables with Romesco Sauce

Romesco Sauce, page 70

1 small cauliflower, broken into florets and steamed

2 carrots, attractively cut, then steamed

3 red potatoes, boiled and sliced

4 small red or golden beets, roasted, peeled, and quartered

3 hard-cooked eggs, quartered

12 Sicilian green olives

Chopped parsley

ROMESCO sauce is as good with winter vegetables as garlic mayonnaise is with summer ones. Both the sauce and the vegetables can be prepared ahead of time.

SERVES 4 TO 6

Thin the sauce with enough water to give it the texture of thick cream. Arrange the cooked vegetables attractively with the eggs and olives, then spoon the sauce over or around them and garnish with the parsley.

Summer Vegetables with Garlic Mayonnaise

Garlic Mayonnaise, page 59

Small new potatoes, steamed or roasted

Tender green or Romano beans, blanched

Carrots, steamed until tender, left whole if small or sliced if not

Cauliflower florets, blanched or steamed until tender

Bell peppers of different colors, cut into strips

Tomatoes, sliced or cut into wedges

Cooked chickpeas or large white beans

Hard-cooked eggs, halved or quartered

Niçoise olives

A PLATTER of summer vegetables with garlic mayonnaise can be an appetizer or an entire meal. Other vegetables that you can use here with great success are radishes, tender salad turnips, and artichoke hearts. For a main course, allow 8 to 12 ounces vegetables and 2 to 4 tablespoons mayonnaise per person.

Make the garlic mayonnaise and set it aside to mellow. Lightly cook the vegetables as suggested. For a first course, cut them rather fine; for a main-course salad, larger pieces are better. Arrange the vegetables on a platter or individual plates, then add the chickpeas, eggs, and olives. Heap the mayonnaise in a mound on the plate and serve.

Salads Featuring Fruits

Fruits as well as vegetables marry well with the savory, pungent flavors found in foods such as salty or buttery cheeses, the bitter chicories, roasted nuts, sharp vinegars, and so on—elements that make fruit into salads as opposed to desserts or compotes. They can open or close a meal or in sufficient quantity can be the center of the meal. As with vegetables, ripe, full-flavored fruits are most fundamental to the success of these salads.

Apple and Celery Salad with Gruyère

SERVES 4 TO 6

3 ounces Gruyère

Salt and freshly milled pepper

1 tablespoon tarragon vinegar

1 small shallot, finely diced

1 tablespoon walnut oil

1 tablespoon sour cream or mayonnaise

1 cup finely diced celery heart

2 crisp apples, unpeeled, finely diced

1/3 cup chopped walnuts or hazelnuts, roasted

2 tablespoons chopped parsley, celery leaves, or a mixture

Dice the cheese into small cubes and put them in a large bowl. Season with a little salt and plenty of pepper. Cover and let stand at room temperature for 1 hour.

Meanwhile, combine the vinegar, shallot, 1/8 teaspoon salt, and pepper to taste in another bowl and let stand for 15 minutes. Whisk in the oil and sour cream, then taste for salt. Add the celery, apples, and nuts to the cheese, pour on the dressing, add the parsley, and toss well.

Persimmon and Hazelnut Salad with Hazelnut Vinaigrette

UNLIKE the acorn-shaped Hachiyas, short, squat Fuyus can be eaten crisp or soft. They're a luscious foil for peppery watercress and striking with red lettuces and radicchio. This is an exuberant first-course salad for a holiday dinner or any festive occasion.

SERVES 4

1/4 cup hazelnuts, roasted

3 Fuyu persimmons, thinly sliced crosswise

3 handfuls mixed lettuces or trimmed watercress

Salt

3 to 4 tablespoons Hazelnut Oil Vinaigrette, page 185

Coarsely chop the hazelnuts. Put the persimmons in a bowl with the hazelnuts and the greens, sprinkle with a few pinches salt, and toss with enough dressing to coat lightly. Divide among salad plates, distributing the nuts and persimmons evenly among the greens.

Variation with Pears: Make the salad using ripe, buttery Comice or Bartlett pears and either the hazelnut dressing or Walnut Oil Vinaigrette, page 185.

Persian Melons with Yogurt and Coriander Dressing

1 cup yogurt

2 pounds ripe Persian, honeydew, or Israeli melon, chilled

3 scallions, thinly sliced

1/2 jalapeño chile, finely diced

Grated zest and juice of 1 lime

2 tablespoons finely chopped mint

1 tablespoon finely chopped basil

1 teaspoon minced ginger or 1/2 teaspoon dried

1/2 teaspoon ground cumin

1/2 teaspoon ground coriander

Salt and freshly milled white pepper

2 handfuls lettuce or mixed greens

SERVE this salad very cold. Bronze-leafed lettuces, like red oakleaf, set it off handsomely. Purslane sprigs and lemon verbena make interesting contributions, too.

SERVES 4 TO 6

Set the yogurt to drain, page 47. Halve the melons, scoop out the seeds, and slice into wedges. Slip a knife under the skin to release the fruit, then cut it into bite-sized pieces.

Mix the yogurt with the rest of the ingredients except the melon and greens. Season with salt and pepper. Adjust the seasonings if needed—they should be on the strong side, the herbs and spices bright and clear. Pour the dressing over the melon and toss. Serve garnished with the greens.

Melon and Cucumbers with Pepper and Lime

1/2 honeydew, cantaloupe, or other melon, chilled

3 cucumbers

2 cups watercress or arugula leaves

Lime and Fresh Mint Vinaigrette, page 187, or juice of 2 limes

Salt and freshly milled pepper

CUCUMBERS and melons are closely related not only botanically but also in texture and sometimes flavor, depending on the variety. Freshly milled pepper is good with both.

SERVES 4

Scoop out the seeds, then slice the melon into narrow wedges and remove the skin. Scrub the cucumbers or peel if the skin is thick; cut into sixths. Make a bed of greens on four plates and arrange the melon and cucumbers on top. Spoon the dressing over the top and season with a little salt and pepper.

Watermelon with Mint, Lime, and Feta

1 pound watermelon

1 tablespoon chopped mint leaves, plus whole sprigs for garnish

1/4 cup diced mild feta or string cheese

Juice of 1 lime

Salt and freshly milled pepper

A sweet-salty-tart fruit salad that's enormously refreshing—and quite surprising. Feta is quite often salty, but the Israeli cow's milk feta is very mild.

SERVES 2

Seed the melon and cut into bite sized pieces. Arrange them on plates and sprinkle with the chopped mint and feta. Season with the lime juice, a pinch of salt, and freshly milled pepper. Serve garnished with sprigs of bright green mint leaves.

Orange, Fennel, and Butter Lettuce Salad

SERVE *this little com-posed salad to conclude a large or spicy meal. Celery can easily step in if fennel is not available.*

SERVES 4

3 navel or blood oranges

Orange Vinaigrette, page 185

1 head butter or Boston lettuce

2 tablespoons chopped fennel greens

10 small mint leaves, thinly sliced

1 small fennel bulb, quartered and thinly sliced

Freshly milled pepper

12 oil-cured black olives

Peel and section the oranges and use the juice in the vinaigrette. Discard the outer leaves of the lettuce. Separate the remaining leaves and keep them whole or tear them into large pieces. Toss the lettuce with 2 or 3 tablespoons of the dressing and half the fennel greens and mint. Then arrange the greens on plates. Toss the oranges, sliced fennel, and remaining herbs with enough dressing to coat lightly, add a little pepper, then tuck them among the lettuce and garnish with the olives.

Mixed Citrus Salad with Avocado

AVOCADOS and citrus fruits grow near each other, their seasons overlap, and their textures and tastes are comple-mentary, so it's hardly surprising that they show up together in salads.

SERVES 4

1 lime

2 tangerines

2 navel or blood oranges

2 ruby grapefruit

2 ripe but firm avocados, preferably Hass

1 shallot, finely diced, or 2 scallions, including an inch of the greens, thinly sliced

1 tablespoon fresh lemon juice

Salt and freshly milled white pepper

1 tablespoon avocado or olive oil

1 tablespoon chopped mint

1 bunch watercress, large stems removed, or the inner leaves of 1 head Boston lettuce

Grate the zest of the lime and one of the tangerines. Peel and section the fruit letting the pieces fall into a bowl. Reserve 1 tablespoon of the juice and drink the rest.

Slice the avocados into the citrus. Combine the shallot with the citrus zest, reserved juice, lemon juice, and $1/8$ teaspoon salt; whisk in the oil. Pour the dressing over the fruit, add the mint and a little pepper, and toss gently. Garnish with the watercress or tuck it among the lettuce leaves.

Mission Figs with Walnuts and Manchego Cheese

1 shallot, finely diced

2 teaspoons balsamic vinegar

1 teaspoon red wine vinegar

Salt and freshly milled pepper

2 handfuls red lettuce, trimmed and torn into pieces, small leaves left whole

1 handful arugula, stems removed

3 tablespoons extra virgin olive or walnut oil

12 ripe figs

8 walnuts in large pieces

Thin shavings of Manchego or dry Jack

ANY variety of fig is fine as long as it's ripe and sweet, but the dense flavor of black Missions is just right with the vinegar and the slightly salty cheese.

SERVES 4

Combine the shallot, vinegars, and ⅛ teaspoon salt in a bowl. Let stand while you prepare the greens, then whisk in the oil. Peel the figs only if the skins are very thick; otherwise, just wipe them with a damp cloth to remove any dust.

Slice the figs into rounds. Toss the lettuce and arugula with half the dressing and arrange on four salad plates. Add the figs and walnuts and season with pepper. Add a few thin shavings of cheese to each salad and serve.

Hearty Salads Based on Pasta, Grains, and Beans

These salads are hearty and filling enough to be served as main dishes, or they can be offered as appetizers as long as the portion sizes are on the small side so that people don't fill up right away. Whether large or small, I find that a healthy garnish of salad greens helps keep them balanced and light.

Regardless of how you serve these salads, take advantage of the fact that most of them can be made well in advance and that they keep and travel well, which makes them good choices for picnics, bag lunches, and buffets. Still, they are usually best when served as soon as they're made and dressed while warm so that the flavors of the vinaigrette are brought strongly to the fore. Any grain, bean, or pasta that holds its shape when thoroughly cooked can be turned into a salad by adding a vinaigrette, and cold leftovers can be steamed back to warmth before dressing. Because these foods are starchy and naturally bland, good strong dressings filled with herbs, mustards, and sharp vinegars are the ones to use.

COOKING GRAINS: To ensure that grains intended for salads come out separate, boil them in a generous amount of salted water until they're done, then drain. Undercook them just a bit so that they finish cooking in their own heat while absorbing the flavors of the dressing. For rice, long-grain varieties are less sticky than short-grain.

BAKING SALAD BEANS: For beans that are tender but will stay intact when tossed, soak them first, then drain and transfer to a shallow baking dish with aromatics, a teaspoon of olive oil, and boiling water to cover by an inch. Cover and bake at 325°F until tender, salting once they've begun to soften, after an hour. A slow cooker is another option. Save the remaining broth for soup.

ALTERNATIVES TO HOME-COOKED BEANS: Although certainly convenient, canned beans tend to be mushy and salty. Some brands are better than others; the organic brands seem to have the best texture, especially the chickpeas, kidney beans, and black beans. If you do use canned beans, give them a rinse first. Frozen baby limas and black-eyed peas strike a happy medium between canned and cooked from scratch—they taste better than the former and don't take as long as the latter.

MIXING GRAINS AND BEANS: Mixing different grains or grains with legumes makes salads with interesting colors and textures. Cook each ingredient separately unless they all cook in the same amount of time, such as brown, wehani, and wild rice. This is where quick-looking legumes, like lentils, the occasional canned bean, or leftovers also can be put to good use.

USING LEFTOVERS: Leftover grains can make good material for salads, but they need to be moistened. Put them in a colander and pour a few cups of boiling water over them or steam them for 5 to 10 minutes.

USING PASTA: Dried pasta is sturdier than fresh, and its ingenious shapes can hold a flavorful dressing or the occasional pea. Salads made with Italian-style pasta taste best warm or at room temperature rather than chilled. Asian noodles, such as soba or cellophane noodles, make excellent cold salads.

FOLDING AND STIRRING: To bring all the elements together without breaking tender grains, beans, or noodles, use a wide, soft rubber spatula to gently fold all the ingredients into each other.

Cool Rice and Cucumber Salad

A SALAD for the dog days of summer. Use white rice for its cool look and mild taste.

SERVES 4 TO 6

1 ½ cups long-grain white rice
Salt
2 to 3 cucumbers, peeled, seeded, and finely chopped
½ cup finely chopped parsley
3 tablespoons chopped dill
2 tablespoons chopped mint

¼ cup finely sliced scallions, including some of the greens
¼ cup champagne vinegar or white wine vinegar
3 tablespoons extra virgin olive oil
½ cup yogurt
Green oakleaf, Boston, or butter lettuce leaves

Bring 2 quarts water to a boil in a medium pan. Add the rice and 2 teaspoons salt and boil until tender, 12 to 15 minutes. Meanwhile, put the cucumbers in a large bowl with the herbs. In a small bowl, combine the scallions, vinegar, oil, and ¼ teaspoon salt.

When the rice is done, pour it into a colander, rinse briefly, then shake off as much water as possible. Put the warm rice into the bowl with the cucumbers, add the dressing and yogurt, and toss gently with a wide rubber spatula. Taste for salt and tartness. Certain types of rice will absorb more vinegar and salt than others. Serve tepid or chilled, mounded on plates and garnished with light green lettuce leaves.

Macadamia Nut and Mixed Rice Salad

½ to 1 cup unsalted or salted macadamia nuts

1 cup wehani rice

½ cup wild rice

½ cup long-grain white rice

½ cup brown basmati rice

2 green bell peppers, finely diced

The Vinaigrette

1 bunch scallions, including some of the greens, thinly sliced

1 garlic clove, minced

1 heaping tablespoon minced ginger

1 jalapeño chile, seeded and finely chopped

Grated zest and juice of 1 orange

2 tablespoons rice wine vinegar

2 tablespoons rice wine (mirin)

1 teaspoon garam masala

2 drops orange oil or 2 teaspoons orange flower water

Salt and freshly milled pepper

½ finely chopped parsley

THE perfume of orange, either from the orange oil (you can find it in specialty stores) or the more floral orange flower water, along with the ginger and the warm spices in garam masala bring the unique flavor of macadamia nuts forward.

SERVES 10

Preheat the oven to 350°F. Roast the nuts on a sheet pan until golden, about 10 minutes. Keep an eye on them; they can brown suddenly. Finely chop half of the nuts and keep the rest in large pieces.

Cook each type of rice separately in salted water, then drain. Combine the ingredients to make the vinaigrette. You may need to fiddle with the seasonings, adding more of this or that to get the balance just right. It should be full of flavor but soft and balanced, not sharp. Combine the cooked rices in a large bowl with the diced peppers. Pour the vinaigrette over the rice and toss with the finely chopped nuts. Just before serving, toss again with the remaining nuts so that they'll be nice and crisp.

Couscous or Quinoa with Pine Nuts and Dried Fruits

1⅓ cups raw couscous or quinoa or 3 cups cooked

Lime-Cumin Vinaigrette, page 187

1 yellow bell pepper, very finely diced

6 dried apricots, finely chopped

3 tablespoons golden raisins

2 tablespoons currants

¼ cup pine nuts, toasted in a small skillet

2 tablespoons chopped cilantro or chives

Salt

Perfect whole lettuce or radicchio leaves

THIS sweet and tangy salad punctuated with succulent bits of pepper and dried fruits is wonderful made with steamed couscous and also fine made with leftovers.

SERVES 4

Cook the couscous or quinoa as described on page 562 or 532. Toss the cooked grain with ¼ cup of the dressing or more to taste, add the remaining ingredients except salt and lettuce, and toss again. Taste and season with salt. Serve it cradled in nicely formed lettuce leaves.

Quinoa Salad with Mangoes and Curry Dressing

SERVES 4

Salt

1⅓ cups quinoa, rinsed thoroughly

2 large mangoes

1 jalapeño chile, seeded and diced

3 scallions, including an inch of the greens, thinly sliced

Curry Vinaigrette, page 187

⅓ cup almonds, roasted

Bring 3 cups water to a boil in a saucepan, then add ½ teaspoon salt and the quinoa. Lower the heat, cover, and simmer until the quinoa is tender, 12 to 15 minutes. Drain.

Cut the mangoes: Stand each one upright and slice down either side of the seed, which you can't see but which runs lengthwise through the center of the fruit. Score the two pieces, then bend the skin. Cut off the squares of mango where they attach to the skin.

Toss the quinoa with the mangoes, chile, scallions, and vinaigrette. Chop the almonds and add them last so that they'll stay crisp.

Bulgur and Green Lentil Salad with Chickpeas

YOU'LL recognize some of the qualities of tabbouleh here, but with the added textures and tastes of lentils and chickpeas. A good winter salad when there's a dearth of good fresh vegetables.

MAKES 5 CUPS

½ cup French green lentils, picked over

1 bay leaf

Salt and freshly milled pepper

¾ cup fine or medium bulgur

5 scallions, including some of the greens, thinly sliced

2 garlic cloves

Grated zest of 2 lemons

6 to 8 tablespoons fresh lemon juice

½ cup extra virgin olive oil

1 teaspoon paprika

1½ cups cooked chickpeas, rinsed if canned

2 cups finely chopped parsley

¼ cup chopped mint or 2 tablespoons dried

COUSCOUS WITH BULGUR

Fine bulgur, like couscous, can also be steamed, which makes it especially light. If you mix bulgur and couscous together, you'll have something interesting—two wheats, similar but different.

Cover the lentils with water in a small saucepan, add the bay leaf and ½ teaspoon salt, and bring to a boil. Lower the heat and simmer until tender but firm, about 25 minutes. Meanwhile, put the bulgur in a bowl, cover with water, and let stand until the liquid is absorbed and the grains are tender, 20 to 30 minutes.

Whisk together the scallions, garlic, lemon zest and juice, oil, paprika, and ½ teaspoon salt in a large bowl. When the lentils are done, drain them and add them to the dressing. Press out any excess water from the bulgur and add it along with the chickpeas, parsley, and mint. Toss gently and thoroughly, then taste for salt and season with pepper. Serve warm or cover and set aside to serve later with a fresh sprinkling of paprika.

> *Variation with Vegetable Garnishes:* In summer, include tomatoes, cucumbers, and peppers, all finely chopped. In winter, toss with a chopped Preserved Lemon, page 82, or rounds of steamed Jerusalem artichoke.

Variation with Purslane: Toss the salad with 1 or 2 handfuls purslane sprigs.

Variation with Walnuts and Tarragon: Replace the mint with 2 tablespoons chopped tarragon. Use half walnut oil in the dressing and add ½ cup chopped roasted walnuts to the salad.

Tabbouleh

1 cup fine or medium bulgur

½ cup fresh lemon juice

1 bunch scallions, including some of the greens, finely sliced

3 or 4 large bunches flat-leaf parsley, finely chopped, about 4 cups

½ cup chopped mint

3 ripe tomatoes, seeded and chopped

6 tablespoons extra virgin olive oil

Salt

Small Bibb or romaine lettuce leaves

TABBOULEH *should be so saturated with parsley that it's moist and intensely green— practically a parsley salad.*

SERVES 4 TO 6

Put the bulgur in a bowl, cover it with water, and let stand until the water is absorbed and the grains are soft, about 30 minutes. Press out any excess liquid, return the bulgur to the bowl, and toss with half of the lemon juice, the scallions, tomatoes, parsley, and mint. Let stand again for 20 to 30 minutes for the grains to soften fully.

Meanwhile, whisk the remaining lemon juice, the oil, and ½ teaspoon salt together. Pour the dressing over the bulgur and toss well. Check the seasoning—it should be lemony and very zesty. Mound the tabbouleh in a shallow serving bowl and surround with the lettuce leaves.

Lentil Salad with Roasted Peppers and Vegetable Garnishes

1 cup French green lentils, picked over

Salt and freshly milled pepper

2 red or yellow bell peppers, roasted, and chopped

Lime-Cumin Vinaigrette, page 187

½ cup chopped parsley

2 tablespoons chopped dill

1 tablespoon chopped mint

2 ripe tomatoes, quartered

½ cup small cubes feta or goat cheese

2 hard-cooked eggs, quartered

12 Kalamata olives

1 cucumber, cut into short spears

WITH *all of its garnishes, this salad can make an entire meal. Try mixing the lentils with 1 cup cooked pasta shells, orzo, or rice—it's not only good but makes legumes more appealing to those not used to eating them.*

SERVES 4 TO 6

Cover the lentils with water in a small saucepan, add ½ teaspoon salt, and bring to a boil. Lower the heat and simmer until tender but still a little firm, 25 to 30 minutes.

Drain the lentils and toss them while warm with the peppers, vinaigrette, parsley, dill, and mint. Taste for salt and season with pepper.

Mound the lentils on a platter and garnish with the tomatoes, cheese, eggs, olives, and cucumber. Serve warm or cold.

Green Lentils with Roasted Beets and Preserved Lemon

THIS salad is inspired by David Tanis, one of my longtime favorite cooks, although he says he doesn't remember it. The concentrated flavors of the beets and lemon make these lentils snap. The salad is good without the preserved lemon too, so don't be deterred if you don't have any.

SERVES 4 TO 6

5 beets, about 1 pound

1 teaspoon olive oil

Salt and freshly milled pepper

1 cup French green lentils

1 carrot, finely diced

1/2 small onion, finely diced

Aromatics: 1 bay leaf, 4 parsley branches, 2 thyme sprigs

1 Preserved Lemon, page 82, or 2 teaspoons lemon zest

Lemon Vinaigrette, page 184

1/3 cup chopped parsley

2 tablespoons chopped mint, plus mint sprigs for garnish

Preheat the oven to 350°F. Peel 4 of the beets and cut them into small cubes. Set the last beet aside for garnish. Toss the cubed beets with the oil, season with salt and pepper, and bake on a sheet pan until tender, about 35 minutes, stirring once or twice. Meanwhile, put the lentils in a pan with water to cover, add the carrot, onion, aromatics, and 1/2 teaspoon salt and bring to a boil. Lower the heat and simmer until tender but still a little firm, about 25 minutes. Drain well.

Cut the preserved lemon into quarters and scrape off the soft pulp. Chop the pulp finely and stir 2 teaspoons into the dressing. Finely chop the remaining skin.

Toss the lentils with the roasted beets and the vinaigrette, the preserved lemon or lemon zest, parsley, and mint. Peel the remaining beet and finely grate it. Put the lentils on a platter and garnish with the grated beet and sprigs of mint.

Black-Eyed Pea and Tomato Salad with Feta

MOSTLY we'll have to use frozen or canned peas, but this is a good salad to make if you've found some fresh black-eyed, purple hull, or crowder peas at a roadside stand. Bean salads often taste most flavorful while warm, but these succulent little beans are good chilled, too.

SERVES 4 TO 6

1 1/2 cups black-eyed peas, fresh, frozen, or canned

2 scallions, including an inch or two of the greens, thinly sliced

1 tomato, seeded and chopped

1 tablespoon chopped parsley

1 tablespoon chopped marjoram or 1 teaspoon dried oregano

Lemon Vinaigrette, page 184

2 to 3 ounces feta cheese, diced or crumbled

Salt and freshly milled pepper

Simmer fresh or frozen peas in salted water to cover in a saucepan until tender; it will take 35 minutes to 1 hour. Give canned peas a rinse and shake off the excess water.

Put the drained cooked peas in a bowl along with the scallions, tomato, parsley, and marjoram. Pour the vinaigrette over the peas and toss gently with a rubber spatula. Add the cheese, some pepper, and toss again. Taste for salt. Serve chilled or at room temperature.

Salad of Black-Eyed Peas, Kidney Beans, Barley, and Corn

1 1/2 cups corn kernels, from 2 large ears

1 cup frozen black-eyed peas

1/2 cup pearl barley

Salt

1 1/2 cups cooked red kidney beans, rinsed if canned

1 green bell pepper, finely diced

1/4 teaspoon red pepper flakes

1/3 cup chopped parsley

2 tablespoons finely diced red onion

3 tablespoons sunflower seed or olive oil

Grated zest and juice of 2 large limes

1/2 teaspoon ground cumin

A CHEERFUL-LOOKING salad that's filled with a variety of textures. Peeled wheat berries would be a delicious substitute for the barley.

SERVES 4 TO 6

Bring a pot of water to a boil. Cook the corn for 1 minute, then scoop it out and set it aside. Add the black-eyed peas, lower the heat, and simmer until tender, about 35 to 40 minutes, then drain. Meanwhile, in a second pot, cook the barley in water to cover with 1/2 teaspoon salt until tender but chewy, about 40 minutes; drain.

Layer the corn, peas, barley, and beans in a shallow glass bowl with the pepper, pepper flakes, parsley, and onion sprinkled in between layers. In a small bowl, whisk together the oil, lime zest and juice, cumin, and 1/4 teaspoon salt; pour it over the salad. When it's time to serve, gently toss the salad with a large rubber spatula.

Red Beans with Walnut Sauce

1/2 cup walnut pieces

1 garlic clove

4 teaspoons red or white wine vinegar

1 tablespoon walnut oil

Salt and freshly milled pepper

Several pinches cayenne

3 scallions, including a few inches of the greens, chopped

3 tablespoons finely chopped cilantro

3 tablespoons finely chopped parsley

2 tablespoons finely chopped basil

1 1/2 cups cooked red kidney beans

ALTHOUGH the flavors in this salad merge better when mixed ahead of time, the presentation is more stunning when the ivory sauce and green herb garnish are added at the last minute. If canned beans are used, rinse them and use water in place of the cooking liquid.

SERVES 4 TO 6

Pulverize the walnuts and garlic in a food processor or with a mortar and pestle, then add the vinegar, oil, and 3 to 4 tablespoons water from the beans, enough to make a smooth dressing. Season to taste with salt, pepper, and cayenne, then stir in half the scallions and half the herbs. Pour the sauce over the beans and garnish with the remaining scallions and herbs. Serve at once or toss and chill until ready to serve. Let come at least partially to room temperature before serving.

White Bean Salad with Tomato Vinaigrette and Olive Croutons

IF possible, use marrow beans, cannellini, or other large white beans for their appealing plumpness.

SERVES 4 TO 6

3 cups cooked white beans, rinsed if canned

Tomato Vinaigrette, page 188

4 scallions, including some of the greens, thinly sliced

¼ cup small basil leaves, thinly sliced

Salt and freshly milled pepper

Olive Paste, page 87

2 small croutons per serving

Frisée, escarole, or butter lettuce leaves

2 hard-cooked eggs, quartered

Basil flowers if available

Put the beans in a spacious bowl or flat dish and pour on the vinaigrette. Add the scallions and basil leaves and mix gently with a rubber spatula. Season with salt and pepper.

Spread the olive paste on the croutons. Place a few salad leaves on individual plates and add the beans. Garnish with the croutons, eggs, and basil flowers.

White Bean Salad with Green Olives and Tarragon

YOUR beans can be cannellini, heirloom Aztecs, navy beans, flageolets, or even frozen limas. A mixture of types is unusual and makes the salad interesting to look at—and to eat.

SERVES 4 TO 6

3 cups cooked white beans, rinsed if canned

2 small celery ribs, thinly sliced

15 Spanish green olives, pitted and sliced

2 tablespoons chopped tarragon

1 tablespoon sherry vinegar

1 garlic clove, minced

½ teaspoon paprika

Salt and freshly milled pepper

4 to 5 tablespoons extra virgin olive oil

Put the beans in a bowl with the celery, olives, and tarragon and gently mix everything together. In a small bowl, combine the vinegar, garlic, paprika, and ¼ teaspoon salt, then whisk in the oil. Taste and adjust the seasonings, then pour the dressing over the beans. Add pepper and mix gently again. Serve at room temperature.

Chickpea and Roasted Pepper Salad

A SPANISH-INSPIRED salad that can be enhanced by surrounding it with olives, hard-cooked eggs, fresh tomatoes, and sliced Manchego.

SERVES 4

2 large red peppers, roasted

3 cups cooked chickpeas, rinsed if canned

¼ cup chopped parsley

2 tablespoons chopped mint

3 tablespoons capers, rinsed

1½ tablespoons fresh lemon juice or red wine or sherry vinegar

Salt

2 garlic cloves, minced

4 tablespoons extra virgin olive oil

Cut the peppers into ½-inch-wide strips and put them in a large bowl with the chickpeas, most of the herbs, and the capers. In a smaller bowl, whisk together the lemon juice, ¼ teaspoon salt, the garlic, and the oil. Pour it over the chickpeas and combine. Cover and refrigerate or serve right away, garnished with the remaining chopped herbs.

Pasta Salads

In general I find pasta salads overrated. Too many are served cold from the refrigerator, where they've been sitting for hours, their flavors dull, their texture stodgy. It's the warmth that brings forth the full potential of the salad, making it sensual and memorable. If you're going to make a pasta salad, try a warm one. Or turn to Asian noodle salads, which are intended to be eaten chilled.

Pasta Salad with Cauliflower and Mustard Vinaigrette

SERVES 4

1 pound cauliflower or broccoli florets
Salt
Mustard Vinaigrette, page 186
4 sun-dried tomatoes, thinly sliced

½ cup chopped scallions, including half of the greens
¼ cup chopped parsley
8 ounces pasta shells or corkscrews
Fresh lemon juice to taste

Cook the cauliflower in a large pot of boiling salted water until barely tender, about 2 minutes. Scoop it out with a strainer, shake off the excess water, and put it in a large bowl with the vinaigrette, tomatoes, scallions, and parsley.

Cook the pasta in the same water, then drain. Add the pasta to the bowl with the rest of the ingredients and toss gently. Serve hot or tepid, with lemon juice to sharpen the flavors.

Ravioli and Tomato Salad with Masses of Basil

1 pound cheese ravioli or tortellini
2 pounds ripe tomatoes
1 6-ounce jar artichoke hearts, drained and halved, optional
1 bunch basil, the leaves torn into pieces

½ cup Niçoise or Greek olives, pitted and cut into large pieces
3 tablespoons capers, rinsed
¼ cup extra virgin olive oil
Salt and freshly milled pepper
Red wine vinegar

THIS dish of tender mouthfuls is inspired by a recipe in Nancy Radke's newsletter from years ago, Ciao! I have often taken this salad on a picnic; when it's finally time to eat, the flavors have mingled nicely.

SERVES 4 TO 6

Bring a large pot of water to a boil for the ravioli. Blanch the tomatoes for 15 seconds, then scoop them out. Peel, seed, and chop them into large pieces. Put the tomatoes and artichokes in a large bowl with the basil, olives, capers, and oil.

Salt the pasta water. Add the ravioli, cook until done, and drain well. Add them to the bowl and toss gently with a rubber spatula. Taste for salt, season with pepper, and sprinkle with vinegar to taste. Serve warm or tepid.

Chilled Mung Bean Noodles with Dulse and Crushed Peanuts

THESE cool, slippery noodles are just the thing on a hot day. They don't require cooking, and they only get better as they marinate in the refrigerator. Dulse is a delicate and delicious sea vegetable.

SERVES 4

About 2½ ounces mung bean noodles

2 carrots, julienned

1 cucumber, seeded and julienned

4 scallions, including a little of the greens, thinly sliced diagonally

¼ cup Japanese rice vinegar

2 teaspoons roasted peanut oil

1½ teaspoons sugar

Salt

1 tablespoon finely chopped ginger

1 jalapeño chile, seeded and finely diced

Several red dulse "leaves," soaked in water for 5 minutes

¼ cup chopped cilantro

½ cup chopped roasted peanuts

Cover the mung bean noodles with boiling water and let stand until softened, about 5 minutes. Drain and put them in a bowl with the carrots, cucumber, and scallions. Whisk the vinegar, oil, sugar, and a pinch of salt together, then add the ginger and chile. Pour over the noodles and toss well. Drain the dulse, coarsely chop, and add it to the noodles with the cilantro and most of the peanuts. Toss again and serve with the remaining peanuts sprinkled over the top.

Mung Bean Noodles

Buckwheat Noodle Salad with Grilled Tofu and Roasted Peppers

THE tofu can marinate for a day or longer, but try to give it at least 1 hour. Buckwheat noodles can be found in Asian markets and many natural food stores. Check the package instructions—they cook more quickly than semolina pasta.

SERVES 4 TO 6

The Tofu and Marinade

1 package Chinese-style firm tofu

⅓ cup hoisin sauce

2 teaspoons dark sesame oil

⅓ cup rice wine (mirin)

3 tablespoons soy sauce

1½ tablespoons dark brown sugar

1½ tablespoons tomato paste

3 garlic cloves, minced or put through a press

1 tablespoon minced ginger

2 pinches red pepper flakes

The Noodles

2 red bell peppers, halved lengthwise and brushed with oil

1 12-ounce package soba noodles

1 bunch scallions, including a little of the greens, thinly sliced

2 tablespoons chopped cilantro

2 tablespoons toasted black or white sesame seeds

Cut the tofu into slabs about ⅜ inch thick and drain briefly on paper towels. Whisk the remaining marinade ingredients together in a pie plate. Add the tofu and turn the pieces so that all are covered with the marinade. Cover and refrigerate until ready to use.

Prepare the grill or heat the broiler. Remove the tofu from the marinade, reserving the marinade. Grill or broil until browned on both sides, then slice into strips. Grill or broil the peppers until the skin blisters, then peel and slice into narrow strips. Boil the noodles in a large pot of salted water until done, according to the package instructions. Drain and rinse under cold water to stop the cooking and shake off excess water. Toss the noodles with the reserved marinade, scallions, cilantro, peppers, and tofu. Sprinkle the sesame seeds over the noodles. Toss again and serve.

Sesame Noodles with Asparagus Tips

The Marinade

¼ cup sesame oil

3 tablespoons dark sesame oil

7 tablespoons soy sauce

3 tablespoons Chinese black or balsamic vinegar

3½ tablespoons dark brown sugar

2 teaspoons salt

2 teaspoons chili oil

1 tablespoon minced ginger

1 garlic clove, finely chopped

¼ cup chopped cilantro

The Noodles and Asparagus

Salt

2 pounds asparagus, trimmed and thinly sliced on a diagonal

1 14-ounce package thin Chinese egg noodles

10 scallions, including the firm greens, thinly sliced

¼ cup sesame seeds, toasted until lightly browned

WHENEVER people ask what they can make a lot of easily and ahead of time for a party, this is what I suggest. It's endlessly versatile—you can vary the vegetable to go with the season, using, for example, snow peas, roasted peppers, grilled eggplant, carrot julienne strips, mung bean sprouts, and fresh or dried shiitake mushrooms.

SERVES 6 TO 8

Mix the marinade ingredients together, stirring to dissolve the sugar.

Bring a large pot of water to a boil. Add salt and the asparagus. Cook until bright green and tender but still firm, just a few minutes. Scoop the asparagus out, rinse it under cold water, and set on a towel to dry.

Pull the noodles apart with your fingers, add them to the boiling water, and give them a quick stir. Boil until tender but not overly soft, tasting them often as they cook. It should take only a few minutes. Pour the noodles into a colander and immediately rinse under cold water. Shake off the excess water.

Toss the noodles with all the marinade and most of the scallions, sesame seeds, and asparagus. Mound them in a bowl or on a platter, then garnish with the remaining asparagus, scallions, and sesame seeds.

Vinaigrettes and Other Dressings

IT'S *the dressing that completes the salad, adding a smooth coating that glides over the ingredients, bringing all the flavors and elements together. Dressing a salad can be the simplest toss in oil and vinegar or glossing with vinaigrettes laden with mustard, shallots, olives and capers, herbs and cheeses. Some salad dressings use buttermilk and yogurt as their base, and a few are sweet, especially those used with fruit, but all have an edge of tartness. No dressing is difficult or time consuming to make. And one of the best dressings—olive oil and lemon juice or vinegar—requires only seconds. Stock your cupboard with a fine olive oil and a few vinegars, and you'll never have to turn to bottled dressing to dress a salad.*

Dressings are formed by bringing together oil and acid (vinegar or lemon) with or without other flavorings. Since vinegar and oil don't naturally merge, vigorous beating with a tiny whisk or a good shake in a covered jar is what convinces them to emulsify into a coherent sauce. As they sit, dressings and vinaigrettes will often separate into these two elements but can quickly be rejoined with a few turns of a whisk. Individual recipes may make more than you need at one time, but the leftovers will keep over the next day or two, refrigerated or at room temperature.

Salad Oils

What's commonly sold as vegetable oil is the last thing you want to put on a salad. Highly refined, odorless, and tasteless, it only makes your salad greasy. Oil is as important an ingredient in a salad as what's dressed, so choose good-quality, delicious oils. Rich heavy nut oils, fragrant roasted sesame and peanut oils, mild sunflower oil, and even more exotic oils—all have their special uses.

BOYAJIAN CITRUS OILS: Only a few drops of these oils are necessary to underline the presence of orange, lemon, or lime in a vinaigrette. Not likely to be in your supermarket, they are found in specialty stores.

DARK SESAME OIL: There's a refined, light sesame oil and a dark, roasted version. The latter should be dark amber in color and have the pronounced perfume of roasted sesame seeds. It's wonderful used as a flavoring for vinaigrettes that coat Asian greens such as tatsoi and Napa cabbage. Kadoya, a Japanese brand, has been my favorite for years.

EXTRA VIRGIN OLIVE OIL: The best extra virgin olive oil, often labeled "estate-bottled" is indeed very expensive, but salads provide one of the best ways to showcase its finesse. Less expensive olive oils labeled "extra virgin," such as Colavita, are also fine.

HAZELNUT OIL: Hazelnut oil made from roasted nuts is rich and viscous. Its nutty flavor complements artichokes, wild rice, pears, and persimmons. Its flavor actually comes through better when it's mixed with olive or another lighter oil.

MACADAMIA NUT OIL: More delicate than hazelnut oil but still rich, that made from roasted nuts, such as Loriva, has the most flavor. It's lovely with salads featuring tropical fruits and with rice salads.

ROASTED PEANUT OIL: The peanut equivalent of extra virgin olive oil, this is saturated with the perfume of roasted peanuts and should be used with that in mind. (Loriva, available at supermarkets and specialty stores, is the best widely distributed brand I know of, although there are also some good Chinese roasted peanut oils available, usually in 1-gallon cans.) I especially like featuring roasted peanut oil in dressings that are seasoned with ginger, soy, and garlic. You can mix roasted peanut oil with lighter, more refined oil or use it straight.

SUNFLOWER SEED OIL: I'm very fond of this oil, especially when it's made from roasted seeds. It has more character than most of the lighter all-purpose oils—its toasty, nutty flavor is definitely present, but it doesn't overwhelm.

WALNUT OIL: Made in France and America, walnut oil should be dark and viscous and redolent of walnuts. If it's pale and bland, it's overrefined. Use walnut oil straight or cut with olive oil or sunflower seed oil in vinaigrettes. Sherry, tarragon, and strong red wine vinegars stand up to its personality. Walnut oil seems to soften bitter greens and complement fall and winter fruits such as pears, apples, and persimmons.

Vinegars

The vinegar you use contributes a great deal to the character of a salad. Vinegars range from sharp to sweet and high acid to low, depending on what they're made from and how they're made. Acidity is expressed in percentage or grains; the information is usually given on the bottle. A sharp, high-acid vinegar would have 65 to 75 grains or 6.5 to 7.5 percent acidity, a low-acid vinegar about 4 percent. Low-acid vinegars require less oil for balance than highly acidic ones.

APPLE CIDER VINEGAR: This has a nicely balanced, lively taste that always seems uniquely American to me. The organic, unfiltered type tends to be more fruity and interesting than the filtered type. A rather all-purpose vinegar, I like it with sunflower seed oil and peanut oils, especially on grains and peas, such as a salad with black-eyed peas.

BALSAMIC VINEGAR: Low-acid, smooth, and complex balsamic vinegar is excellent with fruits (sometimes improving their flavor!) and for tempering the more aggressive red wine and sherry vinegars. Made from the must of white grapes, its unique flavor is gained through successive aging in open wooden barrels over many years. There are three tiers of balsamic vinegar: the first, which is aged for decades, is very costly and exquisite, used by the drop; a second tier of high-quality vinegar, aged 15 to 25 years, is also expensive but not impossibly so; and a third tier, which is syrupy and cloying, is neither aged nor terribly good. Because of its unique flavor and sweetness, balsamic vinegar isn't meant to be used as the sole vinegar in a dressing but as an accent, softening and enriching wine vinegars or enhancing cherries or strawberries by droplets. Unfortunately it has become overused, the poorest quality appearing almost everywhere and on everything. Choose the best you can afford and use it judiciously.

CHAMPAGNE VINEGAR: Champagne vinegar is delicate but has enough strength to support an extra virgin olive oil. Champagne vinegar can also be used by itself, sprinkled over salad greens, by those avoiding oil in dressings. I especially like champagne vinegar with mild tender greens such as butter or Boston lettuce types, oakleaf, salad mixes of baby greens, and so forth.

FRUIT VINEGARS: Fruity and mild, raspberry vinegar was all the rage some years ago. It and other fruit-enhanced vinegars can be used where you want a fruity overtone—with avocados, citrus, pears, green salads with fruit, grains. Use fruit vinegars with discernment. They would not be so good with eggs and cheese, for example.

RED WINE VINEGAR: Frequently used for salads, red wine vinegars vary in body and strength from average to high acid. Aged red wine vinegars ("aged" is designated on the label) are more acidic and are excellent with heavier oils, such as nut oils and extra virgin olive oil, and with dense greens, such as spinach. An excellent full-bodied red wine vinegar is Kimberly's, made from cabernet.

RICE WINE VINEGAR: Japanese vinegar that's extra-mild and sweet, it comes both plain and "seasoned." (The plain is what I have used.) There are also brown rice vinegars. Some, which are aged in open crocks, are as exquisite as a fine balsamic vinegar. Use rice vinegars with toasted peanut and sesame oils, especially those destined for salads including fruit, Japanese noodles, or cucumbers.

SHERRY VINEGAR: Distilled from sherry, this Spanish vinegar has an unmistakable and delicious aroma. It's very acidic and requires much more oil than the standard three-to-one ratio to balance its strength. This is a good vinegar to use with heavier nut oils, and with bitter greens such as radicchio. Mixing in a little balsamic vinegar helps modify its tartness while retaining its rich flavor.

WHITE WINE VINEGARS: Generally a little less aggressive than red wine vinegars, many white wine vinegars come flavored with a branch of tarragon, dill, or other herb—nice when the herb complements the salad. White wine vinegars allow other flavors to come through more in a dressing, such as the particular delicacy of shallots or citrus zest. They're a good choice with lighter-bodied olive oils and more neutral-tasting oils, such as sunflower seed or safflower.

Flavorful Additions

Beyond salt, which is crucial, lots of exciting flavorings can go into dressings. Among them are the following.

For sharpness: capers, olives, green peppercorns, salty cheeses

For liveliness: diced shallots, scallions, snipped chives, and pickled onions

For pungency: fresh garlic pounded to a puree with salt, freshly milled black pepper

For nose tingling: mustard and horseradish

For richness and their ability to smooth out disparate flavors: crème fraîche, sour cream, yogurt cheese, and hard-cooked egg yolk

For smoky sweetness: strained juices from roasted peppers

For exotic fragrance: saffron, a pinch soaked in warm oil or water

For mystery: citrus juices, including tangerine, lime, lemon, and orange, reduced, by simmering, to a concentrated essence

For the spice of life: ginger, cumin, paprika, and coriander; all fresh herbs

For a mild acid nip: seeded and diced ripe tomatoes

Combining Oils and Vinegars

There aren't really any hard-and-fast rules, although some alliances form rather naturally. For example, heavy nut oils need the concentrated strength of an aged red wine or sherry vinegar while a more delicate oil would be overwhelmed by these assertive vinegars. It's not uncommon to mix both vinegars and oils. For example, a little balsamic vinegar tempers a sharper vinegar and adds its sweet note, whereas a little sherry vinegar adds an interesting dimension to a citrus vinaigrette or fruit vinegar. A heavy nut oil can be mixed with a lighter oil, and the nut flavor will carry. The best approach is to experiment and taste. You may find a combination of vinegars and oils that strikes your fancy and becomes your signature dressing.

GARLIC

A subtle presence of garlic can be achieved by letting a crushed, peeled clove rest in the dressing for 10 minutes or so. For a stronger presence, finely chop a clove or pound it in a mortar with a pinch of salt until smooth, then whisk it into the dressing. In its roasted form, garlic is much sweeter.

PROPORTIONS: A basic formula for combining oil and vinegar is one part acid to three parts oil. But, as you can now see, this formula can't work for all vinegar-oil combinations. Sherry vinegar, for example, is so acidic that it may need six parts oil to one, whereas rice wine vinegar can be mixed more like two to three parts to one. You can always start with the three-to-one formula and taste your way from there. When it comes to dressing grains and beans, a sharper dressing is usually in order.

USING ONLY OIL: Some salad combinations are so robust and peppery, such as salads of arugula, watercress, sorrel, and large amounts of herbs, that just a little oil and salt are all that's needed. The spiciness of the greens makes up for the acid, but you can include a few drops of lemon juice too.

USING ONLY VINEGAR: You can also dress a salad with just a little salt and vinegar. Mild low-acid vinegars sharpen the flavor of greens without being overwhelming. Balsamic, rice wine vinegar, champagne vinegar, and low-acid fruit vinegars are ideal. Sprinkle a few drops over salted leaves, toss well, taste, and add more if desired.

TASTING A VINAIGRETTE: First be sure it's well stirred so that there's a unified flavor, not a layer of vinegar on the bottom. So rather than taste it on your finger or from a spoon, taste it on a piece of whatever it will eventually go on—a leaf of lettuce or a slice of orange—then adjust the balance if needed. If the dressing is too tart, add a little more oil; if it's too oily and doesn't have enough bite, add a little more vinegar.

ADDING SALT AND SHALLOTS: Unless you use a fine table variety, salt, especially coarser sea salt, takes a little while to dissolve. And shallots, which I use in many dressings, seem to taste better when they've had a chance to sit for a while in the vinegar before adding the oil. The vinegar sweetens and softens the shallots. To accommodate both, I usually let the salt and/or shallots sit for 15 minutes before whisking in the oil. If you don't do this, the world won't end, but it's an easy habit to get into and results in a better dressing.

Olive Oil Vinaigrette or French Dressing

2 tablespoons white or red wine vinegar
  or fresh lemon juice
1 teaspoon Dijon mustard

Salt and freshly milled pepper
6 tablespoons extra virgin olive oil

THIS basic vinaigrette includes a little mustard to sharpen the flavors.

MAKES ABOUT ¹/₂ CUP

Combine the vinegar, mustard, and ¹/₈ teaspoon salt in a small bowl and let stand for 15 minutes. Then whisk in the oil, adding it in a steady stream. Season with pepper to taste. This is not a mayonnaise, so you can move boldly—it's the whisking that pulls the dressing together. (You can also put everything in a jar with a tight lid and shake until it's quickly blended.) Dip in a lettuce leaf and taste, then adjust the oil, vinegar, or mustard if needed.

Shallot Vinaigrette The delicate onion flavor of shallots is such a worthwhile addition to vinaigrettes that you may find yourself automatically putting them in all your dressings; I certainly do! Peel and finely dice a shallot, then put it in a bowl with the vinegar and salt. Let it stand for at least 15 minutes or longer to sweeten the shallots. It also turns them slightly pink. Stir in mustard or any other flavorings, then whisk in the oil.

Unless they are at the peak of their season, shallots may have a bitter green sprout poking through the top of the bulb. Slice the bulb in half, then lift out the sprout with the tip of a knife. Dice the rest of the shallot finely and cleanly without randomly running your knife back and forth over the pieces. When they haven't been smashed, they seem to have a sweeter flavor.

Lemon Vinaigrette

DICED shallots, mustard, chopped herbs, and capers are all good additions to this vinaigrette. The minced pulp from Preserved Lemons would be delicious here.

MAKES ABOUT ¹/₂ CUP

2 tablespoons fresh lemon juice

1 teaspoon finely chopped lemon zest

Salt and freshly milled pepper

1 shallot, finely diced

5 tablespoons extra virgin olive oil or to taste

Combine the lemon juice, zest, ¹/₄ teaspoon salt, and shallot in a small bowl. Let stand for 15 minutes, then whisk in the oil and season with a little pepper to taste. Taste and correct the balance, adding more oil if needed.

Balsamic or Fruit Vinegar Vinaigrette

A LITTLE red wine vinegar balances the sweetness of the balsamic and fruit vinegars. Especially good on salads with fruits, such as figs or citrus, with tomatoes, or with grilled onions and eggplant.

MAKES ABOUT ¹/₂ CUP

4 teaspoons balsamic, raspberry, or other fruit vinegar

2 teaspoons red wine vinegar

1 shallot, finely diced

Salt and freshly milled pepper

5 tablespoons extra virgin olive oil

Combine both vinegars and the shallot with a few pinches of salt and a little pepper in a small bowl. Let stand for 15 minutes. Whisk in the olive oil. Taste to make sure the balance is right.

Orange Vinaigrette

1 teaspoon finely grated or minced
   orange zest

¼ cup fresh orange juice

2 teaspoons white wine vinegar or
   balsamic vinegar

Salt and freshly milled pepper

3 tablespoons light olive or sunflower
   seed oil

1 tablespoon extra virgin olive oil

2 drops orange oil or 1 teaspoon orange
   flower water, optional

Combine the orange zest and juice, vinegar, and ⅛ teaspoon salt in a small bowl and let stand for 15 minutes. Whisk in the oils and season with a little pepper. Add the orange oil, then taste for salt and adjust the vinegar and oil if needed.

USE this fruit vinaigrette with fennel, beets, and carrots or on a citrus or avocado salad. Blood oranges make a vivid garnet-colored vinaigrette, and the orange oil or orange flower water under-scores the orange flavor.

MAKES ABOUT ½ CUP

Sherry Vinaigrette

1 or 2 garlic cloves, coarsely chopped

Salt and freshly milled pepper

1½ tablespoons sherry vinegar or aged
   red wine vinegar

1 teaspoon Dijon mustard

6 tablespoons extra virgin olive oil

Pound the garlic with ¼ teaspoon salt in a mortar until it breaks down into a puree. Combine the garlic, vinegar, and mustard in a small bowl, then whisk in the oil and season with pepper. Taste and correct the balance.

THIS assertive, garlicky vinaigrette wakes up bland beans and grains. I sometimes pound a hard-cooked egg yolk with the garlic, which smooths and binds these strong flavors.

MAKES ABOUT ½ CUP

Walnut Oil Vinaigrette

1½ tablespoons sherry vinegar or
   tarragon vinegar

2 shallots, finely diced

Salt and freshly milled pepper

1 teaspoon Dijon mustard

6 tablespoons roasted walnut oil or a
   mixture of walnut and extra virgin
   olive oils

Combine the vinegar, shallots, and ¼ teaspoon salt in a bowl and let stand for 15 minutes. Stir in the mustard, then add the oil. Whisk well until the dressing is thick and smooth. Season with pepper. Taste and adjust the amount of vinegar or oil if needed.

THIS dressing is excellent with salads made with frisée, radicchio, esca-role, and spinach, with or without their frequent companions—apples, pears, nuts, and cheeses. Be sure to use an amber-colored oil that has a clear scent of walnuts.

MAKES ABOUT ½ CUP

Hazelnut Oil Vinaigrette As much as I like roasted hazelnut oil, it tastes clearer—and better—when mixed with a portion of light olive oil. Use 2 tablespoons hazelnut oil and ¼ cup olive oil in place of the walnut oil.

Creamy Herb and Shallot Dressing

YOU can use this dressing with a number of foods—delicate garden lettuces, shaved fennel, white beans, and vegetables such as zucchini, asparagus, green beans, or sliced mushrooms.

MAKES ABOUT ¹/₂ CUP

2 tablespoons tarragon vinegar or champagne vinegar

1 shallot, finely diced

Salt and freshly milled pepper

¹/₄ cup extra virgin olive oil or walnut oil

2 tablespoons crème fraîche or sour cream

1¹/₂ tablespoons chopped tarragon

1 tablespoon chopped parsley

1 tablespoon snipped chives

Combine the vinegar, shallot, and ¹/₄ teaspoon salt in a bowl and let stand for 15 minutes. Whisk in the oil and crème fraîche, then stir in the herbs and season with pepper. Taste and correct the balance of oil and vinegar if needed.

Winter Herb Vinaigrette

DRIED herbs and fresh parsley flavor this winter dressing. Use it with steamed or roasted winter vegetables—cauliflower, celery root, turnips, carrots, leeks, and beets.

MAKES ABOUT ¹/₂ CUP

1 garlic clove

Salt

¹/₄ teaspoon black peppercorns

¹/₄ teaspoon fennel seeds

¹/₂ teaspoon dried tarragon

¹/₂ cup chopped parsley

Grated zest of 1 lemon

1 tablespoon capers, rinsed

1 large shallot, finely diced, or ¹/₄ cup thinly sliced scallions, including a little of the green

¹/₃ cup extra virgin olive oil

2 tablespoons champagne vinegar or tarragon vinegar

In a large mortar, mash the garlic with ¹/₄ teaspoon salt, the pepper, fennel, tarragon, and 2 tablespoons of the parsley to make a smooth paste. Add the lemon zest, capers, shallot, oil, and remaining parsley; let stand for 30 minutes. Stir in the vinegar, taste for salt, and add more vinegar if needed for balance.

Mustard Vinaigrette

THE mustard and the vigorous whisking make a very thick dressing. When applied to warm foods, it immediately thins. Use this robust dressing with warm beans (dried or fresh), grated celery root, steamed potatoes, grilled fennel, broccoli, and cauliflower.

MAKES ABOUT ¹/₂ CUP

2 tablespoons aged red wine vinegar, sherry vinegar, or fresh lemon juice

2 shallots, finely diced

1 garlic clove, minced

Salt and freshly milled pepper

1 tablespoon Dijon mustard

2 tablespoons crème fraîche or sour cream

¹/₃ cup extra virgin olive oil

2 tablespoons snipped chives

1 tablespoon chopped parsley

3 tablespoons capers, rinsed

Combine the vinegar, shallots, garlic, and ¹/₄ teaspoon salt in a small bowl. Let stand for 15 minutes, then vigorously whisk in the mustard, crème fraîche, and oil until thick and smooth. Grind in a little pepper, then stir in the herbs and capers. Taste and adjust the seasonings if needed.

Lime and Fresh Mint Vinaigrette

1 teaspoon grated or minced lime zest

2 tablespoons fresh lime juice

Salt

5 to 6 tablespoons sunflower seed or light olive oil

2 scallions, including an inch of the greens, thinly sliced into rounds

2 tablespoons chopped mint or 2 teaspoons dried, crumbled

USE with cucumbers, delicate lettuces, rice, and melon salads.

MAKES ABOUT ½ CUP

Combine the lime zest and juice and ¼ teaspoon salt, then whisk in the oil. Stir in the scallions and mint. Taste and correct the seasonings for balance if needed.

Lime-Cumin Vinaigrette

1 garlic clove

Salt

Grated or minced zest of 2 limes

2 to 3 tablespoons fresh lime or lemon juice to taste

2 tablespoons chopped scallion or finely diced shallot

½ jalapeño chile, seeded and minced

½ teaspoon cumin seeds

½ teaspoon coriander seeds

¼ teaspoon dry mustard

⅓ cup olive oil

2 tablespoons chopped cilantro

CUMIN and lime go especially well with citrus fruits, onions, avocados, and peppers. Roasting and grinding whole spices creates bigger, warmer flavors.

MAKES ABOUT ½ CUP

Pound the garlic with ⅛ teaspoon salt in a mortar until smooth (or put it through a press), then combine it in a bowl with the lime zest, juice, scallion, and chile. Toast the cumin and coriander seeds in a small dry skillet until fragrant, then immediately remove them to a plate to cool. Grind to a powder in a spice mill, then add them to the juice mixture. Whisk in the mustard and oil. Taste and adjust the balance if needed. Let the dressing stand for at least 15 minutes; add the cilantro just before using.

Curry Vinaigrette

1 garlic clove

Salt

2 tablespoons yogurt, mayonnaise, or sour cream

2 teaspoons curry powder

1½ tablespoons fresh lemon juice

5 tablespoons light olive or sunflower seed oil

2 tablespoons finely chopped cilantro

THIS thick, golden dressing is delicious with beets, asparagus, broccoli, and cauliflower and with grain-based salads, especially those made of rice and quinoa. Let it stand for 15 minutes for the full flavor to flower.

MAKES ABOUT ½ CUP

Pound or mince the garlic and ¼ teaspoon salt in a mortar until smooth, or put the garlic through a press. Combine the garlic and salt with the yogurt and curry in a small bowl. Stir in the lemon juice, then whisk in the oil. Let stand for 15 minutes, then stir in the cilantro. Taste for tartness and salt and adjust if needed.

Tomato Vinaigrette

THE *juicy tidbits of tomatoes are an unconventional addition. Use this dressing soon after making it, on green salads, especially spinach salads, and salads based on beans and grains.*

MAKES ABOUT ¹/₂ CUP

1 garlic clove, minced
1 shallot, finely diced
2 tablespoons red wine vinegar
2 teaspoons balsamic vinegar

Salt and freshly milled pepper
4 to 6 tablespoons extra virgin olive oil
3 Roma tomatoes or ¹/₂ cup cherry tomatoes, neatly diced

In a small bowl, combine the garlic, shallot, both vinegars, ¹/₄ teaspoon salt, and pepper to taste. Let stand for 15 minutes, then whisk in the oil and add the tomatoes. Taste and adjust the balance if needed.

Sun-Dried Tomato Vinaigrette: Replace the fresh tomatoes with 6 soft sun-dried tomatoes, finely slivered, then diced.

Tomato Vinaigrette with Olives: Add ¹/₄ cup halved and pitted Niçoise or Kalamata olives, pitted and quartered. Good with grilled vegetables, avocados, fresh goat cheese, and mozzarella.

Saffron Vinaigrette with Basil

FOR *a saffron lover, this dressing will become a favorite. Use it with summer vegetables—roasted peppers and potatoes, grilled zucchini, tomato salads, grilled fennel. Or add finely diced tomatoes to the dressing and spoon it over grilled or roasted eggplants.*

MAKES ABOUT ¹/₂ CUP

3 tablespoons fresh lemon juice
2 teaspoons snipped chives
¹/₂ teaspoon grated or minced orange zest
Salt and freshly milled pepper

¹/₂ cup extra virgin olive oil
Pinch saffron threads
2 tablespoons snipped or torn basil leaves

In a bowl, combine the lemon juice, chives, orange zest, ¹/₄ teaspoon salt, and a few grinds of pepper. Warm 2 tablespoons of the oil right over the heat in a small measuring cup, crumble the saffron threads into it, and let stand for a few minutes. Add this oil to the dressing and whisk in the remaining oil. Add the basil just before using.

Sesame Vinaigrette with Chili Oil

USE *this aromatic dressing with Asian greens such as tatsoi and Napa cabbage, Asian noodles, sweet potatoes, and even fruit—especially mangoes and citrus.*

MAKES ABOUT ¹/₂ CUP

1 garlic clove, minced
1 teaspoon minced ginger
1 shallot, finely diced
3 tablespoons rice wine vinegar
1 teaspoon soy sauce

1 teaspoon light brown sugar
3¹/₂ tablespoons sesame oil
1 tablespoon dark sesame oil
¹/₂ teaspoon chili oil
1 tablespoon chopped cilantro, optional

Combine the garlic, ginger, and shallot in a small bowl, cover with the vinegar, and let stand for 15 minutes. Stir in the soy sauce and sugar, then whisk in the oils. Add the cilantro. Taste and adjust the amount of soy and sugar if needed.

Peanut Dressing with Thai Basil

¼ cup roasted peanut oil

2½ tablespoons rice vinegar or apple cider vinegar

1 tablespoon soy sauce

1 garlic clove, finely minced

½ to 1 serrano chile, diced

2 scallions, including an inch of the greens, thinly sliced

8 mint leaves, finely chopped

2 tablespoons chopped basil, preferably Thai or anise basil

2 tablespoons chopped cilantro

Pinch salt

ROASTED peanut oil makes this dressing highly aromatic. Use it with Napa cabbage and spinach salads, on cubes of silken tofu, or toss with Chinese egg noodles.

MAKES ABOUT ½ CUP

Combine everything in a bowl and whisk together. Taste—the soy sauce may provide enough salt; if not, add some.

Avocado Dressing

¼ cup fresh lime or lemon juice

1 small avocado, peeled and seeded

1 garlic clove, coarsely chopped

1 jalapeño chile, seeded and diced, optional

3 scallions, including an inch of the greens, roughly chopped

¼ cup chopped cilantro

½ cup plus 2 tablespoons olive, avocado, or sunflower seed oil

Salt

USE this thick green dressing with crisp romaine and iceberg lettuce or as a dip for crudités. It will hold well, refrigerated, for several hours. Set plastic wrap directly on the surface to keep it from browning.

MAKES ABOUT 1½ CUPS

Put the lime juice, avocado, garlic, chile, scallions, and cilantro in a blender and puree. Gradually pour in the oil with the machine running. Season with salt to taste.

Variation with Tomatillos: The tartness of tomatillos slices through the richness of the avocado. Remove the husks from 4 large tomatillos, simmer them in water until they turn olive green, then puree. Chill, then stir into the dressing. Add ¼ cup sour cream or yogurt if desired.

Blue Cheese Dressing

6 tablespoons extra virgin olive oil

2 tablespoons sour cream or yogurt

5 teaspoons sherry vinegar or aged red wine vinegar

3 ounces blue cheese such as Maytag, crumbled

1 tablespoon snipped chives

Salt and freshly milled pepper

SPOON over hearts of romaine or serve as a dip for crudités.

MAKES ABOUT ½ CUP

Whisk all the ingredients in a bowl except the salt and pepper, leaving the cheese a little chunky or smooth as you prefer. Taste and add salt if needed—the cheese will be salty—and season with pepper.

Green Goddess Dressing

WITHOUT *the anchovies this isn't a true green goddess dressing, but it's awfully good. Use it with sturdy lettuces, such as iceberg or romaine hearts, or as a spread for sandwiches . Mix it with rice and vegetables for an impromptu summer rice salad.*

MAKES ABOUT 1 CUP

1/2 cup mayonnaise	3 tablespoons chopped chives
1/2 cup sour cream	1 1/2 tablespoons chopped tarragon
1 tablespoon tarragon vinegar	1 garlic clove, coarsely chopped
1/2 cup chopped parsley	1/4 teaspoon salt

Combine all the ingredients along with 2 tablespoons water in a blender or food processor and blend until smooth and pale green. Taste and add more salt if needed.

Dairy-Free Variation: Puree one 10-ounce box of soft silken tofu with 1/2 cup olive oil and the remaining ingredients until smooth.

Feta Dressing with Marjoram and Mint

TRY *this spunky dressing with platters of cucumbers, tomatoes, and peppers, with romaine lettuce, or spooned over warm lentils or beans.*

MAKES ABOUT 2/3 CUP

2 tablespoons aged red wine vinegar	1/3 cup olive oil
1 tablespoon chopped marjoram	1/3 cup crumbled feta cheese
2 teaspoons chopped mint	Salt and freshly milled pepper

Put the vinegar and herbs in a small bowl. Whisk in the oil, then stir in the cheese. Taste for salt—none may be needed because of the feta—and season with pepper. If you prefer a creamier dressing, mash the cheese with the oil first, then combine with the rest of the ingredients.

Buttermilk Dressing with Horseradish

USE *this tangy dressing as a dip or as a topping for roasted vegetables or baked potatoes.*

MAKES ABOUT 1 CUP

1/2 cup buttermilk	2 garlic cloves
1/2 cup yogurt, sour cream, or mayonnaise	Salt
1 tablespoon prepared horseradish	1/4 cup chopped parsley
1/2 teaspoon wasabi or to taste	Fresh lemon juice or white wine vinegar

Combine the buttermilk, yogurt, and horseradish in a bowl. Dilute the wasabi in a little water, then whisk it into the yogurt mixture. Pound the garlic with 1/4 teaspoon salt until smooth, then add the parsley and pound again just to bruise the herbs. Add this to the buttermilk mixture with lemon juice to taste.

Soups from Scratch

A BOWL OF SOUP IS WHOLESOME, COMFORTING, THE ESSENCE OF SIMPLICITY. SOUPS ARE ALSO PRACTICAL BECAUSE THEY'RE RELATIVELY EASY AND QUICK TO MAKE—A GOOD PLACE FOR BEGINNERS TO BEGIN AND FOR MORE PRACTICED cooks to continue. A forgiving food, soup happily accepts a fennel bulb where none was called for, replaces a leek with an onion, provides a home for a tasty leftover. Soup is something we can turn to again and again, and when we don't have time to cook, we're comforted by the pot that awaits us in the refrigerator, for soup always improves with time.

Soup can be a prelude to a meal, the meal itself, or even dessert. Soup can also leave home and travel to lunch in a thermos. The soup that comes before the main course should be light unless the dish that follows is also light. Make sure there's a contrast of color and texture between the two courses. First course soups, often pureed and smooth, are generally more elegant than the homey, comforting soups we turn to again and again. A hearty, full-bodied soup accompanied by bread and followed with a salad makes a wholesome, nurturing meal.

A shallow soup plate—just deep enough to hold soup within its rim—frames a soup perfectly. These elegant plates or small porcelain soup cups are ideal vessels for first-course soups at a sit-down dinner party. Deep bowls or cups are more informal, and their steep sides help the soup retain its warmth. A simple garnish—a swirl of crème fraîche or a spoonful of olive oil, a sprinkling of herbs—is all that's needed to bring out a soup's charm and personality, while more complex garnishes can make an ordinary soup unusual and interesting.

SERVING SIZE: For an appetizer or soup course, $^3/_4$ to 1 cup soup is plenty; for a main-dish serving, $1^1/_2$ to 2 cups soup will do.

STORING STOCKS AND SOUPS: Always refrigerate leftover soup, then bring it to a boil to reheat. Soup often thickens as it stands, so you may have to thin a second-day soup with milk, stock, or water and add chopped herbs or other garnishes to freshen it. Except for yogurt soups and those whose charm depends on being served within moments of completion, all the stocks and soups in this book freeze well. To freeze, divide cooled soup into quantities that make sense for you—$1^1/_2$ cups for a single serving, larger amounts for a family. After defrosting, all the soup needs is reheating and some fiddling—reseasoning and adding a fresh garnish—to come to perfection.

DAIRY-FREE SOUPS: Many soups don't call for butter, cream, or milk, and recipes seldom include eggs. On the other hand, adding a pat of butter, enriching a soup with milk or cream, or swirling in a spoonful of tart yogurt or pungent grated cheese at the end can provide a sharp flavor accent or meld flavors together. Soups that call for butter or small amounts of dairy can be made dairy-free by substituting a suggested oil for the butter and omitting the bit of cheese or sour cream at the end.

Stocks

MOST *of these recipes taste fine made with water, but you may wish to use a stock to add body and depth of flavor to your soup. You have several options when it comes to stock. One is to use the Basic Vegetable Stock, a reliable all-purpose background stock for soups and other dishes. Another is to make a specific stock, such as a mushroom stock, that complements a specific soup. Or you might choose a commercial stock. I find them a little harsh and too salty, but you may not—try them and see. Take whichever approach appeals to you or that you have time for. If you make yourself familiar with the flavor-enhancing stocks in this chapter, as well as the building blocks for improvising, you'll be able to take full advantage of soup's natural flexibility.*

Usually my own preference is to make a Quick Stock—a simple, basic stock that draws on the vegetable trimmings for its supportive flavor. It's effortless, yet your soups will taste deeper and fuller. Preparing it also affords the pleasure of using what might otherwise be discarded.

Stock Options

The generic recipe for vegetarian stock consists of an onion, carrot, celery, and bay leaf, while at the opposite extreme are intense broths made by chefs who can afford to use vast quantities of vegetables and herbs. In between are a host of well-flavored vegetable stocks tailor-made for particular dishes. The methods for all are essentially the same—it's the ingredients that give each stock its unique characteristics.

Making stock isn't difficult, but it is an extra step. Most dishes don't need a stock, but many will be much better with one, and a few actually do require that you make a stock. You'll find that, given even a little experience, making a stock is largely an intuitive process. The following guidelines, and the recipes should free you to approach stock making in a relaxed and spontaneous fashion. Stocks that are uniquely appropriate for a given type of recipe are found throughout the book.

QUICK STOCK, PAGE 196: Used for soups, this stock is made with a few basic ingredients plus trimmings of soup vegetables. It's thin but supportive.

BASIC VEGETABLE STOCK, PAGE 196: An all-purpose, all-season stock that goes practically everywhere and gives depth to dishes like risotto, when water just won't do. It can adapt to the seasons by using those vegetables that are fresh and in season.

ROASTED VEGETABLE STOCK, PAGE 198: A winter stock—the vegetables are roasted first to concentrate their flavors. Hearty enough to be a broth for *pasta in brodo*.

MUSHROOM STOCK, PAGE 197: Full, deep, dark, mushroom-flavored stock—the most impressive and full-bodied of the vegetable stocks. Use it in all dishes that are mushroom based—soups, stews, risotti, pot pies, gratins, and so on.

KOMBU STOCKS, PAGE 232: These stocks replace the traditional Japanese dashi, which includes flaked dried bonito. Kombu, like other seaweeds, has a hint of the sea in it. It's used for miso soups and Japanese noodle dishes.

STOCK FOR STIR-FRIES, PAGE 262: A stock that helps compensate for the flavor traditionally provided by chicken stock in nonvegetarian dishes.

RED STOCK, PAGE 197: A basic quick stock made with herbs and vegetables that harmonize with many Mexican dishes.

HERB AND GARLIC BROTH, PAGE 198: Essentially the Provençal garlic soup *aïgo bouïdo*. Sip this as broth or use it to float filled pasta, cubes of potato, or thin threads of noodles. It's particularly good when used in earthy and robust potato-filled casseroles.

STOCK FOR CURRIED DISHES, PAGE 197: A basic stock made with seasonings appropriate for curries and other Indian dishes.

Elements of Stock Making

When it comes to making stock, it's more useful to know how certain ingredients work with each other than to know a particular recipe. The measurement suggestions, when given, are for 2 quarts of water, 6 cups finished stock.

Basic Ingredients for All Vegetable Stocks

Onions

Carrots

Celery

Thyme

Parsley

Bay leaf

Garlic (a good place to use those little hard-to-peel cloves)

Leek trimmings: roots and leaves

Salt

Oil for the initial sautéing of vegetables

VIRTUALLY all stocks start with these ingredients, which are the backbone ingredients for Basic Vegetable Stock.

Always-Good-to-Include Vegetables

THESE avoid the sweet end of the vegetable spectrum and give depth to stocks.

Chard stems and leaves; beet greens except for red ones

Fresh mushrooms; the soaking water from dried mushrooms

Scallions, in addition to or in place of onions or leeks

Potato parings, preferably organic

Celery root skins, well scrubbed

Parsley root

Jerusalem artichokes

Lettuce

Eggplant

Ingredients to Use for Their Particular Flavors

THESE ingredients have discernible, strong flavors and should be included in stocks that will be used in dishes that incorporate them.

Asparagus: the butt ends

Parsnips: trimmings and cores

Winter squash: the skins and seeds

Fennel: stalks and trimmings

Corn cobs

Pea pods

Cilantro or lovage

Curry spices, cumin, ginger, lemongrass, galangal, saffron

Chinese dried mushrooms

Ingredients to Use in Summer Stocks

INCLUDE any of the following seasonal vegetables and herbs in addition to the basic ingredients.

Zucchini and other squash

Tomatoes

Green beans

Eggplant

Bell peppers, especially red and yellow ones

Corn cobs

Marjoram and basil: stems or leaves

Ingredients to Use in Winter Stocks

SEEK out these additions for your earthy winter vegetable stocks.

Celery root parings, well scrubbed

Parsley root

Leeks: leaves and roots

Garlic, including roasted garlic

Dried sage: 1 or 2 teaspoons per 2 quarts water

Rosemary: about a 1-inch piece

Caramelized Onions, page 396

Mushrooms, fresh and dried

Ingredients to Avoid When Making Stocks

THERE are very few ingredients to avoid scrupulously, and almost all are vegetables in the cabbage family.

Turnips and rutabagas

Cabbages and Brussels sprouts

Broccoli and cauliflower

Red beets, unless you're making a beet soup

Tiny celery seeds, powdered herbs, ground pepper, because they can make stock bitter

Onion skins

Artichoke trimmings

Excessive amounts of greens (more than 4 cups)

Anything you wouldn't eat: no funky or spoiled vegetables

Other Ingredients That Add Depth to Stocks

Sprouted seeds, especially legumes: 1 to 2 handfuls

Lentils and mung beans: ¼ cup, rinsed

Bean broth, especially from chickpeas and white beans, in place of water

Nettles, amaranth, and borage leaves: one or more handfuls

Miso, tamari, soy sauce: a spoonful at a time added at the end to taste

Kombu: a 6-inch piece added at the beginning

Nutritional yeast: 1 to 2 tablespoons to give a "meaty" flavor to stocks; best if cooked first with the vegetables in butter or oil; available in bulk at natural food stores

Nuts, ½ to 1 cup, tied in cheesecloth, cooked in the soup for 20 minutes—they can be retrieved, dried in the oven, and used in cooking, such as in croquettes (Thanks to Tom Ney of *Prevention* magazine for this tip.)

Parmesan cheese rinds: whole chunks added to stocks that will be used for beans

Tips for Making Stocks

- A stock is not a catchall for old or spoiled vegetables, although you can use trimmings, last week's carrots, mushrooms with open caps, and so on. When in doubt, ask yourself, "Would I eat this?" If not, don't put it in the stock.

- Coarsely chop vegetables for stock into pieces about 1 inch square. The more surface area exposed, the more quickly the vegetables will yield their flavors.

- The more vegetables you use, the richer the flavor.

- Unlike meat stocks, vegetable stocks don't benefit from hours of cooking. Quick stocks take 25 to 35 minutes; basic stocks, 45 minutes to 1 hour. When the vegetables have given up their flavors, they have nothing more to offer. Once strained, the flavor of stocks can be concentrated by boiling them, uncovered, until the stock is reduced by half.

- Even after washing, some dirt may remain on vegetables like leeks and celery root. Allow the cooked stock to settle for a few minutes, then strain it carefully through a sieve into a clean container. Once cooked, don't let the stock sit with the ingredients in it—certain herbs turn bitter as they steep.

- Be cautious with unfamiliar herbs and vegetables. Some can turn grassy, like spinach, or bitter, like tiny seeds. If you're not sure about an ingredient, simmer it alone first, then taste the water to see if it's to your liking.

Vegetables and Trimmings

Basic Vegetable Stock

THIS *basic stock is flavor-rich with a golden hue. Include any trimmings from the vegetables you're using that are appropriate. Take a look at "Elements of Stock Making" to tailor this stock to the season.*

MAKES ABOUT 6 CUPS

1 large onion

2 large carrots

2 celery ribs, including a few leaves

1 bunch scallions, including half of the greens

1 tablespoon olive or vegetable oil

1 tablespoon nutritional yeast, optional

8 garlic cloves, peeled and smashed

8 parsley branches

6 thyme sprigs or ½ teaspoon dried

2 bay leaves

Salt

Scrub the vegetables and chop them roughly into 1-inch chunks. Heat the oil in a soup pot. Add the vegetables, yeast, garlic, and herbs and cook over high heat for 5 to 10 minutes, stirring frequently. The more color they get, the richer the flavor of the stock. Add 2 teaspoons salt and 2 quarts cold water and bring to a boil. Lower the heat and simmer, uncovered, for 30 minutes. Strain.

Quick Stock

MAKES ABOUT 6 CUPS

2 teaspoons vegetable or olive oil

1 onion, peeled and coarsely chopped

1 carrot, coarsely chopped

1 celery rib, coarsely chopped

Trimmings from the soup vegetables, rinsed

2 bay leaves and several thyme sprigs or ¼ teaspoon dried

4 or more garlic cloves, peeled and smashed

8 parsley branches, including the stems, or a small handful of stems

Additional herbs and spices appropriate for the soup

Salt

Heat the oil over high heat and add the onion, carrot, and celery. While they're browning, peel the vegetables and add the trimmings to the soup along with the aromatics. Stir occasionally. After about 10 minutes, add 2 teaspoons salt and 2 quarts cold water and bring to a boil, then lower the heat and simmer, uncovered, for 25 to 35 minutes. Strain as soon as the stock is finished.

Quick Stock

Making quick stock is relaxed and improvisational, the steps intermingling with the preparation of the soup vegetables, trimmings added to the pot as you go along. Here's what I do:

Heat a few teaspoons of oil in a large pot. I quickly peel and roughly chop an onion, a carrot, and a celery rib and add them to the pot when the oil is hot. While they're browning, I read through the soup recipe and look for vegetables that have useful trimmings. If I'm using leeks, I chop 2 cups of their inner greens and add them to the pot. If I'm using a celery root, I add the scrubbed skin. As I work, I toss in parsley, smashed garlic cloves, and bay leaves. I look for other ingredients in the recipe that might be amplified in the stock—an herb that's called for (in go extra marjoram, basil, or cilantro stems) or something from the garnish, like scallion greens. Also I check the refrigerator for leftover chopped shallots, a lone mushroom, some chard stems—and add them as I find them.

During the 5 minutes it takes to do all this, I give the pot a stir or two. After 10 minutes, I add salt and water and bring it to a boil. It simmers, uncovered, while I go back to the soup. I like to give the stock about a half hour, then I strain it and add it right to the soup. Still warm, it quickly comes to a boil.

Dark Vegetable Stock Brown the onion before adding the liquid or add 1 tablespoon, or more to taste, light soy or mushroom soy to the finished stock.

Stock for Curried Dishes Make the basic stock, but lightly brown the vegetables in 1 to 2 tablespoons clarified butter, with 1 3-inch cinnamon stick, 4 cloves, 2 teaspoons coriander seeds, 1 teaspoon cumin seeds, and ¼ teaspoon cardamom seeds.

Stock for Mexican Soups and Stews Make the basic, summer, or winter vegetable stock using a safflower or olive oil. Sauté the base vegetables only lightly and include ½ bunch chopped cilantro or the stems from 1 bunch; ½ teaspoon dried oregano, preferably Mexican; several epazote leaves, fresh or dried; 6 garlic cloves, roasted or sautéed in their skins; and 3 tomatoes, broiled until blistered.

Mushroom Stock

½ to 1 ounce dried porcini, about ½ to 1 cup

1½ tablespoons olive oil

1 large onion, chopped

2 carrots, diced

2 celery ribs, diced

4 to 8 ounces white mushrooms, sliced

1 cup chopped leek greens and leek roots, if available

¼ cup chopped walnuts or almonds, optional

2 garlic cloves, roughly chopped

4 thyme sprigs or ¼ teaspoon dried

Aromatics, page 29, including 10 sage leaves or 1 tablespoon dried

2 teaspoons salt

THIS stock adds so much to soups and sauces that it's worth freezing in cubes or 1-cup amounts to have on hand.

MAKES ABOUT 6 CUPS

Shake the dried mushrooms in a sieve to loosen the forest dirt. Heat the oil in a soup pot. Add the onion, carrots, and celery and sauté over medium-high heat, stirring occasionally, until the onion is well browned, about 15 minutes. Scrape the bottom of the pan to loosen the juices that have collected there, then add the dried mushrooms and their soaking liquid, the remaining ingredients, and 9 cups water. Bring to a boil, then lower the heat and simmer, partially covered, for 45 minutes. Strain.

Red Stock

1½ tablespoons vegetable oil

2 onions, sliced

2 celery ribs, diced

2 carrots, chopped

5 white mushrooms, sliced

1 teaspoon dried oregano

½ teaspoon dried thyme

2 tablespoons tomato paste

6 garlic cloves

6 outer lettuce leaves

Stems from 1 bunch cilantro or 1 cup coarsely chopped cilantro

½ cup coarsely chopped parsley

2 teaspoons salt

THIS stock adds great background support to Tortilla Soup and Fideos. In addition to the listed ingredients, you can bolster the flavor by adding a handful of lentils.

MAKES 6 CUPS

Heat the oil in a soup pot over medium-high heat. Add the onions, celery, carrots, mushrooms, and herbs and cook, stirring occasionally, until the onions are browned, about 7 minutes. Add the tomato paste and mush it around the pan for a minute or so, then add the remaining ingredients plus 2 quarts water and bring to a boil. Reduce the heat and simmer, partially covered, for 45 minutes. Strain, pressing out as much liquid as possible.

Herb and Garlic Broth

ESSENTIALLY *this is the Provençal* aïgo bouïdo, *stepped up a bit with a little tomato to make a hearty stock. It's immensely fortifying, good for colds and hangovers, as well as an excellent medium for potato dishes and winter stews.*

MAKES 4 TO 6 CUPS

2 heads garlic, as fresh and firm as possible

1 tablespoon olive oil

1 tablespoon tomato paste

2 bay leaves

10 peppercorns

2 cloves

6 large sage leaves or 2 teaspoons dried

6 thyme sprigs or $1/2$ teaspoon dried

10 parsley branches

2 teaspoons salt

Separate the garlic cloves by pressing down on the heads. Remove most of the papery skins, then smash the cloves with the flat side of a knife to open them up.

Heat the oil in a soup pot, add the tomato paste, and fry over medium heat for about a minute. Add the garlic, remaining ingredients, and 2 quarts water and bring to a boil. Lower the heat and simmer, partially covered, until the garlic cloves are soft, about 45 minutes. Strain. Press the garlic through the strainer with the back of a spoon into the broth or press it into a dish and use for another purpose.

Roasted Vegetable Stock

ROASTING *intensifies the flavors of all vegetables and provides an easy way of bringing added character to what is essentially a basic vegetable stock.*

MAKES ABOUT 6 CUPS

4 carrots

1 large celery rib

3 Jerusalem artichokes

1 large onion, chopped into $1/2$-inch pieces

1 large leek, white part thinly sliced, plus 1 cup chopped inner greens

1 cup diced celery root

6 garlic cloves

2 tablespoons olive oil

2 teaspoons salt

$1/4$ teaspoon peppercorns

$1/2$ cup coarsely chopped parsley

Aromatics, page 29, including 4 sage leaves

1 teaspoon soy sauce or to taste

Preheat the oven to 425°F and scrub the vegetables.

Slice the carrots, celery, and Jerusalem artichokes into $1/4$-inch slices. Put them in a bowl with the onion, the white part of the leek, the celery root, and the garlic. Toss them with the oil, then spread on a sheet pan and roast, turning them every 10 minutes, until browned, about 40 minutes.

Transfer the roasted vegetables to a soup pot and add the remaining ingredients along with 2 quarts water. Bring to a boil, then reduce the heat, cover the pot, and simmer for 40 minutes. Strain, pressing out as much liquid as possible. Taste for salt. A teaspoon of soy sauce may give it a little depth and additional saltiness.

How to Make (Most) Vegetable Soups

10 Basic Steps

CERTAIN *steps in soup making are encountered over and over. Often we don't know why we perform them or what they contribute to the process. Here's what they mean and why we do them—how to make a soup. For a first soup, try the basic Potato Soup. It's a simple illustration of all the steps. After that you should have enough of a feel for the process to move confidently on to the big world of soups.*

1. WARM THE OIL OR BUTTER. . . . Fat captures the perfumes of herbs and garlic (the aromatics) and carries them throughout the body of the soup. It also contributes its own flavor and gets very hot, which is important for searing and browning onions. Most recipes call for 2 tablespoons oil or a mixture of butter and oil, an ample amount for 6 to 8 cups of soup and just a teaspoon or less per serving. Even less can be used, but I encourage you to use *some.* Although diet books suggest using water for sautéing, water is not a substitute for fat because it doesn't contribute or carry flavor. If you must avoid fat, simply simmer the vegetables in stock or water.

2. IN A LARGE, WIDE POT. . . . Give your vegetables a lot of room. A wide soup pot gives a generous surface area for the onions and vegetables to brown. If crowded on top of each other, they'll steam instead. The soup pot should have a heavy bottom so that the vegetables don't burn.

3. ADD THE ONIONS OR LEEKS. . . . Onions, leeks, or scallions are almost always used to start a soup. They're cooked in oil or butter until they soften, often with aromatics such as parsley, bay leaf, thyme, garlic, and sometimes diced carrots and celery. It's important not to rush this step; the longer you give it, the better your soup will be. Browning onions until they're dark gives the soup body, hearty flavor, and rich color. When you want a more delicate flavor, cook the onions or leeks more gently, over lower heat and for less time. Sometimes a little water or stock is added after the first few minutes so that they stew rather than fry. In most of these recipes, we do something in between—letting the onions turn golden but not brown.

4. COOK UNTIL THE ONIONS ARE SOFT, 10 TO 12 MINUTES. . . . Onions take a while to break down, and their softening is inhibited by salt and acids such as tomatoes, wine, vinegar, and lemon juice. It's crucial that the onions be soft before tomatoes are added. If they're not, they'll remain uncooked and raw tasting and in the worst case will float to the surface of the finished soup. Softening takes at least 10 minutes, but to be safe, plan on 12 or more, especially at higher altitudes.

5. ADD THE VEGETABLES AND SALT AND COOK FOR A FEW MINUTES. . . . Since most vegetables don't keep the onions from getting soft, they're added at the beginning when we want them to brown too. Or they're added later and cooked for just a few minutes, to warm them up before the next step. This is a good time to add salt to the soup, for it helps pull out the vegetables' flavors.

6. ADD THE WATER OR STOCK. . . . Now is the time to add the liquid to the vegetables. If you've made a quick stock, it will be warm. If you're using water, just add it cold from the tap.

7. BOIL, THEN SIMMER, PARTIALLY COVERED. . . . The liquid needs to reach a boil, but constant boiling is too violent a motion for a good soup. Once the water boils, lower the heat to a simmer, which produces gentle and constant motion in the pot—hot but not destructive. The pan is covered—but not all the way—so that the soup doesn't escape in the form of steam, nor does it boil over; a little escaping steam keeps it all in check.

8. LET COOL, THEN BLEND OR PUREE. . . . Many soups are pureed. They can be left with some texture or made silken by straining through a fine sieve. You can use a food mill, a hand-held blender, a regular blender with a jar, or a food processor. Very hot soups can sputter and burn, so it's a good idea to let them cool for 5 to 10 minutes before pureeing and to puree with care.

9. TASTE FOR SALT, SEASON WITH PEPPER, AND ADD A LITTLE LEMON OR VINEGAR. . . . If your stock was seasoned and you salted the vegetables, you probably won't need more salt at the end, but it's always a good idea to check right before serving. If the salt seems okay but the soup still needs *something,* often a little lemon juice or a splash of vinegar will bring all the flavors into sudden bright relief. Add freshly milled pepper just before serving too; a lot of pepper added at the beginning can turn bitter.

10. GARNISH AND SERVE. . . . Finally you can ladle out your soup and finish it with a garnish that will add a harmonious or contrasting flavor, color, or texture. If it's very cold or you live at a high altitude where food cools quickly, take a moment to warm the empty soup bowls either in a low oven or with hot water.

SOME QUICK AND EASY SOUPS

Potato Soup and variations • Black Bean Soup • Buttermilk soups and yogurt soups • Chard Soup with Sorrel or Lemon • Melon Soup with Ginger-Cucumber Salsa • Miso soups • Summer squash soups • Red Lentil Soup with Lime

MAIN-DISH SOUPS

Tortilla Soup • Basic Winter Squash Soup with Fried Sage Leaves • Beet Soup with Three Legumes • Lentil Minestrone • A Summer Bean and Vegetable Soup with Pesto • Quinoa Chowder with Spinach, Feta, and Scallions • Split Pea Soup • Winter Vegetable Chowder

FIRST-COURSE SOUPS

Bright Green Spinach and Pea Soup • Cold soups • Corn soups • Cream of Leek Soup with Fresh Herbs and Cheese Croutons • Cream of Tomato Soup • Flageolet Bean and Leek Soup • Parsnip Soup with Ginger and Parsnip "Croutons" • Turnip Soup with Gruyère Croutons • Roasted Red Pepper Soup with Polenta Croutons

Garnishes for Soups

GARNISHES *make plain soups pretty, complete their seasoning, and add texture. Particular garnishes often suggest themselves, but the following suggestions are good with a great many soups and will help you improvise. Use one, two, or even three at a time.*

CHOPPED FRESH HERBS: Parsley, chervil, and chives are always a good choice, but use the herbs that have gone into the soup itself, too.

FRIED HERBS: Sage, parsley, celery, and lovage leaves—fried quickly in olive oil until crisp, then crumbled into the soup—are unusual and tasty.

HERB OR BLOSSOM BUTTERS: Floated or swirled into the soup, these speckled butters, pages 51 to 52, melt, and the herbs and petals spread over the surface.

FRESH GREENS: Slice arugula, lettuce, spinach, or sorrel into very thin ribbons and sprinkle over the soup—these snippets wilt and turn bright green.

COOKED GREENS: Finely chop cooked spinach, beet greens, or broccoli rabe and stir them into soup at the last minute to add vibrant flavor and color. Strong-tasting greens are especially good with bean- and potato-based soups.

VEGETABLES: Lightly cooked carrot julienne strips, slivers of raw radish, and strips of greens used together can rescue a dull-looking vegetable soup or enhance one that's already striking. Stewed leeks, thinly shredded cabbage, or a few chopped tomatoes also can add greatly to a soup's presence.

CROUTONS: Small cubes of crisp bread, toasted baguette slices, or large garlic croutons add textural interest to soups, especially those with uniform textures. Narrow strips of fried or toasted tortillas also add texture as well as their warm corn flavor.

PASTA AND GRAINS: Cooked pasta, rice, or other grains—barley, quinoa, and large grains like spelt—give a soup body and texture. Floating dumplings or cheese and rice molds placed in the bowl before ladling the soup make a special presentation.

CREAM, CRÈME FRAÎCHE, SOUR CREAM, YOGURT, OR WHIPPED CREAM: A spoonful of cream enriches a thin soup or accents a rich one. Crème fraîche dissolves perfectly into a soup, but sour cream and yogurt will curdle if the soup boils, so reheat it carefully. Whipped cream floats on the surface, then gradually melts and is especially pretty when mixed with chopped herbs.

EXTRA VIRGIN OLIVE OIL: Spoon a little of this special oil over the surface of a soup, and the heat will bring out its full aroma. Freshly grated Parmesan cheese and freshly milled pepper are usually welcome where olive oil is. This trio is particularly good with bean soups.

SAUCES: A spoonful of Pesto, Romesco Sauce, or Garlic Mayonnaise—see the sauce chapter—makes a good soup sparkle and helps a soup that is a little bland.

VINEGAR AND LEMON: A few drops of acid often bring a soup's flavors together and make it sing. They also add dimension to soups made with little salt.

Seasonal Vegetable Soups

BY *following the progression of produce through the seasons you can enjoy vegetable soups throughout the year. Vegetables at their peak of ripeness are full of natural sugars, good texture, gorgeous color, perfume, and flavor—especially important in vegetable soups, which are, after all, very simple constructions. The vegetables in season where you live are likely to be the freshest, least expensive, and most rewarding to work with. What's in season varies widely from place to place and doesn't always correspond to what's in the supermarket, so these recipes follow vegetables from A to Z.*

Springtime Asparagus Soup

ASPARAGUS shouts "Spring!" Here's a good place to make a quick stock, using the trimmings from the leeks and the ends of the asparagus.

SERVES 4 TO 6

1 ½ pounds asparagus

1 large leek, white part plus an inch of the green, chopped

6 cups Quick Stock, page 196, or water

1 ½ tablespoons olive oil or butter

1 small onion, chopped

2 tablespoons raw white rice

Salt and freshly milled pepper

Lemon juice to taste

Slice the asparagus into three parts: ends, middles, and tips. Chop the middles and set the tips aside. Use the asparagus ends and leek roots and greens in the stock.

Heat the oil in a soup pot. Add the leek, onion, and rice and sauté over medium-high heat for about 8 minutes, until the onion is slightly colored. Add 1 cup stock and stew for 10 to 12 minutes. Add the chopped asparagus and the remaining stock and simmer, partially covered, for 12 to 15 minutes. Cool briefly, then puree and pass through a food mill to get rid of any fibers. Taste the soup for salt, add a few drops of lemon juice to bring up the flavors, and season with pepper. Return the pot to the stove to keep it warm.

Meanwhile, drop the asparagus tips into boiling salted water and cook until tender, about 4 minutes, then add them to the finished soup.

For the stock　　　　For the soup　　　　For the garnish

Asparagus Soup with Herb Cream Whip ¼ cup cream until stiff and season with a pinch salt, a little white pepper, and 2 tablespoons chopped chervil or tarragon. Stir a spoonful of cream into each bowl of soup.

Asparagus Soup with Fresh Sage Sauté 10 sage leaves with the leek, onion, and rice. Fry 10 more leaves in 2 tablespoons olive oil until they're speckled, about 1 minute, then remove them to a paper towel. Crumble them into the soup just before serving. If the sage is blooming, add a few of the purple flowers to the soup—the essence of spring.

Asparagus and Pea Soup with Basil Peas come into season just as the asparagus is finishing. Boil freshly shelled peas with the asparagus tips and add them to the finished soup along with thinly sliced basil leaves.

Beet Soup

6 cups Quick Stock, page 196, including ½ teaspoon dill seed, ½ teaspoon caraway seed, ¼ cup lentils, and the beet stems, roughly chopped

3 large beets with their greens, about 1½ pounds, peeled and cut into ½-inch cubes

2 onions or 1 onion and 1 leek, white part only, finely diced

2 tablespoons butter or olive oil

1 turnip, peeled and diced

Salt and freshly milled pepper

1 teaspoon lemon juice

Chopped dill

Sour cream or drained yogurt

In spite of the inherent deep flavor of the vegetable, beet soups need a supporting stock. You can make one while preparing the ingredients for the soup. Serve hot or chilled with a dollop of sour cream.

SERVES 4 TO 6

Begin making the stock. As you prepare the soup vegetables, add the beet skins and onion trimmings to the stock. Let it simmer while you begin the soup. Select the best beet greens, chop, and set them aside.

In a soup pot over medium heat, cook the onions in the butter until soft, about 7 minutes, stirring now and then. Add the beets, turnip, and 1 teaspoon salt and cook 5 minutes more, stirring occasionally. Strain the stock—you should have about 6 cups—and add it to the vegetables. Simmer until the beets are tender, about 10 minutes, adding the beet greens during the last 5 minutes. Taste for salt and add the lemon juice to bring up the flavor. Serve the soup sprinkled with dill, seasoned with pepper, with a spoonful of sour cream in each bowl.

Carrot Soups

When carrots are sweet, carrot soups are extraordinary. Unfortunately it's hard to tell by looking, but generally bright color indicates flavor, and big, mature carrots, often overlooked in favor of smaller ones, can taste like candy. For finishing, herbs such as dill, thyme, lovage, and tarragon all make a good match with carrots, but I think their sweetness is best countered with spicy intemperate accompaniments, like chiles and lime. Rice gives the soup body so that it won't separate in the bowl. If the carrots are young, just scrub them with a brush; otherwise, take a moment to peel them.

Carrot Soup with Onion Relish

IF you use pickled red
onions in the relish,
your soup will look very
festive.

SERVES 4 TO 6

2 tablespoons butter, olive oil, or a
   mixture

1 onion, thinly sliced

1 pound carrots, thinly sliced

1 bay leaf

2 tablespoons chopped parsley

3 tablespoons white rice

1 teaspoon sweet paprika

1 teaspoon ground cumin

$^1\!/_2$ teaspoon ground coriander

Salt and freshly milled pepper

7 cups water; or Basic Vegetable Stock,
   page 196, plus 1 cup water

Onion Relish

$^1\!/_3$ cup finely diced white onion or
   Pickled Onion, page 78

1 serrano chile, finely chopped

2 tablespoons chopped cilantro

Few leaves of cinnamon basil, if
   available, or regular basil

Grated zest and juice of 2 limes

**OTHER SPICY
CONDIMENTS FOR
CARROT SOUPS**
Harissa, page 75
Tomatillo Salsa,
   page 103
Chile Butter, page 52
Pureed grilled peppers
   seasoned with cayenne
Chili oil—a few drops
   stirred into each bowl

In a soup pot, melt the butter over medium heat. Add the onion, carrots, bay leaf, parsley, and rice; cook to soften the onion, stirring frequently, about 5 minutes. Add the spices, $^1\!/_2$ teaspoon salt, and some pepper and cook 5 minutes longer. Add the water and bring to a boil, then lower the heat and simmer, partially covered, for 25 minutes.

While the soup is cooking, make the relish by mixing all the ingredients together. Remove the bay leaf from the soup. Puree 2 cups of the soup until smooth, then puree the rest, leaving a little texture and flecks of carrot. Taste for salt and serve each bowl with a spoonful of the relish.

Carrot and Red Pepper Soup

EXCELLENT *chilled as
well as hot, this soup
uses aromatic herbs
rather than spicy season-
ings—another good di-
rection to take with
carrots.*

SERVES 4 TO 6

2 tablespoons butter or olive oil

1 red bell pepper, cut into 1-inch pieces

2 cups diced onion

1 pound carrots, thinly sliced

2 tablespoons white rice

Salt and freshly milled pepper

2 tablespoons chopped parsley

3 tablespoons chopped dill or
   $1^1\!/_2$ tablespoons dried

Grated zest and juice of 1 orange

6 cups water or Basic Vegetable Stock,
   page 196

Finely chopped dill, chopped parsley, or
   Herb Butter, page 51

Melt the butter in a soup pot and add the pepper, onion, carrots, rice, and 1 teaspoon salt. Cook over medium heat, covered, until the onion has softened completely, about 10 minutes, stirring several times. Add a grind of pepper, the parsley, dill, orange zest, juice, and water. Bring to a boil, then simmer, partially covered, until the rice is cooked, about 25 minutes. Cool briefly, then puree all but a cup or two of the soup and return it to the pot. Taste for salt, season with pepper, garnish, and serve.

Chard Soup with Sorrel or Lemon

2 tablespoons butter

1 onion or 2 medium leeks, white parts only, chopped

3 red potatoes, peeled and thinly sliced

1 bunch chard, stems removed, about 10 cups leaves

2 cups sorrel leaves, stems removed, or juice of 1 large lemon

Salt and freshly milled pepper

1/3 cup crème fraîche or sour cream

1/2 cup cooked rice or small toasted croutons

LIGHT-BODIED *but roundly flavored, this is a good soup to begin a large meal. It's quickly made and needs no stock. Chard is available year-round, sorrel mainly in spring. If you can't get sorrel, use fresh lemon juice to give the soup its tart accent.*

SERVES 4 TO 6

Heat the butter in a soup pot over medium-high heat. Add the onion and potatoes and cook, stirring occasionally, until they begin to color, about 8 minutes. Add 1/2 cup water and scrape the bottom of the pot to release the juices that have accumulated. Add the greens and 1 1/2 teaspoons salt. As soon as they wilt down, after 5 minutes or so, add 6 1/2 cups water. Bring to a boil, then lower the heat and simmer, partially covered, for 12 to 15 minutes. Puree the soup, then return it to the pot. Taste for salt and season with pepper. If you didn't use sorrel, add the lemon juice. Mix the crème fraîche with some of the soup to smooth it out, then swirl it into the soup. Serve with rice or croutons in each bowl.

Chard Soup with Cilantro Substitute a small bunch of cilantro, chopped, for the sorrel and add 1 teaspoon paprika to the onions and potatoes. The haunting flavor is hard to place at first but is a must-try for cilantro lovers.

MEASURING GREENS

Since bunches of chard, kale, mustard, and other greens can vary greatly—the stems long on one, short on another—to measure the leaves so that you can anticipate whether your soup will be thin or thick, gently stuff them in a 4-quart measuring cup. Don't fuss about exactitude—this needn't be more than a ballpark guess.

THREE TOOLS FOR PUREEING SOUPS

The blender allows you to control how smooth your soup will be, which is an advantage, but hot soup can spurt meanly out of the jar. It's always recommended that a soup cool for 5 or 10 minutes before being blended. If you're pressed for time, fill the jar only a third full. Always turn the machine on and off in three or four short spurts before you let it run to prevent spattering. Draping a towel over the blender is another good safety precaution, as is covering the blender jar with plastic wrap before placing the lid on top.

An immersion blender, or blender on a stick, brings the blender right into the soup pot. It's easy and safe but best for soups that don't require a major blending. It doesn't have the power of the traditional blender.

The food mill is an especially good choice when a soup has lots of potatoes, which can turn gummy in a blender or food processor. It's also used after blending to ensure a silky smoothness by screening out tiny fibers and seeds.

The food processor works best if you puree the solids, adding the broth as needed to loosen them. Never fill the work bowl all the way to the top and *always* leave the feed tube open so that steam can escape.

Sweet Corn Soup

DON'T *be fooled by the simplicity of this recipe, for corn can be seasoned almost endlessly with herbs and spices. Success depends on using sweet corn, in season; frozen corn needs a supporting stock. I prefer the golden color that yellow corn gives to this soup.*

SERVES 6 TO 8

6 ears corn

1 tablespoon butter or corn oil

1 small onion, thinly sliced

1/2 cup grated waxy potato, such as Yellow Finn

7 cups water; or Quick Stock, page 196, plus 1 cup water

Salt

Half-and-half or milk, optional

Chopped parsley, basil, lovage, tarragon, chives, or dill

Shuck the corn, remove the silk, then slice off the kernels. You should have about 4 cups. Use the flavor-filled cobs in the stock if you're making one.

In a wide soup pot, melt the butter, then add the onion, potato, and 1 cup of the water. Cover the pot and stew over medium heat until the onion is soft, about 10 minutes. Add the corn, 1 teaspoon salt, and the remaining water and bring to a boil. Lower the heat and simmer, partially covered, for 10 minutes. Cool briefly, then puree in a blender in two batches, allowing 3 minutes for each batch. Pass through a food mill or fine strainer, then return the soup to the stove and stir in a little half-and-half to thin it if desired. Taste for salt and serve sprinkled with herbs. When reheating, stir frequently and don't boil or the soup will curdle.

Corn Soup with Flavored Butter Float a thin slice of flavored butter in each bowl of soup. Herb or blossom butters, page 51, are good choices. As the butter melts, the flavors and flecks of herbs and flowers are released into the soup.

Corn Soup with Poblano Chiles and Tortilla Strips Roast, peel, and seed a poblano or other large green chile, then cut it into thin strips. Place some in each bowl with a little crumbled feta or grated Muenster and garnish with chopped cilantro and thin, crisp ribbons of corn tortillas, page 46.

Corn Soup with Tomatoes and Basil Peel, seed, and dice into neat small pieces 1 ripe red or yellow tomato. Slice several basil leaves into thin strips. Place small cubes of fresh mozzarella in each bowl, add the soup, and garnish with the tomato, a shower of basil, and freshly milled pepper.

Roasted Corn Soup Prepare roasted or grilled corn, then remove the kernels. Or sear cut corn kernels in a hot cast-iron skillet until lightly browned. The slightly smoky flavor goes well with additions of minced green chile, lime juice, and tortilla strips.

OTHER SEASONINGS FOR CORN SOUPS

Pureed chipotle chile mixed with sour cream

Lime juice, grated ginger, and curry powder

Pureed roasted sweet or hot peppers

Crème fraîche and chives

Cilantro Salsa, page 56

Corn Chowder with New Potatoes, Golden Peppers, and Basil

1 quart Quick Stock, page 196, or water

1 large leek, white part plus an inch of the green, sliced into thin rounds

Kernels from 6 ears corn, about 4 cups

1 pound new potatoes, peeled and neatly diced

2 branches green or opal basil, 8 leaves plucked, stems reserved

2 tablespoons plus 2 teaspoons butter or vegetable oil

1 large onion, finely diced

1 bay leaf

4 thyme sprigs or ¼ teaspoon dried

Salt and freshly milled white pepper

1 large yellow bell pepper, diced

2 cups milk or additional stock

Finely snipped chives

THIS soup provides lots of good trimmings to use in quick stock—especially the corn cobs.

SERVES 4 TO 6

If you're making the stock, include 2 cups chopped leek greens, the corn cobs, potato peelings, and basil stems.

Melt 2 tablespoons butter in a soup pot and add the onion, leek, bay leaf, and thyme. Cook over low heat until the onion is soft, 10 to 12 minutes, stirring occasionally. Add the potatoes, strained stock, and 1½ teaspoons salt and bring to a boil. Lower the heat and simmer, partially covered, until the potatoes are tender, about 20 minutes. While the soup is simmering, stew the pepper in the remaining butter and a few tablespoons water in a small skillet until tender, about 10 minutes.

Press some of the potatoes against the side of the pot to break them up; then add the corn and milk. Simmer until the soup is heated through and the corn is tender, about 5 minutes.

Thinly slice the basil leaves. Add the stewed peppers to the soup and serve with white pepper, basil, and chives sprinkled over each bowl.

Fennel and Leek Soup with Fennel Greens

THIS chameleon soup accepts Pernod to emphasize the anise, orange to complement it, a little cream to enrich it, and so forth. The ingredients provide excellent material for a quick stock.

SERVES 4 TO 6

2 fennel bulbs, 1 to 1¼ pounds

6 cups Quick Stock, page 196, or water

2 medium leeks, white parts plus an inch of the greens, chopped

1 small potato, peeled and thinly sliced

2 tablespoons olive oil or butter

1 onion, chopped

Salt and freshly milled pepper

⅓ cup cream, optional

Remove the tough outer layers of the fennel and use them in the stock, along with 1 cup chopped stalks, 2 cups chopped leek greens, the leek roots, and the potato skins. Chop ½ cup of the fennel greens and reserve.

Quarter the fennel bulbs, remove the core if tough, and thinly slice crosswise. Warm the oil in a soup pot and add the onion, fennel, leek, potato, 1 teaspoon salt, and 1 cup of the strained stock. Cover and stew over medium heat for 20 minutes, stirring occasionally. Add the remaining stock and bring to a boil. Lower the heat and simmer, partially covered, until the fennel is tender, 15 to 20 minutes more. Stir in the cream and the reserved fennel greens. Taste for salt, season with pepper, and serve.

Leek and Potato Soup

THIS French farmhouse soup—two humble vegetables simmered in water—stands on its own and makes a solid base for a host of other soups. If the potatoes are organic, leave the skins on for flavor and to give the soup the rustic feel it should have.

SERVES 4 TO 6

3 large or 6 medium leeks, white parts only, finely chopped

1½ pounds boiling or Yellow Finn potatoes, scrubbed well

2 tablespoons butter

Salt and freshly milled pepper

Milk or water to thin the soup, if needed

Set the leeks in a bowl of water to soak while you prepare the potatoes, then lift them out with a strainer, letting any sand fall to the bottom. Quarter the potatoes lengthwise and thinly slice them.

Melt the butter in a wide soup pot, add the leeks and potatoes, and cook over low heat, covered, for 10 minutes. Add 7 cups water and 1½ teaspoons salt and bring to a boil. Lower the heat and simmer, partially covered, until the potatoes are soft to the point of falling apart, about 35 minutes. Press a few against the side of the pan to break them up and give the soup body. If needed, thin the soup with milk and heat through. Taste for salt, season with pepper, and serve. (A little cream can replace the milk if you wish to enrich what is really quite a meager soup. If your soup is very thick because of the type of potato used, thin it with milk or water first, then add a small amount of cream at the end to give it fullness.)

Creamed Leek and Potato Soup Pass the soup through a food mill. Thin with milk or water if needed, then add ¼ to ½ cup cream. Serve hot or chilled with finely chopped chives and parsley or chervil. Chilled, it becomes vichyssoise.

Celery Root or Fennel Soup Replace at least half the potatoes with chopped celery root or fennel and cook as described. Use the fennel greens or celery leaves, finely chopped, for garnish.

Potato-Sorrel Soup Add 2 to 4 large handfuls of sorrel leaves, stems removed, to the soup along with the potatoes and leeks. Pass through a food mill or leave chunky and finish with ½ cup cream. This is a delicious, slightly tart, and very refreshing soup, hot or cold.

Watercress Soup Remove and discard the largest stems from a bunch of watercress. Blanch the watercress briefly in salted water. Finely chop or puree it, then add to the soup along with ¼ cup cream or crème fraîche.

Cream of Leek Soup with Fresh Herbs and Cheese Croutons

6 cups Quick Stock, page 196, or water, as needed

6 medium leeks, white parts plus an inch of the greens, sliced into ¼-inch rounds

2 tablespoons butter

1 bay leaf

4 lemon thyme or regular thyme sprigs

Salt and freshly milled pepper

1 tablespoon flour

⅓ cup milk or cream

3 tablespoons chopped herbs: chervil, basil, dill, or tarragon or 1 tablespoon chopped rosemary or lovage

Cheese Croutons, 1 for each bowl

VARY the garnishes to suit the season for this first-course soup.

SERVES 4 TO 6

If you're making stock, chop 3 cups of the green inner leaves of the leeks and use them, plus the roots, in it.

Separate the sliced leeks into rings and soak them in a bowl of water for 5 minutes. Lift them out, letting any sand fall to the bottom. You should have about 4 cups; if not, make up the difference with scallions or onion. Melt the butter in a soup pot and add the leeks, bay leaf, thyme, 1½ teaspoons salt, and 1 cup of the strained stock. Cover the pan and stew over medium heat until the leeks are tender, about 10 minutes. Stir in the flour, then pour in the remaining stock. Bring to a boil, then lower the heat and simmer, covered, for 20 minutes.

Remove the bay leaf and thyme, puree the soup, then return it to the pot. Add the milk and bring to a simmer. Taste for salt and season with pepper. Stir in the fresh herbs and serve with a crouton in each bowl.

Cream of Mushroom Soup

THIS plain-looking soup masks a wealth of flavor that comes from the mushroom stock. An excellent starter for an important winter meal, the servings can be smaller than usual since the soup is both smooth and rich.

SERVES 4 TO 6

1 pound white mushrooms

3 tablespoons butter

1 cup chopped leek or onion

2 garlic cloves, chopped

4 thyme sprigs, leaves stripped from the stems, or 3 pinches dried

Salt and freshly milled pepper

1 tablespoon flour

1 quart Mushroom Stock, page 197

1/2 to 1 cup cream

Finely chopped parsley, chives, or tarragon

Set aside a few nice-looking mushrooms for the garnish and coarsely chop the rest. Melt 2 tablespoons of the butter in a soup pot and add the leek, garlic, thyme, 1 teaspoon salt, and 1/4 cup water. Cover and stew over medium heat for 5 minutes, then raise the heat, add the chopped mushrooms, and cook for 4 to 5 minutes. Stir in the flour, add the stock, and bring to a boil. Lower the heat and simmer, partially covered, for 20 minutes. Puree the soup, return it to the pot, and stir in the cream. Season with salt and pepper. Keep warm over low heat.

Slice the reserved mushrooms. Melt the remaining butter in a small skillet, add the mushrooms, and sauté over high heat until they begin to color, 4 to 5 minutes. Season with salt and pepper. Garnish the soup with the mushrooms and the chopped herbs and serve.

Parsnip Soup with Ginger and Parsnip "Croutons"

I ALWAYS like a parsnip soup but not its dingy color. Mixing it with plenty of carrots gives it a warm, golden glow. The parsnip trimmings and cilantro stems from the garnish make great contributions to the stock.

SERVES 4 TO 6

3 large parsnips, about 2 pounds, peeled

6 cups Basic Vegetable Stock, page 196, or water

1/2 cup chopped cilantro stems plus sprigs for garnish

4 thin slices ginger, unpeeled

3 tablespoons butter or canola oil

1 large onion, roughly chopped

3/4 pound carrots, peeled and thinly sliced

1 1/2 teaspoons ground coriander

1 tablespoon white rice

Salt and freshly milled pepper

1 cup milk, cream, or almond milk to thin the soup, as needed

Cut two of the parsnips crosswise in half, then quarter each half lengthwise. Cut away most of the cores. Reserve the other parsnip. If you're making stock, include the parsnip trimmings, cilantro stems, and one slice of the ginger. Brown the vegetables before adding the water to bring out their flavors.

Heat 2 tablespoons of the butter in a soup pot over medium heat, letting it brown a little. Add the vegetables, remaining ginger, and the coriander. Cook, stirring frequently, until the onion and carrots have begun to brown here and there. Add the rice and 1 1/2 teaspoons salt and cook a few minutes more. Add the strained stock and bring to a boil. Lower the heat and simmer, partially covered, until the vegetables are very soft, about 35 minutes. Remove the ginger, then puree the soup, leaving a little texture or not, as you wish. For a very smooth soup, pass it through a food mill or sieve. Thin if necessary with the milk.

Dice the third parsnip into little cubes and cook in the remaining butter in a skillet, stirring frequently, until golden and tender, about 8 minutes. Season with salt and pepper. Serve the soup with a spoonful of the parsnips added to each bowl. Garnish with sprigs of cilantro.

Roasted Red Pepper Soup with Polenta Croutons

2½ tablespoons olive oil

1 onion, chopped

1 small potato, peeled and thinly sliced

2 garlic cloves, sliced

1 bay leaf

1 tablespoon chopped marjoram, plus extra for garnish

1 tablespoon tomato paste

3 or 4 large red bell peppers, roasted, and coarsely chopped

1 teaspoon sweet paprika

Salt and freshly milled pepper

1 quart water or Basic Vegetable Stock, page 196

Balsamic vinegar to taste

Crisp Polenta Croutons, page 525

A MULTITUDE of garnishes can be used to finish this soup such as Pesto and Olive-Rosemary Butter, but the crunchy polenta croutons are unexpected and good.

SERVES 4

Heat the oil in a soup pot and add the onion, potato, garlic, bay leaf, and marjoram. Sauté over high heat, stirring often, until the potato and onion begin to brown, about 12 minutes. Add the tomato paste and cook for 1 minute. Add the peppers, paprika, and 1 teaspoon salt. Pour in the water and scrape the bottom of the pot. Bring to a boil, then lower the heat and simmer, partially covered, for 25 minutes.

Remove the bay leaf and blend the soup until smooth. Taste for salt, season with pepper, and add a teaspoon or so of vinegar. Serve with the croutons on top and a sprinkling of chopped marjoram.

Potato Soup

FAST *and easy, potato soup costs practically nothing if you stick with ordinary boiling potatoes, a little more if you use fancy ones. And if you've never made soup before, this one is simple to make and will build up your soup confidence. Improvise by including sautéed mushrooms in winter or a diced ripe tomato in summer.*

SERVES 4 TO 6

2 tablespoons olive oil or butter

2 onions, finely diced

3 small bay leaves

2 pounds potatoes, peeled

Salt and freshly cracked pepper

2 tablespoons chopped parsley

Heat the oil in a heavy soup pot over medium heat, add the onions and bay leaves, and cook slowly. Meanwhile, quarter each potato lengthwise, then thinly slice. Irregular pieces are fine—the smaller ones will fall apart, giving body to the soup.

Add the potatoes, raise the heat, and sauté, stirring frequently, until the onions begin to color and a glaze builds up on the bottom of the pan, about 10 minutes. Add 1½ teaspoons salt and 1 cup water. Scrape the bottom of the pot to loosen the solids. Add 2 quarts water and bring to a boil. Lower the heat and simmer, partially covered, until the potatoes are soft, about 30 minutes. Remove the bay leaves, taste for salt, season with pepper, and stir in the parsley. For a soup with more body, pass 1 or 2 cups through a food mill.

Potato and Roasted Garlic Soup Roast 2 heads of unpeeled garlic cloves (they needn't be whole heads) as described on page 377. Add them, skins and all, to the onions and potatoes. Pass the finished soup through a food mill and add a few tablespoons cream. Garnish with snipped garlic chives. A stunning soup.

Potato Soup with Mustard Greens Virtually all greens are good with potatoes, but especially assertive mustard greens. Boil 1 bunch of mustard greens, without their stems, until tender and bright green, 10 to 15 minutes, then drain and coarsely chop them. Stir them into the soup along with 2 or 3 pinches of red pepper flakes. Serve with thin shavings of Parmesan over each bowl.

Potato and Parsley Soup

EASY, *fast, healthful, and good. Parsley roots, also called* Hamburg parsley, *are often available from November through January. They make a tremendous addition.*

SERVES 4 TO 6

1½ pounds potatoes, peeled (can be a mixture of russet and red potatoes)

2 parsley roots if available, scrubbed

1½ tablespoons butter or olive oil

6 shallots or 1 onion, finely chopped

2 bay leaves

½ cup dry white wine

2 cups chopped parsley

Salt and freshly milled pepper

6 cups water or Basic Vegetable Stock, page 196

⅓ cup cream or additional water

Quarter the potatoes lengthwise and thinly slice. Grate the parsley roots. Melt the butter in a soup pot and add the potatoes, parsley roots, shallots, and bay leaves. Cook over medium heat for 5 to 7 minutes, stirring occasionally. Raise the heat, add the wine, and let it reduce until syrupy. Add 1½ cups of the parsley, 1½ teaspoons salt, and the water; bring to a boil. Lower the heat and simmer, partially covered, until the potatoes have broken apart, about 30 minutes. Stir in the cream and remaining parsley and heat through. Taste for salt and season with pepper. Remove the bay leaves and serve.

TIPS FOR USING POTATOES IN SOUP

- Starchy baking potatoes fall apart when boiled, whereas boiling potatoes or waxy varieties, such as Fingerlings, hold their shape. Most soup recipes call for boiling potatoes, but if you include a portion of baking potatoes they'll break down and serve as a natural thickener.

- Much flavor resides in potato skins, which is why they're often left on. But peeled potatoes give the soup a more refined appearance. You can use the skins in the stock, but use organic potatoes because you can't scrub off the chemical residues from conventionally grown ones.

- Greening in the skin and flesh naturally occurs in potatoes through exposure to light. Eating the green parts can make you nauseous, but don't throw out the whole potato—just peel as thickly as necessary to get below the green and use the rest.

- I find the quickest way to peel a potato is with a sharp paring knife rather than a peeler. Cut a slice off each end, then cradle the potato in your hand and remove the skins with five or six swift, long strokes of the knife, going from one end to the other. You'll end up with a nice-looking, quickly peeled potato. This is also true for turnips and rutabagas.

- Use a food mill to puree potato soup. A blender or food processor can turn it into a gummy mass unless used with a very light touch.

Bright Green Spinach and Pea Soup

2 tablespoons olive oil, butter, or a mixture

2 bunches scallions, including half of the greens, coarsely chopped

1 small onion, thinly sliced

3 carrots, thinly sliced

1 celery rib, thinly sliced

1 tablespoon chopped marjoram or basil or 1 teaspoon dried

Salt and freshly milled pepper

10 parsley sprigs, chopped

1 large bunch spinach, stems removed

1 cup peas, fresh or frozen

Lemon juice to taste

For garnish: crème fraîche, small toasted croutons, and calendula petals

BRIEF cooking preserves this utterly simple soup's vivid green. The color lasts only about 10 minutes, so organize yourself to serve the soup right away. Edible flowers, such as yellow calendula petals, would make a cheerful garnish.

SERVES 4 TO 6

Warm the oil in a soup pot and add the scallion, onion, carrots, celery, herbs, 1 teaspoon salt, and ½ cup water. Cover and stew for 5 minutes, then add 5½ cups water and bring to a boil. Lower the heat and simmer, uncovered, for 20 minutes. Add the spinach and peas. Poke the spinach leaves into the soup and cook until they turn bright green, 2 to 3 minutes. Remove from the heat and blend the soup in two batches until perfectly smooth. Taste for salt, season with pepper, and stir in enough lemon juice, starting with ½ teaspoon, to bring up the flavors. Serve immediately with a swirl of crème fraîche, the croutons, and the blossoms floating on top.

Summer Squash Soups

Summer squashes are unassertive, but you can encourage their strengths either by stewing them with seasonings or sautéing them over high heat until they brown a bit. Although a good basic stock provides depth, you can get away with water if your seasonings and garnishes are bright and fresh. Here's a good place to improvise with such finishing touches such as Sorrel Puree, as well as Pesto, Salsa Verde, Cilantro Salsa, herb butters, and herb salts—all in the sauce chapter. Although I've emphasized particular varieties, summer squashes are basically interchangeable.

Summer Squash Soup with Salsa Verde

SERVES 4 TO 6

2 tablespoons olive oil or butter

1¼ pounds zucchini, crookneck, or pattypan squash

1 large onion, chopped

1 bunch scallions, including half of the greens, chopped

2 tablespoons raw white rice

½ cup chopped parsley

6 cups Basic Vegetable Stock, page 196, or water

Salt and freshly milled pepper

Lemon juice

⅓ cup Salsa Verde, page 55

Heat the oil in a soup pot and add the vegetables, rice, and parsley. Stir to coat with the oil, then add ½ cup stock, cover, and stew for 10 minutes over medium heat. (Or heat the oil, add the squash and onion, and sauté over high heat until the squash begins to color, then add the scallions, rice, and parsley.) Add the remaining stock and 1½ teaspoons salt and bring to a boil. Lower the heat and simmer, partially covered, for 25 minutes. Let cool briefly, then puree. Taste for salt, season with pepper, and add lemon juice to taste. Finish the soup by swirling in the salsa verde or pesto.

Zucchini-Cilantro Soup A soup for cilantro lovers. Replace the parsley with 1 cup cilantro leaves. Puree the soup and finish with a squeeze of lime and a spoonful of sour cream.

Summer Squash Soup with Vegetable Garnishes In a small skillet, briefly sauté ½ cup finely diced zucchini, the kernels from 1 ear of corn, and 4 thinly sliced scallions, including an inch of the greens, in 1 teaspoon butter or olive oil. Garnish the soup with the vegetables and finely chopped herbs.

Curried Crookneck Soup Curry is especially good with crookneck squash. If you have time, make the Stock for Curried Dishes, page 197. Sauté the onion and squash in butter or vegetable oil over medium-high heat until they've begun to color, about 10 minutes, then add 1 tablespoon curry powder and proceed as described. Thin the soup if desired with coconut, rice, or almond milk and garnish with cilantro leaves and diced jalapeño.

Winter Squash and Pumpkin Soups

The squashes to use for these golden soups are small hubbards, butternut, and, best of all, any of the dark green–skinned varieties such as Honey Delight and Kabocha. For pumpkins, use those intended for cooking rather than carving. Except for butternut, winter squashes are difficult to peel, so they're halved and baked first—this can be done well in advance. Most winter squash soups don't require a stock, but a quick stock, using the scooped-out seeds, is so easy to make and so flavorful that I generally make one.

Winter Squash Soup with Fried Sage Leaves

2½ to 3 pounds winter squash

¼ cup olive oil, plus extra for the squash

6 garlic cloves, unpeeled

12 whole sage leaves, plus 2 tablespoons chopped

2 onions, finely chopped

Chopped leaves from 4 thyme sprigs or ¼ teaspoon dried

¼ cup chopped parsley

Salt and freshly milled pepper

2 quarts water or Quick Stock, page 196, made with 10 cups water

½ cup Fontina, pecorino, or ricotta salata, diced into small cubes

THE technique used to make this soup can be repeated for other soups, the seasonings—be they sweet or spicy—varied to suit your tastes. Although the soup is good without it, the cheese adds a flavor note that punctuates the natural sweetness of the squash. The Warm Crostini with Blue Cheese and Walnuts are also an excellent accompaniment.

SERVES 4 TO 6

Preheat the oven to 375°F. Halve the squash and scoop out the seeds. Brush the surfaces with oil, stuff the cavities with the garlic, and place them cut sides down on a baking sheet. Bake until tender when pressed with a finger, about 30 minutes.

Meanwhile, in a small skillet, heat the ¼ cup oil until nearly smoking, then drop in the whole sage leaves and fry until speckled and dark, about 1 minute. Set the leaves aside on a paper towel and transfer the oil to a wide soup pot. Add the onions, chopped sage, thyme, and parsley and cook over medium heat until the onions have begun to brown around the edges, 12 to 15 minutes. Scoop the squash flesh into the pot along with any juices that have accumulated in the pan. Peel the garlic and add it to the pot along with 1½ teaspoons salt and the water and bring to a boil. Lower the heat and simmer, partially covered, for 25 minutes. If the soup becomes too thick, simply add more water to thin it out. Taste for salt.

Depending on the type of squash you've used, the soup will be smooth or rough. Puree or pass it through a food mill if you want a more refined soup. Ladle it into bowls and distribute the cheese over the top. Garnish each bowl with the fried sage leaves, add pepper, and serve.

Roasted Butternut and Kabocha Squash

Winter Squash Soup with Lemongrass and Coconut Milk

DRIED *galangal looks like wood chips, but it imparts a delicious flavor to the stock. Butternut squash is easy to peel, so it's not prebaked.*

SERVES 4 TO 6

6 cups Stock for Curried Dishes, page 197

2½ pounds butternut squash, peeled and seeded

1 lemongrass stalk, the tender middle section minced

5 pieces galangal or 3 slices ginger

For garnish: 2 teaspoons *each* finely chopped mint, basil, and cilantro

1 tablespoon roasted peanut oil

1 large onion, diced

2 jalapeño chiles, seeded and diced

1 large garlic clove, crushed

1 cup unsweetened coconut or almond milk

Salt

Juice of 2 limes to taste

Include in the stock the squash skins and seeds, lemongrass trimmings, galangal, and any trimmings from the herb garnish.

Coarsely chop the squash. You should have about 4 cups. Heat the oil in a soup pot, then add the squash, onion, half the chiles, the minced lemongrass, and the garlic. Cook over medium heat for 10 minutes, stirring occasionally. Add the strained stock and bring it to a boil. Lower the heat and simmer, partially covered, until the squash is tender, about 30 minutes. Puree the soup, then return it to the stove and stir in the coconut milk. Taste for salt and add lime juice to sharpen the flavors. Serve garnished with the fresh herbs and the remaining chile.

Summer Tomato Soup

THIS *is the sheer essence of summer and tomato. All you need are shallots, butter, lots of ripe, red, juicy tomatoes, and a few unattended hours. The process is very similar to making fresh tomato sauce.*

SERVES 4 TO 6

3 tablespoons butter

1 cup diced shallots, 8 to 12

5 pounds ripe, red, juicy tomatoes, rinsed and cut into big pieces

Salt and freshly milled pepper

Melt the butter in a wide soup pot over low heat. Add the shallots and let them cook while you prepare the tomatoes. Add the tomatoes to the pot along with 1 teaspoon salt and ½ cup water. Cover and cook for 3 to 4 hours. Give the pot a stir every now and then as you pass through the kitchen to make sure the tomatoes aren't sticking, but if you've used juicy ones there should be plenty of liquid. Pass the tomatoes through a food mill into a clean pot. You should have about a quart of soup. Taste for salt and season with freshly milled pepper.

At this point you can do several things. You can serve small bowls of the soup just as it is, or you can add a few tablespoons to a cup of cream to make gorgeous cream of tomato soup. You can swirl in a tablespoon of butter flavored with shallots and dill, pesto, or basil puree. And if you long for texture in your soup, you can add a few delicate cubed croutons crisped in a little butter. This is also exquisite chilled, served with crème fraîche or diced avocado and lime juice.

Cream of Tomato Soup

2½ tablespoons butter

1 small onion, chopped

1 celery rib, chopped

1½ teaspoons dried basil, crumbled

Pinch ground cloves

2 tablespoons flour

2 15-ounce cans diced tomatoes in puree

Pinch baking soda

2½ cups Basic Vegetable Stock, page 196, or water

1½ cups milk, as needed

Salt and freshly milled pepper

Tomato paste if needed

AN American classic that's made with canned tomatoes. Use one of the good organic brands such as Muir Glen. This quick soup makes a fine pairing with a grilled cheese sandwich or crisp romaine salad.

SERVES 4

Melt the butter in a soup pot over medium heat. Add the onion, celery, basil, and cloves; cook, stirring occasionally, until the onion is limp, about 5 minutes. Stir in the flour, then add the tomatoes, baking soda, and stock; bring to a boil. Lower the heat and simmer, partially covered, for 20 minutes. Let cool briefly, then puree in a blender until smooth. Return the soup to the pot, add the milk, and season with salt. If the soup is too thick, thin it with additional milk or stock. If the tomato flavor isn't as rich as you'd like (if the tomatoes were packed in water instead of puree), deepen it by stirring in a little tomato paste. Reheat and serve piping hot with pepper ground into each bowl.

Fideos—A Mexican Dry Soup

4 to 5 cups Vegetable Stock for Mexican Soups and Stews, page 197, or Red Stock, page 197

2 ancho chiles, stems and seeds removed

2 tablespoons vegetable oil

8 ounces capellini, spaghettini, or skinny egg noodles, broken into 2- to 4-inch lengths

Salt and freshly milled pepper

⅓ cup crumbled feta cheese

⅓ to ⅔ cup grated Monterey Jack

½ cup sour cream or crème fraîche

⅓ cup chopped parsley or cilantro

THIS is too soupy to be pasta, too dry to be soup, and certainly too good to leave alone. A good supper or brunch dish—or even a side dish. Both of the suggested stocks are good. The Red Stock, however, has more body and deeper flavor.

SERVES 4 TO 6

Make either of the stocks. Simmer with the chiles for 15 minutes. Puree in a blender until smooth, then strain again.

Heat the oil in a wide skillet over medium heat. Add the noodles and cook, stirring constantly, until browned, 3 or 4 minutes. Remove them to paper towels.

Add 3½ cups of the stock to the skillet and bring to a boil. Add the noodles and simmer until most of the liquid has been absorbed and the noodles are cooked through, about 10 minutes. If they're still a little crunchy by the time the liquid is absorbed, spoon over another ¼ cup stock and continue cooking. Meanwhile, preheat the broiler.

Season the noodles with salt and pepper and sprinkle the cheeses over the top. Broil until the cheeses have melted. Stir the sour cream with a fork to loosen it, then drizzle it over the top. Sprinkle with parsley and serve.

Tortilla Soup

THIS brick-red broth with its cluster of garnishes is roundly flavorful, even without chicken stock. You do have to make a stock, but it's not a big deal— just your Basic Vegetable Stock plus a few extra ingredients. And although fresh tomatoes are standard, this makes a warming winter soup, and I've had great results using diced canned tomatoes.

SERVES 4

The Broth

6 cups Red Stock, page 197

2 to 3 tablespoons safflower oil

1½ onions, sliced into ½-inch rounds

4 large garlic cloves, unpeeled

2 jalapeño chiles

2 cups canned tomato sauce or 2½ pounds fresh Roma tomatoes

1 teaspoon pureed chipotle chile, or to taste

Salt

The Garnishes

2 pasilla chiles, stem and seeds removed

¼ cup chopped cilantro, plus whole leaves for garnish

1 avocado, diced

Tortilla Strips made from 8 corn tortillas, page 46

Crumbled queso fresco or feta cheese

1 lime, quartered

Start making the red stock. You can prepare everything else while the stock is simmering.

Preheat the broiler. Using about half of the oil, lightly oil the onions, garlic cloves, chiles, and fresh tomatoes. Put them on a sheet pan and broil 4 to 5 inches below the heat. When the onions brown, turn them over and brown the second side. Turn the chiles when they blister. Remove the garlic when browned, then peel. Turn the tomatoes several times so that the skins pucker and brown in places. Remove individual vegetables as they finish cooking. Puree everything in a blender until the sauce is as smooth as possible. (If using canned tomato sauce, puree them with the other vegetables plus an extra ½ cup water to thin the mixture.)

Heat the remaining oil in a wide soup pot over medium-high heat. Add the puree and cook, stirring, until it has thickened, about 5 minutes. Add the strained stock, then simmer, covered, for 25 minutes. Stir in the chipotle chile and taste for salt. At this point, strain the broth if you like a refined, thin soup. If you prefer it thicker and with a little texture as I do, leave it as is.

To toast the chiles, put them in a heavy skillet over medium heat. Press down for 30 seconds or so or until they're fragrant and begin to blister in places. Turn and repeat on the second side, but don't let them burn. When cool, tear or cut them into strips.

Just before serving, add the chile strips and chopped cilantro to the broth and cook for 1 minute. Ladle the broth into bowls and add the avocado, tortilla strips, and crumbled cheese. Garnish with cilantro leaves and serve with the lime wedges.

Turnip Soup with Gruyère Croutons

4 to 6 medium turnips, 1½ to 2 pounds, with their greens if available

3 small boiling potatoes

2 tablespoons butter

2 leeks, white parts only, thinly sliced

1 garlic clove, minced

¼ cup chopped parsley

4 thyme sprigs or ¼ teaspoon dried

Salt and freshly milled white pepper

6 cups water or Basic Vegetable Stock, page 196

½ cup cream or milk

Cheese Croutons, page 209, made with Gruyère cheese

TURNIPS are a hard sell, but they make one of the best soups I know. Take advantage of turnips with nice fresh greens the moment you see them. Their peppery bite offsets the natural sweetness of the roots. Broccoli rabe or mustard greens can easily take their place.

SERVES 4 TO 6

Peel the turnips and potatoes, quarter, and thinly slice them. Discard the stems and any yellowed leaves from the greens. Wash the remaining leaves well.

Melt the butter in a soup pot over medium heat. Add the turnips, potatoes, leeks, garlic, parsley, and thyme. Cook for about 5 minutes, then add 1½ teaspoons salt and the water and bring to a boil. Lower the heat and simmer, partially covered, until the vegetables are tender, about 25 minutes. Puree all or just part of the soup, depending on whether you like a smooth soup or one with some texture. Stir in the cream.

While the soup is cooking, chop the greens into small pieces. There should be about 2 cups, although more is fine. Simmer them in salted water until they're tender, then drain and add them to the finished soup. Taste for salt, season with pepper, and serve with two cheese croutons in each bowl or on the side.

ENSURING SWEETNESS

To ensure a good soup when using turnips that aren't at their peak, thickly peel them, slice them into rounds, and blanch for 1 minute in boiling salted water. Drain and rinse. This keeps them nice and sweet.

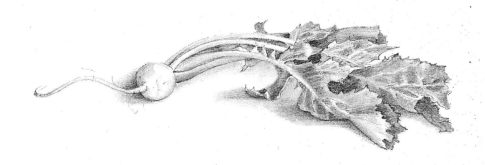

Winter Vegetable Chowder

THIS is a wonderful soup—light but sustaining and full of flavor. The milk is steeped with aromatics, and the vegetables are cooked in water. The whole thing is ladled over cheese-covered toast, which falls apart and thickens the soup. (To make a dairy-free version, use soy milk, cook the vegetables in olive oil, and omit the cheese or use soy-based cheese.)

SERVES 4 TO 6

The Milk

2 cups milk, preferably whole

3 large parsley branches

$^1/_2$ teaspoon dried thyme

2 bay leaves

$^1/_2$ onion, sliced

10 peppercorns, lightly crushed

5 juniper berries, lightly crushed

The Soup

2 tablespoons butter

2 large leeks, white parts plus an inch of the greens, chopped

4 cups chopped winter vegetables—turnips, carrots, celery or celery root, rutabagas, a little parsnip

3 boiling potatoes, about 12 ounces, peeled and diced

2 small bay leaves

2 tablespoons chopped parsley

Salt and freshly milled pepper

2 tablespoons flour

4 to 6 large slices sourdough or country-style bread, toasted

Grated Gruyère or Parmesan cheese

Chopped parsley, tarragon, or lovage

Put everything for the milk in a saucepan, bring it to a boil, then turn off the heat. Cover and set aside while you prepare the vegetables.

Melt the butter in a soup pot over low heat. Add the vegetables, bay leaves, parsley, and $1^1/_2$ teaspoons salt. Cover and cook for 10 minutes. Stir in the flour and add 5 cups water; bring to a boil. Lower the heat and simmer, partially covered, until the vegetables are tender, about 25 minutes. Pour the milk through a strainer right into the soup. Taste for salt and season with pepper. To serve, lay a piece of toast in each bowl, cover it with grated cheese, ladle the soup on top, and sprinkle with parsley.

MAKING SOUPS FROM LEFTOVERS

A cup of pureed vegetables or legumes can make a little soup for one or two people. Vegetable and bean purees, cooked dried beans, plus sautéed greens, roasted peppers, grilled corn, tomato sauce, a bit of pesto—all are good examples of the kinds of leftovers to pay attention to.

10-Minute Soup from Vegetable Puree

HERE'S an example of how to turn a simple vegetable puree into a soup in about 10 minutes.

SERVES 1 OR 2

2 teaspoons olive oil or butter

2 scallions, including some of the greens, thinly sliced

1 small potato, peeled, very thinly sliced, and chopped

Salt and freshly milled pepper

1 cup pureed vegetable, such as broccoli

Water or milk to thin the soup if needed

Warm the oil in a small saucepan, add the scallions and potato, season with a pinch of salt, and sauté over brisk heat, stirring constantly, for 2 minutes to sear the vegetables. Add 2 cups water, scrape the pan to dislodge any tasty bits of potatoes, and bring to a boil. Lower the heat and simmer, covered, until the potato is tender, 8 to 10 minutes. Stir in the puree and add water or milk to thin if needed. Heat through, taste for salt, season with pepper, and serve.

Soups Starring Beans and Grains

THESE solid citizens make especially nourishing, comforting, and filling soups—the perfect medium to persuade people to embrace beans and grains. Mixed with vegetables and aromatic seasonings, the plump tenderness of beans and the robust, chewy textures of grains are easily appreciated.

COMBINING GRAINS AND BEANS: We usually think of bean soups in terms of a single legume, such as black bean chili or lentil soup, but older culinary cultures often mix beans or beans and grains within a single soup. Their contrasting shapes and textures make them much more interesting to eat. Having some cooked beans in the freezer and drawing on canned chickpeas and quick-cooking lentils makes combining beans and grains easy. Since rice, bulgur, and other grains can cook right in the soup, you may have only one legume to cook separately from scratch.

USING THE PRESSURE COOKER: These recipes can easily be adapted to cooking under pressure. A pressure cooker cooks unsoaked beans and large grains in about a third of the time it takes to simmer them. There are two basic approaches. One is to cook the beans, along with aromatics and a few teaspoons of oil (to prevent skins from clogging the gauge), in the pressure cooker while you cut the soup vegetables. Then, when the beans are done, add them and their broth to the vegetables. The second approach is to begin sautéing the vegetables in the pressure cooker pot, then add the beans and liquid and cook the entire soup under pressure. If the soup contains an element that should be fresh, like a garnish of diced tomato, add it once the soup is cooked.

One word of caution: Cooking time for beans is affected by the age of the bean and the hardness of the water. Start with the given time, then release the pressure and check. If the beans are still hard, put the lid back on and return the pot to pressure—it will go up quickly—then cook for another 5 minutes and check again.

BEANS FROM SCRATCH

There are three advantages to cooking your own beans: by the time they're done they're surrounded with a broth that serves as the stock; you can use the exciting heirloom varieties that can't be bought canned; and home-cooked beans taste better and aren't mushy. Canned beans, of course, don't require thinking ahead, and there are times when they can nicely round out a vegetable soup. (The organic brands, such as Eden Foods, are quite good.) While beans take time to cook, the time is unattended for the most part. And with a pressure cooker it's possible to have soup beans—and broth—in only 15 to 30 minutes.

Pinto Bean Soup

PINTO *beans are delicious plain or lavishly garnished. Plain, these are the beans to use for refried beans. Many cooks prefer using the pressure cooker to produce silky smooth beans.*

SERVES 6 TO 8

2 cups pinto beans, soaked for 4 hours or overnight

1 small onion, finely diced

3 garlic cloves, minced

1 teaspoon dried oregano, preferably Mexican

2 teaspoons dried or fresh epazote

Salt

For garnish: slivered scallions or finely diced white onion, diced jalapeño chile, chopped cilantro or mint, sour cream, Tortilla Strips, page 46

Drain the beans, cover them with 2 quarts water, and boil for 10 minutes. Add the onion, garlic, oregano, and epazote. Lower the heat and simmer, partially covered, until the beans are tender, about 1½ hours. Season with salt and serve plain, with the broth, or with two or three of the garnishes. If using a pressure cooker, cook everything together on high for 25 minutes, then release.

Smooth Pinto Bean Soup with Chile, Pine Nuts, and Mint Puree the cooked beans with their broth until smooth and return them to the pot. Thin, if needed, with 1 cup milk or cream and stir in chipotle chile, ground or in adobo sauce, to taste, starting with a teaspoon. Taste for salt. Serve garnished with snipped chives, chopped mint, and toasted pine nuts.

Pinto or Anasazi Bean Soup with Roasted Tomatoes and Garlic Make the soup using pinto or anasazi beans. Puree a portion of the beans and return them to the pot. Make the Grilled Tomato Sauce with Garlic, page 63, including frying it at the end, as described. Stir this into the beans and reheat. Garnish each bowl with a dollop of sour cream or grated Muenster, if desired, and serve with tortillas.

TIPS FOR MAKING BEAN SOUPS

CLEANING: Always sort through beans and lentils and remove any little stones, clumps of earth, chaff, and so on. Even a tiny stone can crack a tooth.

SOAKING: When you're not using a pressure cooker, soaking the beans shortens the cooking time considerably. Soak them from 4 hours to overnight, or cover them with cold water, bring it to a boil, then turn off the heat and soak for 1 hour. In very hot weather, put soaking beans in the refrigerator.

COOKING: After draining the beans, cover with plenty of fresh water and bring to a boil. During the first 10 minutes a scum may form on the surface. Simply skim it off.

SALTING: Don't add salt or acid until the beans have already begun to soften. (Lentils and split peas needn't be soaked, and salt can be added at the beginning.)

PUREEING: To give bean soups a thicker consistency, puree all or just a portion of the beans.

GARNISHING: Croutons, extra virgin olive oil, herb and olive purees, and herb butters are all excellent garnishes for bean soups. Cooked pasta adds texture and interest, as do greens of all kinds.

STORING: Beans sour more quickly than other foods, but a bean soup will keep 4 to 6 days in the refrigerator. To reheat, bring the soup to a full boil. Give it a sniff. If it's spoiled, you'll notice the slightly sour scent of fermentation.

ADDING GRAINS: Wheat berries and other large grains take about 2 hours to cook on top of the stove or 30 minutes in the pressure cooker. Brown rice, wehani, and wild rice take 35 to 45 minutes on the stove. Tiny grains, like amaranth and quinoa, cook in only 15 to 20 minutes and can be cooked directly in the soup.

Barley Soup with Caramelized Onions and Pecorino Cheese

1/4 cup olive oil

3 onions, cut into in 1/2-inch dice

2 quarts Basic Vegetable Stock, page 196, and water

1/2 ounce dried porcini mushrooms, about 1/2 cup

2 tablespoons tomato paste

1 tablespoon minced rosemary or 2 teaspoons dried

1 cup pearl barley, rinsed

1 cup diced celery or celery root

2 carrots, diced

Salt and freshly milled pepper

1/2 cup grated pecorino cheese

PECORINO cheese sets off the sweetness of the onions in this soup. Since it takes a while to brown the onions, you can easily assemble the stock while they're cooking.

SERVES 4 TO 6

Warm the oil in a heavy soup pot. Add the onions, cover, and cook over low heat for 40 minutes. Remove the lid, raise the heat to medium, and cook, stirring frequently, until the onions are browned. While the onions are cooking, make the stock and include the dried porcini. Retrieve them when the stock is done and chop.

Once the onions are browned, add the tomato paste and rosemary and cook for a few minutes more, working the paste into the onions. Add the barley, vegetables, chopped porcini, and strained stock; bring to a boil. Lower the heat and simmer, partially covered, until the barley and vegetables are done, about 25 minutes. Taste for salt, season with freshly milled pepper, and serve with cheese grated over the top.

Beet Soup with Three Legumes

1/2 cup red kidney beans, soaked for 4 hours or overnight

4 medium beets, peeled and diced

1/3 cup brown or green lentils

1 cup cooked chickpeas

2 cups chopped beet greens or chard

Salt and freshly milled pepper

1 bunch scallions, including half of the greens, chopped

2 cups coarsely chopped spinach

1 small bunch parsley, finely chopped

The Garnish

3 tablespoons butter, preferably clarified

1 onion, cut into 1/2-inch squares

1/4 teaspoon turmeric

1/4 teaspoon cayenne

1/4 cup chopped mint

1/2 cup yogurt

THIS soup brings lentils, chickpeas, and beans together in one pot—along with beets. Unlike in most soups, the aromatics are added at the end, breaking the clean surface with a net of golden speckles.

SERVES 6 TO 8

Drain the beans, cover them with 5 cups water, and boil hard for 10 minutes. Lower the heat and simmer, partially covered, until soft, about 1 1/4 hours. Set aside.

Put the beets, lentils, and 7 cups water in a soup pot. Bring to a boil. Lower the heat and simmer, partially covered, for 25 minutes. Add the kidney beans with 2 cups of their liquid, the chickpeas, beet greens, and 2 teaspoons salt; simmer until the greens are tender, about 5 minutes. Add the scallions, spinach, and parsley; cook until the spinach is wilted and bright green. Taste for salt and turn off the heat.

For the garnish, melt the butter in a small skillet over low heat. Add the onion, turmeric, cayenne, and mint; cook until the onion is soft, about 15 minutes, stirring occasionally. Ladle the soup into bowls. Add a spoonful of garnish and yogurt to each serving.

Lentil Soups

Savored over a large part of the world, lentil soups are one of the best-liked, easiest-to-cook, and most varied of soups. The earthy flavor of lentils is complemented by Indian spices, Western herbs, cream, tomato, greens, and anything slightly tart, such as sorrel or lemon.

German brown lentils are the ones we see most commonly, and they make good soups. But the tiny French slate-green Le Puy lentils, available at specialty stores and in bulk at many natural food stores, make the prettiest and most delicious soups. They're entirely worth the slight extra cost, and in my kitchen they are the lentil of choice. Indian red split lentils turn yellow when cooked and fall into a puree, as do other split lentils, which makes them ideal for smooth lentil soups.

Lentils don't need to be soaked, but they do need to be picked over for tiny stones. They cook in just 25 minutes, and salt should be added at the beginning. Like most bean soups, lentil soups taste better a day after they're made.

Hearty Lentil Soup

MUSTARD and vinegar sharpen the flavors in this robust soup.

SERVES 4 TO 6

2 tablespoons olive oil

2 cups finely diced onion

3 large garlic cloves

Salt and freshly milled pepper

3 tablespoons tomato paste

1/3 cup finely diced celery

1/3 cup finely diced carrot

2 bay leaves

1/2 cup chopped parsley

1 1/2 cups French green or brown lentils, sorted and rinsed

1 tablespoon Dijon mustard

1 tablespoon sherry vinegar or red wine vinegar

Chopped celery leaves and parsley

Heat the oil in a soup pot over high heat. Add the onion and sauté until it begins to color around the edges, 5 to 7 minutes. Meanwhile, mince or pound the garlic in a mortar with 1 teaspoon salt. Work the tomato paste into the onion, then add the garlic, celery, carrot, bay leaves, and parsley and cook for 3 minutes. Add the lentils, 2 quarts water, and 1/2 teaspoon salt and bring to a boil. Lower the heat and simmer, partially covered, until the lentils are tender, 25 to 35 minutes.

Stir in the mustard and vinegar. Taste and add more of either as needed. Check the salt, season with plenty of pepper, remove the bay leaves, and serve, garnished with the celery leaves and parsley. The longer the soup sits before serving, the better it will taste.

Cream of Lentil Soup with Croutons Cook until the lentils are soft and mushy, an extra 10 minutes or so. Remove the bay leaves, puree the soup, then pass it through a food mill. Return to the stove and stir in enough milk or cream to thin it to the desired consistency. Serve garnished with chopped celery leaves and small croutons crisped in olive oil or butter.

Lentil Minestrone

2 tablespoons olive oil, plus extra virgin to finish

2 cups finely chopped onion

2 tablespoons tomato paste

¼ cup chopped parsley

4 garlic cloves, chopped

3 carrots, diced

1 cup diced celery or celery root

Salt and freshly milled pepper

1 cup French green lentils, sorted and rinsed

Aromatics: 2 bay leaves, 8 parsley branches, 6 thyme sprigs

9 cups water or Basic Vegetable Stock, page 196

Mushroom soy sauce to taste

1 bunch greens—mustard, broccoli rabe, chard, or spinach

2 cups cooked small pasta—shells, orecchiette, or other favorite shape

Thin shavings of Parmesan, preferably Parmigiano-Reggiano

THIS is one of my all-time favorite soups. It's better when cooked ahead of time, but add the cooked pasta and greens just before serving so that they retain their color and texture.

SERVES 4 TO 6

Heat the oil in a wide soup pot with the onion. Sauté over high heat, stirring frequently, until lightly browned, about 10 minutes. Add the tomato paste, parsley, garlic, vegetables, and 2 teaspoons salt and cook 3 minutes more. Add the lentils, aromatics, and water and bring to a boil. Lower the heat and simmer, partially covered, for 30 minutes. Taste for salt and season with pepper. If it needs more depth, add mushroom soy sauce to taste, starting with 1 tablespoon. (The soup may seem bland at this point, but the flavors will come together when the soup is finished.) Remove the aromatics.

Boil the greens in salted water until they're tender and bright green, then chop them coarsely. Just before serving, add the greens and the pasta to the soup and heat through. Serve with extra virgin olive oil drizzled into each bowl, a generous grind of pepper, and the Parmesan.

Red Lentil Soup with Lime

2 cups split red lentils, picked over and rinsed several times

1 tablespoon turmeric

4 tablespoons butter

Salt

1 large onion, finely diced, about 2 cups

2 teaspoons ground cumin

1½ teaspoons mustard seeds or 1 teaspoon ground mustard

1 bunch chopped cilantro, about 1 cup

Juice of 3 limes or to taste

1 large bunch spinach leaves, chopped into small pieces

1 cup cooked rice

4 to 6 tablespoons yogurt

Put the lentils in a soup pot with 2½ quarts water, the turmeric, 1 tablespoon of the butter, and 1 tablespoon salt. Bring to a boil, then lower the heat and simmer, covered, until the lentils are soft and falling apart, about 20 minutes. Puree for a smooth and nicer-looking soup. (An immersion blender is a great plus here.)

While the soup is cooking, prepare the onion flavoring: In a medium skillet over low heat, cook the onion in 2 tablespoons of the remaining butter with the cumin and mustard, stirring occasionally. When soft, about the time the lentils are cooked or after 15 minutes, add the cilantro and cook for a minute more. Add the onion mixture to the soup, then add the juice of 2 limes. Taste, then add more if needed to bring up the flavors. The soup should be a tad sour.

Just before serving, add the last tablespoon of butter to a wide skillet. When foamy, add the spinach, sprinkle with salt, and cook just long enough to wilt. If the rice is warm, place a spoonful in each bowl. If it's leftover rice, add it to the soup and let it heat through for a minute. Serve the soup, divide the spinach among the bowls, and swirl in a spoonful of yogurt.

Split Pea Soup

1½ cups split green peas, sorted and rinsed

2 tablespoons olive oil

1 large onion, diced

2 carrots, diced

2 large garlic cloves, chopped

¼ cup chopped parsley

1 teaspoon dried marjoram

1 teaspoon fresh or dried chopped rosemary

1 teaspoon paprika

Salt and freshly milled pepper

Aromatics: 2 bay leaves, 8 parsley branches, 6 thyme sprigs

2 quarts Basic Vegetable Stock, page 196, or water

Mushroom soy sauce

Chopped parsley, marjoram, or rosemary

½ cup small croutons browned in olive oil

NOTHING is as comforting in cold weather as a hearty split pea soup. It needn't be thick enough to support the proverbial spoon—in fact it's much better when it's not.

SERVES 4 TO 6

Cover the peas with water and set aside.

Heat the oil in a soup pot over medium heat. Add the onion and carrots and sauté until the onion takes on some color, about 10 minutes. Add the garlic, parsley, herbs, paprika, and plenty of pepper and cook for another few minutes. Drain the peas and add them to the pot along with the aromatics, 1½ teaspoons salt, and the stock. Stir frequently at first to keep the peas from settling to the bottom. Once the soup comes to a boil, lower the heat and simmer, partially covered, until the peas have completely broken down, 1 hour or more. Add extra water if the soup becomes too thick. Remove the aromatics.

Season to taste with soy sauce and/or extra salt as needed. Serve with the chopped parsley and croutons in each bowl.

Split Pea Soup with Spinach or Sorrel Spinach and sorrel add a fresh note. Remove the stems from 1 small bunch of spinach or 4 handfuls of sorrel and cut the leaves into ½-inch ribbons. Roughly chop them so they won't be too long. Stir the greens into the finished soup and cook until wilted.

Cream of Split Pea Soup Both recipes that precede are good creamed. Remove the bay leaves from the finished soup and puree until smooth. Return it to the pot, add 1 cup half-and-half or milk, and heat through. Serve with croutons and chopped parsley mixed with a little minced rosemary.

A Summer Bean and Vegetable Soup with Pesto

ON the first day this Niçoise minestrone is light and brothy, but a day later it's thick and substantial. If you can find fresh shelling beans, use two or three times as many in place of the dried since they don't swell.

SERVES 8 TO 10

1 cup cannellini or other white beans, soaked for 4 hours

Aromatics: 2 bay leaves, 8 parsley sprigs, 4 sprigs of thyme

5 large garlic cloves, 2 sliced, 3 minced

3 tablespoons olive oil

Salt and freshly milled pepper

3 small leeks, white parts plus an inch of the greens, chopped

2 pinches saffron threads

3 carrots, peeled and diced

3 waxy yellow boiling potatoes, chopped

2 turnips, peeled and chopped

3 zucchini, sliced into 1/2-inch rounds or chunks

12 ounces green beans, tipped, tailed, and cut into 1-inch lengths

2 large ripe tomatoes, peeled, seeded, and diced

Pesto or Basil Puree, pages 57 and 507

Rinse the beans, put them in a pot with 3 quarts water, and boil hard for 10 minutes. Add the aromatics, sliced garlic, and 1 teaspoon of the oil. Lower the heat and simmer, partially covered, for 45 minutes. Add 2 teaspoons salt and cook until the beans are tender, 15 to 30 minutes more. Strain the broth, measure, and add water to make 10 cups.

Warm the remaining oil in a soup pot over medium heat. Add the leeks and saffron threads and cook until the leeks look glossy and translucent and the saffron begins to release its aroma, about 10 minutes. Add the vegetables and minced garlic. Cook just to soften the vegetables, 4 to 5 minutes, then add the reserved bean broth and 1 teaspoon salt. Bring to a boil, lower the heat, and simmer until the vegetables are tender, about 30 minutes. Add the beans and taste for salt and season with pepper. Ladle the soup into bowls and stir a spoonful of pesto into each serving.

Flageolet Bean and Leek Soup

THE elegant pale green flageolet bean makes a refined soup. The beans are cooked in stock, so make that first.

SERVES 4 TO 6

1 1/2 cups dried flageolet beans, soaked

3 tablespoons butter

4 medium leeks, including an inch of the greens, chopped

Aromatics: 2 bay leaves, 6 parsley branches, 4 sprigs of thyme

6 cups Basic Vegetable Stock, page 196, or water

Salt and freshly milled white pepper

2 to 3 tablespoons crème fraîche or cream

1/3 cup dry white wine

Chopped tarragon or chervil

Drain the beans. Melt 2 tablespoons of the butter in a soup pot over medium heat. Add two-thirds of the leeks, the aromatics, and 1/2 cup of the stock and stew covered for 5 minutes. Add the beans and the rest of the stock and bring to a boil. Lower the heat and simmer, partially covered, for 45 minutes. Add 1 teaspoon salt and continue cooking until the beans are completely tender, another 15 to 30 minutes. Remove the aromatics, puree 1/2 cup of the beans in some of the broth, then stir the puree back into the soup. Stir in the crème fraîche. Taste the soup for salt.

Melt the rest of the butter in a small skillet and add the remaining leeks and the wine. Stew covered over medium heat until tender, about 15 minutes. Season with salt and white pepper. Ladle the soup into soup plates, add a spoonful of leeks to each bowl, and garnish with the tarragon.

White Bean Soup with Pasta and Rosemary Oil

The Rosemary Oil

1/3 cup extra virgin olive oil

2 tablespoons finely chopped rosemary or 2 tablespoons dried

2 garlic cloves, sliced

The Soup

2 cups cannellini, navy beans, or a mixture

2 tablespoons olive oil

1 tablespoon chopped rosemary or 2 teaspoons dried

1 onion, finely diced

2 carrots, finely diced

1 celery rib, finely diced

5 garlic cloves, sliced

1/3 cup chopped parsley

1 cup diced tomatoes, fresh or canned, with their juices

Salt and freshly milled pepper

1 cup dried small pasta—shells, lumache, or other favorite shape

Thin shavings or freshly grated Parmesan

ROSEMARY-SCENTED oil adds an herbal essence to this soup. Make it first and set it aside to steep while you make the soup. I rather like this made with a variety of white beans so that a single bowl contains beans of different sizes.

SERVES 8 TO 10

Slowly warm the extra virgin olive oil with 2 tablespoons rosemary and 2 garlic cloves until the garlic begins to color, about 3 minutes. Turn off the heat and set aside until needed.

Cover the beans with boiling water and set aside while you prepare the rest of the ingredients.

Heat the oil with 1 tablespoon rosemary in a soup pot over medium heat. Add the onion, carrots, and celery and cook until the onion is softened and starting to color in places, about 10 minutes. Stir in the garlic and parsley and cook for a few minutes more. Drain the beans and add them to the pot along with the tomatoes and 3 quarts water. Bring to a boil, lower the heat, then simmer, covered, until the beans have begun to soften, about 1 hour. Add 2 teaspoons salt and continue cooking until the beans are completely tender, another 30 minutes or so.

Puree half the soup to give it some body—or leave it thin. (For a thicker smooth soup, puree all of it.)

Cook the pasta in boiling salted water, then drain. Strain the rosemary oil. Ladle the soup into bowls and add some pasta to each. Drizzle some of the oil over each bowl and add pepper to taste. Cover with thin shavings of Parmesan.

White Bean and Pasta Soup with Sage Sage is another fine herb with white beans. Replace the rosemary with 2 tablespoons chopped sage or 1 tablespoon dried and add ¼ teaspoon red pepper flakes. For garnish, fry 12 fresh sage leaves in ¼ cup olive oil until they darken. Serve them floating on the soup and the remaining oil drizzled over the top.

White Bean and Pasta Soup with Greens Remove and discard the stems from 1 bunch of chard, spinach, mustard greens, or kale. Coarsely chop the leaves and sauté in a little olive oil with a little chopped garlic and a pinch of red pepper flakes until tender. Add a little water to the pan if it's dry and the greens aren't done. Times will vary, so taste them. Season with salt and stir into the soup just before serving.

Quinoa Chowder with Spinach, Feta, and Scallions

LIGHT, utterly delicious, pretty, and fresh looking, this recipe stems from one in Chef Felipe Rojas-Lombardi's book, The Art of South American Cooking, *that I was drawn to because I simply couldn't imagine it. Now, one of my favorite dishes in any category, it makes a quick, wholesome meal.*

SERVES 4

¾ cup quinoa, rinsed well in a fine sieve

2 tablespoons olive oil

1 garlic clove, finely chopped

1 jalapeño chile, seeded and finely diced

1 teaspoon ground cumin or to taste

Salt and freshly milled pepper

½ pound boiling potatoes, peeled and cut into ¼-inch cubes

1 bunch scallions, including an inch of the greens, thinly sliced into rounds

3 cups finely sliced spinach leaves

¼ pound feta cheese, finely diced

⅓ cup chopped cilantro

1 hard-cooked egg, chopped

Put the quinoa and 2 quarts water in a pot, bring to a boil, then lower the heat and simmer for 10 minutes. While it's cooking, dice the vegetables and cheese. Drain, saving the liquid. Measure the liquid and add water to make 6 cups if needed.

Heat the oil in a soup pot over medium heat. Add the garlic and chile. Cook for about 30 seconds, giving it a quick stir. Add the cumin, 1 teaspoon salt, and the potatoes and cook for a few minutes, stirring frequently. Don't let the garlic brown. Add the quinoa water and half the scallions and simmer until the potatoes are tender, about 15 minutes. Add the quinoa, spinach, and remaining scallions and simmer for 3 minutes more. Turn off the heat and stir in the feta and cilantro. Season the soup with pepper and garnish with the chopped egg.

Black Bean Soup

1½ cups black beans, soaked

2 tablespoons butter or vegetable oil

1 cup finely diced onion

⅓ cup diced celery

⅓ cup diced carrot

1 cup diced green bell pepper

2 bay leaves

2 teaspoons chopped rosemary

1 teaspoon dried thyme

1 tablespoon tomato paste

Salt

½ cup Madeira

½ cup cream or milk

Chopped parsley

AFTER putting chiles in black bean soups for a decade or more, we've forgotten how good these beans are when cooked in a more traditional American style. Although it's simple, you'll find this soup lacks no flavor.

SERVES 4 TO 6

Drain the beans. Melt the butter in a soup pot, add the vegetables and herbs, and cook over medium-high heat for 5 to 7 minutes, until lightly colored. Stir in the tomato paste and cook for 1 minute more, mushing it around in the pan. Add the beans and 2½ quarts water and bring to a boil. Lower the heat and simmer, partially covered, for 1 hour. Add 2 teaspoons salt and continue cooking until the beans are quite soft, another 15 to 30 minutes. Pull out the bay leaves and puree about two-thirds of the soup. Return it to the pot, add the Madeira and cream, and simmer for 5 minutes more. Serve garnished with a little chopped parsley sprinkled over each bowl.

Miso Soup

If you frequent Japanese restaurants, you've certainly begun many a meal with a bowl of cloudy broth garnished exquisitely with tiny cubes of tofu, seaweed, and vegetables. Miso, the basis of this broth, is a paste derived from soybeans and sometimes grains, yet it's nothing like most of the beans and grains we eat. Light yet sustaining, miso soup is inexpensive, essentially instant, noncaloric, and well worth looking into.

The making of miso soup is a valued part of daily life in Japan, where tradition surrounds the various ways of combining the garnishes and different miso varieties according to the seasons. Following are a few basic recipes for kombu stocks, miso soups, and suggestions for garnishes. There are many kinds of miso, and they can be used singly or in blends. The most widely available ones are used here, but try some of the more unusual varieties, such as barley-ginger miso, available at Japanese markets and some natural food stores.

Boiling changes miso's flavor and destroys some of its nutritional value. After adding the diluted miso to the water or broth, heat it only to the simmering point, then serve. Miso soup is made to be eaten at once.

Simple Kombu Stock

KOMBU, a type of kelp, is filled with trace minerals. It comes in long sheets or strips, but only a small piece is used at a time.

MAKES ABOUT 1 QUART

1 4- to 6-inch strip dried kombu

Dash soy sauce

Place 4½ cups water and the kombu in a pot. Cover and simmer for 20 minutes, then add a little soy sauce for flavor.

Kombu Stock with Dried Mushrooms

IT'S hard to get the particular flavor that dried bonito gives to a Japanese stock, but this stock does add greatly to miso soups. You may have to fiddle with the balance, adjusting the saltiness of the soy with the sweetness of the mirin since soy sauces vary. Refrigerated, this will keep for a week.

MAKES 6 CUPS

6 dried Chinese black or shiitake mushrooms

1 bunch scallions, including most of the greens, chopped

1 carrot, thinly sliced

1 4- to 6-inch strip dried kombu

¼ cup soy sauce

2 teaspoons dark sesame oil

2 tablespoons rice wine (mirin)

Salt and sugar to taste

Shake the mushrooms in a strainer to loosen any dirt, then put them in a pot along with 7 cups water and the rest of the ingredients except the salt and sugar. Bring to a boil, then lower the heat and simmer, covered, for 20 minutes. Taste and add a pinch of salt and/or sugar to bring up the flavors. Adjust the balance of soy sauce to mirin if needed. Strain the stock, but retrieve the mushrooms to use in a soup.

Basic Miso Soup

YOU'LL find through experience how much miso is right for you. Usually 2 to 3 teaspoons is plenty for a cup, but it depends on the type of miso. This simplest of miso soups makes an instant pick-me-up.

SERVES 1

2 to 3 teaspoons white or red miso to taste

1 cup boiling water or one of the kombu stocks

Few drops dark sesame oil or chili oil

For garnish: sliced mushroom, slivered scallion, or chopped cilantro, if desired

Put the miso in a cup, add a few tablespoons of the water, and work it into the miso, diluting it to a thick cream. Add the rest of the water, then pour the soup into a bowl or mug. Add a few drops sesame oil, any of the garnishes—or none—and sip.

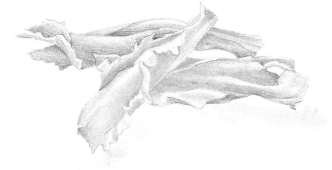

Miso-Tofu Soup with Wakame

8 leaves dried wakame "leaves" or dulse sprigs

4 cups of either kombu stock on page 232, or water

3 tablespoons red or barley miso or a mixture of red with a lighter miso

½ cup finely diced silken tofu, soft or firm

3 scallions, including a little of the greens, thinly sliced

Few drops chili oil

WAKAME is a delicate, leafy sea vegetable that is easy to find at Japanese markets and natural food stores. Dulse, a red seaweed, needs no presoaking and can be used with or in place of wakame—just a sprig per bowl.

SERVES 4

Soak the wakame in lukewarm water until soft, about 15 minutes. Feel for any tough parts and cut them away—there's usually a kind of core. Tear the rest into smaller pieces or slice into thin ribbons. Bring the stock to a boil.

Dilute the miso with 1 cup of the stock. Add the wakame and tofu to the remaining stock and simmer until the tofu has risen to the surface, 4 to 5 minutes. Stir the diluted miso back into the pot and bring nearly to a boil. Add the scallions and chili oil and serve.

MORE GARNISHES FOR MISO SOUPS

The simplest garnishes—a drop of dark roasted sesame oil, the wavy fronds of seaweeds, the translucent rings of a scallion—lend beauty, flavor, and nuance to miso soups. Hard vegetables should be precooked briefly in boiling salted water so that they're tender and bright when added to the soup.

Asparagus, sliced diagonally and blanched

Avocado, thinly sliced

Napa cabbage, thinly sliced

Small watercress sprigs

Spinach leaves, whole if small, thinly sliced if large

Bean sprouts: mung bean, sunflower, and other substantial sprouts

Sweet potatoes, peeled, cubed, and steamed

Fresh mushrooms, thinly sliced

Dried shiitake mushrooms, retrieved from the kombu stock, caps thinly sliced

Snow peas, whole or cut into julienne strips

Carrot, thinly sliced on a diagonal or cut into fine julienne strips

Fried tofu (aburage), thinly sliced

Few drops sake

Cold Soups for Hot Days

OFTEN *smooth and always light, cold soups make a refreshing first course or light meal, a quick pick-me-up, and in the case of fruit soups, a divine summer dessert. Since their flavor improves with time, they're good soups to make in quantity and have on hand during the hot days of summer and fall. A number of soups are made specifically to be eaten cold, such as yogurt soups, avocado soups, and fruit soups; but others—beet, carrot, and chard soups—can be enjoyed either way.*

Avocado-Tomatillo Soup with Lime

TART *tomatillos add a spark to the creamy avocado, which is otherwise too rich and creamy to eat without immediate satiation.*

SERVES 4 TO 6

2 bunches scallions, including most of the greens

1 green bell pepper

2 tablespoons avocado or sunflower seed oil

12 ounces tomatillos, husked and rinsed

1 celery rib, chopped

1 scant tablespoon chopped ginger

2 tablespoons chopped parsley

2 tablespoons chopped mint

2 jalapeño chiles, seeded and diced

1 quart Basic Vegetable Stock, page 196, or water

Salt

2 large avocados

1/2 cup buttermilk or sour cream

For garnish: 2 teaspoons chopped mint and juice of 1 lime

Set aside a few scallions and a quarter of the pepper, then coarsely chop the remainder. Heat the oil in a soup pot and add the tomatillos. Sauté over high heat until they color, about 5 minutes, then add the chopped vegetables, ginger, herbs, and half the chiles. Cook, stirring frequently, until the tomatillos are browned in places, about 10 minutes. Add the stock and 1 teaspoon salt and bring to a boil. Lower the heat and simmer, partially covered, until the tomatillos fall apart, 15 to 20 minutes. Let cool, then puree with the avocados and buttermilk. Chill well. Taste for salt.

Finely dice the reserved scallion and pepper and mix them with the mint, lime juice, a pinch of salt, and the remaining chile. Serve a spoonful scattered over each bowl.

TIPS FOR MAKING COLD SOUPS

- Make a soup early in the day or the day before to allow plenty of time for flavors to mature and for the soup to get good and cold.

- Since cold dulls flavor, the seasonings need to be stronger than the same soup served warm. Always taste a cold soup just before serving to see if it needs a little lemon, salt, or a fresh herb garnish to bring up the flavor.

- To make smooth-textured soups interesting to eat, include some garnish of substance, such as finely diced vegetables and fruits or a salsa.

- Sweet fruit soups are best served as a dessert or over ice as a beverage. Their sweetness can dull the appetite for what's to follow. On the other hand, a sweet soup may be just the thing for a hot day.

Cold Beet Soup

Beet Soup, page 203, made without the
  greens, chilled
Apple cider vinegar or lemon juice

Yogurt or sour cream
Diced cucumber
Snipped dill

ONE *of my grandmother's summer soups, it looks like a raspberry frappé if you whip the soup and yogurt in a blender, then serve it in a tall glass.*

SERVES 4 TO 6

You can leave the beet soup as it is, with its ruby broth and chopped beets, or puree until smooth. In either case, taste it and bring up the flavors with vinegar to taste. Beat the yogurt with a spoon to smooth it out. Ladle the soup into bowls and swirl the yogurt over the top. Add diced cucumber and a shower of dill and serve.

Cold Tomato Soup

4 pounds vine-ripened tomatoes, peeled
  and seeded, juice reserved
Salt and freshly milled pepper
Sugar and/or sherry vinegar

Extra virgin olive oil or sour cream to
  finish
Chopped basil or marjoram
2 scallions, including a few of the
  greens, thinly sliced

THIS soup should be a staple in everyone's August kitchen. It requires only ripe, juicy tomatoes and time in the refrigerator (or good canned tomato juice when fresh tomatoes are lacking). So many flavors flatter tomatoes, this soup is easy to tailor to whatever else you happen to be serving—and to a multitude of garnishes.

SERVES 4 TO 6

Finely chop the tomatoes by hand until they're very fine, almost like a puree. (You can use a blender, but it introduces so much air that the tomatoes turn frothy and pink.) Put the tomatoes in a bowl and add the reserved juice and 2 teaspoons salt. Cover and chill well. Taste and add more salt if needed. If the tomatoes are very tart, add 1 teaspoon sugar and a few drops vinegar to balance the flavors. Taste and continue adjusting until you have it the way you like.

Ladle the soup into bowls and thread a spoonful of olive oil over the top of each. Add pepper and garnish with the basil and scallions.

Cold Tomato Soup with Avocado and Lime Season the soup with lime juice instead of vinegar and garnish with diced avocado, chopped cilantro, and finely diced white onion. Fragrant Mexican marigolds make a stunning aromatic garnish if you have them.

Cold Tomato Soup with Little Garnishes (Gazpacho) Your guests can finish their own soup when presented with little bowls of garnishes set on a tray, as in Spain. Include white onion or scallion, green pepper, cucumber, hard-cooked egg, and tiny croutons crisped in olive oil. Finely dice everything and arrange in mounds or set in individual dishes.

Additional Seasonings Try lightly whipped cream flavored with minced herbs, curry-flavored oil, lemon zest chopped with garlic and parsley or lovage leaves, ribbons of opal basil, cooked rice, or additional diced tomatoes. Almost all of the vinaigrettes and dressings make excellent seasonings for this hospitable soup.

CONVERTING HOT SOUPS TO COLD

Virtually all summer vegetables—eggplant, squash, peppers, onions, tomatoes, corn—are intensified when grilled. Grill them first, then cook them in water or stock and puree for rich-tasting soups, warm or chilled.

Serve cold vegetable soups with fresh garnishes that echo the ingredients—herbs, chiles, spices, and vegetables. With squash soups, sauté (rather than stew) the squash at the beginning until it's golden to bring out its flavor.

Minestrone and bean soups are not as obvious candidates as other soups, but there are times when they're traditionally served chilled. Vinegar or lemon needs to be served alongside. Pureed bean and lentil soups, thoroughly cooked so that there's no trace of chalkiness, can also be served cold with plenty of spicy yogurt and other lively garnishes such as diced tomatoes, relishes, herbs, scallions, and so on.

COLD CARROT SOUP WITH ONION AND PICKLED CARROT RELISH: Make the Carrot Soup with Onion Relish on page 204. Puree and chill well. Make the relish using finely diced Pickled Onions, page 78, and/or Pickled Carrots and Garlic with Cumin, page 79. Add it to the soup just before serving and garnish with sprigs of cilantro. Serves 4 to 6.

COLD CARROT SOUP WITH PEPPER GARNISH: Make the Carrot and Red Pepper Soup on page 204 and chill well. Very finely dice enough bell pepper—orange, yellow, purple, or green—to make $1/2$ cup. (The stem ends, which are often thrown away, are perfect for this.) Combine the peppers with 2 teaspoons extra virgin olive oil and season with salt and a little pepper. Let stand for 15 minutes. Serve the soup with the peppers spooned into each bowl and garnish with thinly sliced basil leaves or a leaf of lemon verbena. Serves 4 to 6.

COLD LEEK AND POTATO SOUP WITH SNIPPED HERBS: Make the Leek and Potato Soup on page 208. Pass all but 2 cups through a food mill, then combine the two soups and chill well. Taste for salt and season with pepper. Assemble a collection of herbs, such as sprigs of chervil, a branch of tarragon, a few chives, a lovage leaf, and sprigs of lemon thyme or lemon verbena. Pluck the leaves off the stems and lightly chop them. You'll need about 3 tablespoons. If there are some chive or thyme blossoms, set them aside. Whisk a few tablespoons crème fraîche until smooth, then drizzle it from a spoon over the top of the soup. Add the herbs and their blossoms and serve. Serves 4 to 6.

COLD CHARD SOUP WITH SOUR CREAM: Chill the tart Chard Soup with Sorrel or Lemon, page 205, and serve with sour cream and diced cucumber in each bowl. Serves 4 to 6.

COLD GRILLED RED PEPPER SOUP WITH BASIL PUREE: Make the Roasted Red Pepper Soup on page 211, grilling both the onion and the peppers first along with an extra orange or yellow pepper and adding $1/2$ cup cream. Peel, seed, and dice the extra pepper. Chill the soup well. Taste for salt and add a little balsamic vinegar or sherry vinegar to sharpen the flavors. Puree a handful of basil leaves with extra virgin olive oil until smooth. Stir the chopped peppers into the soup and garnish each bowl with a swirl of basil puree. Serves 4 to 6.

Yogurt Soups

Smooth and pleasantly tart, yogurt gets along famously with parsley, dill, and mint, chickpeas and wheat, nuts and vegetables. Yogurt soups also make excellent cool drinks or even a summer breakfast for those who like to start their day with savory foods.

The quality of the yogurt you use is crucial since it's the central ingredient. Short of making your own, the best offerings tend to be found at natural food stores, where you can find yogurt free of corn syrup, sugar, gums, and gelatins. Especially good are yogurts made from specific cultures, such as Bulgarian-style yogurt and a divine yogurt with a layer of cream resting on top. Goat milk yogurts have a certain appeal, too.

To my taste, whole-milk or low-fat Bulgarian style makes the best soup. Its texture is loose and silky, and its flavor has just the right amount of tartness. Nonfat yogurt tends to be too sour to make good soups, though there are exceptions. Draining the yogurt first sweetens and greatly improves its flavor. I regularly do this, regardless of the yogurt I use, and then replace the lost whey with buttermilk or regular milk.

If you can't get good, natural, sweet-tasting yogurt, use buttermilk. It makes a great base for all these soups, and its taste is much more reliably balanced.

Yogurt Soup with Rice and Spinach

1 bunch scallions, including half of the greens, chopped

2 tablespoons olive oil

1 onion, chopped

3 garlic cloves, chopped

1 cup chopped parsley

1/3 cup chopped dill or 3 tablespoons dried

Salt and freshly milled pepper

1 large bunch spinach, stems removed

5 cups Basic Vegetable Stock, page 196, enhanced with summer vegetables

1 1/2 cups yogurt, plus extra yogurt or sour cream for garnish

Fresh lemon juice

1 cup cooked long-grain white or brown rice

1 small cucumber, peeled, seeded, and finely diced

A GOOD stock greatly enhances this soup, but if you skip it, be extra-generous with the herbs and allow time for the flavors to marry.

SERVES 4 TO 6

Set aside 2 tablespoons of the scallion for garnish and refrigerate.

Heat the oil in a soup pot and add the onion, garlic, and herbs. Cook over medium heat until the onion is soft, 10 to 12 minutes, stirring occasionally. Add 1 teaspoon salt, the spinach, and the stock and bring to a boil. Lower the heat and simmer just enough to wilt the spinach, a few minutes. Puree, then stir in the yogurt and chill well. When cold, taste again for salt—it will probably need more—or add lemon juice to bring up the flavor. Season with pepper to taste. Serve with rice and diced cucumber in each bowl. Garnish with an additional spoonful of yogurt and the reserved scallions.

Yogurt and Cucumber Soup with Mint

CUCUMBER, parsley, and mint are classically delicious with yogurt.

SERVES 4 TO 6

1 quart yogurt, drained for 25 minutes
1 ½ cups milk or buttermilk
2 garlic cloves
Salt and freshly milled white pepper
2 cucumbers, peeled if waxed

¼ cup chopped parsley
3 tablespoons chopped mint
1 tablespoon extra virgin olive oil
Few drops fresh lemon juice
4 to 6 mint sprigs for garnish

Combine the yogurt and buttermilk in a bowl. Pound the garlic with ½ teaspoon salt in a mortar until smooth. Halve the cucumbers lengthwise, scrape out the seeds, then grate them using the large holes of a grater. Stir the garlic, cucumber, herbs, and oil into the yogurt. Taste for salt and season with pepper and lemon juice. Chill well and serve garnished with mint sprigs.

Yogurt and Cucumber Soup with Scallions and Dill Add 4 finely sliced scallions, including most of the greens, and substitute 3 tablespoons finely chopped dill for the mint.

Yogurt Soup with Crushed Nuts and Garlic Pound ½ cup shelled walnuts, pine nuts, or skinned almonds with the garlic and salt in a mortar until smooth, adding a little of the yogurt or milk to loosen the mixture as you work. Finely dice rather than grate the cucumber and omit the herbs. Garnish with chopped mint.

Buttermilk Soup with Barley or Wheat

JUST as yogurt is often stirred into soups of legumes and grains, different grains and legumes make excellent additions to yogurt or buttermilk soups. Chickpeas, lentils, wheat berries, spelt, bulgur, and couscous—even leftover tabbouleh—are all possibilities.

SERVES 4 TO 6

⅓ cup pearl barley or 1 cup bulgur
1 quart buttermilk or a mixture of buttermilk and yogurt
¼ cup minced scallion, including some of the greens
⅓ cup chopped parsley

2 tablespoons snipped chives
1 teaspoon ground cumin
Salt and freshly milled white pepper
1 tablespoon crushed toasted cumin seeds

Simmer the barley in water to cover in a saucepan until soft, about 35 minutes. If you're using bulgur, cover it with water for 30 minutes, then drain.

Mix together all the ingredients except the cumin seeds. Season with a few pinches salt and pepper to taste; chill well. Serve with the crushed cumin seeds sprinkled on top.

Buttermilk Soup with Chickpeas and Herb Oil

2 garlic cloves

Salt and freshly milled pepper

1 quart buttermilk

1 large cucumber, peeled, seeded, and finely diced

1 15-ounce can chickpeas, rinsed well

1/4 cup extra virgin olive oil

2 tablespoons snipped chives

1/3 cup chopped parsley

3 tablespoons chopped marjoram

Grated zest and juice of 1 lemon

WITH canned chickpeas this soup can be assembled in minutes, then set aside to chill. Serve it with hearty whole-grain bread or rolls.

SERVES 4 TO 6

Pound the garlic with 1/2 teaspoon salt in a mortar until smooth. Combine the buttermilk, garlic, cucumber, and chickpeas in a bowl and chill well. Combine the oil, herbs, a few pinches of salt, and the lemon zest in another bowl. When cold, taste the soup for salt and season with pepper and lemon juice. Serve garnished with the olive oil and herb oil.

Fruit Soups

Cold, smooth, sweet soups are delicious but not everyone's idea of a meal. Try fruit soups as a beverage, poured over ice and served on a hot day. They also make an intriguing dessert and can be given texture by including a chunky fruit salsa or a scoop of fruit sorbet.

Fruit soups are among the easier soups to improvise. Start with sweet, flavorful fruit—nearly overripe fruit is often best. Puree it, season it with complementary spices, tart it a little with lemon or lime juice, and enrich it or not, with cream, yogurt, buttermilk, or the like. A pinch of salt brings up the flavors, as does a little vinegar or lemon juice.

The salsa craze has demonstrated that fruit combines well with acids, chiles, and spices. Bringing some of these elements into play as garnishes for fruit soups gives them a wider role to play in the meal.

Melon Soup with Ginger-Cucumber Salsa

The Soup

1 honeydew, Persian, or casaba melon, about 2 1/2 pounds

Grated zest and juice of 2 limes

1/2 cup yogurt, sour cream, or buttermilk, optional

Salt

Mint or basil sprigs

The Salsa

Reserved wedge of melon, peeled

1/2 small cucumber, peeled and seeded

Grated zest and juice of 1 lime

1 tablespoon minced Thai or regular basil

1 tablespoon chopped mint leaves

1 jalapeño chile, seeded and finely diced

1 small knob of ginger, peeled and coarsely chopped

Salt

WAIT for those juicy, dead-ripe melons to make this soup—the ones sitting on your counter attracting fruit flies are perfect. The spicy salsa adds texture and makes the soup a cooling summer appetizer.

SERVES 4 TO 6

Cut the melon into eighths and set one wedge aside. Seed, peel, and puree the rest. Stir in the lime zest and juice, yogurt, and a few pinches of salt. Cover and refrigerate.

Neatly and finely dice the melon and cucumber and combine with the lime zest and juice, basil, mint, and chile. Force the ginger through a garlic press and add it to the salsa. Season with a pinch of salt and chill.

Serve the soup very cold with the salsa spooned into the middle of each bowl and garnished with mint sprigs.

Watermelon and Blackberry Soup

A FRUIT salad in a pink "broth" of watermelon. It's a little hard to be exact with watermelon— some pieces are full of seeds, others aren't—so you may have to feel your way with amounts.

SERVES 4

6 cups seeded chunks of watermelon
Fresh lemon or lime juice
Salt
2 cups blackberries
3 tablespoons light brown sugar

Rosewater or orange flower water
1 pound *each* red and yellow
    watermelon, approximately
¼ cup pomegranate seeds, if in season
4 mint sprigs

Puree the watermelon chunks and pour the puree into a bowl. Add lemon juice to taste and a pinch of salt and refrigerate, covered. Toss the blackberries with the brown sugar and a few drops of rosewater, cover, and refrigerate for 1 hour. Seed the remaining piece of melon and cut it into bite-sized chunks.

When it's time to serve, flavor the melon juice with rosewater to taste, starting with 1 teaspoon. Divide the juice among chilled soup plates and add the melon pieces, then the berries. If pomegranates are in season, add about 1 tablespoon to each bowl and a squeeze of the juice as well. Garnish with the mint sprigs and serve.

Spiced Plum Soup

HERE'S a perfect use for those tiny plums that are too small to slice or a glut of sweet plums from a prolific tree. Unless the plums are dead ripe, you can expect an astringent edge. This makes a sublime cold drink, poured over ice into tall glasses.

SERVES 4

2 pounds very ripe purple plums
2 large pieces orange zest
1 cup fresh orange juice
1 3-inch cinnamon stick
4 cloves
½ teaspoon ground cardamom

½ teaspoon ground coriander
⅓ to ½ cup mild honey to taste
½ cup buttermilk
Orange flower water
1½ teaspoons balsamic vinegar
Fresh mint leaves

Leave very small plums whole and cut larger ones roughly in half. Don't worry about removing the pits. Put them in a pot with the orange zest and juice, spices, and ⅓ cup honey. Bring to a boil, then lower the heat and simmer, covered, until the flesh easily falls away from the pit, about 30 minutes. Transfer the plums to a food mill set over a bowl and begin to turn it. It will grate against the pits and loosen the flesh. Pick out the pits, cinnamon stick, and cloves with your fingers as you come across them and continue to work the plums through, skins and all. Whisk the buttermilk and 1 teaspoon orange flower water into the plum puree and chill. When the soup is cold, stir in the vinegar;

taste again and correct the seasonings, adding more spice, honey, or orange flower water if needed. Garnish with the mint leaves and serve.

Plum Soup with Wine Use ½ cup orange muscat wine or Japanese plum wine in place of the orange juice and add 1 or 2 drops of orange oil, if available, to the soup.

Bicolored Plum Soup Add the buttermilk to half the soup. Using two ladles simultaneously, pour some of each into the soup bowls. Passing a knife in a zigzag fashion through the lines where the two soups meet makes fancy-looking but easy-to-make swirls.

Winter Soup of Dried Fruits with Pearl Tapioca

¼ **cup large tapioca pearls**

1 **cup dried apricots**

1 **cup dried pitted prunes or Mission figs**

1 **cup dried pears**

½ **cup golden raisins**

½ **cup dried cherries**

2 **3-inch cinnamon sticks**

4 **slices ginger**

1 **quart water or pear juice, plus extra as needed**

Sour cream or drained yogurt, optional

A FRIEND of Norwegian origin served this soup, then shared her recipe with me. The large tapioca pearls are invisible but give it a silky quality. A great winter dish to have on hand, it keeps for weeks refrigerated. Give the pearls a head start with an overnight soak before cooking.

SERVES 4 TO 6

Cover the tapioca and fruit with water and set aside to soak overnight. Drain, then put it in a soup pot with the remaining ingredients except the sour cream. Bring to a boil. Lower the heat and cook slowly, partially covered, until the tapioca pearls are clear, about 2 hours. (Some people like to see a little eye in the center, which gives them their other name, tapioca fish eyes.) Gently give a stir every so often so that nothing sticks to the bottom. If the soup becomes too thick, add water or juice as needed. Serve warm or chilled, for breakfast or dessert, plain or with a spoonful of sour cream or drained yogurt.

Vegetable Stews and Stir-Fries

THE WORD *STEW* USUALLY SUGGESTS A SLOW-COOKED DISH OF ROBUST AND MEATY HEARTINESS. TO ME IT SIMPLY MEANS A MÉLANGE OF INDIVIDUAL INGREDIENTS SIMMERED TOGETHER AT A LEISURELY PACE. *STEW, RAGOUT, BRAISE,* medley—all describe dishes that are composed of seasonal vegetables and their herb companions, simmered and sauced with residual juices. Cooked long enough for their flavors to mingle and marry, these dishes, along with their accompaniments, make an excellent vegetable-based main dish (or a side dish for a meat course if you're not vegetarian).

Vegetable stews are really a varied lot. Here's a cooking approach that unites such diverse dishes as a Cashew Curry, a Tunisian couscous, and a vegetable daube, to name but three. And variety is ever increased if you take into account what seasonal changes themselves suggest. If we think about putting a lid on a stew, we can go a few steps farther and confer dignity on a humble dish. Puff pastry, biscuit dough, and flaky filo all contribute a layer of finesse to seasonal vegetable stews. While I wouldn't hesitate to serve a stew at a casual dinner party, I know that a golden covering of pastry will raise expectations and garner sighs of appreciation.

Stir-fries are also mixtures of elements, but they're better described as two-part dishes with all the cutting done at one end and all the cooking at the other. Unlike a stew, the flavors in a stir-fry are united through a brief but intense exposure to the hot sides of a wok, rendering the vegetables crisp, bright, and shiny. Stews lose some of that color and texture but gain flavor.

Tips for Making Stews

START WITH THE FLAVOR BASE: As with soup, sautéed onions, carrots, celery, and other aromatics provide the flavor base. It's important to the final flavor of the stews not to rush this step. Allow plenty of time for the onions to color, the sugars in the vegetables to caramelize, and the herbs to release their flavors. A good way to keep yourself from rushing is to cut your vegetables while the base is cooking. By the time you're done, it will be too.

LESS IS MORE; COOKING WITH THE SEASONS: Stews work best when they're limited to about five different vegetables in addition to the base. In choosing them, keep in mind a balance of shapes, sizes, colors, and textures as well as flavors.

Choose your vegetables from what's in season; foods that mature at the same time always taste good together: Asparagus, snow peas, and chervil in spring. Artichokes and fava beans in spring too, but artichokes and celery root in fall. Tomatoes, eggplants, and potatoes in summer. Hearty roots and tubers in winter. By *seasonal* I mean the season where you live, not the season of the supermarket, which draws its goods from around the world. If you take your tips from what's grown locally and sold seasonally, it's virtually impossible to put together a poor stew.

BLANCHING: Sometimes it's preferable to cook some of the ingredients separately to preserve their fresh color and texture. Blanching one or more vegetables gives you some control over how your final dish will look since they're cooked separately, then added at the last minute. But don't be afraid to allow at least some of the vegetables to soften—that's often when they taste best. One of the best vegetable braises I've ever eaten was in a Roman restaurant one spring. Asparagus, peas, and fava beans were cooked to nearly a jam-like consistency. By American standards the dish was impossibly overcooked, but it was over the top in terms of sheer flavor.

With practice you'll be able to judge how long individual vegetables take to cook when added to the stew. Start with those that take the longest cooking time and proceed with those that take the shortest time, ensuring that everything will be cooked perfectly at the end.

WINE: Wine gives an acidic lift to the flavors and keeps the vegetables from becoming mushy. A few tablespoons of lemon juice or mild vinegar, such as champagne vinegar, can accomplish the same thing. While dry white wines are good with vegetables, I sometimes prefer a Riesling. Its acidity combined with its sugars doesn't fight the vegetables' natural tendency toward sweetness but harmonizes with them.

ON THE TABLE—PRESENTATION: While satisfying to eat, stews by their nature lack visual definition. This makes presentation a problem, albeit one that's easily solved. Serving stews in a pasta plate or bowl with a wide rim always sets off the food to good advantage.

Other elements of focus are provided by the accompaniments—golden triangles of fried polenta surrounding a mushroom stew, garlic-rubbed croutons framing braised artichokes with leeks and peas, a vegetable-chickpea tagine encircled with pellets of couscous. Stews are best served with something that absorbs their juices and provides a neutral point for the palate to return to. Grains, couscous, polenta, croutons, toast, biscuits, and even waffles are all good candidates. You can give grains more visual definition by packing them into small molds or custard cups, turning them out onto the center of the plate or bowl, and then ladling the stew around them. Toppings of various kinds can turn stews into cobblers and pot pies.

It's also important to cut your vegetables in large, attractively shaped pieces so that the eye will be drawn to identifiable ingredients—a length of carrot, a quartered potato, a whole mushroom—rather than a confusion of small bits. When ingredients in a dish are indistinct and unrecognizable, it's difficult to elicit a receptive response especially from children.

A fresh garnish of chopped herbs, a spoonful of salsa verde, or a diced tomato that's only warmed makes your final vegetable stew look lively and fresh.

Adding a Lid: Turning Stews into Cobblers and Pot Pies

Placing a stew in an ovenproof dish and adding a topping makes the dish more substantial and occasionally elegant. This way it fits with ease into any occasion from family get-togethers to dinner parties to potlucks.

The topping recipes that follow make enough to cover 6 to 8 cups of vegetables. Use a large gratin dish, individual ramekins, or any attractive ovenproof dish. Have the stew at room temperature before adding the top, or the heat will turn the pastry soggy.

Cobbler Topping

1 cup all-purpose flour

1 cup whole-wheat flour

1 tablespoon baking powder

½ teaspoon salt

6 to 8 tablespoons butter, cut into small pieces

1 cup milk

1 egg, beaten, if desired

Using equal parts whole-wheat and all-purpose flour gives this topping character and a good nutty flavor. Any mushroom stew or the Winter Vegetable Stew with Jerusalem Artichokes is a good choice for this topping. Roll out the dough if you like a smooth topping or drop it by spoonfuls to give it a traditional cobbled look.

MAKES ENOUGH FOR A 2-QUART BAKING DISH

Combine the flours, baking powder, and salt in a roomy bowl. Add the butter and work it in with your fingertips until it makes a coarse meal. Add the milk and stir until everything is dampened, then knead the dough a few times right in the bowl until it comes together. Drop the dough by small or large spoonfuls over the stew or roll it out the size of the baking dish, lay it over the stew, and score it attractively with the tip of a knife. Brush it with the egg to make a glaze. Bake at 375°F until the crust is golden, about 35 minutes.

Cheddar Cobbler Topping: Use 6 tablespoons butter. Add ½ to 1 cup grated Cheddar to the dry ingredients.

Dairy-Free Variation: Replace the butter with canola or corn oil. Toss it with the flour, then rub it between your fingers to make a coarse meal. Omit the glaze.

Vegetable Pot Pies Tender golden crust over a vegetable stew never fails to entice. Use the standard Pie Crust, page 693, Galette Dough, page 696, or the yeasted doughs, pages 489 to 490, rolled very thin, or puff pastry. (Commercial frozen puff pastry is perfectly legitimate in my book!) Make sure the vegetable stew is at room temperature. Roll out the dough, cut it to fit the dish, then brush one side of the dough with beaten egg and set it, egg side down, on the vegetables. Flute the edges as you would for a deep-dish pie. Fashion scraps into decorations—leaves, hearts, stars, geometric designs, whatever you fancy—and fasten them to the dough with a bit of egg glaze. Lacking scraps, score the top attractively with the tip of a knife, cutting into but not through the pastry. Brush with beaten egg. Bake at 425°F for 12 minutes, then lower the heat to 350°F and finish baking, about 35 minutes in all.

Filo Covers Allow frozen filo dough to thaw in the refrigerator for 6 to 8 hours. Remove and carefully unfold it. Using the unfilled baking dish as a guide, cut out 8 pieces of filo pastry and cover them with plastic wrap and a barely damp towel. Rewrap the unused portion of filo and return it to the refrigerator.

Brush each of the cut sheets lightly with melted butter, olive oil, or a combination of the two. Stack them on top of each other as you go. You can add flavor and texture by scattering finely chopped toasted nuts between the layers. Score the top into decorative squares or diamonds with a sharp knife or designate portions by cutting completely through the dough. The finished top can be refrigerated until you're ready to use it. Preheat the oven the 375°F. Put the room-temperature cooked stew in the dish, set the filo lid on top, and bake until the filling is hot and the filo is golden, 35 to 40 minutes.

A filo cover would be good with Braised Artichokes with Leeks and Peas, below, or the Corn and Mushroom Ragout with Sage and Roasted Garlic, page 248.

Braised Artichokes with Leeks and Peas

I OFTEN serve this braise with Sautéed Spinach and long thin Garlic-Rubbed Croutons to sop up the juices. Covered with puff pastry, this makes a lovely spring dish for a special occasion.

SERVES 4 TO 6

4 large artichokes

2½ to 3 cups Basic Vegetable Stock, page 196, or water

2 leeks, including an inch of the greens, sliced into ¼-inch rounds

2 fennel bulbs, cut into 1-inch wedges, joined at the root end

2 tablespoons butter

¼ cup diced shallot

½ cup white wine

Salt and freshly milled pepper

12 ounces new red potatoes, scrubbed and cut into quarters

½ to ¾ cup crème fraîche

1 teaspoon Dijon mustard

1 cup shelled peas or fava beans

3 tablespoons chopped fennel greens or parsley

Trim the artichokes as described on page 330, cut into sixths, and set them aside in a bowl of acidulated water until ready to cook. If you're making a stock, be sure to include the trimmings from the leeks and fennel.

Melt the butter in a wide soup pot over medium-high heat. Add the shallot and leeks and cook, stirring frequently, without browning for 3 to 4 minutes. Add the wine, raise the heat, and simmer for 2 minutes.

Drain the artichokes and add them to the pan with the fennel and stock. Season with 1 teaspoon salt, then press a piece of crumbled parchment or wax paper directly over the vegetables. Bring the liquid to a boil, then simmer, covered, until the artichokes are tender, about 25 minutes. Meanwhile, steam the potatoes until tender, 10 to 12 minutes.

When the artichokes and fennel are tender, remove them with a slotted spoon to a dish. Whisk enough crème fraîche and the mustard into the broth and boil briskly to make a thin sauce, 5 to 10 minutes. Add the peas and cook until tender, then return the vegetables and potatoes to the broth. Add the chopped fennel greens, season with pepper, and serve.

Spring Vegetable Stew

Salt and freshly milled pepper

12 baby carrots, or 2 carrots peeled and thinly sliced

½ cup snow peas

6 radishes, including ½ inch of the stems, halved

18 3-inch asparagus tips

6 scallions, including the stems, cut into 3-inch lengths

2 broccoli stems, thickly peeled and sliced diagonally

4 small turnips, or 2 rutabagas and 2 turnips, peeled and cut into sixths

4 tablespoons butter

4 thyme sprigs, preferably lemon thyme

1 tablespoon fresh lemon juice

10 sorrel leaves, sliced into ribbons, optional

1 tablespoon snipped chives

2 teaspoons finely chopped parsley

1 teaspoon chopped tarragon

COOKING the vegetables separately, then combining them, makes it possible to have everything ready in advance. Radishes and broccoli stems may be surprising, but they really give this dish an exceedingly fresh spring look.

While popovers or fresh herb noodles are good accompaniments, I sometimes add some potato gnocchi or cheese tortellini at the end for a soft, surprising mouthful.

SERVES 4

Bring 3 quarts water to a boil and add 1 tablespoon salt. One type at a time, blanch the vegetables until barely tender, then remove to a bowl of cold water to stop the cooking. When all are blanched, reserve 1 cup of the cooking water. Drain the vegetables. (This can be done ahead of time.)

In a wide skillet, melt the butter with the thyme sprigs and reserved liquid. Add the vegetables and simmer until they're warmed through. Add the lemon juice and season with salt and pepper. Add the sorrel and herbs and cook for 1 minute more. Serve at once.

Corn and Lima Bean Ragout

1½ cups fresh or frozen lima beans

2 tablespoons diced onion

Aromatics: 1 bay leaf, 4 parsley branches, and 2 thyme sprigs

Salt and freshly milled pepper

2 tablespoons butter or sunflower seed oil

1 bunch scallions, including 2 inches of the greens, thinly sliced

4 cups corn kernels, fresh or frozen

3 tablespoons chopped parsley

1 tablespoon chopped basil

1 tablespoon chopped thyme

½ teaspoon paprika

½ cup fresh carrot juice or bean broth

2 tomatoes, peeled, seeded, and diced into ½-inch pieces

CARROT juice gives this ragout a soft glow and delicate sweetness. Purple basil leaves and yellow tomatoes also add considerable visual allure, though the usual basil and red tomatoes will be fine. Serve with warm biscuits split in half or over buttered toast.

SERVES 4

Cook the beans in a saucepan over heat with the onion, aromatics, ½ teaspoon salt, and 2 cups water. When tender, after about 15 minutes, drain and reserve the broth. Remove the aromatics.

Melt the butter in a wide skillet or sauté pan over fairly high heat. Sauté the scallions and corn until they begin to color, about 2 minutes, then add the beans, half of the herbs, paprika, and carrot juice. Simmer for 4 minutes, then add the tomatoes and cook for 2 minutes more. Season with pepper, garnish with the remaining herbs, and serve.

Corn and Mushroom Ragout with Sage and Roasted Garlic

ROASTING, grilling, and searing release layers of flavor in these summer vegetables. Make a little stock with the trimmings as you work for the final sauce. Serve with warm popovers, corn bread, or biscuits.

SERVES 4

¼ onion, sliced

10 garlic cloves, 2 peeled, 8 unpeeled

Salt and freshly milled pepper

1 large yellow bell pepper, broiled or roasted

5 ripe but firm tomatoes

3 cups fresh corn kernels and their scrapings, from 4 to 5 ears corn, 1 corn cob reserved

6 ounces shiitake, oyster, or white mushrooms, caps cut into large pieces, stems reserved

3 tablespoons safflower or olive oil

1 small onion, finely diced

8 sage leaves, finely chopped

1 tablespoon chopped parsley

Simmer 3 cups water with the sliced onion, peeled garlic, and ½ teaspoon salt. Add any pepper trimmings, 1 corn cob, broken into pieces, and stems from the mushrooms. Simmer for 25 minutes.

Meanwhile, cut the pepper into pieces about 1 inch long and ½ inch wide, reserving the juices. Heat ½ teaspoon oil in a small skillet over medium heat. Add the unpeeled garlic and cook until the skins are charred and the insides are soft, about 10 minutes. Peel and mash into a paste. Sear the tomatoes in the same pan, turning them frequently, until the skin begins to split. Remove the skins, halve the tomatoes, and squeeze the juice into the stock. Chop the flesh into large pieces.

In a wide skillet, heat 1½ tablespoons oil over high heat. Add the mushrooms and sauté until they begin to color, after 4 to 5 minutes. Set them aside in a bowl. Return the pan to the heat and add 1 tablespoon oil. Sauté the diced onion, garlic, corn, and all but 1 teaspoon of the sage until the corn and onion begin to color, about 5 minutes. Add the reserved mushrooms, peppers, and tomatoes. Season with ½ teaspoon salt and a little pepper.

Strain the stock right into the pan, add any reserved pepper juices, reduce the heat, cover, and simmer for 5 minutes. Serve garnished with the remaining sage and the parsley.

SERVING IDEAS FOR CORN STEWS

Corn stews can take center stage, but they also make a fine accompaniment to frittatas, vegetable soufflés, and puddings. When they're the main attraction, serve them with such accompaniments as popovers, rice timbales, or buttered toast. Make them plain or enrich them with a little grated cheese or cream. Corn stews also make good fillings for other vegetables, such as summer squash, poblano chiles, and bell peppers.

Eggplant Stew with Tomatoes, Peppers, and Chickpeas

1 to 1½ pounds eggplant

6 tablespoons olive oil

1 large red onion, diced into ½-inch squares

1 large yellow or red bell pepper, cut into 1-inch triangles

2 teaspoons paprika

2 plump garlic cloves, thinly sliced

2 tablespoons tomato paste

5 plum tomatoes, peeled, quartered lengthwise, and seeded

1 15-ounce can chickpeas, rinsed

Salt and freshly milled pepper

¼ cup coarsely chopped parsley

THIS summer dish is an easy one to make. Serve it over the Saffron Noodle Cake, a rice pilaf, or with bulgur.

SERVES 4

Cut the eggplant lengthwise into ½-inch slabs, then crosswise into ½-inch sticks. Heat ¼ cup oil in a wide skillet over high heat until hazy. Add the eggplant and stir to distribute the oil. Cook, turning the pieces every few minutes, until golden, about 10 minutes.

Heat the remaining oil in a Dutch oven over medium-high heat. Add the onion, pepper, and paprika and sauté until the onion is lightly browned around the edges, 8 to 10 minutes, adding the garlic during the last few minutes. Stir in the tomato paste, fry it for a minute, then moisten with a few tablespoons water and scrape up the juices from the bottom of the pan. Add the tomatoes, eggplant, chickpeas, 1 cup water, 1 teaspoon salt, and pepper. Lower the heat and simmer, covered, for 20 minutes, stirring once or twice. Stir in the chopped parsley and serve.

Simple Summer Stew with Herb Butter

1½ tablespoons *each* chopped marjoram, basil, and parsley

½ teaspoon grated lemon zest

Salt and freshly milled pepper

4 tablespoons butter, softened

8 ounces green beans, preferably skinny ones, tipped, cut into 3-inch lengths

1 tablespoon olive or sunflower seed oil

1 small onion, finely diced

1 garlic clove, thinly sliced

8 ounces small summer squash, diced or sliced into rounds

1 red or yellow bell pepper, cut into squares

1 large tomato, peeled, seeded, and diced

4 ears corn, shucked, about 3 cups kernels

BY choosing from all the new varieties of beans, squash, and tomatoes that appear in the market during the summer, you can create endless varieties with this single recipe.

SERVES 4

In a small bowl, combine the marjoram, basil, parsley, lemon zest, a pinch of salt, and the butter. Mix thoroughly and set aside.

Bring a pot of water to a boil and add salt. Cook the beans, uncovered, for 2 minutes and then drain.

Heat the oil in a wide pan over high heat with the onion and garlic. Sauté for 1 minute, then add ½ cup water, lower the heat, cover, and simmer for 5 minutes. Add the beans, squash, pepper, tomato, and corn. Season with ½ teaspoon salt, cover, and simmer over low heat for 10 minutes or until tender. Stir in the herb butter, taste for salt, and season with pepper.

Artichoke, Shallot, and Potato Ragout

LOOK to the late summer for baby artichokes, fresh shallots, and new potatoes for this stew. You can dip your bread right into the broth. If you can't find baby artichokes, use full-sized ones, trimmed and quartered.

SERVES 4

16 baby artichokes, trimmed and halved

12 shallots or boiling onions, peeled

3 tablespoons butter, olive oil, or a mixture

3 garlic cloves, peeled and slivered

Aromatics, page 29, including a sprig of rosemary

12 small new potatoes, about 1½ pounds, scrubbed and quartered

4 carrots, cut into pieces about half the size of the artichokes

2 small rutabagas, thickly peeled and cut into sixths

2 tablespoons flour

Salt and freshly milled pepper

¾ cup white wine

3½ cups water or Basic Vegetable Stock, page 196

4 teaspoons chopped parsley

1 teaspoon chopped rosemary

Separate the shallots where natural divisions occur. If you're using boiling onions, cut them in half through the root end.

Warm the butter in a heavy, wide pot over medium heat with the garlic and aromatics. Add the vegetables and cook, stirring occasionally, until they start to color, 7 to 10 minutes. Sprinkle with the flour, then cover and cook for 1 minute. Add 1 teaspoon salt, a few twists of the peppermill, and the wine. Simmer for 3 minutes, then add the water. Cover and cook over low heat until the vegetables are tender when pierced with a knife, about 30 minutes. Taste for salt and pepper and remove the aromatics. Serve in soup plates with the chopped parsley and rosemary scattered over the top.

Artichoke, Pepper, and Chickpea Tagine with Olives and Preserved Lemons

THIS Moroccan-inspired tagine is richly endowed with the reds and golds of fall vegetables. Serve it spooned around a mound of steamed couscous or rice with the bright green chermoula drizzled on the top. The stew can sit while you make the couscous—time only improves it—and the chermoula can be assembled ahead of time.

SERVES 4

5 to 6 medium artichokes, trimmed and quartered

Juice of 1 lemon

Salt

Pinch saffron threads

3 tablespoons olive oil

1 large onion, diced into ½-inch squares

2 large bell peppers, 1 yellow and 1 red, cut into ½-inch pieces

1 tablespoon Harissa, page 75 (see note)

1 15-ounce can chickpeas, rinsed

12 Kalamata or oil-cured black olives

1 small Preserved Lemon, page 82, skin only, diced into small squares

2 tablespoons mixed chopped parsley and cilantro

1 cup dried couscous

Chermoula, page 56

Bring 2 quarts water to a boil, then add the lemon juice and 2 teaspoons salt. Boil the artichokes for 10 minutes, then drain and set aside. Cover the saffron with 1 tablespoon of the boiling water and set aside.

Heat the oil in a large skillet over high heat. Add the onion and peppers, sauté for 1 minute, then add the harissa (or the spices). Reduce the heat to medium and cook for 5

minutes. If you're not using harissa, add the tomato paste and cook for 1 minute, mushing it around the pan. Add the saffron and artichokes and continue cooking, turning the vegetables frequently, until they're coated with the spices and warmed through. Add the chickpeas, olives, lemon skin, herbs, and 2 cups water. Lower the heat and simmer for 15 minutes or until the artichokes are completely tender. Taste for salt.

Cook 1 cup couscous according to your favorite method. Mound it in the center of individual soup plates and spoon the vegetables around it. Drizzle the chermoula over the vegetables and serve.

> *If you don't have any harissa, add the following spices to the onion and peppers, stirring frequently so that none stick to the pan:*
>
> 1/2 teaspoon toasted ground cumin
> 1/2 teaspoon freshly milled pepper
> 1/4 teaspoon ground caraway seeds
> 1/4 teaspoon turmeric
> 1 1/2 teaspoons ground red chile or hot paprika
> 1 tablespoon tomato paste

Braised Turnips with Thyme

1 pound turnips, preferably small

2 rutabagas, thickly peeled and diced into 1/2-inch cubes

1 to 2 tablespoons butter

1 onion, finely diced

3 small garlic cloves, halved

1 carrot, cut into medium dice

4 thyme sprigs or 1/4 teaspoon dried

Salt and freshly milled pepper

2 teaspoons flour

2 tablespoons chopped parsley

1 teaspoon Dijon mustard

1/4 cup cream or crème fraîche

YOU can serve this ragout with buttered toast or make it into little pot pies covered with pie crust or frozen puff pastry.

SERVES 4

If you're using storage turnips, peel them thickly, cut them into sixths, and parboil in salted water for 1 minute. (Tender spring turnips can be scrubbed and left whole.) Parboil the rutabagas for 3 minutes.

Melt the butter in a Dutch oven over medium heat. Add the onion, garlic, rutabagas, carrot, and thyme. Cook for 3 to 4 minutes, then add the turnips. Season with 3/4 teaspoon salt and sprinkle with the flour. Cover and cook over low heat for 4 minutes, then stir in 1 1/2 cups water and the parsley. Simmer, covered, until the turnips are tender, about 15 minutes. Taste for salt, season with pepper, add the mustard and cream, and simmer for 2 minutes more.

Curried Cauliflower and Peas

My friend Kathi Long raved so much about this curry that I asked her to make it for me. It's indeed exceptional—and quite easy—but you do need green mango powder, asafetida, and garam masala, all of which are available at Indian markets. Serve this over steamed rice.

SERVES 4

¼ cup vegetable oil

½ teaspoon toasted ground cumin

¼ teaspoon asafetida

¼ cup peeled and finely diced ginger

4 teaspoons toasted ground coriander

1 teaspoon ground mild red chile or ½ teaspoon cayenne

1 teaspoon turmeric

1 onion, thinly sliced

1 large cauliflower, cut into bite-sized pieces, including the stems

Salt

½ pound sugar snap peas, strings removed

2 teaspoons ground amchoor (green mango) powder

1 teaspoon garam masala

In a wide pot, heat the oil over medium-high heat. Add the cumin and asafetida and cook for 30 seconds, stirring constantly. Add the ginger, coriander, chile, and turmeric and cook for 30 seconds more. Add the onion, lower the heat, and cook until limp, stirring occasionally, about 4 minutes. Next add the cauliflower and 1½ teaspoons salt. Mix everything together, then pour in ½ cup water, cover the pot, and simmer until the vegetables are tender, about 10 minutes. Add the peas and cook for a few minutes more, until they're bright green. Add the amchoor powder and garam masala, stir together, taste for salt, and serve.

Potato and Chickpea Stew

WITH its deep red background and golden potatoes, this stew has become one of my favorites. It multiplies easily and improves with time. Picada, a savory bread crumb mixture, is used to thicken the broth while a bowl of Romesco Sauce infuses it with a rich finish. Steamed spinach or chard can be added directly to the bowl—it gives the dish a fresh element—or served on the side.

SERVES 4

1 pound Yellow Finn, fingerling, or red potatoes

3 tablespoons olive oil

1 large onion, finely diced

2 generous pinches saffron

2 large red bell peppers, finely diced

1 large yellow bell pepper, cut into 1-inch-wide strips

2 large garlic cloves, minced

1 heaping teaspoon sweet paprika

¼ cup chopped parsley, plus extra for garnish

¼ teaspoon red pepper flakes

½ cup medium-dry sherry

2 cups canned crushed tomatoes, plus their juices

2½ cups cooked chickpeas or 2 15-ounce cans, rinsed

3 cups chickpea-cooking broth or water

Salt and freshly milled pepper

Picada, page 35, if needed

Romesco Sauce, page 70

If using fingerling potatoes, scrub, then halve them lengthwise. Large round potatoes can be cut into thick rounds or quartered lengthwise.

Warm the oil in a wide pot with the onion, saffron, peppers, garlic, and potatoes. Cook over medium-low heat, stirring gently every now and then until the potatoes are tender-firm, about 25 minutes. Add the paprika, parsley, and pepper flakes and cook for 3 or 4 minutes. Add the sherry and cook until the juices in the pan are thick and syrupy, about 12 minutes.

Add the tomatoes, chickpeas, and broth to cover. Season with 1½ teaspoons salt and plenty of pepper. Cover and cook over low heat until the potatoes are completely tender, about 20 minutes. If the stew is soupy and you plan to serve it right away, stir in ¼ cup picada (or more, if necessary) to thicken it. If you don't plan to serve the stew for 1 hour or more, it may not need the bread crumbs since it will thicken as it stands. Serve in soup plates with any additional picada sprinkled over the top along with the extra parsley. Add a spoonful of the Romesco sauce to each bowl and pass the rest.

Mushroom Stews

Mushroom stews are versatile, quick to make, and substantial in flavor. They serve extremely well as a main course at any time of year, for mushrooms pair well with wintry herbs, such as rosemary, as well as with the more summery mint and marjoram.

Many markets now carry portobello, cremini, shiitake, and oyster mushrooms. In specialty markets you can even find porcini, morels, and chanterelles. All are pricey, but mushrooms are light, and a few special varieties mixed with white mushrooms make a more interesting dish. A small amount of dried wild mushrooms also adds unique, woodsy flavor notes to these dishes.

When using portobellos, I often remove the gills, unless they're very fresh, since the gills are the first thing to spoil on mushrooms. Always make sure gills are dry and unbroken and have a fresh, sweet smell. A mushroom stock, whether a quick stock or the long-simmered stock adds a great deal of background flavor.

Mushroom stews go well with soft or grilled polenta, popovers, or fresh egg noodles. Drained of their juices, they make an ideal filling for a crêpe or a savory galette. Don't discard those juices; save them to use as a sauce.

Quick Mushroom Stock

¼ cup or more dried porcini

2 teaspoons olive oil

1 onion, coarsely chopped

1 carrot, chopped

1 large garlic clove, sliced

2 mushrooms, sliced, plus any trimmings

2 teaspoons tomato paste

1 tablespoon fresh marjoram or 1 teaspoon dried

½ cup dry white or red wine

1 tablespoon flour

Salt and freshly milled pepper

1 teaspoon red wine vinegar

MAKES ABOUT 1 CUP

Cover the dried mushrooms with 1½ cups hot water and set aside. Heat the oil in a saucepan over high heat. Add the onion, carrot, garlic, and fresh mushroom trimmings. Sauté, stirring occasionally, until well browned, about 10 minutes. Reduce the heat to medium, stir in the tomato paste, marjoram, and wine, and sprinkle on the flour. Cover the pan and cook until the wine is reduced to a syrupy glaze, about 3 minutes. Add the porcini and their soaking water, ½ teaspoon salt, a little pepper, and the vinegar and simmer for 20 minutes. Strain. Remove the dried mushrooms and add them to the stew. If you wish to concentrate the sauce, simmer it in an open pot until it's reduced to the desired strength.

Summer Mushroom Ragout

THE presence of fresh tomatoes, marjoram, and mint gives this ragout a summery aspect. Serve over soft polenta, fresh egg noodles, barley, or rice.

SERVES 4

Mushroom Stock, page 197, or Quick Mushroom Stock, page 253

8 ounces oyster, shiitake, or cremini mushrooms, stems removed

1 pound large white mushrooms, stems trimmed

3 tablespoons olive oil

2 garlic cloves, thinly sliced

4 teaspoons chopped marjoram

2 tablespoons chopped parsley

2 large ripe tomatoes, peeled, seeded, and chopped

Salt and freshly milled pepper

1 teaspoon chopped mint

Make the stock first and include the mushroom trimmings. Slice all but oyster mushrooms about ⅓ inch thick.

Warm the oil and garlic in a wide skillet over medium heat until the garlic is fragrant and golden, about 3 minutes. Remove the garlic. Add the marjoram, parsley, and tomatoes, cook for 1 minute, then raise the heat and add the mushrooms. Season with ½ teaspoon salt and a little pepper. Sauté until the mushrooms begin to color, about 5 minutes. Add the stock, lower the heat, and simmer until the mushrooms are tender and the stock is slightly reduced. Stir in the mint and serve.

Winter Portobello Mushroom Stew

A QUICK and reliable stew with big flavors and many applications. It's best if you can use mushroom stock, but not impossible without it. Serve with soft polenta, mashed potatoes, fresh Rosemary Pasta, or Wehani Rice Pilaf.

SERVES 4

¼ cup olive oil

1 large onion, cut into ½-inch dice

2 teaspoons chopped rosemary

Salt and freshly milled pepper

2 pinches red pepper flakes

½ pound portobello mushrooms, sliced ⅜ inch thick, gills removed

1 pound large white mushrooms, thickly sliced

2 garlic cloves, minced

3 tablespoons tomato paste

1½ cups Quick Mushroom Stock, page 253, or water

1 teaspoon sherry vinegar

2 tablespoons butter, optional

2 tablespoons chopped parsley or tarragon

Heat 1 tablespoon of the oil in a large skillet over medium heat. Add the onion and rosemary and cook, stirring occasionally, until lightly browned, about 12 minutes. Season with salt, pepper, and red pepper flakes and remove to a bowl.

Return the pan to medium heat and add half the remaining oil. When it's hot, add the portobello mushrooms and sauté until nicely browned, about 5 minutes. Add them to the onion and repeat with the remaining oil and white mushrooms. Return everything to the pan and add the garlic, tomato paste, stock, and vinegar. Simmer gently for 12 to 15 minutes, then swirl in the butter. Add the parsley, taste for salt, and season with pepper.

Mushrooms with Paprika and Sour Cream

1 1/2 tablespoons *each* butter and olive oil

1 bunch scallions, including some of the greens, chopped

1 pound large white mushrooms, thickly sliced or quartered

Salt and freshly milled pepper

1 teaspoon flour

1 tablespoon sweet Hungarian paprika

1/2 cup Mushroom Stock, page 197, or Quick Mushroom Stock, page 253

1/2 cup sour cream or a mixture of sour cream and yogurt

SERVE over flat egg noodles, wild rice, buckwheat groats, or barley.

SERVES 3 OR 4

Heat the butter and oil in a wide skillet over high heat. Add the scallions and mushrooms and sauté until the mushrooms begin to color, about 6 minutes. Lower the heat and season with 3/4 teaspoon salt and pepper to taste. Sprinkle the flour and paprika over the mushrooms, add the stock, and simmer, covered, for 3 to 4 minutes. Stir in the sour cream and gently heat through, but do not boil.

Variation with Tofu: Dice a 10-ounce block of firm silken tofu into 1-inch cubes. Simmer in a pan of salted water for 4 minutes, then drain. Add the tofu to the mushrooms once they've colored. The tofu should color as well; move it gently in the pan with a rubber spatula so that all sides are exposed to the heat. Continue the recipe as described, adding a little more stock as needed.

Tunisian Pepper and Potato Couscous

1/3 cup plus 2 tablespoons olive oil

1 large onion, diced in 1/2-inch squares

1 1/2 teaspoons dried mint

1/2 teaspoon crushed red pepper flakes

1 pound boiling potatoes, peeled and cut lengthwise into sixths

2 tablespoons tomato paste

6 garlic cloves, peeled and crushed

1 1/2 cups cooked chickpeas, rinsed if canned

Salt

5 bell peppers, mixed colors, sliced into 1-inch-wide strips

4 tomatoes, peeled, seeded, and chopped

1 1/2 cups couscous

1/3 cup Harissa, page 75

3 tablespoons chopped parsley

THESE summer vegetables yield an excellent broth, part of which is used to cook the couscous pilaf-style.

SERVES 6

In a wide skillet with 2-inch sides, heat 1/3 cup oil over medium heat. Add the onion, mint, pepper flakes, potatoes, tomato paste, and garlic. Cook, stirring occasionally, for 10 minutes, then add the chickpeas, 1 1/2 teaspoons salt, and the peppers. Raise the heat and sauté for 2 minutes. Add the tomatoes and 3 cups water, reduce the heat to low, and simmer, partially covered, until the potatoes are tender, about 20 minutes. When done, remove 2 cups of the liquid for the couscous and set the vegetables aside.

Heat the reserved broth and stir in a teaspoon of the Harissa. Warm the 2 tablespoons oil in a wide pot over medium-high heat. Add the couscous and cook, stirring constantly, for about 1 minute. Turn off the heat and pour in the broth—it will instantly bubble up. When it subsides, shake the pan to even the contents, then cover and set aside for 7 minutes. Fluff the grains with a fork, spoon 1/2 cup water over them, and cover again for 5 minutes. Garnish with parsley and serve remaining Harissa on the side.

Cashew Curry

I am indebted to Joe Evans for this very luxurious dish. Though rich, cashew nuts are composed mainly of monounsaturated fat —and even small portions are filling. The cashews need 6 hours to soak, so plan ahead. Serve with basmati rice. Curry leaves are available at Indian markets.

SERVES 4

½ pound whole cashew nuts

2 tablespoons clarified butter, or ghee

5 shallots, thinly sliced

2 small bay leaves or 5 curry leaves

1 2-inch piece lemongrass or grated zest of 1 lemon

1 tablespoon ground coriander

½ teaspoon turmeric

2 serrano chiles, thinly sliced

2 garlic cloves, chopped

2 slices ginger

Salt

1 15-ounce can unsweetened coconut milk

2 tablespoon chopped cilantro

Soak the cashews for 6 hours, changing the water several times so the nuts will whiten. Drain, then put them in a saucepan with 1½ cups water and simmer until tender, 12 to 15 minutes. Taste them as they cook to make sure they don't become mushy. Drain and set aside.

Heat the butter in a small skillet, add the shallots, and cook over medium heat until golden, stirring occasionally, about 10 minutes. Add the bay leaves, lemongrass, coriander, turmeric, chiles, garlic, ginger, and ½ teaspoon salt. Cook until fragrant, then add the coconut milk, 1 tablespoon cilantro, and cashews. Simmer over moderate heat until the sauce is thickened, stirring occasionally. Remove the bay leaves. Garnish with remaining cilantro.

Spaghetti Squash with Oyster Mushroom and Pearl Onion Ragout

With the little pearl onions and oyster mushrooms, this definitely qualifies as a company dish.

SERVES 4

1 spaghetti squash, about 3 pounds, pierced in several places

1 pound pearl onions

2 tablespoons olive oil

1 tablespoon butter, plus extra for the squash

1 teaspoon sugar

1 parsnip, peeled and finely diced

1 carrot, peeled and finely diced

¼ teaspoon dried thyme

1 teaspoon chopped sage leaves

Salt and freshly milled pepper

1 large garlic clove, minced

1 pound oyster mushrooms, stems removed, or white mushrooms, thinly sliced

4 teaspoons tomato paste diluted with ¼ cup red wine or water

2 tablespoons mushroom soy or regular soy sauce

2 tablespoons chopped parsley

Preheat the oven to 375°F. Set the squash in a pan and bake for 40 minutes. Turn it over and continue baking until completely tender, another 15 to 30 minutes. When done, turn off the oven and let the squash sit until needed.

Meanwhile, cut a sliver off the root ends of the onions. Boil them for 1 minute, then transfer to a bowl of cold water. Peel and cut any larger ones in half.

Heat 1 tablespoon each oil and butter in a large skillet over medium heat. Add the onions, toss to coat, then sprinkle with sugar. Cook, giving the pan a shake now and then, until they start to color, after about 10 minutes. Add the parsnip, carrot, and herbs, season with salt and pepper, and continue cooking until the onions are nicely caramelized, about 10 minutes more.

Set the vegetables aside in a bowl, add another tablespoon of oil to the pan, then add the garlic and mushrooms. Stir quickly, season with salt and pepper, and cook until they begin to color, about 5 minutes. Add the onions back to the pan and add the diluted tomato paste and soy sauce. Cook until the mushrooms are tender, then turn off the heat. (To keep the vegetables moist and to make a little sauce, add water or mushroom stock in small increments.)

Cut the cooked squash in half lengthwise and scoop out the seeds. Pull apart the strands with a fork, toss them with butter to taste, and season with salt and pepper. Pile the squash onto four individual plates, spoon the vegetables around it, garnish with parsley, and serve.

Thai Tofu and Winter Squash Stew

2 to 3 medium leeks, white parts only, about 6 ounces

2 tablespoons roasted peanut oil, plus extra for the tofu, if desired

2 garlic cloves, finely chopped

2 serrano chiles, minced

1 tablespoon finely chopped ginger

1 tablespoon curry powder

1 teaspoon light brown sugar

3 tablespoons mushroom soy sauce

1 15-ounce can unsweetened coconut milk

1 1/2 pounds butternut squash, peeled and diced into 1/2-inch cubes

Salt

1 10-ounce package silken firm tofu, cut into 1/2-inch cubes

Juice of 1 lime

1/3 cup raw peanuts

1/4 cup chopped cilantro

When I was a Zen student, I heard many stories about the monotony of eating boiled tofu and squash in Chinese monasteries. This Thai stew, simmered in a spicy coconut milk broth, is anything but dull, and it's very easy to make. Frying the tofu in roasted peanut oil until golden and crisp adds both flavor and texture. To fry the tofu, drain it while you prepare the ingredients. Heat 1 1/2 tablespoons oil in a non-stick skillet. Dice the tofu, add it to the pan, and fry until golden, 10 to 12 minutes, turning occasionally. You can, however, simmer it directly in the sauce if you prefer to avoid using the extra oil. Serve over basmati or jasmine rice.

SERVES 3 TO 4

Halve the leeks lengthwise, then cut them crosswise into 1/4-inch pieces. Wash well in a bowl of water, then drain.

Heat the oil in a wide soup pot. Add the leeks and cook over fairly high heat, stirring frequently, until partially softened, about 3 minutes. Add the garlic, most of the chiles, and ginger, cook 1 minute more, then add the curry, sugar, and soy sauce. Reduce the heat to medium, scrape the pan, and cook for a few minutes more. Add 3 cups water, the coconut milk, squash, and 1 teaspoon salt. Bring to a boil, then lower the heat and simmer, covered, for 15 minutes. Add the tofu, fried or raw, to the stew once the squash is almost tender, then simmer until it's done. Taste for salt and add the lime juice.

Meanwhile, fry the peanuts in a few drops of peanut oil in a small skillet over medium heat until browned, then coarsely chop. Serve the stew over rice with the cilantro, peanuts, and remaining chile scattered over the top.

Spring Vegetable Ragout

Using a preponderance of artichokes gives this little stew the soft feel of a cloudy spring day, while more peas and asparagus provide a sunnier aspect. In either case, the stew can be completed up to the final step, then finished at the last minute. Serve it with popovers, between rounds of puff pastry, or tucked into six small pre-baked tart shells lined with the Tart Pastry.

SERVES 4 TO 6

1 pound thick asparagus, tough ends trimmed

Salt and freshly milled white pepper

3 large artichokes, trimmed and quartered

Juice of 1 lemon

4 tablespoons butter

1/2 cup finely diced shallots, spring onions, or leeks

4 sprigs thyme, leaves stripped and chopped

2 teaspoons chopped tarragon or basil

1/2 cup white wine

8 ounces white mushrooms, sliced about 1/4 inch thick

1 teaspoon flour

1 cup fresh or frozen peas

Peel the asparagus stalks, then slice them diagonally, leaving the tips 2 to 3 inches long. If the tips are very thick, halve them lengthwise. Bring a quart of water to the boil and add 1 teaspoon salt. Blanch the slivered stalks until bright green and tender-firm, about 2 minutes. Scoop them out and rinse with cold water. Next blanch the tips until tender-firm, about 4 minutes, then rinse and set aside. Thinly slice the quartered artichokes. Add the lemon juice to the water and boil until tender-firm, about 5 minutes. Drain and set aside.

Melt the butter in a 10- or 12-inch skillet or sauté pan. When foamy, add the shallots, thyme, and half the tarragon. Cook over medium heat, stirring occasionally, for 3 to 4 minutes, then add the wine and simmer until it has reduced to a syrupy consistency. Add the mushrooms and 1 teaspoon salt. Raise the heat to high, and sauté, stirring frequently, until they've given up their juices and become tender, after about 5 minutes. Add the artichokes to the pan, sprinkle the flour over the top and carefully fold it into the vegetables. Add 1 cup water or vegetable stock and simmer until the vegetables are heated through. (The stew can be prepared ahead of time up to this point.)

To finish the dish, add the asparagus and peas and continue cooking until they're hot. Taste for salt and season with a little pepper. Add the remaining tarragon and serve.

Winter Vegetable Stew with Sunchokes

An easy stew to assemble, it needs about 30 minutes to cook. Serve over Rosemary Pasta, buckwheat groats, or the Wehani Rice Pilaf or under a pastry lid. If you're a tofu enthusiast, drain 8 ounces firm tofu, cut it into cubes, and then fry in olive oil until browned. Add to the stew during the last 20 minutes of cooking.

SERVES 4

2 tablespoons olive oil

1 large onion, diced

6 garlic cloves, peeled

2 bay leaves

1/4 teaspoon chopped thyme

4 large carrots, cut into 2-inch lengths

2 celery ribs, cut into 2-inch lengths

4 medium boiling potatoes, peeled and quartered

1/2 pound Jerusalem artichokes (sunchokes), scrubbed and cut into 1/2-inch pieces

Salt and freshly milled pepper

1/8 teaspoon grated nutmeg

1 cup dry red wine

1 tablespoon tomato paste

1 tablespoon flour

2 tablespoons parsley chopped with 1 garlic clove

Heat the oil in a Dutch oven over medium heat. Add the onion, garlic, bay leaves, and thyme and cook, stirring occasionally, until the onion begins to brown, about 12 minutes. Add the vegetables and season with 1 1/2 teaspoons salt, pepper, and the nutmeg. Cook for 5 minutes, then raise the heat to high and add the wine. Scrape up any onion bits from the bottom, then simmer until the liquid is reduced by half. Reduce the heat to medium, add the tomato paste, sprinkle with flour, and cook, covered, for 2 minutes.

Stir in 1 cup water and cook until the liquid is again reduced by half. Reduce the heat to low, then simmer, covered, until the vegetables are tender, 20 to 25 minutes. Check the seasonings. Add the chopped parsley and garlic just before serving.

Winter Vegetable Pot Pie

1 sheet frozen puff pastry, thawed

2 cups Herb Béchamel, page 53

1½ pounds butternut squash, peeled and diced into 1-inch cubes

Flour for dredging

2 tablespoons olive oil

2 tablespoons butter

16 shallots or boiling onions, peeled and left whole

1 small celery root

Juice of 1 lemon

3 parsnips, peeled and diced

2 kohlrabi or turnips, peeled and cut into wedges

5 medium carrots, cut into 2-inch lengths

Salt and freshly milled pepper

4 thyme sprigs

½ cup cream or milk

1 egg, beaten

Choose a 2-quart soufflé or gratin dish or four individual 2-cup casseroles. Roll out the pastry between ⅛ and ¼ inch thick and cut it to fit the dish. Cut out leaves or other decorative shapes from the scraps. Refrigerate the pastry until needed. Have the béchamel cooking in a double boiler while you prepare the vegetables.

Toss the squash in flour, letting the excess fall away. Heat the oil and butter in a large skillet and add the squash and shallots. Sauté over medium heat until browned and tender, 20 to 30 minutes, stirring occasionally so that they color evenly. Transfer to the baking dish.

Peel the celery root, dice it into 1-inch cubes, and put them in the bowl with the juice plus water to cover. Parboil the remaining vegetables in salted water until tender but still a little firm. Drain, then parboil the celery root for 1 minute. Combine all the vegetables, season with salt and pepper, and transfer the stew to the dish. Tuck in the thyme sprigs.

Mix the béchamel and cream and pour it over the vegetables, allowing the sauce to fall between the cracks. Refrigerate if baking later, then bring to room temperature before baking.

When ready to bake, preheat the oven to 425°F. Remove the pastry from the refrigerator and lay it on top of the vegetables. Brush the top side with egg, add any decorations, and glaze them, too. Bake for 12 minutes, then lower the heat to 350°F and continue baking until the crust is golden and puffed and the sauce is bubbling, 15 to 20 minutes more. Let settle for a few minutes, then serve.

Dairy-Free Variation: Make the sauce with any vegetable stock, Quick Mushroom Stock, page 253, or soy milk, using 2½ cups in all. Sauté the vegetables in olive oil. Replace the puff pastry with Yeasted Tart Dough with Olive Oil, page 489.

TOPPING a stew with a puff pastry lid makes an impressive dish even if you use frozen puff pastry, which I usually do. The vegetable amounts given here are really suggestions. Salsify, parsley root, and other vegetables are wonderful additions if you have the good fortune to come across them. Oyster mushrooms, Brussels sprouts, fennel, and Jerusalem artichokes are other good candidates for this stew. Except for the oyster mushrooms, the vegetables should be parboiled before being added to the final dish.

This stew is a little more elaborate to make than other dishes, but while the sauce is cooking you can prepare the vegetables, and the whole dish, minus the pastry, can be put together hours or a day in advance of baking.

SERVES 4

Stir-Fries

THE *speed and lightness of the stir-fry have made it one of the most appealing and healthful dishes for home cooks. Many people tell me that they find the singular activity of cleaning and slicing the vegetables to be relaxing at the end of the day. I've always been more of stew person, but as I have learned about stir-frying I have grown to appreciate its rhythm and flavors. I find it's a method that works with a variety of vegetables and non-Asian seasonings, as some of these recipes testify.*

What Is Stir-Frying?

Stir-frying is, in short, a single motion made of three parts:

1. Sautéing the aromatics (chile, garlic, and scallions) in oil

2. Adding the vegetables and stock and, in some cases, steaming them

3. Thickening with cornstarch or adding other sauce ingredients

The first step infuses the oil with flavor. The second step cooks the vegetables. The third concentrates the juices and thickens the sauce.

Stir-frying developed where fuel is scarce—hence the fine slicing and the wok itself. With its thin metal walls, the wok conducts heat rapidly so that flavors are sealed in and the vegetables cook quickly. You may prefer to use a large, lightweight skillet, but the cooking motions will still be fast and energetic. You can expect to make a racket as the utensils—a large metal spatula and ladle—clang against the metal sides of the wok. One of the best ways to get a vivid sense of stir-frying is to go to a Chinese restaurant where you can watch the cooks throw themselves into it. It's exhilarating to watch.

How to Make (Most) Stir-Fries

Some stir-fries are very simple—just a single vegetable—while others have layerings of ingredients such as vegetables, tofu, condiments, noodles, and so on. Nonetheless, these basic techniques pertain to all.

1. Have all your ingredients cut, sliced, blanched when appropriate, measured, and set out in bowls within easy reach of the stove before you begin to cook.

2. Set the wok over high heat before adding the oil, then swirl or push the oil around the sides and heat until a haze forms before you begin cooking. (Author Eileen Yin-Fei Lo heats a slice of ginger in the oil and knows that when it turns light brown the oil is hot enough.)

2. Add the aromatics—scallions, ginger, garlic, red pepper flakes—and immediately begin quickly pushing and moving them around the wok. This process takes 30 seconds to 1 minute.

3. Add the vegetables and a few pinches salt and energetically stir them about the pan with the spatula. Keep moving the food from the center of the wok to the hot sides so it will cook quickly.

4. If called for, add stock or mushroom-soaking water, condiments, soy sauce, tofu, etc. Also if called for, cover the wok and let everything cook until it's sufficiently tender. When the vegetables are done, make a space in the middle and add diluted cornstarch if the recipe calls for it. Once it thickens and darkens, toss to coat the vegetables.

5. Add final seasonings, such as roasted sesame or peanut oil, cilantro, toasted seeds or nuts, etc. Taste and add more salt or soy sauce if needed.

Some Essential Chinese Ingredients

A few staples and some of the wonderful pungent Chinese condiments available in many supermarkets and Chinese groceries will greatly enhance your stir-fries and give them an interesting range of flavors, tastes, and textures. Stir-fry enthusiasts, however, will undoubtedly go far beyond this modest list.

PEANUT OIL: Light and neutral, peanut oil with a high smoke point

ROASTED PEANUT OIL: Richer, with the clear aroma of peanuts, used for the stir-frying or as a flavoring at the end. Two Chinese brands are Lion and Globe; Loriva is American.

DARK SESAME OIL: Dark color and rich, deep flavor make roasted sesame oil an excellent and potent seasoning. A few drops are added to the Stock for Stir-Fries and to a finished stir-fry. Japanese Kadoya brand is excellent. Chili oil is chile-seasoned dark sesame oil.

SOY SAUCE: A visit to an Asian market or even the Asian section of your supermarket will reveal that there's more than one kind of soy sauce. There's thin or light soy, dark soy, a deep mushroom-based soy, and the super-concentrated Japanese tamari. There's also sodium-reduced and lite soy sauce. When it comes to these stir-fries, thin soy sauce or regular Kikkoman are the ones to use for they won't overwhelm the vegetables. The richer sauces, like bigger wines, go better in dishes where meat or fowl are present. However, mushroom soy and tamari do provide deep and hearty flavors. If you like them, just use half the amount called for, then add more, if needed, to taste.

BLACK RICE VINEGAR: A mild vinegar that is uncommonly dark and rich in color. Balsamic or apple cider vinegar can be used in its place.

WHITE RICE VINEGAR: Clear and very mild with a hint of the sweetness of rice. The Japanese version is delicate but not as interesting as some Chinese brands, such as Narcissus and Swatow.

CHINESE WINE (SHAO-HSING): A rich, mellow flavor that isn't easily duplicated by other wines, although pale dry sherry can be used in its place. Keep corked and at room temperature.

CHINESE BLACK MUSHROOMS: These can also be brown. They resemble shiitake, with the familiar mushroom shape. They need to be soaked in warm water for 20 minutes before being used. A longer soak is even better if time allows. Remove the tough stems, carefully pour off the soaking water, and use it in the stir-fry.

CLOUD EARS: These thin fungi do not have a classic mushroom shape, but they have a lovely texture that's a little crunchy and a good flavor that's on the edge of smokiness. Soak them in hot water for 25 minutes, then run your fingers over them and remove any tough knots. Tree ears are similar but larger.

TOFU: Use the Chinese-style firm tofu or the finer silken firm tofu that comes packed in a sealed 10-ounce box. Its taste and texture are more delicate and fragile than the Chinese tofu.

CHILLI PASTE WITH GARLIC OR CHILLI PASTE WITH SOYBEAN (LAN CHI BRAND): These jarred pastes add immediate fire, but fire that's interesting, not just hot.

VEGETARIAN BARBECUE SAUCE: This flavorful condiment is based on mushroom powder with ginger, sesame, soybean sauce, and, I believe, star anise or five-spice powder—at least it tastes that way. A.G.V. brand is the one I use. Nonvegetarian barbecue sauces are based on shrimp and fish.

HOISIN SAUCE: A red, sweet, sometimes pungent spicy sauce, hoisin can now be found in most supermarkets. If at a Chinese market, seek out Ma Ling brand.

SALTED AND FERMENTED BLACK BEANS: Black soybeans partially fermented and preserved with salt add a rich flavor to vegetables, especially asparagus, green beans, and broccoli. Crush them with the flat of a knife before adding them to release their flavor. The best come in a plastic bag with ginger and orange peel.

Stock for Stir-Fries

YOU won't need much—¹/₂ cup or so—but a flavorful stock does add taste to your finished stir-fry. This stock can also serve as a base for miso soup and other Asian dishes. One recipe will give you enough stock for quite a few dishes. It will keep, refrigerated, for a week. If you don't use it that quickly, make it in half the quantity or plan to freeze what you don't use.

MAKES 3 TO 4 CUPS

5 Chinese dried black or shiitake mushrooms

1 bunch scallions, including the greens

1 small onion or leek, finely sliced

2 large carrots, thinly sliced

1 cup mung bean sprouts

¹/₂ cup chopped cilantro stems and leaves

2 ginger slices and 3 garlic cloves, chopped

1 6-inch piece kombu

1 tablespoon soy sauce

1 tablespoon rice wine (mirin)

1¹/₂ teaspoons salt

1 teaspoon dark sesame oil

Put all the ingredients except the sesame oil in a pot with 7 cups cold water. Bring to a boil and cook at a lively simmer for 40 minutes. After 20 minutes, remove the mushrooms and set them aside to use in a stir-fry or miso soup. Strain and return to the stove. Add the oil and taste for salt and soy sauce, adding more to taste if needed.

Chinese Noodle Cake

½ pound thin fresh or dried Chinese egg
   noodles

2 teaspoons dark sesame oil

1½ tablespoons sesame or peanut oil for
   frying

Gently pull the fresh noodles apart with your fingers into a large, loose heap. Boil them in a large pot of salted water until pleasantly firm, 2 to 3 minutes. Drain and rinse under cold water. Shake well, then toss with the dark sesame oil.

Lightly film an 8- or 10-inch nonstick skillet with half the lighter oil. When it's hot, add the noodles, then, with a spatula, neaten the sides and press down lightly on the noodles. Fry over medium heat until they're browned on the bottom, about 5 minutes. Place a plate on top, grasp the skillet, and invert the cake. Return the empty pan to the heat, add the rest of the oil, and slide the cake back in to cook the second side. Serve on a large round platter, topped with or accompanied by a stir-fry.

THESE fat cushiony cakes make an appealing accompaniment to stir-fried vegetables and a nice change from rice. The finished cakes can be held in a low oven if there's a gap in your timing. Chinese egg noodles are usually found in the Asian vegetable section of the supermarket, but spaghettini can be used in their place.

**MAKES ONE
8- TO 10-INCH CAKE**

Vegetable Stir-Fry with Fermented Black Beans

The Aromatics

2 tablespoons roasted peanut oil, plus
   extra to finish

2 teaspoons chopped garlic

3 teaspoons minced ginger

2 tablespoons chopped scallion

2 tablespoons fermented black beans,
   chopped

1 teaspoon red pepper flakes

**The Vegetables (Select 7 to 8 cups
from the following)**

Green beans, sliced diagonally

Broccoli florets and stems, peeled and
   sliced; briefly parboiled

Asparagus, sliced diagonally; briefly
   parboiled

Zucchini, cut into rounds

Snow peas, slivered or left whole

1 cup Stock for Stir-Fries, page 262

1 tablespoon soy sauce

1 tablespoon rice wine (mirin) or sherry

2 teaspoons cornstarch mixed with
   2 tablespoons stock or water

FERMENTED black beans add a pungent, rich flavor to this colorful stir-fry.

SERVES 4 TO 6

Set the wok over high heat, swirl the oil around the sides, and when hot add the garlic, ginger, scallion, black beans, and pepper flakes. Stir-fry 1 minute. Add the vegetables and stir-fry for 2 minutes. Add ½ cup of the stock, the soy sauce, and rice wine and simmer until the vegetables are tender-firm.

Remove the vegetables to a platter, add the rest of the stock to the wok, stir in the cornstarch, and simmer until the sauce is thickened. Pour it over the vegetables and drizzle a little roasted peanut oil over the top.

Stir-Fried Bok Choy with Roasted Peanuts

BOK choy is like two vegetables in one—the crisp stem, the tender leaf. Serve with rice or noodles.

SERVES 2 TO 4

3 tablespoons raw peanuts

2 teaspoons roasted peanut oil

1/4 teaspoon red pepper flakes

Salt

1 1/2 pounds bok choy

2 tablespoons peanut oil

4 garlic cloves, minced

4 teaspoons minced ginger

2 tablespoons soy sauce

1 teaspoon cornstarch mixed with 3 tablespoons Stock for Stir-Fries, page 262, or water

1 teaspoon roasted peanut oil

Fry the peanuts in 2 teaspoons roasted peanut oil until they're golden. Chop with the pepper flakes and a few pinches salt and set aside.

Slice off the bok choy stems and cut them into 1-inch pieces. Leave the leaves whole. Set the wok over high heat. Add the 2 tablespoons peanut oil and roll it around the sides. When hot, add the garlic and ginger and stir-fry for 1 minute. Add the bok choy and a few pinches salt and stir-fry until wilted and glossy. Add the soy sauce and cornstarch and stir-fry for 1 or 2 minutes more or until the leaves are shiny and glazed. Add the crushed peanuts, toss, and serve.

Stir-Fried Mixed Greens

FOR the most interesting stir-fry, use a combination of greens—mustard greens, spinach, romaine lettuce, Napa cabbage, bok choy, and watercress. Serve them with rice or buckwheat noodles garnished with toasted sesame seeds.

SERVES 2 TO 4

1 tablespoon peanut oil

1 teaspoon roasted peanut oil

1 tablespoon minced garlic

1 tablespoon chopped ginger

1/2 teaspoon red pepper flakes

2 tablespoons chopped scallions

10 cups greens, sliced into ribbons about 3/4 inch thick

1/2 cup Stock for Stir-Fries, page 262

Salt

2 teaspoons dark sesame oil

1 teaspoon rice wine (mirin) or medium-dry sherry

1 teaspoon cornstarch diluted with 3 tablespoons water or stock

Heat the wok and add both peanut oils. When hot, add the garlic, ginger, red pepper flakes, and scallions. Stir-fry 30 seconds, then add the greens and stir-fry for 1 minute more. Add the stock, cover, and steam until tender, after 2 or 3 minutes. Season with salt, sesame oil, and mirin.

Letting the juices fall back into the wok, lift the greens with tongs and set them on a platter. Add the cornstarch to the juices left in the wok and boil until thickened. Pour the sauce over the greens.

Stir-Fried Watercress

3 to 4 good-size bunches watercress,
    about 10 cups

Salt

2 tablespoons sesame or peanut oil

1 teaspoon dark sesame oil

1 tablespoon minced ginger

1 garlic clove, minced

1 jalapeño chile, seeded and minced, or
    2 pinches red pepper flakes

NOT just for salads, watercress is wonderful stir-fried. While I'm loath to recommend a vegetable that's usually pricey and of poor quality, occasionally watercress does look glorious. And there are those lucky few who have access to flourishing beds of wild watercress.

SERVES 4

Trim and discard any tough or ragged stems from the watercress. Bring 3 quarts water to a boil and add 1 tablespoon salt, then the watercress. Cook until it turns bright green—1 minute should be fine—then rinse with cold water and pour into a colander. Gently press out the excess water.

Heat the wok, add the oils, and turn to coat the sides of the wok. When a haze forms, add the ginger, garlic, and chile and stir-fry for 30 seconds. Add the watercress and stir-fry until heated through, 2 to 3 minutes.

Cauliflower, Spinach, and Potato Stir-Fry with Coconut Milk

1 small cauliflower, cut into small
    florets

1/2 pound fingerling or red potatoes,
    sliced 1/3 inch thick

Salt

1 bunch scallions sliced, including a few
    inches of the greens

1/2 cup chopped cilantro

1/2 teaspoon turmeric

2 serrano chiles, minced

3 1/2 tablespoons peanut oil

1 large bunch spinach, stems removed

1 15-ounce can unsweetened coconut
    milk

THOUGH stir-fried, this is not a Chinese dish but an Indian-inspired one. Serve over brown or white basmati rice.

SERVES 3 TO 4

Separately boil the cauliflower and potatoes in salted water until tender, then drain. Set aside 2 tablespoons *each* of the scallions and cilantro and puree the remaining cilantro, turmeric, chiles, and 1 1/2 tablespoons of the peanut oil.

Heat the wok, then add 2 teaspoons of the oil and swirl it about the sides. When hot, add the scallions and stir-fry for 1 minute. Add the spinach and stir-fry until wilted and tender. Remove and set aside. Add another 2 teaspoons oil and fry the puree until fragrant. Add the cauliflower and potatoes, season with 1/2 teaspoon salt, and cook until heated through. Pour in the coconut milk and add the spinach. Bring to a boil and simmer for 2 minutes. Taste again for salt and serve garnished with the reserved cilantro and scallions.

Cauliflower with Dried Mushrooms and Bok Choy

The Vegetables

5 large dried shiitake or Chinese black mushrooms

2 cups cauliflower florets

2 carrots, peeled and cut into julienne strips

Salt

1 bok choy, leaves cut into ribbons, stems cut into thin strips

The Aromatics

1 tablespoon peanut oil

1 tablespoon chopped ginger

1 tablespoon minced garlic

1 cup chopped scallions, including a few inches of the greens

$1\frac{1}{2}$ tablespoons cornstarch stirred into $\frac{1}{3}$ cup stock or water

2 teaspoons soy sauce

2 teaspoons dark sesame oil

1 teaspoon chili oil

$\frac{1}{4}$ cup chopped cilantro

2 scallions, including most of the reens, slivered diagonally

Cover the mushrooms with $\frac{1}{2}$ cup warm water and let stand for 20 minutes, until softened. Reserve the water, discard the mushroom stems, and slice the caps. Parboil the cauliflower and carrots separately in salted water until barely tender. Drain and rinse in cold water. Assemble the aromatics.

Heat the wok. Add the peanut oil and swirl it around the pan. When hot, add the ginger, garlic, scallions, and mushrooms. Stir-fry for 2 minutes, then add the cauliflower, carrots, and bok choy stems and leaves. Season with a little salt, add the reserved mushroom water, and simmer, covered, for 3 minutes. Add the cornstarch mixture and simmer until the liquid is thickened and the vegetables are coated nicely. Toss with the soy sauce, sesame and chili oils, and cilantro. Serve garnished with the scallions.

Stir-Fried Carrots, Jícama, and Watercress

I OFTEN use jícama as a substitute for fresh water chestnuts, but here it stands on its own.

2 tablespoons soy sauce

3 tablespoons water or Stock for Stir-Fries, page 262

$\frac{1}{2}$ teaspoon brown sugar

1 teaspoon dark sesame oil

2 tablespoons peanut or light sesame oil

4 teaspoons minced garlic

2 tablespoons chopped ginger

3 carrots, peeled and julienned

Salt

1 pound jícama, peeled and julienned $\frac{1}{4}$ inch thick

1 bunch watercress, large stems removed, the remainder coarsely chopped

2 teaspoons toasted black sesame seeds

In a small dish, combine the soy sauce, water, sugar, and dark sesame oil.

Heat the wok. Add the 2 tablespoons sesame oil and swirl it around. When it's hot, add the garlic and ginger. Stir-fry for 1 minute, add the carrots and a few pinches salt. Stir-fry for 2 minutes, add the jícama and reserved seasonings, and continue to stir-fry until the carrots are tender-firm. Add the watercress and stir-fry for 30 seconds more. Serve garnished with the sesame seeds.

Indian-Style Sauté of Cauliflower and Greens

3 potatoes, peeled and cubed

¼ cup clarified butter or ghee

1 large onion, thinly sliced

1 small cauliflower, quartered and thinly sliced, including the stem

Salt

2 teaspoons chopped garlic

½ teaspoon turmeric

1 teaspoon *each* ground cumin and coriander

1 teaspoon mustard seeds

1 bunch spinach, stems removed

1 bunch watercress, large stems removed

1 small carrot, grated

Juice of 1 lime

Several pinches Garam Masala, page 36

Cilantro sprigs for garnish

AGAIN, I am indebted to Joe Evans for this dish, which marries the rich aromas of a curry with the speedy lightness of a stir-fry. The ghee is important to this dish for its flavor and high heating point. Serve with Naan or pappadums.

SERVES 4

Steam the potatoes until tender. Heat 2 tablespoons of the butter in a wide sauté pan over medium-high heat. Add the onion and sauté until well browned, about 12 minutes. Remove and set aside. Melt the remaining butter in the same pan over high heat. Add the cauliflower, season with salt, and sauté until it begins to color in places, after a few minutes. Return the onion to the pan and add the garlic, spices, and potatoes. Lower the heat and cook until everything is heated through, about 4 minutes. Add the greens, carrot, and ½ cup water. Cover and cook until the greens are wilted, about a minute. Season with lime juice and a few pinches garam masala, then turn onto a platter and garnish with the sprigs of cilantro.

Stir-Fried Roasted Eggplant

THE eggplant is first
roasted in the oven, then
pulled into pieces, a
process that ensures both
tenderness and texture.
It can be done well in
advance of stir-frying,
even a day before. For
eggplant, my favorites
are the plump 8-ounce
Rositas or one of the
slender Asian varieties,
such as Asian Bride.

SERVES 4

1½ to 2 pounds eggplant

2 tablespoons Lan Chi Chilli Bean
   Sauce with Garlic or ½ teaspoon red
   pepper flakes

1 cup Stock for Stir-Fries, page 262

3 tablespoons rice wine (mirin) or sherry

3 tablespoons soy sauce

1½ tablespoons black rice vinegar or
   balsamic vinegar

¼ cup tomato paste

1 tablespoon light brown sugar

1½ tablespoons roasted peanut oil

1 bunch scallions, including most of the
   greens, thinly sliced into rounds

1 tablespoon finely chopped ginger

1 large garlic clove, minced

2 tomatoes, seeded and diced into large
   pieces

Preheat the oven to 400°F. Pierce the eggplant in a few places, put it in a pan, and bake
until very soft when pressed with your fingers, 35 minutes to 1 hour, depending on the
size. As soon as it's cool enough to handle, pull off the skin and pull the flesh into strips
about 1 inch thick. Don't worry about flecks of skin. Combine the chilli sauce, stock,
wine, soy, vinegar, tomato paste, and sugar in a small bowl and set aside.

Heat the wok, add the oil, and swirl it around the sides. Add half the scallions, all of the
ginger, and the garlic and stir-fry for 1 minute. Next add the eggplant and stir-fry for
about 2 minutes. Add the tomatoes and remaining ingredients. Simmer until the eggplant is heated through, 3 to 4 minutes. Garnish with the reserved scallions.

Stir-Fried Brown Rice with Broccoli Rabe

THIS combination of
elements was inspired by
a recipe of Elizabeth
Schneider's. Use cold
leftover rice if possible—
it always seems to come
out better than fresh.
Delicious served with a
miso soup and a Napa
cabbage salad.

SERVES 3 TO 4

1 bunch broccoli rabe or mustard greens

3 tablespoons roasted peanut oil

½ cup Spanish peanuts, skinned

1 bunch scallions, including half of the
   greens, sliced

2 tablespoons finely chopped ginger

1 jalapeño chile, seeded and finely diced

½ cup chopped cilantro

3 cups cooked brown rice

Salt

1 or 2 eggs

2 tablespoons soy sauce

Peel the broccoli rabe stems, then plunge the whole bunch into a pot of boiling salted
water. Cook for 5 minutes, then drain and chop coarsely.

Heat the oil in a large skillet or wok and fry the peanuts over medium-high heat until
golden. Scoop them out, leaving the oil behind. Add the scallions, ginger, chile, and half
the cilantro and stir-fry over high heat for 1 minute. Add the rice and the greens, season
with a few pinches salt, and stir-fry until the rice is hot throughout. Now lower the heat
a little and make a well in the middle. Mix the egg with the soy sauce, add it to the well,

and stir like crazy to distribute the egg. It will cook quickly. Taste and add more soy sauce if needed. Toss with the remaining cilantro and the peanuts and serve.

Fried Rice with Tofu: Instead of or in addition to the eggs, cut one 10-ounce box firm tofu into small cubes and fry it with the scallions until light gold and firm.

Mushrooms and Tofu in Hoisin Sauce

8 to 12 dried Chinese black or shiitake mushrooms

1 block Chinese-style firm tofu, drained, or 2 10-ounce boxes silken firm tofu

2 tablespoons peanut or sesame oil

2 teaspoons chopped garlic

3/4 pound fresh white or shiitake mushrooms, stems removed from the shiitakes, caps quartered

Salt

3 tablespoons rice wine vinegar

Mushroom-soaking water plus Stock for Stir-Fries, page 262, to make 2 cups

2 teaspoons dark sesame oil

1 tablespoon soy sauce

3 tablespoons hoisin sauce

1/2 cup chopped tomato, fresh or canned

2 teaspoons cornstarch dissolved in 2 tablespoons water

2 scallions, including the greens, sliced diagonally

WITH its dark glossy sauce, this stir-fry is especially good over buckwheat noodles and accompanied by a simple vegetable—steamed ribbons of Napa cabbage or slivers of carrots. It can sit in the wok while you finish the accompaniments.

SERVES 4 TO 6

Put the dried mushrooms in a bowl with warm water to cover and let soak for 20 minutes or until soft. Reserve the soaking water, remove the stems, and cut the caps into quarters. Cut the drained tofu into 1/2-inch cubes.

Heat a wok, add the oil, and swirl it around the sides. When it's hot, add the garlic. Stir-fry for 30 seconds. Add the fresh and dried mushrooms and 1/2 teaspoon salt and stir-fry for 2 minutes. Add the vinegar, mushroom water plus stock, dark sesame oil, soy sauce, hoisin sauce, and tomato. Stir everything together, then add the tofu. Lower the heat and simmer for 4 minutes. Add the dissolved cornstarch and cook until the sauce is thickened, another minute or so. Serve garnished with the scallions.

Stir-Fried Broccoli, Mushrooms, and Peppers with Caramelized Tofu

THE *caramelized tofu provides a flavorful, chewy morsel, and the peppers add a needed spot of color. If you have no time to make the tofu, use strips of aburage, fried tofu, or commercially seasoned and pressed tofu.*

SERVES 4

2½ tablespoons roasted peanut oil

2 garlic cloves, minced

1 teaspoon finely chopped ginger

8 ounces broccoli florets

6 ounces fresh shiitake or white mushrooms, stems removed from shiitakes, thickly sliced

1 tablespoon *each* rice wine vinegar, brown sugar, and soy sauce

½ cup water or Stock for Stir-Fries, page 262

1 red bell pepper, cut into long narrow strips

Caramelized Golden Tofu, thinly sliced, page 599

2 scallions, including an inch of the greens, sliced

Add the oil to a heated wok. When hot, add the garlic and ginger and stir-fry for 1 minute. Add the broccoli and mushrooms and stir-fry for 2 minutes. Add the remaining ingredients, except the tofu and scallions, then cover and cook until the broccoli is tender, 4 to 5 minutes. Add the tofu and cook for 2 minutes more. Serve garnished with the scallions.

Dried Mushroom, Leek, and Tofu Stir-Fry with Chinese Barbecue Sauce

CHINESE *vegetarian barbecue sauce is made with mushroom powder and fragrant star anise. I don't know its traditional use, but I think it works very well in producing an exotic and hearty stir-fry.*

SERVES 4

8 dried Chinese black or shiitake mushrooms

3 medium leeks, white parts only

2 tablespoons roasted peanut oil

2 teaspoons chopped fresh ginger

4 scallions, including the greens, chopped

3 teaspoons chopped garlic

Salt

1 cup mushroom-soaking water or Stock for Stir-Fries, page 262

3 tablespoons vegetarian barbecue sauce or hoisin sauce

2 10-ounce boxes silken firm tofu, cut into cubes

Cover the mushrooms with hot water and let stand for 20 minutes to soften. Reserve the liquid, remove and discard the stems from the mushrooms, and thinly slice the caps. Cut the leeks into 2-inch lengths, then slice lengthwise into strips. Wash well.

Heat the wok, add the oil, and, when hot, add the ginger, scallions, and garlic. Stir-fry for 30 seconds. Add the mushrooms, leeks, a few pinches salt and stir-fry for 2 minutes before adding the mushroom water. Cover and cook until the leeks and mushrooms are tender-firm, about 4 minutes. Stir in the barbecue sauce and set the tofu on top. Cover and simmer until the tofu is warmed through and firm, about 5 minutes. Gently stir the mixture to coat the tofu with the sauce, then serve. (For a thicker sauce, add 1 teaspoon cornstarch, diluted in stock or water, at the end.)

Vegetable Stir-Fry with Glass Noodles

2 ounces mung bean noodles

6 dried Chinese black or shiitake
  mushrooms

1 pound vegetables, such as carrots,
  asparagus, broccoli, beans

3 tablespoons sesame or peanut oil

4 teaspoons *each* chopped garlic and
  ginger

1 onion, chopped

1 bok choy, sliced into 1-inch strips

Salt

2 tablespoons soy sauce

¾ cup mushroom-soaking water or
  Stock for Stir-Fries, page 262

2 teaspoons cornstarch diluted in
  3 tablespoons stock or water

1 teaspoon dark sesame, roasted peanut,
  or chili oil

*MADE from mung bean
flour, these noodles (also
called bean threads)
look like a dry bundle of
sticks until they're recon-
stituted in water. When
cooked, they're clear and
slippery.*

SERVES 4

Soak the noodles in warm water for 20 minutes or until soft. Drain. Cover the mushrooms with 1 cup warm water and soak for 20 minutes. Reserve the liquid, discard the
stems, and slice the caps into strips. Thinly slice the vegetables.

Heat the wok, add 2 tablespoons of the oil, and swirl it around. When hot, add the garlic, ginger, onion, and mushrooms. Stir-fry for 1 minute, then add the vegetables. Salt
them lightly and stir-fry for 4 to 5 minutes or until tender-firm. Remove and set aside.
Heat the third tablespoon oil in the wok, add the noodles, soy sauce, and mushroom water, and simmer for 2 minutes. Return the vegetables to the wok, add the diluted cornstarch, and cook until the vegetables are glazed. Toss with the dark sesame oil and serve.

Stir-Fried Peppers with Cloud Ear Mushrooms and Egg Slivers

The Egg Slivers

2 eggs, beaten with 1 teaspoon dark sesame oil

Salt

2 teaspoons peanut oil

The Vegetables and Seasonings

1/4 cup dried cloud ear mushrooms

4 teaspoons roasted peanut or dark sesame oil

1 tablespoon chopped garlic

1 tablespoon chopped ginger

2 tablespoons chopped scallions

1 teaspoon Lan Chi Chilli Paste, or 1 jalapeño chile, seeded and chopped

4 bell peppers, different colors, sliced lengthwise 3/8 inch thick

1 tablespoon soy sauce

1 tablespoon rice vinegar

1 cup mushroom-soaking water or Stock for Stir-Fries, page 262

1 to 2 handfuls mung bean sprouts, rinsed and picked over

2 teaspoons cornstarch diluted in 2 tablespoons mushroom-soaking liquid

Season the eggs with a pinch of salt. Heat the peanut oil in the wok, swirl it around the sides, then add the eggs and immediately swirl them around the sides—don't worry if they lump up in the middle. Cook over medium heat until they're set, then loosen them, turn them over, and cook the other side briefly. Turn the eggs onto a cutting board, roll them up, and cut into ribbons. Set aside.

Soak the mushrooms in 1 cup boiling water to cover for 15 minutes. Remove the mushrooms and reserve the water. Discard the knotty, tough parts of the mushrooms and slice the rest into thin strips.

Wipe out the wok. Add the peanut oil and, when hot, add the garlic, ginger, scallions, and chilli paste. Stir-fry for 45 seconds. Add the peppers and mushrooms, stir-fry 2 minutes, then add the soy sauce, vinegar, and mushroom water. Stir-fry until the peppers are softened, about 3 1/2 minutes. Add the sprouts and cook until they're heated through. Remove everything to a platter with tongs, leaving the juices behind. Thicken the remaining juice with the cornstarch. Pour the sauce over the vegetables and garnish with the egg slivers.

Stir-Fried Sprouts with Cashews

6 Brussels sprouts, trimmed and sliced into ¼-inch strips

6 ounces sprouted lentils, peas, adzuki, or other firm sprouts

1½ tablespoons sesame or mustard oil

¼ teaspoon cumin seeds

3 garlic cloves, finely chopped

1 bunch scallions, including 2 inches of the greens, chopped

1 small onion, quartered and thinly sliced

½ cup toasted cashews

Salt

2 tablespoons lime juice to taste

BHARTI Kirchner, an Indian-born cook, author, and world traveler, offered this unusual stir-fry recipe in her book Indian Inspired, *which has in turn inspired me. Finally, here's a recipe that uses those hearty sprouts made from peas, lentils, and beans to best advantage. This is delicious over brown rice.*

SERVES 2

Steam the Brussels sprouts until barely tender, then rinse and set aside. Steam the sprouted beans until they're tender, 3 to 5 minutes.

Heat the oil in a wok, add the cumin seeds, and fry until they're aromatic and lightly browned. Add the garlic and, as soon as it begins to color, add the scallions and onion. Stir-fry until the onion is translucent, 3 to 4 minutes. Lower the heat and add the Brussels sprouts, sprouted legumes, and cashews. Cook, uncovered, for 1 minute more or until heated through. Remove from the heat and season with salt and lime juice to taste.

Sweet and Sour Stir-Fry with Jícama

The Vegetables

4 carrots, roll-cut or diagonally sliced

3 large stalks broccoli, florets and stems separated, stems peeled and sliced into rounds

1 red or green bell pepper, cut into 1-inch pieces

¼ pound white mushrooms, quartered

½ cup jícama, julienned

The Aromatics

¼ cup chopped tomatoes in sauce

2 tablespoons Chinese black or balsamic vinegar

2 tablespoons light brown sugar

¼ teaspoon red pepper flakes or 2 serrano chiles, minced

Salt

¾ cup Stock for Stir-Fries, page 262

2 tablespoons roasted peanut oil

1 tablespoon chopped garlic

2 teaspoons chopped ginger

1 bunch scallions, including the firm greens, chopped

2 teaspoons cornstarch

3 tablespoons chopped cilantro

THIS sauce is a rich red-brown and pleasantly sweet and sour. With its crunchy, crisp texture, jícama makes a good fresh replacement for water chestnuts.

SERVES 4

Parboil the carrots and broccoli stems in salted water for 3 minutes. Rinse and set aside.

Mix the tomatoes, vinegar, sugar, pepper flakes, ½ teaspoon salt, and ½ cup of the stock in a bowl. Heat the wok, add the oil, and when it's hot, stir-fry the garlic, ginger, scallions, and bell peppers for 1 minute. Add the remaining vegetables, stir-fry for 3 minutes and add the sauce. Cover and simmer for 3 minutes or until the vegetables are hot. Mix the cornstarch with the remaining stock and add to the vegetables along with the cilantro. Cook for 1 minute, then serve.

Mixed Vegetable Stir-Fry with Coconut-Basil Sauce

SOMEWHERE between a stir-fry and a stew, this dish is very aromatic. Serve over basmati rice.

SERVES 3 TO 4

1 pound vegetables—fresh mushrooms, quartered; carrots, roll-cut; asparagus, sliced diagonally; snow peas or string beans, trimmed; jícama or water chestnuts, sliced

6 to 10 dried Chinese black or shiitake mushrooms

1 bok choy, stems sliced and leaves whole

3 garlic cloves

2 tablespoons seeded and diced jalapeños

1 stem lemongrass, minced, or ½ teaspoon finely grated lemon zest

½ teaspoon finely grated lime zest

1 15-ounce can unsweetened coconut milk

Salt

1 teaspoon red pepper flakes

1 tablespoon soy sauce

1 tablespoon fresh lime juice

10 large basil leaves, finely sliced

Parboil the harder vegetables (carrots, asparagus, string beans) one at a time in salted water until tender, then cool. Soak the dried mushrooms in ½ cup warm water until soft. Reserve the water, discard the stems, and slice the caps in half or into strips.

In a mortar or small food processor, make a paste of the garlic, chiles, lemongrass, and zest. Heat a wok, add the coconut milk and the paste, and simmer for 1 minute. Add the vegetables and the reserved mushroom water. Season lightly with salt, then add the pepper flakes and simmer for 5 minutes. Stir in the soy sauce, lime juice, and basil leaves and simmer for 1 minute more.

Gratins and Casseroles:
Hearty Dishes for All Seasons

GRATINS AND THEIR COUSINS, CASSEROLES, ARE ENDURING, UNPRETEN-TIOUS DISHES THAT ARE A BOON FOR ANY COOK SINCE THEY CAN BE MADE AHEAD AND BAKED JUST BEFORE SERVING. IF YOU'RE COOKING FOR BOTH MEAT EATERS and vegetarians, they're a great solution since they can double as a side dish with meat, their traditional role, and as a main-course vegetarian dish, where they do quite well. Besides, everyone enjoys eating gratins, regardless of their food persuasions.

Although French in origin, the gratin is well established here. Certainly we think of scalloped potatoes, scalloped corn, and other scalloped dishes as our very own. Gratins derive their name from the traditional gratin dishes or *tians* of Provence, round or oval earthenware baking dishes with shallow sides that allow for a large surface area to provide plenty of crust covering a soft, creamy interior. While the traditional dishes do make the best gratins, there's no reason not to use another kind as long as it's shallow and has a large surface area. The low, round Spanish earthenware casseroles that have become popular make handsome gratins, and even a pie plate will work.

Like gratins, casseroles are served in the dish they're made in, but the casserole is a deeper dish, fitted with handles and a lid. Traditionally casseroles are those thrifty dishes that extend a small amount of protein-rich food by combining it with more filling grains and beans, reflecting the pyramid model of eating. Or a casserole might consist of vegetables (and other ingredients, such as rice or pasta) bound with eggs, cheese, milk, or a sauce. In the end, the casserole is perhaps a rather vague category, one that includes succulent dishes like moussaka as well as simpler, more impromptu mixtures of vegetables and grains.

Gratin and Casserole Basics

BAKING: Most gratins and casseroles benefit from a gradual cooking at moderate temperatures since high heat toughens cheeses and eggs, ingredients that are often, but not always, included. In general they're quite adaptable and can bake at whatever temperature is convenient. If the top of a gratin isn't brown by the time the rest is done, run the gratin under the broiler until it's golden and crisp.

THE VEGETABLES: Virtually all vegetables can be cooked in gratins.

THE LIQUID: Some vegetables, such as summer squash, have sufficient moisture so no extra liquid is required, but with others a cup or more of liquid provides succulence. The liquid can be cream, milk, soy milk, a thin béchamel sauce, or a good vegetable stock—a strong basic stock, Mushroom Stock, or Herb and Garlic Broth. Eggs can also be included with the liquid. They make a glossy golden topping while adding extra protein to the dish.

TIMING: Gratins and casseroles can be partially or entirely assembled ahead of time. If they're not to be baked for several hours or if they contain eggs, refrigerate them, then allow them to return to room temperature before baking. They can also go directly from the refrigerator to the oven, but allow an extra 15 to 20 minutes of baking time and cover them with foil for the first 25 minutes to help build up the heat. These dishes can linger happily in a warm oven without harm if need be.

To save baking time, slice raw vegetables very thin ($1/8$ to $1/16$ inch). Also, warm the liquid before adding it to the vegetables.

PRESENTATION: Gratins and casseroles are meant to be taken to the table in their serving dishes, which contributes to their homey, relaxed feel. Individual gratin dishes and casseroles make especially handsome main-course presentations—their contained shape naturally graces the dish with formality and focus.

SERVING SUGGESTIONS: I always enjoy gratins served with a salad on the same plate, especially greens dressed with a shallot vinaigrette. The richer the gratin, the better it goes with peppery, sharp greens, like watercress, arugula, and frisée. Casseroles tend to be richer; they can also be served with a salad or with a simply cooked seasonal vegetable.

LEFTOVERS: Leftovers are a treat to take to work, where you can rewarm them in a microwave or oven. Or brown them in a skillet in a little olive oil or butter: Add a few tablespoons water to create steam, cover the pan, and cook over medium heat for 8 to 10 minutes.

MAKING GRATINS LIGHTER

Many gratins are classically creamy and rich. Here are some tips for making gratins work for more health-conscious eating. For every day, use milk—low-fat, whole milk, or soy—instead of cream. Heating it first with aromatics—bay leaf, a few slices of onion, thyme, peppercorns, and a clove of garlic—adds a layer of flavor to the vegetables. A thin béchamel sauce has a creamy consistency without the cream. Nondairy gratins can also be made by replacing the milk with a good vegetable stock, such as the Basic Vegetable Stock, Herb and Garlic Broth, and Mushroom Stock.

Béchamel Sauce for Gratins

2 cups milk or Basic Vegetable Stock,
   page 196
2 slices onion
Aromatics, page 29, plus 1 garlic clove,
   crushed

4 tablespoons butter
3 tablespoons flour
Salt and freshly milled white pepper
Grated nutmeg
½ cup cream, optional

A THIN béchamel sauce can be used interchangeably with cream. Don't skimp on the cooking time; it's really necessary to cook the flour thoroughly. But those 25 minutes of unattended cooking time in a double boiler frees you to prepare the vegetables.

MAKES 2 TO 21/2 CUPS

In a saucepan, slowly heat the milk with the onion, aromatics, and garlic. When it reaches a boil, turn off the heat and set it aside. In another saucepan, melt the butter, stir in the flour, and cook for 1 minute. Whisk in the hot milk at once, including the aromatics. Cook until thickened, then transfer to a double boiler, cover, and cook for 25 minutes. Strain, discard the aromatics, and season with salt, pepper, and a pinch of nutmeg. Stir in the cream.

Artichoke, Celery Root, and Potato Gratin

4 tablespoons butter or olive oil
1 large onion, diced
6 medium or 4 large artichokes,
   trimmed and cut into quarters or
   eighths, page 330
1 large celery root, about 1 pound
   trimmed and thinly sliced
8 ounces potatoes, preferably Yellow
   Finn, peeled and very thinly sliced

Salt and freshly milled pepper
4 cups sturdy white bread without
   crusts, torn into pieces
1 cup milk
½ cup chopped parsley
3 garlic cloves, chopped
½ cup freshly grated Parmesan

THIS is one of my favorite gratins. The homey topping of soaked bread provides moisture for the dish and, eventually, a golden crust. Serve it so the crust stays on top. A somewhat elaborate but nonetheless easily made dish.

SERVES 4 TO 6

Preheat the oven to 375°F. Butter an 8- × 10-inch or slightly larger gratin dish. In a wide skillet, melt 2 tablespoons of the butter, add the onion, and cook over low heat, stirring occasionally. Meanwhile, blanch the artichokes in acidulated water for 10 minutes, then remove to a bowl. Using the same water, cook the celery root for 3 minutes, then the potatoes for 1 minute. Drain and add the celery root and potatoes to the pan with the onion.

Very thinly slice the cooked artichokes, add them to the onion, and stir so that all are coated. Cook until the onion is golden, then turn off the heat and season with 1 teaspoon salt and pepper to taste.

Cover the bread with the milk and soak until it's mushy, about 5 minutes. Squeeze out the excess moisture, then toss it with the parsley, garlic, and Parmesan.

Add the vegetables to the gratin dish—they shouldn't be much more than an inch deep. Cover them with the bread mixture, dot with the remaining butter or drizzle with olive oil, and bake for 35 to 40 minutes. If the top isn't brown, run it under the broiler. Let rest for a few minutes, then serve.

Cabbage and Rye Panade

WITH *layers of vegetables, bread, and broth, a panade lies somewhere between a soup and a gratin. It's just the sort of dish to have on a winter Sunday evening when you want something special but not too demanding. Serve it with the broth, followed by a simple salad, such as Red Lettuces with Radish Sprouts.*

SERVES 4

1 garlic clove and butter for the dish

3 to 4 cups Herb and Garlic Broth, page 198, or Basic Vegetable Stock, page 196, made with 6 extra garlic cloves, crushed, and 6 large sage leaves

3 tablespoons butter

1 small onion, thinly sliced

½ teaspoon juniper berries, crushed

2 tablespoons coarsely chopped sage

About 2 pounds Savoy or green cabbage, quartered and sliced into ribbons

Salt and freshly milled pepper

4 slices rye bread

1 cup grated Gruyère or Teleme

Preheat the oven to 350°F. Rub a 2-quart gratin dish with garlic, then with butter. Make the stock and season it well.

Meanwhile, melt the butter in a wide skillet over medium heat until it begins to brown a little. Add the onion, juniper, and sage and cook until the onion begins to brown. Add the cabbage to the pan, sprinkle on a teaspoon of salt, and add ½ cup water. Cook until the cabbage is tender and browned in places, about 20 minutes, occasionally turning it with a pair of tongs. When done, taste for salt and season with pepper.

Place half the cabbage in the dish, cover it with the bread, followed by the cheese, then the remaining cabbage. Pour the broth over all, and bake until bubbling and the edges of the cabbage leaves are attractively browned, about 45 minutes. Spoon the bread and cabbage into soup plates, then pour the remaining juices around each serving.

Cabbage Gratin

YOU'LL *get a better reception if you call this by its French name,* pain au chou. *"Cabbage loaf" simply fails to suggest how utterly delicate and delicious this country dish is. While good plain, a sauce makes a more finished dish—sour cream flavored with mustard, Fresh Horseradish Sauce, Curry Sauce, or Tomato Sauce with Cream.*

SERVES 4

Butter and freshly grated Parmesan for the dish

1½ pounds green or Savoy cabbage, diced in 2-inch squares

⅓ cup flour

1 cup milk

¼ cup crème fraîche or cream

2 tablespoons tomato paste

3 eggs

3 tablespoons finely chopped parsley or dill

Salt and freshly milled white pepper

Preheat the oven to 375°F. Butter a gratin dish and coat the sides with the cheese. Boil the cabbage, uncovered, in salted water for 5 minutes, then drain. Rinse, then press out as much water as possible. Whisk the remaining ingredients until smooth, add the cabbage, and pour the mixture into the dish. Bake until firm and lightly browned, about 50 minutes.

To Make a Loaf: Bake the cabbage in a loaf pan lined with lightly buttered parchment paper, until firm and lightly colored. Let it rest for a few minutes, then unmold and peel off the paper. The bottom, which is now the top, will be very pale, so either turn it over or cover it with minced herbs or browned bread crumbs.

Celery Root and Potato Gratin

1 garlic clove and butter for the dish	2 teaspoons Dijon mustard
1 celery root, about 1 pound, scrubbed	Salt and freshly milled pepper
1 pound potatoes, preferably Yellow Finn or Yukon Gold	1 cup grated Gruyère
½ cup cream	

Preheat the oven to 375°F. Rub a 2-quart gratin dish with the garlic and then with butter.

Peel the celery root and put the parings in a 3-quart saucepan with 3 cups water and whatever remains of the garlic. Set a steamer over the top and bring to a boil. Quarter the root, then slice it ¼ inch thick. Steam for 5 minutes and remove to a large bowl.

Peel the potatoes, slice them into thin rounds, and steam for 5 minutes or until tender, then add them to the celery root. Strain the cooking liquid, measure 1¼ cups, and mix it with the cream and mustard. Pour it over the vegetables and toss well. Season with ¾ teaspoon salt and pepper to taste. Transfer the vegetables to the gratin dish, smooth them out, and cover with the cheese. Bake until bubbling and browned on top, about 30 minutes.

A BROTH made from the celery root trimmings replaces half of the cream usually found in potato gratins without loss of flavor or texture. Celery root has a haunting flavor that always reminds me of truffles, which are an excellent addition should you be so lucky. (If I were using truffles, I would use all cream in the dish.)

SERVES 4 TO 6

Eggplant Parmesan

2 medium eggplants, about 1½ pounds	8 large basil leaves, torn into pieces
Salt and freshly milled pepper	4 ounces mozzarella, thinly sliced if fresh, grated otherwise
Olive oil	½ cup freshly grated Parmesan
1½ to 2 cups Fresh Tomato Sauce, page 61	

Preheat the oven to 375°F. Lightly oil a 2-quart gratin dish.

Slice the eggplant into rounds about ⅓ inch thick. Unless the eggplant is garden fresh, sprinkle it with salt and let stand for 30 minutes to an hour, then blot dry.

Preheat the broiler. Brush both sides of each round with olive oil and broil 5 to 6 inches from the heat until browned. Broil the second side until browned, then remove and season lightly with salt and pepper. Don't worry if the eggplant has a dry appearance.

Warm the tomato sauce with half the basil. Spread about a third of the sauce over the bottom of the dish, then make an overlapping layer of eggplant. Lay the mozzarella over the top, add the rest of the basil, and sprinkle with the Parmesan. Add the rest of the eggplant and cover it with the remaining sauce. Bake in the middle of the oven until bubbling and hot throughout, about 30 minutes.

EGGPLANT Parmesan used to be the only vegetable entrée one could find on a menu. It was usually breaded and heavy, nothing like the delicate dish that can be made with eggplant in season, fresh mozzarella, and a light summer tomato sauce.

SERVES 4

Golden Gratin of Carrots, Rutabagas, and Turnips

I CAN'T *think of any root vegetable that doesn't bake into a glorious gratin. This trio makes a pretty yellow gratin. Serve as a side dish or a main dish.*

SERVES 4

Butter for the dish
Béchamel Sauce for Gratins, page 277
12 ounces rutabagas, peeled and cut into julienne strips
Salt and freshly milled pepper
1 small onion, finely diced

1 tablespoon butter
12 ounces turnips, peeled and julienned
8 ounces carrots, peeled and julienned
1 cup fresh bread crumbs

Preheat the oven to 375°F. Lightly butter a 2-quart gratin dish. While the sauce is cooking, boil the rutabagas in salted water for 2 minutes and drain. Cook the onion in the butter in a small skillet over medium heat, about 8 minutes; then combine with the rest of the vegetables. Season with salt and pepper and transfer to the gratin dish. Pour the sauce over the top, cover with the bread crumbs, and bake until bubbling and golden on top, about 45 minutes.

Eggplant and Summer Vegetable Gratin

SIMPLE but superb, this is a little slow to put together but not at all difficult. Don't hurry it; the slow cooking guarantees that all the flavors will be richly concentrated.

SERVES 4 TO 6

2 to 2½ pounds globe eggplant, preferably on the small side
Olive oil
Salt and freshly milled pepper
2 large onions, finely diced
3 garlic cloves, chopped
1 large red bell pepper, finely diced

2 large ripe tomatoes, peeled, seeded, and chopped
10 large basil leaves, torn into small pieces
1 cup fresh bread crumbs made from sturdy white bread
¼ cup freshly grated Parmesan

Preheat the oven to 425°F. Slice the eggplant into rounds about ½ inch thick—if it's in season, there's no need to salt them. Brush both sides of each piece with oil and bake on a sheet pan until browned and tender on both sides, about 25 minutes. Season with salt and pepper and set aside. Reduce the heat to 325°F.

Heat 3 tablespoons olive oil in a wide skillet, add the onions and garlic, and cook over medium heat until limp, about 8 minutes. Raise the heat a little, add the pepper and tomatoes, and continue cooking, stirring occasionally, until everything is soft and thickened to a jam, about 20 minutes. Raise the temperature at the end to reduce the juices. Add the basil and season to taste with salt and pepper.

Lightly oil a 2½-quart gratin dish. Make a layer of eggplant in the bottom and spread a third of the tomato-onion mixture over it, followed by another layer of eggplant, half the remaining sauce, then the rest of the eggplant. End with the remaining sauce on top. Cover the dish and bake for 45 minutes. Toss the bread crumbs with olive oil to moisten and the grated cheese. Remove the cover, add the bread crumbs and cheese, raise the oven temperature to 375°F, and bake until the crumbs are nicely browned and crisp on top, about 25 minutes.

Cauliflower Gratin with Tomatoes and Feta

2 to 3 tablespoons olive oil

1 onion, thinly sliced

2 garlic cloves, chopped

1½ teaspoons dried oregano

⅛ teaspoon ground cinnamon

5 fresh tomatoes, peeled, seeded, and diced or 1 15-ounce can diced tomatoes

1 teaspoon honey

1 tablespoon capers, rinsed

Salt and freshly milled pepper

1 large cauliflower, about 1½ pounds, broken into florets

Juice of ½ lemon

2 to 4 ounces crumbled feta

Finely chopped parsley

MY husband asked, "What makes this so zingy?" It's everything really, but especially the honey setting off the tart lemon, capers, and feta. This is so easy to put together you can have it ready for dinner in no time at all. Serve it with a big green salad or a Greek salad and bulgur or rice.

SERVES 4

Preheat the broiler and lightly oil a 2-quart gratin dish.

Heat the oil in a 10-inch skillet over medium heat. Add the onion, garlic, oregano, and cinnamon and cook until the onion is wilted, about 5 minutes. Add the tomatoes, cook for 7 minutes more, then add the honey and capers and season with salt and pepper. Slide the mixture into the dish.

Meanwhile, steam the cauliflower for 5 minutes. Set it on the sauce and season with salt and pepper. Squeeze the lemon juice over the top and add the feta. Place 5 to 6 inches under the broiler until the sauce is bubbling and the cheese is beginning to brown, about 10 minutes. Garnish with the parsley and serve. (If you are assembling the gratin ahead of time, cover and bake it at 400°F until bubbling, about 20 minutes, then brown under the broiler.)

Onion Gratin

EGGS *give this gratin a glossy golden top. The same filling can be baked in a crust to make a savory pie or without the eggs for those who don't eat them.*

SERVES 4

2 tablespoons butter or olive oil

3 pounds white or yellow onions, thinly sliced

1 bay leaf

Pinch ground cloves

1/2 teaspoon dried thyme

Salt and freshly milled pepper

1 cup dry white wine

2 eggs

3 tablespoons flour

1 1/2 cups warm milk or Basic Vegetable Stock, page 196

2/3 cup grated Gruyère or Fontina

3/4 cup fresh bread crumbs

Preheat the oven to 375°F. Lightly butter a 2-quart gratin dish.

Warm the butter in a large skillet over medium heat. Add the onions, bay leaf, cloves, and thyme. Turn the onions over several times to coat, season with salt and pepper, then reduce the heat to low and cook, stirring occasionally, until the onions are golden and soft, 30 to 40 minutes. Add the wine, raise the heat, and cook until it has completely reduced. Remove the bay leaf.

Whisk the eggs with the flour, 1/2 teaspoon salt, and a little pepper, then stir in the warm milk. Combine with the onions and cheese and transfer to the dish. Cover with the bread crumbs and bake until set and the crumbs are browned, about 25 minutes.

Potato and Leek Gratin

FEW *foods elicit the rapturous sighs that a golden gratin of potatoes does. Simmering the potatoes and leeks in milk first ensures that your potatoes end up fully tender. And the leftover milk—thickened with potato starch and well flavored—makes a marvelous base for a soup. Serve with a salad and chilled Applesauce or Apple-Quince Sauce.*

SERVES 4 TO 6

1 garlic clove and butter for the dish

3 pounds russet or Yukon Gold potatoes, peeled and very thinly sliced

1 quart milk

1 bay leaf

3 thyme sprigs or 2 pinches dried

3 garlic cloves, thinly sliced

2 large leeks, white parts only, thinly sliced

Salt and freshly milled white pepper

Grated nutmeg

1 to 2 cups grated Gruyère

2 tablespoons butter, cut into small pieces

Preheat the oven to 375°F. Rub a 9- × 12-inch gratin dish thoroughly with the garlic, then with butter to coat well.

Put the potatoes in a pot with the milk, herbs, sliced garlic, leeks, and 2 teaspoons salt. Slowly bring to a boil, then simmer until the potatoes are barely tender but not to the point of falling apart. Discard the bay leaf and thyme. Drain.

Make a single layer of potatoes, leeks, and garlic in the dish. Season with pepper, a little nutmeg, and cover lightly with cheese. Repeat until all the potatoes and cheese are used up, ending with a layer of cheese. Add enough of the milk to come up to the last layer of potatoes—about 1½ cups—dot with the butter, then bake until a golden crust has formed on top, about an hour.

Variation with Other Cheeses: Try Italian Fontina, Cheddar, Cantal, or, in half the amount, Gorgonzola dolcelatte in place of the Gruyère.

Variation with Other Vegetables: Add these vegetables to the cooked potatoes: thinly sliced, partially cooked celery root or fennel; grated parsley root; a layer of sautéed porcini, chanterelle, or white mushrooms; or trimmed, quartered artichokes, parboiled for 5 minutes, then thinly sliced.

Potato and Mushroom Gratin

1 garlic clove and butter for the dish

1 ounce dried porcini, chanterelles, or morels

2 tablespoons butter, plus extra for the top

1 garlic clove, finely chopped

Salt and freshly milled pepper

1½ pounds waxy yellow or red potatoes, peeled and sliced ¹⁄₁₆ inch thick

¾ pound white mushrooms, thinly sliced

1 cup half-and-half, Quick Mushroom Stock, page 253, or Béchamel Sauce for Gratins, page 277

DRIED wild mushrooms lend their woodsy flavor, and light cream gives the dish a silky texture. For a lighter, nondairy version use the Quick Mushroom Stock.

SERVES 4 TO 6

Preheat the oven to 350°F. Rub a 2-quart gratin dish with garlic, then with butter.

Cover the dried mushrooms with 1¼ cups warm water, let stand for 20 minutes or longer, then run your fingers over the mushrooms to loosen any grit. Strain the liquid carefully and reserve; chop the mushrooms. Heat the butter in a medium skillet and sauté the chopped mushrooms for 3 or 4 minutes. Add the garlic and season with salt and pepper.

Layer half the potatoes in the dish, season with salt and pepper, add the raw mushrooms, and cover with the dried ones. Cover with the remaining potatoes and season again. Heat the half-and-half with the mushroom liquid, then pour it over the top. Bake, uncovered, until the liquid is absorbed and the potatoes are tender and golden, about 1½ hours.

Spicy Potato, Tomato, and Pepper Tagine

INSPIRED by (but many steps removed from) a Moroccan tagine, this late-summer melange goes in an unfamiliar and exciting direction. Use an olive oil with plenty of aroma and flavor.

SERVES 4 TO 6

The Sauce

6 garlic cloves

Salt

2 teaspoons paprika

½ teaspoon ground cumin

¼ teaspoon cayenne

¾ cup chopped parsley

½ cup chopped cilantro

Juice of 1 lemon

3 tablespoons apple cider vinegar

3 tablespoons olive oil

The Vegetables

1½ pounds fingerling, Yellow Finn, or red potatoes, scrubbed

24 2-inch celery pieces

3 large bell peppers—1 red, 1 green, and 1 yellow—cut into 1½-inch squares

4 ripe red or yellow tomatoes, cut into eighths

Salt

Olive oil as needed

In a large mortar, smash the garlic with salt, ½ teaspoon paprika, cumin, and cayenne to make a smooth paste. Add the herbs and pound them to release their flavors; they needn't break down completely. Stir in the lemon juice, vinegar, and oil. Set aside.

Preheat the oven to 375°F. Oil a large earthenware baking dish.

If using fingerlings, slice them in half lengthwise. Quarter other potatoes lengthwise or cut them into chunks. Steam or parboil until barely tender, about 10 minutes, then put them in a bowl with the rest of the vegetables. Season with salt and toss with the sauce.

Transfer the mixture to the baking dish, drizzle oil over the top, cover with foil, and bake for 35 minutes. Remove the foil and continue baking for 15 minutes or until the vegetables are completely tender. Serve with couscous, rice, or cracked wheat.

New Potato Gratin with Tomatoes and Olives

MADE with summer's new potatoes and garden tomatoes, this late-harvest dish is fragrant with herbs and olives. Serve warm or at room temperature, with a wedge of lemon and a spoonful of Garlic or Saffron Mayonnaise.

SERVES 4 TO 6

2 pounds fingerling or any waxy new potato, scrubbed or peeled

Salt and freshly milled pepper

4 large ripe tomatoes

¼ cup olive oil, plus extra for the dish

2 red onions, thinly sliced

¼ teaspoon dried thyme

¼ teaspoon fennel seeds, crushed

⅓ cup Niçoise or Kalamata olives, pitted and coarsely chopped

3 garlic cloves, thinly sliced

8 thyme sprigs, preferably lemon thyme

¼ lemon, thinly sliced

1 tablespoon capers, rinsed

Preheat the oven to 400°F. Oil a 2-quart gratin dish.

Slice the potatoes ⅜ inch thick, lengthwise if they're fingerlings. Boil them in salted water for 4 minutes, then scoop them out, rinse under cold water, and set aside. Plunge the tomatoes into the same water for 10 seconds, then remove and rinse. Peel, halve, and seed. Coarsely chop half of one tomato; slice the rest crosswise.

Warm half the oil in a skillet over high heat and add the onions, dried thyme, fennel, and a little pepper. Sauté until the onions are lightly browned and wilted, about 8 minutes, then transfer them to the gratin dish.

Scatter the chopped tomato, olives, half the garlic, half the thyme sprigs, and half the lemon over the top. Cover with the potatoes, intersperse with the sliced tomatoes, and tuck in the remaining garlic, thyme, and lemon. Season with salt and pepper, scatter the capers over the top, and drizzle with the remaining oil. Cover with foil and bake for 25 minutes, then uncover and bake until the potatoes are fully tender, 20 to 30 minutes more.

Spanish Potatoes with Saffron, Almonds, and Bread Crumbs

2 pounds Yellow Finn or boiling potatoes, peeled and quartered

Salt and freshly milled pepper

2 pinches saffron threads

3 tablespoons olive oil, preferably Spanish

1 slice white country-style bread

½ cup blanched almonds, roughly chopped

2 large garlic cloves, unpeeled

2 cups boiling water or Herb and Garlic Broth, page 198

1 teaspoon paprika

1 tablespoon chopped parsley

THE flavors here are succulent, but be sure to use skinned almonds and white rather than whole-wheat bread to avoid giving this good dish a dingy brown appearance.

SERVES 4

Preheat the oven to 375°F. Lightly oil a gratin dish that's large enough to hold the potatoes in a single layer. Add the potatoes, season them with salt and pepper, and sprinkle with the saffron.

Heat the oil in a small skillet over medium heat, tear the bread into pieces, and fry it with the almonds and garlic until golden. Remove the garlic if it gets too dark. Grind the mixture in a food processor with the paprika, adding a little of the boiling water to make it smooth. Season it with salt and pepper, add it to the potatoes, and pour over the remaining liquid. Cover and bake for 45 minutes, then uncover, gently stir the contents of the dish, and continue baking until the liquid has been absorbed and the potatoes are tender, about 20 to 30 minutes. Brown the top under the broiler and garnish with the parsley.

Spinach Gratin

THIS green gratin can be served as a first course but is filling enough to be a main dish, especially if accompanied with a red pepper or tomato sauce.

SERVES 4 TO 6

Butter for the dish

¹/₂ cup freshly grated Parmesan

3 hefty bunches spinach, about 3 pounds, stems removed

Salt

Béchamel Sauce for Gratins, page 277

¹/₂ cup grated Gruyère

1 cup fresh bread crumbs tossed with 1 tablespoon melted butter or olive oil

Red Pepper Sauce, page 71, or Fresh Tomato Sauce, page 61

Butter a gratin dish or individual ramekins and coat with a few tablespoons of the Parmesan. Preheat the oven to 375°F.

Plunge the spinach into a large pot of boiling salted water and cook until limp. Transfer to a colander, then rinse under cool water. Press out the liquid and finely chop it. Combine the spinach, Béchamel, Gruyère, and remaining Parmesan, then transfer to the prepared dish and cover with the bread crumbs. Bake until browned on top, about 30 minutes. Cut into diamonds or squares and serve with one of the sauces.

Summer Squash, Herb, and Rice Gratin

THIS summery Provençal dish is filling without being at all heavy. Serve it alone or with Fresh Tomato Sauce.

SERVES 4 TO 6

1¹/₂ pounds zucchini, coarsely grated

Salt and freshly milled pepper

1 cup long- or short-grain white rice

2 tablespoons olive oil

2 shallots or ¹/₂ small onion, finely diced

1¹/₂ to 2 cups Herb Béchamel, page 53

¹/₄ cup chopped parsley

2 tablespoons chopped marjoram, plus extra for garnish

¹/₂ cup crumbled ricotta salata or freshly grated Parmesan

Preheat the oven to 375°F and lightly oil a gratin dish. Toss the grated zucchini with 1 teaspoon salt and set it aside in a colander to drain. Boil the rice in 4 cups salted water. When tender, drain it into a colander.

Squeeze the zucchini to rid it of excess moisture. Heat the oil in a wide skillet. Cook the shallots over medium heat until softened, about 3 minutes, then add the zucchini and cook, stirring frequently, until the pan is dry and the squash has begun to color, about 12 minutes. Taste for salt and season with pepper. Combine the rice, zucchini, half the sauce, and the herbs and smooth it into the dish. Add the cheese to the remaining béchamel and spread it over the rice. Bake until the top is golden, about 25 minutes. Add the extra marjoram and serve.

Butternut Squash Gratin with Onions and Sage

¼ cup olive oil

4 cups thinly sliced onion

4 thyme sprigs

2 tablespoons chopped sage or
2 teaspoons dried

Salt and freshly milled pepper

6 cups butternut squash, cut into
½-inch cubes

½ cup flour

2 tablespoons chopped parsley

½ cup grated Gruyère or Fontina

½ cup plus 2 tablespoons heated whole
milk or Herb and Garlic Broth,
page 198

1 cup fresh bread crumbs

A FALL *supper for family or company. Serve with a salad of slightly bitter robust greens.*

SERVES 4

Preheat the oven to 350°F. Lightly oil or butter a 2-quart gratin dish.

Heat half the oil in a skillet over medium heat. Add the onion, thyme, and sage and cook, stirring frequently, until the onions are lightly caramelized, about 15 minutes. Season with ½ teaspoon salt and pepper to taste. Spread in the gratin dish, return the skillet to medium heat, and add the remaining oil.

Toss the squash in the flour, letting the excess fall away. Add it to the pan and cook until it begins to brown in places on both sides, about 7 minutes. Add the parsley, season with salt and plenty of pepper, and cook for 1 minute more. Layer the squash over the onions, cover with the cheese, then add the milk. Cover and bake for 25 minutes, then uncover, add the bread crumbs, and bake until the top is browned and the liquid absorbed, about 25 minutes more.

Turnip and Leek Gratin with Blue Cheese

1 garlic clove and butter for the dish

1 cup half-and-half or Béchamel Sauce
for Gratins, page 277

6 thyme sprigs

1 bay leaf

3 large leeks, white parts only, cut into
¼-inch rounds

Salt and freshly milled pepper

1½ pounds turnips, peeled and sliced
into ¼-inch-thick rounds or half-
rounds

2 ounces Maytag or other blue cheese,
crumbled

I LIKE *this gratin served right on a bed of curly endive or arugula dressed with a walnut vinaigrette. It makes an interesting first course or a small supper. Turnips are sweetest when fresh and small.*

**MAKES 4 MODEST
SERVINGS**

Preheat the oven to 375°F. Rub a 2-quart gratin dish with the garlic, then with butter. Heat the half-and-half with the remains of the garlic, 2 sprigs of the thyme, and the bay leaf. When it's close to boiling, turn off the heat and set aside.

Cook the leeks in 2 quarts boiling salted water for 2 minutes. Scoop them out and put them in a bowl. Add the turnips and cook for 4 minutes, then drain. Layer the vegetables in the dish, intersperse the remaining thyme sprigs among them, season lightly with salt and pepper, and add the blue cheese. Pour the half-and-half through a strainer over the top. Bake, uncovered, until the cream is absorbed and the top is browned, about 30 minutes.

Vegetable Gratin-Soufflé

THIS *simple but dramatic dish combines elements of a gratin and a soufflé. A host of vegetables can be used—celery root, cauliflower, winter squash, broccoli, and turnips. While Gruyère is excellent with all, there's no reason not to use another cheese— Cheddar with cauliflower, for example.*

SERVES 4

Butter for the dish

3 cups vegetables, cut into 1-inch pieces

1/2 cup fresh bread crumbs

3 tablespoons butter

1 cup milk

1/2 small onion or 2 large shallots, finely diced

1/2 cup grated Gruyère

2 eggs, separated

Salt and freshly milled pepper

Pinch grated nutmeg

Preheat the oven to 375°F and lightly butter an 8- × 10-inch gratin dish. Steam or parboil the vegetables until barely tender when pierced with a knife. Drain, rinse under cold water, then finely chop them.

Lightly brown the bread crumbs in 2 tablespoons butter in a small saucepan, then stir in the milk. When it's hot to the touch, turn off the heat. Meanwhile, cook the onion in the remaining butter in a small skillet over medium heat until translucent, about 3 minutes. Combine the onion, vegetables, and bread crumb mixture in a bowl, then stir in the cheese and egg yolks. Season with salt and pepper to taste and the nutmeg. Beat the whites until stiff, then fold them into the mixture. Pour into the prepared dish and bake until puffed and browned, about 25 minutes. Serve immediately.

Cottage Cheese and Spinach Gratin

THIS *gratin can be an appetizer or the center attraction of a meal. Cut it into diamonds and serve warm with a simple tomato sauce or at room temperature garnished with roasted peppers or* Cherry Tomato and Olive Relish. *While spinach is always good with eggs, a mixture of beet greens, escarole, chard, kale, and spinach makes a more interesting and less predictable dish.*

SERVES 6

2 bunches spinach, stems removed

5 eggs, beaten

1/2 cup chopped parsley

1/2 teaspoon dill seeds

1/2 teaspoon ground coriander

2 cups small-curd cottage cheese (nonfat or low-fat is fine)

Salt and freshly milled pepper

Preheat the oven to 350°F. Generously oil an 8- × 10-inch gratin dish.

Cook the spinach with the water clinging to its leaves in a wide skillet over medium-high heat until wilted. Press out the liquid, but reserve it. Finely chop the spinach.

Beat the eggs and add the herbs and cheese along with 1/2 teaspoon salt and a little pepper. Stir in the chopped spinach and the reserved cooking liquid. Pour into the prepared dish and bake until set, about 45 minutes. Let cool for 5 minutes, then cut into diamonds or squares.

Polenta Gratin with Mushrooms and Tomato

Firm Polenta, page 523

2½ tablespoons olive oil, plus extra for the dish

1 large onion, finely diced

2 small bay leaves

½ teaspoon dried thyme

1 teaspoon dried marjoram or basil

12 to 16 ounces mushrooms, sliced

3 garlic cloves, chopped

Salt and freshly milled pepper

½ cup dry red or white white

2 cups tomato puree or crushed tomatoes in puree

1 cup grated provolone or Monterey Jack

¼ cup freshly grated Parmesan

A HEARTY and straight-forward dish, good on a cold night with Braised Carrots and a salad or cooked sauteed greens.

SERVES 6

Lightly oil or butter a 9- × 11-inch baking dish and have a sheet pan nearby. Preheat the oven to 400°F.

Pour half of the hot polenta—just judge it by eye—into the prepared dish and pour the remainder onto a sheet pan. Using a spatula, spread it out to roughly the size of the baking dish, then set it aside.

Heat the oil in a large skillet over medium heat. Add the onion and herbs and cook, stirring frequently, until the onion is browned around the edges, about 10 minutes. Raise the heat to high and add the mushrooms, garlic, and ½ teaspoon salt. Sauté until the mushrooms are browned in places, about 5 minutes. Add the wine, simmer until it's completely reduced, then add the tomato puree. Simmer for 5 minutes, then taste for salt and season with pepper.

Spread half the mushrooms over the polenta in the baking dish. Cover with half the cheeses, then cover with a second layer of polenta. (For ease, cut it into smaller pieces, then place them over the tomato.) Cover with the remaining sauce and cheeses.

Bake until the casserole is bubbling and hot throughout, about 25 minutes.

Enchiladas

CHEESE *enchiladas are the perennial choice for many vegetarians, but here are three offerings that provide a welcome change. Allow two enchiladas per serving and accompany them with black, pink, or pinto beans and simple garnishes such as shredded lettuce or cabbage, jícama, sliced radishes and tomatoes, and pickled onions and carrots. These fillings are also excellent for crêpes and for small stuffed vegetables.*

Corn tortillas are the ones to use for enchiladas. Briefly dipping them into hot oil makes them pliable and protects them from the sauce. If you skip this step, plan to bake your casserole immediately. Although fried tortillas can be filled ahead of time, don't sauce or bake them until you plan to eat. In Mexico, by the way, enchiladas aren't baked in a casserole the way we do here, but are formed, heated, and served immediately.

Crème fraîche or sour cream drizzled over enchiladas provides a modest enrichment and tempers the heat of chiles in some cases. Both should be whisked a little first.

Mushroom Enchiladas with Epazote and Green Chile

EPAZOTE'S *unique flavor is impossible to duplicate. Look for it in Latin and Mexican markets, and if you can't find it, add 2 tablespoons chopped parsley or cilantro to the mushrooms once they're cooked. The Tomatillo Salsa and Red Chile Sauce are also good with these enchiladas.*

MAKES 12 ENCHILADAS

3 tablespoons safflower or peanut oil

1 small onion, finely diced

2 teaspoons chopped garlic

1/2 teaspoon dried oregano, preferably Mexican

1 1/2 pounds mushrooms, finely diced

4 Roma tomatoes, peeled, seeded, and diced

Salt

1/4 cup chopped cilantro

3 serrano chiles, finely diced

2 teaspoons dried epazote

1 cup vegetable oil for frying

12 corn tortillas

2 cups Oven-Roasted Tomato Sauce, page 62

1/2 cup crème fraîche or sour cream

The Filling: Heat the oil in a wide skillet over high heat. Add the onion and sauté for about a minute, then add the garlic and oregano and cook for 2 minutes. Add the mushrooms and tomatoes, season with 1/2 teaspoon salt, and cook, stirring occasionally, until any juices that have been released are absorbed and the mushrooms have begun to color, about 6 minutes. Add the chiles and epazote, then remove from the heat. If you're using cilantro, add it now. Taste again for salt.

The Tortillas: Cover a baking sheet with two layers of paper towels. Heat the oil in an 8- or 10-inch skillet. When hot enough to sizzle a drop of water, fry the tortillas for only 4 seconds on each side. Don't let them crisp. Lay them on the toweling. When done, blot them again to absorb any excess oil.

Filling and Saucing the Enchiladas: Spread 1/4 cup filling on the lower third of each tortilla, making a neat row of filling. Fold the bottom of the tortilla over it and roll. Adjust it so that the seam ends up on the bottom. Place the enchiladas in an ungreased 9- × 13-inch baking dish. Preheat the oven to 375°F. Spoon the sauce over the enchiladas, being sure to cover the ends. Bake until bubbling and heated through, about 20 minutes. Stir the crème fraîche, then drizzle it over the tops of the enchiladas.

Chayote and Corn Enchiladas

2 small chayotes

2 zucchini

1 large red or orange bell pepper

1 white onion

3 tablespoons peanut or safflower oil

1 1/2 cups corn kernels, from 2 ears if fresh

Salt

1 or 2 jalapeño chiles to taste, seeded and diced

2 tablespoons chopped cilantro

1/2 cup grated, then chopped Monterey Jack

1 cup vegetable oil for frying

12 corn tortillas

2 cups Tomatillo Salsa, page 103, Oven-Roasted Tomato Sauce, page 62, or Red Chile Sauce, page 70

1/2 cup crème fraîche or sour cream

You can omit the cheese from these enchiladas, but it does help bind the vegetables and keep them on the fork.

MAKES 12 ENCHILADAS

Dice all the vegetables about 1/4 inch across. Keep them separate. Heat the oil in a wide skillet, add the onion and chayote, and cook over medium-high heat, stirring occasionally, until tender and lightly browned in places, about 5 minutes. Add the pepper, corn, and zucchini, cook for 2 minutes more, then remove from the heat and season with salt. Let cool a little, then add the chiles, cilantro, and cheese.

Fry and fill the tortillas as described in the preceding recipe. Preheat the oven to 375°F and spoon the sauce over the enchiladas. Bake until heated through, about 20 minutes. Serve two on each plate, drizzled with crème fraîche, with a side of black beans and finely shredded jícama with a wedge of lime.

Goat Cheese Enchiladas with Corn and Red Mole

THIS *is a fragrant and complex sauce but not complicated to make. Tomatillo Salsa is also very good here—its tartness sets off the cheese. You can replace a portion of the goat cheese with silken tofu (it completely disappears) if you want a less rich version. Try this filling in stuffed peppers or between two tortillas, as a quesadilla.*

MAKES 12 ENCHILADAS

¼ cup golden raisins

¼ cup pine nuts

2 tablespoons corn or olive oil

1 white onion, finely diced

1 teaspoon minced garlic

1½ cups corn kernels

1½ cups grated Jack or Muenster

2 cups soft goat cheese

⅓ cup chopped cilantro

Salt and freshly milled white pepper

1 cup vegetable oil for frying

12 corn tortillas

Red Chile Mole, recipe follows

½ cup crème fraîche or sour cream

Cover the raisins with warm water and set aside. Brown the pine nuts in a medium dry skillet, then remove. Add the oil to the same skillet and cook the onion with the garlic over medium heat to soften, about 3 minutes, then add the corn and cook for 1 minute more. Drain the raisins and put them in a bowl with the pine nuts, onion-corn mixture, and 1 cup of the Jack, the goat cheese, and cilantro. Mix everything together well and season with salt and a little white pepper.

Fry and fill the tortillas as described on page 290. Make the mole. When ready to bake, preheat the oven to 375°F. Sauce the enchiladas and strew the remaining cheese over the top. Bake until heated through, about 20 minutes. Serve with the crème fraîche spooned over the tops and some of the garnishes suggested on page 290—something fresh and something pickled. Extra sautéed corn is also nice added to the plate.

Red Chile Mole

MAKES ABOUT 2 CUPS

1½ teaspoons coriander seeds

1¼ teaspoons *each* anise seeds, cumin, and dried Mexican oregano

2½ tablespoons vegetable oil

1 small onion, finely diced

1 teaspoon minced garlic

⅓ cup ground mild red chile

1 ounce Mexican chocolate, such as Ibarra, coarsely chopped

Salt

1 teaspoon sherry vinegar

Toast the seeds and oregano in a dry skillet, then remove to a plate as soon as they smell fragrant. Grind in a mortar or spice grinder.

Heat the oil in a 2-quart saucepan and add the onion. Cook, stirring frequently, for about 4 minutes, or until it's brown on the edges, then add the garlic and the ground spices and cook for 1 minute more. Remove from the heat, let the pan cool for a minute, then stir the ground chile into the onions along with 1½ cups water. Return to the stove and bring to a boil, stirring slowly but constantly so that the chile doesn't burn. It will thicken as it cooks, so plan to add another ¼ cup water or more to thin it out a little.

Add the chocolate and stir until it's melted. Simmer for 10 minutes, then stir in the vinegar to bring all the flavors together. Taste and add salt, if needed.

Bread Puddings

MADE *from leftover bread gone stale, savory and sweet bread puddings evolved from times when food was less plentiful. They stand not only for thrift but also for comfort—moist, soft textures punctuated (or not) with nuggets of vegetables and cheese. Bread puddings are easy to make up with what's on hand, as long as you have the one essential ingredient—good bread, preferably a few days old. Now that we're enjoying good bread again, these homey dishes should have a fresh appeal.*

Strata

5 garlic cloves

Salt and freshly milled pepper

3 tablespoons olive oil

1 28-ounce can crushed tomatoes

1 pound white mushrooms, thinly sliced

2 bunches spinach, stems removed, leaves washed but not dried

4 eggs

2 cups milk

1/8 teaspoon grated nutmeg

10 thin slices sourdough or country bread, crusts removed

2 tablespoons chopped marjoram or rosemary

1/2 cup grated Fontina

3/4 cup crumbled Gorgonzola

CALLED a strata because it consists of layers of bread and vegetables, this is a bit of a deal to assemble, but people always like it and it can be set up hours in advance of baking.
A strata makes a fine brunch or supper dish.

SERVES 6 TO 8

Lightly butter or oil a 9- × 12-inch baking dish.

Pound the garlic in a mortar with 1/2 teaspoon salt until smooth. Warm 1 tablespoon olive oil in a skillet over medium heat. Add the tomatoes and a hefty pinch of the garlic. Cook for 20 minutes, stirring occasionally, then season with salt and pepper to taste. Transfer to a dish. Rinse out the skillet and return it to the heat.

Add the remaining oil and turn the heat to high. Add the mushrooms and sauté until they begin to color. Transfer them to a bowl and season with half the remaining garlic and salt and pepper to taste. Return the skillet to the heat, add the spinach, and cook until wilted. Cool, then finely chop, then season with the remaining garlic and salt and pepper to taste.

Beat the eggs and milk with 1/4 teaspoon salt, pepper to taste, and the nutmeg.

Spread 3/4 cup of the tomato sauce in the baking dish. Cover with a layer of bread, followed by the spinach, half the herbs, and half the Fontina. Add a second layer of bread and cover it with tomato sauce, followed by the mushrooms, the rest of the Fontina and herbs, and half the remaining sauce. Add a third layer of bread and cover with the rest of the tomato sauce and the Gorgonzola. Pour the custard over all. The strata can be baked right away, or it can wait for several hours, covered and refrigerated.

Preheat the oven to 375°F and bake until browned and puffed, about an hour. Let cool for 5 minutes before serving.

Bread Pudding with Corn

IN a pinch you can make this comforting supper or brunch dish with frozen corn, but fresh is, of course, far tastier. This pudding can be set up hours in advance of baking. Serve it with a romaine salad.

SERVES 4 TO 6

1 tablespoon corn oil or butter

1 bunch scallions, including half of the greens, sliced into rounds

4 cups corn kernels, fresh or frozen

1/2 teaspoon paprika or ground red chile, plus extra for the top

Salt

1/3 cup chopped parsley or cilantro

1 tablespoon chopped dill or basil

4 eggs

2 cups milk

5 cups cubed bread without crusts

1 cup grated sharp Cheddar

1/2 cup half-and-half or milk

Preheat the oven to 375°F. Butter a 3-quart gratin dish or casserole.

Heat the oil in a wide skillet over medium-high heat. Add the scallions, corn, and paprika and cook until the scallions have softened and the corn is heated through, about 4 minutes. Season with 1/2 teaspoon salt and stir in the parsley and dill.

Whisk the eggs and milk with 1/2 teaspoon salt and pour it over the bread in a bowl. Add the corn mixture and cheese and transfer the mixture to the prepared dish. Pour over the half-and-half. Bake until puffed and browned, about 45 minutes. Add a dash of paprika or chile to the top and serve.

Souffléed Bread Crumb Pudding

HERE bread crumbs are used to make a light and tender pudding, so you'll want to get bite in your meal from a crisp salad. You can have this ready for the oven by the time it's preheated, and if there are only two of you, the recipe is easily cut in half.

SERVES 4 TO 6

4 or 5 slices country bread

3 cups milk

2 cups coarsely grated aged Cheddar or Gruyère

2 teaspoons Dijon mustard

1/8 teaspoon cayenne

4 eggs, separated

Salt and freshly milled pepper

Preheat the oven to 375°F and lightly butter a 2-quart baking or soufflé dish.

Tear the bread into pieces, then make it into coarse crumbs in a blender or food processor. Measure 3 cups and put them in a mixing bowl. Bring the milk to a boil in a saucepan, then pour it over the bread crumbs. Stir in the cheese, mustard, cayenne, and egg yolks, then season with 3/4 teaspoon salt and plenty of pepper. Beat the whites with a pinch of salt until they form firm but soft peaks. Fold them into the bread crumb mixture, pour the batter into the baking dish, and bake until puffed and browned, about 25 minutes.

Beans Plain and Fancy

BEANS, PEAS, AND LEGUMES, OR *PULSES,* AS THEY'RE ALSO CALLED, ARE
ALL SEEDS OF LEGUMINOUS PLANTS, AN EXTREMELY LARGE PLANT FAMILY THAT
FLOURISHES THE WORLD OVER. ALL GROW IN PODS AND ARE SOLD ALMOST
entirely in their dried forms, but when harvested green, they're called *shelling beans.*

One of the least adulterated foods we can buy, legumes have nourished us from
the earliest times and are one of the staple foods of ancient cultures. Because they are considered a simple, humble food, however, they have been largely ignored, at least until recent years. By now almost everyone knows that beans are vital and sustaining. They contain
more protein than any other plant food—especially important for vegetarians. But they're
also beneficial for everyone since they're rich in fiber and aid in reducing cholesterol.

In addition, beans are tremendously versatile. When it comes to color and form,
beans can be truly dazzling. While supermarket shelves have long confined their selection
to only a few of the plainer types, there is a generous wealth of varieties among the newly
introduced heirloom beans that can be as small as a grain of rice or as large as a quail's
egg and display a range of colorful and bizarre markings with names to match. Similarly,
the vast array of lentils and peas found crammed into sacks and bins in any good Indian
or other ethnic market come in every color imaginable.

The subtle virtues of their flavors are best revealed when beans are plainly
cooked. But they can also be teased into fancier fare, as in the Navy Bean and Pasta
Gratin with its pockets of pesto and ricotta, or the delicate Flageolet Beans with Tomatoes and Green Beans. Beans appear as spreads, dips, soups, stews, gratins, salads, side
dishes, and, of course, as soy foods—tofu and tempeh. While I haven't included them
among the desserts, one could. I've certainly enjoyed some extraordinary Japanese
sweets made from beans and other cultures know how to sweeten beans for a meal's ending as well.

How to Select, Prepare, and Cook Beans

SELECTING BEANS: Shop for beans where you think the turnover is brisk. Although beans last virtually forever, with time they become increasingly dry and brittle and require excessive hours on the stove. Beans cooked within the year of their harvest are clearly best. Avoid beans that are chipped, split, and cracked—all signs of long storage.

STORING: Keep beans in a cool cupboard in an airtight container. Because they're so pretty, glass jars are perfect—and they remind you of their presence.

SORTING: All legumes come with some share of the earth—little clumps of dirt, stones, chaff, and whatnot. Spread them out on a cookie sheet, remove any foreign matter as well as discolored beans, then give them a good rinse.

SOAKING: Soaking beans reintroduces moisture, shortens their cooking time, and allows beans that are overdry or immature to float to the surface where they can be skimmed off. Soaking also removes a portion of the complex sugars that cause indigestion. Although beneficial, soaking can be skipped, especially if you're using a pressure cooker, and it's unnecessary with lentils and split peas.

> *Overnight soak:* Beans absorb three to four times their volume in water and swell to two or three times their size. "Soaking beans overnight" means covering them with water at least four times their volume for at least 4 hours, about the time it takes for most beans to absorb the maximum amount of water they can.

> *Quick soak:* When you don't have the time, cover sorted, rinsed beans with four times their volume of water, bring to a boil for a full minute, then turn off the heat, cover, and let stand for an hour.

DRAINING AND PARBOILING: After the beans have soaked, pour off the soaking water, cover them with fresh, and bring to a rolling boil for 5 to 10 minutes. These steps help eliminate the sugars that cause indigestion. *In the recipes that follow, it's assumed that beans have been soaked, covered with fresh water, and boiled hard unless it says otherwise.*

REMOVING THE SCUM: During the parboiling scum frequently forms on the surface. It doesn't represent dirt but the coagulation of proteins. Skim it off before the vegetables or aromatics are added, but if you forget, don't worry—eventually it disappears.

COOKING: A perfectly cooked bean is soft and creamy inside, never hard, its skin intact, not broken. Beans can be cooked on the stove, in a pressure cooker, in the oven, or in a slow cooker. In general, soaked beans take about 1½ hours to cook, although this depends on the type of bean, its age, the altitude, and the quality of water. Old beans, high

altitude, and hard water all add significant time. Size isn't necessarily an indicator. Large beans, like limas, take less time to cook than tiny rice beans.

On the stove: Pour off the soaking water, then cover soaked beans generously with cold water. Boil hard for 10 minutes, remove the scum, then add aromatics—onions, garlic, sage, oil, vegetables, etc. Lower the heat and cook at a simmer. Add salt when the beans are tender but not yet completely cooked, after about an hour.

In the pressure cooker: The pressure cooker is a godsend. Not only does it make the most tender beans, but it makes last-minute beans for dinner possible. Put soaked or unsoaked beans in a pressure cooker with aromatics, a teaspoon oil, and water—at least five times the volume if unsoaked. The oil helps prevent foam or loose skins from clogging the pressure gauge. Bring to high pressure and maintain for 25 minutes unless otherwise indicated. Lower the pressure by quickly releasing the steam. Taste the beans. If they're not quite done, return the lid and bring to pressure for 5 minutes more or simmer until done.

In the oven: Beans baked in the oven smell as good as baking bread. Start with presoaked beans, boil for 10 minutes, then drain and put them in a casserole or gratin dish. Add aromatics and boiling water to cover, then cover. Bake at 325°F to 350°F. It should take about the same amount of time as on the top of the stove. Check to make sure they're only simmering, not boiling. Add salt at the end, uncover, and let them cool in their liquid.

In the slow cooker: The gentle slow heat of slow cookers (Crock-Pots) is ideal for beans. You can soak them or not, but soaking cuts down on the cooking time. Either way, boil beans for 10 minutes, then put them in the pot and cover with three to four times their volume of hot water. Cook on low for 8 hours or on high for 6, approximately. Add aromatics and salt during the last hour or so of cooking.

A Few Additional Tips

REFRIGERATION: In hot weather, soaking beans can actually ferment if left at room temperature. The surface will be covered with fine frothy bubbles and you'll notice a yeasty, sour odor. When it's hot, soak beans in the refrigerator.

SALT: Salt draws out moisture and works against the cooking process, so add it once the beans have gained a degree of tenderness but aren't completely done, about an hour into their cooking. Do not add it to the soaking water.

ACIDS: Tomatoes, wine, vinegar, and other acidic foods inhibit the tenderizing process and for that reason shouldn't be added until after the beans are tender. Once acid is introduced, it's difficult to cook beans to full tenderness.

HARD WATER: Hard, mineral-filled water really slows the cooking time of beans. In the past baking soda was added to soften the water and the skins of the beans. However, it also destroys nutrients and can turn the beans mushy. If you have impossibly hard water and are going to add soda, use just a pinch, or 1/8 teaspoon, per cup of beans. Soft rainwater is wonderful for cooking beans, incidentally.

Other Forms of Beans

CANNED BEANS: As convenient as they are, canned beans are seldom as good as those cooked at home. However, there are times when they can save the day. When it comes to canned beans, you'll do best with natural food brands, such as Eden Foods. They are more expensive than national brands but much better tasting, often organic, and not nearly as salty. All canned beans should be rinsed before being used.

FROZEN BEANS: Frozen peas, black-eyed peas, and lima beans cook fairly quickly, taste good, and are a refreshing alternative to dried.

BEAN FLAKES: These are, basically, precooked beans. They're flat and flaky, like rolled oats. They cook nearly instantly to a mush. They can be added to soups or made into soups and purees.

BEAN PASTAS: The starch from bean and pea flours is used to make pasta—Chinese cellophane noodles are made from mung bean flour, for example. Some new pastas on the market are made Italian style but from bean flours.

BEAN FLOURS: Many legumes are ground to a flour and used to make not only the pasta mentioned above but also crêpes, the Provençal chickpea dish called *socca,* and fermented flatbreads.

BEANS AS DAIRY: Soybeans are eaten most in processed forms—as tofu, soy milk, soy yogurt, and soy-based cheeses—forms that constitute the dairy side of the bean. (See "The Soy Pantry," page 593.)

MAKING SURE THAT BEANS ARE PLEASANT TO EAT

To make beans palatable and pleasant to eat, some cooks insist on soaking, parboiling, and draining before cooking. With equal confidence, others say that beans should never be soaked because valuable nutrients are lost (although if the beans aren't digested, nutrients are also lost). Still others report that nothing you do really makes any difference, and the latest word is that soaking is simply unnecessary. The truth is that people react differently to legumes—some with great sensitivity and others with apparently none, so in the end this is something each person has to work out.

If I'm cooking for someone who is very sensitive to beans, I soak them, discard the soaking water, add fresh water, and always give them a vigorous 5- to 10-minute boil at the start. In addition, I add a teaspoon epazote, a pinch of asafetida, or a 6-inch piece of kelp to the pot—practices followed in bean-eating cultures to make beans digestible. However, I've also found that beans cooked in a pressure cooker with absolutely none of these precautions observed are always pleasant to eat, undoubtedly because they end up so well cooked, which may be the most important factor of all. My advice is, whatever else you do or don't do, always cook beans until they're completely tender. Firm beans may look great on the plate, but they're truly hard to eat, even for the most intrepid bean eater.

Those who are less accustomed to eating beans often find them most appealing when accompanied by vegetables, as in bean and vegetable soups, or by pasta, grains, or a mixture of elements. For that reason, beans occur in many other chapters besides this one, especially in salads and soups.

Quick-Cooking Lentils and Peas

LENTILS: Lentils can be red, green, brown, yellow, pink, and black. There are many more lentil varieties in the world than we're likely to see at home. Most common are the German lentils, actually shades of brown and green, but I much prefer the smaller dark green French lentils from Le Puy. They hold their shape better, which makes them ideal for salads, they have a wonderful deep clean flavor, and they look marvelous on the plate. French green lentils are available at specialty food stores and natural food stores, often in bulk, and they're not much more expensive than regular brown ones. Because they taste and look so good, they're called for in most lentil recipes, but brown lentils can of course be used in their place. Of the more than 50 varieties of colorful Egyptian and Indian lentils, many are also available at natural food stores and Indian and Mediterranean markets. Since they're split, they cook quickly and disintegrate into creamy-textured soups or purees.

Lentils are used endlessly in soups, often punctuated with greens of various kinds. They make wonderful salads and provide an interesting counterpoint when mixed with pasta or rice. Split lentils are cooked into fragrant Indian dals or mixed with rice to make a dish called *kichuri,* and Indian cookbooks are a rich source of lentil recipes. The broth that remains when lentils are drained for salads makes a homely but invigorating drink. Just heat it up and add a teaspoon of cream or milk to each cup along with some snipped chives and parsley. If there's enough to serve as soup, include some thinly sliced croutons or cooked rice. Although usually thought of as winter fare, with the right seasonal accompaniments lentils can be enjoyed year-round.

PEAS: Peas and lentils are often mentioned in the same breath, but peas are botanically and otherwise quite different from lentils. They're round, not flat (unless split), they take longer to cook, and as a group they display a richer variety of sizes and shapes. Some better-known peas are split green peas, black-eyed peas, chickpeas, Swedish brown peas, and yellow peas. Black-eyed peas, crowder, purple hull, and other related peas dear to the South can be found fresh, frozen, and dried. Chickpeas (also known as garbanzo beans) take such a long time to cook that they're treated as beans.

HOW TO COOK: It's not necessary to soak whole lentils and peas, although you can. They take from 25 to 60 minutes to cook. You needn't be fearful about adding salt at the beginning of their short cooking time. In fact, this helps bring out their flavors. Like other legumes, lentils and peas need to be cleaned of debris and rinsed before cooking. French lentils especially seem to come with a good many pieces of chalky pebbles.

Basic Lentils

THIS is the basic method for cooking brown and green lentils. Serve them as a side dish or, keeping them on the firm side, use them for lentil salads.

SERVES 4 TO 6

1 ½ cups brown or green lentils, sorted and rinsed

1 onion, quartered

2 garlic cloves

2 bay leaves

1 carrot, finely diced

1 celery rib, finely diced

Salt and freshly milled pepper

2 tablespoons extra virgin olive oil, roasted walnut oil, or butter

Red wine vinegar

Chopped parsley or chervil

Put the lentils in a soup pot, cover with 6 cups cold water, and bring to a boil. Skim off any foam that rises, then add the onion, garlic, bay leaves, carrot, celery, and 1 ½ teaspoons salt. Lower the heat and simmer until tender but still a little firm—they shouldn't be mushy—about 25 minutes. Strain and reserve the broth for soup stock. Remove the onion, garlic, and bay leaves, taste for salt, and season with pepper. Stir in the oil and add a few drops vinegar to bring up the flavor. Garnish with parsley and serve.

Lentil and Caramelized Onion Croquettes

I THINK of things like lentil cakes as part of our stodgy vegetarian legacy but they also appeared earlier in our history, when meat was far less plentiful. These croquettes date back to 1913. Very simply seasoned, you could certainly include pungent additions such as roasted garlic, but I think they taste good just as they are. Serve with a simple tomato sauce or even ketchup.

MAKES EIGHTEEN 2 ½-INCH CROQUETTES, SERVING 6 AS A MAIN COURSE

2 cups chopped yellow onion

2 tablespoons olive oil, butter, or a mixture

Salt and freshly milled pepper

1 cup lentils, sorted and rinsed

½ cup finely diced celery

½ cup finely diced carrot

2 cups soft bread crumbs

1 egg

Vegetable oil for frying

In a medium skillet over low heat, cook the onion in the olive oil, covered, for 20 minutes. Remove the lid and cook, stirring occasionally, until they're browned, meltingly soft, and full of aroma, about 15 minutes. Season well with salt and pepper.

Meanwhile, combine the lentils, celery, carrot, and 1 teaspoon salt in a saucepan. Add water to cover by 3 inches, bring to a boil, then reduce the heat and simmer until the lentils are soft, about 30 minutes. Drain, reserving the liquid for soup stock. Puree the lentils in a food processor until smooth but still retaining a little texture. Add some of the reserved broth if needed.

Mix the lentils with the onion and half the bread crumbs. Season well with salt and pepper, then stir in the egg. Spread the mixture out on a platter or tray to cool so that it will be easier to handle. Form the mixture into 3-inch ovals or rounds 2 ½ inches across. Spread the remaining bread crumbs on a plate and roll the croquettes in them.

Preheat the oven to 200°F. Pour the oil into a skillet to the depth of ¼ inch and place over medium-high heat. Fry the croquettes in batches until golden brown on both sides, 5 to 8 minutes. Remove them to paper towels to drain and put in the oven to keep warm. Finish frying the others, then serve them all together.

Green Lentils with Wine-Glazed Vegetables

1½ cups French green lentils, sorted
and rinsed

Salt and freshly milled pepper

1 bay leaf

2 teaspoons olive oil

1 onion, cut into ½-inch dice

1 large carrot, cut into ¼-inch dice

1 celery rib, cut into ¼-inch dice

1 garlic clove, mashed or put through a
press

1 tablespoon tomato paste

⅔ cup dry red wine

2 teaspoons Dijon mustard

2 tablespoons butter or extra virgin olive
oil

2 teaspoons chopped parsley or tarragon

IN this dish the vegetables that are usually cooked with the lentils are cooked separately, glazed with tomato and red wine, then added to the lentils. This side dish can easily be transformed into a main dish—see the following variations.

SERVES 4 TO 6

Put the lentils in a saucepan with 3 cups water, 1 teaspoon salt, and the bay leaf. Bring to a boil, then lower the heat to a lively simmer and cook until the lentils are tender but still hold a little texture, about 25 minutes.

Meanwhile, heat the oil in a medium skillet. Add the onion, carrot, and celery, season with ½ teaspoon salt, and cook over medium-high heat, stirring frequently, until the vegetables are browned, about 10 minutes. Add the garlic and tomato paste, cook for 1 minute more, and then add the wine. Bring to a boil and then lower the heat and simmer, covered, until the liquid is syrupy and the vegetables are tender, about 10 minutes. Stir in the mustard and add the cooked lentils along with their broth. Simmer until the sauce is mostly reduced, then stir in the butter and season with pepper. Serve with a flourish of freshly chopped parsley.

Lentil and Wine-Glazed Vegetables with Pastry Crust Adding a lid of puff pastry to these lentils gives them much more focus. (This technique can be applied to most of the bean and vegetable stews in this chapter.) Divide the lentils among four ramekins or a single gratin dish. Roll defrosted puff pastry or pie dough to ⅛ inch thick, then cut it just a hair larger than the dish. Set it over the dish and cut a few decorative slashes for the steam to escape. Bake at 375°F until the pastry is puffed and golden and the lentils are heated through, about 25 minutes.

Lentils with Wine-Glazed Vegetables, Chard, and Garlic-Rubbed Croutons Lentils and greens are a natural pairing. Just before serving, steam or sauté a large bunch chard greens or spinach. Pile the lentils into a flat serving dish, surround them with the greens, or stir the greens into them, and serve with thin Garlic-Rubbed Croutons, page 34.

Green Lentils and Spinach with Hard-Cooked Eggs and Toast

ALL the parts of this rustic one-dish meal can be prepared while the lentils are cooking.

SERVES 4 AS A MAIN DISH

1 cup green lentils, sorted and rinsed

Salt and freshly milled pepper

1 tablespoon extra virgin olive oil

2 to 3 tablespoons butter

2 onions, cut into ¼-inch rounds

1 bunch spinach, leaves only, cut into 1-inch strips

1 garlic clove, minced or put through a press

4 large thin slices toast made from country bread

2 hard-cooked eggs

Put the lentils and 1 teaspoon salt in a saucepan with water to cover by 3 inches. Bring to a boil, then lower the heat and simmer until the lentils are tender, about 25 minutes. Drain, reserving the broth. Meanwhile, heat a tablespoon each olive oil and butter in a wide skillet over high heat. Add the onions and sauté until they're golden, about 10 minutes. Set them aside and add the remaining butter to the pan. Add the spinach, garlic, and a few pinches salt and cook until wilted.

Add the lentils to the pan with the spinach along with a little of the broth and an extra tad of butter if you like. Season with salt and pepper.

Make the toast and cut it into triangles. Peel and chop the eggs. Spoon the lentils into the middle of each plate. Cover with the onions and then the chopped egg. Add pepper and surround with the toasts.

Lentils and Rice with Fried Onions (*Mujadarrah*)

As plain as this sounds, mujadarrah is absolutely one of the best dishes there is. A Jordanian cook I know serves her version accompanied by a chopped vegetable salad that sparkles with parsley and lemon. Although you can cook the onions in a scant amount of oil, it's the oil that makes this otherwise humble dish so very good.

SERVES 4

6 tablespoons olive oil

1 very large onion, sliced into rounds ¼ inch thick

1¼ cups green or brown lentils, sorted and rinsed

Salt and freshly milled pepper

¾ cup white or brown long-grain rice

Heat the oil in a large skillet over medium heat. Add the onion and cook, stirring frequently, until it's a rich, dark brown, about 12 minutes. Meanwhile, put the lentils in a saucepan with 1 quart water and 1 teaspoon salt. Bring to a boil, then simmer for 15 minutes. Add the rice, plenty of pepper, and, if needed, additional water to cover. Cover and cook over low heat until the rice is done, about 15 minutes. Stir in half the onions, then cover and let stand off the heat for 5 minutes. Spoon the lentil-rice mixture onto plates or a platter and cover with the remaining onions.

Lentils with Pasta, Rice, and Buttery Mint Sauce

1 cup farfalle or other dried pasta
  (2 cups cooked)

1 large onion, diced into 1/2-inch squares

2 tablespoons extra virgin olive oil

8 Roma tomatoes, seeded and neatly
  diced

Salt and freshly milled pepper

2 cups cooked lentils, preferably green

1 1/2 cups cooked long-grain white rice

4 to 6 tablespoons butter

3 tablespoons chopped mint leaves

THIS recipe, another favorite of mine, is based on one in Claudia Roden's Mediterranean Cookery. It's the flourish of buttery mint added at the end that makes it so special. Make this when you have leftover rice, lentils, or pasta (or all three). Otherwise it will be excessively complicated, and it should be simple.

SERVES 4 TO 6

Cook the pasta in plenty of salted water, then drain and rinse.

Sauté the onion in the oil in a skillet over medium heat, stirring occasionally, until well browned, 12 to 15 minutes. Add the tomatoes, season with salt and plenty of pepper, and turn off the heat. Heat the lentils, rice, and cooked pasta in a large skillet with 1/2 cup water. Season well with salt and pepper, then add the tomatoes and onion and turn the heat to low. Melt the butter in a small skillet over medium-high heat. When it's sizzling, add the mint leaves and fry for 30 seconds. Grind in plenty of pepper. Pour the butter over the lentil mixture and serve immediately.

Mung Beans and Rice with Spicy Tomatoes

3/4 cup whole green mung beans

1 cup long-grain white rice

1/4 cup chopped cilantro, plus extra for
  garnish

3 garlic cloves

1 tablespoon peeled and roughly
  chopped ginger

1 teaspoon Garam Masala, page 36

1/2 teaspoon turmeric

1/4 teaspoon cayenne

3 tablespoons ghee, mustard oil, or
  clarified butter

1 onion, finely chopped

3/4 teaspoon cumin seeds

1 1/4 teaspoons dill seeds

Salt

1 or 2 jalapeño chiles to taste, seeded
  and finely diced

2 medium tomatoes, cut into wedges

1/2 cup yogurt

THIS mixture of mung beans and rice— kichuri—makes an excellent main dish and any leftovers are delicious browned in a skillet. When tomatoes aren't in season, I replace them with steamed carrot coins seasoned with lime juice.

SERVES 4 TO 6

In separate bowls, cover the beans and rice with water and set aside. Meanwhile, pound or puree the cilantro, garlic, ginger, and spices together.

Heat 2 tablespoons of the ghee in a 3-quart saucepan over medium heat. Add the onion, 1/2 teaspoon cumin seeds, and 1 teaspoon dill seeds. Cook until the onion starts to color, 5 to 7 minutes, then add the cilantro mixture and cook for 3 minutes more.

Drain the beans and add them to the saucepan with 1 quart water and 1 1/2 teaspoons salt. Bring to a boil, then lower the heat and simmer, covered, for 15 minutes. Drain the rice, add it to the pot, and cook for 18 minutes more or until both the rice and beans are tender. Remove from the heat and let stand for 10 minutes.

Heat the remaining ghee in a small skillet over medium heat. Add the remaining cumin and dill along with the chile. Cook until the seeds start to brown, then raise the heat, add the tomatoes, and sauté until they begin to soften, about a minute. Serve the rice and beans garnished with the tomatoes, yogurt, and a sprinkling of chopped cilantro.

Dals

INDIAN *cuisine is filled with lentil-based dishes, or dals. The following few recipes are but a sampling—certainly good tasting and easily doable, but not as complex as they can be. To really explore this dish in its many permutations, seek out a cookbook by an author who really knows the territory, such as Yamuna Devi's* The Art of Indian Vegetarian Cooking.

Dal with Coconut Cream

COCONUT *cream, the thick part that rises to the surface in a can of coconut milk, makes this dal especially good. The next recipe utilizes the milk.*

MAKES ABOUT 2 CUPS

1 cup red lentils, well rinsed
Salt
1 garlic clove
¼ jalapeño chile, chopped

1 tablespoon chopped cilantro stems
2 teaspoons minced ginger
Several tablespoons coconut cream

Combine the lentils, 3 cups water, and ½ teaspoon salt in a saucepan. Bring to a boil, then lower the heat and simmer until they have disintegrated and turned mushy, about 20 minutes. If needed, add more water.

Meanwhile, pound or puree the garlic, chile, cilantro stems, and ginger together. Add them to the cooked lentils. Scoop the coconut cream off the top of a can of coconut milk and stir it into the lentils. Taste for salt and add more coconut cream if desired.

Red Lentil Dal with Aromatics

THIS *dal, which is a little more elaborate than the preceding recipe, uses the coconut milk that lies under the cream. It's delicious served with basmati rice.*

MAKES ABOUT 2 CUPS

1 cup red lentils
1 small onion, finely chopped
2 garlic cloves, sliced
1 jalapeño chile, seeded and chopped
3 tablespoons ghee or clarified butter
½ teaspoon turmeric
1 15-ounce can unsweetened coconut milk, minus the cream

Salt
2 shallots, sliced
1 dried red chile, broken into pieces, or ¼ teaspoon red pepper flakes
3 bay leaves
1 teaspoon mustard seeds

Wash the lentils in several changes of water. In a saucepan over medium-high heat, sauté the onion, garlic, and chile in 2 tablespoons of the ghee for 1 minute. Add the turmeric, lentils, and 3 cups water. Bring to a boil, then lower the heat and simmer, covered, until the lentils are soft, about 30 minutes. Add the coconut milk and simmer for 5 minutes more, stirring occasionally. Taste for salt and remove from the heat.

Heat the remaining ghee in a small skillet over high heat. Add the shallots, red chile, bay, and mustard. Fry until the mustard seeds begin to turn grayish, about 1 minute. Stir this into the lentils and serve.

Yellow Peas and Rice with Onion Relish (Golden Kichuri)

²⁄₃ cup yellow split peas

1²⁄₃ cups basmati rice

3 tablespoons ghee, or vegetable oil

¹⁄₂ teaspoon cumin seeds

¹⁄₄ cup chopped cilantro

¹⁄₂ teaspoon Garam Masala, page 36

¹⁄₂ teaspoon turmeric

3 to 4 cups water or Stock for Curried Dishes, page 197

Salt

Onion Relish

1 white onion, quartered and very thinly sliced

¹⁄₂ teaspoon salt

Juice of ¹⁄₂ lemon

¹⁄₂ teaspoon paprika

¹⁄₂ teaspoon cayenne

2 tablespoons chopped cilantro

ALLOW several hours to soak the peas and rice before cooking.

SERVES 4 TO 6

Soak the peas and rice separately in enough warm water to cover amply—the peas for 3 hours and the rice for 1 hour. Drain.

Heat the ghee over medium-high heat in a heavy skillet or saucepan large enough to accommodate the rice and peas. Add the cumin and cook until fragrant, about 1 minute. Add the peas and rice and stir to coat with the ghee, then add the cilantro, garam masala, turmeric, 3 cups water, and 1 teaspoon salt. Bring to a boil, then lower the heat and simmer, partially covered, until the peas and rice are soft and the liquid has been absorbed, 18 to 20 minutes. If necessary, add more water in ¹⁄₂-cup increments. Turn off the heat and let stand for 10 minutes to steam.

While the peas and rice are cooking, toss the onion with the remaining relish ingredients.

Fluff the peas and rice lightly with a fork, taste for salt, and serve with the onion relish.

Southern Style Black-Eyed Peas

EVERY summer my husband brings me a treat of fresh peas—black-eyed, purple hulls, crowders—from the Little Rock farmers' market. They take slightly less time to cook than dried peas but still require a good hour. Serve these spicy peas, with their juices, over rice with Braised Collard or Turnip Greens.

MAKES 2 CUPS

2 tablespoons safflower or olive oil

1 tablespoon butter

1 onion, diced

1 small green pepper, finely diced

1 celery rib, finely diced

3 bay leaves

1/2 teaspoon dried thyme

2 garlic cloves, minced

1/2 teaspoon ground allspice

1/2 teaspoon ground chipotle chile or red pepper flakes

2 cups fresh or 1 cup dried black-eyed peas

1 quart water or Basic Vegetable Stock, page 196

Salt

Heat the oil and butter in a saucepan or soup pot over medium heat. Add the onion, pepper, celery, bay leaves, thyme, and garlic. Cook for 15 minutes, stirring occasionally, then add the allspice and chile and cook for a few minutes more. Add the peas and water. Bring to a boil, then lower the heat and simmer, partially covered, for 40 minutes. Add 2 teaspoons salt and cook for 20 minutes more or until the peas are tender. Serve with or without the broth.

Swedish Brown Beans (*Bruna Bonor*)

THIS recipe comes from a couple who grow the traditional Swedish brown beans or peas on a small organic farm in Payson, Arizona. You can occasionally find these squarish heirloom peas at farmers' markets. With the molasses, this dish is reminiscent of our Boston baked beans. Serve them with Molasses Buttermilk Bread, a relative to Boston Brown Bread.

SERVES 4

1 1/2 cups Swedish brown peas or navy beans, soaked

1 1/2 teaspoons salt

2 tablespoons blackstrap molasses

1 tablespoon brown sugar

1/4 cup apple cider vinegar

Simmer the peas in 6 cups water, covered, until they're partially tender, about an hour. Add the remaining ingredients and cook until very soft, another 30 minutes or so. When finished, the sauce should be brown and thick. If the beans are tender but the sauce is thin, raise the heat and boil, uncovered, to reduce the amount of liquid. If there isn't enough liquid, add a little water to thin it out.

Chickpeas

ALSO *known as garbanzo beans, chickpeas are an important food in much of the Mediterranean, India, and else-where in the Western Hemisphere. A legume with which most people are comfortably familiar, the chickpea's culinary applications are many. It is featured in salads, soups, stews, pastas, purees, and fritters. Chickpeas are also ground into flour and used to make socca and other flatbreads.*

Canned chickpeas, preferably the organic types, are convenient and quite good. But home-cooked peas provide you with their broth, a valuable ingredient for soups, stews, and stocks.

COOKING TIMES: Chickpeas can take a long time. (At 7,000 feet, in hard mineral water, mine can take 3 hours to cook. But in softened city water at sea level, I've cooked them, without soaking, in less than an hour.) Unless you're using a pressure cooker, plan on soaking them.

Chickpeas

1 cup chickpeas, cleaned and soaked
Aromatics: 1 onion, quartered, 2 parsley sprigs, 4 garlic cloves
1 tablespoon olive oil

6-inch piece kombu or a few pinches asafetida, optional
Salt

IF you use chickpeas a lot, double the amount. You can freeze those that you don't use and have them ready when you are.

MAKES ABOUT 2½ CUPS

Drain the chickpeas. Put them in a saucepan, cover with 2 quarts fresh water, and boil for 10 minutes. Skim off any foam that collects on the surface, then lower the heat. Add the aromatics, oil, and kombu. Simmer, partially covered, until the peas are partially tender, after 45 minutes or so. Add 1½ teaspoons salt and continue cooking until they're completely tender but not mushy. Strain, reserving the delicious broth for soup stock.

In the Pressure Cooker: Times for cooking chickpeas (and other beans) in a pressure cooker are not entirely reliable because of inconsistency in the quality of the peas. My advice is to cook them for less time than you think they need, then finish by simmering.

Bring unsoaked chickpeas, 6 cups water, the aromatics, and the oil up to high pressure. Hold for 25 minutes, then quickly release. Remove the lid and check to see how tender they are. They should be nearly tender. Add salt and simmer until they're fully cooked. (If chickpeas were soaked, cook under high pressure for 15 minutes, then quickly release and check.)

Spicy Chickpeas with Ginger

LOVERS *of chickpeas should look for inspiration to India, where there are many wonderfully lively dishes. This one is inspired by a Bengali dish. Serve with the Yogurt Flatbread (Naan) or basmati rice.*

SERVES 4 TO 6

3 tablespoons mustard oil or vegetable oil

1 large onion, finely diced

1 bay leaf

3 garlic cloves, minced

2 tablespoons grated ginger

2 teaspoons ground coriander

2 teaspoons ground cumin

1/4 teaspoon ground cardamom

Salt and freshly milled pepper

2 tomatoes, peeled and diced

1 1/2 cups chickpea broth or water

3 cups cooked chickpeas or 2 15-ounce cans, rinsed

Juice of 1/2 lemon

For garnishes: little dishes of diced onion, minced jalapeño, chopped cilantro, and diced tomato

Heat the oil in a large skillet over medium heat. Add the onion and cook, stirring frequently, until well browned, 12 to 15 minutes. Lower the heat and add the bay leaf, garlic, ginger, spices, 1/2 teaspoon each salt and pepper, and the tomatoes. Cook for 5 minutes, then add the chickpea broth and chickpeas. Simmer until the liquid is reduced to a saucelike consistency. Taste for salt and season with lemon juice. Serve with the garnishes or scatter them over the chickpeas.

Chickpeas with Harissa Cooked chickpeas mixed with Harissa—Tunisia's pungent red chile paste, page 75—is a good spur-of-the-moment dish, especially if you happen to keep harissa on hand. Warm cooked chickpeas in a pan, stir in harissa to taste along with a little minced garlic and some chopped parsley, season with a little salt, and serve.

Chickpeas with Garlic Mayonnaise The warmth of the chickpeas makes this mixture enormously aromatic. Heat cooked chickpeas in a small pan, then remove and stir in Garlic Mayonnaise, page 59, to coat lightly. Taste and season with salt if needed and freshly milled pepper and toss with chopped parsley or basil. The heat of the chickpeas will thin the mayonnaise to a saucelike consistency. Serve as a warm salad or side dish.

Chickpeas and Greens with Moroccan Spices

1 large bunch chard, stems removed

3 cups cooked chickpeas or 2 15-ounce
  cans, rinsed

6 garlic cloves, coarsely chopped

Salt

2 teaspoons sweet paprika

1 teaspoon whole black peppercorns

1 1/2 teaspoons ground cumin

1/2 teaspoon turmeric

3 tablespoons olive oil

1/4 cup chopped cilantro

2 tablespoons chopped parsley

1 white onion, chopped

1 bell pepper, diced into 1/2-inch squares

1/4 teaspoon dried thyme

1 small dried red chile

4 tomatoes, peeled, seeded, and diced

1 Preserved Lemon, page 82, skin only,
  diced into 1/4-inch pieces, optional

THIS stew is even better the next day. Serve it with couscous, rice, or barley.

SERVES 4

Boil or steam the greens until wilted, then chop coarsely and set aside. Cover the chickpeas with cold water and gently rub them between your hands to loosen the skins. Tip the bowl so that the skins flow off. Drain.

Pound the garlic in a mortar with 1/2 teaspoon salt until smooth or mince it with a knife. Add the dried spices, 1 teaspoon oil to moisten the mixture, and 2 tablespoons of the cilantro and the parsley. Pound until a rough paste is formed.

Heat the remaining oil in a large skillet over medium-high heat. Add the onion, pepper, thyme, and dried chile. Cook for 7 minutes, then stir in the garlic paste, chickpeas, and 1/2 cup water or bean broth. When the onion is soft, add the tomatoes, greens, 1/2 teaspoon salt, and another 1/2 cup water. Reduce the heat to low and simmer for 5 minutes. Stir in the remaining cilantro and the lemon and serve.

Chickpea and Spinach Stew

THIS makes an easy and wholesome dinner. Serve with cracked wheat, bulgur, or rice. If you don't want to bother with the mayonnaise, drizzle the finished dish with extra virgin olive oil instead.

SERVES 4

2 tablespoons extra virgin olive oil

1 small onion, finely chopped

3 garlic cloves, minced

2 pinches red pepper flakes

1 teaspoon paprika

1 teaspoon fresh or dried minced rosemary

1/4 cup chopped parsley

1 cup peeled, diced tomatoes, fresh or canned

3 cups cooked chickpeas or 2 15-ounce cans, rinsed

Salt and freshly milled pepper

2 bunches spinach, stems removed

Garlic Mayonnaise, page 59, or extra virgin olive oil

In a wide sauté pan, heat the oil over high heat. Add the onion, garlic, red pepper flakes, paprika, rosemary, and half the parsley. Sauté for 2 minutes, then lower the heat to medium and cook, stirring frequently, until the onion is soft, about 12 minutes. Add the tomatoes and chickpeas, season with salt and pepper, then cover and simmer for 15 minutes. Meanwhile, cook the spinach in the water clinging to its leaves until tender. Add the spinach to the chickpeas, taste for salt, and season with pepper. Serve in pasta plates, add a spoonful of mayonnaise to each, and garnish with the remaining parsley.

Chickpeas with Potatoes and Tomatoes

THIS Lebanese stew is good served cold, garnished with lemon wedges and black olives, as well as warm.

SERVES 4

1/3 cup extra virgin olive oil

1 large onion, chopped

3 red potatoes, peeled and diced into cubes about the size of the chickpeas

2 carrots, cut into 1/2-inch rounds

1 small dried chile

2 plump garlic cloves mashed with 1/2 teaspoon ground coriander

1 cup peeled, diced tomatoes

3 cups chickpeas, cooked, or 2 15-ounce cans, rinsed

Salt and freshly milled pepper

1/2 cup water or chickpea broth

1/4 cup chopped cilantro

1/2 cup chopped parsley

Heat the oil in a wide skillet over medium heat. Add the onion and cook until it's lightly colored, stirring occasionally, about 8 minutes. Add the potatoes, carrots, chile, and garlic and cook for 5 minutes more. Add the tomatoes and chickpeas, season with 1 teaspoon salt and a few twists from the pepper mill, and add the water. Cover and simmer gently until the potatoes are tender, 15 to 20 minutes. Taste for salt and stir in the chopped fresh herbs.

Chickpeas and Pasta with Sizzling Sage and Garlic

1 large onion, diced

¼ cup extra virgin olive oil

Salt and freshly milled pepper

Large pinch red pepper flakes

3 cups cooked chickpeas or cannellini beans or 2 15-ounce cans, rinsed

8 ounces large farfalle or other dried pasta shapes

2 large garlic cloves, chopped

3 tablespoons chopped sage

THIS homey and simple supper dish is finished with fresh sage and garlic sizzled in olive oil. The same dish is excellent made with cannellini beans

SERVES 4

In a wide skillet over medium heat, fry the onion in 2 tablespoons of the oil until golden, stirring frequently especially toward the end. Season with salt, plenty of pepper, and the pepper flakes. Add the chickpeas and turn the heat to low. Meanwhile, boil the pasta in salted water until al dente, then add it to the chickpeas. Heat the remaining oil in a small skillet over high heat. Add the garlic and sage and fry for 20 seconds. Immediately pour over the dish and serve.

Chickpea Soup with Condiments (Leblebi)

2 cups chickpeas, soaked overnight

1 tablespoon olive oil

2 bay leaves

1 onion, finely diced

6 garlic cloves, roughly chopped

Salt and freshly milled pepper

1½ teaspoons ground cumin

2 tablespoons Harissa, page 75

The Condiments

4 thick slices day-old country bread or pita bread, torn into pieces

6 lemon wedges

1 bunch scallions, including half the greens, sliced into rounds

Capers, rinsed

Harissa, page 75

2 hard-cooked eggs, diced

Pickled turnips, available at Middle Eastern markets

LEBLEBI, a hearty Tunisian breakfast dish that's sold at little stands, is enormously sustaining and a lot of fun to eat. It's one of the best examples I know of good fast food.

SERVES 6 OR MORE

Drain the chickpeas and set them aside. Heat the oil in a soup pot with the bay leaves, add the onion, and cook over medium heat until softened, 5 to 7 minutes. Add the chickpeas and 10 cups water, and bring to a boil. Simmer, covered, until the beans are soft but not completely cooked, about 1 hour.

Meanwhile, pound the garlic in a mortar with 1 teaspoon salt, the cumin, and the harissa until smooth or use a knife to mince. Add to the chickpeas along with another teaspoon salt, then continue cooking until they're fully soft, 15 to 30 minutes.

Put a few pieces of bread in each bowl, ladle the chickpeas along with the broth over it, then serve with the condiments arrayed in little dishes. Dribble in a little extra olive oil and finish with salt and pepper.

Common-Variety Beans and Some New Ones

THE entire bean family is extremely diverse, and thanks to gardeners, farmers, and seed savers working in tandem, a host of new—in the sense of unfamiliar—beans grown by our ancestors have been revived—Jacob's cattle, Christmas limas, marrow beans, Black Valentines, giant scarlet, white, and black runner beans, and many more. These beans display a truly amazing array of colors, bizarre markings, and extraordinary size, ranging from beans the size of grains of rice to beans that swell to the size of quail eggs.

Gradually, such beans are being introduced to the marketplace via specialty stores, farmers' markets, and natural food stores. Heirloom beans can be quite expensive, reflecting their rarity, their appeal, and the fact that many of them involved a great deal of hand work to produce. I always keep a bowl on my kitchen counter, and no one can resist running his or her fingers through them. In spite of their amazing physical markings (which unfortunately fade with cooking), most beans are neutral enough to be used somewhat interchangeably. Still, if you eat them side by side in a comparative tasting, you'll notice their differences in earthiness, sweetness, smoothness, or chalkiness.

Many beans go by several names since they're used world around by cultures that attach different meanings to their markings. To include all the names of a seemingly infinite number of beans is beyond the scope of this book. Those mentioned are limited to those that dedicated foragers are most likely to find. Should you come across some unusual dried bean not described here, give it a try in one of these recipes or just cook it simply to find out how it tastes. After all, all beans are always delicious with nothing more than a little chopped shallot, fruity olive oil, salt, and pepper.

Bean Varieties and Their Cooking Times

As with nearly all foods, cooking times depend on variable circumstances, in this case how old the beans are, how hard the water, how high the altitude. Age, altitude, and the hardness of water all add to cooking time. The times that follow are for dried beans that have been soaked by either the slow or quick method.

Pressure cooker times are for soaked beans cooked at high pressure, the pressure quickly released. Add 5 minutes more for unsoaked beans. Generally it takes a third as long in the pressure cooker as it does to simmer or bake them. If you release the pressure before the beans are fully cooked, it's very easy to return them to pressure and continue cooking until they're done. With practice you'll get the hang of timing. For large beans, such as any of the runner types, I much prefer to cook them either in the oven or on the stove, gently so as to preserve their extraordinary appearance.

In general, dried beans swell 2½ to 3 times their volume when soaked.

ANASAZI BEANS: A small purple and white mottled heirloom bean found in the Mesa Verde ruins in Colorado and cultivated in Colorado. Similar to pinto in flavor; slightly quicker cooking. Cook for 1 to 1½ hours; pressure-cook for 20 minutes or longer as needed.

APPALOOSA BEANS: Small spotted black and white beans; an heirloom variety, also called *Dalmatian,* both being names for spotted animals. Cook in 1¼ hours; under pressure 20 to 25 minutes. Calypso is another small black and white heirloom bean with a creamy texture.

AZTEC BEANS, WHITE AND BLACK: Very large white or purplish black runner beans, apparently retrieved from Indian ruins in Aztec, New Mexico. They cook to extremely plump size and have an earthy flavor. Cook soaked beans for $1\frac{1}{2}$ hours.

BLACK BEANS (TURTLE BEANS, MEXICAN BEANS, *FRIJOLES NEGROS*, VALENTINES): Small, shiny black beans with a cream-colored interior; pronounced earthy taste with sweet tones. Used in Mexican, Caribbean, and South American cooking. They have a rich, vegetal flavor. Black Valentine, an heirloom variety, is exceptionally tasty. Cook soaked beans for about 1 hour; 20 minutes under pressure. A cup of dried beans yields about $2\frac{1}{2}$ cups cooked.

BLACK-EYED PEAS OR BEANS (COWPEAS, CROWDER PEAS, BLACK-EYED BEANS): Popular in the South, these beans have a sweet and mild rather than earthy flavor. They go well with rice and with greens and are the principal component in hoppin' John. They can often be bought in the shell-bean stage (fresh) as well as dried and frozen. Dried beans needn't be soaked, but I always do. They require 40 to 60 minutes of cooking. Be cautious with the pressure cooker—10 minutes should be sufficient. Purple hulls and yellow-eyed peas are closely related to black-eyed peas. A cup dried yields 2 to 3 cups cooked, depending on the variety.

BOLITO BEANS (PINK BEANS): Small round pink beans similar in flavor to pinto beans but faster cooking. Cook for 1 hour or pressure-cook for 20 minutes.

CANNELLINI: Moderately large white kidney-type bean that's very popular in Italy. Excellent for salads, soups, and purees, they have a moist, creamy interior. Cook for 1 to $1\frac{1}{2}$ hours; pressure-cook for 15 minutes, then check.

CRANBERRY BEANS (BORLOTTI, ROMANO): Another bean popular in Italian cooking, the cranberry bean is dusty pink streaked or marked with red strips. About $\frac{1}{2}$ inch long, it's wonderful as a salad bean or cooked with pasta. Sometimes available as a shelling bean in the fall at Italian stores and farmers' markets. Cook for 1 to $1\frac{1}{2}$ hours or pressure-cook for 20 to 30 minutes. Tongues of Fire are another cranberry-type bean.

FAVA BEANS (HORSE BEANS, BROAD BEANS, FOULS, FULS): A staple food in much of the world, favas are large flat beans that have a very distinctive, tart, pungent flavor. (Fuls are a smaller type.) Their skins are tough and require a long soaking and, if possible, removal once they're cooked. In their fresh or shelling form they are popular among chefs for their brilliant green color. Fava beans vary in size from $\frac{1}{2}$ to almost a full inch and in color from green, brown, purple to yellow and splotchy. They can be found at Asian, Mediterranean, and Hispanic markets.

FLAGEOLETS: Known for their refined elegance, flageolets are small ($\frac{3}{8}$ inch) beans that vary from shell white to buff to pale green. They're delicate, fine tasting, and retain their colors. Cook for 1 hour; pressure-cook for 20 minutes. Use flageolets in soups, salads, and gratins; season with fines herbes, buttery sauces, or tomato. Long popular in Europe, especially France, they're now grown widely in the United States.

GREAT NORTHERN BEANS: Larger than navy beans, Great Northerns have a tender creamy flesh; a good bean for stews and gratins. Cook for 1 to $1\frac{1}{2}$ hours; 30 to 40 minutes under pressure.

JACOB'S CATTLE: An American heirloom bean that's kidney shaped, about $\frac{1}{2}$ inch long, cream colored with deep red splotches. These beans need 1 to $1\frac{1}{2}$ hours to cook; 20 to 30 minutes under pressure.

LIMA BEANS (BUTTER BEANS): A flat kidney-shaped bean best known for its role in succotash. Limas, both baby and regular size, have a buttery texture and taste great with butter and herbs. They cook in 45 minutes to 1¼ hours, often more quickly than you expect, so keep an eye on them because they can disintegrate quickly. Using a pressure cooker isn't advised: they're particularly foamy and can clog the valve. If skins are removed once they're cooked, they're even nicer. Fresh and frozen limas are pale green; they dry to white. Christmas limas, an heirloom variety, mottled with purple-red splotches, have a nice nutty flavor.

MARROW BEANS: Small, round white heirloom beans that swell to a substantial-looking nugget. They take 1 to 1½ hours to cook. If cooked carefully, they make a great salad bean.

NAVY BEANS: Small white beans that hold their shape well, navy beans have good, strong flavor and are excellent for salads, simmered dishes, or gratins. They can be used in place of flageolets. They need 1½ hours or possibly longer to cook or 20 to 30 minutes under pressure.

PINTO BEANS: The most popular bean in the Southwest, pintos are small speckled beige and pink beans. They're delicious seasoned with nothing more than a little salt but take well to chile and Southwestern garnishes. Pintos are used for refried beans and chili beans. Cook for 1 to 1½ hours; under pressure 20 to 30 minutes. Giant pintos are runner rather than bush beans and are nearly an inch long. As with all runner beans, a gentle cooking is preferable to the pressure cooker. Pinquito beans are similar to the pinto but pinker and can be used the same way. Often found in Hispanic markets. Pink beans are slightly larger and more kidney shaped than the pinto or pinquito.

RICE BEANS: This skinny little bean resembles long-grain rice. Though packages claim a 40-minute cooking without soaking, my experience says they require much more time—but perhaps mine were old.

RUNNER BEANS (INCLUDING AZTEC, GIANT PINTO, MADEIRA, BLACK, WHITE, AND SCARLET): All these heirloom beans are nearly an inch in length and swell to at least twice their size. Because of their impressive size and the difficulty and expense of obtaining them, they're probably best used where they can be seen and appreciated. A slow careful cooking befits their character. In spite of their size, they often take less than an hour to cook.

SOYBEANS: Soybeans are eaten mostly as tofu, miso, tempeh, oil, flour, soy sauce, and soy dairy products rather than as table beans. They're rather bland and have an exceptionally silky texture as well as more protein and fat than other beans. They're also notably difficult to digest and take an exceptionally long time to cook, at least 3 hours, following a long soak, and so long in a slow cooker that they're likely to ferment before they're done. Their skins loosen easily and can clog a pressure cooker. Soybeans are perhaps better enjoyed in their many processed forms.

WHITE BEANS: These small beans fall, in size, between Great Northern and navy beans and can be used where either of the other is called for. Cook for 1½ hours; 40 to 50 minutes under pressure.

Beans with Aromatics

1 cup beans, cleaned, rinsed, and
    soaked

2 bay leaves

1 small onion, quartered

Several parsley sprigs

1 large garlic clove, sliced

1 teaspoon olive oil

1 piece kombu or pinch asafetida,
    optional

Salt

THIS is a very basic way of cooking virtually any bean, especially good for all varieties of white beans and chickpeas. The aromatics gently infuse the beans and their broth with their flavors yet leave them open to further embellishments.

MAKES ABOUT 2½ CUPS

Drain the beans, cover them with 6 cups fresh water, and bring to a boil. Boil, uncovered, for 10 minutes. Skim off any foam. Lower the heat, add the remaining ingredients except salt, cover, and simmer until the beans are partially tender, 30 minutes to an hour. Add 1½ teaspoons salt and continue cooking until tender but not mushy. Let the beans cool in their broth. Remove the aromatics with a slotted spoon and discard them. Pour off the broth and reserve it for stock. The beans can now be used wherever they're called for.

Beans with Extra Virgin Olive Oil

Beans with Aromatics, preceding recipe

1 large shallot, finely diced, or 3
    scallions, including a little green,
    thinly sliced

1 small garlic clove, minced

3 tablespoons extra virgin olive oil

2 tablespoons chopped parsley

Salt and freshly milled pepper

Lemon wedges

OFTEN it's the simplest treatments that are best, and this way is always wonderful with virtually any type of bean. The warmth of the beans makes the aromas of the parsley, garlic, and pepper explode.

MAKES 2½ CUPS

Put the warm beans in a bowl and add the shallot, garlic, olive oil, and parsley. Turn them gently with a large rubber scraper so as not to break them up. Taste and season with salt if needed and freshly milled pepper. Serve with the lemon wedges.

Variations: Toss warm beans with ⅓ cup Salsa Verde, page 55, or Pesto, page 57. Toss black beans with the Cilantro Salsa, page 56.

White Beans with Tarator Sauce Cook 1 cup Navy or white beans as described on page 314. Drain then toss with ½ to 1 cup Tarator Sauce, page 67, and 2 tablespoons chopped parsley. The warm beans will thin this ivory colored nut sauce, bringing all its aromas to the fore. Accompany with grilled or sautéed artichokes or fennel.

Mixed Beans in Broth with Parsley and Parmesan

HERE'S a good way to use up those odds and ends of beans that tend to accumulate. They won't cook at the same rate—some always fall apart, giving more body to the dish. With a pressure cooker, this is a fast and very easy dish.

SERVES 4 TO 6

2 cups mixed beans

Aromatics: 6 parsley branches, 3 garlic cloves, 1 bay leaf

2 teaspoons olive oil, plus extra virgin to finish

Salt and freshly milled pepper

¼ cup parsley leaves chopped with 1 garlic clove

Freshly grated Parmesan

Put the beans in a pressure cooker with the aromatics, oil, and 2 quarts water. Bring the pressure to high and cook for 25 minutes. Release the pressure, add 1½ teaspoons salt, and if they need more cooking, return the beans to pressure for 5 minutes or simmer until tender. Remove the aromatics. Taste the beans for salt. Serve them, with a little of their broth, in soup bowls with olive oil drizzled over the top, the parsley-garlic mixture, and pepper. Grate the cheese over all or pass it separately.

Beans with Broccoli Rabe and Garlic Croutons

SHARP greens like mustard, turnip, and broccoli rabe provide strong punctuation for white beans, plump runners, and many heirloom varieties—all beans really. Serve thin croutons on the side or make a thick one and spoon the beans, with their greens and sauce, right over them, making a bean and green bruschetta.

SERVES 4 TO 6

Beans with Aromatics, page 315, plus their broth

3 tablespoons olive oil, plus extra virgin to finish

1 onion, finely diced

1 carrot, finely diced

1 bay leaf

1 teaspoon dried oregano

1 bunch broccoli rabe

Salt and freshly milled pepper

2 tablespoons chopped parsley

Garlic-Rubbed Croutons, page 34

Thin slices of Parmesan or dry Jack

While the beans are cooking, warm the oil in a wide skillet over medium heat. Add the onion, carrot, bay leaf, and oregano, lower the heat, and cook, gently stirring every now and then until the onion is soft, about 8 minutes. Peel the tough stems of the broccoli rabe and finely chop them; chop the leaves a little more coarsely. Add both stems and leaves to the pan with the softened onions along with a cup of the bean broth. When they're wilted down, add the cooked beans and simmer, adding more broth as needed, until the greens are done, a good 15 to 20 minutes. Season with salt and pepper and add the parsley. Serve in soup plates with extra virgin olive oil drizzled over the top, a few thin garlic croutons tucked on the side, and paper-thin slices of cheese over all.

Black Beans

Black beans are a recent favorite and much associated with the Southwest, although they're not the traditional bean there; the pinto bean is. Perhaps part of their allure is their color, which has more glamour than the trusty beige pinto. Their texture is pleasantly creamy and their flavor pleasant. Black beans cook fairly quickly, even without soaking, although soaking never hurts. Save the nutrient-rich broth to make a delicious black rice—see page 541.

Basic Black Beans

1 1/2 cups black beans, sorted and rinsed

2 teaspoons fresh or dried epazote or pinch asafetida

1/2 onion

1/2 teaspoon dried oregano

Salt

Drain the beans, cover them with 6 cups fresh water, and boil them hard for 10 minutes, skimming off any foam that collects on the surface. Add the epazote, onion, and oregano. Lower the heat and simmer, partially covered, until the beans are partially tender, about 45 minutes. Add about a teaspoon salt and continue cooking until completely tender, 15 to 30 minutes more.

SERVE these as a side dish or use them in salads, in black bean cakes, or as a filling in enchiladas and burritos. Epazote is traditionally used with Mexican black beans. It lends a distinctive flavor, which can easily become an essential part of the black bean taste.

MAKES 3 TO 4 CUPS

Black Beans with Chipotle and Tomatoes

1 tablespoon safflower oil

1/2 onion, finely diced

Basic Black Beans, preceding recipe, or 1 28-ounce can, rinsed

1 teaspoon chipotle chile in adobo or ground chipotle chile or to taste

1 cup chopped tomatoes

4 cilantro sprigs

Salt

For garnish: crumbled feta cheese, chopped cilantro, and diced serrano or jalapeño chile

Heat the oil in a roomy skillet or saucepan over fairly high heat. Add the onion and sauté for 4 to 5 minutes to soften. Add the beans, chile, tomatoes, and cilantro, lower the heat, and simmer for 15 to 30 minutes. If the beans are dry, add 1 cup or so of water. Taste for salt, then turn the beans into a dish and garnish.

THIS recipe rescues canned black beans from the blahs and does wonders for home-cooked ones. You can build this into a more substantial dish by adding the kernels from three ears of corn at the end.

SERVES 4 TO 6

Black Bean Cakes

MAKE *these cakes from the basic beans or those seasoned with chipotle and tomatoes. If you're using the plainer beans, you might want to add several teaspoons paprika, mild red chile, or pureed chipotle for more intense flavor. Serve with your choice of salsa.*

MAKES TWELVE 3-INCH CAKES, SERVING 6

Black Beans with Chipotle and
   Tomatoes, preceding recipe
2 teaspoons ground cumin
½ cup grated smoked cheese
½ cup chopped cilantro
Salt

Juice of 1 lime or to taste
Vegetable oil for frying
Flour and fine cornmeal for dusting
For garnish: sour cream, cilantro sprigs,
   salsa

Drain the beans and roughly mash or puree them. Add the cumin, cheese, cilantro, and salt and lime juice to taste. Refrigerate for at least 15 minutes, then form into cakes about ½ inch thick and 3 inches across. Dust with flour and place on wax paper. (If they're difficult to handle, return them to the refrigerator until firm.) Heat enough oil in a heavy skillet to generously cover the bottom. Dust the cakes with cornmeal, then fry over medium heat until they form a crust, about 10 to 12 minutes on each side. Keep warm in a 200°F oven until all are done. Garnish with a spoonful of sour cream and sprigs of cilantro and serve with salsa.

Giant Black Beans with Roasted Peppers

CHICKPEAS and white beans are also well matched with peppers and anise, but the giant black runners, an heirloom bean, look and taste spectacular in this simple dish. Serve with chopped fresh parsley or basil and a wedge of lemon.

MAKES ABOUT 3 CUPS

1 cup black runner or other black beans
1 tablespoon olive oil
1 large onion, diced
2 tablespoons chopped basil
½ teaspoon anise seeds
½ teaspoon paprika

¼ cup dry sherry
½ cup bean broth or water
1 large red pepper, roasted and diced
Salt and freshly milled pepper

Cook the beans as for Beans with Aromatics, page 315, using a sprig of epazote, if available, in place of parsley. Warm the oil in a skillet over medium heat. Add the onion, basil, and anise seeds and cook, stirring occasionally, until the onion is soft, about 10 minutes. Add the beans and stir in the paprika, sherry, broth, and roasted pepper. Simmer until the liquid is reduced to a sauce. Taste for salt and season with pepper.

Pinto Beans

2 cups pinto beans, sorted and soaked
½ cup chopped onion

2 teaspoons dried epazote, optional
Salt

PLAIN pinto beans are the usual accompaniment for New Mexican meals. There is a fondness for their unadorned flavor, but they also take well to garnishes such as scallions, grated cheese, toasted pine nuts, chile, and salsas. Anasazi beans can be cooked the same way.

SERVES 4 TO 6

Put the beans in a soup pot, cover them with 2 to 3 quarts water, and boil hard for 10 minutes. Remove any scum, then add the onion and epazote. Lower the heat and simmer, partially covered, until they're partially tender, 30 to 45 minutes. Add 1½ teaspoons salt and continue cooking until they're soft, 15 to 30 minutes more. Serve them with a little of the broth.

Some people think the beans are even better cooked in a pressure cooker. They're remarkably tender and very flavorful. Cook on high for 20 minutes if they've been soaked; 25 if they haven't.

Smoky-Hot Anasazi or Pinto Beans with Broth

1½ cups Anasazi or pinto beans, soaked
½ chipotle chile in adobo sauce, pureed
1 teaspoon dried epazote, optional
2 tablespoons safflower oil
1 onion, finely chopped
2 garlic cloves, chopped

1 teaspoon dried oregano
1 teaspoon toasted ground cumin
1 tablespoon ground mild New Mexican chile or hot paprika
1 tablespoon flour
Salt

YOU can also cook the giant pinto or Madeira beans this way.

SERVES 4

Drain the beans, put them in a soup pot, cover with 6 cups fresh water, and boil for 10 minutes. Remove any foam that collects, then add the chipotle and epazote. Lower the heat to a simmer. While the beans are cooking, heat the oil in a medium skillet over medium heat and cook the onion, garlic, oregano, and cumin for 4 to 5 minutes, stirring frequently. Lower the heat, add the chile and flour, and cook for a few minutes more. Stir in 1 cup water or bean broth and cook until thickened. Add this mixture to the beans.

Continue cooking the beans, partially covered, until they're tender, about an hour in all. Add 1 teaspoon salt about halfway through. When the beans are done, taste for salt again. Serve them in bowls with their broth, accompanied by corn bread or tortillas.

Pinto Beans with Tomatoes and Serrano Chiles

PINQUITOS, *pink beans, pintos, and Anasazis can all be used in this interpretation of the rosy-colored frijoles a la charros. With more broth, this becomes a soup. With less, the beans make a robust filling for warm thick wheat tortillas.*

SERVES 4

2 cups pinto, pinquito, or other beans, soaked

1 small onion, halved and peeled

2 garlic cloves, 1 whole, 1 minced

2 teaspoons fresh or dried epazote, optional

Salt

3 tablespoons vegetable oil

4 tomatoes, peeled and diced

1 to 3 serrano chiles to taste, finely diced

1/4 cup chopped cilantro

2 garlic cloves, minced

Put the beans in a pot with 2 quarts water and boil hard for 10 minutes. Skim off any foam, then add the onion, whole garlic, and epazote. Lower the heat and simmer for 45 minutes. Add 1 1/2 teaspoons salt and continue cooking until the beans are soft, about 30 minutes more. Remove the onion and garlic. (Or pressure-cook unsoaked beans with the onion, garlic, epazote, and 1 teaspoon oil on high for 25 minutes.)

Heat the oil in a skillet over medium heat. Add the tomatoes and their juice, chiles, cilantro, and minced garlic. Cook briskly, pressing on the tomatoes until they break up and thicken into a sauce, about 10 minutes. Add the sauce to the beans and simmer for 15 minutes more.

Serve the beans plain or garnished with crumbled queso fresco or feta, cilantro sprigs, and corn tortillas on the side.

Refried Beans

REFRIED *beans are made with well-cooked beans and their broth. With a pressure cooker you can make these from start to finish in less than an hour. Serve them plain, with the usual bean garnishes, or use them as a base for nachos or as a filling for tacos and burritos.*

MAKES ABOUT 2 1/2 CUPS

1 cup pinto, pinquito, or pink beans, soaked

2 teaspoons fresh or dried epazote, optional

Salt

2 to 3 tablespoons safflower oil

1 small onion, finely diced

1 garlic clove, minced

For garnish: sliced scallions, cilantro, crumbled queso fresco or feta, diced chiles, optional

Put the beans in a pot, cover them with water, and boil hard for 10 minutes. Remove any scum, then add the epazote. Lower the heat and simmer, partially covered, until they're partially tender, 30 to 45 minutes. Add 1 teaspoon salt, then continue cooking until they're very soft. Drain, reserving the broth.

Heat the oil in a nonstick or cast-iron skillet over medium heat. Add the onion and cook, stirring frequently, until it's nicely browned, 8 to 10 minutes, adding the garlic during the last few minutes. Add a third of the beans and 2 cups of the broth. Using a fork or a potato masher, mash the beans as they simmer, working them into the broth. When they're fairly smooth, add another third of the beans and continue mashing. Add more broth if the mixture gets too dry. Repeat with the rest of the beans. Taste them for salt and keep frying until they look dry on the bottom and hold together in the pan. They shouldn't be runny, but they shouldn't be a solid, dry mass either. Roll them out onto a platter, like an omelet, and add the garnishes if you choose.

Red Bean Gumbo with Greens

2 to 3 large bunches greens—one each from mustard, turnip, collards, broccoli rabe, and kale—stems removed and discarded

Salt

1/3 cup safflower oil

6 tablespoons flour

1/2 cup chopped parsley

1 1/2 teaspoons dried thyme

1 1/2 teaspoons dried oregano

1 tablespoon paprika

2 bay leaves

3/4 teaspoon red pepper flakes

3/4 teaspoon freshly milled pepper

2 large onions, chopped

2 bell peppers, chopped into 1/2-inch pieces

3 celery ribs, chopped

5 plump garlic cloves, put through a press or minced

3 cups cooked red kidney beans or 2 15-ounce cans, rinsed

YOU'LL be surprised by the amount of flavor in this dish. If you cook your own beans, by all means use the resulting broth, but I think canned beans taste fine here. Making gumbo is fun and easy going. Serve it over plain boiled or steamed white or brown rice.

SERVES 4 TO 6

Cook the greens in a large pot of boiling salted water until they're tender, about 12 minutes. Scoop them out, reserving the water. Coarsely chop and set aside.

Meanwhile, make the roux: In a wide, heavy soup pot heat the oil over medium-high heat. Whisk in the flour, reduce the heat to low, and cook, stirring constantly with a flat wooden spoon, until the roux is dark reddish brown, 10 to 15 minutes. (This red roux is what gives the gumbo its distinctive rich taste.) Stir in the seasonings, then add the vegetables. Cook for 5 minutes, then stir in the garlic, 2 1/2 teaspoons salt, and 2 quarts water or liquid from the greens or home-cooked beans. Continue stirring until the liquid comes to a boil, then lower the heat and simmer for 20 minutes. Add the beans and greens and cook for 15 minutes more.

At this point, start tasting. I usually find I want more salt as well as more pepper flakes or black pepper to bring up the flavors and the heat, but it may be fine as is for you.

Flageolet Beans with Tomatoes and Green Beans

A DISH for summer when there are slender fresh green beans to use along with the elegant dried flageolets. Although quite good cooked just with the broth, especially if the vegetables are at their peak of flavor, a touch of cream is always good with beans.

SERVES 4 TO 6

1½ cups flageolet beans, soaked
Aromatics, page 29, plus ½ onion
Salt and freshly milled pepper
8 ounces slender green beans
2 tablespoons butter or olive oil
4 shallots, finely diced

½ cup dry white wine
3 ripe tomatoes, peeled, seeded, and neatly diced
2 tablespoons chopped parsley
1 tablespoon chopped marjoram, tarragon, or summer savory

Parboil the drained beans for 10 minutes in 6 cups fresh water. Add the aromatics, lower the heat, and simmer until partially tender, about an hour more. Add 1 teaspoon salt and continue cooking until they're done, 15 to 30 minutes. Drain, reserving the broth. Blanch the green beans in plenty of boiling salted water until barely tender-firm, then drain and rinse with cold water.

Warm the butter in a small skillet over medium heat. Add the shallots and cook until soft, about 8 minutes. Add the wine and tomatoes, bring to a boil, and simmer until the wine is mostly cooked away.

Preheat the oven to 375°F. Lightly butter a gratin dish. Combine the flageolet beans with the green beans and half the herbs and transfer to the dish.

Season with salt and pepper to taste and add enough bean broth or broth and a little cream to moisten the beans. Cover and bake until heated through, about 25 minutes. Garnish with the remaining herbs and serve.

Navy Bean and Pasta Gratin with Basil and Ricotta

FAMILIAR pasta combined with pesto makes this a good dish to serve to reluctant bean eaters. This is an end-of-summer dish when basil and tomatoes are still plentiful. Serve with Roasted Red Pepper Soup with Polenta Croutons (minus the croutons) for a first course and follow with a salad of seasonal greens and a tart vinaigrette.

SERVES 6

1 cup navy, cannellini, or other white beans, soaked
6 tablespoons olive oil
½ onion, finely chopped
1 bay leaf
6 thyme sprigs or ½ teaspoon dried
Salt and freshly milled pepper
3 large garlic cloves, coarsely chopped

2 cups loosely packed basil leaves
1 cup freshly grated Parmesan
1½ cups dried pasta shells, wheels, or other shapes
2 large ripe tomatoes, peeled, seeded, and chopped
1 cup ricotta
1 cup bread crumbs tossed with olive oil to moisten

Parboil the beans in fresh water for 10 minutes, then drain. Heat 1 tablespoon of the oil in a soup pot over medium heat. Add the onion, bay leaf, and thyme. Cook for several minutes, then add the beans and 6 cups water. Simmer, covered, until the beans are nearly tender, about 30 minutes, adding more water if necessary to keep the beans covered. When nearly tender, season with 1½ teaspoons salt and cook for 15 minutes more or until tender. Let cool in their broth.

In a food processor, coarsely chop the garlic and basil. Scrape down the sides, then add the remaining oil and the cheese. Process until you have a coarse puree, then season with salt and pepper to taste.

Preheat the oven to 350°F. Oil a 2-quart gratin dish. Cook the pasta in salted water until more al dente than usual since it will cook further, then drain and rinse under cold water. Combine the pasta, beans, 2 cups of the broth, and the tomatoes in the baking dish. Slip spoonfuls of the pesto and ricotta into the beans, poking them beneath the surface. Lightly press the bread crumbs over the surface, then bake until heated through and browned, about 35 minutes.

All-Bean Chili

2 cups black, red kidney, or other beans, sorted and soaked

2 teaspoons epazote, optional

4 teaspoons cumin seeds

2 teaspoons dried oregano, preferably Mexican

3 onions, finely diced

3 tablespoons vegetable oil

4 garlic cloves, coarsely chopped

Salt

4 teaspoons sweet paprika

2 to 3 tablespoons ground red chile

2 cups peeled, seeded, and chopped tomato, juice reserved

1 to 2 teaspoons pureed chipotle chile

¼ cup chopped cilantro

A dash of red wine or sherry vinegar

Garnish: sour cream, 1 poblano or long green chile, roasted, peeled, and sliced; cilantro sprigs

WHILE there's something especially alluring about black beans, other beans can be used with great success here, such as Jacob's cattle, pinto, or red kidney. Bean chili will keep for 4 to 5 days. To rewarm, thin it with a little water, heat it gently, and be sure to taste before serving. A splash of vinegar will wake it up if it seems dull.

SERVES 6

Drain the beans. Put them in a soup pot, add the epazote and fresh water to cover by 4 inches, and boil for 5 to 10 minutes. Remove any surface scum. Lower the heat and simmer, partially covered. While they're cooking, toast the cumin seeds in a dry skillet over medium heat. When they turn fragrant, add the oregano, shaking the pan so that the herbs don't burn, for about 5 seconds. Turn them onto a plate to cool, then grind to a powder.

Sauté the onions in the oil in a skillet over medium heat for 7 to 8 minutes. Add the garlic, 1½ teaspoons salt, the cumin mixture, paprika, and ground chile. Lower the heat and cook until the onions are soft, another 5 minutes. Add the tomatoes and juice, 1 teaspoon chipotle puree, and the cilantro. Simmer for 15 minutes, then add this mixture to the beans.

Continue cooking until the beans are completely soft, about 30 minutes altogether, making sure the water level stays at least an inch or two above them. Taste and season with more chipotle and salt, if needed, and add a dash of vinegar to the flavors. Ladle the beans into bowls and garnish with a spoonful of sour cream, the chile strips, and a sprig of cilantro.

Giant Lima Beans with Parsley and Sorrel

DESPITE *their size, limas are easy to overcook, so keep an eye on them. This dish can be made into a spring soup by adding the remaining broth as well as any of the starchy residue that falls to the bottom of the pot. If you can't get sorrel, use spinach along with fresh lemon juice. Serves 4*

2 cups large lima beans, soaked

Aromatics: 1 bay leaf, 4 parsley sprigs, 2 thyme sprigs

Salt and freshly milled pepper

1 tablespoon butter

½ cup finely diced leek or onion

1 cup chopped parsley

1 to 2 cups sorrel, stems removed and leaves chopped

¼ cup cream

Drain the beans, then boil them in 1 quart fresh water in a soup pot for 10 minutes. Add the aromatics, lower the heat, and simmer for 30 minutes. Add 1 teaspoon salt and continue cooking until tender, another 15 minutes or so. Drain but reserve the broth. Run your fingers through the beans to loosen the skins, then remove them. This is a fiddly step, but it makes the beans easier to digest and gives them a silky texture.

Melt the butter in a skillet, add the leek and ¾ cup of the parsley, and cook over medium heat until the leek is soft, about 5 minutes. Add the sorrel and cook until it has wilted. Stir in 1 cup of the bean broth and simmer until most of it has evaporated. Add the beans, cream, and remaining parsley. Thin with additional broth if needed. Taste for salt and season with pepper.

White Bean and Vegetable Stew in Red Wine Sauce

I'VE taken liberties with a Troisgros recipe, expanding it into a hearty winter bean and vegetable stew. Cannellini or the plump white Aztec beans make a dramatic, handsome dish. While olive oil is always splendid with beans, it's the butter that gives the dish its silky texture.

SERVES 4 TO 6

2 cups cannellini, Great Northern, or white Aztec beans, soaked

2 bay leaves

½ white onion, stuck with 2 cloves

6 tablespoons chopped parsley

Several thyme sprigs or ¼ teaspoon dried

½ white onion, 1 celery rib, and 1 carrot, finely diced

Salt and freshly milled pepper

4 carrots, cut into 2-inch lengths

3 leeks, cut into ½-inch rounds

1 small celery root, peeled and cut into 1-inch cubes

6 tablespoons butter

3 shallots, finely diced

1 cup dry red wine

1 garlic clove, minced

Drain the beans, add fresh water to cover by at least 2 inches, and boil for 10 minutes. Skim off any foam, then add the bay leaves, onion, ¼ cup of the parsley, the thyme, and the diced onion, celery, and carrot. Lower the heat and simmer, covered, for 1 hour. (Or bake the beans in a 325°F oven.) Season with 1 teaspoon salt and remove the onion and cloves. Add the carrots, leeks, and celery root plus water to cover. Cook until both the beans and vegetables are tender, about 25 minutes. Pour off the excess liquid, but reserve it.

In a medium skillet, melt half the butter with the shallots. Cook over medium heat for about 3 minutes, then add the wine and simmer until only ¼ cup remains and the pan is nearly dry. Add this to the beans, stir in the garlic, season with pepper, and simmer gently for 5 minutes. Cut the remaining butter into small pieces, gently stir it into the beans, and simmer until the butter has emulsified with the wine and broth to make a sauce. If needed, add a few tablespoons of the reserved cooking liquid. Divide among soup plates and serve garnished with the remaining parsley.

Sprouted Beans and Seeds

LONG *one of the clichés of vegetarian cooking, sprouted beans and seeds have virtues that can be enjoyed by all. They're good sources of vitamins, they're easily digested, and they're a fresh, clean food that's available at all times of the year. Anyone who has nosed around food shops in London has seen those uplifting little packages of sprouted cress and mustard seeds looking like miniature green lawns. They're tempting to take home (or to a hotel room), and obviously many people do that. Happily, packaged gardens of sprouted seeds are beginning to be seen here as well.*

In addition to the most common mung bean and alfalfa sprouts, some unusual varieties have begun appearing—fine delicate threads of sprouted radish, leek, and basil seeds that taste vividly of the plants they would have become; big, bold-looking sunflower sprouts that make a strong visual impression in a salad; and an array of sprouted lentils, chickpeas, and other legumes that are great in a stir-fry. Sprouted wheat berries are sometimes added to wheat bread.

WHAT TO LOOK FOR: Whenever possible, try to buy sprouts that are openly displayed in a refrigerated case, where air can circulate freely around them. Tight plastic-wrapped sprouts spoil easily, but if it's all you have to choose from, make sure they look fresh with no signs of browning or spoiling.

HOW TO STORE: Keep sprouts in a loose plastic bag perforated with a few holes so that water doesn't condense. Try to use them as soon as possible.

GROWING YOUR OWN: It's easy to make sprouts at home. Small seeds for sprouting, like radish or basil, can be found at natural food stores, but your own cupboard is probably full of things that can be sprouted—sunflower seeds, chickpeas, whole wheat, lentils, mung beans, and arugula seeds saved from your garden. All seeds sprout—but they do have to be whole. Split peas won't sprout, nor will broken grains. Whatever you decide to sprout, be sure to use seeds that are meant for consumption. Garden seeds are often coated with fungicides, and these are not good to eat. Further, avoid tomato, eggplant, lima beans, and fava beans since their seeds can be toxic.

Soak a few tablespoons of seeds in water overnight.

The next day, pour off the soaking water, rinse them in fresh water until the water runs clear, then drain. Transfer the seeds to a large jar, such as a wide-mouthed quart or half-gallon jar. Place a piece of cheesecloth over the top and fasten it with a rubber band. Gently tip out any excess water (extra water will cause the seeds to spoil) then set the jar on its side and set it on your counter. (Sprouting maven Jody Main says there's no need to bury it in a dark cabinet.) Cover it with a cloth, leaving the screen uncovered.

Rinse and drain the sprouts two to three times a day in normal weather, more often if it's humid, so that they don't spoil. After each rinse, be sure to thoroughly drain off the excess water. Continue until the seeds have sprouted a tail two or three times as long as the seed. (In the case of mung beans and sunflower seeds the sprouts will be two or more *inches* long.) Most sprouts take about 3 days to achieve their desired length—a few take longer, and some take less.

On the last day, take the cloth off and expose the sprouts to the light so that the leaves become nice and green, then store them in the refrigerator. To get the most from your efforts, try to use them as soon after they're ready as possible, when they are most nutritious.

GARDEN SPROUTS: One summer I noticed a lot of very luxurious-looking sprouts in my garden. They turned out to be sunflower seeds that had been kicked aside by the sparrows. I clipped them at the base, gave them a rinse, and used them as I would those cultivated indoors. Similarly, in spring I have a carpet of self-sown arugula and amaranth sprouts, which I either pluck or clip since they need to be thinned in any case. They add a vibrant, piquant accent to an egg salad, a bowl of cottage cheese, or a green salad. If you have a garden, be sure to check it for possibilities.

Vegetables:
The Heart of the Matter

VEGETABLES ARE AT THE HEART OF THIS BOOK. TODAY THERE'S A FETCH-ING PLETHORA AVAILABLE IN FARMERS' MARKETS AND ON OUR MARKET SHELVES, BUT EXPERIENCE TELLS ME MANY SHOPPERS STAY WITH WHAT THEY'RE COMFORT-able with, even when they yearn to experiment. Innumerable times at the market I've been tapped on the shoulder by someone who's dying to know what I'm going to do with that celery root or eggplant. An unfamiliar vegetable *is* intimidating when you haven't a clue to its nature. I've felt that myself in Asian markets when confronted with exotic greens and warty melons; I may be curious, but I'm not inclined to buy without a guide.

This chapter is meant to be just that: a guide to vegetables—both common ones and those that are less so, or common-exotics (they may well be ordinary but are seldom cooked.)

This guide will tell you what the vegetable is and how to cook it, what special handling, if any, it requires; and since every vegetable has its flattering partners—the butters or oils that are most complementary, herbs and spices to use, and cheeses when appropriate, as well as condiments and other vegetables that pair well. The range of pos-sibilities for each vegetable is presented, so you improvise with confidence. Basic recipes are given that can be made without fuss. These dishes are appealing to children, who of-ten prefer plainer tastes, and those who aren't looking for great complications when it comes to dinner, or those looking for simple side dishes.

GRILLED VEGETABLES

One of the best ways to concentrate the flavors of vegetables is through grilling. As in oven roasting, the dry heat of the coals evaporates moisture, concentrates the vegetables' sugars, and deepens their flavors, but grilling adds a smoky flavor to the vegetables. Summer vegetables, which have more moisture than winter ones, are obvious candidates for grilling. Winter vegetables, however, such as squash and sweet potatoes, are good too when grilled either outdoors or over a fireplace grate.

THE TOOLS: Wood fires, charcoal, and gas grills all give good results. Wood smoke adds a little more flavor, but a gas grill is much easier to get going and leaves the heat outdoors in summer. (I use one year-round and grill much more often than if I were relying on a wood fire.) Whatever type of grill you use, from a tiny hibachi to a giant gas grill, always give the rack a vigorous scrubbing when it's hot with a wire brush so that your vegetables don't stick.

A pair of spring-loaded tongs is the ideal tool for picking up and turning vegetables. Long ones allow you to stand well back from the heat and smoke. Special hinged racks allow you to grill small foods that might otherwise fall through the bars, and skewers are a convenient way to grill a number of small items at once.

THE BASIC TECHNIQUE: Make a wood or charcoal fire or preheat your gas grill for 10 to 15 minutes. A wood fire should die down until just small flames and ash-covered coals remain, which takes anywhere from 30 to 45 minutes. Precook the vegetables if necessary and slice them into slabs about ⅜ inch thick or whatever the recipe calls for. Brush both sides with oil to keep them from drying out, season with salt, and place them on the grill, positioning long-cooking vegetables, like eggplant, potatoes, and onions, a little farther from the hottest coals. Turn the vegetables 45 degrees halfway through their cooking time to give them those nice professional-looking grill marks and to compensate for uneven hot or cool spots.

There are many variables in grilling—the heat of the fire, how far the food is above the heat, the thickness of the vegetable, and where on the rack it sits. Perhaps more than any other form of cooking, grilling demands the cook's constant vigilance and judgment to ensure perfectly cooked vegetables.

SAUCES AND SEASONINGS FOR GRILLED VEGETABLES: Virtually all grilled vegetables are perfectly satisfying when brushed with extra virgin olive oil, seasoned with salt and pepper, and garnished with chopped parsley or other herb. But if you want something a little more elaborate, many sauces and seasonings are delicious when spread over grilled vegetables—the oft-mentioned Garlic Mayonnaise, green herb sauces, yogurt sauces, nut-based sauces, herb butters, and seasoned salts, for example. (See the "Sauces and Condiments" and "Foundations of Flavor" chapters.) Those sauces and seasonings suggested in the following pages will naturally be excellent with the same vegetables when grilled. In addition, you can provide a grilled vegetable with more substance by spooning on a tomato and olive relish, crumbled or grated cheeses, crème fraîche, and other rich additions. The eggplant rounds on pages 367 to 368 demonstrate how this can be done.

Leftover grilled vegetables—as well as those fresh off the grill—are enhanced by the vinaigrettes and dressings found in "Salads for All Seasons," such as the Saffron Vinaigrette with Basil over grilled zucchini. They can also be finely diced, dressed, and tossed to make succulent little salads, toppings for croutons and bruschetta, or sandwich fillings. Grilled vegetables can also be converted to soups; grilled pepper or eggplant soup is superb!

Artichokes

To the uninitiated, artichokes, the flower buds of a large thistle, look formidable, but this unusual and delectable vegetable usually becomes a favorite once its acquaintance is made.

Originally brought here by Italians, virtually all artichokes in the United States are grown in California. They're available throughout the year, but their peak seasons are in the spring—March and April—and happily again in the fall, September and October.

TYPES OF ARTICHOKES: The variety we see most is the globe artichoke, but it can assume different appearances. In the spring the buds tend to be round and tightly closed at the top, while in the fall they're more elongated and open. The largest artichokes grow on the tip of the stalk, where they get plenty of light and sun, while the "babies" are found at the shady base. These tiny artichokes weigh as little as a few ounces and don't have a choke. They are typically frozen and marinated but are now sold fresh as well.

WHAT TO LOOK FOR: A fresh artichoke should feel heavy for its size and have fleshy, smooth green leaves that squeak when you press them. Scars and scratches from handling or blisters from frost don't necessarily indicate lack of freshness. In fact, artichokes that have been "kissed" with frost are often sweetest. In any case, the outer leaves usually aren't eaten.

HOW TO STORE: Moisten the tops with water, then store in a plastic bag in the vegetable bin of the refrigerator for up to 2 weeks.

HOW TO USE: Artichokes can be steamed, fried, braised, sautéed, marinated, stuffed, grilled, and roasted. They make a succulent contribution to vegetable stews, pastas, gratins, and risotto. Cooked hearts can be pureed or added to salads. You can freeze your own by trimming them, boiling them in a *blanc* (directions follow) for 5 minutes, then letting them cool before freezing in freezer bags. Commercially frozen artichokes are best used in highly seasoned dishes.

SPECIAL HANDLING: Always use a stainless-steel knife and a stainless-steel or glass pot. Iron or aluminum will discolor artichokes. Never let aluminum foil come into direct contact with them for the same reason.

As you work with artichokes, rub cut areas with a lemon and put trimmed pieces in a bowl with lemon juice or vinegar mixed with water to cover—3 to 4 tablespoons juice to 1 quart. Cooking artichokes in a blanc—the acidulated water mixed with 2 teaspoons *each* flour and olive oil—helps them keep their pale green color.

QUANTITY: Allow three or more baby artichokes or one medium artichoke per person. The hearts of jumbo artichokes are about twice as large as those of mediums.

THE FRAGRANCE OF BAY

A French friend who loves artichokes but not their cooking odor drops a bay leaf in the pot. It's a good trick anytime, for the fragrance of bay perfumes the room as well.

GOOD PARTNERS FOR ARTICHOKES
Olive oil, butter, hazelnut oil, hazelnuts
Tarragon, chervil, thyme, sage, rosemary, garlic, bay
Lemon, orange, capers, fennel seeds, sorrel
Goat cheese, ricotta salata, Parmesan
Peas, beans, potatoes, mushrooms, shallots

SAUCES AND SEASONINGS FOR ARTICHOKES
Melted butter and extra virgin olive oil
Salsa Verde, page 55
Cilantro Salsa, page 56
Garlic Mayonnaise, page 59
Herb-Butter and Olive Oil Sauce, page 51

Preparing Artichokes for Sautéing and Stuffing

FOR QUARTERS AND SLICES: Whether you're using large or baby artichokes, first snap off several layers of the tough outer leaves (to the left) by pulling them downward so that they break off at the base. Stop when the inner leaves become a lighter yellowish green and look tender. Trim the stem and slice off the top third of the artichoke. With a paring knife, smooth the rough areas around the base, removing any dark green parts (below left). Cut the trimmed artichoke into quarters and remove the fuzzy chokes of mature artichokes with a paring knife. (Babies don't have a choke.) Leave in quarters or slice them thinly for sautéing. As you work, put the finished pieces in a bowl of acidulated water to cover.

TO MAKE AN ARTICHOKE CONTAINER: Steam or boil a whole artichoke (see the following recipe), then rinse it under cold water. Reach inside and pull out the cone of inner leaves with a twist of your fingers, then use a spoon to scrape out the choke. Trim the outer leaves if you wish. Now the artichoke can be filled with a salad, filling, or sauce.

Steamed Artichokes

This is the easiest way to cook artichokes, though there are many other ways to enjoy them. Eating a whole artichoke is a leisurely activity and makes a convivial beginning to a meal. You can also boil artichokes, but to my taste they tend to be waterlogged.

Allow 1 medium artichoke per person. If they're scarce or very costly, buy a jumbo one for several friends to share. Clip the thorns from the leaves, slice off the top third of the artichoke, and trim the stem so that it can stand upright, removing as little as possible from the base. Now give them a good rinse, pulling the leaves apart to flush them out. Rub the cut surfaces with a lemon half.

Set the artichokes upside down on a steaming rack over boiling water. Cook until a leaf comes out fairly easily when tugged, 30 to 40 minutes, depending on the size. If you plan to serve cold artichokes, drop them into a bowl of ice water to stop the cooking, then let them drain upside down on a kitchen towel in the refrigerator until ready to eat.

HOW TO EAT AN ARTICHOKE

Almost everyone has a funny or humiliating story about his or her first confrontation with a whole artichoke. To avoid future embarrassment, here's what you do: Pull off each leaf, one by one, dip it into whatever sauce is offered, then slide the leaf between your teeth. The "meat" is at the base of the leaf; the finished leaves get tossed in a bowl in the middle of the table. Don't quit when the leaves are gone, because the best part is next. You'll see a cone of violet-tipped, thin, pale leaves in the center. Pull this off and discard it. Underneath is a fuzzy mat called the choke; slice it off with your knife. What's left is the heart—a large disk of purely edible artichoke—yours to enjoy.

Roasted Artichokes

4 to 6 artichokes
Juice of 1 large lemon
Olive oil as needed
Salt and freshly milled pepper

Aromatics: 4 thyme sprigs and 2 bay leaves
2 tablespoons dry white wine or water

Preheat the oven to 400°F. Lightly oil a gratin dish large enough to hold the artichokes in a single layer. Trim the artichokes as described on page 330 and cut them into sixths. As you work, drop them into a bowl with the lemon juice and water to cover. When all are done, drain, pat dry with a towel, and toss with enough oil to moisten well. Season with ¹/₂ teaspoon salt and pepper to taste. Put them in the prepared dish with the aromatics and wine. Cover with wax paper, then with foil. Bake for 35 minutes, then uncover and bake until crisped around the edges and beginning to brown, about 25 minutes more.

ROASTING makes these artichokes sweet and a little crisp around the edges. Serve them as appetizers, plain or with Garlic Mayonnaise, or spooned over a bowl of soft polenta and covered with thin shavings of Parmesan.

SERVES 4

Grilled Artichokes

Cut the regular artichokes lengthwise in half, set them cut side down on the counter, and press down on them to force the leaves open. (You can leave the babies whole or cut them as well.) Rub them generously with olive oil, pushing it into the leaves. If you like you can work in chopped garlic and parsley as well. Season well with salt and pepper. Set them over the coals and grill on both sides until the base is tender when pierced with a knife, 30 to 45 minutes. Arrange the artichokes on a platter, squeeze lemon juice over them, and serve with lots of napkins. Since they will be at least partially charred, there's no way to eat these neatly.

THESE are unusual and very good and messy to eat. Whether you're using regular or babies, trim the tops and bottoms.

Braised Baby Artichokes

24 baby artichokes, trimmed
Juice of 1 large lemon
¹/₄ cup extra virgin olive oil
6 sage leaves or 6 thyme sprigs
2 strips lemon zest

Salt and freshly milled pepper
1 plump garlic clove, slivered
1 bay leaf
1 tablespoon chopped thyme or parsley

Drop the finished artichokes into a bowl with the lemon juice and water to cover.

Warm half the oil with the sage and lemon zest in a medium sauté pan with a tight-fitting lid. Add the artichokes with 2¹/₂ cups of the lemon water, ¹/₂ teaspoon salt, garlic, and bay leaf. Bring to a boil, then lower the heat, cover, and simmer until the artichokes are tender, 15 to 20 minutes. Scoop them into a bowl, then reduce the remaining liquid until about ¹/₂ cup remains. Pour it over the artichokes and drizzle the remaining oil over the top. Garnish with a little pepper and the chopped herb.

THESE little whole artichokes make a wonderfully tender mouthful. If you can't find them where you live, use five medium artichokes, trimmed and cut into ¹/₂-inch wedges. Serve as a side dish or as a course by themselves, to underscore their specialness.

SERVES 4

Baby Artichoke and Scallion Sauté

THE preparation of the
baby artichokes goes eas-
ily and quickly. If they're
not available, use four to
six medium ones,
trimmed and quartered,
the hearts thinly sliced.
These artichokes are
wonderful tossed with
spaghetti, stirred into
risotto, or spooned over
bruschetta.

SERVES 4 TO 6

20 to 24 baby artichokes
Juice of 2 lemons
2 tablespoons extra virgin olive oil
1 bunch scallions, including an inch of
    the greens, thickly sliced

1/2 cup dry white wine
Gremolata made with 3 tablespoons
    parsley leaves chopped with 1 garlic
    clove and 2 teaspoons lemon zest
1 tablespoon chopped tarragon
Salt and freshly milled pepper

Trim the artichokes as described on page 330, leaving them whole. Put them in a bowl with the lemon juice and water to cover as you work. Drain, then boil them in acidulated water or a blanc until tender-firm, about 10 minutes, then drain again. Slice them lengthwise into halves. (This can be done ahead of time.)

Heat the oil in a large skillet over high heat. Add the artichokes and sauté until they begin to color in places, after several minutes, then add the scallions and wine. When the wine boils off, add 1 cup water and half the gremolata and tarragon. Lower the heat and cook until the artichokes are fully tender, between 5 and 10 minutes, then add the rest of the gremolata and tarragon and season with salt and pepper. Tip them, with their juices, onto a serving plate.

Artichokes Stuffed with Bread Crumbs, Capers, and Herbs

BAKED on a bed of
onions, these artichokes
are best served warm
rather than piping hot.
Accompany with a
spoonful of Garlic
Mayonnaise.

SERVES 4

4 artichokes
1 3/4 cups fresh bread crumbs
1/4 cup extra virgin olive oil
2 garlic cloves, minced or pounded
3 tablespoons chopped parsley
4 teaspoons chopped thyme or marjoram
1/2 cup freshly grated Parmesan

2 tablespoons chopped green olives
2 tablespoons capers, rinsed
1 to 2 teaspoons red wine vinegar
1 Roma tomato, diced
Salt and freshly milled pepper
1 large onion, thinly sliced
1/4 cup dry white wine or water

Prepare artichoke containers as described on page 330. Toss the bread crumbs with half the oil and fry in a skillet over medium heat until crisp and golden. Combine with the garlic, parsley, 1 tablespoon of the thyme, cheese, olives, and capers. Moisten with the vinegar, stir in the tomato, and season with salt and pepper. Pack the mixture firmly into the artichokes.

Preheat the oven to 375°F. In a skillet, sauté the onion in the remaining oil and thyme over medium heat until softened, 8 to 10 minutes. Season with salt and pepper, then transfer to a baking dish large enough to hold the artichokes comfortably. Place the artichokes on the onions and pour the wine into the dish. Cover with parchment or wax paper, then with aluminum foil. Bake until heated through, about 30 minutes, then remove the cover and brown under the broiler.

Asparagus

ASPARAGUS *signifies spring regardless of the weather. In February, asparagus comes from Mexico and California's Imperial Valley, but as the season progresses the crop moves farther north. By mid-June, commercial crops are about finished. When asparagus appears again for the holidays, it's imported from Chile or some equally distant place.*

TYPES OF ASPARAGUS: Asparagus comes thick and thin; green, white, and purple. The most expensive is white, a color achieved through a painstaking blanching process in the fields. Skinny stalks of wild asparagus, which can still be found, have a beguiling vegetable "gaminess." But what most of us are familiar with are either thin (pencil) asparagus or the thicker green stalks. Although the tips are the most succulent part, the whole asparagus stalk can be used. This efficiency compensates for its fairly high price.

WHAT TO LOOK FOR: Once you've found upright, firm-looking stalks, take a moment to examine the tips, particularly if the asparagus is in a bunch. The tips are the best part and the part most likely to break or spoil. They should be closed and compact, appearing neither excessively dry nor damp. The stalks should be firm and smooth, not shriveled in places. Binding asparagus with wire or rubber bands into bunches may be convenient for the grocer, but it's not good for the asparagus. The tightly bound stalks sweat, producing moisture that hastens rotting.

HOW TO STORE: As soon as you get home, remove any bands and wires from bundled asparagus. If it's not to be eaten right away, keep it loose in a plastic bag in the vegetable bin for several days. Set asparagus from the garden, a much rarer treat, in a jar of water with the tops loosely covered with a plastic bag. Be sure to cook it as soon as possible.

HOW TO USE: Asparagus is enjoyed hot, at room temperature, and chilled. Use it for a salad, a side dish, in soups, tarts, omelets, and soufflés. Asparagus can be steamed, boiled, roasted, stir-fried, sautéed, and even grilled. A simple presentation with the sweetest butter or best olive oil suits it just as well as more elaborate treatments.

SPECIAL HANDLING: Because asparagus is grown in fine, sandy soil, it's a good idea to soak it in a basin of water for 15 minutes before cooking to get any grit out of the tips. To trim thin asparagus, hold the stalk with one hand at the bottom and the other hand a few inches away. Bend the asparagus gently and let it snap where the tender and tough parts meet. If it doesn't snap, slide your hands upward a bit and try again. With thick asparagus you're better off cutting it because it will break virtually anywhere on the stalk and you'll end up wasting a lot of good food. If you look, you can usually see a color change in the stalk. Cut it there, and if it seems tough or stringy, make a second cut a little higher up. Many people don't feel it's necessary to peel asparagus, but peeled stalks, especially thick ones, are far more pleasant to eat. Peel them about two-thirds of the way up with an old-fashioned swivel potato peeler.

QUANTITY: Buy as much as you can afford—people like asparagus, and most can easily eat $1/2$ pound if given the chance, especially when it's the first of the season. Allow at least 10 thin stalks and five to six thick stalks per person.

GOOD PARTNERS FOR ASPARAGUS
Butter, extra virgin olive oil, dark sesame and roasted peanut oils
Parmesan, Fontina, eggs
Parsley, basil, fresh sage, chervil, mint, tarragon
Lemon, orange, capers, ginger, soy
Peas, leeks, scallion, artichokes, fava beans

There are plenty of opinions here. Special tall narrow pots are excellent, but they're not good for much else and they take up valuable kitchen space. Plunging asparagus into a big pot of boiling salted water works fine, as does simmering it in a large skillet, which is quickest and I think best. Tying the asparagus into bunches with kitchen twine keeps water from circulating freely to the stalks, but they come out with all the tips facing the same direction, which is nice for presentation. Whatever your vessel, cook asparagus anywhere from 8 to 15 minutes, depending on the thickness of the stalk. Set it on a cloth towel before dressing to wick off any extra moisture, which would dilute your sauce. If it's to be served later, rinse it under cold water first. If you plan to serve it with a vinaigrette but not right away, wait until close to serving to add the acid or it will wash out the color and give it a dull taste.

Skillet Asparagus

CELEBRATE the first asparagus of the year with your finest extra virgin olive oil or sweet, pure butter and maybe a fresh spring herb, such as tarragon, chervil, or a few hothouse basil leaves. This basic cooking method is used in most of the following recipes.

SERVES 4 TO 6

2 to 3 pounds asparagus, trimmed
Salt and freshly milled pepper
3 to 6 tablespoons unsalted butter or
    extra virgin olive oil

2 tablespoons finely chopped herbs

Put the asparagus in a large skillet of cold water with the tips going in the same direction. Bring to a boil, add salt to taste, and simmer uncovered until just tender when pierced with a knife, 8 to 10 minutes, depending on size. Don't wait for a stalk to hang limply when you pick it out of the water, for it will continue to cook. Set the asparagus on a kitchen towel to drain for a minute, then transfer to a large platter. Dot with butter or drizzle with olive oil, season with pepper, and scatter the herbs over. Gently roll the stalks around to coat them, then wipe the edges of the platter and serve.

Asparagus with Salt, Pepper, and Lemon As austere as this sounds, it's perfectly delicious—especially if you can find thin-skinned, perfumed Meyer lemons from California. Season cooked, drained asparagus with salt and pepper and add a squeeze of fresh lemon over the top just before serving.

Roasted Asparagus Roasting asparagus in a hot oven gives it a robust flavor and is convenient when stove space is unavailable. Do this after the shine of the new crop has worn off a little. Preheat the oven to 425°F. Toss trimmed asparagus in olive oil to coat lightly, season with salt and pepper, and set in a shallow baking dish, no more than 2 stalks deep, with a few tablespoons water. Cover and bake 15 minutes. Uncover and continue baking until tender when pierced with a knife, 10 to 15 minutes, depending on its size. Serve on a platter or a bed of arugula greens with lemon wedges, thin shavings of Parmesan, Garlic Mayonnaise, page 59, or Romesco Sauce, page 70.

Asparagus with Peanut Oil and Black Sesame Seeds Dress cooked asparagus with a few teaspoons roasted peanut or dark sesame oil and garnish with toasted black sesame seeds. Snipped garlic chives, if you have them, are a nice touch; chopped cilantro is good too.

SAUCES AND SEASONINGS FOR ASPARAGUS
Green herb sauces, pages
  55 to 57
Orange, Garlic, or Herb
  Mayonnaise, page 59
Beurre Blanc, page 50, or
  Blossom Butter,
  page 51
Hoisin Sauce with Chili
  Paste and Tangerine
  Zest, page 73

Warm Asparagus Vinaigrette Serve warm asparagus dressed with a vinaigrette as a first-course salad or a vegetable. Shallot, Walnut Oil, Lemon, Herb, and Orange Vinaigrettes, pages 183 to 185, are all good choices.

Asparagus Baked with Butter and Parmesan Preheat the oven to 375°F. Simmer 2 pounds or more trimmed asparagus in a skillet until barely tender. Drain, then layer them in a wide, shallow baking dish. Brown 4 tablespoons butter, page 30, and drizzle it over the asparagus, followed by a veil of freshly grated Parmesan. Season with salt and pepper and bake until bubbling, 15 to 20 minutes. Serve hot with lemon wedges.

Slivered Asparagus Sauté with Shallots

1 to 2 pounds thick asparagus, trimmed
 and peeled
2 tablespoons olive oil
Salt and freshly milled pepper
1 large shallot, finely diced

1 small garlic clove, minced
1 teaspoon finely grated lemon zest
2 tablespoons finely chopped parsley
Lemon juice to taste

A QUICK and easy sauté that stretches a limited supply of asparagus. Use this method with sliced artichokes, celery, mushrooms, and zucchini or a mélange of vegetables. Good garnished with thin shavings of Parmesan and bread crumbs crisped in olive oil.

SERVES 4

Slice the asparagus diagonally about ¼ inch thick, leaving the tips about 3 inches long. Heat the oil in a large skillet. Add the asparagus, season with a few pinches salt, and sauté over high heat until nearly tender. Add the shallot, garlic, lemon zest, and parsley; toss well and cook 1 minute more. Season with lemon juice and pepper to taste.

Grilled Asparagus Asparagus, thick or thin, is absolutely delicious grilled. If thick, peel the bottoms of the stalks first and parboil for 1 minute. Drain, roll them in olive oil, and season with salt and pepper to taste. Grill until tender, turning every 3 or 4 minutes. Remove to a platter and drizzle with extra virgin olive oil laced with finely chopped parsley (or other herb) and shallots, Salsa Verde, page 55, or Garlic Mayonnaise, page 59.

Beans

Summer's beans can be as delectable as asparagus or coarse and stringy, depending on whether they're picked young or allowed to mature past their tender prime. They come in different colors, shapes, and sizes, too. As with tomatoes, there's nothing as good as a bean picked warm from the sun.

GOOD PARTNERS FOR
BEANS
*Olive oil, walnut oil,
    butter, crème fraîche,
    dark sesame and roasted
    peanut oils
Basil, parsley, dill,
    tarragon, summer
    savory, ginger
Shallots, garlic, tomatoes,
    olives, and capers*

TYPES OF BEANS: There are many, but here are a few varieties seen most commonly, especially at farmers' markets. Pole beans are varieties that are grown on poles, in contrast to bush beans—varieties like Haricots Verts that grow close to the ground.

Blue Lake Beans: Large, long string beans—succulent if not overgrown. These are what people commonly call *green beans* and *string beans,* although other beans are green as well and most of today's varieties are now stringless.

Haricots Verts: Highly prized, tender, skinny French green bush beans.

Kentucky Wonder Wax Beans: An older variety of pole bean with yellow pods.

Romano Beans: Green beans with flat, thin pods about 4 to 6 inches long.

Royal Burgundy Beans: These deep purple beans turn green when cooked.

Yard-Long Green Beans: A very long Asian bean that tastes a lot like regular green beans. Cut them into more manageable pieces and cook them the same way as other green beans or add them to stir-fries.

WHAT TO LOOK FOR: Lively, tender pods that have good color, are stiff rather than flaccid, and small rather than large.

HOW TO STORE: If you can't eat them right away, store beans in a plastic bag in the refrigerator. They'll keep for days, but cook them as soon as possible.

HOW TO USE: Cooked beans make fine salads and side dishes, and they mix well with other seasonal vegetables in soups and stews.

SPECIAL HANDLING: If the beans are really small, 3 inches or less, remove only the stem end, not the tips. Stringing is seldom necessary now that stringless varieties have been developed. Boil beans uncovered in plenty of salted water. Covering the pot turns them gray. If cooking several varieties at once, cook each type separately since their cooking times will vary. Cooked beans are best eaten right away or at least within a few hours. If dressing beans in advance, wait to add the acid until just before serving.

QUANTITY: Allow 1½ pounds of beans for four to six servings.

Basic Green Beans (and Yellow and Purple)

1 1/2 pounds beans, tipped and tailed

2 tablespoons butter or extra virgin olive oil

Salt and freshly milled pepper

2 tablespoons chopped herbs—parsley, basil, tarragon, summer savory, or dill

ALL tender bush and pole beans can be cooked this way. Dressed with a vinaigrette or yogurt-based sauce, they add a strong element to a composed salad plate.

SERVES 4 TO 6

Cut large beans into pieces 2 to 3 inches long. Drop them by handfuls into a large pot of boiling salted water and cook at a full boil, uncovered, until they're slightly resilient to the tooth. Start tasting them after 3 or 4 minutes, although they may well take longer to cook. When they're done, drain them, shake dry, and spread on a towel. (If they'll be used later, rinse them first under cold water to stop the cooking.) Toss with butter, taste for salt, season with pepper, and toss with the herbs.

Haricots Verts with Garlic Mayonnaise In truth, all beans taste good this way. Toss 1 pound warm beans with 1/2 cup Garlic Mayonnaise, page 59. Add chopped parsley and toss again. Taste for salt and season with pepper. The heat of the beans brings out the garlicky aroma of the mayonnaise and thins it to a saucelike consistency.

SAUCES AND SEASONINGS FOR BEANS

Herb Butter, page 51
Blossom Butter, page 51
Tarator Sauce, page 67
Herb-Butter and Olive Oil Sauce, page 51
Pesto, page 57, or Basil Puree, page 507

Green Beans with Olive Sauce Use your more mature beans with this zesty, somewhat aggressive sauce. Toss 1 pound warm Blue Lake, Romano, or other beans with 1/3 cup Hot and Spicy Tapenade, page 87, or more to taste.

Green Beans with Salsa Verde with Walnuts and Tarragon Toss warm beans with 1/2 cup of this salsa verde, page 55. These are most aromatic when warm.

Green Beans with Yogurt Sauce Toss boiled beans that have cooled for a few minutes with Yogurt Sauce with Cayenne and Dill or Yogurt Tahini Sauce, page 66. Alternatively, drizzle the sauce over them, allowing some of the bright color of the beans to show through, then toss just before serving.

Green Beans Simmered with Tomato

2 tablespoons olive oil

2 small white onions, sliced into thin rounds

1 garlic clove, finely chopped

1 1/2 pounds green beans, tipped and cut into 2-inch lengths

1 large ripe tomato, peeled, seeded, and diced

2 teaspoons chopped parsley

2 teaspoons chopped summer savory, dill, or lovage

Salt and freshly milled pepper

THE tomato disintegrates and turns into a sauce for the beans.

SERVES 4 TO 6

Heat the oil in a medium or large skillet, add the onions, and cook over medium heat until soft and translucent, about 4 minutes. Add the garlic, beans, tomato, and enough water just to cover. Simmer until the beans are tender, then add the herbs and simmer 1 or 2 minutes more. Timing will depend on the age and size of the bean. Season with salt and pepper to taste. Serve hot, tepid, or even chilled.

Beets

THE beet is a wonderful vegetable, but people resist it, partly because of its sweetness. When beets are treated to the acidic nip of vinegar and lemon or the warmth of spices, however, many take to them with enthusiasm. Beets are available year-round but are best from summer to fall, when they're truly in season. The leaves are mild and tender like chard, the roots earthy and sweet.

GOOD PARTNERS FOR
BEETS
*Olive oil, butter, mustard
    oil, yogurt, sour cream
All vinegars, lemon,
    orange, lime
Mustard, horseradish,
    capers, chile
Parsley, dill, tarragon,
    cilantro, cumin, curry
Onions, apples*

TYPES OF BEETS: In the last decade there has been a colorful infusion of variety into the beet world, and many of the new varieties of beets can be found in farmers' and specialty markets. In addition to the basic red beet, here are two new popular varieties.

The skin of the round Chioggia beet is red-orange to bright red, and the flesh inside is ringed with red and white bands. A very striking beet.

Richly colored golden beets are milder than most red beets and don't bleed as red beets do. The leaves look leathery but are tender and sweet.

WHAT TO LOOK FOR: When you can, buy beets with their greens attached. If the greens are to be cooked, they should be free of stems and yellowed or wilting leaves and used as soon as possible. Since the roots store well, the absence of greens doesn't necessarily indicate inferiority, nor does size. What's important is that the roots are firm and the tails fairly smooth.

HOW TO STORE: Beets keep well for weeks in the refrigerator in a paper or perforated plastic bag. The greens also can be stored in a plastic bag, but for only a few days at most.

HOW TO USE: Beets can be eaten raw, roasted, steamed, grilled, boiled, and baked. They are, of course, the featured vegetable in borscht, and they star in all kinds of salads. Cooked beets keep for a week in the refrigerator. The tasty greens can be used in all the ways spinach and chard are.

SPECIAL HANDLING: Regardless of how you cook them, be sure to leave the tail, skin, and at least an inch of the stems attached to keep the valuable juices locked inside. Beets are easier to peel after they're cooked, so just scrub them and cook them with their skins on. Remember, red beets bleed and tint whatever they touch. When making a salad of different-colored beets or combining them with other vegetables, keep red beets separate until the last minute.

QUANTITY: Allow 1 pound trimmed beets for three to four servings; 1 pound of greens serves two to four.

SAUCES AND SEASONINGS
FOR BEETS
*Fresh Horseradish Sauce,
    page 72
Green herb sauces,
    pages 55 to 57
Yogurt Sauce with
    Cayenne and Dill,
    page 66
Romesco Sauce, page 70
Herb salts, pages 75 to 77
Shallot Vinaigrette,
    page 183
Lime-Cumin Vinaigrette,
    page 187*

Roasted Beets In a pan, bake scrubbed unpeeled beets at 400°F or whatever oven temperature is convenient until easily pierced with a knife. A large beet may need an hour to bake, a smaller one 25 to 35 minutes.

Baked Beets Put scrubbed unpeeled beets in a baking dish, add ¼ inch water to the dish, and cover. Bake at 375°F or whatever temperature is convenient. The steaming action speeds the cooking so that a large beet will take about 40 minutes.

Steamed Beets Set scrubbed unpeeled beets in a steaming basket, cover, and steam until tender when pierced with a knife—about 35 to 40 minutes for a large beet, 20 to 25 for smaller ones.

Pressure-Cooked Beets The pressure cooker makes it possible to have beets for supper at the last minute. Put beets in the steaming insert, bring the cooker to pressure, then maintain on high for 10 minutes for large beets, about 7 for smaller ones. Release the pressure quickly. If you find the beets aren't quite done, return the lid and bring the pressure back up. If they're very close, just steam them with the lid loosely closed until done.

Beets with Butter, Salt, and Pepper A very basic vegetable dish but one of the best. Cook beets until tender when pierced with a knife. Slip off the skins when cool enough to handle. Cut them into wedges or rounds and toss with a little butter or olive oil, salt, and freshly milled pepper. Beets are so slick that butter just slides off them rather than becoming absorbed, so you won't need to use much. Serve with lemon wedges or a cruet of vinegar.

Five-Minute Beets

4 beets, about 1 pound
1 tablespoon butter
Salt and freshly milled pepper

Lemon juice or vinegar to taste
2 tablespoons chopped parsley, tarragon, dill, or other herb

GRATED beets cook quickly—if not in 5 minutes, maybe in 8 or 10. The same method, in fact, saves time with other root vegetables as well.

SERVES 4 TO 6

Grate them into coarse shreds. Melt the butter in a skillet, add the beets, and toss them with ½ teaspoon salt and pepper to taste. Add ¼ cup water, then cover the pan and cook over medium heat until the beets are tender. Remove the lid and raise the heat to boil off any excess water. Taste for salt, season with a little lemon juice or vinegar—balsamic or red wine is good—and toss with the herb. If you don't mind the shocking color, you can stir in a tablespoon of yogurt or sour cream, always a good-tasting addition to beets.

Variations: Cook the beets in fresh orange juice or stir in a slice or two of Mustard Butter, page 52, at the end. The herb salts, pages 75 to 77, especially the one with fennel seed, make an interesting change from plain salt.

Vinegared Beets Nested in Their Greens

16 to 24 small beets with their greens, about 2 pounds
1½ tablespoons butter or olive oil

Salt and freshly milled pepper
2 teaspoons balsamic or sherry vinegar

PERFECT for small garden beets about an inch across with fresh tender tops, though you can use larger ones cut into wedges. An assortment of red, striped, and golden beets looks irresistible.

SERVES 4 TO 6

Remove the greens, scrub the beets, and steam them until tender, 15 to 30 minutes. Peel and set aside. Discard any greens that don't look up to snuff, along with the stems. Steam the greens until tender, about 5 minutes, then toss with half the butter and season with salt and pepper. Arrange them in a nest on a plate. In another pan, heat the beets with the remaining butter. Add the vinegar and shake the pan until it evaporates. Spoon the beets into the center of the greens and serve.

Broccoli

BROCCOLI *is a member of the genus* Brassica, *which includes cabbages, cauliflower, and Brussels sprouts, among other plants. Its clusters of buds make broccoli solid, compact, and satisfying to eat. Although available year-round, its usual season is October through May.*

TYPES OF BROCCOLI: In addition to the standard green broccoli, there are some new varieties. It's not always clear what's what with broccoli; some are also called *cauliflowers*. We now have purple broccoli; the chartreuse broccoli Romanesco, whose configuration of spirals forms a pointed head; sprouting broccoli, which gives a longer supply of small sprouts; and broccoflower, which appears to be a combination of broccoli and cauliflower. As different as they look, all can be cooked and seasoned the same way.

WHAT TO LOOK FOR: Look for firm, tight heads, crisp stalks, and perky leaves if any are attached. The greens are quite delicious and can be cooked as you would cook chard or kale. Crowns that are yellowed or have loose or open florets are over the hill; they should be dark green with vibrant, tight buds.

HOW TO STORE: Refrigerate broccoli in loose or perforated plastic bags, preferably in the vegetable bin, where it will keep for several days.

HOW TO USE: Broccoli can be steamed, boiled, sautéed, stir-fried, or braised, but very young broccoli can be eaten raw.

SPECIAL HANDLING: If heads appear to be sandy, soak them for 15 minutes in cold water to loosen the soil, then rinse. Don't overcook broccoli or any of its relatives. When people dislike these vegetables, it's usually because of overcooking, which produces a sulfurous odor (slow braising is the exception). When cooking, steam partially covered and boil uncovered to allow the sulfur compounds to escape.

QUANTITY: Broccoli is usually sold in bunches weighing about $1\frac{1}{2}$ pounds. The crowns plus an inch or two of the stems are also sold loose. The stems are quite edible, although the trimmed broccoli yields more of everyone's favorite part, the tops. One and one-half pounds will yield four very generous side dishes or six more modest ones.

Steamed Broccoli

SERVES 4

$1\frac{1}{2}$ pounds broccoli
Salt and freshly milled pepper

3 to 5 tablespoons butter or Brown
    Butter, page 30
Juice of $\frac{1}{2}$ lemon to taste

Trim the broccoli into large florets with the stems attached. Peel the stems and cut thick ones lengthwise in half so that the heat gets to them from inside and out. Place the broccoli in a steaming basket over boiling water, cover, and steam for 3 minutes. Remove the lid for a moment, then cook, partially covered, until the stems are tender-firm, another 8 to 10 minutes. (Or cook the broccoli in plenty of boiling salted water until tender, 5 to 7 minutes, then drain.) Remove to a platter, season with salt and pepper to taste, and add the butter and a healthy squeeze of lemon.

Broccoli with Mustard Butter and Capers Toss steamed broccoli with Mustard Butter, page 52, 2 tablespoons rinsed capers, and a tablespoon or so of chopped marjoram or parsley.

Broccoli with Garlic, Red Pepper Flakes, and Parmesan Steam or boil 1½ pounds broccoli as described on page 340; drain. Warm 3 tablespoons olive oil with 2 thinly sliced garlic cloves in a large skillet until the garlic begins to color. Add ¼ teaspoon pepper flakes, the broccoli, and salt and pepper to taste. Sauté until heated through. Turn into a dish and cover with paper-thin shavings of Parmesan. The heat of the broccoli will soften the cheese and bring out its flavor.

Warm Broccoli Vinaigrette Warm broccoli tossed with a vinaigrette is intensely fragrant, an excellent salad vegetable. Try broccoli with the vinaigrettes and sauces listed at the right.

Broccoli Stems With their delicate flavor and uplifting color, broccoli stems are quite choice. Use them as a vegetable or as part of a vegetable mixture, be it a soup, salad, or stir-fry. They're exceptionally good—and pretty—with turnips and rutabagas. Peel them thickly, cutting just below the tough outer layer of skin with a paring knife. Slice them into rounds, diagonals, matchsticks, thicker batons, or small squares. Boil in salted water until tender-firm and season as you would broccoli florets.

Broccoli and Scallion Puree

1 bay leaf

Salt and freshly milled pepper

1 to 1¼ pounds broccoli, stems peeled and chopped, florets separated

1 bunch scallions, including an inch of the greens, chopped

2 tablespoons butter

Pinch grated nutmeg

2 teaspoons lemon juice

2 tablespoons cream or crème fraîche, optional

Bring 2 quarts water to a boil with the bay leaf in a saucepan. Add 1 teaspoon salt, then the broccoli and scallions. Cook until the stems are tender, 4 to 6 minutes. Scoop out the vegetables, discard the bay leaf, and reserve the water. Puree in a food processor, leaving a little texture. Add a little of the cooking water if needed to loosen the mixture. Stir in the butter, taste for salt, and season with a little pepper, the nutmeg, and lemon juice. The seasonings should be lively. Stir in the cream if using.

Variation with Sesame Oil: Unexpected but good. Omit the butter and nutmeg and season the puree with 2 teaspoons dark sesame oil.

SAUCES AND SEASONINGS FOR BROCCOLI

Tomato Vinaigrette with Olives, page 188

Lemon Vinaigrette, page 184

Mustard Vinaigrette, page 186

Curry Vinaigrette, page 187

Sesame Vinaigrette with Chili Oil, page 188

Feta Dressing with Marjoram and Mint, page 190

Curry Mayonnaise with Mango Chutney, page 93

A PALE green puree when a soft-textured side dish is called for. Leftovers can be turned into soup in 10 quick minutes or used as the base of a vegetable soufflé.

MAKES ABOUT 2 CUPS, SERVING 4 TO 6

Chopped Broccoli with Lemon

SOMETHING *as simple as chopping the broccoli in- stead of leaving it large changes it completely. The smaller pieces seem to make the tastes meld in your mouth. For a heartier dish, toss more or less equal amounts of boiled diced potatoes, cooked rice, barley, or quinoa with the chopped broccoli.*

SERVES 4 TO 6

1 large bunch broccoli, about 1½ pounds

2 to 4 tablespoons extra virgin olive oil or butter

Salt and freshly milled pepper

Fresh lemon juice to taste

Chop the broccoli into small florets; peel and finely chop the stems. Put the stems in the steaming basket, add the florets, then cover and steam until just a little short of be- ing tender. Toss with olive oil and season with salt, pepper, and lemon juice to sharpen the flavors.

Broccoli Rabe

BROCCOLI *rabe (variously spelled* raab *and* rape) *is a tangy and spicy Italian green with succulent nubbins of florets and yellow flowers. Anyone who has a craving for greens, especially those with an assertive tang, will be drawn to broccoli rabe. You can find it in Italian markets and now even supermarkets. The stems are peeled and eaten along with the leaves. This basic preparation can be enjoyed by itself, over Garlic-Rubbed Croutons, or tossed with pasta.*

Broccoli Rabe with Garlic and Red Pepper Flakes

SERVES 3 TO 4

1 large bunch broccoli rabe, 1½ to 2 pounds

Salt

3 tablespoons extra virgin olive oil

3 garlic cloves, sliced

Several pinches red pepper flakes

Lemon wedges or red wine vinegar

Leaving the leaves and florets attached, peel the large stalks with a paring knife. Drop them into a pot of boiling salted water and cook for 5 minutes, longer if you like your greens well cooked and tender, then drain. Leave it whole or coarsely chop. Heat the oil with the garlic and pepper flakes in a large skillet over medium-high heat until the garlic just begins to color. Add the broccoli rabe and cook, turning it repeatedly so that it's coated with the oil, about 5 minutes. Taste for salt. Serve with lemon wedges or vinegar on the side.

FRONT TO BACK: **Potato and Chickpea Stew** *page 252* and **Romesco Sauce** *page 70*

PREVIOUS PAGE: **Spring Vegetable Stew** *page 247*

Butternut Squash Gratin with Onions and Sage *page* 287

Mixed Beans in Broth with Parsley and Parmesan *page 316*

FACING PAGE: **Baby Artichoke and Scallion Sauté** *page 332*

Braised Fennel with Parmesan *page 374*

FACING PAGE: Carrots with Hijiki *page 352*

FOLLOWING PAGE: Roasted Onions on a Bed of Herbs *page 396*
and Braised Boiling Onions or Shallots *page 395*

Brussels Sprouts

Is there another vegetable that can compete for aggressiveness and lack of subtlety? Poor Brussels sprouts suffer from being picked too large and stored too long, which compromise their possibilities. In addition, master gardener Shepherd Ogden of Cook's Garden told me that the real problem is that because most Brussels sprouts are grown on the mild California coast, they don't get the freeze that makes them the tender and sweet morsels they can be. Despite all this, Brussels sprouts still manage to make their yearly appearance on holiday tables. And when they're good, they're undeniably sweet, mild and utterly delicious—a real treat.

WHAT TO LOOK FOR: Brussels sprouts look just like miniature cabbages, only instead of growing in a cluster of leaves, they cling to a large stalk topped with a shading crown of foliage, somewhat resembling a Dr. Seuss character. Whole stalks can frequently be found at farmers' markets in the fall. They should be dark green and tightly formed. Avoid those whose leaves have unfurled or have begun to yellow. And give them a sniff to make sure they don't have an off-putting odor.

HOW TO STORE: Put them in a plastic bag and refrigerate. Try to use them within a few days at most.

HOW TO USE: When Brussels sprouts are at their best they need just a tad of butter. Otherwise they demand more assertive seasonings to match their own or the tempering effect of cream- and milk-based sauces. All the things that taste good with cabbage (juniper and mustard) and cauliflower (brown butter, capers, and lemon) also go well with Brussels sprouts.

SPECIAL HANDLING: Cutting an × in the bottom brings heat to their centers more quickly, but if you halve or thinly slice Brussels sprouts, they better absorb their tasty sauces and dressings. You can also separate their leaves—attractive and delicious but very time consuming. Soak them in cold water for 15 minutes before cooking. As with broccoli, avoid overcooking.

QUANTITY: Allow 1 pound Brussels sprouts for four to six servings.

GOOD PARTNERS FOR
BRUSSELS SPROUTS
*Butter, olive oil,
    mustard oil
Cream, béchamel, blue
    cheese, Cheddar
Mustard, capers, garlic,
    lemon, vinegar
Caraway, oregano,
    parsley, dill, curry
    spices, juniper*

SAUCES AND SEASONINGS
FOR BRUSSELS SPROUTS
*Curry Sauce, page 71
Cheese Béchamel made
    with sharp Cheddar,
    page 53
Parsley-Caper Sauce,
    page 56
Yogurt Sauce with
    Cayenne and Dill,
    page 66*

Brussels Sprouts with Mustard Butter and Caraway

1 pound Brussels sprouts

Salt and freshly milled pepper

4 tablespoons Mustard Butter, page 52

¹/₂ teaspoon caraway or celery seeds, bruised in a mortar

Bring a large pot of water to a boil. Meanwhile, trim the sprouts, pulling off any wilted leaves, and cut an × in the bottom of each or slice lengthwise in half. Salt the boiling water, add the sprouts, and cook uncovered until tender, 6 to 8 minutes. Drain and shake off the excess water. Toss with the butter and caraway seeds, then season with salt and pepper to taste.

Brussels Sprouts and Walnuts with Fennel and Red Pearl Onions

THIS gorgeous dish was inspired by a picture in Simply French *by Patricia Wells. It's an elaborate preparation for a special meal, but you can cook everything except the Brussels sprouts the day before. Reheat the vegetables, blanch the sprouts, and combine them at the last minute.*

SERVES 8 OR MORE AT A HOLIDAY MEAL

1 cup walnut halves

1 pint red pearl onions or shallots

3 tablespoons butter

1 tablespoon sugar

Salt and freshly milled pepper

1 fennel bulb, julienned, or 5 celery ribs, diced

1 cup Basic Vegetable Stock, page 196, or water

3 tablespoons chopped parsley and celery leaves, mixed

1 pound Brussels sprouts, left whole if small, halved or quartered if not

2 tablespoons walnut oil

2 tablespoons chopped fennel greens and parsley, mixed

Drop the walnuts into a pan of boiling water for 1 minute, then scoop them out. Rub off what you can of their skins with a towel, then dry in a 350°F oven for 7 to 8 minutes. Scald the onions in the same pan for 1 minute, then slip off the outer skins without cutting off the root end. If using shallots, peel and separate, following their natural divisions.

Melt 1 tablespoon butter in an 8- or 10-inch skillet over medium heat. Add the onions, sprinkle with sugar, and season with a little salt and pepper. Cover and cook over low heat, giving the pan a shake every few minutes, until the onions are lightly browned and nearly tender, about 12 minutes. Add the fennel and continue cooking, covered, until tender, 8 to 10 minutes.

In another skillet, melt the remaining 2 tablespoons butter. Add the walnuts and cook over low heat, occasionally giving the pan a shake, until they're golden, 12 to 15 minutes. Add the stock and herbs. Simmer, covered, until the liquid is reduced to a few tablespoons of syrupy juices. Taste for salt and pepper, then combine them with the onions and fennel.

Boil the Brussels sprouts in salted water until tender, 6 to 8 minutes, then add them to the mixture. Add the walnut oil and fennel greens, gently stir everything together, and serve.

Cabbage

WHETHER red or green, smooth or crinkled, cabbage is a mild, sweet vegetable, though we don't generally think of it that way. To keep it sweet and appealing, don't overcook it. And don't save cabbage for winter fare; it's delicious from June on, when the summer varieties come in.

TYPES OF CABBAGE: In addition to color and shape, what differentiates cabbages is whether they're tender, soft summer cabbages or winter varieties. Here are a few common cabbages:

Dutch head cabbages: These smooth green or purple heads are our common everyday cabbages. Some summer varieties are cone shaped, with gently furled leaves.

Savoy cabbage: Vigorously crinkled with dark green outer leaves, this is the sweetest and most dramatic-looking cabbage and the choice variety for stuffing.

Napa or Chinese cabbage: Pale and crinkled, Napa cabbage is a small football-sized loaf, lighter in color and weight than Dutch and Savoy and milder in flavor.

WHAT TO LOOK FOR: All cabbages should have a fresh, firm appearance. Summer cabbage leaves are a bit more open than the leaves of cabbage grown for winter storage. Winter cabbage is firm and heavy, the leaves tightly laid against each other. Ideally, Savoy cabbage should be wreathed in at least some of its outer leaves, though typically it's stripped down to the heart. Napa cabbage should be firm looking, the leaves compact.

HOW TO STORE: Keep cabbage in a plastic bag in your salad crisper. It will keep for weeks, but its nutritive value diminishes with time. If the outer leaves wilt, just remove them before cooking.

HOW TO USE: Cabbage is one of the easiest vegetables to prepare. There's nothing to pare, snip, or remove—just cut it and go. It's used in coleslaws and soups and is delicious braised, boiled, or steamed. Napa cabbage makes an unusual salad and a standard stir-fry ingredient. Its leaves can also be stuffed.

SPECIAL HANDLING: Long sessions in covered pots give cabbage its sulfuric bite and hence its bad reputation. Briefer cooking keeps cabbage sweet and tender. Cooking water seems to cling to it, so wick off excess moisture with a towel to avoid diluting an added sauce. Red cabbage should be cut with a stainless-steel knife, or it will turn a startling blue. Being somewhat coarser than green, it takes a little longer to cook.

QUANTITY: Amounts vary depending on the trimming needed, but a smallish cabbage, weighing about 1½ pounds, yields 6 to 8 cups shredded or chopped cabbage and 4 to 6 cups cooked, enough for four servings.

Boiled Cabbage Nothing sounds so unappealing as boiled cabbage, but when not overcooked it's actually one of the nicest ways to enjoy it. Drop shredded cabbage or wedges into a large pot of boiling salted water. Cook, uncovered, until the leaves are tender, 5 to 10 minutes. Pour into a colander, shake off the water, and press a towel over the cabbage to wick off the excess moisture. Toss with butter or oil, salt and pepper, and any of the seasonings above right—including a dash of apple cider vinegar to bring up the flavors, but not enough to be detectable.

GOOD PARTNERS FOR CABBAGE

Olive oil, butter, brown butter, mustard oil, cream, sour cream
Cheddar, Taleggio, Teleme, Parmesan
Mustard, horseradish, caraway, curry spices, juniper
Dill, marjoram, sage
Apples, apple cider vinegar, lemon juice
Potatoes, buckwheat, pasta

Steamed Cabbage with Butter and Poppy Seeds

SERVES 4

1 small green cabbage, about 1½
    pounds
Salt and freshly milled pepper

2 to 4 tablespoons butter
Poppy seeds

Remove the outer leaves, quarter the cabbage, and cut out the core. (It's quite tasty to nibble on with a bit of sea salt sprinkled over.) Leave the wedges whole or slice them crosswise about ½ inch thick. Steam until tender but not mushy, 5 to 10 minutes. Remove the cabbage to a bowl, blot it quickly with a clean towel, then toss with salt, pepper, butter, and the poppy seeds.

Cabbage Wedges with Chopped Dill

ONE of the fastest, easiest vegetable dishes you can make.

SERVES 4 TO 6

1½ to 2 pounds green cabbage
Salt and freshly milled white pepper

Butter, olive oil, or crème fraîche
2 tablespoons chopped dill

Cut the cabbage into sixths or eighths. Pour about 1 inch water into a wide skillet, add ½ teaspoon salt, and bring to a boil. Add the cabbage and lower the heat to a simmer. Cover and steam until bright green and tender, 8 to 10 minutes. When done, transfer to a platter, add butter or oil to taste, sprinkle with dill, and season with pepper.

Savoy Cabbage with Potatoes and Brown Butter

A RICH and filling cold-weather dish, this combination of flavors is excellent on its own or tossed with buckwheat pasta.

SERVES 4

8 ounces boiling or fingerling potatoes
1½ pounds Savoy cabbage, cut into
    large squares or strips
3 tablespoons Brown Butter, page 30
½ cup diced Taleggio or Teleme

2 tablespoons freshly grated Parmesan
2 tablespoons chopped sage
Salt and freshly milled pepper

Peel the boiling potatoes and cut them into ½-inch chunks or scrub the fingerlings and slice diagonally about ⅜ inch thick. Steam until tender, about 15 minutes, then remove them to a bowl and cover to keep warm. Steam the cabbage until tender, 5 to 10 minutes. Combine the vegetables in a bowl, toss with the brown butter, cheeses, and sage, then season with salt and pepper to taste.

Red Cabbage with Apples

3 tablespoons sunflower seed oil

1 small onion, finely diced

1 tablespoon caraway seeds

1 medium red cabbage, about 2 pounds, quartered, cored, and finely sliced

2 Granny Smith or Pippin apples, quartered, cored, and diced

Salt and freshly milled pepper

Apple cider vinegar

THE combination of cabbage with apples and onions is classic. Vary it by adding boiled, whole chestnuts or toasted walnuts just before serving.

SERVES 4 TO 6

Heat the oil in a large skillet. Add the onion and caraway, give them a stir, then cook for a few minutes over medium heat until the onion is translucent. Add the cabbage and apples and season with 1 teaspoon salt. Cover tightly and cook very slowly until the cabbage is meltingly tender, up to an hour. Taste for salt, season with pepper, and toss with vinegar to taste.

Sweet and Sour Red Cabbage

1 1/2 pounds red cabbage

1/2 teaspoon allspice berries

1 1/2 teaspoons coriander seeds

4 cloves

1 1/2 tablespoons vegetable oil

1 onion, finely diced

3 small bay leaves

1 tablespoon brown sugar or molasses

Salt and freshly milled pepper

1/4 cup diced tomatoes, fresh or canned

1/2 cup juice from the tomatoes or water

2 tablespoons balsamic vinegar

SERVES 4

Using a stainless-steel knife, quarter the cabbage, remove the core, and slice it crosswise into 1/2-inch strips. Bruise the spices in a mortar or grind them in a spice mill. Heat the oil in a wide skillet with the onion, spices, and bay leaves; cook over medium heat until the onion is translucent, about 4 minutes, then add the brown sugar and cook 1 minute more. Lay the cabbage over the onion, season with 1 teaspoon salt, and spoon the tomatoes over all. Pour in the tomato juice, then cover and cook gently until the cabbage is tender, about 15 minutes. Remove the lid and toss everything together. Add the vinegar, raise the heat, and cook until most of the liquid is evaporated, leaving a syrupy glaze. Taste for salt, season with pepper, and serve.

Cabbage with Juniper Berries

JUNIPER is outstanding with cabbage. In this recipe the cream mixes with the juices, turning into a thin sauce. Serve with buckwheat groats (kasha), egg noodles, or soba.

SERVES 4 TO 6

1 small Savoy or green cabbage, about 1½ pounds

Salt and freshly milled pepper

1½ tablespoons butter

1 leek, including an inch of the greens, diced

10 juniper berries, bruised in a mortar

⅓ cup cream

Quarter the cabbage, remove the core, and cut into wide ribbons or squares. Boil, uncovered, in well-salted water for 4 minutes. Drain, rinse under cool water, and squeeze out the excess moisture with your hands.

Melt the butter in a large skillet. Add the leek, juniper, and 1 tablespoon water. Cook over medium heat until the leek is tender, about 5 minutes, then add the cabbage and cream. Taste a piece of the cabbage and add more salt if needed. Cover the pan and cook over low heat for 10 minutes. Taste again for salt and season with pepper.

Napa or Chinese Cabbage This Asian cabbage cooks quickly and is even milder than European varieties. Allow 1½ pounds or more for four servings. Chop the whole cabbage, including the firm white base, into strips of whatever width appeals to you. Heat a few tablespoons water or rice wine in a wide skillet, add the cabbage, and sprinkle with salt. Cook over medium-high heat, turning the leaves with tongs, until wilted. Drain, then toss with dark sesame oil, roasted peanut oil, or butter. Garnish with chopped parsley, cilantro, or dill; snipped chives; toasted sesame seeds; or Gomashio, page 76.

STUFFED CABBAGE

Stuffed cabbages look good on a plate and are substantial but not heavy. They're not hard to make, but they can be time consuming in the context of preparing an entire meal. To make it easy on yourself, plan to have something done ahead of time—the sauce, the cabbage leaves, or another part of the meal. Look to leftover grain dishes, such as pilafs, for fillings—virtually all grains are good with cabbage. Crinkled Savoy cabbage is preferred because of its sweetness and its stunning looks when cooked, but regular green cabbage is delicious, too. Or try Napa cabbage, chard, collard greens, or any other large-leafed vegetable.

To Prepare Cabbage Leaves for Stuffing: Bring water to boil in a stockpot big enough to hold the cabbage. Cut deeply around the core at the base of the cabbage, but don't try to remove it. Immerse the entire cabbage in the boiling water for 4 to 5 minutes, then lift it out, supporting it with a strainer and guiding it with a large fork. Peel off the number of leaves you need or as many as come off easily. Return the head to the water for additional softening and repeat. Before stuffing the leaves, remove the tough white vein at the base of each leaf. You can use the rest of the cabbage in the same or another meal or as part of the filling.

Cabbage Leaves with Rice and Green Herb Filling

1 Savoy or green cabbage, about
  1½ pounds

2 tablespoons butter or olive oil

1 large leek, quartered lengthwise and
  chopped

1 bunch scallions, including a few
  inches of the greens, chopped

1 head butter lettuce, cut into strips and
  chopped

1 large handful sorrel leaves, julienned,
  if available

½ cup chopped parsley

1 teaspoon marjoram

½ teaspoon thyme

Salt and freshly milled pepper

1 cup cooked brown rice, barley, or
  other grain

¼ cup yogurt or pureed silken tofu

¼ cup tomato juice or water

Sorrel Sauce, page 54, or Tomato Sauce
  with Dried Mushrooms, page 64

THE filling uses plenty of greens and herbs, looking optimistically toward spring. A low-fat, high-flavor dish.

SERVES 6

Prepare 12 of the cabbage leaves for stuffing. Preheat the oven to 375°F. Quarter the remaining cabbage, remove the core, cut it into thin strips, then chop finely.

Heat the butter in a wide skillet and add the shredded cabbage, leek, scallions, lettuce, sorrel, and herbs. Season with 1 teaspoon salt, add ¼ cup water, cover, and cook over medium heat until the vegetables are tender, about 15 minutes. Drain, then transfer to a bowl. Add the rice and yogurt and mix well. Season with pepper and additional salt if needed.

Divide the filling by eye into 12 portions. Set the leaves, smooth side down, on the counter. Place a portion on the base of each leaf just above the notched area, fold the ends neatly around it, and roll. Wrap each stuffed cabbage in a towel and twist firmly, forcing it into a ball. Place the balls in a single layer in a baking dish and add the tomato juice. Cover and bake for 30 minutes. Nap each plate with the sauce and place two cabbages on top.

Cabbage-Stuffed Cabbage with Blue Cheese

1 Savoy or green cabbage, about
  1½ pounds

Cabbage with Juniper Berries, page 348

8 ½-inch cubes Gorgonzola or
  Roquefort

I LOVE the filling cooked with juniper berries and cream, but you can also just steam the leaves and season them well with butter, salt, and pepper. Serve these light rolls on a bed of cracked wheat or Wehani Rice Pilaf, surrounded by a tomato sauce or Herb Béchamel.

SERVES 4

Blanch and separate eight cabbage leaves for stuffing as described on page 348. With the rest of the cabbage, make the Cabbage with Juniper Berries or simply steam it, then cool. Place ½ cup cooked cabbage in the center of each leaf and set a cube of the cheese inside that. Roll up the leaf, folding in the sides as you go. Twist the roll in a towel to give it a plump, round shape. Steam until heated through, about 10 minutes, then serve.

Carrots

THESE sweet favorites are always available and easy to prepare. Cook them so they're tender but still have some bite. The moment they get soft, they lose their appeal. Carrots aren't always as sweet as they should be. Their deep orange color (indicating lots of beta-carotene) often, though not always, indicates good flavor. Don't automatically dismiss larger carrots in favor of miniature—often the large ones are best. As always, taste is your surest test.

GOOD PARTNERS FOR CARROTS

Butter, olive oil, cream, dark sesame and roasted peanut oils

Thyme, chervil, lovage, dill, cumin, ginger, mint, chile

Mustard, honey, brown sugar, maple syrup

All root vegetables

TYPES OF CARROTS: Carrots come in a variety of shapes and sizes, from round stubby French market carrots to long pointed or cylindrical varieties, from tiny 3-inch "babies" to immense storage or "horse" carrots. Not all carrots are orange; some, more rarely seen, are white, while others are a gorgeous red.

WHAT TO LOOK FOR: Nicely shaped roots, good color, firmness, and an absence of cracks—cracks usually indicate woody cores. Although not a problem for stocks or juice, cracked carrots aren't so good for eating. Attached greens assure peak freshness.

HOW TO STORE: Remove the greens and keep carrots in a plastic bag in the vegetable bin of the refrigerator for up to about 2 weeks.

HOW TO USE: Enjoy carrots raw and cooked. Use them for salads, soups, purees, and juice. They're also a strong element in stews, stocks, stir-fries, and many vegetable mixtures. Braising and roasting concentrate their flavors.

SPECIAL HANDLING: If fresh from the garden, simply scrub carrots well. Otherwise, peel them. Peeled carrots look much nicer when cooked.

QUANTITY: There are four to five medium carrots in a pound, yielding about 3½ cups chopped. Allow 1 pound carrots for three to four servings.

Steamed Carrots

A BASIC preparation for carrots that will be seasoned later. Add salt, a few sprigs of a favorite herb, and a sliver of onion to the steaming water if you like.

SERVES 4

1½ pounds carrots, scrubbed or peeled
2 tablespoons butter or olive oil to taste
Salt and freshly milled pepper

1 tablespoon minced parsley
2 teaspoons lemon thyme, regular thyme, chervil, dill, mint, or lovage

Leave small carrots whole; cut large carrots into rounds, ovals, matchsticks, or whatever shape you want. Make sure all the pieces are about the same size to ensure even cooking. Steam them, covered, over boiling water until they just yield to the tip of a knife, 5 to 12 minutes, depending on their size. Turn them into a bowl, add the butter or oil, season with salt and pepper, and toss until the butter is melted. Add the herbs and toss again.

Boiled Carrots Cook sliced carrots, uncovered, in plenty of boiling salted water until tender-firm, then drain and season. Start unpeeled whole carrots in cold water, add salt when it boils, then cook until tender. Rinse under cool water, then slip off the skins and finish with any of the suggested sauces and seasonings.

Carrots with Shallots and Parsley Melt 2 tablespoons butter in a medium skillet. Add 3 tablespoons minced shallot and cook over medium heat until it begins to color, after 3 or 4 minutes. Add 1 1/2 pounds steamed or boiled carrots, well drained, and 1/4 cup chopped parsley. Toss well and cook for a few minutes more. Season with pepper and serve. Simple but truly fine.

SAUCES AND SEASONINGS
FOR CARROTS
Salsa Verdes, page 55
*Yogurt Sauce with Cayenne
     and Dill, page 66*
Chile Butter, page 52
Chermoula, page 56
*Indian Salt with Mixed
     Spices, page 77*
*Peanut-Soy Sauce with
     Ginger and Scallions,
     page 73*

Braised Carrots

1 1/2 pounds carrots, scrubbed or peeled

2 tablespoons butter

Salt and freshly milled pepper

2 teaspoons sugar or honey

3 or 4 thyme sprigs

2 tablespoons chopped parsley

BRAISING brings out a fuller range of the carrots' flavor, concentrates their sweetness, and fringes the carrots with a golden glaze. Simple but irresistible.

SERVES 4

Slice the carrots into rounds, ovals, or a roll cut. Heat the butter in a wide skillet. Add the carrots, 1/2 teaspoon salt, a little pepper, the sugar, and thyme. Add water to come to the top of the carrots. Bring to a boil, then cover the pan and simmer until the carrots are tender, 10 to 20 minutes, depending on how they were cut. Uncover the pan, raise the heat, and reduce the liquid until it's syrupy. (If you didn't have enough liquid, or it cooked away too fast, add more while the carrots are cooking.) Continue cooking the carrots until they begin to brown. Check the seasonings and toss with the parsley.

Braised Carrots with Mint and Cider Vinegar

1 1/2 pounds carrots, scrubbed or peeled

1 tablespoon olive oil

10 mint leaves, plus extra for garnish

1 tablespoon chopped lovage or celery
     leaves, plus extra for garnish

1/4 teaspoon celery seeds

Salt and freshly milled pepper

2 tablespoons apple cider vinegar

THE vinegar keeps the texture of the carrots firm. Add lovage if you have it—its distinctive bracing flavor makes it an exciting herb for carrots. These are good warm or cold.

SERVES 4

Slice the carrots into ovals or into rounds about 1/3 inch thick. Warm the oil in a medium skillet with the herbs and celery seeds to bring out their fragrance, then add the carrots, 1/2 teaspoon salt, the vinegar, and water to cover. Bring to a boil, then lower the heat and simmer, covered, until the carrots are tender, about 20 minutes. Remove the lid and reduce any remaining liquid so that the carrots are nicely glazed. Taste for salt, season with pepper, and garnish with the remaining chopped mint and lovage.

Glazed Carrots with Mustard and Honey

HONEYED carrots are usually appealing to children. Parsnips, or parsnips mixed with carrots, are also delicious cooked this way.

SERVES 4 TO 6

1 $\frac{1}{2}$ pounds carrots, scrubbed or peeled	2 teaspoons Dijon mustard
1 tablespoon butter	Salt and freshly milled pepper
1 tablespoon honey or light brown sugar	Chopped parsley

Cut the carrots into 3-inch lengths; halve or quarter the thicker ends so that they'll cook evenly. Steam or boil until tender as described on page 350 or 351.

In a medium skillet, melt the butter with the honey, then stir in the mustard and carrots and season with salt and plenty of pepper. Cook over medium heat for several minutes, until well coated and bubbling, then toss with chopped parsley and serve.

Carrots with Hijiki (or Arame)

SEA vegetables are among the most nutritious plants on earth, and hijiki and arame are two very likable ones, especially in this Japanese dish, which is one of my all-time favorite things to eat. When the mood strikes, I like it with Miso Soup, Golden Fried Tofu, and brown rice, a tradition from my Zen days that has really held up.

SERVES 2 TO 4

2 cups dried hijiki or arame	3 carrots, julienned
Soy sauce or tamari to taste	Salt
2 tablespoons dark sesame oil	Toasted sesame seeds
2 tablespoons slivered ginger	

Cover the hijiki with water and soak for 15 minutes. Drain, then put it in a saucepan with fresh water to cover and 2 tablespoons soy sauce. Bring to a boil, simmer for 15 minutes, then drain again. If using arame, soak for 3 minutes, then drain without parboiling.

Heat the oil in a wide skillet over high heat. Add the ginger and carrots and stir-fry until the carrots begin to color around the edges, about 2 minutes. Add the seaweed and cook 5 minutes more, tossing frequently. Add 1 tablespoon soy sauce and let it cook off. Taste and season with salt and/or soy sauce. Garnish with toasted sesame seeds.

Roasted Carrots with Garlic and Thyme

SINCE the garlic is roasted with the skins on, this is a good time to use all those tiny cloves that are too fiddly to peel. Leftovers are good with a squeeze of lemon.

SERVES 4

1 $\frac{1}{2}$ pounds carrots, peeled	10 or so tiny garlic cloves
2 tablespoons olive oil	Several thyme sprigs
Salt and freshly milled pepper	Chopped thyme or parsley

Preheat the oven to 400°F. Toss the carrots with the oil, then season with salt and pepper. Put them in a roomy baking dish or roasting pan with the garlic and thyme sprigs. Add 2 tablespoons water, cover tightly with aluminum foil, and bake until tender, 25 to 45 minutes. Check at least twice while they're cooking to make sure there's a little moisture in the pan—and give the pan a shake while you're at it. Toward the end, remove the foil and continue roasting until the liquid is reduced and the carrots are browned. Serve garnished with chopped thyme.

Cauliflower

A MASS *of snowy curds wreathed in blue-green leaves, when truly fresh, cauliflower is surprisingly fine and delicate. We think of it mainly as a winter vegetable, but cauliflower is available year-round, and tender small heads from the summer garden are exquisite. Cauliflower is handled and cooked much like its cousin, broccoli.*

TYPES OF CAULIFLOWER: In addition to the familiar white cauliflower, there are lime-green and golden exotics, the crazy green spiraled variety called Romanesco, and broccoflower, which looks like a green cauliflower.

WHAT TO LOOK FOR: Firm, dense heads with tight curds and no bruises, although brown spots can be cut off. Size is not of great importance if the clusters are tight. Sometimes the surface looks fuzzy or bristly; this isn't a problem.

HOW TO STORE: Wrapped in a perforated plastic bag and refrigerated, cauliflower will keep for several days, but it loses its sweetness as it sits. Precut florets should be used within a day or two at most.

HOW TO USE: Tender, fresh cauliflower can be served raw or blanched with seasoned salts and dips. Cauliflower also finds a place in curries and stews, salads and pastas. Don't neglect the leaves and stems, which are quite good cooked alongside the florets.

SPECIAL HANDLING: Handle cauliflower gently to avoid bruising it. If serving it raw, soak the cleaned, trimmed florets in water mixed with a little lemon juice or vinegar to keep them white and tenderize them.

QUANTITY: A medium cauliflower, weighing 1½ pounds, provides about 6 cups florets, enough to serve four to six.

GOOD PARTNERS FOR
CAULIFLOWER
*Butter, brown butter,
  olive oil, mustard oil
Garlic, red pepper flakes,
  paprika, curry, parsley,
  tarragon
Cheddar, Parmesan,
  Gruyére, blue cheese
Strong greens, sun-dried
  tomatoes, saffron, green
  olives*

Steamed Cauliflower

| 1 cauliflower, 1½ to 2 pounds | Salt and freshly milled pepper | SERVES 4 TO 6 |
| 4 tablespoons butter or olive oil to taste | Chopped tarragon or parsley | |

With a sharp paring knife, cut through the stems and pull the florets apart. Trim the ends and peel and dice the stems. Chop any leaves into small pieces. Steam everything over boiling water until the florets are tender but still a little firm when pierced with a knife, 5 to 8 minutes. (A whole head takes 15 to 20 minutes.)

Meanwhile, melt the butter in a wide skillet over medium heat. Add the cauliflower and roll it around in the butter. Cook until the butter begins to smell nutty. Season with salt, pepper, and tarragon to taste.

Cauliflower with Bread Crumbs Brown ¹/₂ cup fresh bread crumbs in 3 table-spoons butter or olive oil in a small skillet over medium heat. Toss steamed cauliflower in the bread crumbs and season with salt and plenty of pepper.

Cauliflower with Mustard Butter and Greens Toss steamed cauliflower with 2 to 4 tablespoons Mustard Butter, page 52. Serve it on a bed of fresh arugula, or cooked chard or mustard greens. A simple but handsome presentation.

Cauliflower with Curry Butter and Toasted Cashews In a medium skillet, heat 2 to 4 tablespoons butter or vegetable oil with 1¹/₂ teaspoons curry powder, the juice of 1 lime, 2 tablespoons snipped chives, and a few tablespoons chopped cilantro. Add steamed cauliflower and toss. Garnish with toasted cashews and serve with brown basmati rice for a quick and easy dinner.

Celery

CELERY *used to be served at almost every meal, presented in a relish tray or celery vase. It is still enjoyed mainly raw, as a crudité and in salads, where its crispness is appreciated. But it's also ubiquitous in soups, stocks, and ragouts and appears frequently in stuffings and stir-fries. The pale leaves make a refreshing seasoning effectively replacing or mixing with chopped parsley, and the clean taste of celery is a surprise to those who have never eaten it cooked. It's so readily available and easy to work with, I urge you to try it. Cooking softens its tendency to be a little bossy, and peeling the outer ribs makes celery more pleasant to eat, whether cooked or raw. A pound of trimmed, peeled celery ribs yields 4 to 5 cups chopped, serving four to six.*

Braised Celery

SERVES 4

1 head celery or 2 packages celery hearts

Several slices leek or onion

1 carrot, thinly sliced

Aromatics, page 29, including ¹/₂ teaspoon peppercorns, and a pinch celery seeds

Salt

3 tablespoons butter

Chopped parsley and celery leaves

Remove the leafy ends of the celery and peel the large outer ribs. Cut all the ribs into 3- to 4-inch lengths. Put the leek, carrot, aromatics, ¹/₄ teaspoon salt, 1 tablespoon of the butter, and 3 cups water in a wide skillet. Bring to a boil, add the celery, cover, and lower the heat to simmer until tender when pierced with a knife, about 30 minutes. Arrange the celery on a platter and strain the liquid into a saucepan. Boil until ¹/₂ cup remains, then whisk in the remaining butter to make a little sauce. Pour it over the celery and garnish with chopped parsley and celery leaves.

Gratinéed Celery Put the braised celery and its sauce in a gratin dish and dust with freshly grated Parmesan, dry Jack, or Gruyère. Broil until the cheese melts, then serve.

Celery Root (Celeriac)

CELERY root, also known as celeriac, is a gnarly, frumpy-looking root, but it has lots of character and a bracingly clean flavor—like celery, only deeper and softer. It's not available everywhere yet, but it is becoming better known. Celery root is a marvelous vegetable, especially enjoyable during the fall and winter months.

WHAT TO LOOK FOR: Firm, bulbous roots with good heft for the size. If they're light but large, the centers will be spongy. If they have their greens, which resemble celery ribs, so much the better—they'll be fresher.

HOW TO STORE: Stored in the refrigerator in a plastic bag, celery root will keep for several weeks.

HOW TO USE: Celery root is best known as the salad *celeri rémoulade*, but it's wonderful in soups and purees and is especially good in gratins. Although expensive, it pairs well with other root vegetables, like potatoes, allowing you to extend it.

SPECIAL HANDLING: Scrub well, then peel a celery root just as you would an orange, page 33. Put cut pieces in water acidulated with lemon juice or vinegar. The parings make an excellent addition to vegetable stocks.

QUANTITY: Commercially available celery roots tend to weigh about 1 pound. Plan to lose a quarter or more of the weight in trimmings. A trimmed 1-pound root will yield only about 2 cups chopped, enough for two to four modest servings—certainly enough to add ample flavor to a gratin, soup, or puree.

Celery Root with Mustard and Chives Peel and dice 1 pound celery root into ¹/₂-inch cubes and boil in salted water to cover until tender, about 5 minutes. Drain, then combine in a skillet with ¹/₄ cup crème fraîche or cream and 1 teaspoon Dijon mustard. Season with salt and freshly milled white pepper. Heat until the cream is hot and slightly thickened, then sprinkle snipped chives on top. Serves 4.

GOOD PARTNERS FOR
CELERY ROOT
*Butter, cream, walnut oil,
   sunflower seed oil*
*Gruyère, walnuts,
   hazelnuts*
Parsley, thyme, mustard
*Potatoes, apples,
   watercress, mushrooms,
   wild rice, truffles*

SAUCES AND SEASONINGS
FOR CELERY ROOT
*Mustard Vinaigrette,
   page 186*
Brown Butter, page 30
*Tarragon Mayonnaise
   with Capers, page 59*
*Creamy Herb and Shallot
   Dressing, page 186*

Celery Root and Potato Puree

CELERY root and potatoes make a most delicious vegetable puree. In addition to serving it as a side dish, you can use it to blanket a shepherd's pie.

SERVES 4 TO 6

2 pounds Yellow Finn or other boiling
    potatoes, peeled

1 celery root, about 1 pound, peeled

Salt and freshly milled pepper

About ½ cup milk, cream, or cooking
    water, warmed

4 to 8 tablespoons butter

Cut the vegetables separately into large pieces. Put each in a saucepan, add cold water to cover and ½ teaspoon salt, and bring to a boil. Simmer until tender, about 15 minutes for the potatoes, 10 minutes for the celery root. Drain, reserving the broth for thinning or to use in making soup. Pass them together through a food mill or mash by hand, adding warm liquid to thin the puree as you go. Season with salt and pepper and stir in butter.

Variations: Flavor the puree with Whole Roasted Garlic, page 377, or include other vegetables in the mix—turnips, parsnips, and fennel are all delicious. Instead of butter, finish the puree with walnut oil or roasted hazelnut oil. Stir in finely chopped parsley or watercress just before serving.

Braised Celery Root with Garlic Croutons

THIS can serve as a light dinner entrée or, without the croutons, as a side dish. Use the trimmings to make a flavorful quick stock.

SERVES 4

2 pounds celery root

Juice of 2 lemons

1 quart Quick Stock, page 196

2 tablespoons butter or olive oil

1 small onion, finely diced

1 carrot, finely diced

1 celery rib, finely diced

Aromatics: 1 bay leaf, 6 parsley sprigs,
    4 thyme sprigs

½ cup dry white wine

Salt and freshly milled pepper

Chopped parsley and thyme

4 large, thin Garlic-Rubbed Croutons,
    page 34

Peel the celery root, quarter it, and slice crosswise ⅜ inch thick. Drop the slices into a bowl of lemon juice and water to cover and set aside. Make the stock, strain it, and return it to the stove to simmer. Preheat the oven to 375°F.

Heat the butter in a medium skillet. Add the diced vegetables and aromatics and cook over medium-low heat, stirring frequently, until softened, about 5 minutes. Add the wine and cook several minutes more, until it has reduced. Season with salt and pepper. Spread the mixture in a gratin dish and cover with the drained celery root. Add simmering stock just to cover.

Press a piece of parchment directly on the vegetables. Bake until the celery root is tender, 50 to 60 minutes. If lots of liquid is left, pour it off, boil until it's reduced to a sauce-like consistency, then return it to the dish. Serve in soup plates topped with chopped parsley mixed with a little thyme and the garlic croutons.

Chard

HERE'S a vigorous green, leafy vegetable that's easy to cook and grow and has a long season. Yet it often arrives at the market looking as if it's gone through a war zone, the leaves shredded and torn. Better to check your farmers' market for vigorous, deep green leaves in their prime. The leaves and their fleshy stalks are often treated as two different vegetables, but when the stalks are barely an inch wide, the two can be cooked as one vegetable.

TYPES OF CHARD: White ribbed (called green) and red chard are the two types most available. A third kind, perpetual spinach chard or beet, is grown more abroad than here. It has small leaves with virtually no stems and so is perfect for those who prefer only the leaves.

WHAT TO LOOK FOR: Vigorous, upright, crinkled dark green leaves on smooth, succulent stalks. The leaves can be extremely large or closer to the size of spinach. Since chard grows rapidly, large leaves don't necessarily imply toughness or lack of flavor, though in general the smaller ones are sweeter and the larger ones take a little longer to cook.

HOW TO STORE: Keep chard refrigerated in a plastic bag until ready to use, preferably within a few days.

HOW TO USE: The stems are typically braised, while the leaves are used as you would spinach—in soups, as braised greens, with eggs, rice, lentils, and in savory tarts. Large leaves can be stuffed. Though treated as two vegetables, there's no reason not to pair the stems and leaves on a plate. To prepare the stems, trim the tops and bottoms, then, with a paring knife, peel off the film of skin and tough fibers that covers the surface. Chard trimmings, particularly the stems, make an excellent contribution to vegetable stocks.

SPECIAL HANDLING: The red stems and veins in the ruby varieties stain, just as beets do, so take that into account when mixing them with other foods and be sure you want their rosy hints. The silver stems discolor, so cook them in acidulated water or a blanc to preserve their whiteness.

QUANTITY: Most bunches of chard weigh about a pound, but they aren't standard. Some bunches have enormous stalks, others are severely trimmed. One pound of leaves yields 12 cups, which cook down to about 3 cups, enough for three to four servings. One pound of stems, trimmed, yields about 4 cups, enough for three to four servings.

Chard Greens with Olive Oil Slice the leaves off the stems, wash them well, then coarsely chop. Drop them into a pot of boiling salted water and cook until tender, 5 minutes or longer if older. Drain, press out the excess moisture with the back of a spoon, then toss with extra virgin olive oil or butter, salt, and pepper. Or turn the cooked, drained greens into a skillet in which you've heated olive oil with a crushed garlic clove and a pinch or two of red pepper flakes. Toss to coat the leaves, season with salt and pepper, and serve with lemon wedges.

GOOD PARTNERS FOR
CHARD
Olive oil, butter
Saffron, garlic, red pepper
  flakes, cilantro, basil
Lemon, red wine vinegar
Tomatoes, potatoes,
  chickpeas, pasta, eggs

Braised Chard with Cilantro

DON'T be put off by the long cooking time—in the end the flavor goes far beyond what's possible with a cursory blanching. A few spoonfuls suffice for a serving, or you can use this effectively as a seasoning for rice or lentils.

SERVES 4

2 large bunches chard, about 2 pounds, leaves sliced into 1-inch-wide ribbons

1 1/2 cups of the chard stems, trimmed and diced

1 onion, finely diced

1/2 cup chopped cilantro

1/3 cup olive oil

1 teaspoon paprika

1 garlic clove pounded with 1 teaspoon salt

Salt and freshly milled pepper

Place all the ingredients in a wide, heavy pot with a few pinches salt. Add 1/4 cup water, cover tightly, and cook over low heat for 45 minutes. Check once or twice to make sure there's enough moisture. If anything is sticking, add a few tablespoons water. When done, taste for salt and season with pepper. The chard should be silky and very fragrant.

Chard Stems with Saffron and Tomatoes

A FINE accompaniment for the Saffron Noodle Cake, or Garlic-Rubbed Croutons.

SERVES 3 OR 4

1 pound chard stems, trimmed and cooked

1 cup cooking water reserved

1 1/2 tablespoons olive oil

1/2 small onion, finely diced

2 teaspoons thinly sliced basil leaves, plus extra for garnish

Pinch saffron threads

Salt and freshly milled pepper

2 tomatoes, seeded and finely diced

2 tablespoons freshly grated Parmesan or Gruyère, optional

Cook the chard stems first—this can be done well ahead of the final baking.

Heat the oil in a 10-inch skillet with the onion, basil, and saffron threads. Cook over medium heat, stirring occasionally, until the onions soften and the saffron begins to yield its color, about 5 minutes. Add the chard stems, season with salt and pepper, then add the reserved cooking water. Simmer, covered, until the stems are fully tender, about 7 minutes. Remove the lid and allow the remaining liquid to reduce to a syrupy consistency. Add the tomatoes and cook for another minute or so to warm them through. Serve with the extra basil strewn over the stems and the grated cheese.

Gratinéed Chard Stems: Transfer the cooked chard stems from either of the two preceding recipes to a small gratin dish. Drizzle extra virgin olive oil over the top, add a little freshly grated Parmesan, and bake at 400°F until the cheese is melted and lightly browned, about 20 minutes.

Chard Stems with Olive Oil

1 pound chard stems, trimmed and
    peeled
2 tablespoons flour
Juice of 1 lemon

Salt and freshly milled pepper
Extra virgin olive oil
Chopped parsley

THE cooking time—from
7 to 20 minutes—really
depends on the tender-
ness of the stems, so test
with the point of a knife
as they cook.

SERVES 3 TO 4

Cut the stems into 3-inch lengths. Whisk the flour into 2 quarts water in a saucepan, bring to a boil, and add the lemon juice and 2 teaspoons salt. Add the stems and boil until tender, about 10 minutes or longer, depending on their tenderness. Drain, then toss with olive oil and parsley. Taste for salt and season with pepper.

Chard Rolls Filled with Winter Vegetables

2 tablespoons olive oil
8 large chard leaves, stems removed and
    finely diced
1 onion, finely diced
3 carrots, finely diced
8 ounces potatoes, finely diced
6 to 8 cups additional finely diced
    vegetables, such as parsnips, parsley
    root, and celery root

1 garlic clove, minced
2 teaspoons chopped tarragon or
    ½ teaspoon dried
Salt and freshly milled pepper
2 tablespoons fresh lemon juice
1 cup water or Basic Vegetable Stock,
    page 196
1 to 2 tablespoons butter

SELECT nice, large leaves
for stuffing. The chard
stems along with root
vegetables fill these
plump bundles.

SERVES 4

Heat the oil in a large skillet. Add the chard stems, onion, other root vegetables, garlic, and tarragon. Season with ½ teaspoon salt and pepper to taste. Cover and cook over medium heat until tender, 20 to 25 minutes. Add the lemon juice.

Plunge the chard leaves into boiling water for 4 minutes, then set on a towel to drain. Cut away the thick part at the base of each leaf. Place the leaves, smooth side down, on the counter. Place 2 heaping tablespoons of filling just above the notch of each leaf, then fold the sides over the filling and roll up the leaves. Keep the remaining filling in the skillet and set the rolls right on top of it. Add the water to the pan, dot the leaves with the butter, and cover. Simmer for 10 minutes. Serve the rolls with the extra vegetables and their juices.

Chicories

(ENDIVE, RADICCHIO, AND ESCAROLE)

WHILE quite different in shape, size, and color, endive, radicchio, and escarole are all chicories—and as such they share a degree of bitterness that turns to sweetness when cooked.

GOOD PARTNERS FOR
CHICORIES
Olive oil, cream, butter
Red pepper flakes, vinegar
Gruyère, Parmesan,
  Asiago

TYPES OF CHICORY: There are a great number of very interesting greens in this family, such as frisée or curly endive, dandelion, and some other salad-type greens. All taste best in the cooler months. Here are some commonly found types:

Belgian endive or witloof is the small cone-shaped head of pale leaves. Some varieties have a pink blush.

Radicchio has deep scarlet leaves, which are sometimes variegated. The variety we see most is compact, like a cabbage, but there are several loose-leafed varieties, seen less frequently in this country.

Escarole roughly resembles loose-leaf lettuce, but the leaves are thick. If properly blanched in the field, the inner hearts will be creamy white.

HOW TO STORE: Keep in a plastic bag in the refrigerator as you would lettuce. It will keep for up to a week, though it's better the earlier it's used.

HOW TO USE: In addition to their uses in salad, chicories can be grilled, seared, and braised.

SPECIAL HANDLING: Chicories bruise where they've been cut, leaving a discolored area, something to consider when they're to be used in salads. Wait until close to serving time to cut. Check the base of the leaves carefully for sand and dirt.

QUANTITY: Allow one Belgian endive for one or two servings; one 6- to 8-ounce head of radicchio for four servings; one head of escarole for two to four servings.

Braised Belgian Endive Melt 2 tablespoons butter in a 10- or 12-inch noncorrosive skillet. Halve six endives and add them, cut sides down. Cook over medium-high heat until well browned. Turn and brown them on their second sides, then turn them back over. Add water to come about ¾ inch up the side of the pan. Simmer, covered, until the endives are tender when pierced with a knife, about 25 minutes. Remove the lid, raise the heat, and evaporate all but a little of the remaining liquid so that a glaze forms on the bottom. Season with salt and a little white pepper. Serves 6 to 12.

Seared Radicchio

2 small firm heads radicchio,
   3 to 4 ounces each
Olive oil as needed
Salt and freshly milled pepper

1 tablespoon chopped parsley
Thin shavings of Parmesan, Asiago, or
   dry Jack

Cut the radicchio into wedges about 2 inches thick at the widest point. Brush them generously with oil, season with salt and pepper, and set aside to marinate for an hour or more. Lightly film a cast-iron skillet with olive oil and set over medium-high heat. When it's very hot, add the radicchio and sear until the leaves begin to brown on the bottom, after a few minutes. Turn and cook the second side, about 5 minutes in all. Transfer to a plate and gently press the wedges to open the leaves. Season with salt and pepper, sprinkle with parsley, and cover with the shavings of cheese.

A DELICIOUS accompaniment for soft polenta, cooked white beans, or an unusual ingredient for a risotto or hearty pasta. Escarole and Belgian endive can also be seared. Use two heads of escarole or two to four endives.

SERVES 4 TO 6

Braised Escarole with Onion

2 heads escarole, about 2 pounds in all
3 tablespoons extra virgin olive oil
1 onion, finely chopped

1 plump garlic clove, minced
Salt and freshly milled pepper
Chopped parsley

Separate the escarole leaves and wash well, taking special care to go over the base of the inner leaves with your fingers where dirt often clings. Drain and coarsely chop. Heat the oil in a wide skillet. Add the onion and cook over medium heat until limp. Add the garlic and cook until it begins to color, but don't let it brown. Add the escarole with any water clinging to the leaves, salt lightly, and cook, covered, until the greens are wilted and tender, 12 to 15 minutes. Season with pepper and toss with the parsley.

IF you've used the tender inner leaves for salads, cook the outer ones like this. Escarole turns a little dingy looking, but its flavor is big and the parsley perks it up.

SERVES 4 TO 6

Grilled Radicchio Though usually treated as a salad green, radicchio is particularly tasty grilled. (Escarole and Belgian endive can also be grilled.) Prepare radicchio for searing as in preceding recipe, and grill until the color has dulled and the radicchio has softened and turned brownish, about 5 minutes on each side. Garnish with chopped parsley, thin shavings of Parmesan, and extra virgin olive oil or serve with Garlic Mayonnaise, page 59. Chopped grilled radicchio also makes an excellent ingredient to add to a risotto with winter squash, to white beans, or as a garnish for polenta or a hearty buckwheat pasta.

Corn

WITH the new supersweet varieties of corn, we no longer need to have a corn patch out back or to add milk and sugar to boiling water to get a tender, sweet ear. Today's corn is bred so that the sugars are slow to turn starchy, which means that even corn that's several days old should be tender. Nonetheless, corn that's superfresh will always be best. When you buy corn from a farmer, don't discard it if there's a worm at the tip or signs of one; just shake it off and trim the ear. Like all sweet vegetables, corn goes with all kinds of seasonings, from sweet herbs to spices to chiles.

GOOD PARTNERS FOR CORN
Butter, cream
*Cheddar, Colby,
   Monterey Jack, feta*
*Dill, basil, parsley, chile,
   Sichuan pepper,
   cumin, sage*
*Squash, beans, peppers,
   tomatoes, lime*

TYPES OF CORN: There are several classes of corn that have very different uses, but for eating fresh we're interested mostly in the new sugar-enhanced and supersweet hybrids. (Some people, I among them, still prefer the older varieties with their chewy texture and "cornier" taste, such as Golden Bantam, to today's sugary ears.) Some older hybrids, like Silver Queen, are delightfully sweet but not cloying.

WHAT TO LOOK FOR: If you can, buy corn in its husks, which protect the kernels from the dry air and also tell you how fresh the corn is. Moist green husks are clearly fresher than dry old brown ones. Rather than pull down a corner of the husks, which is irritating to the farmer because it dries out the corn, run your hands over the ear to be sure the rows are plump and well-filled. Corn smut or fungus (*cuitlacoche* in Spanish) may be alarming to come across, but it's a delicacy with a wonderful wild-mushroom flavor. (To cook, remove it from the ear, slice or chop, then sauté in oil or butter for about 15 minutes.)

HOW TO STORE: If not being cooked right away, corn should be refrigerated in its husks, in a plastic bag. If it's still warm from the sun, cool it under water before storing.

HOW TO USE: Versatile corn is added to soups and stews, pancakes, breads, and puddings. It's delicious sautéed or creamed as well as grilled. Roasted corn kernels add a smoky flavor and chewy texture to corn salads, salsas, and soups.

SPECIAL HANDLING: None, except to use as soon as possible.

QUANTITY: An average ear of corn typically yields about 1/2 to 3/4 cup kernels. If the corn is really good and you're cooking it on the cob, plan to serve two or three ears per person.

SAUCES AND SEASONINGS FOR CORN
*Pesto, page 57, or Salsa
   Verde, page 55*
Cilantro Salsa, page 56
Harissa, page 75
*Sichuan Pepper Salt,
   page 76, or Indian Salt
   with Mixed Spices,
   page 77*
Ground chipotle chile
*Chile Butter, page 52, or
   Herb or Blossom Butter,
   page 51*
Grated Cheddar
*Chopped herbs, such as
   basil, dill, marjoram,
   parsley, cilantro, and
   fresh sage*

Corn on the Cob

Whole ears corn	**Butter**
Salt and freshly milled pepper	

Bring a large pot of water to a boil. While it's heating, pull the husks off the corn, rub off the silk, and cut off any blemished tips. When the water comes to a boil, drop in the ears and cook for 2 minutes. (Don't salt the water—it only toughens the corn.) Pull out the ears with tongs, set them on a towel to drain briefly, then pile on a platter. Pass salt, a pepper mill, sweet butter, and plenty of napkins. Once the season has progressed past the stage where you want your corn pure, start putting out the Chile Butter, page 52, Spicy Moroccan Butter, page 52, salsas, limes, and other condiments.

CORN OFF THE COB

To get corn off the cob, hold an ear with one end resting on the counter or in a large bowl to catch the juices. Using a sharp knife and a sawing motion, slowly slice right down the ear, removing the top one-half to two-thirds of the kernels but leaving their base attached. (It's the fibrous base that gets caught in your teeth.) Then reverse your knife and, using the dull side, press it down the length of the ear to push out the rest of the corn and its milk. These are called the *scrapings*.

If you want corn with a finer texture, grate it on the large holes of a flat grater set over a bowl. Or draw the tip of a sharp knife through the center of each row of kernels, then slice them off as described.

1 ear of corn, sliced, yields $\frac{1}{2}$ to $\frac{3}{4}$ cup kernels

1 ear of corn, grated, yields about $\frac{1}{3}$ to $\frac{1}{2}$ cup kernels

Oven-Roasted Corn Roast whole ears of corn with their husks and silks attached at 450°F for 15 to 20 minutes. If there are no leaves, wrap the corn in foil. When done, remove the husks. The silk will come right off the kernels.

Grilled Corn Keep the stem attached to the ears, pull back the husks, and rub off the silk. Soak for 20 minutes in cold water, then pull the husks back over the kernels, twisting them so they'll stay closed. Grill for 15 to 20 minutes, depending on the heat of the fire, turning the corn every few minutes. As the corn steams, the kernels will turn bright and glossy. Pull back the husks during the last few minutes so that the corn caramelizes just enough to intensify its flavor. Serve with butter, salt and pepper, Sichuan Pepper Salt, Indian Salt with Mixed Spices, or a squeeze of fresh lime juice.

Corn Roasted-in-the-Coals Husk the corn, remove the silk, and wrap the ears in heavy-duty aluminum foil. Lay them right on top of the hot coals and cook for 10 minutes, turning a few times.

Fresh Corn Sauté Allow $1\frac{1}{2}$ to 2 ears per person. Slice off the kernels, then press out the scrapings. Melt a little butter or corn oil in a skillet, add a diced shallot or a few sliced scallions, the corn, its scrapings, and 1 tablespoon water. Sauté until the corn tastes cooked, about 4 minutes. Season with salt and pepper. (For creamed corn, add $\frac{1}{2}$ cup cream at the end and simmer until it has thickened a bit.)

USES FOR LEFTOVER CORN

Sweet nuggets of boiled, roasted, and grilled corn have great potential in the kitchen. Slice the kernels off the cobs and add them to soups and chowders, vegetable ragouts, salads and salsas, muffins and pancakes. You also can slip a few into a spoon bread or polenta.

Succotash

2 cups frozen baby lima beans or fresh shelling beans

6 ears sweet corn, kernels and scrapings removed separately

4 tablespoons butter

Salt and freshly milled pepper

Chopped parsley

Paprika

Put the beans in a saucepan, cover them with water, and simmer until tender, several minutes for frozen beans, about 25 minutes for fresh. Drain, reserving the cooking water. Add the corn kernels to the pan with the butter, $\frac{1}{2}$ teaspoon salt, and enough of the cooking water to barely cover. Cook gently for 3 minutes, then stir in the scrapings. Turn the heat to low and cook, without stirring, until most of the liquid is cooked off, 5 to 10 minutes. Season with pepper, pour into a serving dish, and add the parsley and a dash of paprika. Serve right away.

Corn with Cumin, Chile, and Tomato

SERVES 4 TO 6

6 large ears corn, kernels and scrapings removed separately

1 garlic clove

1 teaspoon ground toasted cumin seeds

Salt and freshly milled pepper

2 tablespoons corn oil or butter

1 onion, finely diced

1 long green Anaheim or New Mexican chile, roasted, and diced

1 large ripe tomato, seeded and diced

1 tablespoon chopped parsley, cilantro, or dill

In a blender, puree 1 cup of the corn kernels with 1 cup water for 3 minutes. Strain, pushing out as much liquid as you can. Meanwhile, pound the garlic, cumin, $\frac{1}{2}$ teaspoon salt, and a little pepper in a mortar until smooth.

Heat the oil in a wide skillet with the onion, pounded garlic, and chile. Sauté over medium-high heat for 4 minutes. Stir in the remaining corn kernels, scrapings, and corn milk. Lower the heat, cover the pan, and simmer for 5 minutes. Add the tomato at the end and cook until warmed through. Taste for salt, stir in the parsley, and serve.

Baked Corn with Cumin and Feta Cheese Make the preceding dish, then transfer it to a lightly buttered gratin dish. Cover with $\frac{1}{2}$ cup crumbled feta—it tempers the sweetness of the corn. Bake at 375°F until bubbling and hot, about 25 minutes. Brown under the broiler, then serve.

Eggplant

EGGPLANT *is the workhorse of the summer kitchen in Mediterranean cuisines. Yet it's still a difficult vegetable for many people, partly because we seldom eat it really fresh, when it's sweet and mild. Eggplant is worth demystifying, for it's highly versatile and has a dense texture that's particularly welcome in the vegetarian kitchen.*

The season for eggplant is summer, and it truly is best then. Fresh eggplants have white or pale green flesh, little seed development, and no trace of the bitterness that often puts people off. Eggplants in season are far superior in flavor to storage eggplants, and you'll find them much easier to cook with since they don't require salting or even peeling.

TYPES OF EGGPLANT: Americans are most familiar with the large purple-black eggplant and some slender Asian varieties. In between, however, are a host of others, from tiny white egg-shaped fruits to plump, short purple ones, to violet, striped, magenta, pure white, and red-orange eggplants. Such variety can be found at farmers' markets but not yet in our supermarkets.

In terms of flavor, the lighter the hue, the milder the eggplant, white eggplants being the mildest, followed by the magenta or purple and white striped varieties, then the dark purple globe eggplants. Red-orange eggplants are quite bitter and intended for pickling. The long Asian eggplants tend to be milder than round varieties and don't require salting.

WHAT TO LOOK FOR: Regardless of variety or color, eggplant should be smooth, firm, and taut. Glossy skin and a bright green stem indicate freshness. There should be good heft in the hand. If it's too light, the flesh may be spongy and seedy, tending toward bitterness.

HOW TO STORE: A cool room (about 50°F) is best, but if you haven't such a place, you can refrigerate eggplant. It's tempting to display eggplants in a voluptuous still life on the table, but of course they deteriorate more rapidly than if cooled. I usually wrap mine in a towel to absorb moisture, then put them in a plastic bag. They will keep for a week, but it's better to use them within a day or two because they quickly lose their mild flavor and begin to turn bitter.

HOW TO USE: The versatile eggplant can be broiled, grilled, fried, roasted, and sautéed. Use it for dips, pasta, soups, stews, casseroles, gratins, and purees. Large pieces can be rolled or layered; whole eggplants can be stuffed.

GOOD PARTNERS FOR
EGGPLANT

*Olive oil, dark sesame,
    and roasted peanut oils,
    cream*
*Parmesan, ricotta, goat
    cheese, Gruyère, feta,
    yogurt, tahini*
*Garlic, basil, peanuts,
    pine nuts, ginger, soy,
    cilantro, saffron*
*Lemon, red wine vinegar,
    balsamic vinegar*
*Tomatoes, peppers,
    onions, summer squash,
    chickpeas, potatoes*

SPECIAL HANDLING: One potential drawback with eggplant is its capacity to absorb oil. This can be overcome, however, by salting. The flesh will shrivel but plump up when cooked. Salting also removes bitterness from mature storage eggplants.

QUANTITY: Yields vary depending on the shape of the eggplant, how you plan to use it— pureed, rolled, stuffed—and whether you peel it. But in general, count on a pound of eggplant yielding about 4 cups chopped, serving two to four.

SALTING EGGPLANT

Eggplant that's freshly picked, harvested before it's full of seeds, and eaten within a few days is naturally sweet and doesn't need salting; nor do the slender Asian varieties. Salting can, however, leach out bitterness from eggplants that have been stored too long or those that are overmature, and moisture for when it is to be fried, since a long salting keeps it from absorbing as much oil. I know some cooks who *always* salt their eggplants and others who *never* do, reflecting perhaps their own sensitivity—or lack thereof—to eggplant.

Sprinkle eggplant slices or cubes lightly with whatever salt you normally use. Let it stand in a colander for at least 30 minutes to reduce bitterness, 1 hour or more to lessen oil absorption. Blot the juices that bead on the surface or quickly rinse the eggplant and blot it dry. When seasoning the eggplant during cooking, taste it before adding more salt to a dish.

Whole Roasted Eggplant

SAUCES AND SEASONINGS FOR EGGPLANT
Yogurt Sauce with Cayenne and Dill, page 66
Cilantro Salsa, page 56
Chermoula, page 56
Sauces Based on Nuts and Seeds, pages 67 to 69
Yogurt Tahini Sauce, page 66
Hoisin Sauce with Chili Paste and Tangerine Zest, page 73

Roasted eggplant has a creamy pale interior, and when charred over the coals it can have a decidedly smoky flavor. Baked to the point of utter collapse, the flesh falls into a near puree that can be served as a vegetable, turned into a savory custard or soufflé, or used as the basis of any of the eggplant spreads starting on page 96. It can also be pulled into shreds, then seasoned, resulting in a coarser texture. Be sure you prick it first in a few places to allow the steam to escape so that the eggplant doesn't explode.

Roasted Eggplant with Garlic Make eight or more small incisions in a globe eggplant and wedge a sliver of garlic into each. Set on a sheet pan and roast at 400°F until tender and collapsed, 20 to 40 minutes, depending on the size. Remove from the oven, let rest several minutes, then slice lengthwise in half. (Eggplant can also be cooked whole on a grill—see page 367.) If the shell is fairly intact, you can cut it in half and serve it seasoned with salt, pepper, and a spoonful of olive oil, a yogurt sauce, pages 65 to 66, or Salsa Verde, page 55. If the shells have collapsed, scoop out the flesh, then season it. One pound of eggplant yields about 1¾ cups roasted eggplant.

Shredded Eggplant Roast the eggplant as described or on a grill, page 367, until tender and soft when you give it a squeeze. Cool in a colander, then pull off the skins and pull the flesh into shreds. Bits of skin are not a problem. Warm or cool, this makes quite a tasty vegetable to use in a pasta salad or as a topping for a bruschetta.

Whole Eggplant Cooked on the Grill Prick an eggplant in several places with a fork. Cook it over the coals or on a covered gas grill until it's tender to the point of collapsing, 20 to 40 minutes, depending on the size and the heat. For a smoky flavor, grill the eggplant until the skin is blackened. Remove it to a bowl and let stand until cool enough to handle. Split lengthwise and scoop out the flesh. Mash it until smooth or pull it into shreds. Season with extra virgin olive oil, minced garlic, and chopped parsley; dark sesame or roasted peanut oil; Salsa Verde, page 55, Tarator Sauce, page 67, yogurt, and so forth. (To cook eggplant in the coals, wrap it in foil, set it on top of the coals, and cook until soft.)

Sautéed Eggplant with Parsley and Pine Nuts

1 ^{1}/$_2$ pounds eggplant, peeled
Salt and freshly milled pepper
^{1}/$_2$ cup olive oil

^{1}/$_4$ cup chopped parsley
1 large garlic clove
2 tablespoons toasted pine nuts

SERVE *this eggplant as a vegetable or use it as a filling for stuffed vegetables. Leftovers make a delicious addition to pilaf or a pasta dish.*

SERVES 4

Cut the eggplant into ^{1}/$_2$-inch rounds, then into ^{1}/$_2$-inch cubes. Sprinkle with salt and set aside for 30 minutes, then blot dry. Heat the oil in a large skillet until nearly smoking. Add the eggplant and stir immediately to coat. Lower the heat to medium and cook, stirring occasionally, until the eggplant is golden and soft, about 15 minutes. Taste, then season with salt and pepper. Chop the parsley and garlic together and toss with the eggplant along with the pine nuts.

Eggplant Rounds

Large rounds or slabs of golden eggplant, simply seasoned, can be served as a side dish, but they also serve as the foundation for other dishes, such as roll-ups and gratins. Use globe eggplant or small, plump Italian varieties. Keep all the skin on or remove it in strips to make a decorative design. Slice the eggplant into rounds or lengthwise into slabs ^{1}/$_2$ to ^{3}/$_4$ inch thick, sprinkle with salt, let stand for 30 minutes, then blot dry. Brush both sides generously with olive oil and season with salt and pepper.

TO BROIL: Broil the eggplant about 4 inches from the heat until browned, about 10 minutes. Turn and broil the second side.

TO BAKE: Bake the eggplant slices on a sheet pan at 425°F until browned on the bottom, 15 to 25 minutes. Turn and bake the second side until browned.

TO GRILL: Cut small, slender eggplants lengthwise in half. Cut larger eggplants into rounds, diagonals, or steaks about ^{3}/$_8$ inch thick. Brush generously with olive oil and lay them on the grill. Leave them for 4 minutes, then turn them 45 degrees and cook another 4 minutes. Turn them over and repeat. Remove and season lightly with salt and pepper. Serve with any of the sauces suggested for whole eggplant, page 367, or use as a base for the more substantial dishes that follow. These make a great filling for a sandwich.

TO FRY: Don't brush the eggplant with oil after salting since it will be fried. Heat ¹⁄₂ inch light olive or vegetable oil in a heavy pan until nearly smoking. Slide in a few eggplant slices without crowding the pan and cook until both sides are nicely colored, 1 minute or so, then drain on paper towels. You can also fry in just enough oil to generously coat the bottom of the pan, but the concentrated heat of the larger amount of oil cooks the eggplant faster, and in the end it may well absorb less oil.

Eggplant Rounds with Cheese and Red Wine Tomato Sauce

THIS combination is substantial enough to serve as a simple main dish.

SERVES 4 TO 6

2 eggplant rounds per person, grilled, broiled, or fried

³⁄₄ cup grated or sliced mozzarella

¹⁄₂ cup crumbled Gorgonzola, or goat cheese, grated Fontina—or a mixture

Red Wine Tomato Sauce, page 64

Chopped parsley or basil

Place the cooked eggplant rounds on a sheet pan and cover with the cheeses. Bake at 375°F until the cheese melts. Serve with 2 or 3 spoonfuls of the sauce on each serving and garnish with the parsley.

Eggplant Rounds with Gremolata First make the Gremolata, a simple mixture of chopped parsley, garlic, and lemon, page 29. Prepare eggplant rounds using whatever method you prefer. As soon as they're cooked, sprinkle the gremolata over them and serve.

Eggplant Rounds with Chermoula and Pine Nuts All green herb sauces can be used this way, but the Moroccan marinade chermoula is especially exciting with eggplant. Prepare eggplant rounds using whatever method you prefer and arrange them on a platter. Spoon Chermoula, page 56, over the slices and let stand 1 hour or longer for the flavors to blend. Just before serving, toast pine nuts and scatter them over the top.

Broiled or Grilled Eggplant with Tarator Sauce Broil or grill two or three eggplant rounds per person. Generously drizzle with Tarator Sauce, page 67, or Walnut Sauce, page 68. Garnish with chopped parsley, toasted pine nuts or walnuts, and, if available, pomegranate seeds. Serve with a garden salad.

Broiled or Grilled Eggplant with Goat Cheese and Salsa Verde Cover broiled or grilled eggplant rounds with crumbled goat cheese and broil until softened. Drizzle with Salsa Verde, page 55, and garnish with neatly diced ripe tomato. A substantial appetizer or light main course.

Eggplant Rounds with Peanut Sauce Broil or grill eggplant rounds, brushing them first with light sesame or peanut oil instead of olive oil. Serve with one of the peanut sauces, pages 69 to 70, and garnish with chopped cilantro, roasted peanuts, and a wedge of lime.

Eggplant Roll-Ups

These fetching bundles of rolled stuffed eggplant make a good dish for entertaining. Fillings can be made from pasta, rice, or, as in the American interpretation that follows, corn bread. The three parts—eggplant, stuffing, and sauce—can all be made in advance, so the actual assembly is quite straightforward. Once assembled, they can be held up to a day before baking. Allow two or three per person for an entrée, one or two as a first course.

Eggplant Rollatini with Corn Bread Stuffing

2 large globe eggplants, about 3 pounds in all

Salt

Corn Bread Stuffing, recipe follows

Red Wine Tomato Sauce, page 64

About ⅓ cup olive or vegetable oil, as needed

Chopped marjoram, basil, or parsley

A SUBSTANTIAL dish for fall when the weather starts to get nippy. An experienced cook can make this from scratch in about 2 hours, but I always like to have something done ahead, such as the corn bread or the sauce.

MAKES 10 TO 12 ROLLS, SERVING 4 TO 6

Slice the eggplant lengthwise no thicker than ⅓ inch or they'll be difficult to roll later. Sprinkle both sides with salt and let stand an hour. Rinse and blot dry. Meanwhile, prepare the stuffing and the sauce if you haven't already.

Brush the eggplant with oil and grill, bake, fry, or broil on both sides until tender. They should be flexible, but if they're dry looking, don't worry. Just stack them on top of each other as they finish cooking—the heat will soften them.

Mound about 2 tablespoons stuffing at the widest end of each piece, roll into a cylinder, and secure with a toothpick. Place seam side down in a lightly oiled baking dish large enough to hold the eggplant rolls in a single layer. Cover the dish with aluminum foil.

When ready to eat, preheat the oven to 400°F. Bake until the eggplant rolls are heated through, about 25 minutes. Spoon a little sauce on each plate and set the rolls on top. Remove the toothpicks and garnish with the chopped herb.

Corn Bread Stuffing

2 tablespoons vegetable oil

1 onion, finely chopped

1 tablespoon chopped sage or
   1 teaspoon dried

½ teaspoon dried oregano

2 cups crumbled Basic Corn Bread,
   page 646

1 egg

Salt and freshly milled pepper

Heat the oil in a medium skillet. Add the onion and herbs and cook over medium heat until soft and lightly browned, about 12 minutes. Mix with the corn bread and egg and season with salt and pepper to taste. Work the mixture together with your hands so that it's evenly moistened. If it seems dry, add a little water.

Eggplant Rollatini with Fresh Mozzarella and Goat Cheese

DELICIOUS served with rice, quinoa, or couscous and a roasted tomato or pepper sauce.

MAKES 10 TO 12 ROLLS, SERVING 4 TO 6

1 cup grated or chopped mozzarella,
   preferably fresh

1 cup crumbled goat cheese

2 scallions, including a few inches of
   the greens, thinly sliced

2 teaspoons minced thyme or rosemary

Salt and freshly milled pepper

2 large globe eggplants, about 3 pounds
   in all, prepared as described in the
   preceding recipe

Red Pepper Sauce, page 71, or Oven-
   Roasted Tomato Sauce, page 62

Combine the cheeses, scallions, and herbs and season well with salt and pepper. If the mixture seems dry and doesn't cohere, add a little milk. Fill the eggplant slices and bake as described in the preceding recipe. Serve with the sauce of your choice.

Rollatini with Capellini

6 ounces capellini or angel hair pasta

1 cup finely diced provolone or mozzarella

3 tablespoons freshly grated Parmesan

2 tablespoons chopped marjoram or basil, plus extra for garnish

Salt and freshly milled pepper

2 large globe eggplants, about 3 pounds in all, prepared as described on page 369

2½ cups Fresh Tomato Sauce, page 61

I FIRST had these scrumptious rollatini in a Los Angeles restaurant, Tuscany, where chef Tommaso Barletta fills them with fine capellini and serves them with a fresh, light tomato sauce.

MAKES 12 PLUMP ROLLS, SERVING 4 TO 6

Boil the capellini in salted water until slightly underdone, then drain. Toss it with the cheeses and marjoram and season with salt and pepper to taste. Divide the pasta among the eggplant slices, then roll them up.

Preheat the oven to 375°F. Spread 1½ cups tomato sauce in a large baking dish and set the rolled eggplant, seam side down, inside. Cover with aluminum foil and bake until the sauce is bubbling and the eggplant is heated through, 25 to 30 minutes. Heat the remaining sauce and ladle some onto each plate. Place the eggplant rolls on the sauce, dust with the extra marjoram, and serve.

Baked Eggplant with Feta Cheese and Tomatoes

4 oblong Asian or Italian eggplants, about 6 ounces each

About ⅓ cup olive oil

Salt and freshly milled pepper

4 ripe tomatoes, peeled, seeded, and chopped

2 to 3 ounces feta cheese

½ teaspoon dried oregano

SERVES 4 TO 6

Preheat the oven to 375°F. Slice each eggplant lengthwise in half and score the cut sides in a crisscross pattern.

Heat 3 tablespoons of the oil in a large skillet. Add the eggplant, cut sides down, and fry over medium-high heat until golden. Fry the second sides for a few minutes, then remove to a plate and season with salt and pepper. Wipe out the pan.

Heat 1 tablespoon fresh oil in the skillet, add the tomatoes, and cook over medium-high heat until they have broken down into a chunky sauce, 5 to 10 minutes. Season with salt and pepper to taste.

Set the eggplants, cut sides up and snugly side by side, in a baking dish. Crumble the cheese over the tops, spoon the tomato over the cheese, and sprinkle with the oregano. Cover and bake until the eggplant is tender, about 40 minutes. Uncover and bake 5 minutes more.

Fava Beans

A FAVORITE *spring shell bean with chefs, fava beans are increasingly available in Italian, Mexican, and farmers' markets. The long, fat green pods surround flat beans, further encased in a skin. The skin needn't be removed when the bean is the size of a thumbnail, but it gets tough when the beans are larger. (To remove, blanch the beans for 1 minute in boiling water, drain, and pinch off the skins with your fingers.) Skinned favas are a brilliant spring green. If you have enough fava beans and enough time, cook them as a side dish. Otherwise, add them to spring vegetable stews and pasta dishes. One pound of pods yields only about ½ cup of beans. They go well with olive oil, yogurt, rosemary, dill, parsley, and thyme.*

Fava Beans with Yogurt, Lemon, and Dill

SERVES 4

4 pounds fresh fava beans in their pods

2½ tablespoons extra virgin olive oil

3 scallions, including some of the greens, thinly sliced

1 teaspoon finely grated lemon zest

1 tablespoon fresh lemon juice

Salt and freshly milled pepper

3 tablespoons finely chopped dill

⅓ cup yogurt, whisked until smooth

Shell the beans and peel them if they're large. Cook them in a medium skillet over medium heat in 1 tablespoon of olive oil until they're tender, about 10 minutes, then stir in the scallions and turn off the heat. Whisk together the remaining oil, lemon zest, juice, and a pinch of salt. Pour it over the beans, add most of the dill, and gently mix everything together. Season with pepper. Pile the beans in a dish, drizzle the yogurt over all, and garnish with the remaining dill. Serve warm or chilled.

Fennel

(Anise, Finocchio, or Florence Fennel)

FENNEL is a plump, pale green bulb that appears in the spring, in summer where the weather is cool, and again in the fall, when it's most delicious. The wild fennel that grows along California roadsides produces a crown of seeds and tall stalks that are splendid for grilling, but it doesn't develop the bulbous root—that must be cultivated. With its soft anise flavor, fennel is sweet, refreshing, and delectable. Because a bulb is a well-defined shape, fennel can assume a strong role on the plate, especially when cooked in halves. It can also be sliced or chopped and sautéed—a good use for the outer leaves, which often come apart from the base.

WHAT TO LOOK FOR: Firm, plump, compact bulbs, preferably with their stalks and some of the feathery greens, which should be lively looking. Small bulbs are preferable for salads since they're more tender, and larger ones are ideal for baking and braising. Avoid any that have begun to crack or bolt, or plan to use them in soups.

HOW TO STORE: Keep fennel refrigerated in a plastic bag, but try to use it within 3 to 4 days. The stalks dry out more quickly than the bulbs, so if you plan to keep them longer, wrap them in a damp towel, then in a plastic bag.

HOW TO USE: Fennel always makes an interesting substitute for celery; it's delicious braised, baked, steamed, sautéed, or grilled and is a fine salad vegetable. Be sure to use the leaves for a garnish or seasoning. I've never found much use for fennel stalks (outside of using them in soup stocks or throwing them in the fire for their aromatic smoke) which is a shame given that fennel is sold by the pound and always comes with lots of stalks. The part closest to the base is sometimes tender enough to add to soups and salads if thinly sliced, but taste it first to make sure it's not too stringy.

SPECIAL HANDLING: Cut off the stalks just where they emerge from the bulb. Fennel has a core, which is visible once you cut it in half. If the bulb is small, it's not necessary to remove it. If the bulb is very large, quarter it and remove the core with a paring knife if it seems tough or stringy. (Taste it to find out.) Remove scarred outer leaves by cutting a thin slice from the base of the bulb, then pulling them off. They can be used, along with the stalks, to make a quick stock, or they can be peeled, then sliced and cooked.

QUANTITY: An average bulb, trimmed, weighs 4 to 6 ounces. Two bulbs yield approximately 1½ cups chopped or sliced, which cooks down to slightly less. Allow one whole bulb for a main-course serving of braised fennel.

GOOD PARTNERS FOR FENNEL
Olive oil, butter
Thyme, bay, parsley, fennel seeds, orange, lemon, saffron
Tomatoes, potatoes, olives, garlic
Parmesan, Gruyère, goat cheese

SAUCES AND SEASONINGS FOR FENNEL
Salsa Verde, page 55
Orange Mayonnaise, page 59
Garlic Mayonnaise, page 59
Saffron Mayonnaise, page 59
Tomato sauces, pages 61 to 64
Parsley-Caper Sauce, page 56

Steamed Fennel

THIS *simple way of cooking fennel leaves it full of flavor.*

SERVES 4

2 medium fennel bulbs, trimmed

1 bay leaf

Salt and freshly milled pepper

Extra virgin olive oil

Chopped fennel greens or parsley

Remove the tough outer leaves and rinse the bulbs. Bring an inch of water to a boil in a large saucepan with some of the fennel stalks and the bay leaf; add a steaming rack. Quarter the bulbs lengthwise and steam, covered, until tender-firm when pierced with a knife, about 20 minutes. Remove to a plate, season with salt and pepper, thread with olive oil, and garnish with the chopped greens.

Braised Fennel with Parmesan

SERVES 4 TO 6

2 tablespoons butter or olive oil

2 to 3 fennel bulbs, trimmed and halved or quartered lengthwise

Salt and freshly milled pepper

½ cup dry white wine or water

⅓ cup freshly grated Parmesan

Chopped fennel greens or parsley

Preheat the oven to 325°F. Rub a baking dish large enough to hold the fennel in a single layer with butter. Steam the fennel for 10 minutes, then arrange in the dish. Dot with butter or drizzle with olive oil, season with salt and pepper, and add the wine. Cover and bake for 20 minutes. Remove the cover, baste the fennel with its juice, then add the cheese and continue baking until the fennel is completely tender, about 10 minutes more. Serve with chopped fennel greens or parsley.

Fried Fennel

SERVE *this as a first course with a wedge of lemon, Saffron Mayonnaise, Garlic Mayonnaise, or Romesco Sauce. A number of pieces of fennel will fall away from the root. You can fry them, too, or use them in a sauté or for fennel soup.*

SERVES 4 TO 6

3 fennel bulbs, trimmed, the root ends intact

1 egg beaten with 1 tablespoon milk

1 cup fine fresh bread crumbs

Olive oil for pan frying

Salt and freshly milled pepper

Slice the fennel lengthwise about ⅜ inch thick or into wedges. In either case, make sure the pieces are joined at the root. Steam until partially tender, about 10 minutes, then remove. Dip the fennel into the egg and milk mixture, then the bread crumbs. (If you don't eat eggs, dip it directly into a plate of flour.) Heat enough oil in a wide skillet to cover generously. When hot, add the fennel in a single layer and lower the heat to medium. Cook on both sides until golden brown. Season with salt and pepper and serve with lemon wedges or one of the suggested sauces.

Braised Fennel with Diced Vegetables

2 large fennel bulbs, trimmed, plus 1
   tablespoon chopped fennel greens

2 tablespoons olive oil

1 carrot, finely diced

1 small onion, finely diced

1 celery rib, finely diced

Several thyme sprigs or ¼ teaspoon
   dried

1 bay leaf

Salt and freshly milled pepper

½ cup dry white wine

1 tablespoon butter

THIS is a most delicious treatment of fennel—a bit more complex than the preceding recipes and with correspondingly greater stature. Served with a spoonful of Saffron Mayonnaise, it makes an elegant first course or light entrée.

SERVES 2 TO 4

Peel the outer leaves of the fennel; if they're badly bruised, remove them. Keeping the root end intact, halve each bulb lengthwise.

Heat the oil in a large skillet, add the diced vegetables and herbs, and sauté over medium-high heat until the onion begins to color, after several minutes.

Move the vegetables to one side of the pan and add the fennel halves, cut sides down. Spoon the vegetables over and around them, season with salt and pepper, and pour in 1 cup water. Lower the heat to medium, cover, and cook until the liquid has evaporated, 10 to 12 minutes. Give the diced vegetables a stir and add ½ cup water. Cover and cook until the fennel is tender-firm when pierced with a knife, 15 to 20 minutes. By this time it should be nicely browned on the bottom.

Remove the vegetables and the fennel to a serving dish, placing the fennel cut sides up. Return the pan to the heat, add the wine and butter, and scrape the caramelized bits from the bottom of the pan. When the wine and butter have reduced by half, add the fennel greens, taste for salt, and season with pepper. Spoon the sauce over the fennel and serve.

Grilled Fennel Fennel is one of my favorite vegetables to grill. Cut the stalks from a fennel bulb. If the bulb is small, cut it in half lengthwise. If it's large, cut into ½-inch slices, making sure that each slice has a piece of the root attached. Steam for 10 minutes, then brush generously with olive oil and season with salt. Grill for 5 to 6 minutes on each side. Serve with Garlic Mayonnaise, page 59, Salsa Verde with Walnuts and Tarragon, page 55, Sea Salt with Fennel Seeds and Thyme, page 77, or Mustard Vinaigrette, page 186.

Garlic

GARLIC is a vegetable as well as a pungent seasoning. But in either case garlic heads should be hard and tight, the cloves free from bruises and sprouts. A succession of crops appears in our markets for a good portion of the year—Mexican red garlic comes in late spring, followed by California garlic, and then local garlic everywhere. Elephant garlic, a relative, has very large, mild-tasting cloves that lack the feisty character of true garlic. Green garlic refers to newly formed garlic heads still attached to their greens—usually a local specialty. Their cloves are milky and the flavor extremely mild and delicious; it's really another vegetable altogether. Green garlic should be refrigerated, but dried heads can be stored at room temperature on the counter or in special perforated clay jars that allow air to circulate.

SPECIAL HANDLING: To open a head of garlic, set it top side down on a counter and press down on it with your palm to force the cloves apart. Regardless of how you plan to use garlic, the dried, knotty bit at the base should be removed, brown spots should be cut out deeply, and bitter green sprouts, which are prevalent in winter garlic, should be removed with the tip of a paring knife.

Fresh, new garlic is easy to peel with a knife. Cut off the dried core at the base of the clove, put the blade of your knife underneath the skin, and it should practically pop off. If your garlic is going to be chopped, minced, pounded, or thrown into a soup stock, lay the flat side of a chef's knife on the garlic and give it a whack to loosen the skin.

SAFETY NOTE: Garlic tastes best when it's freshly chopped, but if you want to hold it for a few hours, put it in a bowl with olive oil to cover to keep it fresh tasting and prevent oxidation. While it may be tempting to store it this way for days or weeks, botulism can grow without the presence of acid, even when refrigerated. It's simply not worth taking a chance, so throw out any that's left over.

FRESH GARLIC PUREE: Pounding garlic in a mortar makes it smooth and sweet tasting, whereas the garlic press, though useful, can leave a metallic off taste unless it's made of ceramic. Coarsely chop peeled garlic, then put it in a mortar with a little salt. The salt grabs at the garlic and speeds the process of breaking it down by pulling out its moisture. Pound it with the pestle until smooth, a matter of just a minute. The resulting puree can be stirred into a mayonnaise, sauce, soup, vegetable puree—wherever you want the flavor but not chunks. It shouldn't be fried since it will burn almost instantly.

ROASTED GARLIC PUREE: The puree that forms within the skins of roasted garlic (the following recipe) can be used as a flavoring just the way fresh can, but roasted garlic has a deeper and softer dimension. To get the puree, work the softened cloves in a sieve with a rubber spatula to force it through. Instead of roasting, you can simmer garlic cloves in a little water, olive oil, and herbs until tender. An average head of garlic yields only about a heaping tablespoon, but a little goes a long way.

Whole Roasted Garlic

1 head garlic per person   **Olive oil or butter**

Preheat the oven to 350°F. Rub off the outer papery skins, leaving the cloves encased in the last layer. Set the heads upright in an oiled baking dish, spoon a little olive oil over them or place a knob of butter on each, then add a few tablespoons of water to the dish. Cover tightly with foil. Bake for 45 minutes, then remove the foil and bake 30 minutes more, until the garlic is completely soft inside. Squeeze a clove open just to be sure.

LONG cooking sweetens pungent garlic. Squeezed out of each clove, the soft garlic is eaten with potatoes or spread over toast. The garlic must be of the best quality—rock hard with no bruises or sprouts.

Greens

COOKING greens have similar qualities yet distinctive personalities. It's mainly southerners who know greens, but the popularity of foods from other cultures, especially Asia and Italy, has given us all a new appreciation for them. So has the calcium content, especially in the "difficult" greens—dandelion, turnips, collards, and kale.

TYPES OF GREENS: Mild, tender, quick-cooking greens include spinach, chard, beet greens, bok choy, and other Asian greens. More aggressive examples are collards, turnip, broccoli rabe, mustard, dandelion, and turnip greens. Kale is somewhere in between. All greens require the same consideration from selection through storing.

WHAT TO LOOK FOR: Good greens should have a lively, bouncy look, bursting with vitality. Smaller leaves are sweeter and more tender than large ones, but large leaves once cooked will be tender, too. Yellowing, limpness, and spotting indicate age and a loss of vitality. In this state they often have a slightly sour smell and a bitter taste.

HOW TO STORE: Cook greens as soon after picking or purchasing as possible. Until then, refrigerate them in plastic bags.

HOW TO USE: Serve greens simply cooked as a side dish. They're also delicious in soups and exceedingly good combined with neutral foods, such as potatoes, pasta, and beans. Some, like chard, can be wrapped around savory fillings or themselves chopped and used as fillings for pastas and crêpes. If tender enough, they can be added to salads.

SPECIAL HANDLING: Many greens are grown in fine, sandy soil. Rain splashes onto the leaves, leaving a fine but gritty deposit, so they must be washed carefully, sometimes in two or three changes of water. Trim them first, then give the leaves a rinse under the tap. Fill a sink or large bowl with plenty of water, add the greens, and gently agitate the leaves to loosen the dirt. Let them soak for a few minutes while the dirt settles to the bottom, then lift them up without stirring up the dirty water below. Repeat until they're really clean. Taste to make sure; grit will ruin the finest dish. Tough stems need to be removed in their entirety; more tender stems should be cut at the base of the leaves by slicing them off, your knife going the length of the stem.

QUANTITY: All greens diminish greatly in volume once cooked. For two generous servings, allow 1 pound greens, usually the weight of one well-filled bunch.

*GOOD PARTNERS FOR
GREENS
Olive oil, roasted peanut
    and dark sesame oils,
    mustard oil, butter
Parmesan, Asiago, dry
    Monterey Jack
Red pepper flakes,
    vinegar, pepper sauce,
    garlic
Potatoes, legumes, pasta*

A Glossary of Greens

BEET GREENS, SPINACH, AND CHARD: These three greens are closely related botanically and can be used more or less interchangeably. They cook quickly, are tender and sweet in the mouth, and are highly versatile. Each type is treated separately in this chapter.

BOK CHOY, CHOY SUM: These mild members of the cabbage family are delectable. Bok choy has fleshy white stems and green leaves, both of which are used in stir-fries. One bunch will make two or three servings. Choy sum, which looks like a miniature bok choy, can be treated the same way or cooked whole. Allow one or two per person.

COLLARDS: These are the big, round, flat-leafed greens that encircle thick, inedible stalks. They're often milder than mustard and kale but take longer to cook, 15 to 20 minutes. They don't cook down too much so that one bunch, weighing slightly less than a pound, can serve two. Include collards in soups or treat them as a vegetable.

KALE: Kale's hearty flavor is enjoyed in winter soups, especially those with potatoes and beans, and as a vegetable. The stems are as tough as ropes, so slice the leaves all the way off. The kale we see most commonly has intensely ruffled gray-green leaves that are fairly tough, needing 12 to 15 minutes to cook. Red Russian kale has flat blue-green leaves that are somewhat more tender. Even though it cooks down, kale manages to hold much of its volume. A bunch weighing about a pound yields 1½ to 2 cups cooked. Ornamental kales are more to look at than to eat, although I've sometimes used the most tender leaves, torn in small pieces, in salads.

MUSTARD GREENS: Light green, crinkled, more tender than kale, these greens have a hot mustardy punch. Remove the stems and ribs if tough, then simmer until tender, 10 to 20 minutes, although some cook mustard for hours. The longer it cooks, the softer its flavor becomes. Briefly cooked, it's tender but spicy. Allow a 1-pound bunch for two servings.

TURNIP GREENS: These are assertive tasting with a rough texture when raw, but many people find turnip greens delicious. Southern style demands a long cooking time, which makes them silky and deep tasting. Turnip greens are wonderful combined with their roots in soups. A bunch weighing about a pound will serve two.

WATERCRESS: Usually used for salads, when you can get it in quantity, try it sautéed or stir-fried—it's simply delicious. Remove the larger stems before cooking and allow a standard bunch for a single serving.

OTHER GREENS: Amaranth, orach, Good King Henry, and wild spinach are all tender, vitamin-rich greens. They're most likely to be found in the wild, at farmers' markets, or grown at home. They can be eaten raw, in salads, or cooked. Long stems should be removed; the remaining leaves will cook down to about half their volume.

Boiled Greens Efficient for a large, awkward amount of greens. Bring a large pot of water to a boil and add 1 teaspoon salt per quart. Drop the greens into the water and cook, uncovered, until tender, 5 to 20 minutes, depending on the variety and how you like them. Some people cook them far longer. Drain, press out excess moisture, then toss with olive oil or butter, salt, and pepper. If you're using them for a filling, rinse under cold water, squeeze out the excess water, then finely chop.

Skillet Greens Using less water results in a nutrient-rich broth that can more easily be recaptured in a soup stock. Bring 1 quart water to a boil in a skillet, then add 1 teaspoon salt and the greens. Simmer, uncovered, turning the leaves until all are tender, 5 to 20 minutes. Drain, then toss them with butter or olive oil and season with salt and pepper. If you're using them later, quickly rinse them under cold water to stop the cooking.

Simmered Choy Sum These tender little vegetables cook in their entirety within minutes, look absolutely stunning, and are so delicious that you can allow one or two per person. Cut four choy sum in half lengthwise, soak them in a bowl of water for 15 minutes, then rinse carefully, giving special attention to the base. Place them cut sides down in a skillet of simmering salted water and cook until bright green and tender, about 4 minutes. Remove with tongs to a platter and drizzle a tiny bit of dark sesame oil or roasted peanut oil over all.

Braised Collards or Turnip Greens

4 bunches collards or turnip greens,
    long stems and tough ribs removed
Salt
¼ cup Brown Butter, page 30

1 onion, diced
2 garlic cloves, thinly sliced
½ teaspoon red pepper flakes
Pepper Sauce, page 74

THIS is my approximation of southern greens. After some practice, I've settled on brown butter to give them their special taste, although it's not the traditional flavor that bacon provides.

SERVES 4 TO 6

Plunge the greens into a large pot of boiling salted water, cook them for 10 minutes, then remove to a bowl. Reserve ½ cup of the cooking water. Heat the butter with the onion, garlic, and pepper flakes in a wide skillet over medium heat, stirring occasionally, until the garlic is lightly colored and the onion is soft. Add the greens, their reserved cooking water, and 1 teaspoon salt. Cook for 30 minutes and taste again for salt. They can use a lot. Serve with the sauce on the side.

Collards with Pepper Sauce Cook two bunches collard greens, 1½ to 2 pounds, as for Skillet Greens, above. Coarsely chop or leave in large pieces, then toss with 2 to 3 tablespoons extra virgin olive oil, salt and pepper to taste, and a dash of Pepper Sauce, page 74. Serves 4.

Collards with Peanuts Sauté the simmered collards, preceding recipe, briefly in roasted peanut oil, then toss with chopped Roasted Chile-Peanuts, page 88.

Greens with Tomatoes and Asiago

SERVES 2

1 large bunch collard greens or chard stems removed, leaves cut into large pieces

2 tablespoons olive oil

1 garlic clove, thinly sliced

2 tomatoes, peeled and diced

Several pinches dried oregano

Grated Asiago

Simmer or boil the greens in salted water as described on page 379, then drain. Put them in a wide skillet with the oil, garlic, and tomatoes. Season with the oregano, and cook over high heat until the tomatoes are heated through. Serve with cheese grated over the top.

Greens with Crisped Bread Crumbs

CRISPED bread crumbs accomplish the same thing as bacon bits—they provide a contrast of texture and bites of intensity. Roasted chopped nuts, especially peanuts, are also good for crunch—and flavor.

SERVES 4

½ cup coarse fresh bread crumbs

1 tablespoon butter or oil

2 bunches greens, trimmed and washed

2 tablespoons extra virgin olive, roasted peanut, or dark sesame oil

Salt and freshly milled pepper

Sauté the crumbs in the butter in a small skillet until crisp and golden. Meanwhile, boil or simmer the greens as described on page 379, then drain. Toss with oil, and season with salt and pepper. Serve with the bread crumbs sprinkled over the top.

Greens with Potatoes

THIS is a homey, unpretentious-looking dish but one that's full of taste and comforting.

SERVES 4

4 boiling or Yellow Finn potatoes, about 1 pound

Salt

1 to 2 pounds greens, trimmed and coarsely chopped

2 tablespoons extra virgin olive oil, plus extra for drizzling

1 large garlic clove, thinly sliced

½ teaspoon red pepper flakes

2 tomatoes, if in season, peeled and diced

Cover the potatoes with cold water, add salt to taste, and bring to a boil. Cook until tender, about 25 minutes. Drain, then peel and coarsely chop. Simmer the greens in a large skillet, as described on page 379, until tender, then drain. You may need to do this in two batches. Return the skillet to the stove, add the oil, and heat with the garlic and pepper flakes. When you can smell the garlic, add the greens, potatoes, and tomatoes. Cook over medium heat, breaking up the potatoes with a fork and mashing them into the greens to make a kind of rough hash. Taste for salt and serve with olive oil drizzled over the top.

Kale with Olives

1 bunch kale, green or Red Russian,
stems and ribs removed

2 to 4 tablespoons olive oil

$^1/_3$ cup pitted Kalamata olives, coarsely
chopped

$^1/_4$ teaspoon red pepper flakes

Salt

1 lemon, quartered

SERVES 2 TO 3

Simmer the kale leaves, as described on page 379, until tender, about 10 minutes. Drain
and press out excess moisture with the back of a spoon. Toss immediately with the oil,
olives, pepper flakes, and salt to taste. Serve with the lemon wedges.

Kale with Cannellini Beans

1$^1/_2$ to 2 pounds kale or mixed greens,
stems and ribs removed

Salt and freshly milled pepper

1 small onion, finely diced

1$^1/_2$ tablespoons olive oil

2 plump garlic cloves, minced

Pinch red pepper flakes

2 teaspoons chopped rosemary

$^1/_2$ cup dry white wine

1$^1/_3$ cups cooked cannellini, rinsed well
if canned

Freshly grated Parmesan, optional

*ADDING white beans to
greens makes a hearty,
unpretentious, and fast
supper. Serve with or
over Garlic-Rubbed
Croutons or topped with
bread crumbs crisped in
olive oil.*

SERVES 2 TO 4

Simmer the kale, as described on page 379, in salted water until tender, 7 to 10 minutes. Drain, reserving the cooking water, and chop the leaves. In a large skillet, sauté the
onion in the oil with the garlic, pepper flakes, and rosemary for about 3 minutes. Add the
wine and cook until it's reduced to a syrupy sauce. Add the beans, kale, and enough
cooking water to keep the mixture loose. Heat through, taste for salt and season with
pepper, and serve with a dusting of Parmesan.

ACID TIP FOR GREENS

A splash of vinegar or a squeeze of lemon is often the secret element that brings a dish to
life by heightening all the other flavors. This is true even with foods that are naturally strong
tasting, like the more aggressive greens. That squeeze of lemon or light dousing of vinegar
magically sweetens, softens, and sharpens, making everything taste better. A bit of hot chile
will do the same. In fact, pepper sauce, the ubiquitous seasoning of the South, neatly combines both elements in a single jar.

Mixed Greens with Cumin and Paprika

EVERYONE seems to love greens cooked this way, warm or cold as a salad. Be sure to use at least one assertive green for character.

SERVES 3 OR 4

12 cups mixed greens—kale, broccoli rabe, chard or beet, escarole, mustard greens

Salt

4 large garlic cloves

1 cup chopped parsley

1 cup chopped cilantro

3 tablespoons olive oil

2 teaspoons paprika

2 teaspoons ground cumin

For garnish: oil-cured black olives, wedges of lemon and tomato

Discard any inedible parts of the greens, such as kale stems and tough ribs. Set the leaves in a steamer—the tougher ones on the bottom, the most tender on top—and cook until tender. Or boil each type separately in salted water, then drain. Chop into pieces about 1 inch square.

Pound the garlic with ½ teaspoon salt in a mortar until smooth, then work in the parsley and cilantro and pound them briefly to release their flavors.

Warm the oil with the paprika and cumin in a wide skillet over medium heat until they release their fragrances. Don't let them burn. Stir in the garlic, then add the greens and cook until any extra moisture has evaporated. Taste for salt. Pile into a dish and garnish with the olives, lemon, and tomato.

FIVE IDEAS FOR LEFTOVER GREENS

• Toss them with chickpeas, pasta, diced tomatoes, and freshly grated Parmesan.

• Toss them with boiled diced potatoes and mix in a little grated Gruyère. Or stir them into mashed potatoes.

• Mix finely chopped cooked greens with cooked rice, barley, quinoa, or pasta.

• Add greens to potato, lentil, and bean soups at the end of the cooking.

• Chop and combine greens with feta, ricotta salata, or Gruyère, black olives, and capers and use them to fill empanadas or spread over toast.

Jerusalem Artichokes

(SUNCHOKES)

A TRUE *American native, the Jerusalem artichoke is neither from Jerusalem nor an artichoke. A more accurate name is* sunchoke, *because these tubers form beneath a sunflower. They have a sweet, nutty flavor. They're delightfully crisp, like water chestnuts, but during cooking they can quickly and unpredictably turn mushy, so they demand a watchful eye. The knob-shaped variety is most widely available and usually comes trimmed into more or less uniform pieces. Look for firm, unblemished tubers and store them in a plastic bag in the refrigerator for up to 2 weeks. Scrub them vigorously rather than peel them. Jerusalem artichokes can be eaten raw, cooked in winter soups and stews, roasted, and sautéed. They can also be difficult to digest, so start out eating them gradually. Avoid cooking them in cast iron, which causes them to discolor. One pound is enough for four to six servings.*

Roasted Jerusalem Artichokes

1 pound Jerusalem artichokes, sliced
   into ¹/₂-inch rounds or left whole

1 to 2 tablespoons sunflower seed oil

Salt and freshly milled pepper

A few rosemary or thyme sprigs

SERVES 4 TO 6

Preheat the oven to 400°F. Toss the Jerusalem artichokes with the oil and ¹/₂ teaspoon salt. Bake them in a shallow gratin dish with the herb for 20 to 30 minutes. Pierce them with the tip of a knife—they should be mostly tender but offer some resistance. Season with pepper.

Sautéed Jerusalem Artichokes with Sunflower Seeds

1 pound Jerusalem artichokes, sliced
   into ¹/₄-inch rounds

2 tablespoons sunflower seed oil

Salt and freshly milled pepper

3 tablespoons toasted sunflower seeds

2 tablespoons chopped parsley

1 teaspoon chopped thyme

SERVES 4 TO 6

Sauté the Jerusalem artichokes in the oil in a large skillet over high heat until lightly browned and tender but still a bit crisp. Taste them as they cook; they can be done in 5 minutes or as long as 10. Season with salt and pepper, add the sunflower seeds, parsley, and thyme, and toss well.

Wine-Glazed Jerusalem Artichokes with Rosemary

SERVES 4

1½ tablespoons olive oil

1 pound Jerusalem artichokes, sliced into rounds

1 garlic clove, finely chopped

Salt and freshly milled pepper

2 teaspoons chopped rosemary

½ cup dry white wine

Heat the oil in a wide skillet. Add the Jerusalem artichokes and garlic and sauté for about 1½ minutes. Season with salt and pepper, add the rosemary and wine, and continue to cook over high heat until the wine is reduced to a few tablespoons. Add 1 tablespoon water, cover, and cook for a minute more or until tender-crisp. (Although they can turn mushy in an instant, it can also take as long as 10 minutes before they're done.) Boil the excess liquid, if any, down to a glaze.

Kohlrabi

WITH *stems branching out of purple or green globes, kohlrabi is a strange-looking vegetable. Harvested small, it's mild and sweet, like a young turnip, and altogether pleasant. It's available in summer and fall and sometimes in winter. Look for small, firm vegetables with purple or pale green skin just slightly larger than a golf ball. Keep stored in a plastic bag in the refrigerator until ready to use. Kohlrabi can be prepared any way turnips are. It's delicious sliced into thin wedges and sprinkled with sea salt or grated into salads. To cook, cut it in quarters, rounds, or matchsticks then steam or roast it. Kohlrabi goes well with butter, sour cream, dill, mustard, and horseradish. A pound will serve four.*

Kohlrabi with Horseradish

SERVES 4

4 or 5 kohlrabi, about 1 pound, peeled

2 to 4 tablespoons crème fraîche or sour cream

Prepared horseradish in vinegar

2 teaspoons chopped dill

Salt and freshly milled pepper

Slice the kohlrabi into julienne strips or wedges. Steam until tender, 5 to 8 minutes, then remove to a bowl and toss with the crème fraîche, horseradish, and dill. Season with salt and pepper to taste.

Leeks and Scallions

DELICATE-FLAVORED *leeks are becoming increasingly available and can now be found pretty much year-round. Milder and more subtle than onions, leeks are also more costly. When I say "leek or onion" in a recipe, it's mainly to spare you the expense or bother of trying to find leeks where they're unavailable. But when a dish is based on leeks, it should be made with them. Scallions, which are also tender and mild, and nearly always inexpensive, can be used in some of the ways that leeks are—especially in soups.*

WHAT TO LOOK FOR: The edible part of the leek is the white part plus an inch or two of pale green. With scallions it's the white plus whatever greens are firm and crisp. The roots and leaves of both are excellent for stocks. Some varieties of leek have a short, stubby shank, or white part, while others are very long. You'll want leeks that have the largest proportion of white to green. The more tender the leek, the more suitable it is for braising or grilling. Very large leeks are better for soups and stews. When overmature, they develop a tough core of leaves at their centers.

HOW TO STORE: Store leeks and scallions in a plastic bag in the vegetable bin for a week. If the outer leaves turn yellowish, just strip them off; usually the rest will be edible.

HOW TO USE: Leeks can be served as salads, grilled, or featured in soups, stews, gratins, savory galettes, and tarts. When scarce, they can be stretched with scallions. Scallions are delicious stewed, grilled, and used raw as a seasoning. They make an excellent base for a soup in place of onions.

SPECIAL HANDLING: Perhaps due to new growing techniques, leeks are cleaner than in the past. But traditionally leeks do have a lot of sand and dirt lodged between their leaves. They need to be washed thoroughly but gently. Cut off the greens an inch above the white part and slice off the roots, leaving a thin piece attached so that the leaves remain joined at the base. Halve the leeks lengthwise down to an inch from the root end or all the way through. Swish them back and forth several times in a sink full of water to loosen the dirt, then soak for 15 minutes. Rinse under gently running water. Fan the leaves open so that the water can get to the base. Wash chopped leeks after cutting.

When using leeks at the start of a recipe, as a soup base for example, don't brown them as you would onions or they'll lose the delicacy that sets them apart. They don't caramelize well.

Scallions need only be trimmed of their roots and flabby greens, then rinsed.

QUANTITY: For a vegetable dish, plan on one medium leek, trimmed, per person. One pound of trimmed leeks yields four servings or about 4 cups chopped, 2 cups cooked. A bunch of scallions weighing 4 to 6 ounces, trimmed of most of its greens, yields about 1 cup chopped.

Steamed Leeks Allow one or two leeks per person. Halve them lengthwise, leaving the root end intact, and wash well. Steam them, cut sides down, until tender when pierced with the tip of a knife, 8 to 20 minutes, depending on their size. Remove to a platter and dress with extra virgin olive oil or one of the recommended sauces.

GOOD PARTNERS FOR LEEKS
AND SCALLIONS
Butter, olive oil, hazelnut oil, cream, crème fraîche
Parmesan, goat cheese, Gruyère, Cheddar
Capers, wine, olives, mustard, curry spices
Thyme, parsley, chervil, tarragon, fines herbes, saffron
Potatoes, fennel, celery, eggs

SAUCES AND SEASONINGS
FOR LEEKS AND SCALLIONS
Romesco Sauce, page 70
Garlic Mayonnaise, page 59, or Tarragon Mayonnaise with Capers, page 59
Green herb sauces, pages 55 to 57
Mustard Vinaigrette, page 186
Herb-Butter and Olive Oil Sauce, page 51

Braised Leeks

SERVE *warm alone or as a side dish.*

SERVES 4

Salt and freshly milled pepper

Aromatics, page 29, plus ¹/₂ teaspoon peppercorns

2 carrots, thinly sliced

1 celery rib, sliced

4 leeks, trimmed, halved, and rinsed

Butter or extra virgin olive oil

chopped herbs—fines herbes, chives, marjoram, tarragon, or parsley

Bring 3 quarts water to a simmer in a deep skillet or Dutch oven with 2 teaspoons salt, the aromatics, carrots, and celery. Slip the leeks into the pan and cook gently until tender when pierced with a knife, 15 to 25 minutes. Lift them out and arrange them, cut side up, on a platter. Glide a piece of butter over the top or drizzle with olive oil, then cover lightly with herbs and season with salt and pepper. Or serve with any of the suggested sauces and seasonings. The cooking liquid makes an excellent broth for risotto and soups.

Grilled Leeks with Parmesan and Olive Croutons

A PERFECT *first course or an elegant light lunch.*

SERVES 4

8 Grilled Leeks, page 387

thin shavings of Parmesan or Gruyère

8 croutons spread with Olive Paste, page 87

2 hard-cooked eggs, quartered

Chopped parsley or chervil

Salt and freshly milled pepper

Arrange two grilled leeks on individual plates, lay the cheese shavings over them, and place two small olive croutons and two egg quarters on each plate. Sprinkle parsley over all and season with salt and pepper.

Leeks Simmered in Wine

USE *three or four very thin leeks per person or two larger ones, about an inch across.*

SERVES 4

2 tablespoons butter

8 leeks, about an inch in diameter, trimmed, halved lengthwise and rinsed

¹/₂ cup dry white wine

Salt and freshly milled pepper

Aromatics: 2 bay leaves, 6 parsley sprigs, 3 thyme sprigs, ¹/₂ teaspoon peppercorns

Chopped chervil, tarragon, or parsley

In a skillet that will hold the leeks comfortably, melt the butter over medium heat. Add the leeks and cook until they begin to color a little. Add the wine and cook until it's reduced by half, then add 2 cups water, ¹/₂ teaspoon salt, and the aromatics. Simmer, partially covered, until the leeks are tender, 10 to 20 minutes. Remove them to a platter. Continue cooking the liquid until it's the consistency of light syrup, then pour it through a strainer over the leeks. Season with salt and pepper and garnish with the chopped herb.

Gratinéed Leeks You can set these delicious leeks up in advance of baking. Steam or braise eight to 12 small leeks, page 385 or page 386, then put them in a lightly buttered baking dish. Add ½ cup cream, season with salt and white pepper, and cover with 2 tablespoons freshly grated Parmesan cheese. Bake at 400°F until bubbling and browned, about 15 minutes.

Grilled Leeks Slice trimmed leeks in half lengthwise and rinse well. Steam them, cut side down, until barely tender, then brush with olive oil and season with salt. Grill on both sides until light grill marks appear, turning as necessary. Serve with extra virgin olive oil mixed with finely chopped parsley or chervil spooned over the leeks, Mustard Vinaigrette, page 186, or Romesco Sauce, page 70, on the side.

Mushrooms

Being a fungus rather than a true vegetable, mushrooms are different from the rest of the plants we eat. But they're highly prized for their woodsy flavor and they're versatile, quick to prepare, and exceptionally satisfying.

TYPES OF MUSHROOMS: A mixture of cultivated mushrooms and exotics is affordable and makes standard mushroom dishes more exciting. In some places it's possible to buy fresh wild mushrooms. Like their dried counterparts, they bring an exquisite note to any dish.

White Mushrooms: Also called *domestic, brown, cultivated, button* when small, *stuffers* when large, these are our everyday mushrooms. Buying them loose is preferable unless they look particularly fresh in their packages.

Portobellos: A giant newcomer with a smooth brown cap, thick stem, and black gills. Large enough to grill and stuff. Use the stems in stocks.

Cremini: Also called *Italian field mushrooms*, cremini are similar to white mushrooms but a little rounder and larger with tan or brown caps.

Shiitake: Long enjoyed as Japanese or Chinese dried mushrooms, shiitake are now available fresh. The flesh is tight and strong, the flavor rather intense. Discard the tough, knotty stems or use them in stocks.

Enoki: Little clusters of pale, skinny mushrooms, these make a pretty garnish for miso and other clear soups.

Oyster: Pale, clustered mushrooms joined at the base. They have a delicate flavor and can be combined with other mushrooms or enjoyed alone. Discard the tough stems.

GOOD PARTNERS FOR
MUSHROOMS
Butter, sour cream, cream, olive oil, dark sesame oil
Garlic, parsley, lemon, rosemary, tarragon, cumin, paprika
Pine nuts, bread crumbs
Wine, sherry, Madeira
Onions, potatoes, leeks, barley, rice

WHAT TO LOOK FOR: All mushrooms should be firm, have a sweet earthy smell, and be pleasant to touch—dry and firm, never slimy. Lots of cooks prefer market mushrooms with their caps tightly closed, but the mushroom flavor actually deepens as they age and the caps open. If open, the gills should look fresh—especially in portobellos. If the gills are matted down with moisture, they're likely to have a funky smell, which can affect the taste. Give them a whiff before using. Portobellos are large enough that you can simply slice off the gills. At the other extreme, excessive dryness doesn't mean they're spoiled, although such mushrooms aren't so attractive. Shiitakes are sometimes like this—but they revive when cooked, have more flavor, and make an excellent contribution to stocks.

HOW TO STORE: Store fresh mushrooms in a closed paper bag or in their cardboard container, the plastic replaced with a barely damp paper towel. You can keep them in a perforated plastic bag for 1 or 2 days. Much longer and they begin to turn a little slimy.

HOW TO USE: Mushrooms can be sautéed, marinated, grilled, broiled, cooked in parchment, added to stuffings, or stuffed themselves. They're wonderful cooked simply, and they provide the basis for many stews and soups. They also make fine salads and sandwiches and are a common element in stir-fries. Except for shiitake and portobello mushrooms, the stems can be cooked along with the caps.

SPECIAL HANDLING: To clean, wipe off domestic mushrooms with a damp cloth or plunge them into a basin of water, run your hands over them, and drain quickly. Portobellos should just be wiped. Enoki and oyster mushrooms don't usually need any cleaning. I usually slice the gills off portobellos before cooking since they bleed a dark juice into the dish.

For good color, sauté mushrooms in a roomy skillet over high heat. They quickly absorb any fat but eventually release it along with their juices, then brown.

QUANTITY: Allow 1 pound for four small servings or two main-dish servings.

Sautéed Mushrooms with Garlic and Parsley

VERY simple and fast, this is one of the most basic—and best—ways to cook mushrooms. Mushrooms are delicious cooked in either butter or olive oil—or a mixture of both.

SERVES 4

1 pound mushrooms, one or several
   varieties, cleaned

3 to 5 tablespoons butter, olive oil, or a
   mixture

Salt and freshly milled pepper

1/2 lemon

2 tablespoons chopped parsley

1 large garlic clove, minced

Cut the mushrooms into halves, quarters, or slices about 1/4 inch thick. Melt the butter in a wide skillet over high heat. Add the mushrooms all at once and immediately move them around the pan so they all pick up a little of the fat. Keep sautéing even though the pan appears to be dry. Once the mushrooms yield their juices and then reabsorb them, they'll begin to color nicely. When golden, season well with salt and pepper. Add a squeeze of lemon, then toss with the parsley and garlic and serve.

Roasted Mushrooms with Pine Nuts

1 pound cremini or large white
   mushrooms, sliced ⅓ inch thick

Salt and freshly milled pepper

2 to 3 tablespoons olive oil

3 tablespoons chopped parsley

2 garlic cloves

2 pinches red pepper flakes

3 tablespoons toasted pine nuts

ROASTING concentrates the earthy-woodsy flavor of mushrooms. Pine nuts are always good with mushrooms, but especially when roasted.

SERVES 4

Preheat the oven to 400°F. Put the mushrooms in a wide, shallow baking dish, season with salt and pepper, and toss with the oil. Bake until sizzling, about 25 minutes. Meanwhile, chop the parsley and garlic together. When the mushrooms are done, toss them with the parsley and pepper flakes. Scatter the pine nuts over the top and serve.

INTERESTING MUSHROOM CUTS

Instead of cutting mushrooms into even halves or quarters or slicing them in parallel lines, angle your knife to make the cuts irregular. Doing this reveals the interesting shapes and markings that even the most common mushrooms have, giving them more panache on the plate.

Mushrooms with Tarragon and Cream

2 tablespoons butter

1 pound mushrooms, sliced at an angle,
   about ⅓ inch thick

Salt and freshly milled pepper

½ cup dry white wine

¼ cup cream

¼ cup crème fraîche or sour cream

2 tablespoons chopped parsley

1 garlic clove

2 teaspoons chopped tarragon

A GREAT dish to know when you need something nice in a hurry. Serve over toast, noodles, or barley.

SERVES 2 TO 4

Heat the butter in a large skillet over high heat, add the mushrooms, and sauté until they're nicely colored. Season with salt and pepper, add the wine, lower the heat, and simmer until the wine is reduced by half. Add the creams and simmer until thickened slightly. Chop the parsley, garlic, and tarragon together, add them to the mushrooms, and serve.

USING DRIED MUSHROOMS TO ENHANCE FLAVOR

The unique flavor of dried wild mushrooms enhances all mushroom sautés and ragouts. Use ½ ounce or even more if you have them. Cover them with warm water and set them aside to soak anywhere from 15 minutes to several hours. Drain but reserve the flavorful water. Chop the mushrooms and sauté them with fresh ones; use the liquid, carefully decanted, in place of stock or water in your dish.

Pan-Seared Portobello Mushrooms

PORTOBELLOS seared in a cast-iron skillet taste grilled. Enjoy them as a side dish, spooned over Garlic-Rubbed Croutons, in a sandwich, or on a bed of spinach.

SERVES 2

1 large portobello mushroom, about 8 ounces, stem removed

Olive oil as needed

Salt and freshly milled pepper

Shallot Vinaigrette, page 183, sherry vinegar, or balsamic vinegar

Slice the cap ½ inch thick at an angle so that you'll have plenty of surface area, then brush both sides of each slice lightly with oil. Set a cast-iron skillet over high heat, film it thinly with oil, then add the mushroom slices. Sear for 4 to 5 minutes, then turn and sear the second side. Eventually they will begin to brown. Remove them to a platter and season with salt and pepper. Brush with vinaigrette or drizzle a few drops of vinegar over the top.

Grilled Portobello Mushrooms These meaty mushroom slices are wonderful tucked into a sandwich or simply by themselves. You can turn them into a substantial entrée by placing a whole cap over a mound of braised or sautéed greens. Carefully remove the stems from 1 pound (two large) portobello mushrooms and wipe the caps. Chop 3 tablespoons parsley, 1 teaspoon dried oregano, and 2 garlic cloves together and stir into ¼ cup extra virgin olive oil. Brush part of this mixture over the mushrooms, then grill until the mushrooms begin to brown and are soft to the touch, 8 to 10 minutes on each side. Slice the mushrooms on a slant to expose a wide band of flesh, then pile them on a platter, season with salt and pepper, and drizzle with the remaining parsley mixture.

Sautéed Mushrooms with Spinach and Pepper

THIS is one of those utterly simple dishes that's so easily made it should be part of everyone's repertoire. It makes a fine side dish, but mounded on an English muffin or toasted country bread it quickly becomes an informal main dish. It's the butter that nudges it toward excellence, but you can make quite a good dish with olive oil, too.

SERVES 2 TO 4

4 tablespoons butter or olive oil

8 ounces white mushrooms, sliced ¼ inch thick

Salt and freshly milled pepper

1 garlic clove, slivered

1 hefty bunch spinach, about a pound, stems removed

Melt 2 tablespoons of the butter in a roomy skillet, add the mushrooms, and cook over high heat until they've released their juices and browned, about 6 minutes. Season with salt and plenty of pepper and set aside on a plate.

Return the pan to the heat and add the remaining butter and the garlic. When the butter is foaming, add the spinach, sprinkle with salt, and cook until tender and most of the liquid has evaporated, about 4 minutes. Return the mushrooms to the pan and toss with the spinach. Taste for salt and check to be sure everything is good and peppery.

WILD MUSHROOMS AND TRUFFLES

Wild mushrooms are a joy to cook with because they bring such exotic flavors to the table. They have so much character, in fact, that just a few go far, effectively flavoring eggs, soufflés, soups, and pasta. Though our fields and forests are full of these prizes, it's safest to procure those brought to local markets by knowledgeable foragers. If they seem too pricey, you can stretch them by mixing them with more neutral white mushrooms. Should you find yourself with a bounty, however, you can use them in any of the recipes given for white varieties.

Choose wild mushrooms that are neither too dry nor too heavy with moisture—full and plump with a firm texture. Store them in the refrigerator, spread out on a tray and covered with a barely damp cloth, until ready to use.

BOLETES: *Boletus edulis,* whose Italian name is *porcini* and French name is *cèpe,* also grows in American forests and is often called a *bolete.* Looking a little like a large bun with silky grayish tan skin and dense white meat, this mushroom is truly impressive, whether fresh or dried. Instead of having gills, the bottom surface of this mushroom resembles a sponge. It should be pale and firm. Boletes enjoy an erratic season during the summer and fall months that's tied closely to the rains. Before using them, brush off any dirt and cut out any areas where bugs or needles have bored. Fresh boletes can be cut into thick slabs and grilled, sautéed, stewed, roasted—essentially cooked any way white market mushrooms are. Extras can be sliced and set on a tray to dry or dried in a dehydrator. Dried porcini are available in many groceries and specialty stores. Their price per pound is startling, but it takes just ½ ounce or so to add their magic to a dish.

CHANTERELLES: Mostly golden-orange in color, chanterelles can range in size from a large carpet tack to a tiger lily, which their shape resembles. Their scent is sweet and fruity, almost like apricots or spices, and their seasons are spring, late summer, and fall. They often throw off quite a lot of liquid during cooking; simply strain it off and continue cooking the mushrooms until they're done. Use the juice to flavor sauces or soups. You can dry them or freeze cooked chanterelles in their cooking liquid. They can also be purchased dried.

MORELS: Distinguished by their honeycombed surface, these comely mushrooms look like they stepped out of a fairy tale. Since they're mainly a spring mushroom, they're often paired with asparagus, fiddlehead ferns, and peas. Their flavor may remind you of very lightly smoked tea as well as the woods. They're lovely to cook whole, but cut a few open first to see if they're really clean. If not, you might want to slice them lengthwise instead and shake or pick out the forest debris. Dried morels are also available.

TRUFFLES: Nothing has quite the haunting perfume of truffles. They're extremely expensive but also one of the greatest pleasures to cook with and eat. Many traditional recipes that feature truffles are simple— truffles are sliced thinly over eggs, risotto, polenta, and other such humble foods whose simplicity sets off the splendor of the truffle to its fullest.

Italian white truffles and French black ones from Périgord are considered the best, and I would be happy with either. There are some American truffles, but they don't really compare to the European ones. A truffle for Christmas Day is better than any turkey. Store your truffle in a bowl of risotto rice and bury some eggs in it as well. The scent will penetrate both, and you can enjoy truffled eggs and risotto as well as the truffle itself. In lieu of fresh truffles, you can buy them jarred. They can be good, but they never seem to have the elusive quality of the fresh ones.

Okra

A LONG, *pointed pod with fine ridges extending the length of its body, okra's other name,* lady fingers, *suggests the refinement of its shape. Its African name,* gombo, *recalls okra's best-known role in the dish of the same name,* gumbo. *By any name, okra is slimy, and rather than try to ignore this fact, perhaps it's best just to admit that's how things are. Okra has its virtues—thickening gumbos or stews and binding vegetable juices into a sauce—but crisp texture isn't one of them.*

Look for green or red pods 2 to 3 inches long. This isn't just a nicety—larger okra can be as tough as ropes. Okra doesn't keep well for more than a few days. Keep it wrapped in paper or a plastic bag in the refrigerator; don't let it get wet, and use as soon as possible. Okra can be pickled, steamed, stewed, deep-fried, and even grilled. To keep its gumminess to a minimum, avoid cutting into the pods. A pound could feed a crowd, depending on how people feel about it, or as few as three or four.

Steamed Okra The pods look stunning. Rinse 1 pound okra, leave them whole, and steam them for 4 to 6 minutes. Arrange them on a plate and serve warm with clarified butter to dip into and lemon wedges to squeeze over, or cold with Lemon Vinaigrette, page 184, or mayonnaise flavored with curry powder. Serves 4 to 8.

Fried Okra This remains one of the most popular ways to eat okra, probably because the crisp coating mitigates the slippery texture. Serve with spicy Green Chile Mayonnaise, page 60, or as a garnish for a summer stew of corn and beans. Slice 1 pound small okra into rounds about 1/4 inch thick and toss with 1 cup fine cornmeal or crushed cracker crumbs—saltines are fine—mixed with 1 teaspoon salt. Heat 1/2 inch peanut oil in a heavy skillet until it's just short of smoking. Toss the okra in a large sieve to shake off the excess cornmeal, then fry in small batches until golden. Transfer to paper towels to drain briefly, but serve hot. (You can also fry whole pods.) Serves 4 to 6.

Grilled Okra Grilling is one of the best things a person can do with okra. For ease of handling, skewer four or five pods onto two parallel skewers, like a ladder. Brush with vegetable oil and sprinkle with salt. Grill on both sides until lightly marked. Eat hot off the grill with a squeeze of lemon or a dash of Indian Salt with Mixed Spices, page 77, add it to a sauté of corn and tomatoes, or use to garnish a plate of black-eyed peas and rice.

Onions

THIS is the workhorse vegetable in the kitchen, for there's hardly a dish that doesn't begin with onions. Onions, like leeks, also have their own role to play as a vegetable. Onions should not be overlooked for they're generally very easy to prepare, inexpensive, and good to eat.

TYPES OF ONIONS: We see these basic onions in our markets throughout the year:

Yellow Onions: The most ubiquitous cooking onions, yellow onions are readily available, inexpensive, and often very pungent but become sweet when cooked.

White Onions: Milder and not as sweet as yellow onions; preferred when you don't want to add more sweetness to a dish—and when affordable.

Red or Purple Onions: Often disk shaped, sweet red onions are milder than white or yellow ones. They're excellent for pickles and for grilling.

Torpedo Onions: Long, oval onions with red flesh and brown papery skin, torpedo onions are also good for roasting and grilling.

Boiling Onions: Almost as big as golf balls, boiling onions, also called *creaming onions*, are perfect for cooking whole or slicing into small, compact rounds.

Cipolline: Slightly larger than boiling onions and disk shaped, these seasonal Italian summer onions are sweet and mild, perfect for roasting and braising.

Pearl Onions: Actually little bulbettes, pearl onions are beautiful cooked whole in a vegetable braise but are time-consuming to peel.

Sweet Onions: Walla Walla, Maui, and Vidalia onions are extrasweet, low in sulfur, and juicy. They're available only when fresh, and they don't keep for much longer than a week. They are the very best onions to use for salads and sandwiches.

Shallots: Small, brown-skinned bulbs with a mild onion flavor, shallots are sold mostly in packages of two or three and used for vinaigrettes. However, they are delicious braised and roasted, and if you find a good source at a farmers' market, by all means try them in quantity.

WHAT TO LOOK FOR: Onions should be firm and fresh smelling with dry papery skins. Avoid those that are sprouting or have a sooty appearance (wash them well if you've no choice), look greenish, or have woody-looking stems. Remove any sprouts inside. Freshly harvested onions are shiny and moist looking and haven't formed their papery skins. They're frequently mild and sweet in spite of their initial sulfur bite—a treat in the summer kitchen.

HOW TO STORE: Store onions in a cool, dry place where there's plenty of air circulating around them. This can be on your counter. Keep onions far from potatoes—they're incompatible and cause each other to spoil.

HOW TO USE: Onions can be sautéed, grilled, roasted, braised, pickled, stuffed, deep-fried, and cooked to a savory jam.

SPECIAL HANDLING: To keep from crying when you cut onions, use a very sharp knife and/or chill them in a bowl of cold water for 15 to 30 minutes before cutting. Always wrap cut onions well so that their smell doesn't permeate your butter and cheese—fats absorb odors. Save leftovers—chopped onions keep for a day or two in a sealed container, and having some on hand is always a great convenience when it's time to make dinner.

QUANTITY: An average medium yellow or white onion weighs between 4 and 6 ounces and yields approximately 1 cup sliced or chopped. Large onions can weigh up to 1 pound, smaller ones as little as 2 or 3 ounces. Onions can cook down to half—or less—of their volume, depending on how long they cook. As a vegetable, allow 1 pound of onions for three or four servings.

Baked Whole Onions in Their Jackets

Allow one firm onion per person. Put them, unpeeled, in a baking dish, add ½ inch water, and cover with aluminum foil. Bake at 375°F for 1 hour. Uncover and continue baking until tender when pierced with a knife, 15 to 30 minutes more, depending on the size. Cut them in half and serve them in their jackets or pull back the skins and slice off the root end. Season with salt, lots of freshly ground pepper, butter or olive oil, and finely minced parsley, thyme, or tarragon.

Grilled Onions

One of my favorite ways to cook onions. I prefer fresh red or white onions from the farmers' market, but storage onions work well, too. Peel large onions, slice them into ½-inch-thick rounds, and secure each slice with one or two toothpicks to keep the rings from separating. Brush both sides with olive oil and season with salt and pepper. Grill for 8 to 10 minutes, until they're nicely marked, then turn them carefully and cook the second side until well marked and softened. Arrange the onions on a platter. Serve with butter or olive oil and lots of freshly ground pepper, with a splash of your favorite vinegar, or sprinkle with ground chipotle chile. Leftovers make such good additions to salads and sandwiches that it's worth planning for extras.

A QUICK VINEGAR SAUCE FOR ONIONS

Vinegar has a keen affinity for onions. Serve this sauce with baked or grilled onions or over an onion frittata. Melt 3 tablespoons butter in a small skillet over high heat. When it foams, add 2 tablespoons sherry vinegar and boil it rapidly, shaking the pan back and forth, until it's emulsified, then pour it directly over the onions. Step back when you add the vinegar—the fumes are quite powerful.

Sautéed Onions

2 tablespoons olive oil or a mixture of
oil and butter

1 large onion, sliced about ½ inch thick

Salt and freshly milled pepper

Heat the oil in a wide skillet. Add the onion and sauté, flipping often but letting them rest in the pan long enough to brown, about 5 minutes in all. Season with salt and pepper and serve right away.

COOKING onions over brisk heat produces one of the best anticipatory smells I know. Sautéed onions add much to simple foods, such as a grilled cheese sandwich or a plate of macaroni and cheese.

SERVES 2 TO 3

Braised Boiling Onions or Shallots

1 pound boiling onions, cipolline,
shallots, or a mixture

2 tablespoons butter or olive oil

2 small bay leaves

2 thyme sprigs

2 teaspoons sugar

Salt and freshly milled pepper

½ cup dry white wine or vermouth

A HANDSOME dish when made with a mixture of shallots, white and red boiling onions, and cipolline.

SERVES 4 TO 6

Blanch the onions in boiling water for 2 minutes, then drain and remove the outer skin. If using shallots, peel them raw and pull them apart at their natural divisions. Melt the butter in a skillet with the bay leaves and thyme and add the onions and sugar. Cook over medium heat, shaking the pan occasionally, until browned in places, 10 to 15 minutes. Season with ½ teaspoon salt and pepper to taste and add the wine. Bring to a boil, then lower the heat, cover, and simmer until the onions are tender, 15 to 20 minutes. Check once or twice during cooking, and if the pan is dry, add a few tablespoons water. Remove the lid and reduce the remaining juices to a syrupy glaze.

Roasted Onions with Vinegar and Rosemary

4 to 5 onions, sliced into ½-inch rounds

2 tablespoons olive oil

2 tablespoons balsamic vinegar

1 tablespoon finely chopped rosemary

Salt and freshly milled pepper

SERVE these easily prepared onions as a side dish, but keep any leftovers in mind when planning subsequent meals. You can add them, chopped, to arugula or spinach salad or spoon them over bruschetta with slivered Manchego or Parmesan cheese.

SERVES 4 TO 6

Preheat the oven to 400°F. Toss the onions with the oil, vinegar, and rosemary. Season with salt and pepper. Put them in a baking dish with a few tablespoons water. Cover and bake for 30 minutes, then uncover and continue baking until the onions are browned around the edges and tender, about 30 minutes more. Give them a stir every 10 minutes or so toward the end.

Roasted Onions on a Bed of Herbs

A SPECTACULAR-looking dish for minimal effort—perfect for the holidays. Look for onions with crisp, papery skins. They're fine without the herbs, too.

SERVES 6

2 tablespoons butter

2 tablespoons olive oil

3 large yellow onions, halved and peeled

Salt and freshly milled pepper

4 sage sprigs and several thyme sprigs

1 cup dry white wine or water

Heat the butter and oil in a wide skillet, then add the onions, cut sides down. Cook over medium-high heat until well browned, about 15 minutes. Check their progress occasionally—those on the outside of the pan usually take longer to cook, so partway through switch them with those in the middle. When browned, turn them over and cook on the curved side for a few minutes. Season well with salt and pepper.

Preheat the oven to 375°F. Line the bottom of a 10-inch earthenware dish such as a round Spanish casserole with the herbs. Place the onions, browned side up, on the herbs and pour in the wine. Cover with aluminum foil and bake until tender when pierced with a knife, 1 hour or slightly longer. Serve warm with or without the Quick Vinegar Sauce for Onions, page 394.

Fried Onion Rings   Slice peeled yellow onions into rounds about ½ inch thick. Separate the rings, dip them in a bowl of milk, then in flour seasoned with salt and pepper. In a deep fryer, heat peanut oil to about 350°F or until it sizzles a chunk of bread to gold in about 1 minute. Add the onions a handful at a time and fry until golden, about 3 minutes. Lift them out with a strainer, drain briefly on paper towels, then sprinkle with salt or ground red chile. Repeat until all are done, then serve.

Caramelized Onions

THIS heavenly jam of caramelized onions takes about 1½ hours of cooking, but most of it is unattended. I make these when I'm doing something that calls for breaks. Every 20 minutes or so I stir them. Caramelized onions are wonderful as a filling for buckwheat crêpes, or tossed with pasta, walnuts, and rosemary.

MAKES ABOUT 3 CUPS

4 tablespoons butter

3 pounds onions, sliced ¼ to ⅓ inch thick

4 thyme sprigs

Salt and freshly milled pepper

1 cup dry white wine

1 tablespoon sherry vinegar

In a wide, deep skillet or Dutch oven, melt the butter over medium heat, letting it color a little. Add the onions and thyme, stir them about, and cover. Cook until they turn limp and reduce in volume, about 5 minutes, then turn the heat to low and toss the onions with 1¼ teaspoons salt. Cover, cook for 20 minutes, then add the wine and cover again. Every 20 minutes or so, give them a stir. After an hour or so the onions will begin to brown. You can hear them start to sizzle. Now start stirring them more frequently so that they don't burn. When they're a rich golden brown, stir in the vinegar and turn off the heat. Taste for salt and season with pepper.

Parsnips

LIKE many root vegetables grown for animal fodder, parsnips are unjustly underestimated, for the fragrant strength of these roots is considerable. Though sweet enough to be eaten for breakfast, their usual place is as a vegetable side dish. Parsnips are available from fall to early summer, but those dug after the first frost are always the sweetest.

WHAT TO LOOK FOR: Parsnips are a firm, tapering, ivory-colored root; they should not be flaccid, flabby, split, or shriveled, all signs of poor care. The best parsnip I ever ate was huge, dug out from under a covering of March snow, so size isn't necessarily a deterrent to goodness. Freshness is the key; if too old or not well stored, parsnips can turn bitter. Unless they're to be chopped, choose vegetables that are more or less the same size so they'll cook evenly.

HOW TO STORE: Keep parsnips in a plastic bag in the vegetable bin. Cold temperature, close to 32°F, helps sweeten them.

HOW TO USE: Steamed, boiled, baked, roasted, or sautéed, parsnips are delicious with just butter, salt, and pepper. They can be stewed with other winter vegetables, added to potato puree, and made into a good soup. Parsnips are related to carrots, and they can be used in most carrot recipes to good effect. Since their flavor always dominates, use them only where you really want it.

SPECIAL HANDLING: Parsnips have a clearly demarcated core. You don't have to remove it unless it's obviously woody. Probe it with the tip of a knife to see. Peel parsnips before cooking or boil them first, then slip off the skins. Because the tops are thick and the bottoms skinny, they don't cook evenly unless cut into equal pieces.

QUANTITY: Allow 2 pounds parsnips for four to six servings.

GOOD PARTNERS FOR PARSNIPS
Butter, brown butter, curry
Honey, maple syrup, brown sugar, mustard
Ginger, curry, parsley, thyme, tarragon, chives
Onions, apples, other root vegetables

Buttered Parsnips

1½ to 2 pounds parsnips, peeled
2 tablespoons butter or Brown Butter, page 30

Salt and freshly milled pepper
Chopped parsley or tarragon

ALTHOUGH they're tough-looking roots, parsnips turn soft quickly—keep an eye on them.

SERVES 4

Cut the parsnips into pieces of equal length, then halve or quarter the thicker ends so they'll be approximately the same thickness as the rest. Steam or boil in salted water until tender-firm, 7 to 10 minutes, checking after 5 minutes. Drain and toss with the butter, season with salt and pepper to taste, and toss with chopped parsley.

Parsnips with Bread Crumbs Melt 1 tablespoon butter in a skillet, add ¼ cup fresh bread crumbs, and fry until golden and crunchy, a few minutes. Toss them with the boiled or steamed parsnips in the preceding recipe.

Sautéed Parsnips Slice 2 pounds peeled parsnips into ¼-inch rounds. Sauté in 2 tablespoons canola oil, sunflower oil or butter in a skillet over medium heat until tender and beginning to brown, about 6 minutes. Season with salt and pepper and toss with chopped parsley. Serves 4 to 6.

Roasted Parsnips Preheat the oven to 400°F. Peel 2 pounds parsnips. Leave them whole if small or cut them into batons or chunks. Toss with 2 tablespoons oil or melted butter and season with salt and pepper. Roast in a large gratin dish or roasting pan, uncovered, until browned and tender, 20 to 30 minutes. Give them a stir every 10 minutes so that they color evenly. Serves 4 to 6.

Pureed Parsnips

YOU can sharpen the flavor of this puree with buttermilk or soften it with cream. Vegans can use the rich-flavored cooking water for thinning and omit the butter.

SERVES 6

1½ pounds parsnips, peeled
½ pound boiling potatoes, peeled
Salt and freshly milled pepper

½ cup buttermilk, cream, or cooking water as needed
4 tablespoons butter

Chop the parsnips and potatoes into pieces, the potatoes about half the size of the parsnips. Put them in a saucepan with cold water to cover and 1 teaspoon salt. Bring to a boil, then lower the heat and simmer until tender. Drain, reserving the liquid. Pass the vegetables through a food mill or beat by hand into a puree. Add enough buttermilk to make the mixture smooth and easy to work. Stir in butter, taste for salt, and season with pepper.

> *Variation:* Cook parsnips with other root vegetables, such as carrots, celery root, turnips, rutabagas, parsley root, a chopped leek or onion, then puree. Grated Swiss or Gruyère makes a good addition.

Curried Parsnips with Yogurt and Chutney

YOU can make this a main dish if you serve it on a bed of braised greens or sautéed spinach.

SERVES 4

1½ pounds parsnips, peeled and chopped into even-sized pieces
2 to 3 tablespoons butter or canola oil
1 onion, thinly sliced
2 apples, cored and thinly sliced
1 teaspoon curry powder

Salt and freshly milled pepper
¼ cup yogurt
¼ cup Apricot and Dried Fruit Chutney, page 81, Apple-Pear Chutney, page 81, or a commercial mango chutney
2 tablespoons chopped cilantro

Steam the parsnips until barely tender, about 7 minutes. Melt 2 tablespoons of the butter in a medium skillet. Add the onion, apples, and curry powder and cook over medium heat, stirring frequently, for 10 minutes. Add the parsnips, season with salt and pepper, and cook 5 minutes more with the additional tablespoon butter to help them brown. Turn off the heat, then stir in the yogurt, chutney, and cilantro and serve.

Peas

PRECIOUS and fleeting, peas occupy a tiny window in time in late spring and early summer. The minute heat sets in they're finished, but until then they are one of the most delectable treats in the vegetable world. Little need be done except to cook them as soon as you can. Unlike today's corn, their sugars quickly turn to starch once picked.

TYPES OF PEAS:

Pod Peas: Also called *English peas* or *shelling peas,* these are the old-fashioned peas that are shucked from their pods. If they're not starchy, they can be eaten raw.

Snow Peas: Eaten whole, these are the flat, pale green pods sometimes called *Chinese peas.* The peas themselves are barely formed; the pods are tender.

Sugar Snap Peas: A newer variety, these are plump-podded peas that resemble shelling peas, but the pods themselves are sweet, tender, and crisp. They're cooked and eaten whole.

Pea Shoots: Found in Asian markets, these tender vines can be sautéed or stir-fried and eaten right along with the peas.

Winged Peas: Also called *winged beans* or *asparagus peas,* these are another vegetable altogether, but they resemble a small sugar snap pea—with wings. They should be small, no more than 1/2 inch thick. Cook them as you would peas or green beans.

WHAT TO LOOK FOR: Bright green color and a crisp, fresh look is what you want in all peas. Yellowing tells you that they've begun to turn starchy. If you can, bite into one raw to make sure it's tender. While scars may detract from a pea's visual perfection, they usually disappear when cooked.

HOW TO STORE: If you must store them, keep them in a plastic bag in the refrigerator, but try to use them as soon as you can.

HOW TO USE: Peas can be steamed, boiled, stir-fried, made into soups, and tossed shelled and uncooked into salads and pastas. They are so special and their season is so brief that they beg for simple treatments.

SPECIAL HANDLING: Strings should be removed from pods. With a paring knife, cut into the stem end, lift the string that binds the pea like a zipper, and pull down to the blossom end. Turn and pull out the second string on the other side. Very small peas needn't be strung.

QUANTITY: Allow 1 pound pod peas for 1 cup shelled, serving two or three. For edible-pod peas, 1 pound should serve four.

GOOD PARTNERS FOR
PEAS
*Butter, dark sesame and
   roasted peanut oils
Dill, chives, chervil,
   parsley, basil, mint,
   ginger, garlic
Shallots, onions,
   asparagus, turnips, fava
   beans, scallions*

An Assemblage of Peas

SINCE *shelling peas and edible-pod peas cook quickly and I often find myself with some of this kind and a few of that, I simply cook them together. They look marvelous and taste just fine!*

SERVES 2 TO 4

1 pound peas, different varieties
Salt and freshly milled white pepper

Butter to taste
Chopped mint, basil, chives, or dill

String the snow peas and edible-pod peas; shuck any shelling peas. Bring a pot of water to a boil, add salt, and drop in the peas. Boil until they're bright green and tender, a minute or two. Drain, shake dry, then return to the empty pan, where they'll finish drying in its heat. Stir in a small piece of butter, a little pepper, and whatever fresh herb appeals to you. If you have pea shoots, cook them with the peas.

Peas with Peanut Oil: Omit the butter from the preceding recipe and toss the cooked peas with a few teaspoons roasted peanut or dark sesame oil and snipped chives.

Sugar Snap Peas with Scallions and Dill

THIS basic dish is easy to vary: Use shallots instead of scallions. A handful of peeled fava beans, pea shoots, and slivered asparagus tips added to the peas turns it into a spring vegetable sauté.

SERVES 4

1 pound sugar snap peas, strung, or winged peas
6 scallions, including a few inches of the greens, finely sliced
Salt and freshly milled pepper

1 tablespoon butter or olive oil
2 tablespoons chopped dill or another favored herb

Put the peas in a skillet with the scallions, a few pinches salt, the butter, and enough water just to cover the bottom. Cook until bright green and tender, after a minute or two—taste one to be sure. If using olive oil, add a little to the pan now. Taste for salt, season with a little pepper, and add the dill.

Stir-Fried Peas with Sichuan Pepper Salt

THE spicy, aromatic salt is delicious with peas, but if you haven't any, use plain sea salt. I like snow peas plump and whole, but you can slice them diagonally to give the dish a more dynamic play of shapes.

SERVES 4 TO 6

1$\frac{1}{2}$ tablespoons roasted peanut oil
1 garlic clove, chopped
1 pound snow or sugar snap peas, strung

$\frac{1}{2}$ to 1 teaspoon Sichuan Pepper Salt, page 76, to taste

Heat a wok or large skillet, then dribble in the oil. When the oil is hot, add the garlic and stir-fry for 30 seconds. Add the peas and stir-fry until they turn bright green. Turn off the heat, sprinkle with the salt, toss again, and serve.

Peppers

ONE *of the greatest gifts of late summer is the wealth of glossy, brightly hued peppers available in the garden and at farmers' markets. Peppers are filled with juicy sweetness, have an appealing, crisp texture, and merge splendidly with all the vegetables and herbs of the season.*

TYPES OF SWEET PEPPERS: Color indicates stage of ripeness and, in some cases, variety. Although bells are what we see most, many other kinds are widely available:

Banana Peppers: The sweet version of Hungarian hot peppers, about 5 inches long and pale yellow with blushes of pink, banana peppers can be used for stuffing, although they don't stand upright.

Bell Peppers: Left on the plant, green peppers eventually turn red, but some varieties are selected for their red, yellow, orange, or purple pigmentation. Green and purple peppers have a tarter flavor than their red and yellow cousins. Mexibells look like green bell peppers but are hot. Stuffers are squat green bell peppers that stand upright easily. They're often sold wrapped in packages of four or six.

Cubanelles: These large sweet peppers are long, narrow, and oddly creased. They can be extremely sweet and are wonderful grilled and salted.

Italian Sweet Peppers: These look more like what we call a chile than a bell pepper, but they're mild. They're delicious lightly grilled and salted.

Pimientos: These heart-shaped peppers come to a pointed tip and are deep red when ripe, with a rich, concentrated flavor.

WHAT TO LOOK FOR: Smooth, firm flesh with no wrinkles or soft spots.

HOW TO STORE: If not using them right away, store peppers in a plastic bag in the refrigerator. They'll keep for a week or more, but accumulated moisture eventually causes peppers to spoil.

HOW TO USE: Unwaxed garden peppers are a treat to enjoy as a crudité or in salads. Peppers find their way into soups, spreads, salads, purees, sauces, and stews. They can also be stuffed, sautéed, or grilled.

GOOD PARTNERS FOR
PEPPERS
Olive oil
Saffron, fennel, anise,
  basil, marjoram, garlic
Balsamic vinegar, sherry
  vinegar, olives, capers
Mozzarella, Fontina, goat
  cheese, Parmesan
Tomatoes, eggplant,
  onions, summer squash,
  corn

SPECIAL HANDLING: Almost all commercial peppers are waxed. Grilling, roasting, and broiling peppers removes the wax along with the skins, gives them extra flavor and makes them supple. You can also wash them in a weak solution of soapy water, then rinse.

When slicing peppers, open them up, then cut from the inside of the pepper rather than from the outside. A knife can bounce off the outer hard surface, whereas the porous cell walls inside tend to grab the blade—far safer, especially for inexperienced cooks or those using dull knives.

To prepare a pepper for slicing, slice off the top and a small piece off the bottom, then make a cut down the side. Open the pepper up, slice off the veins, scrape out the seeds, then cut it into strips, triangles, or whatever is called for. The tops can be added to stocks or diced into small pieces for salads or salsas.

QUANTITY: Peppers can vary greatly in size and weight, but an average bell pepper weighs about 6 to 8 ounces and holds about 1 cup of filling. Trimmed and seeded, it will yield approximately 1½ cups thinly sliced or chopped. Roasted and peeled peppers yield slightly less since the softened peppers will collapse.

Sautéed Peppers

A DISH that can be used in many ways, these will keep, refrigerated, for a week. The high heat sears the onions and peppers and gives them almost a smoky edge.

MAKES 3 TO 4 CUPS

4 large bell peppers—red, yellow, and/or orange

3 tablespoons olive oil

1 small red onion, quartered and thinly sliced crosswise

2 garlic cloves, thinly sliced

1 tablespoon tomato paste diluted with ¼ cup water

Salt and freshly milled pepper

1 tablespoon balsamic vinegar, to taste

1½ tablespoons chopped marjoram or 2 tablespoons sliced basil leaves

Slice the peppers into wide or narrow strips as you prefer. Heat the oil in a wide skillet, add the onion, and sauté over high heat until translucent and beginning to color around the edges, 4 to 5 minutes. Add the garlic and peppers and continue to cook, stirring every so often, until the peppers are singed on the edges, about 10 minutes. Add the diluted tomato paste, lower the heat to medium, and continue cooking until the peppers are soft, about 10 minutes more. Season with salt and pepper to taste, add the vinegar, and raise the heat to high. Cook, stirring frequently, until the peppers are glazed, then stir in the marjoram.

USES FOR SAUTÉED PEPPERS AND PEPERONATA

Enjoy sautéed peppers warm, tepid, or even chilled. Serve them as a side dish or stir them into omelets and scrambled eggs; spoon them over grilled polenta or pasta or the Saffron Noodle Cake, page 457; toss leftovers with hot rice and Parmesan or crumbled Gorgonzola. Use them to top crostini, bruschetta, and pizzas or tuck them into crêpes. Include them on an antipasto plate accompanied by sliced fresh mozzarella, olives, capers, and crudités.

ROASTING AND PEELING PEPPERS AND CHILES

Peppers that are best for roasting are those with thick walls and flat, smooth surfaces. They should be meaty and feel heavy in the hand. Green peppers are often too thin to roast well—but not always. Varieties vary. Try to judge by their heft if you're not sure.

Roasted and peeled peppers can be kept for a week or so in the refrigerator. Put them in a clean jar, cover with olive oil, and seal.

ON THE GRILL OR BURNER: Place whole peppers directly on a gas burner or gas or charcoal grill. If you have an electric burner, an *asador,* a small mesh grill that sits right over the element, is a great help. (It can go right over gas burners, too, and can be used for grilling other vegetables as well as warming tortillas.) Roast the peppers until the skin becomes wrinkled and loose, turning them frequently with a pair of tongs. If you want the peppers to be soft and slightly smoky, roast them until the skins are completely charred. Set the peppers in a bowl, put a plate on top, and let them steam at least 15 minutes to loosen the skins.

If you wish to grill bell peppers for eating, without peeling them, slice off the top and the tip of the pepper, open it up, and remove the veins and seeds. Brush with olive oil or Lemon Vinaigrette, page 184, and grill, skin side facing the coals, until the skins are puckery and lightly marked but not charred. Turn and grill on the second side for a few minutes, then remove and season with salt and pepper. Leave the peppers in large pieces or cut them into strips as desired. Skinny peppers and chiles can be brushed with oil, grilled whole until just blistered, then sprinkled with salt.

IN THE OVEN: Use this method when you want to peel the peppers without cooking them too much. Cut off the top of the pepper, then slice it in half lengthwise, remove the seeds and veins, and press down on each half to flatten. Brush the skins with oil, then set them skin side up on a sheet pan. Bake at 400°F or broil 5 to 6 inches under the heating element until the skins are wrinkled but not charred, 10 to 20 minutes. Remove and stack the peppers on top of each other to steam for 15 minutes.

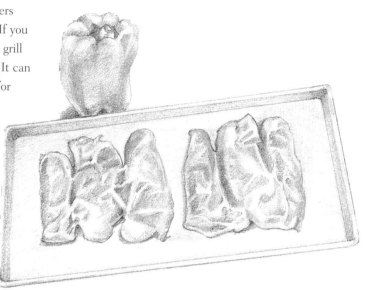

PEELING PEPPERS: First reserve any juice that has collected from the steaming peppers in the bottom of the bowl or tray. Concentrated and sweet, it makes a wonderful addition to vinaigrettes and sauces. Next rub off the skins with your hand or a paper towel. Don't worry about getting every little fleck of skin. Although rinsing the peppers is faster, you'll wash away their good flavor, so try to be patient and do it by hand. Open the peppers and scrape out the seeds, then cut as desired.

Peperonata

IN THIS *Italian dish the peppers are stewed with fresh tomatoes until soft, rather than seared as in the preceding recipe. The resulting dish is tender and juicy, but it can be used the same ways as sautéed peppers—see the following note.*

SERVES 4 TO 6

¼ cup olive oil

2 onions, diced

3 garlic cloves, thinly sliced

2 bay leaves

1 teaspoon chopped thyme

5 or 6 bell peppers—red, yellow, and green—diced or sliced

Salt and freshly milled pepper

5 ripe tomatoes, peeled, seeded, and neatly diced

Heat the olive oil in a wide skillet. Add the onions, garlic, bay leaves, and thyme and cook over medium-high heat, stirring frequently, until the onions are soft and lightly colored, about 10 minutes. Add the peppers, season with ½ teaspoon salt, and raise the heat. Cook briskly until the peppers begin to soften, then add the tomatoes and reduce the heat to medium. Simmer, stirring occasionally, until the excess water from the tomato has cooked away, about 15 minutes. Taste for salt and season with pepper.

Roasted Pepper Strips and Onions (*Rajas*)

RAJAS *are strips of roasted chile. Here they are mixed with bell peppers. They can be served as a vegetable or used in quesadillas, enchiladas, or omelets.*

MAKES ABOUT 1½ CUPS

2 poblano chiles

2 large bell peppers—1 red and 1 green

1 small onion, thinly sliced

1 teaspoon minced garlic

1 tablespoon vegetable oil

Salt

Fresh lime juice or sherry vinegar

Roast and peel the poblanos and bell peppers as described on page 403. Cut the chiles and peppers into strips about ½ inch wide, put them in a bowl, then strain the juices over them.

Sauté the onion and garlic in the oil in a medium skillet over medium-high heat just until the onion begins to brown around the edges, about 5 minutes. Combine with the pepper strips and season with salt. When ready to serve, add a little lime juice to sharpen the flavors. These will keep in a covered container in the refrigerator for several days.

Tunisian Tomato and Pepper Stew

2 to 3 yellow onions, diced

1 garlic clove, slivered

¼ cup olive oil

2 pounds tomatoes, peeled, seeded, and chopped, juices reserved

4 bell peppers—red, green, and yellow—chopped into 2-inch pieces

2 teaspoons Harissa, page 75

2 teaspoons sweet paprika

Salt

1 tablespoon chopped parsley or basil

THIS succulent Tunisian dish is seasoned with Harissa, which tempers the sweetness of the summer vegetables. Serve at room temperature as a side dish or hot with couscous or pasta.

SERVES 4 TO 6

Sauté the onions and garlic in the oil in a wide skillet over medium heat until softened, about 5 minutes. Add the tomatoes, peppers, harissa, paprika, and ½ teaspoon salt. Cook for several minutes, then add ½ cup water or juices from the tomatoes. Simmer, stirring occasionally, until the tomatoes have thickened to a sauce and the peppers are tender, about 25 minutes. Taste for salt and stir in the parsley.

FRESH CHILES

Certain parts of the country enjoy many more chiles than others but here are four chiles that are relatively easy to find almost everywhere. If you live in the Southwest, chances are you know a lot about the chiles that are popular in the area.

Green chiles eventually ripen to red on the vine. With ripening, their flavor naturally sweetens as the sugar content rises, just as with bell peppers. The capsaicin, the source of the chiles' heat, is concentrated around the veins and seeds. If you want to minimize heat, these are the parts to remove. If you're sensitive to chiles' volatile oils, wear gloves while handling them and avoid touching your eyes, nose, and mouth. Small chiles, like jalapeños and serranos, can be grilled but are most often eaten diced and raw. Larger chiles are always grilled, then peeled because their skins are quite tough and hard to digest.

JALAPEÑOS: Once consistently hot, a strain of this stubby plump short chile has been bred for mildness, so now you have to taste one to find out if it's hot. If you want heat, keep the veins and seeds; otherwise it's easy to cut the flesh away. Jalapeños are plump enough to stuff, grill, fry, or pickle.

LONG GREENS: Anaheims and New Mexican are two of several chiles described as *long greens.* Bright green with a hint of yellow rather than dark tones, these chiles are usually, though not always, mild and good multipurpose chiles. They always taste better roasted; then they can be made into *rajas* or stuffed.

POBLANO CHILES: A luscious heart-shaped, large, dark green chile with black patches on its wide shoulders, the poblano is hot and very tasty (although sometimes you'll get one that's mild). It's often used for making *rajas, chile rellenos,* and sauces. As with long green chiles, its flavor is improved by roasting.

SERRANO: The small—about 2 inches long—slender cylindrical chile is bright dark green. It's hot with a good chile flavor rather than a green pepper taste. Plan to use serrano chiles with their seeds because they're difficult to remove. You can use these interchangeably with jalapeños, but you may find you prefer the flavor of one over the other.

Red Peppers Stuffed with Corn and Fresh Mozzarella

THIS filling can also be used for zucchini or tomatoes. Serve with a fresh, summery tomato sauce.

SERVES 2 TO 4

2 red bell peppers, halved lengthwise

2 tablespoons butter

1 bunch scallions, including the firm greens, thinly sliced

2½ to 3 cups kernels from 5 ears of corn

2 tomatoes, peeled, seeded, and diced

1 fresh mozzarella cheese, 4 to 5 ounces, finely diced, or 1 cup grated Cheddar or Monterey Jack

2 tablespoons finely sliced basil leaves

⅔ cup fresh bread crumbs

Salt and freshly milled pepper

Paprika

Preheat the oven to 375°F. Lightly butter a baking dish just large enough to hold the peppers.

If the red peppers won't stand upright, slice them lengthwise in half, leaving the stem end intact. Steam them for 5 minutes and set aside.

Melt the butter in a large skillet. Add the scallions, corn, and tomatoes and cook for 3 minutes over medium heat. Turn off the heat and stir in the cheese, basil, and half the bread crumbs. Season with salt and pepper. Fill the peppers and top with the remaining bread crumbs. Set them in the prepared dish, add a few tablespoons water to the dish, cover, and bake until the corn is hot and the peppers are cooked, about 25 minutes. Uncover and brown the tops under the broiler. Dust with paprika and serve.

Potatoes

FILLING, versatile, and still inexpensive, potatoes are such a perennial favorite that in some cookbooks they have a chapter of their own. They're still delectable today, especially now that we're finally becoming reacquainted with some of the delicious heirloom varieties our ancestors knew. We've also become acquainted with another treat— freshly dug summer potatoes. These are real new potatoes and so delicious you can enjoy them with almost nothing on them at all. Many of our old potato favorites gain a renewed lease on life when made with some of the new varieties—as well as new potatoes.

TYPES OF POTATOES: It's not always easy to figure out which potatoes to use for what. For a long time our market choices were limited to a baker, two boilers, and a few all-purpose potatoes, so we're simply out of practice when it comes to making sense of the exciting varieties that are now surfacing. Essentially potatoes vary in their starch content, and it's the starch that makes one type of potato more suitable for a dish than another.

Potatoes come in a startling array of shapes, sizes, and colors. Some are unique to particular regions where growing conditions are ideal—hence the Idaho or Maine potato. The more interesting heirloom potatoes, long the darlings of chefs, are becoming increasingly available in farmers' markets, specialty, and natural food stores. By all means try them if you see them!

Blue Potatoes: Any blue vegetable is a novelty, but some of the new varieties of these Peruvian potatoes, such as Purple Vikings and All Blues, have a surprising amount of flavor that's a little nutty and often very sweet. Bake, roast, or steam them and use in salads.

Yellow Finns: A pretty oval potato with buttery-looking yellow flesh. These make golden mashed potatoes, are delicious roasted and baked in gratins, but tend to fall apart in a salad.

Red Russian, Banana, Rose Fir, fingerlings: Looking roughly like large fingers, their dense, waxy flesh makes them the best for potato salads and good in gratins and stews. They're also delicious steamed or roasted with garlic and herbs. They needn't be peeled, only scrubbed.

Russet Burbanks: These potatoes are some of the best bakers, yielding flaky white or golden flesh. They also make excellent fries and grated potato cakes.

Gold Rush, Yukon Gold, Caribes: These potatoes are good bakers too, but are also good in other roles, making them basically all-purpose potatoes. Caribes have a blush in the skin and deep eyes—a very pretty potato.

New Potatoes: Although they're often spoken of as if they were a variety, and even sold as such, all potatoes are new potatoes when they're dug, regardless of their size or type. This is when potatoes are most delicate and sweet. New potatoes are a summer vegetable. Their papery thin skins need only be scrubbed, and the potatoes are superb steamed over water laced with herbs.

WHAT TO LOOK FOR: Potatoes should be firm and have a sweet, earthy smell. Eyes are not a problem. Some of the tastiest varieties of potatoes have deep eyes from which the sprouts eventually appear. Simply cut them out with the tip of an old-fashioned potato peeler—that's what it's for. Sprouts indicate that the potato has started to grow; its texture is diminished, gradually turning soft and spongy.

HOW TO STORE: Keep potatoes in a cool, dark place, such as a loosely closed paper bag in a cupboard, away from onions. Moisture causes them to spoil, and light turns them green. Don't refrigerate and don't plan on keeping new potatoes for more than a few weeks.

HOW TO USE: Perhaps the most versatile of vegetables, potatoes can be used in soups, stews, salads, gratins, omelets, and baked goods; they can be pureed, fried, sautéed, baked, roasted, grilled, boiled, and mashed.

SPECIAL HANDLING: If potatoes show any greening, cut it away with a knife. It will nauseate you if you eat it, but the rest of the potato can be eaten safely.

QUANTITY: Peeled and sliced, 1 pound of potatoes yields about 2½ cups. Mashed, 1 pound yields a scant 2 cups. If potatoes are offered as a side dish, allow 1 pound for three or four servings; if they've been mashed, they may well serve only three since this form is so popular.

GOOD PARTNERS FOR
POTATOES
Butter, olive oil, cream,
   sour cream
Chervil, chives, basil,
   lovage, sage, rosemary,
   thyme
Mustard, sorrel, curry
   spices, saffron, pepper
Goat cheese, Cheddar,
   Cantal, Fontina,
   Gruyère
Tomatoes, greens,
   peppers, onions, garlic,
   leeks, root vegetables

WHICH POTATOES ARE FOR WHAT

Potato varieties not only differ in starch content, they also change once they're picked—growing more starchy as time passes. A chef friend of mine goes through seasonal agonies as his usually reliable Castle Rocks that he uses for French fries become less reliable for no apparent reason except time out of the ground. Potatoes can be baffling.

HIGH-STARCH POTATOES FOR BAKING AND FRYING:
Starchy potatoes have dry, mealy flesh. That's what makes a baked potato fluffy and a fried one light and crisp. If you boil a baking potato, it falls apart. Potato cakes are made from raw, shredded potatoes, and are held together by the starch. Some cooks don't like the sometimes gluey quality, so they rinse it off and rely on eggs instead to hold the shreds together. Good varieties for baking and frying are:

> Burbank russets (the Idaho potato) and all other russets
>
> Bintje, Castle Rock

LOW-STARCH BOILING POTATOES: Potatoes that boil well hold their shape, these are the ones to use in salads, stews, and gratins—they absorb liquids, dressings, and sauces without falling apart. They're waxy fleshed, moist, and dense, rather than powdery and dry. Some familiar boiling potatoes are:

> Red Bliss, Red Dale, and Norland (your supermarket boiling potatoes)
>
> Red Pontiac, Peruvian Purple, Purple Viking, All Blue
>
> Red La Soda, Yellow Finn, White Rose
>
> Rose Fir, Red Russian, Banana, and other fingerling types

ALL-PURPOSE POTATOES: The moderates fall somewhere in the middle, which makes them more or less adequate for all cooking methods. To mention a few: Katahdin, Kennebec, Superior.

A TEST TO TELL: If you're not sure what kind of potato you've got, slice one with a sharp knife. If the knife is covered with a foamy substance or the potato grabs onto the knife, then it's starchy and a baker. If not, it's a boiler. So-so, it's all-purpose.

SAUCES AND SEASONINGS FOR POTATOES
Romesco Sauce, page 70
Garlic Mayonnaise,
  page 59
Chile Butter, page 52
Sichuan Pepper Salt,
  page 76
Tomatillo Salsa, page 103
Pesto, page 57
Fresh Horseradish Sauce,
  page 72
Green Goddess Dressing,
  page 190
Chermoula, page 56

Steamed Potatoes A perfect treatment for tender new potatoes. Bring an inch of water to a boil in a saucepan. Scrub the potatoes and set them in a steaming basket over the water. Cover and steam until tender when pierced with a knife, 25 minutes or longer, depending on their size. Remove and toss with butter or extra virgin olive oil, salt, and freshly milled pepper.

Boiled Potatoes Put scrubbed or peeled potatoes in a saucepan, cover with cold water, and bring to a boil. Add a little salt, then lower the heat and simmer until the potatoes are tender when pierced with a skewer or knife, 15 to 30 minutes, depending on their size.

Broiled Potatoes Cut steamed or boiled potatoes lengthwise in half and score the tops with the tip of a knife. Brush them with oil or butter and broil, cut side facing the heat, until bubbling and browned. Remove and garnish with garden herbs, Golden Mustard Barbecue Sauce, page 74, or freshly milled pepper and sea salt.

Add herbs, garlic, and other aromatics to boiling or steaming water—their flavors will be taken up by the absorbent and neutral potatoes. To absorb moisture from cooked potatoes, cover them with a clean towel. Adding warm rather than cold liquid to mashed potatoes makes them light. When adding potatoes to hot oil, make sure they're absolutely dry so the oil doesn't spatter.

Mashed Potatoes

3 pounds russet or Yukon Gold potatoes, scrubbed

Salt and freshly milled pepper

4 to 8 tablespoons butter or olive oil

About 1 cup milk, cream, buttermilk, or cooking water, warmed

Pinch grated nutmeg

AN old adage says that starchier varieties make the lightest, fluffiest potatoes. In general this is true, although I've made divine mashed potatoes with spuds just one or two days from the field. The liquid that thins the potatoes can be the water they're cooked in, low-fat milk, whole milk, or cream. If you like a little tartness, try buttermilk. Leftovers are endlessly useful. Pipe them over a vegetable stew to make a shepherd's pie; form them into cakes and fry until golden on both sides; dilute them with water or stock to make a soup; or use them in bread and biscuits.

MAKES ABOUT 6 CUPS

Don't peel the potatoes—the peels give flavor to the cooking water. Put the potatoes in a large saucepan, cover with cold water, add 2 teaspoons salt, and boil until tender, 15 to 30 minutes depending on size. Remove the potatoes from the water, reserving the water for soup, bread, or thinning the potatoes. Holding the potatoes in a towel, peel them, then break them into chunks and mash with an old-fashioned potato masher, a handheld mixer, a food mill with large holes, or a ricer. (The food processor makes them gluey.) Beat in as much butter as you want to use—potatoes can absorb an infinite amount. Gradually beat in the warm liquid until the potatoes are smooth, moist, and light. Season with salt, pepper, and nutmeg. It's best to serve them right away, for they become stiff once cooled. If you must, hold them in a double boiler or a bowl set over a pan of simmering water and covered loosely with foil.

Saffron Mashed Potatoes: Crumble two hearty pinches saffron threads into a few tablespoons of warm cooking water and steep for 5 minutes. Add it to the potatoes along with the warm liquid.

Mashed Potatoes with Basil Puree: Serve mashed potatoes with Basil Puree, page 507, drizzled over them. Or just before serving, stir ½ cup puree into the potatoes, leaving it streaked with green.

Mashed Potatoes with Roasted Garlic: Roast one or two large heads of garlic until tender, page 377. Squeeze out the softened garlic and stir into the potatoes.

Mashed Potatoes with Herbs and Olive Oil: Add to the cooking water a bay leaf, a few slices onion, 6 thinly sliced garlic cloves, and several thyme sprigs. Peel and mash the potatoes, using olive oil in place of butter and thinning them with the reserved liquid. At the end, stir in 2 tablespoons chopped herbs—parsley, thyme, rosemary, or sage.

Mashed Potatoes with Root Vegetables: Replace half the potatoes with turnips, rutabagas, parnips, fennel, or celery root, and your mashed potatoes will have a lot more character. Peel and chop the vegetables into large pieces and cook together with the potatoes. Mash, using the cooking water, and finish with butter or olive oil.

Baked Potatoes

A baked potato is unthinkably easy and rather comforting. No wonder many people make a meal of one. Large Idaho russets are the ones to use for the classic baked potato. Buy organic ones if you like to eat the skin. Don't wrap your potato in foil—it creates steam by holding in the moisture. You want it to escape so that the finished potato will be fluffy and dry.

Preheat the oven to 425°F. If baking more than one, choose potatoes that are approximately the same size. Scrub them and pierce them in a few places with a fork or run a large "potato" nail through the middle, which will release steam and bring heat more quickly to the center. Bake until tender, about 1 hour, depending on the size. When it's done, slice the potato along its length and once crosswise in the middle. Push the ends together to open it up. Serve with any of the following:

Stuffed Baked Potatoes One of the least complicated and homiest suppers, but a step above a plain baked potato. Bake one russet potato per person. Slice the top third off the length of the potato and scoop out the inside from both pieces with a spoon, leaving the skin intact. Mash with milk, season with salt and pepper, and moisten with butter or olive oil; or mix with any of the sauces and seasonings for baked potatoes just listed. Return the filling to the potato skins and serve.

Potato Skins If you like them crisp and crunchy, snip the skins left from baked potatoes into wide strips, brush them with olive oil, season with salt and pepper, and bake at 425°F until crisp.

Grilled Potatoes Slice steamed or boiled potatoes in half if they're small, diagonally into pieces about ¹/₂ inch thick if large. Brush with olive or vegetable oil and grill, turning them 45 degrees after about 7 minutes. Cook on both sides or on just one. Season with salt and pepper and serve with Golden Mustard Barbecue Sauce, page 74, or any of the peanut sauces on page 69.

Roasted Potatoes

ONIONS, parsnips, celery root, turnips, and artichokes are also good roasted and can be cooked right alongside the potatoes. You can use any type of potato in this dish.

SERVES 4 TO 6

1 ¹/₂ **pounds potatoes, peeled and cut into chunks more or less the same size**

Olive oil
Salt and freshly milled pepper

Preheat the oven to 425°F. Toss the potatoes with enough oil to coat them lightly, 1 teaspoon salt, and a little pepper. Bake in a shallow pan in a single layer until tender when pierced with a knife, 25 to 40 minutes, depending on the size. Stir them a few times so that they brown evenly.

Roasted Potatoes with Garlic and Herbs

1½ pounds Yellow Finn, fingerling, or
   regular boiling potatoes

1 head fresh, firm garlic cloves,
   separated but unpeeled

2 tablespoons olive oil

4 teaspoons chopped rosemary or sage

2 bay leaves

4 thyme sprigs

Salt and freshly milled pepper

*THIS easy dish highlights
the special plain
goodness of potatoes.*

SERVES 4 TO 6

Scrub the potatoes well, then put them in a bowl of water with a few tablespoons salt and let stand for 15 minutes. Meanwhile, preheat the oven to 400°F and lightly oil a shallow baking dish. Drain the potatoes and pat dry with a towel. Toss them with the garlic, oil, and herbs, then season with salt and pepper. Arrange them in the prepared dish and bake, uncovered, until the potatoes are tender when pierced with a knife, 25 to 40 minutes, depending on their size. Turn them several times while they're cooking so that they brown evenly. Eat them with the softened cloves of garlic squeezed out of their paper cases.

Fingerlings with Slivered Garlic

3 tablespoons butter or olive oil, plus
   extra for the dish

1 pound fingerling or other potatoes,
   scrubbed and sliced lengthwise into
   halves or thirds

6 garlic cloves, thinly sliced

Salt and freshly milled pepper

*THESE potatoes end up
moist and succulent un-
less you continue baking
them once they're tender
—then they'll crisp on the
bottom, and that's
delicious too. These hold
their heat well in the
baking dish, so you can
bake them an hour or so
ahead of time and hold
them in the warm oven.*

SERVES 4

Preheat the oven to 400°F. Lightly butter a shallow baking dish. Layer the potatoes in the dish with the garlic and small pieces of butter or a drizzle of oil and season with salt and pepper. Make sure there's butter or oil for the top.

Add a few tablespoons water to the dish, then cover and bake until tender, 40 to 50 minutes. Remove the foil and bake for 15 minutes longer to brown the top.

Oven-Roasted French Fries These are irresistible. Preheat the oven to 450°F and lightly oil a cookie sheet. Peel two russet potatoes, then cut them into large batons or French fries. Toss with enough oil to coat them lightly, then set them on the pan in a single layer. Bake for 10 minutes and turn them over. Bake for 20 minutes more, turning them several times so that they color on all sides. When golden and tender, sprinkle with salt and serve piping hot. Accompany with spicy Romesco Sauce, page 70, with mayonnaise flavored with Harissa, page 75, or dust them with cayenne. Serves 4.

Roasted Potatoes and Root Vegetables

ROASTING vegetables requires little more than washing, peeling, and tossing them with olive oil and herbs. Medium-sized vegetables are best since they have the maturity needed for flavor yet are small enough to be tender. To ensure even cooking and browning, use a pan large enough to hold the vegetables in a single layer. Serve these showered with any of the herb salts, with fresh Horseradish Sauce, or balsamic vinegar.

SERVES 4 TO 6

2½ pounds mixed root vegetables—potatoes, carrots, turnips, parsnips, beets, sweet potatoes, small onions or whole shallots

1 head garlic, separated into cloves but unpeeled

Several short rosemary sprigs or 10 sage leaves

3 bay leaves

Olive oil

Salt and freshly milled pepper

Preheat the oven to 450°F. Peel the vegetables, onions, and shallots. Cut everything into pieces roughly the same size except for the parsnips, sweet potatoes, and turnips, which cook faster and can be slightly larger than the rest. Toss the vegetables, garlic, and herbs with oil to coat lightly, then season with salt and pepper. Put everything in a roomy pan. Bake, uncovered, in the top third of the oven for 20 minutes, shaking the pan once or twice. Reduce the heat to 375°F and continue baking until the vegetables are tender when pierced with a knife, 20 to 30 minutes, depending on how large they are. Remove the bay leaves. If using one of the herb salts or vinegar, sprinkle it over the vegetables as soon as they come out of the oven.

Golden Pan-Fried Potatoes

SERVES 4

1 pound red or white boiling potatoes

2 tablespoons clarified butter, olive oil, or vegetable oil

Salt and freshly milled pepper

Peel and thinly slice the potatoes. Heat the butter in a wide, heavy skillet—cast iron is fine—over high heat. Add the potatoes and fry without disturbing them until they begin to color on the bottom, about 5 minutes. Turn them over and fry on the second side until the potatoes are golden and tender, about 15 minutes in all. Season with salt and pepper and serve.

Potato Cakes

Many countries have their own potato cakes, all of which are made a little differently. The potatoes can be raw, boiled, or mashed; some are bound with eggs, others not. Other root vegetables sometimes join the potatoes, as do enrichments of herbs, garlic, and cheese. Virtually any kind of potato can be used, but if you use a high-starch potato—any of the russets, for example—rinse the cut potatoes in cold water to get rid of the bulk of the starch. Although some people say it's the starch that holds them together, I find that potato starch leaves an unpleasant texture. A rinse or two will leave sufficient starch to lightly bind the potatoes.

Latkes: Potato Pancakes with Eggs and Onions

2½ pounds russet potatoes, peeled

3 eggs or 1 egg and 2 egg whites, beaten

1 white onion, grated or very finely chopped

¼ cup flour, toasted bread crumbs, or cracker crumbs

Salt and freshly milled pepper

3 tablespoons clarified butter, vegetable oil, or a mixture

LATKES are the traditional food of Hanukkah but are loved year-round. They're as good for supper as for brunch, accompanied by sour cream and chilled applesauce or set on a nest of pungent salad greens.

SERVES 6 TO 8

Peel the potatoes and coarsely grate them by hand or in a food processor. Put them in a bowl of water as you work. When ready to cook, drain the potatoes and wrap them in a towel to squeeze out the excess water. Return the potatoes to the bowl and add the eggs, onion, flour, 2 teaspoons salt, and pepper to taste.

Preheat the oven to 200°F. Film a heavy skillet with some of the butter and set it over medium-high heat. When hot, drop in the batter by spoonfuls and cook over medium heat until browned, about 6 minutes. Repeat on the second side. Put the finished ones on a plate and keep them in the oven until all are done. Serve with sour cream and applesauce or sour cream covered with a sprinkling of snipped chives.

Straw Potato Cake

1½ to 2 pounds potatoes, peeled

3 to 4 tablespoons clarified butter, olive oil, or vegetable oil

Salt and freshly milled pepper

THESE irresistible crisp golden cakes can be made with russets, boilers, Yukon Golds, or Yellow Finns. Delicious on their own, they also make a beguiling base or accompaniment for a vegetable sauté.

SERVES 4 TO 6

Slice the potatoes into fine julienne strips by hand or on a mandoline or grate them on the large holes of a grater. If using high-starch potatoes, rinse them in cold water and towel-dry.

In a 10-inch cast-iron or nonstick skillet, melt half the butter over medium heat. When hot, add half the potatoes, making a layer about ½ inch thick. Season with salt and pepper, then cover with a second layer the same thickness. Neaten the edges, press down on the cake, and reduce the heat to low. Cook until the bottom is golden, 10 to 15 minutes. (The potatoes will become translucent as they cook.) Turn the potatoes onto a plate, add the remaining butter to the pan, and slide them back in. Cook until the second side is golden. Turn the cake onto a platter, cut into wedges, and serve.

Potato–Celery Root Cakes: Replace half the potato with peeled and finely grated celery root. Serve garnished with finely chopped celery leaves mixed with sliced scallions or chives. Grated parsley root and salsify also make excellent additions.

Stuffed Potato Cakes: Add half the potatoes to the pan, then cover with a layer of one or more of the following fillings. Season with salt and pepper, add the remaining potatoes, and cook as described.

Chopped thyme, marjoram, rosemary, or fried sage leaves
Grated raclette, Fontina, fresh mozzarella, Teleme, Cheddar
Snipped chives or sliced scallions
Sautéed Onions, page 395, or Caramelized Onions, page 396
Sautéed Mushrooms with Garlic and Parsley, page 388

Mashed Potato Cakes

HERE'S where leftovers come into their own. Serve these with apple-sauce, Sautéed Onions, and cooked greens or with fried eggs and salsa.

MAKES TWELVE 4-INCH CAKES

2½ cups Mashed Potatoes, page 409

1 cup dried bread crumbs or sesame seeds

Clarified butter or olive oil for frying

Shape the potatoes into 12 round or oval cakes about ¾ inch thick. Coat them with bread crumbs or sesame seeds and set on wax paper. Film a heavy skillet with some of the butter and set over medium heat. When hot, add the cakes and cook until golden, about 5 minutes. Turn and fry on the second side. Repeat until all are done.

Walnut and Potato Croquettes

THIS recipe was inspired by one I found in a 1913 cookbook. It was de-scribed as something to make when meat was scarce, but it's delicious in its own right. Go ahead and serve the croquettes with ketchup.

MAKES 10 TO 12, SERVING 4 TO 6

1½ tablespoons butter

½ cup grated onion

1 cup finely chopped walnuts

1 cup Mashed Potatoes, page 409

2 cups fresh bread crumbs

1 egg

Salt and freshly milled pepper to taste

1 tablespoon chopped sage, rosemary, or parsley

Vegetable oil and/or clarified butter for frying

Melt the butter in a small skillet, add the onion, and cook over medium heat until browned, stirring frequently. In a bowl, mix the onion, walnuts, potatoes, half the bread crumbs, and the egg. Season with 1 teaspoon salt, a little pepper, and the sage. Scoop up 2 heaping tablespoons of the mixture at a time and shape into an oval. Spread the re-maining bread crumbs on a plate and roll the croquettes in them to coat evenly.

Preheat the oven to 200°F. Heat ⅛ inch oil in a wide skillet and place over high heat. Add as many of the croquettes as will fit comfortably, reduce the heat to medium, and cook on both sides until golden, about 10 minutes in all. Remove them to paper towels and place in the oven while you finish frying the rest.

Comforting Stewed Potatoes

1 1/2 pounds mixed boiling and baking
   potatoes
8 scallions, including a few inches of
   the greens, chopped
2 to 3 tablespoons butter

Salt and freshly milled pepper
Water or milk
3 tablespoons chopped parsley

SOMETIMES *the plainest
foods are most satisfying.
Soft and almost soupy,
this is a dish to sup on
alone or with a close
friend. As good as it
tastes, it's not a dish for
company.*

SERVES 4

Peel the potatoes and cut them into 1/2-inch chunks. Put them in a heavy saucepan with the scallions and butter, 1 teaspoon salt, and enough water or milk to cover. Bring to a boil, then lower the heat and simmer, covered, until the potatoes are tender and the liquid has been absorbed, about 25 minutes. Taste and season with salt and pepper. Toss with the parsley and serve.

Steam-Roasted Potatoes

1 1/2 pounds small red potatoes, scrubbed
   well
3 tablespoons melted butter or olive oil

Salt and freshly milled pepper or one of
   the herb salts, pages 75 to 77
Chopped parsley or fines herbes

THESE *roasted potatoes
are creamy inside, crisp
on the outside. For best
results, use the small
golf-ball-sized red
potatoes sold as "new"
potatoes.*

SERVES 4 TO 6

Remove a band of skin around the middle of each potato and steam until tender but shy of being done when pierced with a knife, 15 to 20 minutes. Preheat the oven to 425°F. Put the potatoes in a baking dish and roll them around with enough butter or olive oil to coat lightly. Bake until the skin is golden brown, about 40 minutes, giving the pan a shake a couple of times so the potatoes will brown evenly. Season with salt and pepper and roll them around in the chopped parsley.

Potatoes Baked in Salt

2 pounds kosher or coarse sea salt
1 1/2 pounds fingerling or small round
   potatoes, scrubbed

Several rosemary sprigs

THE *salt leaves a distinct
film of flavor but doesn't
make the potatoes salty.
Select potatoes that are
the same size, on the
small side, and leave
them whole. The salt can
be reused many times—
and you'll want to, these
are so good.*

SERVES 4

Preheat the oven to 400°F. Make a base of salt about 1 inch deep in a Dutch oven or other baking dish large enough to hold the potatoes in a single layer. Set the potatoes and rosemary on the salt and add more salt to cover. Bake until the potatoes can be pierced easily with a knife, about 35 minutes. Keep the potatoes embedded in the salt until ready to serve, then scrape away the top layer and gently pull them out.

Radishes

THERE are several different types of radishes—the round red ones, long French breakfast radishes, multicolored Easter egg radishes, Spanish black radishes, snowy Icicle radishes, and giant Asian daikon. While all are usually eaten raw, they can also be braised.

Braised Red Radishes

SERVES 4

20 plump radishes, red or multicolored
1 to 2 tablespoons butter
1 shallot, diced

1 teaspoon chopped thyme or several pinches dried
Salt and freshly milled pepper

Trim the leaves from the radishes, leaving a bit of the green stems, and scrub them. If the leaves are tender and in good condition, wash them and set aside. Leave smaller radishes whole and halve or quarter larger ones.

Melt 2 to 3 teaspoons butter in a small sauté pan. Add the shallot and thyme and cook for 1 minute over medium heat. Add the radishes, a little salt and pepper, and water just to cover. Simmer until the radishes are tender, 3 to 5 minutes. Add the leaves if using and cook until they're wilted and tender, 1 minute more. Remove the radishes to a serving dish. Boil the liquid, adding a teaspoon or two more butter if you like, until only about ¼ cup remains. Pour it over the radishes and serve.

ALSO *known as oyster plant because of a supposed similarity to oysters, salsify is an old-fashioned root vegetable that's enjoying a minor comeback thanks to some adventurous farmers. The long, thin roots are not, to my taste, particularly oysterlike, but they are subtle and delicious, more nutty than sweet. Salsify browns the moment it's peeled, so have a bowl of water mixed with plenty of lemon juice right next to you as you work. Once it's peeled and cut, boil salsify for about 20 minutes, then dress it with butter, brown butter, or cream or with lemon, shallots, and parsley. There's a bit of waste in the peelings, so 1 pound provides only three to four small servings.*

Salsify with Shallots and Parsley

Juice of 2 lemons
1 pound salsify
1 tablespoon flour
Salt and freshly milled pepper

1 large shallot, finely diced
2 tablespoons butter
Chopped parsley

SERVES 3 TO 4

Set aside ¹/₂ lemon and squeeze the juice from the rest into a bowl. Peel the roots one at a time and cut into desired lengths or julienne strips. Quickly put the finished pieces in the lemon juice and add water, as needed, to cover. Bring 2 quarts water to a boil in a saucepan and add the juice of the remaining ¹/₂ lemon, the flour, and 2 teaspoons salt. Drain the salsify, add it to the pot, and boil until tender when pierced with a knife, 15 to 25 minutes. Drain again.

Cook the shallot in the butter in a medium skillet for a few minutes, then add the salsify and cook until golden, about 5 minutes more. Toss with parsley and season with salt and pepper.

Spinach

SPINACH has so many things going for it—it's delicious, it's readily available, it's easy to prepare, and it can be used in myriad ways. Spinach can be used interchangeably with beet greens, chard, and other spinachlike plants, such as New Zealand spinach, orach, amaranth, and so on. I have no trouble using several bunches a week.

GOOD PARTNERS FOR
SPINACH

*Butter, cream, olive oil,
    dark sesame oil*
*Red pepper flakes, garlic,
    parsley, dill, basil,
    curry, nutmeg*
*Lentils, onions, chickpeas,
    mushrooms, pine nuts*
Yogurt

TYPES OF SPINACH: The three basic types of spinach are the dark green, crinkled varieties, such as Bloomsdale; the pointed, smooth-leafed kind we see often in bunches in supermarkets; and some broader round-leafed types.

WHAT TO LOOK FOR: Look for whole leaves that are dark green, free of yellowed spots and bruises. (Bruises have a watery, dark appearance.) For salads, small tender leaves are choice, but larger ones will do as long as they aren't tough. You can tell by looking at the stems—if they're thick, the plant has been in the ground a while and that spinach is best for cooking.

HOW TO STORE: Stored dry in a plastic bag in the vegetable bin, spinach should keep for 3 to 4 days. Never store spinach wet.

HOW TO USE: Spinach is used in salads, as a cooked vegetable, and as a filling for pasta, crêpes, cannelloni, omelets, and other foods like soufflés and savory pies. It makes delicious soup or an addition to soup, and its lustrous color sets off some of the duller-looking legumes. Discard the long stems, which are hard to eat. The crowns, which are the last few inches of stems joined at the root, are edible and quite good eating. Steam or blanch them.

SPECIAL HANDLING: Take special care in washing spinach. It's grown in fine sandy soil, which is invariably splashed on the leaves. It's not always visible, so test a leaf by taking a bite. After discarding the stems, sort through the leaves and discard any that are yellowed or show excessive bruising. Never cook spinach in aluminum; it ruins its color and taste.

QUANTITY: Allow one bunch of spinach, weighing a scant pound, for two servings. It takes 1 to 1½ pounds spinach leaves for 1 cup cooked.

Cooked Spinach
This is the best way to cook spinach greens that will be seasoned afterward or used in another dish. Remove the stems and wash the leaves, but don't dry them. Put the leaves directly into a large skillet with the water still clinging to the leaves. Add a few pinches of salt and cook over high heat, turning occasionally until the leaves are wilted and bright green, about 3 to 5 minutes. If the spinach is to be used later, rinse under cold water to stop the cooking. Before using, gently squeeze out the excess moisture. If it's to be used right away, simply drain it, shake off the excess water, then transfer it to a skillet and season according to one of the recipes that follow.

Spinach with Sesame Oil and Toasted Sesame Seeds
Blanch two bunches trimmed and washed spinach leaves in boiling salted water. Drain, then toss with 1 tablespoon dark sesame oil and a few drops rice vinegar to taste. Season with salt and toss again with 1 tablespoon toasted sesame seeds. Serves 4.

Buttered Spinach

1 large bunch spinach, cooked until tender

2 to 6 tablespoons butter, cut into pieces

Salt and freshly milled pepper

Grated nutmeg

Once the spinach is wilted, add the butter and begin picking up the spinach with tongs until the butter melts and coats the leaves. Season with salt, pepper, and a small grating of nutmeg.

BUTTER and spinach seem to be made for each other—a generous coating makes spinach unbelievably silky. But how much butter to use I leave to you. Piled on an English muffin or a Garlic-Rubbed Crouton, this makes a simple supper for two.

SERVES 2

Sautéed Spinach

2 tablespoons olive oil or butter

1 garlic clove, thinly sliced

1 large bunch spinach, stems removed, leaves washed but not dried

Salt and freshly milled pepper

A DISH in itself, this is also another basic way to cook spinach.

SERVES 2 TO 3

Heat the oil in a wide skillet with the garlic. Cook over medium-high heat until the garlic turns light gold, then add the spinach, salt it lightly, and cook until bright green and limp, just a few minutes. Move the leaves around the pan, picking them up and turning them over as they cook. Season with pepper and serve.

Spinach with Croutons: If your spinach eaters are wary of its silky texture, toss buttered or sautéed spinach with small croutons sautéed in olive oil or butter until crisp or simply crisped in the oven.

Spinach with Mushrooms: Or call it mushrooms with spinach—it's about equal amounts of each and exquisite in either case. See the recipe on page 390.

Creamed Spinach with Toast

1/4 to 1/2 cup cream

1 garlic clove, smashed

1 large bunch spinach, preferably small leaves, stems removed

2 teaspoons butter

Salt and freshly milled white pepper

Grated nutmeg

2 pieces of thin white or wheat toast, cut into triangles, or toasted levain bread

THIS smooth and soothing old-fashioned dish is one to enjoy once in a while. Use any leftover spinach in an omelet or scrambled eggs.

SERVES 2

Heat the cream with the garlic until fine bubbles form on the surface, then turn off the heat and set aside. Cook the spinach as described on page 418. Rinse, then squeeze out the excess water and finely chop. Melt the butter in a skillet, add the spinach, and cook until the pan is dry. Pour the cream through a strainer directly into the pan and simmer until it thickens slightly. Taste for salt and season with pepper and a few scrapings of nutmeg. Set the toast on plates and mound the spinach over them.

Spinach or Chard Catalan Style

RAISINS and pine nuts are what make this side dish Catalan, but the same ingredients appear in the south of France and Italy—parts of the same culinary world.

SERVES 4

2 bunches spinach or 1 large bunch chard, stems removed, leaves blanched

2 tablespoons olive oil

1 large garlic clove, sliced

⅓ cup dark or golden raisins

⅓ cup pine nuts

Salt and freshly milled pepper

Coarsely chop the cooked spinach. Warm the oil with the garlic in a wide skillet over medium heat. When the garlic is golden, remove it. Add the raisins and pine nuts and cook until the raisins are plumped and the pine nuts are golden. Add the greens and cook until they're heated through. Season with salt and pepper to taste.

Sautéed Spinach with Garlic and Red Pepper

MOST greens taste great cooked in this Roman style.

SERVES 4

2 tablespoons olive oil

2 garlic cloves, chopped

2 pinches red pepper flakes

2 bunches tender spinach, stems removed, leaves blanched

Salt

Juice of ½ lemon or a few teaspoons red wine vinegar

Heat the oil with the garlic and pepper flakes in a wide skillet over medium-high heat until the garlic begins to color. Add the cooked spinach and toss to coat it with the oil. Add ½ cup water and cook until it's absorbed and the greens are heated through. Season with salt and a little lemon juice or vinegar.

Spinach or Chard with Scallions, Parsley, and Dill

SERVES 4

2 bunches spinach or chard, stems removed, leaves blanched

2½ tablespoons olive oil

2 bunches scallions, including 2 inches of the greens, sliced

3 tablespoons chopped parsley

3 tablespoons chopped dill

Salt and freshly milled pepper

Coarsely chop the blanched spinach or chard. Warm the oil in a wide skillet over medium heat, then add the scallions and herbs. Cook gently until wilted and fragrant, then add the spinach and continue cooking until it's heated through. Season with salt and pepper.

Summer Squash

SUMMER squashes are thin skinned, tender, quick cooking, and versatile—a staple vegetable in the summer kitchen. With tender young squash the simplest preparations are sufficient. Don't be afraid to really cook summer squash. Brief cooking preserves its texture, but longer cooking brings out much more of its good squash flavor.

TYPES OF SUMMER SQUASH: Small to medium squash are always preferable, for large ones tend to be seedy, watery, and altogether less flavorful.

> **Zucchini:** Long, straight, and cylindrical, zucchini are dark green, light green, variegated, or bright yellow-gold.
>
> **Round Zucchini:** Green skin streaked with white and paler green flesh. The French variety Ronde de Nice is good up to about 6 inches in diameter. Calabacitas, a type of squash native to the Southwest, is light green and white striped.
>
> **Scallop or Pattypan Squash:** Shaped like a flying saucer with a scalloped edge running around the equator, scallop and pattypan squash come golden, pale green, dark green, and garishly splashed with green and gold. After a long absence, these pretty delectable squash are making a comeback.
>
> **Yellow Crookneck or Gooseneck:** Named for its crook-shaped neck, this summer squash usually has large seeds but also one of the best squash flavors. Some varieties have taken the crook out of the neck, and some have a warty appearance, but all are quite tasty.

WHAT TO LOOK FOR: Freshly picked summer squash have bright, shiny skins. Look for firm, glossy-looking vegetables, small to moderate in size.

HOW TO STORE: Store summer squash in a perforated plastic bag in the vegetable bin or in a large plastic container covered with a towel and then with a lid. This way they'll keep well for 4 to 5 days. Don't let moisture bead up on squash.

HOW TO USE: Use summer squash in stir-fries, sautés, stuffed, grilled, in frittatas, soups, pastas, timbales, and summer stews. Zucchini, always overabundant in the garden, has been known to find its way into baked goods and desserts.

SPECIAL HANDLING: Salting, an optional step, improves texture and flavor by removing excess water. Toss coarsely grated or diced squash with a small amount of salt, let it

GOOD PARTNERS FOR SUMMER SQUASH
Olive oil, butter, yogurt
Parmesan, Gruyère, goat cheese
Garlic, parsley, basil, marjoram, thyme, dill, mint, lemon
Walnuts, pine nuts,
Tomatoes, corn, peppers, eggplant, chile

SAUCES AND SEASONINGS
FOR SUMMER SQUASH
Blossom Butter, page 51
Olive-Rosemary Butter,
  page 51
Salsa Verde, Chermoula,
  Cilantro Salsa, or
  Pesto, pages 55 to 56
Parsley-Caper Sauce,
  page 56
Lemon Vinaigrette,
  page 184
Yogurt Sauces, pages 65
  to 66
Walnut Sauce, page 68
Fresh Tomato Sauce,
  page 61
Tarator Sauce, page 67

stand in a colander for 15 to 30 minutes, then rinse and squeeze dry. It's amazing how much liquid is exuded and how much more concentrated the final squash flavor is.

QUANTITY: An average zucchini, about 6 inches long, weighs between 4 and 6 ounces. Allow 1½ pounds for four generous servings. One pound of squash yields approximately 4 cups grated, shrinking to 2 cups if salted—or about 3½ cups diced or sliced.

Steamed Squash Slice 1½ pounds squash and steam until tender, 5 to 8 minutes, depending on size. When cooked, it will take on a shiny, translucent look. Toss with butter or olive oil and chopped fresh herbs and season with salt and pepper. Serves 4 to 6.

Boiled Squash Drop diced, sliced, or chopped squash into a large pot of boiling salted water and boil until tender, 3 to 5 minutes, depending on size. Drain, shake off the excess water, toss with butter or oil, and season with salt and pepper.

Grilled Summer Squash Slice zucchini lengthwise into thirds or halves. Brush each side with olive oil and season with salt. Grill on both sides until browned, turning 45 degrees once. Arrange on a platter and brush with any of the sauces suggested for squash, especially Yogurt Sauce with Cayenne and Dill, page 66.

Crookneck Squash with Scallions

SERVES 4 TO 6

2 pounds small crookneck squash

2 tablespoons olive oil, butter, or a mixture

8 scallions, including some of the greens, thinly sliced

Salt and freshly milled pepper

Halve the squash lengthwise and leave whole if very small or if larger slice into ½-inch-thick rounds or diagonals. Heat the oil in a wide skillet, add the squash, and sauté over high heat until lightly colored around the edges, about 4 minutes. Add the scallions and 2 tablespoons water, then lower the heat, cover, and cook until the squash is fully tender, 6 to 7 minutes. Season with salt and pepper to taste.

Sautéed Zucchini with Garlic and Lemon

SERVES 4 TO 6

2 tablespoons olive oil

2 garlic cloves, sliced

1½ pounds zucchini, thinly sliced or diced into small cubes

Salt and freshly milled pepper

2 teaspoons finely grated lemon zest

2 tablespoons chopped herbs, such as dill, marjoram, and basil

Heat the oil in a wide skillet, add the garlic, and cook over medium heat until it begins to color. Raise the heat, add the zucchini, and sauté until heated through. Lower the heat and continue to cook, turning occasionally, until tender and golden around the edges, 8 to 10 minutes. Season with salt and pepper, toss with the lemon and herbs, and serve.

Zucchini Matchsticks with Yogurt Sauce

1 ½ pounds zucchini
Salt

2 tablespoons olive oil
½ cup Yogurt Sauce with Cayenne and
    Dill, page 66

Trim the ends of the zucchini, slice each one crosswise in half, then into long slabs about ⅓ inch thick. Angling your knife, cut the slabs into strips, also ⅓ inch wide. Toss them with 1 ½ teaspoons salt, set them in a colander, and let stand for 30 minutes. Rinse and pat dry. Meanwhile, prepare the sauce. Heat the olive oil in a wide skillet, add the zucchini, and sauté over high heat until lightly browned in places, about 5 minutes. (If you prefer to avoid the oil, steam the zucchini instead.) Turn into a bowl and serve the sauce spooned over the top.

EACH of these large, bold batons is tipped with green. Yogurt Sauce with Cayenne and Dill is excellent here. If you shred the zucchini instead of cutting it, you get more of a "hash." It's not as pretty, but the flavors are better amalgamated, and it makes a great filling for a crêpe or omelet.

SERVES 4

Slow-Cooked Zucchini Coins with Chopped Herbs and Crumbled Feta

2 to 3 tablespoons olive oil or butter
1 ½ pounds zucchini, thinly sliced
1 garlic clove, thinly sliced
Salt and freshly milled pepper

¼ cup chopped mixed herbs—dill, basil,
    parsley, and cilantro
½ cup crumbled feta

Heat the oil in a wide skillet, then add the zucchini and garlic. Sprinkle lightly with salt and cook over low heat for 20 to 30 minutes, stirring every so often. The finished squash should have a light golden glaze over the surface and be caramelized in places. Taste for salt and season with pepper. Toss with the herbs and cheese and serve.

A RELAXED, slow cooking brings out the zucchini's full squash flavor, which quick cooking eclipses. Serve these golden coins as a side dish, over hot rice, or with pasta.

SERVES 4 TO 6

Crosshatched Zucchini An attractive way to present tender young squash as well as small eggplants. Cut squash lengthwise in half. Using the tip of a small knife, score the cut surfaces in a crisscross pattern without cutting through the skin. Brush lightly with olive oil and season with salt and pepper. Heat a cast-iron skillet over medium-high heat, then brush a film of olive oil over the surface. Set the zucchini cut side down in a single layer and cook until golden. Turn, add a few tablespoons water to create a little steam, and cook on the second side until tender when pierced with a knife. Serve cut side up with a wedge of lemon, Harissa thinned with water, page 75, Tomato-Basil Pesto, page 57, or any of the sauces suggested for summer squash on page 422.

Whole Flowering Zucchini You may come across young squash attached to their blossoms hidden in your own vines or brought to the farmers' market by an enterprising grower. Although the flowers suggest stuffing, here's another way. Allowing three or four squash per person, separate the flowers and cut them into strips. Slice the squash lengthwise into halves or thirds. Heat a little olive oil in a wide skillet, add the squash, and sauté over high heat. As soon as it begins to color and soften, add the flowers, a splash of water, and cover for 30 seconds. Season with salt and pepper to taste and scatter finely chopped basil over the top. Serve warm as an appetizer or as a garnish for an omelet, a vegetable custard, or a rice gratin.

Zucchini and Fresh Herb Fritters

SIMPLY delicious! Serve plain or with a yogurt sauce, Salsa Verde, or a dollop of Garlic or Green Chile Mayonnaise. (For a vegan version, replace the eggs with ¹/₂ cup pureed silken tofu.)

SERVES 4

Salt and freshly milled pepper

2 pounds green or golden zucchini, coarsely grated

2 eggs, beaten

1 bunch scallions, including an inch of the greens, thinly sliced

1 cup dried bread crumbs

2 garlic cloves, finely chopped

¹/₂ cup chopped parsley

1 tablespoon chopped marjoram or basil

1 teaspoon chopped mint

Olive oil as needed

Lightly salt the zucchini and set it aside in a colander to drain for 30 minutes. Meanwhile, mix the remaining ingredients together except the oil and pepper. Quickly rinse the squash, squeeze out the excess water, then stir it into the batter. Taste for salt and season with pepper.

Film two large skillets with olive oil. When hot, drop in the batter—¹/₄ cup makes a fritter about 3¹/₂ inches across—and cook over medium heat until golden on the bottom. Turn and cook the second side. Serve hot.

Squash Fans on an Onion Bed

¼ cup olive oil

1 large red or yellow onion, thinly sliced

2 bell peppers, 1 red and 1 yellow, thinly sliced

1 teaspoon chopped thyme or several thyme sprigs

2 bay leaves

1 tablespoon chopped marjoram

1 cup dry white wine

Salt and freshly milled pepper

2 short, fat zucchini, calabacitas, or Ronde de Nice

2 plump Asian or Italian eggplants, 5 to 7 inches long

4 tomatoes, halved and sliced crosswise ⅜ inch thick

12 Niçoise olives, pitted

4 garlic cloves, thinly slivered

Heat 2 tablespoons of the oil in a large skillet over medium heat. Add the onion, peppers, and herbs and cook, stirring occasionally, until lightly browned, 8 to 10 minutes. Add ½ cup wine, simmer for 5 minutes, then season with ½ teaspoon salt and plenty of pepper. Put the onion mixture in a baking dish large enough to hold the vegetables in a single layer.

While the onions are cooking, slice the zucchini and eggplants lengthwise in half. Placing the cut side on the counter, make two incisions starting about ½ inch below the stem end, dividing the vegetable lengthwise into three even pieces. Work the tomatoes into the spaces and stuff the empty spots with olives and slivers of garlic. (Add any leftover tomato, olives, or garlic to the onions.) Run two toothpicks through the end of each vegetable to hold everything together, then set the stuffed vegetables on the onions. Brush with the remaining oil and pour the rest of the wine over all.

Preheat the oven to 400°F. Cover the dish with foil and bake until the vegetables are tender when pierced with a knife, about 45 minutes for the squash, slightly longer for the eggplant. Serve warm or tepid with the onions and peppers.

INSPIRED by a recipe of Richard Olney's, fanning and stuffing the interstices of short, fat summer squash and plump eggplant gives these vegetables drama. And a mixture of squash and eggplant looks particularly nice. Measurements are relaxed and variable. While I have sometimes used only garlic for the filling, sautéed artichoke hearts, ricotta salata, or Olive Paste can also be tucked inside the crevices.

SERVES 4 OR 8

Broiled Zucchini Stuffed with Gruyère and Feta

THIS is quick, easy, and makes a nice presentation for a first course or light main dish.

SERVES 4

4 medium zucchini, about 6 ounces each

2 teaspoons butter

Salt and freshly milled pepper

1/3 cup feta

1/4 cup cottage cheese or ricotta

1/4 cup grated Gruyère

1 egg

1 tablespoon chopped parsley

2 teaspoons chopped marjoram

1 teaspoon flour

Preheat the broiler. Lightly oil a baking dish large enough to hold the squash in a single layer. Prepare the zucchini for stuffing, halving each one and scooping out the flesh. Finely chop the flesh and cook it in the butter in a skillet, stirring frequently, until browned in places. Season with salt and combine with the remaining ingredients.

Fill the zucchini and set them side by side in the prepared baking dish. Broil about 6 inches from the heat until the filling is browned and heated through, about 20 minutes.

Zucchini with Corn and Squash Filling

THE round summer squash are perfect containers for this filling. Otherwise, use zucchini.

SERVES 4

4 calabacitas, Ronde de Nice, or zucchini, about 6 ounces each

1 cup finely diced zucchini

2 teaspoons butter or corn oil

Kernels from 2 ears corn, about 1 1/2 cups

1 cup cooked quinoa or rice

2 tablespoons grated Muenster

4 scallions, including some of the greens, thinly sliced

1 jalapeño chile, seeded and minced

2 tablespoons chopped cilantro, parsley, or basil

Salt

Preheat the oven to 375°F. Prepare the squash for stuffing, slicing off the top third for a lid. Sauté the diced zucchini in the butter in a skillet over high heat until tender, about 4 minutes. Mix with the remaining ingredients, seasoning with salt to taste. Fill the squash, replace the tops, and set in a baking dish. Add water to come about 1/4 inch up the sides of the dish and cover with aluminum foil. Bake until tender when pierced with a knife, about 25 minutes.

STUFFED SUMMER SQUASH

First boil whole squash for 5 minutes to soften, then rinse under cold water. Halve zucchini lengthwise and scoop out the centers with a pointed spoon. Or slice off the top third and scoop out the flesh of the larger bottom piece. Use it, with or without the lid, as a zucchini "boat." Pattypan or scallop squash can be treated the same way. Always leave the shell at least 1/3 inch thick so that it's strong enough to hold its shape. Use the flesh that's been removed in the stuffing or in a soup stock.

Scallop Squash with Saffron Rice

6 scallop or pattypan squash, 6 to 8
  ounces each

Pinch saffron threads steeped in 1
  tablespoon boiling water

¾ cup cooked long-grain white rice

3 scallions, including some of the
  greens, thinly sliced

3 tablespoons finely diced mozzarella,
  preferably fresh

3 tablespoons chopped basil leaves or
  Pesto, page 57

1 teaspoon grated lemon zest

Salt and freshly milled pepper, to taste

THE bright yellow Sunburst variety makes particularly pretty containers. Make sure they can stand firmly— slice a little piece off the bottom if necessary. Serve with a fresh or roasted tomato sauce.

SERVES 6

Preheat the oven to 375°F. Prepare the squash for stuffing as described on page 425. Rinse, then slice off ½ inch or so from the top and set it aside. Hollow out the insides of the squash and chop the flesh. Add the saffron to the rice and add the remaining ingredients, including the chopped squash, seasoning well with salt and pepper. Fill the squash and replace the lids. Set in a baking dish, pour water into the dish to come about ¼ inch up the sides of the dish, then cover with foil and bake until the squash feels tender, about 25 minutes.

Sweet Potatoes

WE have long been in the habit of calling sweet potatoes yams, although the true yam, a tropical vegetable, is seldom seen outside of Latin markets. What we call yams at the supermarket are, in fact, the paler, drier-fleshed sweet potatoes. Regardless of what we call them, what we mean are delectable sweet-fleshed tubers.

TYPES OF SWEET POTATOES: Sweet potatoes come with light tan, orange, and purple skins. Their flesh ranges from pale buff to dark, rich orange. In general, the darker the flesh, the sweeter and moister it is once cooked.

> **Garnet and Jewel:** Two new varieties, often found labeled with their names. Both have deep orange-red skins and flesh and tend to be on the small side.

> **Louisiana:** Sweet, moist-fleshed sweet potatoes—the standard.

> **Jersey:** Light-colored sweet potatoes that tend to be on the dry side. Sometimes they resemble chestnuts in flavor.

WHAT TO LOOK FOR: Firm roots with pointed ends and no bruises. Although sweet potatoes look tough, they're actually easily damaged. Bruises result from even minimal rough handling. Once bruised, spoilage quickly spreads below the surface and ruins the entire vegetable.

HOW TO STORE: In spite of their sturdy appearance, sweet potatoes are not terribly good keepers, so plan to use them within a week of purchase. Your grocery is better equipped for longer storage than your home. Keep them in a cool cupboard, if you have one, or on the counter. They *can* be refrigerated in a perforated plastic bag, but they don't love the cold and they mustn't freeze.

*Butter, dark sesame and
roasted peanut oil
Ginger, allspice, orange,
chile, nutmeg,
cinnamon
Brown sugar, molasses,
maple syrup, bourbon,
pecans, black walnuts*

HOW TO USE: Sweet potatoes are delicious simply baked or steamed and served in their jackets or in the traditional candied versions served during the holidays. They make excellent purees that can also be used in savory and sweet foods, from custards and pies to breads and waffles, and are good roasted and grilled.

SPECIAL HANDLING: Scrub well before cooking. If you want to eat the skins, look for organically grown sweet potatoes. Once peeled and sliced, put them in a bowl of water to prevent oxidation if you aren't planning to cook them for a while—lemon isn't necessary. Sweet potatoes don't have enough starch to behave the same way regular potatoes do, so they're not really interchangeable with potatoes unless you use some of both.

QUANTITY: Sweet potatoes can weigh as little as 4 ounces or as much as 1 pound. A pound yields 3 to 4 cups chopped or about 1⅓ cups mashed. Allow at least 4 ounces for a serving.

Baked Sweet Potatoes Nearly every time I bite into a roasted sweet potato, I ask myself if anything can be more delicious. With a spinach salad, a roasted sweet potato makes an easy dinner that's rich in green and yellow vegetables. Preheat the oven to 400°F. Choose sweet potatoes of similar size if cooking more than one. Scrub well and bake until very tender when pierced, 50 to 60 minutes for a 12-ounce potato. To serve, slice lengthwise, break up the flesh with a fork, and add the traditional pat of butter, Chile Butter, page 52, or even a little dark sesame oil. Season with salt and pepper.

Steamed Sweet Potatoes Scrub sweet potatoes and leave them whole or cut them into large pieces. Steam, covered, over boiling water until tender when pierced with a knife, 30 to 50 minutes, depending on size.

Grilled Sweet Potatoes Slice steamed or boiled potatoes in half if they're small or diagonally into ½-inch-thick pieces if large. Brush with vegetable oil and grill, turning them 45 degrees after about 7 minutes. Cook on both sides or just one. Season with salt and pepper and serve with Golden Mustard Barbecue Sauce, page 74, and Thai Peanut Sauce, page 69.

Boiled Sweet Potatoes For best results, leave unpeeled potatoes whole. If cut into chunks before cooking, they tend to become waterlogged. Cover with cold water and bring to a boil. Lower the heat and simmer until tender when pierced with a knife. Peel once cooked. Slice or mash and serve with butter, salt, and pepper.

Sweet Potatoes in the Pressure Cooker Put scrubbed whole sweet potatoes on a steaming rack in a pressure cooker, add ½ inch water, lock on the lid, and bring to pressure. Maintain on high 12 minutes for an 8-ounce potato, 25 minutes for 14 ounces, then quickly release the pressure. Pierce the potato with a knife at the thickest spot. If it's not fully tender, either return to pressure for 2 minutes and check again or loosely cover and steam until done.

Mashed Sweet Potatoes Leaving their skins on or not as you wish, mash 2 pounds baked, boiled, or steamed sweet potatoes with 1 teaspoon grated orange or tangerine zest, the juice of an orange or tangerine, and butter to taste. Season well with salt and pepper and serve. Or try using any of these traditional seasonings: bits of pineapple, candied ginger, toasted pecans or black walnuts, bourbon, a few pinches nutmeg or cinnamon, allspice, and cloves. (Leftovers can be used in Sweet Potato Muffins with Candied Ginger, page 644, or waffles.) Serves 4 to 6.

Mashed Sweet Potatoes with Ginger and Sesame Boil 2 pounds whole sweet potatoes with five slices ginger until completely soft. Discard the ginger, peel the potatoes, and puree or pass through a food mill. Season with salt. Stir in 1 teaspoon ground coriander, butter, or dark sesame oil to taste. Heap in a bowl and garnish with toasted black sesame seeds. Serves 4 to 6.

Broiled Sweet Potatoes Slice cooked sweet potatoes lengthwise in half or into diagonals $1/2$ inch thick, allowing one or two halves per person. Brush lightly with vegetable oil and broil until sizzling. Serve with salt and pepper or with a peanut sauce, pages 69 to 70, Sesame Marinade, page 604, or Golden Mustard Barbecue Sauce, page 74.

Candied Sweet Potatoes

$3^1/2$ **pounds sweet potatoes, scrubbed**

1-inch knob of ginger, peeled and thinly sliced, optional

6 tablespoons butter

Salt and freshly milled pepper

$1/3$ **cup maple syrup or dark brown sugar**

$1/2$ **cup apple juice or water**

THESE are still a holiday favorite and are even better the next day with leftover cold cranberries. Use your favorite type of sweet potato or mix all varieties in a single dish.

SERVES A HOLIDAY CROWD

Boil the potatoes until tender but still slightly firm when pierced with a knife. Drain. When cool enough to handle, remove the skins. Cut them lengthwise into slices about $3/8$ inch thick.

Preheat the oven to 375°F. Butter a large, shallow casserole and make a layer of potatoes. Scatter a few ginger slices over them, dot with butter, season with salt and pepper, and drizzle some of the syrup on top. Repeat until all the potatoes are used. Dot the last layer with butter and pour in the juice. Cover with aluminum foil and bake for 1 hour. If the oven is being used for other things and is set at a lower temperature, simply bake them longer.

Tomatoes

PEOPLE *are passionate about tomatoes, one of the true joys of summer. Good tomatoes require conditions oppo-site to commercial needs—hand-picked, vine-ripened fruits grown from seeds that predict flavor rather than ship-ping capabilities—which is why they're so hard to come by in the supermarket. There are, however, some rare exceptions. An organic cooperative in Baja, Mexico, imports scrumptiously sweet cherry tomatoes that satisfy tomato lust in spring, long before our tomato seasons begin in middle to late summer. The general rule, though, is that tomatoes are best when they're grown locally, in season, and picked when ripe.*

GOOD PARTNERS FOR TOMATOES
Butter, olive oil, cream
Parmesan, mozzarella, Cheddar, goat cheese
Basil, parsley, tarragon, lovage, chives, oregano, garlic
Vinegar of all kinds
Peppers, squash, eggplant, legumes, corn, shallots

TYPES OF TOMATOES: It's hard to keep up with all the exciting heirloom and new hy-brid tomato varieties that are introduced each year, but here are some types we're most likely to see. Curiously, many are named after fruits.

Plum and Roma Tomatoes: In some parts of the country these tomatoes are known as *Romas*, in other parts *plum tomatoes*. But by either name they are oval, 3 to 4 inches long, thick fleshed, and dry rather than juicy. Since there's little juice to cook off, they are particularly suitable for sauces and are called for in recipes where meatiness, rather than juiciness, is desired.

Pear and Cherry Tomatoes: Pear-shaped and small spheres, red or yellow, these petite tomatoes are charming on a crudité plate or in a composed salad. Cherry tomatoes were once mostly one size—about the size of a cherry—but now these include the tiny currant tomatoes as well as more standard varieties. They can be made into sauces and sautéed, as well as nibbled raw.

Slicing Tomatoes: This is your classic tomato. Marmande is a French variety that's bright red, round, and full of flavor—the essence of tomato. Early Boy and Early Girl are two standard American varieties that are also round, red, and juicy. In between are a host of unusual heirloom varieties with exotic colors, markings, and shapes—folds, creases, and pleats—that delight the eye and in no way compromise flavor.

Beefsteak: The king of tomatoes, these giant fruits—some can weigh up to $2\frac{1}{2}$ pounds—are the ultimate tomato for a summer salad. The Mortgage Lifter, an heirloom variety, is an excellent example of this type.

Yellow Tomatoes: Tomatoes of yellow hue, whether pale or deep, vibrant or matte, are low in acid. Often people who don't like or can't eat red tomatoes find that they enjoy these low-acid varieties.

Green Tomatoes: This usually refers to unripe tomatoes, but there are also some green varieties that are ripe while they're green, such as the Zebra tomato, and Green Grape.

WHAT TO LOOK FOR: Regardless of shape, color, or size, good aroma and perfume are the keys to a good-tasting tomato. They should be firm but not rock hard. It's all right if the skin has a slightly tacky feel to it.

HOW TO STORE: Keep tomatoes at room temperature or in a cool place, but not in the refrigerator unless a glut makes it impossible to do otherwise. Cold kills everything about them that's good.

HOW TO USE: Ripe tomatoes are mostly enjoyed raw, but they make a great cooked vegetable, too. Use tomatoes for soups, salads, sauces, or juice or sauté, stuff, or bake them. They're an important addition to stews and stir-fries, adding a bit of acid that lifts the surrounding flavors.

SPECIAL HANDLING: None, except to avoid cold. Peeling isn't necessary for raw tomatoes, except for refinement—removing the skins makes their texture silkier. Peeling is advisable when cooking for longer than a brief sauté, since the skins roll up into jagged shards. Removing the seeds is also a matter of refinement—it makes a dish look and feel nicer.

QUANTITY: One pound, or 4 medium raw tomatoes, is ample for three to four servings, two to three servings when cooked, or 1 cup peeled, seeded, and diced tomatoes.

PEELING, SEEDING, AND CHOPPING TOMATOES

To peel a tomato, slash a little × at the base with a knife, then drop it into a pan of boiling water. When you see the edges of the × begin to loosen and roll back, after 10 to 20 seconds, scoop it out and drop it into a bowl of cold water to cool. Now you can easily slip off the skin. With ripe tomatoes the skin may quickly split in other places as well. Remove the tomato as soon as that happens.

To seed the tomato, cut it in half around its equator. Hold a half in one hand and pull out the seeds with your fingers while squeezing gently.

If a tomato is to be used for a sauce, coarsely chop it. If you want to add visual panache to a dish, separate the walls of the tomato from the core and use just the flat pieces. The cores can be finely diced and used in another or the same dish.

Tomatoes Glazed with Balsamic Vinegar

A VERY easy thing to do with tomatoes. The vinegar reduces with the butter, leaving the tomatoes glistening with a shiny glaze. Serve as a side dish or with toast and chopped parsley for a quick supper.

SERVES 4

1½ pounds ripe but firm tomatoes
2 tablespoons butter
3 tablespoons balsamic vinegar

1 plump shallot, finely diced
Salt and freshly milled pepper

Core the tomatoes, then cut them into wedges about 1½ inches across at the widest point. In a skillet large enough to hold the tomatoes in a single layer, heat the butter until it foams. Add the tomatoes and sauté over high heat, turning them over several times, until their color begins to dull, about 3 minutes. Add the vinegar and shallot and shake the pan back and forth until the vinegar has reduced, leaving a dark, thick sauce. Season with salt and plenty of pepper.

Herb-Baked Tomatoes

SERVES 4

4 ripe but firm slicing tomatoes
Salt and freshly milled pepper
Extra virgin olive oil

Herbs—2 tablespoons chopped marjoram, lovage, dill, and/or basil or 1 teaspoon dried oregano

Preheat the oven to 375°F. Lightly oil a large, shallow baking dish. Cut the tomatoes around their equators and set them upright in the baking dish. Sprinkle with salt, drizzle with oil, cover with the herbs, and season with pepper. Bake until hot and beginning to color on top, about 20 minutes. Serve carefully, making sure they're not stuck to the pan.

Variation: Prepare the tomatoes as described above, but reserve the herbs. Bake at 300°F until shriveled and glazed, about 2 hours, adding the herbs for the last 30 minutes. Serve them as a vegetable or perched on a thin round of mozzarella or a slice of toast. Leftovers make a rich addition to a summer soup or sauce.

Tomatoes Provençal

PARSLEY, garlic, and tomato are a timeless combination.

SERVES 4

4 medium or 8 small firm, ripe tomatoes
3 to 4 garlic cloves to taste
1 cup parsley leaves, preferably flat-leaf
3 tablespoons chopped basil

¾ cup bread crumbs made from day-old bread
Salt and freshly milled pepper
Extra virgin olive oil

Preheat the oven to 400°F. Lightly oil a gratin dish. Cut the tomatoes in half around their equators and gently remove the seeds with your fingertips. Chop the garlic, parsley, and basil together, then mix them with the bread crumbs and season well with salt and pepper. Lightly fill the tomatoes with this mixture, set them in the gratin dish, and thread olive oil generously over their tops. Bake for 30 minutes. They'll be soft, so remove them carefully from the dish.

Moroccan Stuffed Tomatoes A few years ago, I enjoyed these at a seaside café in Morocco. Though called tomatoes Provençal on the menu, instead of parsley the filling was rich with the flavors of mint and cilantro. Fill the tomatoes with Chermoula, page 56, cover with bread crumbs and/or grated cheese, then bake as described. (To make this more substantial, fill the tomato with rice or couscous first and spoon the sauce over the top.) Serves 4.

Stuffed Tomatoes Choose ripe but fairly firm tomatoes for stuffing so that they'll hold up to the oven's heat. If necessary, slice a sliver off the bottom so that they can stand, slice a quarter off the top, and gently scoop out the seeds and pulp with your fingers. Discard the seeds and use the pulp in the filling.

Fried Green Tomatoes

4 medium green (unripe) tomatoes

¾ cup fine cornmeal

3 to 4 tablespoons vegetable oil or clarified butter

Salt and freshly milled pepper

3 tablespoons chopped basil, tarragon, or parsley, or Green Chile Mayonnaise, page 60

SERVE these as a first course or side dish, use them in a sandwich or pasta, or serve them as a garnish for a stew of corn and late summer vegetables.

SERVES 4

Slice the tomatoes crosswise ⅓ to ½ inch thick. Press each piece into a plate of cornmeal to coat on both sides. Heat the oil in a wide skillet over high heat until hot enough to sizzle a drop of water. Add the tomatoes, reduce the heat to medium, and fry on both sides until golden. Remove to a plate, season with salt and pepper, and serve with the chopped herbs or mayonnaise.

Tomatoes Stuffed with Herbed Grains

4 medium to large ripe but firm tomatoes

1 cup cooked rice, couscous, quinoa, or other grain

½ cup toasted pine nuts or chopped toasted almonds

2 garlic cloves, minced

3 tablespoons finely chopped parsley

2 tablespoons finely chopped dill or basil

3 tablespoons grated Parmesan

Salt and freshly milled pepper

Extra virgin olive oil

SERVES 4

Preheat the oven to 375°F. Trim the tomatoes, chop the pulp, and mix it with the rice, nuts, garlic, herbs, and cheese. Season well with salt and pepper and fill the tomatoes. Replace the tops, brush them with oil, and set closely together in a small, oiled baking dish. Bake until the filling is hot, about 25 minutes. Carefully remove the tomatoes with a spatula to a serving plate.

Turnips and Rutabagas

TURNIPS and rutabagas are often treated as versions of the same vegetable. While what's good for a turnip is good for a rutabaga, rutabagas are drier fleshed and need to cook longer. If you want to interchange them, just allow extra time for the rutabagas. If both are used in the same recipe—and the creamy yellow of the rutabaga is stunning with the white turnip—parboil the rutabagas for 10 minutes to give them a head start.

GOOD PARTNERS FOR
TURNIPS AND RUTABAGAS
Butter, cream
Gruyère, blue cheeses
Thyme, savory, tarragon,
  rosemary
Watercress, roasted garlic,
  leeks, other root
  vegetables

TYPES OF TURNIPS AND RUTABAGAS: For many people, the only turnips ever seen are large storage turnips, scarred from handling, their greens long discarded, their flesh sometimes bitter. Rutabagas are even worse off, with their heavy coatings of preservative wax. But both turnips and rutabagas have their shining moments. Turnips in their youth, small and firm with shiny white skin and fresh tender greens, are nothing short of exquisite. Rutabagas are rarely sold with their greens, but if you can find them freshly pulled in the fall, they too are an excellent vegetable. Both can be found in their prime at farmers' markets. However, storage turnips and rutabagas shouldn't be overlooked, for they can be a valuable addition to the winter kitchen and their limitations are manageable.

WHAT TO LOOK FOR: In spring and summer, look for small, fresh turnips with smooth creamy skins. Greens are a bonus. Avoid giant rutabagas or vegetables that are shriveled or cracked.

HOW TO STORE: Stored in a plastic bag in the refrigerator, storage turnips and rutabagas will keep for several weeks; fresh turnips a few days.

HOW TO USE: Serve fresh turnips raw, with sea salt, as a crudité. Turnips and rutabagas can be included in winter vegetable stews and soups, steamed, pureed, cut into julienne strips and combined with other vegetables, or roasted.

SPECIAL HANDLING: Tender garden turnips needn't be peeled unless you wish to. To sweeten older turnips, thickly peel and slice them, then cook them in boiling salted water for 1 minute. Drain and rinse with cold water. Rutabagas should be thickly peeled.

QUANTITY: One pound, or 4 to 6 small to average turnips or rutabagas, yields 3 to 4 cups chopped, enough for four to six servings.

Spring Turnips with Their Greens

SERVES 4

12 or more small turnips, scrubbed, greens trimmed and washed

Salt and freshly milled pepper

2 to 4 tablespoons butter

Several thyme or lemon thyme sprigs, leaves plucked

If they're really tender and small, it's not necessary to peel the turnips. Bring 3 quarts water to a boil for the greens and set a steaming basket over salted water for the turnips.

Add 1½ teaspoons salt, add the greens, and simmer until tender, 8 to 10 minutes. Meanwhile, steam the turnips until they're tender-firm, 10 to 12 minutes. Drain the greens, press out excess moisture with the back of a spoon, toss them with half the butter, and season with salt and pepper. Arrange them on a plate. Toss the turnips with the remaining butter, a few pinches salt, a grind of pepper, and the thyme. Pile the turnips on the greens and serve them together.

Buttered Turnips and Rutabagas with Mixed Herbs

1½ pounds turnips and/or rutabagas, peeled

Salt and freshly milled pepper

2 tablespoons butter or sunflower oil

1 tablespoon chopped parsley

2 teaspoons chopped tarragon or thyme

2 tablespoons snipped chives

1 garlic clove, minced

½ cup fresh bread crumbs browned in 1 tablespoon butter or oil

THIS recipe, inspired by British writer Jane Grigson, has long been a favorite of mine.

SERVES 4 TO 6

Dice the turnips and rutabagas into ½-inch cubes. Boil them separately in salted water until they're tender-firm, about 12 minutes for the turnips and 20 minutes for the rutabagas. Drain. Melt the butter in a wide skillet. When foamy, add the vegetables and sauté over medium-high heat, stirring frequently, until golden. Toss with the herbs and garlic, taste for salt, and season with pepper. Remove to a serving dish and scatter the crisped bread crumbs over the top.

Roasted Turnips or Rutabagas

1½ pounds turnips or rutabagas, peeled and quartered

Salt and freshly milled pepper

Canola or safflower oil

3 small bay leaves

2 rosemary sprigs or 6 thyme sprigs

A GOOD dish for colder weather. Larger turnips can be used.

SERVES 4 TO 6

Preheat the oven to 375°F. Lightly oil a shallow roasting pan or baking dish. Boil the turnips in salted water for 3 minutes and drain. Wick off the extra moisture with a towel. If using rutabagas, parboil them for 15 minutes or until barely tender. Toss with enough oil to coat them lightly, then season with salt and pepper. Transfer them to the dish with the herbs and bake, uncovered, until tender when pierced with a knife and browned, 25 to 30 minutes.

Julienned Turnips or Rutabagas with Savory

1¹/₂ to 2 pounds turnips, peeled and
    julienned

Salt and freshly milled pepper

1 tablespoon butter

1 tablespoon olive or canola oil

1 teaspoon finely minced savory or
    ¹/₂ teaspoon dried

1 tablespoon chopped parsley

Sprinkle the turnips lightly with salt and set aside in a colander for 30 minutes. Squeeze out the excess moisture.

Warm the butter and oil in a skillet over medium heat. Add the turnips and savory. Cook gently, stirring occasionally, until tender, 12 to 15 minutes. Add the parsley, taste for salt, season with pepper, and toss again before serving.

(If you wish to make this dish with rutabagas, don't salt them, but add them directly to the pan with the butter and oil. Once they're warmed through, add ¹/₂ cup water, cover, and cook for 10 minutes. Uncover and continue cooking until tender and browned in places.)

Turnip or Rutabaga Puree with Leeks

RUTABAGAS tint a puree butter yellow, and the potato helps make the texture creamy.

SERVES 4 TO 6

1 small russet potato, peeled

2 pounds turnips and/or rutabagas,
    thickly peeled

2 medium leeks, white parts only,
    chopped

1 garlic clove, thinly sliced

Salt and freshly milled pepper

2 tablespoons or more cream,
    buttermilk, or milk

2 tablespoons butter

2 teaspoons chopped thyme

Chop the potato and turnips the same size. If using rutabagas, chop them about half the size of the potato. Put the vegetables, leeks, and garlic in a pot with cold water just to cover, add ¹/₂ teaspoon salt, and simmer, partially covered, until tender, 15 to 20 minutes. Drain, reserving the liquid.

Mash the vegetables with a fork for a rough-textured puree or pass them through a food mill. Add 2 tablespoons or more cream or reserved broth to thin the puree. Stir in the butter and thyme and season with salt and pepper to taste.

Variations: Stir 1 cup grated Gruyère cheese into the puree. Or simmer the vegetables in milk instead of water. Add a tablespoon Whole Roasted Garlic, page 377, and a teaspoon finely chopped rosemary to the puree. Or enrich the puree with a little crème fraîche and stir in 1 cup watercress sprigs that have been blanched briefly in boiling water, then finely chopped.

Rutabaga Fries Peel and slice rutabagas into long batons or French fries. Soak them in water for 30 minutes, then drain and towel-dry. Toss with vegetable oil to coat lightly and a few pinches salt. Spread them on a sheet pan and bake at 400°F, turning occasionally, until golden and tender, 30 to 40 minutes. When done, toss them with a little finely minced rosemary, sea salt, and freshly cracked pepper.

Winter Squash and Pumpkins

Winter squash is the name given to those cucurbits that develop tough skins, which allow them to be stored and kept over the winter. Once limited to a few varieties, there is now a plethora of these squashes, including some stunningly rich-tasting ones. While they differ in size, shape, color, and density, nearly all winter squash have a sweet yellow or orange flesh. With the exception of pumpkins grown specifically for eating, squash always makes a better vegetable than pumpkin.

TYPES OF SQUASH: The names and types of squash are ever changing, but these are reliably available.

Acorn: This is one winter squash most Americans know—acorn shaped with smooth skin that's dark green, orange, or a splashy mixture of the two. The flavor can be a little bland, which may be one reason it's often sweetened.

Banana Squash: This is the squash you find cut into slabs and wrapped in plastic at the market. Whole, it's much too huge for most people to lift, carry, store, or cook. But once cut, it's an easy squash to work with. The skin is light pinkish tan, the flesh yellow, and the flavor rather mild.

Buttercup: Perfection, Honey Delight, Black Forest, Red Kuri, and the Japanese Kabocha are squat and round and usually dark green except for the Kuri, which is red-orange. All these squash have dense flesh, which is extraordinarily sweet. You'll be asked if you added sugar to your soups. Although the shape suggests fillings of broth and cream, these are not particularly good for that purpose since the flesh readily absorbs liquids.

Butternut: This buff-skinned squash has a long, straight solid neck and a round bottom that contains the seeds. Not only does it have exceptionally good flavor, but butternut squash is easy to peel, which makes it ideal for gratins and other dishes. An excellent all-purpose winter squash.

Delicata: Yellow, orange, or cream-colored with dark green strips, oblong and usually slender, these delicious squash are generally small, weighing about a pound, though toward the end of the season, they can get fairly large. Their shape makes them good shallow containers, and their skins are easy to peel. Once peeled, they can be cut into rounds and sautéed. A similar squash—upright and lighter in color—is Sweet Dumpling.

GOOD PARTNERS FOR WINTER SQUASH AND PUMPKINS
Olive oil, butter, brown butter, sunflower seed oil
Fontina, Gruyère, pecorino Romano, Parmesan
Sage, rosemary, garlic, red pepper flakes, chile, cumin, coriander
Brown sugar, coconut milk, ginger, lime, lemongrass, curry
Onions, radicchio, apple, quince

Hubbard: Orange, blue-skinned, or slate-colored, large, ungainly, and covered with "warts," this old-fashioned squash is nonetheless one of the best for eating. Fortunately new varieties, such as Queensland Blue, are small enough for the home cook to handle.

Mini Squash and Pumpkins: Sweet Dumplings, Jack-be-Littles, and other tiny varieties can be stuffed, baked, or steamed. One squash is perfect for one person, especially a child who will love having his or her own baby pumpkin. They're cute, convenient, and quite good to eat, too.

Spaghetti Squash: Oval and yellow-skinned with pale yellow flesh, this squash is so coarse that its cooked flesh can be pulled into long strands resembling spaghetti. It's somewhat bland but good treated just as spaghetti, with sauces. Chilled cooked squash can be tossed with a vinaigrette and served as a winter salad.

Turban Squash: With their high striped "hats," these look very exotic but are not nearly as pleasant to eat as to look at. Better for decorations and doorstops.

WHAT TO LOOK FOR: Winter squash and pumpkins should be firm and hefty for their size. The heavier they are, the denser and moister the flesh. There may be rough patches on the skin, but the only real problem is soft, spongy spots; avoid them if you can or cut them out if you can't.

HOW TO STORE: Keep whole squash in a cool, dry place that has plenty of ventilation—a back porch would be ideal. If you like to keep them out where they can be seen, try to use them within a week or two, before they dry out. Cut squash can be wrapped and re-frigerated for up to a few days.

HOW TO USE: Winter squash are easy to bake, roast, or steam. They can be made into purees and soups and used in pies, breads, and cakes. Slices and chunks can be fried, sautéed, or baked in gratins and simmered in stews. The skins and seeds are effective in soup stocks.

SPECIAL HANDLING: Cutting large squash can be difficult. A heavy knife or cleaver and a rubber mallet are useful tools. Whack the knife into the squash, then bear down or tap it with the mallet to open the squash. Cut next to the stem rather than through it—it'll be easier on your knife. Or bake squash whole until they begin to soften, then cut them. Spaghetti squash needs to be punctured in several places before baking, or it will explode in the oven. Some nonchalant cooks I know drop large squash on the floor to break them open—advisable only when all else fails.

QUANTITY: Allowing for the seeds and skins, a 1-pound squash, halved and baked, is adequate for two servings, and 1 pound of peeled, seeded squash yields approximately 2 cups pureed. Whole weights and trimmed weights will vary from one squash variety to another, so it's difficult to give absolute quantities. However, those who love squash will wish for large portions, and leftover cooked squash is always easy to reheat.

Baked Winter Squash A practical approach to preparing squash for any number of uses. Cut a squash in half, then scoop out the seeds and fibers. Brush the cut surfaces with a thin film of oil and set the squash, cut side down, on a sheet pan. Bake at 375°F or whatever oven temperature is convenient, until the squash looks wrinkled, soft, and about to collapse, usually about 30 minutes. The cut side should be richly glazed. Place upright on a serving plate, season with salt and pepper, a tad of butter, and serve. Or scoop out the flesh, mash it with butter, and return it to the shell. You can also use this squash to make a puree, soup, or pie filling.

Sometimes squash exudes a clear, sweet liquid. If you let it sit for about 15 minutes, the liquid will become reabsorbed into the flesh as it cools.

Baked Whole Squash If a squash is too tough to cut into pieces or too large to handle easily, bake it whole at 350°F or so until it feels soft when pressed, 30 minutes or longer, depending on size. Remove, then halve and scrape out the seeds. Return it to the oven and continue cooking until it's done.

Steamed Squash Cut winter squash into halves, quarters, or wedges, scrape out the seeds, and place in a steamer basket over boiling water. Steam, covered, until tender, 30 to 40 minutes, depending on size. Season with butter, salt, and pepper or scrape out the flesh and use for other dishes.

Grilled Winter Squash or Pumpkin This is for those who like to grill in all seasons. If you plan to leave the skins on, you can use any variety of winter squash. If peeling them is important, stick to butternut or Delicata squash. Cut squash into slices a scant ¹/₂ inch thick, remove fibers and seeds, and steam until barely tender. Combine 2 minced garlic cloves with 1 teaspoon each chopped rosemary and thyme and ¹/₃ cup olive oil. Brush it over the squash and season with salt and pepper. Grill on both sides until marked and tender, then serve with a dash of apple cider vinegar or a spicier condiment such as Harissa, page 75.

Winter Squash Puree Easy, versatile, and useful, leftovers can fill ravioli, turn into a soup, or be added to muffins, breads, biscuits, and waffles. Halve, seed, and bake 3 pounds squash until tender. Scrape the flesh away from the skin, then beat until smooth by hand with a large wooden spoon. This should be easy unless the squash is stringy, in which case use a food processor or food mill. Stir in butter to taste and season with salt and pepper. Makes about 2 cups.

To enrich the puree, grate Gruyère, Fontina, or Emmenthaler into it. Crumble fried sage leaves, on top. Add mascarpone and freshly grated nutmeg to taste. Flavor with extra virgin or dark sesame oil, or mix in Sautéed Onions, page 395.

Roasted Winter Squash or Pumpkin Use a squash that's easy to peel, such as butternut or banana. Preheat the oven to 400°F. Peel and seed 2¹/₂ to 3 pounds squash and cut into 2-inch cubes. Toss it with olive or vegetable oil to coat lightly and season with salt and pepper. Spread the squash in a large baking dish or sheet pan. Roast for 15 minutes, turn the pieces, and roast for 15 minutes more. Turn again and bake until the squash is completely tender, 10 to 15 minutes longer. Serves 4 to 6.

Baked-Steamed Acorn Squash Preheat the oven to 375°F. Cut an acorn squash in half from stem to tip and remove the seeds. Brush with oil and place cut side down in a baking dish. Add ¹/₂ inch water and bake until soft, about 30 minutes. By this time the water will have evaporated and the bottom will have begun to color. Serve with butter, salt, and pepper, or Spicy Moroccan Butter, page 52, or sweeten with a spoonful of maple syrup, honey, or brown sugar and a dash of cinnamon, nutmeg, or allspice.

Baked Delicata Squash Delicata is one of the easiest squashes to handle and one of the quickest to cook. Preheat the oven to 350°F. Allow one 8- to 12-ounce squash per person. Place a large knife on one of the green grooves that run down the surface of the squash, bear down, and cut the squash in half lengthwise. Scrape out the seeds, brush the cut surface with olive oil, season with salt and pepper, and set, cut side up, in a baking dish. Add about ⅓ inch water, cover with aluminum foil, and bake until tender, 25 to 35 minutes.

Delicata Squash Rings

THESE *take just 10 to 12 minutes to cook and when finished are glazed with a rich caramel coating from the natural sugars in the squash. Serve these as a side dish or add them as an attractive garnish to winter vegetable stews.*

SERVES 2 TO 4

2 Delicata squash, 12 to 16 ounces each
1½ tablespoons olive or vegetable oil
Salt and freshly milled pepper

Chopped parsley, Gremolata, page 29, or any of the suggested sauces and seasonings on page 438

Peel the squash with a vegetable peeler, slice off the ends, and scoop out the seeds with a teaspoon. Cut the squash into rings about ⅓ inch thick. Heat the oil in a wide skillet, add the squash, and fry over medium heat until richly colored on the bottom, about 6 minutes. Turn and cook on the second side until tender. Remove to a serving plate, season with salt and pepper, and garnish with parsley.

Butternut Squash Coins

BUTTERNUT *squash is the easiest—and prettiest of the squashes to use because of its long, smooth neck. Serve these squash coins with Sautéed Onions, drizzled with Chermoula or Salsa Verde, or simply with plenty of freshly milled pepper and a few drops of apple cider vinegar or balsamic vinegar.*

SERVES 4 TO 6

1 large butternut squash, about 3 pounds
4 to 6 tablespoons olive oil or sunflower seed oil

Salt and freshly milled pepper

Slice the neck from the squash where it joins the bulb. Peel it with a vegetable peeler or a knife, using long, even strokes. Reserve the bottom for another use. Slice the neck crosswise about ¼ inch thick. Preheat the oven to 200°F.

Heat 2 tablespoons of the oil in a wide skillet over medium-high heat. Add a single layer of squash and fry until golden and flecked with brown, about 10 minutes. Turn and fry the second side. Remove to paper towels to drain and keep warm in the oven. Repeat with the rest, adding oil as needed. Season with salt and pepper. Serve drizzled with vinegar, smothered with Sautéed Onions, page 395, or with one of the suggested sauces.

Baked Spaghetti Squash with Gruyère and Parsley

1 spaghetti squash, about 3 pounds, punctured

1 cup grated Gruyère

2 to 4 tablespoons butter

¼ cup parsley chopped with 1 garlic clove

Salt and freshly milled pepper

Preheat the oven to 375°F. Bake the squash until the flesh is yielding and soft, an hour or more. Slice the squash in half and scrape out the seeds. Now drag a fork through the flesh, pulling the strands apart. Toss them with the parsley, cheese, and butter. Season with salt and pepper and serve.

Spaghetti Squash with Tomato Sauce Tomato sauces of all kinds are good with spaghetti squash. Toss the strands lightly with olive oil, salt, and freshly milled pepper, then pile them on a platter. Make a nest in the middle for 1 to 2 cups tomato sauce. Toss, then serve. Pass Parmesan cheese at the table.

Spaghetti Squash with Mushroom Ragout Serve spaghetti squash with any of the mushroom ragouts or with Sautéed Mushrooms with Garlic and Parsley, page 388. Season the squash with butter or olive oil, salt, and pepper, then mound it on a platter and surround with the mushrooms. Toss before serving.

A SIMPLE and very satisfying combination of flavors. Be sure to puncture the squash in at least a few places, or it will explode in the oven and make a truly amazing mess—I know this from experience. Even when properly cooked, the strands of squash will be a little crunchy.

SERVES 4

Provençal Winter Squash Gratin

2 to 2½ pounds butternut squash

5 garlic cloves, finely chopped

½ cup chopped parsley

Salt and freshly milled pepper

3 tablespoons flour

Extra virgin olive oil

Preheat the oven to 325°F and oil a shallow earthenware baking dish. Peel the squash and cut it into even-sized cubes, from ⅓ inch to 1 inch. Toss it with the garlic, parsley, salt, and pepper. Add the flour and toss again until the pieces are coated lightly, letting the excess fall to the bottom. Pile the squash into the dish and drizzle oil generously over the top. Bake, uncovered, until the squash is browned and tender when pierced with a knife, about 2 hours. When served, the individual pieces will collapse into a puree.

A LONG, slow baking intensifies the already deep flavor of the squash. In his book Simple French Food, *Richard Olney suggests cutting the squash into tiny cubes. For special meals I make it his way—it's marvelous looking with the crusty cubes of squash tinged brown on the edges. But for every day, I cut the squash into larger pieces.*

SERVES 4 TO 6

Pasta, Noodles, and Dumplings

PASTA IS PERFECT FOR BUSY PEOPLE WHO WANT TO EAT WELL AND SIMPLY
AT HOME. A PLETHORA OF DISHES CAN BE MADE FROM A POUND OF NOODLES AND
A FEW VEGETABLES—OFTEN IN THE AMOUNT OF TIME IT TAKES TO BOIL WATER
and cook the pasta. Pasta dishes that are to be baked can be set up hours ahead of time
so that they're ready to heat when you're ready to eat. More elaborate pastas, such as
ravioli, cannelloni, and layered lasagne, are dishes worthy of a special occasion.
Dumplings, a close relative, are tender morsels that rank among the most comforting
foods we know, and the increasing bounty of Asian noodles takes us into entirely new
realms of possibilities.

Certainly one of the beauties of pasta is that it pairs endlessly well with vegetables, adapting with blissful ease to the nuances of the changing seasons. Pasta is
equally good with spring's asparagus, summer's ripe tomatoes, or the pungent greens of
fall and winter.

DRIED PASTA: Dried pasta has good flavor, good bite, and it's absolutely practical. Italian brands like De Cecco and Delverde have long been considered the best, but American brands, now being made with hard durum wheat, are beginning to challenge the
imports in pasta tastings.

Beyond Italian pasta there are American egg noodles, Greek orzo, thin Mexican
noodles or fideos, Japanese soba, Chinese mung bean threads, Thai rice sticks, and
many more varieties. The health food industry has introduced wheat-free pastas made
from quinoa, kamut, amaranth, spelt, ground artichokes, and corn flours. Without the
gluten from the hard wheat, these tend to have a crumbly texture that makes it almost
impossible to find that moment when they're perfectly cooked. Pasta made from spelt
flour stands out as being closest to wheat in both texture and flavor. Asian noodles,

which are altogether different in taste and texture from our Western pasta, are often made from nonwheat ingredients such as mung bean starch, yam starch, rice flour, and buckwheat.

FRESH PASTA: Fresh egg pasta has a completely different quality from dried; its texture is silky and tender rather than toothsome. It's wonderful for lasagne and essential for filled pastas, such as ravioli. If you're making your own, you can add flavorings such as saffron, pepper, herbs, spinach, and other essences to make fragrant doughs of colored hues. In many cities it's possible to buy commercial fresh pasta, including sheets to use for ravioli and lasagne. Though a timesaver, they're never quite as fine as homemade.

SERVING SIZES: Four ounces of pasta, fresh or dried, is more than adequate for a main course serving. In truth, I find that three ounces is ample. If you're serving pasta for a first course or making a very rich pasta which you'll eat in smaller quantity, then two ounces should be plenty. Of course, serving sizes relate to what else you're having in the meal—how much and how rich it is.

Making Fresh Pasta

IT'S *easy to get the hang of making pasta, and it's always amazing to see the noodles that accumulate from your rather minimal efforts. For equipment, all you need is a relatively inexpensive hand-cranked pasta machine. For ingredients, use all-purpose flour, good quality eggs, olive oil and sea salt. Throughout the book I've used large eggs, but for pasta, extra large seem to provide just the right amount of moisture. If your climate is very dry, you may need to use a little extra liquid—beaten egg, olive oil, milk or water. Although a wet dough is easy to knead, it's harder to handle later on because it will stick to itself when you roll it out. Make it soft enough to knead with ease, but try not to make it overly moist. A dry dough will smooth out as you pass it through the pasta machine.*

Egg Pasta

MAKES ABOUT 1 POUND

2 cups flour

2 extra large eggs

2 teaspoons olive oil or water if needed

¼ teaspoon salt

By Hand: Put the flour on a clean counter, shape it into a mound, and make a well in the center. Put the eggs, oil, and a few pinches salt in the center, break them up with a fork, then gradually begin pulling in the flour from the sides. Bring in as much flour as you can and still have a smooth mass of dough that doesn't stick to your hands.

When you can't add any more flour, pass the flour remaining on the counter through a strainer, returning it to the counter; discard the lumps. Knead the dough, picking up as much of the flour on the counter as it will hold, until it's silky and moist but not sticky, 3 to 4 minutes. Slip the dough into a plastic bag and set it aside to rest for 10 to 15 before rolling it out. If your dough is dry and difficult to knead, this resting period will help soften it.

In the Mixer: You'll need a heavy-duty mixer with a paddle attachment. Mix the flour and salt in the bowl. Beat the eggs and oil together with a fork in a cup. With the mixer on low, add the eggs and oil and mix until the flour is absorbed. It will look rather lumpy. Grasp it with your hand, form it into a ball, and knead until smooth and pliant. Cover and let rest for 10 to 15 minutes.

In the Food Processor: Combine the flour and salt in a food processor and turn on the motor. Add the oil, then the eggs. Work until little pealike particles are formed, then turn the dough out, gather it together, and knead until smooth. Cover and let rest for 10 to 15 minutes.

Rolling Out the Dough

The pasta machine is essentially foolproof and will knead the dough to smoothness even if your own kneading techniques are weak.

Flatten the dough out with your hands to make a piece of the width that will fit your machine. (If you're increasing the recipe to make 1½ pounds, divide the dough into two pieces.) Set the machine at the widest setting (the lowest number) and feed the dough through once. Now fold the dough into thirds, press down any excessively thick parts, and run it through again with the open edges going through first. Repeat this process until the dough is smooth, four or five times.

Go to the next notch on the machine and run the dough all the way through without folding it. (With this and every pass through the machine, lightly dust the dough with flour or semolina.) Turn the gear to the next notch and pass the dough through once. Continue through the next-to-the-last setting. The dough should be very thin. If it isn't (machines differ), go on to the last setting.

To make the increasingly long piece of dough easier to handle, you can cut it into smaller lengths at any point and roll each one separately, but it's surprisingly resilient and will tolerate being flipped back and forth over the machine. The dough can now be cut into noodles.

Cutting the Noodles

You may want to use your machine's cutting attachment, but cutting by hand leaves a rougher edge—better for catching the sauce.

Fold a piece of dough roughly 15 inches long into thirds, then cut firmly across the folds into the width you want your pasta to be. Toss the strands in a little flour or semolina to separate them and keep them from sticking. You can cook the pasta right away or set it aside on a floured surface covered with a cotton towel for up to several hours, or to cook the next day.

EGG PASTA AMOUNTS

- 1 cup flour + 1 extra large egg yields 8 ounces or enough for 2 large and 4 medium portions

- 2 cups flour + 2 extra large eggs yields 1 pound pasta or enough for 4 large or 6 medium portions, or a lasagne recipe

- 3 cups flour + 3 extra large eggs yields 1½ pounds pasta or enough for a lasagne recipe for 6 large or 8 medium portions

FLAVORED PASTAS

The following amounts are for 1 pound of pasta, using the Egg Pasta recipe on page 444.

Saffron Pasta: Crumble 3 pinches saffron threads and steep them in 2 tablespoons hot water until the water cools. Add it to the flour when you add the eggs.

Red Pepper Pasta: Add 1 tablespoon ground red chile, red pepper flakes, or paprika to the flour.

Black Pepper Pasta: Add 2 tablespoons coarsely milled pepper to the flour.

Spinach Pasta: Wash and dry 2 cups lightly packed spinach leaves, then puree them with the eggs. Use this as the liquid for the pasta. You may need to add a little extra flour to the dough, which will be emerald green.

Rosemary Pasta: Add 3 tablespoons minced fresh rosemary to the dough.

Green Herb Pasta: Chop 1/4 cup assorted fresh herbs, such as thyme, marjoram, parsley, basil, arugula, and/or sage. Blanch them for 10 seconds in boiling water, squeeze dry, then finely chop. Add them, with the eggs, to the flour. Emphasize a single herb or make a mixture.

Whole-Wheat Pasta: Use 1 each cup whole-wheat and white flour.

Seven Steps to Cooking Pasta

1. BRING A LARGE POT OF WATER TO A ROLLING BOIL. Whether the noodles are fresh or dried, long or short, using a large pot of water gives them lots of room to swim around so they don't stick to each other. The volume also helps maintain the rolling boil that keeps the pasta aloft and in motion. For 1 pound, use 6 quarts of water. If you're parboiling vegetables, use the same water and cook the vegetables first.

2. ADD SALT, THEN THE PASTA. Add plenty of salt—at least a teaspoon for each quart of water. Add it just before you add the pasta since salty water is slower to boil and the salt can develop an odd taste after a short time. It isn't necessary to add oil to the water.

3. BOIL UNTIL THE PASTA IS AL DENTE. Part of the charm of dried pasta is its texture. It needs to have a little bite, to be firm to the tooth, which is what *al dente* means. Cooking time is always relative to the size of the pot, the vigor of the boil, and your altitude. Instead of relying on the clock, taste the pasta as it cooks, until it is tender but retains a pleasant firmness. There shouldn't be a chalky core at the center of the pasta, which indicates rawness. The moment between rawness and perfection is brief, so be on your toes. Pasta with holes in it may cook more quickly than you anticipate since it cooks from both the inside and the outside. Pasta made from grains other than wheat also cooks differently, so consult the instructions before starting, but rely on your taste. Fresh egg pasta cooks in just a few minutes and doesn't achieve the same degree of toothiness as dried.

4. DRAIN THE PASTA. You can drain pasta into a colander, scoop it out with a strainer or lift it out with a pair of tongs (just hold the tongs upright so the scalding water doesn't flow down your arm). If your sink is filled when the crucial moment comes, a strainer will be very useful. A large flat Chinese strainer works well, as does the special oval Italian scoop that you can slide in right next to the edge of the pot. If it's important that the pasta be dry so as not to dilute the sauce, use a colander.

5. PUT THE PASTA DIRECTLY INTO THE SAUCE, LETTING SOME OF THE COOKING WATER DRIP INTO THE PAN. Often I let some of the water drip into the pasta vegetables—it seems to add just the right amount of moisture to thin the sauce and keep the noodles from sticking. There is no need to rinse pasta unless you need to stop the cooking at once, as for baked pasta dishes that will be finished later. In this case, toss the cooked, cooled noodles with a little olive oil to prevent them from sticking.

6. SERVE IN HEATED PASTA PLATES. Pasta cools quickly, and as it loses its heat it becomes increasingly less wonderful. So just before serving pasta, ladle some of the boiling water into the serving bowl or pasta plates to warm them or have the dishes warming in a low oven. Bowls designed specifically for pasta and soup plates are the perfect shape and size.

7. PASS A PIECE OF CHEESE WITH THE GRATER. While you might add a little cheese to the pasta when you toss it, you don't want to add so much that the noodles cling together. Instead, have a chunk of hard grating cheese on a plate with a small grater and pass it around the table. Freshly grated cheese is always preferable to pregrated—it has better flavor.

Spaghetti with Artichokes

4 to 6 medium artichokes, trimmed and quartered	3 tablespoons chopped tarragon or rosemary
Juice of 2 large lemons	1/2 cup dry white wine
1/3 cup olive oil	Salt and freshly milled pepper
1 large onion, finely diced	1 pound spaghetti
4 garlic cloves, chopped	Freshly grated Parmesan, plus a chunk of Parmesan for the table
2 small bay leaves	

ARTICHOKES have one season in the spring and a second in the fall. A spring dish might be seasoned with fresh tarragon, a fall dish with rosemary and toasted walnuts or with bread crumbs crisped in olive oil.

SERVES 4 TO 6

Thinly slice the artichoke quarters and put them in a bowl with the lemon juice and water to cover. Start heating a large pot of water for the pasta.

Heat 3 tablespoons of the oil in a wide skillet with the onion. Drain and add the artichokes. Sauté over high heat, stirring frequently, until they're well colored, about 7 minutes. Lower the heat and add the garlic, bay leaves, half the tarragon, and the wine. Simmer, scraping the pan, until the wine is reduced. Add 1 cup water and 1/2 teaspoon salt and cook until the artichokes are tender, about 10 minutes. Taste for salt.

Cook the spaghetti in boiling salted water until al dente. Scoop it out and add it to the artichokes with the remaining oil and tarragon. Season with salt and freshly ground pepper and toss well. Serve the pasta lightly covered with grated cheese, then pass the cheese and grater at the table.

Linguine with Asparagus, Lemon, and Spring Herbs

A MINIMAL but true pasta primavera. Should they come your way, stew a handful of peas or fava beans with the scallions as well. This dish can be made with butter or olive oil or a mixture.

SERVES 4 TO 6

2 tablespoons olive oil

2 tablespoons butter

1 large bunch scallions, including half of the greens, thinly sliced

2½ teaspoons grated lemon zest

1 tablespoon finely chopped thyme, sage, or tarragon

Salt and freshly milled pepper

2 pounds asparagus, tough ends removed

1 pound linguine

4 tablespoons pine nuts, toasted in a small skillet

3 tablespoons chopped parsley

2 tablespoons snipped chives, plus blossoms if available

Freshly grated Parmesan, optional

While water is heating for the pasta, heat half the oil and butter in a wide skillet over low heat. Add the scallions, lemon zest, thyme, and a few pinches salt and cook slowly, stirring occasionally.

Meanwhile, slice 3-inch tips off the asparagus, then slice the remaining stalks diagonally or make a roll cut. When the water boils, salt it, add the asparagus, and cook until partially tender, 3 to 4 minutes. Scoop it out, add it to the scallions, and continue cooking. Cook the pasta, then add it to the pan with some of the water clinging to the strands. Raise the heat and stir in the remaining oil, the pine nuts, parsley, chives, pepper to taste, and a few tablespoons cheese. Divide among pasta plates, grate a little cheese over each portion, and garnish with the chive blossoms.

Spinach Fettuccine with Arugula and Tomatoes

As they mature, arugula leaves get large, hot, and spicy. They're too robust for salads, but when cooked their pungency softens, leaving just enough to add zest to the pasta.

SERVES 4 TO 6

1 pound spinach fettuccine

Salt

4 tablespoons olive oil, plus extra virgin to finish

3 garlic cloves, chopped

2 small dried red chiles, broken in half, or several pinches red pepper flakes

6 or more cups mature arugula leaves, large stems removed, leaves coarsely chopped

4 Roma tomatoes, seeded and diced

3 tablespoons chopped parsley

Freshly grated Parmesan or pecorino Romano

Drop the pasta into plenty of salted boiling water and cook until al dente.

Meanwhile, heat the oil in a large skillet, add the garlic and chile, and cook over medium heat until the garlic turns light gold. Add the arugula, season with a few pinches salt, and sauté until wilted. Stir in the tomatoes and parsley and turn off the heat. When the pasta is done, scoop it out and add it directly to the pan. Toss well and serve with a dusting of cheese and extra virgin olive oil drizzled over the top.

Whole-Wheat Spaghetti with Arugula, Walnuts, and Ricotta Salata

Make the pasta as described but with whole-wheat spaghetti and without the tomatoes. Toss it with ½ cup toasted chopped walnuts and thin shavings of ricotta salata.

Pasta and Beans

There's a reason pasta with beans (pasta e fagioli) is a classic. The toothiness of the pasta and softness of the beans make an exceptionally congenial pairing. With all the different beans as well as pasta shapes now available, the possibilities for putting the two together should be nearly endless, but here are some pairings that are timeless.

Butterflies with Chickpeas

3 tablespoons olive oil

1 plump garlic clove, minced

3 tablespoons chopped parsley

¹/₄ teaspoon red pepper flakes

1¹/₂ cups cooked chickpeas, rinsed if canned

8 ounces farfalle or orecchiette

Salt and freshly milled pepper

3 tablespoons mixed freshly grated Parmesan and pecorino Romano

¹/₂ cup bread crumbs crisped in olive oil or toasted in the oven

NOTHING could be quicker to make than this dish, and since it's quite likely you already have chickpeas and pasta and good olive oil on hand, it makes a great last-minute supper.

SERVES 2 TO 4

Warm half the oil in a large skillet with the garlic, parsley, and pepper flakes. Add the chickpeas and ¹/₂ cup water and simmer gently over medium heat. Meanwhile, cook the pasta in plenty of salted boiling water until al dente. Drain and add it to the chickpeas. Toss, taste for salt, season with pepper to taste, and add the remaining oil. Serve covered with a sprinkling of the cheeses and/or the toasted bread crumbs.

Shells with Baby Lima Beans and Rosemary

2 cups frozen baby lima beans

3 tablespoons olive oil or butter

1 onion, quartered and thinly sliced crosswise

1 tablespoon minced rosemary or summer savory

2 tablespoons finely chopped parsley

Salt and freshly milled pepper

8 ounces medium conchiglie (shells)

Freshly grated Parmesan

IT'S so hard to get fresh lima beans that I usually use the frozen baby ones. Some of the beans find their way into the cavities of the shells—a sweet surprise in the mouth.

SERVES 2 TO 4

Bring water for pasta to a boil, add the lima beans, and cook until they're tender. Scoop them out and set aside. Warm 2 tablespoons of the oil in a large skillet, add the onion and rosemary, and sauté over medium heat until just lightly browned, about 8 to 10 minutes. Add a ladleful of pasta water, the cooked beans, and the parsley. Season with salt and pepper and turn off the heat.

Add salt to the pasta water and cook the shells until al dente. Scoop them out and add them to the beans. Add the final spoonful of oil and grate a little Parmesan over the top.

Lumache with Broccoli and Capers

A FAST *little pasta for busy nights—although there's nothing second rate about this dish, with its succulent bits of vegetable nestled inside pasta.*

SERVES 4 TO 6

2 garlic cloves, peeled

Salt and freshly milled pepper

1/3 cup extra virgin olive oil

1/2 teaspoon red pepper flakes

1/4 cup capers, rinsed

1 1/2 pounds broccoli

1 pound lumache, conchiglie, or gnocchi

Freshly grated Parmesan

Mince or mash the garlic with 1/2 teaspoon salt until smooth, then put it in a large bowl with the oil, pepper flakes, and capers. Thickly peel the broccoli stems. Cut both the crowns and stems into small bite-sized pieces.

Bring plenty of water to a boil for the pasta. When it boils, add salt, add the broccoli, and cook, uncovered, until tender, 4 to 5 minutes. Scoop it out, shake off the water, add it to the bowl, and toss with the oil. Cover. Cook the pasta until al dente, then drain and add it to the broccoli. Toss well, season with plenty of pepper, and toss with the cheese.

Variations: Broccoflower or broccoli Romanesco is delicious in place of or along with the broccoli. Also good with these vegetables are finely slivered sun-dried tomatoes, diced roasted red peppers, Salsa Verde, page 55, pitted black olives, and fresh marjoram, dill, or a few pinches dried oregano.

Orecchiette with Broccoli Rabe

ORECCHIETTE, *the little ear-shaped pasta, is traditionally combined with robust broccoli rabe. I make this at least once a week when broccoli rabe is available, and when it's not, I find the Chopped Broccoli is delicious here, too.*

SERVES 3 TO 4

1 bunch broccoli rabe, about 1 1/2 pounds

12 ounces orecchiette

Salt

4 tablespoons olive oil, plus extra virgin to finish

3 garlic cloves, thinly sliced

1/2 teaspoon red pepper flakes

Freshly grated Parmesan

Lemon wedges

While the pasta water is heating, peel the lower stems of the broccoli rabe, then add the whole bunch to the boiling water. Boil for 5 minutes, then remove it with a strainer and coarsely chop. Start cooking the pasta in boiling salted water.

Meanwhile, warm the oil with the garlic and pepper flakes in a wide skillet over medium heat until fragrant. Add the broccoli rabe and cook gently, occasionally adding a little pasta water to the pan so it doesn't dry out. Drain the pasta, add it directly into the greens, and toss with a spoonful of the extra virgin olive oil, salt to taste, and a little grated Parmesan. Toss well and serve with an additional dusting of cheese and a wedge of lemon on each plate.

Pasta with Broccoli Rabe and Tomatoes Add 2 or 3 tomatoes, seeded and diced, to the greens toward the end of their cooking, then add the pasta and season as described. Toast a few tablespoons pine nuts in a small skillet until golden, then scatter them over the top. Serve with or without the lemon.

Fusilli with Cauliflower, Olives, and Herbs

1 large head cauliflower, broccoflower, or a mixture

Salt and freshly milled pepper

1 bunch scallions, including most of the greens, thinly sliced

1 bunch parsley, stems removed, leaves finely chopped

2 tablespoons finely chopped tarragon

1/2 cup pitted and chopped Spanish green olives

1/3 cup extra virgin olive oil

1 pound fusilli, rotelle, or other sturdy pasta

Coarsely grated ricotta salata or Manchego

I LIKE cauliflower accompanied by strong, clean tastes like those provided by olives and herbs. Broccoflower looks and tastes wonderful with the cauliflower, or you can use either one alone.

SERVES 4 TO 6

Bring a large pot of water to a boil. Cut the cauliflower into small florets, then peel and dice the stems. Salt the water, add the cauliflower, and boil until partially tender, 3 to 5 minutes. Scoop the cauliflower into a large bowl and add the scallions, herbs, olives, and oil. Cover to keep warm. Cook the pasta in the salted boiling water, then drain, add it to the bowl, and toss well. Taste for salt and season with pepper. Add the cheese, toss again, and serve.

Spaghettini with Cauliflower, Butter, and Pepper

Salt and freshly milled pepper

1 cauliflower, cut into tiny florets, stems peeled and chopped

4 tablespoons butter

1/2 cup finely chopped parsley

1 teaspoon coarse mustard

1/4 teaspoon red pepper flakes

1 pound spaghettini, orecchiette, or small conchiglie

1/2 cup freshly grated Parmesan, pecorino Romano, or a mixture

1/2 cup fresh bread crumbs, toasted until golden and crisp

THE simplicity of this dish is deceiving. It's very good—full of warm, lively flavors.

SERVES 4 TO 6

Bring a large pot of water to a rolling boil. Salt it to taste, add the cauliflower, and cook for 3 minutes. Scoop the cauliflower into a large pasta bowl and add the butter, parsley, mustard, and pepper flakes. Add the pasta to the salted boiling water and set the bowl over the pot to keep it warm, leaving a crack so the water doesn't boil over, while the pasta cooks. Drain it when it's done and add it to the cauliflower. Grind a generous amount of pepper over all, then toss with the cheeses and crumbs.

Summer Spaghetti with Corn and Tomatoes

THOSE with allergies to wheat can try this untraditional summer pasta with corn-flour spaghetti and take advantage of the parallel flavors. Don't expect corn-flour pasta to have the same texture as wheat.

SERVES 3 OR 4

12 ounces corn-flour or regular spaghetti

Salt and freshly milled pepper

2 tablespoons corn oil or butter

1 bunch scallions, including half of the greens, chopped

2 cups corn kernels, from 3 ears corn

1 bell pepper, any color, finely diced

1 jalapeño chile, seeded and diced

3 tomatoes, halved, seeded, and diced

½ cup chopped cilantro

2 ounces queso fresco or feta

1 lime, quartered

Cook the pasta in plenty of salted boiling water until al dente. Meanwhile, heat the oil in a large skillet and add the scallions, corn, bell pepper, and chile. Sauté over high heat for 3 minutes, then add the tomatoes, most of the cilantro, and a ladle of the pasta water. Season with ½ teaspoon salt and a little pepper and turn the heat to low. Drain the pasta, shaking off the excess water. Add it to the vegetables and toss well. Divide among pasta plates, crumble the cheese over the top, and add the remaining cilantro. Serve with a wedge of lime.

Spaghetti with Garlic, Parsley, and Bread Crumbs

A DISH for all seasons that's made from pantry staples. The ubiquitous Roman trio—garlic, olive oil, and red pepper flakes—seasons this simplest of pastas.

SERVES 4 TO 6

1 pound spaghetti

Salt and freshly milled pepper

⅓ cup extra virgin olive oil

4 garlic cloves, chopped

½ teaspoon red pepper flakes

½ cup chopped flat-leaf parsley

½ cup mixed freshly grated Parmesan and pecorino Romano

½ cup fresh bread crumbs crisped in 1 tablespoon olive oil

Cook the spaghetti in plenty of salted boiling water. Meanwhile, warm the oil with the garlic and pepper flakes in a wide skillet over medium heat. As soon as the garlic starts to color, remove the pan from the heat.

Drain the spaghetti, shaking off the excess water, and put it in a warmed pasta bowl. Pour the oil mixture over the top and toss with the parsley and cheese. Taste for salt, season with pepper, and serve with the bread crumbs scattered on top.

Fusilli with Garden Vegetables and Tarragon

3 ripe tomatoes

3 slender carrots, peeled and thinly sliced into rounds

4 small summer squash, thinly sliced or cubed

½ cup peas or a handful sugar snap peas

1 small red onion, quartered and thinly sliced crosswise

1 yellow or red bell pepper, quartered and thinly sliced crosswise

2 garlic cloves, minced

2 tablespoons chopped tarragon

3 tablespoons extra virgin olive oil

Salt and freshly milled pepper

12 ounces fusilli or penne

THIS *pasta dish is also good at room temperature with a dash of balsamic or tarragon vinegar.*

SERVES 3 OR 4

Bring a large pot of water to a boil. Blanch the tomatoes for 10 seconds, then peel, seed, and neatly dice them. Put them in a large bowl. Blanch the carrots and summer squash for 2 minutes and the peas for 1 minute. As they finish cooking, scoop them out with a strainer, shake off the excess water, and add them to the tomatoes along with the onion, bell pepper, garlic, tarragon, and oil. Add salt to the water and cook the pasta until al dente. Scoop it out, add it to the vegetables, and toss well. Taste for salt, season with pepper, and serve.

Linguine with Tomato Sauce

2 garlic cloves

⅓ cup olive oil

2 cups tomato sauce, made from fresh or canned tomatoes, pages 61 and 63

2 tablespoons chopped basil

2 tablespoons chopped parsley

Salt and freshly milled pepper

12 ounces linguine or spaghetti

Red pepper flakes

THIS *Neapolitan pasta shows that good food is often the simplest. In this case it's also very easy to make. A fresh summer tomato sauce is really a treat, but canned tomatoes in purée can make a very respectable sauce when you can't use fresh—which is, after all, most of the time.*

SERVES 4

Start heating a large pot of water for the pasta. Meanwhile, whack the garlic with the flat side of a knife and remove the skins. Warm the oil in a large skillet over medium heat, add the garlic, and cook gently until the cloves are golden. Remove them and discard. Add the tomato sauce and herbs and simmer gently over medium heat, stirring occasionally. Season with a few pinches salt. If the sauce looks a little dry, add a ladle of the pasta water. Cook the pasta in the boiling water until al dente, drain, and put it in a serving bowl. Add the sauce and toss well. Season with pepper to taste and pass red pepper flakes at the table.

Spaghetti with Tomatoes, Olives, and Capers

THIS summer spaghetti has lots of spirit. While delectable with fresh tomatoes, it's enjoyable in the winter too: I make it with 1½ cups diced canned tomatoes in place of the fresh.

SERVES 4 TO 6

⅓ cup olive oil

3 large garlic cloves, 2 sliced and 1 chopped

1 pound Roma tomatoes; peeled, seeded, and chopped; 1 pint cherry tomatoes, quartered; or 1 15-ounce tomatoes, chopped

24 Kalamata olives, pitted and coarsely chopped

¼ cup capers, rinsed

½ teaspoon red pepper flakes

1 tablespoon chopped marjoram

Salt and freshly milled pepper

1 pound spaghetti

½ cup chopped parsley

Heat the oil with the garlic slices in a wide skillet over medium heat. When the garlic is golden, remove and discard it. Add the chopped garlic, tomatoes, olives, capers, pepper flakes, and marjoram. Simmer briskly for 10 minutes and season with salt and pepper. Cook the spaghetti in plenty of boiling salted water, drain, and add it to the sauce along with the parsley. Toss well and serve.

> *Variation with Roasted Peppers:* Add a red and yellow bell pepper, roasted, or 1 cup bottled roasted peppers, peeled, seeded, and chopped, to the skillet with the tomatoes.

Penne with Tomatoes, Olives, Lemon, and Basil

THE tomatoes cook by the heat of the pasta, which leaves them fresh but fully aromatic. Peeling them is optional, but it makes their texture silky. This summer dish couldn't be easier to make or give more in return for such little effort.

SERVES 2 TO 4

1½ pounds ripe tomatoes, 1 or more varieties

3 tablespoons finely diced shallot or onion

3 tablespoons torn basil leaves

1 tablespoon chopped parsley

20 Niçoise olives, pitted and chopped

Grated zest of 1 lemon

2 garlic cloves, minced

2 pinches red pepper flakes

3 tablespoons extra virgin olive oil

Salt and freshly milled pepper

8 ounces penne, conchiglie, or rigatoni

Bring a large pot of water to a boil for the pasta. Plunge in the tomatoes for 10 seconds, then peel, halve, gently squeeze out the seeds, and chop into ½-inch pieces. Combine the tomatoes in a large bowl with the shallot, basil, parsley, olives, lemon zest, garlic, pepper flakes, and oil. (This sauce can sit for an hour before being used.) Add salt to the boiling water and cook the pasta until al dente. Drain and add it to the tomatoes. Toss gently with a wide rubber scraper. Divide among pasta plates, season with pepper, and serve.

Perciatelli with Roasted Tomatoes, Saffron, and Garlic

3 pounds Roma tomatoes, halved lengthwise

¹/₃ cup extra virgin olive oil

1 large slice white sourdough or country bread

4 plump garlic cloves, coarsely chopped

Salt and freshly milled pepper

3 pinches saffron threads

1 pound perciatelli or spaghetti

¹/₃ cup coarsely chopped parsley

Preheat the broiler. Set the tomatoes cut side down in a baking dish in a single layer. Brush them with some of the oil and broil about 6 inches from the heat until the skins begin to char, about 5 minutes. Turn them over with a spatula and broil the second side until browned in places. Don't worry if they start to fall apart.

Brush both sides of the bread with oil and broil until golden on both sides. Break it into large pieces and pulse in a food processor with 1 garlic clove to make fine crumbs. Pound the remaining garlic in a mortar (a large one if you have one) with ¹/₂ teaspoon salt and the saffron until smooth. Stir in a tablespoon of hot water and the remaining oil, then add the tomatoes one by one and pound to make a sauce with a slightly rough texture. (This last step can also be done in a food processor.)

Cook the pasta in plenty of boiling salted water until al dente. Drain, then put it in a warm serving bowl. Toss with most of the sauce, then divide among pasta plates. Spoon the remaining sauce over each portion and finish with the bread crumbs, pepper, and parsley.

PERCIATELLI—SPAGHETTI with a hole down the middle—is ideal for high altitudes since it cooks from both the inside and the outside, taking less time as a result. This pasta is a late-summer favorite in our house.

SERVES 4 TO 6

Broken Lasagne with Fried Green Tomatoes and Parsley

2 pounds green tomatoes, sliced ¹/₃ inch thick

¹/₂ cup fine cornmeal

Salt and freshly milled pepper

Vegetable oil for frying

4 tablespoons extra virgin olive oil

4 garlic cloves, finely chopped

1 heaping cup coarsely chopped parsley

1 pound lasagne noodles, broken into large pieces

Freshly grated Parmesan, dry Jack, or Asiago, if desired

Coat the tomatoes with cornmeal seasoned with salt and pepper. Heat about ¹/₈ inch vegetable oil in a skillet. When hot, add the tomatoes and fry over medium heat until browned but not soft, about 30 minutes on each side. Remove to paper towels to drain.

Put the olive oil, garlic, and parsley in a wide pasta bowl. Cook the lasagne in plenty of boiling salted water until al dente, then drain it, add it to the bowl, and toss with the oil. Season with plenty of pepper. Divide among heated plates, cover with the tomatoes, add more pepper, and grate the cheese lightly over all.

STRONG, curly-edged pieces of lasagne stand up well to fried green tomatoes. Though this one is not a traditional recipe there are a number of traditional lasagne dishes that are tossed rather than layered. Lasagne doesn't always need to be a laborious effort.

SERVES 4 TO 6

Spaghetti with Zucchini and Basil

A VISITOR *from Naples cooked this dish for a group of us at our local cooking school. The zucchini was simmering in olive oil—no scant tablespoon here—and her pasta water was very salty. But the finished dish was neither oily nor salty, and not a single strand remained on our plates. The milk gave the sauce a certain substance.*

SERVES 4 TO 6

1½ pounds small or medium zucchini

⅓ to ½ cup olive oil to taste

2 garlic cloves, thinly sliced

Salt and freshly milled pepper

½ cup half-and-half or milk

1 pound spaghetti

½ cup mixed freshly grated Parmesan and Romano

Handful basil leaves, torn into small pieces

Start heating a large pot of water for the pasta. Quarter the zucchini lengthwise, then cut into ½-inch chunks. Warm the oil with the garlic in a wide skillet. Add the zucchini and season with salt and pepper. Cook gently over medium heat, stirring every so often, until the squash is soft and browned in places, about 20 minutes. Add the half-and-half and cook for 10 minutes more, stirring more frequently.

Meanwhile, add salt to the boiling water and cook the pasta. Drain and toss it with the zucchini, cheeses, and basil. Taste for salt and season with pepper.

Rosemary Pappardelle with Roasted Winter Vegetable and Red Wine Ragout

YOU can cook the vegetables for this hearty pasta a day or two in advance since they don't suffer with time, but plan to add water to thin the sauce. The root vegetables should be cut slightly smaller than the other vegetables.

SERVES 4 TO 6

1 ounce dried porcini, about 1 cup

1 large onion, chopped into ½-inch pieces

1 large red bell pepper, chopped into ½-inch pieces

½ pound mushrooms, preferably shiitake, chopped into ½-inch pieces

4 cups root vegetables cut into small dice—carrots, celery root, turnips, parsnips

2 garlic cloves, chopped

2 tablespoons olive oil

Salt and freshly milled pepper

1 tablespoon tomato paste

Aromatics: 8 sprigs parsley, 4 sprigs thyme, 1 bay leaf, 1 3-inch branch rosemary

1½ tablespoons flour

2 cups dry red wine

1 pound Rosemary Pasta, page 446

3 tablespoons butter

Chopped rosemary or parsley

Preheat the oven to 450°F. Cover the dried mushrooms with 1 cup warm water and set aside for 20 minutes, then drain. Reserve the liquid and chop the mushrooms.

Toss all the vegetables with the oil and 1 teaspoon salt. Roast them on a sheet pan until browned in places, about 25 minutes. Remove the vegetables to a wide skillet set over medium heat and add the chopped mushrooms, tomato paste, and aromatics. Stir in the flour, then add the wine and reserved mushroom water. Simmer, partially covered, for 30 minutes. Season with salt and pepper. Remove the aromatics just before serving.

Meanwhile, make the pasta, roll it out, and cut it into ½-inch-wide strips, or pappardelle. Cook the pasta in plenty of boiling salted water until done, then drain. Toss the pasta with the butter and half the vegetables in a wide pasta bowl. Divide it among individual plates and spoon the remaining vegetables over the top along with the rosemary.

Spaghettini with Salsa Verde

1 cup Salsa Verde, page 55, at room
  temperature

1 pound spaghettini or long fusilli

Salt

Freshly grated Parmesan

GREEN *and pungent
with flecks of parsley,
tart capers, and garlic,
the sauce can be made
ahead of time.*

SERVES 4 TO 6

Put the salsa verde in a pasta bowl. Cook the pasta in plenty of boiling salted water until al dente, then drain and shake off the water. Add it to the bowl and toss well. Grate a little Parmesan over the top or pass around separately.

Variation with Zucchini: Dice 8 ounces tender green zucchini into small cubes and boil in the pasta water until tender, about 4 minutes. Scoop it out, shake off the water, and add to the bowl with the salsa verde. Cook the pasta and toss it with the sauce and zucchini.

Saffron Noodle Cake

2 tablespoons olive oil

2 pinches saffron threads

8 ounces saffron pasta, linguine,
  or spaghettini

Salt and freshly milled pepper

2 eggs, beaten

1/2 cup freshly grated Parmesan
  or Asiago

1 bunch scallions, including an inch
  of the greens, finely sliced

1/2 cup finely chopped parsley

1/3 cup finely chopped basil or marjoram

2 tablespoons butter, olive oil, or
  a mixture of butter and oil

THIS enormously versatile and attractive dish goes well with spring and summer vegetables. The eggs bind the cake and give it more substance but vegans can omit them. You can make Saffron Pasta or buy dried saffron linguine. If you use the latter, omit the saffron from the recipe.

Accompany with the Cherry Tomato and Olive Relish and crumbled goat cheese; Garlic Mayonnaise and roasted peppers; or serve with garlicky braised greens and any spring or summer vegetable ragout.

SERVES 3 OR 4

Warm the oil in a small metal measuring cup, add the saffron, and set aside. Cook the pasta in plenty of boiling salted water until al dente, then drain. Rinse under cold water and shake dry. Combine it with the saffron oil, eggs, cheese, scallions, and herbs and mix well—your hands will be the best tool. Season with salt and plenty of pepper.

Heat half the butter in an 8- or 10-inch nonstick skillet. Add the pasta, pat it down, and even the edges. Cook over medium heat until golden on the bottom, about 5 minutes. Turn the cake out onto a plate, add the remaining butter to the pan, slide the cake back in, and cook until the second side is crisp and golden. Cut into wedges and serve.

Saffron Noodle Cake with Cheese Center Add just half the noodles to the skillet, then cover with a layer of fresh mozzarella, provolone, or Fontina, leaving a 1/2-inch margin around the edge. Cover with the rest of the noodles and finish cooking. When you slice the cake, there will be a thin, succulent layer of cheese in the center.

Saffron Noodle Cake with Pepper Filling Spread 2 cups Peperonata, page 404, over the bottom layer of noodles, then cover with the remainder.

Butterflies with Sautéed Mushrooms

THIS is a pasta for any night of the week—it's pleasant to make and requires few ingredients. Start the mushrooms when you start heating the water for the pasta.

SERVES 4 TO 6

1 pound farfalle

2 tablespoons olive oil

1 tablespoon butter, plus extra to finish

1 pound mushrooms, thinly sliced

¹/₂ lemon

Salt and freshly milled pepper

¹/₂ cup dry white wine

2 garlic cloves, finely chopped

1 small bunch parsley, finely chopped

Freshly grated pecorino Romano or Parmesan, optional

Bring a large pot of water to a boil for the pasta. Meanwhile, heat the oil and butter in a large skillet. Add the mushrooms and sauté over high heat until browned around the edges, 4 to 5 minutes. Squeeze the lemon over them, season with salt, then lower the heat to medium and cook 5 minutes longer, stirring occasionally. When the pan becomes dry, add the wine with the garlic and half the parsley. Season with salt and pepper and reduce the heat to low.

Salt the pasta water, add the pasta, and cook until al dente. Scoop it out and add it to the mushrooms, allowing a little of the water to drip into the pan. Raise the heat and add the rest of the parsley and a little additional butter to finish. Serve with or without the cheese—it's good either way.

Portobello Mushrooms with Pappardelle

EVEN if you make the pasta yourself, this is an easy but impressive, bold dish. The pasta can be made several hours in advance, or you can use dried pasta.

SERVES 2 TO 4

8 ounces Egg Pasta, page 444, cut into ¹/₂-inch-wide noodles or 8 ounces dried pappardelle

2 portobello mushrooms, about 1 pound

2 tablespoons olive oil

1 small onion, finely diced

Salt and freshly milled pepper

2 cloves garlic, finely chopped

1 tablespoon tomato paste

¹/₂ cup dry white or red wine

¹/₃ to ¹/₂ cup cream to taste, optional

¹/₄ cup chopped parsley

2 teaspoons minced rosemary or marjoram

2 tablespoons toasted bread crumbs

Freshly grated Parmesan

Make the pasta first and set it aside. Start heating a large pot of water for the pasta. Meanwhile, remove the stems and gills from the portobellos and slice the caps into ¹/₂-inch strips. Cut the larger pieces in half.

Heat the oil in a large skillet, add the onion, and cook over medium heat until lightly colored. Raise the heat, add the mushrooms, and sauté until they begin to brown, about 4 to 5 minutes. Season with salt and pepper and add half the garlic. Mix the tomato paste and wine and add it to the mushrooms. Lower the heat and cook for 5 minutes more. If the pan dries, add a little pasta water.

Cook the pasta in the boiling salted water, then drain and add it to the mushrooms along with the cream, herbs, and remaining garlic. Toss, correct the seasonings, and divide among warm serving plates. Scatter the bread crumbs and a very light dusting of freshly grated cheese over each serving.

Linguine with Onions, Peas, and Basil

3 tablespoons butter

1 red onion, quartered and thinly sliced
    crosswise

1¹/₂ pounds fresh peas, shucked,
    or 2 cups frozen

Salt and freshly milled white pepper

8 ounces fresh or dried linguine

¹/₄ cup small basil leaves, plucked
    into pieces

3 tablespoons freshly grated Parmesan

NEW onions from the summer garden and fresh peas make a delicate dish for late spring or early summer. Butter and olive oil are both good with peas—although I prefer the butter here.

SERVES 2 TO 4

Start heating a large pot of water for the pasta. Meanwhile, melt 1 tablespoon of the butter in a wide skillet. Add the onion and a few spoonfuls water and stew over low heat until the onions are soft, 8 to 10 minutes. Add the peas and cook until they're bright green and tender, a minute or two. Season with salt and a little pepper.

Cook the pasta in the boiling salted water, then scoop it out and add it to the peas, allowing a little water to fall into the pan. Add the basil and remaining butter, then toss with a large fork and spoon. Distribute the pasta among heated plates, then go back for the peas that have stayed behind and spoon them over the pasta. Add a dusting of Parmesan to each plate.

Fettuccine with Sautéed Peppers and Parsley

4 large bell peppers—red, yellow, and
    orange or all one color

4 tablespoons olive oil

Salt and freshly milled pepper

1 pound fettuccine

²/₃ cup chopped parsley

Freshly grated Parmesan, optional

COLORFUL and uncomplicated, and the peppers echo the shape of the fettuccine.

SERVES 4 TO 6

Start heating a large pot of water for the pasta. Meanwhile, cut the peppers into strips about as wide as the fettuccine. Heat the oil in a large skillet over high heat, then add the peppers; give a stir, let them sit for a few minutes, and stir again. Continue cooking in this fashion for about 10 minutes. The peppers should caramelize here and there along the edges, soften, and yield their juices but not lose their skins. They'll smell very sweet. Season with salt and pepper, add a ladle of the pasta water, and turn the heat to low.

Add salt to the boiling water and cook the pasta until al dente. Scoop it out and add it to the peppers, allowing some of the water to drip into the pan. Raise the heat and toss the pasta and peppers with the parsley. Distribute the pasta among the plates, then go back to the pan for the peppers that have fallen aside. Grate a little cheese over the top and serve.

Variation: Toss 1 pound rigatoni or other sturdy dried pasta shape with ¹/₂ cup Saffron or Garlic Mayonnaise, page 59, then add the peppers. This makes a very luscious dish of pasta.

Pasta and Cheese

Cheese has always been an irresistible partner for pasta. When the heat of the pasta meets the crumbles and shards of cheese, there's an explosion of fragrance that's truly sensational. Cheeses are an immensely enjoyable food, and they can support a good wine—important for wine fanciers who don't eat meat. Cheese is especially appealing in cold weather—appropriate for winter festivities and celebrations. Don't try to make these pastas with less of anything to save calories and fat—just enjoy them fully on special occasions.

Fettuccine with Parmigiano-Reggiano

EVERY mouthful of this classic pasta is a treasure. Though simple, it relies on care each step of the way, starting with the ingredients—the best butter you can get, golden Parmigiano-Reggiano, and fresh egg pasta.

4 TO 6 SMALL SERVINGS

8 ounces Parmigiano-Reggiano, in chunks, at room temperature

¼ pound unsalted butter, in small pieces, at room temperature

1 pound Egg Pasta cut as fettuccine, page 444

Salt and freshly milled pepper

Allow time to grate the cheese finely by hand. Have the wine opened, the table set, and the plates warmed before you begin. Also have a large shallow bowl at hand since you'll need plenty of room to toss the cooked pasta. (This applies to all pasta dishes, but here you especially don't want to waste the perfection of your ingredients.)

Put half the butter in the bottom of the bowl. Cook the pasta in plenty of salted boiling water until done, drain it in a colander, and add to the bowl. Add about ½ cup cheese and begin lifting the strands of pasta with a fork and spoon, working quickly and letting the strands fall back into the bowl. Continue until the butter is melted and the strands are coated.

Add the rest of the butter and another ½ cup cheese and repeat until the strands of pasta are coated with the sauce formed by the melting butter mingling with the cheese. Scatter the rest of the cheese over the top and serve. Pass a pepper mill at the table.

Fettuccine with Gorgonzola

1 garlic clove, thinly sliced

8 ounces Gorgonzola dolcelatte, broken into chunks

2 tablespoons unsalted butter

¼ cup cream or milk

Salt and freshly milled pepper

12 ounces fettuccine

Start heating a large pot of water for the pasta. Meanwhile, set a large bowl with the garlic, cheese, butter, and cream over the pot. As the water heats, the butter and cheese will soften. Don't worry about lumps of cheese—the heat of the pasta will smooth everything out. When the water comes to a boil, remove the bowl and salt the water. Add the pasta and cook the pasta until done. Drain, add it to the cheese, and toss everything with a fork and spoon until the pasta is coated with the sauce. Taste for salt, season with pepper, and serve on warmed pasta plates.

Fettuccine with Goat Cheese Replace the Gorgonzola with 8 ounces fresh goat cheese. Cook as described but toss with chopped thyme or rosemary.

Macaroni Smothered with Onions

3 tablespoons clarified butter or 1 tablespoon each butter and vegetable oil

2 large onions, thinly sliced into rounds

Salt and freshly milled pepper

4 boiling potatoes, peeled and cut into ½-inch chunks

1 pound macaroni

1 cup grated Gruyère

4 tablespoons chopped parsley

Start heating a large pot of water for the pasta. Meanwhile, melt the butter in a wide skillet. Add the onions and cook over medium heat, stirring occasionally, until nicely browned, about 20 minutes. Salt the boiling water, add the potatoes, and boil until tender, about 8 minutes. Scoop them out and put them in a warmed pasta bowl. Add the pasta to the boiling water and cook until al dente. Drain and add to the potatoes. Toss with the cheese and parsley and season with salt and plenty of pepper. Serve smothered with the onions.

Baked Pastas

Baked pasta dishes usually consist of a number of elements—the pasta, vegetable, cheese if using, and plenty of sauce to keep everything moist. Some preparations are very straightforward, others far less so. Lasagne made from scratch can be quite involved, but a tossed lasagne gratin is not. The advantage of all of them is that they can be put together long before they're baked. They're wonderful to come home to when you've been out all day, and they're great dishes for gatherings when you don't want to be in the kitchen.

Angel Hair Pasta and Cheese Soufflé

THE finest of pasta strands, angel hair or capellini is used to make these airy pasta gratins. Bake this gratin in a standard soufflé dish, individual gratin dishes, or a single large one.

SERVES 4

Béchamel Sauce, page 53, using 2½ cups milk, 5 tablespoons butter, salt and pepper, ⅛ teaspoon grated nutmeg

3 eggs, separated

½ cup grated Gruyère

½ cup freshly grated Parmesan

8 ounces capellini

Salt and freshly milled pepper

Begin making the béchamel sauce. While it's cooking, preheat the oven to 450°F. Butter a 2-quart soufflé dish, gratin dish, or four individual dishes. Whisk a little of the sauce into the egg yolks to warm them, then whisk in the rest along with the Gruyère and all but 2 tablespoons of the Parmesan.

Cook the pasta in plenty of boiling salted water until barely al dente, then drain and rinse under cold water. Combine the pasta with the sauce in a roomy bowl. Whisk the egg whites until they hold stiff peaks, then fold them into the pasta. Scrape everything into the prepared dish and sprinkle the remaining Parmesan over the top. Bake until puffed and golden brown, about 25 minutes.

Pasta and Mushroom Soufflé Sauté 8 ounces chopped mushrooms in 1½ tablespoons olive oil over high heat until they release their juices and begin to brown, about 5 minutes. Season with salt, pepper, and 2 teaspoons finely chopped marjoram or rosemary. Stir this mixture into the béchamel sauce and proceed as described. You can replace a portion or all of the milk with Mushroom Stock, page 197.

Pasta and Spinach Soufflé Remove the stems from 1 large bunch spinach, wash well, and cook in the water clinging to its leaves until wilted and tender. Chop finely, add to the béchamel sauce, and proceed as described.

BAKING PASTA IN A MOLD

To give baked pasta dishes a more finished look, brush the bottom and sides of an 10-inch springform pan generously with butter or oil, then coat with fine dried bread crumbs or ground almonds. Place the pan on a cookie sheet. Add 2 beaten eggs to the pasta to ensure that its form will hold, then add the pasta to the mold. Bake at 350°F for 25 minutes until hot. To serve, transfer the pan to a large plate, gently loosen the sides, and remove. Slice into wedges.

Ziti with Sharp Cheddar and Mushrooms

3 tablespoons butter, olive oil, or
    a mixture of oil and butter

1 celery rib, finely chopped

8 ounces mushrooms, chopped

2 leeks, white parts only, quartered
    lengthwise and sliced

1 teaspoon dried marjoram

1/4 cup flour

3 cups milk, warmed

Salt and freshly milled pepper

1/8 teaspoon grated nutmeg

1 heaping tablespoon mustard

1 pound ziti, macaroni, or mostaccioli

1 1/2 cups grated sharp Cheddar

1 cup fresh bread crumbs

ZITI, a tubular pasta, comes in both long strands and short tubes. The long coils are a lot of fun to work with, but macaroni or mostaccioli can also be used.

SERVES 6

Warm the butter in a saucepan. Add the celery, mushrooms, leeks, and marjoram and cook over medium heat for about 5 minutes. Stir in the flour and cook for 1 minute, then quickly whisk in the milk. Simmer for 15 minutes, stirring occasionally. Season the sauce with 1 teaspoon salt, pepper to taste, the nutmeg, and the mustard.

Preheat the oven to 350°F and lightly butter or oil a 3-quart baking dish. Cook the ziti in plenty of salted boiling water until barely done. Drain it in a colander, then rinse under cold water. Combine the pasta with the sauce and cheese, then pour it into the baking dish and cover with the bread crumbs. Bake until bubbling and browned on top, 25 to 30 minutes.

Penne with Eggplant and Mozzarella

1 1/2 to 2 pounds eggplant

Salt and freshly milled pepper

5 tablespoons olive oil

1 onion, finely diced

1/2 teaspoon dried thyme

1/4 teaspoon red pepper flakes

3 garlic cloves, minced

1 28-ounce can crushed tomatoes

1/4 cup chopped basil or marjoram

1 pound penne or macaroni, cooked
    until al dente and rinsed under cold
    water

1 cup grated mozzarella

1 cup grated Gruyère

THE tomato sauce here is quite straightforward, but if you have a little extra time or wish to make this without the cheese, prepare the more robust Red Wine Tomato Sauce—and include the olives as suggested in the variation. You'll need 3 to 4 cups sauce.

SERVES 4 TO 6

Slice the eggplant into rounds or ovals 1/2 inch thick, then into 1/2-inch-wide strips about 2 inches long. Unless the eggplant is very fresh, lightly salt it and set aside while you make the sauce.

Warm 1 1/2 tablespoons of the oil in a medium skillet, add the onion, thyme, and pepper flakes, and cook over medium heat until the onion has softened, about 10 minutes. Add the garlic and cook for a few minutes more. Add the tomatoes and simmer for 30 minutes. Season with salt and pepper.

Preheat the oven to 375°F. Oil a 3-quart baking dish. Pat the eggplant dry. Heat the remaining oil in a large skillet, add the eggplant, and cook over medium heat until golden and tender, stirring occasionally, about 20 minutes. Season with pepper and toss with the herb. Mix the eggplant with the tomato sauce, pasta, and cheeses in the baking dish, then cover with aluminum foil and bake for 35 minutes or until heated through.

Noodle Kugel

ANN *Katzen's kugel and its reputation among Santa Fe friends long preceded our meeting. Slightly sweet, kugels are often served as if they were savory, though you can certainly serve this as dessert. I like this one with Chilled Apple or Quince Sauce and a simple watercress salad.*

SERVES 6 TO 8

1 pound wide egg noodles

2 cups nonfat cottage cheese

2 cups sour cream

4 eggs, lightly beaten

½ cup sugar

½ cup golden raisins

1 cup grated tart apple or ½ cup diced apricot

Topping

1 cup fresh bread crumbs

1 teaspoon *each* ground cinnamon and coriander

1 teaspoon light brown sugar

6 tablespoons butter, melted

Butter a 3-quart baking dish and preheat the oven to 350°F. Cook the noodles in boiling salted water just until they're done, then drain and rinse to stop the cooking. Combine the remaining ingredients in a bowl, stir in the noodles, then turn them into the baking dish. Mix the topping ingredients, then cover the surface with the topping and bake until the top is browned, 45 to 55 minutes. Let it rest for 10 minutes, then turn onto a platter and serve.

Lasagne

Lasagne is not just a casserole to serve to a crowd but an elaborate and very special dish. While lasagne can be relatively simple—some dishes are tossed rather than layered, such as the Tossed Spinach Lasagne and Goat Cheese Gratin—making a lasagne dish is always a bit of work and expense whether you're using dried pasta or fresh, layering it or not. The filling needn't be thick—lasagne is still a pasta dish, after all. Although six layers of pasta are deep and dramatic, I usually use just four, especially if I'm using dried pasta.

Dried, instant, and fresh are the three choices for pasta. Dried pasta tends to be thick. I strongly favor De Cecco, because its wider, shorter sheets are much easier to work with than the usual long, skinny ones. I usually use 10 to 12 ounces for a four-layer lasagne, a pound for six layers, using an 8½- × 11-inch baking dish. Instant or no-boil pasta, a recent product, doesn't require precooking, ends up more like fresh lasagne, and greatly simplifies this complicated dish. (If you parboil it for 30 seconds before layering, it's even better.)

FRESH EGG PASTA FOR LASAGNE: Make a 1½-pound batch of Egg Pasta, page 444, using with 3 cups flour, 3 extra large eggs, 1 tablespoon olive oil or water if needed and ½ teaspoon salt. This may make more than you need, but you can dry the leftover dough and use it another time.

Roll the dough through to the last setting on your pasta machine. Cut the sheets into lengths that equal the length—or width—of your pan. Let the strips rest on lightly floured towels while you continue preparing the dish. They can stand for up to 2 hours before being cooked.

To cook the pasta, bring a large pot of water to a boil and add salt. Have a large bowl of cold water next to the stove. Add a few strips of pasta to the pot at a time, cook for 1 minute, then scoop them out and immediately transfer to the cold water. As you assemble the dish, remove the pieces you need and let them dry briefly on a clean towel. (If using dried pasta, follow the package instructions.)

AHEAD OF TIME Lasagne can be completely formed then allowed to rest for a few hours in the refrigerator before baking. It can also be frozen at this point. But according to Clifford Wright, who has made more lasagne than anyone I know because he's the author of *Lasagne* (Little, Brown, 1995), lasagne is even better upon rebaking. Cover well with foil, keeping it tented over the center. Bake the lasagne just short of the final browning, then let it cool to room temperature, refrigerate it, or even freeze it. Allow time to let it return to room temperature, then cover with foil and bake at 325°F for 45 minutes or until the center is hot.

Tossed Spinach Lasagne and Goat Cheese Gratin

1 pound fresh Spinach Pasta, page 446

2 cups Herb Béchamel, page 53

$1/2$ cup cream

8 ounces goat cheese, crumbled

Salt and freshly milled pepper

1 tablespoon chopped thyme

$1/2$ cup freshly grated Parmesan or aged goat cheese

2 tablespoons cold butter, thinly shaved

HOMEMADE noodles make this dish light and extraordinary. Tossing them with the sauce is not just for speed—it also results in charmingly irregular strata, with small mountains of pasta that rise above the rest, turning crisp and golden.

SERVES 6

Make the pasta dough and, while it's resting, make the béchamel. Add the cream and goat cheese to the sauce. Don't worry about lumps of cheese—they're wonderful to bite into.

Preheat the oven to 375°F. Lightly butter a 3-quart gratin dish. Roll the dough through to the thinnest setting on your pasta machine, then cut it into strips about 8 inches long and 2 inches wide. Parboil them for 1 minute in plenty of salted water, transfer the strips to cold water, then drain. Toss the pasta with the sauce, thyme, pepper, and all but 2 tablespoons of the Parmesan. Pile it in the gratin dish and cover with the remaining cheese and shaved butter. Bake until bubbling and browned here and there on top, 30 to 40 minutes.

Eggplant Lasagne with Garlic Béchamel

THIS *lasagne is packed with summer's sweet eggplant. I might accompany the squares of lasagne with Oven-Roasted Tomato Sauce or a sauté of cherry tomatoes. It can use both the color and the acid bite.*

SERVES 4 TO 6

3 pounds eggplant, sliced lengthwise about ⅓ inch thick

Olive oil, as needed

Salt and freshly milled pepper

1 pound instant lasagne or Egg Pasta dough, page 444, cut for lasagne

2 fresh mozzarella balls, about 8 ounces

½ cup freshly grated Parmesan

6 basil leaves, torn into pieces

Garlic Béchamel

2½ cups milk

3 garlic cloves, smashed with the flat side of a knife, then peeled

4 tablespoons butter

¼ cup flour

½ cup cream or half-and-half

Salt and freshly milled white pepper

Salt the eggplant unless it's garden fresh, then set it aside for 30 minutes. Preheat the oven to 425°F. Blot the eggplant dry and brush both sides with the oil. Set the slices on sheet pans and bake until browned on the bottom, 15 to 20 minutes. Turn the slices over and bake until the second side is browned, another 15 to 20 minutes. The eggplant will look rather dry but will become moist as it sits. Season with salt and pepper. Make the béchamel.

Slowly heat the milk with the garlic in a saucepan. When it comes to a boil, cover the pan, turn off the heat, and set aside to steep for 15 minutes. Melt the butter in another saucepan over medium heat, stir in the flour, and cook for 2 minutes. Pour in the milk all at once through a strainer and stir until the sauce is thickened. Cook over very low heat or in a double boiler over simmering water for 20 minutes, stirring occasionally. Pour in the cream and season with salt and pepper to taste.

Lightly butter an 8- × 10-inch baking dish. Spread ½ cup sauce over the bottom. Add a layer of pasta and cover with ⅓ cup sauce. Lay down one-third of the eggplant, cover with one-third of the mozzarella, 2 tablespoons Parmesan, and two of the basil leaves, torn into small pieces. Repeat with two more layers. Top with a final layer of pasta and cover it with the remaining sauce and Parmesan. Cover with foil. Preheat the oven to 400°F. Bake for 25 to 30 minutes or until heated through. Remove the foil and bake for 10 to 15 minutes more. Let stand for a few minutes before serving.

Mushroom Lasagne

1 ounce dried porcini or morels

Béchamel Sauce, page 53, using 2½ cups milk, 4½ tablespoons butter, 4½ tablespoons flour, salt and white pepper, ⅛ teaspoon grated nutmeg

1 pound portobello mushrooms, stems removed and caps thinly sliced

¼ cup olive oil

4 tablespoons butter

1 pound white mushrooms, thinly sliced

⅓ cup chopped parsley

3 large garlic cloves, finely chopped

Salt and freshly milled pepper

1 pound instant lasagne, dried lasagne, or Egg Pasta, page 444, cut for lasagne

¾ cup freshly grated Parmesan

YOU can have this fragrant mushroom lasagne ready for baking in less than an hour if you use instant lasagne. I make only four layers of mushrooms with dried lasagne; with fresh, which is thinner, I prefer to make six.

SERVES 4 TO 6

Cover the porcini with 1 cup warm water and set aside to soak. Make the béchamel sauce. Cook it in a double boiler over simmering water or over low heat along with the stems from the portobello mushrooms. After 30 minutes, remove the stems. Strain the porcini and add the liquid to the sauce.

Coarsely chop the porcini. Heat half the oil and butter in a wide skillet over high heat. Add half the white mushrooms and sauté until they begin to color around the edges and soften, about 5 minutes. Toss them with half the parsley and garlic, season with salt and pepper, and remove them to a bowl. Repeat with the remaining mushrooms, including the porcini. Add any juices that collect to the sauce.

If using fresh pasta, prepare it as described on page 446. If using dried pasta, parboil it as directed on the box. Instant lasagne needs no attention at this point.

Butter a 9- × 12-inch baking dish. Cover with a layer of pasta, then with ½ cup béchamel sauce, one-fourth of the filling, and 2 tablespoons grated cheese. Repeat this layering until you have four layers of filling. Spread the final layer of pasta with the remaining sauce and cheese.

When ready to eat, preheat the oven to 400°F. Cover the lasagne with foil and bake for 20 to 30 minutes or until heated through. Remove the foil and continue baking until browned in spots on top, 10 to 15 minutes more.

Lasagne-Mushroom Gratin In this variation the same ingredients are tossed together rather than layered. I love the visual effect of the jumbled noodles. Prepare the mushrooms and sauce as described. Cook fresh egg lasagne, then toss everything together but a fourth of the cheese. Bake at 425°F in a large buttered gratin dish—a large earthenware Spanish casserole is especially attractive—covered with the remaining cheese, until bubbling and browned on top.

Lasagne with Eggplant and Chard

1 ½ pounds Egg Pasta, page 444, or 1 box dried

1 cup Fresh Tomato Sauce, page 61, or Quick Canned Tomato Sauce, page 63

1 ½ pounds eggplant, sliced crosswise ¼ inch thick

2 tablespoons olive oil, plus extra for the eggplant

2 tablespoons butter

½ onion, finely diced

3 garlic cloves, finely chopped

1 bunch green chard, about 1 ½ pounds, stems removed

Salt and freshly milled pepper

½ cup dry white wine

1 cup ricotta

1 egg

¾ cup grated pecorino Romano

8 ounces fresh mozzarella, thinly sliced

Prepare the pasta dough and tomato sauce. Roll and cut the dough, set it aside on towels to dry while you prepare the vegetables, then parboil as described on page 464. Unless it's garden fresh, salt the eggplant, let stand 30 minutes, then blot dry.

Preheat the oven to 400°F. Brush both sides of the eggplant lightly with oil. Place the slices on a sheet pan and bake, turning once, until browned on both sides, about 30 minutes in all. Chop coarsely.

Heat 2 tablespoons oil and the butter in a large skillet. Add the onion and garlic and cook over medium heat for about 3 minutes, stirring frequently. Add the chard, sprinkle with ½ teaspoon salt, and cook until wilted, about 5 minutes. Add the wine, cover, and cook until the chard is tender and the pan is dry, about 10 minutes. Turn the mixture out onto a cutting board and finely chop. In a bowl, mix together the ricotta, ⅓ cup water, and the egg, then stir in the chard. Taste and season with salt and freshly ground pepper.

Oil a 9- × 12-inch baking dish. Spread ⅓ cup tomato sauce over the bottom and cover with a layer of pasta. Scatter a quarter of the grated cheese over the top and add a quarter of the eggplant, ricotta mixture, and mozzarella. Follow with another layer of pasta and repeat for three more layers. End with a layer of pasta and the remaining sauce. Cover with foil, tenting it above the surface.

Preheat the oven to 400°F. Bake 20 to 30 minutes or until heated through. Remove the foil and bake for 5 to 10 minutes more.

Ravioli and Cannelloni

As grateful as we are for frozen ravioli, it's the fresh, supple dough and unusual fillings that make the homemade versions so beguiling. Handmade pastas are eminently suitable for special occasions, and the process is fairly straightforward for those with reasonable pasta-making skills.

MAKING FILLED PASTAS: To make these dishes go smoothly, here are a few things to keep in mind. Cheese fillings are easy to make, and since vegetable fillings should be cool, they can be made hours in advance. If you have a shop that sells fresh sheets of *thin* pasta, you can bypass making your own.

Wonton wrappers also come in handy for making ravioli. Use these paper-thin squares, found in the produce section of your supermarket usually near the Asian vegetables, as you would fresh pasta. Egg roll wrappers can be used for cannelloni.

The sauces, which are generally simple, can be made ahead of time unless they're the last-minute type, in which case they're usually quite fast and better made *à la minute*. And once formed, the pasta can be held for several hours before being cooked, providing another window of time.

As always, take a moment to study the recipe before you start and look for lag times, such as the half hour it takes to bake a squash for winter squash ravioli, that you can use for another part of the dish, the meal, or something else altogether.

Tips for Making Small Filled Pastas

Well liked because of their curious shapes and succulent fillings, these stuffed pastas make a very special first or main course. You can float them in a roasted vegetable broth or wild mushroom stock, and although untraditional, I find that a few crescent-shaped agnolotti or cheese-filled ravioli slipped into a vegetable stew add an unexpected luscious bite. Making the pasta, filling, and sauce takes 2 hours at the most for complicated fillings; an hour or less for a simpler one.

AMOUNTS: A 1½-pound recipe of egg pasta (using 3 cups flour, 3 extra large eggs, and 1 tablespoon olive oil and ½ teaspoon salt) makes enough for 36 to 48 filled pastas or four to six servings. (This depends in part on whether you roll your pasta to the last or next-to-the-last setting as well as on the size and shape.) Each ravioli takes a mounded teaspoon of filling, so you'll need 1½ to 2 cups filling.

TO FORM RAVIOLI: Dust the counter lightly with flour. Divide the dough into two or three pieces so that it's easy to handle and roll out one piece at a time, using a pasta machine. It should be thin, but not so thin that it tears easily. Cut the final long strip into smaller lengths so that it's easy to handle. Cover the strips with plastic wrap to keep them supple until you can shape them. Work quickly so that the pasta dough doesn't dry out.

There are many ways to form and shape stuffed pastas. For square ravioli, crease a

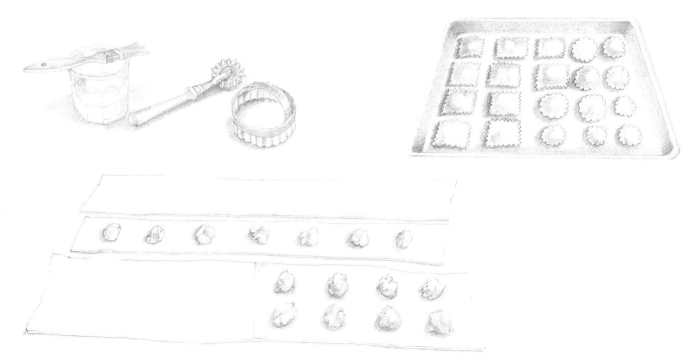

strip of dough lengthwise, then dot it with evenly placed mounds of filling as each recipe suggests. Alternatively, crease a length of dough crosswise, lay out a double row of filling on one half, then bring the second half over the top. You can also place one narrow strip on top of a second strip, dotted with the filling. Some people find that using ravioli forms saves them time.

Always dampen the dough before sealing it tightly. I find a finger does the job best; a pastry brush can also be used, but watch that it doesn't leave too much moisture. Pinch the edges to form a seal. If you're not cooking them within a short time, cover them loosely with a piece of wax paper and then a towel. You can refrigerate them, but preferably no more than an hour or two; otherwise the moisture from the filling will cause the dough to soften on the bottom.

TO COOK RAVIOLI: Using a wide Chinese strainer or cotton towel, lower all the ravioli at once into a pot of gently boiling salted water. If the ravioli have air pockets in them—a not-uncommon occurrence—they'll float to the top, but that doesn't indicate that they're done. Check by tasting a bit of the edge after about 4 minutes. They need 4 to 5 minutes to cook—possibly longer if your dough is on the thick side. When done, lift them out with the strainer rather than dumping them into a colander.

Unlike other pasta, ravioli, which are more fragile, don't need to be in a large quantity of boiling water. Instead they can be cooked in a wide soup pot in salted water that's only gently boiling so that they don't break apart.

MAKING RAVIOLI AHEAD OF TIME: Ravioli can be placed on wax paper and refrigerated, uncovered, for a few hours before cooking. Because their fillings are moist and the dough is fragile, they won't keep much longer than that. They can be frozen, however: Spread them on a cookie sheet and freeze until they're hardened, then transfer them to freezer bags.

Gorgonzola Ravioli with Tomato Sauce

SERVES 4 TO 6

1 ½ pounds Egg Pasta, page 444

Fresh Tomato Sauce, page 61

1 cup ricotta

1 cup crumbled Gorgonzola

¼ cup freshly grated Parmesan, plus
    extra to finish

1 egg

Salt and freshly milled pepper

⅛ teaspoon grated nutmeg

1 tablespoon finely chopped parsley or
    mixed rosemary and parsley

Make the pasta dough and tomato sauce and set aside. Beat the cheeses and egg together until smooth, then season with salt, pepper, and nutmeg.

Roll out the pasta dough and form the ravioli as described. To cook, drop the ravioli into a pot of gently boiling salted water and cook for 4 or 5 minutes. Warm the sauce and pour about ½ cup into each warmed pasta bowl or plate. Scoop out the ravioli and shake off the water. Set them on top of the sauce, then spoon a little extra sauce over the top. Grate a veil of Parmesan over the top and garnish with the parsley.

Variation with Tomato-Cream Sauce: A few tablespoons of cream will smooth and enrich the sauce. Add it once the sauce is finished and cook to heat it through. Add the cooked ravioli to the sauce, swirl them about, then serve.

Spinach Tortellini with Walnuts, Parsley, and Pecorino

1 ½ pounds Egg Pasta, page 444

½ onion, finely diced

1 garlic clove, minced

1 tablespoon *each* olive oil and butter

1 large bunch spinach, about 1 pound, stems removed, leaves roughly chopped

Salt and freshly milled pepper

1 cup ricotta

1 egg

⅛ teaspoon grated nutmeg

Walnut Sauce

½ cup walnuts, roasted and finely chopped

2 tablespoons pine nuts, toasted in a small skillet and finely chopped

1 garlic clove, minced

½ cup chopped parsley

2 tablespoons butter

3 tablespoons extra virgin olive oil

¼ cup grated pecorino Romano or Parmesan, plus extra for garnish

THIS *nut sauce is a quick enhancement for store-bought or homemade pastas alike. The shape of this pasta catches the nuts and shards of cheese in its fold, but you can make a simpler square ravioli if you prefer.*

SERVES 4 TO 6

Make the pasta dough and set it aside to rest.

Cook the onion and garlic in the oil and butter in a skillet over medium heat until the onion is softened, about 6 minutes. Add the spinach, season with ½ teaspoon salt, and cook until tender. Raise the heat to evaporate the remaining juices, then remove and finely chop. Mix with the ricotta and egg and season with the salt, pepper, and nutmeg to taste.

Roll out the dough and cut it into 2-inch squares or circles. Place a dab of filling—about ½ teaspoon—in the center of a square. Fold the square corner to corner, forming a triangle. One side should fall just a little short of the other. Press the edges together. Pick up the triangle and hold it with the long side facing the counter. Wrap the two lower corners around your finger, lapping one over the other, and press to secure them. Repeat with the rest.

Start heating water for the pasta. Meanwhile, in a large bowl combine the nuts, garlic, parsley, butter, olive oil, ¼ cup cheese, a pinch of salt, and pepper to taste. Cook the tortellini in the gently boiling salted water for 4 or 5 minutes and add them to the walnut sauce. Gently mix them into it to melt the butter, then serve lightly dusted with additional cheese.

Eggplant Agnolotti with Tomato Sauce

IF you have a mortar that's large enough, use it for the eggplant. It goes just as quickly as a food processor and leaves a little texture. The eggplant mixture—minus the eggs—makes an excellent spread for crostini.

SERVES 4 TO 6

1 pound eggplant, peeled and thinly sliced

Vegetable or olive oil as needed

1/3 cup walnuts

1 cup ricotta

1/2 cup grated pecorino Romano, plus extra for garnish

2 eggs, beaten

2 tablespoons chopped basil

2 tablespoons chopped parsley

4 teaspoons chopped mint

Salt and freshly milled pepper

1 1/2 pounds Egg Pasta, page 444, or Saffron Pasta, page 446

Fresh Tomato Sauce, page 61

1/4 cup roughly chopped or torn basil leaves

Preheat the oven to 400°F. Brush both sides of the eggplant slices with oil, set on a sheet pan, and bake until browned on the bottom, about 20 minutes. Turn and brown the other side, about 20 minutes more. Pound the walnuts in a mortar or grind in a food processor, then work in the eggplant until fairly smooth. Remove the mixture to a bowl and add the cheeses, eggs, and herbs. Season to taste with salt and pepper. Set aside to cool.

Meanwhile, make the pasta dough. While it's resting, make the tomato sauce. To form the agnolotti, roll out the pasta dough and cut out 3-inch circles with a fluted biscuit cutter. Place the filling on one half of a circle. Brush the edges with water, fold in half and press together. With your fingers, gently bend the half-circle to form a crescent. Cook them in gently boiling salted water for 4 or 5 minutes. Scoop them onto a platter, interspersed with the sauce, basil, and additional grated cheese.

Butternut Squash Ravioli with Toasted Pecans and Sage

THIS is one of my favorite winter pasta dishes, but you might consider it a model for other vegetable-filled ravioli. Sweet potato can be substituted for the squash, or you can go in an entirely different direction, using a potato and winter vegetable puree,or pureed peas, asparagus, or cauliflower.

SERVES 4 TO 6

1 butternut squash, about 2 pounds

Vegetable oil for the squash

2 tablespoons butter

Salt and freshly milled pepper

1/2 cup freshly grated Parmesan

1/2 cup dried bread crumbs

1 1/2 pounds Egg Pasta, page 444

Brown Butter with Pecans and Sage

4 to 6 tablespoons butter

1 garlic clove, thinly sliced

2 tablespoons chopped sage leaves

2 tablespoons chopped parsley

2 teaspoons chopped thyme

1/3 cup pecans, toasted and coarsely chopped

Freshly grated Parmesan or pecorino Romano

Preheat the oven to 375°F. Slice the squash in two, remove the seeds, and brush the cut surfaces with oil. Bake cut side down on a sheet pan until soft, 30 to 40 minutes. Scoop out the flesh and measure 2 cups. Beat it with the butter until smooth and season well with salt and pepper. (If the squash seems watery, dry it out by stirring it in a skillet over high heat to get rid of extra moisture.) Add the cheese and bread crumbs and mix well.

Roll out the dough and form into 2-inch ravioli, circles, or crescents as described in the preceding recipe. In a skillet large enough to hold the finished pasta, melt the butter with the sliced garlic, sage, and 1 tablespoon parsley, and thyme and cook over heat until the butter is lightly browned and has a nutty aroma. Cook the ravioli in the gently boiling salted water for 4 or 5 minutes, then drain. Add the pecans to the skillet with the remaining parsley, then add the ravioli to the sauce. Cook for 30 seconds, then serve dusted with Parmesan.

Cannelloni

Cannelloni are squares of pasta rolled around a filling, blanketed with a protective layer of sauce, and baked. Traditional fillings tend to be based on ricotta cheese or on greens—the same fillings used for ravioli. Like ravioli, cannelloni are traditionally served as a first course but here they're featured as the main event, garnished with vegetables that harmonize with the filling.

PASTA FOR CANNELLONI: Egg pasta made with 1 cup flour, 1 extra-large egg, 1 teaspoon olive oil, and a pinch of salt makes enough pasta for 12 cannelloni, which serves four generously or six modestly. Roll the dough to the thinnest setting on the pasta machine and cut the strips into 12 pieces 5 inches long. Parboil two or three squares at a time until they rise to the surface. Transfer them to a bowl of cold water to stop the cooking, then lay them on a clean kitchen towel to dry for about 10 minutes before filling.

FORMING THE CANNELLONI: Spoon or pipe 2 tablespoons filling through a pastry tube along one of the long edges of a pasta square, going almost to the end. Loosely roll the pasta to form a tube, like a cigar. Place the stuffed pastas in a lightly buttered baking dish so that they're just touching but aren't crowded. Keeping the flap side facing up makes them easier to remove. Make only a single layer of cannelloni and cover with béchamel sauce.

MAKING CANNELLONI AHEAD OF TIME: Cannelloni can be formed a day ahead of baking, covered with plastic wrap, and refrigerated. They can also be frozen, but it seems a shame to go to so much effort for frozen food. Either way, allow the cannelloni to come to room temperature before baking.

Cannelloni with Ricotta, Pesto, and Sautéed Tomatoes

SERVES 4 TO 6

8 ounces Egg Pasta, page 444

Béchamel Sauce, page 53, made with 1$\frac{1}{2}$ cups milk, 3 tablespoons butter, 3$\frac{1}{2}$ tablespoons flour, salt, and white pepper

1$\frac{1}{2}$ cups ricotta

$\frac{1}{2}$ cup freshly grated Parmesan, plus extra for the dish

$\frac{1}{4}$ cup Pesto or Basil Puree, page 57 or 507

1 egg

Salt and freshly milled pepper

Sautéed Tomatoes

2 large ripe tomatoes, peeled and seeded

1 tablespoon butter or extra virgin olive oil

1 teaspoon balsamic vinegar

Make the pasta dough and set it aside to rest. Make the béchamel sauce. Combine the ricotta, Parmesan, pesto, and egg. Season with salt and pepper. If you wish a more pronounced basil flavor, add a little more of the pesto or basil puree to pick it up.

Roll out the pasta and form 12 cannelloni as described on page 473. Lay them in a buttered gratin dish, cover with the sauce, and grate a little extra Parmesan over the top. Preheat the oven to 375°F and bake until hot, about 30 minutes. Meanwhile, neatly dice the tomatoes, discarding the core. Heat the butter in a medium skillet over high heat. When foamy, add the tomatoes and quickly sauté them just long enough to warm them through. Season with salt and pepper, add the vinegar, and swirl the pan over the heat for a few seconds. Serve the tomatoes scattered around each portion of cannelloni.

Green Cannelloni with Ricotta and Peppers

A PARTICULARLY attractive white, green, and red pasta dish.

SERVES 4 TO 6

8 ounces Spinach Pasta, page 446

Béchamel Sauce, page 53, made with 1$\frac{1}{2}$ cups milk, 3 tablespoons butter, 3$\frac{1}{2}$ tablespoons flour, salt and white pepper, and $\frac{1}{8}$ teaspoon nutmeg

2 large red bell peppers, roasted

Salt and freshly milled pepper

1 tablespoon thinly sliced basil leaves

Olive oil

1 cup ricotta

1 cup freshly grated Parmesan

1 egg

2 tablespoons chopped parsley

Make the pasta dough and set it aside to rest. Meanwhile, make the béchamel sauce. While it's cooking, finely dice the peppers and toss them with salt and pepper, the basil, and enough olive oil to moisten. Set aside.

Beat the cheeses with the egg and parsley and season with $\frac{1}{2}$ teaspoon salt and a few twists of the peppermill. Shape and fill 12 cannelloni as described on page 473. Lay them in a lightly buttered baking dish, then spoon the béchamel sauce over them.

Preheat the oven to 375°F. Bake the cannelloni for 25 minutes. Let stand for a few minutes, then serve, garnished with the roasted peppers.

Green Cannelloni with Sautéed Mushrooms Sautéed mushrooms are another vegetable that flatters these cannelloni. Thinly slice a pound of mushrooms, then sauté them in butter and olive oil. Add a little chopped garlic and parsley once they're cooked, then spoon them around the cannelloni.

Saffron Cannelloni with Chard Filling and Chard Stem Garnish

8 ounces Saffron Pasta, page 446

Béchamel Sauce, page 53, made with 1½ cups milk, 3 tablespoons butter, 3½ tablespoons flour, salt, and white pepper

2 large bunches chard, stems removed but reserved

1½ tablespoons olive oil

1 white onion, finely diced

¼ cup finely chopped parsley

1 cup ricotta

½ cup freshly grated Parmesan

2 tablespoons mascarpone or crème fraîche

1 teaspoon grated lemon zest

Salt, freshly milled pepper, and grated nutmeg

Fresh lemon juice

Butter or extra virgin olive oil

HERE the chard stems, so often thrown away, are finely diced and used to garnish the cannelloni.

SERVES 4 TO 6

Make the pasta dough and set it aside to rest while you make the béchamel sauce. Cook the chard leaves in boiling salted water until tender, about 5 minutes. Drain, rinse under cold water, then press out the excess moisture and finely chop. Put the chard in a bowl.

Heat the oil in a small skillet over medium heat. Add the onion and parsley and cook until the onion is translucent, about 5 minutes. Add the onion to the chard and mix with the ricotta, half of the Parmesan, the mascarpone, lemon zest, and ⅛ teaspoon nutmeg. Season with ½ teaspoon salt or more to taste and a little pepper.

Shape and fill 12 cannelloni as described on page 473. Preheat the oven to 375°F. Arrange them in a buttered gratin dish and cover with the béchamel sauce and remaining cheese. Bake until browned and bubbling, 25 to 30 minutes. Meanwhile, trim the chard stems, then go over them lightly with a vegetable peeler. Dice them into small cubes—you'll need about a cup—then put them in a pan with water to cover, a tablespoon lemon juice, and ½ teaspoon salt. Simmer until tender, about 7 minutes, then drain. Toss them with a little butter or olive oil and season with pepper. Serve the cannelloni with the chard stems scattered around them.

Cannelloni with Greens and Sautéed Artichokes

THESE *greens have plenty of character. They also make a good filling for empanadas. If artichokes aren't in season, you can omit them entirely and serve the cannelloni with diced tomatoes warmed in a little butter or olive oil or Oven-Roasted Tomato Sauce.*

SERVES 4 TO 6

8 ounces Egg Pasta, page 444

Béchamel Sauce, page 53, made with 1½ cups milk, 3 tablespoons butter, 3½ tablespoons flour, salt and white pepper, ⅛ teaspoon grated nutmeg

1½ pounds mixed greens, such as chard, kale, watercress, beets, spinach, arugula, stems removed

3 tablespoons chopped parsley

3 tablespoons chopped basil

2 tablespoons chopped marjoram

2 garlic cloves, finely chopped

1 cup ricotta

1 egg

¼ cup fresh bread crumbs

Salt, freshly milled pepper, and grated nutmeg

Sautéed Artichokes

3 medium artichokes, trimmed and quartered

Juice of 1 large lemon

2 tablespoons olive oil

Salt and freshly milled pepper

2 tablespoons parsley chopped with 1 small garlic clove

Make the pasta and set it aside to rest. Make the béchamel sauce. While it's cooking, boil the greens in plenty of salted water until tender, about 5 minutes. Drain, rinse under cold water, then squeeze out the excess moisture and finely chop them. Mix the greens with the herbs, garlic, ricotta, egg, and bread crumbs. Season to taste with salt, pepper, and a few pinches grated nutmeg.

Preheat the oven to 375°F. Shape and fill 12 cannelloni as described on page 473. Arrange them in a lightly buttered gratin dish and cover with the béchamel sauce. Bake until lightly browned on top and heated through, about 30 minutes. Meanwhile, dice the artichoke hearts into ½-inch pieces. As you work, toss the pieces with lemon juice. Heat the oil in a wide skillet. Drain the artichokes, add them to the oil, and sauté over high heat until golden and tender, about 7 minutes. Season with salt and pepper and toss with the parsley-garlic mixture. Serve the cannelloni with the artichokes spooned around them and over the top.

Dumplings

I THINK of dumplings as tender little mouthfuls that are ultimately soothing, the way soft and starchy foods should be. We don't make dumplings much anymore but they're so good they deserve a fresh look. You can make them out of nothing fancier than your cupboard items, like flour and semolina, milk, and perhaps eggs.

Semolina Coins

3½ cups milk

2 pinches saffron threads, optional

Salt

1 cup plus 2 tablespoons semolina

4 tablespoons butter

3 eggs or 2 whole eggs and 2 egg yolks

½ cup grated Gruyère

½ cup freshly grated Parmesan

⅛ teaspoon grated nutmeg

2 tablespoons melted butter

Lightly butter a sheet pan and a 2- or 3-quart gratin dish and set aside.

Heat the milk in a spacious saucepan, crumble in the saffron, and add 1 teaspoon salt. When it's almost boiling, whisk in the semolina, adding it in a fine, steady stream. Stir constantly as the milk comes to a boil, then cook until stiff enough to support a spoon, about 3 minutes. Remove from the heat. Beat in the butter and then the eggs, one at a time. Then stir in the Gruyère, half the Parmesan, and the nutmeg. Pour the mixture onto the sheet pan and spread it out to a thickness of ⅓ inch. It will cover about half the pan. Let stand until set, about 2 hours or overnight. Cover with plastic wrap if longer than 2 hours.

Preheat the oven to 375°F. Using a juice glass or wine glass, cut out 2-inch circles of the firm semolina, pick them up with a spatula, and overlap them in the baking dish. (Mine never look very even at this point, but they end up just fine.) Reserve the scraps. With the scraps you can form oval dumplings by scooping it up in one teaspoon and shaping it with a second, then baking them in a gratin dish. Or pack the scraps into buttered ramekins and bake them later, then turn them onto a plate with a little tomato sauce, sautéed mushrooms, or surrounded by a vegetable stew. Drizzle the melted butter and scatter the rest of the Parmesan.

Bake until hot, bubbling, and beginning to color on top, 20 to 25 minutes. Run them under the broiler at the end until the top is golden.

EVERYONE is happy to eat these little dumplings. The batter can be made and cut hours before they're baked. (If you don't want to bother with the cutting, you can just pour the warm semolina directly into the dish, then cut it nicely when you serve.) Accompany with a light tomato sauce, kale or other skillet greens, Sautéed Peppers, or an Herb-Baked Tomato.

SERVES 4

Potato Gnocchi

GNOCCHI is one of those foods that can be heavenly or ghastly. The art is in getting the feel of the dough. Practice before making them for company and follow these tips: Use baking potatoes and bake rather than boil them; pass them through a ricer or a food mill so they'll stay light and fluffy; and don't beat or mash them. There are two stages at which the gnocchi can rest before baking.

MAKES ABOUT 100 LITTLE DUMPLINGS, SERVING 4 TO 6 AS A MAIN COURSE, 8 AS AN APPETIZER

2 large russet potatoes, about 2 pounds
1¼ cups flour or more if needed
Salt and freshly milled pepper

3 tablespoons cold butter
½ cup freshly grated Parmesan

Preheat the oven to 400°F. Pierce the potatoes and bake until tender when a knife is inserted, 45 minutes to an hour, depending on the size. Peel them while they're hot and pass them through a food mill or ricer, letting them fall into a large bowl. They should be light and fluffy. Let cool for 15 minutes, then sprinkle with the flour and 1 teaspoon salt. Using your hands, gently work until you have a smooth, soft dough. If it seems sticky, add a few tablespoons more flour, but don't knead or overwork it.

Take a quarter of the dough and roll it into a long rope about ½ inch thick. Cut it diagonally into pieces about ¾ inch long. You can either roll them into little balls or press one side against the tines of a fork. Set them in a single layer on a baking sheet lightly dusted with flour. Repeat with the remaining dough, then cover with a towel and refrigerate for a few hours if you aren't ready to cook them.

To cook, bring a wide casserole or skillet of water to a boil and butter a large gratin dish. Add salt to the water, then lower the heat to a simmer. Add a batch of 10 or 15 gnocchi and cook gently until they rise to the top. Count 10 seconds, then lift them out with a strainer and remove them to the dish. Finish cooking the rest. (This can be done ahead of time.) When you're ready to eat, preheat the oven to 400°F. Shave the cold butter over the top and cover with a thick veil of cheese. Bake until bubbling and the cheese is beginning to brown in places, about 25 minutes. Add fresh pepper and serve.

Variations: Instead of baking the gnocchi, use two pans, simmer them all at once, then gently lift them out of the water into a serving bowl. Pour on melted butter and add the cheese or serve them with a light Fresh Tomato Sauce, page 61. A few gnocchi make a tender addition to a spring vegetable stew.

Saffron Dumplings

THESE little dumplings, based on a classic cream puff batter, can be added to vegetable stew or broiled. Serve with Sautéed Spinach and Tomatoes Glazed with Balsamic Vinegar.

SERVES 3 TO 4

1 cup milk
2 pinches saffron threads
3 tablespoons butter
3 tablespoons minced herbs—parsley with chives, marjoram, or basil

Salt and freshly milled pepper
1 cup flour
4 eggs

Preheat your broiler and lightly butter a large gratin dish.

Heat the milk with the saffron threads, butter, herbs, ¾ teaspoon salt and a little pepper. When boiling and the butter has melted, stir in flour all at once, then remove the pan from the heat and beat it vigorously with a wooden spoon to make a smooth paste. Return the pan to a low heat and continue beating until the paste leaves a film on the bottom of the pan. Turn off the heat, and beat in the eggs, one at a time, until smooth and completely incorporated. (In a mixer, use a paddle attachment.)

Bring a wide, deep skillet of water to a simmer and add 1 teaspoon salt. Drop the batter by tablespoons (smaller, if they're for soup), into the water and cook for 6 minutes. Turn and cook on the second side for 6 minutes more. (Don't let the water boil—the dumplings will far apart.) When done, remove them to the prepared dish. Drizzle the melted butter over the top, dust with cheese, and broil until golden and sizzling.

Asian Noodles

LIKE *Italians, Asians are enthusiastic noodle eaters. Unlike Italian noodles, however, Asian noodles are made from all kinds of flour, not only the wheat that is prevalent in China but also yam, potato, rice, and other starches. Their shapes and textures range from clear and silky mung bean threads to green-tea and buckwheat soba to thick, plump rice noodles. There are probably hundreds of different Asian noodles, a number of which are available at Asian groceries, natural food stores, and even supermarkets.*

One of the frustrations of Asian noodle dishes for many strict vegetarians is the ubiquitous presence of fish sauce, oyster sauce, and dried bonito. If you use these products, more flavors are available to you. In the following recipes, these popular seasonings have been replaced by others that leave the finished dish just as flavorful.

Cooking Asian Noodles

Asian noodles are cooked differently from Italian pasta. First, the water isn't salted, and second, the noodles are cooked until tender, not al dente. In the case of Japanese soba, somen, and udon, the water foams and rises when the water returns to a boil, then cold water is added to make it subside. After this happens three or four times, the noodles are usually done—taste them to be sure. Depending on thickness, they cook in 5 to 7 minutes. Rice noodles and mung bean noodles are soaked to tenderness rather than cooked.

Asian noodles are often drained, rinsed well to wash off the starch, then added to the dish and reheated, unlike Italian pastas, which are best added directly from the cooking pot to the sauce.

CELLOPHANE OR BEAN-THREAD NOODLES: Made from mung bean starch, these wrinkled nests of silvery, thin noodles become clear and soft once soaked. Soak dried noodles in a bowl of warm water for about 15 minutes if they are to be cooked further, 30 minutes if not. Snip the strands to shorter lengths with scissors. If the dried noodles are thrown into hot oil, they'll instantly puff up into white, crunchy strands resembling shredded Styrofoam. They make a dramatic bed—or garnish—for stir-fries.

CHINESE EGG NOODLES OR MEIN: Sold both fresh and dry, these noodles most resemble Western pasta—in fact, linguine and fettuccine are often suggested as substitutes for thin and wide mein, but their flavor is unique. The fresh noodles come tightly packed and wrapped in plastic. Before cooking, you'll need to pull all the strands apart, fluffing them as you go. When loosened, a small package becomes quite a large pile. Dried egg noodles look something like bedsprings. They're cooked in unsalted boiling water. When they begin to soften, start pulling the strands apart with a pair of chopsticks.

RICE NOODLES OR RICE VERMICELLI OR RICE STICKS: These are the noodles used for *pad thai* and other dishes from Southeast Asia and southern China. Sold dried outside of large Asian communities, rice sticks are whitish, either wavy or straight, and about as long as a chopstick. Rather than cooked, thin noodles or rice sticks are soaked in warm water for 10 to 15 minutes until soft, then added to soup or stir-fried. Wider flat rice noodles are covered with boiling water and then allowed to soften. Like mung bean noodles, rice sticks can be thrown into hot oil, which turns them crisp and light within moments. When fresh, rice noodles are called *fun*.

SOBA OR BUCKWHEAT NOODLES: These Japanese noodles are very refined, their taste both delicate and earthy. Some of the fancier varieties are quite elegant and very expensive. Soba is served cold during the sultry Japanese summers or hot in winter. You also can use soba to replace the Italian buckwheat pasta, pezzoccheri, which is hard to find here.

UDON AND SOMEN: These Japanese noodles are made from wheat flour and come packaged in little 8-inch-long bundles. They are usually served in broth with accompanying garnishes. Some varieties are extremely fine. Those about the thickness of a toothpick are served chilled with cucumbers. Others are large, some smooth and machine made, others rougher looking. I especially like the latter, for they have a very handmade look when cooked.

Noodles in Thai Curry Sauce

PREPARED *Thai curry pastes, available at many natural food stores and some supermarkets, deliver enormous amounts of flavor with ease and make a good staple for your cupboard. Serve these noodles hot or tepid.*

SERVES 4

8 ounces fresh or dried Chinese noodles or linguine

1½ tablespoons roasted peanut oil

3 garlic cloves, minced

1 teaspoon minced ginger

2 large shallots, thinly sliced into rounds, or ½ onion, diced

1 15-ounce can unsweetened coconut milk

1 to 3 teaspoons red Thai curry paste

2 tablespoons soy sauce

2 scallions, thinly sliced into rounds

Fresh basil leaves, Thai basil, if possible, and small cilantro sprigs for garnish

Cook the noodles in plenty of boiling water until tender—about 2 minutes for fresh, 4 to 6 minutes for dried, and slightly longer for linguine. Drain and rinse well to stop the cooking.

Heat the oil in a wok or a skillet until just short of smoking. Add the garlic, ginger, and shallots and stir-fry over high heat until softened, about 2 minutes. Add the coconut milk, curry paste, and soy sauce and stir to break up the paste. Lower the heat and simmer until everything is well blended, 3 to 4 minutes. If serving hot, add the noodles and toss until they're warmed through. If serving cold, toss with the sauce once it's cool. Turn the noodles onto a platter and garnish with the scallions, basil, and cilantro.

Burmese Noodles

The Curry Paste

½ onion, chopped

2 large garlic cloves

2 ¼-inch rounds fresh ginger

1 teaspoon paprika

½ teaspoon turmeric

½ teaspoon salt

2 red bird chiles, chopped, or
    ½ teaspoon red pepper flakes

The Noodles and Vegetables

5 dried shiitake or Chinese black
    mushrooms

8 ounces fresh Chinese egg noodles or
    fettuccine

⅓ cup chopped roasted peanuts

2 tablespoons roasted peanut oil

1 large tomato, seeded and cut into
    ½-inch pieces

½ can unsweetened coconut milk, the
    cream reserved

1 handful snow peas, trimmed

2 scallions, including most of the
    greens, cut into 1-inch pieces

2 tablespoons soy sauce

Cilantro, basil, and mint leaves for
    garnish

A FRIEND with a passion for Asian food created this vegetarian version of one of his favorite dishes for me. The fresh noodles soak up the sauce and all its rich flavors.

SERVES 2

Using a mortar and pestle or a food processor, work all the curry paste ingredients into a rough paste and set aside.

Soak the mushrooms in warm water in a small bowl for 15 minutes or longer; drain, reserving the liquid. Discard the stems and slice the caps into strips. Pull the noodles apart with your fingers. Prepare the peanuts.

Heat the oil in a wok over high heat, add the curry paste, and move it around the pan for 30 seconds. Lower the heat to medium and cook for 12 to 15 minutes, stirring frequently and adding small amounts of water from time to time to keep it from sticking. When it begins to release some of the oil, add the tomato, raise the heat, and add the mushroom liquid and coconut milk. Simmer for a minute, then add the mushrooms, snow peas, scallions, and soy; turn off the heat.

Cook the noodles in plenty of boiling water until tender, about 4 minutes for fresh noodles. Scoop them out, shake off the excess water, and add them to the wok. Lift several times to coat thoroughly with the sauce. Pile the noodles onto platter and garnish with the reserved coconut cream, the peanuts, and the herbs.

Soba with Hijiki and Stir-Fried Vegetables

HIJIKI, a delicious black sea vegetable, garnishes this robust cold-weather pasta.

SERVES 3 TO 4

¼ cup dried hijiki, soaked for 30 minutes and drained

3½ tablespoons soy sauce

2 teaspoons sugar

6 ounces soba

1½ tablespoons peanut oil

1 bunch scallions, whites thinly sliced into rounds and greens sliced diagonally

4 teaspoons chopped fresh ginger

1 large garlic clove, chopped

2 carrots, cut into julienne strips

5 large mushrooms, thinly sliced

Salt

1 tablespoon rice wine (mirin)

4 cups Napa cabbage leaves sliced into ½-inch ribbons

2 teaspoons dark sesame oil

2 tablespoons sesame seeds, toasted in a small skillet

Chili oil

Put the hijiki in a saucepan with 2 tablespoons of the soy sauce, the sugar, and water to cover. Simmer for 15 minutes or until soft, then drain, reserving the liquid.

Cook the soba in plenty of boiling water until tender, 5 to 7 minutes. When the water foams up, add a cup of cold water to bring it down and repeat if necessary. Drain and rinse well under running water.

Place the peanut oil in a wok and heat until hot but short of smoking. Add the white parts of the scallions, ginger, and garlic and stir-fry over high heat for 45 seconds. Add the carrots and mushrooms and stir-fry for 1 minute, then add ½ teaspoon salt, the remaining soy sauce, and the mirin. Toss, then cover the pan and cook for 1 minute. Add the soba, cabbage, and most of the hijiki and toss until the noodles are heated through. Turn off the heat and toss once more with dark sesame oil and sesame seeds. Remove to a platter and garnish with the remaining hijiki, the scallion greens, and drops of chili oil to taste.

Somen in Broth with Silken Tofu and Spinach

A LIGHT, brothy noodle dish—so simple and clean. A small cluster of enoki mushrooms would make an aesthetically appealing garnish here—or use one or two white mushrooms, thinly sliced.

SERVES 2

3 cups Stock for Stir-Fries, page 262, or Kombu Stock with Dried Mushrooms, page 232

Few drops soy sauce, preferably mushroom soy

1 tablespoon rice wine (mirin) or to taste

2 ounces somen

½ 10-ounce package silken tofu, finely diced

2 mushrooms, thinly sliced

12 spinach leaves, cut into wide ribbons

½ teaspoon dark sesame oil

2 scallions, thinly sliced

2 teaspoons toasted sesame seeds

Chili oil

Make the stock and taste it. You may need to build the flavor by adding a little soy sauce and mirin to taste.

Cook the somen in plenty of boiling water until tender, 3 to 5 minutes, adding cold water when it begins to foam to the top of the pot. Drain and rinse thoroughly under cold water. Shake dry.

Add the tofu, mushrooms, spinach, and sesame oil to the stock and simmer gently for about 3 minutes. Add the somen and simmer until it's heated through. Divide between two bowls and garnish with the scallions and sesame seeds. Add a few drops chili oil if you like the heat.

Soba in Broth with Spinach, Purple Dulse, and Silken Tofu

Kombu Stock with Dried Mushrooms, page 232

6 ounces soba

2 clumps dulse or wakame

1 slender carrot, very thinly sliced on the diagonal

1 10-ounce box silken tofu, diced into small cubes

2 cups small spinach leaves, stems removed

2 scallions, diagonally sliced

16 cilantro leaves

Chili oil

A VERY light, fresh, and pretty noodle dish. Purple-colored dulse, a kind of seaweed, is gorgeous in the bowl. You can also use wakame, a similar but slightly more substantial sea green. Take a few dried clumps of either and soak them briefly in cool water. The leaves will open up. Separate them if joined at the base.

SERVES 4

Make the kombu stock and strain it carefully. Remove the stems from the mushrooms and thinly slice the caps. Cook the noodles in plenty of boiling water until tender but slightly undercooked since they will be reheated later. Rinse under cold water. Cover the dulse with cool water and run your fingers over it to loosen any tiny seashells or sand. Pull the leaves apart with your fingers.

Bring the stock to a boil in a saucepan. Add the mushrooms and carrot and simmer for 1 minute. Add the noodles and tofu and simmer very gently until both are heated through, after several minutes. Finally add the spinach and cook until the it's wilted. Divide the noodles among heated bowls, then ladle the broth and vegetables over them. Drain the dulse and add it to the bowls as well. Garnish with the scallions and cilantro and serve with a few drops chili oil in each bowl.

Udon with Stir-Fry and Five-Spice Tofu

*AN exceptionally flavor-
ful plate of noodles. The
tofu, available at natural
food stores, is baked and
flavored with five-spice
powder. It's perfectly seasoned for this dish.*

SERVES 2 TO 4

The Sauce

¹/₃ cup Stock for Stir-Fries, page 262,
  or water

3 tablespoons hoisin sauce

1¹/₂ tablespoons soy sauce

1¹/₂ tablespoons tomato paste

2 garlic cloves, minced

2 jalapeño chiles, seeded and finely
  chopped

1 tablespoon grated lemon zest or
  minced lemongrass

The Noodles and Vegetables

1 7- or 8-ounce package udon

2 tablespoons roasted peanut oil

¹/₂ package five-spice tofu, thinly sliced

2 medium leeks, white parts only,
  julienned

1 red bell pepper or ¹/₂ *each* red and
  green, thinly sliced into long strips

4 mushrooms, thinly sliced

Salt and freshly milled pepper

Coarsely chopped cilantro for garnish

Mix all the sauce ingredients together and set aside.

Cook the noodles in plenty of boiling water until tender, 5 to 7 minutes. When the water foams up, add a cup of cold water to make the foam subside and repeat if needed. Drain and rinse when done.

Heat the wok with the oil until hot but not smoking. Add the tofu and stir-fry over high heat until it's sizzling, about 1 minute. Remove and set aside. In the same oil, stir-fry the leeks and bell pepper for 1 minute. Add the mushrooms and cook for 1 minute more, then season with a few pinches salt. Return the tofu to the wok and add the sauce. Cook for 30 seconds and turn off the heat.

Drain the udon, shake it dry, and put it on a platter with the vegetables and tofu over the top. Season with pepper and garnish with the cilantro.

Glass Noodles with Spinach

*IN The Modern Art of
Chinese Cooking,
Barbara Tropp sings the
praises of this dish. She
calls for a rich chicken
stock, but I use vegetable
stock in its place. Keep
this dish in mind when
spinach is tender and
young.*

SERVES 3 TO 4

2 bunches young spinach

Salt

2 ounces bean-thread or cellophane
  noodles

1 cup Basic Vegetable Stock, page 196

1¹/₂ tablespoons peanut oil

¹/₂ teaspoon sugar

2 teaspoons dark sesame oil

Bring a medium pot of water to a boil. Meanwhile, separate the clumps of spinach, remove the leaves, and trim the root ends to about 1¹/₂ inches in length. These are called the *crowns*. Wash both leaves and crowns in plenty of cold water. Flush out the roots under running water. Add salt to the water and blanch the crowns until the colors glow, then scoop them out. Blanch the leaves until wilted and bright green. Drain and rinse along with the crowns under cold water. Gently press out the excess liquid.

Soak the noodles in hot water until softened, about 3 minutes, then drain and snip them into 5-inch lengths. Simmer the noodles in the stock until tender and silky, 3 to 5 minutes. They will have absorbed most of the stock.

Warm a wok, then add the peanut oil and heat until almost smoking. Add the spinach leaves and crowns and stir-fry for 30 seconds. Add $1/2$ teaspoon salt and the sugar and continue to stir-fry until the leaves are hot. Add the noodles and sesame oil, stir a few more times, taste for salt, and serve.

Chinese Dumplings with Shredded Cabbage, Mushrooms, and Leeks

1 pound Napa cabbage

Salt

$1/4$ cup dried black Chinese mushrooms

$1/4$ cup dried tree ear mushrooms

6 fresh mushrooms, finely chopped

2 tablespoons chopped leek or scallion

1 teaspoon minced garlic

1 teaspoon minced ginger

1 teaspoon rice wine vinegar

Sichuan Pepper Salt, page 76, or salt and freshly milled white pepper

24 wonton wrappers

THESE dumplings are surprisingly easy to make. Steaming produces a more flavorful dumpling, but they can also be fried, as for potstickers. Serve with one of the Asian dipping sauces.

MAKES APPROXIMATELY 20 DUMPLINGS

Slice the cabbage leaves into strips $1/2$ inch wide and the base about $1/8$ inch wide. Measure 4 cups into a colander. Sprinkle lightly with salt, toss, and set aside for an hour. Squeeze out the excess moisture. It shouldn't be necessary to rinse it, but taste to make sure. Meanwhile, cover the dried mushrooms generously with boiling water and let soak for 15 minutes. Squeeze dry, remove the stems, and slice the caps into thin strips. Reserve the soaking liquid.

Combine the cabbage, dried and fresh mushrooms, leek, garlic, ginger, and vinegar. Add Sichuan pepper salt to taste and more vinegar if needed to bring up the flavors. Put a spoonful of the filling in the middle of a wonton wrapper, paint the edges with water, and fold the opposite corners together. Use as much filling as you can and still be able to close the dumpling. Make two or three pleats on each side, then set the dumpling down firmly to make a solid, flat bottom. Repeat with the remaining filling and wrappers. Cover with a barely damp towel until ready to cook.

To steam the dumplings, lightly oil the surface of the steamer, set the dumplings on top, and bring the water to a boil. Cover and steam for 7 minutes.

To fry the dumplings, coat a 12-inch cast-iron skillet generously with peanut oil, add the dumplings, and fry over medium-high heat until golden on the bottom. Add enough of the reserved mushroom soaking liquid, plus water if needed, to come about one-third up the side of the dumplings—stand back—and cover until the hissing subsides. Boil briskly until the liquid is reduced and the potstickers begin to fry again. Now is when they stick to the pot. Turn off the heat and gently loosen them with a thin metal spatula.

Savory Tarts, Pies, Turnovers, and Pizzas

EVERYONE LIKES A PIE. TARTS, FLANS, GALETTES, TURNOVERS, AND PIZZAS—ALL THE WAYS CRUSTS AND FILLINGS ARE COMBINED—HAVE UNIVERSAL APPEAL. IF YOU'RE WONDERING WHAT TO SERVE A GUEST WHOSE EATING disposition runs away from vegetarian dishes, try one of these recipes. Pies are trusty and familiar, and always welcome.

There's quite a range of possibilities when it comes to pairing crusts with fillings. Some savory tarts are silky smooth—such as the Tender Tomato Tart, a tender tart of garden vegetables, or the resounding Roasted Eggplant and Tomato Tart. Their flaky crusts provide an important textural contrast to the smooth filling, but you could easily bake these in ramekins without a crust and provide texture elsewhere, with a leaner crouton or a crisp vegetable. Other tarts are naturally full of texture, and some use vegetables as a crust in place of pastry—such as the Spinach and Herb Torta in a Potato Crust.

Some of these pies are affectionately called *galettes,* rustic fabrications of dough folded over vegetable fillings. They're rather flat and informal and can be big or sized for a single serving. I used to make them only as desserts, until one day I figured out that they were just as good with savory fillings. Tender, golden yeasted doughs—essentially glorified pizza doughs—come into play here as well as standard pie dough.

Pizza is another kind of pie, a very familiar one that everyone enjoys. Easy to improvise, pizzas are not merely the realm of sophisticated adults but the kind of food that children can happily get involved in without taxing their parents too much. Calzones and their close relations, empanadas, are essentially folded pizzas or turnovers, a casual food with enormous appeal. They can be filled with rustic mixtures of greens and olives as well as cheeses.

Because there are always two parts to these dishes—a crust and a filling—they can be a little time consuming. I wouldn't suggest making them on the spur of the moment for a weekday dinner unless you're comfortable in the kitchen and a speedy cook. Being familiar with pastry certainly helps move things along, too. Doughs and their fillings, however, can often be made ahead of time, and all that's left to do at the last minute is to assemble and bake your pie.

Tips for Savory Pies

THE DOUGH: The flakiest crusts are made with butter, but you can use an oil-based pastry or one of the less rich yeasted doughs. (Pie dough recipes are in the dessert chapter; yeasted doughs in this chapter.) Since dough takes only a few minutes to make, make it first, then let it rest while you gather the filling ingredients.

PREBAKING TART AND PIE SHELLS: Prebaking tart shells or pie crusts without a filling (or blind) long enough for the crust to set creates a finished pastry whose crust is thoroughly cooked and crisp. The easiest way I've found to do this is to first put the formed tart or pie shell in the freezer until it hardens, at least 15 minutes. Once the oven is preheated to 400°F, I put the shell on a sheet pan (so I won't have to handle it later—crusts on tart shells are fragile) and bake until it is lightly browned, about 25 minutes. Because the dough is frozen, it will hold its shape without the cumbersome addition of pie weights. Check once or twice while baking and if any bubbles have formed, deflate them with the tip of the paring knife. If you've saved a scrap of the dough, you can use it to patch any holes as soon as the shell comes out of the oven. Just gently rub a piece of the soft dough into any holes. To remove the rim from a filled, finished tart, see page 698.

SERVING: These savory tarts and pies are best served warm from the oven, but some of them keep surprisingly well. Many are good at room temperature, and some are sturdy enough to take on a picnic or withstand the rigors of the buffet table. When it comes to leftovers, the crust may lose its crispness, but they're easily reheated and very nearly as good.

TRANSFORMING TARTS AND GALETTES INTO SAVORY FLANS

If making a crust involves too much time, too many calories, or anything else that's problematic, you can omit it altogether, changing the dish from a tart to a timbale or a flan. To make up for the lost texture of the crust, grace the top of the dish with fresh bread crumbs crisped in olive oil or butter.

To bake a savory timbale or flan, select a glass or ceramic loaf pan, gratin dish, or four to six ramekins. Butter them well. Add two or three beaten eggs to the vegetable mixture if it doesn't have any binder and increase the seasonings by half. Pour the mixture into the buttered dish. Set the flan in a larger dish and add warm water to come halfway up the sides. Bake at 375°F until well set, and the top is beginning to brown, for 20 to 35 minutes, depending on the size of the dish. When a toothpick comes out clean, the flan is done.

YEAST-RISEN *doughs require less fat than standard short crusts do because the yeast provides the tenderness and elasticity. The yeast also gives them good flavor. Angelic to handle, these doughs make gorgeous pies, tarts, and galettes, with golden sculpted surfaces. The only trick is to roll them very thin. If you don't, your crust will end up bready. There will be more dough than you need, but you can always use the extra dough to make a few breadsticks or rolls.*

These malleable doughs make enough dough for one 9-, 10-, or 11-inch tart, pie, or galette.

Yeasted Tart Dough with Olive Oil

2 teaspoons active dry yeast

$^1/_2$ teaspoon sugar

$^1/_2$ cup warm water

3 tablespoons olive oil

1 egg, lightly beaten

$^3/_8$ teaspoon salt

1$^3/_4$ cups flour, as needed

Dissolve the yeast and sugar in the water in a medium bowl and let stand until bubbly, about 10 minutes. Add the oil, egg, and salt, then stir in the flour. When the dough is too stiff to work with a spoon, turn it onto the counter and knead until smooth and elastic, about 4 minutes. Add more flour if necessary to keep it from sticking. Set the dough in an oiled bowl, turn it over to coat, cover with a towel, and let rise until doubled in bulk, 45 minutes to an hour. Turn the dough out. Roll it into a thin circle and use it to line a tart or pie pan or to make a free-form galette. (For individual tarts, divide it into 6 pieces, shape into balls, and let rest under a towel for 15 minutes before rolling them out.)

THE egg contributes to the strength and suppleness of the dough. If you don't eat eggs, leave it out and add an additional 3 tablespoons water with 1 tablespoon oil.

MAKES ONE 9-, 10-, OR 11-INCH TART, PIE, OR GALETTE, 6 TO 8 INDIVIDUAL SHELLS

Yeasted Tart Dough with Butter

2 teaspoons active dry yeast

$^1/_2$ teaspoon sugar

$^1/_2$ cup warm milk or water

1 egg at room temperature

$^1/_4$ teaspoon salt

2 cups flour, approximately

4 tablespoons soft butter

Dissolve the yeast and sugar in the milk in a mixing bowl and let stand until bubbly, about 10 minutes. Stir in the egg and salt, then begin adding the flour $^1/_2$ cup at a time. After you've added a cup, beat in the butter, then continue adding flour until the dough pulls away from the edge of the bowl. Turn it out onto a counter and knead until shiny and smooth, after a few minutes. Add more flour as needed to prevent sticking.

Transfer the dough to a lightly buttered bowl, cover with a towel, and let rise until doubled in bulk, 45 minutes to an hour. Turn the dough out and roll it into a 13- to 14-inch circle. Use it to line a large tart or pie pan or to make a free-form galette. (Or divide the dough into 6 smaller pieces for individual pastries. Shape into balls, then let them rest under a towel for 15 minutes before rolling them out.)

THIS dough is both tender and sturdy. Slightly sticky and needing a good beating when the butter is added, it's best made using a mixer with a paddle attachment. Work in as much flour as you can before kneading so that it will be easy to handle.

MAKES ONE 10- TO 12-INCH TART, PIE, OR GALETTE SHELL

Yeasted Pastry for Desserts: Proof the yeast and water, then stir in 2 tablespoons sugar, 1/2 teaspoon vanilla extract, and 1 teaspoon grated lemon or orange zest along with the egg. For a more tender tart, use 6 tablespoons.

Yeasted Pastry for a Double-Crusted Tart Increase the milk or water from the preceding recipe to 1 cup, the butter to 6 tablespoons, and the flour to 3 cups or more, as needed. To form the tart, follow the directions on the previous page.

Roasted Eggplant and Tomato Tart

THE *somewhat dull color of this tart makes it hard to imagine the fullness of its flavor. Some sprigs of opal basil help set it off to best advantage. The eggplant and tomatoes can be roasted well in advance of baking.*

MAKES ONE 9-INCH TART

Tart Pastry, page 694
1 pound eggplant, any variety
3 Roma or plum tomatoes
2 eggs
1 cup half-and-half

Salt and freshly milled pepper
1/8 teaspoon grated nutmeg
1 tablespoon finely chopped basil
Several basil sprigs for garnish, preferably opal basil

Make the tart dough, then roll it out and line a 9-inch tart pan. Set in the freezer to harden.

Puncture the eggplant in several places, then roast on a sheet pan in a 375°F oven until it's completely soft and collapsed, 30 to 40 minutes. Broil or grill the tomatoes until lightly charred. When cool enough to handle, remove the eggplant skins and puree the flesh with the whole tomatoes. Beat the eggs in a bowl, then stir in the eggplant puree and cream. Season with 1/2 teaspoon salt, a little pepper, the nutmeg, and the chopped basil.

Preheat the oven to 400°F. Remove the tart shell from the freezer, set it on a sheet pan, and bake until lightly colored, about 25 minutes. Remove. Lower the temperature to 375°F. Add the filling to the shell and bake until set and a knife comes out clean, 25 to 30 minutes. Let rest for 10 minutes, then remove the rim, set the tart on a platter, and serve, garnished with sprigs of opal basil.

Fresh Herb Tart

Tart Pastry, page 694

1 small garlic clove, smashed with a knife

2 whole eggs

2 egg yolks or another whole egg

1/2 cup cream or half-and-half

2 ounces fresh goat cheese, crumbled

1/2 cup finely chopped herb leaves—a mixture including flat-leaf parsley, chervil, tarragon or marjoram, lemon thyme, sorrel

Salt and freshly milled white pepper

Make the tart dough, roll it out, and line a 9-inch tart pan. Freeze it for at least 15 minutes, then set on a sheet pan and bake it in a 400°F oven until lightly browned, 20 to 25 minutes. Remove and reduce the temperature to 350°F.

Spear the garlic with a fork and use it to beat the eggs, egg yolks, cream, and goat cheese together. Let it steep in the custard while you chop the herbs, then remove it. Pour the custard through a sieve into a bowl, then add the herbs and season with 1/2 teaspoon salt and a little pepper. Pour the custard into the shell and bake until set and golden, about 30 minutes. Let cool to tepid or room temperature, then remove from the rim and place on a platter.

THIS *quivering, herb-flecked tart is one of the true glories of the summer garden. I have been making it since Geraldene Holt arrived from England with the gift of her beautiful book,* Recipes from a French Herb Garden. *My American garden is a good herb provider as well. Serve this tart warm or at room temperature surrounded by sliced tomatoes and crisp new lettuces.*

MAKES ONE 9-INCH TART

Tender Tomato Tart

2 tablespoons olive oil

2 small celery ribs

1 carrot, finely diced

1 1/2 pounds ripe tomatoes, coarsely chopped

1 onion, finely diced

1 garlic clove, minced

2 tablespoons chopped parsley

5 large basil leaves

Tart Pastry, page 694

Salt and freshly milled pepper

3 eggs, well beaten

Warm the oil in a heavy pot, add the vegetables and herbs, and stew, covered, over low heat for 1 hour. Occasionally give the pot a stir to make sure nothing is sticking, adding a few tablespoons water if the pot seems dry. Pass the vegetables through a food mill or puree. While they're cooking, prepare the pastry, line a 9-inch tart pan, and prebake as described on page 488 until lightly colored.

Lower the temperature to 400°F. Season the puree with 1/2 teaspoon salt and a little pepper. Stir in the eggs and taste for salt. Pour the filling into the shell and bake until it appears set and a cake tester comes out clean, 25 to 35 minutes. Let cool for 10 minutes before serving.

A LUSCIOUS, *tender tart made with summer's sweetest vegetables. In this case you might prefer to start the vegetables first since they need an hour on the stove. Something crunchy and acidic enhances this tart, like a salad of chopped vegetables dressed with olive oil and a dash of vinegar or lemon.*

MAKES ONE 9-INCH TART

Tomato and Red Pepper Tart

WITH crisscrossed strips of peppers and olives, this is one of my favorite late summer dishes. There's not a speck of cheese, egg, or cream— it's just a jam of sweet seasonal vegetables. The filling is also stellar in small turnovers or baked in a galette. Serve with a green salad, followed by a cheese plate.

MAKES ONE 10-INCH TART

Yeasted Tart Dough with Olive Oil, page 489

2 red onions, finely diced

3 tablespoons olive oil, plus extra for the crust

1 1/2 pounds ripe tomatoes, preferably Roma

3 large red bell peppers

3 large garlic cloves, minced

1/8 teaspoon saffron threads

1/4 teaspoon anise seeds

Salt and freshly milled pepper

2 tablespoons chopped basil

16 Niçoise or 8 small Kalamata olives, halved and pitted

Make the dough and set it aside to rise. Cook the onions in the oil over medium heat until soft, about 12 minutes, stirring occasionally. While they're cooking, peel, seed, and finely chop the tomatoes. Roast the peppers. Set aside two-thirds of one pepper and finely chop the rest. Add the garlic, tomatoes, and diced peppers to the onions, crumble the saffron and anise seeds into the mixture, and season with 1/2 teaspoon salt and a little pepper. Cook for 30 minutes, stirring occasionally, especially toward the end. The mixture should be quite thick. Taste for salt and stir in the basil leaves.

Preheat the oven to 400°F. Roll out the dough and drape it over a 10-inch tart pan. There will be plenty of overhang. Trim it and crimp the dough around the rim. Add the filling. Cut the reserved pepper into narrow strips and use them to make a lattice design over the top. Place the olives in the spaces formed by the peppers. Bake for 35 minutes. Remove and brush the rim of the crust with olive oil. Unmold the tart onto a platter and serve.

Tomato Tartlets with Rosemary

THESE little free-form tarts are full of Provençal flavors. Use tomatoes in season, mixing varieties and colors. Serve them warm from the oven or at room temperature. These are durable enough to take on a picnic.

MAKES 6 INDIVIDUAL TARTS

Galette Dough, page 696, or either Yeasted Tart Dough, page 489

2 tablespoons finely chopped rosemary

1 pound tomatoes, approximately, thinly sliced

18 Niçoise olives, pitted and halved

Extra virgin olive oil

Salt and freshly milled pepper

2 tablespoons finely grated Parmesan, optional

Preheat the oven to 425°F. Divide the dough into six equal pieces and roll each piece into a circle about 1/8 inch thick. Sprinkle 1/2 teaspoon rosemary over each circle and gently roll it into the dough. Overlap five or six slices of tomato on each round, leaving a 1-inch border around the edge. Tuck in the olives, sprinkle more rosemary on top, drizzle with oil, and season with salt and pepper. Fold the edges of the dough over the tomatoes, creasing every inch or so. Cup your hands around the tarts and press together to make a firm little package. Brush the tops lightly with olive oil.

Bake until the crust is golden, 20 to 25 minutes. Add the cheese during the last 5 minutes. Serve hot, warm, or at room temperature. To reheat, place in a hot oven for about 8 minutes.

Green Herb Tart (*Torta d'Erbe*)

Yeasted Pastry for a Double-Crust Tart, page 490

2 bunches chard, or chard and beet greens to make 12 to 16 cups chopped leaves

2 tablespoons butter or a mixture of butter and olive oil

2 to 3 ounces sorrel leaves, 1 to 1½ cups, if available

2 bunches scallions, including half the greens, finely chopped

½ cup chopped parsley

1 cup chopped arugula

2 tablespoons chopped basil or anise hyssop

Salt and freshly milled pepper

1 cup ricotta

2 eggs, lightly beaten

½ cup milk

½ cup grated Gruyère

2 tablespoons freshly grated Parmesan

⅛ teaspoon grated nutmeg

THIS *large golden pie filled with greens and herbs—chard, sorrel, arugula, anise hyssop leaves, beet greens, and so forth—truly celebrates spring. This looks impressive and holds well. Rest assured, the double crust is easy to make and form.*

MAKES ONE 11-INCH TART, SERVING 8 TO 12

Make the dough and set it aside to rise.

Meanwhile, chop the chard into bite-size pieces and wash. (It will look like a huge amount, but it cooks down.) Melt 2 tablespoons of the butter in a large skillet over medium heat. Add the chard with the water clinging to its leaves, or as much as will fit, sprinkle with 1 teaspoon salt, and cook, turning it as it wilts, until it has cooked down and is tender. If the pan becomes dry, add a few tablespoons water, as needed.

Heat the remaining butter in a medium skillet. Add the scallions, sorrel, arugula, and basil, and cook over medium heat until tender, about 5 minutes. Add them to the cooked chard and taste for salt and season with pepper.

Beat the ricotta, all but 2 tablespoons of the beaten eggs, and milk until smooth, then stir in the cheeses and greens. Taste for salt and season with pepper and the nutmeg.

When the dough has doubled in bulk, preheat the oven to 375°F. Divide the dough into two pieces. Roll one piece out no thicker than ⅛ inch and drape it over an 11-inch tart pan with a removeable rim, or shallow pie plate. Ease the dough into the edges of the pan without stretching and trim the edge so that it's a little larger than the pan. Add the filling. Roll out the second piece of dough and cut out a circle the same size as the surface of the tart. Place it right on the filling, then fold the longer piece of dough over it. Crimp the edges. Using the tip of a paring knife, score the top of the tart in a crisscross design without cutting through the dough. Brush it with the reserved egg.

Bake for 35 minutes or until the top crust is well browned. Carefully remove the rim, then return the tart to the oven for 10 minutes more to brown and crisp the edges. Let cool for 10 minutes, then transfer to a platter. Serve warm or tepid.

Variation: Add ½ cup chopped dill and replace the Gruyère with feta. Don't add salt to the cheese mixture.

Spinach and Herb Torta in a Potato Crust

IT'S a little simpler to put the filling in a pie crust, but I think golden potatoes make a more interesting container, and they taste so right with the spinach. This is equally wonderful warm or at room temperature, for appetizers or a main dish.

SERVES 4 TO 8

3 large russet potatoes, about 1 1/4 pounds

About 2 tablespoons olive oil

1 bunch scallions, including the firm greens, sliced

1 tablespoon chopped dill or 2 teaspoons dried

1/2 cup chopped parsley

1/2 cup chopped cilantro

Salt and freshly milled pepper

2 bunches spinach, leaves only, coarsely chopped

2 eggs, beaten

1 cup small-curd cottage cheese

1/3 to 1/2 cup crumbled feta to taste

Grated zest of 1 lemon

Neatly peel the potatoes with a paring knife. Slice two of them crosswise about 1/8 inch thick. Slice the third potato lengthwise, also 1/8 inch thick. Brush some olive oil in a wide skillet and set it over high heat. When the oil is hot, reduce the heat to medium. Make a layer of potatoes and cook, turning them once, until golden on both sides and tender when pierced with a knife after a few minutes. Repeat until all are done. Remove them to a paper towel as they finish cooking.

Add 1 tablespoon oil to the pan. Add the scallions, dill, parsley, and cilantro and cook over medium heat until the scallions are wilted and bright green, about 4 minutes. Season with salt and remove to a bowl. Add the spinach to the same pan with the water clinging to its leaves (or add 1/4 cup water if it's dry). Cook over high heat until the leaves are wilted and tender, about 4 minutes. Transfer the spinach to a sieve and press out any excess water, then add it to the scallions. Add the eggs, cheeses, and lemon zest and stir well. Taste for salt and season with pepper.

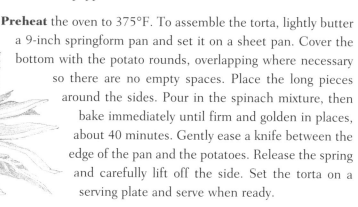

Preheat the oven to 375°F. To assemble the torta, lightly butter a 9-inch springform pan and set it on a sheet pan. Cover the bottom with the potato rounds, overlapping where necessary so there are no empty spaces. Place the long pieces around the sides. Pour in the spinach mixture, then bake immediately until firm and golden in places, about 40 minutes. Gently ease a knife between the edge of the pan and the potatoes. Release the spring and carefully lift off the side. Set the torta on a serving plate and serve when ready.

Eggplant Torta

3½ pounds eggplant, sliced lengthwise ⅓ inch thick

3 tablespoons olive oil plus extra oil or butter for the pan

Salt and freshly milled pepper

1 large bunch chard, stems discarded

1 onion, finely diced

2 pinches saffron threads

2 large garlic cloves, minced or put through a press

¼ cup chopped basil

⅓ cup grated Gruyère

¾ cup fresh goat cheese, about 3 ounces

3 tablespoons freshly grated Parmesan

3 eggs, beaten with 1 tablespoon water

Fresh Tomato Sauce, page 61, or Goat Cheese Sauce, page 72

THIS *is definitely a dish to make when presentation counts. It's not particularly difficult, but it does involve at least an hour to make and assemble the parts. The torta holds its heat well and needn't be served piping hot. In fact, it's excellent at room temperature.*

SERVES 6 TO 8

Preheat the oven to 425°F. Unless it's garden fresh, salt the eggplant, let stand 30 minutes, then blot dry. Brush both sides of the eggplant with oil, lay them on a sheet pan, and bake until the bottom is browned, after about 12 minutes. Turn and bake to brown the second side, about 10 minutes. Remove and season with salt and pepper.

Meanwhile, finely chop the chard. Heat 3 tablespoons oil in a wide skillet over medium heat, add the onion, and sprinkle on the saffron. Cook slowly, stirring occasionally, until the onion is quite soft, about 12 minutes, then stir in the garlic and chard with the water clinging to its leaves. Sprinkle over ½ teaspoon salt and cook slowly, stirring occasionally with tongs, until the chard is fully tender, about 15 minutes. If the pan seems dry at any point, add water about ⅓ cup at a time. When tender, stir in the basil, taste for salt, and season with plenty of pepper.

To form the torta, brush a 9-inch springform pan with oil or butter. Arrange five or six slices of eggplant around the edge, overlapping them as you go. They need to come at least 2 inches up the side. Next make overlapping layers of the eggplant to cover the bottom of the pan. Trim the eggplant slices, if needed, to make them fit, and use any odd pieces to fill in the gaps. The eggplant may be higher in the center than at the rim.

Sprinkle the eggplant with half of the Gruyère, then make a layer with half of the chard. Cover the chard with half the goat cheese and a tablespoon of Parmesan. Use half of the remaining eggplant to make a layer—the trimmings are fine—and cover with the rest of the Gruyère, followed by the remaining chard and goat cheese. Sprinkle with a tablespoon of Parmesan.

Now slowly pour the beaten eggs over the torta, letting them seep into the vegetables. Make a final layer of eggplant, arranging the slices attractively since this is the side that will be seen. Cover with the remaining Parmesan and bake until the custard is set, 35 to 40 minutes. Let cool for 10 or 15 minutes, then run a knife around the edge and carefully dislodge the springform. Set the torta on a serving plate if you plan to serve it whole. Or slice it into wedges and surround with the sauce.

Rice and Ricotta Tart

THIS sturdy, reheatable tart can easily be varied with the addition of different cheese and even types of rice. Heavier rices, like wild rice, will tend to fall to the bottom, however.

SERVES 4 TO 6

Pie Crust with Bran, page 693, or
   Yeasted Tart Dough with Butter,
   page 489
1/2 cup rice
Salt and freshly milled white pepper
1 cup ricotta

2 eggs
1/2 cup milk
1/8 teaspoon grated nutmeg
1/2 cup freshly grated Parmesan

Fit the dough into a 9-inch tart pan or shallow pie pan. Freeze until firm. Preheat the oven to 400°F and bake the frozen crust until lightly colored and set, about 25 minutes. Remove and lower the temperature to 350°F.

Boil the rice in 3 cups water with 1/2 teaspoon salt. When cooked but still just a bit firm, pour it through a sieve, reserving the water. Beat the ricotta with the eggs and milk until smooth, then add 1/4 teaspoon salt, the nutmeg, the Parmesan, and the rice. Pour the filling into the shell and bake until golden and set, about 40 minutes. (The rice water is viscous and naturally sweet. It makes a soothing and delicious chilled drink, plain or flavored with a drop of almond extract or almond syrup. It's a boon to someone who's been suffering an upset stomach or sore throat.)

Ricotta Tart with Saffron and Herbs

AN aromatic and pretty golden tart. The bran in the crust makes a nice nutty foil for the mild cheese.

SERVES 4 TO 8

Pie Crust with Bran, page 693
2 pinches saffron threads
2 tablespoons butter
1 large shallot, finely diced
1/4 cup white wine
2 cups ricotta

2 eggs
1/4 cup freshly grated Parmesan or dry
   Jack
2 tablespoons chopped parsley
1 1/2 tablespoons chopped marjoram
Salt and freshly milled white pepper

Fit the pie crust into a 9-inch tart pan. Freeze until hard while you preheat the oven to 400°F. Bake, on a sheet pan, until lightly browned, about 25 minutes. Remove and lower the temperature to 350°F. Cover the saffron threads with a tablespoon boiling water and set aside.

Melt the butter in a small skillet over medium-high heat. Add the shallot and cook, stirring frequently, for about 2 minutes. Add the wine and simmer until it's reduced. Beat the ricotta and eggs in a mixer or food processor until smooth, then, by hand, stir in the diluted saffron, cheese, shallot, and herbs. Season with 1/2 teaspoon salt and a little pepper. Transfer to the tart shell and bake until set on top and golden, about 25 minutes.

Savory Vegetable Galettes

THESE savory flat pies occupy a place somewhere between pizzas and tarts. Their free-form crusts are entirely for-giving, for ragged edges and lopsided circles are part of their charm—but they can be made perfectly round with evenly trimmed edges for those who prefer symmetry.

Thin slices of galette can be served as appetizers or first courses, while larger portions make an excellent veg-etable entrée. Galettes can also be made into individual pastries that take center stage with authority. Less fragile than their larger siblings, individual galettes can be made a few hours ahead of time and reheated in a hot oven.

ACCOMPANIMENTS: Individual pastries can be surrounded by braised greens or a com-plementary vegetable finely cut so that it encircles the pastry. I particularly like galettes set on a bed of salad, such as watercress or frisée, dressed with a shallot-rich vinaigrette. The salad offers a fresh contrast to the galette, while the heat of the pastry brings out the flavor of the shallots.

QUANTITY: A recipe for galette dough makes one 10-inch or six individual galettes. One large pie serves 8 to 10 as a first course, or 4 to 6 as a main course. A recipe for yeasted dough makes enough for two fairly open or an enclosed tart.

MAKING GALETTES: First make the filling and allow it to cool to room temperature. This can be done ahead of time. Make the dough of your choice. Roll it into a circle about 14 inches across and $1/4$ inch thick, leaving the edges rough or trimming them. Place the dough on a cookie sheet or the back of a jelly roll pan so that when done it can be slid easily onto a serving plate.

Spread the filling in the middle of the dough, leaving a $1^{1}/2$- to 3-inch border around the edge. The wider the border, the more the filling will be covered. Slide your hand under the edge of the dough and bring it up over the filling, going all the way around the galette, overlap-ping the folds. You can make neat, sharply defined pleats or soft, irregular folds. Yeasted dough lends itself much more to soft, rounded edges than galette dough. Brush the galette dough with melted butter or an egg wash to give it sheen and color, then bake right away.

For individual galettes, divide the dough into six equal pieces and shape them into disks. Roll into circles between 6 and 8 inches across, add the filling, and gently pleat all the way around. Or roll the dough into a square and fold the edges over the filling like a four-sided envelope.

MAKING AHEAD OF TIME: Doughs for galettes can be rolled out in advance and refrig-erated—useful if you're planning on making several at once for a party. Fillings can also be made a day or two ahead. Plan ahead and at the last minute you need only combine the shell and the filling and bake them. While galettes are always best freshly baked, left-overs can be reheated. Set pieces directly on a pizza stone or cookie sheet and warm them in a hot oven.

Cabbage and Mushroom Galette with Horseradish Sauce

A TENDER yeasted tart dough is good with this winter filling. Serve with wild rice or buckwheat groats and julienne strips of kohlrabi, steamed and tossed with chopped tarragon or dill.

SERVES 4 TO 6

Yeasted Tart Dough with Butter, page 489, or Galette Dough, page 696

2 tablespoons butter

1 large onion, finely diced

4 ounces fresh shiitake mushrooms, stems discarded, caps thinly sliced

1 teaspoon chopped thyme or $1/2$ teaspoon dried

1 teaspoon chopped tarragon or $1/2$ teaspoon dried

1 tablespoon chopped dill or 1 teaspoon dried

6 cups thinly sliced cabbage, preferably Savoy, or 4 cups cabbage plus 2 cups other greens, such as beet, chard, or kale

Salt and freshly milled pepper

$1/4$ cup chopped parsley

1 hard-cooked egg, chopped

$1/4$ cup sour cream or yogurt

1 teaspoon tarragon vinegar

2 tablespoons melted butter

Fresh Horseradish Sauce, page 72

Make the dough and set aside to rise or chill while you make the filling.

Heat the butter in a large skillet over medium heat. Add the onion, mushrooms, and herbs and cook until softened, about 10 minutes. Add the cabbage, 1 teaspoon salt, and $1/2$ cup water. Cover and cook slowly until the cabbage is tender, 15 to 20 minutes, turning it occasionally. Add more liquid. When tender, uncover and raise the heat to evaporate any excess moisture. The mixture should be fairly dry. Stir in the parsley, egg, and sour cream. Season with vinegar and taste for salt and pepper.

Preheat the oven to 400°F. Roll the dough into a large, thin circle and set it on the back of a sheet pan, or a cookie sheet. The edges will hang over the sides. Add the filling, making a mound 7 to 8 inches across, then fold the edges over and brush with the melted butter. Pour any extra butter into the vegetables. Bake until browned, 25 to 30 minutes. Carefully slide it onto a serving plate. Serve with the horseradish sauce on the side.

Leek and Goat Cheese Galette

THIS galette takes plenty of leeks to make it plump, so if they're hard to come by, use a mixture of leeks and scallions. Served on a salad of peppery watercress, it makes one of my favorite spring dinners. If you don't want to use cream, leave it out rather than replacing it with milk.

SERVES 6

6 large leeks, including an inch of the green

3 tablespoons butter

1 teaspoon chopped thyme

$1/2$ cup dry white wine

$1/2$ cup cream or crème fraîche

Salt and freshly milled pepper

1 egg, beaten

3 tablespoons chopped parsley or 1 tablespoon chopped tarragon

Galette Dough, page 696

$1/2$ to 1 cup soft goat cheese to taste, about 4 ounces

Thinly slice and wash the leeks. You should have about 6 cups.

Melt the butter in a medium skillet. Add the leeks, thyme, and $1/2$ cup water. Stew over medium heat, stirring frequently, until the leeks are tender, about 12 minutes. Add the wine and continue cooking until it's reduced, then add the cream and cook until it just coats the leeks and little liquid remains. Season with salt and plenty of pepper. Let cool 10 minutes, then stir in all but 1 tablespoon of the beaten egg and 2 tablespoons of the parsley.

Preheat the oven to 400°F. Roll out the dough for one large or six individual galettes. Spread the leek mixture on top, leaving a 2-inch border around the edge. Crumble the cheese over the top then fold the dough over the filling. Brush with the reserved egg and bake until the crust is browned, 25 to 30 minutes. Remove, scatter the remaining parsley over the top, and serve.

Mushroom Galette

Galette Dough, page 696

2 cups Quick Mushroom Stock, page 253

2 to 3 teaspoons Dijon mustard to taste

Aged red wine vinegar or sherry vinegar

1/4 cup olive oil

1 large onion, cut into 1/2-inch dice

2 teaspoons minced rosemary or 1 teaspoon dried

Salt and freshly milled pepper

2 pinches red pepper flakes

1/2 pound portobello or shiitake mushrooms

1 pound large white mushrooms

2 garlic cloves, minced

3 tablespoons tomato paste

1 tablespoon butter

2 tablespoons chopped parsley

2 tablespoons melted butter or beaten egg for the glaze

THIS is a dish I'd choose for a special occasion. It's a production, requiring a mushroom stock for the sauce, a filling, and a crust. But all the parts can be made well in advance of the final baking.

SERVES 6

Make the dough.

Season the stock with a few teaspoons mustard and just enough vinegar to sharpen the flavors. Set it aside.

Heat 1 tablespoon of the oil in a large skillet. Add the onion and rosemary and cook over medium heat until the onion is lightly browned, about 12 minutes. Season with 1/2 teaspoon salt, a little pepper, and the red pepper flakes. Remove to a bowl.

Heat half the remaining oil in the same skillet over high heat. Add half the mushrooms and sauté until browned, then season with salt and pepper. Remove to the bowl with the onions, then repeat with the remaining mushrooms. Return everything to the pan, add the garlic and tomato paste diluted with a few spoonfuls of the stock, and a teaspoon of the vinegar. Add the remaining stock, bring to a boil, then stir in the butter and the parsley. Cook for 5 minutes, then drain, reserving the juices.

Preheat the oven to 400°F. Roll out the dough for one large or six individual galettes, then add the mushrooms. Loosely fold the dough over the filling and brush it with melted butter or egg. Bake until the crust is browned, about 25 minutes. Heat any reserved juices and spoon them into the mushrooms.

Winter Squash Galette

THIS is one of my favorite cold-weather dishes. The cheese and sweet squash make an intriguing combination, and a yeasted dough is particularly good here. You might serve this with the Watercress Salad with Slivered Endive.

SERVES 6

Yeasted Tart Dough with Olive Oil or Butter, page 489, or Galette Dough, page 696

2¹/₂ pounds winter squash, such as butternut

1 small head garlic, cloves separated but not peeled

1 tablespoon olive oil, plus extra for the squash

1 onion, finely diced

12 fresh sage leaves, chopped, or 2 teaspoons dried

¹/₂ cup freshly grated pecorino or Parmesan

Salt and freshly milled pepper

1 egg, beaten

Make the dough. Preheat the oven to 375°F. Cut the squash in half, scrape out the seeds, and brush the cut surface with oil. Stuff the garlic into the cavities and place the squash cut side down on a sheet pan. Bake until the flesh is tender, about 40 minutes. Scoop out the squash and squeeze the garlic cloves. Mash them together with a fork until fairly smooth, leaving some texture.

Warm 1 tablespoon oil in a skillet over medium heat. Add the onion and sage and cook until the onion is soft and beginning to color, about 12 minutes. Add it to the squash along with the grated cheese and season with salt and pepper to taste.

Roll out the dough into a 14-inch circle and spread the filling over it, leaving a border of 2 inches or more. Pleat the dough over the filling, then brush the edges with beaten egg. Bake until the crust is golden, about 25 minutes.

Onion Galette with Mustard Cream

A SLIGHTLY slimmer version of the creamier quiche of years past. The sweetness of the onions needs the pungent, salty accent of the cheese and herbs.

MAKES ONE 10-INCH GALETTE

Galette Dough, page 696, or Yeasted Tart Dough with Butter, page 489

3 tablespoons butter

6 cups thinly sliced yellow onion

1 tablespoon chopped thyme or rosemary

¹/₂ cup dry white wine

Salt and freshly milled pepper

2 eggs, beaten

1 tablespoon Dijon mustard mixed with ¹/₄ cup cream

¹/₂ cup fresh bread crumbs

¹/₄ cup grated pecorino Romano or Parmesan

Make the dough and set it aside.

Melt the butter in a large skillet over medium heat. Add the onion and thyme and cook, stirring occasionally, until they soften and turn golden, about 15 minutes. Add the wine, cook until it has reduced, then season with salt and pepper.

In a bowl, combine all but 2 tablespoons of the egg with the mustard and cream. Stir in the onion, bread crumbs, and cheese.

Preheat the oven to 400°F. Roll the dough into a 14-inch circle. Put the onion on the dough, leaving a 2- to 3-inch edge. Fold the dough over the onion and brush with the reserved egg. Bake until shiny and golden, about 25 minutes.

Folded Pastries: Turnovers and Empanadas

FOLDED *filled pastries appear the world over, known in their various tongues and guises as calzone, Cornish pasties, empanadas, tacos, and so forth. They make a portable meal, easy to carry away and eat elsewhere, whether across the room at a cocktail party or to a grassy riverbank.*

Virtually any savory filling you like can be tucked into the folds of pastry just as long it's not too moist. Certainly most of the fillings used for the galettes and vegetable tarts will work well. After all, it's not a far cry from a galette to an empanada—it's even the same dough, with the folds extended and sealed so that the filling is entirely contained.

Making Turnovers

DOUGHS: For turnovers you can use Galette Dough, Pie Dough, and the yeasted doughs, including pizza dough. One recipe Galette Dough yields twelve 3-inch turnovers, each one holding 1 1/2 to 2 tablespoons filling. Twelve ounces pizza or other yeasted dough, one recipe, yields 12 to 16 pieces.

SHAPING THE TURNOVERS: Divide the dough into the number of pastries you want to make and roll each one separately into circles about 1/8 inch thick. (With stretchy yeast dough you can roll out the entire amount, then cut out 3-inch circles with a biscuit cutter.) Set the circles on a sheet pan, cover, and refrigerate until you're ready to fill them. Let them warm up for 5 minutes to soften.

Place 1 1/2 to 2 tablespoons filling on the lower half of each circle, then fold the top half down to form a crescent. Too much filling makes it difficult to seal the pastry, as experience will quickly show. If you're having trouble getting floury dough to stick to itself, paint the edge with water or beaten egg, then use your fingers to press them together. Working your way around the edge, fold the dough into little pleats or press the edges with the tines of a fork to seal them. Brush the turnovers with beaten egg, dust them with poppy or sesame seeds if you like, and bake at 375°F until they're golden and glossy, about 25 minutes. They can be served hot, warm, or at room temperature.

MAKING AHEAD OF TIME: Turnovers can be prebaked, then returned to the oven to rewarm for 5 to 10 minutes. If well wrapped, they can be frozen for a month or so, either cooked or uncooked.

OTHER FILLINGS FOR TURNOVERS

Turnovers are easy to improvise using a number of recipes that appear elsewhere in the book. The preceding galette fillings given are particularly easy to adapt.

Blue Cheese and Walnut Spread, page 106: use for small pastries only

Goat cheese mixed with ricotta and rosemary

Winter squash puree with caramelized onions: Sautéed Mushrooms with Garlic and Parsley, page 388

Sautéed Peppers, page 402, mixed with shredded mozzarella or goat cheese

Mixed Greens with Cumin and Paprika, page 382

Feta Cheese and Herb Turnovers

SERVE *the small ones for appetizers. Large ones, set hot on a plate of* Herb Salad, *make a nice little dinner entrée.*

MAKES 12 SMALL OR 4 TO 6 LARGE TURNOVERS

Galette Dough, page 696

1/4 pound feta

1/4 pound farmers' cheese

3 scallions, including an inch or two of the greens, thinly sliced

1 tablespoon *each* chopped dill and marjoram

2 large lemon thyme or regular thyme sprigs, leaves only

Freshly milled pepper

1 egg yolk, beaten with 1 tablespoon milk

Sesame or poppy seeds

Divide the dough into 4, 6, or 12 pieces and roll each into a ball. Dust the counter lightly with flour and roll each ball into a circle about 1/8 inch thick.

Work the cheeses, scallions, herbs, and pepper to taste together—the mixture needn't cohere. Divide the filling among the pieces of dough, fold the edges over, then crimp them with your thumbs, making small pleats around the edge, or seal with a fork.

Preheat the oven to 375°F. Brush the pastries with the beaten egg, sprinkle with sesame or poppy seeds, and bake for about 25 minutes, until browned all over. Let cool for 5 or 10 minutes before serving.

Mushroom Turnovers

MAKES 6 TO 12 TURNOVERS

Yeasted Tart Dough with Olive Oil or Butter, page 489, or Galette Dough, page 696

12 ounces mushrooms

2 tablespoons olive oil

1/4 cup finely diced onion

1 garlic clove, minced

1 tablespoon chopped tarragon or dill

2 tablespoons chopped parsley

1 1/2 tablespoons tomato paste

Salt and freshly milled pepper

2/3 cup toasted bread crumbs

1 egg, beaten

1/2 cup sour cream

Divide the dough into the number of turnovers you'll be making and roll each into a ball. Dust the counter lightly with flour and roll each ball into a circle about 1/8 inch thick. Preheat the oven to 375°F.

Finely chop half the mushrooms and thinly slice the rest. In a wide sauté pan, heat half the oil over high heat. Add the onion and finely chopped mushrooms and sauté until the mushrooms release their juices, about 5 minutes. Toss in the garlic and cook until the mixture is dry. Stir in the herbs and tomato paste, season with salt and pepper, and remove to a bowl.

Using the same skillet, heat the remaining oil. Sauté the sliced mushrooms over high heat until browned, after a few minutes. Add these to the bowl and mix with the bread crumbs, all but a tablespoon of the egg, and the sour cream. Season with salt and pepper to taste. Let cool, then fill the turnovers, fold and seal the edges, and brush the tops with the reserved egg mixed with 1 tablespoon water. Bake until nicely browned, about 15 minutes.

Empanadas with Greens and Olives

Galette Dough, page 696, or Yeasted
   Tart Dough with Butter or Oil,
   page 489

2 teaspoons sweet paprika

10 cups mixed greens, such as beet
   greens, chard, spinach, kale

2 tablespoons olive oil

1 small onion, finely diced

2 garlic cloves, chopped

2 bay leaves

1/4 cup chopped parsley

1/4 teaspoon red pepper flakes

1/2 cup pitted olives, such as Kalamata

1/2 cup grated provolone

1 beaten egg

Salt and freshly milled pepper

A ROBUST little pastry based on greens, olives, and a paprika-flavored dough.

MAKES 12 PASTRIES

Make the dough, adding the paprika to the flour. Divide it into 12 pieces and roll each into a 3- to 4-inch circle. Set on a sheet pan and refrigerate. Preheat the oven to 375°F.

Wash the greens, but don't dry them. Heat the oil in a wide skillet over fairly high heat. Sauté the onion with the garlic, bay leaves, parsley, and pepper flakes until the onion begins to color a little, about 4 minutes. Add the greens and cook until they're tender, 8 to 12 minutes, turning them with tongs as they cook. If there's a lot of moisture when they're done, press it out with the back of a spoon. Finely chop the greens, then mix them with the olives, cheese, and half of the egg. Season to taste with salt and pepper.

Place 1 1/2 tablespoons filling on the lower half of each dough circle, then fold the pastry over and seal the edges. Brush with the remaining egg. Bake for 20 minutes or until nicely browned. Serve warm or at room temperature.

Escarole Calzone

ESCAROLE, *a large let-tucelike chicory, has a pleasant bitter edge that is tempered here with walnuts and cheeses. These calzones are large enough to make a meal*

MAKES 4 CALZONE

Pizza Dough, page 506

$^{1}/_{2}$ cup walnuts

Salt and freshly milled pepper

2 bunches escarole, separated at the base

2 tablespoons olive oil, plus extra to finish

4 garlic cloves, chopped

$^{1}/_{2}$ teaspoon red pepper flakes

$^{1}/_{2}$ cup pitted Kalamata or Niçoise olives

2 tablespoons capers, rinsed

$^{3}/_{4}$ cup grated mozzarella

$^{3}/_{4}$ cup grated Fontina

2 tablespoons freshly grated Parmesan

1 to 2 teaspoons balsamic vinegar

Make the pizza dough and set it aside to rise. Preheat the oven to 350°F. Roast the walnuts on a sheet pan for 5 minutes, then season them with salt and pepper. Finely chop. Turn the oven up to 450°F. If you have a baking stone, heat it at the same time.

Discard any escarole leaves that are yellowed. Wash, then coarsely chop them. Heat the oil in a wide skillet over medium-high heat with the garlic and pepper flakes. When the garlic is fragrant, add the escarole and sauté, turning it frequently with tongs until tender, about 7 minutes. (It may work best to do this in two batches.) Remove to a colander and press out as much liquid as possible. Combine with the remaining ingredients except the oil, seasoning to taste with vinegar and plenty of pepper.

Divide the dough into 6 pieces. Use two to make into rolls or breadsticks. Roll the rest into four thin $6^{1}/_{2}$-inch circles and set them on a floured pizza peel or the back of a sheet pan; see page 506. Let them rest for 15 minutes. Place the filling over half of each circle, leaving a 1-inch border. Brush the edge with water, fold the top down, then crimp the edges. Slide the calzone onto the baking stone and bake until browned on top, 15 to 20 minutes. Brush with olive oil to make them shine.

Calzone with Mozzarella and Goat Cheese Filling

CHEZ *Panisse's famous calzone with goat cheese and prosciutto is the departure for this scrumptious all-out cheesy pastry.*

MAKES 6 CALZONE

Pizza Dough, page 506

2 cups grated mozzarella, about 8 ounces

1 cup crumbled goat cheese, about 4 ounces

2 tablespoons parsley chopped with 2 garlic cloves

$^{1}/_{4}$ cup finely sliced scallion, including some greens

Salt and freshly milled pepper

Olive oil

Finely grated Parmesan

Make the pizza dough and divide it into six pieces. Shape them into balls, then roll into thin circles about $6^{1}/_{2}$ inches across. Let them rest on the counter, dusted with flour, while you make the filling. Preheat the oven to 450°F. Combine the remaining ingredients, except the oil and Parmesan, seasoning with salt and pepper to taste.

Mound 3 heaping tablespoons filling on the bottom half of each circle. Paint the edges with water, then fold the top down, press the dough together, and crimp the edges. Bake until browned on top, 15 to 20 minutes. Brush the top with olive oil, sprinkle with Parmesan, and serve.

> *Pizza Pie Variation:* Instead of the crescent shape, roll out two circles the same size and place the filling over one, leaving a ½-inch border. Place the second round on top and crimp the edges together. Bake until browned, then brush with olive oil. These can be made in individual portions or as a single large pie, cut into wedges.

Pizza

WHILE making pizza isn't as fast as ordering it on the phone, what arrives in a box doesn't compare to what comes out of your oven. Pizza appeals to everyone, especially kids, and pizza making is a pleasantly chaotic activity that enjoys the special excitement of anticipation. Pizza's the kind of food that draws everyone to the kitchen. Everyone can take part. While the cook is busy baking, family and friends can be put to work pitting olives, slicing mushrooms, grating cheese, arranging the toppings. Or they can just relax. (I met my husband over an olive-pitting pizza session so you never know what might come out of it!) Unlike boxed pizzas, homemade pizzas always bear a personal stamp. Spare and elegant, loaded with chiles, rough and tumble or whatever—if you enjoy informality plus made-to-order cooking with drama and flair, then pizzas are probably for you.

Some pizzas have thick, bready crusts, others are crisp crusted and thin, and some are folded to make the calzones that precede. Most of the pizzas described here are the thin-crusted variety. If you prefer a breadier pizza, use half again as much dough, roll it about ½ inch thick, and allow an additional 10 to 15 minutes for baking.

SPECIAL EQUIPMENT: Two pieces of equipment help make excellent pizzas and hearth breads: a pizza stone and a peel—a large, flat paddle made of wood or metal. A stone provides intense bottom heat that burns off moisture, giving the crust a firm, crisp texture. The peel allows you to slide the pizza directly onto the stone, but you can use the back side of a baking sheet almost as easily.

THE DOUGH: Pizza dough is essentially a bread dough enriched with olive oil. It's easy and straightforward to make and can be ready to use in about an hour. Leftover dough can be frozen, but it needs more time to thaw than it takes to make it fresh. You can always bake extra into rolls or a little focaccia.

THE TOPPINGS: Be generous with the toppings, but don't forget that a heavily laden piece of dough is difficult to slide into the oven. Cheese smells irresistible and tastes wonderful, but a light hand keeps it from overwhelming the other ingredients. Good pizza cheeses are fresh mozzarella, Fontina, Gorgonzola, and goat cheese, with freshly grated Parmesan, dry Jack, or pecorino providing a sharper accent. Regular mozzarella and soy-based cheeses are improved if moistened with fruity olive oil, seasoned with pepper, and allowed to stand 15 minutes before being used. Herbs really come into their glory on pizzas. Tossed on the pie as it comes out of the oven, their volatile oils leap to life. Olives, capers, and a good pinch of red pepper flakes provide pungent, sharp accents.

Cheese can be grated, vegetables sliced and sautéed, garlic and herbs chopped while the dough is rising.

THE OVEN: Oven temperature is most important to the success of your pizza. It takes a hot oven to make a crisp, brown crust without drying out the top. Preheat your oven to 500°F, allowing 30 minutes rather than the usual 10. Adjust your rack to the center or top third of the oven. If you're using a pizza stone, make sure it's already in the oven when you turn it on since it takes 30 minutes to heat up fully.

USING A PEEL: To use a peel, first dust it with semolina, flour, or fine cornmeal—coarse polenta is too gritty. Place the dough on the peel and work up the edges a bit to make a rim. Jerk the peel back and forth to make sure the dough is loose. If it isn't, take it off and dust it again. When you're satisfied that the dough can slide easily, add the toppings, open the oven door, and tip the peel at the back edge of the baking stone. Give it a jerk as you pull the peel away, easing the pizza onto the stone. When the pizza is done, slide the peel back under it and take it out of the oven. Or, if you've another pizza on the peel, just lift it out with a spatula.

Pizza Dough

THERE'S nothing complicated about pizza dough. It's simply a bread dough that includes some olive oil, like the focaccia dough on page 670. If you're new to yeast doughs, you can take a look at pages 656 to 660 first to learn about what makes them work, or you can just plunge ahead.

MAKES ENOUGH DOUGH FOR EIGHT 6-INCH PIZZAS, FOUR 10-INCH PIZZAS, OR TWO 12- TO 14-INCH PIZZAS

1½ cups warm water	1½ teaspoons salt
2 teaspoons active dry yeast	½ to 1 cup whole-wheat flour, to taste
2 tablespoons extra virgin olive oil	3 to 3½ cups flour

Pour ½ cup of the water into a mixing bowl, stir in the yeast, and set aside until foamy, about 10 minutes. Add the remaining water, olive oil, and salt, then beat in the whole wheat flour followed by enough white flour to form a shaggy dough. Turn it out onto the counter and knead until smooth, adding more flour as needed to keep it from sticking. For a crisp, light crust, pizza dough should be on the moist side, which means it will be slightly tacky.

Put the dough into an oiled bowl, turn it once to coat, then cover with a towel and set aside to rise until doubled in size, 40 to 60 minutes. Turn the dough onto the counter and divide into the number of pizzas you want. Shape each piece into a ball, set on a lightly floured counter, cover with a towel, and let rise for another 20 to 30 minutes.

Shaping the Dough Taking one ball at a time, flatten it into a disk, pushing it outward with your palm. Working from the middle, push the dough out with your fingers until it's about ¼ inch thick and fairly even, thickening slightly at the edge. Or roll the dough into a circle, then push up the sides to make a slight rim. Dust the peel or pan with semolina, fine cornmeal, or flour, set the dough on top, cover with a towel, and let it rest for 10 or 15 minutes before you add the toppings.

Tomato Sauce for Pizza

2 tablespoons olive oil
2 garlic cloves, thinly sliced
Salt and freshly milled pepper

1 28-ounce can crushed tomatoes in
   sauce

*THE sauce needs to be
fairly thick, or the crust
will come out soggy.*

**MAKES ABOUT 3 CUPS,
ENOUGH FOR FOUR 10-
INCH PIZZAS**

Warm the oil over medium heat in a wide skillet with the garlic and a little black pepper. Add the tomatoes and a pinch of salt and raise the heat. Cook, stirring frequently, until the juices are evaporated and the sauce that remains is thick enough to mound on a spoon with no surrounding watery liquid. Taste and correct the seasonings.

Basil Puree

3 garlic cloves
½ cup extra virgin olive oil

2 cups basil leaves
½ teaspoon salt

*SINCE cheese is usually
included on pizza, I drizzle this puree instead of
pesto over the pizza
when it comes out of the
oven.*

MAKES ABOUT ¾ CUP

Pulverize the garlic with the oil in a blender, then add the basil by handfuls, followed by the salt. Puree until smooth. The mixture should be thin enough that you can easily spread it over the dough or drizzle it over the top.

Pizza Tips

It's easy to make several kinds of pizza at once. For example, choose two of the simpler pizzas and one or two of the heartier, more involved ones, keeping in mind an interesting balance of flavors, particularly in the cheese department. To devise your own combinations, keep in mind that delicious bit of Salsa Verde, page 55, or that tag end of Gorgonzola hiding in the refrigerator. Sautéed mushrooms, caramelized onions, and other cooked toppings can be prepared well ahead of the time.

    If you're using a pizza stone, you can make only one large pizza at a time. But this is perfect—while one is in the oven, you can roll out the dough for the next, set it on the peel, and let it rest while you assemble the toppings. It all flows together.

    I find that many cheeses are fine baked for the entire time, which is, after all, very short. Other cheeses, such as goat cheese or Parmesan, are better added during the last 2 or 3 minutes—just enough to warm them up and bring out their flavors.

    These recipes are for 10-inch pizzas, which use 8 ounces or a quarter of the dough. Of course you can make smaller—or larger—pizzas, adjusting the toppings accordingly.

Pizza Margherita

THIS *classic Italian pizza combines the timeless good flavors of tomato, mozzarella, and basil.*

MAKES ONE 10-INCH PIZZA

$^1/_4$ recipe Pizza Dough, page 506

$^3/_4$ cup Tomato Sauce for Pizza, page 507

4 ounces fresh mozzarella, thinly sliced

Extra virgin olive oil

8 fresh basil leaves, torn into small pieces

Preheat the oven to 500°F.

Roll or stretch out the dough to make a 10-inch circle, place it on a floured peel or pizza pan, and let it rest for 10 minutes. Spread the tomato sauce over the dough, leaving a $^1/_2$-inch border around the edge. Lay the mozzarella over the sauce and drizzle a little oil over all. Bake on a pizza stone or in the pan until the crust is browned, 7 minutes, then remove and brush the crust with a little oil and scatter the torn basil leaves over the top.

Pizza with Tomato, Mozzarella, and Olives

THE *success of a simple pizza, like this one, depends on the quality of your oil and herbs—which should be fruity and fragrant, respectively.*

MAKES ONE 10-INCH PIZZA

$^1/_4$ recipe Pizza Dough, page 506

$^3/_4$ cup Tomato Sauce for Pizza, page 507

3 to 4 ounces mozzarella, diced into small cubes

12 Gaeta, Niçoise, or Kalamata olives, pitted and quartered

1 tablespoon chopped marjoram

Freshly milled pepper

Extra virgin olive oil

Preheat the oven to 500°F.

Roll or stretch out the dough into a 10-inch circle, place it on a floured peel or pizza pan, and let rest for 10 minutes. Spread on the tomato sauce, leaving a $^1/_2$-inch border around the edge. Scatter the cheese and olives over the sauce, then add half the marjoram and a little pepper. Drizzle a little oil over all. Bake on a stone or in the pan until the pizza is bubbling, about 10 minutes, then remove and add the remaining marjoram.

White Pizza (*Pizza Bianca*)

¼ recipe Pizza Dough, page 506

Extra virgin olive oil

4 ounces fresh mozzarella, very thinly sliced or cubed

2 tablespoons freshly grated pecorino or Parmesan

8 basil leaves, torn into small pieces, or ¼ cup Basil Puree, page 507

Freshly milled pepper

As the name suggests, this is a cheese pizza, flavored with basil. The cheese should be the delicate fresh mozzarella accented with a sharper pecorino or a good Parmesan.

MAKES ONE 10-INCH PIZZA

Preheat the oven to 500°F.

Roll or stretch the dough into a 10-inch circle, set it on a floured peel or pizza pan, and let rest for 10 minutes. Brush a little oil over the dough, then cover with the mozzarella. Drizzle a little more oil over the top and bake on a stone or in the pan until bubbling, about 7 minutes. Add the grated cheese, return to the oven for 2 minutes more, then remove and scatter the basil and some pepper over the top. Or, less traditional but also good, drizzle the basil puree over the top.

Black and White Pizza Covering the dough with a thin layer of Olive Paste, page 87, instead of the olive oil adds a pungent note. Thyme, marjoram, or dried oregano as well as basil is a good herb to use.

Pizza with Tomato and Gorgonzola

¼ recipe Pizza Dough, page 506

¾ cup Tomato Sauce for Pizza, page 507

3 ounces Gorgonzola, crumbled

2 tablespoons freshly grated Parmesan

1 tablespoon finely chopped rosemary

Salt and freshly milled pepper

THIS pizza contains the combined delights of tomato, rosemary, and Gorgonzola. Use the Gorgonzola dolcelatte or, if you can't find it, Cambazola or Saga blue.

MAKES ONE 10-INCH PIZZA

Preheat the oven to 500°F.

Roll or stretch the dough into a 10-inch circle, set it on a floured peel or pizza pan, and let rest for 10 minutes. Cover it with the tomato sauce, then the Gorgonzola. Bake on a stone or in the pan until the cheese is melted and bubbling and the crust is browned, about 7 minutes. Add the Parmesan and rosemary and bake for 2 minutes more. Remove and season with a little salt and pepper.

Pizza with Grilled Eggplant, Tomato, and Basil Puree

SMALLER, *oblong egg-plant varieties—Italian or Asian—are the best size and shape here, but large ones can also be used, cut lengthwise into quarters, then into wedges.*

MAKES ONE 10-INCH PIZZA

3 small oblong eggplants, sliced into rounds $1/3$ inch thick

Extra virgin olive oil

Salt and freshly milled pepper

$1/4$ recipe Pizza Dough, page 506

$1/4$ cup Basil Puree, page 507

2 Roma or plum tomatoes, sliced into $1/4$-inch rounds

2 tablespoons freshly grated Parmesan

Brush each side of the eggplant with oil and broil or grill on both sides until nicely colored and tender. Season with salt and pepper.

Preheat the oven to 500°F.

Shape the dough into a 10-inch circle, set it on a floured peel or pizza pan, and let rest for 10 minutes. Brush a little of the basil puree over the bottom, leaving a $1/2$-inch border, then cover with overlapping slices of the eggplant and tomatoes. Bake for 6 minutes, then add the cheese and return to the oven for 2 minutes more. Drizzle with the remaining puree and season with pepper.

Pizza with Eggplant and Dried Oregano

MAKES ONE 10-INCH PIZZA

3 tablespoons extra virgin olive oil

8 to 12 ounces eggplant, diced into $1/2$-inch cubes

2 tablespoons parsley chopped with 1 garlic clove

Salt and freshly milled pepper

$1/2$ teaspoon dried oregano

$1/4$ recipe Pizza Dough, page 506

4 ounces mozzarella, preferably fresh, diced into small cubes

Preheat the oven to 500°F.

Heat 3 tablespoons of the olive oil in a wide skillet over medium-high heat. Add the eggplant and sauté, stirring every few minutes, until golden and tender, about 15 minutes. Meanwhile, roll or stretch the dough into a 10-inch circle, set it on a floured peel or pizza pan, and let it rest for 10 minutes.

Remove the skillet from the heat, add the parsley-garlic mixture, and season with salt, plenty of pepper, and the oregano. Toss the eggplant with the cheese.

Cover the dough with the eggplant and cheese and bake on a stone or in the pan for 7 to 8 minutes or until the crust is browned.

Mushroom Pizza with Tomato and Smoked Cheese

1/4 recipe Pizza Dough, page 506

2 tablespoons olive oil

6 ounces mushrooms, thinly sliced

Salt and freshly milled pepper

1/2 cup Tomato Sauce for Pizza, page 507

1 tomato, seeded and diced

2 to 3 ounces smoked mozzarella or provolone, coarsely grated

2 tablespoons freshly grated Parmesan

2 tablespoons parsley chopped with 1 garlic clove

Red pepper flakes

I LIKE to use big fleshy mushrooms, like porto-bellos or, with luck, porcini.

MAKES ONE 10-INCH PIZZA

Preheat the oven to 500°F.

Roll the dough into a 10-inch circle, set on a floured peel or pizza pan, and let rest for 10 minutes. Heat the oil in a wide skillet over high heat. Sauté the mushrooms until browned, about 5 minutes. Season well with salt and pepper.

Spread the tomato sauce over the dough. Add the diced tomato, then the mushrooms. Bake for 5 minutes, add the cheeses, and bake for 3 minutes more. Remove and scatter the parsley-garlic mixture and pepper flakes over the top.

Pizza with Mozzarella, Olives, and Salsa Verde

1/4 recipe Pizza Dough, page 506

3 ounces mozzarella, diced into small cubes

3 Roma or plum tomatoes, seeded and diced

20 Niçoise or 10 Kalamata olives, pitted and chopped

Freshly milled pepper

1 teaspoon olive oil

2 tablespoons freshly grated Parmesan

2 tablespoons Salsa Verde, page 55

MAKES ONE 10-INCH PIZZA

Preheat the oven to 500°F.

Roll the dough into a 10-inch circle, set it on a floured peel or pizza pan, and let it rest for 10 minutes. Combine the cheese, tomatoes, and olives and season with a little pepper and the olive oil. Spread this over the dough and bake on a stone or in the pan for 6 minutes. Add the Parmesan and bake for 2 minutes more. Remove and drizzle with the salsa verde.

Pizza with Sautéed Artichoke Heart and Fontina

PREPARE *the artichoke before you make the pizza.*

MAKES ONE 10-INCH PIZZA

1 large artichoke, trimmed, the heart thinly sliced

3 tablespoons olive oil

Juice of ½ lemon

Salt and freshly milled pepper or red pepper flakes

¼ recipe Pizza Dough, page 506

2 tablespoons tomato paste

⅓ cup grated Fontina

2 teaspoons capers, rinsed

2 tablespoons freshly grated Parmesan

2 teaspoons chopped parsley

Preheat the oven to 500°F.

In a medium skillet over high heat, sauté the artichoke heart in 2 tablespoons olive oil until tender and browned, 10-12 minutes. Squeeze lemon juice over the artichokes and season with salt and pepper.

Roll or stretch the dough into a 10-inch circle, set it on a floured peel or pizza pan, and let it rest for 10 minutes. Dilute the tomato paste with the remaining oil and spread it over the dough. Lay the artichokes on top, then add the cheese and capers. Bake for 6 minutes, add the Parmesan, and bake for 2 minutes more. Remove, scatter the parsley over the top, and season with pepper or a pinch of red pepper flakes.

Potato and Roasted Pepper Pizza

PEOPLE are usually surprised by the idea of putting potatoes on pizza, but it is done in Italy and is especially good made with summer's moist and tender new potatoes.

MAKES ONE 10-INCH PIZZA

¼ recipe Pizza Dough, page 506

1 red or yellow bell pepper, roasted, page 403

4 teaspoons extra virgin olive oil

Salt and freshly milled pepper

6 ounces new fingerling or other potatoes, scrubbed

1 garlic clove, minced

2 teaspoons chopped thyme

2 ounces smoked mozzarella or provolone, grated

2 teaspoons capers, rinsed

15 Niçoise olives, pitted and chopped

Red pepper flakes

Preheat the oven to 500°F.

Roll or stretch the dough into a 10-inch circle, set it on a floured peel or pizza pan, and let it rest for 10 minutes.

Finely dice the pepper, moisten it with a teaspoon of the oil, and season it with salt and pepper. Thinly slice the potatoes. Heat a tablespoon olive oil in a wide skillet over medium heat. Add the potatoes and a few tablespoons water, cover, and cook until tender, about 5 minutes. Season with salt, pepper, the garlic, and the thyme. Toss the potatoes with the cheese, peppers, capers, and olives.

Cover with the potato mixture and bake for 7 minutes. Remove and add a few good pinches of red pepper flakes.

Zucchini Pizza with Cherry Tomatoes and Goat Cheese

¹/₄ recipe Pizza Dough, page 506

3 small-to-medium zucchini, thinly sliced into rounds

Olive oil for sautéing, plus extra virgin for the top

Salt and freshly milled pepper

4 ounces cherry tomatoes, approximately

1 garlic clove, finely chopped

4 basil leaves, torn into small pieces or very thinly sliced

2 ounces mozzarella, thinly sliced or diced

2 ounces goat cheese or feta, crumbled

USE any mix of small, sweet tomatoes—cherry, currant, and pear.

MAKES ONE 10-INCH PIZZA

Preheat the oven to 500°F.

Roll or stretch the dough into a 10-inch circle, set it on a floured peel or pizza pan, and let it rest for 10 minutes.

Sauté the zucchini in 1 tablespoon olive oil in a skillet over medium heat until tender and beginning to color, about 4 minutes. Season with salt and pepper. Slice the tomatoes into halves or quarters and toss them with the garlic, a little olive oil, some pepper, and half the basil.

Distribute the mozzarella and zucchini over the dough, then add the tomatoes. Bake on a stone or in the pan for 5 minutes, then add the goat cheese and bake for 3 minutes more. Remove, drizzle with a little extra virgin olive oil, and sprinkle on the rest of the basil leaves.

Roasted Pepper Pizza

¹/₄ recipe Pizza Dough, page 506

1¹/₂ cups roasted bell peppers, in thin strips

1 jalapeño chile, seeded and finely diced

8 oil-cured black olives, pitted and torn into small pieces

Salt and freshly milled pepper

1 scant cup shredded or thinly sliced mozzarella, optional

1 tablespoon olive oil or Basil Puree, page 507

ROAST the peppers and have them ready before you assemble this pizza. A mixture of colors—red, yellow, and orange—is gorgeous. I often throw in a diced jalapeño as well, for its snappy presence. The cheese can be left out, and you'll still have a moist and richly flavorful pizza.

MAKES ONE 10-INCH PIZZA

Preheat the oven to 500°F.

Roll or stretch the dough into a 10-inch circle, set it on a floured peel or pizza pan, and let it rest for 10 minutes.

Toss the peppers, chile, and olives together and season with salt and pepper. Lay the cheese over the dough, leaving a ¹/₂-inch border, then cover with the peppers. Bake for 7 minutes, then remove and drizzle with the oil or basil puree.

Pizza with Other Peppers: Use the Peperonata, page 404, or Sautéed Peppers, page 402, mixed with 2 teaspoons rinsed capers. Bake as described, using cheese or not as you prefer. Serve garnished with a flourish of chopped parsley or basil. Or cover a pizza with Roasted Pepper Strips and Onions (Rajas), page 404, and garnish with Cilantro Salsa, page 56, or chopped cilantro.

Another Mushroom Pizza

ONE of my favorite summer pizzas. If you have access to more exotic mushrooms—cremini, oyster, porcini—use them as well or instead.

MAKES TWO 10-INCH PIZZAS

½ recipe Pizza Dough, page 506

1 pound shiitake and portobello mushrooms, mixed

3 tablespoons olive oil

¼ cup finely diced white onion

6 plum tomatoes, seeded and diced into ¼-inch pieces

3 tablespoons chopped thyme

2 tablespoons red wine vinegar or to taste

Salt and freshly milled pepper

2 cups grated Fontina

½ cup freshly grated Parmesan

Preheat the oven to 500°F.

Roll or stretch the dough into two 10-inch circles, set on peels or in pizza pans, and let rest for 10 minutes.

Wipe the mushrooms, remove their stems, then thinly slice the caps. Heat the oil in a wide skillet over medium-high heat. Add the onion and cook, stirring occasionally, until it has softened, about 4 minutes. Raise the heat, add the mushrooms, and sauté until they begin to look soft and shiny, about 5 minutes. Stir in the tomatoes and thyme and season with vinegar. Turn off the heat and season with salt and pepper.

Spread most of the Fontina over the dough, add the mushroom mixture, then cover with the remaining Fontina and the Parmesan. Bake on a stone or in the pans until the cheeses have melted and the edge of the pizza is browned, about 10 minutes. Remove and serve.

Grains:
Kernels and Seeds of Life

GRAIN IS AT THE CENTER OF NEARLY EVERY CIVILIZATION, SO MUCH SO THAT FOOD CULTURES ARE PRACTICALLY DEFINED BY THEIR GRAINS: THE RICE AND MILLET OF ASIA, THE CORN OF THE AMERICAS, THE AMARANTH OF THE AZTECS AND quinoa of the Incas, the oats of the Scots, the wheat of Italy, and so forth. Although Americans are big consumers of grain, we don't consume it directly, for most of our grains are fed to animals, used in industry, or made into alcohol. Until recently we've rather ignored grain as primary food, but as we better understand its importance to our health and its ability to feed so many, grain is beginning to regain its lost status.

The variety of grains now commonly available to us is far more diverse than it ever has been. Grains like quinoa, amaranth, spelt, kamut, and bulgur can show up on the table as easily as rice has in the past. Couscous has become commonplace, and when it comes to rice there are all kinds of varieties unknown even a relatively short time ago—scented grains like jasmine and pecan rice, black rice, popcorn rice, and new hybrids like wehani. And of course, risotto has made significant headway into our kitchens, often assuming a major role in the vegetarian kitchen.

We've yet to center our meals around grain the way Chinese make everything else on the plate relate to a bowl of rice. But given their immense diversity and the possibility of appearing in any course of any meal—in our own way, we end up eating grain throughout the day.

The Parts of a Grain

STARTING *from the outside of the kernel, grains are made up of a protective fibrous hull called the* bran, *then the* starchy endosperm, *and at the heart the* germ. *In the refining process, we lose the bran, which contains most of the minerals, fiber, and much of the riboflavin inherent in grains. The oil-rich germ, which can quickly turn rancid, is frequently removed as well. What we end up eating is the starchy middle, which has the most carbohydrate and the fewest vitamins and minerals. Although lost nutrients are added to refined grains through enrichments, whole grains retain more fiber and trace minerals, which is why they're considered nutritionally superior. In the health food industry, for example, whole-wheat flour, wheat germ, and bran have always been featured in baked goods, flours, and cereals because of the contributions they make to our health and diet.*

Knowing Your Grits from Your Groats

WHOLE GRAINS (GROATS): These grains do not undergo processing or refining and contain their bran, germ, and endosperm. They also take the longest to cook—except buckwheat (kasha), the tiny quinoa, amaranth, and teff—and are generally very chewy. While nutritionally beneficial, whole groats—whether oats, wheat, barley, or spelt—tend to be the least appealing form of grain, especially if served alone. They cook much better when they're combined with other foods and used in casseroles, soups, croquettes, salads, and other dishes.

POLISHED GRAINS: The tough husk, along with some or all of the bran, is removed from these grains, which include wheat berries, brown rice, and pearl barley. Polished grains cook more quickly than those with the husks still intact, but they still take a good 40 minutes or longer.

GRITS, MEAL, AND CRACKED GRAINS: When, during the milling process, grains are further broken down in size, they become grits. Examples include hominy or corn grits, cracked wheat, and steel-cut oats. Some are derived from whole grains; others are more refined. Their textures are toothy and substantial.

FLAKES: When sliced groats or cracked grains are steamed and rolled, they become flakes. Rolled oats, or oatmeal, is one flake we all know, but rolled barley, wheat, rye, and spelt are others. Flakes cook quickly and are light, fluffy, and easy to digest. They are good as a side dish, not just as a morning cereal. Wheat bran and oat bran are not rolled; they're just naturally light and flaky.

FLOUR: Finally, with further milling, grain becomes flour. When the bran and germ are left in wheat, it's whole-wheat flour. The equivalent exists for corn and other flours as well. Depending on the type of wheat and the milling, whole-wheat flour can be flaky with large bits of bran; grainy and dense; or soft and fine, almost like white flour. Whole-wheat pastry flour is the finest of all. Enriched flour has nutrients added back into it. When using white flour, my preference is for unbleached all-purpose flour, but today's whole-wheat pastry flours can be used more or less interchangeably with all-purpose white.

How to Select, Store, and Cook Grains

SELECTING: Organically grown stone-ground grains and flours can be found in many supermarkets and most natural food stores, in packages and in bulk. Buy 1-pound bags of grains you use only occasionally and replace them more frequently. When buying grains and their flours from bins, make sure they have a nice, fresh smell, and have not turned rancid.

STORING: Because the germ of whole grains contains oil, they deteriorate more quickly than refined ones. To keep them fresh, store grains in tightly covered glass jars in a cool place. Three to four months is a reasonable period for keeping whole or cracked grains. Oil-rich flours and meals, such as stone-ground cornmeal made from whole corn that has not been degerminated, should be kept in the refrigerator or freezer.

SOAKING: Like beans, large grains and short-grain brown rice cook more quickly and are more easily digested if soaked before cooking. Although this is not entirely necessary, soaking them in cool water anywhere from an hour to overnight does help to soften them. Basmati rice is soaked to plump and lengthen the grains.

COOKING: A 2-quart saucepan with a tight-fitting lid is ample for cooking 1 to 2 cups of raw grains. A nonstick surface makes it easier to clean the pans, but if grain does stick to the pan, a short soak should be sufficient to loosen it.

After the grains have cooked, let them stand for 5 to 10 minutes to continue absorbing moisture. To produce fluffy, separate grains, put a clean towel under the lid once they've finished cooking, then let stand. The towel, rather than the grain, will absorb the steam.

USING A PRESSURE COOKER: A pressure cooker is a great timesaver with long-cooking grains such as brown rice, spelt, kamut, wheat berries, and other whole groats. Cook them without soaking at high pressure for one-third the time suggested for regular cooking. If they're not done, return to pressure and continue cooking for another 5 to 10 minutes. Smaller grains are usually quick cooking and, in my opinion, too delicate for the pressure cooker.

SALTING: Salt doesn't seem to be as necessary to bring out the flavor of grains as it is for other foods. You'll find you can use it in small amounts—$^1/_4$ to $^1/_2$ teaspoon for 1 cup uncooked grain. When cooking large, whole grains, add salt during the last 30 minutes just as you do with beans.

Making Grains Attractive and Appealing

MANY *people resist the earthy brown tones and hearty, chewy textures of grains. Grains, by themselves, just don't have the sensual appeal of glossy peppers or a bunch of fragrant herbs, plus they're more often than not piled on a plate in plain, ungainly portions. So to make the most of grains' considerable virtues, consider these approaches:*

- When you plan a grain dish, make sure there's plenty of color and contrast on the plate, not all brown foods. Peppers, asparagus, greens, carrots, and zucchini are just a few colorful vegetables to consider.

- Accompany grains with lively garnishes. Sautéed tomatoes, braised greens, yogurt, chopped fresh herbs, salsas, and toasted nuts are delicious as well as attractive.

- Gradually add grains to your menu. Mixing cooked brown and white rice together makes a dish that's lighter and more familiar than all brown rice. Or start with grits, rice, and polenta, which are soft, comforting, and easy to like. Add a cup of leftover cooked grains to your favorite muffin or pancake recipe.

- I've found that by themselves the large kernels of oats, wheat, kamut, and spelt are the most difficult grains for people to warm up to; they're just too dense. However, they are enjoyable when added to soups—a cup or so of cooked grain to a pot—where their chewy texture provides a welcome contrast to softer elements. Kamut, spelt, tiny amaranth, and quinoa are also available as flours which can easily be added to breads, muffins, and other baked goods.

Barley

UNTIL *recently, barley was used mostly in soup, especially the classic mushroom-barley soup or Scotch broth. Today we enjoy it cooked like risotto as well. Barley is usually polished, or pearled, as it's commonly called. It's bland but pleasantly textured and toothsome—easy to serve in place of rice and a nice change. Barley grits make a good breakfast cereal. Malted barley is a sweetener that can be used in place of sugar or honey in bread baking.*

Barley with Butter or Roasted Nut Oil

SERVE *simply cooked, soft, chewy barley with a winter vegetable stew or a mushroom ragout. The additions for kasha— browned onions, pasta, and leeks with rosemary oil—are also good with barley.*

MAKES ABOUT 3¹/₂ CUPS

3 cups water, Basic Vegetable Stock, page 196, or Mushroom Stock, page 197

Salt and freshly milled pepper
1 cup pearl barley, rinsed
Butter or walnut or hazelnut oil

Bring the water to a boil in a 2-quart saucepan. Add ¹/₄ teaspoon salt and stir in the barley. Lower the heat, cover the pan, and simmer until tender, 25 to 30 minutes. Let stand for 5 minutes before serving. Serve tossed with a little butter and pepper or season with one of the delicious roasted nut oils.

Savory Barley Flakes

2 cups barley flakes
Salt and freshly milled pepper

Butter or roasted nut oils

Toast the flakes in a dry skillet over medium heat, stirring frequently, until they smell good. Bring 2 cups water to a boil in a saucepan. Add $^1/_2$ teaspoon salt, then the flakes. Cover the pot, lower the heat, and cook for 5 minutes. Turn off the heat and let stand for 5 minutes more. Fluff with a fork, add butter to taste, and season with pepper.

READY in 10 minutes, barley flakes are light and easy to digest. With a bit of butter and a shower of pepper, they're simply delicious—a great change from rice. And you can substitute wheat, spelt, or rye flakes.

SERVES 4

Barley-Mushroom Pilaf with Sautéed Mushrooms

$^1/_2$ to 1 ounce dried porcini, about $^1/_2$ to 1 cup
1 pound white mushrooms
5 tablespoons olive oil or a mixture of oil and butter
Salt and freshly milled pepper
2 garlic cloves, chopped

$^1/_2$ cup dry white or red wine
1 onion, finely chopped
1 cup pearl barley, rinsed
$^1/_4$ cup chopped parsley mixed with a little tarragon or rosemary

A HEARTY side dish or a good filling for stuffed cabbage. This recipe makes enough for 12 cabbage rolls.

SERVES 4 TO 6

Cover the dried mushrooms with 3 cups warm water. Set aside to soften for at least 15 minutes, then remove and finely chop. Reserve the liquid and add enough water to make 3 cups, if necessary. Meanwhile, chop half the fresh mushrooms and slice the rest.

Heat 2 tablespoons of the oil in a wide skillet over high heat. Add the chopped fresh mushrooms and cook, stirring frequently, until well colored, about 5 minutes. Season with salt and pepper, then add the dried mushrooms, garlic, and wine. Reduce the heat to medium and cook until the wine is absorbed and the pan is nearly dry, about 2 minutes.

In a 3-quart saucepan, heat a tablespoon of the remaining oil. Add the onion and cook over medium heat until limp, 5 minutes. Add the barley, stir in the cooked mushrooms, reserved mushroom liquid, and $^1/_2$ teaspoon salt. Bring to a boil. Lower the heat and simmer, covered, until tender, 35 to 40 minutes.

Meanwhile, sauté the sliced mushrooms in the remaining oil over high heat until golden, about 5 minutes. Season with salt and pepper. Loosen the cooked barley with a fork, toss it with the herbs, and pile it into a serving dish. Garnish with the sautéed mushrooms.

Green Barley and Kale Gratin

NOT a dowdy dish at all—the kale turns the barley bright green. Bake it in a gratin dish or individual ramekins.

SERVES 4 TO 6

²/₃ cup pearl barley, rinsed

Salt and freshly milled pepper

1 large bunch kale, about 1¼ pounds, stems entirely removed

2 tablespoons butter

3 tablespoons flour

1½ cups milk or Basic Vegetable Stock, page 196

¼ teaspoon allspice

⅛ teaspoon grated nutmeg

½ cup grated Gruyère or provolone

In a saucepan, add the barley to 1 quart boiling water with ½ teaspoon salt and simmer, uncovered until tender, about 30 minutes. Drain. While it's cooking, cook the kale in a skillet of boiling salted water until tender, 6 to 10 minutes. Drain, then puree with ¼ cup of the cooking water until smooth.

Preheat the oven to 375°F. Melt the butter in a small saucepan, whisk in the flour, then add the milk. Cook, stirring constantly over medium heat, until thick. Season with allspice, nutmeg, salt, and pepper. Combine all the ingredients, check the seasonings, then transfer to a lightly buttered baking dish or ramekins.

Bake until lightly browned on top, about 30 minutes. If you've used ramekins, run a knife around the edges, then unmold them by giving them a sharp rap on the counter. Present them browned side up.

Barley Risotto

As with short-grain rice like Arborio, the starch in barley makes its own creamy sauce, which allows it to be cooked the way risotto is. The technique is basically the same as that for risotto, and you can use any of the condiments suggested for risotto. Artichokes and mushrooms are especially good choices.

SERVES 4

6 cups Basic Vegetable Stock, page 196, or Mushroom Stock, page 197

2 tablespoons olive oil

1 small onion, finely diced

2 garlic cloves, finely chopped

1 cup pearl barley

¾ cup dry white wine

2 tablespoons butter

½ cup freshly grated Parmesan or pecorino Romano

¼ cup finely chopped parsley or fines herbes

Juice of 1 lemon or to taste

Salt and freshly milled pepper

Have the stock at a simmer. Heat the oil in a heavy wide pan or soup pot. Add the onion and garlic and cook over medium heat until the onion is translucent, about 4 minutes. Add the barley and cook for 1 minute, stirring to coat the grains. Raise the heat a little, add the wine, and cook, stirring frequently until the wine is nearly absorbed. Add 2½ cups of the stock, cover the pot, and simmer until the stock is nearly absorbed. Now start adding stock ½ cup at a time, stirring more or less constantly and waiting for each addition to be absorbed before adding more. After about 40 minutes the barley should be tender and the dish thick and creamy. You may not need to use the full amount of stock. Stir in the butter, cheese, half the parsley, and lemon juice to taste. Taste for salt and season with pepper. Serve garnished with the remaining parsley.

Buckwheat (Kasha)

BUCKWHEAT *isn't a true grain, but a fruit. However, we treat it as if it were a grain. We know buckwheat groats as kasha and buckwheat flour as the special element in buckwheat pancakes or blini and in Japanese soba noodles. Buckwheat groats are sold both roasted (as used in the following recipes) and unroasted. Unroasted buckwheat groats are pale and bland, but when roasted, they become dark and their earthy flavor blossoms. Buckwheat is light and quick-cooking. An egg—or just the white—stirred into the kernels before adding the liquid keeps the texture light and fluffy. If you omit the egg coating, the grains remain separate, falling off your fork, rather than clinging together.*

Kasha (Buckwheat Groats)

2 cups water or Basic Vegetable Stock,
  page 196

1 egg or 2 egg whites

1 cup roasted buckwheat groats

1 tablespoon butter

Salt and freshly milled pepper

SERVE *this fluffy grain with roasted root vegetables, steamed kohlrabi, or braised cabbage. It makes a good filling for stuffed cabbage, too.*

SERVES 4

Bring the water to a boil in a 3-quart saucepan. Beat the egg in a bowl with a fork, then stir in the groats. Heat a wide skillet over medium heat, add the groats, and cook, stirring constantly until the grains are dry and separate, about 3 minutes. Add them to the water with the butter and ½ teaspoon salt. Lower the heat and simmer, covered, until all the liquid is absorbed, 7 to 12 minutes—some brands cook more quickly than others. Let stand for 5 minutes, then lightly fluff with a fork and season with pepper before serving.

Kasha with Fried Onions Sauté 3 cups sliced onion in 2 tablespoons clarified butter or oil in a skillet until well browned, 12 to 15 minutes. Season with salt and pepper and serve strewn over the kasha along with chopped parsley for color.

Kasha Varnishkes (Kasha with Bow Ties) When I tested this recipe, I realized how long it had been since I last had this Eastern European classic—and what I had been missing. Time your cooking so that the noodles and onions are done when the kasha is—they take about the same time to cook.
    Boil 1 cup of bow tie noodles or farfalle pasta in salted water until done, then drain them. Sauté 1 large onion, chopped, in 2 tablespoons butter or oil in a skillet over medium heat until lightly browned, about 12 minutes. Season well with salt and pepper. When the kasha is done, toss it with the noodles and onions and serve.

Kasha with Toasted Walnuts and Scallions This simple garnish gives textural variation and a fresh element to either the Kasha or Kasha with Bow Ties. Melt 1 or 2 tablespoons butter or sunflower seed oil in a medium skillet. Add 1 cup chopped walnuts, 1 bunch of sliced scallions, including half the greens, and cook over medium heat until everything smells toasty and the nuts have begun to color, about 5 minutes. Season well with salt and pepper, then add thyme and parsley. Gently stir this mixture into the finished kasha.

Corn

CORN is America's native grain, and there's a great deal to be said about corn—its history and lore, its enormous prevalence in the food industry, and our romance and fascination with it. While there are many types and forms of corn, we eat most of it unknowingly in processed foods where it appears as a sweetener, a starch, and an oil. Of course, we also enjoy corn as a fresh vegetable (see the vegetable chapter) as well as in other forms such as cornmeal, polenta, grits, hominy or posole, and popcorn. Corn is also milled into flour.

While I'm quite certain that we lead the world in the number and variety of corn recipes, it's fallen to Italy to make that unsavory-sounding dish, cornmeal mush, a star in the culinary sky by calling it polenta.

CORNMEAL (POLENTA): Cornmeal can be white, yellow, or blue; the color comes from the different varieties of corn. Regardless of color, the most nutritious cornmeal still contains the germ. Because it's rich in oil, whole-grain meal should be refrigerated once opened. Degerminated cornmeal, found boxed in the baking section of your market, needn't be refrigerated. It usually announces itself as "degerminated" on the label so you know what you're getting.

Cornmeal can be very fine, almost like flour, or coarse and gritty, varying from brand to brand. I use cornmeal that has a little texture but isn't floury in dishes like spoon bread, sometimes for polenta, and certainly for hot cereal.

Polenta

Polenta is essentially grits or coarse cornmeal. In fact, one company labels its yellow and white corn grits parenthetically as polenta. The Italian name certainly teases the imagination more than our cornmeal mush does. But wherever corn is eaten, cornmeal mush exists. And regardless of what it's called, it makes a practical and highly versatile dish. Polenta can even put in an appearance for dessert when served with a spoonful of mascarpone and drizzled with molasses, a recollection of our own worthy Indian pudding, or garnished with sour cream, warm honey, and poppy seeds.

American cornmeal cereal isn't usually cooked longer than 20 minutes, but when it comes to polenta, tradition calls for 45 minutes of constant stirring. Averse as we are to giving time to simple tasks, it's the time spent cooking that brings out the full corn flavor. I find 30 minutes makes good-tasting polenta. Using a double boiler eliminates the need for constant stirring, but I don't mind the stirring if I'm not rushed. I find it provides a quiet time to catch up on some reading—I just put my book near the stove and read while I stir. There is also an instant Italian polenta which cooks in about 10 minutes. It has very good flavor and rich golden color.

If you plan to serve soft polenta, use 4 parts water to 1 part polenta; for firm polenta the ratio is closer to 3 parts water to 1 part polenta. However, these ratios have to be taken with a grain of salt, for you may find yourself adding more water just to make the polenta easier to stir. In general, for firm polenta, use less water.

Traditional Polenta

2 cups coarse cornmeal, preferably
   stone-ground, or a mixture of coarse
   and fine cornmeal

1 1/2 teaspoons salt or to taste
2 to 6 tablespoons butter, optional

IF the polenta erupts into volcanic spurts at any point, wrap a napkin around your stirring hand and charge ahead. This is the polenta to make if you wish to let it harden for another use.

SERVES 6

Bring 6 to 8 cups water to a boil in a large, heavy saucepan and add the salt and then the cornmeal in a steady stream, stirring constantly with a whisk to avoid making lumps and having the meal seize up within the first few minutes. (You can also use 2 cups of the water, cold, to make a slurry with the meal, then whisk it in all at once.) Lower the heat and cook, stirring more or less constantly, for 30 to 45 minutes. If the polenta seizes up into a hard mass, add small increments of boiling water while it cooks, to smooth it out. When done, taste for salt and then turn off the heat and stir in butter to taste. Serve soft polenta immediately or keep it warm over boiling water until ready to serve.

Firm Polenta When cooled, polenta firms up quickly. It can then can be sliced and broiled, grilled, fried, or baked into casseroles and gratins. Make the Traditional Polenta using 6 cups water to make a stiffer, drier polenta. As soon as it's done, pour it onto a clean counter, sheet pan, a large baking dish, loaf pan, or two pie plates. Using a spatula or knife dipped in cold water, immediately spread the polenta out to a thickness of 3/8 inch or so. Let it cool until firm, about 15 minutes or slightly longer if you've poured it into a loaf pan. Cut the firm polenta into desired shapes. Covered with plastic, firm polenta will hold for 1 or 2 days in the refrigerator.

Double Boiler Method for Soft Polenta

1 1/2 teaspoons salt or to taste
2 cups coarse cornmeal, preferably
   stone ground

2 to 6 tablespoons butter, optional

THIS technique produces good soft polenta without requiring constant attention. It does, however, take longer since it doesn't cook directly over the heat. For a richer polenta, replace half or all of the water with milk.

SERVES 6

Bring a few inches water to a boil in the lower half of a double boiler, then lower the heat. Bring 8 cups water to a boil in the top part of the double boiler directly over the heat, then add the salt and cornmeal as for traditional polenta. Cook, stirring constantly, until the consistency is even, then place the pan over the simmering water and cover. Cook for 1 1/2 hours. If you're in the kitchen, give it a stir every now and then, but it will come out all right if left unattended. Taste for salt, turn off the heat, and stir in butter. To hold, lower the heat so that the water barely simmers and let stand until ready to use.

Polenta with Cheese

THE *flavor of corn is remarkably well suited to cheese. The choice of cheese can be deliberate or simply be a way to use scraps of good cheeses. Gorgonzola, Fontina, and Parmesan are traditional Italian enrichments, while Cheddar gives a much more American taste. Smoked cheeses provide a heartiness that contributes a great deal to a vegetarian meal. Eight cups cooked polenta can easily absorb between 1 and 2 cups.*

SERVES 6

Cooked Polenta, page 523

1 to 2 cups grated Fontina

½ cup freshly grated Parmesan, plus extra for garnish

Butter

Freshly milled pepper

Make the polenta. When it's done, turn off the heat, stir in the cheeses, and add butter to taste. Season with pepper and serve with an additional sprinkle of grated Parmesan.

Polenta with Browned Onions and Thyme   The addition of onion gives a larger range of flavor and texture to polenta. While the polenta is cooking, heat 2 tablespoons butter or olive oil in a medium skillet. Stirring occasionally, cook 1 large, finely diced onion with 2½ teaspoons chopped thyme (or rosemary) until soft, about 15 minutes. Season with salt and pepper. Stir it into the polenta during the last 10 minutes or so that the polenta is cooking. When done, turn off the heat and stir in 1 cup grated Parmesan. Taste for salt and season with pepper.

Soft Polenta with Gorgonzola and Bread Crumbs

A LUXURIOUS treatment of a humble food, this makes an utterly delicious, informal, easy meal.

SERVES 6

Cooked Polenta, page 523

1 cup milk

1 cup freshly grated Parmesan

6 to 8 ounces Gorgonzola

¾ cup bread crumbs crisped in butter

¼ cup chopped parsley

Freshly milled pepper

When the polenta is done, stir in the milk and Parmesan. Pour it into individual serving bowls, crumble the Gorgonzola over the top, and garnish with the bread crumbs and parsley. Pepper liberally and serve.

Grilled or Broiled Polenta This makes a substantial accompaniment to vegetable ragouts and sautés, or it can be simply served with a tomato sauce and crumbled Gorgonzola or goat cheese.

Cut firm polenta into squares, diamonds, rectangles, or other shapes. Brush both sides lightly with olive oil. Make sure your grill is very clean so that the polenta won't stick. Grill until lightly marked, then turn and grill the second side. Or broil the polenta on both sides until browned in places.

Golden Polenta Cakes Cut firm polenta into desired shapes, then coat each piece with bread crumbs, semolina, or fine cornmeal. Fry in olive oil or clarified butter on both sides until golden. Sprinkle lightly with salt and serve.

Polenta Cakes with Parsley Salad For an appetizer or first course, make the golden polenta cakes and top with a small mound of Parsley Salad with Parmesan, page 144.

Crisp Polenta Sticks and Croutons A tasty, hot appetizer to serve with sea salt, herb salt, or sauce, such as Red Chile Mayonnaise, page 60, or Romesco Sauce, page 70. Slice firm polenta into pieces about 3 inches long and ³/₈ inch wide. Heat an inch or so of peanut or olive oil in a cast-iron or nonstick skillet until it's hot enough to sizzle a crumb of polenta. Add several sticks at a time to the pan and fry until crisp. They won't brown much, and they'll probably clump together, but don't worry. Remove them to paper towels to drain for a moment, then pry them apart. Dust lightly with salt or ground red chile and serve. To make a crisp crouton for a soup, cut firm polenta into cubes and fry in the same way.

Polenta Croquettes with Tomato Sauce

Firm Polenta, page 523
2 eggs, beaten with ¹/₄ cup milk
Salt and freshly milled pepper
1 cup fresh bread crumbs

Olive oil for pan frying
2 cups tomato sauce
Chopped parsley

SERVE these croquettes with a Fresh Tomato Sauce in summer or a more robust one in winter, such as the Red Wine Tomato Sauce with Olives.

MAKES 10 OR MORE

Cut firm polenta into 3-inch circles, squares, or other shapes. Beat the eggs and milk with a few pinches salt and a little pepper. Dip the polenta into the egg mixture, then coat it with the bread crumbs. Heat oil about ³/₈ inch deep in a medium skillet over medium-high heat until hot enough to quickly sizzle a bread crumb. Fry the croquettes until crisp and pale gold on both sides, turning them once. Remove them briefly to paper towels, then arrange them on a platter or individual plates. Top each croquette with the tomato sauce and garnish with parsley.

Polenta Cheddar Croquettes Stir 1 to 1¹/₂ cups grated sharp Cheddar, 6 thinly sliced scallions, including some of the greens, 3 tablespoons chopped parsley, and a few pinches red pepper flakes into cooked polenta. Let cool, then make into croquettes, as above. Serve with a dab of Olive-Rosemary Butter, page 51, a spoonful of the Corn-Tomato Relish or the Cherry Tomato and Olive Relish, page 78.

Polenta Dumplings with Warm Sage and Garlic Butter

THIS *simple polenta dish is very attractive baked in individual gratin dishes. If they're not available, though, individual portions can be served from a larger dish.*

MAKES 6 APPETIZER SERVINGS

½ recipe Firm Polenta, page 523

Butter for the dish

½ cup grated Parmesan

Warm Sage and Garlic Butter, page 50

Freshly milled pepper

Cut the cooled, firm polenta into 2½-inch rounds. Butter individual gratin dishes or a single large one. Overlap the rounds of polenta, allowing 3 to 4 per serving. Sprinkle with the Parmesan, drizzle with the sage butter, then broil about 6 inches from the heat until the cheese is bubbling and the polenta is hot, 3 to 5 minutes. Remove from the oven, season with pepper, and serve.

Polenta Gratin with Tomato, Fontina, and Rosemary

THE *fragrance of the rosemary and the warm cheese in this layered gratin is irresistible. The tomato sauce can be of the simplest kind, and the dish can be assembled ahead of time and then reheated when needed.*

SERVES 4

Firm Polenta, page 523

1 to 1½ cups grated Fontina

2 tablespoons butter

1½ cups Fresh Tomato Sauce, page 61

1 tablespoon finely chopped rosemary

Salt and freshly milled pepper

½ cup Gorgonzola

Chopped parsley

Make the polenta. During the last few minutes of cooking, stir in half the Fontina and the butter, then spread it, about ⅜ inch thick, on a clean counter or sheet pan to harden. Slice into rectangles or rounds—the exact size doesn't matter. This can be done hours in advance.

Heat the tomato sauce with half of the rosemary. Taste and season with salt, if needed, and a little pepper.

Preheat the oven to 400°F. Spread ¾ cup of the tomato sauce in a 3-quart gratin dish, then overlap the pieces of polenta with the remaining Fontina. Spoon the remaining sauce carefully in bands over the polenta, leaving the edges exposed. Crumble the Gorgonzola over the top and sprinkle with the rest of the rosemary and the parsley.

Bake, uncovered, for about 30 minutes or until the gratin is hot and bubbly. Garnish with the parsley, season with a little pepper, and serve.

Corn and Hominy Grits

White or yellow, corn grits are prepared and served much the way polenta is—warm with butter, enriched with cheese, allowed to cool, then fried, and so forth. Hominy grits are milled from corn that has been soaked with lime to soften the skins, a treatment that gives them an unusual flavor. Old-fashioned stone-ground grits are the best-tasting grits by far. They take about 40 minutes to cook as opposed to fast-cooking yet bland instant grits, but they can cook in a double boiler without much attention from you.

Grits

1 quart water or 2 cups *each* water and milk

1 cup stone-ground grits

Salt and freshly milled pepper

Butter to taste

THIS is about as complicated as some people like them. This recipe is written for stone-ground grits. For instant grits, follow the package instructions.

SERVES 4

Bring the water to a boil in the top of a double boiler, then stir in the grits and add ½ to 1 teaspoon salt. Cook, stirring constantly until the grits thicken, about 5 minutes, then set them over simmering water. Cover and cook until they're tender, about an hour. If you're not using a double boiler, cook the grits over very low heat, stirring frequently, for at least 35 to 40 minutes. (The longer they cook, the better grits taste. If they get too thick, just add water to thin them.) You can nurse them along for hours! Stir in as much butter as you like and season with pepper.

Breakfast Grits Skip the pepper and add a spoonful of sorghum, molasses, or maple syrup to each bowl along with cold milk.

Cheese Grits Add 1 cup grated Cheddar or Longhorn into the hot grits and add a few shakes of Tabasco or other favorite hot sauce.

Fried Grits

Cheese Grits, preceding recipe

1 egg beaten with 1 tablespoon water or milk

About 2 cups fresh bread crumbs

Vegetable oil for pan frying

SERVE these golden croquettes with greens and fried eggs, with salsa and beans, or alongside a summer vegetable stew.

MAKES SIXTEEN 2-INCH CROQUETTES

Pour the cooked grits into an 8-inch square pan or whatever is convenient and let cool until firm, 30 minutes or so. Cut into 16 fingers, squares, or triangles. Dip them into the beaten egg, then roll them in the bread crumbs. (They can be refrigerated at this point, but allow them to return to room temperature before frying.)

Heat ¼ inch of oil in a cast-iron skillet until it's hot enough to sizzle a drop of water. Add the grits and fry in a single layer on both sides until golden brown. Keep the finished ones warm in the oven until all are done, then serve.

Hominy Grits Pudding

THIS pudding holds well in the oven and is one of those dishes you can enjoy for breakfast, brunch, or a casual supper. If you add whole, plump hominy kernels, they'll give your teeth something to bite into.

SERVES 4

4 tablespoons butter

Cheese Grits, page 527

1 cup milk

2 eggs, beaten

¼ teaspoon cayenne or 1 teaspoon paprika

Freshly milled pepper

1 15-ounce can white or golden hominy, rinsed, optional

Preheat the oven to 350°F and lightly butter a 2-quart casserole or soufflé dish. Stir the butter into the grits. Cool for 5 minutes, then stir in the milk and eggs and season with cayenne and pepper. Add the hominy. Pour into the casserole and bake until the pudding is firm and a knife inserted in the center comes out clean, about 45 minutes. Serve with honey or strawberry jam for breakfast or accompanied with a tomato-onion salad for supper.

Souffléed Grits Pudding In the preceding dish, use 4 eggs, separated. Whip the whites until they hold soft but firm peaks, then fold them into the grits. Pour into the dish, set it in a pan, and add boiling water to come partially up the sides. Bake until risen and firm, 40 to 50 minutes.

IMPROVISING GRAIN PUDDINGS

Millet, barley, grits, rice, quinoa—virtually all cooked grains will set into a pudding when eggs and milk are added, as in the grits pudding or the souffléed variation. Cooked this way, they emerge light and tender and comforting, the way a pudding should be.

Hominy and Posole

Hominy and posole are whole kernels of corn that have been treated with lime or the ashes of certain plants. The alkali solutions loosen the skins, which are scrubbed off and

washed away; then the corn is either frozen or dried. The rich and unique flavor of posole (it's called *pozole* in Mexico) is the same as that in tamales or in corn tortillas, both of which are made from flour ground from lime-treated corn. Canned hominy, the southern version, is precooked, but in a pinch it can take the place of posole. Posole is very popular in New Mexico, where it's available in white, yellow, blue, and even red varieties.

Posole with Red Chile Pods

2½ cups dried posole

½ onion, diced

2 large garlic cloves, peeled and smashed

3 dried red New Mexican chile pods or guajillo chiles

1 teaspoon dried oregano, preferably Mexican

Salt and freshly milled pepper

Garnishes: finely shredded cabbage, thin tortilla strips, page 46, diced avocado, lime wedges, chopped cilantro, diced white onion, toasted dried oregano, crumbled queso fresco or feta

ALTHOUGH *simmered only with onion, oregano, and dried red chiles, this rustic dish bursts with flavor. It's the kind of dish I like to have on hand to heat up at a moment's notice for a quick meal.*

SERVES 4 TO 6

Cover dried posole with boiling water and let stand for at least an hour or overnight. Drain the posole and combine 4 quarts water with all the ingredients, except the salt, pepper, and garnishes, in a soup pot. Bring to a boil, then lower the heat and simmer, covered, until the posole is tender and many of the kernels have opened up or flowered, like popcorn, about 2 hours. (This flowering gives it another name—popcorn soup.) Time can vary a great deal from brand to brand—it could be done in 1½ hours or take as long as 3.) Season with 2 teaspoons salt about halfway through, then season with salt and pepper to taste when finished.

Ladle the posole into bowls with some of the broth. Pile a lofty nest of shredded cabbage or tortilla strips over each bowl of posole, then spoon the remaining garnishes around the sides. Or arrange the garnishes on a platter and let your guests help themselves.

Posole with Red Chile Sauce Once the posole is tender, stir in Red Chile Sauce, page 70, to taste, starting with ½ cup. Serve with any of the suggested garnishes, including grated Jack or crumbled goat cheese.

FROZEN POSOLE

Frozen posole can be found in bags in the meat cases of many supermarkets in the Southwest. It cooks much more quickly than dried posole and doesn't require soaking. If using frozen posole, use 2 pounds or 4 cups and 3½ quarts water. It should be done in about an hour.

Posole with Pumpkin Seed Mole and Garnishes

THIS dish is more elaborate than the preceding one, and its main garnish is a pumpkin seed–based mole or sauce. If you can, assemble the ingredients for the sauce close to serving, and it will be a delicate green. After a while it loses its vibrant color, but still tastes just as good.

SERVES 6

Posole with Red Chile Pods, page 529

¾ cup hulled pumpkin seeds

1 pound tomatillos, papery husks removed

10 romaine lettuce leaves, cut into strips

2 jalapeño chiles, roughly chopped

½ cup chopped cilantro

1 tablespoon vegetable oil

Salt

Garnishes: tortilla strips made from 2 blue corn tortillas, page 46, finely diced white onion, lime wedges, toasted oregano, preferably Mexican, 1 avocado, diced, sour cream or crème fraîche

Cook the posole as described but without the red chiles. When it's done, drain and reserve 5 cups of the broth.

To make the mole, toast the pumpkin seeds in a dry pan until they begin to pop. Remove to a plate to cool, then grind as finely as possible in a food processor.

Put the tomatillos in a saucepan with water to cover, bring to a boil, then simmer until soft and dull colored, about 12 minutes. Drain, then puree them in a blender with the lettuce, chiles, cilantro, and 1 cup of the reserved broth.

Heat the oil in a cast-iron skillet, add the puree, and fry, stirring frequently, over brisk heat for 5 minutes. Add the ground pumpkin seeds and cook until the sauce is thickened, about 10 minutes. Work the mole through a strainer, then taste for salt. When ready to serve, heat the posole with the remaining reserved broth, then stir in the mole. Serve fully garnished or with the garnishes set out in small bowls.

Green Hominy Stew An approximation of this dish can be made with canned hominy if posole isn't available. Use 5 to 6 cups drained. Add 5 cups water and simmer with a finely diced onion, a chopped garlic clove, and salt to taste for 20 minutes. Add the mole and serve.

USING SORREL LEAVES

Mexican culinary maestra Diana Kennedy recommends using sorrel instead of the lime for tartness. I've done this whenever I've had sorrel, and it is delicious. Use 15 to 20 leaves with the stems removed instead of the lettuce and omit the limes in the garnish.

A ROUND *golden grain that resembles couscous, millet remains the primary grain in much of Asia and parts of Africa. Americans know it mostly as birdseed, yet it deserves a place at our tables for its light, pleasant taste. Millet is a rich source of B vitamins, surpassing even brown rice and whole wheat.*

Millet can be a bit quirky to cook. Unless you steam it for an hour, as you would couscous, millet doesn't cook into even, separate grains. Some grains will be soft, like mashed potatoes, while others are still crunchy. I find the textural variations to be part of millet's appeal.

Toasted Millet

1 cup millet   Butter   **MAKES ABOUT 3 CUPS**
Salt and freshly milled pepper

Give the millet a quick rinse to wash off any dust, then drain, shaking off as much moisture as possible. Toast it in a large skillet over medium heat until the grains are dry, separate, and smell good. Bring 3 cups water to a boil in a 2- or 3-quart saucepan, add ½ teaspoon salt, then stir in the millet.

Lower the heat and simmer, covered, for 30 minutes. Turn the millet into a bowl, season with pepper, and stir in butter to taste.

Millet with Pan-Roasted Corn and Tomatillo Salsa

1½ tablespoons corn oil
1 large onion, chopped
½ teaspoon ground cumin
3 garlic cloves, finely chopped
1 cup millet, rinsed
Salt

3 cups corn kernels, fresh or frozen
3 Anaheim or New Mexican chiles, roasted
¼ cup chopped cilantro
Tomatillo Salsa, page 103
Sour cream

YOU might serve this with a big colorful array of grilled summer vegetables or use it to stuff peppers or as a filling for stuffed chard leaves.

SERVES 4 TO 6

Heat the oil in a wide soup pot over medium heat. Add the onion and cumin and sauté, stirring frequently, until softened, about 5 minutes. Add the garlic and cook for 1 minute more. Stir in the millet, 1 teaspoon salt, and 2¾ cups water. Cover and simmer for 25 minutes, then let stand for 10 minutes. Remove the millet to a large bowl and fluff with a fork.

While the millet is cooking, sear the corn in a dry cast-iron skillet over high heat, stirring constantly until the kernels take on a parched smell. Peel, then chop chiles. Toss the millet, chile, corn, and cilantro together. Serve with the salsa and sour cream on the side.

Millet and Chickpea Pilaf with Saffron and Tomatoes

SINCE *millet doesn't separate into distinct grains when cooked, I always enjoy it more when it's mixed with foods of contrasting texture, such as chickpeas. Serve this with lots of garlicky braised chard or spinach. Leftovers are delicious browned in olive oil.*

SERVES 4 TO 6

2¹/₂ tablespoons olive oil

1 cup millet, rinsed

¹/₂ onion, finely diced

¹/₂ teaspoon dried basil

Pinch saffron threads

1¹/₂ cups cooked or 1 15-ounce can chickpeas, rinsed

1¹/₂ cups diced tomatoes, fresh or canned

1 teaspoon sweet paprika

Salt and freshly milled pepper

2¹/₂ cups boiling water or a mixture of water and tomato juice

2 tablespoons finely chopped parsley

3 tablespoons grated Parmesan or Gruyère, optional

Heat 1¹/₂ tablespoons of the oil in a heavy 10-inch skillet, add the millet, and cook over medium heat until the grains begin to color, 4 to 5 minutes. Scrape the millet into a bowl, return the pan to the heat, and add the remaining tablespoon oil along with the onion, basil, and saffron. Cook over medium-high heat until the onion begins to color, 5 to 7 minutes.

Reduce the heat to low and add the millet, chickpeas, tomatoes, and paprika. Season with 1 teaspoon salt and add the boiling water. Cover and cook until the liquid is absorbed and the millet is done, about 35 minutes. If it's still a little raw, add ¹/₄ cup water and continue cooking. Gently break up the grains with a fork. Taste for salt, season with pepper, then stir in the parsley and cheese.

Quinoa

ONCE *the staple food of the Incan civilization, quinoa has twice been introduced to the United States, and it has finally caught on. Pronounced* keen-wa, *these tiny grains are generally met with enthusiasm. Quinoa is light, pleasant tasting without textural idiosyncrasies—and it cooks in 15 minutes. Often called a superfood, quinoa is a good source of plant protein and iron, potassium, magnesium, and lysine.*

You can find both the grain and flour forms of quinoa at your natural foods store. Since the flour is low in gluten, it should be mixed with wheat flour for baking. Quinoa's many uses have been well described by one of its main champions, Rebecca Wood, whose book, *Quinoa: The Supergrain,* contains hundreds of recipes.

Quinoa is naturally covered with a protective coating called *saponin.* In the fields, bitter saponin keeps the seed safe from birds and insects. Although much of it is removed before you buy it, always give quinoa a thorough rinsing in a fine sieve under cold water to ensure that it's sweet, not bitter or soapy tasting.

One especially unusual feature of quinoa is that when cooking, a tiny opaque spiral appears, encircling the grain and curling into its center. Expect to see this and know that everything is as it should be.

Quinoa

1 cup quinoa

2 cups water or Basic Vegetable Stock, page 196

Salt and freshly milled pepper

1 tablespoon butter or sunflower oil

Rinse the quinoa several times in a bowl of cold water to remove the saponin, draining it each time in a fine sieve. Bring the water to a boil in a small saucepan, then add ¼ teaspoon salt and the quinoa. Lower the heat, cover the pan, and simmer until the liquid is absorbed and the spiral of the germ is visible, 12 to 15 minutes. Let stand for 5 minutes. Toss with butter and season with pepper.

SERVE this as a side dish, put it under a stir-fry in place of rice, or use it as a filling for stuffed vegetables or as a crunchy addition to muffins, pancakes, and breads.

MAKES ABOUT 3 CUPS

Spicy Quinoa and Potato Croquettes

1 large russet potato, about 10 ounces

1 cup cooked quinoa

1 small onion, finely diced

2 tablespoons sunflower seed oil, plus oil for cooking

2 teaspoons paprika

1 teaspoon ground coriander

1 teaspoon ground cumin

½ teaspoon dried oregano

2 garlic cloves, minced

¼ cup chopped parsley and/or cilantro

1 egg

⅓ cup cottage cheese, grated Jack, or mashed tofu

Salt

1 cup fresh or dried bread crumbs

CHEESE adds substance and flavor, but it can be omitted or replaced with soy-based cheese or even mashed tofu. Serve these croquettes with salsa, sour cream, and finely shredded salted cabbage or Jícama and Cucumbers with Chile and Lime.

SERVES 4

Boil or steam the potato until tender, then mash it with a fork and mix it with the quinoa. Sauté the onion in 2 tablespoons oil in a small skillet over medium heat for 2 minutes, then add the spices and oregano. Cook over medium heat, stirring frequently, until the onion is soft, about 8 minutes, then add the garlic and cook for 1 minute more. Add this to the potato-quinoa mixture along with the parsley, egg, cheese, and salt to taste.

Work the mixture together, then divide it into four large or eight smaller portions and shape them into ovals. Press each croquette gently into the bread crumbs. Generously film a nonstick skillet with the oil and set over medium heat. When hot, add the croquettes and cook on both sides until nicely browned.

Quinoa and Fresh Corn with Scallions

SERVE as a side dish or use as a filling for chard leaves, tomatoes, or zucchini. If you have time, make a quick stock using the flavorful corn cobs.

SERVES 4

3 plump ears of corn
2 cups Quick Stock, page 196, or water
1 cup quinoa, thoroughly rinsed
Salt and freshly milled pepper

1 tablespoon butter or canola oil
1/2 cup thinly sliced scallions, including some of the greens
1/3 cup crumbled feta or grated Cheddar

Shuck the corn, slice off the kernels, and set them aside. Reverse your knife and scrape the cobs to get the milk. Bring the stock to a boil in a saucepan; add the quinoa, corn scrapings, and 1/2 teaspoon salt. Lower the heat, cover, and simmer for 15 minutes. Turn off the heat and let stand for 5 minutes. Melt the butter in a small skillet, add the scallions and corn kernels, and cook over medium-high heat until the scallions are bright green, about 3 minutes. Toss them with the quinoa. Season with pepper and serve, garnished with the crumbled cheese.

Curried Quinoa with Peas and Cashews

CARROT juice gives this one-dish meal a vibrant color and flavor.

SERVES 4

2 tablespoons canola oil or butter
1 onion, 1/4 finely diced, 3/4 coarsely chopped
1 cup quinoa, thoroughly rinsed
2 teaspoons curry powder
Salt and freshly milled pepper
2 zucchini, diced into small cubes

1 cup carrot juice
1 cup peas
1/4 cup thinly sliced scallions, including a little of the greens
1/2 cup cashews, roasted and coarsely chopped
2 tablespoons chopped cilantro

Heat half the oil in a small soup pot, add the finely diced onion, and cook over medium heat for about 3 minutes. Stir in the quinoa, 1/2 teaspoon curry powder, and 1/4 teaspoon salt and cook for 2 minutes. Add 2 cups boiling water then lower the heat. Cover and cook for 15 minutes.

Meanwhile, heat the remaining tablespoon oil in a 10-inch skillet. Add the chopped onion, zucchini, and remaining 1 1/2 teaspoons curry powder. Cook, stirring frequently, over medium heat for 5 minutes. Add 1/2 cup water, the carrot juice, and 1/2 teaspoon salt. Cover and simmer for 5 minutes, then add the peas and scallions and cook for a few minutes more. Stir the vegetables and cashews into the quinoa. Taste for salt and season with pepper. Serve in soup plates, garnished with cilantro.

Fingerlings with Slivered Garlic *page 411*

CLOCKWISE FROM TOP: **Tomato and Red Pepper Tart** *page 492*,
Winter Squash Galette *page 500*, and **Baked Winter Squash** *page 438*

FACING PAGE • CLOCKWISE FROM TOP LEFT: **Tossed Spinach Lasagne and Goat Cheese
Gratin** *page 465*, **Fideos (A Dry Mexican Soup)** *page 217*, and **Saffron Noodle Cake** *page 457*

Posole with Red Chile Pods *page 529*

Chard and Onion Omelet (*Trouchia*) *page 576*

Giant Cheddar Soufflé *page 580*

FACING PAGE: **Winter Citrus Compote in Tangerine Syrup** *page 684*

FRONT TO BACK: **Prune Tart in Almond Custard** *page 699* and **Fresh Cream Cheese** *page 709*

Quinoa Timbales with Currants and Pine Nuts

¾ cup quinoa, thoroughly rinsed

Salt and freshly milled pepper

1 tablespoon olive or sunflower oil

1 red onion, finely diced

¾ teaspoon ground cumin

¼ teaspoon ground cinnamon

¼ teaspoon ground ginger

¼ teaspoon ground coriander

⅛ teaspoon turmeric

¼ cup chopped cilantro or parsley

¼ cup currants

3 tablespoons pine nuts or almonds, toasted and chopped

1 teaspoon grated orange or lemon zest

Cook the quinoa in 1½ cups water with ¼ teaspoon salt as described on page 533. Meanwhile, warm the oil in a small skillet. Add the onion, spices, and several grinds of pepper, and cook gently until softened, about 10 minutes. Season with salt.

Drain the quinoa when it's done and toss it with the onion mixture along with the cilantro, currants, pine nuts, and orange zest. Pack servings of the mixture into timbale molds, cups, or ramekins, then immediately turn them out onto individual plates.

TIMBALES refer to those little drum-shaped metal molds found in good cookware stores. If you don't have them, ramekins, custard cups, or tea cups will do. Pressing quinoa and other grains into a mold, then turning them out, gives them visual appeal and a starring role on the plate. Surround them with black beans, braised greens, peas, or your chosen accompaniment.

SERVES 4 TO 6

Two Tiny Grains: Amaranth and Teff

Just as quinoa was the mother grain of the Incas, amaranth was the principal food of the Aztecs, and teff dates back more than 3,000 years to Egyptian civilization. These grains are now being cultivated in the Western mountain states. Their nutritional qualities far surpass those of wheat, rice, and corn. One of the easiest ways to use these grains is in baked goods, for both are made into flour.

AMARANTH: Containing more of the essential amino acids than almost any other plant food, amaranth is second only to quinoa in iron and is a strong provider of calcium. It requires neither soaking nor a lengthy turn on the stove. Its texture is pleasantly crunchy and its flavor both sweet and peppery, with molasseslike tones.

When cooked, it has a slightly gelatinous quality. In fact, amaranth can be used to thicken soups. It makes a delicious breakfast cereal and in flour form can be added to baked goods. The grains can also be sprouted or popped in a dry skillet to make miniature "popcorns."

TEFF: Remarkably minuscule—according to the box, 150 grains of teff weigh as much as a single grain of wheat—teff is high in calcium and protein, but its minute size makes it a little difficult to enjoy as a side dish of any substantial proportions. In grain form, it is best used as a breakfast cereal or mixed with other grains. As a flour, combine it with wheat or use it to make the Ethiopian flatbread injera.

About Rice

RICE is the most consumed grain, in its natural grain form, in the United States. We usually treat it as a side dish, but for much of the world rice is the center of the plate, garnished with vegetables and small amounts of meat or fish. In its whole form, rice is a good source of B vitamins, which are the most difficult to obtain in a plant-based diet. Otherwise rice is not particularly nutritious unless it's combined with beans, greens, and other vitamin-rich foods. Rice is, however, easily digested, free of gluten, and versatile.

The shape of the grain, which is related to its starch content, affects how rice cooks: long-grain rice, which has the lowest amount of starch, emerges separate and fluffy; medium-grain rice is moister, tenderer, and somewhat chewier than long-grain varieties; and short-grain rice, which is nearly round, either clumps together or remains separate but bound with its own smooth, starchy sauce, depending on how it's cooked.

Rice, especially white rice, is the chameleon grain, easily taking on any flavor you care to introduce. Try adding a slice of frozen herb butter or other flavored butter to a pot of hot rice or a teaspoon dark sesame oil, roasted peanut, or roasted walnut oil to impart flavor. A few teaspoons grated lemon zest or grated ginger and a tablespoon of soy sauce take it in another direction altogether. Saffron, bay leaves, fresh herbs, spinach, or a few tablespoons salsa verde, pesto, or salsa added to cooked rice make it very aromatic and flecked with green. Use your imagination and look out for choice, highly seasoned leftovers in your refrigerator.

HOW RICE IS PROCESSED: Rice is classified according to how it's milled and processed, both of which affect cooking time and nutritional value.

Brown rice has only its husk removed during the milling process. Because the bran stays intact, it's richer in fiber, trace minerals, and those all-important B vitamins. Brown rice takes the longest time to cook, 30 to 40 minutes.

White rice has the husk, bran, and most of the germ removed during milling, which reduces the amount of fiber and vitamins. Its flavor is mild, its texture soft, and the cooking time is shorter by half.

Enriched rice compensates for what's lost in the milling of white rice by having nutrients added back to the rice the form of a coating. In the end it may be more nutrient rich than brown rice, but it lacks fiber. Enriched rice shouldn't be rinsed.

Converted or parboiled rice has been steamed under pressure before milling to force some of the nutrients into the endosperm to preserve them. Converted rice is also enriched. When cooked, the texture is fluffy and somewhat peculiar. The same is true of instant rice, which is precooked, dehydrated, then cooked again, which means all of the rice's flavor is gone.

HOW TO COOK RICE: Rice needn't be rinsed unless it looks dusty and needs picking over for pebbles, which is rare nowadays. Enriched, converted, or instant rice should never be rinsed. Soaking basmati rice for 30 minutes produces delicate, elongated grains. In general, brown rice, especially short-grain, takes about twice as long to cook as white rice. As with beans, the cooking time can be reduced if the grain is soaked first or is cooked in a pressure cooker.

Boiled Rice: Add rice to a pot of (unmeasured) boiling salted water and cook like pasta until done, which means tasting frequently after 12 to 15 minutes. Cooking rice this way is call *free boiling,* and this method is used for rice salads. Although the rice won't stick, water-soluble-vitamins and enrichments are lost, and the unique texture of starchy Italian and Spanish rice is completely destroyed by this method.

Steamed Rice: Add rice to measured boiling salted water—twice the amount of water to white rice and two-and-a-half times for brown. Butter and seasonings can be included as well. Cover the pan and cook for 15 to 20 minutes for white rice, 35 to 45 for brown.

Pilaf Style: Sauté rice in oil or butter with seasonings, stirring the rice to make sure all the grains are coated. Add the water and follow the directions for steamed rice. When done, cover the pan with a towel and a lid, then let stand for 5 to 10 minutes. The towel will absorb the steam and keep the grains separate.

Rice Cooker Method: An electric rice cooker, a staple in many Asian homes and restaurants, provides an extremely reliable way to cook perfect rice. The rice stays warm for hours. Originally intended for Asian white rice, it can be adapted to other grains as well, although it may take a few attempts to figure out the exact times and amounts.

Rice Varieties

Increasingly more varieties of rice are being exported to and grown in the United States. Ethnic markets carry exotic varieties, such as the glutinous sweet rices or golden Egyptian rice. Most natural food stores and many supermarkets are well stocked with a number of varieties, especially fragrant ones like jasmine and basmati rice.

BROWN RICE: The brownness is actually a result of the milling process, not the variety. Before polishing, all rice is brown. Mottled, flecked, long-grain or short-grain, this is the most wholesome form of rice. Its well-pronounced flavor is nutty and its texture chewy. Brown rice is better known in America than in rice-eating cultures, where white rice is preferred. During a stay in Japan, I tried to describe brown rice to my hosts, who, thinking I wished to eat it, responded by serving white rice colored brown with soy sauce. They had never seen brown rice.

CAROLINA RICE: This long-grain white rice has been grown in South Carolina since the 18th century.

FRAGRANT RICES: These have subtle floral or nutty nuances. Basmati rice from Pakistan, India, and the Middle East has a very long grain and is soaked to extend its length. In India basmati is considered a luxury rice. Basmati is now grown in Arkansas and Texas, under the trade name Texmati. Another basmati hybrid is pecan rice, whose flavor suggests pecans. Jasmine rice from Thailand is more floral, with a smooth, silky texture. Popcorn rice is another aromatic variety.

ITALIAN AND SPANISH RICE: Arborio is the best known of the short-grain rice varieties from northern Italy, but Carnaroli and Vialone Nano are also popular. Valencia rice is the Spanish equivalent. Very round and starchy, these are the rices used for risotto and paella. When they are cooked in these dishes, the starch is released but a firm core remains, which gives the rice an exciting combination of textures. Such rice should never be rinsed or boiled and drained, or its creamy starch will be wasted.

SWEET (OR GLUTINOUS) RICE: Another short, round grain with a high starch content, this Asian rice is sticky and sweet. It is used to make mochi, rice that is pounded into a glutinous mass, then formed into white pillows, dumplings, sweet puddings, and

Leftover rice can be made into fried rice, added to soups for a toothsome garnish, cooked with eggs, and added to breads, pancakes, muffins, and other baked goods. If the rice is short-grain and a little sticky, simmer it in water or milk, top with cinnamon and raisins, and enjoy as a breakfast cereal. If the grains are separate, toss them with a vinaigrette and bits of vegetables, herbs, cheese, and other odds and ends. Cooked wehani, brown, or wild rice can be frozen and thawed as needed.

restorative soups called *congee*. Its unique flavor and texture distinguish it from other varieties.

WEHANI: A new hybrid grown in California, wehani is a long-grain, mahogany-hued rice with a very rich, nutty, and slightly floral flavor. It's grown by the Lundberg Family Farms, rice growers in northern California, who also grow a superior short-grain organic brown rice.

WILD RICE: Neither a true rice nor always wild, this long black grass is native to North America and was once a staple food of native North Americans. Chewy and very earthy tasting, wild rice has more B vitamins and proteins than true rice. It's a very labor-intensive crop to harvest—in some places it's still hand-gathered. When cooked, it expands greatly, which helps offset its high price.

White Rice

A GENERAL all-purpose method that showcases the flavor nuance of each variety. Long-grain rice, whose grains come out separate and distinct, is ideal for salads. Medium and short grains, which are starchier, tend to stick together.

MAKES ABOUT 2¹/₂ CUPS

¹/₄ to ¹/₂ teaspoon salt

1 tablespoon butter, optional

1 cup white rice

Bring 1³/₄ to 2 cups water to a boil in a saucepan, add the salt and butter, then stir in the rice. (Use the larger amount of water for softer rice or if cooking at higher altitudes.) Lower the heat, cover the pot, and cook without looking, for 15 to 20 minutes. Carefully fluff the grains with a fork.

   Checking Rice for Doneness. Altitude, hardness of water, whether the rice has been soaked or not at all affect the cooking time of rice. If the water has been absorbed but the rice isn't as tender as you'd like, sprinkle 1 to 2 tablespoons water over the top, cover, and return to the heat for 5 minutes more. Repeat if necessary. If the rice is done but there is a little extra water, wait for a few minutes—it will be absorbed. If there's a lot of extra water, drain it.

White Basmati Rice

USE this rice with Indian dishes. Rinsing and soaking the grains before cooking allows the rice to lengthen, yielding exceptionally fine long grains.

MAKES ABOUT 3 CUPS

1 cup white basmati rice

¹/₄ teaspoon salt

Wash the rice in a bowl of cold water, gently swishing it back and forth with your fingers. Let the rice settle to the bottom, then pour off the water to remove any bits of bran as well as excess starch so that the grains will be separate and springy when cooked. Repeat until the water runs almost clear, then drain. Cover the rice with a few cups of water and let stand for 30 minutes. Drain, reserving 1³/₄ cups. Combine the rice and reserved water in a 2-quart pot, add the salt, and bring it to a boil. Reduce the heat to low, cover, and cook until the water is absorbed and the rice is tender, about 15 minutes. Let rest for 5 minutes, then fluff with a fork.

Brown Basmati Rice

1 cup brown basmati rice
1/4 teaspoon salt

Rinse and soak the rice, as for white basmati rice, but measure out 2⅛ cups of the soaking water. Cook as described for 30 to 40 minutes. Taste a grain. If it isn't quite done but the water has been absorbed, sprinkle with 2 tablespoons water and cook for 5 to 10 minutes more. Let stand for 5 minutes, then fluff with a fork and serve.

MORE perfumed than regular short-grain brown rice.

MAKES ABOUT 3 CUPS

Wehani Rice

1 cup wehani rice
Salt

If you have time, let the rice soak in water to cover for an hour to swell the grains; drain. Bring 2½ cups water to a boil in a saucepan, stir in the rice, cover, and cook over low heat until the rice is tender, about 40 minutes. Let stand for 5 to 10 minutes, then fluff it with a fork. Add salt to taste.

RUSSET grains or wehani rice are especially nice mixed with white rice, barley, or wild rice.

MAKES ABOUT 2½ CUPS

Basic Brown Rice

1 cup brown rice
Salt

Rinse the rice in a bowl of water and drain. (If time allows, first soak it for an hour or overnight in water to cover.) Bring 2⅛ cups water to a boil in a saucepan and add the rice. Lower the heat, cover tightly, and cook over low heat without disturbing the lid for 40 to 50 minutes. Salt to taste after the rice is cooked.

ENHANCE brown rice with butter, salt, and pepper as well as sesame salt (gomashio) or other herb salts and soy sauce.

MAKES ABOUT 2½ CUPS

Brown Rice or Wehani Rice in the Pressure Cooker

1 cup long- or short-grain brown rice
2 cups water or Basic Vegetable Stock, page 196

1 tablespoon vegetable oil or butter
Salt

Combine the rice, water, oil, and a few pinches salt in a pressure cooker. Bring the pressure to high, then lower the heat to maintain it. Cook for 20 minutes, then turn off the heat and quick-release for long-grain rice. For short-grain rice, allow the pressure to drop slowly on its own.

THE pressure cooker works for short- or long-grain brown rice, brown basmati, and wehani rice. They can even be cooked together. The pressure cooker method produces slightly stickier rice than other methods.

MAKES ABOUT 2¼ CUPS

Seasoned Brown Rice Those who are new to brown rice may like it better when cooked with seasonings. Add ½ teaspoon dried marjoram and a pinch of thyme to the pot along with 2 tablespoons diced onion and a little butter or olive oil. Cook as for basic brown rice or in the pressure cooker.

Sesame Rice Cook the rice with 2 teaspoons dark sesame oil and serve with Gomashio, page 76.

Lacquered Rice Add 1 tablespoon tamari or soy sauce to the pot. The tamari will turn the rice a deep, lacquered hue and impart a rich taste, especially when the rice is cooked in the pressure cooker.

Calico Rice Here's a way to introduce the heartier brown rices to your family or extend expensive wild rice. Cook long-cooking rice—brown rice, wehani, and wild rice—together. Separately cook white rice, then combine them. Toss with butter and season with salt and pepper. (Keep this in mind for when you have leftover brown or wild rice.)

Mexican Green Rice with Roasted Chiles

USE leftovers, if there are any, as filling for summer vegetables, such as tomatoes, peppers, and squash. Add a little crumbled queso fresco or feta to the top and bake.

SERVES 3 TO 4

2 cups Stock for Mexican Soups and Stews, page 197, or water
1 celery rib, finely chopped
½ white onion, chopped
1 garlic clove, chopped
½ cup parsley leaves, large stems removed
5 tablespoons coarsely chopped cilantro

Salt
1 tablespoon vegetable oil
1 cup white rice
3 Anaheim or New Mexican green chiles, roasted
5 mint leaves, chopped

Simmer the stock with the celery, onion, garlic, parsley, and 2 tablespoons of the cilantro until the celery is tender, about 5 minutes. Puree and return it to the pan. Season to taste with salt.

Heat the oil in a 2-quart saucepan over medium heat. Add the rice and cook, stirring constantly, for several minutes, until clear and pale gold. Add the warm stock and bring to a boil. Cover and cook over low heat for 15 minutes. Let stand for 5 to 10 minutes. Meanwhile, peel, seed, and chop the chiles. Add them to the pan along with the remaining cilantro and the mint and gently fluff them into the rice with a fork.

Variation with Peas: Add 1 cup fresh or frozen peas while the rice is standing. The heat of the rice should cook them.

Red Rice: Cook white rice in the Red Stock, page 197, according to the recipe on page 538.

Rice Cooked in Black Bean Broth

2 tablespoons safflower or other
  vegetable oil

1/2 white onion, finely diced

1 1/4 cups white rice

2 garlic cloves, finely chopped

1/8 teaspoon anise seeds

2 cups broth from cooked black beans
  or broth plus water

1 cup peeled, diced tomatoes, fresh or
  canned

Salt

Garnishes: queso fresco, diced jalapeño
  chiles, chopped cilantro, slivered
  scallions, chopped tomatoes, and/or
  sour cream

THE nutritious broth that remains from cooking black beans makes a flavorful, rich broth for cooking rice. Although motivated by common sense not to waste this delicious broth, I was delighted to find that using the broth this way is also a Mexican tradition.

SERVES 4

Heat the oil in a 3-quart saucepan. Add the onion and sauté over medium-high heat for 4 to 5 minutes. Add the rice, garlic, and anise and stir to coat the rice. Cook until it's light gold, 3 to 4 minutes, then add the broth, tomatoes, and 1/2 teaspoon salt and bring to a boil. Cover and cook over low heat until the rice is done, 15 to 18 minutes. Turn into a dish and serve with any or all of the garnishes.

Rice with Spinach, Lemon, and Dill

2 tablespoons olive oil, butter, or a
  mixture

1 cup finely chopped scallions,
  including an inch or two of the
  greens

1 cup long-grain white or brown rice

1 large bunch spinach leaves, finely
  chopped

2 tablespoons chopped dill or
  2 teaspoons dried

Grated zest and juice of 1 lemon

Salt and freshly milled pepper

COOKING the spinach with the rice adds character, but don't expect its color to be bright green. Augment the protein in this dish by stirring in 1/2 cup crumbled feta or 1 cup large-curd cottage cheese or by garnishing it with cubes of Fried Kasseri and toasted pine nuts.

SERVES 4

Warm the oil in a saucepan over medium heat. Add the scallions and cook, stirring frequently, until wilted, 3 to 4 minutes. Add the rice, spinach, dill, lemon zest, and 1/2 teaspoon salt; cook until the spinach has wilted. If you're using white rice, add 1 3/4 cups water; for brown rice, add 2 1/4 cups. Bring to a boil, then lower the heat, cover, and cook until the liquid is absorbed, 15 to 18 minutes for white rice, 30 to 40 minutes for brown. Add the lemon juice and gently loosen the grains with a fork. Cover and let stand for 5 minutes. Season with pepper and serve.

Rice Pilafs

The preliminary sautéing with onions sets pilaf apart from risotto and other rice dishes. Using long-grain rice, whether white or brown, ensures that the finished dish is light, the grains separate, though you can certainly make a decent pilaf with medium-grain rice. The rice is first cooked in a little butter or olive oil, then finished in simmering water or stock. A 2- to 3-quart heavy, ovenproof pot or saucepan with a tight-fitting lid is best for pilafs. You'll find that improvisation when making pilafs is tempting—and entirely appropriate.

Basic Rice Pilaf

2 tablespoons butter, olive oil, or a mixture

1 small onion, finely diced

1¼ cups long-grain white or brown rice

2 cups simmering water or stock for white rice, 2½ cups for brown

1 small bay leaf

Salt and freshly milled pepper

Heat the butter with the onion in a 2- or 3-quart saucepan and cook over medium heat until the onion is translucent, about 3 minutes. Add the rice, stir to coat, and cook for 2 minutes. Add the water, bay leaf, ½ teaspoon salt, and a little pepper. Cover, lower the heat as much as you can, and cook until the rice is done—about 20 minutes for white rice, 40 for brown. (If cooking brown rice and the pan seems dry but the rice isn't done, dribble 2 to 4 tablespoons water over the surface, return the lid, and cook for 10 minutes more.) When the rice is done, put a towel under the lid, turn off the heat, and let it stand for 5 to 10 minutes to finish steaming. Gently break the grains apart with a fork, discard the bay leaf, and serve.

Baked Rice Pilaf Preheat the oven to 375°F. After adding the water or stock, transfer the covered pot to the oven and bake for 30 minutes for white rice, 45 minutes for brown, until the liquid is absorbed.

Rice Pilaf with Mushrooms Add 1 cup chopped mushrooms to the onion and cook for 4 to 5 minutes before adding the rice. To emphasize the flavor, use Mushroom Stock, page 197, or the dried mushroom soaking water. Garnish with fresh parsley or tarragon.

Curried Rice Pilaf with Opal Basil

THIS is especially good made with basmati rice. Plum-colored opal basil leaves dramatically set off the tan-colored rice, but use green basil if opal isn't available.

Basic Rice Pilaf

1 tablespoon butter or canola oil

2 teaspoons curry powder

⅓ cup golden raisins

¼ cup chopped mixed parsley and cilantro

2 tablespoons thinly sliced basil

¼ cup slivered almonds or pine nuts, toasted

Cook the onion for the Basic Rice Pilaf using the extra tablespoon butter, curry powder, and raisins. Add the rice, then proceed as described. When done, add the herbs and toasted almonds and separate the grains with a fork.

Rice Pilaf with Saffron and Spice

2 tablespoons olive oil or clarified butter

1/2 small onion, finely diced

1/2 teaspoon ground cardamom

2 pinches saffron threads

1 3-inch cinnamon stick

5 whole cloves

1 1/2 cups basmati rice, soaked for 30 minutes and drained

1/2 teaspoon salt

1 tablespoon finely chopped parsley

WITH this method the rice sits unattended for 40 minutes, but even if you use that time to prepare the rest of the meal, the rice will still be quite warm at serving time. This pilaf is fragrant with whole spices.

SERVES 4

Warm the oil in a 2- or 3-quart saucepan. Add the onion and spices and cook over low heat, stirring frequently, for about 3 minutes. Add the rice and stir to coat, then add 3 cups water and salt. Increase the heat to medium and simmer, uncovered, until the liquid is absorbed and holes have appeared over the surface. Turn off the heat, put a clean towel over the pot, and cover with a tight lid. Set on the back of the stove for 40 minutes. When ready to serve, gently fluff the rice with a fork and scatter the parsley on top.

Wehani Rice Pilaf

1 1/2 cups wehani rice

1 1/2 tablespoons oil or butter

1/2 cup finely diced onion

1 bay leaf

1/2 teaspoon dried marjoram

1/4 teaspoon dried thyme

1/3 cup dry red wine

Salt and freshly milled pepper

WEHANI is a dense grain —consider stirring in another cooked grain at the end, such as long-grain brown or white rice, barley, or quinoa to lighten it.

SERVES 4

Rinse the rice, then cover it with 5 1/4 cups boiling water and let stand for 15 minutes.

Heat the oil in a heavy 2- or 3-quart saucepan. Add the onion and herbs and cook over medium heat until the onion is translucent, about 8 minutes. Add the wine, raise the heat, and cook until reduced to a syrupy consistency. Add the rice with its soaking liquid and 1/2 teaspoon salt and bring to a boil. Lower the heat, cover, and cook for 45 to 50 minutes. (If you're using a pressure cooker, bring to pressure and cook for 20 minutes, then let the pressure fall rather than using the quick release.) Separate the grains with a fork, season with pepper, and serve.

Rice and Chickpea Pilaf with Pine Nuts and Currants

SERVE this light pilaf with grilled or braised vegetables or use as a filling for eggplant, zucchini, stuffed cabbage, or grape leaves.

SERVES 4

1 large onion, grated or minced

3 tablespoons olive oil

½ cup toasted pine nuts

1 teaspoon allspice

1 cup white or brown rice

⅓ cup currants

¼ cup chopped parsley

3 tablespoons chopped mint leaves

3 tablespoons chopped dill or 1 tablespoon dried

Salt and freshly milled pepper

Juice of 1 lemon

1 15-ounce can chickpeas, drained and rinsed

Put the onion in a wide saucepan with the oil, pine nuts, and allspice. Cook over medium heat until the onion is soft, 6 to 8 minutes. Add the rice, currants, and herbs and cook for a few minutes more. Season with ½ teaspoon salt and a little pepper, then add the water—2 cups for white rice, 2¼ cups for brown—and the lemon juice. Bring to a boil. Cover the pan, reduce the heat to low, and cook until the liquid is absorbed and the rice is tender, 18 to 20 minutes for white, 40 minutes or longer for brown. Toss gently with the chickpeas, cover, and let stand for 10 minutes for the chickpeas to heat through.

Variation with Lentils: In place of all or a portion of the chickpeas, use cooked lentils, preferably the French green ones.

Baked Spanish Rice

PAELLA is the inspiration for this baked red rice dish. The simple, quick stock and the stewing of the onions are essential for rice's deep flavor, but this is a comfortable, puttering sort of dish. Serve with a bowl of heady Garlic Mayonnaise.

SERVES 4 TO 6

The Stock

1 large onion, coarsely chopped

1 tablespoon olive oil

2 tablespoons tomato paste

1 teaspoon fennel seeds

1 head garlic, outer skin removed

2 teaspoons sweet paprika

¼ teaspoon turmeric

1½ teaspoons salt

The Rice:

¼ cup olive oil, preferably a fruity Spanish oil

1 large onion, diced

10 sun-dried tomatoes, dry or drained oil-packed, snipped into strips

3 garlic cloves, chopped

3 tablespoons chopped parsley, plus extra for garnish

2 teaspoons sweet paprika

1 teaspoon turmeric

Pinch red pepper flakes

2 pinches saffron, steeped in 2 tablespoons hot water

Salt and freshly milled black pepper

1½ cups Valencia or Arborio rice

For the stock, sauté the onion in the oil in a saucepan until partly browned, then add the tomato paste and 1 cup water. Scrape up the juices from the bottom of the pot and break up the tomato paste. Add the remaining ingredients plus 6 cups water, bring to a boil, then simmer, partially covered, for 25 minutes. Set aside the garlic, then strain, pressing out as much of the broth as you can. Add water if needed to make 5 cups liquid.

For the rice, heat the oil in a wide soup pot over medium heat. Add the onion and tomatoes, lower the heat, and cook, stirring every so often, until the onion is browned, 20 to 30 minutes. Meanwhile, while it's cooking heat the stock and lightly oil a shallow earthenware casserole about 12 inches across. Preheat the oven to 350°F.

Add the chopped garlic, seasonings, $^1/_2$ teaspoon salt, and the rice to the browned onion. Stir to coat the rice, then raise the heat to medium, add the stock and cook, stirring occasionally, for 10 minutes. Transfer the mixture to the casserole, nestling the reserved head of garlic in the center. Bake for 25 minutes or until the rice is tender. Remove the casserole, cover it with a cloth, and let stand for 10 minutes. Garnish with the parsley and serve.

> *Variation with Vegetables:* Add 2 cups of the following to the rice when you add it to the onions—tiny cauliflower florets, diced roasted red peppers, chopped fennel (use the stalks in the stock), or peas.

Indonesian Fried Rice (*Nasi Goreng*)

1 small white onion or several large
shallots, thinly sliced

2 serrano chiles, diced

3 to 4 tablespoons roasted peanut oil

2 tablespoons soy sauce mixed with
1 tablespoon brown sugar or molasses

1 teaspoon ketchup or tomato sauce

Salt

4 cups cooked white or brown basmati
rice

Caramelized Golden Tofu, page 599 or
Marinated and Fried Tempeh,
Indonesian Style, page 609, or
commercially prepared spiced tofu,
diced into small cubes

$^1/_2$ cup peas or a handful snow peas

1 bunch scallions, including some of the
greens, diagonally sliced

LIKE all fried rice dishes, nasi goreng is best made with cold rice. Depending on your time and resources, this can be very simple or elaborately garnished.

SERVES 4

Pound the onion and chiles in a mortar or work in a small food-processor to make a paste. Heat the oil in a wok, add the onion paste, and stir-fry over high heat for a minute. Add the sweetened soy sauce and ketchup. Season with a few pinches salt, add the rice, and stir-fry until heated through. Add the tofu, peas, and most of the scallions and stir-fry for 1 minute more. Heap the rice onto a platter and garnish with the remaining scallions or with any of the following: Roasted Chile-Peanuts, page 88, crushed; pea shoots; long fine strips of cucumbers and carrots; finely shredded napa cabbage; thinly sliced water chestnuts or jícama.

Three Rice Gratins

Instead of serving rice *and* a vegetable, combining the two and binding them with a light béchamel sauce makes a more substantial main dish. Like vegetable gratins, rice gratins can be made ahead of time and baked later. They can even be made from leftover rice. These gratins are easy to multiply and to improvise using vegetables and grains other than those suggested or by adding a covering of bread crumbs for contrasting texture. Leftovers can be cut into squares and heated in an oven or in a skillet. Allow 25 to 35 minutes for baking, depending on whether or not the ingredients are warm or chilled from the refrigerator.

Béchamel for Rice Gratins

$1/4$ cup minced shallot or onion

3 tablespoons butter

2 tablespoons flour

$1 1/2$ cups milk, scalded

Salt and freshly milled white pepper

$1/2$ teaspoon grated nutmeg

Cook the shallot in the butter in a small saucepan over low heat for 3 minutes. Stir in the flour and cook for 2 minutes more. Whisk in the hot milk all at once, then cook for 20 minutes, stirring frequently, or for 30 minutes in the top of a double boiler. Season with $1/2$ teaspoon salt, a little pepper, and the nutmeg.

Rice and Winter Squash Gratin

SERVES 4

Béchamel for Rice Gratins, preceding recipe

1 cup long-grain brown or white rice, boiled or steamed, page 537

1 tablespoon butter or olive oil

1 tablespoon chopped sage or 2 teaspoons crumbled dried

2 to 3 cups coarsely grated butternut or other winter squash

Salt and freshly milled pepper

2 garlic cloves, chopped

$1/4$ cup chopped parsley

$1/2$ cup grated Gruyère or Fontina

Preheat the oven to 400°F. Lightly butter a 6- to 8-cup gratin dish or 4 individual ramekins. Make the sauce and cook the rice unless you're using leftovers.

Heat the butter with the sage in a wide skillet over medium-high heat. Add the squash, $1/2$ teaspoon salt, and sauté until the squash begins to brown in places, about 8 minutes. Toward the end, stir in the garlic and parsley. Combine the rice, sauce, squash, and cheese. Taste for salt and season with pepper. Turn into the dish and bake until hot and beginning to form a crust on top, 25 to 35 minutes.

Rice and Summer Squash Gratin

1 cup white rice, boiled or steamed

Béchamel for Rice Gratins, page 546

1 tablespoon olive oil

1 pound zucchini, coarsely grated

1 garlic clove, minced

1 tablespoon chopped marjoram or
   2 tablespoons chopped basil

Salt and freshly milled pepper

¼ cup freshly grated Parmesan

½ cup grated mozzarella

Red Pepper Sauce, page 71, or Fresh
   Tomato Sauce, page 61

HERE'S a summer variation of the preceding recipe.

SERVES 4

Preheat the oven to 400°F. Lightly butter or oil a 2- to 3-quart gratin dish. Cook the rice and make the béchamel sauce. Heat the oil in a wide skillet. Add the zucchini and sauté, stirring frequently, over high heat until dry and beginning to color in places, about 12 to 15 minutes. Toward the end, add the garlic and marjoram and season with salt and pepper. Combine the rice, zucchini mixture, cheeses, and béchamel sauce. Turn into the dish and bake until firm and golden, about 25 minutes. Serve with either sauce.

Rice and Spinach Gratin

Béchamel for Rice Gratins, page 546

2 bunches spinach leaves

2 tablespoons olive oil or butter

½ cup finely chopped scallions,
   including an inch or two of the
   greens

2 small garlic cloves, minced

2 tablespoons *each* chopped parsley,
   dill, and marjoram

Salt and freshly milled pepper

1 cup white or brown rice, cooked

1 cup ricotta, optional

SERVE warm with a sauce of tomatoes or peppers, or cold with Saffron Mayonnaise or Salsa Verde.

SERVES 4

Preheat the oven to 400°F and lightly butter or oil a baking dish. Make the béchamel sauce. Cook the spinach in a wide skillet in the water clinging to its leaves until limp, just a few minutes. Rinse it quickly, then squeeze out the water and finely chop.

In a wide skillet, cook the spinach in the oil with the scallions, garlic, and parsley mixture for about 3 minutes. Season with salt and pepper to taste. Combine the rice with the spinach, sauce, and ricotta, if using. Turn into the dish and bake until puffed and lightly browned, about 25 minutes.

Rice and Eggs: Wholesome Fast Food

Made from ingredients anyone's likely to have on hand, this combination makes a fast, nourishing dish that is homey and comforting. The heat of the rice cooks the egg—and any hot grain or noodle would do the same. One cup cooked rice to one egg is a reasonable proportion. Embellishments include a little grated cheese, a spoonful of pesto, a handful of chopped herbs, toasted nuts, cooked greens or artichokes, roasted peppers, sautéed mushrooms, or peas.

Rice and Eggs

SERVES 4 TO 6

1 1/2 cups rice

1 or 2 eggs

Salt and freshly milled pepper

2 tablespoons butter

1/2 to 1 cup grated provolone

Boil or steam the rice as described on page 537. Beat the eggs until light and frothy, with a few pinches salt and plenty of pepper. When the rice is done, drain it and shake off the water if boiled and return it to the pot. Rapidly stir in the beaten egg, butter, and cheese. If you work quickly, the egg should cook evenly and be invisible except for its shine.

Rice and Eggs with Peas and Herbs

SERVES 4 TO 6

1 cup fresh or frozen peas

4 scallions, including some of the greens, thinly sliced

Rice and Eggs, preceding recipe, using 1/2 cup freshly grated Parmesan instead of provolone

3 tablespoons chopped chervil, basil, or sage

Grated zest of 1 lemon

Freshly grated Parmesan

Pea shoots, if available

Cook the peas and scallions in a little water until tender, then add them to the rice and eggs along with the herbs and lemon zest. Serve dusted with grated Parmesan and garnished with pea shoots.

Rice and Eggs with Pesto, Pine Nuts, and Tomatoes

Rice and Eggs, page 548, without cheese

1/3 cup Pesto, page 57, or Basil Puree, page 507

2 tablespoons pine nuts, toasted until golden

1/4 cup finely diced feta or freshly grated Parmesan

1 ripe tomato, seeded and diced

THIS summer version is good hot or tepid. Use pesto or any other favorite herb sauce, such as the Cilantro Salsa or Salsa Verde with Walnuts and Tarragon, in which case omit the pine nuts from the recipe.

SERVES 4

Make the rice and eggs as described, then add the pesto, pine nuts, and cheese. Serve with the tomatoes scattered over the top.

Brown Rice and Eggs with Pungent Greens and Walnuts

1 1/2 cups brown rice

Salt and freshly milled pepper

2 bunches mustard greens, stems removed

1 large garlic clove, minced or pressed

2 tablespoons extra virgin olive oil

1 or 2 eggs

1/2 cup toasted chopped walnuts or Salt and Pepper Walnuts, page 89

Grated pecorino Romano, optional

SERVES 4 TO 6

Boil the rice in salted water until tender, 30 to 50 minutes, depending on whether it's long- or short-grain. Meanwhile, cook the greens in 2 quarts salted boiling water until tender, 5 to 7 minutes. Drain, then press out the liquid and coarsely chop them. Toss the greens with the garlic and oil and season with salt to taste. When the rice is done, drain it, then return it to the pot and rapidly stir in the eggs until well coated. Add the greens and walnuts and toss again. Serve with a light covering of grated cheese.

Risotto

Like pasta, these creamy grains of rice serve as a backdrop for an array of vegetable seasonings. While perhaps most comforting in colder weather, risotto can move gracefully through the seasons, especially where summers are cool. Spring starts with a risotto of asparagus and saffron, then moves on to summer with tiny cubes of tender squash. Fall follows with a robust wild mushroom and red wine risotto, and winter is the season for a scarlet beet risotto or a luxurious risotto gratin.

The most important ingredient in risotto is the rice itself, which must be a short, plump, starchy grain. Italian Arborio rice can be found at gourmet stores and even some supermarkets. The way the rice is cooked enables the starch to form a velvety sauce, yielding a marvelous combination of silky and chewy textures—at once comforting and titillating.

How to Make Risotto

This method applies to virtually all risotto dishes. Once you've grasped these basics, you'll see how quickly improvisations suggest themselves.

1. HAVE YOUR STOCK SIMMERING ON THE STOVE. . . . For one recipe, you'll need 5½ to 6½ cups stock. Use a well-made stock that's full of flavor and seasoned with salt. The Basic Vegetable Stock, page 196, fortified with extra vegetables plus generous trimmings from the risotto vegetables, will do fine. Season it with salt and have it simmering on the stove when you begin.

2. MELT THE BUTTER IN A WIDE POT. . . . In risotto, butter is a seasoning as well as a cooking medium, although it is possible to use oil. You need a wide pot so that the broth can cook sufficiently quickly. A narrow, tall pot just won't work; a wide skillet is a better choice.

3. ADD THE ONION AND COOK UNTIL SOFTENED. . . . As with a soup, onion helps create a flavor base. It should take just 3 to 4 minutes over medium heat to soften; it needn't brown.

4. ADD THE RICE TO THE POT. . . . Stir it around for a minute or so to thoroughly coat the grains with the butter. (And never rinse the rice, or you'll lose the starch that's essential to the dish.)

5. ADD THE WINE AND STIR UNTIL IT'S ABSORBED. . . . Wine gives risotto an acid note that lifts up the flavors. If you cook two risottos, one with and one without wine, you can readily taste the difference. If you don't want to use wine, bring up the flavors at the end with just a little lemon juice.

6. BEGIN ADDING THE SIMMERING STOCK. . . . When you add the stock, the heat should be high enough to maintain a lively bubble. There are two ways to incorporate it into the rice. The most traditional way is to add it in ½-cup increments. With constant stirring and the right heat, each increment should take about 2 minutes to be absorbed. The other way is to start by adding 2 cups of the stock and letting it simmer, stirring only occasionally, until it's absorbed by the rice. The remainder of the stock is then added in ½-cup increments until the risotto is done, stirring continually. While less traditional, this method gives you a little grace period at the beginning of the cooking if something else comes up, and it makes perfectly good risotto. You can also use a pressure cooker, but I think that one of the nice things about making risotto is actually standing there, stirring, and seeing it come, as if by magic, together.

7. ADD THE FINAL BROTH, VEGETABLES, AND SEASONINGS. . . . The timing of the last two additions is a fiddly stage that requires tasting and adjusting to make sure the grain is cooked and the sauce is right. The risotto should be pourable but not thin. The vegetables, cheese, cream, and herbs are added during the last few minutes. Once they've gone in, turn off the heat and stir more energetically to combine them. Taste for salt and, if adding lemon, do so now. Serve right away in heated soup plates.

ALTITUDE: At altitudes higher than 5,000 feet you'll need to increase your cooking time by 5 to 15 minutes to make up for the lower temperature of the boiling stock. This also means that you'll need an extra cup or so of stock.

TIMING: Risotto is best when you make the dish from start to finish without a pause. Before you begin, have the table set, soup plates warmed, and everyone ready to eat. However, most restaurants have a trick that you can use at home. You will need an extra cup of stock.

Cook the risotto up to the last two additions of stock, then spread it out on a sheet pan and refrigerate immediately to stop the cooking. When you're ready to resume, return it to the pan and add the extra cup of stock to loosen the grains. Finish the risotto as you would normally, making the last two additions plus the vegetables and seasonings.

Artichoke Risotto

4 large artichokes, trimmed, quartered, and thinly sliced, page 330

2 tablespoons olive oil

Salt and freshly milled pepper

5 1/2 to 6 1/2 cups Basic Vegetable Stock, page 196

2 tablespoons butter

1/2 cup finely diced onion

1 garlic clove, minced

1 1/2 cups Arborio rice

1/2 cup dry white wine

1/2 cup mascarpone, crème fraîche, or cream

3/4 cup freshly grated Parmesan

1/2 cup finely chopped parsley

MAKE this at the peak of artichoke season —during April and again in September. If you aren't able to get mascarpone, use crème fraîche in its place.

SERVES 4

Prepare the artichokes, then drain and pat them dry. Heat the oil in a wide skillet. Add the artichokes and sauté over medium-high heat until golden and tender, 10 to 12 minutes. Season with salt and pepper and set half of them aside. Chop the remainder. (This can be done ahead of time.)

Have the stock simmering on the stove. Melt the butter in a wide soup pot. Add the onion and cook over medium heat until softened, about 4 minutes, adding the chopped artichokes and the garlic halfway through. Add the rice and cook and stir for 1 minute. Pour in the wine and simmer until it has been absorbed.

Add 2 cups stock, cover, and cook at a lively simmer until it's absorbed. Begin adding the stock in 1/2-cup increments, stirring constantly until each addition is absorbed before adding the next. When the rice tastes done, stir in the mascarpone, 1/2 cup of the Parmesan, and all but 2 tablespoons of the parsley. Taste and season with salt and pepper. Warm the remaining artichokes in their pan during the last few minutes of cooking, then spoon them over the rice and serve garnished with the Parmesan and parsley.

Fresh Mushroom Risotto

Mushroom Stock supplies this risotto with a huge amount of flavor. You can have it ready ahead of time.

SERVES 4

The Mushrooms

2 tablespoons butter

1 tablespoon olive oil

¹/₂ cup finely diced white onion or shallot

12 to 16 ounces white or portobello mushrooms, thinly sliced

1 large garlic clove, finely chopped

Salt and freshly milled pepper

¹/₂ lemon

The Rice

5¹/₂ to 6¹/₂ cups Mushroom Stock, page 197

2 tablespoons butter

¹/₃ cup finely diced onion or shallot

1¹/₂ cups Arborio rice

¹/₂ cup dry white wine or Marsala

¹/₃ to ¹/₂ cup cream

¹/₂ cup freshly grated Parmesan

¹/₄ cup chopped parsley

Heat the butter and oil in a wide skillet, add the white onion, and cook over medium heat for about 5 minutes, stirring frequently. Add the mushrooms, raise the heat, and sauté until browned around the edges, about 5 minutes. Add the garlic, season with salt and pepper, and squeeze the lemon juice over all. Turn off the heat and set aside.

Have the stock at a simmer. Melt the butter in a wide pot. Add the onion and cook over medium heat to soften, 3 to 4 minutes. Add the rice, stir to coat, and cook for 1 minute. Add the wine and simmer until it's completely absorbed. Add 2 cups stock, cover, and cook at a lively simmer until it's absorbed. Begin adding the stock in ¹/₂-cup increments, stirring constantly until each addition is absorbed before adding the next one. About halfway through, add the mushrooms. After the last addition, add the cream and stir with more vigor. Taste for salt and season with pepper. Stir in the Parmesan and parsley and serve.

Dried Wild Mushroom Risotto

The mushroom stock combined with the red wine makes a risotto with flavor to match its mahogany color. A good choice for a company meal.

SERVES 4

1 ounce dried porcini

5¹/₂ cups Mushroom Stock, page 197

2 tablespoons butter, plus extra to finish

3 plump shallots, finely diced

1¹/₂ cups Arborio rice

¹/₂ cup dry red wine

3 tablespoons chopped parsley

¹/₂ cup freshly grated Parmesan

Salt and freshly milled pepper

Soak the dried mushrooms in 1 cup warm water for 30 minutes, then lift them out and strain the liquid. Add it to the stock and bring to a simmer. Finely chop the mushrooms.

Heat the butter in a wide soup pot, add the shallots, and cook over medium heat until translucent and soft, 3 to 5 minutes. Add the rice and cook, stirring frequently, for 1 minute. Add the mushrooms and wine and simmer until the wine is absorbed, stirring a few times, then add 2 cups stock, cover, and cook at a lively simmer until it's absorbed. Begin adding the stock in ¹/₂-cup increments, stirring constantly until each addition is absorbed before adding the next. When the rice is cooked, stir in the parsley, cheese, and an additional tablespoon or two of butter. Taste for salt and season with pepper.

Beet Risotto with Greens

5½ to 6½ cups Basic Vegetable Stock, page 196, including beet or chard stems

3 tablespoons butter or a mixture of butter and olive oil

½ cup finely diced onion

1½ cups Arborio rice

½ cup dry white wine

2 tablespoons chopped parsley

2 tablespoons chopped basil or 1 tablespoon dried

2 to 3 medium beets, peeled and grated, about 2 cups

2 to 3 cups greens—beet, chard, kale, or spinach—stems removed, finely chopped

Salt and freshly milled pepper

Grated zest and juice of 1 lemon

½ cup freshly grated Parmesan

If you're wary of beets—I ordered my first beet risotto with great doubts—be assured that this risotto has not only an incredible jewellike color but also a delicious, deep taste, tempered by the greens, lemon, and Parmesan.

SERVES 4

Have the stock simmering on the stove. Heat the butter in a wide pot, add the onion, and cook over medium heat for 3 minutes, stirring frequently. Add the rice, stir to coat it well, and cook for 1 minute. Add the wine and simmer until it's absorbed, then stir in half the parsley, the basil, grated beets, and the chard or kale. Add 2 cups stock, cover, and cook at a lively simmer until the stock is absorbed. Begin adding the remaining stock in ½-cup increments, stirring constantly until each addition is absorbed before adding the next. When you have 1 cup left, add the beet greens or spinach. Taste for salt, season with pepper, then stir in the lemon zest and juice to taste. Serve dusted with the cheese and the remaining parsley.

Risotto with Scallions, Lemon, and Basil

4 bunches scallions, including a few inches of the greens

3 tablespoons butter

Salt and freshly milled pepper

5½ to 6½ cups Basic Vegetable Stock, page 196

⅓ cup finely diced shallot or white onion

1½ cups Arborio rice

½ cup dry white wine

½ cup cream or crème fraîche

1 cup finely chopped parsley

4 thinly slivered basil leaves

2 teaspoons finely grated lemon zest

⅓ cup freshly grated Parmesan

Scallions, lemon zest, a few hothouse basil leaves—these simple ingredients taste bright and springy, making this a dish to turn to when the weather is drab. Be sure to use the scallion roots and extra greens in the stock.

SERVES 4

Trim and thinly slice the scallions. Cook them in 1 tablespoon of the butter until softened, 3 to 4 minutes, then season with salt and pepper and set aside.

Have the stock simmering on the stove. Melt the remaining butter in a wide pot. Add the shallot and cook over medium heat for 3 to 4 minutes, stirring frequently. Add the rice, stir to coat the grains, and cook for 1 minute. Add the wine and simmer until it's absorbed. Add 2 cups stock, cover, and cook at a lively simmer until it's absorbed. Begin adding the rest in ½-cup increments, stirring constantly until each addition is absorbed before adding the next. When the rice is nearly finished cooking, stir in the scallions and cream and cook for 1 minute. Add the parsley, basil, and lemon zest. Taste for salt, season with pepper, and serve with a dusting of cheese.

Risotto with Garden Peas, Basil, and Saffron

THE last of the peas and the first of the tomatoes are captured in this early summer risotto. This is one of the nicest ways to feature garden peas. Use a few handfuls of the pods in the vegetable stock.

SERVES 4

2 pounds fresh pod peas or 2 cups frozen

6 cups Basic Vegetable Stock, page 196

2 tablespoons butter

½ cup finely chopped shallot or onion

2 pinches saffron threads, ground in a mortar

1½ cups Arborio rice

½ cup dry white wine

½ cup mascarpone or crème fraîche, optional

½ cup freshly grated Parmesan, plus extra to finish

3 tomatoes, peeled, seeded, and diced

8 large basil leaves, thinly sliced

Salt and freshly milled pepper

Snipped chives

Shuck the peas if using fresh ones. Have the stock simmering on the stove.

Melt the butter in a wide pot. Add the shallot and saffron and cook over low heat, stirring occasionally, until the shallot has softened and the saffron has released its color, about 3 minutes. Stir in the rice and cook for 1 minute. Raise the heat, add the wine, and cook until it's absorbed. Add 2 cups stock, cover, and cook at a lively simmer until it's absorbed. Begin adding the stock in ½-cup increments, stirring constantly until each addition is absorbed before adding the next. When the rice is nearly done and only two more additions remain, stir in the peas. Add the last of the stock, then stir in the mascarpone, Parmesan, tomatoes, and basil. Taste for salt, season with pepper, and serve with extra cheese and chives strewn over the top.

Vivid Parsley and Pea Risotto

THESE ingredients are so simple, yet the overall effect is stunningly green and fresh tasting. The parsley sauce can be made a day ahead. I always add four or five lovage leaves for their unusual, beguiling flavor.

SERVES 4

2 large bunches parsley, preferably flat-leaf

Salt and freshly milled white pepper

4 to 5 lovage leaves

4½ to 5 cups Basic Vegetable Stock, page 196, or water

2 tablespoons butter

⅓ cup diced onion or leek

1½ cups Arborio rice

½ cup dry white wine

1½ cups fresh or frozen peas

½ cup cream or mascarpone, optional

½ cup freshly grated Parmesan

With a sharp knife, shave off most of the parsley leaves. Using your fingers, break off the larger stems and use them in the vegetable stock. Measure 3 cups leaves, well packed but not crammed.

Bring 1½ cups water to a boil. Add ¼ teaspoon salt, the parsley, and the lovage. Boil for 1 minute. Turn off the heat, let stand for 5 minutes, then puree in a blender at high speed until smooth. Taste for salt and season with pepper.

Have the stock simmering on the stove. If the parsley sauce has been refrigerated, bring it to a boil, then turn off the heat.

Melt the butter in a wide pot. Add the onion and cook over medium heat until softened, 3 to 4 minutes. Add the rice and cook, stirring frequently for 1 minute, then pour in the wine and simmer until it's absorbed. Add 2 cups stock, cover, and simmer, stirring occasionally until it's absorbed. Begin adding the remaining stock in ½-cup increments, stirring constantly until each addition is absorbed before adding the next. When all has been absorbed and the rice is very nearly done, add the parsley sauce. Raise the heat and cook briskly while stirring until the rice is done and most of the sauce has been absorbed. Add the peas and cream. Taste for salt and season with pepper. Turn off the heat and stir in half the cheese. Serve dusted with the remaining cheese.

Sizzling Risotto Gratin

3½ cups Basic Vegetable Stock, page 196

4 tablespoons butter, plus butter for the dish

1 small red onion, finely diced

1¾ cups Arborio rice

1 cup dry white wine

8 ounces Italian Fontina, cut into tiny cubes, about 2 cups

1 cup cream, chilled

Few pinches freshly grated nutmeg

Salt and freshly milled white pepper

THIS glorious and utterly luxurious recipe is inspired by Nancy Radke, who published it years ago in her newsletter Ciao! It hails from the Val d' Aosta, a region near the Italian Alps that's famous for its creamy Fontina. Unlike most, this risotto is cooked in advance and then finished in the oven. It makes a stunning winter supper, preceded by an array of grated vegetable salads and followed by a citrus compote.

SERVES 4 TO 6

Have the stock simmering on the stove. Butter a 2-quart gratin dish.

Melt the butter in a wide pot. Add the onion and cook over medium heat until soft and translucent, about 3 minutes. Add the rice, raise the heat a little, and cook, stirring constantly, for about 3 minutes. Add the wine, raise the heat to high, and simmer until it's completely absorbed. Add half the stock, adjust the heat so that the liquid is simmering briskly, and cook, stirring occasionally until it is mostly absorbed, about 12 minutes. Add the remaining stock in ½-cup increments, stirring constantly, until each addition is absorbed before adding the next.

Remove the rice from the heat and stir in the cheese, cream, and nutmeg. Taste and adjust the seasonings if needed, then pour the rice into the gratin dish. Cover with plastic wrap and leave at room temperature until you're ready to serve.

Preheat the oven to 500°F and set the oven rack in the top third of the oven. Bake the risotto until it's sizzling and golden, about 15 minutes. If it's not browning, turn on the broiler for a final minute so that the surface is a rich gold. Serve immediately.

Risotto Croquettes

CROQUETTES *made with leftover risotto are so good that you might actually start out with them in mind rather than hope for leftovers. They make a charming vegetarian main dish set on a plate surrounded with salad greens, a sauce, or a simple vegetable accompaniment such as those suggested here.*

SERVES 4 TO 6

2 eggs
¹/₂ cup milk
Salt and freshly milled pepper
3 cups fresh bread crumbs

Risotto, any of the preceding recipes, chilled
Clarified butter or light olive oil for pan frying

Beat the eggs with the milk in a pie plate and season with salt and pepper. Put the bread crumbs in another pie plate. Scoop the risotto up with a spoon and form it into a flattened oval about 3 inches long. (Or simply divide the rice into the number of portions you need.) Using one hand, slide the croquettes into the egg, then scoop them out and put them in the dish with the bread crumbs. Using the other hand, roll them around so that they're covered, then transfer to a large plate.

If you're not planning to cook them right away, cover with wax paper and refrigerate, but allow them to come to room temperature before cooking. Fry them in clarified butter or oil until crisp and golden. Serve hot.

Risotto-Stuffed Vegetables If you'd rather avoid breading and frying, use leftover risotto to fill stuffed peppers, tomatoes, eggplants, cabbage, or chard leaves. Mound the filling, but don't pack it, then bake at 375°F until heated through, about 25 minutes.

Wild Rice

WILD *rice is savored for its long black grains and earthy flavor. It can be served alone, combined with other varieties of rice, or used in stuffings, salads, and as an exotic addition to pancakes and waffles, breads, and even soups.*

MAKES ABOUT 3 CUPS

1 cup wild rice
Salt and freshly milled pepper

1 tablespoon butter or roasted hazelnut oil

Cover the rice with cold water, remove any bits of chaff or other odd particles that float to the surface, and drain. Bring 1 quart water to a boil in a saucepan and add the rice and ¹/₂ teaspoon salt. Lower the heat, cover, and cook until the rice is done, 45 to 50 minutes. Take a taste—it should have a little bite, and many of the grains will have blossomed or split. If there's any extra water, simply pour it off. Return the cover and let the rice stand for 5 to 10 minutes. Fluff the grains with a fork. Taste for salt, season with pepper, and stir in the butter.

Wild Rice with Walnut and Scallions Sauté

1 tablespoon olive oil or butter

1/2 cup coarsely chopped walnuts

2 bunches scallions, including half the greens, sliced in 1/4-inch rounds

2 tablespoons thinly sliced tarragon

Salt and freshly milled pepper

Grated zest of 1 lemon

1 tablespoon roasted walnut oil

3 cups cooked wild rice

I MUCH prefer wild rice mixed with other grains or seasoned with something fresh and highly aromatic, like this scallion sauté.

SERVES 4 TO 6

Heat the oil in a medium skillet over high heat. Add the walnuts and cook for a minute or so, then add the scallions and tarragon. Season with salt and pepper and sauté until the scallions are bright green and soft, after a few minutes. Stir in the lemon zest, then toss the mixture with the rice. Drizzle with the walnut oil and toss again.

Wild Rice and Celery Root Gratin

Béchamel for Rice Gratins, page 546

1 tablespoon butter

1 small celery root, peeled and grated

Juice of 1 lemon

1 garlic clove, minced

2 tablespoons chopped parsley, plus extra for garnish

Salt and freshly milled pepper

3 cups cooked wild rice or Calico Rice, page 540

1/2 cup grated Gruyère

1/4 cup freshly grated Parmesan

YOU can make a very good version of this gratin without dairy by using Mushroom Stock in the béchamel sauce and omitting the cheese. In place of the cheese, add 1/2 cup toasted ground walnuts or almonds.

SERVES 4 TO 6

Preheat the oven to 400°F. Lightly butter or oil a baking dish and make the béchamel. Melt the butter in a medium skillet over medium heat. Add the celery root with the lemon juice, garlic, and 2 tablespoons parsley and cook until tender, about 5 to 7 minutes. Season with salt and pepper to taste. Combine the wild rice, celery root, and sauce and stir in the cheeses. Turn into the dish and bake until firm, about 25 minutes. Sprinkle with chopped parsley and serve.

Wheat: New and Ancient Forms

WHEAT *is the principal cereal consumed throughout the world. Most of it is eaten in its milled form in bread and pasta, but is also enjoyed as cracked wheat and bulgur, wheat flakes, wheat berries, semolina, and couscous (which is actually a pasta).*

There are many varieties and strains of wheat. Three common ones are hard, soft, and durum wheat. Hard wheat is preferred for bread baking because its gluten content is the highest. (Gluten allows dough to stretch and capture the gases that make bread rise.) Soft wheat has less gluten and is preferred for pastries that aren't kneaded and worked, such as pies and cakes, cookies, muffins, and so forth. Durum wheat, which is also hard, produces the flour that's so prized for pasta making.

In addition to contemporary wheat, two ancient strains—spelt and kamut—are the antecedents to our modern hybrids. Spelt and kamut are of special interest to those who have wheat intolerances, for they contain a more digestible form of gluten. Yet in terms of flavor and texture, they behave enough like wheat to make them a successful alternative ingredient in some processed foods, such as pasta. Kamut and spelt are also sold as whole grains and as flour.

Wheat Berries

Frozen cooked wheat berries are a convenient item to have on hand, so cook enough to have some left over. If you have time to soak wheat berries overnight, they'll cook more quickly and be easier to digest.

MAKES ABOUT 4 CUPS

1 cup wheat berries, soaked overnight and drained   Salt

On the Stove Put the wheat berries in a pot with plenty of water to cover by a few inches. Bring to a boil, then lower the heat, cover the pot, and simmer until they're tender, 1 to 2 hours. Add ½ teaspoon salt once they've started to soften.

In the Pressure Cooker Combine unsoaked wheat berries, 2 quarts water, and ½ teaspoon salt. Bring to pressure and cook for 30 minutes. Let the pressure drop slowly or release, then check for doneness. If they're still a little hard, cover the pot and simmer until they're soft.

Peeled Wheat Kernels

THESE skinned grains of wheat cook more quickly and tenderly than wheat berries, but finding them might be difficult. I buy mine at a Middle Eastern market, where they're sold as golden peeled wheat.

MAKES ABOUT 3 CUPS

1 cup peeled wheat, soaked overnight and drained   Salt

Put the wheat in a saucepan with water to cover by several inches and bring to a boil. Lower the heat, cover the pan, and simmer until the grain is tender, 30 to 40 minutes. Add ½ teaspoon salt after 15 minutes. If it cooks for the longer amount of time, it will become glutinous, like barley, making a soothing morning cereal, pudding, or addition to baked goods. Cooked slightly less, it remains distinct and can be added to soups and other grain dishes.

Whole Wheat with Chickpeas, Lentils, and Tarragon

1 $\frac{1}{2}$ tablespoons olive oil

1 onion, diced

1 green bell pepper, finely chopped

1 tablespoon chopped tarragon

$\frac{3}{4}$ cup French green lentils, sorted and rinsed

Salt and freshly milled pepper

2 cups cooked wheat berries or peeled wheat

1 $\frac{1}{2}$ cups cooked chickpeas, rinsed if canned

Additional extra virgin olive oil or roasted walnut oil to finish

HERE'S where those frozen wheat berries can come in handy. If you use canned chickpeas, you can make this dish in about 25 minutes.

SERVES 4 TO 6

Heat the oil in a small soup pot. Add the onion, pepper, and tarragon and cook over medium heat, stirring frequently, until the onion begins to color, about 7 minutes. Add the lentils, 5 cups water, and 1 $\frac{1}{2}$ teaspoons salt and bring to a boil. Lower the heat and simmer, covered, until nearly tender, about 20 minutes. Add the wheat berries and chickpeas; continue cooking until they're warmed through and the lentils are tender, about 5 minutes. Drain (reserve the liquid for stock) and pour the grains into a serving dish. Taste for salt, season with pepper, and drizzle generously with olive or walnut oil.

Variations: A splash of fresh lemon juice, chopped parsley, and additional fresh tarragon transform this dish into a salad. Any left over can be tossed with pasta, such as farfalle, along with fresh herbs and toasted chopped walnuts.

Whole Spelt and Kamut These very large, dense grains are best added to soups, mixed with other grains, or used in grain-based salads. Both benefit from an overnight soaking. They take 1 to 2 hours to cook, 40 minutes in a pressure cooker, or overnight in a slow cooker. As with dried beans, add salt toward the end of cooking.

> 1 cup spelt yields about 2 $\frac{1}{4}$ cups cooked
>
> 1 cup kamut yields about 2 $\frac{3}{4}$ cups cooked

Rolled and Flaked Spelt In this form, spelt is easy and fast to cook, perhaps more accessible than the same grain in its longer-cooking whole form. Cover 1 cup flaked spelt with 2 cups boiling water, cover, and allow to stand for 10 minutes or until the liquid is absorbed. Season with a pinch of salt, freshly milled pepper, and a little butter, olive oil, or nut oil. Also see Savory Barley Flakes, page 519, for another use for spelt.

Bulgur

Spelled many ways and often mistaken for cracked wheat, bulgur is wheat that has been steamed whole, then dried and cracked into grits. The steaming precooks the grain, making bulgur very quick to prepare, a yet-to-be discovered boon for today's busy cooks.

Bulgur comes in three sizes. Very fine bulgur is used for tabbouleh, and the coarsest size is used for pilafs. The medium size can go in either direction. Bulgur needs only to be soaked to become tender, but it can also be cooked. Middle Eastern markets as well as natural food stores are good sources for bulgur, especially the fine size and bulgur in bulk.

Light but roundly flavored, bulgur is excellent on its own or mixed with rice, chickpeas, and lentils in salads, soups, or side dishes.

Cooked Bulgur

ANYONE *looking for a quick grain to prepare need look no further.*

SERVES 4

1 cup fine or medium bulgur

Salt and freshly milled pepper

1 tablespoon butter, extra virgin olive oil, or roasted walnut oil

Garnishes: chopped parsley, dill or tarragon; toasted pine nuts or walnuts; currants, dried cherries, or pomegranate seeds, optional

Rinse the bulgur to remove any dust. Put it in a bowl with a few pinches salt and pour on 2½ cups boiling water. Cover and let stand for 15 minutes for fine bulgur, 25 minutes for medium. If there's any excess water, pour the bulgur into a strainer. Toss with butter. Taste for salt, season with pepper, and toss with any of the garnishes.

Steamed Bulgur To make the most delicate salad grain, steam bulgur as described for Steamed Couscous, page 565. It will take about 30 minutes in all.

Bulgur Pilaf with Pine Nuts and Currants

NOT *only a quick-cooking side dish, this pilaf also makes an excellent filling for cabbage, chard, and grape leaves.*

MAKES 4 CUPS

1 to 2 tablespoons olive oil

1 small onion, very finely diced

1 garlic clove, minced

1 tablespoon chopped dill or 1 teaspoon dried dill

½ teaspoon ground allspice

1 cup bulgur, rinsed

Salt

⅓ cup currants, dried cranberries, or dried cherries

⅓ cup toasted pine nuts

Heat the oil in an 8-inch skillet or a 3-quart saucepan over medium heat. Add the onion, garlic, dill, and allspice and cook, stirring frequently, until the onion is translucent, 3 to 4 minutes. Add the bulgur and ¼ teaspoon salt and cook for 1 minute more. Pour in 1¼ cups water, bring it to a boil, then lower the heat and cook, covered, for 10 minutes. Stir in the currants, remove from the heat, cover, and let stand for 5 minutes more. Fluff with a fork, add the pine nuts, and fluff again.

Cracked Wheat

Cracked wheat resembles bulgur, but the whole kernels have not been steamed previously, so it needs to be cooked rather than soaked. Cracked wheat comes in two sizes—medium and coarse. Medium is what we usually see. Cracked wheat doesn't take long to cook, and like bulgur, it's very good mixed with legumes, especially chickpeas and lentils, as well as with pasta and rice.

Cracked Wheat

1 cup cracked wheat

Salt and freshly milled pepper

1 tablespoon butter or extra virgin olive
    oil, to taste

2 tablespoons chopped parsley

THE flavor of this grain may remind you of Wheatena or Bear Mush cereal. You can cook this right in a deep skillet. If you don't have one with 2-inch sides, add the toasted wheat to the water in a saucepan.

SERVES 4 TO 6

Toast the wheat in a dry skillet with 2-inch sides over medium heat. Stir constantly, until it gives off a warm, nutty aroma, after a few minutes. Stir in 2½ cups boiling water and ½ teaspoon salt. Lower the heat and simmer, covered, until the grain is tender, about 15 minutes. Set a cloth under the lid and let stand for 5 to 10 minutes. Fluff in the butter and parsley with a fork and season with pepper.

Cracked Wheat Pilaf with Tomato and Cinnamon

2 tablespoons olive oil or butter

1 onion, finely diced

1 cup cracked wheat

¼ teaspoon ground cinnamon

Salt and freshly milled pepper

1 cup finely diced tomatoes, juice
    reserved

¼ cup chopped parsley

SERVE this pilaf with a yogurt sauce and accompany with grilled eggplant, golden zucchini coins, or a vegetable stew, especially one based on eggplant and chickpeas. Millet and rice can also be cooked this way.

SERVES 4 TO 6

Heat the oil in a heavy saucepan over medium heat. Add the onion and cook, stirring frequently, until it begins to color, about 10 minutes. Add the cracked wheat, cinnamon, and ½ teaspoon salt and stir to coat the grains. Stir in the tomatoes and the reserved juice plus enough water to make 2½ cups, and bring to a boil. Lower the heat, cover the pot, and simmer until the liquid is absorbed and the wheat is tender, about 15 minutes. Remove from the heat and let stand for 5 minutes. With a fork, lightly stir in the parsley. Taste for salt and season with pepper.

    Variation: After the cracked wheat is cooked, toss in 1 to 2 cups cooked chickpeas, lentils, pasta, or green peas. Cover the pan and let stand for 10 minutes. Season with chopped tarragon or dill mixed with or in place of the parsley.

Couscous

Although we treat it as a grain, couscous is actually a small, granular pasta made of semolina. It's become a new standard in our pantry, but most people know it only in its instant just-add-water form. Traditionally couscous is steamed, which renders it wonderfully light and delicate and nothing like the instant. Steaming is very much worthwhile when you have the extra time it takes. The pilaf method—toasting the grains in oil before adding liquid—also produces couscous with distinctly separate grains; not as light as steamed, but a clear improvement over the box method and certainly more possible on a regular basis.

Couscous comes in different sizes: very fine, medium, and large pearls that resemble tapioca. The extra-fine and large grains are seldom seen outside of Middle Eastern markets, but the medium is easy to find in boxes or bulk bins. Couscous sold in bulk seems to be fresher than the packaged, which I've found to be stale and offputting on more than one occasion. Whole-wheat and light-colored couscous cook in the same amount of time.

Incidentally, other grains and even pasta can be steamed. Steamed bulgur makes the most delicate tabbouleh imaginable, and combining it with couscous makes a more interesting salad than if just one grain is used. Small grains and bulgur cook in about the same time as couscous, and the method is the same.

In *Couscous and Other Good Food from Morocco,* Paula Wolfert describes how to steam couscous, and I more or less follow her method. I admit that I was intimidated before I actually did it. But once you see how it works, you can do it without giving it a second thought.

There's a special two-part pot for cooking couscous, but you can easily improvise your own setup as described below.

Steamed Couscous

ALLOW 50 minutes in all from start to finish. You can leave the second steaming until just before serving.

MAKES ABOUT 5 CUPS

Put 2 cups whole-wheat or regular couscous in a large shallow bowl, cover it with water, and swish it about with your fingers. Pour off the water, let it stand for 15 minutes, then rake the couscous with your fingers to break up any lumps.

If you don't have a *couscousière,* place 3 inches water in a large pot. Set a colander or steaming unit on top and wrap a piece of damp cheesecloth around the seam where the units meet to seal them. If they're not very tight, dip the cloth in flour first—the steam will cook the paste, making a tighter seal. Bring the water to a boil.

When steam is rising through the colander holes, dribble in the couscous. Steam, uncovered, for 20 minutes. Loosen the seal, then empty the couscous into a shallow dish and spread it out with a fork. Gradually sprinkle over 1 cup water in which you've dissolved 1 teaspoon salt. Lightly oil your hands and again rake the grains with your fingers, breaking apart any lumps. Let it stand for 10 minutes or until you're ready to finish cooking your meal.

Check the water in the steamer to make sure it's boiling. Rejoin the two units, add the couscous, and repeat the steaming process for another 20 minutes. If there's more couscous than you think you'll eat, set some aside to use later. If you're serving it with a stew, turn the couscous into a round, shallow serving dish, fluff it with a fork, then rake it into a mound. Spoon your accompanying vegetables around it, then spoon the sauce over the couscous or pass it separately.

Excessive Clumping Some brands of couscous tend to form a large number of tight lumps. If this is the case with yours, add 2 to 4 tablespoons olive oil to the couscous first, gently working it in with your fingers. Add the water and let the couscous stand for 30 minutes before the first steaming. It will absorb the water as it stands.

Couscous by the Pilaf Method

3 cups water or vegetable broth
1 to 2 tablespoons butter or olive oil

1 cup fine or medium couscous
Salt

Bring the water to a boil. Meanwhile, melt the butter in a 10-inch skillet over medium heat. Add the couscous, stir to coat the grains, and cook for 1 to 2 minutes. The grains will color slightly. Remove from the heat, add ½ teaspoon salt, and pour in 2 cups of the water. It will instantly bubble up. When it subsides, shake the pan to even the contents, cover, and set aside for 7 minutes to steam. Fluff the grains with a fork, pour in the last cup of the boiling water, cover, and let stand for 5 minutes. Remove the lid and fluff the couscous before serving.

THIS couscous won't swell as much as when steamed, but the grains come out nice and separate, and it's easy to do. If you're making a vegetable stew that has yielded a broth, use it in place of water.

MAKES ABOUT 4 CUPS

Eggs and Cheese

EGGS ARE OFTEN DESCRIBED AS THE PERFECT FOOD. THEY PROVIDE SOLID NOURISHMENT AT MODEST COST IN A FORM THAT CAN BE USED SIMPLY AND QUICKLY. PARENTS WOULD DO A GREAT SERVICE TO THEIR OFFSPRING BY TEACH-ing them how to scramble an egg or make an omelet. Surely no home-cooked food is faster to make than a plate of eggs; nothing is more comforting than a custard; and only eggs can create the magical loft of a soufflé or put a glossy glaze on a bread or pastry. Simply put, eggs do things in the kitchen that other foods just can't do.

We tend to forget that eggs aren't just for breakfast. Sometimes it takes visiting another country to see their potential. In Spain there's the ubiquitous tortilla, or potato frittata, available everywhere from bars to museum cafeterias from morning until night. In Italy, you can add a slice of frittata to your antipasto plate or slurp a warm froth of zabaglione. Occasionally here at home one can still find a basket of hard-cooked eggs on a bar or deli counter for quick sustenance. In short, eggs are perfectly suitable for any hour of the day. If you can't or don't eat eggs, but you remember them fondly, turn to egg substitutes or scrambled tofu or ricotta to fill a similar role, especially for breakfast.

While cheese is a very different food altogether, it too is a ready source of solid nourishment. Eggs and cheese flatter one another on such a regular basis that it makes sense for them to reside in the same chapter. A cheese soufflé represents the perfect marriage of eggs and cheese with the eggs providing height, lightness, and strength and the cheese contributing its unique flavor, but these two foods meet in other dishes too—in omelets, flans, custards, savory puddings, timbales, and so forth.

Egg Basics

Hens' eggs come in colors from white and brown to pale green and blue, depending on the breed of the chicken. Nutritionally, however, they're the same, as are fertile and non-fertile eggs. When cracked, a fresh egg looks perky, and the yolk and white are bound closely together. As eggs age, they flatten out, and older ones are better for baking than for scrambling, frying, or boiling since their flavor is no longer at its best. Floating an egg in a bowl of water is one way to tell if an egg is fresh: old eggs float; fresh ones sink.

The color of the yolks reflects what chickens have been eating. Chickens I've known that peck at this kernel of corn and that fresh green plant, bug, or blossom as they wander over the yard have eggs with bright yellow yolks. A friend in New Mexico feeds chile scraps to her hens, and their yolks are an alarming shade of orange! The flecks of blood that sometimes appear on the yolk aren't harmful; they indicate that the egg has been fertilized, but you can lift them out with the edge of a shell for aesthetic reasons.

ORGANIC EGGS: While organically raised food is always preferable to use, it's especially important with eggs. Those that come from chickens that aren't crammed into small cages and given boosters of hormones to encourage laying and antibiotics to compensate for the disease crowding fosters are simply better all around. They look lively and healthy, the yolks are bright yellow, and the chickens who laid them are healthier, too. Organic eggs are more expensive but not only do they taste better, I never worry about salmonella when I use them.

CARE AND HANDLING: It's best to store eggs in the refrigerator, preferably in their insulated cartons, at 45°F or less. Eggs are porous and absorb the flavors of nearby foods, so keep them away from onions and other strong foods. To avoid any possibility of salmonella, discard cracked eggs and handle eggs with clean hands.

Extra egg whites and yolks can be refrigerated for several days. Cover yolks with a little water so that they don't form a skin, then cover with a lid. Egg whites need just a lidded container, whether refrigerated or frozen.

SIZES: Size is determined by weight. A large egg weighs 2 ounces. Five large eggs (or four extra-large or six medium or seven small) equal 1 cup. The yolk is a third of the egg's volume. Large eggs are what I usually buy and are used in the recipes in this book, except for pasta. There I use extra-large eggs.

TO SEPARATE THE YOLK FROM THE WHITE: Sharply crack an egg on the edge of a glass or metal bowl, then pry open the shell and let the whites fall into the bowl as you pass the yolk back and forth from shell to shell. The cautionary cry not to have even a speck of yolk in the whites is, in my experience, somewhat exaggerated. Most often, whites will whip up fine even with a speck of yolk present. But as a precautionary measure, break each white into a cup, then add it to the rest. That way, if a lot of yolk gets into one white, you can discard the offending egg without losing the entire batch.

EGG WHITES: Egg whites don't have the richness or flavor of yolks, but they contribute protein and structure to a dish. Beaten whites expand and trap air, adding volume, lightness, and loft to cakes, soufflés, puffed omelets, etc. To reach their maximum volume, they should be at room temperature: cover cold eggs with hot tap water for about 5 minutes to bring them to room temperature, then separate them. Or separate cold eggs, then take the bowl with the whites and swirl it about 4 inches over a burner. Test them frequently with your finger and stop as soon as they feel warm.

When beating whites, avoid using plastic bowls and make sure that all utensils are clean and free of grease, for that's what prevents whites from expanding. Use a whisk, hand mixer, or heavy-duty mixer with a balloon whisk. Begin electric mixers on low speed until the eggs are foamy, then raise the speed to high.

Most recipes will direct you to whisk whites into either soft or firm peaks. Soft peaks droop a little when a clump is taken up on the end of a whisk or a spoon, whereas stiff whites stand straight out. Their look should be glossy and uniform, not dry. When dry, the whites clump and are difficult to fold without overworking and losing loft. I find it's better to err on the side of slightly underbeating whites than overbeating them so that the eggs can be folded in quickly without loss of volume.

EGG YOLKS: Yolks contribute moisture, tenderness, richness, and color—if they themselves have color—to food. One of their other functions is to thicken sauces, such as a béchamel sauce when it becomes the base for a soufflé. To keep egg yolks from curdling in hot liquid, they must first be tempered: Whisk the yolks together in a small bowl and gradually add ½ cup or so of the hot liquid until the mixture is warm, then return the mixture to the pot.

EGG SUBSTITUTES: Eggs act as binders in foods and contribute moisture and tenderness. A few foods mimic these qualities and can be used in their place. For one egg, substitute:

½ cup mashed banana, applesauce, or pureed prune in muffins, quick breads, and pancakes

2 tablespoons cornstarch or arrowroot added to the dry ingredients or dissolved in a few tablespoons water

3 ounces silken tofu, pureed until smooth

Crumbled firm tofu or ricotta for scrambled eggs

A NOTE ABOUT SALMONELLA: The bacterium *Salmonella enteridis* can cause illness and, in very extreme cases, death. While a bout with salmonella is bound to be unpleasant, even avian scientists are divided about what to recommend. Outbreaks always cause alarm, but data suggest that it's out of proportion to the actual probability of contracting salmonella poisoning. Outbreaks are also usually traced to mishandling of eggs in institutional settings, where practices are used that home cooks don't usually encounter, such as pooling raw eggs and holding cooked ones. How we respond in our own kitchens is, I believe, a personal matter. I feel confident in the eggs I buy, which are from small free-range flocks raised locally without added hormones and antibiotics. But if I didn't have this option, lived in a part of the country where outbreaks of salmonella poisoning are numerous, or cooked for an elderly or ill person, I might well take the precautions suggested by the American Egg Board: Avoid using raw eggs and cook eggs adequately.

Cooking induces pasteurization, which takes place at 140°F if held for 3½ minutes, killing harmful bacteria. Instant-read thermometers (dip them in boiling water first to make them most effective) are best for checking temperatures, but also just cook your eggs until the whites are set and the yolk has begun to thicken.

Eggs:

To end up with tender eggs rather than rubbery ones, keep the cooking temperature moderate. Heat makes proteins hard, and egg whites are pure protein. The exception is the omelet, which goes into a hot pan of sizzling butter, but it's cooked so quickly that the eggs remain tender.

Boiled Eggs People tend to boil an egg as they were taught at home. Some prick the end of the egg with a pin so that pressure doesn't build up and crack the shell. Some start eggs in cold water; others lower them into a pot that's already simmering. It really doesn't matter as long as you don't actually boil or overcook them—that's what makes them dry and hard and surrounds the yolks with a green ring.

The times given are for large eggs cooked at sea level. Above 5,000 feet, water boils at increasingly lower temperatures, so cooking times will be longer. In spite of altitude conversion formulas, I've found that some experimentation is necessary to figure out exact time for high-altitude eggs.

Incidentally, peeling hard-cooked eggs that are very fresh can be a nightmare—the shell breaks into pieces, sticks to the membrane, and when you finally get a piece to come off, a good chunk of the white comes off as well. In the end, the peeled egg looks pockmarked. If you don't mind eating the egg right out of the shell, this isn't a problem. But if you need perfectly peeled eggs, older eggs are preferable.

Soft-Boiled Eggs The white solidifies but is tender; the yolk is warm and runny. Bring a small saucepan of enough water to cover the egg to a gentle boil, just above a simmer. Set the egg on a spoon, lower it into the pot, and cook for 3 to 3½ minutes. If you're cooking several eggs at once, lower them into the water in a basket so that they'll all begin cooking at the same time.

Medium-Boiled Eggs These aren't quite as loose as the soft-boiled variety; the egg white is firmer, the yolk soft but not so runny, and the whole thing is actually peelable. Bring water to a gentle boil, lower the egg into the pan, turn off the heat, add a lid, and let stand for 5 minutes.

Hard-Boiled (Hard-Cooked) Eggs These are the eggs to eat warm with a pinch of sea salt and pepper, to use for egg salads or composed salad plates. When cut in half, the yolk should have a dime-sized moist dot in the center. The boiling time is very minimal so that the cooked egg will be tender and moist rather than hard and dry.

Put eggs in a pot with cold water to cover. Bring them to a gentle boil and boil for 1 minute. Turn off the heat, cover, and let stand for 6 minutes. (At 7,000 feet I find it takes 10 minutes.) If you're not eating them right away, plunge them into cold water to stop the cooking. Leftover eggs can be refrigerated for days.

Poached Eggs Those little oval-shaped poaching tins on legs are reliable, but what you get isn't a true poached egg. A real poached egg swims freely in a swirling water bath. A little vinegar added to the cooking liquid aids in setting the whites, especially when the eggs are very fresh.

Cover an egg with hot water to bring it to room temperature. Put 2 to 3 inches water in a small skillet, bring it to a boil, and add ½ teaspoon vinegar and a few pinches salt. Lower the heat to a simmer. Break the egg on a plate. Stir the water in a circular direction, then slip the egg into the whirlpool. The swirling motion keeps the whites from floating away like rags. Baste the yolks by spooning the water over them until they turn opaque and are set, about 3 minutes or longer for a firmer yolk. Remove the egg with a slotted spoon and set on a slice of waiting toast.

Fried Eggs Melt a few teaspoons butter in a small nonstick skillet. When it's foaming, break one or two eggs into the pan and set the heat to medium. Cook until the whites are set and the yolks are partially set, about 3 minutes. Serve them sunny side up or give the pan a shake to loosen the eggs and turn them over. Fry on the second side briefly or until the yolk is firm.

Steam-Fried Eggs, Sunny Side Up Fry an egg as described, but when the white is set, add a few tablespoons of water, cover the pan, and cook over medium heat until the yolk loses its shine, about 2 minutes.

Steam-Fried Eggs with Chipotle Chile and Grated Cheese These are breakfast eggs with strength! Make steam-fried eggs, but before adding the water, sprinkle them liberally with grated Jack or Cheddar and ground chipotle chile or cayenne. The cheese melts, the chile runs into it, and it's very good.

THE EGG TIMIN' SONG

I found this little story in a community cookbook called *Treasured Alabama Recipes*.

"Back in the days when cooks sang in the kitchen while they worked, our Thurza improvised her own musical accompaniment for every task. When cooking boiled eggs, she always sang 'Amazing Grace.' She called it her 'egg timin' song,' and she explained, 'Folks say they want a 3-minute egg, I sing all 4 verses. They order an egg doner, I sing all four and repeat the first verse. They don't want the egg so done, I leaves off the last verse. Singing is more pleasantsome than watching a clock.'"

Scrambled Eggs

PROPERLY *made, scram-
bled eggs are soft and
tender curds. They're
wonderful piled on a
crisp English muffin or
a toasted slice of country
bread, accompanied by a
mound of spinach or a
baked tomato. They're
also generously receptive
to additions of fresh
herbs, cheeses, asparagus
tips, or sautéed diced
mushrooms—as long as
they're in small pieces.
Allow two to three large
eggs per person or, if you
want to eliminate some
of the yolks, replace them
with extra whites.*

SERVES 2

4 to 5 eggs

2 tablespoons water or milk

Salt and freshly milled pepper

1 tablespoon butter or more to taste

Briskly beat the eggs in a bowl with the water and a few pinches salt and pepper. Melt the butter in an omelet pan or a small nonstick skillet. When it's sizzling, reduce the heat to low, add the eggs, and slowly begin to stir with a flat-bottomed wooden spoon. Drag the spoon over the bottom of the pan, pulling the cooked egg up with it. As soon as the eggs are as dry or as wet as you like them—or even a moment before—remove them to a warm plate. Scrambled eggs continue to cook from their own heat.

Scrambled Eggs with Fines Herbes Add 2 teaspoons *each* chopped chives, parsley, and chervil to the eggs before cooking.

Scrambled Eggs with Cheese Have ready $1/4$ to $1/2$ cup grated cheese near the stove, then add it after the eggs are in the pan. All kinds of cheeses go well with eggs— strong Cheddar, mild Jack, cottage cheese, goat cheese, Fontina, Gruyère, and smoked cheeses.

Deluxe Scrambled Eggs Scramble the eggs with cheese and snipped chives or other favored herb, then stir in a few tablespoons small croutons.

Scrambled Eggs with Vegetables In a tablespoon butter, sauté 2 to 3 table-spoons diced cooked artichoke hearts, mushrooms, or small cooked asparagus tips. Add mushrooms or asparagus to the eggs once they're in the pan; artichokes should be added at the very end so that they don't discolor the eggs.

Scrambled Eggs with Harissa If you like your morning eggs with some spice, try these. Beat 2 to 3 teaspoons Harissa, page 75, into the eggs and cook them in a com-bination of olive oil and butter. Garnish with a few pinches chopped parsley.

Baked or Shirred Eggs

Butter for the dish   **Salt and freshly milled pepper**
12 eggs

Preheat the oven to 400°F. Butter an 8- × 12-inch or equivalent gratin dish. Carefully break the eggs into it, placing them next to each other, then season with salt and pepper. Bake, covered or open, until the yolks are nearly set, anywhere from 6 to 10 minutes. The exact time depends on how quickly the dish conducts the heat, so check them after five minutes. The eggs will continue cooking when removed from the oven.

Baked Eggs with Herbs Add a sprinkling of chopped parsley, chervil, tarragon, or basil to the eggs as soon as they come out of the oven.

Baked Eggs with Cheese and Bread Crumbs Loosely cover the bottom of the dish with grated cheese, crack the eggs on top, and cover with additional cheese mixed with several tablespoons fresh bread crumbs and chopped herbs, if desired. Season and bake as described.

Chile Baked Eggs Spread a little Harissa, page 75, in the bottom of the baking dish along with butter or olive oil. Instead of black pepper, sprinkle ground red chile or paprika over the eggs, then bake as described.

Baked Eggs on Peperonata Brush the baking dish with olive oil. Heat Peperonata—stewed peppers and tomatoes, page 404, in a saucepan, then spread it thinly or thickly in the dish. Make 12 small depressions, break the eggs into them, then bake as described.

Baked Eggs with Feta, Tomato, and Marjoram Butter or oil the dish and add the eggs. Crumble a few tablespoons of feta over the top followed by a scattering of finely diced tomatoes. Season with pepper (the feta will be salty enough that you don't need to add more). Bake as described, then remove, and sprinkle freshly chopped marjoram over the top.

A RELIABLE, easy method for beginners or those who get the willies when it comes to cooking eggs for more than one or two. And that's what this recipe is for, for it doesn't make sense to take the time or trouble to heat up an oven for just a single serving. Use a shallow ovenproof dish that can be brought to the table, so that the eggs nestle next to each other.

6 SERVINGS

Omelets

AN omelet makes a fine meal, regardless of the hour. From start to finish, an omelet takes just minutes to make. Since they're best when made with just two to three eggs—the heat of the butter and depth of the eggs being easiest to control in small amounts—it's easy to make several omelets in a row when feeding a group. Large omelets aren't impossible to make, but they lose in finesse. Read the instructions first for "A Simple Omelet" if you're not familiar with the technique, because there won't be time to study once you begin.

There are different styles of omelet making. A French omelet is made by simultaneously scrambling the eggs and jerking the pan until the eggs, barely set, can be rolled onto a plate. Another style, so charmingly executed to a Joplin rag in the Japanese movie *Tampopo*, consists of rolling the eggs once they've set by hitting the handle and jerking the pan so that they're thrown to the far edge of the pan. When the whites are separated and beaten then folded into the yolks you have the makings of a puffy souffléd omelet. I, however, prefer the method described in the following recipe.

A Simple Omelet

2 to 3 eggs   1 tablespoon butter
Salt and freshly milled pepper

Using a fork or whisk, beat the eggs in a small bowl with a few pinches salt and pepper just to blend—about 20 strokes. It shouldn't be a uniform mixture. Melt the butter over high heat in an 8-inch omelet pan or nonstick skillet, rotating the pan so that butter coats the bottom and the sides. Allow the butter to sizzle and the foam to subside, then add the beaten eggs and let them sit for 2 to 3 seconds. With a fork or rubber spatula if using a nonstick pan, begin to draw the lightly cooked egg toward the center of the pan. As you do so, tilt the pan so that uncooked beaten eggs flow into the bare part of the pan. Continue working your way around the pan, pulling the cooked egg in and tilting the pan. When there's just a little moist egg puddled on top, add your filling, if using one, then tilt the pan away from you. Give a few raps on the handle and the far edge should fall back on itself, then turn the pan over the plate so that the folded omelet falls out. It should be golden on the outside, soft and moist inside.

Omelet Fillings Except for herbs, which are beaten right into the eggs, add omelet fillings just before you fold the eggs and turn them onto a plate. Fillings can be sautéed vegetables, small croutons, and/or cheese. In Japan they often put rice in omelets and serve them with ketchup—it sounds awful but tastes good, at least there, when eaten in context. Here's a place for improvisation—as a glance at any diner breakfast menu will show you. Avoid overstuffing omelets with too many ingredients, too much bulk, or too-wet fillings.

Cheese Omelet Sprinkle a few tablespoons crumbled or grated cheese over the eggs—Gruyère, Emmentaler, Cheddar, goat, feta, whatever your pleasure.

Herb Omelet Whisk a tablespoon of finely chopped herbs into the eggs—fines herbes, marjoram, flat-leaf parsley, or an exotic combination of parsley, dill, cilantro, and scallions. The Sorrel Purée, page 40, is practically meant for eggs.

Omelet with Tiny Croutons Lightly brown several tablespoons small fresh bread cubes in a tad of butter or teaspoon of olive oil and add them to the omelet just before folding it. They provide a wonderful contrast to the smooth eggs. I sometimes add a little Gruyère as well.

Mushroom Omelet Sauté ³/₄ cup sliced mushrooms in butter or olive oil and season with a little minced garlic and chopped parsley or marjoram. Spread them over the eggs before folding or serve them on the side.

Vegetable Omelets Add ¹/₂ cup steamed or blanched vegetables, seasoned and tossed in a little butter. Try asparagus tips, braised spinach, sautéed onions, broccoli florets, sautéed artichokes, grilled peppers, and so forth.

Egg White Omelet with Spinach

2 teaspoons butter or olive oil

2 cups spinach or chard leaves

Salt and freshly milled pepper

3 egg whites, beaten with ¹/₂ teaspoon chopped marjoram or chives

ANYTHING YOU can put in a regular omelet can be added to this one, but avocado, in particular, gives it some of the rich, soft feel that yolks have.

SERVES 1

In a small nonstick skillet, melt half the butter, add the spinach, and cook until it's wilted. Season with salt and pepper, then move it to a plate. Add the second bit of butter to the pan, then pour in the whites. Tilt the pan to spread them out, then cook over medium heat until they're set. Season with a pinch of salt and pepper, arrange the spinach over a third of the eggs, then gently prod the eggs over it to make a rolled omelet.

Stuffed Green Chile Omelet

2 large green chiles—Anaheim, New Mexican, poblano—roasted, page 403

¹/₄ cup or more grated Cheddar, Jack, goat cheese, or Muenster

2 tablespoons chopped cilantro

2 tablespoons sliced scallion

3 eggs

Salt

2 teaspoons butter or oil

A ROUGH-AND-READY plate of eggs in which roasted green chiles are stuffed loosely with cheese and cooked within the omelet.

SERVES 1 OR 2

Slip the skins off the chiles, cut a slit in the middle of each one, and carefully pull out the seeds. Mix the cheese, cilantro, and scallion together and loosely stuff the chiles. Whisk the eggs with salt and stir in any leftover cheese mixture.

Preheat the broiler. Heat the butter in a 10-inch skillet and set the chiles in it slit side up. Cook over high heat for a few minutes, then pour in the eggs. Go around the edge of the pan several times with a fork, pulling the cooked egg in toward the center and mounding it around the chiles. When no more of the egg is fluid, slide the pan 6 inches under the broiler and leave until golden and barely set. Serve the omelet with warm tortillas, black beans or plain pinto beans, and a side of salsa.

Frittatas

FRITTATA is the Italian—and most common—name for a flat, opened-faced omelet, but similar egg dishes are found in many other Mediterranean countries: Spain's tortilla, Tunisia's tagine, Persian kuku, Provence's trouchia. These thick, sturdy omelets are saturated with vegetables, herbs, and other substantial additions. Extremely versatile, they can be enjoyed warm or at room temperature, and they can also be made thin, stacked on top of each other, and bound with a layer of mayonnaise. Cut them into small squares and serve as appetizers, slice them into wedges and place on a composed salad plate, take them on picnics, serve them for brunch, and so forth.

HOW TO COOK A FRITTATA: Whisk the eggs just to break them up, add salt, pepper, herbs, garlic, and cheese if called for, then stir in the prepared vegetables. Heat butter, olive oil, or a combination in a nonstick skillet. Its size determines the thickness of the frittata. The thicker the frittata, the more slowly you need to cook it so that it will cook through without burning. For six eggs, an 8- to 10-inch skillet should be fine. Once the fat is hot, tilt the pan to coat it, then add the eggs and lower the heat. Allow the eggs to sit for a minute, then give the pan a gentle shake to make sure they aren't sticking. If they are, loosen them carefully with a thin rubber spatula. Cook the eggs over low to medium heat until they're set and the top is nearly dry, about 10 minutes.

FINISHING IN THE PAN: Place a large plate over the skillet, secure both plate and skillet with your hands, and invert the entire thing. Add a little more butter or oil to the pan, slide the eggs back in, and finish cooking, just 2 to 3 minutes. When done, invert onto a serving plate.

FINISHING UNDER THE BROILER: Once the eggs are nearly set, put the frittata under the broiler 4 to 6 inches from the heat, to brown and finish cooking, a matter of just a few minutes. Remove, then invert the frittata onto a serving plate.

Zucchini Frittata with Marjoram

THIS frittata can serve as the blueprint for the recipes that follow, except that you don't have to salt other vegetables. (Grating and salting the squash draws out its moisture, which keeps the eggs from becoming watery.) Zucchini is so amenable to variations that you can enjoy different versions of this frittata all summer long.

SERVES 4 TO 6

1¼ pounds zucchini, coarsely grated
Salt and freshly milled pepper
3 tablespoons olive oil
6 eggs

1 large garlic clove, crushed or minced
1 tablespoon chopped marjoram
⅓ cup freshly grated Parmesan or
  dry Jack

Toss the zucchini with 1 teaspoon salt and set it aside in a colander for 20 to 30 minutes. Rinse briefly, then squeeze dry.

Warm half the oil in a wide skillet over medium-high heat. Add the zucchini and cook, stirring frequently, until it's dry and flecked with gold in a few places, about 6 minutes. Transfer the zucchini to a bowl and wipe out the pan.

Preheat the broiler. Beat the eggs with a few pinches of salt and some pepper, then stir in the garlic, zucchini, marjoram, and cheese. Add the remaining oil to the pan and, when it's hot, add the eggs. Lower the heat, cook for a minute or so, then give the pan a few jerks to make sure the eggs are loose on the bottom. If they're sticking, loosen them carefully with a thin rubber spatula. Cook over medium-low heat until the eggs are set and the top is nearly dry, about 10 minutes. Put the frittata 4 to 6 inches under the broiler to finish cooking the top.

Zucchini Frittata with Basil Basil is another wonderful herb with squash. Add a few tablespoons chopped basil leaves to the eggs in place of the marjoram—or stir in a few tablespoons Pesto, page 57, and omit the cheese.

Zucchini Frittata with Ricotta Add ¹/₂ to 1 cup ricotta cheese to the eggs.

Zucchini Frittata with Salsa Verde In place of the chopped fresh herbs, stir ¹/₄ cup Salsa Verde (or any of its variations), page 55, into the eggs.

Zucchini Frittata with Walnuts or Pine Nuts Once the top of the frittata is nearly set, cover it lightly with toasted walnuts or pine nuts.

Onion Frittata with Vinegar and Walnuts

1 ¹/₂ **pounds onions, peeled and quartered**
1 ¹/₂ **tablespoons olive oil**
2 **tablespoons sherry vinegar**
Salt and freshly milled pepper
¹/₈ **teaspoon ground cloves**

6 **eggs**
2 **tablespoons chopped parsley**
2 **tablespoons butter**
¹/₂ **cup walnuts, roasted**

IT'S easy to overlook an onion omelet, but it makes your house smell so inviting, especially when the sizzling sherry vinegar and butter are added at the end. Remember, sharp knives and cold onions don't cause tears.

SERVES 4 TO 6

Slice the onions crosswise about ¹/₄ inch wide. Warm the olive oil in a 10-inch skillet, add the onions, and cook over medium heat, stirring occasionally, until they're golden and soft, about 30 minutes. Add half the vinegar, let it reduce, then season well with ³/₄ teaspoon salt, pepper to taste, and the cloves. Preheat the broiler.

Whisk the eggs, season them with a few pinches salt, then add the onions and parsley. Melt a tablespoon butter in a 10-inch skillet until it's sizzling, then add the eggs and lower the heat. Scatter the walnuts on top and cook until the eggs are set and nicely browned on the bottom, 8 to 10 minutes. Slide the pan 4 to 6 inches under the broiler to finish cooking the top, but take care not to burn the walnuts.

Loosen the frittata and tilt it onto a serving platter. Return the pan to the stove and raise the heat. Add the remaining butter and, when it begins to foam, add the remaining vinegar. Slide the pan back and forth to combine the two, then pour it over the eggs.

Chard and Onion Omelet (*Trouchia*)

THESE *Provençal eggs, laced with softened onions and chard, never fail to elicit sighs of appreciation. I'm forever grateful to Nathalie Waag for making trouchia when she came to visit—it has since become a favorite. The trick to its success is to cook everything slowly so that the flavors really deepen and sweeten.*

SERVES 4 TO 6

3 tablespoons olive oil

1 large red or white onion, quartered and thinly sliced crosswise

1 bunch chard, leaves only, chopped

Salt and freshly milled pepper

1 garlic clove

6 to 8 eggs, lightly beaten

2 tablespoons chopped parsley

2 tablespoons chopped basil

2 teaspoons chopped thyme

1 cup grated Gruyère

2 tablespoons freshly grated Parmesan

Heat 2 tablespoons of the oil in a 10-inch skillet, add the onion, and cook over low heat, stirring occasionally, until completely soft but not colored, about 15 minutes. Add the chard and continue cooking, stirring occasionally, until all the moisture has cooked off and the chard is tender, about 15 minutes. Season well with salt and pepper.

Meanwhile, mash the garlic in a mortar with a few pinches of salt (or chop them finely together), then stir it into the eggs along with the herbs. Combine the chard mixture with the eggs and stir in the Gruyère and half the Parmesan.

Preheat the broiler. Heat the remaining oil in the skillet and, when it's hot, add the eggs. Give a stir and keep the heat at medium-high for about a minute, then turn it to low. Cook until the eggs are set but still a little moist on top, 10 to 15 minutes. Add the remaining Parmesan and broil 4 to 6 inches from the heat, until browned.

Serve trouchia in the pan or slide it onto a serving dish and cut it into wedges. The gratinéed top and the golden bottom are equally presentable.

Ricotta Frittata

MADE *with good quality ricotta, this frittata is very delicate. Since it contains no vegetables, serve some on the side, like Grilled Asparagus in spring, Roasted Root Vegetables in winter, Tunisian Tomato and Pepper Stew in summer, or Mushrooms with Tarragon and Cream any time of year.*

SERVES 4 TO 6

4 to 6 eggs

Salt and freshly milled white pepper

1 cup ricotta

1/4 cup freshly grated Parmesan

1 1/2 tablespoons chopped marjoram

1 small garlic clove, crushed

2 tablespoons of a mixture of olive oil and butter

1/2 cup bread crumbs, crisped in olive oil or butter

Preheat the broiler. Beat the eggs with 3/4 teaspoon salt and white pepper to taste. Stir in the cheeses, marjoram, and garlic. Heat the oil and butter in an 8- or 10-inch skillet, add the egg mixture, and lower the heat. Cook until set, about 12 minutes, then brown 4 to 6 inches under the broiler. When done, slide the frittata onto a plate, sprinkle with the bread crumbs, and serve.

Spaghettini and Parsley Frittata

6 to 8 eggs

1 heaping cup chopped parsley

2½ tablespoons chopped marjoram

2 garlic cloves mashed with ¼ teaspoon salt

½ teaspoon finely grated lemon zest

½ cup freshly grated Parmesan

Salt and freshly milled pepper

4 ounces dried spaghettini or linguine (2 to 3 cups cooked)

2 tablespoons butter or olive oil, plus oil to finish

Beat the eggs with a fork, then stir in all but a tablespoon of the herbs, the garlic, lemon zest, and cheese. Season with salt and pepper and let stand while you cook the pasta. When the pasta is done, drain, then rinse with cold water to cool; you should have 2 to 3 cups. Shake off the excess and add it to the eggs.

Preheat the broiler. Heat the butter in a large nonstick skillet until foamy, then pour in the egg mixture. Lower the heat, gently shake the pan back and forth a few times to distribute the pasta, then cook until the eggs are firm, 8 to 10 minutes. Place 4 to 6 inches under the broiler until the top is browned. Loosen the frittata with a rubber spatula and slide it onto a serving dish. Mix the reserved tablespoon of herbs with a little olive oil and brush this mixture over the top right before serving.

A GREAT way to use left-over pasta. Finish as described here or melt 2 tablespoons of butter in a small skillet, add as much white wine vinegar, and swirl it over the heat until the sauce emulsifies. Pour over the omelet and serve.

SERVES 4 TO 6

Tunisian Eggs with Grilled Peppers and Harissa

4 bell peppers—2 red, 1 green, and 1 yellow, grilled and roasted, page 403

1 garlic clove, minced

Salt

6 eggs

2 to 3 teaspoons Harissa, page 75

2 tablespoons chopped parsley

1 tablespoon olive oil

THESE eggs, streaked red with spicy harissa, really get the day started or keep it going!

SERVES 4 TO 6

Cut the peeled peppers into ¼-inch strips and dice them finely. Mix them with the garlic and a pinch of salt. Beat the eggs with a few pinches salt, then stir in the harissa, parsley, and peppers. Heat the oil in a 10-inch nonstick skillet. When hot, pour in the eggs, lower the heat, and cook until set, 8 to 10 minutes. Invert onto a plate, return the eggs to the pan, and finish cooking the second side, about 3 minutes.

Spanish Potato and Onion Frittata
(*Tortilla Español*)

THIS cushionlike golden omelet is present in Spanish bars everywhere, providing a nourishing boost for flagging energy from morning through night. The generous amount of olive oil gives the potatoes a velvety, tender texture. The finished dish should be completely moist and golden, not the least bit dry.

SERVES 6 TO 8

Scant ½ cup fruity olive oil, Spanish if you have it

2 pounds white or red potatoes, peeled and very thinly sliced

1 large onion, thinly sliced or diced

Salt and freshly milled pepper

6 to 8 eggs, beaten

Warm 5 tablespoons of the oil in a very wide nonstick or cast-iron skillet. Add the potatoes and cook over medium heat, stirring frequently, until they're cooked through and golden, about 20 minutes. When done, the potatoes will have lost their opaque white centers. Separate any slices that stick together so that they'll cook evenly. When done, transfer the potatoes to a bowl with a slotted spoon. If there's no oil remaining in the pan, add another tablespoon and sauté the onions until they're lightly browned. Add them to the potatoes and season well with salt and pepper. Pour in the beaten eggs.

Wipe out the pan with a towel, then return it to the stove and add 2 tablespoons oil. Pour in the egg mixture, smooth down any potatoes that stick up, and cook over low heat until golden on the bottom, about 10 minutes. Invert the omelet onto a plate, slide it back into the pan, and cook until set, a few minutes.

Potato Frittata with Rosemary Add 2 teaspoons minced rosemary to the potatoes while they're frying.

Potato Frittata with Smoked Cheese Add ½ cup grated smoked cheese—mozzarella, gouda, Cheddar. This makes a good dish for fall or winter, served with sautéed apples or applesauce flavored with quince.

Frittata with Tomatoes and Feta

USE tomatoes that aren't too juicy—meaty plum or Roma are best here. If fresh marjoram isn't available, use dried oregano in its place— a scant teaspoon in the eggs and extra on top.

SERVES 4 TO 6

6 eggs

Salt and freshly milled pepper

1 bunch scallions, including an inch of the greens, finely sliced

1 garlic clove, minced

¼ cup chopped parsley

1 tablespoon chopped marjoram, plus extra for garnish

1 tablespoon each butter and olive oil, or a mixture

4 Roma tomatoes, halved, seeded, and diced

2 ounces feta, thinly sliced

Beat the eggs with a few pinches salt, then add the scallions, garlic, and herbs. Preheat the broiler.

Heat the butter and oil in an 8- or 10-inch skillet until foaming. Pour in the eggs, lower the heat, and distribute the tomatoes and feta evenly over the top. Cook until the eggs are set, then slide the pan 4 to 6 inches under the broiler and brown the top. Instead of inverting the omelet, slide it onto a large platter, keeping the top side up. Garnish with the additional marjoram and serve.

FEW dishes are as dramatic as a soufflé. The whole dish swells like an enormous inhalation—then, within moments of serving, collapses. In spite of such drama, soufflés are not at all difficult to make. You simply make a stiff béchamel, beat in egg yolks, add cheese and/or other fillings, and finally fold in billowy whisked egg whites. Vegetable soufflés incorporate a cup or so of pureed vegetable into the base. They don't rise quite as high but are still impressive. A pudding soufflé is the same dish baked in a water bath, which tempers the rise but also slows the fall, giving the cook some leeway for serving as well as the further advantage of reheating. Roulades are soufflés baked flat in sheet pans (jelly roll pans), then rolled around a filling and sliced or, if you prefer, cut into strips, stacked, and served like a soft, savory Napoleon.

Goat Cheese Soufflé with Thyme

Butter, plus 2 tablespoons freshly grated Parmesan, for the dish

1¼ cups milk or cream

Aromatics: 1 bay leaf, several thyme sprigs, 2 thin onion slices

3 tablespoons butter

3 tablespoons flour

Salt and freshly milled pepper

Pinch cayenne

4 egg yolks

1 cup (about 4 ounces) crumbled goat cheese, preferably a Bucheron or other strong-flavored cheese

6 egg whites

Several plump thyme sprigs, leaves only

Preheat the oven to 400°F. Butter a 6-cup soufflé dish or an 8-cup gratin dish and coat it with the Parmesan. Heat the milk with the aromatics until it boils. Set it aside to steep for 15 minutes, then strain.

Melt the butter in a saucepan. When foamy, stir in the flour and cook over low heat for several minutes. Whisk in the milk all at once and stir vigorously for a minute or so as it thickens, then add ¾ teaspoon salt, a few twists of pepper, and the cayenne. Remove from heat. Beat in the egg yolks one at a time until well blended, then stir in the cheese. Don't worry about getting it smooth.

Beat the egg whites with a pinch of salt until they form firm peaks, then stir a quarter of them into the base to lighten the mixture. Fold in the rest, transfer to the prepared dish, then put in the center of the oven and lower the heat to 375°F. Bake for 30 minutes or until golden and just a bit wobbly in the center. Remove, scatter the thyme over the top, and serve immediately.

Gruyère Soufflé This is every bit as enticing as a goat cheese soufflé. Omit the aromatics and add a pinch of nutmeg to the base along with the cayenne. In place of goat cheese, stir in 1 cup coarsely grated Gruyère.

OF all soufflés, this is my favorite. The enticing aroma of goat cheese is very seductive, and the little pockets of melted cheese are found treasures. Although a classic soufflé dish forms a high, puffed crown, I often bake this and other soufflés in a large shallow gratin dish instead. It still looks marvelous, it bakes more quickly, and this way there's plenty of crust for everyone.

SERVES 4

Vegetable Soufflés When making the base for the Goat Cheese Soufflé, cook a diced shallot (or 3 sliced scallions, including just a little of the green) in the butter for a few minutes before adding the flour.

While spinach and eggs form a classic alliance, other vegetables make handsome additions to a soufflé base too. It should be cooked, seasoned, and finely chopped or pureed before being folded into the base along with the egg yolks. Add the cheese, whisk in the whites, and bake in a 6-cup soufflé dish, individual ramekins, or a gratin dish as described.

Spinach Soufflé Cook a large bunch of spinach leaves with the water clinging to them until tender, then finely chop and season with salt, pepper, and a pinch of nutmeg. For cheese, stay with the goat cheese or use Fontina, Gruyère, or Cheddar. You can use other greens as well—chard and tender Red Russian kale come to mind.

Broccoli Soufflé Stir 2 teaspoons Dijon mustard into the béchamel base, then fold in 1 cup finely chopped cooked and seasoned broccoli. For cheese, use ¹/₂ cup grated sharp Cheddar.

Asparagus Soufflé Fold ³/₄ cup finely chopped asparagus tips into the base. For the cheese, use Fontina or Gruyère.

Winter Squash Soufflé Fold in 1 to 2 cups pureed baked winter squash (or sweet potatoes) into the base and for cheese use Fontina or Gruyère. Crumble fried sage leaves over the top as soon as it comes out of the oven.

Giant Cheddar Soufflé

THIS grand-looking souffle is baked in a round Spanish terra-cotta casserole—13 to 14 inches across and a little over 2 inches high—or an equivalent-sized ovenproof dish. You can make the base ahead of time, guide a small pat of butter over the surface, set a piece of plastic directly on top, and hold until needed. Before using, rewarm the base in the top of a double boiler set over simmering water.

SERVES 6 TO 8

Butter, plus 2 tablespoons freshly grated Parmesan, for the casserole

5 tablespoons butter

6 tablespoons flour

2 cups warm milk

6 egg yolks

1³/₄ cups grated aged Cheddar

Salt

1 teaspoon paprika or ground red chile

10 egg whites

Preheat the oven to 400°F. Butter a 12-cup gratin dish and dust the sides with Parmesan.

Melt the butter in a saucepan, whisk in the flour, and cook over low heat for several minutes. Whisk in the warm milk all at once, lower the heat, and cook for 1 minute, stirring. Remove from the heat and beat in the yolks two at a time. Stir in the cheese. Season with ³/₄ teaspoon salt and the paprika.

Beat the whites with a pinch of salt until they hold firm peaks. Fold them into the yolk mixture, then pour into the casserole. Put in the center of the oven and lower the heat to 375°F. Bake until the soufflé has risen and is golden brown all over the top, about 30 minutes. A slight quivering in the middle and firmness around the edges mean that the center will be loose enough to provide a creamy sauce. If you prefer a firmer center, bake 5 minutes longer. In either case, serve it as soon as it's ready.

Rolled and Stacked Soufflés

Everyone will wonder how you did it, but you don't have to say how easy it is to make a rolled soufflé, or roulade. All you do is bake your soufflé on a four-sided sheet pan or jelly roll pan, then add a filling and roll it up. These versatile roulades can be served hot or cold; they can be made hours in advance of serving; they're an ideal dish for a brunch and sturdy enough to be carried to a picnic. If you're preparing a roulade to be served later, securely wrap it in plastic wrap and refrigerate until ready to use. Remove 20 minutes or so before reheating, brush it with milk or cream, cover lightly with a folded piece of foil, and bake for 25 to 30 minutes at 400°F.

Roulades don't always have to be rolled into large logs. You can divide the base in two and make smaller, more delicate rolls that, when sliced, are an ideal size for an appetizer or as an element on a composed salad plate. You can also cut the base into same-size long rectangles once it's covered with its filling and then stack the roulade pieces on top of each other, which is a very attractive way to present this dish.

Roulade Base

4 tablespoons butter

5 tablespoons flour

1 1/2 cups warm milk

Salt and freshly milled white pepper

Pinch cayenne

5 eggs, separated and at room temperature

1/2 cup freshly grated Parmesan or Gruyère

MAKES ENOUGH FOR A ROULADE SERVING 6 TO 12

Preheat the oven to 400°F. Dab the corners of a 10- × 15-inch sheet pan or jelly roll pan with a little butter, then line with wax paper or parchment, including the edges. Lightly butter, then flour the paper or mist with cooking spray.

Melt the butter in a saucepan, stir in the flour, and cook for 1 minute. Whisk in the warm milk, then turn the heat to low and cook, stirring constantly, for 3 to 4 minutes more. Season with salt, a few twists of pepper, and the cayenne. Whisk 1/2 cup of the base into the yolks, then whisk the yolks back into the base and stir in the cheese.

Beat the egg whites with a pinch salt until they form smooth, firm peaks, then fold them into the base. Spread the batter evenly over the sheet pan, reaching into the corners—an offset spatula is ideal here. Bake in the middle of the oven until the top is lightly browned, puffed, and starting to crack in places, about 15 minutes. Don't underbake it, but don't let it get dry either. Let cool in the pan for 10 minutes, then slide the soufflé off the pan on its paper and flip it over onto a counter lined with wax paper. Peel off the paper.

Spread the filling over the top and roll tightly toward or away from you, whichever feels most natural. When you come to the end, roll the paper tightly around the roulade, slide it onto your outstretched arm to support it, and set it in the refrigerator. Reheat if required. To serve, slice it into 1-inch rounds. Or form the soufflé as suggested, using small rolls or stacked.

SERVING SUGGESTIONS: For appetizers, cut the soufflé base in half lengthwise, roll each of the pieces to make very small roulades, and serve them, thinly sliced, as pass-arounds or set on a piece of rye or sourdough bread. Slice full-sized roulades 1/2 to 1 inch wide, arrange two pieces on a plate at a jaunty angle to each other, then surround them with salad greens tossed with a Shallot Vinaigrette, page 183. Spoon a little of the vinaigrette onto the roulade.

Roulade with Tomatoes, Ricotta, and Basil

SERVES 6 TO 12

6 firm but ripe tomatoes, seeded and finely diced

Salt

1 cup ricotta

1/2 cup mayonnaise or sour cream

4 scallions, including some of the greens, thinly sliced

1/2 cup chopped parsley

10 large basil leaves, sliced into thin ribbons

Salt and freshly milled pepper

Roulade Base, preceding recipe

Sprinkle the tomatoes with 1/2 teaspoon salt and let them stand in a colander to drain for 20 minutes. Beat the ricotta until smooth with mayonnaise to thin it, stir in the scallions and herbs, and season with salt and pepper. Spread evenly over the roulade, cover with the tomatoes, and roll. Serve right away or chilled, surrounded with very finely sliced spinach leaves tossed with Mustard Vinaigrette.

Roulade with Chipotle and Cilantro Season the ricotta mixture with 2 to 3 teaspoons pureed chipotle chile in adobo sauce. Instead of the basil, use 1/4 cup chopped cilantro leaves.

Roulade with Ricotta, Cucumbers, and Dill In place of tomatoes, salt 2 large peeled, seeded, and diced cucumbers for 30 minutes, then squeeze dry before scattering them over the base. Serve with a salad of butter lettuce and mint or nasturtium leaves.

Roulade with Roasted Peppers and Tomato Sauce

USE just red peppers or a mixture of colors. Accompany with an arugula salad.

SERVES 6 TO 12

Roulade Base, page 581

About 1 cup Saffron Mayonnaise, page 59

3 large red and/or yellow peppers, roasted and finely diced

Fresh Tomato Sauce, page 61

Red wine or balsamic vinegar

Spread the roulade base with a layer of saffron mayonnaise, cover with the peppers, then roll or layer as described. Chill the tomato sauce and season with a few drops of vinegar to brighten the flavor. Serve the roulade chilled or at room temperature with the sauce pooled on the plate.

Roulade with Yogurt Cheese and Fresh Herb Filling

½ cup cream cheese or soft fresh goat cheese

3 tablespoons mayonnaise

1 cup Yogurt Cheese, page 47

Salt and freshly milled pepper

Roulade Base, page 581

4 scallions, including a little of the green, finely sliced, or 3 shallots, diced

½ cup chopped parsley

¼ cup chopped dill

¼ cup chopped basil

2 tablespoons chopped cilantro

Grated zest of 1 large lemon

1 teaspoon olive oil

I LIKE this roulade surrounded with watercress or tender red mustard greens, tossed with a finely diced tomato and a Shallot Vinaigrette.

SERVES 6 TO 12

Beat the cream cheese with a few tablespoons mayonnaise until smooth, then stir in the yogurt. Taste for salt, season with pepper, then spread over the roulade. Mix the scallions, herbs, and lemon zest together in a bowl, add a pinch of salt, and toss with a teaspoon of olive oil. Sprinkle them evenly over the yogurt cheese mixture, then roll tightly or stack.

Corn Pudding Soufflé

2 cups corn kernels, preferably fresh, from about 3 ears

1 cup milk

3 tablespoons butter

2 tablespoons finely diced shallot or scallion

3 tablespoons flour

½ cup crumbled goat cheese, Cheddar, or feta

Salt and freshly milled white pepper

3 eggs, separated

Cilantro Salsa, page 56

THIS pudding forms a soufflé's crown but is slower to fall. Serve plain or with a spoonful of Pesto, Salsa Verde, or other salsa of your choosing. For a summer dinner, serve the pudding accompanied with Tomatoes Glazed with Balsamic Vinegar, grilled zucchini, and a side of black beans.

SERVES 4

Preheat the oven to 375°F. Butter a 6-cup soufflé dish. Puree 1½ cups corn with the milk for a full 3 minutes, then pour it into a fine sieve and press out the liquid with a soft rubber scraper. Set aside.

Melt the butter in a saucepan, add the shallot, and cook over heat for 1 minute. Stir in the flour, then whisk in the corn-milk and cook over medium heat, stirring constantly, for 5 minutes. Remove, stir in the remaining corn, the cheese, ½ teaspoon salt, and a little pepper. Warm the yolks with ½ cup of the mixture, then return them to the pan, stirring briskly.

Beat the whites until they hold firm peaks, then fold them into the base. Pour the batter into the dish and set in a baking pan with boiling water to come halfway up the side. Bake until a golden puffy crown has emerged and the pudding is sturdy, about an hour. Serve warm with the sauce.

Cheese and other Dairy Products

ALONG with eggs, beans, and grains, dairy foods are the cornerstones of virtually all traditional cuisines—Asian cuisines being the main exception. As with eggs, many dairy foods are shunned because of their fat and now the presence of growth hormones, but to many, dairy foods are still an integral part of our food culture. Dairy foods retain an important place in our diet as a source of not only calcium and protein but also pleasure. Cheeses are divine examples of human culture as well as bacterial cultures, and there's nothing like the aroma of good butter or the feel in your mouth of softly whipped cream or the velvety tang of crème fraîche or tart, refreshing yogurt. I believe that if you like a food, moderation and balance are still the best guidelines for its use.

A number of dairy products are now made fat-reduced. This is fine when it comes to milk—low-fat milk has been used in nearly all the recipes that call for milk—but not so fine when it comes to butter and sour cream. Reduced-fat butter is extremely watery, for example, and cannot be used in baking. Other reduced-fat products won't give you the taste or texture, especially when cooked, that you're accustomed to.

ALTERNATIVES TO DAIRY: There are now quite a few alternatives to cow's milk. Soy milk, rice milk, and almond milk are commonly available milk substitutes, and soy milk is now made into yogurt, sour cream, and even cheese. Soy cheeses use calcium caseinate, a protein derived from cow's milk that makes cheese stretchy and elastic, which, strictly speaking, also makes these cheeses unacceptable to vegans. Some use these cheeses to avoid cholesterol and fat, but the *Vegetarian Journal* points out that most cheeses are not that high in cholesterol anyway, and many soy cheeses have a high sodium count as well. As for taste and texture, they don't taste like cheese, nor do they melt well. Cheese alternatives aren't inexpensive either—for the same price you can buy decent real cheese.

BOVINE GROWTH HORMONE: Bovine growth hormone, referred to as rBGH or rBST, is injected into dairy cows to increase their milk production. Among its side effects is increased stress for the cows, resulting in more occurrences of udder infections in the cows and a subsequent need for more antibiotics. Many small dairies do not use the growth hormone and they are now allowed to print on their cartons that the milk comes from cows *not* treated with rBST. Due to pressure from consumers, many natural food stores post information about their milk or have information available on request. If you buy national brands of milk, cheese, and butter, however, it will probably come from cows given growth hormones. Large manufacturers draw from milk pools whose dairies have in part, if not all, used the hormone. The growth hormone is not used in Europe, and you'll usually find that small, local dairies do not use it.

Some Favorite Cheeses

There are many wonderful cheeses in the world, and fortunately, there are some excellent cheese books that go into great detail about what is available here and overseas. But here are those that I tend to turn to over and over again, partly because they are what's most readily available where I live and because I like them. Of course, when opportunity arises through travel, I enjoy trying cheeses that are hard to find in the American Southwest.

BLUE CHEESE: Roquefort, Maytag, Gorgonzola, Saga, and Stilton, among others, have strong though differing characters. The French Roquefort and American Maytag are robust and crumbly, the former a little salty, both excellent eating cheeses. Gorgonzola seems to be everybody's favorite blue these days. The dolcelatte, or sweet milk type, is the creamy one. It should be an ivory color with no pink or beige tones and no puddling in its wrapper. It's a superb cheese for eating and cooking, but getting a piece in prime condition can be difficult. Always try to taste it first and buy it cut from the wheel rather than wrapped. The other Gorgonzola is more crumbly and less creamy—heartier and more robust. There is now an excellent Gorgonzola of this type made in Wisconsin (Bel Gioso), but most American-made Gorgonzolas don't have the intrigue and nuance of the Italian ones. Saga is a rather mild, creamy-textured blue, a dessert cheese to enjoy with pears. There's also the magnificent Stilton, with its crumbly texture and big bold flavor, a great cheese for hearty red wines, sherry, and port. The Bleu D'Auvergne also pairs well with red wines of strong character.

CHEDDAR: Americans as well as the English are good makers of Cheddar cheeses. (*Cheddaring* refers to the process of cutting and stacking the curds.) Dense in texture, Cheddars range from mild to tangy and sharp. They become more complex and deep with age. (I recently enjoyed a 10-year-old Wisconsin Cheddar that was absolutely superb!) Cheddars can be white—Vermont's Grafton Village Cheddar, for example, or yellowed with annatto seed as in Wisconsin Cheddars. Cheddar is always good with eggs, in baked dishes of all kinds, in sandwiches, and also with fruits and nuts. To me the Cheddar is always a distinctly American taste, but often a good goat or Gruyère can be used where Cheddar is called for with excellent results. I always find Cheddars a good match for crisp, fall apples or hard cider and freshly cracked walnuts, pecans, or, best, hickory nuts. Cheddar is also good paired with rye breads and berry jams. A slice goes nicely with grape as well as apple pie.

COTTAGE CHEESE: So common as to be practically forgotten except as an ingredient, cottage cheese is still a wonderful fresh-style cheese, creamy but with tang and texture. Try it with olive oil and pepper, page 587, pureed with watercress, page 93, or mixed with yogurt and topped with fruit.

FETA: Greek, French, Bulgarian, and Israeli versions have slightly different personalities, depending on, among other things, the type of milk used. But overall feta provides a sharp accent to everything from eggs and vegetable salads to vegetable gratins. A slice of feta drizzled with a few drops extra virgin olive oil and cracked pepper makes a fine bite to enjoy with a glass of wine, and you can enjoy it in sandwiches too. When baked, feta softens and becomes more perfumed. Dried oregano, mint, and fresh marjoram are particularly complementary with feta. If yours is very salty, a few brief soakings in cold water helps reduce the saltiness.

FONTINA: True Italian Fontina is superb. It's wonderfully creamy, and its flavor is almost fruity with nutty overtones. True Fontina Val d'Aosta has the image of a jagged mountain in a circle stamped on top. Danish and domestic versions are rather bland, but, like Italian Fontina, they melt well, which is one of this cheese's virtues. They're far more available and less expensive than true Italian Fontina, but try the real thing if you have a chance. Fontella and Fontinella are Fontina-like cheeses, also produced in northern Italy.

GOAT CHEESE: Most American goat cheese is fresh, tangy, and very mild. But there are other forms that are more interesting, from aged goat cheeses to more robust cheeses made in the French style, especially Bucheron. Whether sharp and assertive or fresh and delicate, goat cheese always adds character to a dish. It pairs uncommonly well with levain breads, roasted peppers, and eggplant, while rosemary, thyme, garlic, and olive oil are its natural seasonings. Fresh goat cheese makes an excellent grilled cheese sandwich and a heavenly soufflé. But don't leave it just to the savory realm. The slight tang of mild fresh goat cheese is interesting with fruit and nut breads, dates, pears, and other sweet partners. When it comes to more interesting styles such as the Banon, Crottin, or Pyramide, I enjoy those made by Capriole, Coach Farms, and Laura Chenel.

GRUYÈRE: Gruyère has a classic goodness that draws me back to it year after year. It's dense and rich, at first grainy but quick to soften on the tongue. It has a nutty, buttery quality that makes it a natural to serve with pears, apples, and quince preserves. It's wonderful in omelets and soufflés, gratins and soups. It makes a superb grilled cheese sandwich and is excellent in other sandwiches as well or on bruschetta. Try it thinly sliced and accompanied by fine butter on French bread or walnut bread.

MOZZARELLA: Delicate and milky, fresh mozzarella is classically paired with tomatoes and is also excellent with olive paste, roasted peppers, or simply a good fruity olive oil, cracked pepper, and fresh herbs. Unlike the processed version, fresh mozzarella does not turn rubbery when heated but melts into tender strands. It's glorious in a lasagne or gratin but also enjoyable as a delicate dessert cheese.

MEXICAN CHEESES: These are becoming increasingly easy to find, especially now that Mexican-style cheeses are being made in Wisconsin. Here are some you're likely to find and use:

> **Queso Blanco:** A fresh white cheese, somewhat similar to the Indian panir. Mild but a bit salty and tangy, its texture is somewhat spongy. When cooked it softens but doesn't melt.

> **Queso Fresco:** This popular fresh cheese is more crumbly then queso blanco. In fact it is used as a sharp accent, crumbled over salads, tacos, refried beans, fideos, and other dishes. A mild feta can be used in its place.

> **Asadero and Queso Chihuahua:** Both are good melting cheeses, the ones used in quesadillas. Monterey Jack and Muenster can successfully take their place, however.

> **Cotija:** A hard grating cheese to use with fideos, chilaquiles, and enchiladas. Parmesan or Asiago can be used in its place.

MONTEREY JACK AND DRY JACK: This is a true American cheese. The anonymous mass-produced Jacks are not particularly remarkable, but Vella's Bear Flag Jack from Sonoma County, California, and the Vivianis' Sonoma Jack are really delightful, smooth, soft white cheese with tiny eyes, delicacy, and mild acidity or tang. Dry Jack is aged for up to 10 months and protected with dark brown rind. Its crumb and intensity will make you think of Parmesan. It's excellent for grating or eating.

PARMESAN: We are finally enjoying a love affair with the real thing—Parmigiano-Reggiano, the cheese that many connoisseurs have described as the world's greatest cheese. This grainy, straw-colored cheese comes to us through years of tradition and adherence to numerous restrictions that must be observed if it's to be given the name, which is, by the way, stamped on the rind. The flavor of this cheese is big and complex. A little goes far, but it must be treated well. Cut off what you need, let it come to room temperature, and grate it as you use it. Don't buy it grated; its flavor will have dissipated. Wrap well what you haven't used, and please don't waste this treasure by using it to improve the flavor of an inferior food, like low-fat mayonnaise. Just enjoy it for its own sake. Many may not realize that Parmesan is an excellent eating cheese. Try it shaved or slivered over a salad or with pears and a dessert wine. When you buy Parmesan, whether Reggiano or another type, avoid hard dry pieces with a great deal of rind. The rind isn't edible, but it does add flavor to a bean soup or minestrone—just throw a piece in the pot.

PECORINO: Pecorino cheeses are made from sheep's milk, and pecorino Romano is a classic example that's easy to find here. Most pecorinos share two characteristics— pronounced sharpness and sheepiness that may or may not be to your liking. Pecorino from Umbria is one exception; it is mild and sweet, an excellent eating cheese. Pecorino is used mostly as a grating cheese and often in company with Parmesan. I find it particularly pleasing with roasted walnuts and arugula, especially if it's grated into shards and allowed to come to room temperature.

RICOTTA: More versatile than you might think, ricotta doesn't only go into lasagne and ravioli but makes a delicate filling for a sandwich or a crêpe. It can go in a sweet direction too if you drizzle it with honey or rum, dust it with cocoa or combine it with richer cheeses to make a coeur à la crème. It can also be scrambled and baked. Ricotta should be sweet, delicate, and smooth, not at all grainy. Whole-milk ricotta tends to have a better texture. Otherwise, quality varies depending on where you are in the country. It's generally much better on the East Coast than in the Southwest and West until you find an Italian neighborhood. Ricotta salata is ricotta that has been salted and pressed. Its texture is dense, and it can be thinly sliced. Use it with salad greens, tomatoes, cucumbers, avocado, and grilled vegetables or crumble it over pasta.

TELEME: Another true American cheese, Teleme is both buttery and tangy, practically flowing when it's at room temperature. Look for the words *rice washed* or *rice rind* on the label. (The less expensive Teleme that doesn't say *rice washed* on the label just doesn't have the magic.) Teleme makes a particularly wonderful grilled cheese sandwich, and it's a fine cheese to serve with French bread.

YOGURT CHEESE: Thick and tangy, this can often take the place of sour cream, and it can be spread on bread or toast. It goes well with the same foods yogurt is good with— cucumbers, tomatoes, eggplant, hummus, or spicy chickpea spread. You can find it in Middle Eastern markets, but to make your own, see page 47.

Skillet Cheese

A VERY *fast bite that makes a substantial snack or a light meal when accompanied by warm pita bread and sliced tomatoes. Be ready to serve the cheese immediately; it neither waits nor reheats.*

SERVES 1

Olive oil

1/2-inch slice scamorza, provolone, or processed mozzarella

Freshly milled pepper

Warm a serving plate. If you're serving accompaniments, have them ready. Film a small skillet with olive oil. Set over medium heat. When the oil is hot, add the cheese and cook until it begins to soften and the bottom is golden. Turn it over and cook on the second side until soft but not melted. Remove to a plate and shower with freshly milled black pepper.

Baked Cheese on Toast with Wine

ADD *a salad and a piece of fruit, and you'll dine quickly and well.*

SERVES 2 TO 4

2 cups grated Gruyère or Emmentaler

2 eggs, lightly beaten

1/2 cup dry white wine

4 slices country bread or wheat bread

2 tablespoons butter

Dash cayenne

Preheat the oven to 400°F. Mix the cheese, eggs, and half the wine and spread the mixture over the bread. Melt the butter in a heavy skillet large enough to hold all four slices. Swirl in the remaining wine, then settle the bread into the pan. Add cayenne. Bake until the cheese melts, 12 to 15 minutes.

Ricotta and Spinach Fritters

THESE *little fritters are just delicious and so easy to put together. Serve them for lunch with a platter of tomatoes or as a first course at dinner. You can certainly include herbs here if you like.*

MAKES EIGHT 2 1/2-INCH FRITTERS

1 bunch spinach, leaves only

1 cup ricotta

2 eggs

1/2 teaspoon salt and freshly milled white pepper

1/8 teaspoon grated nutmeg

1/4 cup flour

1/2 cup grated Gruyère

2 tablespoons freshly grated Parmesan

Butter or olive oil for frying

Wilt the spinach in a skillet over heat in the water clinging to its leaves. When tender, after 4 to 5 minutes, remove, squeeze out any water, chop finely, then combine with the rest of the ingredients except butter.

Lightly film a skillet with butter. When hot, drop the batter by spoonfuls and fry slowly, over medium heat, until browned on the bottom, about 5 minutes. Turn and cook on the second side. Arrange on a platter and serve warm.

Cottage Cheese with Olive Oil and Black Pepper

This is one of the fastest dishes ever—plus it's delicious. If you can find it (I fear it's hardly ever made anymore, at least in the Southwest), use large-curd cottage cheese, preferably made from wholesome organic milk. Put some on a plate, season it with some freshly ground sea salt and coarse black pepper, then drizzle a little extra virgin olive oil over the top. No need to embellish further, although you can do so by sprinkling on some snipped chives, a favorite herb, or chopped watercress or arugula. Enjoy this with a whole-grain bread or cracker, some crisp celery, and a few olives or purely by itself.

Savory Custards and Timbales

These dishes are generally quick to assemble and require 30 minutes or so for baking— a useful window of time for making a salad and setting the table. They're excellent for a brunch, a Sunday supper, and other low-key food events, but they also make a refined first course at the beginning of a more elaborate dinner. Custards in their various forms are smooth, subtle, and soothing, good when you need warmth and nourishment but aren't in the mood for a culinary challenge.

Using a water bath, or *bain-marie,* is important with all custards to ensure tenderness. To make a water bath, place a dish that's larger than your baking dish in a preheated oven, then add hot to near-boiling water to come at least halfway up the sides of the filled baking dish. The water modulates the heat so that the custard cooks evenly and smoothly. A pair of spring-loaded tongs is useful for removing small ramekins easily from the water bath.

To unmold individual ramekins, let them stand for 5 minutes, then run a knife around the edge and turn them out onto a wide spatula, like a pancake turner. Turn them over once more so that the golden surface is upright and place them on individual serving plates.

To reheat custards and timbales, brush them with milk or cream, cover them with foil, and bake at 375°F for 15 to 25 minutes. The milk moistens the tops and allows them to swell, becoming fresh and tender again. Cream works even better.

Goat Cheese Flan

8 ounces goat cheese, preferably Bucheron or other strong goat cheese, or a mixture of fresh goat cheese and a few tablespoons grated aged goat cheese

3 eggs

1 cup cream or half-and-half

1 cup crème fraîche

Salt and freshly milled white pepper

1 teaspoon chopped thyme

Preheat the oven to 350°F. Generously butter six ½-cup ramekins.

Cream the goat cheese with the eggs, then stir in the cream and crème fraîche. Pour this mixture through a strainer, then stir in ¼ teaspoon salt, a few twists of the peppermill, and the thyme. Divide the custard among the ramekins, place them in a dish, and add near-boiling water to come halfway up the sides. Bake until the custards are well set except for a small circle in the center, about 20 to 25 mintes. Remove and let stand for 10 minutes. Serve them in the ramekins or carefully run a knife around the edge and turn them out onto individual plates. Surround with a salad if this your main dish, or Roasted Potatoes and Root Vegetables, page 412.

FOR years one of my favorite foods was a warm goat cheese tart, but now I find I prefer the silky custard baked in a ramekin, turned out and served with a salad (watercress, for example), instead of in a buttery crust. Yes, you can use milk, but the cream gives these flans an ethereal silken texture. If you wish, use a 9- or 10-inch tart pan lined with Tart Pastry and partially baked.

MAKES SIX ½-CUP FLANS

Savory Cheese Custards

ACCOMPANY *these tender custards with crackers or toast and a tossed green salad with plenty of chopped vegetables.*

SERVES 4

3 eggs

1 1/2 cups milk

Salt and white pepper

1/2 cup grated Fontina

1/3 cup freshly grated Parmesan

2 pinches cayenne

2 teaspoons snipped chives

Preheat oven to 350°F. Lightly butter four 1-cup ramekins or custard cups. Beat the eggs with the milk, 3/4 teaspoon of salt, and a little pepper. Strain into a bowl, then stir in the remaining ingredients, except the chives. Pour into the ramekins and sprinkle the chives over each one. Bake the ramekins in a water bath until golden on top and set, except for a dime-sized quivery center, about 20 minutes. Remove, let stand 5 minutes and then serve.

Cheddar Custards Replace the Fontina with a sharp, aged Cheddar and dust the unbaked custards with paprika.

Vegetable Custard

THOSE *who partake of chawan-mushi in Japanese restaurants won't find the notion of a savory custard strange. This is a comforting, easy supper dish that can be put together with leftover vegetables in about a minute.*

SERVES 4 TO 6

1 1/2 cups milk

3 whole eggs or 4 egg whites

Salt and freshly milled white pepper

Pinch grated nutmeg

2 cups chopped cooked vegetables, such as spinach or chard, broccoli, cauliflower, shredded zucchini or corn

1/2 cup grated cheese, such as Cheddar, Gouda, or Swiss

2 tablespoons freshly grated Parmesan

Preheat the oven to 350°F. Lightly butter a 1 quart soufflé dish or six 1-cup ramekins.

Whisk the milk and eggs until smooth, then add the rest of the ingredients. Pour the batter into the prepared dish and set it in a pan with near-boiling water to come halfway up the sides. Bake until the custard is set and a knife inserted comes out clean, 40 to 50 minutes for a single large custard, 25 minutes for individual ones. Let cool for 5 minutes before serving.

Corn Custard with Sichuan Pepper Salt

3 eggs

2 tablespoons flour

1 cup milk or light cream

Salt

3 cups fresh corn kernels, from about
   5 ears corn

4 scallions, thinly sliced

2 tablespoons chives, sliced into rounds

Sichuan Pepper Salt, page 76

SICHUAN pepper adds an intriguing twist to a traditional Shaker dish, but if you don't have it, simply use white pepper, which also has a floral quality.

SERVES 4

Preheat the oven to 325°F. Lightly butter a 6-cup casserole or four 1-cup ramekins.

Whisk together the eggs, flour, milk, and ½ teaspoon salt, then stir in corn, scallions, and chives. Pour the batter into the prepared dish, set it in a pan, and add enough boiling water to come at least halfway up the sides. Cover loosely with aluminum foil and bake until firm when shaken gently or until a knife inserted in the center comes out clean, about 1½ hours, an hour for individual custards. Remove the foil during the last 20 minutes of cooking. Serve warm with the pepper salt sprinkled over the top.

Zucchini Timbales with Red Pepper Sauce

1½ pounds zucchini, coarsely grated

Salt and freshly milled pepper

2 tablespoons olive oil

1 small onion, finely diced

2 garlic cloves, minced

3 tablespoons chopped parsley

1 tablespoon chopped marjoram

1 teaspoon chopped mint

3 eggs

1 cup milk, preferably whole

⅓ cup freshly grated Parmesan

Red Pepper Sauce, page 71

MAKE the pepper sauce while the timbales are cooking—or, if you prefer, use one of the fresh tomato sauces or the Sorrel Sauce.

SERVES 6

Preheat the oven to 350°F. Lightly butter six 1-cup ramekins. Toss the zucchini with 1 teaspoon salt, set it in a colander for 30 minutes, then squeeze out the excess moisture.

Warm the olive oil in a skillet and add the onion. Cook over medium heat for 2 minutes, then add the zucchini and continue cooking, stirring frequently, until the moisture has cooked away, about 20 minutes. Add the garlic and herbs and season with salt and pepper to taste. Beat the eggs and milk, then stir in the zucchini mixture and the cheese. Divide among the ramekins, set in a pan, and add hot water to come at least an inch up the sides. Bake until the custards are set and lightly browned on top, about 45 minutes. Let cool for 5 minutes, then run a spatula around the edge and turn them out onto your hand, then onto serving plates. Serve with the sauce and garnish with a generous smattering of herbs.

Winter Squash Flans with Greens and Red Wine–Shallot Sauce

THIS *fall dish is inspired by restaurateur Kathy Cary of Lilly/La Pêche in Louisville. She served this dish on a night we cooked together (with two other women chefs) as a first course, topped with foie gras, but it stands quite well on its own. Have the squash cooked ahead of time, and both the flans and sauce will hold or can be reheated. I would start with a soup or a salad, then the flans, and for dessert, a selection of blue cheeses with walnuts and pears.*

SERVES 6

The Squash Flans
2 cups pureed cooked winter squash
¹/₄ teaspoon ground cumin
¹/₄ teaspoon ground cinnamon
2 eggs
1 teaspoon salt
¹/₃ cup cream or milk

The Sauce
4 tablespoons butter
6 plump shallots, sliced
5 juniper berries, slightly crushed
¹/₂ teaspoon peppercorns, crushed
1¹/₂ cups Merlot or Zinfandel
Few drops balsamic vinegar

The Greens
1 tablespoon butter
1 tablespoon vegetable oil
6 cups chopped greens—chard, baby kale, spinach—washed and chopped
Salt

Preheat the oven to 375°F. Lightly butter six 1-cup ramekins.

Combine the flan ingredients, divide them among the ramekins, and set in a baking pan. Pour boiling water halfway up the sides of the ramekins and bake until the custards are set and pulling away from the sides a bit, 30 to 40 minutes. Remove them from the oven, let rest for 5 minutes, then slide a knife around the edges. If you're not serving right away, leave them in the pan with the water and a piece of foil over the top to keep them warm. They'll hold their heat for about 30 minutes.

Meanwhile, make the sauce. Melt half the butter in a medium skillet and add the shallots and spices. Cook over medium heat until the shallots are golden, about 6 to 8 minutes, then add the wine. Simmer until it's reduced by about half, then whisk in the remaining butter and the vinegar.

Heat the butter and oil in a wide skillet, add the greens, and sauté over high heat until wilted and tender, 4 to 6 minutes. Season with salt. If the sauce is cold, warm it, while whisking, over low heat.

Turn the warm custards out onto individual plates. Place the greens around the custards, then spoon the sauce over and around the greens.

The Soy Pantry

THE COW OF THE ORIENT, PROVIDING MANY FORMS OF NOURISHING HIGH-PROTEIN FOODS, JUST AS CATTLE DO. IN ASIA, SOYBEANS ARE ENJOYED NOT AS BEANS PER SE BUT IN ALTERED FORMS, WHICH ARE MORE EASILY digested. When ground with water, cooked, then strained, soybeans yield a milky liquid called *soy milk*. With the addition of coagulants and heat, soy milk can be turned into tofu, which itself comes in many forms. The quest in America for dairy substitutes has spawned an industry that has succeeded in converting soy milk into yogurt, sour cream, ice cream, and cheese. Tempeh, a high-protein fermented Indonesian soy food, has a dense, meaty quality. It can be used to simulate strips of bacon and other such foods or prepared more simply. Fermentation of soybeans creates miso, a flavor paste that forms the base of many soups, and the more familiar seasoning, soy sauce. All in all, the soybean has a huge sphere of culinary influence in Asia, which is now being explored and pushed to new horizons in America. Anyone who wants a reliable nonmeat protein source will be naturally interested in the many forms of the soybean.

Many soy products, including tofu, have gotten a bad rap, not always unjustifiably. Some soy foods, like TVP (textured vegetable protein), a sawdustlike by-product used to replace meat, lie near the bottom of my culinary list. But many soy foods are fine, high-quality foods.

In my experience, soy succeeds best when it's prepared in traditional ways. Most people enjoy a bowl of miso soup, a tofu stir-fry, or a crispy tempeh dish without a second thought when eating in Japanese, Chinese, and Thai restaurants. It's when soy foods are converted into Western forms, like soy cheese, tofu "dogs," or a miso-based barbecue sauce, that all but diehard enthusiasts tend to shy away. Often it's simply because these foods don't taste like the food they're supposed to mimic. I like tofu, but not in my lasagne. The recipes I tend to enjoy best are, for the most part, those that come out of the host cultures of Asia, and these are the recipes that I've chosen to feature, along with some "Western" interpretations that taste good to me and that I think you will like too.

Soy Milk

THIS *milk substitute is used by people who are lactose intolerant or by anyone who wants an alternative to cow's milk. When my recipes call for milk, soy milk is included in the spectrum of offerings, along with skim, whole, 1 percent, etc. Soy milk behaves like cow's milk in cooking and baking; you can even sour it by adding a tablespoon of vinegar to make a substitute for buttermilk.*

Though virtually lacking in calcium and higher in fat content than skim milk, soy milk *is* higher in protein. Brands differ in taste and color, but overall the quality has improved greatly in recent years. Today there are many brands that I find quite acceptable for pouring over cereal, for making into smoothies, and for using in baking. Soy milk is not difficult to make from scratch, but it is somewhat tedious. Fortunately soy milk is available virtually everywhere now, except for truly isolated areas. Antiseptically packaged, it keeps, unrefrigerated, on the pantry shelf for months, until opened.

MORE RECIPES INCLUDING TOFU, SOY MILK, AND MISO

STEWS, SOUPS, AND CASSEROLES
Winter Vegetable Stew with Jerusalem Artichokes
Mushrooms with Paprika and Sour Cream
Goat Cheese Enchiladas with Red Mole
Miso soups
Thai Tofu and Winter Squash Stew
Mushrooms and Tofu in Hoisin Sauce

SAUCES
Sesame Sauce with Tofu
Peanut-Tofu Sauce
Green Goddess Herb Dressing, dairy-free version
Tofu "Mayonnaise"
Tofu Garlic "Mayonnaise"

Nondairy Béchamel Sauce

PASTA AND NOODLES
Soba in Broth with Spinach, Purple Dulse,
    and Silken Tofu
Udon with Stir-Fry and Five-Spice Tofu
Spring Rolls with Napa Cabbage and Tofu

OTHER
Smoothies
Scrambled Tofu
Tofu Salad Spread
TLT—Tempeh, Lettuce, and Tomato Sandwich
Tempeh on Rye Sandwich

Tofu

A GOOD *source of protein and satisfying to eat, tofu can stand in for meat and to some extent can replace dairy products and eggs. Serious tofu enthusiasts use it to replace everything from ricotta to ground beef. Personally, I find it annoying to see bland tofu masquerading as pungent feta cheese, but in some instances—the enchilada filling or the Sesame Sauce with Tofu—its presence goes completely unnoticed.*

Tofu is also good on its own. Silken tofu has a remarkably soothing, custard-like texture, while Chinese-style tofu offers chewy satisfaction that is often missed in vegetarian food. Tofu is also incredibly fast and eay to prepare. It's something like the vegetarian equivalent of the chicken breast—amenable and ready to go, a blank canvas for many wonderful pungent Asian sauces and some Western ones as well. If you think you don't like tofu, remember that you've probably enjoyed it many times in Asian restaurants.

Tofu is made when soy milk is heated and stirred with coagulants. It solidifies into curds, which are pressed together to make blocks of tofu. Depending on the coagulant and the screening method, tofu can be very firm or have the silky texture of a flan.

Since tofu is so easy to buy today, I am not giving a recipe for how to make it from scratch. The process is similar to making cheese, and like homemade cheeses, homemade tofu is usually more subtle and delicious than store-bought. If you want to try making tofu, see Bill Shurtleff's tofu guide *par excellence, The Book of Tofu* (Ballantine Books, 1975).

Types of Tofu

In addition to these commonly seen forms of tofu, there are countless other more esoteric forms to be found in Asian markets—tofu skins, freeze-dried tofu that resembles sponges, fermented tofu, and so forth, for which you'll need a more complete guide.

CHINESE-STYLE FIRM TOFU: Dense, firm, somewhat coarse-looking but smooth when cooked, this tofu comes packed in water in sealed plastic cartons. The meatiest type of tofu, it can withstand long marination, frying, and grilling. This is the kind to use on brochettes or to freeze. Chinese-style tofu usually comes in 1-pound cartons. Sometimes the piece is solid; sometimes it's sliced into slabs.

SILKEN TOFU: Flawlessly smooth, this silky-textured tofu (both soft and firm) is more fragile and tender than the Chinese style. It's best for miso soups, tofu salads, pureeing, mock mayonnaise, egg substitutes, and so forth. But it can be baked, sautéed, or broiled if handled carefully. It comes in antiseptically sealed boxes that keep indefinitely at room temperature. Once opened, silken tofu should be refrigerated and used within a few days.

MARINATED BAKED TOFU: At natural food stores and Asian markets you can find different kinds of marinated baked tofu. Made from Chinese-style tofu, they are very firm and are seasoned with five-spice powder; peanut and sesame seeds; barbecue sauce; and so forth. All have a meaty, chewy texture, and their flavor is improved if they're sautéed first in a little peanut or sesame oil. They make an excellent addition to stir-fries and Asian pasta dishes, like dumplings and spring rolls.

FROZEN TOFU: Japanese freeze-dried tofu has a rather pronounced flavor, and its spongy texture makes it difficult to fall in love with. However, freezing your own tofu results in a product that's easier to use, especially for those who want to use tofu to replace meat. Its network of holes draws seasonings and marinades into it, and its toughness allows for good texture, yet its flavor remains rather neutral. Just crumble it up and treat it the way a recipe featuring ground meat would ask, only plan to increase the seasonings. Frozen tofu shouldn't be deep-fried (it absorbs too much oil) or used in any of the pureed forms (it's too tough).

To freeze tofu, cut it into eight 1-inch slabs if it's a solid block, then drain it briefly, put it in a plastic bag and freeze. To use, let it thaw, then squeeze out the moisture.

TOFU BURGERS AND DOGS: Tofu and other soy products are also fashioned into those symbols of casual, stress-free eating, burgers and dogs. This is a boon, especially for vegetarian children who want to eat the same things their peers do. Fortunately, you needn't struggle to make them. Mimicking meat is hard work, but others, gratefully, have done it for you.

Buying and Storing

Freshness is as essential with tofu as it is with milk. Always check the dates and keep it refrigerated—the Japanese tofu too once it's opened. Chinese tofu keeps best if covered with water and changed daily. Tofu should smell pleasantly sweet, mild, and faintly nutty. Once it begins to take on a sour smell, which you will easily be able to detect after 4 days or so, it's not as good to eat. You will find the very freshest tofu in Chinese markets, floating in large plastic tubs, where each batch is usually sold out every day.

Draining

Getting rid of the water in tofu makes room for a marinade to penetrate or allows the tofu to be fried without sputtering. A big fuss is often made about this step. However, effective draining can be as quick as a cursory blotting. Unless you're deep-frying, this step shouldn't deter you from cooking tofu.

Just put a few paper towels on a cutting board, cut the tofu into slabs, and place them on the towels. Usually I simply blot the top surface with more towels. If I'm planning to fry it, I cover the tofu with a towel, put a weight like a can of tomatoes on it, and tilt the board toward the sink to drain for 15 minutes or so. Sturdy Chinese-style firm tofu can take this handling; silken tofu, which is more fragile, should be treated the first way.

Firming and Precooking

Many recipes call for shallow- or deep-frying tofu in oil to give it a chewy texture and an attractive color. Once fried, it can be marinated and then broiled, used in stir-fries, or added to stews. Another way to firm up tofu is to drop cubes into a pot of simmering water for about 5 minutes. In both cases heat makes the proteins firm so that cubes of tofu won't fall apart when cooked further.

Marinating Tofu and Tempeh

Both tofu and tempeh benefit by a turn in a marinade before being cooked. Tempeh absorbs much better than tofu, becoming flavor saturated in about 20 minutes. With tofu only the outside is really affected by the marinade. Tempeh should be steamed for 15 to 20 minutes, then put in a shallow dish, like a pie plate, with the marinade. For tofu, drain it well, or its moisture will dilute the marinade. Slice and cover with the marinade. Tofu can rest, refrigerated, for several days in its marinade.

AMOUNTS: All recipes make enough for a 1-pound block of Chinese-style tofu, two 10-ounce packages of silken tofu, or two 8-ounce pieces of tempeh.

Hot Mustard Marinade

2 teaspoons minced garlic

2 teaspoons grated onion

3 tablespoons hot mustard

½ teaspoon cayenne

3 tablespoons roasted peanut oil

3 tablespoons balsamic vinegar or
Chinese black rice vinegar

1½ tablespoons unsulfured molasses

*HOT, spicy, and a little
sweet. The molasses
makes a rich caramel
glaze, especially on
tempeh.*

MAKES ABOUT ¾ CUP

Combine the ingredients, then brush over sliced, drained tofu or steamed tempeh. Both
can be sautéed, broiled, or baked, and the marinade used as a sauce.

Sesame-Ginger Marinade

2 large garlic cloves, minced or put
through a press

4 teaspoons finely chopped ginger

½ teaspoon red pepper flakes

1 tablespoon dark sesame oil

2 tablespoons sesame oil

4 teaspoons brown sugar

3 tablespoons soy sauce

*USE this as a marinade
for silken-firm or
Chinese-style tofu.*

MAKES ABOUT ½ CUP

Combine the ingredients in a bowl, then pour over drained, sliced tofu or steamed tempeh. Gently push the pieces around so that all are covered. Refrigerate until ready to use.
Grill or broil, using the extra marinade as a sauce.

Thai Coconut Marinade and Sauce

1 tablespoon finely chopped ginger

5 garlic cloves

½ cup chopped cilantro

½ cup canned unsweetened coconut
milk

1½ tablespoons soy sauce or
1 tablespoon mushroom soy

2 tablespoons roasted peanut oil

2 tablespoons brown sugar

1 to 2 teaspoons Thai green curry paste
or 2 serrano chiles, chopped

2 shallots or 1 bunch scallions,
including an inch of the greens,
finely diced

MAKES ABOUT ¾ CUP

Puree or pound everything but the shallots into a paste. Add the shallots. Brush half over
steamed tempeh or drained tofu. Marinate for 20 minutes for tempeh, an hour or more
for tofu. Grill or broil and serve the remaining marinade as a sauce.

Hoisin Marinade

HOISIN sauce can be found at most supermarkets and Asian groceries. Use the marinated tofu with Chinese noodles or in stir-fries.

MAKES ABOUT ³/₄ CUP

¹/₄ cup hoisin sauce

¹/₄ cup rice wine (mirin)

2¹/₂ tablespoons soy sauce

1¹/₂ tablespoons brown sugar

1¹/₂ tablespoons ketchup

3 garlic cloves, finely minced or pounded until smooth

Combine the ingredients in a small bowl. Spread over tofu or steamed tempeh and marinate for several hours or overnight.

Golden Tofu

GOLDEN, meaty, and chewy, this is one of the easiest ways to prepare tofu. Use it in stir-fries, serve it with sea salt, soy sauce, or one of the sauces listed in the preceding recipe.

SERVES 2 TO 4

1 1-pound package Chinese-style firm tofu, cut into slabs about ³/₄ inch thick

2 tablespoons peanut oil

Salt

Drain, then blot the tofu with paper towels. Cut it into ³/₄-inch cubes. Heat the oil in a medium nonstick skillet over fairly high heat. Add the tofu and fry until golden. It takes several minutes to color, so let it cook undisturbed while you do something else, then come back and turn the pieces. While they should color, don't let them get dry and hard. Drain briefly on paper towels, then slide onto a heated serving dish and salt lightly.

Golden Tofu with Quick Peanut Sauce Always a popular dish in Thai restaurants, this is unthinkably easy to make, including the sauce. Fry the tofu as described. If it's for an appetizer, cut it into cubes; if it's your main dish, cut it into slabs. While it's cooking, make the Quick Peanut Sauce on page 69. Serve the tofu with the sauce spooned over the top and garnish, if you wish, with thinly sliced scallions, cilantro sprigs, or toasted sesame seeds.

Gently Simmered Tofu If you wish to cook tofu with no oil, simply cut it into cubes without bothering to drain it, then lower it into a pot of lightly salted simmering water or the Stock for Stir-Fries, page 262. Simmer gently for 5 minutes. Remove with a slotted spoon, drain briefly on paper towels, then serve, warm or chilled with Gomashio, page 76, Toasted Nori with Sesame Seeds, page 76, or tamari. Or arrange the tofu in individual dishes and serve with any of the following sauces spooned over the top: Hoisin Sauce with Chili Paste and Tangerine Zest, page 73, Peanut-Soy Sauce with Ginger and Scallions, page 73, Sesame-Soy Sauce, page 73, or Sesame-Ginger Marinade, page 597.

Caramelized Golden Tofu

Golden Tofu, page 598
2 tablespoons soy sauce

3½ tablespoons light brown sugar

While the Golden Tofu is cooking, mix the soy sauce and sugar in a small bowl. Heat a wok or heavy skillet, add a tablespoon of the oil used to fry the tofu or fresh peanut oil, and swirl it around the wok. When hot, add the soy mixture, reduce the heat to medium, and add the tofu. Toss well, then simmer for 2 minutes. Add 3 tablespoons water and cook until the sauce coats the tofu with a syrupy glaze. Turn off the heat. Let the tofu cool in the syrup for 10 minutes, then transfer to a serving dish.

INSPIRED by chef Barbara Tropp, this process transforms the Golden Tofu into richly lacquered pieces that are delicious in stir-fries and Chinese noodles. Cut it into triangles about ½ inch thick, as Barbara does, and serve with slivered scallions and toasted sesame seeds.

MAKES ABOUT 1½ CUPS

Sweet and Sour Tofu

Golden Tofu, page 598, or Gently
  Simmered Tofu, page 598
1 bunch scallions, including the firm
  greens
¼ cup diced canned tomatoes
2 tablespoons Chinese black rice vinegar
  or balsamic vinegar
2 tablespoons light brown sugar
2 serrano chiles, minced

Salt
2 teaspoons dark sesame or roasted
  peanut oil
1 tablespoon chopped garlic
2 teaspoons chopped ginger
¾ cup Stock for Stir-Fries, page 262,
  or water
1½ tablespoons cornstarch dissolved in
  ½ cup water

KIDS especially like sweet and sour foods. Made with the Golden Tofu, this dish is both pretty and easy to make.

SERVES 4

While the tofu is cooking, slice two of the scallions diagonally, set them aside for a garnish, and chop the rest into ½-inch pieces. Combine the tomatoes, vinegar, sugar, chiles, and ½ teaspoon salt in a bowl.

Heat the wok, then add the oil and swirl it around the sides. Add the garlic and ginger, and stir-fry for 1 minute. Add the tomato mixture, chopped scallions, and stock. Simmer for about 4 minutes, then add the tofu and cornstarch mixture. Cook until the sauce is thickened and the tofu is heated through, several minutes more. Garnish with the reserved scallions and serve.

Tofu in Curry-Coconut Sauce

FAST and resoundingly flavorful, this Vietnamese dish traditionally calls for frying the tofu until it's firm and golden—a process that adds texture and luster, but you can simmer it instead.

SERVES 2 TO 3

1 tablespoon roasted peanut oil

1 small onion, thinly sliced

1 small green or red bell pepper, thinly sliced

2 serrano chiles, minced

1 to 2 teaspoons Thai curry paste or curry powder

1/2 cup canned unsweetened coconut milk

1/2 cup Stock for Stir-Fries, page 262, or water

Salt

Golden Tofu, page 598, or Gently Simmered Tofu, page 598

1/3 cup cilantro leaves, coarsely chopped

3 tablespoons roasted chopped peanuts

Heat a wok, add the peanut oil, and, when it's hot, add the onion, pepper, and chiles and stir-fry for 1 minute. Stir in the curry paste, then add the coconut milk, stock, 1/2 teaspoon salt, and the tofu. Simmer for 2 minutes more or until the tofu is heated through. Serve over rice or noodles garnished with the cilantro and peanuts.

Tofu in Coconut Sauce with Ginger and Lemongrass

THIS spicy-sweet Vietnamese sauce is delicious with tofu and with cubes of golden fried tempeh. Although complex-tasting, its cooking time is about 20 minutes. Serve over jasmine rice or rice noodles.

SERVES 4

1 1-pound package Chinese-style firm tofu, drained

3 tablespoons peanut oil

8 shallots, thinly sliced, or 1 small white onion

Salt and freshly milled white pepper

1 bunch cilantro, the leaves plus a little of the stems

1 tablespoon finely diced fresh ginger

2 tablespoons minced lemongrass, from the middle of the stalk, or grated zest of 1 lemon

1 jalapeño chile, seeded and diced

1 15-ounce can unsweetened coconut milk, plus water to make 2 cups

3 pieces galangal, optional

1 teaspoon soy sauce, preferably mushroom soy

Cilantro sprigs for garnish

Drain the tofu, then dice it into 1/2-inch cubes. Heat 2 tablespoons oil in a medium skillet, add the shallots, and cook over medium heat until lightly browned, about 10 minutes. Season with a few pinches salt, then add half the cilantro. Remove from the heat and set aside.

Heat a wok, add the remaining oil, and swirl it around the sides. When hot, add the ginger, lemongrass, and jalapeño. Stir-fry for about 30 seconds, add the coconut milk mixture and galangal and bring to a boil. Lower the heat, add the tofu, and simmer gently until heated through and the sauce has thickened, about 10 minutes. Add the soy, season with plenty of pepper, then add the shallots and remaining cilantro. Serve garnished with the cilantro sprigs.

Tempeh in Coconut Sauce: Cut an 8-ounce package of tempeh into 1-inch cubes or ¹⁄₂-inch strips. Steam for 10 minutes, then fry in peanut oil over medium-high heat about 5 to 7 minutes, until golden and crisp. Add to the coconut sauce when you would add the tofu.

Spicy Stir-Fried Tofu with Coconut Rice

The Rice

1³⁄₄ cups basmati rice

4 teaspoons roasted peanut oil

1 small onion, finely diced

1 tablespoon minced ginger

1 garlic clove, minced

¹⁄₄ teaspoon turmeric

Salt

1 15-ounce can coconut milk

3 leaves kaffir lime leaves or ¹⁄₂ teaspoon lime zest

The Tofu

2 10-ounce boxes silken-firm or extra-firm tofu or 1 pound Chinese-style firm tofu

1 tablespoon ground coriander

1 tablespoon ground cumin

¹⁄₂ teaspoon paprika

¹⁄₄ teaspoon cayenne

2 teaspoons sugar

2 tablespoons peanut oil

4 scallions, including half of the greens, coarsely chopped

2 tablespoons fresh lime juice

¹⁄₂ cup cilantro, chopped

THIS dish consists of two parts, fragrant coconut rice and spicy tofu.

SERVES 6

Gently wash the rice in a bowl, soak for 30 minutes, then drain. Warm the oil in a 3-quart saucepan with the onion, ginger, garlic, and turmeric. Cook over medium-low heat for 8 minutes, then add the rice and ¹⁄₂ teaspoon salt. Stir to coat the grains, then add the coconut milk, 2 cups water, and the lime leaves. Bring to a boil, turn the heat to low, cover, and cook until the rice is done, 15 to 18 minutes, stirring twice during cooking. Turn off the heat and set it aside while you prepare the tofu. It will look a little wet at first, but the liquid will be absorbed by the time you're ready.

Drain the tofu, then cut it into ¹⁄₂-inch cubes. Combine the spices, 1 teaspoon salt and the sugar in a bowl, add the tofu, and toss gently with a rubber spatula. Heat the oil in a wok or skillet, add the tofu, and stir-fry until crispy and golden, about 5 to 7 minutes. Add the scallions and cook just until they're wilted, then add the lime juice. Serve the tofu on the rice, garnished with the cilantro.

Malaysian-Inspired Tofu Curry

THIS dish is very simple to make and full of sweet and spicy flavors. Tamarind, which provides tartness, is available at many natural food stores and Indian groceries. Serve this curry over Chinese egg noodles, linguine, or rice.

SERVES 3 TO 4

1 1-pound package Chinese-style firm tofu or 2 10-ounce boxes silken-firm or extra-firm tofu

2 15-ounce cans unsweetened coconut milk, or 1 can coconut milk mixed with 1 cup water

2 teaspoons light brown sugar

Salt

1 tablespoon ground coriander

2 teaspoons curry powder

1/2 teaspoon turmeric

1/4 teaspoon cayenne

1 teaspoon taramind paste

2 large garlic cloves, minced

1 tablespoon finely chopped ginger

4 Roma tomatoes, seeded and diced

4 scallions, including the firm greens, chopped

Juice of 1 lime

Cilantro, chopped

Drain, then dice the tofu into 1/2-inch cubes. Combine the coconut milk, sugar, 1/2 teaspoon salt, spices, tamarind paste, garlic, and ginger in a medium skillet. Boil for 1 minute, then add the tofu. Lower the heat and simmer for 10 minutes. Add the tomatoes and scallions and simmer for approximately 10 minutes more. Add the lime juice and taste for salt. (I sometimes find a little mushroom soy sauce makes a good addition.) Serve garnished with chopped cilantro.

Marinated Grilled Tofu with Hoisin Sauce

KEN Hom is the inspiration for this blend of flavors. Use the Chinese-style firm tofu if you intend to grill it and give the tofu plenty of time to sit in the marinade. A day or two isn't too long, but if a half hour is all you have, don't be deterred. Accompany with a salad of finely ribboned spinach or Napa cabbage dressed with Sesame Vinaigrette with Chili Oil.

SERVES 2 TO 4

1 1-pound package Chinese-style firm tofu

1/3 cup hoisin sauce

2 teaspoons lemon thyme, chopped or regular thyme

1 teaspoon marjoram, chopped or 2 pinches dried

1/4 cup dry sherry

2 tablespoons olive oil

1 large garlic clove, crushed

1/2 teaspoon freshly milled pepper

1 tablespoon toasted black or white sesame seeds

2 scallions, including the greens, sliced into rounds

Cut the tofu into rectangles or triangles 1/2 inch thick. Set on paper towels to drain. Combine the hoisin sauce with the herbs, sherry, olive oil, garlic, and pepper. Place the drained tofu in a baking dish and score the tops, making diagonal cuts about halfway through each piece. Brush the marinade generously over the tofu, cover, and refrigerate until ready to cook.

To broil, place the tofu 4 or 5 inches under the heat and broil until the top is bubbling and the tofu is heated through, 7 to 10 minutes. For grilling, brush both sides with the marinade and grill on both sides, about 15 minutes in all. Serve with the sesame seeds and scallions over the top.

Golden Fried Bean Curd with Tomatoes

1 1-pound package Chinese-style firm tofu, drained

1 cup peanut oil for frying

4 shallots, thinly sliced

4 garlic cloves, thinly sliced

1¼ pounds ripe tomatoes, seeded and diced into ½-inch pieces

Vegetarian Nuoc Mam, recipe follows

1 tablespoon light brown sugar

½ cup Stock for Stir-Fries, page 262

1 teaspoon rice wine vinegar

2 scallions, including the greens, sliced diagonally

2 tablespoons cilantro leaves

Drain the tofu, then cut it into cubes about ¾ inch across. Heat the oil in a wok or skillet. When hot enough to sizzle a drop of water, fry the tofu in two batches until golden and firm, about 7 minutes. Carefully pour off the oil and save it to use again.

Return the wok to the heat and add 1 tablespoon peanut oil. When hot, add the shallots, stir-fry for 30 seconds, then add the garlic and stir-fry for 1 minute more. Add the tomatoes, 2 tablespoons of the sauce, and the sugar. Stir-fry for 1 minute, then lower the heat and simmer, covered, for 15 minutes. Pour in the stock, add the tofu, and cook until the tofu is heated through, about 5 minutes. Season to taste with the rice wine vinegar and additional sauce. Transfer to a bowl, garnish with the scallions and cilantro, and serve.

Vegetarian Nuoc Mam

2 garlic cloves, minced

1 or 2 serrano chiles, minced

2 tablespoons light brown sugar

2 tablespoons fresh lime juice

¼ cup rice wine vinegar

¼ cup mushroom soy sauce

Stir everything together in a small bowl.

Herb-Crusted Tofu

1 1-pound package Chinese-style tofu or 2 10-ounce boxes silken tofu

1 cup fine bread crumbs, fresh or dried

½ cup freshly grated Parmesan, Asiago, or other hard cheese

1 tablespoon chopped parsley

1 teaspoon dried basil or marjoram

½ teaspoon dried thyme

½ teaspoon dried savory

1 egg, beaten with 2 tablespoons milk

Olive oil for frying

Slice the tofu into slabs about ⅓ inch thick and set them on paper towels to drain. Meanwhile, combine the bread crumbs, cheese, and herbs in a flat dish. Dip each piece of tofu into the egg mixture, then the bread crumbs.

Film a skillet with the oil. When hot, add the tofu and fry over medium heat on both sides until golden, 10 to 12 minutes in all.

Sesame Tofu

SERVE this tofu over brown rice for a very easy weekday meal. If you haven't marinated the tofu ahead of time, you can still make the dish, and the strength of the sauce will carry it. The marinade also makes an excellent sauce for grilled eggplant and Chinese noodles.

SERVES 3 TO 4

1 1-pound package Chinese-style firm tofu or 2 10-ounce boxes silken tofu

Sesame Marinade, recipe follows

1 tablespoon dark sesame oil

1 tablespoon toasted sesame seeds

Chopped cilantro

Cut the Chinese-style tofu into slabs and blot well with paper towels. For silken tofu, blot the whole squares, then slice, making a total of eight slabs. Make the marinade and pour half into a pie plate. Add the drained tofu, then the rest of the marinade. Cover and let stand for an hour or as long as you have time for.

When ready to cook, pour off the marinade and set it aside. Heat a nonstick skillet with the oil, add the tofu, and fry until firm and browned, about 5 minutes on each side. Add the marinade to the pan and cook until bubbling and hot. Serve the tofu and the sauce over brown rice and garnish with sesame seeds and chopped cilantro.

Sesame Marinade

2 tablespoons sesame oil

1 tablespoon dark sesame oil

$1/4$ cup soy sauce

5 teaspoons balsamic or rice wine vinegar

$1 1/2$ tablespoons sugar or to taste

$1/2$ teaspoon red pepper flakes or chili oil

2 tablespoons finely chopped scallion

$1 1/2$ tablespoons chopped cilantro

Combine the ingredients in a bowl and stir until the sugar is dissolved. Taste and adjust for sweetness if needed. Depending on the type of soy sauce you've used, you may need to add more sugar for balance.

Tofu and Steamed Cabbage with Rice and Peanut Sauce

THIS dish is light and quick if the peanut sauce is already prepared. The rich Sesame Sauce or Marinade is also delicious here.

SERVES 2

1 cup brown basmati rice

1 pound Savoy or napa cabbage, quartered and cored

Salt

1 10-ounce box silken-firm or extra-firm tofu, diced into $1/2$-inch cubes

3 tablespoons chopped cilantro

Quick Peanut Sauce, page 69

1 tablespoon roasted peanuts

If using basmati rice, first soak it for 30 minutes, then drain and cook, page 539. Cut the cabbage into $1/4$-inch ribbons. If using napa cabbage, thinly slice the base as well. Set a steaming basket in a saucepan over boiling water. Lay the cabbage over the bottom, sprinkle lightly with salt, then set the tofu on top. Cover and steam until the cabbage is bright green and tender, 8 to 10 minutes. Carefully remove and arrange over the cooked rice. Garnish with the cilantro, drizzle with peanut sauce, and garnish with peanuts.

Variation with Golden Tofu: If you want a little more punch to this dish, fry the tofu as described on page 598, then season with salt or Gomashio, page 76. Serve on top of the cabbage.

Baked Tofu with Braised Peppers and Olives

The Tofu and Vegetables

1 1-pound package Chinese-style tofu, well drained

2 tablespoons olive oil

2 onions, thinly sliced

1 teaspoon chopped thyme or $\frac{1}{2}$ teaspoon dried

1 tablespoon chopped marjoram or basil

$\frac{1}{4}$ cup chopped parsley

3 bell peppers—red, yellow, and green— thinly sliced

1 cup thinly sliced mushrooms

1 garlic clove, minced

Salt and freshly milled pepper

$\frac{1}{2}$ cup dry white wine

20 Niçoise olives, halved and pitted

$\frac{1}{4}$ cup freshly grated Parmesan

The Sauce

2 tablespoons olive oil

2 tablespoons sherry vinegar or red wine vinegar

1 tablespoon tomato paste

1 teaspoon Dijon mustard

2 garlic cloves, minced

Freshly milled pepper to taste

$\frac{1}{2}$ teaspoon tamari or soy sauce

HERE tofu is smothered extravagantly with a stew of summer vegetables and herbs. For a vegan dish that has lots of flavor, omit the cheese or use soy cheese. Start with a salad, then serve the tofu with grilled polenta, rice, or spinach pasta. End with a slice of chilled ripe melon.

SERVES 4

Preheat the oven to 375°F. Cut the drained tofu into triangles or slabs about $1\frac{1}{2}$ inches wide. Set them in an ungreased pie plate and bake until they're slightly firm and liquids are released, about 20 minutes. Pour off the excess liquid if any remains.

Heat the oil in a wide skillet, add the onions, and sauté over high heat for 2 minutes. Add the herbs, peppers, mushrooms, and garlic, sauté for 2 minutes more, then lower the heat to medium and cook until the onions have softened, stirring occasionally, about 6 minutes. Season with salt and pepper. Add the wine and olives and simmer until the vegetables are coated with a syrupy sauce, about 8 minutes. Spread them in a lightly oiled casserole or gratin dish and wiggle the tofu into the vegetables.

Whisk the ingredients for the sauce together, then pour it over the vegetables and tofu. Bake, covered, until heated through, about 25 minutes. Serve with Parmesan grated over the top.

Tofu with Paprika and Sour Cream

SERVE *this stew over kasha (buckwheat groats) or wide egg noodles garnished with freshly chopped parsley and poppy seeds.*

SERVES 4 TO 6

2 blocks silken tofu

3 tablespoons butter and canola oil

2 large onions, chopped

2 celery ribs, finely diced

1 teaspoon fennel or caraway seeds, bruised

2 tablespoons sweet paprika

1 tablespoon flour

Salt and freshly milled pepper

1 green bell pepper, diced

2 teaspoons tomato paste

1 cup water or Basic Vegetable Stock, page 196

$^{1}/_{2}$ to 1 cup sour cream

Cut the tofu into cubes or strips and simmer them in water until firm, 4 to 5 minutes. Remove with a strainer and set aside.

Heat the butter in a wide skillet. Add the onions, celery, and fennel seeds and cook over medium heat until golden, about 10 minutes. Add the paprika, flour, 1 teaspoon salt, pepper, and tomato paste. Stir well, then add the water and tofu. Bring to a boil, then lower the heat, cover, and simmer for 15 minutes. Remove the lid, stir in the crème fraîche, and heat through.

Blackened Tofu

THIS *was my husband's idea, and it works. The melted butter is essential for the right flavor—as are powdered garlic and onion, ingredients I never use otherwise. Because of the extreme heat and volatility of the spices, it's best to cook blackened anything out-of-doors or under a good fan. A covered gas grill works fine. Serve with Coleslaw with Buttermilk-Horseradish Dressing.*

SERVES 4 TO 6

2 1-pound blocks Chinese-style firm tofu

Salt

1 tablespoon sweet paprika

1 teaspoon onion powder

1 teaspoon garlic powder

$^{1}/_{2}$ to 1 teaspoon cayenne to taste

$^{3}/_{4}$ teaspoon ground white pepper

$^{3}/_{4}$ teaspoon black pepper

$^{1}/_{2}$ teaspoon dried thyme

$^{1}/_{2}$ teaspoon dried oregano

6 to 8 tablespoons butter, melted

Cut the tofu into slabs about $^{1}/_{2}$ inch thick and set them on paper towels to drain for at least 30 minutes, preferably with a weight on top. They need to be very dry. Mix $2^{1}/_{2}$ teaspoons salt and the spices and herbs in a bowl. Brush each piece of tofu with melted butter, then dredge with the spice mixture, patting it firmly into the tofu. This can be done ahead of time.

Preheat the oven to 250°F and have a platter and spatula at hand. Heat a cast-iron skillet on the stove or covered gas grill until it's white-hot, about 15 minutes. Pour a teaspoon of melted butter onto each piece of tofu, then place it, butter side down, into the hot skillet and step back. Wait 2 minutes, then turn it over and repeat on the second side. Remove to a platter and keep in the oven until all are cooked.

Tempeh

A HIGH-PROTEIN *food from Indonesia, tempeh is made from cooked soybeans that are inoculated with a spore and then fermented. It looks like a firm, flat cake, mottled with small brown and gray spots. While tempeh readily accepts seasonings, it also has a pronounced taste of its own. Its texture is chewy, its flavor nutty, but it can be faintly bitter unless cooked thoroughly. Most tempeh is not precooked; it needs to be steamed for 20 minutes or simmered in a marinade; then it can be taken in a number of different directions. Its ability to absorb flavors and its texture, which allows for slicing, braising, frying, and crumbling, make tempeh quite versatile. At any stage tempeh can be cut into strips, wedges, and chunks or crumbled and used like ground meat. Many vegetarians like tempeh's ability to pass for hamburger or bacon, while others find this use unnecessary. Traditionally, tempeh isn't used as a mock meat but as a highly nutritious food with its own properties and flavors.*

TEMPEH NUTRITION: Tempeh's protein is about equal to that of meat but without the cholesterol. It's a good source of vitamin B, has little fat and plenty of fiber. A 4-ounce portion has 200 calories, 17 grams of protein, and 4 grams of fat. And 4 ounces is quite a generous portion because of its density.

TYPES OF TEMPEH: Though traditionally a soy product, tempeh can also be made from rice, millet, sesame, peanuts, and quinoa; some are even flavored with Italian herbs. The traditional all-soy tempeh holds its shape best and, to my taste, has the best flavor. Added seasonings tend to get lost; you can more effectively add your own. Tempeh can be found frozen at your natural food store in 8- or 10-ounces packages. Once defrosted, it's best used within 5 days. Cooked, it will keep for several days in the refrigerator.

PRECOOKING TEMPEH: Steaming is a way of precooking tempeh. Once steamed, it can be fried, crumbled, or added to a marinade. Cut tempeh into desired shapes or leave whole, then steam over boiling water, covered, for 20 minutes. You can also precook tempeh directly in a broth or in a thin marinade. Simmer it slowly for 15 to 20 minutes in any thin marinade, such as the Rich Sesame Sauce or Marinade, page 68.

Tempeh Simmered in Broth

1 8- or 10-ounce package tempeh

2 garlic cloves, put through a press

A few onion slices

2 bay leaves

¼ cup thin soy sauce or 2 tablespoons thin soy and mushroom soy

Optional additions: chipotle chile, red pepper flakes, thyme sprigs, sliced ginger, rosemary, dried mushrooms, tomato paste, and so forth

IF THERE'S a particular flavor you're planning to use later with the tempeh—such as oregano or ginger—tailor the broth to your needs by adding a pinch or slice.

SERVES 2

Quarter the tempeh or cut it into the shape you'll be using later. Put everything in a skillet just large enough to hold the tempeh, bring it to a boil, then cover and simmer slowly until the broth has been absorbed, about 15 minutes. Turn it over once during the cooking.

Tempeh Strips in a Smoky Molasses Marinade

THIS *tempeh has a delicious smoky-sweet flavor that's reminiscent of bacon.*

MAKES 18 TO 20 STRIPS

1 8- or 10-ounce package tempeh
Broth ingredients, from preceding recipe
4 thin slices ginger
1 clove

$^1/_4$ teaspoon pureed chipotle chile or a few drops liquid smoke
2 tablespoons molasses
1$^1/_2$ teaspoons tomato paste
1 tablespoon vegetable oil

Slice the tempeh crosswise into thin strips. Combine the remaining ingredients in a small skillet, bring them to a boil, and add the tempeh. Simmer slowly, covered, for 15 minutes, remove the lid, and continue cooking until all the liquid has been absorbed. At this point the tempeh will begin to fry in the oil. Cook until it's glazed and browned, about 5 minutes.

Barbecued Tempeh

SERVES 2 TO 4

1 8- or 10-ounce package tempeh, cut into strips $^1/_2$ inch thick

1 cup Golden Mustard Barbecue Sauce, page 74, or favorite commercial sauce

Steam or simmer the tempeh in broth for 20 minutes, then put it in a dish and cover with barbecue sauce. Turn it over so both sides are coated, then cover and refrigerate until ready to eat or overnight. Grill or broil for about 5 minutes on each side.

Fried Tempeh

FRIED *tempeh makes a good snack with a little sea salt sprinkled over the top and is excellent served with peanut sauce.*

SERVES 2 TO 4

1 8- or 10-ounce package tempeh, steamed for 20 minutes

$^3/_4$ cup peanut or canola oil

Cut the steamed tempeh into triangles, thin slices, nuggets, or whatever shape works for your dish. Heat the oil in an 8-inch skillet until it sizzles a bread crumb, then add the tempeh a few pieces at a time. When golden, remove to a paper towel to drain.

Marinated and Fried Tempeh, Indonesian Style

1 8- or 10-ounce package tempeh

1½ teaspoons tamarind paste

½ onion, thinly sliced

3 slices ginger

1 teaspoon ground coriander

1 bay leaf

⅛ teaspoon red pepper flakes

1 teaspoon brown sugar

2 pieces galangal, optional

¾ cup peanut oil

BOTH marinating and frying are used in this traditional dish.

SERVES 2 TO 4

Cut the tempeh into slices about ½ inch thick or a little less. Combine 1½ cups water with the remaining ingredients except the oil and bring to a boil. Add the tempeh, then lower the heat and simmer, covered, for 30 minutes or until all the liquid is absorbed. Heat the oil in a medium skillet. When hot enough to sizzle a bread crumb, add the tempeh and fry in batches over high heat until golden and crisp, about 3 to 5 minutes. Drain briefly on paper towels, then serve with sea salt, a chutney, one of the peanut sauces, or Western style Golden Mustard Barbecue Sauce.

Baked Tempeh or Tofu with Mustard-Honey Marinade

2 8- or 10-ounce packages tempeh or
   1 1-pound package Chinese-style
   firm tofu

3 tablespoons mild honey

1 tablespoon molasses

1 tablespoon peanut oil

1 teaspoon soy sauce

3½ tablespoons mustard

2 teaspoons curry powder

Salt and freshly milled pepper

THE marinade can also serve as a sauce to accompany rice or noodles.

SERVES 4

If using tempeh, cut it into ½-inch slabs and steam for 10 minutes. If using tofu, cut it into cubes or slabs and set on paper towels to drain while you mix the remaining ingredients for the marinade in a bowl. Place the tempeh or tofu in a pie plate and brush the marinade over it. Let stand for at least 20 minutes or as long as overnight. Preheat the oven to 400°F. Bake until sizzling and hot, about 20 minutes, basting midway through the cooking. Serve with any extra marinade on the side.

Breakfast Anytime

IF YOU WANT TO SEE DIVERSITY IN OUR POPULATION, JUST THINK ABOUT THE AMERICAN BREAKFAST FOR A MOMENT. YES, THERE'S AN UNDERLYING BELIEF THAT THIS IS NOT THE MEAL TO SKIP BECAUSE A GOOD BREAKFAST GIVES YOU WHAT YOU need for a day of clear thinking. But when it comes to eating breakfast, whole family units cease to cohere. Each member heads off in a different direction. Some eat on the run; others insist on a real meal; some—perhaps many or most—just skip it and grab something later.

Breakfast is a sensitive meal. Not everyone is ready to face food in the morning. A piece of toast, preferably around 10 o'clock, may well be enough. My husband has learned not to ask if he can fix me anything, although sometimes it turns out that I'm frying an egg for myself only moments after he's made an omelet. No one's offended. When it comes to breakfast, we go our own ways, occasionally colliding and sitting down together.

Largely it's hectic morning schedules that make breakfast such a hit-or-miss affair. Yet breakfast is an important meal, especially for children, and an enjoyable one to share. The opportunity for sharing doesn't often come until the weekend, and that's when breakfast turns into that strange hybrid called *brunch,* a meal that includes not only breakfast foods but dishes you might well serve for dinner or dessert. Recipes that are suitable for brunch are scattered throughout the book, but a list of them follows.

Conversely, many of the foods we associate with the morning hour are great for dinner. How many of us have turned to a bowl of cereal when we've come home late at night, hungry but tired? Who doesn't enjoy an omelet for lunch or pancakes and fried eggs for supper? There's a calming, easy feeling about eating breakfast for dinner, as if it doesn't really count somehow. It's backward and fun, like taking a holiday or leaving work early.

Certainly eggs are one of our traditional breakfast foods, but they're such a quick and easy food to cook for other meals that they have their own chapter. Look to the "Eggs and Cheese" Chapter for most egg recipes, including those breakfast basics like scrambled and fried eggs.

One of the obstacles to eating wholesome breakfasts, of course, is time. But a little planning and some ingenious uses of common household appliances may help make eating breakfast possible again—and enjoyable.

Brunch

Brunch allows for a variety of foods that don't bear relationship to each other at other meals. Brunch breaks the rules, like eating pancakes for dinner. Without compunction you can serve a coffee cake, a fruit compote, an egg dish, a salad, and a dessert, thus allowing for both sweet and savory inclinations or an indifferent mixing of the two. Here are some dishes from other chapters that are good for brunch. The menu arrangements I leave to your own whims and fancies.

SWEETS (IN ADDITION TO COFFEE CAKES, PANCAKES, AND MUFFINS)
Cinnamon–Brown Sugar Rolls (Sticky Buns) • Rosemary-Lemon Bread • Little Lemon Biscuits Angel Biscuits • Fruit compotes • Crisps, cobblers, and fruit galettes • Nutmeg Pie • Brown Sugar-Yogurt Tart in a Nut Crust • Simple fruit desserts • Rhubarb Tart with Orange Custard • Stovetop Rice Pudding • Fresh Cream Cheese served with fruits.

SAVORIES
Fideos, A Mexican Dry Soup • Avocado Toasts • Cheese or vegetable soufflés, • Goat Cheese Flans Old-Fashioned Spoon Bread with Condiments • Strata and other bread puddings • Frittatas Roulades • Savory galettes • Olives • Sliced tomatoes and cucumbers • Vegetable salads • Watercress with Slivered Endive • Lacy Corn Cakes with Pepper Relish

Breakfast Fruits

FOR *a weekday meal breakfast fruit, if it exists at all, probably consists of a banana or an apple grabbed on the run. Certainly when time allows, breakfast fruits can be prepared somewhat more elaborately, but a good piece of fruit needs little fiddling. Tropical resorts, for example, do little more for their breakfast fruit than to thinly slice and then skillfully fan a papaya or pineapple and accompany it with wedges of lime. Compotes are certainly attractive for brunches or breakfasts when one has more time for cooking. Once made, they keep for many days in the refrigerator to be drawn from throughout the week. Virtually all of the simple fruit desserts and compotes are just as good for breakfast or for more elaborate brunches.*

APPLESAUCE: A perennial favorite, cold or warm, applesauce is a soothing breakfast fruit to enjoy alone, with cottage cheese, yogurt, and a dash of nutmeg or cinnamon. Applesauce couldn't be easier to make, page 681.

SAUTÉED APPLES OR PEARS: Both a simple dessert and a morning fruit, these can be made in moments and are delicious by themselves or served over oatmeal. See page 680.

BERRIES: Sprinkle berries lightly with brown sugar and serve them with sour cream, Yogurt Cheese, page 47, or yogurt, or simply have them available to add to the cereal bowl.

GRAPEFRUIT: Grapefruit is a winter fruit, and the old-fashioned way of preparing it is still good today. Cut it in half across the equator, then, using a grapefruit knife, cut along each section. Serve like this or sprinkle with brown sugar and place under the broiler until the sugar is melted.

MANGOES: Make a "porcupine mango." Slice a mango lengthwise about 1/3 of the way in. You'll have 2 pieces plus the center, which contains the seed. (This piece is for you.) Score the flesh of the 2 remaining pieces in a crisscross fashion, cutting down to the skin but not through it. Pull the ends toward you, forcing the center out to reveal little cubes of mango ready to eat. Serve with wedges of lime or lime juice squeezed over the fruit. Or peel then slice the mangoes into a bowl of blackberries, raspberries, or Rhubarb, Strawberry, and Mango Compote, page 685.

MELONS: An unchallenging breakfast fruit in every respect. Rather than serving entire half melons, slice a melon into whatever size wedge seems appropriate, then scoop out the seeds. Slide a knife just between the fruit and the rind to loosen it, then slice the melon crosswise into bite-size pieces. If it's a very wide piece, slice it lengthwise down the center as well. Serve with a wedge of lemon or lime or salt and pepper. Or, slice the melon into very thin slices and fan them on a platter. Serve plain or intersperse berries and lime or lemon wedges.

PAPAYA: Slice a papaya in half and remove the seeds. Squeeze lime juice over the fruit or serve with lime wedges. The seeds are crunchy and quite edible. Try rinsing a few and using them to garnish the fruit. Or fill the papaya center with raspberries and squeeze passion fruit over them.

DRIED FRUITS AND NUTS

A plateful of dried fruits—figs, dates, prunes, apples, pears—and nuts, cracked or in their shells, couldn't be easier to assemble for breakfast or to take to work.

Poached Prunes with Lemon

POACHED dried fruits are good at any meal in my opinion. Serve them plain or with yogurt, a spoonful of mascarpone, or heavy cream.

SERVES 4 TO 6

1 lemon or small orange

1 12-ounce package dried prunes

1 3-inch cinnamon stick

Remove several long bands of zest from the lemon, then slice them into thin strips. Combine everything in a saucepan and add water to cover. Bring to a boil, then lower the heat and simmer gently until the prunes are tender and plump, about 25 minutes. Serve warm or cold with their juices.

Poached Gingered Apricots In place of prunes, cook dried apricots as described, adding several slices of fresh ginger to the pot and omitting the cinnamon.

Stewed Rhubarb

COLD stewed rhubarb with a smidgen of cream or yogurt makes bracing breakfast fruit.

SERVES 4 TO 6

1 1/2 pounds rhubarb

1/2 cup sugar or honey or to taste

3 cloves

Grated zest and juice of 1 orange or lemon or 2 tangerines

Chop the rhubarb into short pieces and put in a heavy pan with the sugar, cloves, zest, and juice. Cook over low heat until the rhubarb has broken down, about 10 minutes. Taste and sweeten if needed.

Variations: Add whole or halved strawberries, sections of blood orange or tangerine, sliced kumquat, or sliced mango to the fruit once it's cooked. Season the compote with a few drops of orange oil or a few teaspoons, to taste, of orange flower water.

Winter Breakfast Compote

FRUIT syrups, such as passion fruit—available in specialty stores—add exotic flavors as well as a little extra sweetness to this breakfast compote.

SERVES 4 TO 6

2 grapefruits, 1 white and 1 red

2 navel oranges

2 large tangerines

2 small red bananas or 1 yellow banana

2 kiwi fruit

1/2 cup pomegranate seeds, optional

1/2 cup passion fruit or pomegranate syrup, or 1/4 cup warmed orange honey

1/2 cup shredded coconut

Peel and section the citrus fruits and place them in a serving dish. Squeeze the pulp over them to get the juice. Slice the bananas diagonally, peel and slice the kiwifruit, and tuck them among the citrus sections; cover with the pomegranate seeds. Drizzle the syrup over the fruit and chill until ready to serve. Toast the coconut in a dry pan until lightly browned, then remove to a plate to cool. Serve the compote with the coconut dusted over the top.

Morning Beverages

ASIDE from coffee, tea, and juice, there are a number of delicious drinks to enjoy for breakfast and brunch—or even later in the day, when the addition of club soda or mineral water turns them into sparkling coolers.

While beverages are usually accompaniments to food, they also make a soothing breakfast for many. A fruit smoothie, for example, makes a perfectly good start to the day. If you're looking for ways to eat more soy foods, soy milk fits right into a smoothie, as do protein powders or other such boosters. If you don't eat dairy, rice milk, coconut milk, and almond milk as well as soy milk can be used in place of cow's milk. On the other hand, yogurt and buttermilk make thick, pleasantly tart, creamy-textured smoothies. Almost any fruit can be used, not only fresh, ripe fruits but unsweetened frozen berries, peaches, and cherries and cooked dried fruits such as prunes and apricots. For flavoring, vanilla is always good—I practically pour it in—but so are almond extract and orange flower water. Here are some ideas to get you started.

Almond Milk

½ cup blanched and peeled almonds

6 tablespoons light honey or sugar

A few drops almond extract

1 tablespoon orange flower water or to taste

THIS almond milk, which is nothing like its commercial counterpart, makes a very restoring and refreshing drink. Serve it chilled and plain or mix with mineral water to make a cooler.

MAKES ABOUT 3 CUPS

Put 3 cups cold water in a blender, turn it to high speed, and gradually add the almonds. Blend until well pulverized—about 5 minutes—then strain through cheesecloth into a saucepan. Stir in the honey, bring to a boil, and simmer for 2 minutes. Turn off the heat and let cool. Stir in the almond extract and orange flower water and refrigerate until well chilled. To serve, mix in a glass with ice. If the mixture is too thick, add a little water or mineral water.

Variation: Omit the orange flower water and flavor the milk with ¼ teaspoon or more ground cardamom or nutmeg or with ½ to 1 teaspoon ground cinnamon and the finely grated zest of a lemon.

Banana Smoothie

1 ripe banana

¾ cup milk

¼ cup yogurt or buttermilk

1 teaspoon honey or sugar

½ teaspoon vanilla

SERVES 1

Puree the banana, milk, yogurt, and honey in a blender, then add enough vanilla to give it a good flavor.

White Grape Juice with Orange and Basil

THIS fragrant drink is a gentle eye-opener in the morning or, come evening, a sparkling cooler.

SERVES 4

1 quart grape juice

1 large orange, thinly sliced

10 sprigs lemon basil or lemon verbena, plus extra for garnish

Sparkling mineral water, if desired

Combine the juice, orange and herbs in a pitcher and steep for several hours or overnight in the refrigerator. Strain and serve chilled, with a few ice cubes and a fresh sprig of basil in each glass. For fizz, add mineral water to each glass to taste.

Honeydew and Lime Juice with Mint

DEAD-RIPE melons make superlative drinks. Lime and mint are classic with melon, but try ginger, lemon verbena, or lemon balm as well.

SERVES 4

$1/2$ large ripe green or pink honeydew melon

Juice of 2 to 4 large limes

$1/2$ cup mint leaves

Club soda or sparkling mineral water, if desired

Puree the honeydew in a blender with the lime juice and mint leaves. Chill or serve right away, over ice with a dash of club soda.

Nectarine-Mango Frappe

SERVES 2 TO 3

2 nectarines or peaches

1 large mango

$1^{1}/_2$ cups yogurt or buttermilk

A few drops vanilla

6 ice cubes

Fresh lemon or lime juice to taste

Peel and slice the fruit, then puree in a blender or food processor with the yogurt, vanilla, and ice until smooth. Add the lemon or lime juice to taste and serve.

Mango-Orange Cooler

A LUSCIOUS orange beverage to remember when mangoes are plentiful.

SERVES 4

2 ripe mangoes, weighing about 1 pound each

2 cups orange juice

8 ice cubes

Juice of 2 to 3 limes

Sparkling water, if desired

Mint sprigs or lime wedges

Peel the mangoes and cut as much of the flesh off the pits as possible. Add the orange juice and ice and puree until smooth. Add lime juice to taste. Pour into a pitcher over ice cubes and let the foam settle a few moments, then thin with sparkling water and serve with a sprig of mint or lime wedges.

Pear Smoothie

1 cup pear juice

1 ripe pear

2 drops almond extract

1 cup yogurt or buttermilk

SERVES 1 TO 2

Puree everything in a blender until smooth, then pour over ice.

Pineapple-Coconut Milk Drink

2 cups chopped fresh or canned
   pineapple

1 15-ounce can unsweetened coconut
   milk

1 banana

1 teaspoon orange flower water

*IF you're ending a day of
leisure with this drink,
add a splash of rum.*

SERVES 2 TO 4

Blend all the ingredients plus ½ cup water together and pour over ice.

Banana-Pineapple Frappé

2 ripe bananas

1 tablespoon honey

2 tablespoons buttermilk, milk, or yogurt

1 cup fresh pineapple or pineapple juice

Pineapple sage or mint sprigs for
   garnish

*For more tropical flavor,
add the pulp of one or
two passion fruits or passion fruit syrup.*

SERVES 2 TO 3

Puree the bananas in a blender with the honey, milk, and pineapple juice. Pour over ice and garnish with sprigs of pineapple sage if available.

Protein Drink

1 cup soy milk

¼ cup yogurt, optional

2 tablespoons protein powder

½ cup fruit—berries, peach, mango,
   banana

1 tablespoon honey

2 teaspoons orange flower water

1 teaspoon vanilla

*OF course you can add a
serving of protein pow-
der to any smoothie, or
start with this recipe and
then improvise.*

MAKES 1 LARGE SERVING

Combine everything in a blender and puree until frothy and smooth.

Breakfast Cereal

FOR *cereal, you might take a second look at some old American favorites like Wheatena, Farina, Roman Meal, oatmeal, and puffed rice, or new ones such as buckwheat, couscous, amaranth, spelt flakes, and grits made not just from hominy but also from corn, barley, and brown rice. In short, plenty of good choices are available, and while many packaged cereals, especially cold ones, are pricey, those sold in bulk and most hot cereals are quite reasonable. Certainly one of our national food embarrassments is packaged cereal. The sheer volume of it, coupled with the high cost and its great quantities of added sugar, must surely discourage any well-intentioned shopper trying to put something wholesome on the breakfast table. But among the junk offerings there are many delicious cereals of excellent quality.*

TIPS FOR MAKING HOT CEREALS: The smaller the grain, the more quickly it cooks. Chewy groats can take as long as 2 hours, stone-ground grits 45 minutes, but fine cream of wheat cooks in minutes. If you're in a hurry, use the smaller-sized grains or flakes, such as rolled oats.

Depending on whether the grain is coarse, fine, or flaked, the ratio of water to cereal differs. While packaged cereals have their own cooking instructions, all cereal is made the same way: Stir the cereal into lightly salted boiling water, usually one part cereal to three parts water, then cook over medium-low heat, stirring occasionally, until it has thickened and tastes cooked. If the finished cereal is too thick for your liking, simply stir in more liquid. If it's too thin, you can even whisk in additional cereal—as long as you give it time to cook through. Some people like lumps, but if you prefer to avoid them, be sure to add the cereal gradually to water, whisking while you do so.

Although fine cereals, like cream of rice, thicken quickly, their flavor emerges more fully if you can give them extra 5 to 10 minutes on the stove. Not only will the cereal taste better, but it will be more digestible too.

Water is the usual cooking medium for cereal, but milk and juice are other possibilities—oatmeal cooked in apple juice or cream of wheat cooked in milk, for example. A little butter or sweetener can be stirred in at the end or not. While we generally prefer sweetened cereals, savory toppings, such as sesame salt (Gomashio, page 76) or grated cheese are also good.

Multigrain cereals are popular today. You can make your own just by cooking your cereal odds and ends together. Leftover rice, wheat berries, quinoa, and other grains also make interesting additions to cooked cereals. Add them once the cereal has thickened.

Tips for Cooking Breakfast Cereals

TOASTING CEREALS: All grains and flakes can be given a flavor boost by toasting. Put cereal in a dry skillet set over medium heat and stir frequently until they begin to smell toasty and take on a little color. Remove to a plate as soon as they're toasted so they don't burn. Cook the grains as you normally would.

USING A DOUBLE BOILER: A double boiler cooks cereal perfectly without your attention, so you can shower and dress, make lunches, or tend to other things while it's cooking. Cornmeal, noninstant oats, multigrain cereals, and steel-cut oats are good cereals for this method, although any cereal can be cooked this way. Cook the cereal in the top part of the double boiler directly over the heat just until it begins to thicken, then set it over simmering water, cover, and cook for 20 minutes (40 for steel-cut oats).

USING A SLOW COOKER: The slow cooker is ideal for grits and long-cooking grains like steel-cut oats. Combine the ingredients the night before, set the cooker on low, and awake to the aroma of hot cereal.

USING A THERMOS: This method is suitable for most every cereal. Fill a wide-mouth thermos with hot water and set it aside. Meanwhile, cook cereal in boiling water just until it has begun to thicken. Drain the thermos, add the cereal, screw on the lid, and leave it until morning. If you have no time to eat before leaving, you can take it with you.

Hot Breakfast Cereal

1 quart water   1 cup coarse cereal
Salt

Bring water to a boil, add ¼ to ½ teaspoon salt, then gradually whisk in the cereal. Lower the heat and simmer, partially covered. Give it a stir every now and then to keep it from sticking or boiling over. Most cereals thicken before the grain is actually cooked, but you can detect its raw taste. Cook until the cereal actually tastes done, 25 to 40 minutes, depending on the grain.

USE this formula for grit-sized cereals— polenta, barley, and rice grits, seven-grain or any other fairly coarse cereal.

MAKES ABOUT 4 CUPS

Fine Breakfast Porridge.

3 cups water   1 cup cereal
Salt

Bring water to a boil, add ¼ teaspoon salt, and gradually whisk in the cereal. Lower the heat and cook over low heat, stirring frequently, until thickened, 10 to 20 minutes.

FINE meals, like cream of rice and wheat, and fine cornmeal, absorb less water and cook more quickly than grits.

MAKES ABOUT 3 CUPS

TOPPINGS FOR COOKED CEREALS

Brown sugar, maple syrup, molasses, sorghum, or honey	Ground flax seeds
Milk, including soy milk, rice and almond milk, buttermilk	Raisins, currants, chopped dates, chopped dried apricots
Fruit juices, especially apple and pear	Stewed prunes, especially in cream of wheat, rice, and couscous
Butter, yogurt, or sour cream, especially when combined with molasses	Sautéed apples, especially on steel-cut oats and toasted barley flakes
Grated Cheddar, especially on grits	
Toasted nuts and seeds	Spice, especially cinnamon, nutmeg, cardamom

Quick Cooking Oats and Other Rolled (or Flaked) Grains

BECAUSE of their flattened appearance, rolled grains are also called flakes. Other grains can be cooked just as oatmeal is, although they end up with varying textures.

MAKES ABOUT 3 CUPS

3 cups water
Salt

1¼ cups rolled grains

Bring water to a boil, add ¼ teaspoon salt, then stir in the grain. Lower the heat and simmer until the cereal is thickened, about 5 minutes. Cover and let stand for 5 minutes before serving.

Cornmeal with Vanilla and Molasses

IT'S the splash of vanilla that makes this cereal so good. Cornmeal needs to be a little gritty to avoid lumps. If what you have looks more like corn flour, mix it into half the water before heating. Stir this slurry into the remaining water when it boils and simmer until done.

MAKES ABOUT 4 CUPS

1 cup fine white or yellow cornmeal, preferably stone-ground
1 quart boiling water
Salt

2 teaspoons vanilla
Butter
Unsulfured molasses

Gradually whisk the cornmeal into boiling water. Add a few pinches salt, lower the heat, and cook until thickened. Stir frequently, especially at the beginning. Fine cornmeal will be done in 4 to 5 minutes, coarse grits in 30 to 40. When done, stir in the vanilla and butter to taste. Serve with molasses.

Fried Cornmeal Mush Today we call this polenta, but many of us who enjoyed this as children know it as mush. My father always made extra cornmeal for breakfast, then poured the leftovers into a loaf pan to cool for the next day.

Cut cooled, cooked cornmeal cereal into ½-inch slices and fry it in a little oil or butter. You can give it a little more substance by dipping it first into beaten egg, then into cornmeal, *then* frying until golden and crisp. Serve with molasses, honey, or jam. Oatmeal is also good prepared this way.

Maple-Nut Cereal

THE combination of maple syrup and toasted nuts is always welcome on wheat-based and mixed-grain cereals.

MAKES ABOUT 4 CUPS

1 quart water
Salt
1 cup cracked wheat, cream of wheat, or multigrain cereal

½ teaspoon ground cinnamon
½ cup toasted pecans or walnuts
Maple syrup

Bring water to a boil, add the salt, and stir in the cereal and cinnamon. Stir for a few minutes, then lower the heat, cover the pan, and cook until thick, about 7 minutes. Pour into bowls, serve with the toasted nuts on top, and rim the edge with maple syrup. Serve with a pitcher of milk.

Hot Cereal with Sesame Salt Gomashio, page 76, toasted sesame seeds ground with salt, is a popular Japanese condiment that's eaten with rice and all sorts of other foods. It really is quite delicious and is just the thing for those who don't care for sweetened cereals and for those who prefer to skip the milk. If you like its nutty flavor, you'll find that Gomashio tastes wonderful on all grains.

Steel-Cut Oats

5 cups water
Salt

1¾ cups steel-cut oats

Bring water to a boil, add ½ teaspoon salt, then gradually stir in the oats. Return to a boil until the mixture thickens, after a few minutes, then transfer them to the top of a double boiler and cook, covered, over simmering water until tender but still a little chewy, about 35 minutes. Or combine the ingredients and add them to a slow cooker and cook overnight over low heat. The next morning, spoon out the cereal.

Another suggestion, from *The Breakfast Book* by Marion Cunningham, is to simmer the oats in the top of a double boiler for 5 minutes the night before, cover the pot, and go to bed. Next morning, just reheat them over simmering water.

THESE hearty oats, also called Scotch or Irish oats, take longer to cook than most cereals and are ideal candidates for the slow cooker and the double boiler. Leftovers make such a wonderful chewy addition to pancakes, muffins, and breads.

MAKES ABOUT 4½ CUPS

Breakfast Grits

1 quart water
Salt

1 cup stone-ground corn grits

Bring water to a boil, add ½ teaspoon salt, and whisk in the grits. Stir for the first minute or so, then lower the heat and cook for 35 to 40 minutes, giving an occasional stir. Or cook them in a slow cooker or double boiler as described on pages 618 to 619. If you like texture in your cereal, add whole hominy, drained and rinsed, to breakfast grits.

These have a reassuring, simple appeal that's more interesting than cream of wheat yet not overly challenging. Enjoy grits with a spoonful of molasses and butter or with Cheddar and a dash of Tabasco sauce.

MAKES ABOUT 4 CUPS

Breakfast Couscous with Honey and Dates

2 cups water
1 cup milk
Salt

1 cup fine or regular couscous
8 dates, pitted and chopped
Butter, cinnamon, and honey

Combine the water and the milk in a saucepan with a pinch of salt and bring to a boil. Stir in the couscous and add the dates. Cook for about 30 seconds, then turn off the heat, cover the pan, and let stand until the liquid is absorbed, 10 to 15 minutes. Serve with a pat of butter and a dash of cinnamon and drizzle with honey.

THIS breakfast pudding is quite easy to elaborate on. Prunes are always good with wheat, while a teaspoon of orange zest or orange flower water lends fragrance. You could cook the couscous in water and pour almond milk over the top and serve with toasted slivered almonds.

SERVES 4

Sweet Rice Breakfast Soup

SHORT-GRAIN *rice turns soft and creamy—soothing when you're recovering from the flu or a cold. Use the Japanese sweet rice, either white and brown, Arborio, or other short-grain rice.*

MAKES ABOUT 3 CUPS

1/2 cup short-grain white or brown rice

3 cups water or almond milk

Salt

1 short cinnamon stick

Butter, brown sugar, and cold milk

Put rice , water, 1/2 teaspoon salt, and cinnamon stick in a pot, bring to a boil, then simmer slowly until the mixture is creamy and thick, 20 minutes for white rice and about an hour for brown. Remove the cinnamon stick and serve with a tad of butter, brown sugar, and cold milk.

Savory Rice Soup

A RICE *soup makes a savory and invigorating start to the day. You can make it even more so by adding diced serrano chiles or chili oil.*

MAKES ABOUT 3 CUPS

Sweet Rice Breakfast Soup, preceding recipe, without the cinnamon

1 sheet nori

Soy sauce or tamari

1 or 2 scallions, thinly sliced

Chopped cilantro

Toasted sesame seeds or Gomashio, page 76

While the rice is cooking, toast a sheet of nori by passing it back and forth through a flame or over an electric burner. After several passes it will become crisp. Season the cooked rice with it with a little soy sauce to taste. Stir in the scallions, then crumble the toasted nori over the top and top with cilantro and toasted sesame seeds.

Cooked Amaranth

THE *tiny seeds cluster and float on the surface at first, but eventually they absorb the water. Amaranth turns slightly gelatinous.*

MAKES ABOUT 1 1/2 CUPS

1 1/2 cups water

1/2 cup amaranth

Salt

Combine water, the amaranth, and a pinch of salt in a small saucepan, bring to a boil, and then reduce the heat to a simmer. Cover and cook over low heat for 25 minutes or until the water is absorbed, about 15 minutes.

> ***Variation with Mixed Tiny Grains:*** Mix teff, amaranth, and quinoa, the latter thoroughly rinsed, and cook as described.

Millet Porridge with Currants and Almonds

PORRIDGE *offers one of the best ways to take advantage of millet's nutritional virtues.*

MAKES ABOUT 3 CUPS

1/2 cup millet

3 cups water

Salt

Small handful currants or raisins

A few tablespoons slivered almonds, toasted in a small skillet

Butter or sour cream

Rinse the millet. Bring the water to a boil, add 1/4 teaspoon salt, the millet, and the currants, and simmer over low heat for 30 minutes. Serve with the almonds and a pat of butter or sour cream.

Cold Cereals

WHEN *you look at the sugared cereals on our supermarket shelves it's hard to believe that cold cereals began as an invention of health-food enthusiasts. However, there are always alternatives to the mainstream offerings, many of which are easily within reach. Here are a few alternatives for homemade cold cereals that you might also enjoy.*

Scots Crowdie This is something I thought I made up on my own, but it turns out that it's actually a Scottish dish. Simply cover uncooked rolled oats with thick, cold buttermilk and add a spoonful of honey, berries, or a sliced banana if you wish. If you don't like buttermilk, try it with yogurt. Both have the tang that's just right here.

Bircher Muesli

2 cups rolled oats or 1 cup rolled oats
    and 1 cup mixed barley, rye, wheat,
    or spelt flakes

¹/₄ cup wheat germ

¹/₄ cup sunflower seeds, almonds, or flax
    seeds

1 grated apple or ¹/₂ cup dried fruits—
    raisins, cranberries or cherries

Preheat the oven to 375°F. Mix the oats, wheat germ, and seeds on a cookie sheet and bake for 10 minutes. Let cool, then combine with the apple. For one portion, mix ¹/₂ cup of the toasted grains and top with the grated apple, then add milk. Sweeten to taste with maple syrup or honey.

A HIGH-PROTEIN high-fiber Swiss cereal invented by Dr. Bircher-Brenner. It differs from granola in that the grains are not pretoasted or mixed with oil or sweetener.

MAKES ABOUT 2 CUPS

Granola

6 cups flaked or rolled grains

1 cup chopped nuts

1 cup wheat germ

1 teaspoon grated nutmeg

1 tablespoon ground cinnamon

Salt

1 cup raisins

¹/₂ cup safflower or canola oil

³/₄ cup honey, golden syrup, or maple
    syrup

Preheat the oven to 300°F. Toss the dry ingredients but not the raisins together, then add the oil and sweetener and toss again to coat them thoroughly. Spread the mixture on two sheet pans and bake until golden, turning every 10 minutes so that it browns evenly. When done, after about 30 minutes, add the raisins and let cool. As the granola cools, it will lose its stickiness and become crunchy. Store in a tightly covered jar.

Low-Fat Granola Omit the oil and toast everything as suggested. Keep the sweetener or reduce it. It *does* give the cereal a nice crunch and is perhaps a better idea than simply passing the sugar bowl.

ANOTHER early health food that has gone mainstream and is no longer so healthy. Nowadays, the oil and honey that make it smell like cookies when it comes out of the oven make granola more suspect than healthful. Use this version if you're trying to wean kids away from sugary pops and loops or as a topping for yogurt and fruit.

MAKES ABOUT 8 CUPS

Granola with Vanilla and Fruit Juice

ANOTHER way to make granola—using juice instead of oil.

MAKES ABOUT 6 CUPS

4 cups rolled flakes—oat, wheat, spelt, barley

1 cup quinoa, rinsed well

2 teaspoons ground cinnamon

1 teaspoon grated nutmeg

1/2 cup sliced or slivered almonds

1 teaspoon vanilla

1 cup pear or apple juice

1/2 cup honey or maple syrup

1/2 cup raisins or dried cherries

Preheat the oven to 300°F. Mix the flakes, quinoa, spices, and almonds together, then add the vanilla, juice, and honey. Toss well to moisten evenly, then toast on a sheet pan until browned, about 30 minutes, stirring a few times. Add the dried fruit once the cereal is cooked.

ADDITIONS TO GRANOLA

Except for adding dried fruits after the granola is baked so that it won't turn rock hard, there are no hard-and-fast rules about ingredients. All of these can be used in granola mixtures.

Oat, wheat, spelt, barley, or rye flakes

Cashews, walnuts, pecans, pumpkin seeds, macadamia nuts, almonds

Sesame seeds, sunflower seeds, popped amaranth, or toasted quinoa

Flaked coconut, banana chips

Chopped dates, dried cranberries, cherries, apples, pears, or papaya slices

Wheat, rice or oat bran, wheat germ

Vanilla or almond extract

Cinnamon, nutmeg, cardamom, mace

Breakfast Burritos

THE *breakfast burrito is standard southwestern fare, although the particulars vary from place to place. Some versions contain scrambled eggs with trimmings (potatoes, grated cheese, bacon, red or green chile) or an entire omelet. At our farmers' market, some farmers sell breakfast burritos filled with home-grown squash, corn, or beans. In restaurants they're likely to come smothered with red or green chile or a side of salsa. While this is clearly an improvisational sort of dish, here's a rough idea of how to make a tasty, straightforward breakfast burrito.*

Breakfast Burrito with Scrambled Eggs and Cheese

2 large wheat tortillas

4 eggs, beaten with 1 tablespoon water

Salt

2 tablespoons butter

¹/₂ cup grated Monterey Jack

1 serrano chile, finely chopped

2 scallions, including half of the greens, chopped

Chopped cilantro

MAKES 2 BURRITOS

Place the tortillas, one on top of the other, in an ungreased skillet over low heat. As the bottom one warms, flip them over to warm the second one. Reverse the tortillas and repeat for the other sides.

Meanwhile, season the eggs with ¹/₂ teaspoon salt. Heat the butter in a nonstick skillet over medium heat until it sizzles. Add the eggs and scramble them. When they're nearly done, turn off the heat and stir in the cheese, chile, scallions, and cilantro. Scoop the eggs into the warm tortillas, fold them over, and serve.

Breakfast Burritos with Tofu If you don't eat eggs, fill the burritos with Scrambled Tofu, page 627. Since tofu is on the dry side, plan to add a tablespoon or two of your favorite salsa. You can also fill your burrito with the Scrambled Ricotta Cheese with Salsa on page 626.

Migas

MIGAS, a Tex-Mex dish, are eggs scrambled with tortilla crisps, preferably homemade ones, making a hearty, rustic plate of eggs. I never pass up the chance to enjoy them when I'm in Texas.

SERVES 2

2 to 3 corn tortillas or a few handfuls broken tortilla chips, plus extra tortillas for serving

1 tablespoon oil or butter

2 scallions, including the greens, chopped

1 jalapeño chile, finely diced

4 eggs, beaten with 1 tablespoon water

2 plum or Roma tomatoes, chopped

1/2 cup grated Monterey Jack or Cheddar

Chopped cilantro

Salt

Salsa

Cut the tortillas into strips or triangles and bake or fry them until crisp, page 46. Break them into bite-sized pieces. Heat the oil in a nonstick skillet. Add the scallions and chile and sauté until the scallions are limp. Pour in the beaten eggs and start stirring them. Just before they're finished cooking, add the chips, tomatoes, cheese, and cilantro. Finish cooking, then season with salt to taste. Serve with warm tortillas and salsa on the side.

Variations: There's nothing hard-and-fast about migas except the presence of the tortilla chips. You can fry a little onion and bell pepper to start, use a tomato-based salsa in place of the fresh tomato; double the cheese or leave it out. Unless I have a great salsa on hand, I nearly always end up adding a good dusting of hot and smoky chipotle chile powder.

Scrambled Ricotta Cheese with Salsa

I NEVER even thought of doing this until I saw a recipe in Diana Kennedy's The Art of Mexican Cooking. Now I prepare my own version. It makes a great fast filling for warm corn or wheat tortillas.

SERVES 2

2 tablespoons vegetable oil

1/4 cup finely diced onion

2 serrano chiles, minced

1 1/2 cups ricotta

A few tablespoons crumbled feta or Cheddar

Salt

1/2 cup Pico de Gallo, page 102, or commercial salsa

Heat the oil in an 8-inch skillet over medium heat. Add the onion and chiles and cook for a minute or so without letting them brown. Add the ricotta and feta, taste, then season with salt. Raise the heat to medium and cook, occasionally moving the cheese about the pan, until it becomes firm and the bottom has begun to color, about 5 minutes. Turn out and serve with the salsa.

Variations: Leave out the chiles and add 3 tablespoons chopped herbs such as those used in the Scrambled Tofu with Herbs and Cheese, page 627.

Scrambled Tofu

1 tablespoon vegetable oil

3 tablespoons thinly sliced scallion or onion

1 10-ounce box silken tofu

¼ teaspoon turmeric

Salt and freshly milled pepper

Heat the oil in a small skillet, add the scallion, and sauté over medium heat until soft, 2 or 3 minutes. Crumble in the tofu, add the turmeric, season well with salt and pepper, and cook over high heat, stirring frequently, until the curds have firmed up and are heated through.

WHATEVER gets added to scrambled eggs can go into tofu. Turmeric gives tofu a yellow egglike hue, but use it with restraint—it is bitter in quantity. Roll up in a warm tortilla or serve with toast.

SERVES 2

Scrambled Tofu with Herbs and Cheese

1 tablespoon olive or safflower oil

2 teaspoons butter

2 10-ounce packages silken tofu

2 tablespoons chopped parsley

2 tablespoons chopped tarragon, basil, or marjoram

2 tablespoons finely sliced scallion

½ cup grated Cheddar, Muenster, goat cheese, or feta

Salt and freshly milled pepper

Paprika

SERVES 4

Heat the oil and butter and, when hot, crumble the tofu into the pan. Cook over high heat, stirring frequently, until it begins to look firm, after several minutes. Add the herbs and cheese, taste and season with salt, then season with pepper. Serve with a dash of paprika over the top.

Scrambled Tofu with Tomatoes and Salsa

1½ tablespoons safflower or canola oil

3 tablespoons diced onion or scallion

1 or 2 serrano chiles to taste, diced

½ teaspoon ground cumin

¼ teaspoon dried oregano

2 10-ounce boxes silken tofu

3 tablespoons chopped cilantro

Salt to taste

½ cup grated Cheddar

Warm tortillas

Salsa of your choosing

SERVE in corn or wheat tortillas.

SERVES 4

Heat the oil in a skillet, add the onion, and sauté over high heat for 1 or 2 minutes to sear it. Add the chiles, cumin, and oregano and cook for 1 or 2 minutes more. Crumble in the tofu and cook, stirring frequently, until it's firm and hot. Stir in the cilantro, season with salt, remove from the heat, and add the cheese. Serve with warm tortillas and plenty of salsa.

Hash Brown Potatoes

SOME *versions of this American breakfast staple start with raw potatoes, others with boiled grated ones. I always think they taste better when the potato has been precooked—something you can do the night before. If you start with raw grated potato, allow a little extra time for it to cook all the way through and brown.*

SERVES 4 TO 6

1½ pounds russet potatoes
¼ cup finely diced onion, if desired

3 tablespoons clarified butter, olive oil, or vegetable oil
Salt and freshly milled pepper

Cover the potatoes with cold water, boil until nearly tender, then drain. When cool, remove the skins and grate coarsely. Mix with the onion.

Heat the butter in a cast-iron skillet. When hot enough to sputter a drop of water, add the potatoes. Season them with salt and plenty of pepper, lower the heat, and fry until golden on the bottom, about 5 minutes. While they cook, press them lightly with a spatula and give the pan a shake once or twice to make sure they're not sticking. Turn them over and fry on the second side. Or, if you don't want them in a cake form, just stir them around the pan every few minutes, letting them stand between stirrings, until browned all over.

Hash Browns with Green Chile and Cheese Add 3 to 4 tablespoons roasted green chile—jalapeño, poblano, or Anaheim—and several chopped scallions to the cooking potatoes. Once the potatoes are lightly browned, stir in a few tablespoons chopped cilantro and ½ cup grated Jack, Cheddar, Muenster, or even large-curd cottage cheese.

Hash Browns with Melted Cheese and Ground Chipotle Chiles Finish the potatoes by grating a little Monterey Jack or Teleme cheese over the top and dust generously with ground chipotle chile. Serve alongside your eggs, or scramble an egg, put it on top, and wrap the whole thing in a large tortilla for a sensational breakfast burrito.

Eliot's Breakfast Parsnips

MASTER *organic gardener Eliot Coleman made these parsnips for me one cold spring Vermont morning with monster-sized roots dug from the under the snow-covered ground. They were the best parsnips I've ever tasted.*

SERVES 4

3 tablespoons unsalted butter
1 pound parsnips, as fresh and plump as possible, peeled and sliced into thin rounds

½ cup toasted chopped walnuts or pecans
Warm maple syrup

Melt the butter in a heavy skillet over medium heat. Don't let it get too hot. Add the parsnips and a pinch of salt. Cook, stirring frequently, until golden all over from their caramelizing sugars, 7 to 10 minutes. Serve covered with the nuts and maple syrup.

Pancakes, Griddle Cakes, and Hot Cakes

PANCAKES, *griddle cakes, and hot cakes—they're the same thing, really—are a hallowed Sunday morning tradition for many families. The assembly is the same as for quick breads: Combine dry ingredients in one bowl, the wet ingredients in another, then mix them together with a few strokes of fork or spoon. Don't overwork the gluten by mixing too hard—any lumps always seem to take care of themselves. If the batter is too thick, gently stir in additional milk or water. For extra-light, fluffy pancakes beat the egg whites separately, then fold them into the batter.*

Cook pancakes in a heavy skillet or on a griddle heated gradually over medium-high heat. When hot, add the batter, then reduce the heat to medium so that the cakes will be cooked by the time they brown. If you cook your cakes in a little butter or oil, they'll come out crisper on the outside with a golden, lacy fringe. Cooking them in a dry pan yields a more uniform-looking cake.

Buttermilk Pancakes

1 1/2 cups all-purpose flour or whole-wheat pastry flour

1 to 3 tablespoons sugar

Salt

1 teaspoon baking soda

2 teaspoons baking powder

1/4 teaspoon grated nutmeg

2 eggs

3 tablespoons butter, melted, or oil

1 1/2 cups buttermilk

1 teaspoon vanilla

THE classic American pancake is light, white, and tender. Serve them with fruit, syrup, or yogurt or vary them with the addition of fruit, nuts, and different flours.

MAKES FOURTEEN 4-INCH CAKES

Mix the dry ingredients in one bowl. In a second bowl, beat the eggs and add the butter, buttermilk, and vanilla. Pour the wet ingredients into the dry and stir just enough to combine.

For each pancake, drop 1/4 cup batter onto a nonstick griddle or skillet set over medium-high heat. Cook, without disturbing until fine bubbles appear over the surface after a few minutes. Flip them over and cook until browned on the second side, about 1 minute. Refrain from patting them or turning them a second time—both actions will make the pancakes lose their lightness.

When done, remove to a platter and serve right away or keep warm in a low (200°F) oven until all are finished.

Whole-Wheat Pancakes Use whole-wheat flour, 1 cup whole-wheat flour mixed with 1/2 cup wheat bran, or whole-wheat pastry flour.

Mixed-Grain Pancakes These are light and ethereal with a nice play of textures and flavors. Use 1/2 cup flour, 1/2 cup cooked grain such as rice or quinoa, 1/4 cup cornmeal, and 1/4 cup rye or buckwheat flour, or improvise a mixture of your own. Other grains to consider are semolina, mixed-grain cereals, oats and other flaked grains, and toasted millet or amaranth for crunchiness.

DOING WITHOUT BUTTERMILK

What's nice about buttermilk is that it gives pancakes tenderness and tang. When you don't have any, add a tablespoon vinegar to a cup of milk and let it stand for 10 minutes. It will curdle slightly. If you prefer to use regular milk, just omit the baking soda from the recipe.

Banana-Nut Pancakes Add two thinly sliced bananas and ½ cup lightly toasted chopped pecans or walnuts to the batter.

Apple or Pear Pancakes Thinly slice one or two apples or pears and stir them into the batter. Flavor the batter with ¼ teaspoon ground cardamom, or ½ teaspoon ground cinnamon or grated nutmeg. Serve with applesauce or its variations, page 681.

Quince Cakes Grate a ripe, fragrant quince and add it to the batter.

Berry Pancakes Berries always make a wonderful addition to griddle cakes. Use ½ to 1 cup berries and either fold them into the batter or distribute them over the top of the cakes while the first side is cooking. Serve with maple syrup and yogurt or sour cream or dust with powdered sugar and drizzle with fresh lemon juice.

Rice Pancakes For a chewy, substantial accent, fold ½ to 1 cup cooked wild rice, brown rice, or white rice into the batter.

Corn Cakes Replace ½ cup of the flour with cornmeal and stir 1 cup corn kernels into the batter. If using fresh corn, be sure to include the corn milk and scrapings too. Delicious with honey or molasses.

Quinoa Cakes For a feathery light cake with delectable texture and taste, fold in ½ to 1½ cups cooked quinoa or as much as the batter will hold. The tiny grains will pop in your mouth.

Lacy Buttermilk Corn Cakes with Pepper Relish

WITHOUT *the relish, these tender cakes are pliable, easy to wrap around molasses and ricotta for a breakfast crêpe or sautéed cherries or plums for dessert.*

**MAKES SIXTEEN
5-INCH CAKES**

¾ **cup stone-ground cornmeal**

2 **eggs, beaten**

1½ **cups buttermilk**

4 **tablespoons butter, melted, or oil**

¼ **teaspoon salt**

2 **teaspoons baking powder**

½ **teaspoon baking soda**

1 **cup flour**

Sour cream

Whisk 1 cup boiling water with the cornmeal until smooth, then set it aside while you gather the remaining ingredients. Stir in the eggs, buttermilk, and butter, then whisk in the remaining dry ingredients.

For each pancake, drop ¼-cup batter onto a heated nonstick skillet to make a 5-inch cake. Immediately bubbles will form on the surface. Turn, just once, as soon as the cake begins to look a little dry on top and cook the second side until golden. Top each cake with a dab of sour cream and a spoonful of pepper relish.

Pepper Relish

1 ripe tomato, seeded and finely
    chopped

½ red bell pepper, finely diced

½ yellow bell pepper, finely diced

2 scallions, including half of the greens,
    finely sliced

3 tablespoons chopped parsley

2 teaspoons chopped marjoram

Salt and freshly milled pepper

Dash vinegar or to taste

Combine the relish ingredients and adjust seasonings.

Buckwheat Flapjacks

¾ cup buckwheat flour

¾ cup all-purpose flour

1 teaspoon baking powder

½ teaspoon baking soda

½ teaspoon salt

¼ cup unsulfured molasses

2 eggs

3 tablespoons vegetable oil, plus extra
    for the pan

1¾ cups buttermilk

Turbinado sugar

Molasses Butter, following recipe

BUTTERMILK, buckwheat, and molasses are naturals together. A sprinkle of turbinado sugar on top provides crackle and crunch.

**MAKES FOURTEEN
4-INCH PANCAKES**

Whisk the dry ingredients together in a large bowl. In a second bowl, combine the molasses, eggs, oil, and buttermilk. Pour the wet ingredients into the dry and stir together briskly to combine.

Make the molasses butter while the batter rests. For each pancake, drop ¼-cup batter onto a lightly greased nonstick skillet or griddle. Cook over medium heat until covered with bubbles, then flip once and cook about ½ minute more. Serve with the molasses and butter and a sprinkling of raw sugar.

Molasses Butter Heat ⅓ cup unsulfured molasses in a pan with 2 tablespoons butter until the butter is melted. Turn off the heat and whisk in ⅓ to ½ cup crème fraîche until smooth.

Cottage Cheese and Nutmeg Pancakes

2 eggs, separated

1 cup buttermilk

1 cup cottage cheese

4 tablespoons butter, melted

1 teaspoon vanilla

½ teaspoon grated nutmeg

1 tablespoon sugar

¼ teaspoon salt

½ teaspoon baking soda

1 cup flour

Oil or butter for the pan

THESE are wonderful! They tend to stick a little, so plan to add some oil or butter to the pan each time. Serve with sour cream and strawberry jam or a compote of dried cherries and golden raisins.

**MAKES TWELVE 4-INCH
PANCAKES**

Whisk the yolks and buttermilk together in a bowl. Stir in the cottage cheese, butter, and vanilla. Add the dry ingredients and whisk them together in a few swift strokes. Beat the egg whites until they form soft peaks, then fold them into the batter.

For each pancake, drop ¼-cup batter onto a griddle or large skillet set over medium heat. Cook until the surface is thoroughly laced with bubbles, about 4 minutes, then turn once and cook briefly on the second side. These generally take a little longer to cook than other cakes.

Oatmeal Pancakes

THESE *don't have the usual cakelike crumb that most cakes do, but they taste wonderful. Use coarse-textured rolled oats for the best texture and serve with applesauce or sautéed apples and thick yogurt.*

MAKES FOURTEEN 4-INCH PANCAKES

1½ cups rolled oats

2 cups buttermilk

2 eggs

1 teaspoon vanilla

2 tablespoons brown sugar or maple syrup

¼ cup canola oil

½ teaspoon salt

½ cup flour

¼ teaspoon grated nutmeg

½ teaspoon baking soda

Stir the oats and buttermilk together and let stand for 20 minutes. Beat the eggs with the vanilla, sugar, and oil, then stir in the soaked oats. Combine the dry ingredients and add them to the oat mixture as well. For each pancake, drop ¼ cup batter onto a heated griddle or skillet and cook over a medium-low heat until the tops are covered with holes. Turn the cakes over and cook the second side. Because of the moisture in this batter, the cakes need to cook slowly, but turn them only once.

Oatmeal-Buttermilk Pancakes with Fruit Gently stir a cup of blackberries, raspberries, or mulberries into the batter, then cook as described. Or serve oatmeal pancakes with a mound of blackberries sweetened with brown sugar and a dollop of yogurt.

Oatmeal-Buttermilk Pancakes with Steel-Cut Oats Soak steel-cut oats overnight in the buttermilk so that they'll soften. Next morning, add the rest of the ingredients as given.

Waffles

MODERN *waffle irons are a breeze to use with their nonstick coatings and reliable thermostats. This is one time I'm delighted to have the guesswork removed—the old kinds offered quite a challenge unless well seasoned. Most pancake batters work for waffles, though you may want to thin the batter with extra milk and add an extra 2 tablespoons oil or melted butter. The extra butter helps give waffles their crisp exterior. For very light waffles, separate the whites, beat them until they hold soft peaks, and fold them into the batter. Waffles needn't be just for breakfast—they can include corn or grated cheese, or they can be served alongside a vegetable ragout or bean stew. They can make a dessert, too, embellished with fresh or poached dried fruits, dessert sauces, and yogurt or whipped cream.*

Basic Waffles

MAKES 8 WAFFLES

3 eggs, beaten

$1^1/2$ cups milk or buttermilk

$^1/4$ cup canola oil or butter, melted

1 teaspoon vanilla extract

2 cups flour

1 teaspoon baking powder

$^1/2$ teaspoon baking soda

$^1/4$ teaspoon salt

In a bowl, mix the wet ingredients together. In another bowl, stir together the dry ingredients. Pour the wet ingredients into the dry and combine them with a fork. The batter should on the thin side or your waffles will be too cakey. Test a spoonful to be sure and add more milk if it's too thick. Cook according to your waffle iron's instructions.

Multigrain Waffles For the flour, use 1 cup all-purpose or whole-wheat pastry flour and $^1/4$ cup each wheat or oat bran, cornmeal, rye, and soy or quinoa flour. Sometimes I add just a tablespoon or two of odds and ends, including cereal mixes, such as seven grain, in place of one of the other flours.

Pecan Waffles Stir 1 cup finely chopped pecans (or other nuts) into the batter or sprinkle the nuts over the batter as soon as it's poured into the waffle iron.

Rice Waffles Stir 1 cup cooked, drained wild rice, basmati, or brown rice into the batter to give your waffles chewiness and character. Cooked quinoa and millet are also good additions.

Savory Corn Waffles

TRY corn waffles for a Sunday night supper or brunch served with chile butter, salsa, or Pepper Relish with Anise Seeds, and crumbled feta.

MAKES 10 TO 12 WAFFLES

1½ cups whole-wheat pastry flour

1¼ cups fine cornmeal

2 teaspoons baking powder

½ teaspoon baking soda if using buttermilk

1 teaspoon salt

3 eggs, separated

2½ cups buttermilk or milk

6 tablespoons corn oil or butter, melted

Kernels from 2 ears of corn, or 1½ cups frozen corn

Combine the dry ingredients in one bowl. In a second bowl, whisk together the egg yolks, milk, and oil. In a third bowl, whisk the whites until they hold soft peaks. Make a well in the dry ingredients, pour in the wet ingredients and stir to combine, then fold in the whites along with the corn kernels. Cook according to your waffle iron's instructions, then serve with an array of condiments.

Yeasted Waffles and Pancakes

RAISING pancakes and waffles with yeast is an old American tradition that predates the invention of baking powder. The overnight proofing develops the flavor of the flours, and the yeast ensures lightness even for heavier grains. The batter keeps well, covered and refrigerated, for several days.

MAKES 10 TO 12 WAFFLES

2¼ teaspoons or 1 package active dry yeast

1 teaspoon sugar

2 cups lukewarm milk

½ teaspoon salt

1½ cups flour

1 cup whole-wheat, quinoa, toasted barley, or other flour

2 tablespoons sugar

5 tablespoons canola oil or butter, melted

2 eggs, beaten

½ teaspoon baking soda

In a small bowl, sprinkle the yeast into ¼ cup warm water and stir in the sugar. Let stand until foamy, about 10 minutes. Put the warm milk and salt in a large bowl, then add the yeast mixture and whisk in the flours. Cover and refrigerate overnight if the weather is warm or leave out on the counter if it's cool. Next morning, add the sugar, oil, eggs, and soda. Cook according to your waffle iron's instructions or on a preheated griddle.

French Toast

While French toast provides a way to use slightly stale bread, you can certainly use fresh bread. Serve French toast with powdered sugar, warm maple syrup, applesauce, berries—whatever toppings you like on pancakes.

SERVES 2

2 eggs

1 tablespoon sugar

½ teaspoon orange flower water, optional

1½ teaspoons vanilla extract

½ teaspoon ground cinnamon

1 cup milk

4 slices bread

Butter or oil for the skillet

Whisk the eggs with the sugar and flavorings, then stir in the milk. Pour the batter into a pie plate and put in two pieces of bread. Let stand for 3 minutes, then turn it over and let stand again to absorb the batter. Really stale bread will take longer. Press on it with your fingers—you can tell if it's still dry. Melt a little butter in a large nonstick skillet. When it's bubbling, pick up the bread and put it in the skillet. Cook both sides until nicely browned. Repeat with the remaining bread and batter.

Breakfast Breads

COFFEE *cakes, sticky buns, and fruit- and nut-studded breads are part of weekend or special holiday breakfasts, as are simpler fare, like muffins and biscuits. Those recipes that depend on a yeasted dough or are served at other meals—cinnamon rolls, muffins, and biscuits, for example—can be found in the bread chapter. Croissants, Danish pastries, and brioche fortunately can be found in bakeries. Here are some quick breads that are eminently suitable for breakfast and brunch, quick and easy to prepare.*

Applesauce Spice Bread

¼ **pound (1 stick) butter**

½ **cup white sugar**

¾ **cup light brown sugar, packed**

2 eggs at room temperature

A mixture of 1 cup applesauce with 1½ teaspoons baking soda

2 cups cake flour or all-purpose flour

½ **teaspoon salt**

2 teaspoons ground cardamom or cinnamon

½ **teaspoon grated nutmeg**

½ **teaspoon ground ginger**

¼ **teaspoon ground cloves**

THIS tender loaf is more cakelike than many quick breads due to the use of cake flour. Serve it plain or drizzled with a powdered sugar glaze. The batter is also very good over an upside-down cake featuring apples or pears. A narrow bread pan (4 × 10 inches), available at specialty stores, makes an especially fine-looking bread.

MAKES ONE 4- × 10-INCH LOAF

Preheat the oven to 375°F. Lightly butter a bread pan. Line it with wax paper or parchment paper, then butter and flour it. (A spray hasn't worked well for me in this recipe.)

Cream the butter with the two sugars in a mixing bowl until light and fluffy. Add the eggs one at a time, scraping down the sides in between additions, then stir in the applesauce mixture. Stir the dry ingredients together in a bowl, then add them to the butter mixture and stir just enough to combine well.

Turn into the pan and bake in the top third of the oven until firm and a cake tester comes out clean, about 50 minutes. Let cool in the pan for 5 minutes, then carefully turn out onto a rack to finish cooling.

Variations: In place of the applesauce, use 1 cup pureed persimmon, mixed with the baking soda as described. Applesauce made with quince or pear, page 681, makes a more exotic cake. Omit the ginger and clove and half the remaining spices to allow the more subtle flavor of the fruit to come through.

Sweet Corn Coffee Cake with Berries

THIS moist coffee cake is studded with berries and dusted with powdered sugar.

MAKES ONE 8-INCH ROUND CAKE

1¹⁄₃ cups flour
³⁄₄ cup cornmeal, any color
¹⁄₂ cup plus 2 tablespoons sugar
1 teaspoon baking soda
2 teaspoons baking powder
¹⁄₂ teaspoon salt
1 cup buttermilk

Grated zest of 1 lemon
2 teaspoons vanilla extract
2 eggs
¹⁄₃ cup butter, melted, or corn oil
1 to 2 cups raspberries, blackberries, or blueberries
Powdered sugar

Preheat the oven to 375°F. Butter and flour or spray an 8-inch springform cake pan or an 8-inch square pan.

Whisk the dry ingredients together in a bowl. In a second bowl, combine the wet ingredients. Quickly stir them together, then scrape into the pan. Scatter the berries over the top and bake in the center of the oven until the cake is browned and beginning to pull away from the sides of the pan, about 45 minutes. Remove the rim if you've used a springform pan, transfer the cake to a serving plate, and dust with powdered sugar. Serve warm.

Cranberry-Nut Bread

FOR this delicious breakfast bread or tea cake, you can start with fresh cranberries, as described here, or use 1 cup cooked cranberries.

MAKES ONE LOAF OR 18 MUFFINS

2 cups raw cranberries
¹⁄₂ cup sugar
Grated zest of 1 orange plus 1 tablespoon orange juice
6 tablespoons butter
³⁄₄ cup light brown sugar, packed
2 eggs at room temperature
1 cup buttermilk

2¹⁄₂ cups all-purpose or whole-wheat pastry flour
¹⁄₈ teaspoon ground cloves
1 teaspoon baking soda
1¹⁄₂ teaspoons baking powder
¹⁄₂ teaspoon salt
1 cup pecans or walnuts, finely chopped

Preheat the oven to 375°F. Spray or butter and flour a bread pan or 18 muffin cups.

Put the cranberries in a saucepan with the sugar, orange zest, and juice. Cook over high heat, stirring frequently, until most of the berries burst and the sugar is dissolved, 4 to 5 minutes.

Cream the butter and sugar in a mixing bowl until light and fluffy, then add the eggs one at a time and beat until smooth. Add the buttermilk. Combine the dry ingredients except the nuts and stir half into the batter. Add the cranberries, then the remaining flour, and fold in the nuts. Spoon the batter into the pan and bake in the center of the oven until well browned on top and a toothpick comes out clean, about an hour and 10 minutes. Turn out onto a rack to cool.

Oat and Brown Sugar Coffee Cake

1 cup rolled oats, preferably noninstant

1/4 pound (1/2 cup) butter

1 cup light brown sugar, packed

2 eggs at room temperature

1 1/2 teaspoons vanilla

1 teaspoon ground cinnamon

1 teaspoon baking powder

1/2 teaspoon baking soda

1/2 teaspoon salt

1 1/2 cups flour

1 cup Pecan Streusel, page 643

TENDER, with good oat flavor, this is an old American coffee cake that one doesn't see much anymore.

SERVES 6 TO 8

Preheat the oven to 375°F. Spray or butter and flour a 9- × 12-inch baking dish.

Pour 1 1/2 cups boiling water over the oats and set them aside. Cream the butter and sugar until light and fluffy, then add the eggs one at a time. Scrape down the bowl and continue beating until the mixture is smooth, then add the vanilla, cinnamon, and oats. Combine the dry ingredients and stir them in with a rubber scraper or wooden spoon. Pour into the prepared baking dish, cover with streusel, and bake until a skewer comes out clean—about 35 minutes.

Orange and Dried Fruit Coffee Cake

1/4 pound (1/2 cup) butter

Grated zest and juice of 1 large orange

3/4 cup light brown sugar, packed

2 eggs at room temperature

1/2 teaspoon salt

1 teaspoon baking powder

1 teaspoon baking soda

2 1/4 cups flour

3/4 cup buttermilk

1 cup dried cherries, cranberries, chopped dates, or chopped prunes

1/2 to 1 cup chopped pecans or walnuts

THIS is a favorite recipe for an old-fashioned dessert that I have modified by omitting the sugar glaze and some of the sugar in the cake and including a wider variety of fruits.

MAKES ONE 9- × 13-INCH CAKE

Preheat the oven to 350°F. Butter and flour a 9- × 13-inch baking pan or a kugelhopf pan.

Cream the butter with the orange zest and sugar until light and fluffy. Add the eggs, one at a time, and beat until smooth, then stir in the juice and the salt, baking powder, and soda. Alternately add the flour and buttermilk, in thirds, beating just until smooth, then fold in the dried fruits and the nuts. Bake until lightly browned and firm to the touch and a skewer comes out clean, about 45 minutes.

Babka with Dried Cherry and Almond Filling

THIS is my grand-
mother's and mother's
recipe for a silken dough
that makes the most
luxurious, tender sweet
rolls. You can make this
dough the day before you
plan to bake it, then give
it 2 hours to return to
room temperature. An
electric mixer with a
paddle attachment is a
great help in mixing this
soft, sticky dough.

The cherry-almond
filling is one of many
wonderful fillings you
can use. A classic poppy
seed filling is another,
there are fillings based
on prunes and raisins, or
you can treat the dough
as for cinnamon rolls.

MAKES 1 LARGE BREAD,
SERVING 10

2$\frac{1}{4}$ teaspoons (1 envelope) active dry yeast

$\frac{1}{2}$ cup warm milk

$\frac{1}{3}$ cup plus 1 teaspoon sugar, plus extra for the top

$\frac{1}{4}$ pound ($\frac{1}{2}$ cup) butter, preferably unsalted, at room temperature

$\frac{1}{2}$ teaspoon salt

2 eggs at room temperature

$\frac{1}{2}$ cup sour cream

3 to 3$\frac{1}{2}$ cups all-purpose flour

Cherry-Almond Filling

1$\frac{1}{4}$ cups whole or slivered almonds, toasted

$\frac{1}{4}$ pound ($\frac{1}{2}$ cup) butter, preferably unsalted, at room temperature

$\frac{1}{2}$ cup packed light brown sugar

$\frac{1}{2}$ teaspoon vanilla

$\frac{1}{4}$ teaspoon almond extract

1 egg at room temperature

1 cup dried cherries or a mixture of cherries and golden raisins

Stir the yeast, milk, and 1 teaspoon of the sugar together in a small bowl and set aside until foamy, about 10 minutes. Meanwhile, in a mixing bowl, beat the butter with the remaining sugar and the salt until creamy. Add the eggs one at a time, followed by the sour cream and yeast. Add the flour by the cup until it clears the sides of the bowl, then turn it out and knead until the dough feels silky and smooth. Transfer to a buttered bowl, place a piece of plastic wrap directly over the surface, and set aside to rise until doubled in bulk. Or refrigerate overnight.

Make the filling. Cover the dried fruit, if hard, with hot water until softened, 10 to 15 minutes. Drain, squeeze dry, and set aside. Grind almonds finely. Cream the butter with the sugar until smooth, then add the flavorings, egg, and ground almonds.

Punch down the dough, then roll it into a rectangle approximately 1 × 2 feet. (If you've refrigerated it, leave it at room temperature for about 2 hours before rolling. It will still feel a little cold.) Cover with the almond filling, leaving a 1$\frac{1}{2}$-inch border all the way around, then scatter the cherries on top. Roll it up tightly and transfer to a lightly buttered cookie sheet. Form it into a crescent, with the ends pointing toward the center, or slice crosswise to make individual rolls. Set aside, covered with a towel until doubled in bulk, about an hour.

During the last 15 minutes, preheat the oven to 375°F. Brush the bread with the glaze, sprinkle generously with sugar, then bake in the center of the oven until golden brown and cooked through, about 1 hour. If it gets too dark while baking, cover it loosely with foil. Let cool on a rack, but serve warm.

Breads By Hand

NOTHING CONVEYS THE FEELING OF HOME AND HEARTH LIKE THE SMELL OF BAKING BREAD OR THE WARMTH OF A BASKET OF BISCUITS BEING PASSED AROUND THE TABLE. IN FACT, THE SIGHT AND SMELL OF HOMEMADE bread have always evoked a sense that all is well and that, I'm convinced, is behind the popularity of bread machines. Good bread is not as difficult to find for sale today as it once was, but still we make our own so we can wake up or come home to the reassuring smell of bread baking.

Many people think that their lives are too busy to include baking bread, but conveniently, breads fall into two categories—quick breads, which depend on fast-working baking powder and baking soda, and yeast breads which often need several hours or more to rise before baking. These different leavenings and ways of using them give us a number of options for baking strategies that make sense for our lives. For example, most quick breads (muffins, corn bread, biscuits) can be assembled by the time the oven is heated, and that, indeed, is quick. If you have 25 minutes to an hour or so for baking, you can fit them in. Yeasted risen pancakes and waffles take longer to ready, but they can be started the night before, plus they gain in flavor as they spend the night rising. Yeasted breads, like sandwich breads, spread their several stages over a number of hours, but it's easy to accommodate them to our schedules. On the other hand, some yeasted breads can be baked without pausing for kneading or a second rise, which makes them far quicker to make than conventionally thought. Small batches of dough rise more quickly than large ones and flatbreads, like pita, naan, and foccacia can be ready for the oven within an hour. So regardless of whether they're quick or long-rising, we can find some type of baked good that works with our lives.

Quick Breads

SINCE *they rely on baking powder, baking soda, and often eggs to gain their rise, muffins, scones, pancakes, biscuits, and tea cakes can be made from start to finish in an hour or less. Even a novice can assemble these batters and doughs in the time it takes the oven to preheat. While many quick breads are breakfast favorites, most are equally enjoyable at other meals as well. Freshly made biscuits and corn bread turn an otherwise ordinary meal into a special one.*

FLOUR: All-purpose unbleached white flour makes the light, high baked goods that are the trademark of American baking. Today whole-wheat pastry flour, which behaves just like white flour without making breads stodgy or heavy, is also available. Graham flour—whole-wheat flour with flakes of bran—also makes a fairly light but more wholesome bread. Other flours—rye, barley, corn, amaranth, quinoa, spelt, and buckwheat—contribute flavor, texture, and nutrition, but they need to be blended with wheat flour, which contains gluten, the stretchy substance that allows doughs to rise.

To measure flour, spoon it into a dry cup measure, one that's calibrated to the top, then sweep off the excess with a knife. Don't pack the flour down.

SWEETENERS: Sweeteners include sugar, honey, molasses, barley malt syrup, sucanat, and sorghum. Grains have their own inherent sweetness, so I find that just a small amount of sweetening, if any, is sufficient. Others, however, may prefer to go to the higher end of the range offered in recipes.

EGGS: Eggs bind, tenderize, and enrich quick breads while helping them rise. Those who wish to can replace the yolks with extra whites or use low-cholesterol eggs. You *can* also leave them out entirely, but your breads will be more crumbly and dry. To maintain moisture, you can replace eggs with fruit purees and pureed silken tofu volume for volume, about 3 tablespoons per large egg.

FAT: Oils can be used successfully in many quick breads, but where you want a more cakelike product, use butter and cream it with the sugar to incorporate air. I like to use enough fat to keep my baked goods moist and tender. With less, I've noticed that people just add more butter at the table.

LIQUIDS: I'm an ardent fan of buttermilk (low-fat is fine) because of its tangy note and the tenderness it produces in baked goods. Dried buttermilk, found in the baking section of supermarkets, can be added to the flour mixture in place of fresh, and natural yogurts (without added gums) can also replace buttermilk. Fermented milk products such as buttermilk and yogurt always require baking soda for leavening. If you're using regular milk, omit the soda and add an extra $1/2$ teaspoon baking powder. Other liquids that can be used in quick breads are fruit juices and rice, soy, or almond milk.

If you don't have buttermilk on hand, add 1 tablespoon distilled vinegar or lemon juice to 1 cup warm cow's milk or soy milk, stir until it curdles, then let stand 5 minutes before using. Chemically, it will behave just like buttermilk, requiring soda for the best rise.

Mixing and Baking Quick Breads

Have the ingredients at room temperature so that the batter will begin its rise as soon as it enters the oven. The only exception to this rule are biscuits or any bread where cold solid fat is worked into the flour. To bring eggs to room temperature, cover them with hot tap water and they will lose their chill after a few minutes.

Whisk together the dry ingredients before adding the wets so that they're well blended and there are no lumps of baking soda or powder. And don't forget to mix well from the bottom of the bowl up.

Quick bread batters are more resilient than we're led to believe, but avoid overmixing them. Light handling makes a lighter product. If you feel a batter has been overworked, let it stand for 10 to 15 minutes before baking to allow it to relax. Double-acting baking powder starts its second rising action when it enters the oven, so resting won't keep the bread from rising.

BAKING: Quick breads generally bake at around 375°F and should be baked in the center or top third of the oven. When baking several pans at once, leave a few inches between them so that air can circulate and an even temperature can be maintained. Turn them once during baking so that they'll brown evenly. Test a bread for doneness by inserting a long straw or thin skewer in the middle; it should come out dry and clean.

BAKING STONES: A pizza stone, also called a *baking stone,* is wonderful not only for getting a good crust on a pizza but for many breads as well. Since I always leave my stone in the oven, I've come to explore its possibilities. Biscuits, scones, and soda breads can be baked directly on the hot stone if you like a crisp bottom crust, or you can bake them on a sheet pan on top of the stone.

COOLING AND STORING: Quick breads are tempting to eat warm, but they slice more easily when cool. Always let loaves and muffins cool in their pans for 5 to 10 minutes before turning them out on a rack to finish cooling. Baked goods that contain fruit and vegetable purees keep well for days, wrapped and at room temperature. Breads that have gone a little stale can be moistened with water, put in a paper bag, and reheated at 375°F. All quick breads are great toasted.

Having muffins and breads on hand in the freezer can be a boon to a busy cook. To freeze baked goods, wrap cooled breads in a layer of plastic wrap followed by foil. Muffins can just go right into a zippered plastic bag. Let them thaw at room temperature or in the refrigerator before unwrapping. To reheat, wrap them loosely in foil and put in a 350°F oven for 15 to 20 minutes.

Muffins

MUFFINS may be our favorite quick bread. They're easy and versatile, and they make a tidy little bread that freezes well. Streusel, the crunchy, sweet toppings on page 643, makes them Sunday morning special. Not all muffins are sweet, though—look to the cheese and corn-rye muffins as savory accompaniments for soups or a savory breakfast.

Basic Buttermilk Muffins

A PLAIN, moist muffin that you can add to or embellish with ease.

MAKES 12 MUFFINS

2 ½ cups all-purpose or whole-wheat
    pastry flour
2 teaspoons baking powder
1 teaspoon baking soda
½ teaspoon salt
½ to ¾ cup packed light brown sugar

2 eggs, lightly beaten
1 ⅓ cups buttermilk
⅓ cup canola oil or butter, melted
1 ½ teaspoons vanilla extract

Preheat the oven to 375°F. Spray, oil, or butter muffin tins. Mix the dry ingredients in one bowl and the wets in a second bowl, then combine them with a few swift strokes. Using a rubber spatula, stir the batter up from the bottom of the bowl to make sure that there aren't any pockets of flour. Don't beat the batter and don't worry about a slightly uneven appearance. Spoon or scoop the batter into the tins, going nearly to the top for a nicely rounded muffin. Bake in the upper third of the oven until browned and well risen, about 25 minutes. Turn out the muffins and serve.

High-Protein Flour Muffins Replace up to 1 ¼ cups flour with quinoa or amaranth flour or ¾ cup flour with soy flour or untoasted wheat germ.

Spice Muffins Add 2 teaspoons ground cinnamon, 1 teaspoon grated nutmeg or ½ teaspoon ground cardamom, ⅛ teaspoon ground clove, and 1 teaspoon powdered ginger to the dry ingredients.

Fresh Fruit Muffins Add 1 cup of any of the following fruits to the batter: raspberries, blackberries, blueberries, tossed with a tablespoon of flour; apples or pears, finely diced; cranberries or finely diced rhubarb, tossed with 1 teaspoon orange zest; quince, grated; or pineapple, chopped into small pieces. Be sure to mix it thoroughly from the bottom so that the fruit doesn't become lodged in a single spot.

Dried Fruit Muffins Add 1 cup raisins, currants, chopped dates, dried cherries, or chopped prunes to the wet ingredients. If the fruit is hard, soften it first in hot water to cover for 10 to 15 minutes, then drain. Chopped nuts are always an excellent choice with dried fruits. Use up to 1 cup per recipe.

Dried Apricot and Ginger Muffins Dice 1 cup dried apricots into raisin-sized pieces and put them in a bowl with boiling water to cover. Let stand for 10 minutes or until soft, then drain. Add 1 1/2 teaspoons ground ginger to the dry ingredients and 1/2 cup diced candied ginger. Combine the wets and dries, then stir in the apricots. Add 1/2 cup chopped nuts or a streusel topping for a fancy muffin.

Date-Nut Muffins Add 1 cup chopped pitted dates and 1 cup chopped pecans or walnuts to the batter. Cover the muffins with pecan or orange streusel topping.

Fresh Corn Muffins Substitute 1 cup fine stone-ground cornmeal for the all-purpose flour and stir in 1 1/2 cups uncooked corn kernels.

Streusel Topping for Muffins and Coffee Cakes

Sprinkle these mixtures over muffins, coffeecakes, or baked fruits before baking for a sweet, crunchy topping. Leftovers freeze well, and it's always nice to have some ready to use. Use cold butter and mix the ingredients together in a small bowl with your fingers or in a food processor until crumbly. Sprinkle over the batter, pressing them lightly into it, just before they go into the oven.

AMOUNTS: These recipes make enough for a dozen muffins. Double the recipe to cover a coffee cake.

Basic Streusel

1/4 cup packed light brown sugar

1/2 cup flour or 1/4 cup *each* flour and rolled oats

1/2 teaspoon grated nutmeg or ground cinnamon

4 tablespoons cold butter

Orange Streusel

1 1/2 tablespoons finely grated orange zest

1/3 cup packed light brown sugar

1/2 teaspoon ground cinnamon or 1/4 teaspoon ground cardamom

4 tablespoons butter

1/2 cup flour

Pecan Streusel

1/2 cup packed brown sugar

2 teaspoons flour

1/2 teaspoon ground cinnamon

1/4 teaspoon grated nutmeg

3 tablespoons butter

2/3 cup chopped pecans

Banana Oat Muffins

A TENDER, low-fat muffin for banana bread lovers.

**MAKES 9 PLUMP
MUFFINS**

2 large ripe bananas, mashed

¾ cup buttermilk

⅓ cup packed light brown sugar

1 whole egg or 2 egg whites

2 tablespoons canola oil or melted butter

1 cup rolled oats

1½ cups all-purpose or whole-wheat pastry flour

1 teaspoon grated nutmeg

1½ teaspoons baking soda

Preheat the oven to 375°F. Spray or oil muffin tins.

In one bowl, mix the bananas with the buttermilk, sugar, egg, and oil, then add the oats. In another bowl, combine the flour, nutmeg, and baking soda. Pour the wet ingredients into the dry and quickly stir them together. Fill the muffin tins two-thirds full. (Put a little water in the empty cups.) Bake until golden brown and springy when pressed lightly with a finger, about 25 minutes. Run a knife around the edge of each muffin and remove.

Sweet Potato Muffins with Candied Ginger

CHUNKS of candied ginger make these particularly good. If you don't have ginger readily at hand, replace it with chopped dates, raisins, or fresh pineapple. Serve these with Brie or other mild cheese, butter, or cream cheese.

**MAKES 10 TO
12 MUFFINS**

⅓ cup chopped candied ginger or chopped pineapple, dates, or raisins

¼ cup butter, melted, or vegetable oil

⅓ cup unsulfured molasses

½ cup packed light brown sugar

1 cup mashed cooked sweet potato or winter squash

2 eggs

½ cup buttermilk

1¾ cups flour

1 teaspoon baking powder

1 teaspoon baking soda

½ teaspoon salt

1 teaspoon ground cinnamon

Preheat the oven to 375°F. Oil or spray muffin tins. Mix the ginger and wet ingredients in a bowl until smooth; mix the dry ingredients in a second bowl. Combine the two, mixing gently until well blended. Spoon the batter into the muffin tins and bake on the middle shelf until lightly browned, 25 minutes.

Corn-Rye Muffins

MULTIGRAINED and filling, these are good, hearty lunch muffins. The batter can also be baked as a quick bread.

MAKES 10 MUFFINS

1 cup whole-wheat flour

½ cup rye flour

½ cup stone-ground cornmeal

2 teaspoons baking powder

2 to 4 tablespoons unsulfured molasses

½ teaspoon salt

2 eggs or 1 whole egg and 2 egg whites

1 cup milk

⅓ cup corn oil

Preheat the oven to 375°F and spray or oil muffin tins. Mix the dry ingredients in one bowl, the wets in another, then combine them and stir together quickly. Fill muffin cups about two-thirds full and bake until risen and lightly browned, about 25 minutes.

Cheese Muffins

1¼ cups flour
½ cup stone-ground cornmeal
2½ teaspoons baking powder
½ teaspoon salt
2 eggs

1 cup milk
2 tablespoons corn oil
1½ tablespoons honey
1 to 2 cups grated Cheddar

SERVE *these savory muffins with summer soups made of corn, tomato, or roasted peppers or with the All Bean Chili.*

MAKES 10 MUFFINS

Preheat the oven to 400°F. Oil or spray muffin tins. Combine the dry ingredients in one bowl and the eggs, milk, oil, and honey in another. Pour the wet ingredients into the dry, stir them quickly together, then stir in the cheese. Fill the muffin cups about three-quarters full, then bake until the muffins are browned and springy, about 25 minutes.

Cheese Muffins with Herbs: Add 2 tablespoons chopped dill and 1 teaspoon toasted ground cumin seeds or caraway seeds to the batter.

Cheese-Corn Muffins: Add 1 cup uncooked corn kernels to the batter with the cheese. If you like it hot, include ½ cup chopped roasted green chiles.

Quinoa Muffins

1 cup cooked or ½ cup raw quinoa
1 cup whole-wheat pastry flour
1 cup quinoa flour
¼ teaspoon salt
1 teaspoon baking soda

½ cup packed light brown sugar
1 egg
¼ cup butter, melted, or vegetable oil
1¼ cups buttermilk or yogurt
1 teaspoon vanilla extract

THESE *are crunchy and so good! If you have no leftover quinoa, remember that you can cook fresh in practically the time it takes to preheat the oven.*

MAKES 9 TO 12 MUFFINS

Preheat the oven to 375°F. Spray or oil muffin tins.

If cooking quinoa, rinse it well, put it in a small saucepan with 1 cup water, and bring to a boil. Simmer, covered, until the water is absorbed, about 15 minutes, then drain.

Meanwhile, combine the flours, salt, soda, and sugar in a mixing bowl. Beat the egg with the oil, buttermilk, and vanilla. Stir the wet ingredients into the dry, add the quinoa, and mix with a spatula, scraping up from the bottom so that the flour is mixed in thoroughly. Scoop the batter into the muffin cups and bake until firm and light brown on top, 25 to 30 minutes.

Molasses-Buttermilk Bread

DARK, *crumbly, and moist with the tangy flavor of buttermilk, this is a close cousin of Boston brown bread. Serve with whipped cream cheese, fresh ricotta, or a mild cheese, such as St. André or Explorateur.*

MAKES ONE 4- × 8-INCH LOAF OR 10 MUFFINS

½ cup rye flour

½ cup fine stone-ground cornmeal

1 cup all-purpose or whole-wheat pastry flour

½ teaspoon baking soda

1 teaspoon baking powder

¾ teaspoon salt

1 cup buttermilk

3 tablespoons vegetable oil or butter, melted

½ cup unsulfured molasses

2 whole eggs or 3 egg whites

¾ cup raisins, chopped dates, or currants

Preheat the oven to 350°F and spray or butter and flour a bread pan. Combine the dry ingredients in a mixing bowl; whisk the wet ingredients together in a second bowl. Pour the wet ingredients into the dry and stir quickly to combine. Stir in the fruits. Transfer to the prepared pan and bake for 45 minutes or until a cake tester comes out clean. Let cool for at least 15 minutes in the pan before turning out onto a rack or serving.

Corn Breads

This American favorite can be whipped together by the time the oven is heated. Corn breads are most accommodating. You can use white, yellow, or blue cornmeal; buttermilk or sweet milk; butter or corn oil, which enhances the flavor of corn. Stone-ground cornmeal, whatever the color, will make the best-tasting breads.

Basic Corn Bread

MAKES ONE 8-INCH SQUARE PAN OR 10-INCH SKILLET

2 tablespoons butter

1 cup stone-ground cornmeal

1 cup all-purpose or whole-wheat pastry flour

½ teaspoon salt

2 teaspoons baking powder

2 eggs

¼ cup corn oil or butter, melted

2 to 4 tablespoons honey to taste

1 cup milk

Preheat the oven to 425°F. Put the butter in an 8-inch square baking pan and set in the oven while it's heating. Meanwhile, stir the dry ingredients together and make a well in the center of the bowl. In another bowl, whisk together the wet ingredients. As soon as the oven is hot, remove the pan and brush the butter around the edges. Pour any excess into the wet ingredients. Quickly mix the wet and dry ingredients together, then pour the batter into the pan and bake in the middle of the oven until golden brown on top and beginning to pull away from the edges, about 25 minutes. Serve hot right from the pan.

Green Chile and Cheese Corn Bread Add ¹/₂ cup grated Jack or Cheddar and ¹/₄ cup or more diced roasted green chiles to the batter.

Vanilla Corn Bread Vanilla sets off the sweetness of corn and is good when you want a slightly sweeter breakfast bread. Add 1 teaspoon vanilla extract to the wet ingredients and use the larger amount of honey.

Corn-Husk Muffins For a popular southwestern effect, moisten 10 dried corn husks, the kind used for tamales, in hot water. Place one in the bottom of each muffin cup. Secure them with a dab of the batter and leave one end sticking up several inches. Bake at 375°F for 20 to 25 minutes.

Muffins with Corn Kernels Stir 1 cup fresh or frozen corn kernels into the batter for a little extra crunch.

Buttermilk Skillet Corn Bread

3 tablespoons butter

1 cup flour

1 cup stone-ground white or yellow cornmeal

1 teaspoon baking powder

¹/₂ teaspoon baking soda

¹/₂ teaspoon salt

2 eggs, beaten

2 tablespoons sugar or honey

2 cups buttermilk

A BIG, tender golden cake baked in a cast-iron skillet.

SERVES 6

Preheat the oven to 375°F. Put the butter in a 10-inch cast-iron skillet and place in the oven while you get everything else together: Sift the dry ingredients in one bowl and mix the eggs, sugar, and buttermilk in another. Remove the pan from the oven, brush the butter over the sides, then pour the rest into the wet ingredients. Combine the wet and dry ingredients, and stir long enough to make a smooth batter. Pour the batter into the hot pan and bake until lightly browned and springy to the touch, 25 to 30 minutes.

Marion's Custard Corn Bread A first-rate Sunday morning or supper bread. Pour a cup of cream over the batter just as the bread goes into the oven, but don't stir it. It will settle into the bread while baking, leaving a custardy layer on top. Delicious drizzled with molasses, honey, or blackberry jam.

Spoon Bread

A CROSS *between corn bread and a pudding, practical spoon bread uses ordinary ingredients, is easy to make, and is comforting and nourishing. Serve it any time of day, with butter and molasses, or with savory accompaniments.*

SERVES 4

³/₄ cup fine stone-ground white or yellow cornmeal

2 teaspoons baking powder

Salt and freshly milled white pepper if savory

4 tablespoons butter, cut into chunks

4 eggs, beaten

³/₄ cup milk

Preheat the oven to 375°F. Lightly butter a 2-quart soufflé or other baking dish. Stir the cornmeal, baking powder, and ³/₄ teaspoon salt together, then add the butter and pour 1¹/₂ cups boiling water over all. Stir to break up any lumps, then let stand until the butter is melted. Add the eggs and milk, pour into the baking dish, and bake until puffed, golden, and set, 45 to 50 minutes. Serve hot.

Cheese and Chile Spoon Bread Stir ¹/₃ to ¹/₂ cup chopped roasted green chiles into the batter and scatter ¹/₂ cup finely grated Muenster or Jack over the top before baking.

Spoon Bread with Condiments Mentioned in Huntley Dent's classic work *The Feast of Santa Fe,* this is a great way to enjoy spoon bread for brunch or supper. Arrange a variety of condiments in little bowls: salsas; Red Chile Sauce, page 70; chopped cilantro and chopped scallion; diced jalapeño chile or chopped roasted green chile; grated Jack or Muenster or crumbled goat cheese. Serve the bread with a large spoon to make a neat mound, then let each person scatter condiments over the top.

Biscuits

Basic biscuits are easy and fast to make—the oven won't even be hot by the time you're ready to pop them in. If you're reheating soup for dinner, biscuits will make it special. Here are a few things to know about making good biscuits:

- The less the dough is worked, the more tender the biscuits will be. Knead the dough just until it comes together in a smooth ball—about a dozen kneadings. Gently rework the scraps and use them too.

- Placing biscuits close together makes them rise higher and the steam coming off them keeps them from drying out. Placed an inch apart or more, they'll be crustier. Biscuits baked directly on a heated pizza stone have an especially good crust.

- If you don't have a biscuit cutter, a drinking glass, wineglass, shot glass—a glass of any kind will do. Biscuits can also be cut with a knife into diamonds or squares.

- Enjoy them while they're still warm from the oven. Biscuits aren't meant to be kept around, but leftovers are good toasted.

Basic Buttermilk Biscuits

2 cups all-purpose or whole-wheat
    pastry flour

2 teaspoons baking powder

1/2 teaspoon baking soda

1/2 teaspoon salt

6 tablespoons butter

1 cup buttermilk

BUTTERMILK biscuits are exceptionally tender with a slightly tangy edge.

**MAKES 12 TO
16 BISCUITS**

Preheat the oven to 450°F. If you have a baking stone, heat the oven for an extra 10 minutes. Otherwise, lightly grease a sheet pan and set it aside.

Combine the dry ingredients in a bowl and cut in the butter with your fingers or two knives until the mixture looks like coarse meal. Pour in the buttermilk and stir it with a fork until the dry ingredients are evenly moistened. Lightly flour the counter, turn out the dough, and pat it into a circle about 3/4 inch thick. Cut into rounds or another shape. Reassemble the scraps and cut them out as well. Bake the biscuits directly on the hot baking stone or on the sheet pan until light brown, 15 to 20 minutes.

Baking Powder Biscuits Instead of buttermilk, use regular milk and omit the baking soda.

Biscuits Made with Oil In place of butter and shortening, use the same amount of oil—canola, sunflower seed, or other vegetable oil. Stir the oil into the milk, then add this mixture to the dry ingredients. Stir just until the dough leaves the sides of the bowl and don't worry about its lumpy appearance. Flour the counter, knead briefly or simply pat it into a circle, then cut out the biscuits and bake.

Dropped Biscuits Increase the liquid in the Basic Buttermilk Biscuits or Baking Powder Biscuits to 1 1/3 cups. Instead of rolling it out, drop the dough by spoonfuls onto the sheet pan. They will be rough and cobbled looking rather than smooth, but just as good.

Seeded Cheese Biscuits To the dry ingredients for Buttermilk Biscuits or Baking Powder Biscuits, add 1 cup coarsely grated, then chopped cheese, such as sharp Cheddar or Gruyère. Roll them out, brush the tops of the biscuits with beaten egg, and sprinkle generously with poppy or sesame seeds before baking.

Whole-Wheat Biscuits A coarse-milled flour filled with bran, such as graham flour, makes a light but very substantial biscuit—one that will hold you all morning. Replace white flour with graham flour or 1 1/2 cups whole-wheat flour mixed with 1/2 cup wheat bran.

Angel Biscuits

THREE *kinds of leaven-ing raise these heavenly biscuits. Although they contain yeast, they aren't kneaded and they require only as much time as it takes to preheat the oven. Make them small and serve them with a spot of good jam, a thin slice of Gruyère cheese, or any of the flavored butters.*

MAKES ABOUT FIFTY 1-INCH OR TWENTY-FOUR 2-INCH BISCUITS

2¼ teaspoons (1 envelope) active dry yeast

2 teaspoons sugar

4 cups all-purpose flour

2 teaspoons baking powder

1 teaspoon baking soda

1½ teaspoons salt

½ pound butter (1 cup)

1½ cups buttermilk

1 egg, beaten

Stir the yeast into ¼ cup warm water with 1 teaspoon sugar in a small bowl and set aside to proof. Meanwhile, mix the remaining sugar with the flour, baking powder, soda, and salt in a mixing bowl, then cut in the butter with your fingers or two knives until coarse crumbs are formed. Stir in the yeast mixture and the buttermilk and bring it together with a fork.

Turn the dough out onto a counter and knead lightly until smooth, then roll it out about ⅜ inch thick. Cut out the biscuits any size you like. I like using a cordial or sherry glass so that they're small—one or two bites—good for a cocktail biscuit or brunch where there's lots of other food. Transfer them to a lightly buttered sheet pan, brush with beaten egg, and let rise for 15 minutes while you preheat the oven to 375°F. Bake until the biscuits are browned, about 20 minutes.

Yeasted Potato Biscuits

UNLIKE *the Angel Bis-cuits, these exceptional biscuits do require rising time, so they're not for last-minute baking. The potato combined with the yeast makes them feather-light and tender, with a delectable fragrance.*

MAKES TEN 2-INCH BISCUITS

2¼ teaspoons (1 envelope) active dry yeast

½ cup buttermilk or regular milk

2 tablespoons butter, cut into small pieces

1 tablespoon sugar

½ cup warmed mashed potatoes (about 1 medium potato)

1 teaspoon salt

2½ cups all-purpose or bread flour

Beaten egg, milk, or cream, for glazing

Stir the yeast into ¼ cup warm water in a small bowl and set it aside. Slowly warm the buttermilk with the butter and sugar in a small pan. (Buttermilk may curdle, but it will smooth out in the end.) When the butter has melted, pour the liquid into a bowl and beat in the potatoes, salt, ¼ cup of the flour, and the proofed yeast. Cover and let stand until light and foamy, about 30 minutes.

Stir in the remaining flour until no more can be added easily, then knead the dough un-til smooth and elastic. Cover and let rise until doubled in bulk, 45 minutes to an hour. Turn it out, then roll into a circle about ⅓ inch thick and cut into 2-inch rounds. Place on a lightly greased sheet pan, cover, and let rise again until nearly doubled, 45 minutes to an hour.

Preheat the oven to 400°F. Brush the biscuits with the beaten egg and bake until the biscuits are golden, about 20 minutes.

Oat Scones

1 cup rolled oats, plus extra for the counter

1½ cups all-purpose or whole-wheat pastry flour

3 tablespoons brown sugar

2 teaspoons baking powder

½ teaspoon salt

7 tablespoons cold butter, cut into small pieces

1 egg

½ cup plus 2 tablespoons milk or cream

½ teaspoon vanilla extract

Preheat the oven to 425°F. If you have a baking stone, heat it for an extra 10 minutes.

Mix the dry ingredients together, then cut in the butter with your fingers or two knives until coarse crumbs are formed. Beat the egg with the milk and vanilla and stir it into the dough. Mix just enough to moisten the dry ingredients evenly. Scatter some oats on the counter and turn the dough out on top of them. Pat into a circle about ½ inch thick, then cut into eight wedges and place each piece on the hot baking stone, if using, or on a sheet pan. Bake until nicely browned, 15 to 18 minutes. Serve warm.

SCONES, *closely related to biscuits, are usually enriched with an egg, frequently sweeter, and sometimes richer. Serve these tender oat scones with bitter marmalade, strong honey, or apple butter and Tangy Whipped Cream. For variety, try rye, barley, or other flakes in place of the oats.*

MAKES 8 SCONES

Ginger Cream Scones

½ to 1 cup candied ginger, chopped to the size of a raisin

2 cups flour

2 teaspoons baking powder

1 tablespoon sugar, plus extra for the top

½ teaspoon salt

4 tablespoons cold butter, cut into small pieces

2 eggs

½ cup plus 1 tablespoon cream or a mixture of milk and cream

½ teaspoon vanilla

Preheat the oven to 425°F. If you have a baking stone, heat it for an extra 10 minutes. Or lightly butter a sheet pan.

Toss the ginger with a tablespoon of the flour. Mix the remaining flour with the baking powder, sugar, and salt, then cut in the butter with your fingers or two knives until the mixture resembles meal. Combine the eggs, cream, and vanilla, then stir it into the flour mixture along with the ginger. Turn the dough onto a floured board and lightly knead 8 to 10 times. Pat or roll the dough into a circle about ¾ inch thick, then brush the top with the remaining cream and sprinkle with sugar. Cut into 12 wedges or into small circles and bake directly on the stone or on the sheet pan until glazed with gold, about 15 minutes. Serve warm.

Some Other Flavorings for Scones: The following are always good additions whether you're making the hearty oat or cream scones: 1 heaping teaspoon grated orange or lemon zest; ⅓ cup currants, dried cherries, berries, or raisins, plumped in warm water and then squeezed dry; ⅓ cup chopped dates; ½ cup chopped pecans, walnuts, or roasted hazelnuts; caramelized pecans or walnuts; grated nutmeg or ground cinnamon.

WHEN *I was pastry chef at Cafe Escalera in Santa Fe, I used to make these for early-morning customers who wanted just a little something with their coffee. It's the cream that makes them melt in your mouth like nothing else does. Ginger scones make an exceptional base for strawberry, peach, or dried winter fruit compote shortcake.*

MAKES 12 SCONES

Irish Soda Bread with Bran and Oats

THERE are many kinds of Irish soda bread, but this one, filled with honest ingredients—flaky bran and rolled oats—is one of my favorites. If you have a baking stone, bake the bread right on it, but allow 25 minutes for it to preheat. This bread is very good with cheeses of all kinds—from aged Cheddar to St. André or mild goat cheese—and strong, bitter marmalade.

SERVES 6

1 cup all-purpose flour
1 cup whole-wheat flour
$\frac{1}{2}$ cup wheat bran
$\frac{1}{2}$ cup rolled oats

$1\frac{1}{2}$ teaspoons baking soda
5 tablespoons cold butter
$1\frac{1}{4}$ cups buttermilk
2 tablespoons molasses or honey

Preheat the oven to 400°F. If you have a baking stone, heat it for an extra 10 minutes. Otherwise lightly butter or oil a sheet pan.

Mix the dry ingredients in a bowl, then cut in the butter with two knives (or use a food processor) until it's crumbly and fine. Stir in the buttermilk and molasses, bringing everything into a ball, then turn the dough onto a floured counter and knead until smooth but still soft, no more than a minute. Shape into a disk 7 or 8 inches across, then slash an X in the center. Set directly on the hot baking stone or on the pan and bake until browned, about 35 minutes. Though it's very tempting to eat the bread piping hot, it tastes better if it can cool on a rack for at least 30 minutes.

Corn Tortillas

I REMEMBER my adventurous parents coming home from the store with a bag of masa harina (flour made from lime-treated corn) so that we could make our own tortillas. We tried slapping out tortillas with our hands the way we'd seen Mexican women do. Dough flew around the kitchen, and we never did really get a tortilla, which is probably why it took me so long to get around to making corn tortillas again—this time with a press.

Although corn tortillas are easily available, your own hot-off-the-press tortillas—as well as anything made with them—will be exquisite.

MAKES ABOUT SIXTEEN 6-INCH TORTILLAS

2 cups masa harina (Quaker or Maseca brand, available at supermarkets and Mexican markets)

1 cup plus 3 tablespoons hot water

Stir the masa harina and hot water together in a bowl, then cover and let stand for 30 minutes. Add cool water, a tablespoon at a time, working the dough with your hands until the dough is soft and pliable but not so wet that it's sticky.

Divide the dough into 16 pieces and roll them into balls. Cover them with a barely damp towel or plastic wrap so that they don't dry out. Heat a large griddle or a couple of cast-iron skillets over medium heat.

To make the tortillas, line the bottom of a metal tortilla press with plastic wrap or a plastic bag. Place a ball of dough in the center, flatten it a little with your hand, then cover with a second plastic bag. Bring the top of the press down and press firmly but not too hard. You're looking for a tortilla between 5 and 6 inches across and just slightly less than $\frac{1}{8}$ inch thick. It will take a few tries to figure out just how hard to press.

Quickly peel the plastic off the top of the tortilla, flip it into your hand, and quickly remove the plastic from what is now the top. Now ease the tortilla off your hand and onto the griddle. Let it sit for 15 seconds before trying to turn it over. Cook on the second side until it's speckled on the bottom, 30 to 45 seconds. Stack the finished tortillas in a cloth-lined basket. They'll retain their heat for about 30 minutes.

If the dough was moist enough, the tortillas should have swelled like pita bread, which gives them a wonderful light texture. If your first tortillas are heavy, dry, and cracked around the edges, knead a little more water into the remaining dough.

Flour Tortillas

2 cups flour, preferably pastry flour,
white or whole wheat

1½ teaspoons baking powder

1 teaspoon salt

2 teaspoons vegetable oil, such as
safflower

¾ cup water or milk

Stir together the flour, baking powder, and salt in a large bowl. Sprinkle on the oil, then work it into the flour with your fingers until combined evenly. Stir in the water and work with your fingers again to form a somewhat sticky ball.

Flour your counter, turn out the dough, and knead it vigorously until smooth and soft, about a minute. By now it should be smooth and, as my friends Bill and Cheryl Jamison, experts in all things Southwestern, say, about the texture of your earlobe. Press a piece of plastic wrap onto the dough or cover the bowl with a damp towel and let the dough rest for 15 minutes. (If you used all-purpose flour, let it rest for 30 minutes to relax the gluten.) Divide the dough into eight pieces and roll each one into a circle about ¼ inch thick, handling it as little and lightly as possible.

Heat an ungreased griddle or cast-iron skillet over medium-high heat. Let the heat really build up, then lay a tortilla into the pan and cook for 40 seconds or until flecked on the bottom. Flip and cook on the second side for 40 to 60 seconds. Stack in a basket lined with a napkin and serve warm.

In New Mexico, flour tortillas are made with whole-wheat as well as white flour. Size depends on where in the Southwest or Mexico you are and how you're going to use the tortillas. If you can buy good tortillas, you don't need to make your own. But if you can't, you might want to try. A soft flour that doesn't have too much gluten is preferable for these thick New Mexican–style tortillas.

MAKES EIGHT 8-INCH TORTILLAS

Wheat Thins

1½ cups flour

½ cup wheat bran

½ teaspoon salt, plus extra for the top

¼ pound butter (½ cup)

Preheat the oven to 425°F. Combine the flour, bran, and salt in a bowl, then cut in the butter with your fingers or two knives until it looks like coarse crumbs. Lightly stir in 5 tablespoons ice water, or more as needed, until the dough clings together when pressed with the hands. Roll it out as thin as you can manage on a lightly floured surface. If you want a salty cracker, sprinkle the surface with salt and gently press it in with the rolling pin. Dock the surface with the tines of a fork, then cut into squares or diamonds and transfer to a baking sheet.

Bake until lightly browned on top, 8 to 10 minutes. Let cool briefly, then serve. Store in an airtight tin or freeze.

FLAKY and irresistible, these crackers have a rich flavor thanks to wheat bran. Make the dough by hand or with a mixer fitted with a paddle attachment.

MAKES ABOUT SEVENTY 1-INCH SQUARES

Seed Crackers

CERTAINLY *there are many good crackers on the market, but none will look or taste like these. The dough takes about 2 minutes to make in a food processor plus 15 minutes to rest, and, once rolled and cut, 10 minutes to bake. Use half the dough at a time and freeze the rest if you need just a few dozen crackers.*

**MAKES ABOUT
50 CRACKERS**

1 cup all-purpose or whole-wheat pastry flour

¹/₂ teaspoon salt, plus extra for sprinkling

2 tablespoons butter

1 teaspoon mustard

1 heaping cup Cheddar, grated

¹/₃ cup freshly grated Parmesan

2 eggs

2 tablespoons seeds, such as caraway, cumin, sesame, poppy, fennel, and black mustard seeds

Red pepper flakes, optional

Mix the flour and salt in a bowl, then work in the butter with your fingers until small crumbs are formed. Add the mustard, cheeses, and eggs and work the dough lightly so that it forms a coherent mass. Wrap in plastic, press into a disk, and let rest for 15 minutes in the refrigerator.

Preheat the oven to 375°F. Divide the dough into two pieces. Lightly flour your work surface and roll each piece into a rectangle about 10 × 14 inches. Scatter the extra salt, seeds, and pepper flakes over the top and lightly press them into the dough with the rolling pin. (Make a mixture of seeds or visually divide the dough into strips and use just one kind of seed on each strip.) Cut into squares, diamonds, or strips, transfer to a sheet pan, and bake until golden brown and slightly puffed, 8 to 10 minutes. Serve within the day or store in an airtight container until needed. Reheat frozen crackers for about 5 minutes in a 350° oven to freshen them.

Crêpes

ALTHOUGH *not as popular as they once were, crepes are always well received. They can make simple foods special and they're not difficult to make. Consider too, this decade's romance with the wrapper—certainly the crêpe is that if nothing else. Here are a few things to know about making crêpes:*

1. After being mixed, the batter needs to rest so that it can relax and absorb the flour, ensuring that the crêpes will be supple and tender when cooked. Although you'll be able to use the batter within 30 minutes, it's better if it can rest for 2 hours, or overnight.

2. Start heating the pan over a fairly high heat, then reduce the temperature to medium once the pan is hot. If the pan gets too hot, just wave it back and forth in the air several times to cool it down.

3. If the batter is the right consistency, it will coat the pan quickly and evenly. If it's too thick, it will be sluggish. Thin a too thick batter by gently stirring in additional milk or water until it's the right consistency. The first crêpe usually never turns out, so just throw it out and go onto the second, which will probably be fine. You don't need to oil the pan each time, only the first time.

Crêpe Batter

2 eggs
1 cup milk
½ cup water
½ teaspoon salt

1 cup all-purpose flour
3 tablespoons melted butter
　　or vegetable oil

Combine all the ingredients in a blender or food processor and blend until smooth, about 5 seconds. Scrape down the sides, then blend 5 seconds more. Cover and set aside set in the refrigerator to rest.

Heat a crêpe pan (a 7 to 10-inch lightweight skillet with sloping sides) then brush it with a little oil or butter as soon as it's hot. When it sizzles, pour in a little more than 2 tablespoons batter (for a 7-inch pan) and immediately swirl it around the pan. Cook until golden on the bottom, about 1 minute. Slide a knife under an edge to loosen the crêpe, grab it with your fingers and flip it over. The second side need only cook until it's set, about 30 seconds.

Set the finished crêpe on a plate, then continue making the rest. If you stack the finished crêpes on top of each other they'll hold their heat quite well until all are done.

How to Use Crepes Filling needn't be more than a little cheese grated over top and freshly peppered, or, for dessert, a squeeze of lemon juice and a dusting of sugar. More elaborate preparations of course are to be considered too. Some savory fillings can be formed from many of the simpler recipes in the book, such as the following:

　　Sautéed Spinach with ricotta cheese and a spoonful of pesto
　　Sautéed Mushrooms with Garlic and Parsley
　　Mushrooms with Tarragon and Cream
　　Mushroom Stews
　　Skillet Asparagus with Warm Sage and Garlic Butter
　　Roasted Asparagus and Fontina Cheese
　　Corn and Mushroom Ragout with Sage and Roasted Garlic
　　Simple Summer Stew with Herb Butter
　　Chopped Broccoli
　　Sautéed Zucchini with Garlic and Lemon
　　Corn and Lima Bean Ragout

Crêpe Shapes Crêpes can be rolled, folded into quarters, folded into packages, quartered then rolled into cones, or filled then rolled and sliced. Always place your filling on the second (paler) side so that when finished, the golden side is exposed. Filled crêpes can be brushed with butter and heated in a 350°F oven for 12 to 15 minutes or browned in a skillet.

Variations to the Batter Substitute half the flour with other more interesting flours, such as buckwheat, corn flour, masa, quinoa, rye, and so forth. Or add two pinches saffron threads diluted first in 1 tablespoon hot water to the batter, or ¼ cup chopped herbs—parsley, basil, thyme, marjoram, rosemary are some good ones.

Breads Made with Yeast

Bread baking is a life-renewing experience. For many, the very act of baking—bringing dry granules of yeast and flour into a living dough, working it under your hands, and inhaling its good smells while it bakes—is its own reward. But many people also bake because of the quality and kinds of bread they can make at home. While good bread is getting much easier to find, good bakeries don't yet exist in every community. To have breads based on whole grains and interesting flours and leavenings, many still have to make them at home.

In addition to our traditional American breads, we are now baking a host of new favorites—flatbreads and coarse, chewy country breads based on slow-developing wild yeasts. There's no shortage of information for the aspiring home baker on how to make these challenging new—or, rather, *ancient*—breads, for many good bakers have written extensively about their craft. This chapter is a sampler of both basic and new breads that fit our needs and wants today and isn't meant to cover the entire vast territory of bread baking.

While many have found the bread machine an answer to the problems of time and scheduling, bread machines have their own recipe requirements and formulations. The recipes in this chapter are the conventional, hands-on variety and shouldn't be used in bread machines.

Yeasted Bread Basics

Bread baking is not difficult, but it helps to understand how the ingredients you'll be using function. If you're new to bread baking, take a look at this section before you start.

YEAST: Yeast is a living organism that gives bread life, loft, and character. Because it's alive, its allure is very powerful. Beginners are often afraid of killing the yeast, but it's actually easy to make it thrive—and difficult to kill. Usually the first attempt is successful, but if it isn't, remember that all you've lost is some water, yeast, and a little flour.

Yeast comes in two forms: compressed cakes and dried granules. Cake yeast, which used to be common, is now rather hard to find. More common and convenient is dry yeast. It can be found in the baking section of your supermarket in small foil packets, but it's far cheaper and more convenient to buy it in bulk at a natural food store and measure it out as needed.

In general, a ¼-ounce package, which contains about 2¼ teaspoons yeast, will raise 6 cups flour mixed with 2 cups liquid. At high altitudes, where breads tend to rise too high and too fast, you might use 2 teaspoons instead. Using less yeast also means the dough develops more flavor during its extended rise.

Getting Yeast Growing: Yeast comes alive in a warm environment. Its life usually begins when it's dissolved in warm water that's pleasant to the touch, between 100 and 115 degrees on a thermometer, or baby bottle temperature. If you're just starting out, take the temperature of the water the first time so you can see what it is; sprinkle it on your inner wrist to see how it feels, then use the skin test thereafter. You'll get the feel of it quickly.

Proofing: Yeast wasn't always as reliable as it is today, so it had to be proved (or proofed) to make sure it would work. That's what we're doing when we stir it into a small amount of warm water, sometimes with a pinch of sugar. If it's alive, it will begin to foam in 5 to 10 minutes. Today's commercial yeast is virtually fail-safe, and new fast-rising yeasts are added directly to the flour. If using fast-rising or instant yeasts, read the instructions—they often call for smaller amounts.

SUGAR AND SALT: Sugar in any form (malt syrups, honey, molasses, and so on) feeds the yeast and speeds its growth. Whole grains contain natural sugars that also provide food for the yeast. Salt keeps the yeast from growing too fast or too much, and of course it gives flavor to bread.

FLOUR: The type of flour you use determines how a bread looks, tastes, and handles. Gluten, a protein found in wheat, has elasticity that allows the dough to rise by trapping the released gases from the yeast. Gluten is developed by kneading and beating. Flour milled from hard winter wheat, called *bread flour,* has more gluten than pastry flour, which is made from soft wheat. All-purpose flour, made from a blend of wheats, has enough gluten to give bread its rise but not so much that it can't also be used for quick breads and pastries. Special flours like rye, soy, corn, barley, quinoa, have virtually no gluten, so they need to be blended with a portion of wheat flour—at least half.

Usually 3 cups flour, or about a pound, requires 1 cup liquid. Some special flours, like buckwheat, require more liquid, and flour in dry climates will also need more liquid. This is why the last bit of flour is held back, to be kneaded in as required.

In addition to wheat, interesting textural and flavor additions are gained by adding bran, wheat berries, cracked wheat, cooked rice, oats, flakes, bulgur, and cornmeal. Mashed potatoes, nuts, dried fruits, olives, cheese, and herbs are other additions that find their way into specialty breads.

A NOTE ABOUT WHOLE-WHEAT FLOUR

Whole-wheat flours differ from one another according to how they're milled. Most are fine and powdery, just like white flour. In fact, there is a white whole-wheat flour, although most are brown. However, I am particularly fond of a coarser type with visible flecks of bran. Its roughness makes a lighter, less dense product but one with character. A small mill in New Mexico (Valencia) produces just such a flour, but of course it's not available nationwide. You can achieve a similar effect by using graham flour, which is usually coarser than regular whole wheat, or by replacing up to a quarter of the flour with wheat bran. Keep your eye out for small mills in your area that aren't nationally known—you may find just the flour you like.

LIQUID: Water is usually the liquid in yeasted breads. Milk (including buttermilk) is used when you want a softer dough with a fine crumb. Other liquids you can use for bread are the whey that separates from yogurt when you're making yogurt cheese; the water left from boiling potatoes; and beer. Eggs are added to the liquid for richer breads.

FAT: Most breads do not depend on fat for structure. However, it does contribute flavor and tenderness and also helps keep breads moist—important in dry climates. If fat isn't called for and you wish to include some, add 2 to 4 tablespoons when you add the proofed yeast to the water (for a recipe calling for 5 to 6 cups flour). If leaving out fat where it's called for, be sure to replace its volume with water or milk.

BAKING EQUIPMENT: Not a great deal of equipment is needed for bread baking. Most of what's needed are kitchen fixtures—a small bowl or teacup for proofing yeast, a large bowl, and a large bowl for mixing the dough, preferably heavy ceramic or pottery, which holds its warmth, although stainless and glass are also fine. Aside from measuring spoons and cups, you'll want a wooden spoon for mixing doughs and a dough scraper—a metal 4- × 6-inch dull blade with a handle—for scraping dough up off the counter or for assisting in working wet, sticky doughs.

A kitchen scale is useful for weighing rolls and loaves so they'll be equal in size, although you'll do well using your eyes. Sheet pans and a baking stone are used for baking rolls and free-form breads. For standard loaves, you'll want two bread pans, $8\frac{1}{2} \times 4\frac{1}{2}$ inches or, my favorite, 4×10 inches (available at good kitchen stores). A spray bottle is handy for introducing moisture to the oven to develop the crust, and a pastry brush is for brushing on glazes.

A stand-up mixer with paddle attachment certainly isn't necessary for baking bread, but it's very nice to use if you have one. My KitchenAid is my best-loved kitchen luxury, and I use it all the time for baking.

10 Basic Steps to Making Yeasted Breads

Most recipes for yeasted breads follow these steps. Variations are always given in the particular recipes where they occur.

1. PROOF THE YEAST IN $\frac{1}{4}$ CUP WARM WATER. This step proves to you that the yeast is active and ready to work. Stir the yeast into warm tap water and let it stand until it's covered with foamy bubbles, which takes about 10 minutes. If nothing happens in 15 minutes, throw it out and start over.

2. COMBINE THE LIQUIDS AND SALT, THEN BEGIN WORKING IN THE FLOUR. Using either a wooden spoon or an electric mixer with a paddle attachment, work in as much flour and other dry ingredients such as whole grains and milk powders. Beat vigorously until you have a shaggy, heavy dough that pulls away from the sides of the mixing bowl.

3. TURN THE DOUGH ONTO A COUNTER AND KNEAD THE DOUGH UNTIL SMOOTH. Kneading is the heart of bread baking. The steady, rhythmic motion of folding, pressing, and turning develops the strands of gluten and determines the fineness of the crumb. Since kneading involves pushing, try to work at a height where you can comfortably lean into it, using your whole body, not just your arms.

Dust your counter or bread board lightly with flour, then turn out the dough, scraping everything out of the bowl. The dough will be rough and sticky. Have the flour you haven't used in a mound on the counter and a metal dough scraper for moving wet doughs and scraping it off your fingers.

Dust some flour over the top, then gather the dough into a mass and bring the far portion of it toward you, folding it over. Press on it with both hands, where the folded part meets the bulk of the dough, and push it away from you. Push at the rate the dough will accept the pressure—don't try to force it into any particular speed. When you've pushed it out, give the dough a quarter turn, then repeat. As you knead, brush in small amounts of flour if it feels damp and sticky. Usually 5 to 8 minutes is enough time. Don't worry about working in all the flour. Just work in enough so that by the time you've finished kneading, the dough is smooth and elastic but still a bit tacky rather than dry.

4. PUT THE DOUGH INTO AN OILED BOWL, TURNING ONCE TO COAT THE TOP. Use a deep bowl with room for the dough to double in size. Oil (or butter) prevents the dough from sticking to the bowl and keeps the dough from drying out and forming a crust. Always prepare your bowl as you're setting up since it's awkward to stop in midstream.

5. COVER WITH A DAMP TOWEL. Covering with a damp cotton kitchen towel or a piece of plastic wrap stretched over the bowl keeps a crust from forming over the surface. You can also use a thin plastic produce bag—just lay it directly on the dough, pressing it over the sides so that when the dough expands it will remain protected from the drying effects of the air.

6. SET IN A WARM PLACE TO RISE UNTIL DOUBLED IN BULK. A warm spot can be near the stove, in an oven with the pilot light or lightbulb on, or on top of a hot water heater. In cold weather I've even put dough in my car, a highly effective incubator, to rise. It usually takes about an hour and a little more for the dough to rise until it's twice its size. Doughs containing eggs and lots of butter are more sluggish. "Double in bulk" gives you a visual suggestion. A properly risen dough should be very soft and hold a depression when poked with a finger.

Don't use a place that's too warm, or the yeast will grow too fast. It's better to take more time at a cooler temperature than to rush the dough. A cool, slow rise develops different layers of flavors in bread. In fact many European breads are made with less yeast to ensure a slow rise.

Dough can remain overnight, even for days, in the refrigerator, but you need to allow at least a few hours for it to come to room temperature before completing its rise.

7. PUSH THE DOUGH DOWN. This step deflates the dough and strengthens it. Push your fist into the dough in several places to knock the air out of it, then turn it out onto a lightly floured counter. At this point, if you're too busy to shape the dough, just return it to the bowl, cover, and let rise again. It will double again but in about half the time.

8. SHAPE THE DOUGH AND LET IT RISE A SECOND TIME. You can now shape the dough into loaves (or rolls or buns) and put them into their pans or on the back of a peel if baking on a stone. Once shaped, cover again and let them rise. This rise will take less time than the first, but it's important not to rush it, especially with breads made with heavy flours. If you press the side of a round bread gently with your fingers, it should be very soft and tender, like a relaxed calf or arm muscle. Breads in loaf pans should have risen to the top of the pan, swelling noticeably in the center. Preheat the oven during the last 15 minutes of this rise.

9. SCORE THE BREADS. Slashing the tops of the breads before they go into the oven allows steam to escape. With loaf breads this isn't always necessary, but if you don't score free-form breads, they'll make their own vents by tearing at the base. The designs for scoring are often deliberate, not merely decorations, although they are indeed attractive. At this point you can brush the surface with a glaze to give your dough a burnished surface and provide a surface for seeds to adhere to.

10. BAKE UNTIL BROWNED AND PULLING AWAY FROM THE SIDES OF THE PAN. Bake bread in the middle of a preheated oven. Breads gain their full rise right away—called *oven spring*—then they brown. Most loaf breads take between 45 and 55 minutes to bake through. If the tops get too brown, lay a piece of foil loosely over them. When done, the bread will have shrunk a little from the sides of the pans, and when you turn them out, the sides should be firm and brown. If they're pale looking, return the breads to the oven without their pans for 5 to 10 minutes more. One test for doneness is to tap the loaves on the bottom and listen for a hollow sound rather than a dull thud, but unless you bake a lot, it's not always easy to tell one sound from the other. Although it's tempting to eat bread hot from the oven, it slices better if you let it cool on a rack for at least an hour, preferably longer.

Trouble Spots

Making yeasted breads is generally a trouble-free activity, but there are a few things that just might go wrong, some of which are easy to correct.

THE DOUGH WON'T RISE: Chances are your yeast was too old. (If using foil packets, check their expiration date.) But if you proofed it first in warm water to make sure it was alive, it could be that your general atmosphere plus the added liquid was too cold. If that's the case, turn on the oven for 10 minutes, turn off the heat, then put the dough in. Its warmth should get it going. If it still doesn't rise, and the yeast proofed, your liquid might have been too hot. This is the one time you just have to give up and start over.

OVERPROOFING: If you let your dough rise too long, it will begin to get puckery looking on top and eventually will collapse. Just punch it down and let it rise again. If you bake it without doing this, the bread will have a flabby, rippled appearance on top.

THE DOUGH IS READY BUT YOU'RE NOT: Bread dough is very forgiving if something comes up and you can't attend to your risen dough—just punch it down to press out the air and let it rise again. If you need more time than the 20 minutes or so that its rise will take, or you can't get to it until much later, put a piece of plastic wrap over the top and stick it in the refrigerator. Since it takes a while for the mass of dough to cool, it may still obtain its rise rather quickly. Just punch it down again. Eventually it will cool and settle down. Allow an hour or more for it to return to room temperature before resuming.

YOU'VE SHAPED YOUR BREADS AND THEN CHANGED YOUR MIND. You want three breads instead of two, or one looks funny, or you suspect a bread is too big for the pan. Reportion the dough, give it 15 minutes or so to relax, then reshape it as you wish.

Glazes for Breads, Pies, and Other Pastries

Glazes give a glossy coat and finished appearance to baked goods, not only breads but also scones, pies, biscuits, and galettes. They also make a surface amenable to making seeds stick. When glazing yeasted breads, reserve a little so that once the breads have expanded, about 15 minutes into the baking, you can brush the newly exposed areas as well. When glazing sweet pastries, adding a few teaspoons sugar to the glaze increases the luster and shine of the finished product.

Egg White Glaze

1 egg white

1 tablespoon water or milk

Pinch salt (or sugar for sweet bread)

Whisk the ingredients until well blended. Use this on seed breads and country breads or on any bread if you want to avoid using the yolk.

Egg Glaze

1 egg yolk or 1 whole egg

1 tablespoon water, milk, or cream

1 teaspoon sugar for sweet breads

Whisk everything together until smooth.

Melted Butter: Melted butter also gives a lustrous dark appearance and good texture to crusts. For two loaves, melt 3 tablespoons butter and spread it over the breads just before baking. Reserve a little and add it once the oven spring has taken place.

The yolk makes a glaze that's far more lustrous, giving the bread a richly burnished look. Use with egg breads and white breads, including the basic sandwich loaf.

Classic Sandwich Bread

2¼ teaspoons (1 envelope) active dry yeast

1½ cups warm water

½ teaspoon sugar

1 cup warm milk

1 tablespoon honey

¼ cup vegetable oil

2½ teaspoons salt

2 cups all-purpose flour

3 to 4 cups bread flour

Egg Glaze

HIGH, fine-grained, and white, this is our basic white sandwich bread. You can use the same dough for dinner rolls, bread sticks, and cinnamon buns.

MAKES 2 LOAVES

In a small bowl, stir ½ cup of the water and the yeast together, add the sugar, and set aside until foamy, about 10 minutes. In a larger bowl, combine the milk, remaining water, the honey, oil, and salt, then stir in the proofed yeast. Using a wooden spoon or the paddle attachment of an electric mixer, work in the flour a cup at a time until you have a shaggy, heavy dough that leaves the sides of the bowl. Turn it out onto a lightly floured counter and gradually knead in the remaining flour until the dough is smooth and resilient, about 5 minutes. Put it in a deep oiled bowl, turning it so that the top is oiled too. Cover with a damp towel and set in a warm place to rise until doubled in bulk, an hour or longer.

Deflate the dough by pressing down on it, then divide it into two equal pieces, shape into balls, cover, and let rest for 10 minutes. Meanwhile, oil two bread pans. Flatten the dough into two rectangles the length of the pan. Roll it up tightly, pinch the seams together to seal the ends, and place in the pans, seam side down. Cover again and let rise until the dough is just above the edge of the pan, about 35 minutes. Preheat the oven to 375°F. Leave the dough as is or score the top with three diagonal slashes. Brush with the egg glaze and bake until browned and pulling away from the sides, 40 to 45 minutes. If the tops get too dark, cover loosely with foil. Turn the bread out, tap the bottom to make sure it has a hollow sound, not a thud, then set on a rack to cool.

Using Dried Milk Use 2 cups water instead of milk and water and add ½ cup non-fat dry milk to the flour.

Buttermilk Sandwich Bread Heat buttermilk instead of regular milk—it will separate but will smooth out in the end. Or add ½ cup dried buttermilk to the dry ingredients.

Seeded Sandwich Bread Brush the shaped loaves with a beaten egg, then coat with poppy or sesame seeds. Be particularly generous around the edges so that the seeds will roll down the newly exposed dough as it bakes.

Dill Bread Add 2 tablespoons dried dill weed and 1 tablespoon dill seed to the dry ingredients. Glaze with egg and sprinkle with dill seeds.

Cheddar Bread Knead 2 cups coarsely grated sharp Cheddar in with the flour. It has a tantalizing aroma, especially when added to buttermilk bread.

Using Specialty Flours While we're fond of white breads, they lack the fiber that whole grains have. Nonetheless, it's possible to improve them by including other flours that can't be used alone because they lack gluten. Quinoa, amaranth, spelt, and kamut are all high-protein flours. Use them in place of the all-purpose white flour. If using soy flour, don't use more than a third. Expect to gain less rise than if you were to use all wheat.

Whole-Wheat Sandwich Bread

EVEN made with 100 percent whole-wheat flour, this bread is fine and light, perfect for sandwiches. The gluten flour helps develop the lightness, as does taking the time to make a sponge, a two-step approach to making whole-grain breads. (If you don't have time to make a sponge, follow the basic directions given in the preceding Classic Sandwich Bread recipe, using half or all whole-wheat flour.)

MAKES 2 LOAVES

The Sponge
2¼ cups warm water

1 scant tablespoon (1 envelope) active dry yeast

¼ cup unsulfured molasses

⅔ cup nonfat dry milk or dried buttermilk

½ cup gluten flour

2 cups whole-wheat flour

The Bread:
⅓ cup vegetable oil

2½ teaspoons salt

3½ cups whole-wheat flour

Stir the warm water, yeast, molasses, dry milk, gluten flour, and the 2 cups whole-wheat flour until smooth. Scrape down the sides of the bowl, cover with a damp cloth, and set aside in a warm place for an hour until it's foamy on top and doubled in volume.

Gently stir down the sponge, then add the oil, salt, and 1 cup of the flour and beat until smooth. Begin adding the remaining flour by ½-cup increments until you have a shaggy, heavy dough. Turn it out onto a lightly floured counter and knead in as much flour as the dough will take, adding it a few tablespoons at a time. Knead until the dough is smooth but still a little tacky, 3 to 5 minutes.

Place the dough in an oiled bowl, turn it to coat the top, then cover and set in a warm place to rise until doubled in bulk, about 1½ hours or possibly longer. Deflate the dough, then divide it in two, shape into loaves, and place them seam side down in two greased 4½- × 8½-inch bread pans. (If you like a rustic look, roll the loaves into wheat bran or wheat flakes before putting them in the pans.) Cover again and set aside until the dough has risen to the edge of the pans, about 45 minutes. During the last 15 minutes, preheat the oven to 375°F. Bake in the center of the oven until browned, 45 to 50 minutes. Let cool completely before slicing.

Cracked Wheat–Honey Bread

¼ cup warm water

1 teaspoon sugar

2¼ teaspoons (1 envelope) active dry yeast

1½ cups hot water

1¼ cups milk or buttermilk

¼ cup unsulfured molasses or honey

3 tablespoons vegetable oil

2 teaspoons salt

1 cup fine or medium bulgur or cracked wheat

2 cups whole-wheat flour

2 to 3 cups bread flour or all-purpose white flour

THIS *ratio of whole-wheat to white flour makes a moderately high sandwich bread, while the cracked wheat gives it textural strength. I actually prefer bulgur to cracked wheat since it's precooked and not as hard.*

MAKES 2 LOAVES

Combine ¼ cup warm water with the sugar and yeast in a small bowl and set aside until foamy, about 10 minutes. Prepare two 8- × 4-inch bread pans and oil a bowl for the dough.

In a mixing bowl, combine 1½ cups hot water and the milk, then stir in the molasses, oil, and salt. Add the yeast and bulgur, then begin beating in the flour, adding as much as you can until the dough leaves the sides of the bowl. Turn onto a lightly floured counter and knead until smooth, about 5 minutes, adding flour a little at a time. Put it in an oiled bowl, turn once to coat the top, then cover and set aside to rise until doubled in bulk, about 1¼ hours.

Push the dough down, then turn it out and divide it in two. Form two loaves and set them in oiled or sprayed 4½- × 8½-inch bread pans. Cover again and let rise until the dough has risen to the top of the pan, about 40 minutes. Preheat the oven to 375°F. Bake for 45 minutes or until well browned.

Potato Bread

MASHED *potatoes make bread moist, tender, and exceptionally flavorful. This makes delicious toast and fine dinner rolls as well as bread. If you don't have mashed potatoes on hand, simply boil a peeled, sliced baking potato in plenty of water until soft enough to mash.*

MAKES 2 LOAVES

¼ cup warm water

2¼ teaspoon (1 envelope) active dry yeast

½ teaspoon sugar

1½ cups hot water

1½ cups buttermilk

3 tablespoons butter, softened

2 teaspoons salt

1 cup mashed potatoes

4 cups bread flour

3 cups all-purpose flour

Egg Glaze, page 661

Poppy seeds or sesame seeds

Stir the yeast and sugar into ¼ cup warm water in a small bowl and let stand until foamy, 10 minutes. Meanwhile butter or spray two 8- × 4-inch bread pans and oil a bowl for the dough.

In a mixing bowl, combine the buttermilk, 1½ cups hot water, butter, salt, and potatoes. Stir in the yeast, then beat in the flour by cupfuls, starting with the bread flour, until it leaves the side of the bowl. Turn the dough out onto the counter and knead until smooth, working in as much flour as the dough will hold and still be a little tacky. Transfer the dough to an oiled bowl, turn it to coat the top, then cover and set aside until doubled in bulk, about 1¼ hours.

Push the dough down, shape into two loaves, and set it in two greased 4½- × 8½-inch pans. Cover and let rise again until doubled in bulk, about 45 minutes. Preheat the oven to 375°F. Brush the egg glaze over the top, cover with poppy seeds, and bake until nicely browned, about 45 minutes.

Oat Bread

A LOAF *with a rustic-looking crust covered with oats and bran.*

MAKES 1 LOAF

¼ cup warm water

½ teaspoon sugar

2¼ teaspoons (1 envelope) active dry yeast

1 cup warm water or milk

¼ cup honey

2 tablespoons butter, softened, or canola oil

1½ teaspoons salt

1 cup whole-wheat flour

1 cup rolled oats

1 cup oat or wheat bran

2 to 3 cups bread flour or all-purpose flour

Additional oats and bran for the top

Combine ¼ cup warm water, the sugar, and the yeast in a small bowl and set aside until foamy, about 10 minutes. Meanwhile, butter or spray a 9 × 5-inch loaf pan and oil a bowl for the dough.

In a mixing bowl, stir together the warm water, honey, butter, and salt. Stir in the yeast, then add the whole-wheat flour, oats, and bran. Beat in the bread flour until the dough pulls away from the bowl. Turn it out onto a lightly floured counter and knead for 5 minutes, adding as much of the remaining flour as it will hold and still be a little tacky. Put the dough in the oiled bowl, turn it once, then cover and set aside until doubled in bulk, about an hour.

Push down the dough, then shape it into a loaf. Roll it into a mixture of bran and oats to coat the top, then set it in a 5- × 9-inch loaf pan. Cover and let rise until again doubled, about 35 minutes. Preheat the oven to 375°F during the last 15 minutes. Bake for 45 minutes or until the bread pulls slightly away from the sides of the pan.

Light Rye Bread

A MILD, moist, light-colored bread. Without caraway seeds it won't seem like rye bread to those who always associate the two.

MAKES 1 LOAF

The Sponge

1 ½ cups water

2 ¼ teaspoons (1 envelope) active dry yeast

1 ½ tablespoons unsulfured molasses

1 ¼ cups whole-wheat or bread flour

¼ cup nonfat dry milk or dried buttermilk

The Bread

2 tablespoons vegetable oil

2 teaspoons salt

1 ½ cups rye flour

¾ to 1 cup bread flour or all-purpose flour

Cornmeal for the pan

Egg White Glaze, page 660

Mix together everything for the sponge in a bowl, then cover and let rise for 2 hours. It should be foamy.

Stir down the sponge, then add the oil, salt, and rye flour. Beat in the bread flour until the dough is shaggy and pulls away from the side, then turn it out onto a lightly floured counter and knead in the remainder. You can expect it to be a little stickier to handle than all-wheat flour doughs.

Transfer to an oiled bowl, cover, and set in a warm place until doubled in bulk, about 1 hour. Push the dough down, then shape into an oval loaf about 10 inches long. Scatter cornmeal over a baking pan or peel if you're using a baking stone. Place the bread on it, cover, then let rise until doubled in bulk, about 40 minutes. Preheat the oven to 375°F during the last 15 minutes. Make three diagonal slashes across the top and brush with the glaze. Bake for 45 to 50 minutes or until browned.

Seeded Rye Knead 1 tablespoon caraway or fennel seeds into the dough. Shape into a 5- × 9-inch loaf or free-form oblong loaf, brush with an egg glaze, sprinkle with additional seeds, and make several diagonal slashes in the top.

Molasses Bread with Cooked Grains

LEFTOVER *cooked cereal worked into yeasted breads makes them moist and dense. The amount of flour will be more variable than usual because of the wetness of the cereal.*

MAKES 2 LOAVES

2$\frac{1}{4}$ cups warm water

2$\frac{1}{4}$ teaspoons (1 envelope) active dry yeast

$\frac{1}{2}$ teaspoon sugar

$\frac{1}{4}$ cup unsulfured molasses

3 tablespoons corn or sunflower seed oil

2$\frac{1}{2}$ teaspoons salt

1$\frac{1}{2}$ cups cooked cracked wheat, rice, oatmeal, seven-grain cereal, etc.

2 cups all-purpose flour

3 to 4 cups whole-wheat flour

Stir the yeast into $\frac{1}{4}$ cup of the warm water with the sugar. Set aside until foamy, about 10 minutes. Meanwhile butter or spray two 8 × 10 loaf pans and oil a bowl for the dough.

In a mixing bowl, combine the remaining 2 cups warm water, molasses, oil, salt, and cooked cereal. Add the yeast, then beat in the white flour, followed by a cup at a time of the whole-wheat flour until the dough leaves the sides of the bowl. Turn out the dough and knead until smooth but still a little tacky, adding flour as needed.

Turn the dough into the oiled bowl, cover, and set aside to rise until doubled in bulk, about 1$\frac{1}{4}$ hours. Preheat the oven to 375°F during the last 15 minutes. Turn it out and shape into loaves. Cover and set aside until doubled in bulk, about 40 minutes. Bake the bread for 50 minutes.

Multigrain Bread with Sunflower Seeds

MULTIGRAIN *mixes containing flax seeds and a variety of cracked grains work well in this bread. Extra sunflower seeds make this delicious loaf even better.*

MAKES 2 LOAVES

The Sponge

1 cup uncooked multigrain cereal

1$\frac{1}{2}$ cups hot water

1 cup buttermilk

2$\frac{1}{4}$ teaspoons (1 envelope) active dry yeast

2 tablespoons honey or malt syrup

1 cup whole-wheat flour

The Bread

2$\frac{1}{2}$ teaspoons salt

2 tablespoons sunflower seed oil, plus extra for glazing

$\frac{3}{4}$ cup sunflower seeds

4 cups whole-wheat, all-purpose, or bread flour

Combine everything for the sponge in a mixing bowl, cover loosely, and set aside for an hour to soften the grains and proof the yeast.

Stir down the sponge, then stir in the salt, oil, and sunflower seeds. Begin beating in the flour until the dough is too heavy to stir, then turn out the dough and knead in the rest by hand until the dough is smooth and supple but still a little tacky. Turn the dough into an oiled bowl, cover well with plastic wrap, and set aside until doubled in bulk, about 1$\frac{1}{2}$ hours.

Push down the dough, divide it into two pieces, and shape into loaves. Place in two sprayed or buttered and floured 4$\frac{1}{2}$- × 8$\frac{1}{2}$-inch bread pans and let rise until doubled again, about 45 minutes. During the last 15 minutes, preheat the oven to 375°F. Slash the bread and brush it with the extra sunflower seed oil. Bake in the center of the oven until the loaves are golden brown and well risen and firm, about 45 minutes.

Amaranth Cornmeal Bread

The Sponge

1 1/2 cups warm water

2 1/4 teaspoons (1 envelope) active dry yeast

1 1/2 tablespoons honey

1 1/2 cups bread flour

2 tablespoons nonfat dry milk

The Dough

2 tablespoons corn oil

1 1/2 teaspoons salt

1/2 cup whole amaranth

1/2 cup amaranth flour

3/4 cup stone-ground cornmeal, plus extra for the top

1 cup whole-wheat flour

1 cup bread flour

THIS bread features two grains of the new world—amaranth and cornmeal. Whole amaranth is very nutritious and very tiny. You can use it whole or pop it first, as you would popcorn, in a dry skillet.

MAKES 1 LOAF

Stir together everything for the sponge until smooth, then cover and let rise for 1 hour.

Stir the oil and salt into the sponge, then begin beating in the remaining ingredients except the glaze. When the dough is shaggy, turn it out onto a counter and knead until smooth and elastic, 6 to 8 minutes. (Because of the amaranth, the gluten needs to be worked a little more than usual.) Cover and let rise until doubled in bulk, about 1 hour, then deflate and shape the dough into a loaf. Place in an oiled or sprayed 4 1/2- × 8 1/2-inch bread pan and let rise until doubled again, about 30 minutes. Preheat the oven to 375°F during the last 15 minutes. Slash the top with a knife, making three diagonal cuts, then brush the bread with the glaze and dust the top with cornmeal. Bake until browned and pulling slightly away from the pan, about 45 minutes.

Peppered-Cheese Bread

1 1/3 cups warm milk or water

2 1/4 teaspoons (1 envelope) active dry yeast

1 1/2 teaspoons salt

2 teaspoons coarsely ground black pepper

1 teaspoon red pepper flakes

1 egg, well beaten

3 cups all-purpose flour or a mixture of whole-wheat and white

1 cup grated or finely diced Cheddar

A GOOD party bread—it looks so festive and pretty with its shiny golden crust. Made with white flour, the bread is tender and soft; with whole wheat it's more robust and hearty—or you can use a mixture.

MAKES 1 ROUND LOAF

Put the milk in a large bowl and stir in the yeast. Let stand until foamy, about 10 minutes, then whisk in the salt, pepper, pepper flakes, all but 1 tablespoon of the beaten egg, and 1 cup of the flour. When smooth, start adding the remaining flour. When the dough gets too heavy for the spoon, turn it out and knead until smooth.

Flatten the dough with your hands and scatter half the cheese over it. Knead it into the dough, then repeat with the rest of the cheese. Place the dough in a lightly oiled bowl, turn once, then cover and set aside until doubled in bulk, 45 minutes to an hour.

Push the dough down, then turn it out onto the counter. Shape it into a tight ball. Cover and set aside until doubled in bulk, about 45 minutes, preheating the oven to 375°F during the last 15 minutes. Slash a large X in the top, then brush it with remaining beaten egg. Bake for 45 minutes, then turn onto a rack to cool.

Walnut Bread

DENSE with wheat and walnuts, this crusty free-form bread derives its excellent flavor from roasted walnut oil as well as from the nuts. This is a wonderful bread to serve with soft cheese of all kinds—Fontina, Taleggio, St. André, a homemade ricotta or ricotta-goat mixture, or cream cheese. A coarse whole-wheat flour containing lots of bran is the best choice. If yours is fine, add a cup of wheat bran and decrease the whole-wheat flour by 1 cup.

MAKES 2 OR 3 ROUND LOAVES

2¹⁄₂ cups warm water

2¹⁄₄ teaspoons (1 envelope) active dry yeast

¹⁄₄ cup roasted walnut oil

1 tablespoon honey or malt syrup

¹⁄₂ cup nonfat dry milk

2 teaspoons salt

1 cup wheat bran if whole-wheat flour is smooth

3 to 4 cups whole-wheat flour

About 2 cups all-purpose flour

1¹⁄₂ cups chopped walnuts, preferably blanched and roasted, page 41

Melted butter for the top

Stir the yeast into ¹⁄₄ cup warm water in a small bowl and set it aside while you gather your ingredients.

Put 2¹⁄₄ cups warm water in a mixing bowl and stir in the oil, honey, dry milk, and salt. Add the bran and whole-wheat flour. Beat well until the batter is smooth. Add enough all-purpose flour to make a heavy dough that pulls away from the sides of the bowl, then add the walnuts. Turn the dough out onto a counter and knead until smooth, adding more white flour as needed to keep it from sticking. Put the dough in an oiled bowl, turn it once, cover with plastic wrap, and set aside to rise until doubled, about 1¹⁄₂ hours.

Turn the dough out and cut it into two or three pieces. Shape each piece into a tight ball, cupping your hands around the dough to give it a plump, round shape. Place each ball on an oiled baking sheet, cover, and set aside until doubled in bulk, about 45 minutes. During the last 15 minutes, preheat the oven to 375°F.

Slash the breads, making three or four parallel cuts across the loaves, then brush with melted butter. Bake until a rich brown crust is formed and the bread is done, about 40 minutes.

Challah

WHEN I was in high school, our neighbor used to bake it every Friday for Sabbath. The smells that wafted over the fence were so enticing they pulled me right into her kitchen. She showed me what to do, then I made this bread every weekend for a year. Leftovers make great French toast and bread pudding, both sweet and savory.

MAKES 2 LARGE BRAIDS

2¹⁄₄ cups warm water

2¹⁄₄ teaspoons (1 envelope) active dry yeast

3 tablespoons sugar

3 eggs, beaten, 2 tablespoons reserved

¹⁄₄ cup vegetable oil

1 tablespoon salt

6 to 7 cups all-purpose flour

Poppy seeds

Mix the yeast with ¹⁄₄ cup warm water and a teaspoon of the sugar in a small bowl. Set aside until foamy, about 10 minutes, then stir it into 2 cups warm water in a mixing bowl along with the rest of the sugar, the eggs, oil, and salt. Add the flour a cup at a time, stirring to make a smooth batter. When it becomes heavy, turn it onto the counter and knead in the rest of the flour until the dough is satiny smooth, about 8 minutes. Set it in an oiled bowl, turn once, then cover. Set aside until doubled in bulk, about an hour. Push down the dough, divide it in half, then divide each half into three equal pieces.

To shape the bread, roll each piece of dough into a rope 10 to 12 inches long. Cross the strands over each other in the middle, then begin braiding the strands, moving toward you. When you finish one end, turn the bread and braid the other end. Tuck in the ends to make them look smooth and finished. (You may find it easier to join the ropes at one end and then braid.)

Place the braids on an oiled sheet pan. Cover them with a damp towel and set aside until doubled, about 45 minutes. Preheat the oven to 375°F during the last 15 minutes. Beat the reserved egg with a tablespoon of water, then brush most of it over the breads and sprinkle with poppy seeds. Once the bread has risen, brush the remaining egg wash into newly exposed areas. Bake until the bread is burnished gold, about 45 minutes, then cool on a rack.

Buckwheat-Raisin Bread

The Sponge

1¼ cups warm water

2¼ teaspoons (1 envelope) active dry yeast

1⅓ cups bread flour

½ cup dried buttermilk or nonfat dry milk

3 tablespoons unsulfured molasses or honey

The Bread

2 tablespoons oil or butter, melted

1¾ teaspoons salt

1½ cups dark raisins, large monukkas if possible

2 teaspoons cinnamon

1 cup chopped walnuts

1 cup buckwheat flour

1 to 1¼ cups bread flour or all-purpose flour

Egg Glaze, page 661

BUCKWHEAT flour bakes quite nicely into breads as long as it's mixed with wheat to provide gluten. This is a dark loaf, warmed with cinnamon and studded with fruit. Serve with cream cheese and apple butter or use to make a breakfast grilled cheese sandwich and serve with sautéed apples or applesauce.

MAKES 1 LOAF

Mix everything for the sponge in a bowl until smooth, then cover and set in a warm place for 1 hour.

Stir down the sponge, then add the oil, salt, raisins, cinnamon, and nuts. Stir in the buckwheat, then work in the bread flour until you can't add any more. Turn the dough onto a counter and knead until smooth and resilient, about 6 minutes. Put in an oiled bowl, turn once, cover, and let rise until doubled, 1 to 1½ hours.

Push the dough down and form it into a loaf. Place in a buttered or sprayed 4½- × 8½-inch bread pan, cover, and let rise until doubled again, about 40 minutes. Preheat the oven to 375°F during the last 15 minutes. Brush the bread with the glaze or dust with buckwheat flour. Bake until browned and pulling away from the sides of the pan, about 45 minutes.

Focaccia

FOCACCIA has found a secure footing in America during the last 10 years, and whole books are devoted to this famous Italian flatbread. This recipe makes one plump little focaccia, enough to serve six at dinner, or eight as an appetizer. Offering fresh bread at a meal is a nice touch, and this one can be ready to bake in a scant hour.

SERVES 6 TO 8

1 ¼ cups warm water

2 teaspoons active dry yeast

½ teaspoon sugar

1 teaspoon salt

2 tablespoons fruity olive oil, plus extra for the top

2 ½ to 3 cups all-purpose flour or a mixture of whole-wheat and white

Cornmeal if using a stone

1 ½ teaspoons coarse sea salt

Dissolve the yeast and sugar in ¼ cup warm water in a small bowl and set aside until bubbly, about 10 minutes. Meanwhile oil a bowl for the dough.

In a mixing bowl, combine 1 cup warm water with the proofed yeast, then add the salt, oil, and as much flour as the dough will hold. Turn it out onto a floured surface and knead until smooth, working in enough flour to make it easy to handle, about 5 minutes. Place in the oiled bowl, turn once, and cover with a damp cloth. Set in a warm place to rise until doubled in bulk, about 45 minutes to an hour.

Turn out the dough and roll it into circle or oval about ½ inch thick. Leave it whole or slash it decoratively in several places, then pull on the dough to open the cuts. Place on the back of a sheet pan or a wooden peel dusted with cornmeal, brush with olive oil, and sprinkle with coarse salt. Cover and let rise again, about 30 minutes.

Meanwhile, preheat the oven to 400°F with a baking stone if you have one. Bake the bread in the middle of the oven until the bread is browned, about 30 minutes. To develop a crisp crust, spray the bread with water two or three times during the first 10 minutes in the oven.

Focaccia with Fennel Seeds Crush 1 teaspoon fennel seeds in a mortar or with the dull side of a knife just to bruise them and knead them into the dough. When it's time to roll out the dough, sprinkle whole fennel seeds over the top, then roll them in with a rolling pin.

Herb Focaccia Very finely mince 2 tablespoons fresh rosemary or sage leaves. Knead half into the dough and sprinkle the remainder on top, along with the salt, just before baking. If using sage leaves, set aside some whole ones for garnish and add them when the bread comes out of the oven.

Focaccia with Caramelized Onions Thinly slice 1 large onion and cook it in 2 tablespoons olive oil over medium heat until soft and dark gold, about 20 minutes. Stir more frequently as the pan begins to dry. Season with salt and pepper. Spread the onions over the risen focaccia and sprinkle with dried oregano or chopped rosemary. (Pitted Gaeta or Niçoise olives are good too; their salty tang sets off the sweetness of the onions. Walnuts are also good with onions and olives.)

Focaccia with Blue Cheese and Walnuts After the rolled dough has risen, press your fingertips over the top to make indentations. Crumble Gorgonzola over the top and bake. Take the bread out after 25 minutes, add a sprinkling of chopped walnuts, and return it to the oven for 5 minutes more. Serve with pepper cracked over the top and a scattering of chopped parsley. I've also made this bread successfully using leftover Blue Cheese and Walnut Spread, page 106.

Foccacia Sandwich Rolls Divide the dough into four to six pieces and knead each piece into a round. Press or roll it out into a disk a scant ¹/₂ inch thick. If the dough doesn't want to be worked, let it rest for 5 or 10 minutes, then go back to it. Cover and let rise, then bake at 400°F until the rolls are well browned, about 30 minutes. Spray them with water when they go into the oven and once or twice more during the baking. Remove from the oven and brush with oil.

Sandwich Focaccia with Rosemary

2 cups warm water

2¹/₄ teaspoons (1 envelope) active dry yeast

1 teaspoon sugar

3 tablespoons fruity olive oil, plus extra for the top

1¹/₂ teaspoons salt

1 to 2 tablespoons finely minced rosemary

1 cup whole-wheat flour

5 cups all-purpose or bread flour

THIS focaccia is thick enough to slice in half for sandwiches, or it can be served as bread, cut into squares or rectangles. Add any of the toppings used for focaccia—sautéed onions, fennel seeds, crumbled Gorgonzola.

**MAKES ONE
10- × 15-INCH BREAD**

Stir the yeast into 2 cups warm water with the sugar in a mixing bowl and set aside until foamy, about 10 minutes. Meanwhile oil a bowl for the dough.

In a larger mixing bowl, mix the water with the yeast, stir in the olive oil, salt, rosemary, and whole-wheat flour. Gradually add the remaining flour until it's too heavy to work, then turn out the dough and knead until smooth. Place it in the oiled bowl, turn it once, then cover and let rise until doubled in bulk, about 1¹/₄ hours.

Lightly dust a counter with flour. Lightly oil a sheet pan and dust it with fine cornmeal. Roll out the dough to more or less fit the pan. Press it so that the thickness is more or less even. Cover and let rise for another hour or until tender to the touch. Preheat the oven to 400°F during the last 15 minutes. Dimple the dough by poking it with your fingertips, then brush it generously with olive oil. Bake in the bottom third of the oven until nicely browned, about 30 minutes.

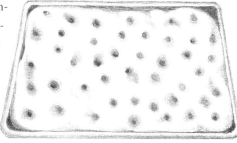

Pita Bread

HOMEMADE *pita bread is fragrant, and tender— just as enchanting as any other homemade bread. It's also relatively quick (for a yeasted bread) and very enjoyable to make. Pita bread should puff, but if it doesn't, it's still delicious and can be used as a wrapper or a dipping bread. A table of appetizers becomes truly special when warm, fresh pitas are added. Using bread flour helps to give your bread loft.*

**MAKES TEN
8-INCH BREADS**

1¹/₂ cups warm water

2¹/₄ teaspoons (1 envelope) active dry yeast

1 teaspoon honey or barley malt syrup

1³/₄ teaspoons salt

2 tablespoons olive oil, plus extra for the griddle if using

1¹/₂ cups whole-wheat flour, preferably coarsely ground with flakes of bran, or 1 cup whole-wheat flour mixed with ¹/₂ cup wheat bran

2 cups bread flour

Put 1¹/₂ cups warm water in a mixing bowl, stir in the yeast and honey, and set aside until foamy, about 10 minutes. Meanwhile oil a bowl for the dough.

Stir in the salt and olive oil, then beat in the whole-wheat flour and bran until smooth. Add the remaining flour in small increments until the dough is too heavy to stir. Turn it onto a counter and knead until you have a smooth, supple dough, after a few minutes, adding more flour as required. Put it in an oiled bowl, turn to coat, then cover and set aside until doubled in bulk, 50 minutes to an hour.

Punch the dough down and divide into 10 pieces for 8-inch breads. Roll each piece into a ball, then cover them with a damp towel. If baking in the oven, preheat it now with a baking stone or sheet pans in it to 475°F. Let the dough relax while the oven heats, about 15 minutes, then roll each piece into a circle a little less than ¹/₄ inch thick. Don't stack the rolled breads.

Baking Pita in the Oven: Pitas will almost always balloon when baked in the oven, but they won't have the pretty mottled appearance they get when cooked on a griddle. Drop the rounds of dough directly onto the stone or heated pans and bake for 3 minutes. They should be completely puffed. Remove them from the oven and cover with a towel to help them deflate.

Baking Pitas on the Stove: Cooked this way, my pitas don't swell in a very predictable fashion. However, they end up beautifully mottled and are pliable enough to wrap around a filling. Heat a cast-iron skillet or griddle over high heat. When hot, turn the heat to medium, then brush a little oil over the surface. Set a circle of dough in the middle. Let it sit for 30 seconds, then turn it over. Slowly the bread should begin to puff. You can encourage its puffing by gently pressing the bubbles to spread the hot air outward. Once the bread has swollen, after a minute or two, turn it over to brown the top side—another minute or so. Put the finished breads under a towel or in a plastic bag to keep them soft.

Barley-Sesame Flatbreads

1³/₄ cups warm water

2¹/₄ teaspoons (1 envelope) active dry yeast

1 cup barley flour

2 tablespoons barley malt syrup or honey

2 tablespoons dark sesame oil

2 teaspoons salt

¹/₂ cup nonfat dry milk or dried buttermilk

³/₄ cup whole-wheat flour

¹/₄ cup wheat bran

2 cups bread flour

¹/₂ cup sesame seeds

Olive or sesame oil for frying

Sprinkle the yeast into ¹/₄ cup warm water in a small bowl and set aside until bubbly. Meanwhile, toast the barley flour in a dry skillet over medium heat, stirring occasionally until it has a good smell and has turned from white to light brown.

In a mixing bowl, combine 1¹/₂ cups warm water with the malt syrup, oil, salt, and yeast. Stir in the dry milk, then begin adding the flours in the order given. When the dough becomes too heavy to mix, turn it out and knead until smooth. Place it in an oiled bowl, turn once to coat the top, then cover with a damp towel and set in a warm place to rise until doubled in bulk, about 1¹/₂ hours.

Push the dough down and divide it into eighteen 2-ounce pieces. Roll them into balls, then cover them with a towel and let rest for 15 minutes. Press the balls into disks, scatter sesame seeds on the counter, and roll out each piece of dough to make a circle about ¹/₄ inch thick. Turn them once, scatter sesame seeds on the second side, and press them in with your hands. Cover with a towel and let rise for 20 to 30 minutes.

Film a cast-iron skillet or griddle with the oil. When the pan is hot, add as many breads as will fit and reduce the heat to medium-low. Cook slowly so that the breads have time to cook through as they brown—5 to 7 minutes on each side. Serve warm.

TIBETAN barley bread, a dense sustaining loaf, used to be a favorite of residents of Tassajara Zen Mountain Center in the late sixties. This version, baked in the style of an Afghani flatbread, is still substantial but a little less dense, and the entire surface is coated with golden, crunchy sesame seeds. Enjoy these warm from the pan and serve them, cut into wedges, with yogurt cheese, olives, and Herb Salad.

MAKES 18 TO 20 SMALL BREADS

Yogurt Flatbread (*Naan*)

NAAN *are flatbreads that are found, in varying forms, throughout Central Asia. This particular recipe, taught to me by Joe Evans, is made with yogurt, which makes the breads tender and slightly sour.*

Serve these breads warm with a vegetable stew or dipped into a spicy yogurt sauce or a salsa of green chiles and fresh coriander.

MAKES 8 TO 10 SMALL BREADS

¹/₄ cup warm water

2¹/₄ teaspoons (1 envelope) active dry yeast

³/₄ cup hot water

³/₄ cup plain yogurt, preferably whole-milk

¹/₄ cup ghee or clarified butter

1¹/₂ teaspoons salt

1 cup whole-wheat flour

¹/₄ cup wheat bran, unless flour is bran-flecked

3 cups all-purpose or bread flour

Sprinkle the yeast over ¹/₄ cup warm water in a small bowl and set aside until foamy, about 10 minutes. Meanwhile, combine ³/₄ cup hot water, the yogurt, ghee, and salt in a bowl, then stir in the yeast, whole-wheat flour, and bran. Work in enough white flour to form a heavy dough, then turn it out and knead, adding more flour if needed, until smooth but slightly tacky. Put the dough in an oiled bowl, turn it to coat the top, then cover and put in a warm place until doubled in bulk, about 1 hour.

Preheat the oven to 450°F with a pizza stone or a sheet pan. Turn out the dough onto a lightly floured counter and divide into 8 or 10 pieces. Roll them into balls, cover with a towel, and let rest for 10 minutes.

Here are two options for shaping the dough:

1. Pat the dough into a circle using your fingertips to dimple it all over. Then gently pull it in opposite directions to make a dimpled oblong. The texture will be uneven, providing crisp and bready parts. Place right on the baking stone or hot sheet pan and bake until browned on top, 12 to 15 minutes. (This is based on the traditional "snowshoe" naan, a much larger bread.)

2. Pat or roll the dough into a circle about ¹/₄ inch thick. Make five short knife cuts, radiating from the center like a sand dollar, then transfer to the baking stone and bake until browned. (This idea comes from Naomi Duguid, author of *Flatbreads*). You can also make plain rounds, like pita breads, but this cut bread is very pretty.

When the breads are done, stack them on top of each other and serve, warm if possible. I sometimes brush a little softened butter over them and sprinkle them very lightly with freshly milled sea salt.

Stuffed Flatbreads

INDIAN *restaurants always have a variety of irresistible stuffed flatbreads. Here the dough is rolled over a stuffing of seasoned minced onion—moist and very tasty.*

MAKES 8

Yogurt Flatbread, preceding recipe

1 cup finely minced onion

2 garlic cloves, minced

¹/₂ teaspoon salt

¹/₂ teaspoon ground cumin

¹/₄ teaspoon cayenne

¹/₃ cup chopped cilantro

Make the dough and mix the remaining ingredients together. Roll the dough into 8 circles and spread 2 tablespoons filling over half of each one. Fold the dough over the filling and gently roll or pat it out again, forming a thin cake, then bake.

Dinner Rolls

Dinner rolls were once seen much more frequently on the American table than they are today. I don't think we serve bread as much as we used to, and when we do, it's apt to be a sliced loaf rather than a roll. Still, a tender roll served warm is such a nice refinement, it's a pleasure to revive this tradition on occasion. Beautifully shaped, well-glazed rolls always give the impression that they were made especially for you. But the real joy is for the baker, for rolls are a delight to shape and bake.

Refrigerator rolls were once a busy cook's way of having fresh rolls on the table every night with little effort. A bowl of bread dough would sit at the ready in the refrigerator for 4 or 5 days. The cook would lop off a piece as needed, form it into rolls, and let them rise while dinner preparation was under way. As the dough aged, it would acquire a little sourness and, with it, character.

Today we're mildly amazed if we get dinner on the table every night, and fresh rolls are certainly far above anyone's expectations. However, if the desire seizes you at any time, know that rolls can be made from any bread dough. A batch of dough made with 3 cups flour will make:

1 loaf of bread

10 to 12 2-ounce dinner rolls

4 to 6 4-ounce sandwich-sized rolls

To make rolls from any bread dough, make the bread through its first rise, then push it down. Divide the dough into pieces the size you wish. You can make very tiny 1-ounce rolls, more typical dinner-sized 2-ounce rolls, or even something as large as a miniature bread.

If the dough is too springy to work and doesn't want to cooperate, let it rest for 15 minutes, then try shaping it again. Set the shaped doughs on a lightly greased sheet pan seam side down, cover with a towel, and let them rise until doubled, 30 to 45 minutes. (At this point you can decoratively slash round or oval rolls.) For a burnished look, brush the rolls with one of the egg glazes on pages 660 to 661, or with melted butter. Now is the time to scatter any seeds over the top since they'll stick to the glaze.

Bake rolls in a preheated 375°F oven until risen and golden, 15 to 25 minutes, depending on their size.

ROUNDS: To shape dough into rounds, cup your hand tightly over a piece, then move your hand rapidly around in a circle, keeping it close in at the base and pressing downward as you move. These actions will force it into a sphere. Once risen, slash a cross in the top, make two or three parallel cuts with a sharp knife, or make two snips of the scissors to provide air vents. A single sphere makes a pretty little bread, but you can also make three marble-size rounds and stick them together, either on a sheet pan or in a buttered muffin tin to make a classic cloverleaf roll.

OVALS: Using your hands, shape a loosely formed round into an oval torpedo-like shape. Make three scissor snips down the top or slash the rolls diagonally with a razor blade or sharp knife.

TWISTS AND KNOTS: Roll each piece of dough into a snake about ½ inch thick and, if using a standard 2-ounce piece, about 8 inches long. Try tying it into a knot, tucking the ends underneath for a complicated-looking roll. Or bend it in the middle, then twist the two ends like a rope. Or coil the dough around it-self to make a snail shape or simply have fun creating shapes that catch your fancy. No slashing is necessary with twists and knots; seeds look wonderful.

MAKING REFRIGERATOR ROLLS: After shaping rolls, cover them with lightly buttered or oiled plastic wrap and refrigerate them for up to a few hours or overnight. Remove from the refrigerator an hour or even as little as 30 minutes before baking if they haven't been chilled for more than a few hours.

More traditionally, make the dough but don't shape it. After it has been kneaded, in-stead of letting it rise, place it in a well-oiled or buttered spacious bowl, turned so that the top is coated. Put the bowl in a plastic bag or cover it securely with plastic wrap and refrigerate. If you happen to notice that the dough has risen, just punch it down and re-turn it to the refrigerator.

To use, remove as much dough as you need—a scale will give you a good idea if you don't feel confident judging by eye—and shape it into rolls. Since the dough will be very cold after a long stay in the refrigerator, allow at least 2 to 3 hours for it to warm up and begin to rise.

Corn-Rye Buttermilk Rolls

BECAUSE of the non-glutenous flours and their limited rising pow-ers, I prefer this fine-crumbed dough for rolls, although you can bake it into a bread—just don't expect it to rise as high as others. Slightly rough stone-ground flours make the tastiest rolls.

**MAKES TEN
3-INCH ROLLS**

2¼ teaspoons (1 envelope) active dry yeast

2¼ cups warm water, whey, or potato water

¼ cup corn oil, preferably unrefined

¼ cup molasses

1 tablespoon salt

½ cup dried buttermilk or nonfat dry milk

1 cup whole-wheat flour

1 cup rye flour

1 cup fine stone-ground cornmeal

3 cups all-purpose or bread flour

Wheat bran for coating

Stir the yeast into ¼ cup warm water in a small bowl and set aside until foamy. Mean-while, oil a bowl for the dough.

Put 2 cups warm water in a mixing bowl and add the oil, molasses, salt, and yeast. Whisk in the dry milk, then beat in the whole-wheat flour, rye flour, and cornmeal until smooth.

Begin adding the all-purpose flour ½ cup at a time. When you can't work in any more, turn it out onto a counter and knead until smooth and springy, about 3 minutes. The dough should be a little tacky. Set it in an oiled bowl, turn it once, cover, and set aside to rise until doubled in bulk, 1½ to 2 hours.

Divide into equal pieces, depending on the size roll you want, and shape each piece into a ball. Roll them in the wheat bran, then set them on a baking sheet and slash to make a cross. Cover with a towel and set aside until doubled in size and soft to the touch, 40 minutes to an hour. During the last 15 minutes, preheat the oven to 375°F. Bake the rolls for 25 minutes, until browned.

Little Lemon Biscuits

¹/₄ cup warm water

2¹/₄ teaspoons (1 envelope) active dry yeast

3 tablespoons sugar or honey, plus extra sugar for the tops

¹/₂ cup crème fraîche or buttermilk

6 tablespoons melted butter

Finely grated zest of 1 lemon

¹/₄ cup cornstarch

³/₈ teaspoon salt

2¹/₄ to 2¹/₂ cups all-purpose flour

In a mixing bowl, scatter the yeast over ¹/₄ cup warm water and stir in a teaspoon of the sugar. When it has proofed, after 10 to 15 minutes, stir in the remaining sugar, crème fraîche, 4 tablespoons of the melted butter, and the lemon zest. When smooth, add the cornstarch and salt, then begin beating in the flour. When the dough is too heavy to mix with a spoon, turn it out and knead in the remaining flour. The dough should be smooth and shiny and still a little tacky. Turn it into a buttered bowl, cover the top, and set aside to rise until doubled in bulk. Although the amount of dough is small, because of the crème fraîche and butter it will take at least an hour to rise.

Turn the dough onto a lightly floured counter and roll it out about ³/₈ inch thick. Cut out the cakes with a small biscuit cutter or a glass so that they measure 1 to 2 inches across. Reroll the scraps and cut them out too. Arrange the cakes on a sheet pan about an inch or more apart. Remelt the remaining butter, brush the tops, and sprinkle with fine sugar. Let them rise until doubled in bulk while you preheat the oven to 375°F. Bake the cakes until they're deep gold, high, and crisp. Remove and serve warm.

WHEN I saw a picture of these little yeasted cakes in The Flavors of France *by Jean Conil and Fay Franklin, I couldn't wait to try them. They're tender, golden, and fragrant—completely divine. Cornstarch makes them feather-light, but a day later they'll be inedibly dry. You can, however, roll and cut them out, and refrigerate them the night before.*

MAKES TWELVE 2-INCH TO TWENTY 1-INCH BISCUITS

Rosemary Holiday Bread

1 cup milk, preferably whole

5 tablespoons butter, cut into small chunks

¹/₄ cup honey

2 teaspoons finely chopped rosemary

Finely chopped zest of 1 large lemon

2 eggs, beaten

¹/₄ cup warm water

2¹/₄ teaspoons (1 envelope) active dry yeast

³/₄ teaspoon salt

1 cup toasted pine nuts or chopped walnuts

1 cup golden raisins

4 cups all-purpose flour

Egg Glaze, page 661, or melted butter

2 tablespoons crystal sugar or granulated sugar

In a small saucepan, warm the milk over medium heat with the butter, honey, rosemary, and lemon zest. Stir to help the butter melt, then pour into a mixing bowl and set it aside until the milk has cooled to lukewarm. Beat in the eggs.

Meanwhile, sprinkle the yeast over ¹/₄ cup warm water and let stand until foamy, 10 to 15 minutes. Stir it into the milk mixture and add the salt, nuts, and raisins. Vigorously

THE rosemary in this holiday bread suggests pine or angelica more than it does savory flavors. Bake this pretty bread in a large bundt pan, a 9-inch springform, or two brioche pans. This bread makes delicious toast. Serve for breakfast or later in the day with a glass of dessert wine, sherry, or coffee.

MAKES 1 LARGE HOLIDAY BREAD OR 2 LOAVES

beat in the flour one cup at a time until it clears the sides of the bowl. Turn it out onto a counter and knead for several minutes until smooth. Place in a buttered bowl, cover, and set aside to rise until doubled in bulk, 1 to 1½ hours. Meanwhile, generously butter a baking pan (or pans), going all the way up the sides. Punch down the dough once it has risen, form it into a ball, and place in the pan(s). Let it rise again until very soft to the touch and doubled in bulk, another hour. During the last 15 minutes, preheat the oven to 350°F. Brush the bread with the glaze and sprinkle with sugar. Bake until golden and high, about 45 minutes. Gently release the bread from the pan and let cool on a rack.

Cinnamon Rolls

THESE classic morning rolls can be made with the basic dough for Classic Sandwich Bread or the silky rich Babka dough. If using the bread dough, cut the recipe in half or make the full amount and use half for bread. The mixture of butter, sugar, and syrup is what makes these buns sticky. You can omit it if you wish and have very good plain cinnamon rolls.

MAKES 16 TO 20 ROLLS

Classic Sandwich Bread, page 661, or
  Babka, page 638
1 tablespoon ground cinnamon
½ cup packed brown sugar

½ cup chopped pecans or walnuts
½ cup raisins or currants
2 tablespoons melted butter

While the dough is rising, mix the cinnamon, brown sugar, nuts, and raisins in a small bowl.

Push the dough down. If using the bread dough, divide it in half and use one half to make a loaf of bread. Roll the remainder (or the babka dough) into a 12- × 16-inch rectangle. Brush it with the melted butter, sprinkle the sugar mixture over the surface, and tightly roll up lengthwise. Slice into rounds about 1 inch wide and set them in the butter-coated pan, cut side facing up. Don't hesitate to cram them together. Let rise for 30 minutes.

Preheat the oven to 375°F. Bake the rolls in the center of the oven until well risen and browned, about 30 minutes. Invert them onto a serving plate—the sugar will have caramelized and coated the rolls. You can also serve them baked side up if you prefer.

Sticky Buns Beat 6 tablespoons butter with ¾ cup dark brown sugar and 1½ tablespoons dark corn syrup until smooth, then spread it in a 9-inch pie plate or baking dish. Set the rolled buns, cut sides facing up, on this mixture, let rise for 30 minutes, then bake. Turn them out onto a serving plate while they're still warm, before the syrup cools and hardens.

Desserts:
Ending on a Sweet Note

I LOVE MAKING DESSERTS—SO MUCH THAT I HAVE WORKED, ON MORE THAN ONE OCCASION, AS A PASTRY CHEF. BUT I AM MOST ATTRACTED TO DESSERTS THAT ARE BASED ON FRUIT, RATHER THAN ELABORATE PASTRIES AND TOWERING CON-fections, because I enjoy the same qualities in fruits that I do in vegetables—their aromas, their vivid or subtle flavors, their sensuality, and their seasonality, which marks our own passage through the year. I also enjoy the interplay that fruits enjoy with one another and with those foods that accompany them, such as spices and nuts, wines and liqueurs.

If we were able to count on good-tasting fruits throughout the year, we would be able to enjoy, without effort, the most simple and healthful of desserts. Unfortunately the hardest part about assembling a worthy fruit plate is finding the fruit. I suspect that because we generally lack the fruit that delivers breathtaking pleasure, we have become a nation that's excessively fond of pastry. But as with vegetables, good fruit can be found if you keep a watchful eye out for what grows where you live and eat within the season.

Many desserts break those health rules that people strive to live by. The desire to have our cake and eat it too has spawned an industry that produces desserts and sweets based on ersatz fats and sugars, foods that only distantly mirror the real thing. I don't have desserts often, but I like real ones when I do—cakes made with butter, flaky pie crusts, whipped cream on the side, fine cheeses. The desserts I've chosen to include are honest indulgences to be savored and enjoyed, leaving cravings and longings satisfied instead of merely teased.

In addition to the desserts found in this chapter, there are some delectable yeasted buns and a rosemary lemon cake in the bread chapter that can double as desserts, especially when paired with soft cheeses or fruit compotes.

Fruit: The Perfect Dessert

WITHOUT *a doubt, the healthiest dessert is a fine piece of fruit. Sadly, fruits suffer even more than vegetables at the hands of pickers, shippers, and rough-handed stockboys. Modern agriculture isn't beneficial to fruit the way hands-on, careful cultivation is. If fruit were as good as it could be or as it looks, we wouldn't need a bit of convincing to eat it. So try to search out fruit that's grown near where you live—you may be rewarded with flavor that's far beyond your expectations. Once you've sat down to a really fine nectarine, a tree-ripened fig, or a crisp fall apple, you can easily understand why serving fruit at the end of the meal has long been the European tradition.*

SERVING FRESH FRUIT: A bowl or basket of fruit arranges itself beautifully regardless of what we do to it. It matters not whether it's a silver bowl of red apples lined with golden fall leaves, a baroque assembly of grapes, persimmons, muskmelons, and nuts, or just a plate of sliced watermelon. Just select the best fruit you can and let everyone choose a piece. Provide fruit knives and small plates for pits and peels. Peeling, coring, and slicing, then eating bite by bite, slows us down, allowing us to really taste the fruit.

Since cold deadens flavors, fruit is most aromatic and fragrant when it's at room temperature—with certain exceptions. A chilled orange or melon, both of which are exceptionally sweet, can be wildly refreshing. And a crisp fall apple picked off the tree is also good cold. But stone fruits—peaches, apricots, plums, cherries, and nectarines—tropical fruits, and berries are always better at room temperature.

Spur-of-the-Moment Fruit Desserts

Often a little cooking or a few added ingredients make fruit seem more like a proper dessert for those who aren't entirely happy just reaching for an apple. They also bring out flavors in fruits that are less than stellar.

Sautéed Apple Rings with Raisins and Pine Nuts

YOU can also make this with firm, ripe pears. They'll give up more juices than apples do, making a nice little sauce for a scoop of ice cream.

SERVES 4

4 apples, cored and peeled

1 tablespoon butter

1 tablespoon sugar

$^1/_4$ cup golden raisins or currants

$^1/_4$ cup toasted pine nuts

3 tablespoons applejack, apple brandy, or *membrillo* (a quince liqueur)

Slice the apples into rounds about $^3/_8$ inch thick. Heat the butter in a large skillet, add the apples, and toss with the sugar. Cook over high heat, flipping the apples in the pan every 30 seconds or so, until they have begun to caramelize, about 12 minutes. Poke one with a knife; if they're not tender, add $^1/_4$ cup water to create a little steam. When tender, add the raisins and pine nuts, cook for another few minutes, then add the applejack and cook until it has evaporated. Serve warm with ice cream.

Applesauce

3 pounds apples, quartered

Honey or sugar

Fresh lemon juice

$\frac{1}{2}$ teaspoon ground cinnamon, cardamom, or allspice or a pinch ground cloves, optional

If *you're using a food mill,* put the apples in a pot, add $\frac{1}{3}$ cup water, cover securely, and cook until the apples are completely tender, about 20 minutes. Or put them in a pressure cooker with 3 tablespoons water, bring the pressure to high, and cook for 10 minutes. Release the pressure or let it fall by itself. Pass the cooked fruit through the food mill into a clean pot. Taste and sweeten with honey if the sauce is tart or add the lemon juice if the apples are too sweet. Add the spices. Simmer for 5 minutes, then cool. *If you're not using a food mill,* peel and core the apples first, then cook until they're broken down into a sauce.

Quince or Pear Sauce Quinces and pears give applesauce an elusive perfume, and quinces turn it rosy pink. Add 2 quinces to the apples. If cooking in a pressure cooker, cut the quinces into sixths. If not, thinly slice them, chop, then stew them with the apples. Or add 3 or 4 ripe pears to the apples and cook, seasoning with cardamom or nutmeg. There's no reason not to combine all three fruits in a single sauce. In fact, it's a delectable combination that makes a common food rather exotic.

APPLESAUCE can begin as a soothing breakfast fruit and end as a dessert, tucked inside a buckwheat crêpe or made into the glorious dessert.

The pressure cooker in tandem with the food mill eliminates the need to peel and core the apples. You can have applesauce in 15 minutes. Fresh fall apples are especially great, but don't overlook those older ones whose texture is no longer good for eating out of hand. And include some with red skins—they tint the sauce pink.

MAKES ABOUT 1 QUART

Applesauce Bread Crumb Pudding

4 cups applesauce (see preceding recipe)

$\frac{1}{2}$ teaspoon freshly ground cardamom

5 tablespoons butter

$2\frac{1}{2}$ cups fresh bread crumbs made from sturdy white sandwich bread

$\frac{2}{3}$ cup quince, raspberry, or lingonberry preserves

1 cup whipping cream

Honey

Pinch freshly ground cardamom

Preheat the oven to 325°F. Butter a 6-cup soufflé mold or glass baking dish.

Season the applesauce with $\frac{1}{2}$ teaspoon cardamom. Melt the butter in a medium skillet over medium heat. Stir in the crumbs. They'll lump up, but keep stirring until they're golden brown, at which point they'll separate again. Put a quarter of the bread crumbs in the dish, add a third of the sauce, and dot with a third of the preserves. Repeat twice more, ending with a layer of crumbs. Bake for 25 minutes.

Whip the cream and sweeten it with just a little honey to taste and a pinch of cardamom. Serve the dessert warm and pass the whipped cream in a bowl.

THIS Danish-American dessert appears fairly regularly in community cookbooks. A quince- or pear-flavored applesauce, is much more haunting, but apple is delicious too. Bake this ahead of time, then hold it in a low oven during dinner.

SERVES 8

Dates with Mascarpone This combination is exquisite. Serve in winter when dates are in season and at their best—moist and soft. Include a few walnuts or toasted pecans alongside or on top for their contrasting texture. Allow 2 or 3 large, moist dates per person and about a teaspoon of mascarpone, cream cheese, or Yogurt Cheese, page 47, per date. Slit the dates in half lengthwise and remove their seeds. Spread, spoon, or squeeze a little of the mascarpone into each date half. Serve the dates on a plate, resting in paper cases if you like. Or simply put out a plate of dates and a bowl of cheese and let everyone make their own.

Caramelized Figs with Orange Flower Water

AN intense and fragrant dessert.

SERVES 4

12 to 16 mission or other fresh figs, sliced lengthwise

½ cup sugar

3 tablespoons cream or crème fraîche

1 to 2 teaspoons orange flower water to taste

Dip each fig into the sugar on a plate, heavily coating the cut surface. Heat a cast-iron skillet and add the figs, cut sides down. Cook over medium-high heat until the sugar begins to melt and caramelize, turning an amber color. Turn them over and cook for a minute more, then remove them to a serving dish. Turn off the heat and immediately whisk the cream into the pan, stirring to dissolve the sugar. This should take less than a minute. Add the orange flower water, pour the sauce over the figs, and serve.

Broiled Figs

SERVE these with Frozen Honey Mousse, a spoonful of mascarpone, or honey.

SERVES 2

4 plump, ripe fresh figs, any variety

1 teaspoon sugar

Preheat the broiler. Slice the figs in half lengthwise, lay them on a sheet pan, and sprinkle with the sugar. Set them about 4 inches under the heat until they begin to brown, 2 to 3 minutes. Serve them warm with any of the suggested accompaniments.

Sautéed Nectarines

SERVE with a spoonful of cold cream poured over each, Tangy Whipped Cream, or ice cream.

SERVES 4

4 ripe but firm nectarines or peaches

2 teaspoons butter

1 tablespoon light brown sugar or maple syrup

1 tablespoon maraschino liqueur or marsala

Wash the fruit but leave the skins on. Cut them into quarters or sixths and discard the stones. Melt the butter in a skillet over medium heat. Add the sugar, then the nectarines. Cook for about 4 minutes, carefully turning the fruit a few times, then add a few tablespoons water and let the fruit simmer. When the skins look as if they're going to slip off, add the liqueur and cook for 30 seconds more. Serve warm with the juices.

Caramelized Pineapple

1 large ripe pineapple

About 2 teaspoons butter

About 3 tablespoons sugar, as needed

3 tablespoons maraschino liqueur, kirsch, or rum, optional

Squeeze of lime juice, optional

THIS is one of my favorite last-minute fruit desserts. Serve it warm from the pan with Frozen Honey Mousse, whipped crème fraîche, or vanilla ice cream. Leftovers make a luscious addition to a crème brulée. You can speed things along by buying a peeled fresh pineapple.

SERVES 6 TO 8

Slice the skin off the pineapple and remove the eyes with the tip of a potato peeler. Cut it into rounds or half-rounds about ½ inch thick. Carefully remove the core from each piece.

Melt the butter in a wide skillet, sprinkle some of the sugar evenly over it in a thin layer, and add the pineapple. Cook over high heat until the sugar has caramelized and the bottom side is richly glazed, 4 to 5 minutes. Sprinkle the tops with sugar, turn the pineapple over, and cook until the second side is caramelized, another 4 to 5 minutes. Remove it from the pan and serve. Or add the liqueur and a squeeze of lime juice, scrape the bottom, reduce until syrupy, and pour the sauce over the pineapple.

Oranges with Pomegranate Seeds

6 navel oranges

1 lemon

1 pomegranate

10 mint leaves, plus extra for garnish

⅓ cup sugar or honey

1 2-inch cinnamon stick

5 cloves

POMEGRANATES appear in the late fall, around Thanksgiving, and are generally still available when oranges comes into season. Inside their leathery-looking skins are ruby seeds and a sweet-tart juice.

SERVES 4

Using a zester, remove long strands of the zest from one of the oranges and the lemon. Plunge the zest into boiling water for 10 seconds, then drain and set aside. Peel the oranges, page 33, slice them into ¼-inch rounds, and put them in a dessert bowl. Slowly cut a pomegranate in half, peel back the skin, and remove the seeds from half of it. Add the seeds to the oranges with the mint. Juice the remaining half by placing it in a bowl in the sink and leaning down hard on it to force out the juices.

Put 1 cup water, the sugar, spices, and zest in a saucepan and bring to a boil. Stir to dissolve the sugar and simmer for a few minutes. Remove from the heat and add the pomegranate juice. Pour the syrup, with the spices, over the oranges and refrigerate. Serve chilled, garnished with fresh mint leaves.

Compotes and Poached Fruits

Mixtures of fruits sweetened and suspended in syrups, compotes are one of the best ways of presenting both perfect fruits and those that don't have quite the flavor or sweetness to stand on their own. Compotes provide us with desserts that avoid added crusts, fillings, and creams. Just a spoonful of crème fraîche or whipped cream sets off the fruit beautifully. Most compotes are best chilled, accompanied, if at all, with a simple cookie or a slice of cake. Leftovers are wonderful for breakfast or brunch.

Many compotes leave a residue of tinted fruit-flavored syrup. It keeps more or less indefinitely, refrigerated, and can be used to sweeten iced tea, mixed with club soda or champagne, or spooned around a scoop of vanilla ice cream or yogurt.

Apricot and Berry Compote for Early Summer

LUSCIOUS *is the word that describes this bowl of fruit. If fresh apricots aren't available, you can use canned ones or 1 cup dried, simmered in the water and sugar for 25 minutes or until they're tender.*

SERVES 6

8 large apricots, ripe but still firm, about 1 1/2 pounds

1/2 cup sugar

1 cup raspberries

1 cup blackberries or boysenberries

1/2 vanilla bean, split lengthwise

Cut the apricots into halves or quarters. Bring the sugar and 2 cups water to a boil in a 2-quart saucepan. Add the apricots, lower the heat, and simmer just until they're tender and the skin is getting loose, 3 to 4 minutes. With a slotted spoon, transfer them to a serving bowl and add the berries. Boil the syrup for 3 or 4 minutes to reduce it, then remove from the heat. Scrape the seeds from the vanilla bean into it, pour it over the fruit, then chill. Serve the compote in individual bowls or use it to accompany vanilla or apricot cream or a slice of sponge cake.

> *Variations:* Mangoes are often ripe at the same time apricots and berries are. Peel one or two, cut them into small chunks, and add them to the compote. Just before serving, slice a red banana into the fruit. Pitted cherries are another seasonal addition that look and taste wonderful here.

Winter Citrus Compote in Tangerine Syrup

THIS *cheerful-looking compote makes a perfect end to a winter meal or beginning to a festive brunch. You can be very extravagant and use every conceivable variety of citrus fruit or just a few kinds. Following are some suggestions —improvise with what you have. Some special fruits to keep your eye out for are small pink Texas grapefruit, blood oranges, Honeybells, Satsumas, and kumquats.*

SERVES 6

3/4 cup fresh tangerine juice or a mixture of tangerine and orange juices

3 tablespoons sugar

6 large kumquats, sliced into rounds

2 tablespoons zest removed from any of the citrus below

1 teaspoon orange flower water

3 small pink grapefruit

3 navel oranges or tangelos

3 blood oranges

3 tangelos, Honeybells, or other citrus

Sprigs of mint leaves

Bring the juice and sugar to a boil in a small saucepan. Add the kumquats and zest, then lower the heat and simmer for 10 minutes. Stir in the orange flower water and set aside.

Peel the grapefruit, oranges, and tangelos as described on page 33. If the grapefruits are small ones, slice them into rounds; otherwise section them. Slice the remaining fruits into rounds about 1/3 inch wide. Place the fruit and juices in a serving bowl or deep platter. Pour the syrup with the kumquats and zest over the fruit and chill until ready to serve. Serve garnished with sprigs of mint.

> *Variations:* Other fruits happily complement citrus and add to the luster of this dish. Add thinly sliced small star fruits or kiwifruit, or drizzle the contents, seeds and all, of one or two passion fruits over the compote.

Rhubarb, Strawberry, and Mango Compote

1½ pounds rhubarb, cut into ½-inch lengths

1 cup sugar

⅛ teaspoon ground cloves

Grated zest and juice of 1 large orange

1 pint strawberries, sliced in half or left whole if small

1 mango, peeled and cut sliced into small pieces

Toss the rhubarb with the sugar, cloves, and orange zest and juice, then put it in a wide skillet or pot. Cook over medium heat, stirring occasionally. As soon as the rhubarb is tender—so some pieces will have fallen apart while others are still whole—transfer it to a bowl and stir in the strawberries and mango. Toss gently, then cover and chill. As it cools, its red juices will be released.

Rhubarb Compote with Citrus Add sections of 2 blood oranges to the chilled compote. Or cook the rhubarb with 6 kumquats, sliced into thin rounds, seeds removed.

Rhubarb Compote with Star Anise Make the compote as given, with 2 pieces of star anise in addition to the cloves.

NOT an elegant compote—the rhubarb loses its shape and turns mushy—but it's thick and red with plenty of juice and chunks of yellow mango. Serve it, chilled, with a slice of the Yeasted Sugar Cake or Little Lemon Biscuits, and a dollop of whipped cream. This is also a good breakfast fruit.

SERVES 6

Poached Pears

One of our most reliable winter fruits, pears are immensely versatile, especially once they've been poached. A whole pear can stand impressively alone, and halves can be combined with other fruits in compotes, tarts, and upside-down cakes or as an accompaniment to rice puddings. In turn, the pears can be accompanied by a scoop of ice cream, Frozen Honey Mousse, or Fresh Cream Cheese. Poached pears keep for weeks in the refrigerator, ready to use for an impromptu dessert.

A special tool called a *pear corer,* a coil of sharp metal that's wider at one end than the other, makes it very easy to remove the core and the stem fibers without breaking the pear.

Fall Compote with Pears, Persimmons, and Figs

Pears Poached in Riesling, or Pears Poached in Vanilla Syrup, page 686

¼ cup golden raisins

Zest of 1 lemon, removed with a zester

2 Fuyu persimmons

6 fresh figs, halved

½ pint raspberries

24 muscat grapes

Pour the syrup off the pears, put it in a small pot, and simmer with the raisins and lemon zest until the raisins are plumped. Pour it back over the pears and refrigerate until cool.

Arrange the pears in a large bowl or in individual soup plates. Serve two halves per person or slice the halves into strips, leaving them joined at the top and fan them into the dish. Thinly slice the persimmons crosswise and divide them among the dishes along with the figs, raspberries, and grapes. Spoon the raisins, lemon zest, and juice over each and serve.

FOR persimmons, use the small squat Fuyus rather than the acorn-shaped Hachiya. They can be eaten when crisp whereas the Hachiyas make your mouth pucker unless they're very soft.

SERVES 4 TO 6

Pears (and Other Fruits) Poached in Vanilla Syrup

SERVES 4 TO 6

Use this light syrup with peaches, apricots, nectarines, and other fruits.

1 1/2 cups sugar

Several 2-inch pieces lemon zest, removed with a vegetable peeler

1/2 vanilla bean

4 to 6 ripe but firm pears, such as Winter Nelis, Bartletts, Bosc, or Anjou

Bring 1 quart water to a boil with the sugar, lemon zest, and vanilla bean. Stir to dissolve the sugar, then lower the heat to a simmer.

Neatly peel the pears in long even strokes, then cut them in half. Remove the cores and stem ends with a pear corer. As you work, add them directly to the simmering syrup. Cook gently until they begin to look translucent around the edges, anywhere from 20 to 40 minutes, depending on the type of pear. Remove them with a slotted spoon to a bowl.

Scrape the seeds of the vanilla bean into the syrup and pour the syrup over the pears, along with the vanilla bean. Later you can dry it and use it to flavor sugar. Cover and refrigerate until needed.

> *Variations:* In place of or along with the vanilla bean, you can flavor the syrup with 3 star anise, 4 cloves, a 3-inch cinnamon stick, or several pieces of thinly sliced ginger.

Pears Poached in Riesling

SERVES 6

3 cups Riesling

1 cup water or fresh orange juice

1 large piece orange zest, removed with a vegetable peeler

1/4 cup sugar

6 ripe firm pears, such as Winter Nelis, Bartletts, or small Bosc

1 tablespoon honey

Combine the wine, water, orange zest, and sugar in a 3-quart saucepan and gradually bring to a boil. Meanwhile, peel the pears. If small, leave them whole; if larger, halve them lengthwise and remove the core and stem with a pear corer. Simmer until the pears are translucent around the edges, 20 to 40 minutes. Transfer the pears to a bowl. Add the honey to the wine and simmer until amber colored and syrupy. Pour over the syrup, lay a piece of plastic wrap directly over the pears to keep them from browning, and refrigerate. Serve the pears with their syrup, accompanied by Frozen Honey Mousse, page 709, a spoonful of mascarpone, or softly whipped cream.

Pears in Red Wine For 4 to 6 pears, simmer 2 cups red wine—a light Côtes-du-Rhône or Zinfandel—with 2 cups water, 1 1/2 cups sugar, 3 cloves, a strip of orange or lemon zest, and 1/4 vanilla bean. Peel and core the pears and cook as described.

686   VEGETARIAN COOKING FOR EVERYONE

Winter Compote with Wine-Poached Pears and Dried Fruits

Poached Pears, any of the preceding
   recipes

1/4 cup monukka or golden raisins

1/4 cup dried cherries

Zest of 1 orange, removed with a zester
   or finely slivered

8 dried prunes or apricots, soaked in
   warm water for 15 minutes

1/2 cup whipping cream

1 tablespoon sugar

1/2 teaspoon ground cinnamon

A STUNNING jewellike compote, especially with the giant monukka raisins (available at natural food stores). The pears, as well as the rest of the fruits, can be poached many days in advance—and, in fact, they're better that way.

SERVES 6 TO 8

Pour 1 cup of the syrup from the pears into a saucepan and add the raisins, cherries, zest, and prunes. (Leave enough liquid to cover the pears or lay a piece of plastic wrap directly on them to keep them from browning.) Simmer, covered, until the fruits are soft, about 20 minutes. Chill. Whip the cream with the sugar and cinnamon until soft peaks are formed.

Arrange the pears in a large bowl or individual serving plates. Add the dried fruits and zest along with their syrup. Add a spoonful of the cream to each plate and serve with Cardamom Cookies, page 715, or the Yeasted Sugar Cake, page 702.

Warm Baked Fruit and Honey Compote

1 1/2 cups dried apricots

1/2 cup dried pears

1/4 cup dried cherries

1/4 cup currants

Zest of 1 lemon

4 kumquats sliced into rounds

3 tablespoons honey

1 cup fresh orange juice

2 tablespoons butter

SERVE these fruits for dessert with the Ginger-Oat Shorties, or for breakfast with the Ginger Cream Scones.

SERVES 4 TO 6

Cover the apricots, pears, and cherries with warm water and set aside to steep for 4 hours or overnight. The next morning, pour off the soaking water and put them in a baking dish with the currants, lemon zest, and kumquats. Mix the honey with the orange juice, pour over the fruits, and dot the top with butter.

Preheat the oven to 375°F. Cover and bake for 20 minutes, then remove the cover and continue baking for 15 minutes. Serve warm or at room temperature.

   Variation with Bananas: Many people like the taste of cooked bananas. Try using the big red ones or little finger bananas; their flavor is slightly sharper than the yellow ones. Peel 2 or 3, slice them into rounds about 1/2 inch thick, and add them to the fruit just before baking.

Dried Mission Figs in Red Wine with Anise

THESE poached figs with their hint of anise make a good accompaniment to rice pudding, or you can serve them alone, accompanied by something creamy and cold—whipped crème fraîche would be good. Prunes are also delicious cooked this way, with or without the anise.

SERVES 4 TO 6

12 ounces dried mission figs	$1/2$ cup honey
$1^1/2$ cups red wine, such as Merlot or Cabernet	3 large strips lemon zest
	4 cloves
$1/2$ cup water	$1/2$ teaspoon anise seeds

Cut the knotty stems off the figs. If the figs are very hard, cover them with warm water and let stand until they're soft, 30 minutes to an hour, then drain. Put them in a saucepan with the remaining ingredients. Bring to a boil, then simmer, partially covered, until the figs are tender, about 30 minutes. Remove the figs to a dish with a slotted spoon, then simmer the liquid until it's syrupy, after several minutes. Pour the syrup back over the figs and chill before serving.

Dried Fruit Gratin with Pistachio-Walnut Topping

THE scent of the vanilla permeates this assemblage of fruits, and the nut-crumb topping provides a fine crunch. It's the perfect dessert when just a bite of something sweet is wanted. Serve it with a mound of yogurt cheese or a spoonful of mascarpone.

SERVES 4 TO 6

1 cup dried apricots	3 tablespoons sugar
1 cup pitted dried prunes	$1/4$ cup mixed nuts—peeled pistachios, walnuts, hazelnuts
$1/2$ cup dried cherries or cranberries	
$1/2$ vanilla bean, split lengthwise	1 tablespoon butter

Cover the dried fruits with warm water and set them aside until they've plumped up, about 20 to 30 minutes. Drain.

Preheat the oven to 350°F. Lightly butter a shallow baking dish and set the vanilla bean on the bottom.

Arrange the fruit loosely in the dish. Mix $3/4$ cup hot water with 2 tablespoons sugar, pour it over the fruit, cover the dish with foil, and bake for 25 minutes. Chop the nuts with the remaining sugar and mix with the butter. Uncover the fruit, sprinkle the topping over it, and return to the oven until the nuts are lightly browned, about 10 to 15 minutes more.

Fruit Crisps

As American as apple pie, crisps are among our best-loved desserts. They're so easy to put together, and the crumb topping gives them the succulence of pie without the trouble of making a crust. Everyone knows apple crisp, but peaches, apricots, plums, cherries, berries, pears, rhubarb, cranberries, plus combinations of fruits also make prime crisps. Improvisation is easy here. If crisps are popular in your house, make the crisp topping in large amounts and store it in the freezer until you're ready to bake.

Crisps bake best in a 2-inch-high baking dish or gratin dish. Set your crisp on a cookie sheet to catch any drips.

Crisp Topping

6 tablespoons butter, cut into ½-inch chunks

¾ cup brown sugar, packed

⅔ cup flour

½ cup rolled oats or chopped nuts

¼ teaspoon salt

½ teaspoon grated nutmeg

1 teaspoon ground cinnamon, optional

MAKES ENOUGH FOR ONE 8- × 10-INCH CRISP

Using your fingers or the paddle attachment of a mixer, work the butter with the rest of the ingredients so that each piece is coated and you have a coarse, crumbly mixture. Use it to cover a shallow gratin dish of sliced fruit.

> *Variation Made with Oil:* In place of butter, use 6 tablespoons canola or a mixture of canola and a rich-flavored nut oil, such as walnut or hazelnut.

Peach, Raspberry, and Blackberry Crisp

Crisp Topping, preceding recipe

2 pounds ripe peaches

1 cup blackberries

1 cup raspberries

½ cup sugar

3 tablespoons flour

THE combination of peaches and berries is superb. Serve it with the classic accompaniment —vanilla ice cream. Peaches vary in juiciness, and this amount of flour is right for ripe, juicy fruits. If your peaches aren't juicy, reduce the flour by a tablespoon.

SERVES 4 TO 6

Preheat the oven to 375°F. Butter a 2- to 2½-quart baking dish. Make the topping and set aside. To peel the peaches, drop them into a pan of boiling water for 10 seconds, then remove them to a bowl of cold water. Their skins should slip right off.

Slice the peaches into a large bowl, in wedges ½ inch thick; discard the stones. Add the berries, sugar, and flour and toss gently. Transfer the fruit to the baking dish and cover with the topping. Set it on a baking sheet to catch the juices and bake until the top is well browned and the peaches are tender when pierced with a knife, about 45 minutes.

Apricot and Cherry Crisp with Almond Topping

Crisp Topping, above, made with chopped almonds instead of rolled oats

2½ pounds ripe apricots

1 pound cherries, dark red Bing or sour pie cherries

2 tablespoons sugar

1½ tablespoons minute tapioca

⅛ teaspoon almond extract

IF pressed to choose, this crisp might be my favorite. These juicy fruits are also good baked under a cobbler topping.

Apricots are frequently uneven in their ripening—the part facing the sun can be as soft as jam, the opposite side still quite firm.

SERVES 4 TO 6

Preheat the oven to 375°F. Lightly butter a 2½-quart gratin dish. Make the topping.

Pit the apricots and cut into quarters. Pit the cherries and slice them in two or leave whole. Toss both fruits with the sugar, tapioca, and almond extract. Lay the fruit in the prepared dish and cover with the topping. Set the dish on a baking pan to catch the juices and bake until the top is browned and the juices have thickened around the edge. Serve warm with vanilla or honey ice cream.

Rhubarb-Apple Crisp

YOU *need the apples for*
texture, but they also
temper the natural
tartness of the rhubarb.

YOU need the apples for
texture, but they also
temper the natural
tartness of the rhubarb.

SERVES 4 TO 6

Crisp Topping, page 689
1 1/2 pounds apples, peeled and cored
2 pounds rhubarb, diced into 1-inch
    pieces

1 1/4 cups sugar
1/4 cup flour
1 teaspoon ground cinnamon
Pinch ground cloves

Preheat the oven to 375°F. Make the topping and set it aside. Dice the apples, then put them in a bowl and toss with the remaining ingredients. Arrange the fruit in a 2-quart gratin dish and cover with the topping. Set the dish on a sheet pan to catch any drips and bake until the juices from the fruit are bubbling and the topping is brown, about 1 hour and 10 minutes.

Blueberry Crisp Six cups tossed with 1/4 cup light brown sugar and 1 teaspoon finely grated lemon or lime zest.

Plum Crisp Three pounds, quartered and tossed with 1/4 cup sugar, 1 teaspoon grated orange zest, and a pinch ground cloves.

Nectarine and Raspberry Crisp: A scant 3 pounds nectarines, peeled and sliced 1/2 inch thick, tossed with 2 tablespoons sugar and a pint or more raspberries.

Pear Crisp 2 1/2 pounds peeled, cored, and sliced ripe but firm pears, about 1/2 inch thick, tossed with 1/2 teaspoon grated nutmeg or ground cardamom and covered with an almond crisp topping. Pears are also good mixed with blackberries, raspberries, and apples.

Apple Crisp Two and one-half pounds, peeled, cored, and thinly sliced apples, tossed with 1 teaspoon ground cinnamon, 1 teaspoon grated lemon zest, 1 tablespoon fresh lemon juice, and 2 tablespoons sugar.

Fruit Cobblers

Warm fruit cobblers are another classic American dessert. They're especially good made with juicy fruits since the dough on top draws up the juices just as a dumpling does. Cobblers are easy to make for a crowd. They hold their heat well, so they can be baked just before or during dinner and still be warm enough to melt a scoop of ice cream when it's time for dessert.

The basic recipe for fruit cobbler serves four generously or six modestly. It uses 6 to 8 cups fruit, sweetened and seasoned when appropriate with lemon or spice and covered with a biscuit dough. Dropping the dough by small spoonfuls gives the finished dish a cobbled appearance; hence its name. A shallow gratin dish or pie plate gives plenty of crust in proportion to fruit. I prefer a tender, tangy buttermilk biscuit dough, but if your preference is for sweet milk or cream biscuits, use the appropriate liquid and omit the baking soda.

Cobbler Topping

1½ cups all-purpose or whole-wheat pastry flour

⅓ cup sugar

1 teaspoon baking powder

½ teaspoon baking soda

½ teaspoon salt

6 tablespoons cold butter, cut into small pieces

½ cup buttermilk

½ teaspoon vanilla

MAKES ONE 8- × 10-INCH COBBLER

Mix the dry ingredients together, then cut in the butter using your fingers or two knives until it forms coarse crumbs. Stir in the buttermilk and vanilla with a fork until dough clings together when grabbed with your hand. If too dry, add a little more buttermilk until all the flour is moist enough to cohere. Spoon the dough over the fruit using a small spoon to give the surface a cobbled appearance. For a smoother look, you can roll the dough and cut out biscuits or simply lay the whole sheet of dough over the fruit.

Stone Fruit Cobbler

6 to 8 cups sliced peeled ripe peaches, plums, apricots, or nectarines

½ cup light brown sugar, plus extra for the top, if desired

1 teaspoon ground cinnamon or ½ teaspoon ground nutmeg or cardamom

¼ cup flour

Grated zest of 1 lemon

1 tablespoon fresh lemon juice

Cobbler Topping, preceding recipe

1 egg, beaten, or 1 tablespoon cream or milk, optional

SERVES 4 TO 6

Preheat the oven to 375°F. Lightly butter an 8- × 10-inch baking dish.

Toss the fruit with the sugar, spice, flour, zest, and juice. Put the fruit in the dish, then cover it with the topping. Brush the top with the beaten egg and sprinkle it with sugar for a shiny, sparkly crust. Bake until the fruit is cooked and bubbling around the edges, about 25 minutes. Let the cobbler sit for a while before serving, but serve it warm with cream, yogurt, or ice cream.

Blueberry Cobbler Toss 6 cups blueberries with ¼ cup flour, ⅓ cup packed brown sugar, 1 tablespoon molasses, the grated zest of 1 lemon, and 1 tablespoon fresh lemon juice.

Spiced Peach Cobbler Toss sliced peeled peaches with ¼ cup white or packed light brown sugar, ⅛ teaspoon *each* ground ginger, cloves, and nutmeg, 1 teaspoon ground cinnamon, and 2 tablespoons flour.

Good Fruit Combinations for Cobblers Try blueberries with peaches; peaches, nectarines, and plums; apricots and cherries; rhubarb and apples; cranberries and apples; or any of the combinations suggested for crêpes.

A Few Favorite Tarts and Galettes

THERE'S *nothing like a piece of warm pie for dessert or the same pie reheated for breakfast. American pies are deep and hearty, while tarts tend to be less so. Galettes are free-form pies that have a rustic appearance. But regardless of what you call your pie, you have to start with the pastry.*

ABOUT THE PASTRY: I made my first pie when I was 13, and I can vividly recall my frustration as the crust split, tore, and crumbled. I was in tears—it was to be a peach pie for my mother, and it was a mess. I didn't really grasp how to make pie dough until, many years later, I found myself baking a lot of pies in a row for a benefit. After a dozen pies I began to get it! Pie dough is one of those things where the wisdom of your hands must be allowed to develop. Words, in the end, are really no replacement for experience. Nonetheless, my advice is to use a light but firm hand as you work. You don't want to be rough with your dough, but don't be too timid either. You have to take charge and be respectful at once.

INGREDIENTS: Fat provides flavor and flakiness. A mixture of butter and shortening provides for both, but because I don't like to use hydrogenated oil I tend to use all butter in my crusts. Oil can be used, but it is much more difficult to make a tender crust with it, though not impossible. When it comes to flour, you want an all-purpose flour with only a moderate amount of gluten so that the dough doesn't become too stretchy.

The more fat in proportion to flour, the easier the dough is to handle. The leaner the dough, the greater the likelihood of its being difficult to work. That's why classic pie dough takes more practice to make well than short tart doughs.

In the case of pie and galette doughs, the butter and water are cold. This helps to create a flaky texture when the dough bakes. Cutting in the butter so that a mealy texture remains—described as coarse crumbs or like cornmeal—also helps ensure lightness and flakiness. Classic tart dough, which has much more butter in proportion to flour, can be made with the butter at room temperature, and it's almost impossible to overwork it. Egg yolks also help bind a crust and make it tender, as well as enrich its flavor. If you're nervous about making dough, add an egg yolk along with the butter.

Always use just as much water as you need to bring your dough together and no more. Add it gradually and handle the dough lightly. Although using a lot of water makes the dough easy to roll out, when baked it will be tough and shrunken. (If you live where the air is dry, you can expect to use extra water. Don't worry about it—in this instance it will be fine.)

ROLLING THE DOUGH: Once your dough comes together into a ball, gently press it into a disk. It will be easier to roll this way. When it comes to rolling out dough, there's no reason to refrigerate it first unless it's a hot day and the butter or shortening has become squishy. In this case, slip it into a plastic bag and refrigerate for 15 minutes.

Place your disk of dough on a lightly floured work surface or a special cloth made for pie dough. Roll the dough from the center, going in the four cardinal directions, then in between. In the end the dough should be large enough to fit the pan easily if it's intended for one (galettes don't require pans), and it should about ⅛ inch thick.

The easiest way to move the dough is to fold it into quarters, pick the whole thing up, and set it down with its point at the center of the pan. Then you simply unfold it. Always ease the dough into the pan rather than stretch it since the dough will shrink when it bakes. Trim the edges before or after filling the shell, then crimp them, using your thumb and forefingers or a fork. For a galette you can leave the edges ragged or trimmed.

Pie Crust

1 1/2 cups flour
1/2 teaspoon salt

1/4 pound cold butter
3 to 5 tablespoons ice water, as needed

MAKES ONE 9-INCH PIE
SHELL

Mix the flour and salt in a bowl, then cut in the butter, using your fingers or two knives, until it resembles coarse meal. Lightly stir in the water a tablespoon at a time until you can bring the dough together in a ball. If crumbs remain on the bottom, add a few drops of water so that you can pull them together as well. Shape the dough into a disk and roll it out into a circle 1/8 inch thick. If the dough is so warm that it's sticky, refrigerate it for 15 minutes, then roll it out.

Pie Crust with Bran

1 1/4 cup flour
1/4 cup wheat bran
1/4 teaspoon salt

1/4 pound butter, cut into small pieces,
     or a mixture of butter and shortening
3 to 5 tablespoons ice water, as needed

THE nutty flavor of bran is always particularly good with custard or ricotta fillings, whether sweet or savory.

MAKES ONE 9-INCH PIE
SHELL OR 10-INCH TART
SHELL

Combine the flour, bran, and salt in a bowl, using your fingers or two knives, then cut in the butter, until the mixture resembles coarse meal. Lightly work in enough water for the dough to cohere when brought together with the hands. Gently flatten the dough into a disk. Slip it into a plastic bag and let rest for 15 minutes in the refrigerator if the dough feels too soft or overworked; otherwise, immediately roll it out into a circle 1/8 inch thick.

Pie Crust Made with Oil

1 1/2 cups flour
1/2 teaspoon salt

1/2 cup canola oil
2 tablespoons milk, soy milk, or water

I HAVE had absolutely wonderful tender crusts made with oil by some-one else, but I honestly think it takes a lot of practice to succeed. Fortunately, even if yours is less than tender, it will still taste good.

MAKES ONE 9-INCH PIE
SHELL

Mix the flour and salt together in one bowl, the oil and the milk in another. Gently stir the liquids into the flour until the dough comes together. Shape the dough into a flat disk, then roll it out between two sheets of wax paper, 1/8 inch thick. Peel off the top sheet of paper, invert the dough into a pie pan, and carefully remove the second sheet. If any tears occur—and they probably will—simply press the dough back together.

Tart Pastry

A TENDER European-style crust for lining those French tart pans with a removable bottom. Because the dough is so short, it's virtually impossible to overwork it.

MAKES ONE 9-INCH TART SHELL

1 cup plus 2 tablespoons flour

¹/₄ teaspoon salt

1 tablespoon sugar

¹/₂ cup butter at room temperature, cut into small pieces

A mixture of ¹/₂ teaspoon vanilla extract and 3 tablespoons water (omit for savory tarts)

Stir the flour, salt, and sugar together in a bowl, then work in the butter with two knives, your fingers, or a mixer until it makes fine crumbs. Don't let it become completely smooth, though. Stir in enough vanilla-water to pull the dough together. Wrap in plastic wrap and let rest in the refrigerator for 15 minutes.

To line the pan, roll the dough out into a 9-inch circle then set it in the pan. Using the heel of your palm, press the dough up the side. If some pieces are too long, break them off and add them, as needed, to areas that are too short. The sides should be about ¹/₄ inch thick, rise ¹/₄ inch above the rim, and be slightly thinner at the base of the pan. This way, when the dough slumps during the baking, this shallow space will be filled evenly instead of being overly thick and underbaked. Carefully set the tart shell in the freezer to harden.

Tart shells are nearly always prebaked before filling. To prebake a tart shell, preheat the oven to 400°F. Place the frozen shell on a sheet pan and bake until set and lightly browned, about 25 minutes. Check it several times for swells and prick any large bubbles with the tip of a knife.

Alsatian Tart Dough

THIS batter bakes into a tender, almost cakelike crust with a rich, eggy flavor. Not only does it go particularly well with fruits (it's used in the Rhubarb Tart), but it's very easy to make, and great for anyone who's intimidated by pie crust.

MAKES ONE 11-INCH TART

¹/₂ cup unsalted butter

¹/₂ cups sugar

¹/₈ teaspoon salt

3 eggs, at room temperature

¹/₂ teaspoon vanilla extract

2 teaspoons grated orange zest

1 cup flour

Cream the butter, sugar, and salt until light and fluffy, then add the eggs one at a time and beat until smooth after each addition. Add the vanilla and orange zest, then stir in the flour and salt. Using a spatula, smooth the batter into the tart pan, pushing it up against the edges to make a slight rim. Fill and bake.

Nut Crust

½ cup almonds, pecans, or walnuts

¾ cup white or whole-wheat pastry flour

¼ teaspoon salt

3 tablespoons light brown sugar

5 tablespoons butter, cut into small pieces

½ teaspoon vanilla mixed with 2 tablespoons water

A RICH, crunchy crust —the ideal lining for a smooth-textured tart such as the Brown Sugar–Yogurt Tart.

MAKES ONE 9-INCH TART OR PIE SHELL

Preheat the oven to 350°F. Toast the nuts on a sheet pan until they smell good, about 8 minutes. Cool, then chop half the nuts finely and the other half coarsely. Toss all the nuts, flour, salt, and sugar in a bowl, then cut in the butter using your fingers or two knives. Add the vanilla-water bit by bit. Use your hands to bring the dough together into a ball.

Press the dough into a tart shell or pie pan, building it evenly up the sides. Freeze until firm before filling and baking.

Three Fruit Galettes

For these rustic open-faced pies, the dough is rolled out in a free-form fashion, left untrimmed, the edges loosely draped over the fruit. They don't require crimping, weaving, or other manipulations of the dough. You can use all kinds of fruit—apricots, nectarines, grapes, cherries, and prune plums. If the fruit promises to be juicy, scatter ½ cup or more toasted bread crumbs or crushed *amaretti* under them to absorb the juice. Form your galette on a cookie sheet or on the back side of a jelly roll pan so that you can slide it off onto a serving plate once it's done.

Galette Dough

MAKES ONE LARGE
GALETTE OR TWELVE
3-INCH TURNOVERS

2 cups all-purpose or whole-wheat
    pastry flour

½ teaspoon salt

1 tablespoon sugar

12 tablespoons cold, unsalted butter,
    cut into small pieces

⅓ to ½ cup ice water as needed

Mix the flour, salt, and sugar together in a bowl. Cut in the butter by hand or using a mixer with a paddle attachment, leaving some pea-sized chunks. Sprinkle the ice water over the top by the tablespoon and toss it with the flour mixture until you can bring the dough together into a ball. Press it into a disk and refrigerate for 15 minutes if the butter feels soft.

To form a galette, roll it out on a lightly floured counter into a 14-inch irregular circle about ⅛ inch thick. Fold it into quarters and transfer it to the back of a sheet pan or a cookie sheet without sides. Unfold it. It will be larger than the pan.

Add the fruit according to the recipe, leaving a border 2 to 4 inches wide. Fold the edges of the dough over the fruit, overlapping them as you go. Depending on how much of an edge you have left, the galette will be partially or completely covered, almost like a two-crust pie. Brush the top with melted butter—it will take about a tablespoon—or an egg beaten with a little milk or cream. Sprinkle it heavily with sugar—using about 2 tablespoons—then bake according to the recipe instructions.

Fresh Fig and Honey Galette

THE figs must be sweet and nearly overripe with thin, splitting skins. Serve with Fresh Cream Cheese, goat cheese, or Frozen Honey Mousse.

SERVES 6

Galette Dough, above, or Yeasted Tart
    Dough with Butter, page 489

3 to 4 tablespoons butter as needed

½ cup fresh white bread crumbs if using
    galette dough

12 to 16 large ripe purple figs, stems
    removed

2 tablespoons honey

⅛ teaspoon ground cloves

¼ teaspoon ground anise

1 tablespoon sugar

Preheat the oven to 400°F. Roll the dough into a large circle and drape it on a flat cookie sheet pan or over the back of a sheet pan.

If you're using the galette dough, melt 1 tablespoon of the butter in a small skillet, add the bread crumbs, and cook over low heat until they're golden and crisp. Scatter them in the center of the dough, making an 8-inch circle.

Cut the figs in half and lay them over the bread crumbs, cut side up. Heat the honey with 1 tablespoon of the butter and the spices in a small pan, then drizzle it over the figs. Fold the edge of the dough over the top. Melt the remaining tablespoon of butter in the same pan, brush it over the dough, and sprinkle with the sugar. Bake until the crust is nicely browned, 35 to 40 minutes.

Apricot Galette

Galette Dough, page 697
⅓ cup crushed amaretti, biscotti, or dry bread crumbs

12 large ripe apricots, sliced in half
3 tablespoons butter, melted
3 tablespoons sugar or more to taste

Preheat the oven to 425°F. Roll the dough into a 14-inch circle and drape it over the back of a sheet pan. Leaving a border of 2 inches or so, cover the center of the dough with the crumbs. Arrange the apricots over the crumbs, cut side down, making a single layer or overlapping them if they're very large or if you have extra fruit. Fold the edges of the dough over the fruit, overlapping it to make wide pleats. Brush the dough with butter and drizzle any remaining butter over the fruit. Sprinkle both the crust and apricots generously with sugar. Bake for 15 minutes, then reduce the heat to 375°F and continue baking until the fruit is tender and the crust is browned, 20 to 25 minutes more. Remove and let cool to lukewarm before serving. Slice into wedges and serve with crème fraîche, a scoop of honey ice cream, or vanilla ice cream.

Apple Galette with Pine Nuts and Candied Lemon

Candied Lemon, following recipe
Galette Dough, page 696
1½ to 2 pounds apples, peeled, cored, and halved
⅓ cup currants, golden raisins, or monukka raisins

2 tablespoons sweet sherry or Calvados
¼ cup toasted pine nuts
¼ cup sugar
½ teaspoon ground cinnamon
2 tablespoons butter, melted

First make the candied lemon slices. Make the dough, roll it into a large circle ⅛ inch thick, and set it on the back of a sheet pan or on a cookie sheet without sides. Preheat the oven to 400°F.

Thinly slice half of the apples crosswise and toss them with the currants, sherry, pine nuts, 4 teaspoons of the sugar, and the cinnamon. Finely chop the remaining apples, then toss them with 4 teaspoons sugar. Mound them in the center of the dough, forming a 7-inch circle, and arrange the sliced apples over the top. Add the juice from the bowl. Cut about half the lemon slices in half and tuck them among the apples.

Fold the edges of the dough over the fruit, pleating it as you go, partially covering the apples. Brush with the melted butter and sprinkle with the remaining sugar. Pour any extra butter over the apples. Bake until the crust is richly glazed and the apples are tender, about 45 minutes. Serve warm with Tangy Whipped Cream, page 717.

Candied Lemon Slices: Bring a cup of water and a cup of sugar to a boil in a small heavy saucepan. Add 2 thinly sliced lemons and simmer, covered, for 25 minutes. Let cool, then transfer to a covered container. They will keep for at least a month, refrigerated.

Tip for Handling Tart Shells

To make tart shells easy to handle, always bake them on a sheet pan. That way it's easy to remove them from the oven without accidentally damaging the edges or loosening the bottom.

To remove the rim from a finished tart, first make sure the crook of your arm is covered if the tart is still hot. Carefully move one hand under the pan, then, with the other hand, ease the rim down your arm and let it rest there. Tilt the far edge of the tart toward the serving plate, then lower the pan nearly all the way down. Before slipping your hand out, rest the pan on the tip of a knife, then let it down onto the plate. This way you won't crumble the pastry.

Blueberry Custard Tart

HUCKLEBERRIES and blueberries from the wild are especially choice in this tart. If you're picking them yourself, remember it takes only 2 cups of fruit—really not that much.

MAKES ONE 9-INCH TART

Tart Pastry, page 694
1 pint blueberries or huckleberries
1 tablespoon flour
3 tablespoons unsulfured molasses
1 teaspoon finely grated lemon zest

1 egg
$^2/_3$ cup sour cream or crème fraîche
$^1/_2$ teaspoon vanilla
$^1/_8$ teaspoon grated nutmeg

Line a 9-inch tart pan with the tart pastry and freeze it until it's hard. Preheat the oven to 425°F. Set the frozen shell on a sheet pan and bake until lightly browned, about 25 minutes.

Sort through the berries and remove any stems or badly bruised fruits. Toss them with the flour, molasses, and lemon zest and arrange them loosely over the bottom of the tart shell. Mix the remaining ingredients together and pour over the berries. Bake until the custard is browned and puffed, about 35 minutes. Let cool before serving.

Brown Sugar–Yogurt Tart in a Nut Crust

WHOLE-MILK yogurt, such as Brown Cow brand, makes the most luxurious tart, but you can use low-fat yogurt, too, preferably drained to rid it of its whey, or even buttermilk. Serve the tart still slightly warm, plain or accompanied by sweetened blackberries.

MAKES ONE 9-INCH TART

Nut Crust, page 695
1$^1/_4$ cups yogurt, preferably whole-milk, drained, page 47
2 eggs
3 tablespoons butter, melted

1$^1/_2$ teaspoons vanilla extract
$^2/_3$ cup dark brown sugar, packed
2 tablespoons flour

Make the dough and line a 9-inch tart pan or shallow pie pan. Refrigerate until firm while you preheat oven to 350°F. Whisk together the yogurt, eggs, butter, vanilla, and sugar, then stir in the flour. Set the shell on a sheet pan, pour in the batter, and bake until set and browned, 30 to 35 minutes. Serve warm.

Prune Tart in Almond Custard

Tart Pastry, page 694

12 ounces pitted prunes

1 cup crème fraîche

1 egg

1 tablespoon orange flower water

¼ cup sugar

1 cup finely ground almonds or walnuts

3 tablespoons Armagnac or brandy

Powdered sugar

No one believes prunes can make an exquisite pastry until they eat this tart. I wouldn't hesitate a moment to serve this for an important winter meal. It's best when still a little warm.

SERVES 8 TO 10

Make the pastry, line a 9-inch tart pan, and prebake in a 400°F oven as described on page 694.

Simmer the prunes in water until tender, about 25 minutes. Drain them well, then arrange them on the tart shell. Whisk together ½ cup crème fraîche, the egg, orange flower water, sugar, and ground nuts. Pour this custard over the prunes. Bake until the custard is set, puffed, and golden, about 35 minutes. Remove it from the oven and immediately spoon the Armagnac over the top. Before serving, loosen the remaining crème fraîche with a fork. Dust the edge of the tart with powdered sugar and serve with a spoonful of crème fraîche on the side of each piece.

Prune Galette You can also make this tart into a galette. After folding the pastry over the prunes, slowly pour the custard into the galette. You may not be able to use all of it. Brush the dough with melted butter, sprinkle with sugar, and bake at 425°F until browned, about 30 minutes. Spoon the Armagnac into the fruit while hot, then allow the galette to cool before serving.

Plum Turnovers with Crushed Pecans

1 1-pound package frozen puff pastry, defrosted overnight in the refrigerator

2½ cups quartered pitted plums

1 cup finely chopped pecans or walnuts

⅓ cup light brown sugar, packed

½ teaspoon ground cinnamon

1 teaspoon grated orange zest

½ teaspoon orange flower water, optional

1 egg, beaten

I LIKE to use Santa Rosa or late-season Italian prune plums in these pastries. The latter are unusually easy to slice and pit. Serve these turnovers warm with Frozen Honey Mousse or Tangy Whipped Cream.

MAKES 8 TURNOVERS

Roll each sheet of puff pastry dough into a 12-inch square. Cut each piece into four 6-inch squares.

Toss the remaining ingredients except egg in a bowl. Add more sugar if the plums are tart. Divide the filling among the pieces of pastry, laying it across the center. Moisten the edges of the dough with the beaten egg, then fold the top half of the pastry over the lower to make a triangle. Crimp the edges with a fork. You can decoratively score the tops by carefully dragging a sharp paring knife over the dough, but not cutting through it. Transfer the turnovers to a sheet pan and brush them with the remaining egg. Refrigerate until ready to bake.

Preheat the oven to 375°F. Bake the turnovers until golden on top and the pastry well puffed, about 25 minutes. Serve warm.

Nutmeg Pie

A DELICATE *cottage cheese pie that blossoms with spice. Perfect for a brunch or a modest dessert, accompanied by sweetened berries in summer or a spoonful of the Spiced Dried Fruits in Wine Syrup in winter.*

MAKES ONE 9-INCH PIE

Nut Crust, page 695, or Pie Crust with
    Bran, page 693
2 cups small-curd cottage cheese
1/2 cup sour cream or yogurt

3 eggs
1 teaspoon grated nutmeg
1/8 teaspoon salt
1/3 cup light honey or sugar

Line a 9-inch pie or tart pan with the dough and freeze until hardened. Preheat the oven to 425°F. Set the frozen shell on a sheet pan and bake until the crust is set and lightly colored, about 25 minutes. Remove and lower the oven temperature to 350°F.

Whisk the remaining ingredients together until smooth. Pour the filling into the shell and bake in the center of the oven until puffed, barely firm, and starting to color in places, 30 to 40 minutes. Serve warm or at room temperature.

Cinnamon Tart Substitute 1 teaspoon freshly ground cinnamon for the nutmeg. This tart makes a soothing ending to meals that are heavily flavored with chile and spice.

Rhubarb Tart with Orange Custard

BAKED *in a large French tart pan, this rosy tart isn't overly sweet so you can serve it for brunch as well as for dinner. If you don't like making pie dough, you'll be greatly relieved to know that the crust is actually a batter.*

MAKES ONE 11-INCH TART

1 1/2 pounds rhubarb
1/2 to 3/4 cups sugar to taste
1/8 teaspoon ground clove
1 tablespoon orange flower water
Alsatian Tart Dough, page 694

1 egg
1/2 cup crème fraîche or cream
1 tablespoons Grand Marnier
Powdered sugar

Lightly butter and 11-inch tart pan. Preheat the oven to 375°F.

Peel the rhubarb if it's tough and stringy and dice it into small squares, about 1/3-inch across. Toss it with the sugar, using the larger amount for a sweeter tart, clove, and orange flower water and set aside. Meanwhile, make the batter and line the tart pan.

Beat the egg in a 2-cup measure, then add the juices that have collected from the rhubarb with enough cream to make 1 cup. Distribute the rhubarb over the batter, keeping it within the rim. Pour the custard over the fruit and bake until set and lightly browned, about 45 minutes. Remove from the oven and immediately spoon the Grand Marnier over the surface. Serve the tart warm, dusted with powdered sugar.

Five Favorite Cakes

THERE *are occasions when a great cake makes a celebratory statement that other desserts, as good as they might be, just don't do. I'm very fond of elaborate cakes, especially when they're made by someone else, but my home repertoire relies largely on these five cakes that, while varied in texture and feature, are far simpler to make than the multilayered marvels of the professional. They are cakes that fill a number of our needs when it comes to pastry. The poppyseed cake, that's especially enjoyable during the cooler months, stays moist for days, feeds many, and is one to enjoy with a cup of coffee or tea. At the opposite end of the spectrum, the yeast-risen sugar cake might make its etheral appearance at the table in the company of fresh fruits, clouds of cream, and a glass of sparkling wine. The olive oil cake introduces a mysterious new flavor and the fine texture of the chiffon cake, while polenta appears as the featured ingredient in a moist pound cake that can be enjoyed year around. Lastly, that favorite American confection, the upside-down cake, takes on a host of new appearances with the fragrant almond batter supporting a variety of seasonal fruits.*

Poppyseed Cake

1 cup poppyseeds stirred into ½ cup hot milk

2 cups flour

1 teaspoon baking powder

1 teaspoon baking soda

³⁄₈ teaspoon salt

3 eggs, separated

½ cup unsalted butter

1 cup sugar

2 teaspoons vanilla

1 cup sour cream or buttermilk

No mere sprinkling of seeds here—this cake is dense with poppyseeds that have been allowed to swell in hot milk. You can let them steep for several hours and the cake will be better for it, but if you decide to make this at the last minute, just start them soaking first thing, then drain off any milk that didn't get absorbed before adding the poppyseeds to the batter. Serve this cake dusted with powdered sugar and accompanied with whipped cream and sliced strawberries—or just plain.

MAKES 1 9-INCH CAKE, SERVING 10 TO 12

Set the poppyseeds aside to soak in the milk until needed. Preheat the oven to 375°F. Lightly butter and flour (or spray) a 9-inch springform pan. Mix the dry ingredients together and set them aside.

In a bowl beat the egg whites until they form firm but moist peaks and set aside. In another bowl cream the butter with the sugar until light and fluffy. Add the vanilla, then beat in the yolks one at a time until smooth. Scrape down the bowl, then stir in the sour cream and drained poppy seeds. Add the dry ingredients in thirds. (If using a mixer, this can be done on low speed.) Scrape up the batter from the bottom of the bowl to make sure it's well mixed, then stir in a quarter of the beaten egg whites before folding in the rest. Smooth the batter into the pan, then bake until golden, firm, and beginning to pull away form the sides of the pan, about 50 minutes. Remove from the oven, set the cake on a rack, and gently remove the rim so that the cake can cool.

Olive Oil Cake

WHEN *baked, olive oil has a rich and somewhat mysterious flavor. This cake is high and handsome, much like a chiffon cake. In fact, call this a chiffon cake—people often balk at the idea, but not the taste, of an olive oil cake. Serve this delicate confection with a dessert wine or sherry and accompany with sliced nectarines, pears, berries, and whipped cream flavored with apricot preserves.*

MAKES A TALL 10-INCH CAKE, SERVING 10 TO 12

4 eggs, separated, plus 1 egg white, at room temperature

1 cup sugar

1 teaspoon vanilla

1 tablespoon orange flower water

Finely grated zest of 1 large orange and 1 lemon

¹/₂ teaspoon salt

¹/₂ cup plus 2 tablespoons olive oil

1¹/₃ cups milk

2¹/₂ cups sifted cake flour

2 teaspoons baking powder

Powdered sugar

Preheat the oven to 375°F. Oil or butter and flour a 10-inch springform or bundt pan.

Beat the egg whites until they form soft peaks, then gradually add ¹/₃ cup of the sugar and continue beating until firm peaks are formed. Scrape them into a large bowl and set aside. In the same mixing bowl—don't bother to rinse it—beat the yolks with the remaining sugar until thick and light colored. Lower the speed, add the flavorings and salt, then gradually pour in the oil. The batter will be thick, like mayonnaise. Slowly add the milk, then whisk in the flour and baking powder. Reach thoroughly around the bottom of the bowl to make sure everything is well mixed. Fold in the egg whites. Scrape the batter into the prepared pan.

Bake in the center of the oven for 25 minutes. Reduce the temperature to 325°F and bake for 40 minutes more or until a cake tester comes out clean and the cake has begun to pull away from the sides. (It's better to err on the side of overbaking than underbaking this cake.) Let cool in the pan for 10 minutes. Remove the rim or invert, if using a bundt pan, onto a cooling rack. When cool, gently transfer the cake to a cake plate and dust with powdered sugar.

Yeasted Sugar Cake

COVERED *with a cracked sugar crust, this cake is fragrant with butter—yet it uses far less than most cakes. And although it's made with the yeast, the rising time is brief. I love this cake at any time of day, with raspberries, with fruit compotes of all kinds, and in place of shortcake with strawberries and cream.*

SERVES 10 TO 12

The Cake

2¹/₄ teaspoons (1 envelope) active dry yeast

¹/₄ cup sugar

2 cups flour, plus extra for the counter

¹/₂ teaspoon salt

¹/₂ cup warm milk

2 eggs, at room temperature

4 tablespoons butter, at room temperature

The Topping

2 tablespoons butter, softened

¹/₄ cup light brown or white sugar

Stir the yeast and 1 teaspoon of the sugar into ¹/₄ cup warm water in a small bowl and let stand until foamy, about 10 minutes. Combine the flour, remaining sugar, and salt in a mixing bowl. Add the yeast, milk, and eggs and beat until smooth. Add the butter and beat vigorously until the batter is silky. Scrape down the sides, then cover and let rise until doubled in bulk, about 45 minutes.

Lightly butter a 9-inch tart pan or cake pan. Stir down the dough, turn it onto a lightly floured counter, and gently shape it into a disk. Set it in the pan and flatten it with your hands. Rub the softened butter all over the top, then cover with the sugar, using all of it. Let rise for 30 minutes. During the last 15 minutes, preheat the oven to 400°F.

Bake the cake in the center of the oven until well risen and the sugar has begun to melt and brown, about 25 minutes. The surface should be covered with cracks. When done, let it cool briefly, then unmold and serve, still a little warm, with fruit and softly whipped cream.

Variations: Add 1 teaspoon finely grated lemon zest to the batter along with ½ teaspoon vanilla extract or ½ teaspoon crushed anise seeds. A half cup of finely ground almonds and a drop of almond extract are also good additions.

Polenta Pound Cake

¼ pound butter, preferably unsalted

1 cup sugar

Finely grated zest of 1 lemon

3 eggs, at room temperature

1 teaspoon vanilla

½ teaspoon almond extract

½ cup sour cream or yogurt

½ cup plus 2 tablespoons cornmeal

1 cup flour

½ teaspoon baking powder

¼ teaspoon salt

½ cup pine nuts

Powdered sugar

CORNMEAL pound cakes are popular in Santa Fe, and this is one I made when I was cooking at Cafe Escalera. It's a great year-round cake and the perfect accompaniment to seasonal fruit compotes.

MAKES 1 LOAF CAKE, SERVING 8 TO 10

Preheat the oven to 350°F. Brush a 4- × 10-inch or 5- × 8-inch loaf pan with butter and dust it with flour.

Cream the butter, sugar, and lemon zest until light and fluffy, about 3 minutes. Add the eggs one at a time, then the flavorings and sour cream. Stir in the cornmeal followed by the flour, baking powder, and salt.

Spoon the batter into the pan, smooth the top, then give the pan a sharp rap to remove any air pockets. Scatter pine nuts over the top and gently press them into the batter. Bake in the center of the oven until the top is firm to the touch and golden brown or a cake tester comes out clean, about an hour. Let cool for 10 minutes then turn out onto a rack. Serve dusted with powdered sugar.

Upside-Down Cakes

Easy to make, fetching to look at, and universally popular, upside-down cakes can be made with virtually any fresh fruit and many canned ones. (Plums, green figs, and apricots are some I turn to in a pinch.) Upside-down cakes are my spur-of-the-moment dessert when I have unexpected company, but there's nothing about them that's second-class.

Pear-Almond Upside-Down Cake

THE almonds are in the cake. For a fine, feathery texture, grind them in a hand-cranked grinder rather than a food processor. Serve with softly whipped cream flavored with a little almond extract or orange zest or with a scoop of honey ice cream.

SERVES 6 TO 8

The Pears
3 tablespoons butter
³/₄ cup light brown sugar, packed
2 large Comice or Bartlett pears

The Almond Cake
¹/₄ pound (¹/₂ cup) unsalted butter at room temperature
³/₄ cup granulated sugar
1 teaspoon vanilla

¹/₄ teaspoon almond extract
3 eggs at room temperature
²/₃ cup blanched almonds, finely ground
1 cup flour
1 teaspoon baking powder
¹/₄ teaspoon salt

Preheat the oven to 375°F. Heat the butter with the brown sugar in a 10-inch cast-iron skillet over medium heat until the sugar is melted and smooth, then remove the pan from the heat. Peel, halve, and core the pears. Set one of the halves aside and cut the other three lengthwise into slices about ¹/₄ inch thick, angling your knife around the pears so that all the slices are the same thickness. Overlap the slices in the sugared pan, going around the outside. Slice the remaining half crosswise and fan it into the center.

For the cake, cream the butter and sugar until light and fluffy, then add the vanilla and almond extract. Beat in the eggs one at a time until smooth. Stir in the nuts, followed by the remaining dry ingredients. Spoon the batter over the fruit and smooth it out with an offset spatula.

Bake in the center of the oven until the cake is golden and springy when pressed with a fingertip, 35 to 40 minutes. Let cool in the pan for a few minutes, then set a cake plate on top of the pan, grasp both the plate and the pan tightly, and turn it over. Carefully ease the pan off the cake. If any fruits have stuck to the pan, simply pry them off and return them to the cake.

Peach Upside-Down Cake Peel and halve 5 freestone peaches. Place them cut side down on the sugared surface as described. Fill the spaces in between with ¹/₃ cup chopped pecans and cover with the almond batter in the preceding recipe. Bake as described and serve warm with whipped cream or Buttery Bourbon Sauce, page 718.

Apple Upside-Down Cake Peel and core 3 apples, then halve them lengthwise. Slice them crosswise about ¼ inch thick. Overlap the apples around the outer edge of the sugared pan, then, reversing directions, fill in the center. Cover with batter, page 704, and bake as described. Serve with Caramel Nut Sauce, page 719.

Winter Jewel Upside-Down Cake with Pomegranate Compote

The Fruit

3 tablespoons butter

1 cup light brown sugar

⅔ cup dried apricots

⅓ cup dried prunes

2 tablespoons each dark raisins, golden raisins, and dried cranberries

Seeds of one pomegranate

1 tablespoon sugar

1 teaspoon orange flower water

whipped cream flavored with 2 teaspoons grated orange zest

The Batter

1 cup *each* cake flour and all-purpose flour

1 teaspoon baking powder

1 teaspoon baking soda

⅜ teaspoon salt

¼ pound (½ cup) butter

1 cup sugar

1½ teaspoons vanilla

⅛ teaspoon almond extract

2 eggs, at room temperature

1 cup buttermilk

This jewel-like cake is covered with a buttermilk cake and served with sweetened pomegranate seeds and softly whipped orange flavored cream.

MAKES 1 10-INCH CAKE

Melt the butter in a 10-inch cast-iron pan over medium heat. Stir in the sugar, cook until it's dissolved, then remove the pan from the heat.

Cut some of the apricots into quarters and leave the rest whole. Put all the dried fruits in a saucepan, add water to cover, and simmer until softened, about 15 minutes. Drain, gently squeezing out the moisture. Arrange them over the bottom of the pan.

Preheat oven to 375°F. Mix the dry ingredients for the cake batter together. Cream the butter with the sugar until light and fluffy. Add the flavorings, then beat in the eggs one at a time until smooth. Scrape down the bowl, stir again to blend in any bits of butter, then stir in the buttermilk. Add the dry ingredients, in thirds, to the butter mixture. (If using a mixer, this can be done on low speed.) Scrape up the batter from the bottom of the bowl to make sure it's well mixed. Smooth the batter over the fruit.

Bake in the center of the oven until springy to the touch and beginning to pull away from the pan, about 35 minutes. Let cool for a few minutes, then invert onto a cake plate. While the cake is baking, cut the pomegranate in quarters, remove the seeds to a bowl, and sprinkle them with a tablespoon sugar and the orange flower water. Refrigerate. Softly whip the cream, sweeten it to taste, and add the orange zest. Serve the cake warm with the chilled pomegranate seeds and whipped cream

Chocolate Terrine

8 ounces bittersweet or semisweet chocolate

1/4 cup freshly brewed espresso or strong coffee

1/2 pound (1 cup) unsalted butter, cut into small pieces

2 eggs, separated

2 tablespoons sugar

1 cup ladyfingers or Petite Beurre brand cookies, broken into 1/2-inch pieces

1 cup chopped toasted almonds

2 tablespoons brandy

Softly whipped cream

Lightly oil a 4- × 10-inch bread pan, a 2-quart bowl, or another container that will look attractive when unmolded.

Melt the chocolate and espresso in the top of a double boiler with half the butter, stirring occasionally. Remove from the heat and beat in the remaining butter and the egg yolks.

Beat the whites until they hold soft peaks, then add the sugar and continue beating until they're glossy and firm. Fold them into the chocolate, then stir in the ladyfingers, almonds, and liquor. Transfer the mixture to the prepared pan. Refrigerate until firm, about 6 hours or overnight.

To unmold, carefully hold the dessert in a large bowl of very hot water until the edges are melted. Invert it onto a platter and give the pan a sharp tap. If it doesn't come out right away, wrap the pan in a steaming hot towel for a few minutes and try again. Serve sliced into thin wedges, accompanied by lightly sweetened whipped cream.

Variations: Substitute hazelnuts and Frangelica liqueur for the almonds and brandy; crushed amaretti for the ladyfingers and Amaretto for the brandy. If you like the contrast of fruit with chocolate, include 1/2 cup dried cherries, raisins, or chopped prunes, macerated first in brandy to cover for 20 minutes. Or accompany the terrine with fresh raspberries. Orange is always good with chocolate, too. Include 2 teaspoons finely grated orange zest or 1/2 cup chopped candied orange peel and use Grand Marnier instead of brandy.

Puddings

PUDDINGS can be made of most anything and served warm or chilled, but they're universally tender and soft, which makes them at once comforting and homey, always well received by children and adults alike.

Pear Pudding with Almond Topping

Butter for the dish

3 eggs

$^1/_3$ cup sugar or $^1/_4$ cup honey

$1^1/_2$ teaspoons vanilla

$^1/_4$ teaspoon almond extract

$^1/_8$ teaspoon salt

$^1/_4$ teaspoon grated nutmeg or ground cardamom

$1^1/_2$ cups milk

$^1/_3$ cup flour

4 firm but ripe pears, such as Comice or Bartlett

$^1/_2$ cup crumbled *amaretti* or Crisp Topping, page 689, made with almonds

Cream, optional

Preheat the oven to 375°F. Generously butter a 2-quart gratin dish or pie plate. Combine the eggs, sugar, extracts, salt, nutmeg, milk, and flour in a blender and puree until smooth. Scrape down the sides and blend for a few seconds more. Set aside until ready to use.

Peel, halve, and core the pears then slice them thinly into the baking dish. Pour the batter over the top, add the crushed amaretti, and bake in the center of the oven until puffed and golden, about 50 minutes. Serve warm, accompanied by a pitcher of cream.

THIS dessert merges the French clafouti with the crunchy surface of a crisp. Since this pudding is best warm from the oven, have the batter and fruit ready, then combine them at the last minute and bake while everyone's eating. If you like Amaretto, sprinkle a few tablespoons over the top as soon as it comes out of the oven.

SERVES 6

Stovetop Rice Pudding

1 cup medium- or long-grain rice or $^3/_4$ cup Arborio rice

1 3-inch cinnamon stick or vanilla bean, halved lengthwise

1 tablespoon grated orange zest

$^1/_4$ teaspoon salt

3 cups milk

$^1/_3$ to $^1/_2$ cup sugar or honey to taste

Ground cinnamon

In a small saucepan, simmer the rice in $2^1/_2$ cups water with the cinnamon stick, orange zest, and salt until the liquid is absorbed, 15 to 20 minutes. Add the milk and stir in the sugar, starting with the smaller amount. Bring to a boil, then lower the heat and simmer, stirring frequently, until thickened but still a little soupy, about 30 minutes. Taste for sweetness and add more sugar if desired. (I sometimes add a tablespoon of strong chestnut honey for flavor as well as sweetness.) Serve warm or chilled with a dash of cinnamon on top. Accompany with a spoonful of the Spiced Dried Fruits in Wine Syrup, page 721, or other wine-poached fruits such as pears, figs, and prunes.

MANY know rice pudding as a warm, slow-baked comfort food, but it can also be a cool, refreshing dessert. Although medium-grain rice is traditional, you can also use the fat, starchy risotto rice or even long-grain rice, though it won't be so starchy. Almond and rice milk make fragrant substitutes for milk.

SERVES 4 TO 6

Rice Pudding with Anise Use lemon instead of orange zest, and add 1 heaping teaspoon anise seeds, lightly crushed between your fingers, to the milk. Serve warm or chilled, with the Dried Misson Figs in Red Wine with Anise, page 688.

Rice Pudding with Sherry Add ½ cup cream sherry to the pudding during the last 10 minutes.

Rice Pudding with Meringue A satiny meringue lightens the pudding and gives it a more glamorous feel. Whisk 3 egg whites, at room temperature, until they form soft peaks, then gradually add ⅓ cup sugar. Continuing beating until the peaks are firm and glossy, then fold them into the warm rice pudding. Leave plenty of airy, sweet pockets and streaks.

Cream Cheese Pudding Soufflé

PLAN the rest of your meal so that there aren't too many last-minute details to attend to. You can have the base ready to go, then beat the whites and complete the dish. Serve plain, with sugared berries or with any fresh fruit sauce. I like the Warm Cherry Sauce. If you prefer to bake this in a single dish, scoop two large spoonfuls onto each plate, garnish with fruit, and dust the top with powdered sugar.

SERVES 4

Butter and sugar for the dishes

4 egg whites at room temperature

5 tablespoons powdered sugar, plus extra for the top

2 to 4 egg yolks

8 ounces cream cheese

1 teaspoon vanilla

1 teaspoon orange flower water

2 teaspoons finely grated orange zest

1 cup sugared blackberries, sliced blood oranges, Warm Cherry Sauce, or fresh fruit sauces, pages 719 to 721

Preheat the oven to 400°F. Butter four 1-cup ramekins and dust them with sugar.

Whip the whites until they hold soft peaks. Add 2 tablespoons of the sugar and continue beating until the peaks are stiff but not dry. Remove them to a large bowl. Put the cream cheese in the same mixing bowl (no need to wash it) and beat until smooth. Add the yolks one at a time, followed by the remaining ingredients except fruit. Stir a quarter of the whites into the mixture to lighten it, then fold in the rest.

Divide among the ramekins and set them in a baking pan. Add hot water to come halfway up the sides and bake until golden, about 25 minutes. There should be a little cap, and the soufflés should be set.

Serve each soufflé in its dish or slide a knife around the edge, then turn each out onto your hand, reverse it, and put it on a plate. Dust with powdered sugar and serve plain, with the suggested accompaniments.

Frozen Honey Mousse

1 cup whipping cream

3 egg yolks

1/2 cup strongly flavored honey

Finely grated zest of 1 tangerine or 1/2 orange

1/4 cup peeled pistachios, coarsely chopped

1 tablespoon orange flower water

Whip the cream until it holds soft but firm peaks. Scrape it into another bowl and refrigerate. Without rinsing the mixing bowl, beat the yolks and honey until they thicken and turn pale, 8 to 10 minutes at high speed. Add the zest, pistachios, and orange flower water, then fold in the cream and whisk at low speed until everything is well combined. Freeze in individual ramekins or a single container. It will take about 3 hours for the mousse to set, although you can serve it at any time. Before serving, allow it to stand at room temperature for 5 to 10 minutes to soften to the right consistency.

A COLD *and creamy accompaniment that seems perfect with all fruits, but especially the Caramelized Pineapple or anything made with figs. You can reverse the order by freezing the mousse in individual ramekins and serving them garnished with fruit, and you can also serve it soft instead of frozen.*

SERVES 8

Fresh Cream Cheese

3/4 cup crème frâiche or whipping cream

8 ounces cream cheese

2 tablespoons honey or 1/4 cup powdered sugar

Extra cream and vanilla sugar for serving, if desired

Line a small colander, basket, or perforated heart-shaped molds with a double layer of damp cheesecloth. There should be enough cloth to hang over the rim by several inches.

Whip the crème fraîche until stiff and scrape it into a bowl. Add the cream cheese and honey to the mixing bowl (no need to rinse it out) and beat until light. Stir a quarter of the whipped cream into the cream cheese and beat until smooth, then fold in the remaining cream. Scrape the mixture into the colander and fold the ends of the cheesecloth over the top. Set the colander in a bowl and refrigerate for 24 hours. Check several times and pour off any liquid that has drained to the bottom of the bowl.

To serve the cheese whole, unfold the cloth, turn the cheese onto a serving plate, and peel off the cheesecloth. Or simply lift out a portion with a soupspoon, then place it on each dessert plate. Serve, if you wish, with a little cream poured over the top and a sprinkle of vanilla sugar, along with fruit or a fruit sauce.

Variation with Goat Cheese Mild, fresh goat cheeses give another kind of tang to this cheese. Follow the same procedure, but use cream instead of crème fraîche and 6 ounces each cream cheese and goat cheese.

WHEN *molded in heart-shaped molds, this becomes* coeur à la crème. *Serve this mousse-like cheese, one of the simplest and most flexible of desserts, with fresh berries, fruit purees, poached fruit, Caramelized Pineapple, or alongside a piece of warm prune tart. Since this consists of little more than cream and cheese, use the finest, most natural ingredients possible. Make it a day before serving so that it can firm up.*

SERVES 6 TO 8

Vanilla Custard

IN its simplest form, mother's custard, as this used to be called, is made by the formula 1 cup milk to 1 egg, a tablespoon or so of sugar, and a splash of vanilla. Additional yolks make it richer and more tender, and cream instead of milk does the same.

SERVES 4 TO 6

2 cups milk or any combination of milk and cream or half-and-half

½ vanilla bean or 1 teaspoon vanilla

¼ cup sugar

2 whole eggs

1 egg yolk, optional

Grated nutmeg or ground cinnamon

Heat the milk with the vanilla bean and sugar in a small saucepan over low heat without letting it boil. Meanwhile, preheat the oven to 325°F. Have ready a single baking dish or four to six custard cups. Stir the milk several times to make sure the sugar is dissolved.

Beat the eggs and egg yolk in a 1-quart measuring cup, then gradually whisk in the hot milk. Scrape the seeds from the vanilla bean into the custard. If using vanilla extract, stir it in. Pour the custard through a strainer into the dish. Set in a baking pan and grate a little nutmeg over the top. Add warm water to come at least an inch up the sides, then bake until the custard is set and a knife inserted comes out clean, about 35 minutes for small custards, 45 to 50 minutes for a single custard. Chill. Serve plain or accompanied by fruit, especially berries, poached dried fruits, or a citrus compote.

Ices

ICES, be they granitas, sorbets, or sherbets, fill the role of a light and sweet ending to a meal. Fruit ices are not difficult to improvise, as the following formula illustrates, but the secret to making these simple desserts memorable rests, not surprisingly, on the quality of the fruit. Since fruit ices consist only of fruit, except for some sugar, the fruit really has to taste good to start with.

Serve ices on plates, in ice cream dishes, or tucked into champagne flutes or wineglasses. (Champagne or Prosecco drizzled over a flute full of ice is wonderfully festive.) A sprig of mint or other flattering herb, such as lemon verbena, rose geranium leaves and their flowers, or lemon verbena sprigs, makes a pretty garnish, as do extra fruit, candied citrus peels, and, of course, cookies.

A General Formula for Making Fruit Ices and Sorbets

I learned this years ago from Lindsey Shere, Chez Panisse's esteemed pastry chef, and it has stood me in good stead ever since. With it in hand, you can improvise with whatever fruits you have. Just be sure to taste your final puree before freezing to adjust the amount of acidity if needed, since fruits vary in sweetness. Sometimes a squeeze of lemon balances everything nicely. This proportion provides enough sugar to make a smooth-textured sorbet if eaten within the first day. After that, it will get chalkier and more crumbly, the trade-off for using less sugar.

1. Juice or puree your fruits. Some fruits yield more flavor—and pulp—if cooked first, such as apricots and plums: Just put them in a pan with a little water and cook until they've fallen off their pits. Skins, pits, and small seeds can be removed by passing them through a food mill.

2. Measure the amount of fruit puree, then divide by four to determine how much sugar to use. If you have 4 cups of puree, you'll need 1 cup of sugar.

3. Put the sugar in a small saucepan and add just enough puree to moisten it, about ¹/₂ cup. (There's no need to heat the entire amount; besides, color is lost when it's heated.) Heat, stirring frequently, until clear. When you rub a drop between your fingers, it should feel perfectly smooth. If it feels grainy, cook for a few minutes more, then test again.

4. Combine the syrup with the remaining puree and add your flavorings—citrus zest, a few drops of liquor, or a bit of fresh lemon or lime juice.

5. Freeze according to the directions for your ice cream maker.

Strawberry Ice

1 quart ripe red strawberries, rinsed
About 1 scant cup sugar

Few drops kirsch
4 to 6 perfect small berries, for garnish

Hull the berries, pulling out the core using the tip of a vegetable peeler, then puree them in a blender or food processor. Measure the puree, divide by four, and measure out that much sugar. It will probably be about ⁷/₈ cup sugar. Put the sugar in a saucepan, add ¹/₃ cup of the puree or water, and heat, stirring until the sugar is dissolved and the mixture doesn't feel grainy when rubbed between your fingers. Combine the syrup with the rest of the puree and chill. Stir in the kirsch and set aside ¹/₂ cup, if desired, to spoon over the finished sorbet.

Freeze according to your ice cream maker's instructions. Serve with the reserved sauce drizzled over the top. Garnish with sprigs of mint or another sweet herb and a perfect fresh berry.

THIS sounds so ordinary, but it's so good when it's homemade. You can set aside some of the sweetened strawberry puree to drizzle over the finished ice if desired.

MAKES ABOUT 1 QUART

Pink Grapefruit Sorbet

1 tablespoon finely grated grapefruit zest
3 cups grapefruit juice, from 3 or 4 ruby grapefruits

Juice of 1 lemon
³/₄ cup sugar

Put the zest in a bowl and add the grapefruit and lemon juice. If there are seeds in the juice, pour it through a coarse sieve so that the small bits of pulp will still go through. Put the sugar in a saucepan, add ¹/₂ cup juice, and simmer until the sugar is completely dissolved. Add the syrup back to the juice and chill. Freeze according to the instructions of your ice cream maker.

ONE of the most refreshing endings to a filling winter's meal I can imagine. If you're inclined to make candied citrus peels, be sure to serve a few alongside.

SERVES 6

Grapefruit Coupe with Champagne Serve the sorbet in champagne flutes, then pour champagne over the top. Serve with candied grapefruit peels.

Grapefruit Sorbet with Lime and Tequila Serve the sorbet with a splash of tequila and a wedge of lime on the glass.

Grapefruit-Campari Slush The Campari underscores the rosy color of the grapefruit. Add ½ cup to the chilled sorbet mixture, then freeze. The alcohol will make this a little slushier than usual. Garnish with a flourish of mint.

Lemon Verbena Sherbet

LEMON verbena gives another citrus dimension to this old-fashioned dessert. If you don't have the herb, though, omit it and you'll still have a classic milk sherbet. Serve with Warm Cherry Sauce spooned over the top.

MAKES 3 CUPS, SERVING 4 TO 6

2 cups milk, preferably whole
2 cups lemon verbena leaves, rinsed
½ cup plus 2 tablespoons sugar

Pinch salt
½ cup fresh lemon juice
Lemon verbena leaves for garnish

Put the milk, lemon verbena, sugar, and salt in a saucepan and slowly bring to a boil. Turn off the heat and let stand for an hour, stirring occasionally to dissolve the sugar. Strain, then stir in the lemon juice. The mixture will curdle, but it doesn't matter—it smooths out when frozen. Freeze in an ice cream maker according to the manufacturer's instructions. Serve garnished with fresh verbena leaves or violets.

Mango Sherbet

MANGO makes a sherbet with intense color and flavor. It's wonderful alone and even better served with blackberries, raspberries, or sliced mangoes splashed with tequila or rum.

SERVES 4

2 ripe mangoes, 8 to 10 ounces each
½ cup light brown sugar, packed
½ cup buttermilk, yogurt, or water

Juice of 2 limes
Pinch salt

Peel the mangoes, cut the flesh into a bowl, then squeeze the pits to get off as much flesh and juice as possible. Puree the mango. Heat the sugar with ½ cup of the puree until smooth to the touch. Combine it with the remaining puree, buttermilk, lime juice, and salt. Freeze according to the manufacturer's instructions. Left soften before serving.

Cinnamon-Lemon Ice Milk with Espresso (*Blanco y Negro*)

3 cups milk, preferably whole

1 cup cream

Zest of 2 lemons, removed with a zester

4 3-inch cinnamon sticks

³/₄ cup sugar

Pinch salt

3 egg whites

Garnishes: warm or chilled espresso, whipped cream, toasted slivered almonds

Very slowly heat the milk and cream with the lemon zest, cinnamon sticks, ¹/₂ cup sugar, and the salt. When nearly boiling, turn off the heat and let it steep until cool to allow the flavors of the lemon and cinnamon to be absorbed thoroughly.

Beat the whites until soft peaks form. Add the remaining ¹/₄ cup sugar and continue beating until they're glossy but still soft. Strain the milk into a bowl and fold in the whites. Freeze according to your ice cream maker's instructions. (I prefer to make this only a few hours before serving so that it doesn't have a chance to become stone hard.)

To serve, pour a little espresso into the bottom of a champagne flute, add a few spoonfuls of the ice, then pour in more espresso. It will fall down the glass and cover the ice. Top with a spoonful of sweetened whipped cream, add a few toasted almonds, and serve.

ESPRESSO poured over champagne flutes of delicate ice milk topped with a cloud of whipped cream makes a magnificent little ice cream float. Blanco y Negro neatly fills the gap when good fresh fruits aren't available, but it's really excellent at any time of year. A Little Nut Cookie, on the side is the perfect accompaniment.

MAKES ABOUT 1 QUART

Cardamom Ice

3 cups milk, preferably whole

1 cup cream

Zest of 1 lemon, removed with a zester

2 or 3 large strips orange zest

1 cup sugar or ²/₃ cup sugar plus 3 tablespoons honey

3 3-inch cinnamon sticks

1 teaspoon hulled cardamom seeds, coarsely crushed

4 cloves

1 teaspoon each finely grated orange and lemon zest

¹/₄ cup peeled pistachios, chopped

Put the milk, cream, coarse citrus zest, sugar, and spices in a saucepan and very slowly bring to a boil. Turn off the heat and let stand for an hour or longer for the flavors to develop. Strain. Stir in the finely grated zest and pistachios. If still warm, cool in the refrigerator or over ice. Freeze in an ice cream maker according to the manufacturer's directions.

THIS light and fragrant ice is best served the day it's made, or it tends to turn crumbly. My favorite accompaniment is a plate of crispy Filo Cigars.

MAKES ABOUT 1 QUART

Cookies on the Side

CRISP, *crumbly, and buttery, cookies are often just the thing to complete the simpler desserts like sliced fruit or compotes, ices and ice creams, fresh cheeses, or custard. They needn't be big or elaborate—just a rich little bite to bring a meal nicely to its conclusion. Of course cookies are also great to enjoy with cup of tea or coffee at midday or to find tucked into a bag lunch. If you make a batch for dinner but don't want the extras tempting you, just put them in an airtight container and freeze them for another time.*

A Little Nut Cookie

THIS *is the easiest cookie in the world to make. You can drop the dough, roll it out between your hands, or roll it into a log and freeze it to slice and bake later. You can also vary it. Roasted nut oil underscores the flavor of the nuts.*

MAKES 3 DOZEN 2-INCH COOKIES

¼ pound (½ cup) unsalted butter

1 tablespoon roasted nut oil—walnut, hazelnut, macadamia—optional

¾ cup light brown sugar, packed or a mixture of white and brown sugar

1 egg

1 teaspoon vanilla

¼ teaspoon salt

1¼ cups flour

1 cup finely chopped nuts—walnuts, hazelnuts, macadamia nuts, pecans

Powdered sugar

Preheat the oven to 375°F. If you're using the nut oil, take away a tablespoon of the butter. Cream the butter, oil, and sugar until smooth and light. Beat in the egg, then add the vanilla and salt. With the mixer on low, stir in the flour, then stir in the nuts.

Drop the dough by teaspoons onto cookie sheets, about 2 inches apart. Or, for a more evenly shaped cookie, roll the dough between your palms. Bake until lightly browned on top and slightly browner on the bottom, 8 to 10 minutes. Let cool on a rack., then dust with powdered sugar.

Spice Nut Cookies Add ½ teaspoon ground cinnamon or grated nutmeg when you add the flour.

Almond Cookies Finely grind 1 cup lightly toasted almonds—peeled or not. Reduce the vanilla to ½ teaspoon and add ¼ teaspoon almond extract.

Chocolate Nut Cookies A sophisticated tollhouse cookie. Coarsely chop 1 to 2 ounces bittersweet chocolate and stir it into the batter. For mocha cookies, add 1 teaspoon powdered espresso to the dough as well.

Cardamom Cookies

¼ pound unsalted butter (½ cup)

½ cup powdered sugar, plus extra for tops

2 tablespoons granulated sugar

1 egg yolk

1 teaspoon ground cardamom

⅜ teaspoon salt

1¼ cups flour

Cream the butter and sugars until light and fluffy, then beat in the egg yolk. Stir in the cardamom, salt, and flour. Divide the dough in two, roughly shape each piece into a log about 1 inch thick, then roll in plastic wrap or wax paper. Pull each log through your thumb and first finger to make it even and, if you prefer, longer and narrower. Refrigerator until firm or freeze until ready to use.

Preheat the oven to 375°F. Cut the dough into ¼-inch rounds or diagonals and set them on cookie sheets at least 1 inch apart. Bake until pale golden on top and lightly browned around the edges, 8 to 10 minutes. Cool. Serve plain or dusted with confectioners' sugar.

CARDAMOM is a perfect spice for pears and is lovely with all fruits. While peeling and pounding your own cardamom pods will make the spice practically explosive, I've found that commercial ground cardamom is quite good as long as it's fresh.

MAKES 3 DOZEN 2-INCH COOKIES

Filo Cigars

½ pound frozen filo pastry

2 cups blanched almonds

¾ cup sugar

¼ teaspoon ground cardamom

2 tablespoons orange flower water

4 tablespoons butter, melted

Put frozen filo pastry in the refrigerator the night before you make these, allowing it to thaw gradually.

Preheat the oven to 400°F. Grind the almonds in a hand-cranked grinder so that you end up with a light powder or finely chop them by hand. Toss with the sugar, cardamom, and enough orange flower water to dampen the mixture slightly.

Unroll the filo and cut it crosswise into strips 5 to 7 inches wide. Stack the strips in a pile and cover with a barely damp towel. Place a piece of pastry on the table, heap 2 teaspoons almond mixture at one end, then fold over the outer edges and roll it up. Brush the surface with butter. Bake on ungreased cookie sheets until golden brown, about 12 minutes.

Filo Cigars II For a crunchier pastry that can be baked ahead of time, sprinkle 2 tablespoons of the almond mixture over the entire surface of each filo strip. Fold in the long edges by ½ inch. If the dough is brittle and won't bend without breaking, brush a little butter on it to make it pliable. Roll, then brush the surface with a little butter. Bake for 8 to 10 minutes, until nicely browned.

MAKE these fragrant almond pastries short and plump or long and skinny. They can be formed ahead of time, but the filling hardens as it cools, so they're best baked close to serving. A second version, which can be baked in advance, follows. Allow ample time to defrost the filo pastry.

MAKES 24 TO 30 COOKIES

Ginger-Oat Shorties

BOTH ground and candied ginger give these cookies their zing. Serve with fresh melon or melon sorbets in summer or poached figs or apricots in winter.

MAKES TWENTY-FOUR 2-INCH SQUARES

³/₄ cup rolled oats
¹/₂ pound unsalted butter (1 cup)
1 cup light brown sugar, packed
¹/₄ teaspoon salt

1 teaspoon ground ginger
1¹/₂ cups flour
¹/₂ to 1 cup chopped candied ginger

Preheat the oven to 350°F. Put the oats in a blender or food processor and process briefly so that some of the oats are broken and others remain whole. Set aside.

By hand or in a mixer fitted with a paddle attachment, beat the butter with the sugar until light and fluffy, then add the salt, ground ginger, and oats. Work in the flour, then add the candied ginger. Use your hands to mix in any flour left in the bottom of the bowl.

Press the dough evenly into a 9- × 12-inch pan, then score the surface, marking off squares, diamonds, or skinny rectangles. Bake until lightly browned on the surface, 30 to 35 minutes. Remove and cut again along the score lines, then set aside to cool. The cookies will crisp as they cool. Store in an airtight tin.

Jam Bars or Tart

EVERYONE needs a dessert to fall back on in a pinch, and this is one. If you bake the dough in a tart pan, you can cut it into wedges and serve it as a tart. Otherwise, cut it into small squares.

SERVES 10

¹/₄ pound (¹/₂ cup) unsalted butter
¹/₂ cup powdered sugar
¹/₂ cup packed light brown or white sugar
1 teaspoon vanilla
1 egg
¹/₂ teaspoon baking powder

¹/₂ teaspoon ground cinnamon
1¹/₂ cups flour
¹/₄ teaspoon salt
¹/₂ to ³/₄ cup preserves, such as fig, raspberry, or marmalade
³/₄ cup chopped walnuts, pecans, or rolled oats

Preheat the oven to 350°F. Cream the butter with the sugars until light and fluffy. Add the vanilla and egg, beat until smooth, then add the dry ingredients except the nuts.

Set aside approximately ³/₄ cup of the dough and press the rest evenly into an 8- × 10-inch baking pan or a 9-inch tart pan with a removable bottom or pie plate. Spread the preserves over the top. Mix the reserved dough with the nuts and crumble it over the top. Bake until lightly browned on top, about 40 minutes. Let cool, then cut into squares. Or serve as a tart, cut into thin wedges.

Whipped Cream and Other Dessert Sauces

SIMPLE desserts are made special by the simple enhancement of softly whipped cream and sauces based an old favorites such as caramel, chocolate, bourbon, and fruit. All are easy to make, and they can do a great deal to upgrade a pint of ice cream or an unfrosted cake. In some cases they can go right over pancakes and waffles, too.

Crème Chantilly (Softly Whipped Cream)

¹/₂ cup whipping cream

2 to 3 teaspoons powdered sugar to taste, or slightly less granulated sugar

¹/₂ teaspoon vanilla or other flavoring, such as a few drops almond extract, orange flower water, liqueur, jam, or pureed fruit

THIS is such a ubiquitous garnish, yet all too often it ends up stiff instead of mounding into soft drifts. Just take care not to overbeat the cream. If you do, just stir in some extra to soften it.

MAKES ENOUGH FOR 4 TO 6 SERVINGS

With a whisk or a mixer, beat the cream until it forms soft, billowy peaks. Add the sugar and any flavorings that go with your dish. If you're not ready to use the cream, cover it well and refrigerate. If the cream has returned to liquid on the bottom, give it a few turns with the whisk.

Cinnamon Cream Stir in ¹/₂ teaspoon or more ground cinnamon.

Ginger Cream Stir in ¹/₄ to ¹/₂ teaspoon ground ginger and a few tablespoons finely diced candied ginger.

Tangy Whipped Cream

¹/₂ cup whipping cream

¹/₂ cup crème fraiche or sour cream

1 tablespoon light brown sugar or powdered sugar or to taste

1 teaspoon vanilla or other flavoring, such as a few drops almond extract, orange flower water, liqueur, jam, or pureed fruit

CRÈME fraîche or sour cream gives a tart and silky dimension to whipped cream. I especially like this with warm fruit galettes, cobblers, and crisps.

MAKES ENOUGH FOR 4 TO 6 SERVINGS

Combine the creams in a bowl and whisk until soft and billowy. Stir in the sugar and your chosen flavoring.

Yogurt Topping with Orange Zest

1 cup yogurt, drained for 25 minutes, page 47

Honey or maple syrup to taste

1 teaspoon orange or lemon zest

¹/₂ teaspoon freshly grated nutmeg or ground cinnamon

MAKES 1 CUP

Combine everything in a bowl.

Apricot Sauce

TRY *this sauce with crêpes, pancakes, and French toast as well as with ice cream.*

MAKES ABOUT 1¹/₂ CUPS

1 cup dried apricots, roughly chopped

¹/₂ vanilla bean, split lengthwise

2 to 4 tablespoons sugar or honey

A few drops fresh lemon juice

In a saucepan, bring the apricots, 2¹/₂ cups water, and the vanilla bean to a boil. Lower the heat and simmer until the fruit is soft. Scrape the seeds out of the vanilla bean with a knife. Puree the apricots and return them to the heat. Add sugar or honey to taste—apricots can have an edge of tartness—and cook until there's no granulation. Add a few drops of lemon juice.

Maple Rum-Raisin Sauce

A GREAT *choice for ice cream—not just vanilla, but coffee ice cream too.*

MAKES ABOUT 1¹/₂ CUPS

¹/₂ cup raisins

3 tablespoons dark or light rum

1 cup maple syrup

¹/₄ cup brown sugar, packed

Grated nutmeg

2 tablespoons butter

Cover the raisins with the rum and set aside to soften for 15 minutes. Heat the syrup and sugar in a saucepan with a tablespoon of water. Add the raisins and the rum and season with a little nutmeg. Simmer for 2 minutes and whisk in the butter.

Buttery Bourbon Sauce

A BOOZY *enhancement for peaches and/or ice cream, topped with toasted pecans.*

MAKES ABOUT 1 CUP

1 cup light brown sugar, packed

¹/₄ pound unsalted butter (¹/₂ cup)

¹/₂ cup cream or half-and-half

2 tablespoons bourbon, such as Maker's Mark

Put the sugar, butter, and cream in a saucepan and stir to dissolve the sugar. Cook over medium heat until smooth and hot, then stir in the bourbon.

Caramel Nut Sauce

½ cup pecans or walnuts

1 cup light brown sugar, packed

½ cup light or dark corn syrup

1 cup cream

Pinch salt

½ teaspoon vanilla

A CLASSIC nut-studded caramel sauce to spoon over ice cream, baked bananas, or Oats and Brown Sugar Coffee Cake.

MAKES ABOUT 2 CUPS

Preheat the oven to 350°F. Toast the nuts for 5 minutes, then coarsely chop them. Combine the sugar and corn syrup in a saucepan with the cream. Cook over medium heat, stirring frequently, until the mixture is smooth. Add the salt and cook until it has thickened a little more, about 5 minutes. Stir in the vanilla and nuts.

Chocolate Sauce

8 ounces bittersweet chocolate, coarsely chopped

¼ cup water or freshly brewed strong coffee

½ cup cream

2 tablespoons unsalted butter

1 teaspoon vanilla

2 teaspoons brandy, Grand Marnier or Chartreuse

THIS sauce is thin, rich, and very chocolaty. The better the chocolate, the better the sauce.

MAKES ABOUT 1½ CUPS

In a heavy saucepan set over low heat, combine the chocolate, water, and cream, stirring frequently, until the chocolate is melted. Remove from the heat and stir in the butter, vanilla, and brandy. Cool slightly, then drizzle over ice cream or fruits.

Mango Puree

2 large ripe mangoes

½ cup fresh lime juice or orange juice

Freshly grated nutmeg

SPOON this vivid sauce over fresh fruit or blend it with buttermilk or ygurt for smoothies.

MAKES ABOUT 1½ CUPS

Peel the mangoes and slice off as much flesh from the seed as possible. Puree it with the lime juice. Add a little freshly grated nutmeg to taste.

Berry Sauces

Berry purees provide a lustrous garnish for desserts that cry out for the bright flavor of fruit. While fresh fruit is preferable, frozen berries will work too, and sometimes they are, sad to say, better than many fresh ones. Use the blender just long enough to break up the fruit—you don't want to puree the seeds, or they'll give your sauce a slightly bitter edge and gritty texture.

Raspberry or Strawberry Sauce

THIS carmine-colored sauce is wonderful with peaches, sliced pears, and figs—especially when the raspberries predominate.

MAKES ABOUT 1 1/3 CUPS

1/4 to 1/2 cup sugar to taste

2 cups fresh or frozen raspberries, strawberries, or a mixture

1 teaspoon kirsch or framboise or to taste

Boil 1/4 cup water and the sugar, using the larger amount if the berries are tart, in a small saucepan until no graininess remains when you rub a drop between your fingers. Set aside to cool. Crush or puree the berries, then press them through a fine sieve with a soft rubber scraper until all the juice is forced out and only the seeds remain. Stir in the cooled syrup, then add kirsch to taste. If the berries were lackluster, you might use framboise to bolster the raspberry flavor.

Blackberry Sauce Try this sauce not only on ice cream but drizzled over chunks of cold watermelon as well. Substitute blackberries, fresh or frozen, for the raspberries and 3 tablespoons light brown sugar for the granulated. If the berries were very sweet, add a few drops lemon juice to the sauce to sharpen their flavors. Stir in Grand Marnier, Cointreau, or orange flower water to taste.

Blueberry Sauce

THIS makes a striking purple sauce. I always find that lime does wonders for blueberries—it sparks them, but gently—as does ginger and even a touch of molasses. I use this on pancakes and over lemon sherbet or ginger ice cream.

MAKES ABOUT 1 2/3 CUPS

3 cups blueberries, stems removed

2 teaspoons molasses

1/3 to 1/2 cup sugar to taste

1 teaspoon ground cinnamon or ginger or 1/2 teaspoon grated nutmeg

Juice of 1 lime to taste

Rinse the berries and put them in a saucepan with the water clinging to them. Add the molasses and sugar, starting with the lesser amount, and the spice. Bring to a boil, stirring occasionally. The berries should burst and fall apart. Taste, add the rest of the sugar if needed, and stir in the lime juice. At this point you can serve the sauce as it is, warm and textured with fruit, or you can force it through a strainer to make it smooth and serve it warm or chilled.

Warm Cherry Sauce

1 pound ripe, dark red cherries, pitted

¼ cup sugar or as needed

1 tablespoon kirsch or to taste

A few drops lemon juice or balsamic vinegar

FRESH warm cherries, swimming in their juices, can grace a slice of cake, go over ice cream or rice puddings, and flatter a heart-shaped Fresh Cream Cheese or most anything chocolate.

MAKES ABOUT 2 CUPS

Put a single layer of the cherries in a large sauté pan over high heat. Sprinkle 2 tablespoons sugar over them and cook, shaking the pan back and forth, until the sugar melts and the cherries begin to release their juices, after just a few minutes. Transfer to a bowl and repeat with the rest. When done, stir in the kirsch and a few drops lemon juice.

Spiced Dried Fruits in Wine Syrup

The Syrup

2 cups muscat or Riesling

1½ cups sugar

½ vanilla bean

1 3-inch cinnamon stick

Zest of 1 orange or lemon, removed with a zester

The Fruit

½ cup dried apricots, cut into small pieces

½ cup whole dried apricots

1 cup pitted prunes

1 cup mixed raisins: monukka, muscat, or golden

½ cup currants

¼ cup dried cherries or cranberries

DURING the winter this is a very handy item to have on hand to garnish a simple cake, embellish poached pears, or spoon over custard or rice pudding. It will keep, refrigerated in a tightly covered container, for up to 2 months.

MAKES 3 CUPS

Bring 2 cups water, the wine, and the sugar to a boil in a saucepan with the spices and citrus zest. When the sugar has dissolved, add the fruits. Reduce the heat and simmer, partially covered, until the fruits are tender and the sauce syrupy, about 30 minutes. Let cool, then transfer to a container with a tight-fitting lid. Store in the refrigerator.

Cheese

INSTEAD of sweets, cheese is favored by many at the close of a meal. I find that this is the best time to savor these unique, often hand-crafted foods. Since hunger has already been sated, one can really taste for enjoyment, slowly enjoying the range of flavors and textures that fine cheeses offer.

There are different ways to approach serving cheese. You can simply choose one that you like, make a random assortment from whatever looks good, or select a number of cheeses made in the same style such as blue cheeses, or with the same kind of milk, such as goat's milk. A grouping of goat cheeses might include a goat blue, a goat Cheddar, a tangy fresh cheese as well as an aged one.

Very delicate cheeses, such as a ricotta or other fresh cheese, can be served with honey or sweetened dried fruits or combined with other cheeses, to make a coeur à la crème and served with a handful of ripe berries. There are the sensational triple creams, like St. André, which are lovely to eat with freshly cracked walnuts, pears, or fresh cherries. Aged cheeses, such as a golden wedge of Parmigiano-Reggiano, shouldn't be overlooked as dessert cheeses; aged cheeses often exhibit great character as eating cheeses—they aren't just for grating.

Regardless of the cheese you choose, what's most important is to serve cheese at room temperature—with the exception of ricotta and yogurt cheeses. A cold cheese is deadened. It needs to warm up for its flavor to emerge and bloom. In winter this can take several hours, so arrange your cheese tray ahead of time. Fine cheese is rare and expensive, and it's a great waste to eat it cold.

CHOOSING CHEESES: Although each cheese has its own particulars to consider, you always want a cheese that's not only interesting but has a fresh, clean, appetizing smell. Avoid cheeses that have an ammoniated or other off-putting odor. Sniff cheese, ask to taste it, and try to have a piece cut for you from a wheel rather than settle for one that has been cut, wrapped, and allowed to stand until liquids separate from the cheese. When it comes to knowing about particular cheeses, it's a good idea to consult a good guide, such as Vivienne Marquis and Patricia Haskells's *The Cheese Book* (Simon and Schuster, 1964) or, more recently, Steven Jenkins's *Cheese Primer* (Workman, 1996). Food magazines are frequently a good resource for information on small dairies producing excellent farmhouse cheeses and how to get them.

MAKING YOUR OWN: There are a number of fresh-style cheeses that are not at all difficult to make. If you enjoy things like making bread and sprouting seeds, you may find it very exciting to make your own cream cheese, mascarpone, ricotta, panir, and other simple cheeses. Something as simple as cream cheese becomes exquisite when homemade, especially if you have access to milk from a local dairy. Contact the New England Cheese Making Supply Company (Box 85, Ashfield, MA 01330-0085; 413-628-3808). The company carries equipment, cultures, and advice that really works.

Some Cheese Combinations

Try fresh cream cheese, ricotta, or yogurt cheese drizzled with honey and served with Whole-Wheat Biscuits to Eat with Cheese, dried fruits, and a glass of dessert wine. Or serve a small mound of ricotta with the Spiced Dried Fruits in Wine Syrup, page 721.

Fresh Cream Cheese or coeur à la crème is classically served with a little cream poured over the top, a sprinkling of vanilla sugar, and a handful of tender, sweet berries.

Fresh goat cheese, ricotta, or mascarpone is delicious served with ripe figs and new-crop walnuts.

Stilton and English blues are wonderful with apples, especially when the apples are at the peak of their season. Cox Orange Pippin, Golden Russet, Mutsu, and Braeburn are some favorites. Buttery Comice or Bartlett pears are also good with blue cheeses. Try Gorgonzola dolcelatte with pears, apples, or apple-pears. This cheese is especially interesting when thinly sliced, drizzled with warm honey, and served with lightly roasted almonds. Cabrales—a marvelously fortifying Spanish blue cheese that is at last beginning to appear in our markets—is wonderful with toasted Walnut Bread, page 668, or freshly cracked walnuts and sherry. (Before the meal, serve it with a drier sherry or a full-bodied Spanish red wine.)

Aged Cheddars are also wonderful served with crisp fall apples or apple-pears, hard cider, and a handful of cracked walnuts or, even better, buttery hickory nuts. Wisconsin produces some excellent aged Cheddars as well as an aged Gruyère, a yellow Muenster made from Guernsey milk, and other fine cheeses, available from Atlas Delicatessen in Madison, Wisconsin. (Call John Taylor at 608-256-0606 to find out what's available; he'll ship. He doesn't yet have a catalog.)

With cream cheese, Manchego, or ricotta salata, try a slice of pink, jellied quince paste or a slice of fruit bread, such as the Applesauce Spice Bread. Mascarpone, yogurt cheese, ricotta, or a mild goat cheese, are excellent with moist fresh dates.

Try double and triple cream cheeses with cherries and a glass of kirsch, with Walnut Bread, page 668 or a date nut bread.

Whole-Wheat Biscuits to Eat with Cheese

1 cup all-purpose flour
1 1/4 cups whole-wheat flour
1/2 cup wheat bran
1 teaspoon baking powder
1/2 teaspoon baking soda

1/2 teaspoon salt
1/4 cup light brown sugar, packed
1/4 pound (1/2 cup) cold unsalted butter, cut into small pieces
1 egg, beaten with 1/2 cup buttermilk or water

NOT too sweet, these biscuits are a good accompaniment for all kinds of cheese, from triple cream to blue to Fresh Cream Cheese made with goat cheese.

MAKES ABOUT 60 2-INCH BISCUITS

Preheat the oven to 375°F. Combine the dry ingredients together in a mixing bowl. Add the butter and mix with a paddle attachment or rub between your fingers until it resembles coarse meal. Stir in the egg mixture until distributed evenly. Squeeze a handful of dough; if it clings, the dough is ready. If it's too crumbly, add more buttermilk—by drops—until it coheres. Shape into a disk and let rest for 10 minutes.

Roll the dough out on a lightly floured surface 1/8 inch thick for a thin, crisp wafer or 1/4 inch thick for a thicker, more crumbly one. Cut out the cookies with a biscuit cutter or a glass 2 inches across. Prick the tops in several places with a fork, then set them on an ungreased cookie sheet and bake until lightly browned, 12 to 15 minutes.

Resources

DATES:
ARIZONA DATE GARDENS (fresh dates, including Black Sphinx, Medjools, and Khadrawis)
P.O. Box 1921
Tempe, AZ 85281
(602) 921-9685

HEIRLOOM BEANS:
PHIPPS COUNTRY STORE AND FARM
P.O. Box 349
Pescadero, CA 94060
(415) 879-0787
(800) 279-0889 mail order only

ELIZABETH BERRY
Gallina Canyon Ranch
Box 706
Abiquiu, NM 87510
Send $1.00 and a self-addressed stamped envelope for catalog

BAKING GOODS AND EQUIPMENT: Specialty flours; good tools for baking, including saffron by the ounce, Boyajian citrus oils, dried buttermilk, and food mills.

KING ARTHUR FLOUR COMPANY
The Baker's Catalog
P.O. Box 876
Norwich, VT 05055-0876
(800) 827-6836

FALLS MILL (stone-milled grits)
134 Falls Mill Road
Belvidere, TN 37306
(615) 469-7161

OILS:
OMEGA NUTRITION (makes high-quality organic apple cider vinegar, hazelnut and walnut oils, pumpkin seed oil, Brazil nut oil, and other oils)
(800) 661-3529

LORIVA OILS (excellent high-quality roasted nut oils—peanut, hazelnut, macadamia, sesame, and sunflower)
20 Oser Avenue
Hauppauge, NY 11780
(800) 945-6748

ZINGERMAN'S (excellent range of olive oils, vinegars, farmhouse cheeses, and other good things to eat and cook with)
422 Detroit Street
Ann Arbor, MI 48104
(313) 769-1625

CHEESES:
JOHN TAYLOR (rare farmhouse cheeses from Wisconsin)
Atlas Delicatessen
1923 Monroe Street
Madison, WI 53711
(608) 256-0606

CAPRIOLE, INC. (makes some of the most interesting goat cheeses in the United States, including a fine aged goat)
10329 Newcut Road
Greenville, IN 47124
(812) 923-9408

HERBS AND SPICES:
PENZEYS, INC. (incredibly fresh spices including Turkish bay leaves, saffron, a variety of curry powders, cinnamons, and gingers)
P.O. Box 933
Muskego, WI 53150
(414) 574-0277

SOUTHWESTERN INGREDIENTS:
COYOTE CAFE GENERAL STORE
132 West Water Street
Santa Fe, NM 87501
(505) 982-2454
(800) 866-HOWL (4695)

Index

Chayote and corn enchiladas, 291
Cheddar cheese, 585, 723
  Cheddar cobbler topping, 245
  custards, 590
  grilled sandwich with onion, 122
  peppered-cheese bread, 667
  polenta Cheddar croquettes, 525
  soufflé, giant, 580
  ziti with mushrooms and, 463
Cheese(s). *See also specific varieties*
  about, 31, 565, 584–87; grated, 28;
    serving suggestions, 722–23
  and angel hair pasta soufflé, 462
  baked cheese on toast with wine, 588
  biscuits, seeded, 649
  bread, peppered, 667
  and chile spoon bread, 648
  custards, savory, 590
  and green chile corn bread, 647
  grits, 527
  muffins, 645
  omelet, 572
  for sandwiches, 124
  sandwich recipes, 121–22
  skillet cheese, 588
  toasts, 106
Cheese substitutes, 31, 584
Chermoula, 56; eggplant rounds with, 368
Cherry:
  and apricot crisp, 689
  sauce, warm, 721
Cherry tomato(es):
  and olive relish, 78
  sauce, 62
  zucchini pizza with goat cheese and,
    513
Chervil, 38
Chickpea(s), 299, 307
  basic, 307; in pressure cooker, 307
  bulgur and lentil salad with, 172
  butterflies with, 449
  buttermilk soup with herb oil and, 239
  eggplant stew with tomatoes, peppers,
    and, 249
  with garlic mayonnaise, 308
  and greens with Moroccan spices, 309
  with harissa, 308
  and millet pilaf with saffron and toma-
    toes, 532
  and pasta with sizzling sage and garlic,
    311
  with potatoes and tomatoes, 310
  puree, spicy, 99
  and rice pilaf, 544
  soup, with condiments (leblebi), 311
  spicy, with ginger, 308
  sprouting, 325
  stew: with potatoes, 252; with spinach,
    310
  tagine with artichokes, peppers, olives,
    and preserved lemons, 250
  whole wheat with lentils, tarragon, and,
    559
Chicories, 137, 360. *See also* Belgian en-
    dive; Escarole; Radicchio
Chile(s):
  about, 32–33; roasting and peeling,
    403; varieties, 405

chile butter, 52
chile cheese toasts, 106
chipotle(s), 32; hash browns with
    cheese and, 628; mayonnaise, 60;
    roulade with cilantro and, 582;
    steam-fried eggs with cheese and,
    569
  green, 405; avocado sandwich with
    olive paste and, 118; cheese and
    chile spoon bread, 648; and cheese
    corn bread, 647; mayonnaise, 60; and
    mint salsa, 103; stuffed green chile
    omelet, 573
  pepper sauce, 74
  red, 32, 33; baked eggs with, 571;
    harissa, 75; mayonnaise, 60; mole,
    292; posole with, 529; romesco
    sauce, 70; sauce, 70
  roasted: Mexican green rice with, 540;
    pepper strips and onions (rajas), 404
Chile colorado, 70
Chili, all-bean, 323
Chili oil, sesame vinaigrette with, 188
Chilli paste:
  Chinese, 262
  hoisin sauce with tangerine and, 73
Chinese cabbage. *See* Cabbage, napa or
    Chinese
Chinese dumplings, with shredded cab-
    bage, mushrooms, and leeks, 485
Chinese ingredients, 261–62
Chinese noodle cake, 263
Chinese noodles, 479, 480
Chinese parsley. *See* Cilantro
Chipotle(s). *See* Chile(s), chipotle(s)
Chives, 38
  romaine hearts with pecans and, 142
Chocolate:
  chocolate nut cookies, 714
  sauce, 719
  terrine, 706
Chopping techniques, 22–24, 39, 137
Chowder:
  corn, with potatoes, peppers, and basil,
    207
  quinoa, with spinach, feta, and scal-
    lions, 230
  winter vegetable, 220
Choy sum, 378, 379
Chutney(s), 33
  apple-pear, 81
  apricot and dried fruit, 81
Cilantro, 38
  beets with lemon, mint, and, 151
  braised chard with, 358
  chard soup with, 205
  mustard-cilantro sauce, 72
  roulade with chipotle and, 582
  salsa, 56
Cinnamon:
  -lemon ice milk with espresso, 713
  rolls, 678
  tart, 700
Citrus fruit, 33. *See also specific varieties*
  compote: with rhubarb, 685; in tanger-
    ine syrup, 684; winter breakfast, 614
  mixed citrus salad with avocado, 168
Citrus oils, 43, 180

Cloud ear mushrooms, 262
  stir-fried peppers with egg and, 272
Cobblers:
  fruit, 690–91
  vegetable, 245
Coconut:
  cream, dal with, 304
  marinade, Thai, 597
  milk, 34; cauliflower, spinach, and
    potato stir-fry with, 265; pineapple-
    coconut milk drink, 617; winter
    squash soup with lemongrass and,
    216
  rice, spicy stir-fried tofu with, 601
  sauce(s): coconut-basil, mixed vegetable
    stir-fry with, 274; curry-coconut, tofu
    in, 600; tempeh in, 601; Thai, 597;
    tofu in, with ginger and lemongrass,
    600
Coeur à la crème, 722, 723
Coffee cake(s):
  oat and brown sugar, 637
  orange and dried fruit, 637
  streusel toppings for, 643
  sweet corn, with berries, 636
Coleslaw:
  with buttermilk-horseradish dressing,
    152
  cabbage slaw with spicy greens, 152
Collards, 378
  braised, 379
  with peanuts, 379
  with pepper sauce, 379
  with tomatoes and asiago, 380
Compotes, fruit, 614, 683–88
Condiments, 49, 74. *See also* Chutney(s);
    Relish(es)
  herb salts, 75–77
  pepper sauce, 74
  preserved lemons, 82
Cookies:
  almond, 714
  cardamom, 715
  chocolate nut, 714
  filo cigars, 715
  ginger-oat shorties, 716
  jam bars, 716
  nut, 714
  spice nut, 714
Coriander, 38
  fresh. *See* Cilantro
  and yogurt dressing, Persian melons
    with, 167
Corn, 362, 363
  baked, with cumin and feta, 364
  bread(s), 646 (*see also* Corn muffins);
    amaranth cornmeal, 667; basic, 646;
    buttermilk skillet, 647; corn-rye but-
    termilk rolls, 676; custard corn
    bread, Marion's, 647; green chile and
    cheese, 647; spoon bread, 648; stuff-
    ing, eggplant rollatini with, 370;
    vanilla, 647
  bread pudding with, 294
  cakes, 630; lacy buttermilk, with pepper
    relish, 630
  coffee cake, sweet, with berries, 636
  with cumin, chile, and tomato, 364

mayonnaise (aïoli), 59
pickled carrots and, 79
roasted: mashed potatoes with, 409;
potato soup with, 212; spread with
white beans and sage, 101; whole,
377
and sage butter, warm, 50
Ghee, 30
Ginger:
cream scones, 651
-cucumber salsa, melon soup with,
239
mashed sweet potatoes with sesame
and, 429
-oat shorties, 716
peanut-ginger dressing, cabbage salad
with, 153
sesame-ginger marinade, 597
sweet potato muffins with, 644
tofu in coconut sauce with lemongrass
and, 600
Glass (cellophane or bean-thread) noodles. See Noodle(s), glass
Glazes, for breads and pastries, 660–61
Gluten, 558
Gnocchi, potato, 478
Goat cheese, 124, 585–86, 723
croutons, warm, salad with, 140
enchiladas, with corn and mole, 292
fettuccine with, 461
flan, 589
fresh cream cheese with, 709
and leek galette, 498
log, dusted with herbs, 114
and mozzarella, calzone with, 504
pizza with zucchini, cherry tomatoes,
and, 513
rounds, with pepper and herbs, 113
sauce, 72
soufflé, with thyme, 579
and spinach lasagne gratin, 465
Gomashio, 76
hot cereal with, 621
Gorgonzola, 723. See also Blue cheese
fettuccine with, 461
pizza with tomato and, 509
ravioli, with tomato sauce, 470
sauce, warm, 72
soft polenta with, 524
Grain(s). See also specific grains
about, 515–18; in salads, 169, 170; in
soups, 221
puddings, improvised, 528
Granola, 623–24
Grapefruit(s), 33, 613
pink grapefruit sorbet, 711–12
Grape juice, white, with orange and basil
or lemon verbena, 616
Gratin(s), 275, 276
artichoke, celery root, and potato, 277
barley and kale, green, 520
butternut squash, 287
cabbage, 278
cabbage and rye panade, 278
carrots, rutabagas, and turnips, 280
cauliflower, 281
celery root: with potato, 279; with wild
rice, 557

cottage cheese and spinach, 288
dried fruit, with pistachio-walnut topping, 688
eggplant, 279, 280
lasagne-mushroom, 467
leek: with potatoes, 282; with turnips
and blue cheese, 287
mushroom: and lasagne, 467; and
potato, 283
navy bean and pasta, 322
onion, 282
polenta: with mushrooms and tomato,
289; with tomato, Fontina, and rosemary, 526
potato: and celery root, 279; and leek,
282; and mushroom, 283; Spanish,
with saffron, almonds, and bread
crumbs, 285; spicy potato, tomato,
and pepper tagine, 284; with tomatoes and olives, 284
rice: with spinach, 547; with summer
squash, 286, 547; wild, with celery
root, 557; with winter squash, 546
risotto, sizzling, 555
rutabaga, carrots, and turnips, 280
spinach, 286; and cottage cheese, 288;
and rice, 547
spinach lasagne and goat cheese, 465
summer squash: with herbs and rice,
286; with rice, 547
turnip: with carrots and rutabagas, 280;
with leeks and blue cheese, 287
vegetable gratin-soufflé, 288
winter squash: with onions and sage,
287; Provençal, 441; with rice, 546
Greek salad, 164
Green bean(s), 336
basic, 337
as crudité, 91
flageolets with tomatoes and, 322
with garlic mayonnaise, 337
with olive sauce, 337
potato salad with eggs and, 160
salads, warm, 149
with salsa verde with walnuts and tarragon, 337
simmered with tomato, 337
with yogurt sauce, 337
Green chile(s). See Chile(s), green
Green goddess dressing, 190
Green herb tart (torta d'erbe), 493
Green peppercorns, 44
Greens. See also Salad greens; specific
types
about, 377–78, 381; leftover, 382; measuring, 205
beet risotto with, 553
boiled, 379
brown rice and eggs with walnuts and,
549
with cannellini beans, 381
cannelloni with artichokes and, 476
cauliflower with mustard butter and,
354
and chickpeas with Moroccan spices,
309
with crisped bread crumbs, 380
empanadas with olives and, 503

Indian-style sauté of cauliflower and,
267
mixed: with cumin and paprika, 382;
stir-fried, 264
with potatoes, 380
red bean gumbo with, 321
skillet, 379
spicy, cabbage slaw with, 152
with tomatoes and asiago, 380
white bean and pasta soup with, 230
winter, with fennel and mushrooms,
140
winter squash flans with, 592
Green salads, 136–42
Green tomatoes. See Tomato(es), green
Gremolata, 29
eggplant rounds with, 368
Grilled cheese sandwiches, 121–22
Grilled vegetable(s), 127, 328. See also
specific vegetables
grilled vegetable heroes, 127
Grits, 516. See also Polenta
basic and variations, 527
breakfast, 527, 621
puddings, 528
Groats, 516, 517. See also Kasha
Gruyère cheese, 124, 586
apple and celery salad with, 166
soufflé, 579
Guacamole, 94
toasts with pickled onions, 104

Haricots verts. See also Green bean(s)
with garlic mayonnaise, 337
Harissa, 75
chickpeas with, 308
scrambled eggs with, 570
Tunisian eggs with peppers and, 577
Havarti cheese, 124
Hazelnut(s), 41
and persimmon salad, 166
sauces: romesco, 70; tarator, 67
Hazelnut oil, 43, 180
vinaigrette, 185; persimmon and hazelnut salad with, 166
Herb(s), 36–40
aromatics (bouquet garni), 29
butter, 51
-crusted tofu, 603
and feta cheese turnovers, 502
fines herbes, 29
focaccia, 670
and garlic broth, 193, 198
green herb pasta (dough), 446
gremolata, 29
herb-butter and olive oil sauce, 51
mayonnaise, 59
omelet, 573
persillade, 29
roulade with yogurt cheese and, 583
in salad dressings, 182, 186
in salads, 137, 143, 144
salts, 75–77
sauces, 54, 55–57
and spinach torta, 494
tarts: fresh herb, 491; green herb (torta
d'erbe), 493
High-altitude cooking, 24–25

Hijiki:
  carrots with, 352
  soba with stir-fried vegetables and, 482
Hoisin sauce, 262
  with chili paste and tangerine zest, 73
  hoisin marinade, 598
  marinated grilled tofu with, 602
  mushrooms and tofu in, 269
Hominy, 516, 528. *See also* Grits; Posole
  green hominy stew, 530
Honeydew melon and lime juice with mint, 616
Honey mousse, frozen, 709
Horseradish:
  buttermilk dressing with, 190
  kohlrabi with, 384
  sauce, fresh, 72

Ices, 710–11
  cardamom ice, 713
  cinnamon-lemon ice milk with espresso, 713
  lemon verbena sherbet, 712
  mango sherbet, 712
  pink grapefruit sorbet, 711
  strawberry ice, 711
Indian salt with mixed spices, 77
Indian-style sauté of cauliflower and greens, 267
Indonesian fried rice, 545
Indonesian-style tempeh, 609
Ingredients, 28; mail-order sources, 724
Irish soda bread with bran and oats, 652

Jack cheese, 586; quesadilla with, 123
Jam bars or tart, 716
Jerusalem artichokes (sunchokes), 383
  roasted, 383
  sautéed, with sunflower seeds, 383
  wine-glazed, with rosemary, 384
  winter vegetable stew with, 258
Jícama:
  as crudité, 92
  and cucumbers with chile and lime, 111
  salad with avocado and orange, 149
  stir-fries: with carrots and watercress, 266; sweet and sour, 273

Kale, 378
  and barley gratin, green, 520
  with cannellini beans, 381
  with olives, 381
Kamut, 517, 518, 558, 559, 662
Kasha, 516, 521
Kasseri cheese, fried, 114
Kichuri, golden, 305
Kidney beans:
  red bean gumbo with greens, 321
  salad with black-eyed peas, barley, and corn, 175
  with walnut sauce, 175
Knives, 14–15
Kohlrabi, 384
  as crudité, 92
  grated celery and, with mustard vinaigrette, 155

with horseradish, 384
Kombu stock, 193, 232

Lasagne, 464–65
  broken, with fried green tomatoes and parsley, 455
  eggplant, with garlic béchamel, 466
  eggplant and chard, 468
  mushroom, 467; gratin, 467
  tossed spinach lasagne and goat cheese gratin, 465
Latkes, 413
Leblebi, 311
Leek(s), 209, 385
  braised, 386
  creamed, on walnut toast, 134
  and goat cheese galette, 498
  gratinéed, 387
  gratins: with potato, 282; with turnips and blue cheese, 287
  grilled, 386, 387
  in mustard vinaigrette, 158
  simmered in wine, 386
  soup(s), 208–9; cold leek and potato, 236; with flageolet beans, 228
  sprouts, 139
  steamed, 385
  stir-fry with mushrooms, tofu, and Chinese barbecue sauce, 270
  turnip or rutabaga puree with, 436
Leftovers:
  greens, 382
  rice, 537
  soups from, 220
Lemon(s), 33
  candied slices, 697
  chard soup with, 205
  cinnamon-lemon ice milk with espresso, 713
  preserved, 82
  vinaigrette, 184
Lemon balm, 38
Lemongrass:
  tofu in coconut sauce with ginger and, 600
  winter squash soup with coconut milk and, 216
Lemon verbena, 38
  sherbet, 712
  white grape juice with orange and, 616
Lentil(s), 299
  basic, 300
  dals, 304–5
  green: and bulgur with chickpeas, 172; and spinach with hard-cooked eggs and toast, 302; with wine-glazed vegetables, 301
  and onion croquettes, 300
  with pasta, rice, and buttery mint sauce, 303
  red: dals, 304–5; soup, with lime, 226
  and rice with fried onions, 302
  salads, 172–74
  soups, 224–26; beet soup with three legumes, 223
  sprouting, 325
  whole wheat with chickpeas, tarragon, and, 559

Lettuce, 136, 137
  mixed green salad, 138
  red, with radish sprouts, 139
  romaine salads, 142
  sprouts, 139
Lima bean(s), 314
  and corn ragout, 247
  giant, with parsley and sorrel, 324
  pasta shells with rosemary and, 449
  succotash, 364
Limburger sandwich, 121
Lime(s), 33
  -cumin vinaigrette, 187
  and fresh mint vinaigrette, 187
  honeydew and lime juice with mint, 616
  red lentil soup with, 226
Linguine:
  with asparagus, lemon, and herbs, 448
  with onions, peas, and basil, 459
  with tomato sauce, 453
Lovage, 38–39
Lumache with broccoli and capers, 450

Macadamia nut and mixed rice salad, 171
Macadamia nut oil, 180
Macaroni smothered with onions, 461
Malaysian-inspired tofu curry, 602
Manchego cheese, 723
  figs with walnuts and, 169
Mango(es), 613
  nectarine-mango frappé, 616
  -orange cooler, 616
  quinoa salad with curry dressing and, 172
  rhubarb, strawberry, and mango compote, 685
  sauce, 719
  sherbet, 712
Maple-nut cereal, 620
Maple rum-raisin sauce, 718
Marinade:
  hoisin, 598
  hot mustard, 597
  mustard-honey, tempeh or tofu with, 609
  sesame, 604; rich, 68; sesame-ginger, 597
  smoky molasses, tempeh strips in, 608
  Thai coconut, 597
Marjoram, 39
  feta dressing with mint and, 190
  potato salad with pickled onions and, 160
  zucchini frittata with, 574
Mascarpone, dates with, 682, 723
Mayonnaise:
  basic, 58
  curry, with mango chutney, 93
  tofu, 60
  variations, 59–60
Melon(s), 613
  and cucumbers with pepper and lime, 167
  honeydew, and lime juice with mint, 616
  Persian, with yogurt and coriander dressing, 167

chopped, with feta dressing, 163
citrus, mixed, with avocado, 168
couscous, with pine nuts and dried
   fruits, 171
cucumber, 156–57
dandelion greens with garlic croutons
   and hard-cooked egg, 141
fall, with walnuts and walnut oil, 144
farmers' market, 163
fennel, 157–58, 168
figs with walnuts and Manchego, 169
fruit, about, 148, 166
with garden herbs, 144
grated, 154–55
Greek, 164
green, 136–42
green bean, warm, 149
greens for, 136–37, 143
herb (sabzi), 143
kohlrabi and celery, grated, with mustard vinaigrette, 155
leeks in mustard vinaigrette, 158
lentil, 172–74
macadamia nut and mixed rice, 171
melon, 167
mixed green, 138
mushroom, grilled, with watercress, 158
noodle, 178–79
orange: with avocado and jícama, 149;
   with fennel and butter lettuce, 168
parsley, with Parmesan, 144
pasta, 170, 177
pear, fennel, and endive, 158
pepper: with broccoli and tomato vinaigrette, 151; with chickpeas, 176;
   with Fontina, 159; with preserved
   lemon and cumin, 159; with saffron
   vinaigrette, 159
persimmon and hazelnut, 166
pita bread, toasted, with vegetables and
   herbs (fattoush), 164
potato, 160–61
quinoa, 171–72
ravioli and tomato with basil, 177
red lettuces with radish sprouts, 139
rice, 170–71
romaine hearts, 142
spinach, 143, 144, 146–47
sprouts on, 139
summer vegetables with garlic mayonnaise, 165
tabbouleh, 173
tatsoi with sesame oil vinaigrette, 139
tomato, 162–63; with arugula and olive
   croutons, 146; with black-eyed peas
   and feta, 174; and ravioli, with
   masses of basil, 177; with spinach
   and basil-walnut dressing, 147
turnips and celery, grated, with mustard
   vinaigrette, 155
with warm goat cheese croutons, 140
watercress, with slivered endive, 140
watermelon with mint, lime, and feta,
   167
winter greens with fennel and mushrooms, 140
winter vegetables with romesco sauce,
   165

Salad dressing(s), 148, 180–83. See also
   Vinaigrette(s)
avocado, 189
basil-walnut, spinach and tomato salad
   with, 147
blue cheese, 189
buttermilk, with horseradish, 190
feta, with marjoram and mint, 190
French, 183
green goddess, 190
herb and shallot, creamy, 186
peanut, with Thai basil, 189
peanut-ginger, cabbage salad with, 153
yogurt and coriander, Persian melons
   with, 167
Salad greens, 136–37, 143
Salmonella, 59, 567
Salsa(s). See also Relish(es)
cilantro, 56
ginger-cucumber, melon soup with, 239
green chile and mint, 103
pico de gallo (salsa Mexicana, salsa
   cruda), 102
salsa verde, 55
tomatillo, 103
tomato-avocado, 102
Salsify with shallots and parsley, 417
Salt, 28, 44–45, 183
herb salts, 75–77
potatoes baked in, 415
Sandwich breads, 661–63
Sandwiches, 117–18
avocado, 118–19
braised spinach with tomatoes and
   sautéed onion on focaccia, 131
bruschetta, 132–33
canapés, 103–4
cheese, 121–22
cheeses for, 124
cucumber, 119
egg salad, 128–29
focaccia, 126, 671
fried egg, 129
frittata, 104, 129
grilled cheese, 121–22
heroes, grilled vegetable, 127
marinated tofu, 130
onion, 120
pan bagnat, 126–27
pita, 125
portobello mushroom, grilled, 120
supper sandwiches, 131–34
tempeh, 130
tofu salad, 129
tomato, 120, 126, 127, 131
Sandwich rolls, focaccia, 671
Sauce(s), 49. See also Salsa(s); Sauces,
   dessert
barbecue: Chinese, 262; golden mustard, 74
béchamel, 53; garlic, 466; for gratins,
   277; walnut, 54
beurre blanc or rouge, 50
chermoula, 56
coconut, tofu in, with ginger and
   lemongrass, 600
curry, 71
curry-coconut, tofu in, 600

flavored butters, 51–52
goat cheese, 72
Gorgonzola, warm, 72
herb-butter and olive oil, 51
hoisin with chili paste and tangerine
   zest, 73
horseradish, fresh, 72
mayonnaise, 58–60
mint, buttery, lentils with pasta, rice,
   and, 303
mustard barbecue sauce, golden, 74
mustard-cilantro, 72
parsley-caper, 56
peanut. See Peanut(s), sauce(s)
pepper, 74
pesto, 57; artichoke, 95; tomato-basil,
   57
red chile, 70
red chile mole, 292
red pepper, 71
red wine, white bean and vegetable
   stew in, 324
red wine-shallot, winter squash flans
   with, 592
red wine tomato, eggplant rounds with
   cheese and, 368
rice wine vinegar with garlic, 73
romesco, 70
sage and garlic butter, warm, 50
salsa verde, 55; with walnuts and tarragon, 55
sesame: rich, 68; sesame-soy, 73; with
   tofu, 67
sorrel, 54
tahini with lemon and garlic, 67
tarator, 67
Thai coconut, 597
tofu "mayonnaise," 60
tomato, 60–64
vinegar, for onions, 394
walnut, 68; béchamel, 54; salsa verde
   with, 55
yogurt, 65–66
Sauces, dessert, 717–21
Savory, 40
Savoy cabbage. See Cabbage, savoy
Scallion(s), 209, 385
and baby artichoke sauté, 332
and broccoli puree, 341
crookneck squash with, 422
quinoa chowder with spinach, feta, and,
   230
risotto with lemon, basil, and, 553
spinach or chard with, 420
and walnut sauté, wild rice with, 557
Scallop squash with saffron rice, 427
Scones:
ginger cream, 651
oat, 651
Scots crowdie, 623
Sea salt with fennel seeds and thyme, 77
Sea vegetables (seaweed), 352. See also
   Arame; Dulse; Hijiki; Kombu; Nori;
   Wakame
Seeds, 41. See also Sesame; Sunflower
   seeds; Tahini
brine-soaked, 90
seed crackers, 654